THE GOOD FOOD GUIDE 2012

Distributed by Littlehampton Book Services Ltd
Faraday Close, Durrington, Worthing, West Sussex, BN13 3RB

Base mapping by Cosmographics Ltd
Data management and export by AMA DataSet Ltd, Preston
Printed and bound by Charterhouse, Hatfield

A catalogue record for this book is available from the British Library

ISBN: 978 1 84490 123 4

Consultant Editor: Elizabeth Carter
Managing Editor: Rochelle Venables

The Good Food Guide makes every effort to be as accurate and up to date as possible. All inspections are anonymous, but every Main Entry has been contacted separately for details.

As we are an annual Guide, we have strict guidelines for fact-checking information ahead of going to press, so some restaurants were dropped if they failed to provide the information we required. Readers should still check details at the time of booking, particularly if they have any special requirements.

Please send updates to: editors@thegoodfoodguide.co.uk or The Good Food Guide, 2 Marylebone Road, London, NW1 4DF

We would love to hear your feedback on any restaurant. To have your say, please visit www.thegoodfoodguide.co.uk/feedback.

*"You can corrupt one man.
You can't bribe an army."*

Raymond Postgate, founder of
The Good Food Guide, 1951

Please turn to the page number listed to find restaurant reviews for the corresponding region.

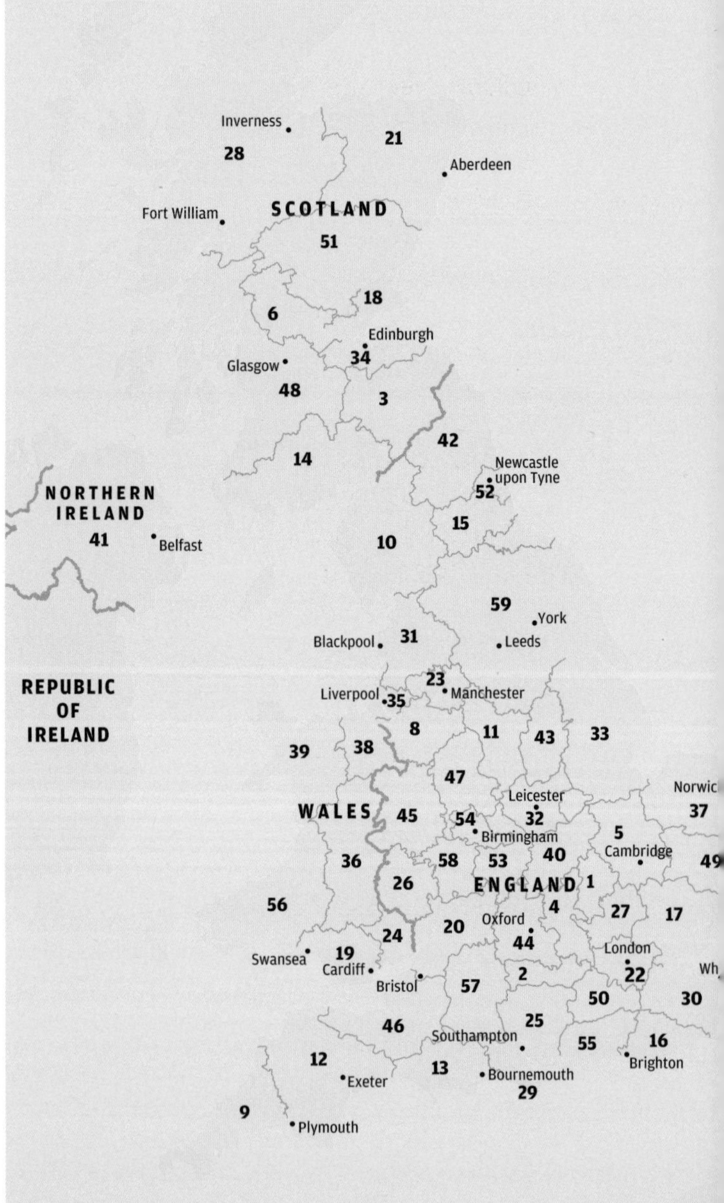

Contents

Introduction

Welcome to the 2012 edition of *The Good Food Guide*. Each year the Guide is re-researched and written from scratch. All our entries are based on anonymous, expert inspections and bolstered by feedback from readers, the unique combination of which gives a balanced view of what a restaurant is really like. The perennial strength of this much-loved book is that every single entry represents a range of meals eaten by genuine restaurant customers – people who claim no free meals, special service, recompense or reward. Where there is doubt, the restaurant is left out. We aim to present to you the very best of what the UK has to offer. And our standards are exacting.

Our origins lie in The Good Food Club founded by Raymond Postgate, 'Public Stomach Number One', who famously campaigned against 'cruelty to food'. Reports from the club's members soon resulted in the publication of *The Good Food Guide* in 1951, and over the years we have built up a meticulous, thoroughly comprehensive reporting system that casts a critical eye over Britain's cafés, pubs, bistros and restaurants. Although much has changed over the years, the ethos of the original Guide remains: we are completely impartial, and we don't accept any sponsorship or free meals. It is because of this, and because the Guide will always be the voice of the consumer, not the restaurant industry, that *The Good Food Guide* remains the UK's most trusted, best-loved restaurant bible. And in this digital age, where advice from blogs, forums and websites abounds, that long-established, dependable voice is needed now more than ever.

Everyone's talking about…

On the food front it has been a fascinating year. The ongoing UK recession doesn't seem to have been felt much on London's restaurant scene. Our capital has become a magnet for big money from Asia, the Middle East, Europe and the US, ensuring that London's restaurant outlook has remained dynamic and vibrant – even expansionist – with high-profile British chefs opening second or third restaurants, and international superstars keen to set up camp. London's event-openings have dwarfed anything happening in the rest of the UK since the last edition of this Guide.

And who would have thought that a top-scoring chef would be offering food from Britain's culinary past with such pride. But at Heston

Blumenthal's Dinner, the exploration and modernisation of historic British dishes has put down a marker for the coming years. Already Marcus Wareing has followed suit with nostalgic British classics at his second restaurant, the Gilbert Scott.

At the very top, change is being brought about by the passionate commitment of a highly individual group of chefs who are beginning to dominate the UK's dining scene. They are redefining ideas on what constitutes 'good food' and have made their way through the Guide's ratings at an electric pace. Twenty-five years ago *The Good Food Guide* coined the phrase 'Modern British' cooking to describe a revolution taking place in kitchens across the UK; a revolution this generation of chefs grew up with. They have built on the themes of that movement which were spelled out in the 1987 edition: regionality; the produce market; relishes and spices; tradition.

At the very top, change is being brought about by the passionate commitment of a highly individual group of chefs.

But while chefs including Simon Rogan, Sat Bains, Jason Atherton, Nathan Outlaw and even that honorary Englishman Claude Bosi, can be seen as a collective, each chef's outlook is unique and their style of cooking is hard to pigeonhole. Some have brought their Modern British cooking closer to its immediate environment, using fiercely regional, native ingredients to fantastic effect; others take a Google Earth approach, sourcing the very best produce from home and European markets. The bottom line – the common ground – lies in the exploration of quality produce through classical skills and modern methods: it is the vividness of the imagination displayed by each chef that is so exciting.

Gastropub RIP…

It's the time of the pub, again, and 'gastropub' is no longer a fitting description – from this edition we will no longer use the word. As a catch-all it was frequently synonymous with restaurant ambitions: 'Have you booked?' is not the sort of greeting you expect in a pub. The ongoing recession is hitting pubs hard, and they can no longer afford to ignore drinkers or diners looking for flexible eating options and value for money. It's time for a return to good old-fashioned hospitality; and what better words to express those values than 'pub' and 'inn'.

We are seeing a plethora of pubs actively courting drinkers with the welcome return of the bar snack, especially where pork pies, Scotch eggs and pork scratchings are made in house. Good-value lunches respect tradition and quality, with time-honoured British classics such as meat pies, sausages, and ham and eggs. In the evening, chefs let loose with more ambitious dishes.

And in an intriguing twist to the pub revolution, those pubs that have been influenced so strongly by the influx of successful restaurateurs into the business are now, in their turn, influencing restaurants. Traditional dishes, so ingrained in the British taste, have taken the reverse path from pub to restaurant: a mini shepherd's pie accompanying a prime lamb cut; a new way of looking at the gammon and pineapple theme; variations on the burger; even pork scratchings make an acceptable nibble with drinks in smart restaurants.

Over to you...

Back in austere, post-war Britain, Raymond Postgate's aim was to help those who wanted to find places serving half-decent food. Now we have lots of choice, and lots more very decent places to eat – and we need more help than ever in finding them. In buying and using the Guide you are supporting its aim to improve standards of food and service; for this is a book to be used and, overall, enjoyed. We hope you take great pleasure in the restaurants featured in it, and that you will find time to tell us about your experiences. If you would like to contribute, please log on to: www.thegoodfoodguide.co.uk. We collect, read and count every piece of feedback – and we may well use some of your recommendations in next year's edition. Until then, happy eating.

Elizabeth Carter, Consultant Editor

Editors' Awards

Every year *The Good Food Guide* team recognises excellence across the restaurant industry with its Editors' Awards. For the 2012 edition, the team is delighted to confer the following awards:

Best New Entry 2012
Pollen Street Social, London

Pub of the Year
The Duke of Cumberland Arms, Henley, West Sussex

Wine List of the Year
ramsons, Ramsbottom, Greater Manchester

Chef of the Year
Angela Hartnett, Murano, London

Up-and-Coming Chef of the Year
Paul Foster, Tuddenham Mill, Tuddenham, Suffolk

Fish Restaurant of the Year
Café Fish, Isle of Mull, Scotland

Best Value for Money
Kitchen, Sheffield, Yorkshire

Alfresco Restaurant of the Year
Vineyard Café, Ashprington, Devon

1

2

3

4

5

6

7

8

9

10

Readers' Awards

The Good Food Guide has always championed excellence and good service at restaurants throughout the UK. The Good Food Guide Readers' Restaurant of the Year award, run annually in the spring, is a chance for our readers to nominate their favourite local eatery, with the criteria that restaurants should offer regional produce where possible, are independently run and consistently deliver top-notch service. The Awards attracted thousands of nominations via our online feedback form (www.thegoodfoodguide.co.uk/feedback) and by post. From the shortlist of regional winners, The Good Food Guide team picked an overall Restaurant of the Year. This year the winner was Orwells in Shiplake, and their award was presented by our 2011 Lifetime Achievement recipient, Raymond Blanc.

The Readers' Restaurant of the Year 2012
Orwells, Shiplake

1. WALES - Cwtch, Pembrokeshire
2. EAST ENGLAND - Roger Hickman's, Norwich
3. LONDON - Retro Bistrot, Teddington
4. SOUTH EAST - Orwells, Shiplake
5. SOUTH WEST - The Mill Tea & Dining Room, Lyme Regis
6. MIDLANDS - Edmunds, Birmingham
7. NORTHERN IRELAND - Molly's Yard, Belfast
8. NORTH EAST - Salvo's, Leeds
9. NORTH WEST - Spire, Liverpool
10. SCOTLAND - Ondine, Edinburgh

Longest-serving restaurants

The Good Food Guide was founded in 1951. The following restaurants have appeared consistently since their first entry into the Guide.

The Connaught, London, 59 years
Gravetye Manor, East Grinstead, 55 years
Porth Tocyn Hotel, Abersoch, 55 years
Sharrow Bay, Ullswater, 51 years
Le Gavroche, London, 42 years
The Capital, London, 41 years
The Hungry Monk, Jevington, 41 years
Ubiquitous Chip, Glasgow, 40 years
Plumber Manor, Sturminster Newton, 39 years
The Druidstone, Broad Haven, 39 years
The Waterside Inn, Bray, 39 years
Isle of Eriska Hotel, Isle of Eriska, 38 years
Airds Hotel, Port Appin, 36 years
Farlam Hall, Brampton, 35 years
Corse Lawn House Hotel, Corse Lawn, 33 years
Hambleton Hall, Hambleton, 33 years
The Pier at Harwich, Harbourside Restaurant, Harwich, 33 years
Grafton Manor, Bromsgrove, 32 years
Magpie Café, Whitby, 32 years
RSJ, London, 31 years
The Seafood Restaurant, Padstow, 31 years
The Sir Charles Napier, Chinnor, 31 years
Kalpna, Edinburgh, 30 years
Le Caprice, London, 30 years
Little Barwick House, Barwick, 30 years
Inverlochy Castle, Fort William, 29 years
Ostlers Close, Cupar, 29 years
The Cellar, Anstruther, 28 years
Brilliant, London, 27 years
Clarke's, London, 27 years
Le Manoir aux Quat'Saisons, Great Milton, 27 years
Roade House, Roade, 27 years
Blostin's, Shepton Mallet, 26 years
Read's, Faversham, 26 years
The Castle at Taunton, Taunton, 26 years
The Three Chimneys, Isle of Skye, 26 years
Wallett's Court, St Margaret's-at-Cliffe, 26 years
Northcote, Langho, 25 years
ramsons, Ramsbottom, 25 years
Weavers, Haworth, 24 years
The Old Vicarage, Ridgeway, 24 years
Le Champignon Sauvage, Cheltenham, 23 years
Kensington Place, London, 23 years
Quince & Medlar, Cockermouth, 23 years
Silver Darling, Aberdeen, 23 years
Bibendum, London, 22 years
The Great House, Lavenham, 22 years
Ynyshir Hall, Eglwysfach, 22 years

Top 50 restaurants 2012

A placing within *The Good Food Guide's* Top 50 listing is greatly coveted by chefs and restaurateurs. This year, we have seen some changes at the top.

1. The Fat Duck, Berkshire (10)
2. L'Enclume, Cumbria (9)
3. Restaurant Sat Bains, Nottinghamshire (9)
4. Gordon Ramsay, Royal Hospital Road, London (9)
5. Restaurant Nathan Outlaw, Cornwall (8)
6. Le Manoir aux Quat'Saisons, Oxfordshire (8)
7. Marcus Wareing at the Berkeley, London (8)
8. Pollen Street Social, London (8)
9. Hibiscus, London (8)
10. The Square, London (8)
11. Le Champignon Sauvage, Gloucestershire (8)
12. Adam Simmonds at Danesfield House, Buckinghamshire (8)
13. Whatley Manor, The Dining Room, Wiltshire (8)
14. Le Gavroche, London (8)
15. Alain Ducasse at the Dorchester, London (8)
16. Restaurant Martin Wishart, Edinburgh (8)
17. The Ledbury, London (8)
18. The Waterside Inn, Berkshire (7)
19. Dinner by Heston Blumenthal, London (7)
20. Robert Thompson at the Hambrough, Isle of Wight (7)
21. Midsummer House, Cambridgeshire (7)
22. Murano, London (7)
23. John Campbell at Coworth Park, Berkshire (7)
24. Fraiche, Merseyside (7)
25. Gidleigh Park, Devon (7)
26. Bohemia, Jersey (7)
27. Fischer's Baslow Hall, Derbyshire (7)
28. The Crown at Whitebrook, Gwent (7)
29. The Pass, West Sussex (7)
30. Michael Wignall, the Latymer at Pennyhill Park Hotel, Surrey (7)
31. Hambleton Hall, Rutland (7)
32. The Old Vicarage, Derbyshire (7)
33. Andrew Fairlie at Gleneagles, Tayside (7)
34. Harry's Place, Lincolnshire (7)
35. The Kitchin, Edinburgh (6)
36. Tyddyn Llan, Denbighshire (6)
37. Artichoke, Buckinghamshire (6)
38. Purnell's, West Midlands (6)
39. Mr Underhill's, Shropshire (6)
40. The Hand & Flowers, Buckinghamshire (6)
41. Anthony's Restaurant, West Yorkshire (6)
42. The Greenhouse, London (6)
43. Simon Radley at the Chester Grosvenor, Cheshire (6)
44. The Sportsman, Kent (6)
45. The Creel, Orkney (6)
46. ramsons, Greater Manchester (6)
47. The Yorke Arms, Ramsgill, North Yorkshire (6)
48. Club Gascon, London (6)
49. The Royal Oak, Paley Street, Berkshire (6)
50. Galvin La Chapelle, London (6)

How to use the Guide

Each year *The Good Food Guide* is completely rewritten and compiled from scratch. Our research list is based on the huge volume of feedback we receive from readers; the list of many of our contributors at the back of the book is testimony to their dedication. This feedback, together with anonymous inspections, ensures that every entry is assessed afresh. To everyone who has used our feedback system (www.thegoodfoodguide.co.uk/feedback) over the last year, many thanks, and please keep the reports coming in.

Symbols

Restaurants that may be given Main Entry or Also Recommended status are contacted ahead of publication and asked to provide key information about their opening hours and facilities. They are also invited to participate in the £5 voucher scheme. The symbols on these entries are based on this feedback from restaurants, and are intended for quick, at-a-glance identification. The wine bottle symbol is an accolade assigned by the Guide's team, based on their judgement of the wine list available.

 Accommodation is available.

 It is possible to have three courses (excluding wine) at the restaurant for less than £30.

 The restaurant has a separate vegetarian menu.

£5 OFF The restaurant is participating in our £5 voucher scheme. (Please see the vouchers at the end of the book for terms and conditions.)

 The restaurant has a wine list that our inspector and wine expert have deemed to be exceptional.

£XX The price indicated on each review represents the average price of a three-course dinner, excluding wine.

Scoring

We believe that the restaurants included in *The Good Food Guide* are the very best in the UK; this means that a score of 1 is a significant achievement.

We reject many restaurants during the compilation of the Guide. Obviously, there are always subjective aspects to rating systems, but our inspectors are equipped with extensive scoring guidelines, so that restaurant bench-marking around the UK is accurate. We also take into account the reader feedback that we receive for each restaurant, so that any given review is based on several meals.

- 1/10 Capable cooking, with simple food combinations and clear flavours, but some inconsistencies.
- 2/10 Decent cooking, displaying good basic technical skills and interesting combinations and flavours. Occasional inconsistencies.
- 3/10 Good cooking, showing sound technical skills and using quality ingredients.
- 4/10 Dedicated, focused approach to cooking; good classical skills and high-quality ingredients.
- 5/10 Exact cooking techniques and a degree of ambition; showing balance and depth of flavour in dishes, while using quality ingredients.
- 6/10 Exemplary cooking skills, innovative ideas, impeccable ingredients and an element of excitement.
- 7/10 High level of ambition and individuality, attention to the smallest detail, accurate and vibrant dishes.
- 8/10 A kitchen cooking close to or at the top of its game – highly individual, showing faultless technique and impressive artistry in dishes that are perfectly balanced for flavour, combination and texture. There is little room for disappointment here.
- 9/10 This mark is for cooking that has reached a pinnacle of achievement, making it a hugely memorable experience for the diner.
- 10/10 It is extremely rare that a restaurant can achieve perfect dishes on a consistent basis.

You will notice that not all restaurants are scored: Also Recommended reviews are not scored but are worth a visit. Readers Recommend reviews are supplied by readers. These entries are the local, up-and-coming places to watch and represent the voice of our thousands of loyal followers.

London Explained

London is split into six regions: Central, North, East, South, West and Greater. Restaurants within each region are listed alphabetically. Each Main Entry and Also Recommended entry has a map reference.

The lists below are a guide to the areas covered in each region.

London — Central

Belgravia, Bloomsbury, Covent Garden, Fitzrovia, Green Park, Haymarket, Holborn, Hyde Park, Lancaster Gate, Leicester Square, Marble Arch, Marylebone, Mayfair, Oxford Circus, Piccadilly, Soho, Trafalgar Square, Westminster

London — North

Archway, Belsize Park, Camden, Euston, Golders Green, Hampstead, Islington, Kentish Town, King's Cross, Primrose Hill, Stoke Newington, Swiss Cottage, Willesden

London — East

Arnold Circus, Barbican, Bethnal Green, Blackfriars, Canary Wharf, City, Clerkenwell, Dalston, Farringdon, Moorgate, St Paul's, Shoreditch, Spitalfields, Tower Hill, Wapping, Whitechapel

London — South

Balham, Bankside, Battersea, Bermondsey, Blackheath, Brixton, Clapham, East Dulwich, Elephant and Castle, Forest Hill, Greenwich, Putney, South Bank, Southwark, Tooting, Wandsworth, Wimbledon

London — West

Belgravia, Chelsea, Chiswick, Earl's Court, Ealing, Fulham, Hammersmith, Kensal Rise, Kensington, Knightsbridge, Notting Hill, Paddington, Pimlico, Shepherd's Bush, South Kensington

London — Greater

Barnes, Croydon, Crystal Palace, East Sheen, Gants Hill, Harrow-on-the-Hill, Kew, Richmond, Southall, Teddington, Sutton, Twickenham, Wood Green, Walthamstow

LONDON

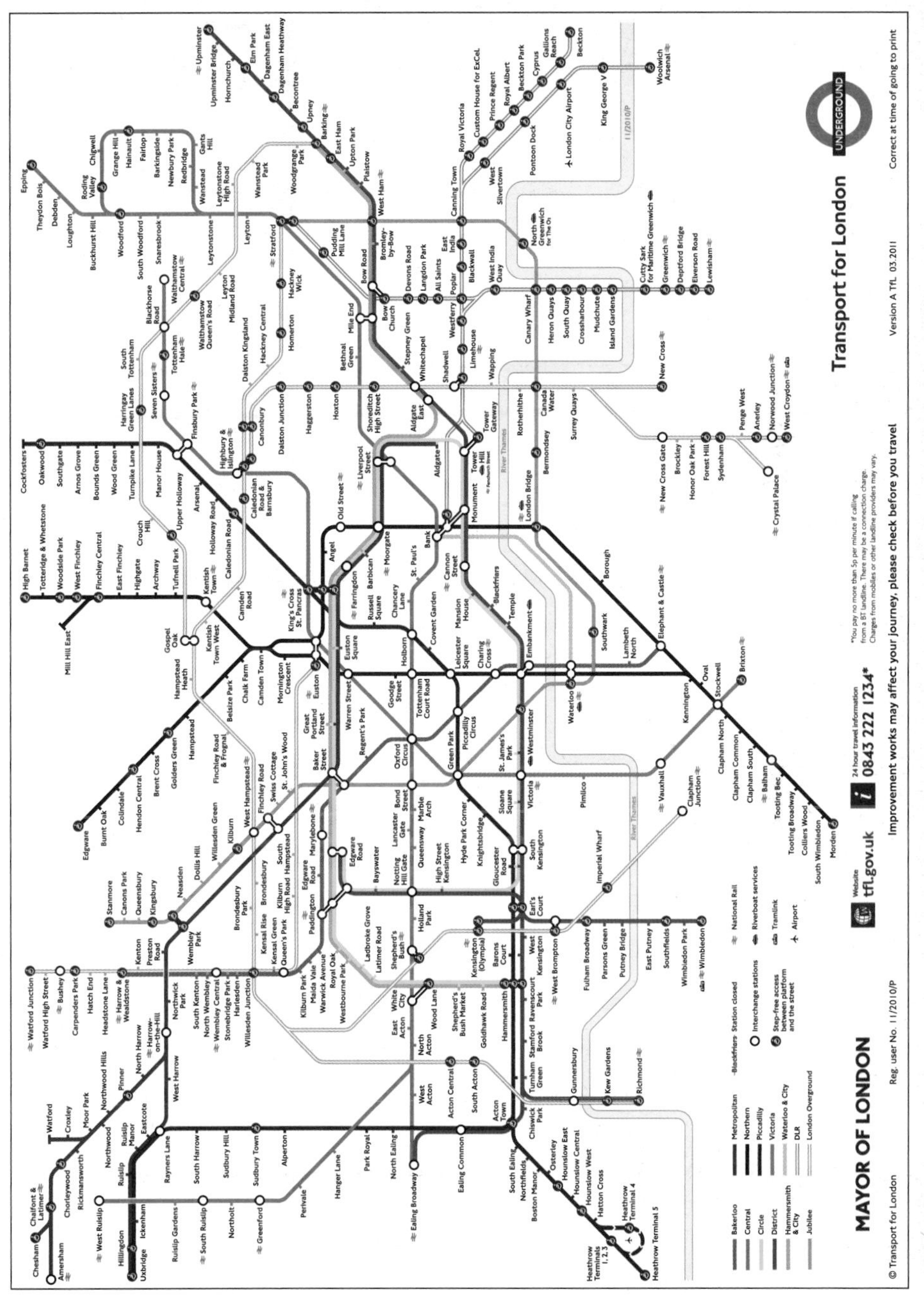
Transport for London
UNDERGROUND
MAYOR OF LONDON
tfl.gov.uk
24 hour travel information
0843 222 1234*
Improvement works may affect your journey, please check before you travel
Version A TfL 03.2011
Correct at time of going to print
Reg. user No. 11/2010/P
© Transport for London

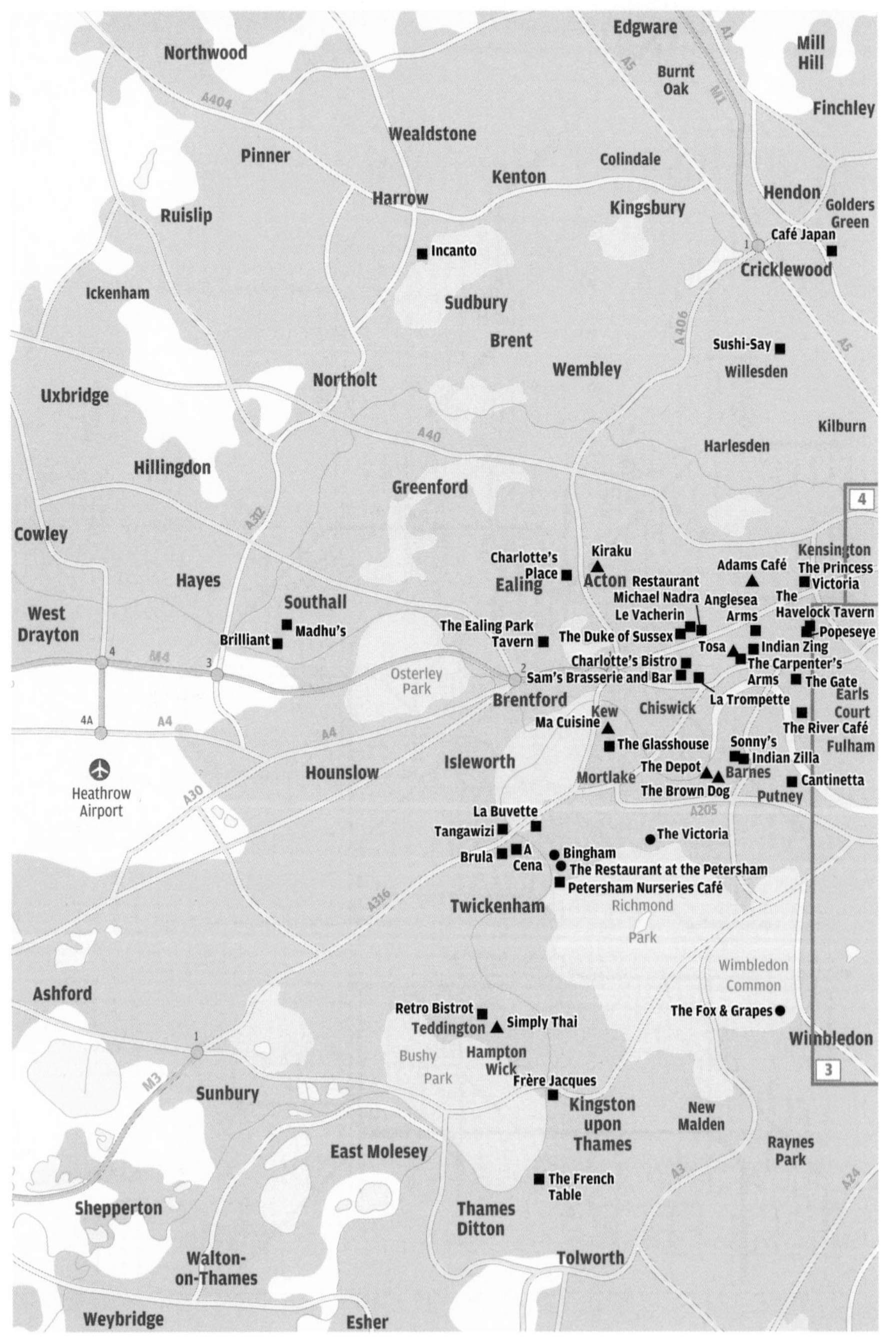
Northwood
Edgware
Burnt Oak
Mill Hill
Finchley
Pinner
Wealdstone
Colindale
Kenton
Harrow
Kingsbury
Hendon
Golders Green
Ruislip
Café Japan
Incanto
Cricklewood
Ickenham
Sudbury
Brent
Sushi-Say
Wembley
Willesden
Uxbridge
Northolt
Kilburn
Harlesden
Hillingdon
Greenford
Cowley
Charlotte's Place
Kiraku
Kensington
Adams Café
The Princess Victoria
Hayes
Ealing
Acton
Restaurant Michael Nadra
Anglesea Arms
The Havelock Tavern
West Drayton
Southall
Le Vacherin
Madhu's
Brilliant
The Ealing Park Tavern
The Duke of Sussex
Popeseye
Tosa
Indian Zing
Charlotte's Bistro
The Carpenter's Arms
Osterley Park
Sam's Brasserie and Bar
The Gate
Brentford
Chiswick
La Trompette
Earls Court
Kew
Ma Cuisine
The River Café
Heathrow Airport
The Glasshouse
Sonny's
Fulham
Isleworth
Indian Zilla
Hounslow
The Depot
Mortlake
Barnes
Cantinetta
The Brown Dog
Putney
La Buvette
Tangawizi
The Victoria
Brula
A Cena
Bingham
The Restaurant at the Petersham
Petersham Nurseries Café
Twickenham
Richmond Park
Wimbledon Common
Ashford
Retro Bistrot
The Fox & Grapes
Teddington
Simply Thai
Wimbledon
Bushy Park
Hampton Wick
Frère Jacques
Sunbury
Kingston upon Thames
New Malden
East Molesey
Raynes Park
The French Table
Shepperton
Thames Ditton
Walton-on-Thames
Tolworth
Weybridge
Esher

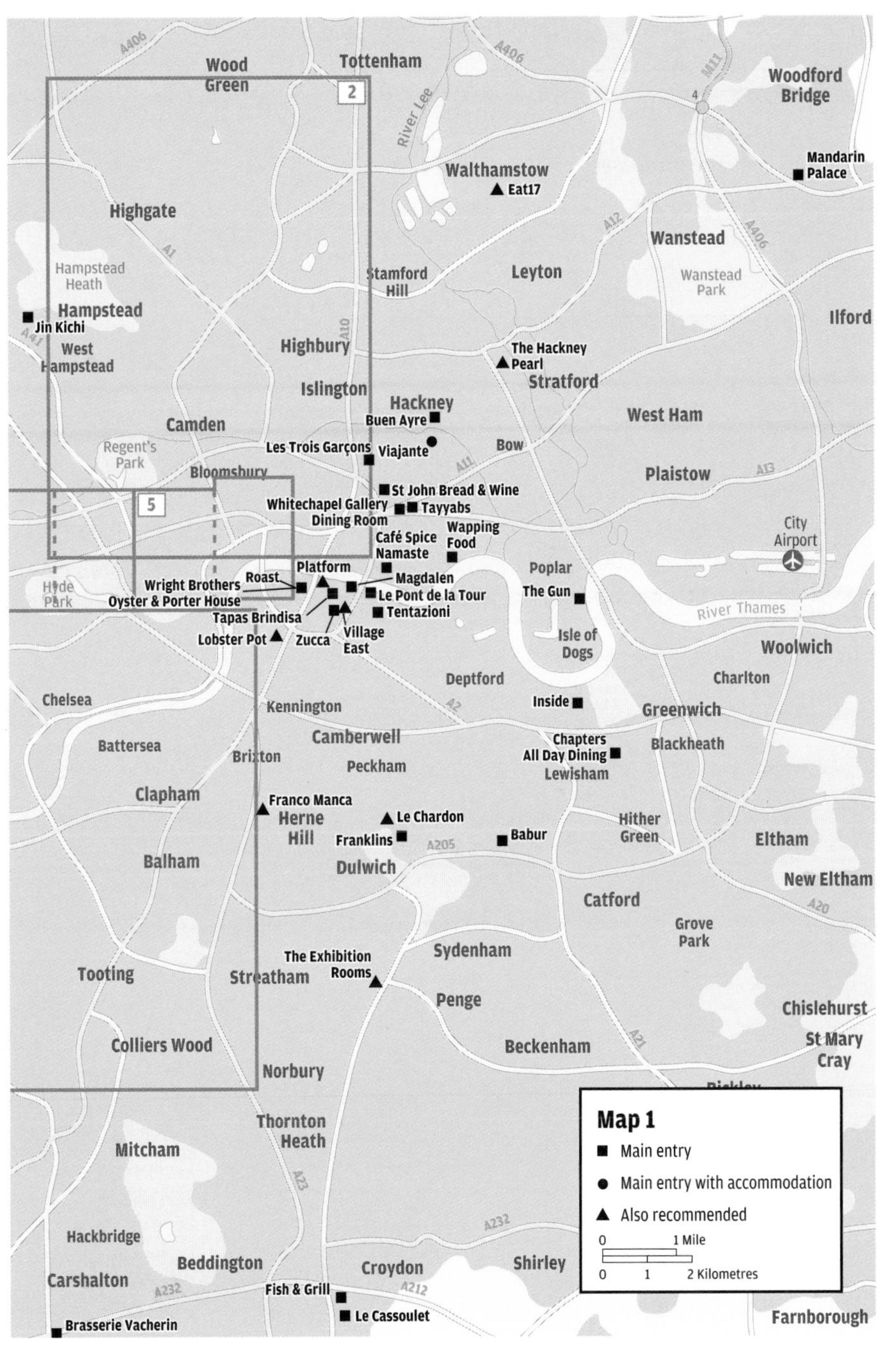
Wood Green
Tottenham
Woodford Bridge
Mandarin Palace
Walthamstow
Eat17
Highgate
Wanstead
Wanstead Park
Hampstead Heath
Stamford Hill
Leyton
Hampstead
Jin Kichi
West Hampstead
Ilford
Highbury
The Hackney Pearl
Stratford
Islington
Hackney
Buen Ayre
Camden
West Ham
Regent's Park
Les Trois Garçons
Viajante
Bow
Bloomsbury
Plaistow
St John Bread & Wine
Whitechapel Gallery Dining Room
Tayyabs
Wapping Food
Café Spice Namaste
City Airport
Platform
Poplar
Roast
Magdalen
Hyde Park
Wright Brothers
Oyster & Porter House
Le Pont de la Tour
The Gun
Tapas Brindisa
Tentazioni
River Thames
Lobster Pot
Zucca
Village East
Isle of Dogs
Woolwich
Deptford
Charlton
Chelsea
Inside
Kennington
Greenwich
Battersea
Camberwell
Chapters All Day Dining
Blackheath
Brixton
Peckham
Lewisham
Clapham
Franco Manca
Herne Hill
Le Chardon
Hither Green
Franklins
Babur
Eltham
Balham
Dulwich
New Eltham
Catford
Grove Park
The Exhibition Rooms
Sydenham
Tooting
Streatham
Penge
Chislehurst
Colliers Wood
Beckenham
St Mary Cray
Norbury
Thornton Heath
Mitcham
Hackbridge
Beddington
Croydon
Shirley
Carshalton
Fish & Grill
Le Cassoulet
Farnborough
Brasserie Vacherin
Map 1
Main entry
Main entry with accommodation
Also recommended
0 1 Mile
0 1 2 Kilometres

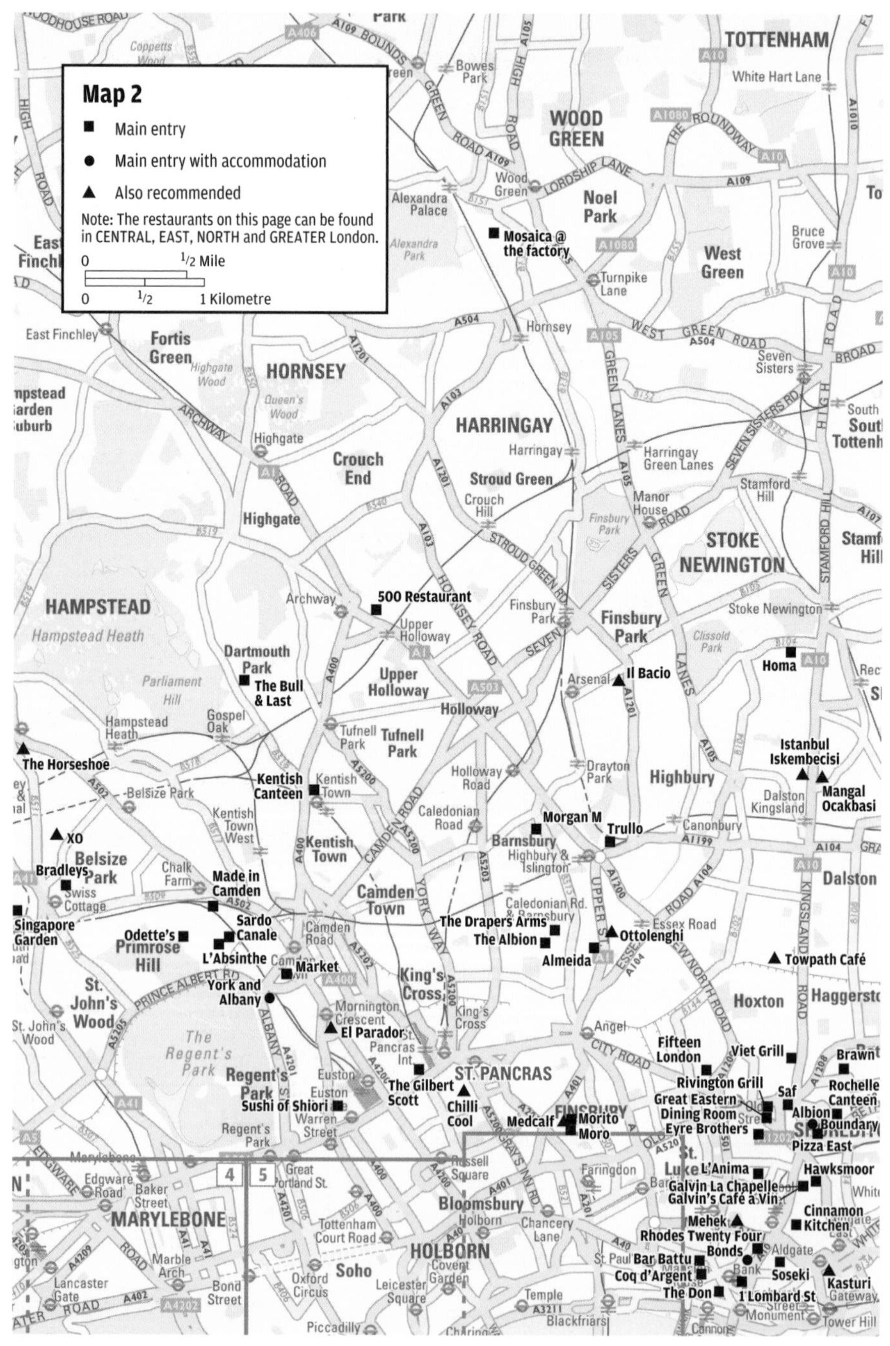
Map 2
Main entry
Main entry with accommodation
Also recommended
Note: The restaurants on this page can be found in CENTRAL, EAST, NORTH and GREATER London.
0 1/2 Mile
0 1/2 1 Kilometre
Mosaica @ the factory
500 Restaurant
The Bull & Last
Il Bacio
Homa
The Horseshoe
Istanbul Iskembecisi
Mangal Ocakbasi
Kentish Canteen
XO
Bradleys
Morgan M
Trullo
Made in Camden
Singapore Garden
Sardo Canale
Odette's
L'Absinthe
Market
The Drapers Arms
The Albion
Almeida
Ottolenghi
Towpath Café
York and Albany
El Parador
Fifteen London
Viet Grill
Brawn
The Gilbert Scott
Chilli Cool
Rivington Grill
Saf
Rochelle Canteen
Sushi of Shiori
Great Eastern Dining Room
Albion
Boundary
Medcalf
Morito
Moro
Eyre Brothers
Pizza East
L'Anima
Hawksmoor
Galvin La Chapelle
Galvin's Café a Vin
Mehek
Cinnamon Kitchen
Rhodes Twenty Four
Bonds
Bar Battu
Coq d'Argent
Soseki
Kasturi
The Don
1 Lombard St
HAMPSTEAD
HORNSEY
HARRINGAY
WOOD GREEN
TOTTENHAM
STOKE NEWINGTON
MARYLEBONE
HOLBORN
ST. PANCRAS
Highbury
Hoxton
Dalston
Camden Town
King's Cross
Regent's Park
Soho
Bloomsbury

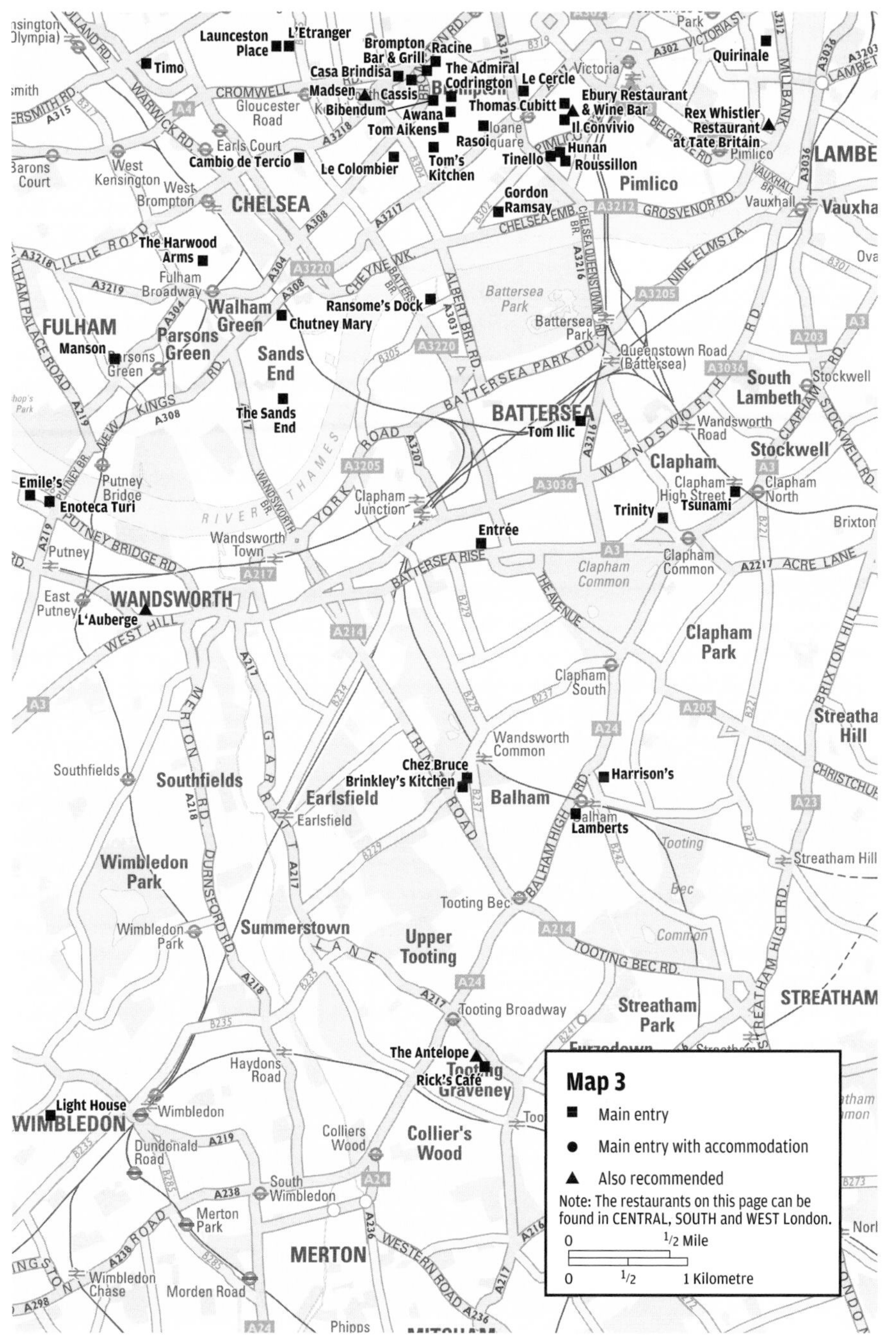
Launceston Place
L'Etranger
Brompton Bar & Grill
Racine
Timo
Casa Brindisa
The Admiral Codrington
Le Cercle
Madsen
Cassis
Bibendum
Awana
Thomas Cubitt
Ebury Restaurant & Wine Bar
Il Convivio
Quirinale
Rex Whistler Restaurant at Tate Britain
Tom Aikens
Rasoi
Hunan
Tinello
Roussillon
Cambio de Tercio
Le Colombier
Tom's Kitchen
Gordon Ramsay
The Harwood Arms
Ransome's Dock
Chutney Mary
Manson
The Sands End
Tom Ilic
Emile's
Enoteca Turi
Trinity
Tsunami
Entrée
L'Auberge
Chez Bruce
Brinkley's Kitchen
Harrison's
Lamberts
The Antelope
Rick's Café
Light House
CHELSEA
FULHAM
Walham Green
Parsons Green
Sands End
Pimlico
BATTERSEA
South Lambeth
Stockwell
Clapham
Clapham Park
WANDSWORTH
Southfields
Earlsfield
Balham
Wimbledon Park
Summerstown
Upper Tooting
Streatham Park
STREATHAM
Tooting Graveney
Collier's Wood
WIMBLEDON
MERTON
RIVER THAMES
Battersea Park
Clapham Common
Map 3
Main entry
Main entry with accommodation
Also recommended
Note: The restaurants on this page can be found in CENTRAL, SOUTH and WEST London.
0 1/2 Mile
0 1/2 1 Kilometre

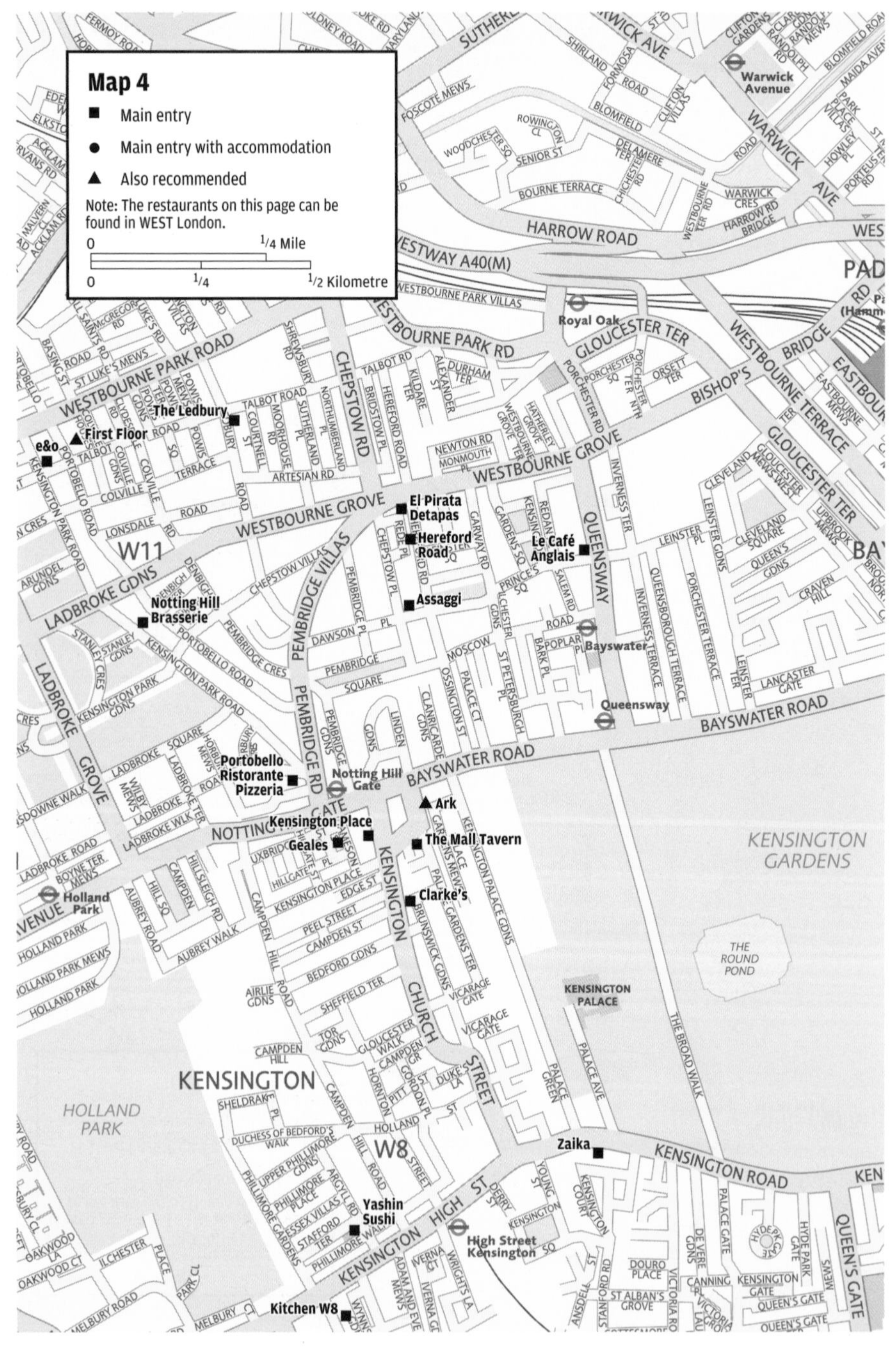

Map 4
Main entry
Main entry with accommodation
Also recommended
Note: The restaurants on this page can be found in WEST London.
0
1/4 Mile
0
1/4
1/2 Kilometre
The Ledbury
First Floor
e&o
El Pirata Detapas
Hereford Road
Le Café Anglais
Assaggi
Notting Hill Brasserie
Portobello Ristorante Pizzeria
Notting Hill Gate
Ark
Kensington Place
Geales
The Mall Tavern
Clarke's
Holland Park
Zaika
Yashin Sushi
High Street Kensington
Kitchen W8
Warwick Avenue
Royal Oak
Bayswater
Queensway
W11
W8
KENSINGTON
HOLLAND PARK
KENSINGTON GARDENS
THE ROUND POND
KENSINGTON PALACE
HARROW ROAD
WESTWAY A40(M)
WESTBOURNE GROVE
WESTBOURNE PARK ROAD
BAYSWATER ROAD
KENSINGTON ROAD
KENSINGTON HIGH ST
KENSINGTON CHURCH STREET
QUEENSWAY
LADBROKE GROVE
PEMBRIDGE VILLAS
CHEPSTOW RD

Note: The restaurants on this page can be found in CENTRAL and WEST London.

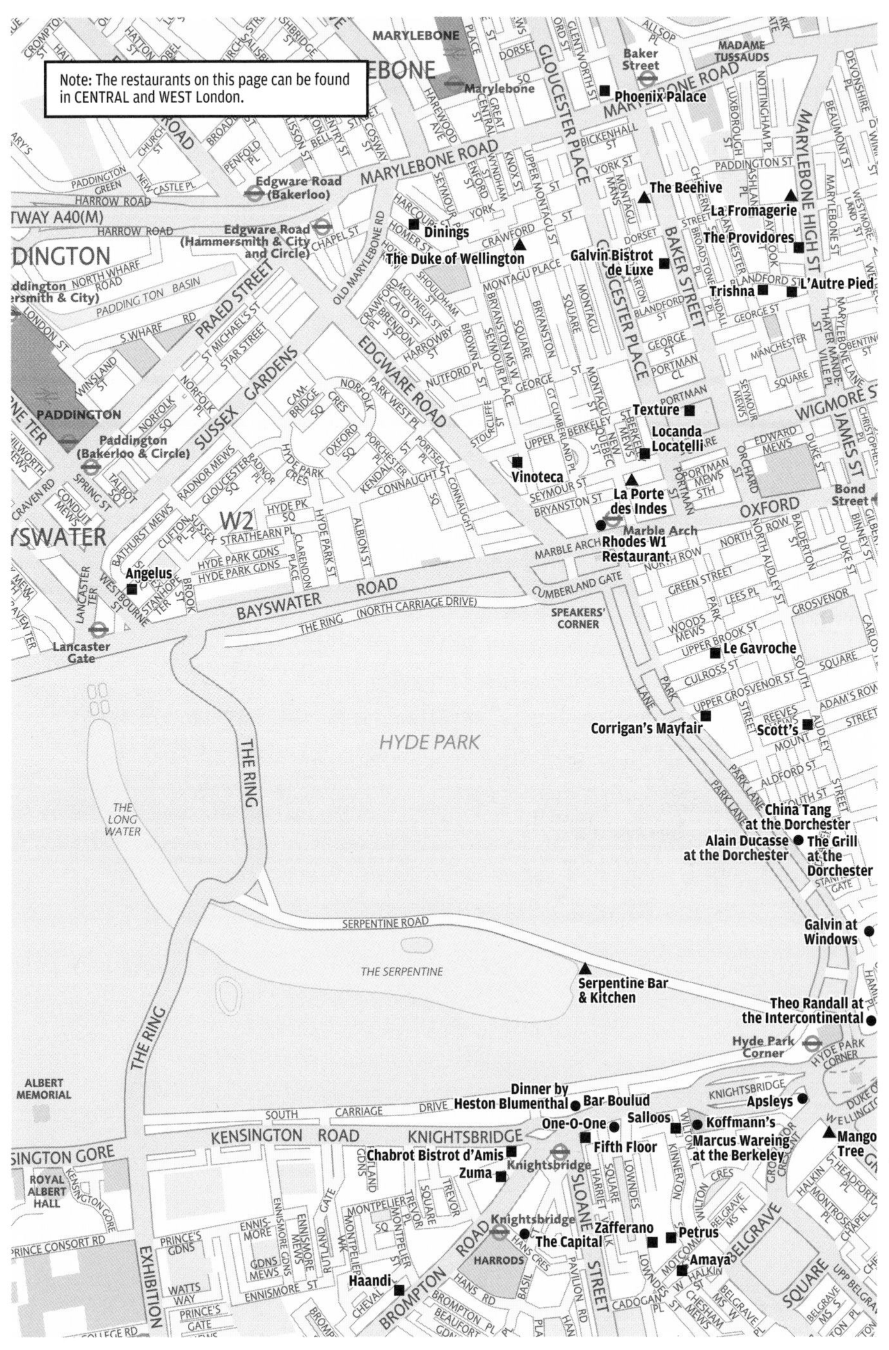

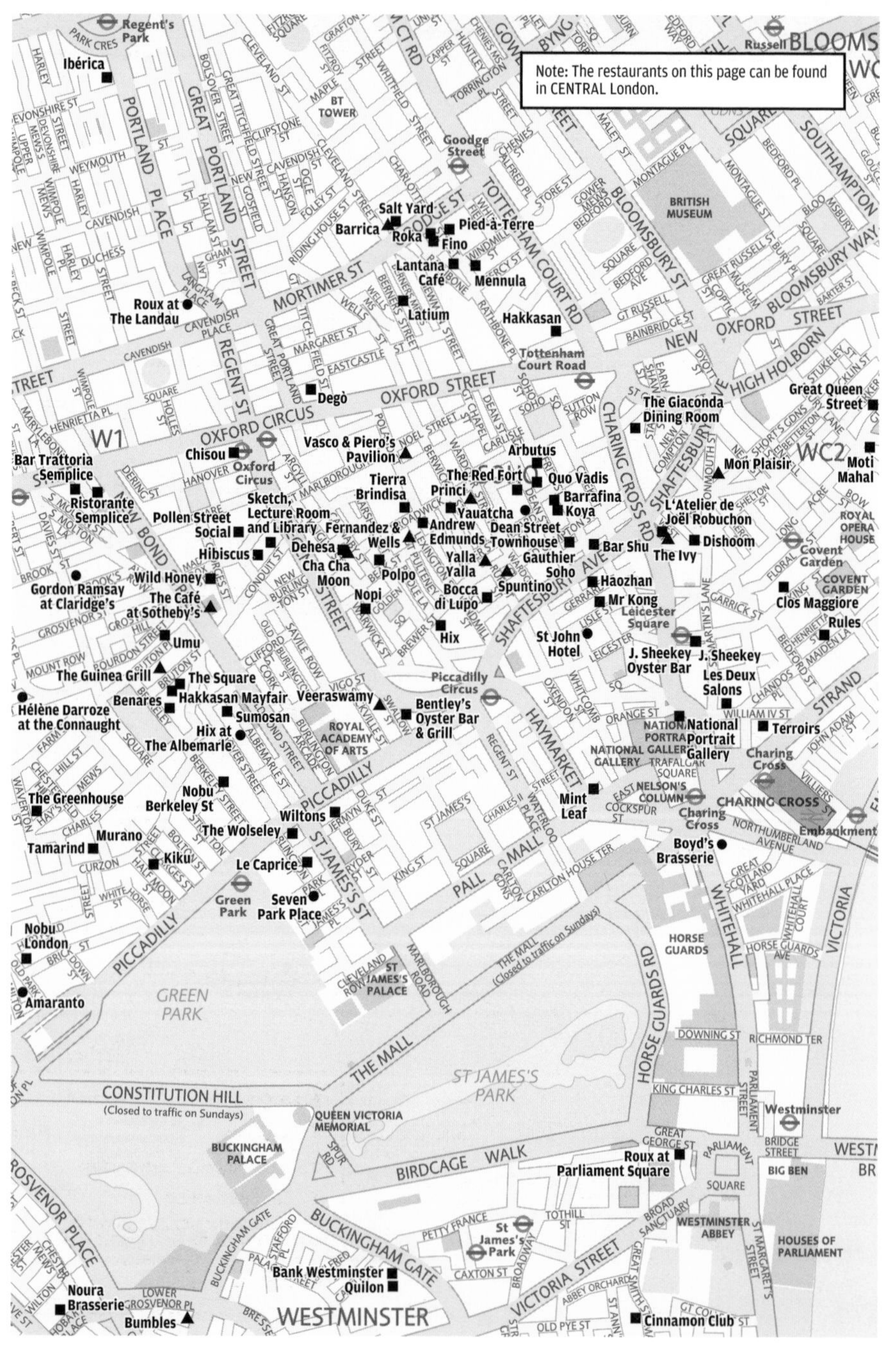
Note: The restaurants on this page can be found in CENTRAL London.
Regent's Park
Ibérica
BT TOWER
Goodge Street
BRITISH MUSEUM
Salt Yard
Barrica
Roka
Pied-à-Terre
Fino
Lantana Café
Mennula
Roux at The Landau
Latium
Hakkasan
Tottenham Court Road
Dego
The Giaconda Dining Room
Great Queen Street
W1
WC2
Oxford Circus
Chisou
Vasco & Piero's Pavilion
Arbutus
Bar Trattoria Semplice
Ristorante Semplice
Tierra Brindisa
The Red Fort
Quo Vadis
Mon Plaisir
Moti Mahal
Pollen Street Social
Sketch, Lecture Room and Library
Princi
Barrafina
Koya
L'Atelier de Joël Robuchon
Yauatcha
Fernandez & Wells
Andrew Edmunds
Dean Street Townhouse
Bar Shu
Dishoom
Hibiscus
Dehesa
Cha Cha Moon
Polpo
Yalla Yalla
Gauthier Soho
The Ivy
Covent Garden
ROYAL OPERA HOUSE
Gordon Ramsay at Claridge's
Wild Honey
Spuntino
Haozhan
Bocca di Lupo
Nopi
Mr Kong
The Café at Sotheby's
Leicester Square
Clos Maggiore
Rules
Umu
Hix
St John Hotel
J. Sheekey Oyster Bar
J. Sheekey
The Guinea Grill
The Square
Les Deux Salons
Benares
Hakkasan Mayfair
Veeraswamy
Piccadilly Circus
Bentley's Oyster Bar & Grill
Hélène Darroze at the Connaught
Sumosan
ROYAL ACADEMY OF ARTS
National Portrait Gallery
NATIONAL GALLERY
Terroirs
Hix at The Albemarle
TRAFALGAR SQUARE
Charing Cross
Nobu Berkeley St
NELSON'S COLUMN
Mint Leaf
CHARING CROSS
The Greenhouse
Wiltons
Embankment
The Wolseley
Murano
Tamarind
Boyd's Brasserie
Kiku
Le Caprice
Green Park
Seven Park Place
Nobu London
HORSE GUARDS
ST JAMES'S PALACE
GREEN PARK
Amaranto
THE MALL (Closed to traffic on Sundays)
ST JAMES'S PARK
CONSTITUTION HILL (Closed to traffic on Sundays)
QUEEN VICTORIA MEMORIAL
Westminster
BUCKINGHAM PALACE
BIRDCAGE WALK
Roux at Parliament Square
BIG BEN
St James's Park
WESTMINSTER ABBEY
HOUSES OF PARLIAMENT
Bank Westminster
Quilon
Noura Brasserie
Bumbles
WESTMINSTER
Cinnamon Club
OXFORD STREET
PICCADILLY
REGENT ST
HAYMARKET
PALL MALL
STRAND
WHITEHALL
VICTORIA STREET
BUCKINGHAM GATE
GROSVENOR PLACE
HORSE GUARDS RD
CHARING CROSS RD
SHAFTESBURY AVE
NEW OXFORD STREET
HIGH HOLBORN
TOTTENHAM COURT RD
GREAT PORTLAND STREET
PORTLAND PLACE
MORTIMER ST

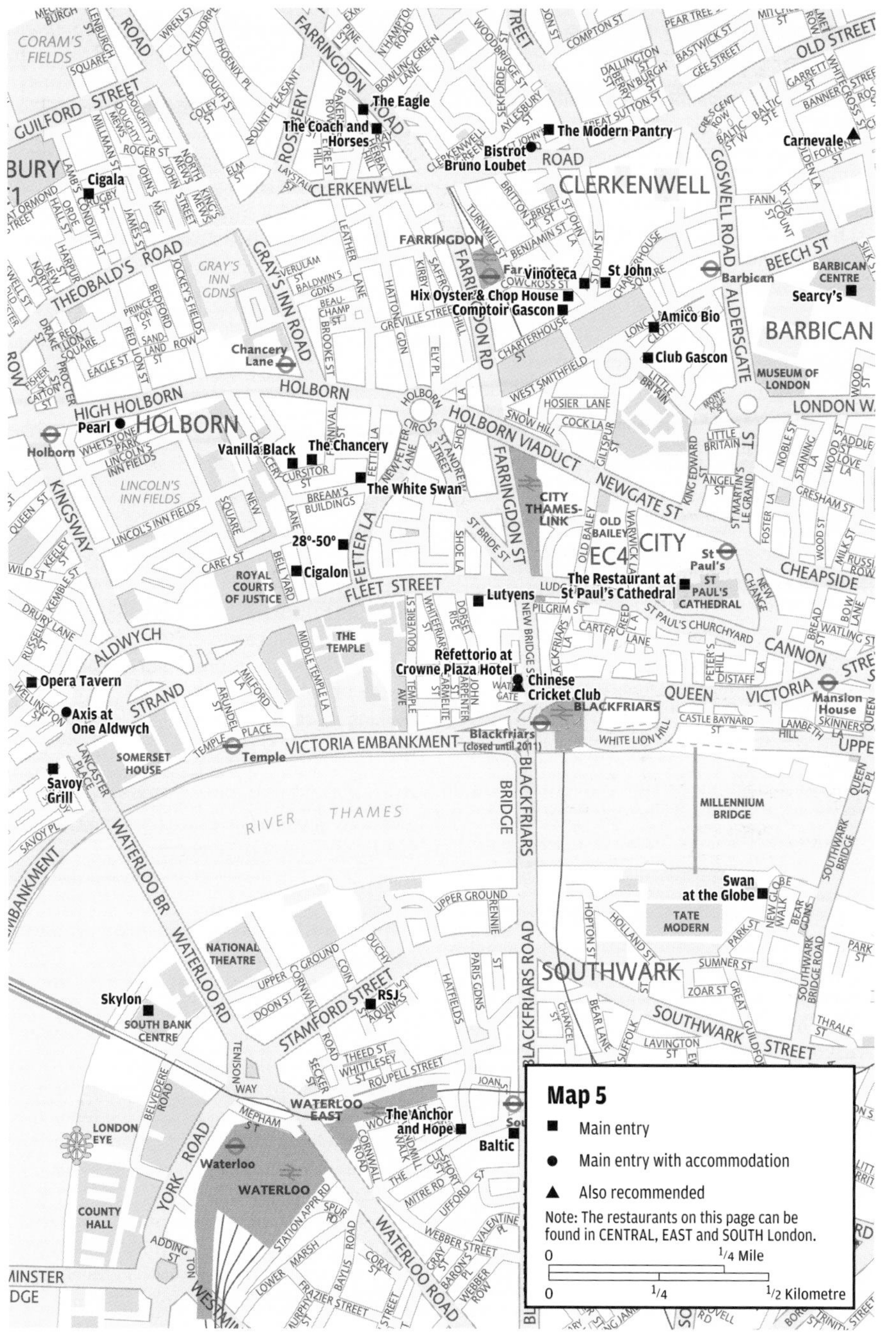
The Eagle
The Coach and Horses
The Modern Pantry
Bistrot Bruno Loubet
Carnevale
Cigala
CLERKENWELL
Vinoteca
St John
Hix Oyster & Chop House
Comptoir Gascon
Searcy's
Amico Bio
Club Gascon
BARBICAN
MUSEUM OF LONDON
Pearl
HOLBORN
Vanilla Black
The Chancery
The White Swan
28°-50°
Cigalon
CITY
EC4
The Restaurant at St Paul's Cathedral
ST PAUL'S CATHEDRAL
Lutyens
ROYAL COURTS OF JUSTICE
THE TEMPLE
Refettorio at Crowne Plaza Hotel
Chinese Cricket Club
BLACKFRIARS
Opera Tavern
Axis at One Aldwych
SOMERSET HOUSE
Savoy Grill
RIVER THAMES
MILLENNIUM BRIDGE
Swan at the Globe
TATE MODERN
NATIONAL THEATRE
SOUTHWARK
Skylon
SOUTH BANK CENTRE
RSJ
The Anchor and Hope
Baltic
LONDON EYE
COUNTY HALL
WATERLOO
Map 5
Main entry
Main entry with accommodation
Also recommended
Note: The restaurants on this page can be found in CENTRAL, EAST and SOUTH London.
0
1/4 Mile
0
1/4
1/2 Kilometre

Alain Ducasse at the Dorchester

Definitive gastronomic destination
The Dorchester Hotel, 53 Park Lane, Hyde Park, W1K 1QA
Tel no: (020) 7629 8866
www.alainducasse-dorchester.com
⊖ Hyde Park Corner, map 4
Modern French | £78
Cooking score: 8

V

The Dorchester lobby makes you think of an elongated Bedouin tent; stepping out of its Rococo extravagance, you then enter a world of beige contemporary conformity, hidden by a perforated shapeless screen, with a half-frosted extension area looking on to Park Lane at the front. Alain Ducasse has come in for some pointed criticism internationally in recent years, not all of it scrupulously fair. The operation here, headed by Jocelyn Herland, seems poised between a commitment to classical hauteur and modern demotic, neither quite the one nor the other, and often difficult – as many readers feel – to grasp. Consistency remains a bugbear. Impact might veer wildly within one meal, as was the verdict of the reporter who praised a superbly timed piece of richly sauced sea bass, and a definitive lime soufflé with fromage blanc sorbet, but found the lobster and shrimp ravoli in ginger consommé 'underseasoned and bitter'. At inspection a pork main plate featured a so-so piece of the fillet, some poorly rendered belly, fantastic black pudding, and a fascinating side dish of bits of ear and tongue. It lacked overall focus, but then there may be precisely cooked salmon with Swiss chard and a delightfully well-judged ponzu sauce. The 'lunch hour' deal, which includes a couple of glasses of wine, featured in May a pitch-perfect dish of Kentish lamb in an almost mulligatawny-like, Indian-spiced jus, with an underlay of farro risotto, the grains swollen to a delirious savoury intensity – a distinct upswing after a starter of a soft-boiled egg on a spoonful of lovely brandade. Breads and petits fours are amazing, the heap of peppery gougères a generous way of getting you started. Service is by a cast of thousands, professionally solicitous in all, but they need to wait for a pause in your conversation rather than invariably cutting in. The wine list is for other people, when even wines by the glass are all in double figures (from £11, bottles from £30), but the lunch selections are good.

Chef/s: Jocelyn Herland. **Open:** Tue to Fri L 12 to 2, Tue to Sat D 6.30 to 10. **Closed:** Sun, Mon, 26 to 30 Dec, 22 to 25 Apr, 8 to 31 Aug. **Meals:** Set L £50. Set D £78. Tasting menu £115 (8 courses) to £180. **Service:** 12.5% (optional). **Details:** Cards accepted. 82 seats. Wheelchair access. Music. Children allowed.

NEW ENTRY

Amaranto

Lavishly conceived Italian hybrid
Four Seasons Hotel, Hamilton Place, Park Lane, Mayfair, W1J 7DR
Tel no: (020) 7319 5206
www.fourseasons.com
⊖ Hyde Park Corner, Green Park, map 5
Italian | £40
Cooking score: 4

Amaranto's huge marble dining tables and generous personal space are testament to the fact this lavishly conceived restaurant/bar hybrid is in a five-star Mayfair hotel. But it's not all pomp and pomposity, thanks largely to helpful, unfussy service. The menu promises a fairly ambitious take on Italian cucina, and the chef is up to the task: a scallop platter, for example, includes the bivalve classically wrapped in pancetta alongside a tartare with blood orange and a carpaccio with tiny cubes of spiced potato, all set off by a winsome spoonful of carbonara sauce. Elsewhere, langoustines are paired with astonishingly light gnocchi and a shot of vibrant pesto, while mains might deliver a decent chunk of properly aged beef or spot-on fritto misto beautifully presented with hummus, lemons and capers. The Italian-accented wine list is suitably sumptuous, although just about everything is offered by the glass (from around £10). Don't miss cocktails in the sexy bar/salon or the chance of eating alfresco on Park Lane.

Chef/s: Davide Degiovanni. **Open:** all week L 11.30 to 2.30 (3 Sat and Sun), D 6.30 to 10.30. **Meals:** alc (main courses £10 to £30). Set L £19.50 (2 courses) to £26. **Service:** 15% (optional). **Details:** Cards accepted. 58 seats. 20 seats outside.

Andrew Edmunds

Good-value food and rocking wine
46 Lexington Street, Soho, W1F 0LW
Tel no: (020) 7437 5708
⊖ Oxford Circus, Piccadilly Circus, map 5
Modern European | £26
Cooking score: 2

There is every reason to keep this historic place in the Guide – with due warning. Although it's not presented in a modern way, the food is well bought, well cooked, has a strong feeling for seasonality and is reasonably priced. The warnings centre on service, which has been unusually shambolic of late. On the credit side, the dark, candlelit interior, with cramped seating upstairs and down, evokes another era, the menu is a sensible evolution of the traditional – ham hock persillade and celeriac rémoulade, Dorset crab spaghettini with tomato, rocket and chilli, vanilla cheesecake with berry compote – and the wine list rocks. Andrew Edmunds is a wine buff and his list offers a good variety at prices few would balk at. House selections start at £16.50.

Chef/s: Roberto Pieggesi. **Open:** all week L 12.30 to 3 (1 Sat, 1 to 3.30 Sun), D 6 to 10.45 (10.30 Sun). **Closed:** 24 Dec to 2 Jan, Easter. **Meals:** alc (main courses £10 to £19). **Service:** 12.5% (optional). **Details:** Cards accepted. 55 seats. 4 seats outside. No music. No mobile phones. Children allowed.

Angelus

Bells-and-whistles flavours of France
4 Bathurst Street, Lancaster Gate, W2 2SD
Tel no: (020) 7402 0083
www.angelusrestaurant.co.uk
⊖ Lancaster Gate, map 4
Modern French | £48
Cooking score: 4

'Fantastic', exclaimed one reader after dining at this suave modern French restaurant that's been shoehorned into a former pub. The quietly stylish interior makes much of the original Georgian fittings – fireplaces, dark panelling and stained glass are all in situ – and flexibility means that Angelus is a great local asset: a brunch menu is served all day (omelettes, steak baguette, assiette of charcuterie) alongside the carte. Top-drawer ingredients provide the backbone for immaculately produced dishes such as garlic and herb-crusted loin of lamb and confit shoulder lyonnaise served with crushed Jersey Royals, mint and niçoise vegetables. There are, of course, rich and indulgent notes to be seen, in a signature starter of foie gras crème brûlée with caramelised almonds and an impeccably made warm mint chocolate chip soufflé with chocolate sauce and mandarin sorbet. France is explored in depth on a wide-ranging list, with house wine £25.

Chef/s: Martin Nisbet. **Open:** all week 10am to 11pm (10pm Sun). **Closed:** 24 Dec to 3 Jan. **Meals:** alc (main courses £20 to £29). Set L £40. **Service:** 12.5% (optional). **Details:** Cards accepted. 40 seats. 12 seats outside. Separate bar. Wheelchair access. Music. Children allowed.

NEW ENTRY

Apsleys

Jaw-droppingly glamourous Italian

The Lanesborough, Hyde Park Corner, Hyde Park, SW1X 7TA

Tel no: (020) 7333 7254

www.lanesborough.com

⊖ Hyde Park Corner, map 4

Italian | £70

Cooking score: 6

V

The name above the door is that of Heinz Beck, one of Rome's finest chefs – and a reporter who has enjoyed Beck's sublime food in the Eternal City says 'his standards are met' by the kitchen at the Lanesborough outpost. The 'jaw-dropping glamour' of the room, with its modern chandeliers and glass atrium, is reflected in the jaw-dropping expense of the experience. The most economical way in is the monthly changing 'menu del giorno' [sic]. The Italian kitchen team creates 'superbly vibrant and authentic' modern Italian cuisine. Antipasti of fish crudo or warm seafood salad (the highlight of a conservative set menu) create the tone – elegant and light, just the way the jet set likes it. Pasta primi are among London's best; the carbonara fagottelli is quite unmissable. Suckling pig to follow, roast and braised, benefits from assured saucing and 'savoury notes like you will not believe'. Desserts such as classic rum baba are strongly praised, too. Service could be smoother (two 'good evening' greetings at lunchtime suggested staff on autocue) and the cheesy music is too vulgar for a dining experience that's anything but. The cheapest bottle is £30 on a list of big-hitting Italians and four-figure grands crus.

Chef/s: Massimiliano Blasone. **Open:** all week L 12.30 to 2.30, D 7 to 10.30. **Meals:** alc (main courses £29 to £38). Set L £25 (2 courses) to £ 35. Set D £65 (5 courses). **Service:** 12.5% (optional).
Details: Cards accepted. 100 seats. Separate bar. No mobile phones. Wheelchair access. Music. Children allowed. Car parking.

Arbutus

Unfettered modern food with style

63-64 Frith Street, Soho, W1D 3JW

Tel no: (020) 7734 4545

www.arbutusrestaurant.co.uk

⊖ Tottenham Court Road, map 5

Modern European | £35

Cooking score: 6

Manning the front line of British gastronomy, Arbutus has stuck to its guns and flourished triumphantly since launching in 2006. From the very start, founders Will Smith and Anthony Demetre bucked the trend, discarding tablecloths, reining in their prices and ditching the fripperies of 'fine dining' – but never compromising on quality. Whether you are sitting at one of the big box tables or perched at the American-style 'eating bar', the message is clear: this is unfettered modern food, 'red in tooth and claw', delivered with real style and bags of confidence. The daily menu mines a rich vein, allowing ingredients (lordly or otherwise) to shine through – be it braised pig's head with potato purée and caramelised onion ravioli or luscious beef tartare served on a mighty 'muffin' of sourdough bread. The squid and mackerel burger with zingy razor clams and sea purslane remains a 'brilliantly dressed' showpiece, melting beef bavette comes with a separate copper pot of oozing, buttery dauphinoise, and 'pieds et paquets' comprises two pieces of sheep's stomach, a little casserole of richly sauced tripe and a plate of toast topped with chopped trotters: 'I didn't know where to start', confessed one reader. As for dessert, few can resist the prospect of an oh-so-beautiful île flottante (the size of a 'hockey puck') with crunchy pink pralines and vanilla-flecked custard. The drinker-friendly wine list makes its own statement, with everything available by the 250ml carafe and bottles from £14.50.

Chef/s: Alan Christie. **Open:** all week L 12 to 2.30 (3 Sun), D 6 to 11 (11.30 Fri and Sat, 10.30 Sun). **Closed:** 25 and 26 Dec, 1 Jan. **Meals:** alc (main courses £15 to £20). Set L £16.95. Pre-theatre set D £18.95. **Service:** 12.5% (optional). **Details:** Cards accepted. 70 seats. No music. Children allowed.

L'Atelier de Joël Robuchon

Thoroughbred food from a super-chef
13-15 West Street, Covent Garden, WC2H 9NE
Tel no: (020) 7010 8600
www.joel-robuchon.com
⊖ Leicester Square, map 5
Modern French | £50
Cooking score: 6

V

Once past the discreet frontage, the sultry black of the ground-floor dining room, set off by bright reds and a living wall of greenery, may not be to everyone's taste, but it is undoubtedly impressive. The best seats are at the counter, looking straight into the open-plan kitchen, but if high bar stools don't appeal, there is a more conventional dining room on the first floor (similar menu, less atmosphere) as well as a top-floor bar. This is super-chef Joël Robuchon's thoroughbred world of contemporary French cuisine seen through highly original tasting plates. Flavours and balance are precisely considered, from fabulous langoustine fritters with basil pistou to a renowned combo of free-range quail stuffed with foie gras and served with those famed truffle-mashed potatoes – the latter as hard to bypass as the signature dish of beef and foie gras mini-burgers with lightly caramelised bell peppers, served with a tiny portion of crispy fries. For a more conventional three courses, the carte obliges with Scottish lobster salad 'à la minute', and pork ribs confit with mustard, spätzle, baby gem and onions, while 'visually stunning' desserts such as a pear, pistachio and vanilla-filled chocolate 'boule surprise' will simply amaze. As will the final bill. Service can be patchy, but is well-meaning. Wines from £28.
Chef/s: Olivier Limousin. **Open:** all week L 12 to 3, D 5.30 to 11 (10.30 Sun). **Closed:** 25 and 26 Dec, 1 Jan. **Meals:** alc (main courses £21 to £39). Set L and pre-theatre D £22 (2 courses) to £27. Tasting menu £125. **Service:** 12.5% (optional). **Details:** Cards accepted. 43 seats. Separate bar. Wheelchair access. Music. Children allowed. Car parking.

L'Autre Pied

Confident little Marylebone flyer
5-7 Blandford Street, Marylebone, W1U 3DB
Tel no: (020) 7486 9696
www.lautrepied.co.uk
⊖ Bond Street, map 4
Modern European | £40
new chef

V

Lauded as one of the classiest little eateries in the neighbourhood, L'Autre Pied has always scored highly with its confident, user-friendly style and tight-knit conviviality (think close-packed bare tables, silk panels and chinoiserie). It has also gained a reputation for bold contemporary food, intelligent ideas and sympathetic seasonal resonance: confit pork ravioli with white bean ragoût, Jerusalem artichoke and horseradish foam; fillet of hake with a summery assemblage of pea shoots, broad beans and lemon oil emulsion, and desserts such as poached pear and cinnamon mille-feuille with pear purée and acacia honey ice cream are typical of the house style. Head chef Marcus Eaves was due to step into Shane Osborn's shoes at Fitzrovia sibling Pied-à-Terre (see entry) as the Guide went to press, and the Blandford Street kitchen was being handed over to his deputy Andrew McFadden (a graduate of multi-gonged Restaurant Oud Sluis in the Netherlands). McFadden will no doubt put his own spin on things, although it's unlikely that the cooking will veer far from its current course. As for the wine list, expect a trustworthy selection from reputable sources across the globe, with prices from £25 (£5 a glass). Reports please.
Chef/s: Andrew McFadden. **Open:** all week L 12 to 2.45 (3.30 Sun), Mon to Sat D 6 to 10.45. **Closed:** 24 Dec to 2 Jan. **Meals:** alc (main courses £22 to £28). Set L and D £18.95 (2 courses) to £22.50. Sun L £29.50. Tasting menu £49.50 (5 courses) to £62 (8 courses). **Service:** 12.5% (optional). **Details:** Cards accepted. 51 seats. 9 seats outside. Music. Children allowed.

Axis at One Aldwych

Thrilling interiors and straight-talking food
1 Aldwych, Covent Garden, WC2B 4BZ
Tel no: (020) 7300 0300
www.onealdwych.com
⊖ Covent Garden, map 5
Modern British | £35
Cooking score: 2

Readers consider the pre-theatre menu at this radically designed, subterranean space beneath the One Aldwych hotel to be one of the better deals in town. There has been praise for 'beautiful' warm bread and for devilled chicken livers followed by beetroot risotto with whipped goats' cheese, honey, toasted walnuts and parsnip crisps that proved to be both 'tasty and light enough to allow sitting through a show after the meal'. Others arriving later to sample the carte have not fared so well, citing overcooked wood pigeon and 'poor service'. However, unfussy beef bourguignon and a simple, citrusy lemon tart are redeeming factors. Wines from £20.

Chef/s: Tony Fleming. **Open:** Tue to Fri L 12 to 2.30, Tue to Sat D 5.30 to 10.30 (5 Sat). **Closed:** Sun, Mon, 25 Dec. **Meals:** alc (main courses £14 to £36). Set L and D £16.75 (2 courses) to £19.75. **Service:** 12.5% (optional). **Details:** Cards accepted. 90 seats. Separate bar. Wheelchair access. Music. Children allowed.

Bank Westminster

Easy-eating brasserie food
45 Buckingham Gate, Westminster, SW1E 6BS
Tel no: (020) 7630 6644
www.bankrestaurants.com
⊖ St James's Park, map 5
Modern European | £40
Cooking score: 2

Set inside the Victorian pile that is the Crowne Plaza Hotel, overlooking a pretty courtyard and with enough glass and daylight to create a conservatory feel, Bank merrily continues as a long-standing fixture on the Westminster dining scene. Menus are long enough to ensure that most tastes are catered for. They show occasional inventive touches, but generally play it safe with a repertoire of broadly contemporary dishes. To start, there might be chilli squid with Thai noodle salad or mushroom risotto, followed by salmon fishcakes or lamb cutlets from the tandoor clay oven. House wine is £15.60.

Chef/s: David Ferguson. **Open:** Mon to Fri L 12 to 5, Mon to Sat D 5 to 11. **Closed:** Sun, 25 to 27 Dec, bank hols. **Meals:** alc (main courses £12 to £49). Set L and D £37.50 to £47.50. **Service:** 12.5% (optional). **Details:** Cards accepted. 170 seats. 18 seats outside. Separate bar. Wheelchair access. Music. Children allowed.

Bar Shu

Red-hot Szechuan trailblazer
28 Frith Street, Soho, W1D 5LF
Tel no: (020) 7287 8822
www.bar-shu.co.uk
⊖ Leicester Square, map 5
Chinese | £25
Cooking score: 4

Londoners are getting a taste for the red-hot thrills of Szechuan cooking, thanks in part to this trailblazing Soho restaurant spread over three floors. Conditions are pretty cramped inside, but home comforts aren't an issue once the food arrives. The cuisine is famed for its lip-tingling use of chillies and uncompromising way with body parts, although the pictures on Bar Shu's menu may settle any nerves before you order a plate of 'pepper-fragrant kidney slices' or 'pock-marked old woman's beancurd'. Szechuan is a landlocked province, but it also has a strong tradition of seafood cookery – witness sliced sea bass in a soup of pickled mustard greens or 'red robe' hairtail with whole garlic and shiitake mushrooms. Newcomers may find it all a bit scary, but the kitchen manages the X-rated flavours with admirable finesse and sensitivity. Special green-tea drinks soothe the palate; otherwise try the wine, from £20.90.

Bar Shu's sibling, Ba Shan is at 24 Romilly Street, while Baozi Inn at 25 Newport Court is perfect for an ultra-cheap fix.
Chef/s: Mr Xiao Zhong Zhang. **Open:** all week 12 to 11. **Closed:** 24 and 25 Dec. **Meals:** alc (main courses £9 to £29). **Service:** 12.5%. **Details:** Cards accepted. 100 seats. Wheelchair access. Music. Children allowed.

Bar Trattoria Semplice

Straightforward Italian home cooking
22-23 Woodstock Street, Mayfair, W1C 2AR
Tel no: (020) 7491 8638
www.bartrattoriasemplice.com
⊖ Bond Street, map 5
Italian | £27
Cooking score: 2

'Excellent food, well prepared and served', noted a visitor to this just-round-the-corner spin-off from Ristorante Semplice (see entry). Best described as a smart café that's 'pleasant, modern and comfortable', it makes a fitting background for some shrewdly sourced ingredients presented with the minimum of fuss. Dishes that have satisfied include grilled vegetables served with fried scamorza cheese, a seafood platter of scallops, squid and king prawns served with avocado and crème fraîche mousse, and 'delicately flavoured and decidedly al dente' fusilli teamed with Italian sausage and broccoli. The Italian wine list starts at £13.50.
Chef/s: Marco Torri. **Open:** all week L 12 to 3, D 6 to 10.30. **Closed:** 25 and 26 Dec, bank hols. **Meals:** alc (main courses £9 to £19). Set L £16.95 (2 courses) to £18.95. **Service:** 12.5%. **Details:** Cards accepted. 70 seats. 30 seats outside. Separate bar. Music. Children allowed.

Also recommended entries are not scored but we think they are worth a visit.

Barrafina

A tiny tapas treasure
54 Frith Street, Soho, W1D 4SL
Tel no: (020) 7813 8016
www.barrafina.co.uk
⊖ Tottenham Court Road, map 5
Spanish | £28
Cooking score: 4

Brothers Sam and Eddie Hart continue to keep the standards of London's Spanish food scene high with this postage-stamp of a tapas bar. It's perennially popular, so you'll need to arrive exceptionally early to avoid queuing, but once seated at the glossy L-shaped counter you'll realise it's worth the wait. Creamy ham croquetas and perky Padrón peppers showered with sea salt pique the interest ahead of plates of Ibérico ham – 'my personal highlight' notes a regular – large grilled prawns in garlic, the popular suckling pig, and lamb cutlets. Almondy Santiago tart proves 'a pleasing finale'. The menu could be updated a little more often: one fan noted 'there were a few specials, but I'm sure they were the same as on previous visits', but then conceded that 'everything is so good'. Cava, sherry and mainstream Spanish grape varieties dominate the wine list (from £19), with plenty of choice to complement the food.
Chef/s: Nieves Barragan Mohacho. **Open:** all week L 12 to 3 (1 to 3.30 Sun), D 5 to 11 (5.30 to 10 Sun). **Closed:** 25 and 26 Dec, 1 Jan, bank hols. **Meals:** alc (main courses £5 to £16). **Service:** 12.5% (optional). **Details:** Cards accepted. 23 seats. 12 seats outside. No music. Children allowed.

ALSO RECOMMENDED

▲ Barrica

62 Goodge Street, Fitzrovia, W1T 4NE
Tel no: (020) 7436 9448
⊖ Goodge Street, map 5
Spanish

The bar is buzzy, but tables towards the back of this long, narrow room are more sedate, and the tapas on offer is 'very tasty, with an interesting selection'. Ingredients are all, and are given centre-stage prominence in the likes of specially imported jamón Ibérico (acorn-fed hams from £6.75) or daily specials such as English asparagus with Manchego and olive oil (£5.95). Charcoal-grilled squid is simple but done well, and spinach with brown garlic and olive oil is 'moreish'. Service veers between friendly and brusque. House wine is £15. Closed Sun.

▲ The Beehive

126 Crawford Street, Marylebone, W1U 6BF
Tel no: (020) 7486 8037
www.thebeehive-pub.co.uk
⊖ Baker Street, map 4
British

Befitting its status as one of Marylebone's oldest hostelries, the Beehive exudes a real sense of tradition, still functioning firmly as a boozer for those just wanting a drink, with the added bonus of decent all-day food. Expect to find a mix of bistro and pub classics – mussels in white wine sauce (£8.90) and pork fillet with potato rösti and caramelised onion (£14.95) alongside fish and chips with tartare sauce or beef burger with bacon, cheese and fries. House wine is £15.90. Open all week.

Benares

Refined Indian cooking
12a Berkeley Square, Mayfair, W1J 6BS
Tel no: (020) 7629 8886
www.benaresrestaurant.com
⊖ Green Park, map 5
Indian | £55
Cooking score: 4

Upstairs on Berkeley Square, Atul Kochhar's luxurious bar and restaurant promises refined Indian cooking with the odd European detail. The room is windowless but classy, lined with banquettes and a cool white relief. Smooth, helpful service uses almost-discreet hand signals. To start there are tiny, feather-light poppadoms, then perhaps the favourite chicken tikka pie or a green mango and coconut soup. Wonderfully sour, its pleasures are mitigated by an unnecessary accompaniment of pasty corn cakes with pickled red cabbage. Reporters comment on a lightness of touch, which is certainly evident in the delicate sesame peanut sauce served with spiced roast venison, skilfully cooked with a cumin and coriander crust and served with a matching biriyani. Dessert might be thick yoghurt with rose crisps and hibiscus sorbet, pretty and perfumed. Amid all this luxury, there is an undertow of naffness: the vegetables delicately spiced but presented in a stuffed courgette, and the illustrated wine list. Split into Old and New World, including India, this starts at £16 – a misleadingly low entry point. Since the sommelier's matches don't always work, follow your instincts.

Chef/s: Jitin Joshi. **Open:** all week L 12 to 2.30 (3 Sun), D 5.30 to 11 (6 to 10.30 Sun). **Closed:** 23 to 26 Dec, 1 Jan. **Meals:** alc (main courses £24 to £54). Set L and D £24 (2 courses) to £29. Grazing Menu £79 (4 courses). **Service:** 12.5% (optional). **Details:** Cards accepted. 120 seats. Separate bar. Music.

Bentley's Oyster Bar & Grill

Re-energised seafood institution
11-15 Swallow Street, Piccadilly, W1B 4DG
Tel no: (020) 7734 4756
www.bentleys.org
⊖ Piccadilly Circus, map 5
Seafood | £45
Cooking score: 4

£5 OFF

Richard Corrigan's update of this Victorian Gothic building retains the rich heritage of the famed original, which opened in 1916. The ground floor, with its solid marble counter and red leather banquettes, is the setting for the buzzing oyster bar where diners feast on an all-day menu of bivalves, crustacea and suchlike. A more formal atmosphere prevails in the smartly appointed upstairs grill, although seafood remains the predominant theme: top-notch ingredients are simply prepared in exemplary dishes of dressed crab, grilled Dover sole or lobster and basil macaroni, while other ideas such as steamed Cornish fish with Thai spices, golden pineapple and cardamom demonstrate the kitchen's open-minded approach. Meanwhile, meat eaters can fill up on grills or ballottine of guinea fowl with pearl barley. High prices attract an expense-account crowd, as does the extensive food-friendly wine list, which offers a terrific choice from some of the world's elite producers. Bottles start at £19.50, or you can pick from around 20 wallet-friendly selections by the glass or carafe.

Chef/s: Michael Lynch. **Open:** Grill: Mon to Fri L 12 to 3, Mon to Sat D 6 to 11. Oyster Bar: all week 12 to 12 (10 Sun). **Closed:** 25 Dec, 1 Jan. **Meals:** alc (main courses £19 to £30). **Service:** 12.5% (optional). **Details:** Cards accepted. 140 seats. 50 seats outside. Separate bar. Music. Children allowed.

Bocca di Lupo

Big-hitting trendy trattoria
12 Archer Street, Piccadilly, W1D 7BB
Tel no: (020) 7734 2223
www.boccadilupo.com
⊖ Piccadilly Circus, map 5
Italian | £30
Cooking score: 4

There's a touch of Italian vernacular about the name (which means 'the mouth of the wolf'), and Bocca di Lupo strikes quite a pose on shabby Archer Street – a 'raunchy location' for a big-hitting trattoria that reverberates with noisy, Soho-style dolce vita, in the heart of theatreland. Elbow your way to the bar and watch the kitchen action, or procure a table in the slightly cramped dining room hung with paintings. Either way, expect a trendy menu that ditches conventional courses in favour of small and large plates bursting with bold regional flavours. Nip to Liguria for nettle and borage pansotti with walnut sauce, stop off in Rome for tripe with guanciale (bacon made from pig's cheeks), and wind down in Abruzzo with some challenging sanguinaccio (a sweet 'pâté' composed of pig's blood and chocolate). Also check out the deli delights of fried crescentine with finocchiona (fennel-flavoured salami) and soft, tangy squacquerone cheese. The all-Italian wine list is a regional thriller with oodles by the glass or carafe. Bottles start at £15.50.

Chef/s: Jacob Kenedy. **Open:** all week L 12.30 to 3 (4 Sun), Mon to Sat D 5.15 to 10.45. **Meals:** alc (main courses £14 to £25). **Service:** 12.5% (optional). **Details:** Cards accepted. 60 seats. Music. Children allowed.

Boyd's Brasserie

Brasserie with a sense of occasion
8 Northumberland Avenue, Covent Garden, WC2N 5BY
Tel no: (020) 7808 3344
www.boydsbrasserie.co.uk
⊖ Charing Cross, map 5
British | £45
new chef

£5 OFF

Statement chandeliers and smart upholstery have jazzed up the spacious and elegant brown marble foyer of the old Victoria Hotel to create a brasserie with a sense of occasion. Despite its proximity to Trafalgar Square, it feels quite removed from the action – one doesn't just stumble upon Boyd's. As we went to press head chef Richard Hawthorne had just left, to be replaced by David Colison and Sebastiaan Moors – too late for us to receive any feedback on the cooking. But the 'terrific-value set meal' and 'decent house wine' (£17) were still featuring on the menu. Staff 'who looked like they didn't want to be there' seemingly have 'charming' and 'efficient' days, too. Reports please.

Chef/s: David Colison and Sebastiaan Moors. **Open:** Mon to Fri L 12 to 3, Mon to Sat D 5 to 10. **Closed:** Sun, 25 and 26 Dec. **Meals:** alc (main courses £10 to £25). Set L £15.90 (2 courses) to £19.90. Set D £19.90 (2 courses) to £24.90. **Service:** 12.5% (optional). **Details:** Cards accepted. 80 seats. Separate bar. Wheelchair access. Music. Children allowed.

ALSO RECOMMENDED

▲ Bumbles

16 Buckingham Palace Road, Belgravia, SW1W 0QP
Tel no: (020) 7828 2903
www.bumbles1950.com
⊖ Victoria, map 5
Modern British £5 OFF

This long-established but modern British restaurant not far from Victoria station is as reliable as ever – delivering sound cooking, reasonable prices and a homely and friendly atmosphere. Rabbit 'head to toe' (roasted saddle, slow-cooked shoulder, confit legs) and sea bass with Oxsprings cured ham, curry cream and pickled carrots are typical of the set-price menu (two/three courses £19.50/£23.50). House French is £12.90. Closed Sat L and Sun.

▲ The Café at Sotheby's

34–35 New Bond Street, Mayfair, W1A 2AA
Tel no: (020) 7293 5077
www.sothebys.com
⊖ Bond Street, Oxford Circus, map 5
Modern European

The open aspect of this stylish café just off Sotheby's foyer ensures a generous amount of foot traffic, especially on auction days, and helps to maintain the bustling atmosphere. The never-off-the-menu lobster club sandwich (£18.75) is one way to approach lunch, but crab linguine with lemon and chilli oil (£8.50) or calf's liver with braised radicchio, soft polenta, crispy San Daniele ham and sage (£17.50) are equally promising. Sotheby's Serena Sutcliffe MW selects the wine; prices from £19. Breakfast and afternoon tea, too. Open Mon to Fri.

Le Caprice

Iconic Mayfair brasserie
Arlington House, Arlington Street, Mayfair, SW1A 1RJ
Tel no: (020) 7629 2239
www.le-caprice.co.uk
⊖ Green Park, map 5
Modern British | £35
Cooking score: 4
V

The vintage Mayfair hangout that gave Caprice Holdings its name has been around for decades, seducing generations of star-seekers, celebs and grown-up hedonists with its ever-so-glamorous demeanour, riffing piano player and iconic David Bailey photos. The monochrome look may now seem dated, but Caprice delivers the goods when it comes to slick service and approachable brasserie food. London's culinary legends still queue up on the menu – the salmon fishcakes with sorrel sauce, the crispy duck salad (with coriander and shiso cress these days), the iced berries with chocolate sauce and, of course, the Caprice burger. But the kitchen also runs with the zeitgeist by offering the likes of sautéed foie gras with dandelion leaves and pomegranate or Devon duck with white asparagus and spiced sour cherries. Sunday brunch and theatre deals are fair value, although readers have been outraged by the 'totally unnecessary' cover charge levied on each table. The well-chosen wine list has a pricey French heart, with precious little below £30.

Chef/s: Andrew McLay. **Open:** Mon to Sat L 12 to 3 (4 Fri and Sat), D 5.30 to 12. Sun 11.30am to 11pm. **Closed:** 25 Dec. **Meals:** alc (main courses £15 to £27). Pre/post-theatre set D £17.25 (2 courses) to £22.25. **Service:** 12.5% (optional). **Details:** Cards accepted. 74 seats. Separate bar. No mobile phones. Wheelchair access. Music. Children allowed. Car parking.

ALSO RECOMMENDED

▲ Cha Cha Moon

15-21 Ganton Street, Soho, W1F 9BN
Tel no: (020) 7297 9800
www.chachamoon.com
⊖ Oxford Circus, map 5
Pan-Asian £5 OFF

Alan Yau's canteen-style noodle bar promises to go beyond 'noodle pop culture' to serve up authentic pan-Asian dishes, from Hong Kong street food to Thai chicken curry. Be willing to queue and expect to sit shoulder-to-shoulder at communal tables with views of staff working at speed in the glass-fronted kitchen. Typical choices take in Taiwan beef noodles (£7.30), jasmine tea-smoked chicken lao mian, and seafood ho fun (£8.30). Drinks include cocktails, Tsingtao beer and a handful of wines, starting at £14.90 a bottle. Open all week.

The Chancery

Chic bolt-hole in lawyerland
9 Cursitor Street, Holborn, EC4A 1LL
Tel no: (020) 7831 4000
www.thechancery.co.uk
⊖ Chancery Lane, map 5
Modern European | £35
Cooking score: 4

The corner site in Holborn is a compact but smartly designed white-walled space, full of buzz (especially at lunchtimes), with a kitchen producing some ingeniously creative food. A piece of pork cooked sous-vide to melting intensity is accompanied by batons of apple, artichoke hearts and puréed Jerusalem in an expressively savoury opener, while the sweetbreads and a lamb's kidney are gently shoehorned into mille-feuille pastry layers, and sparingly sauced with mustard sabayon. After that, the level might drop a little, a serving of so-so duck breast, sliced too finely, rescued by a crisp spring roll of the leg confit with carrot and beansprouts, but a serendipitous bit of 1980s nostalgia arrives in the form of paupiettes of plaice, brilliantly timed, rolled around creamed leek, alongside pomme mousseline and a buttery Champagne sauce. Dessert might be a wodge of perfectly rendered carrot cake, topped with cream cheese and served with gorgeous butternut squash ice cream. Wines are very gently priced for the area; bottles start at £17.50.

Chef/s: Stephen Englefield. **Open:** Mon to Fri L 12 to 2.30, Mon to Sat D 6 to 10.30. **Closed:** Sun, 24 Dec to 3 Jan. **Meals:** Set L and D £28 (2 courses) to £34.50. **Service:** 12.5% (optional). **Details:** Cards accepted. 70 seats. 10 seats outside. Separate bar. Music. Children allowed.

China Tang at the Dorchester

A glamorous slice of high-camp glitter
The Dorchester Hotel, 53 Park Lane, Hyde Park, W1K 1QA
Tel no: (020) 7629 9988
www.thedorchester.com
⊖ Hyde Park Corner, map 4
Chinese | £75
Cooking score: 3
V

Dreamed up by the lifestyle guru and entrepreneur Sir David Tang, this subterranean dining room below the Dorchester triggers echoes of old colonial Shanghai and Hong Kong with its silken swathes, sumptuous chinoiserie and staff in white 'ocean-liner' uniforms. It's a glamorous slice of high-camp glitter, with prices that will make your eyes water as surely as an overdose of Szechuan chilli. However, there's nothing scary about an orthodox menu that pads its way confidently through dependable dim sum, Peking duck, steamed sea bass with ginger and spring onion, Singapore noodles and suchlike. Braised lobster, abalone and plenty more luxury dishes besides are on hand for those who want to flash the platinum – an accessory that's also essential if you're considering the wine list (£30 is the bottom line).

Chef/s: Chong Choi Fong. **Open:** all week L 11 to 3.30 (4 Sat and Sun), D 5.30 to 12. **Closed:** 25 Dec. **Meals:** alc (main courses from £14 to £150). Set L

£15 (2 courses) to £75. **Service:** 12.5% (optional). **Details:** Cards accepted. 200 seats. Separate bar. No music. Wheelchair access. Children allowed.

Chisou

Style and substance in perfect harmony
4 Princes Street, Mayfair, W1B 2LE
Tel no: (020) 7629 3931
www.chisou.co.uk
⊖ Oxford Circus, map 5
Japanese | £50
Cooking score: 4

This modest Japanese restaurant in a quiet street not far from Oxford Circus has something of the bustle and enthusiasm of a Tokyo eating house. The extensive menu encompasses all manner of traditional and contemporary dishes, with sparkling fresh sushi playing a major role (a seat at the sushi bar is a popular option); yellowfin tuna, sea bass, sea urchin, flying-fish roe and more have passed the quality test. The menu also takes in various 'inside-out' rolls and sashimi, as well as salads and soups, tempura, teriyaki and the like, while familiar appetisers, from edamame beans to agedashi tofu (fried bean curd), start the ball rolling. Now in its tenth year, Chisou remains a most reliable destination, popular with the Japanese community. Wines are from £20, otherwise drink tea, shochu or saké. A second branch is at 31 Beauchamp Place, SW3 1NU; tel (020) 3155 0005.
Chef/s: Kodi Aung. **Open:** Mon to Sat L 12 to 2.30 (12.30 to 3 Sat), D 6 to 10.30. **Closed:** Sun. **Meals:** alc (main courses £5 to £24). Set L £14.50 (2 courses) to £19.50. Set D £45 (2 courses) to £55. **Service:** 13% (optional). **Details:** Cards accepted. 60 seats. 6 seats outside. Music. Children allowed.

Visit us Online
To find out more about *The Good Food Guide*, please visit www.thegoodfoodguide.co.uk

Cigala

Lively Spanish hangout
54 Lamb's Conduit Street, Bloomsbury, WC1N 3LW
Tel no: (020) 7405 1717
www.cigala.co.uk
⊖ Holborn, Russell Square, map 5
Spanish | £30
Cooking score: 1

£5 OFF

'The place hasn't changed in 11 years', was one reporter's observation about this unpretentious Spanish hangout, which remains as busy as it did when it first opened. Chef/proprietor Jake Hodges was one of the original chefs at Moro (see entry) and he follows a similar no-nonsense approach to Hispanic food. Feed on tapas in the lively downstairs bar or fill up on paella, grilled shoulder of Iberian pork or grilled whole plaice in the dining room. Wines from £16.95.
Chef/s: Jake Hodges. **Open:** all week 12 to 10.45 (12.30 to 10.45 Sat, 12.30 to 9.30 Sun). **Closed:** 24 to 26 Dec. **Meals:** alc (main courses £12 to £19). Set L £16 (2 courses) to £18. **Service:** 12.5% (optional). **Details:** Cards accepted. 60 seats. 20 seats outside. Separate bar. No music. Children allowed.

NEW ENTRY
Cigalon

Provence on a plate
115 Chancery Lane, Holborn, WC2A 1PP
Tel no: (020) 7242 8373
www.cigalon.co.uk
⊖ Chancery Lane, map 5
French | £26
Cooking score: 3

Word has spread, and Cigalon (named after the 1935 Marcel Pagnol film) is going great guns. Diners revel in the 'welcoming, impeccable service' and the rustic, robust Provençal style that inspires both the restaurant and the menu. The result is the kind of food that, via Elizabeth David, introduced many people to French cuisine in bygone days – simple things like a 'beautiful' salade niçoise with 'perfectly cooked eggs and wonderfully

fresh tuna', and salt cod poached in vegetable broth with 'a lovely silky, garlicky aïoli'. More contemporary pairings get an airing too, as in spelt and smoked pumpkin risotto with sage or pork tenderloin with confit belly and roasted beetroot and salsify. Bread is good, but desserts are not a strong suit. House wine £19.
Chef/s: Julien Carlon. **Open:** Mon to Fri L 12 to 2.30, D 6 to 10. **Closed:** Sat, Sun, last week Dec, first week Jan, bank hols. **Meals:** alc (main courses £11 to 27). Set L £19.50 (2 courses) to £26.50. Set D £35. **Service:** 12.5% (optional). **Details:** Cards accepted. 68 seats. Separate bar. Music. Children allowed.

Cinnamon Club

Exciting new-wave Indian
30-32 Great Smith Street, Westminster, SW1P 3BU
Tel no: (020) 7222 2555
www.cinnamonclub.com
⊖ Westminster, map 5
Indian | £50
Cooking score: 3
£5 OFF

Embedded within the Victorian opulence of the Old Westminster Library, the Cinnamon Club is a magnet for MPs, political journos and expensive suits who appreciate its gentlemanly attributes, discreet countenance and exciting food. Executive chef Vivek Singh is a serious player on the new-wave Indian scene and his cooking is a palate-jangling ride across the east-west culinary divide, with intriguingly spiced possibilities at every turn. Roast saddle of Oisin deer with fenugreek and onion sauce is a signature dish, but his imagination also turns to lamb's sweetbread bhajis, tandoori chicken suffused with sandalwood, and a dish of herb-crusted black bream with Jerusalem artichoke 'podimas' and lemony tomato sauce. Needless to say, prices are a world away from your local curry joint, but choose carefully from the gilt-edged wine list and you should leave happy. House recommendations start at £26.
Chef/s: Vivek Singh and Hari Nagaraj. **Open:** Mon to Sat L 12 to 2.45, D 6 to 10.45. **Closed:** Sun. **Meals:** alc (main courses £15 to £32). Set L £19 (2 courses) to £22. Set D £24 (2 courses) to £28. Tasting menu £75. **Service:** 12.5% (optional). **Details:** Cards accepted. 130 seats. Separate bar. No music. Children allowed.

Clos Maggiore

Romantic restaurant with good set deals
33 King Street, Covent Garden, WC2E 8JD
Tel no: (020) 7379 9696
www.closmaggiore.com
⊖ Covent Garden, map 5
French | £38
Cooking score: 2

'It was like walking into *A Midsummer Night's Dream*,' noted a visitor to this sought-after destination for theatregoers and those seeking respite from chain-bound Covent Garden. Others have agreed, liking the drama of the décor, the 'great romantic atmosphere' and the friendly staff. The food takes a broadly French perspective, perhaps duck foie gras with a crisp confit duck leg, pain d'épices, roasted hazelnuts and poached rhubarb, then braised Charolais beef cheek with a bay leaf and Hermitage sauce, and vanilla and praline cream Vacherin to finish. The set menu is good value. House wine is £18.50.
Chef/s: Marcellin Marc. **Open:** all week L 12 to 2.15, D 5 to 11 (10 Sun). **Closed:** 25 Dec. **Meals:** alc (main courses £18 to £20). Set L and pre-theatre menu £19.50. Set D £22.50. Post-theatre menu £27.50 (2 courses). Tasting menu £59 (6 courses). **Service:** 12.5% (optional). **Details:** Cards accepted. 70 seats. Music.

Corrigan's Mayfair

Food with flash and panache
28 Upper Grosvenor Street, Mayfair, W1K 7EH
Tel no: (020) 7499 9943
www.corrigansmayfair.com
⊖ Marble Arch, map 4
Modern British | £48
Cooking score: 6
£5 OFF **V**

The address, just off Park Lane, could hardly be more opulent, a suitable location, perhaps, for a chef whose food has always been about flash and panache. The interior design is meant to be 'contemporary hunting lodge' but the result is weirdly muted – a rather dull, monochrome space. Let's call it 'understated'. What isn't understated is the cooking, which retains the stamp of Richard Corrigan's seasonally led modern British approach, with big, bold, primary flavours registering strongly throughout. A salad of game bird meats and wet walnuts with romesco dressing might be a typical starter, while main courses take a robust line with fish (red mullet with salt cod, chorizo and parsley) and the gentler cuts of meat, as in the red anchovy butter, peppered bone marrow and garlic confit that come with a piece of beef fillet. Nor is there any need to recline into creamy blandness at dessert stage when quince tart with whisky ice cream is to hand. Seasonal market menus and deals are a lure, and the lunch deal, which includes a 250ml carafe of wine, is reckoned fine value. The wine list offers as extensive and handsome a choice as Mayfair expects, in a commendable food-led format. Prices start at £27.

Chef/s: Richard Corrigan and Chris McGowan. **Open:** Sun to Fri L 12 to 3 (4 Sun), all week D 6 to 11 (9.30 Sun). **Closed:** 25 to 27 Dec, 1 Jan. **Meals:** alc (main courses £24 to £38). Set L Mon to Fri £27. Sun L £27. **Service:** 12.5% (optional). **Details:** Cards accepted. 85 seats. Separate bar. Wheelchair access. Music. Children allowed.

Dean Street Townhouse

Boisterous Soho brasserie
69-71 Dean Street, Soho, W1D 3SE
Tel no: (020) 7434 1775
www.deanstreettownhouse.com
⊖ Tottenham Court Road, map 5
Modern British | £35
Cooking score: 3

V

Take one cream-painted Georgian town house deep in old Soho, kit out its upper floors with boutique bedrooms and throw open the rest to the chattering classes, media types, celebs and Joe Public in general. Welcome to DST – a boisterous, all-hours brasserie for the twenty-first century, full of fun and gregarious babble. The zinc bar gets rammed – likewise tables in the elbow-to-elbow dining areas, where British sensibilities are writ large on the menu. 'Mince and potatoes' is the dish of the moment, but also come here if your fancy turns to pea and lovage soup, veal kidney with roast cauliflower and devilled sauce or porterhouse steak and chips. DST's first six months were a PR-fuelled triumph, but some reports suggest it has gone off the boil (clumsy flavours, a cynical 'mass-produced' feel and lackadaisical service ruined it for one reporter). Breakfast and brunch are a boon to the neighbourhood (if you can find room to breathe), and the wine list promises decent quaffing from £18.50.

Chef/s: Stephen Tonkin. **Open:** all week 7am to midnight (1am Fri, 8am to 1am Sat, 8am to midnight Sun). **Meals:** alc (main courses £12 to £33). Set early D £19.50. **Service:** 12.5% (optional). **Details:** Cards accepted. 120 seats. 26 seats outside. Separate bar. Wheelchair access. Music. Children allowed.

NEW ENTRY

Degò

Sassy, upbeat Italian
4 Great Portland Street, Fitzrovia, W1W 8QJ
Tel no: (020) 7636 2207
www.degowinebar.co.uk
⊖ Oxford Circus, map 5
Italian | £36
Cooking score: 4

£5 OFF

It may be pitched just off Oxford Circus, but Degò is anything but a 'tourist board' pizza/pasta joint. Combining a cool, street-level wine bar and low-lit basement dining room, this place looks the business in its sassy black and red garb, with leather-textured wall tiles, cocktails and glass-fronted wine cellar. Chef Dario Schiavo has worked with some starry names and his 'on-cue' cooking delivers a raft of imaginative, well-constructed and snappily dressed dishes with a strong Venetian accent. Baccalà mantecato (creamed cod) is a classic, likewise homemade spaghetti with duck ragù, but also look for the 'unlayered' aubergine

Parmigiana (served 'warm' in summer), sole terrine with grilled pepper, or lamb cutlets with fennel salad and minted courgettes. Desserts reject tiramisu clichés in favour of more interesting sweet hits: try the semifreddo perfumed with rose petals or chocolate and caramel meringue with ginger sauce. Degò's owner is also a knowledgeable sommelier and his inspiring, all-Italian wine list includes a cracking selection by the glass and many unusual names (note the Villa Franciacorta). Bottles start at £19.

Chef/s: Dario Schiavo and Massimo Mioli. **Open:** Mon to Fri L 12 to 3 (3.30 Fri), all week D 6.30 to 10.30 (11 Fri, 5.30 to 11 Sat, 5.30 to 10 Sun). **Closed:** 25 and 26 Dec, bank hols. **Meals:** alc (main courses £8 to £16). Set L £15 (2 courses) to £23. Tasting menu £35. **Service:** 12.5% (optional). **Details:** Cards accepted. 45 seats. 20 seats outside. Separate bar. Wheelchair access. Music. Children allowed.

Dehesa

Impeccable tapas
25 Ganton Street, Oxford Circus, W1F 9BP
Tel no: (020) 7494 4170
www.dehesa.co.uk
⊖ Oxford Circus, map 5
Spanish/Italian | £27
Cooking score: 3

One of a trio of informal tapas eateries (see entries for Salt Yard and Opera Tavern), this elegant corner site draws in diners with its appealing, populist repertoire. It's not your average tapas joint. Inspiration comes from Italy as well as Spain, with impeccable charcuterie and cheese selections from both countries served alongside hot dishes that could be as simple as chorizo à la plancha or tortilla, and as intricate as duck breast with candied beetroot, green beans and jamón-truffle dressing or red mullet and gurnard cacciucco (Italian fish stew) on bruschetta. Courgette flowers with Monte Enebro cheese and honey has become the group's trademark. The well-chosen Spanish/Italian wine list is arranged by style and opens at £15.35.

Chef/s: Giancarlo Vatterori. **Open:** Mon to Fri L 12 to 3, D 5 to 11. Sat 12 to 11, Sun 12 to 5. **Closed:** 10 days Christmas. **Meals:** alc (tapas £4 to £10). **Service:** 12.5% (optional). **Details:** Cards accepted. 40 seats. 16 seats outside. Music. Children allowed.

NEW ENTRY

Les Deux Salons

Big brasserie bristling with chart-toppers
40-42 William IV Street, Covent Garden, WC2N 4DD
Tel no: (020) 7420 2050
www.lesdeuxsalons.co.uk
⊖ Charing Cross, map 5
Modern French | £30
Cooking score: 4

Having conquered Soho and Mayfair with Arbutus and Wild Honey respectively (see entries), Messrs Anthony Demetre and Will Smith have stormed resurgent Covent Garden for their latest venture – a big, bold brasserie spread over two floors, with smoky mirrors, tiled floors and a sociable hubbub downstairs, plus a more intimate 'salon' above. In trademark fashion, the kitchen makes the most of meaty cheap cuts for a menu that bristles with potential chart-toppers: lemony goats' curd and cavolo nero encased in 'ravioli' of thinly sliced rose veal could become as iconic as Demetre's squid and mackerel burger, likewise a 'fabulous' crusty pie stuffed with juicy bacon and succulent snails. Elsewhere, pitch-perfect calf's liver with roast onions and lamb's sweetbreads 'bouchée à la reine' have knocked spots off insipid ribeye with chips – although textbook rum baba and gâteau opéra restore the balance. If there's an Achilles' heel it's the service, which often seems unable to cope with the crowds. Everything on the admirable 60-bin wine list is available by the carafe (from £4.75); bottles start at £14.50.

Chef/s: Anthony Demetre. **Open:** all week L 12 to 3, D 5 to 11. **Closed:** 25 and 26 Dec, 1 Jan. **Meals:** alc (main courses £12 to £24). Set L and pre-theatre D £15.50. **Service:** 12.5% (optional). **Details:** Cards accepted. 150 seats. Separate bar. No music. Wheelchair access. Children allowed.

Dinings

Dinky Japanese thriller
22 Harcourt Street, Marylebone, W1H 4HH
Tel no: (020) 7723 0666
www.dinings.co.uk
⊖ Marylebone, map 4
Japanese | £48
Cooking score: 3

Squeezed into a poky Marylebone town house, Dinings is one of those teeny-weeny places where food matters more than comfort or attitude. Aficionados watch the art of sushi demystified at the street-level counter, although most punters seek out the utilitarian basement 'bunker'. Owner Tomonari Chiba honed his skills at Nobu London (see entry) before peeling away from the mother ship, so it's no surprise that the menu brings much more than Japanese tradition to the table. The big theme here is 'tapas' – captivating small plates of immaculately assembled food shot through with clear, assertive flavours and vivid contrasts: salmon tataki with sweet mustard miso, char-grilled Iberian pork shoulder with tomato yuzu sauce, and luxurious morsels of seared Wagyu beef sushi topped with truffle salsa and ponzu jelly. High prices pay for serious culinary skills, prime ingredients and the odd slice of foie gras. The wine list opens at £19.

Chef/s: Masaki Sugisaki. **Open:** Mon to Fri L 12 to 3, Mon to Sat D 6 to 10.30 (11 Sat). **Closed:** Sun, 25 Dec to 3 Jan. **Meals:** alc (main courses £9 to £28). Set L £17.50 (2 courses). **Service:** 10.5% (optional). **Details:** Cards accepted. 28 seats. Music. Children allowed.

Please send us your feedback

To register your opinion about any restaurant listed in the Guide, or a new restaurant that you wish to bring to our attention, please visit the web address at the bottom of the page. Your feedback informs the content of the book and will be used to compile next year's reviews.

NEW ENTRY

Dishoom

Striking all-day Indian café
12 Upper St Martin's Lane, Covent Garden, WC2H 9FB
Tel no: (020) 7420 9320
www.dishoom.com
⊖ Leicester Square, Covent Garden, map 5
Indian | £25
Cooking score: 3

Flaunting a striking mix of checkerboard and wood floors, dark panels and marble-topped tables, this capacious all-day Indian café serving Bombay street food, more familiar curry house dishes and a few Anglo-Indian ideas, makes quite an impact on touristy Upper St Martin's Lane. The menu takes a broad sweep from 'very good, quite delicate and gently spiced' calamari with lime and chilli to a much-praised dill salmon tikka, and lamb chops rubbed with crushed black pepper and chillies. Homemade pickles and chutneys, breads, slow-cooked black dhal, and desserts of mango kulfi or pomegranate and chilli ice have also found favour. Expect mostly small plates, with the recommendation to order three dishes each. House wine is £18.90, otherwise drink lassi or house chai.

Chef/s: Naved Nasir. **Open:** all week 8am to 11pm (9am Sat, 9am to 10pm Sun). **Closed:** 25 Dec. **Meals:** alc (main £7 to £10). Set L and D £18 to £25. **Service:** 12.5% (optional). **Details:** Cards accepted. 120 seats. 20 seats outside. Separate bar. Wheelchair access. Music. Children allowed.

ALSO RECOMMENDED

▲ The Duke of Wellington

94a Crawford Street, Marylebone, W1H 2HQ
Tel no: (020) 7723 2790
www.thedukew1.co.uk
⊖ Marylebone, Baker Street, map 4
Modern British

Always buzzing, this updated pub is an asset to the Baker Street area. Eat in the lively bar or make your way to the first-floor dining room; either way expect an unfussy, contemporary menu. Dressed crab on toast (£7.75) is a favourite, by all accounts, while typical main courses are braised veal cheeks with saffron risotto and Little Gem, or grilled monkfish with a warm salad of chorizo, clams and courgettes (£19.50). Finish with vanilla pannacotta and rhubarb 'Jammie Dodger'. Wines from £15. Open all week.

▲ Fernandez & Wells

43 Lexington Street, Soho, W1F 9AL
Tel no: (020) 7734 1546
www.fernandezandwells.com
⊖ Piccadilly Circus, Oxford Circus, map 5
Spanish

This buzzy wine bar is part of a triumvirate of cool Soho pit-stops owned by Jorge Fernandez and Rick Wells, which also includes an espresso bar in St Anne's Court and a café on Beak Street. The small, functional room gets uncomfortably crowded at times, but grab a stool and choose from the piles of 'bocadillos' on the oak counter or order Padrón peppers (£3.50), 36-month cured jamón Ibérico, grilled Alejandro chorizo (£6.50) or cider-marinated Cornish sardines. House wine £21. Open all week.

Fino

Stellar, sharp-shooting tapas
33 Charlotte Street (entrance in Rathbone Street), Fitzrovia, W1T 1RR
Tel no: (020) 7813 8010
www.finorestaurant.com
⊖ Goodge Street, map 5
Spanish | £25
Cooking score: 3

Accessed via a discreet entrance on Rathbone Street, this tapas big hitter is a study in understated Anglo-Hispanic chic. The basement room is a minimalist hubbub of noise and chatter, but sharp staff keep things on track and the kitchen seldom falters. Cheeses and charcuterie are sourced with proper care, and the daily menu always includes an array of vivid seasonal plates: tortillas and seafood from 'the plancha' might be joined by punchy morcilla Ibérica with piquillo peppers and spinach, lamb cutlets with Jerusalem artichoke purée or Monte Enebro goats' cheese with broad beans on toast. Specials such as white asparagus with romesco sauce are worth a go, and you can ease down with a fluffy Santiago tart. Sherry is given due consideration and there are plenty of juicy Spanish wines from £18.

Chef/s: Nieves Barragan Mohacho. **Open:** Mon to Fri L 12 to 2.30, Mon to Sat D 6 to 10.30. **Closed:** Sun, 25 and 26 Dec, bank hols. **Meals:** alc (tapas £9 to £23). Set L £15.95 (2 courses) to £17.95. **Service:** 12.5% (optional). **Details:** Cards accepted. 85 seats. Separate bar. Wheelchair access. Music. Children allowed.

ALSO RECOMMENDED

▲ La Fromagerie

2-6 Moxon Street, Marylebone, W1U 4EW
Tel no: (020) 7935 0341
www.lafromagerie.co.uk
⊖ Baker Street, Bond Street, map 4
Modern European £5 OFF

Bag a table at the deli/café attached to La Fromagerie and you will find yourself surrounded by a veritable takeaway feast, but the kitchen also shows its mettle with a seasonal repertoire of brasserie staples such as confit duck leg (£10.50) or handmade agnolotti filled with braised veal (£9.50). Fresh, inventive soups, sandwiches and salads exemplify the straightforward approach, breakfasts are recommended, and it goes without saying that the cheese plates are seriously tempting. Desserts are mainly excellent cakes and tarts. Wines from £16.80. Open all week, shop hours.

Also Recommended

Also recommended entries are not scored but we think they are worth a visit.

Galvin at Windows

Ambitious French food and fabulous views
Hilton Hotel, 22 Park Lane, Mayfair, W1K 1BE
Tel no: (020) 7208 4021
www.galvinatwindows.com
⊖ Hyde Park Corner, Green Park, map 4
French | £65
Cooking score: 6

A reporter with a head for heights reckoned that this restaurant rivals the one halfway up the Eiffel Tower, and certainly, before one eats or drinks anything, it's worth taking stock of that panoramic view through full-drop windows over central London and beyond. It makes a fine setting for ambitious contemporary French cooking. Some of the earthier ingredients in the French repertoire are brought into play for the likes of parsley velouté with snail persillade, garlic purée and a poached egg, or slow-cooked pork cheeks with caramelised apple, purple potato and red wine sauce, on the menu du jour. It's on the menu prestige that the kitchen really takes wing, offering lobster raviolo with monk's beard in a nage of sea vegetables, followed perhaps by John Dory with orange-braised endive, raisins and curry oil, or loin and shoulder of venison with red cabbage, smoked pomme purée and sauce Grand Veneur. Dessert can be as classique (rum baba, tarte Tatin) or as 'good-grief' (dark chocolate soup, whipped white chocolate ganache and tonka and honey jelly) as you like. The wine list is big in the headline regions, but finds a little space for some rarities. How about a barrel-aged Pinot Blanc from Luxembourg at £52? A good selection by the glass starts at £5.

Chef/s: André Garrett. **Open:** Sun to Fri L 12 to 2.30 (3 Sun), Mon to Sat D 6 to 10.30 (11 Thur to Sat). **Closed:** bank hol Mon. **Meals:** Set L £22 (2 courses) to £27. Set D £65. **Service:** 12.5% (optional). **Details:** Cards accepted. 109 seats. Separate bar. No music. No mobile phones. Wheelchair access. Children allowed. Car parking.

Galvin Bistrot de Luxe

Unbridled jollity and persuasive Gallic charms
66 Baker Street, Marylebone, W1U 7DJ
Tel no: (020) 7935 4007
www.galvinrestaurants.com
⊖ Baker Street, map 4
French | £34
Cooking score: 5

'There is a certain swagger here', observed one reporter – no doubt referring to Galvin's black leather banquettes, mahogany panelling and stone floors as well as its noisy, unbridled jollity and persuasive Gallic charms. If in-house puffing was still legal, this wonderfully atmospheric room would reek of Gauloises. Chris Galvin has the brasserie mode down to a T, dishing up exemplary renditions of steak tartare, escargots à la bourguignonne and calf's liver with pomme purée, Alsace bacon and sauce diable as well as veering into voguish territory for the likes of yellowfin tuna escabèche with saffron dressing. Lasagne of Dorset crab is a surefire winner here – the gossamer-like pasta packed with fresh white meat and rounded off with a silky shellfish bisque – and the kitchen cranks up its refined rusticity for a dish of tender pot-roasted Landaise chicken served with a fricassee of broad beans and morels, plus some tarragon velouté for added lustre. Desserts such as a textbook tarte Tatin are as French as you can get, while strong coffee with a 'delightful' pistachio financier guarantees a happy ending. Pricing is sensible, set menus are a steal and wines (from £19.75) stay mostly in La Belle France, with plenty by the glass or 'pot lyonnais'.

Chef/s: Chris and Jeff Galvin. **Open:** all week L 12 to 2.30 (3 Sun), D 6 to 10.30 (11 Thur to Sat, 9.30 Sun). **Closed:** 25 and 26 Dec, 1 Jan. **Meals:** alc (main courses £16 to £19). Set L £17.50. Set D £19.50. **Service:** 12.5% (optional). **Details:** Cards accepted. 128 seats. 12 seats outside. Separate bar. No music. Wheelchair access. Children allowed.

Gauthier Soho

Excellent cuisine and exceptional value
21 Romilly Street, Soho, W1D 5AF
Tel no: (020) 7494 3111
www.gauthiersoho.co.uk
⊖ Leicester Square, map 5
French | £35
Cooking score: 6
£5 OFF **V**

Alexis Gauthier, formerly of Roussillon (see entry), continues his excellent cuisine in the intimate town house that was once Richard Corrigan's domain. Praise for this venture comes thick and fast, a favourite topic being the exceptional value for money on offer here. In the first-floor dining room a real fire adds character and warmth to whiteness that verges on clinical. The menu is built on seasonal ingredients cooked 'the French way' and served small so you can create your own tasting menu. There's nothing fussy or gratuitously showy; just assured cooking with clear and classic flavours. Expect a 'brilliant bread board' and confident openers such as peanut twirls with guacamole and salsa dip or egg with Parmesan tuiles. At inspection, a starter of pumpkin soup with chanterelles was thick and velvety, while the buttery excesses of foie gras and sweet mango were whipped into shape by a verjus reduction. The balance of decadence and restraint held true in a main course of tender fillet of Black Spot pork with pork jus, red pepper, kale and creamy gratin dauphinois. Reporters agree that desserts are a high point – from Alexis' famous and 'sublime' dessert Louis XV to the sophisticated comforts of roasted spiced pear with brioche perdu and yoghurt sorbet. The wine list is worth perusing for its literary value as well as for the superb Francophile-goes-global approach, starting at £22.

Chef/s: Alexis Gauthier and Gerard Virolle. **Open:** Mon to Fri L 12 to 2.30, Mon to Sat D 5.30 to 10.30. **Closed:** Sun, 21 to 30 Aug, bank hols. **Meals:** Set L £18 (2 courses) to £25. Set D £35. Tasting menu £70. **Service:** 12.5% (optional). **Details:** Cards accepted. 45 seats. Separate bar. No music.

Le Gavroche

Gems from the haute cuisine jewel box
43 Upper Brook Street, Mayfair, W1K 7QR
Tel no: (020) 7408 0881
www.le-gavroche.co.uk
⊖ Marble Arch, map 4
French | £85
Cooking score: 8

Le Gavroche is a traditional French restaurant in Mayfair. That description alone, which may once have applied unremarkably to dozens of places, is gradually heading towards the status of a USP in the twenty-first century. What it offers, within the confines of an elegant basement room, is a service and a style of cooking that hark back to an era of Lucullan magnificence, when dining out might be a full-scale occasion in every sense. Given the economics, many people come here for the long-standing fixed-price lunch, which still includes wine, coffee and water. Loyal supporters praise the precision and the unrestrained opulence that might produce the famous quenelles of pike in lobster cream sauce, Provençal fish soup with Gruyère and aïoli, lambs' tongues on pomme mousseline, and a chicken leg braised in red wine with risotto, before desserts of apple charlotte and a bouquet of sorbets round off a highly satisfactory enterprise. Others detect a surprisingly prosaic lack of ambition – underseasoned mackerel tartare, and a main course that didn't quite rise above the reader's designation of 'roast chicken with good gravy'. Wandering into the realms of the eight-course menu exceptionnel, you should reliably find the dazzle and flash you've come for, perhaps in the form of monkfish in red wine with balsamic-braised salsify, or the fabulous beef fillet with its potato croquette in shallot sauce – relatively simple dishes that nonetheless stand out in three dimensions. French and British farmhouse cheeses are mostly brilliant, and desserts can get positively avant-garde, as when Amadei chocolate truffle turns up with puffed rice, a praline biscuit, bitter chocolate sorbet and golden rum jelly.

Service is fascinating in its balletic precision, until it comes to this sort of caper: 'The waitress poured a little [wine] to taste herself, a practice that always irritates us.' It shouldn't be difficult to see why that might be annoying, but beyond such silly theatrics, there is a vinous treasure-house of mostly French stars at prices that take no prisoners. Start at £20 for white and £30 for red.

Chef/s: Michel Roux. **Open:** Mon to Fri L 12 to 2, Mon to Sat D 6.30 to 11. **Closed:** Sun, 22 Dec to 5 Jan, bank hols. **Meals:** alc (main courses £27 to £59). Set L £50. Tasting menu £100. **Service:** 12.5% (optional). **Details:** Cards accepted. 68 seats. Separate bar. No music. No mobile phones. Children allowed.

The Giaconda Dining Room

Instantly appealing food
9 Denmark Street, Soho, WC2 H8LS
Tel no: (020) 7240 3334
www.giacondadining.com
⊖ Tottenham Court Road, map 5
Modern European | £29
Cooking score: 3

'Affable, relaxed and unharrassed' don't normally spring to mind when talking about edgy Denmark Street (aka Tin Pan Alley), but this unprepossessing dining room bucks the trend with its good-time mix of buzz, bonhomie and fairly priced sustenance. Once the Giaconda Café (legendary haunt of rock stars and wannabe musos), it has taken on a new, cosmopolitan persona, thanks to Aussie chef/proprietor Paul Merrony. Instantly appealing food is the deal: a 'gratifying saucerful' of marinated salmon with fennel, cucumber and grated salt cod, duck confit with lyonnaise potatoes, and a rich crumble of mushrooms and creamed shallots set off by a meringue-like swirl of horseradish cream have all hit the spot. Crisp chips show that caring touch, emollient milk and almond sorbet is 'good for the soul', and luscious chocolate and praline mousse cake delivers spoonfuls of deliciousness. Quaffable wines from £19.

Chef/s: Paul Merrony. **Open:** Tue to Fri L 12 to 2.15, Tue to Sat D 6 to 9.15. **Closed:** Sun, Mon. **Meals:** alc (main courses £12 to £17). **Service:** not inc. **Details:** Cards accepted. 32 seats. No music. Children allowed.

Gordon Ramsay at Claridge's

Aristocrat à la mode
Brook Street, Mayfair, W1K 4HR
Tel no: (020) 7499 0099
www.gordonramsay.com
⊖ Bond Street, map 5
Modern European | £70
Cooking score: 5

As a slice of stately, special-occasion glitz, Claridge's is up there with the best in town and you can soak up some of its Art Deco majesty as you saunter through the grand foyer on your way to the flagship restaurant. This was Gordon Ramsay's first foray into the world of top-hatted London hospitality and current chef Steve Allen knows how to deliver GR finesse in spades – although the dining room's orangey-peach walls, OTT three-tiered light fittings and purple chairs are something of an acquired taste. The kitchen sends out highly varnished food, with powders, essences, foams and daubs strewn deliberately over just about everything, and plenty of newfangled thinking when it comes to matching ingredients on the plate: sautéed Scottish scallops might appear with pan-seared watermelon and morel velouté, while halibut from the Isle of Gigha has been seen in company with braised rabbit and a mélange of hazelnuts, pickled shallots and red wine jus. There's also room for some canny reinvention: beef Wellington with Parma ham and smoked potato purée, for example, or roast rack and loin of Highland venison with a wintry garland of creamed Brussels sprouts, chestnut, beetroot and endive. Desserts are given the full contemporary treatment, with elaborately adorned parfaits, soufflés and brûlées on display, alongside lashings of Valrhona chocolate. The wine list is a Ramsay heavyweight, with class on every page; top-

dollar Champagnes and vintage French thoroughbreds are augmented by superior names from the New World, and it pays to invest serious money. Prices start at £24 (or go by the glass, from £6).
Chef/s: Steve Allen. **Open:** all week L 12 to 2.45 (3 Sat and Sun), D 5.45 to 11 (6 to 11 Sat, 6 to 10.30 Sun). **Meals:** Set L £30. Set D £70. Menu Prestige £80 (6 courses). **Service:** 12.5% (optional). **Details:** Cards accepted. 150 seats. No music. Wheelchair access. Children allowed.

Great Queen Street

Gregarious eatery with no-frills British grub
32 Great Queen Street, Covent Garden, WC2B 5AA
Tel no: (020) 7242 0622
⊖ Covent Garden, map 5
British | £30
Cooking score: 1

Only the fittest survive on the frenetic, mean streets of Covent Garden, and reports suggest this gregarious eatery is struggling to maintain its 'wow' – although brisk, clued-up staff still keep the theatre crowds happy, dishing up plates of unreformed British grub without fuss or furbelows. Seasonality rules in the shape of soused herrings, celeriac and Crozier Blue soup or breast of lamb with haggis and swede mash; chicken pie is a treat to share, but save room for some rhubarb and custard. Wines from £13.50.
Chef/s: Tom Norrington-Davies and Sam Hutchins. **Open:** all week L 12 to 2.30 (3.30 Sun), Mon to Sat D 6 to 10.30. **Closed:** Christmas, New Year, bank hols. **Meals:** alc (main courses £10 to £26). **Service:** not inc. **Details:** Cards accepted. 60 seats. 12 seats outside. Separate bar. No music. Wheelchair access. Children allowed.

Also Recommended

Also recommended entries are not scored but we think they are worth a visit.

The Greenhouse

Romance, urban chic and artful cooking
27a Hay's Mews, Green Park, W1J 5NX
Tel no: (020) 7499 3331
www.greenhouserestaurant.co.uk
⊖ Green Park, map 5
French | £75
Cooking score: 6
V

Reached through an immaculate, shadowy garden in an otherwise undistinguished mews, the Greenhouse is a world apart from surrounding Mayfair. The smart minimalist interior makes the most of that green view between the tall buildings and continues the theme with pale greens and browns, a winding leaf motif here and a wall of twigs there. Antonin Bonnet's cooking fits the bill perfectly; artful and inventive, it pushes the boundaries without losing touch with its classic French roots. Dishes are shaped by the cycle of the seasons – on a winter visit, a starter of seared foie gras with spicy red wine glaze, beetroot and rhubarb was generous and warming, while a main course of tender Pyrenean milk-fed lamb with apple and tamarind purée, potato fondant and a pork and lamb caillette perfectly balanced comfort with creativity. That blend of classic and clever continues at dessert, when choices range from the famous 'snix' (a sumptuous ode to the Snickers bar) to homely apple tarte Tatin with vanilla ice cream. Fixed-price lunches have been appreciated for value and performance – perhaps 'a very fine and substantial' ballottine of rabbit and foie gras with green lentils, a 'perfectly cooked and presented' roast pigeon breast with celeriac purée, and 'a divine' Taneka chocolate confection with banana sorbet. The sky's the limit on the illustrious global wine list, which nevertheless throws in some impressive offerings from £22.
Chef/s: Antonin Bonnet. **Open:** Mon to Fri L 12 to 2.30, Mon to Sat D 6.30 to 11. **Closed:** Sun, bank hols. **Meals:** Set L £25 (2 courses) to £29. Set D £65 (2 courses) to £75. Tasting menu £75 (7 courses) to

£90. **Service:** 12.5% (optional). **Details:** Cards accepted. 60 seats. No music. No mobile phones. Wheelchair access. Children allowed.

The Grill at the Dorchester

Confident food and baronial splendour
The Dorchester Hotel, 53 Park Lane, Hyde Park, W1K 1QA
Tel no: (020) 7629 8888
www.thedorchester.com
⊖ Hyde Park Corner, map 4
Modern British | £45
Cooking score: 4

The Grill Room, as it used to be known, has been serving the great and the good with foursquare British food since 1931. Its present livery, by a French designer, pays homage to that tradition with its rich tartan fabrics, heroic murals and magenta table lamps. It's a gloriously unreconstructed backdrop for a menu that is actually more exciting than standard heritage fare – perhaps not quite as avant-garde as what they're eating over in the Alain Ducasse room (see entry), but well-executed and consistent anyway. The eponymous grill might produce a Dover sole or a pork chop with parsnip drop scones and cidery onions, while more cutting-edge thinking sees lamb loin poached and served with its caramelised sweetbread in consommé. Desserts still push the right buttons, with chocolate and mint parfait, or coffee layer cake and Bailey's ice cream. Wines from a classical list start at £28 (£7 a glass).

Chef/s: Brian Hughson. **Open:** all week L 12 to 2.30 (12.30 to 3 Sat, 3.30 Sun), D 6.30 to 10.30 (11 Sat, 7 to 10.30 Sun). **Meals:** alc (main courses £20 to £55). Set L £23 (2 courses) to £27. Set D £31 (2 courses) to £35. Sun L £38. Tasting menu £60 (5 courses) to £80. **Service:** 12.5% (optional). **Details:** Cards accepted. 84 seats. Separate bar. Wheelchair access. Music. Children allowed. Car parking.

ALSO RECOMMENDED

▲ The Guinea Grill

30 Bruton Place, Mayfair, W1J 6NL
Tel no: (020) 7409 1728
www.theguinea.co.uk
⊖ Bond Street, map 5
British

Mayfair isn't all stratospheric haute cuisine. You can still get a decent (nay, 'award-winning') steak and kidney pie amid the ambience of an old London boozer, as at this Young's pub just near Berkeley Square. Go posh to start, if you will, with crayfish and crab cocktail (£11.75), before sinking into one of those pies or perhaps pan-roasted salmon with grilled veg and new potatoes, or one of the dry-matured steaks (from £21.50 for a 12oz rump). Wines from £17.40. Closed Sat L and Sun.

Hakkasan

Ice-cool Chinese jet-setter
8 Hanway Place, Fitzrovia, W1T 1HD
Tel no: (020) 7927 7000
www.hakkasan.com
⊖ Tottenham Court Road, map 5
Chinese | £50
Cooking score: 5

The location is nothing to write home about, but descend the staircase and you enter a sultry, subterranean world suffused with moody indigo lighting and black lacquered panels. It may be ice-cool, but noise levels can be deafening – especially if punters have fuelled up at the cocktail bar before settling in. An extended list of dim sum pulls the lunchtime crowds, and the kitchen moves quickly from textbook chiu chow dumplings to more edgy ideas including crispy smoked duck and pumpkin puffs, sweet black sesame balls or mixed bean cakes with 'prosciutto rustico'. The full carte promises other sensations, including the famed roast silver cod with Champagne and Chinese honey, as well as baked quail in lotus leaves and braised organic pork belly with plum sauce, kumquats and lily bulbs. If money is no object, place an advance order for a right royal marriage of Peking duck with beluga caviar (£165 at the last count!). Wines, sakés and sherries are fastidiously tailored to the food, and every bottle is a winner. Prices start at £25 (£7.20 a glass).

Chef/s: Tong Chee Hwee. **Open:** all week L 12 to 3.15 (4.15 Sat and Sun), D 6 to 11.15 (12.15 Thur to Sat). **Closed:** 24 and 25 Dec. **Meals:** alc (main courses £12 to £61). **Service:** 13% (optional). **Details:** Cards accepted. 210 seats. Separate bar. Wheelchair access. Music. Children allowed.

NEW ENTRY

Hakkasan Mayfair

Slinky setting for opulent Chinese food
17 Bruton Street, Mayfair, W1J 6QB
Tel no: (020) 79071888
www.hakkasan.com
⊖ Green Park, Bond Street, map 5
Modern Cantonese | £70
Cooking score: 4

Having cracked a decidedly unfashionable location in Hanway Place, the Hakkasan roadshow rolled into Mayfair to lay claim to its spiritual home; the Rolls Royce showroom next door signals that the entry level will be high. At heart, a cool dining room and lively bar, slinkily done out in blacks and reds with minimal lighting, it's the perfect backdrop for a fashionable take on Chinese cooking – nominally Cantonese, with impeccable ingredients. The food can be revelatory: exquisite dim sum, spicy prawn with lily bulb and almond, and char-grilled quail in foie gras sauce. Chilean sea bass in Chinese honey was the star of one visit, with homemade tofu, aubergine and mushroom in a chilli and black bean sauce proving itself more than just mere makeweight. East-meets-west desserts are not a strong point, and drinking is expensive, with the thoroughly opulent wine list opening at £33.

Chef/s: Tong Chee Hwee. **Open:** all week L 12 to 3.15, D 6 to 10. **Meals:** alc (main courses £10 to £80). **Service:** 13%. **Details:** Cards accepted. 220 seats. Separate bar. Wheelchair access. Music. Children allowed.

Haozhan

Blazing a trail in Chinatown
8 Gerrard Street, Soho, W1D 5PJ
Tel no: (020) 7434 3838
www.haozhan.co.uk
⊖ Leicester Square, map 5
Chinese | £29
Cooking score: 3

A smart little number decked out in black and green, Haozhan is blazing a trail for a modern style of oriental dining in the heart of Chinatown. The uncluttered interior sets the tone for a menu that successfully combines influences from China, Malaysia and Japan, but it's worth noting that you can find traditional favourites (crispy aromatic duck, sweet-and-sour chicken) alongside the fusion dishes. Haozhan specialities include black cod siu mai dumplings topped with tobiko and served with homemade chilli vinegar oil, and grilled lamb cutlets with cocoa sauce. Reporters have praised the chilli quail and soft-shell crab starters, and the traditional Taiwanese sanpei chicken. For great value at lunch, ask to see the special menu. A creditable selection of wines starts at just £13.50.

Chef/s: Weng Kong Wong. **Open:** all week L 12 to 5, D 5 to 11.30 (12 Fri and Sat, 11 Sun). **Closed:** 24 and 25 Dec. **Meals:** alc (main courses from £10 to £41). Set L £8 (2 courses) to £10. Set D £14.50 (2 courses) to £32. **Service:** 12.5% (optional). **Details:** Cards accepted. 80 seats. Music. Children allowed.

Hélène Darroze at the Connaught

Avant-garde, complex, thrilling
16 Carlos Place, Mayfair, W1K 2AL
Tel no: (020) 3147 7200
www.the-connaught.co.uk
⊖ Bond Street, Green Park, map 5
French | £75
Cooking score: 6

V

Following an excursion into jazzy patterns a few years ago, the Connaught dining room is back to the oak-panelled sobriety with which it has always felt comfortable. It's an oddly comforting atmosphere indeed, all subdued lighting and murmured solicitations, and it's a cleverly muted backdrop for the snap, crackle and pop of Hélène Darroze's cooking. There is a sense of studied Parisian intellectualism about this food, announced in the borderline-incoherent menu descriptions, which may start in French and drift into 'anglais de pidgin' with blurts of adventitious Hispanic. The result is dishes that are not titled, as such, but inventoried, as though a rummage through the fridge might have produced Racan pigeon with a crust of pralines from Pralus, grilled duck foie gras from Les Landes, glazed beetroots, wild strawberries, baby sorrel, intense jus with Mexican mole – the least successful dish at an inspection, as it didn't rise above its defiant heterogeneity. This slip is the rule-proving exception though, as most of what turns up is powerfully impressive, stunning even. A first course of a single fat scallop bathed in tandoori spices, alongside a more Thai-informed spring carrot and citrus mousseline, is a sensational burst of flavours, while the superb milk-fed Pyrenean lamb at main might be anatomised into saddle, kidney, cutlets and even foot, all worked up with an anchovy-garlic jus that references pissaladière, accompanied by a pot of Béarn beans and piquillo peppers. Desserts allow a gentle coming back to earth, perhaps with a glass of textured apple elements surrounding a fragile pannacotta, pungently redolent of sage. Service is A1, especially from the young sommelier, who is readily clued-up about the tonnage of fine wine that the place trades in. Glass selections include a fine mature Bordeaux, Château Pibran 2004, at £17, while bottles start at around £35.

Chef/s: Hélène Darroze. **Open:** Tue to Sun L 12 to 2.15 (11 to 3 Sat and Sun), Tue to Sat D 6.30 to 10.15. **Closed:** Mon, first week Jan, 2 weeks Aug. **Meals:** Set L £35. Set D £75. Tasting menu £85 (7 courses). **Service:** 12.5% (optional). **Details:** Cards accepted. 62 seats. Separate bar. No music. No mobile phones. Wheelchair access. Children allowed. Car parking.

Hibiscus

Affluence, stature and breathtaking cooking
29 Maddox Street, Mayfair, W1S 2PA
Tel no: (020) 7629 2999
www.hibiscusrestaurant.co.uk
⊖ Oxford Circus, map 5
Modern French | £80
Cooking score: 8
V

A Mayfair restaurant to be reckoned with and a serious contender on the international food scene, Claude Bosi's Hibiscus purrs contentedly, sure of its stature, affluence and pedigree. The dining room itself may seem rather cool and featureless, apart from the odd touch of glamour, but it's the food that people come to appreciate. There are dishes here that live on the outer reaches of modern French gastronomy, without plunging into the 'molecular' abyss – just consider Shropshire rose veal with aubergine and peanut butter caviar, boulangère potato, white miso and bonito jus, or even roast hand-dived scallops with pork pie sauce, pink grapefruit and wood sorrel. It also takes considerable nerve and brio to serve foie gras terrine with a compote of green mango and aloe vera. Bosi's kitchen knows how to swim confidently in the mainstream too – delivering a trademark amuse of mushroom velouté blended with a little scrambled egg and coconut (brought to the table in an eggshell) as well as a fabulous main course of plaice 'with just a hint of translucence in the middle', sharpened with a tangy clementine sauce and surrounded by earthy roasted salsify and mushrooms. Other ideas are harder to pin down: one reporter found unmistakable hints of American BBQ in long-cooked, 'fork-cutting tender' pork shoulder with glorious smoked potato mash, sweetcorn and other embellishments; and what about Cornish black bream stuffed with morels and Kaffir lime, in company with new season's soya beans and coffee. Desserts see Bosi breaking the rules again, especially when it comes to savoury flavours – witness a refresher of Granny Smith apple sorbet accompanied by finely diced celeriac and cumin crisp, a dark chocolate tart daringly paired with white miso ice cream and fresh goats' cheese or a mille-feuille of ginger, Puy lentils and wild lime. Some consider the carte way too pricey for its own good, but set lunches always deliver supreme quality and high levels of gustatory stimulation for a relatively modest outlay: recent standouts have included squid (served raw and cooked) with coffee, olives and yuzu ('one of the best things I've eaten all year') and a must-try Amalfi lemon tart ('worth the price of entry alone'). Nothing jars here, staff know how to engage and respond warmly while retaining their formal poise, and the wine list is a treasure trove – especially if your first vinous love is France. Otherwise you can go rustic on Corsica or pay handsomely for a trip to Tuscany or Australia's Eden Valley. Prices start at £26 (£6 a glass) for a 'version nature' from Provence.

Chef/s: Claude Bosi. **Open:** Tue to Sat L 12 to 2.30, Mon to Sat D 6.30 to 10 (6 Fri and Sat). **Closed:** Sun, 10 days Dec to Jan. **Meals:** Set L £29.50. Set D £60 (2 courses) to £80. Tasting menu L £85 (6 courses), D Fri and Sat £80 (4 courses) to £100 (8 courses). **Service:** 12.5% (optional). **Details:** Cards accepted. 45 seats. No music. No mobile phones. Wheelchair access. Children allowed.

Hix

Flavours that ring out
66-70 Brewer Street, Soho, W1F 9UP
Tel no: (020) 7292 3518
www.hixsoho.co.uk
⊖ Piccadilly Circus, map 5
British | £30
Cooking score: 4
V

Mark Hix opened this chic Soho venue in late 2009, bringing his trademark style of direct, modern, unfussy British food to a restaurant-rich slice of central London. You can head downstairs to Mark's for bar snacks and cocktails, or stay on the ground for a menu of well-rendered brasserie dishes served in a cool, no-nonsense atmosphere, where bespoke mobiles by the likes of Damien Hirst and Sarah Lucas hover over proceedings. Trad starters embrace options such as prawn cocktail or smoked salmon and soda bread, and there's also a hearty mussel and cider broth. One or two less familiar accompaniments crop up among mains – sea purslane with the cod, buttered sprout tops and a game dumpling with roast woodcock – while presentations keep things neat and straightforward, the better to let flavours ring out. Finish with pear and almond tart. A useful selection of wines by the glass kicks off at £4.75 for a sturdy Tempranillo.

Chef/s: Kevin Gratton. **Open:** all week 12 to 11.30pm (10.30pm Sun). **Closed:** 25 Dec. **Meals:** alc (main courses £15 to £28). Set L and D £17.50 (2 courses) to £22.50. **Service:** 12.5% (optional). **Details:** Cards accepted. 80 seats. Separate bar. Music. Children allowed.

Hix at the Albemarle

Invigorated old-school charmer
Brown's Hotel, 30 Albemarle Street, Mayfair, W1S 4BP
Tel no: (020) 7518 4004
www.thealbemarlerestaurant.com
⊖ Green Park, map 5
British | £33
Cooking score: 4
🛏 V

A liberal application of trendy Brit art – courtesy of Tracey Emin et al – helps to dispel any patrician gloom in this invigorated, old-school dining room with its dark panelled walls, pillars and green leather seating. Clubby masculinity also meets racy new blood in the kitchen, where food-hunting patriot Mark Hix is introducing a new generation to the native thrills of soused alexanders, boxty pancakes, snail pie and rape greens. This is home-grown gastronomy with a vengeance and it can yield terrific results: gutsily seasoned ham hock with chunky piccalilli; pheasant with creamed Brussels sprouts, bacon and chestnuts; wild rabbit braised in Burrow Hill cider, and an inspired dish of pollack with Cornish mussels and punchy Bath Pig chorizo. For afters, reel in the

years with sparkling party treats including rhubarb jelly with ice cream, buttermilk pudding or ginger parkin. Wines are knowledgeably sourced but pricey; house selections start at £28 (£8 a glass).
Chef/s: Mark Hix and Marcus Verberne. **Open:** all week L 12 to 3 (12.30 to 4 Sun), D 5.30 to 11 (7 to 10.30 Sun). **Meals:** alc (main courses £16 to £27). Set L and pre-theatre D £27.50 (2 courses) to £32.50. Sun L £37.50. **Service:** not inc.
Details: Cards accepted. 80 seats. Separate bar. No music. Wheelchair access. Children allowed.

Ibérica

Impeccable Spanish all-rounder
195 Great Portland Street, Fitzrovia, W1W 5PS
Tel no: (020) 7636 8650
www.ibericalondon.com
⊖ Regent's Park, Great Portland Street, map 5
Spanish | £30
new chef

£5 OFF

Modern Spanish cooking served in a light, sleekly designed space has proved a winning formula for this tapas bar-cum-restaurant and it has accrued a strong following. But right on our deadline we learnt of the departure of Santiago Guerrero. New chefs are Neftali Cumplido and Cesar Garcia (who worked for a year with executive chef Nacho Manzano at his high-ranking Casa Marcial in Asturias). It is unlikely that there will be any dramatic changes to a cooking style that embraces the creative touches one might find in the new Spain. Revised menus were unavailable as we went to press, but the tapas bar will continue to be strong on cured hams and cheeses. The wine list is an all-Spanish affair.
Chef/s: Neftali Cumplido and Cesar Garcia. **Open:** all week 11.30am to 11.00pm (12 to 6 Sun). **Closed:** 25 Dec. **Meals:** alc (main courses £5 to £38). **Service:** 12.5% (optional). **Details:** Cards accepted. 125 seats. Wheelchair access. Music. Children allowed.

ALSO RECOMMENDED

▲ The Ivy

1-5 West Street, Covent Garden, WC2H 9NQ
Tel no: (020) 7836 4751
www.the-ivy.co.uk
⊖ Leicester Square, map 5
Modern European

The Ivy sails on, a West End bolt-hole where one still scans the room for stars of stage and screen, and the brasserie menu still delivers plenty of unpretentious choice. The kitchen's version of kedgeree (£13.25 as a starter) gets the nod from one satisfied reader. Mains take in roast devilled veal kidneys with cauliflower mash (£17.50), with sides such as Parmesan courgettes, and there's blood orange trifle with 'wild' chocolate to finish. Wines from £25. Open all week.

J. Sheekey

Theatreland's seafood star
28-32 St Martin's Court, Covent Garden, WC2N 4AL
Tel no: (020) 7240 2565
www.j-sheekey.co.uk
⊖ Leicester Square, map 5
Seafood | £37
Cooking score: 4

Don't be intimidated by the top-hatted doorman, the frosted windows or the masculine, wood-panelled dining room – they are all part of Sheekey's inimitable charm. Set up by seafood trader Josef Sheekey in 1896, this theatreland evergreen became part of Caprice Holdings in 1998. Whether you are looking for a clubby, deal-brokering den or an eminently civilised, pre/post-show pit-stop, it satisfies all demands. Bivalves and crustacea 'au naturel' are the kitchen's stock-in-trade, its fish pie is legendary, and there are always tempters for those wanting something more challenging than pan-fried slip soles. Check the specials for, say, char-grilled squid with capers and preserved lemon or hake fillet with Exe mussels, wild garlic and kale mash. If fish isn't an option, order herb-roasted corn-fed chicken or a steak, and leave room for some treacle tart or cheesecake ice cream. Patrician Old World names dominate the wine list, with prices from £21.75.

Chef/s: Richard Kirkwood. **Open:** all week L 12 to 3 (3.30 Sun), D 5.30 to 12 (6 to 11 Sun). **Closed:** 25 Dec. **Meals:** alc (main courses £15 to £40). Sun L £26.50. **Service:** 12.5% (optional). **Details:** Cards accepted. 93 seats. Separate bar. No music. No mobile phones. Wheelchair access. Children allowed.

J. Sheekey Oyster Bar

Bushy-tailed Sheekey offspring
33-34 St Martin's Court, Covent Garden, WC2N 4AL
Tel no: (020) 7240 2565
www.j-sheekey.co.uk
⊖ Leicester Square, map 5
Seafood | £26
Cooking score: 4

If you don't have the time or inclination for a full-dress Sheekey experience, this bushy-tailed offspring should fit the bill for a couple of plates of seafood and a drink. Pitched right next door to the esteemed original (see entry) it echoes the style, with wood panelling, photos of stage stars and a classy horseshoe-shaped counter at the heart of things. The kitchen takes its cue from Sheekey senior, but concentrates its efforts on manageable, affordable items ranging from Strangford Lough oysters and dressed crab to razor clams with sea purslane, sautéed octopus with chorizo and broad beans or salmon ceviche with peppered lime and endive. If something more filling is required, consider a bowl of squid and wild boar cassoulet or Cornish fish stew, and finish with a helping of nostalgia – maybe Welsh rarebit or steamed sponge pudding with Yorkshire rhubarb and custard. Everything on the snappy wine list is sensibly offered by the glass or carafe, with bottles from £17.25.

Chef/s: Richard Kirkwood. **Open:** all week noon to midnight (11pm Sun). **Closed:** 25 Dec. **Meals:** alc (main courses £7 to £13). **Service:** 12.5% (optional). **Details:** Cards accepted. 32 seats. No mobile phones. Wheelchair access. Music. Children allowed.

Kiku

Calming Japanese retreat
17 Half Moon Street, Mayfair, W1J 7BE
Tel no: (020) 7499 4208
www.kikurestaurant.co.uk
⊖ Green Park, map 5
Japanese | £30
Cooking score: 4

The name means 'chrysanthemum', and there's something reassuringly Zen-like about Kiku's clean lines, stone floors and oriental blinds – no wonder it has established itself as a calming retreat for Mayfair's corporate crowd and lovers of traditional Japanese cuisine. Sushi fans should head straight for the vast bar, where chefs deliver sparklingly fresh nigiri of the highest order and all manner of intriguing hand-rolls, from yamagobo (with mountain burdock) to sakekawa (salmon skin) and unagi kyuuri (grilled eel and cucumber). Alternatively, move into the dining room where you can submit to the measured rituals of a kaiseki banquet or order from carte; either way, stimulate your appetite with nameko oroshi (Japanese mushrooms on grated mooli) or dengaku konnyaku (devil's tongue plant topped with sweet miso paste) before tackling teriyaki salmon, a casserole of taro and aubergines, or deep-fried lemon sole. Shabu-shabu hotpots and noodle-based udonsuki are good for sharing, and there are pretty little daifuku rice cakes to finish. Wines start at £15.50.

Chef/s: H Shiraishi, Y Hattori and M Anayama. **Open:** Mon to Sat L 12 to 2.30, all week D 6 to 10.15. **Closed:** Sun, 25 and 26 Dec, 1 Jan. **Meals:** alc (main courses £10 to £39). Set L £15 (2 courses) to £20. Set D £20 (2 courses) to £50 (8 courses). **Service:** 12.5%. **Details:** Cards accepted. 100 seats. No mobile phones. Wheelchair access. Music. Children allowed.

NEW ENTRY

Koya

Noodles with oodles of love and care
49 Frith Street, Soho, W1D 4SG
Tel no: (020) 7434 4463
www.koya.co.uk
⊖ Tottenham Court Road, map 5
Japanese | £15
Cooking score: 2

It requires something special to stand out on foodie Frith Street, and the love and care that Koya lavishes on its udon noodles gives it just that. The basic dining room has a four-stool counter out back overlooking the kitchen, providing a grandstand view of the chefs at work. Choose from an 'honest, authentic' selection including mushroom with walnut miso, mixed seaweed or prawn and vegetable tempura. Alternatively, blackboard specials offer the likes of baby clam and sea aster salad and there are various rice bowls with miso soup. Expect to queue; charming waiters will squeeze you in – often at a shared a table, but that adds to the buzz. Wine is £21.50, but saké, shochu or beer may be preferable.
Chef/s: Junya Yamasaki and Shuko Oda. **Open:** Mon to Sat L 12 to 3, D 5.30 to 10.30. **Closed:** 25 and 26 Dec. **Meals:** alc (main courses £6 to £13). **Service:** 10% (optional). **Details:** Cards accepted. 48 seats. No music. Children allowed.

Lantana Café

Brilliant for brunch
13 Charlotte Place, Fitzrovia, W1T 1SN
Tel no: (020) 7637 3347
www.lantanacafe.co.uk
⊖ Goodge Street, Tottenham Court Road, map 5
Eclectic | £15
Cooking score: 1

This casual, likeable Aussie café is one of those places that is creatively redefining what we expect of eating out in the capital. It's open daily for a reasonably priced, flexible menu that ranges from breakfasts of Spanish-style baked eggs with chorizo, spinach, fresh basil and spicy tomato sauce to lunches of brown sugar-cured salmon with braised fennel, baked polenta and salsa verde – no wonder there are queues at the weekend. Corn fritters and banana bread are must-haves, and the coffee is superb. House French is £17.
Chef/s: Tim Dorman. **Open:** all week 8 to 6 (9pm Thur and Fri, 9 to 5 Sat and Sun). **Closed:** 25 Dec to 2 Jan, bank hols. **Meals:** alc (main courses £4 to £13). **Service:** not inc. **Details:** Cards accepted. 25 seats. 8 seats outside. Music. Children allowed.

Latium

Accomplished Italian
21 Berners Street, Fitzrovia, W1T 3LP
Tel no: (020) 7323 9123
www.latiumrestaurant.com
⊖ Goodge Street, Oxford Circus, map 5
Italian | £34
Cooking score: 3

The smart atmosphere of this accomplished Italian restaurant with its crisply dressed tables and vibrant paintings suits the area well. For all that its feet may be in Fitzrovia, its heart is in Lazio – and indeed in other parts of the Italian peninsula too. Campania bresaola with green beans and lemon oil is a zesty antipasto, while pasta options take in crab tagliolini in aubergine salsa, as well as myriad ways with ravioli. Mains include benchmark osso buco with polenta and glazed baby onions, and there's a good coffee-foamed tiramisu to finish. Italian thoroughbreds dominate a wine list that starts at £16.
Chef/s: Maurizio Morelli. **Open:** Mon to Fri L 12 to 3, Mon to Sat D 6.30 to 10.30 (11 Sat). **Closed:** Sun, 24 Dec to 3 Jan, bank hols. **Meals:** Set L £15.50 (2 courses) to 20.50. Set D £28.50 (2 courses) to £33.50. **Service:** 12.5% (optional). **Details:** Cards accepted. 65 seats. Wheelchair access. Music. Children allowed.

Locanda Locatelli

Ritzy, seductive Italian flagship
8 Seymour Street, Marble Arch, W1H 7JZ
Tel no: (020) 7935 9088
www.locandalocatelli.com
⊖ Marble Arch, map 4
Italian | £56
Cooking score: 4

The epitome of Italian cool for many West End A-listers, imperious Giorgio Locatelli's flagship sails on, seducing everyone with its leather surrounds, etched glass screens and the promise of clear-flavoured regional 'cucina'. Fresh tones and understatement abound, from 'delightfully tender' char-grilled squid pointed up with chilli, garlic and rocket to a sublime combo of burrata with oven-dried tomatoes, basil breadcrumbs and red wine vinegar. Homemade pasta is a star turn and the kitchen rings the seasonal changes, delivering beautifully fashioned pappardelle with chicken livers and sage as well as malfatti parcels with pumpkin and amaretti. Steamed hake with garlic, parsley and fennel salad is a typically straight main, while desserts include a take on Eton mess involving Amalfi lemons. Despite its ritzy, sharp-suited demeanour and grown-up exclusivity, Locanda Locatelli also fits well as an unstuffy family destination – even if staff are sometimes short on smiles. Meanwhile, the wine list reads like a 'Serie A' league table of Italian viniculture; premier league growers abound and there's plenty for those on a tight budget, with prices from £12 (£3.50 a glass). Mind-boggling grappas, too.
Chef/s: Giorgio Locatelli. **Open:** all week L 12 to 3, D 6.45 to 11. **Closed:** 24 to 26 Dec, 1 Jan. **Meals:** alc (main courses £17 to £33). **Service:** 12.5% (optional). **Details:** Cards accepted. 82 seats. No music. No mobile phones. Wheelchair access. Children allowed.

ALSO RECOMMENDED

▲ Mango Tree

46 Grosvenor Place, Belgravia, SW1X 7EQ
Tel no: (020) 7823 1888
www.mangotree.org.uk
⊖ Victoria, Hyde Park Corner, map 4
Thai £5 OFF

The opulent setting, on one of the perimeter roads of Buckingham Palace Gardens, is a prime site for one of central London's more dazzling Thai restaurants. Coffee-coloured banquettes and a bright, airy atmosphere make a pleasing backdrop for exotic cocktails and sound Thai cookery. Barbecued pork with cucumber and nam jim sauce (£7.25), textbook tom yum soup with shimeji mushrooms, stir-fried king prawns with peppers, onion and chilli (£17), and the house-special beef sirloin with ginger, garlic and oyster sauce are the business. Wines from £19. Open all week D only.

Mennula

A hearty Sicilian workout
10 Charlotte Street, Fitzrovia, W1T 2LT
Tel no: (020) 7636 2833
www.mennula.com
⊖ Goodge Street, map 5
Italian | £35
Cooking score: 3

'Sicilians believe their food is the best in the world', writes one who knows, and there's no shortage of regional pride at this patriotic venue deep in W1 medialand. The island's fulsome flavours and ingredients are given a hearty workout here, starting with a mini feast of stuzzichini including 'little balls of ambrosia' in the shape of arancini stuffed with cream cheese. Dill-flavoured lasagne with sardines is a speciality, although the kitchen also dishes up thick slabs of monkfish with pitch-perfect saffron risotto and samphire, lamb shank with root vegetable mash and balsamic juices, and some wildly inviting, 'big statement' desserts including wondrous cassata, cannoli and almond (mennula) semifreddo. Exemplary service comes with 'exactly the right amount of reserve', but space is tight and the muzak can grate. There have also been gripes about 'underwhelming' vibes, lacklustre flavours and far-from-cheap prices. The wine list is packed with regional Italian goodies, including a heady Sicilian contingent from £16.50.

Chef/s: Santino Busciglio. **Open:** Sun to Fri L 12 to 3, all week D 6 to 11 (9 Sun). **Closed:** bank hols. **Meals:** alc (main courses £14 to £29). Set L and D £17.50 (2 courses) to £19.50. **Service:** 12.5% (optional). **Details:** Cards accepted. 40 seats. 8 seats outside. Music. Children allowed.

Mint Leaf

Cool subterranean Indian
Suffolk Place, Haymarket, SW1Y 4HX
Tel no: (020) 7930 9020
www.mintleafrestaurant.com
⊖ Piccadilly Circus, Charing Cross, map 5
Indian | £40
Cooking score: 2

Black-uniformed waiters strut their stuff along the raised 'catwalks' between the tables of this dimly lit contemporary Indian yards from Trafalgar Square. To the gentle thrum of chill-out music they parade back and forth, bringing jewel-bright cocktails and European-influenced versions of Indian dishes. Scottish scallops are pan-fried and flavoured with star anise and green peppercorns, while a seekh kebab sees minced lamb pepped up with saffron and basil. Most customers skip the well-constructed wine list (bottles from £22) in favour of cocktails with risqué names. A second Mint Leaf, open weekdays only, is at 12 Angel Court, Bank EC2R 7HB; tel (020) 7600 0992.

Chef/s: Gopal Krishnan. **Open:** Mon to Fri L 12 to 3, all week D 5.30 to 11 (10.30 Sat and Sun). **Closed:** 25 and 26 Dec, 1 Jan. **Meals:** alc (main courses £13 to £28). Set L and D £13.95 (2 courses) to £17.95. **Service:** 12.5% (optional). **Details:** Cards accepted. 200 seats. Separate bar. Wheelchair access. Music. Children allowed.

ALSO RECOMMENDED

▲ Mon Plaisir

21 Monmouth Street, Covent Garden, WC2H 9DD
Tel no: (020) 7836 7243
www.monplaisir.co.uk
⊖ Covent Garden, map 5
French

Little changes at this unreservedly French institution. The menu deals in precisely the kind of dishes one expects and the kitchen makes a good fist of most of them: 'fantastic' French onion soup (£6.75), 'delicious' sea bream with mustard sauce, 'old-fashioned' coq au vin (£16.95), and a 'very good' cheese selection (£8.95) were components of a satisfying dinner for one group of reporters. Pre- and post-theatre menus (£15.95 for two courses) are good value. House French is £18. Closed Sun.

Moti Mahal

Regional Indian cooking
45 Great Queen Street, Covent Garden, WC2B 5AA
Tel no: (020) 7240 9329
www.motimahal-uk.com
⊖ Covent Garden, map 5
Indian | £50
Cooking score: 3

When restaurants are imported from overseas they often lose something in translation, but this smart Covent Garden outpost of a Delhi stalwart produces some of the best Indian food in the capital. The menu takes its inspiration from the Grand Trunk Road as it works its way 2500km from Bengal to Pakistan's North-West Frontier, so expect plenty of regional specialities. Feast on lamb chops roasted with Kashmiri chillies from Peshawar or nibble on crispy fried courgette flowers stuffed with whiting, a Bengali favourite. A glass-fronted kitchen affords a view of the breadmaker as he turns out perfect tandoor-baked naans and rotis. Cleverly compiled tasting menus help to narrow down your selections and the lunch offer is a steal for cooking of this calibre. House wine is £28.

Chef/s: Anirudh Arora. **Open:** Mon to Fri L 12 to 3, Mon to Sat D 5.30 to 11. **Closed:** Sun, 25 to 28 Dec Dec, 1 Jan. **Meals:** alc (main courses £9 to £28). Set L £15 (2 courses) to £18. Set D £19 (2 courses) to £23. **Service:** 12.5% (optional). **Details:** Cards accepted. 100 seats. Wheelchair access. Music. Children allowed.

Mr Kong

Chinatown beacon with plenty of hits
21 Lisle Street, Soho, WC2H 7BA
Tel no: (020) 7437 7341
www.mrkongrestaurant.com
⊖ Leicester Square, map 5
Chinese | £20
Cooking score: 2

You may feel spoiled for choice in Chinatown, but the random approach is not the best one. Instead, seek out the beacons of quality such as Mr Kong, where amid traditional décor and on-the-ball, friendly service the kitchen oversees a regionally eclectic menu that scores plenty of hits. Staples such as spring rolls and crispy duck are utterly dependable, and among main dishes king prawns with fried squid or black-pepper chicken show up well. Venturing further into the water, you might try sizzling frogs' legs in chilli and black bean, or, from the chef's specials, steamed crab in rice wine with glass noodles. An extensive menu of vegetarian dishes – a rarity in most Chinese restaurants – is proving popular. House French is £10.50.

Chef/s: Kwai Kong and Y Wai Lo. **Open:** all week noon to 2.45am (1.45am Sun). **Closed:** 24 and 25 Dec. **Meals:** alc (main courses £8 to £30). Set L and D £10.50 (2 courses) to £24.80 (4 courses). **Service:** 10% (optional). **Details:** Cards accepted. 110 seats. No music. No mobile phones. Children allowed.

Also recommended entries are not scored but we think they are worth a visit.

★ CHEF OF THE YEAR ★ ANGELA HARTNETT

Murano

Angela wows the crowds again
20 Queen Street, Mayfair, W1J 5PP
Tel no: (020) 7495 1127
www.angela-hartnett.com
⊖ Green Park, map 5
Italian | £65
Cooking score: 7

V

Angela Hartnett's star is waxing ever more strongly since she bought herself out of the Gordon Ramsay stable and made herself the sole owner of Murano, an elegant, über-cool room done out in neutral colours, with carefully judged lighting and well-spaced tables. Copious praise continues to pour in from readers, whether singling out generous pre-nibbles of deep-fried arancini balls and charcuterie, the excellent bread or simply expressing delight with service that is as 'attentive and friendly as ever'. The cooking has its roots in regional Italian cuisine, but also shows a broader affection for Mediterranean flavours, fabulous seasonal ingredients and modern ideas. The kitchen sends out perfectly ripe San Marzano tomatoes well-matched by smoked ricotta and black olive powder, or a perfect raviolo stuffed with breast and confit of quail, served with a delicate sauce lifted by orange zest (pronounced 'lovely'). This confidence is matched by the thoughtfulness of assemblies – for one reporter a 'mouthwatering'chicken with citrus and garlic 'worked a treat'. Timings are generally careful, and dishes have an inherent simplicity and coherence which gives them a timeless feel: a perfectly cooked piece of halibut, for example, served with delicate gnocchi, sticky glazed chicken wings, white asparagus and hazelnut velouté. Fine judgement is applied to desserts, which can achieve a simplicity that belies the effort that created them – a textbook apricot and biscotti soufflé served with Amaretto anglaise, say. With all the incidentals (appetisers, pre-dessert of exquisitely flavoured mini-sorbets, petits fours and so forth), you will leave Murano having gone through a lot of food – yet the lightness of touch is such that you aren't likely to feel outfaced. And it's worth noting that these incidentals arrive with the excellent-value set lunch, too – making it one of London's bargains. The 27-page wine list explores Italy, France and the Iberian Peninsula in detail, but mark-ups are high. Drink by the glass from £5.50.

Chef/s: Angela Hartnett. **Open:** Mon to Sat L 12 to 3, D 6.30 to 11. **Closed:** Sun, 25 and 26 Dec. **Meals:** Set L £30. Set D £65 (3 courses) to £75. Tasting menu £85 (8 courses). **Service:** 12.5% (optional). **Details:** Cards accepted. 56 seats. Separate bar. No music. No mobile phones. Wheelchair access. Children allowed.

National Portrait Gallery, Portrait Restaurant

Flexible menus and top views
St Martins Place, Trafalgar Square, WC2H 0HE
Tel no: (020) 7312 2490
www.searcys.co.uk
⊖ Leicester Square, Charing Cross, map 5
Modern British | £30
Cooking score: 2

'What a view over London!' exclaimed one reporter, but another bemoaned the fact that hard surfaces make the National Portrait Gallery's top-floor dining room one of the capital's noisiest restaurants. Maybe not the best location for an intimate tryst, but in all other aspects just what's needed to complement the gallery's cultural offerings. Flexibility is there in the form of breakfasts and afternoon teas, with a greatest hits list of modern British cooking in between. Crab mayonnaise, devilled kidneys, confit duck leg and pork belly with red cabbage are typical of the output – and good quality is to the fore. Wines from £17.70.

Chef/s: Katarina Todosijevic. **Open:** all week L 11.45 to 2.45, Thur, Fri and Sat D 5.30 to 8.30. **Closed:** 24 to 26 Dec. **Meals:** alc (main courses £14 to £21). Set L £20 (2 courses) to £25. Pre-theatre set D £16.50 (2 courses) to £19.50. **Service:** 12.5% (optional). **Details:** Cards accepted. 90 seats. Separate bar. No music. Wheelchair access. Children allowed.

Nobu Berkeley St

Über-cool fashionistas' hangout
15 Berkeley Street, Mayfair, W1J 8DY
Tel no: (020) 7290 9222
www.noburestaurants.com
⊖ Green Park, map 5
Japanese | £66
Cooking score: 5

V

The Nobu group still draws on a loyal fan base of smart West Enders, who understand the drill perfectly by now, happily bending to the system of time-limited tables and packing the ground-floor bar in noisy throngs, before floating upstairs to sit on black bentwood chairs and let the menus work their magic once more. If there is anybody still unsure what to expect, it's exquisitely rendered versions of classical Japanese dishes – donburi, kushiyaki, maki and tempura variations – overlaid with South American fire in the form of chillied-up anti-cucho skewers or crossover dishes such as seared toro tuna with yuzu miso and jalapeño salsa. A Japanese wood-burning oven confers the precisely judged 'empyreumatic' note on many dishes, while the freshness of the seafood (all-important in sushi and sashimi offerings such as cuttlefish, razor clam and sea urchin) is beyond reproach. Set dinners, perhaps based on a teriyaki dish, are a good way of exploring the range. To finish, get to grips with warm chocolate ganache with crema catalana ice cream, candied pistachio garapiñados and mixed berry coulis. Organic juice blends such as blueberry, apricot, orange and sage head up the quality drinking, which embraces a treasure-trove of classic western wines from £32, as well as sakés of every grade and style.

Chef/s: Mark Edwards. **Open:** Mon to Fri L 12 to 2.15, all week D 6 to 11 (12 Thur to Sat, 9.15 Sun). **Closed:** bank hols. **Meals:** alc (main courses £5 to £32). Set L £26 to £29. Set D £23 to £26.25. **Service:** 15% (optional). **Details:** Cards accepted. 200 seats. Separate bar. Music.

Nobu London

Japanese fusion pioneer
Metropolitan Hotel, 19 Old Park Lane, Mayfair, W1K 1LB
Tel no: (020) 7447 4747
www.noburestaurants.com
⊖ Hyde Park Corner, map 5
Japanese | £75
Cooking score: 5

It may have been overtaken in the glamour stakes by its effervescent sibling on Berkeley Street (see entry), but Nobu's original London outlet can still turn heads – even if some die-hard fans think the white-walled dining room now looks as jaded as an 'airport cafeteria'. The paparazzi have moved on, but Mark Edwards' food is as emphatic as ever – although it hardly feels revolutionary these days. His once-daring black cod in miso has been bastardised across the land, but a first taste of fabulously delicate 'new style' sashimi, tuna tataki with ponzu or a bowl of silkily dressed rock shrimp tempura can still send sensory shock waves through the system. Nobu's trump card was the introduction of vivacious Latin flavours to the time-honoured conventions of Japanese cuisine – weird and wonderful ceviches, fiery 'anti-cuchos' skewers and crossovers such as langoustines with red chilli and shiso salsa – and it also likes to pile on the luxury with slabs of high-grade Wagyu beef, foie gras gyoza and blobs of caviar. When it comes to dessert, freaky lollipops and chocolate bento boxes are just the start: how about diving headlong into a plate of 'huevo' (calamansi parfait, shiso and Thai basil sponge with pistachio ice cream, lychee coulis and a chocolate shell). Extras such as the whacking 15 per cent service charge can grate (especially when table-turning is ruthlessly enforced), and the high-end wine list takes no prisoners. Growers and vintages are peerless, but you'll struggle to find anything below £30 (and that includes half-bottles).

Chef/s: Mark Edwards. **Open:** all week L 12 to 2.15 (12.30 to 2.30 Sat and Sun), D 6 to 10.15 (11 Fri and Sat, 10 Sun). **Closed:** 25 and 26 Dec, 1 Jan. **Meals:** alc (main courses £10 to £36). Set L £60 to £70 (5 courses). Set D £80 to £95 (6 courses). **Service:** 15% (optional). **Details:** Cards accepted. 160 seats. No music. Wheelchair access. Children allowed.

NEW ENTRY

Nopi

Clean, vibrant food from sunnier climes
21-22 Warwick Street, Soho, W1B 5NE
Tel no: (020) 7494 9584
www.nopi-restaurant.com
⊖ Piccadilly Circus, map 5
Middle Eastern/Mediterranean | £36
Cooking score: 3
V

Yotam Ottolenghi has extended his café/deli empire (see entry, Ottolenghi) with the opening of this two-tiered restaurant on the edge of Soho. With white-painted walls, pale wood and brass light fittings, it's the very definition of understated chic. It's suggested that each person choose three savoury dishes to share, but, as one reporter points out, 'not all of them lend themselves to the idea, and others are too good to share'. The kitchen fuses Mediterranean and Middle Eastern culinary traditions, and the result is clever, fresh and very effective, as in perfectly char-grilled broccolini with skordalia (a thick garlic sauce) and chilli oil; grilled mackerel with red lentils, smoked labneh (yoghurt cheese) and mint sauce, and miso quail with red shallots, grapes and verjus. Home-baked sourdough and aubergine spread is delicious, cardamom rice pudding with rose syrup and pistachio makes a perfect finish. Wines from £19.

Chef/s: Sarit Packer. **Open:** Mon to Fri 8am to 2.45, D 5.30 to 11.30. Sat 9am to 11.30pm, Sun 10am to 4pm. **Meals:** alc (main courses £7 to £12). **Service:** 12.5% (optional). **Details:** Cards accepted. 98 seats. Music. Children allowed.

Noura Brasserie

Spicy Lebanese favourite
16 Hobart Place, Belgravia, SW1W 0HH
Tel no: (020) 7235 9444
www.noura.co.uk
⊖ Victoria, map 5
Lebanese | £35
Cooking score: 3

 **V**

As the original London branch of the Noura chain, this upscale brasserie has a reputation to uphold and it does the job, thanks to polite, suited staff, smart surrounds and emphatically spiced food. There's a spirit of generous hospitality about the cooking, from the harvest festival of raw vegetables presented as an opener to the vast array of hot and cold mezze that form the backbone of the menu: creamy moutabal with a hefty whack of tahini is a 'standout', and readers have also gorged themselves on bowls of hummus, crisply coated kibbeh and grease-free fatayer pastries. Mains are all about moist, chunky skewered meats served with salad and a dollop of toum (Lebanese aïoli), while sticky-sweet baklava ranks as the textbook finale – although rosewater ice cream is also recommended. House wines are £24.

Chef/s: Badih El Asmar. **Open:** all week 11am to 11pm (10.30 Sun). **Meals:** alc (main courses £13 to £24). Set L £22.50. Set D £32. Sun L £32. **Service:** 12.5% (optional). **Details:** Cards accepted. 130 seats. 30 seats outside. Wheelchair access. Music. Children allowed.

NEW ENTRY

Opera Tavern

A nice line in charcuterie and tapas
23 Catherine Street, Covent Garden, WC2B 5JS
Tel no: (020) 7836 3680
www.operatavern.co.uk
⊖ Covent Garden, map 5
Spanish/Italian | £25
Cooking score: 4

'A wine list to keep everyone happy' with its enticing by-the-glass selection of sherries, stickies, sparklers and excellent Italian house-pours (from £3.90 a glass) isn't all Opera Tavern has to offer. This two-storey theatreland pub conversion – 'a great addition to the area and good value' – also does a nice line in charcuterie and original Spanish/ Italian tapas (not unlike sister venues Dehesa and Salt Yard, see entries). Three dishes are recommended per person, though we'd throw in some nibbles (say pig's ears or a mini Ibérico pork burger) for a more substantial meal. At inspection, our fennel salami was on the turn, but things picked up over small plates of mackerel escabèche with hazelnuts and beets, and salt marsh lamb with nutty wild garlic farro. Pudding might be poached meringues with rhubarb, saffron cream and honeycomb, all flavours exquisitely balanced. Request a downstairs table for more atmosphere.

Chef/s: James Thickett. **Open:** all week L 12 to 3, Mon to Sat D 5 to 11.30. **Closed:** 24 Dec to 1 Jan. **Meals:** alc (tapas £4 to £14). **Service:** 12.5% (optional). **Details:** Cards accepted. 53 seats. 10 seats outside. Separate bar. Wheelchair access. Music. Children allowed.

Pearl

Eye-popping delights and affordable decadence
252 High Holborn, Holborn, WC1V 7EN
Tel no: (020) 7829 7000
www.pearl-restaurant.com
⊖ Holborn, map 5
Modern French | £60
Cooking score: 5

£5 OFF V

If you've ever dreamt of dwelling 'in marble halls', this grandiose slice of heritage real estate might just bring it all to life. Once home to Pearl Assurance, the lofty space is now a sparkling playground for beautiful people; Ionic columns provide the necessary gravitas, arty strings of pearly baubles dangle from above and romance is in the air. Service is 'simply lovely' and Jun Tanaka's food regularly hits the high notes, as you would expect from a chef steeped in the sensual world of mackerel fondant, stuffed pig's trotters and salt-crusted venison. His cooking is built on pin-sharp technique and meticulous detail, although he never forgets that flavour comes first: his tomato jelly immediately transported one recipient to 'the Italian coast'. He also knows how to conjure up eye-popping visual delights: a colour blast of hot-smoked salmon with chicory tart, beetroot purée and blood orange vinaigrette. for example. Meanwhile, seasonal alliances could yield braised pig's cheek with crisp belly, white polenta, confit ceps and quince purée at the year's end, or lemon sole with roast white asparagus, razor clams, samphire and shrimps come summer. Those who make it to dessert can expect further stunners in the shape of, say, a peanut and caramel chocolate dome with hazelnut ice cream. Meals are fleshed out with ample amuse-bouches and a plethora of petits fours, while the wine list is a weighty tome pitched at big spenders; prices rise sharply from £24.
Chef/s: Jun Tanaka. **Open:** Mon to Fri L 12 to 2.30, Mon to Sat D 6 to 10. **Closed:** Sun, 23 Dec to 4 Jan, Easter, last 2 weeks Aug. **Meals:** Set L £26.50 (2 courses) to £29.50. Set D £50 (2 courses) to £60. Tasting menu £70. **Service:** 12.5% (optional). **Details:** Cards accepted. 77 seats. Separate bar. Wheelchair access. Music. Children allowed.

Phoenix Palace

Delightful dim sum
3-5 Glentworth Street, Marylebone, NW1 5PG
Tel no: (020) 7486 3515
www.phoenixpalace.co.uk
⊖ Baker Street, map 4
Chinese | £35
Cooking score: 2

£5 OFF

At its best, this stylish 280-seater Chinese can perform as well as most of its rivals in the capital, especially at lunchtime when dim sum feature an array of delights such as delicate steamed prawn dumplings and pork and prawn turnip patties. The kitchen also handles the standard Cantonese repertoire well, with a few regional detours, and seafood is a strength: Dover sole, perhaps grilled with ginger and garlic soy sauce or steamed with tangerine peel. However, there have been worrying gripes from reporters in recent months concerning shambolic service. Let's hope this is a blip. Chilean house wine is £17.
Chef/s: Marco Li. **Open:** all week 12 to 11.30 (11 to 10.30 Sun). **Closed:** 25 Dec. **Meals:** alc (main courses £9 to £48.80). Set D £27.80. **Service:** 12.5% (optional). **Details:** Cards accepted. 280 seats. Separate bar. No mobile phones. Wheelchair access. Music. Children allowed.

Pied-à-Terre

Serious dining for serious people
34 Charlotte Street, Fitzrovia, W1T 2NH
Tel no: (020) 7636 1178
www.pied-a-terre.co.uk
⊖ Goodge Street, map 5
Modern French | £75
new chef

£5 OFF V

Synonymous with pedigree, precision and cultured poise, Pied-à-Terre also makes a virtue of discretion, going about its gilt-edged culinary business in a bijou Charlotte Street town house. The dining room's narrow dimensions and its restrained detailing – a glass screen here, a refined flower arrangement there – create a mood of intimate comfort that concentrates the senses wonderfully. For the past 11 years serious-minded foodies have beaten a path to its door for a taste of Shane Osborn's perfectly orchestrated, exquisitely calibrated food, but in 2011 the Aussie star announced that he was hanging up his whites and 'going travelling' for an extended sabbatical. His replacement took over too late for us to assess properly, but Marcus Eaves is no stranger to the Fitzrovia kitchen: he was Osborn's protégé before becoming top dog at its Marylebone sibling L'Autre Pied (see entry). Expectations are high, but Eaves' track record suggests that his confidence, assertive technique and sheer culinary class will be more than up to the challenge. Thankfully, Pied-à-Terre's stupendous cellar remains, allowing diners the additional pleasure of fabulous drinking from exemplary growers. 'Suggested wines' (from £28) offer a tempting snapshot of the list, or you can sip by the glass (from £5). Reports please.

Chef/s: Marcus Eaves. **Open:** Mon to Fri L 12.15 to 2.30, Mon to Sat D 6 to 10.45. **Closed:** Sun, last week Dec, first week Jan. **Meals:** Set L £23.50 (2 courses) to £29.50. Set D £60 (2 courses) to £75. Tasting menu £85 (10 courses) to £95. **Service:** 12.5% (optional). **Details:** Cards accepted. 44 seats. Separate bar. No music. Children allowed.

★ BEST NEW ENTRY 2012 ★

NEW ENTRY

Pollen Street Social

Utterly brilliant big-city eatery
8-13 Pollen Street, Mayfair, W1S 1NQ
Tel no: (020) 7290 7600
www.pollenstreetsocial.com
⊖ Oxford Circus, map 5
Modern British | £55
Cooking score: 8
V

Quitting Gordon Ramsay's Maze seems to have done Jason Atherton a power of good, judging by the energy, confidence and good vibrations oozing from his new gaff. Secreted on a discreet Mayfair alleyway, Pollen Street Social consists of a pulsating bar where fabulous cocktails and tapas plates are the order of the day, nestled cheek-by-jowl with a dining room that screams West End class – proper leather, proper wood trim, original artwork and a centrepiece floral display. It feels genuinely user-friendly and the whole place fairly bristles with life; 'mingling' comes with the territory (it's not called Social for nothing) and there's no 'please be seated' formality, although razor-sharp staff know the drill when it comes to the niceties of twenty-first century dining. In all, PSS is the kind of playful big-city eatery you would kill for as your local: 'I'd love to be a regular', confessed one convert, 'popping in every week and knowing everyone'. Maze was famed for its grazing dishes, but Pollen Street's approach is more conventional – although you can still build your own tasting menu from the admirably flexible carte. There's also a brilliant-value set lunch, which must rank as one of London's top bargains. Atherton is no absentee exec chef, either – he puts in the hours and his food is utterly brilliant. Ideas are cross-fertilised, inventive strokes of genius abound and British ingredients loom large, although there's an increasing nod to his beloved Spain. Consider pearly white halibut dressed with slices of fatty ham, sprouting broccoli and mussel stock accompanied by a copper pan filled with the most flavoursome paella imaginable, or an incredibly complex, 'sweetly acidic' riff on tomatoes involving fresh heirloom 'fruit', a sorbet and creamed burrata with a vanilla-tinged gazpacho poured over it.There are also a few reminders of the Maze glory days – notably the unctuous 'tongue 'n' cheek' with caper and raisin purée served in a pot with a side of wickedly buttery mash for mopping up all that richness ('maximum flavour, maximum satisfaction'). One dish, however, steals the show – a stunning study in monochrome involving tiny pieces of almost-milky squid cut and cooked to look like 'risotto' rice grains, sitting on discs of mooli stained with squid ink and surrounded by tiny crisp black nuggets and crunchy shavings of raw cauliflower, all bathed in golden squid stock. And then there's the dessert bar – a trump card if ever there was one. Perch at the counter, park your bag on the little stool provided and watch the chefs as they assemble all manner of captivating delights. It's like sushi for the sweet-toothed. On offer: anything from a Lilliputian deconstructed peanut butter and jam confection with rice puffs to the year's most outrageous visual pun – slices of ingeniously transmuted watermelon made to look like pata negra 'ham', intermingled with candied goats' curd and an intense basil sorbet. Meanwhile, the supremely confident sommelier (ex-Maze) proffers advice honestly when it comes to the tremendous 500-bin wine list. Treasures abound (Bott Geyl Mettis from Alsace, for example), half bottles are numerous and prices start at £24.

Chef/s: Jason Atherton. **Open:** Mon to Sat L 12 to 3, D 6 to 11. **Closed:** Sun, 25 and 26 Dec, 1 and 2 Jan, bank hols. **Meals:** alc (main courses £20 to £30). Set L £22 (2 courses) to £25. Tasting menu £70. **Service:** 12.5% (optional). **Details:** Cards accepted. 68 seats. Separate bar. Wheelchair access. Music. Children allowed.

Polpo

Riotous Italian 'tapas'
41 Beak Street, Soho, W1F 9SB
Tel no: (020) 7734 4479
www.polpo.co.uk
⊖ Piccadilly Circus, Oxford Circus, map 5
Italian | £18
Cooking score: 3

They don't take bookings in the evening, so you'll need to join the scrum at this riotous Italian venue – Russell Norman's ridiculously trendy take on a Venetian 'bacaro'. Every detail has been nailed here, from the obligatory zinc bar to the brick walls, terracotta paintwork, bare lights and deliberately 'distressed' feel. The menus double as brown-paper placemats and the open kitchen sends out quick-fire, tapas-style 'cicheti', little plates of cod cheeks and lentils 'with a fantastic sharp dressing', crumbed ox tongue with balsamic, deep-fried arancini balls, and 'sweet things' such as mischievous rum and raisin doughnuts. Be warned: noise levels are 'painful' and getting served can be a problem. House vino is £10.80 a litre. Baby sibling Polpetto is squeezed above the French House at 49 Dean Street, W1D 5BG; tel (020) 7734 1969, and da Polpo is at 6 Maiden Lane, WC2E 7NA; (020) 7836 8448.

Chef/s: Tom Oldroyd. **Open:** all week L 12 to 3 (4 Sat and Sun), Mon to Sat D 5.30 to 11. **Closed:** 25 Dec to 1 Jan. **Meals:** alc (tapas £5 to £8). **Service:** 12.5% (optional). **Details:** Cards accepted. 60 seats. Separate bar. Wheelchair access. Music. Children allowed.

ALSO RECOMMENDED

▲ La Porte des Indes

32 Bryanston Street, Marble Arch, W1H 7EG
Tel no: (020) 7224 0055
www.laportedesindes.com
⊖ Marble Arch, map 4
Indian

This bastion of Indian dining has been around for years and while some suggest it's 'resting on its laurels', others claim it's a 'unique dining experience'. The décor is certainly something to marvel at – a sprawling playground of tropical plants, complete with a cascading waterfall. An extensive menu features all the usual suspects, though the kitchen takes pride in dishes from India's former French colonies: richly spiced seafood stew, crab and corn cakes fragrant with curry leaves (£9.25), or duck breast in tamarind sauce (£17.50). Sunday brunch is popular, too. Wines start at £20. Open all week.

Symbols

- Accommodation is available
- £30 Three courses for less than £30
- V Separate vegetarian menu
- £5 OFF £5-off voucher scheme
- Notable wine list

LAURE PATRY
Pollen Street Social

When did you first know you wanted to be a sommelier?
I went to catering school and after that became a commis sommelier. I really enjoyed learning more about wine and visiting vineyards and decided that it would be my career.

Name three qualities needed to be a successful sommelier.
You need to be knowledgeable, likeable and have great attention to detail.

What is the most difficult part of your job?
The hours. And the fact that you're always standing.

What is your favourite food and wine combination?
There are many. At the moment I like our squid with Wild Ferment Assyrtiko, tiramisu with Lillypilly, foie gras with our Madeira Boal Barbeito, and blue cheese with Sauternes or icewine.

Which product, person or innovation has been the most influential in your field of expertise?
For me, I'm most influenced by meeting the wine producer and visiting the vineyard. It's the best way to learn.

▲ Princi

135 Wardour Street, Soho, W1F 0UT
Tel no: (020) 7478 8888
www.princi.co.uk
⊖ Tottenham Court Road, Piccadilly Circus, map 5
Italian

An all-day pit-stop in Soho, Princi opens for breakfast at 7am, with freshly baked croissants and banana bread toast, and for the famished, a full Italian (think full English, but call the bacon 'pancetta', for £8.50). The hungry lunchtime and evening stampedes are fed with pizza, from £9, pasta dishes and meaty stews, as well as focaccia sandwiches. It's hard to leave without having at least looked at the patisserie, which is so copious an array – from chocolate and walnut tart to zuppa inglese. Wines from £17. Open all week.

The Providores

Exhilarating fusion trailblazer
109 Marylebone High Street, Marylebone, W1U 4RX
Tel no: (020) 7935 6175
www.theprovidores.co.uk
⊖ Baker Street, Bond Street, map 4
Fusion | £46
Cooking score: 3

Peter Gordon has kept fusion alive and kicking for over a decade at his first-floor Marylebone restaurant, where inspired combinations have the potential to keep 'palates consistently entertained'. While dishes such as beef fillet with pickled shiitakes, chilli-glazed carrots and béarnaise butter prove his uncontested flair, tuna carpaccio with crispy squid, tobiko and olive oil jelly has been 'an incongruous mismatch of ingredients' – when you factor in eye-watering prices, there's no room for error. The ground floor, no-reservations Tapa Room is a cheaper way to dine, though it's cramped and decibel levels are astoundingly high. Happily there's less to criticise on the wine list – an impressive romp through Gordon's native New Zealand (from £22 for a good Marlborough Sauvignon

Blanc) with 20 options by the glass and carafe. Kopapa, 32-34 Monmouth Street, WC2, tel (020) 7240 6076 is Gordon's latest venture.

Chef/s: Peter Gordon and Cristian Hossack. **Open:** all week L 12 to 3, D 6 to 10. **Closed:** 24 Dec to 4 Jan, Easter Mon. **Meals:** alc (main courses £8 to £24). **Service:** 12.5% (optional). **Details:** Cards accepted. 42 seats. 6 seats outside. Music. Children allowed.

Quilon

Heaven-sent South Indian flavours
41 Buckingham Gate, Westminster, SW1E 6AF
Tel no: (020) 7821 1899
www.quilon.co.uk
⊖ St James's Park, Victoria, map 5
Indian | £40
Cooking score: 4

A sultry tropical mural, floral displays and pastel colours do their best to disguise the fact that Quilon is a corporate hotel dining room – albeit one with heaven-sent South Indian food. Chef Sriram Aylur understands every nuance of the region's cuisine and brings considerable technique and cheffy know-how to the table, with seafood as the top shout. Chunks of halibut simmered in coconut milk with raw mango, a take on caramelised black cod employing thick, spiced molasses instead of miso, and a mustard-laced casserole of monkfish, shrimps and scallops are just some of the delights on offer. However, if Kerala's richly fragrant maritime harvest doesn't appeal, you can always order guinea fowl with tomato masala or one of the fascinating veggie options. Also pay full attention to the details: soft-cooked rice with yoghurt curd, wonderfully crisp appam pancakes, and okra pachadi in particular. Saké is a surprising addition to the list of spice-friendly wines (note the Indian Chenin Blanc). Prices start at £22.

Chef/s: Sriram Aylur. **Open:** Sun to Fri L 12 to 2.30 (12.30 to 3.30 Sun), all week D 6 to 11 (10.30 Sun). **Closed:** 25 Dec. **Meals:** alc (main courses £16 to £29). Set L £24. Set D £41. Sun L £24. **Service:** 10% (optional). **Details:** Cards accepted. 83 seats. Separate bar. Wheelchair access. Music.

Quirinale

Statesmanlike Italian
1 Great Peter Street, Westminster, SW1P 3LL
Tel no: (020) 7222 7080
www.quirinale.co.uk
⊖ Westminster, map 3
Italian | £36
Cooking score: 3

Proximity to the Houses of Parliament means the clientele is likely to include huddles of men in suits, but this surprisingly light, modern basement restaurant has a lot more to offer than well-spaced tables designed for power broking. Ten years on, Stefano Savio's approach to food remains consistent – namely vibrant Italian dishes based on fresh seasonal ingredients, delivered by confident staff. He exacts maximum flavour across the board, opening the show with antipasti of Parma ham with glazed veal sweetbreads before going on to top-drawer pasta such as lamb lasagne with artichokes. Veal cutlet 'alla milanese' is a well-rendered classic, or you could try monkfish with speck and Castelluccio lentils. The wine list is predominantly Italian, with cross-border forays into France. Prices start at £21.

Chef/s: Stefano Savio. **Open:** Mon to Fri L 12 to 2.30, D 6 to 10.30. **Closed:** Sat, Sun, 24 Dec to first Mon in Jan, Aug, bank hols. **Meals:** alc (main courses £16 to £28). Set L £19 (2 courses) to £23. **Service:** 12.5% (optional). **Details:** Cards accepted. 50 seats. Music. Children allowed.

Quo Vadis

A place that's forever Soho
26-29 Dean Street, Soho, W1D 3LL
Tel no: (020) 7437 9585
www.quovadissoho.co.uk
⊖ Tottenham Court Road, map 5
Modern British | £34
Cooking score: 2

A dining institution since the 1920s, Quo Vadis has enjoyed a few makeovers in recent years, but behind the striped awning is a place that's forever Soho, all neon signage and stained glass, now carefully nurtured by the Hart

brothers (of Fino fame, see entry). A menu of robust, modern British brasserie cooking takes in ham hock terrine with piccalilli, crisp-fried calf's brains with tomato compote, and red gurnard with mussels and sea beet. The kitchen also accommodates everything from Dorset rock oysters to Rutland-reared, grass-fed Longhorn steaks, and the cooking aims for satisfaction rather than aesthetic statements. Finish with Pimm's jelly and lemon granité. Wines start at £23.
Chef/s: Jean Philippe Patruno. **Open:** Mon to Sat L 12 to 2.30, D 5.30 to 10.45. **Closed:** Sun, 24 to 26 Dec, bank hols. **Meals:** alc (main courses £12 to £35). Set L and D £17.50 (2 courses) to £19.50. **Service:** 12.5% (optional). **Details:** Cards accepted. 70 seats. Separate bar. No music. Children allowed.

The Red Fort

Regal dishes and subtle spicing
77 Dean Street, Soho, W1D 3SH
Tel no: (020) 7437 2115
www.redfort.co.uk
⊖ Tottenham Court Road, map 5
Indian | £35
Cooking score: 2
£5 OFF

Since opening in 1983, the Red Fort has survived a major fire and several changes of chef, but it continues to offer contemporary, upmarket interpretation of 'Mughal Court cooking'. The plush décor and smartly attired staff are mirrored by regal dishes with subtle spicing and a use of quality British ingredients that sets it apart from many of its contemporaries. Expect stone bass fillet cooked with mustard seed, coconut milk and curry leaf or Scottish lamb, which makes an appearance in a rogan josh flavoured with nutmeg, mace, cinnamon and bay leaf. Wines are not cheap, with bottles from £25.
Chef/s: M. A. Rahman. **Open:** Mon to Fri L 12 to 2.30, all week D 5.30 to 11.30 (10.30 Sun). **Closed:** 25 Dec. **Meals:** alc (main courses £16 to £34). Set L £14 (2 courses) to £25. Set D £18 (2 courses) to £40. **Service:** 12.5% (optional). **Details:** Cards accepted. 80 seats. Separate bar. Wheelchair access. Music. Children allowed.

ALSO RECOMMENDED

▲ Rex Whistler Restaurant at Tate Britain

Millbank, Westminster, SW1P 4RG
Tel no: (020) 7887 8825
www.tate.org.uk
⊖ Pimlico, map 3
Modern British

Wines are a fundamental part of a meal at this long-standing gallery restaurant, with plenty on the list to tempt, including an impressive 60 or so by the half-bottle. Well-chosen bottles from across France and Europe, with a decent selection from the New World, are backed up by fair pricing, starting at £16.50. To eat, razor clams with samphire (£7.50), herb-crusted venison loin with venison pudding (£19.50) and lemon posset come with 'charming service' and the superb Rex Whistler mural as a backdrop. Open all week, L only. Note: closed for refurb early in 2012.

Rhodes W1 Restaurant

Glitz, glamour and highfalutin food
Great Cumberland Place, Marble Arch, W1H 7DL
Tel no: (020) 7616 5930
www.rhodesw1.com
⊖ Marble Arch, map 4
Anglo-French | £50
Cooking score: 5

The principal Rhodes-branded dining room at the Cumberland Hotel near Marble Arch (there's a Brasserie in here too) is not to be missed. It's an eye-poppin', jaw-droppin' Kelly Hoppen room with light-fittings in dripping crystal and antique French chairs for parking yourself on. The Anglo-French fusion of the interior reflects something roughly similar going on in the kitchen. Paul Welburn is a skilled interpreter of this style, mixing classical and modern technique to memorable effect. A bowl of Jerusalem artichoke velouté contains a slow-cooked duck egg and much more besides (cannellini beans, bacon and wild mushrooms), while the smoked salmon, which is served warm, comes with gravadlax, sour apple, celeriac and hazelnuts for an interesting savoury array. Mains, too, are carefully balanced somewhere mid-Channel, as when a caramelised breast and slow-cooked leg of squab pigeon arrives with seared foie gras and pickled blackberries. Dessert could be Yorkshire rhubarb in a number of guises, with a gingery flapjack to boot, or else textbook prune and Armagnac soufflé with vanilla ice cream. Wines start at £24.50.

Chef/s: Paul Welburn. **Open:** Tue to Fri L 12 to 2, Tue to Sat D 7 to 10. **Closed:** Sun, Mon, 2 weeks Jan, 2 weeks Aug. **Meals:** Set L £19.95 (2 courses) to £24.95. Set D £39.90 (2 courses) to £49.90. **Service:** 12.5% (optional). **Details:** Cards accepted. 45 seats. Separate bar. Wheelchair access. Music.

Ristorante Semplice

Suave metropolitan Italian
9-10 Blenheim Street, Mayfair, W1S 1LJ
Tel no: (020) 7495 1509
www.ristorantesemplice.com
⊖ Bond Street, Green Park, map 5
Italian | £45
Cooking score: 5

Step through the doors of this gilded, burnished and glossy Italian just off Bond Street and you are in foodie heaven. Chef Marco Torri's food achieves a distinct blend of creativity and fashion, backed up by proper grounding in the old ways. He also knows his clients and ratchets up the impeccably sourced components, tempting the assembled crowd with a salad of scallops, candied ginger and faux pink pepper from Peru, an oh-so-simple pan-fried goats' cheese with red beetroot and balsamic vinegar, and a splendid rendition of a classic – vitello tonnato. From a long list of recommended dishes comes examples of the kitchen's mightily impressive capabilities: Gragnano linguine with Piedmontese rabbit ragù and fresh chilli; roast milk-fed Piedmontese veal with shiitake mushrooms, courgettes, Taggiasca olive and sweet potato sauce; wild sea bass served with sautéed spinach and a sauce of Spello chickpeas. Competitively priced set-lunch menus lure more than just Mayfair shoppers with plates of homemade spaghetti alla chitarra with amatriciana sauce, roast duck breast with lentils and Swiss chard, and orange salad with dark chocolate sorbet. The likeable wine list explores Italy with insightful selections arranged by region. House wines are from £17.50.

Chef/s: Marco Torri. **Open:** Mon to Fri L 12 to 2.30, Mon to Sat D 7 to 10.30 (11 Fri and Sat). **Closed:** Sun, bank hols, 25 to 31 Dec. **Meals:** alc (main courses £12 to £30). Set L £27.50 (2 courses) to £31. Tasting menu £85 (7 courses). **Service:** 12.5% (optional). **Details:** Cards accepted. 55 seats. Separate bar. No music. Wheelchair access. Children allowed.

Roka

Chic sushi and robata fireworks
37 Charlotte Street, Fitzrovia, W1T 1RR
Tel no: (020) 7580 6464
www.rokarestaurant.com
⊖ Goodge Street, map 5
Japanese | £50
Cooking score: 4

A big-city eatery right down to its thumping soundtrack, sharing dishes and below-stairs Shochu Lounge, Roka is cool, energetic and full of pulsating action. A robata grill holds centre stage, and the best seats in the house are around its grainy, wood-planked perimeter: watch as chefs do the business on everything from Korean-spiced lamb cutlets and de-boned quail to hotate (skewered scallops with wasabi and shiso). Sparkling fresh sushi and sashimi are top shouts, and the kitchen's penchant for seafood also shows in creative plates of butterfish tataki with white asparagus and yuzu dressing, or spicy yellowfin tuna with cucumber, chives and tempura flakes. Service is 'amazingly good' – given that the place is virtually non-stop from noon to around midnight – and it's worth taking advice when it comes to the fascinating list of sakés, shochu and style-driven wines (from £24). A second branch feeds the City throngs at 40 Canada Square, Canary Wharf, E14 5FW; tel (020) 7636 5228.

Chef/s: Hamish Brown and Nicholas Watt. **Open:** all week L 12 to 3.30 (12.30 to 4 Sat and Sun), D 5.30 to 11.30 (10.30 Sun). **Meals:** alc (dishes from £5 to £15). **Service:** 15%. **Details:** Cards accepted. 88 seats. 24 seats outside. Separate bar. Wheelchair access. Music. Children allowed.

Roux at Parliament Square

Assured food in measured surroundings
Parliament Square, Westminster, SW1P 3AD
Tel no: (020) 7334 3737
www.rouxatparliamentsquare.co.uk
⊖ Westminster, St James's Park, map 5
Modern European | £60
Cooking score: 4

A hit with politicians and the business crowd, Michel Roux Jr's second self-named restaurant (see also Roux at the Landau) strikes a statesmanlike pose, while the kitchen gets the thumbs-up for its assured food. Toby Stuart, previously sous chef at Galvin at Windows (see entry) now heads the kitchen and he pulls off ideas from the modern European repertoire with aplomb. Fish is sensitively handled, the treatments maximising its exemplary freshness – witness 'carefully cooked' steamed halibut served with asparagus, good morels and lemon thyme mousseline. Pigeon appears as a richly flavoured 'Kiev', featuring foie gras rather than garlic butter, with Madeira sauce, peas, beans, mousserons and courgette flowers. Crab raviolo with leeks, Avruga caviar and Champagne velouté could open proceedings, while a 'very well made' blackberry and apple crumble soufflé with a light green apple and Calvados sorbet might bring them to a close. Wines from £25.
Chef/s: Toby Stuart. **Open:** Mon to Fri L 12 to 2, D 6.30 to 10. **Closed:** Sat, Sun, 24 Dec to 4 Jan. **Meals:** Set L £29.50. Set D £50 (2 courses) to £60. Tasting menu £70. **Service:** 12.5% (optional). **Details:** Cards accepted. 56 seats. Separate bar. No mobile phones. Wheelchair access. Music. Children allowed.

Roux at the Landau

A grand hotel touting contemporary food
Langham Hotel, Portland Place, Oxford Circus, W1B 1JA
Tel no: (020) 7965 0165
www.thelandau.com
⊖ Oxford Circus, map 5
Modern European | £55
Cooking score: 5
V

The dining room at the Langham Hotel is an oval space, wood-panelled and chandeliered, with a view of All Souls church opposite. In late 2010, Chris King was transported from the deep-rooted classicism of Le Gavroche to head up the more obviously modern European repertoire here. Effective dishes have included a trio of Orkney scallops topped with truffle strands and matched with Jerusalem artichoke purée, a plate of sea bass with salsify, brown shrimps and braised lettuce in a smear of meaty jus, and a horseradish-crusted serving of the fashionable featherblade of beef, with creamy mash and a deep red wine jus. There is a secure understanding of the inherent potential and flavours within each component in these dishes, allied to a technical sensitivity which ensures that nothing is forced into a form that doesn't suit it. The pairing of chorizo-stuffed rabbit with langoustine, served with saffron rice, therefore recalls classic paella, while a more North African mood hovers over the rack of lamb with cracked wheat and olives. Dessert might be William pear and walnut soufflé, a combination that appears to work against its airborne inclinations, with fine bitter chocolate sorbet. The wine list is a rather snooty roll call of classics, with prices from £30 (glasses from £7.25).
Chef/s: Chris King. **Open:** Mon to Fri L 12.30 to 2.30, Mon to Sat D 5.30 to 10.30. **Closed:** Sun, bank hols. **Meals:** alc (main courses £18 to £42). Set L and D £47.50. **Service:** 12.5% (optional). **Details:** Cards accepted. 90 seats. Separate bar. Wheelchair access. Music. Children allowed.

Rules

Britannia rules in Covent Garden
35 Maiden Lane, Covent Garden, WC2E 7LB
Tel no: (020) 7836 5314
www.rules.co.uk
⊖ Covent Garden, Leicester Square, map 5
British | £42
Cooking score: 3

Now into its third century, London's oldest restaurant continues to delight 'hearty diners who want traditional comfort food' – with the odd grilled squid with Puy lentils or lamb curry inputting colour to the bare-bones Britishness of it all. It would be wrong to say that everything here is fantastic, but the setting is magical and the quality of the raw materials is first-class. Game and beef are the sensible things to order and are done well: from the famous grouse to fillet of red deer (with roast beetroot and chanterelles); from slabs of rare Belted Galloway beef or aged Aberdeen Angus to an 'intensely flavoured' steak and oyster pie. Puddings mean puddings – golden syrup, sticky toffee, steamed chocolate. Wines from the Rhône Valley are a speciality, with house French at £24.50.

Chef/s: Harvey Ayliffe. **Open:** all week 12 to 11.30 (10.30 Sun). **Closed:** 24 to 27 Dec. **Meals:** alc (main courses £18 to £28). Bar menu available. **Service:** 12.5% (optional). **Details:** Cards accepted. 95 seats. Separate bar. No music. No mobile phones. Children allowed.

Salloos

Bastion of Pakistani cooking
62-64 Kinnerton Street, Knightsbridge, SW1X 8ER
Tel no: (020) 7235 4444
⊖ Knightsbridge, map 4
Pakistani | £35
Cooking score: 3

Muhammad Salahuddin's exceedingly likeable, long-standing, family-run restaurant in a quiet Belgravia mews is reckoned to be one of the best Pakistani restaurants in the capital, its reputation hinging on consistency and top-quality raw materials. Tandooris form the backbone of a menu that sees no need to change, among them the kitchen's signature marinated lamb chops as well as shish kebabs, chicken tikka and superb naan and paratha breads. Specialities range from chicken or prawn karahi (with tomato, ginger, coriander and chillies) to slow-cooked curries like hallem akbari (shredded lamb over wheatgerm, lentil and spices) and the order-in-advance showpiece, raan masala (leg of lamb marinated with mild spices) for four to six people. Interesting vegetable sides, traditional desserts and above-the-norm service are all part the excellent package. Wines from £20.

Chef/s: Abdul Aziz. **Open:** Mon to Sat L 12 to 2.30, D 7 to 11.15. **Closed:** Sun, 25 and 26 Dec. **Meals:** alc (main courses £17 to £20). **Service:** 12.5%. **Details:** Cards accepted. 45 seats. No music. No mobile phones.

Salt Yard

Lively tapas hot spot
54 Goodge Street, Fitzrovia, W1T 4NA
Tel no: (020) 7637 0657
www.saltyard.co.uk
⊖ Goodge Street, map 5
Spanish/Italian | £30
Cooking score: 2

Tables are closely packed in the ground floor and stark basement dining rooms (the former is the preferred space) of this lively Fitzrovia hot spot. While modern tapas means wide-reaching cooking styles and influences, invariably there are Spanish basics, perhaps tortilla or chorizo and marinated peppers, supplemented by seasonal treats such as crispy squid with sea purslane and shellfish aïoli or char-grilled neck fillet of lamb with crushed Jerusalem artichokes and salsa verde. Courgette flowers stuffed with goats' cheese and drizzled with honey is a never-off-the-menu signature of the whole group (see entries for Dehesa and Opera Tavern). Spanish and Italian wines start at £15.35.

Chef/s: Andrew Clarke. **Open:** Mon to Fri L 12 to 3, Mon to Sat D 6 to 11 (5 Sat). **Closed:** Sun, 10 days Christmas, bank hols. **Meals:** alc (tapas £4 to £10).

Set L and D £27.50 (2 courses) to £32.50. **Service:** 12.5% (optional). **Details:** Cards accepted. 73 seats. 8 seats outside. Music. Children allowed.

NEW ENTRY

Savoy Grill

Showing respect for tradition
The Savoy, Strand, Covent Garden, WC2R 0EU
Tel no: (020) 7592 1600
www.gordonramsay.com
⊖ Charing Cross, map 5
Anglo-French | £45
Cooking score: 4

The Savoy Hotel was born again in late 2010, the no-expense-spared makeover having taken four years to complete. But the Grill just needed freshening up, and there has been no change to the oddly comforting atmosphere, the glossy wood-panelled sobriety and subdued lighting. Here, chef Andy Cook has shown respect for tradition on his long menu of brasserie favourites from both sides of the Channel. Primarily, this is a place 'that's all about meat'; here you can eat spectacular T-bone steaks, veal chops, Herdwick lamb cutlets, as well as duck breast with duck and cep sausage and sherry bacon sauce, and perhaps the best steak and kidney pudding in London. The cooking can undoubtedly reach great heights, but standards generally seem variable and several reporters have registered disappointments – fish cookery, for example, has been hit and miss. From a strong base in France, the wine list turns up interesting bottles from all corners of the world, starting at £22.

Chef/s: Andy Cook. **Open:** all week L 12 to 3 (4 Sun), D 5.30 to 11 (6 to 10.30 Sun). **Meals:** alc (main courses £17 to £39). **Service:** 12.5% (optional). **Details:** Cards accepted. 100 seats. No music. Wheelchair access. Children allowed.

Scott's

Gorgeously sleek, with soothing seafood
20 Mount Street, Mayfair, W1K 2HE
Tel no: (020) 7495 7309
www.scotts-restaurant.com
⊖ Green Park, map 4
Seafood | £45
Cooking score: 4
V

Scott's gorgeously sleek, high-gloss dining room cleverly blends a Parisian brasserie look with up-to-the-moment metropolitan chic – diners sit on green leather banquettes at white-clad tables amid oak panelling, Art Deco mirrors and contemporary art. The appeal of the menu is not hard to spot. It delivers good renditions of dishes that soothe rather than challenge; a well-considered mix of fish and shellfish, with a few upmarket brasserie ideas for those in the mood for meat. The straightforwardness of the cooking is another confidence booster – the repertoire runs from dressed crab and simply grilled sardines to sautéed cod cheeks with bacon, broad beans and wild garlic, or skate wing with capers and nut brown butter. It also presses the comfort button with chicken, ham and leek pie and navarin of lamb (and possibly vodka Martini jelly with bergamot lemon ripple). Only 'offhand' service niggles. Plenty of thought has been put into the wine list, which opens at £24.

Chef/s: David McCarthy. **Open:** all week 12 to 10. **Closed:** 25 Dec. **Meals:** alc (main courses £17 to £29). **Service:** 12.5% (optional). **Details:** Cards accepted. 120 seats. 28 seats outside. Separate bar. No music. No mobile phones. Wheelchair access. Children allowed.

ALSO RECOMMENDED

▲ Serpentine Bar & Kitchen

Serpentine Road, Hyde Park, W2 2UH
Tel no: (020) 7706 8114
www.serpentinebarandkitchen.com
⊖ Hyde Park Corner, map 4
Modern British

Sitting outdoors on the eastern edge of the Serpentine, you might almost imagine yourself out in the country. It's a lovely location for this informally run eatery with its chunky bare tables and wood-fired oven. Order at the bar from a choice that might take in pigeon breast with honey-roast parsnip and braised lentils (£7.50), sea bream with stem broccoli and brown shrimp butter (£14.50) or breast of corn-fed chicken with crispy rosemary polenta and oyster mushroom sauce. Wines from £16. Open all week.

Seven Park Place

Modern French cuisine in all its glory
St James's Hotel and Club, 7-8 Park Place, Mayfair, SW1A 1LS
Tel no: (020) 7316 1600
www.stjameshotelandclub.com
⊖ Green Park, map 5
Modern French | £49
Cooking score: 6

If you're looking for casual sustenance, go elsewhere: this freestanding restaurant embedded in the 'wedding cake' surroundings of the St James's Hotel drips good manners and sobriety. Warm up (if that's the right phrase) in the yellow Art Deco bar before graduating to the dining room – a dense amalgam of patterned carpets, patterned banquettes and dramatic patterned wallpaper. This is home to chef William Drabble – 'one of London's finest', and a true exponent of modern French cuisine in all its buttery, finicky glory. Like the place itself, his food is meticulously restrained; at best it's also 'utterly memorable', even if dishes sometimes lack that elemental 'zing'. An iconic starter of seared scallops with Jerusalem artichoke purée and crispy bacon harks back to Drabble's days at the now-defunct Aubergine, and it sets the bar high. After that, loin of veal accompanied by ravioli of ceps and foie gras, braised lettuce and Madeira jus is silky richness on a plate, while poached brill fillet with celeriac, apples, mussels and chives makes its impact with lighter, gentler flavours. To finish, it's all about cool excess – an 'over-sugared' assiette of chocolate or poached cherries with tiny beignets, almond ice cream and shortbread, say. Service is pitch-perfect for such a grand show – deferential, assiduously attentive and designed to make everyone feel 'spoilt'. The wine list is aimed at those who are prepared to pay for quality; choice is global, growers and vintages are hard to fault, and there are interesting 'seasonal discoveries' too. House selections start at £6.80 a glass.

Chef/s: William Drabble. **Open:** Tue to Sat L 12 to 2, D 7 to 10. **Closed:** Sun, Mon. **Meals:** Set L £24.50 (2 courses) to £29.50. Set D £43 (2 courses) to £49. **Service:** 12.5% (optional). **Details:** Cards accepted. 26 seats. Separate bar. No music. Children allowed.

Sketch, Lecture Room & Library

Extravagant pleasure palace
9 Conduit Street, Mayfair, W1S 2XG
Tel no: (020) 7659 4500
www.sketch.uk.com
⊖ Oxford Circus, map 5
Modern European | £100
Cooking score: 6

V

The best advice at Sketch: go with it. Without willingness on the part of the diner, Sketch, and particularly the top-floor, top-end Lecture Room & Library, might seem ridiculous, overdone, obscenely expensive. But if one accepts that, occasionally, every dining room needs flower vases taller than a man, décor in tones of hot sand, hordes of attendants and a 'housemaid' who's only there to open the door of the crystal-encrusted loos, indulgence is possible – indeed, highly likely. Each course, designed by Pierre Gagnaire and cooked by Jean-Denis Le Bras, is a multiple play on ideas and ingredients; readers love the

experimental approach. Expect several bowls, which might bear the different components of a scallop and morel starter: a crisply caramelised mollusc served with a dark mushroom paste; scallop mousse, airy beneath creamed morels with the heat of Arbois wine; cold osso buco-style sweetbreads; a grapefruit sorbet with an unwise pool of creamy cold velouté. Textures, especially liquid ones, can be a challenge – black pudding 'soup' doesn't work, even with a fabulous pork chop and buttery gratin of chard and ham. Gagnaire's calling card is, of course, pastry. The main component of a chocolate dessert – a shallow soufflé into which a square of chocolate-coated blackcurrant parfait is plunged – works fabulously, though the extra frills seem just that. Wine, from a serious and extensive list, starts at £21, and one of the pleasing details is a real choice of half-bottles and glasses.
Chef/s: Jean-Denis Le Bras and Pierre Gagnaire. **Open:** Tue to Fri L 12 to 2.30, Tue to Sat D 6.30 to 10.30. **Closed:** Sun, Mon, 2 weeks Dec, 2 weeks Aug. **Meals:** alc (main courses £35 to £55). Set L £30 (2 courses) to £35. Tasting menu from £75 (7 courses) to £95. **Service:** 12.5% (optional). **Details:** Cards accepted. 50 seats. Separate bar. No mobile phones. Wheelchair access. Music. Children allowed.

ALSO RECOMMENDED

▲ Spuntino

61 Rupert Street, Soho, W1D 7PW
www.spuntino.co.uk
⊖ Piccadilly Circus, map 5
Tapas

'Scores highly in the cool stakes, and tattooed servers only add to the edge', noted a visitor to this recent arrival from the people behind Soho big hitter Polpo (see entry). It's a fun place and 'refreshingly different for London' with its transatlantic take on the Italian 'tapas' theme. The short, sharp menu takes in the likes of truffled egg toast, zucchini pizzeta (£6), bone marrow and meatball 'sliders', and 'piping hot' mac and cheese (£8). House wine is £16.50. Open all week. Note: 'no telephone, no bookings'.

The Square

Harmonious top-end cuisine
6-10 Bruton Street, Mayfair, W1J 6PU
Tel no: (020) 7495 7100
www.squarerestaurant.com
⊖ Green Park, map 5
Modern French | £80
Cooking score: 8
V

An unashamed Mayfair thoroughbred, the Square looks pitch-perfect for a serious, high-end restaurant in the moneyed environs of W1: lofty ceilings, perfect lighting above carefully arranged tables, full-drop windows looking out onto Bruton Street and a few discreetly arranged pieces of artwork on the walls make it ideal for corporate lunches and special-occasion dinners. Its mood of supreme confidence and reliability is sustained by effortlessly efficient staff who know when to chat and when to keep their distance. Chef/patron Philip Howard is one of few top-rated chefs who values cooking more than celebrity status or media grandstanding – and it shows in his extraordinarily harmonious, disciplined food. Many dishes greet diners like old friends: the legendary lasagne of Dorset crab with a cappuccino of shellfish and Champagne foam; the sauté of Scottish langoustines with Parmesan gnocchi enriched with a potato and truffle emulsion; the roast foie gras with a tarte fine of endive, 'ice wine' glaze, Seville orange purée and honeycomb, for example. Occasionally, the kitchen constructs disconcertingly 'new' flavours (hot and cold oysters with smoked mackerel, squid ink pearls, sea water jellies, lemon oil and caviar), although it's on safer ground serving up broad-shouldered offerings such as monkfish with pearl barley, braised lettuce and lardo di Colonnata, or an evocatively autumnal dish of venison with salt-baked beetroot, stuffed celeriac and a port-glazed pear. The gargantuan cheese trolley receives glowing endorsements, while desserts aim to impress by virtue of their meticulous artistry – perhaps a 'perfectly formed' Brillat-Savarin cheesecake with passion fruit and banana

sorbet. Given its gilt-edged credentials, mark-ups on the aristocratic wine list are quite charitable – especially when it comes to finer vintages. Everything is chosen with real authority and oenophile knowledge, from exclusive small-house Champagnes to rare dessert tipples. Prices start around £25 (£8 a glass).
Chef/s: Philip Howard. **Open:** Mon to Fri L 12 to 2.30, all week D 6.30 to 10 (10.30 Sat, 9.30 Sun). **Closed:** 24 to 27 Dec, 1 Jan, bank hols. **Meals:** Set L £30 (2 courses) to £35. Set D £80. Tasting menu £105 (9 courses). **Service:** 12.5% (optional). **Details:** Cards accepted. 70 seats. No music. No mobile phones. Wheelchair access. Children allowed.

NEW ENTRY
St John Hotel

No-frills native food in tourist central
1 Leicester Street, Leicester Square, WC2H 7BL
Tel no: (020) 3301 8069
www.stjohnhotellondon.com
⊖ Leicester Square, map 5
British | £40
Cooking score: 4

Manzi's old-school seafood restaurant stopped operating a few years ago, but the site and the edge-of-Chinatown area received a shot in the arm when British food champions Fergus Henderson and Trevor Gulliver moved in. This third link in the St John chain (see entries) continues the exploration of our native larder. The food is as plain and unadulterated as the restaurant itself – a white-painted room with the barest of fittings and little decoration save for an open-plan kitchen. A tersely written menu promises the likes of tripe, peas and mint or bacon and beans (for two), and while the cooking can appear deceptively simple, it works because of the quality of the ingredients. Mussels come shelled in a rich, thick tomato and dill sauce on toast, while a comforting dish of lamb sweetbreads with butter beans is invigorated by a side of watercress salad. To conclude, the famous custard tart vies with blancmange or strawberry trifle. Service is attentive. House wine is £26.
Chef/s: Tom Harris. **Open:** all week L 12 to 3, D 5.30 to 2am. **Meals:** alc (main courses £14 to £24). **Service:** 12.5% (optional). **Details:** Cards accepted. 50 seats. Separate bar. No music. Wheelchair access. Children allowed.

Sumosan

Classy modern Japanese
26b Albemarle Street, Mayfair, W1S 4HY
Tel no: (020) 7495 5999
www.sumosan.com
⊖ Green Park, map 5
Japanese | £40
Cooking score: 4

Glimpsed behind a vast expanse of glass, Sumosan has occupied its swish Mayfair site for 10 years and remains as well turned out as its chic clientele. As well as the dining area, the space is divided into several bars, including a sushi counter and a glamorous cocktail den in the basement. While the kitchen can focus on traditional Japanese cuisine, it also veers off into fusion fancies, say duck in lingonberry sauce or turbot on a bed of cauliflower and broccoli with wasabi risotto. Otherwise, appetisers range from edamame to tuna tataki, and the repertoire encompasses salads and soups, chicken yakitori, tempura and the like, though various tasting and set menus make choosing easier. Desserts are only superficially Japanese, perhaps white and dark chocolate fondant with green tea ice cream. The wine list opens at £28 and there is a good selection of saké.
Chef/s: Bubker Belkhit. **Open:** Mon to Fri L 12 to 2.45, all week D 6 to 11.30 (10.30 Sun). **Closed:** 25 and 26 Dec, Easter Mon. **Meals:** alc (main courses £8 to £65). Set menus from £24.90. **Service:** 15% (optional). **Details:** Cards accepted. 120 seats. Separate bar. Wheelchair access. Music. Children allowed.

Tamarind

A masterclass in Moghul cuisine
20 Queen Street, Mayfair, W1J 5PR
Tel no: (020) 7629 3561
www.tamarindrestaurant.com
⊖ Green Park, map 5
Indian | £50
Cooking score: 5

£5 OFF **V**

It's appropriate that this high-ranking contemporary Indian should go about its business in one of the capital's smartest ethnic dining rooms – a lustrous basement with highly polished floors, shimmering gold-hued columns and extravagant floral arrangements. All is inviting and exceedingly tasteful, and Alfred Prasad's team deliver a masterclass in rich Moghul cuisine from the northern reaches of the subcontinent. The region's benchmark specialities appear in all their luxuriously spicy glory, from peshawari champen (lamb cutlets marinated with garlic, paw-paw, paprika, fennel and cream) to murgh makhni (chicken tikka in a sauce of creamed tomatoes spiked with green chillies and fenugreek leaves). But this is an open-minded, inventive kitchen with a talent for fashioning new ideas out of well-tried themes – perhaps dressing a salad of spiced duck breast and avocado with orange and chaat masala or matching sea bass with asparagus, raw mango and a mustard-tinged tomato sauce. Vegetable sides such as slow-cooked black dhal or a spicy mélange of shiitake mushrooms, sugar snaps and peas are a revelation, and the kitchen is on top form when it comes to breads (try the date and poppy seed naan). Prices are a world away from your average local curry house, but so is the quality. Also be prepared to spend if you open the wine list; bottles start at £26.50.
Chef/s: Alfred Prasad. **Open:** Sun to Fri L 12 to 2.45, all week D 5.30 to 11 (6 to 10.30 Sun). **Closed:** 25 and 26 Dec, 1 Jan. **Meals:** alc (main courses £18 to £28). Set L £17.50 (2 courses) to £19.50. Pre-theatre D £27.50. Sun L £32. Tasting menu £56 to £68. **Service:** 12.5% (optional). **Details:** Cards accepted. 88 seats. Music.

Terroirs

Crowd-pulling bistro with French classics
5 William IV Street, Covent Garden, WC2N 4DW
Tel no: (020) 7036 0660
www.terroirswinebar.com
⊖ Charing Cross, map 5
French | £25
Cooking score: 3

With the atmosphere of a 'buzzy Paris bistro', Terroirs continues to pull in the Covent Garden crowds. The menu recreates French classics using well-sourced British produce, all beautifully presented – perhaps rich, homely cassoulet in an earthernware pot, or a knockout tarte Tatin still caramelising as it comes to the table in a cast-iron pan. Elsewhere are wooden boards layered with charcuterie or seasonal cheeses and Poilâne bread plus an undeniably delicious roast Landaise chicken fragranced with sweet garlic. Happily the emphasis is on sharing, so there's plenty of opportunity to try it all. The wine list is no less delightful, well-chosen and keenly priced (from £17). There's always a spirited crowd, particularly upstairs where things are a little bit more casual. The only downside is the high decibel levels.
Chef/s: Ed Wilson. **Open:** Mon to Sat L 12 to 3, D 6 to 11. **Closed:** Sun, 25 and 26 Dec, 1 Jan, bank hols. **Meals:** alc (main courses £12 to £16). **Service:** 12.5% (optional). **Details:** Cards accepted. 130 seats. 6 seats outside. Separate bar. Music. Children allowed.

Texture

Big-statement dining with Nordic nuances
34 Portman Street, Marble Arch, W1H 7BY
Tel no: (020) 7224 0028
www.texture-restaurant.co.uk
⊖ Marble Arch, map 4
Modern French/Nordic | £55
Cooking score: 4

 **V**

The gorgeously sleek, high-gloss Champagne bar and seriously handsome dining room cleverly dovetail nineteenth-century elegance with up-to-the-moment metropolitan chic – just the ticket for Agnar Sverrisson's confident take on the cuisine of his native Iceland. He favours a clean-cut approach, but weaves in a few details from the contemporary French style – Anjou pigeon, for example, is teamed with sweetcorn, shallot, bacon popcorn and red wine essence. Top-drawer ingredients provide the backbone for immaculately pretty, clean-as-a-whistle dishes ranging from organic salmon (smoked and 'graflax') with excellent horseradish to a main dish of shoulder and best end of lamb with wild Icelandic herbs and mustard sauce. Crispy cod skin nibbles and 'hearty bread' have been praised, as has the 'really excellent-value' set lunch. Desserts dazzle – white chocolate mousse and ice cream served with dill and cucumber was the 'standout of the meal' for one reporter. It's also worth musing over the heavyweight wine list, a deeply serious slate that explores France in depth but also scours the world's major growing areas. Prices start at £18. Texture's latest opening is 28°-50° (see entry).

Chef/s: Agnar Sverrisson. **Open:** Tue to Sat L 12 to 2.30, D 6.30 to 10.30. **Closed:** Sun, Mon, 2 weeks Aug, 3 weeks Dec. **Meals:** alc (main courses £28 to £32). Set L £19.90 (2 courses) to £24. Tasting menu £54 (6 courses) to £68. **Service:** 12.5% (optional). **Details:** Cards accepted. 55 seats. Separate bar. No mobile phones. Wheelchair access. Music. Children allowed.

Theo Randall at the InterContinental

Big, bold Italian cooking
InterContinental London Hotel, 1 Hamilton Place, Mayfair, W1J 7QY
Tel no: (020) 7318 8747
www.theorandall.com
⊖ Hyde Park Corner, map 4
Italian | £50
Cooking score: 6
V

The corporate expanses of Park Lane's InterContinental Hotel might seem far removed from the byways of Italian regional cooking, but Theo Randall has made this restaurant very much his own since arriving in 2006. As one of the unsung heroes of the River Café (see entry) he knows all about seasonality, sourcing and the wonders of wood-fired ovens, so it's no surprise that his bold, uncluttered food resonates with ingredients-driven rusticity. If the chic, moneyed surrounds suggest effete culinary mannerisms, think again – there's not a wisp of foam or a daub of edible 'paint' to be seen. Instead, dishes arrive heroically unadorned, from an invigorating salad of Italian leaves with two kinds of tomato, fresh basil and caprino fresco cheese to a heap of curly squid with Lamon borlotti beans and a hit of chilli and anchovy. As you might expect, seasonal pasta is a surefire success, bringing bowls of bouncy handmade tagliatelle with fresh peas, prosciutto and mint in summer, or cappelletti stuffed with slow-cooked veal, porcini and trompettes de mort as autumn descends. But it's Randall's beloved oven that really steals the show, working at full tilt to deliver mighty slabs of pearly turbot on the bone or marinated Anjou pigeon cooked on pagnotta bruschetta with pancetta and treviso tardivo. When it comes to dessert, the signature Amalfi lemon tart is hard to trump, although ricotta cheesecake with vanilla-marinated pears runs a close second. Lofty prices reflect the snazzy address and wines aim for jet-setting international appeal, although there are a few gutsier Italian offerings too. Bottles start at £25.

Chef/s: Theo Randall. **Open:** Mon to Fri L 12 to 3, Mon to Sat D 5.45 to 11. **Closed:** Sun, 25 and 26 Dec, bank hols. **Meals:** alc (main courses £23 to £36). Set L £25 (2 courses) to £29. **Service:** 12.5%. **Details:** Cards accepted. 120 seats. Separate bar. Wheelchair access. Music. Children allowed. Car parking.

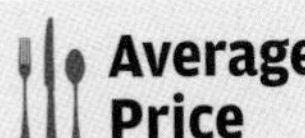

The average price listed in main-entry reviews denotes the price of a three-course meal, without wine.

Tierra Brindisa

Premium Spanish provisions
46 Broadwick Street, Soho, W1F 7AF
Tel no: (020) 7534 1690
www.tierrabrindisa.com
⊖ Oxford Circus, map 5
Spanish | £19
Cooking score: 3

Competition is fierce in the bustling streets of Soho, but this Spanish pit-stop more than holds its own. The rather cramped dining room and lighter, more attractive bar and open kitchen deal in premium Spanish produce. The Brindisa trademarks include superb Iberian charcuterie, boquerones, ham and chicken croquetas, grilled sardines with pipirrana salad (a form of gazpacho), and potato, chorizo and pepper tortilla. Elsewhere, there's Ibérico pork fillet with sage, morcilla de Burgos and apple purée, or sea bass with escalivada (roasted vegetables). Commence business with exquisite Gordal olives tinged with orange and oregano, and finish with a Manchego semi-cured cheese. Both go down well with a glass of something from the fine selection of sherries. Keenly chosen Spanish wines start at £17.
Chef/s: Russell Jeff. **Open:** all week 12 to 11 (4 to 9 Sun). **Closed:** 25 and 26 Dec, 1 Jan. **Meals:** alc (tapas £7 to £11). Set L and D £25 (2 courses). **Service:** 12.5% (optional). **Details:** Cards accepted. 48 seats. 6 seats outside. Separate bar. Wheelchair access. Music. Children allowed.

Trishna

Indian seafood star
15-17 Blandford Street, Marylebone, W1U 3DG
Tel no: (020) 7935 5624
www.trishnalondon.com
⊖ Marylebone, Bond Street, map 4
Indian/Seafood | £30
Cooking score: 3

£5 OFF **V**

The cool London sister of a famous seafood restaurant in Mumbai, this sleek Marylebone favourite continues to impress with its innovative Indian dishes conjured with mainly British seafood. 'Really excellent' was one reporter's description of the potato chaat (chickpeas, tamarind, sweet yoghurt, shallots, red chilli), which was followed by a 'well-made' seafood biryani of sea bass and shellfish. Other popular main courses include South Indian lamb curry heady with curry leaf, cinnamon and coconut. Spiced chocolate torte with poached pear and pistachio milkshake is one of the fragrant desserts made on the premises. The menu matches every dish with a different wine, and wine flights are also on offer. The list starts at £20.
Chef/s: Karam Sethi. **Open:** all week 12 to 2.45 (12.30 to 3.15 Sun), D 6 to 10.45 (6.30 to 9.45 Sun). **Closed:** 25 and 26 Dec, 1 and 2 Jan. **Meals:** alc (main courses 6 to £20). Set L £15 (2 courses) to £18. Tasting menu £35.50 (5 courses) to £44. **Service:** 12.5% (optional). **Details:** Cards accepted. 65 seats. 10 seats outside. Music. Children allowed.

Umu

Gilt-edged Kyoto cuisine
14-16 Bruton Place, Mayfair, W1J 6LX
Tel no: (020) 7499 8881
www.umurestaurant.com
⊖ Green Park, Bond Street, map 5
Japanese | £100
Cooking score: 5

Press the touchpad in Umu's wood-panelled entrance and the door slides open to reveal a calming sanctuary of modern Japanese style. Everything from the handmade wallpaper and silk drapes to the glassware and staff uniforms has been carefully selected to create a feeling of tranquillity and refinement – and the same goes for the food. Based on the haute cuisine of the former imperial city of Kyoto, it's precise and beautifully presented. To fully appreciate the top-end cuisine, opt for one of the rigorously defined, eight-course kaiseki banquets based on the traditional Japanese format. Dishes highlight different cooking techniques and meals always proceed in a certain order: an appetiser is followed by a clear, palate-cleansing broth and rice comes before dessert. Ingredients from home and away are also given five-star treatment on the contemporary carte – perhaps langoustines with amber tomato jelly, egg-yolk vinegar and caviar, Wagyu beef with Himalayan rock salt, wasabi and soy, or wild Scottish lobster with seven-pepper shichimi, tofu miso bisque and yuzu foam. Lunchtime bento boxes provide a cheaper introduction to the cuisine; alternatively, nab a spot at the sushi counter and watch as the chefs display their craft in studied silence. The classy global wine list is supplemented by a bewildering array of sakés, although a sommelier is on hand to help guide you. House selections start at £30.

Chef/s: Yoshinori Ishii. **Open:** Mon to Sat L 12 to 2.30, D 6 to 11. **Closed:** Sun. **Meals:** alc (main courses £18 to £65). Set L from £25. Tasting menu £95. **Service:** 12.5% (optional). **Details:** Cards accepted. 60 seats. Separate bar. Wheelchair access. Music. Children allowed. Car parking.

ALSO RECOMMENDED

▲ Vasco & Piero's Pavilion

15 Poland Street, Soho, W1F 8QE
Tel no: (020) 7437 8774
www.vascosfood.com
⊖ Oxford Circus, map 5
Italian

One of the more enduring of Soho's old-school Italians, this Guide stalwart delivers straightforward and comforting cuisine rather than culinary fireworks. Umbrian dishes dominate a menu that rolls out in traditional format: mini plates of carpaccio of tuna and avocado; antipasti of crostini with chicken livers; handmade tagliatelle with Umbrian beef ragù (£9.50) and strips of calf's liver and onions with sautéed cabbage (£19.50). Pricey, but pre-theatre deals offer the best value. House wine is £17.50. Closed Sat L and Sun.

Also recommended entries are not scored but we think they are worth a visit.

▲ Veeraswamy

Victory House, 99-101 Regent Street, Piccadilly, W1B 4RS
Tel no: (020) 7734 1401
www.veeraswamy.com
⊖ Piccadilly Circus, map 5
Indian

Born in 1926, Britain's 'oldest Indian restaurant' has glammed-up its looks in recent years, with silver jali screens, swathes of gold-leaf granite, multicoloured lights and exotic fabrics. The kitchen has also moved with the times and now sends out crab and ginger kebabs, crispy chicken lollipops (£8.75) and Keralan chicken stew with lacy 'appam' pancakes (£19.75) alongside its tikkas, biryanis and masala lamb chops. To finish, try something wacky such as 'home-style' mango vermicelli or tandoori fruit with pistachio ice cream. Wines from £23. Open all week.

NEW ENTRY

Vinoteca

Rustic-chic bolt-hole with terrific wine
15 Seymour Place, Marylebone, W1H 5BD
Tel no: (020) 7724 7288
www.vinoteca.co.uk
⊖ Marble Arch, map 4
Modern European | £26
Cooking score: 2

Like its chart-topping parent in Farringdon (see entry), the youthful Marylebone Vinoteca is a 'terribly informal', rustic-chic bolt-hole for chattering lunches or wine-sipping assignations. The combination of a shop, on-view kitchen and convivial dining room is immediately appealing, while assorted culinary influences jostle on a menu that's geared for casual satisfaction: Spanish cured meats sit alongside British cheeses, croquetas appear next to new season's asparagus, and bigger plates might include aromatic leek and wild mushroom tart, a springtime dish of whole plaice with bacon, broad beans and peas, or grilled bavette with triple-cooked chips (all with wine-matching suggestions). To finish, 'tongue-tingly' rhubarb jelly with

amaretti biscuits has gone down a storm. Vinoteca's ever-evolving wine list is full of irresistible opportunities at irresistible prices, whatever your global preferences; a weekly by-the-glass selection offers great sampling from £3.50 and bottles start at £14.50.
Chef/s: William Leigh. **Open:** all week L 12 to 3 (4 Sat and Sun), Mon to Sat D 6 to 10. **Closed:** 25 to 27 Dec, 1 Jan. **Meals:** alc (main courses £9 to £16). **Service:** 12.5% (optional). **Details:** Cards accepted. 60 seats. 6 seats outside. Separate bar. Music. Children allowed.

The White Swan

Foodie boozer with sound credentials
108 Fetter Lane, Holborn, EC4A 1ES
Tel no: (020) 7242 9696
www.thewhiteswanlondon.com
⊖ Chancery Lane, map 5
British | £32
Cooking score: 3

A beacon of quality since it opened in 2004, the White Swan's reputation has spread far beyond its immediate locale – a foodie boozer combining pubby credentials with a kitchen that's capable of delivering some accomplished food. Crowds may pack the bar, where sustenance includes ploughman's, fishcakes and sausage, mash and onion gravy, but the smartly appointed top-floor dining room is the place for more interesting dishes with plenty of clever modern touches, say grilled red mullet with salt cod brandade and pipérade or breast of duck and braised leg with a blood orange tarte fine and purple sprouting broccoli. A modish chocolate bavarois with candied orange and a dollop of Chantilly cream makes a perfect finale. Wines from £16.
Chef/s: Jon Coates. **Open:** Mon to Fri L 12 to 3, D 6 to 10. **Closed:** Sat, Sun, 25 and 26 Dec, bank hols. **Meals:** alc (main courses £13 to £24). Set L £26 (2 courses) to £29.75. Bar menu also available. **Service:** 12.5% (optional). **Details:** Cards accepted. 42 seats. Separate bar. Music. Children allowed.

Wild Honey

Impressive Francocentric bistro
12 St George Street, Mayfair, W1S 2FB
Tel no: (020) 7758 9160
www.wildhoneyrestaurant.co.uk
⊖ Bond Street, Oxford Circus, map 5
Modern European | £35
Cooking score: 6

The middle sibling in Will Smith and Anthony Demetre's trio of restaurants (see entries for Arbutus and Les Deux Salons) has an altogether more Bond Street ambience, as befits its top-notch location, with a wood-panelled room extending elegantly back from the bar area. Sit up at the counter for an in-out lunch or informal evening assignation, and you'll gain, among other things, an appreciation of how efficiently the place is run. The same commitment to straightforwardly described and presented modern Francocentric bistro dishes informs the kitchen at all three addresses. Combinations inspire: start with a salad of soused mackerel, broccoli and peanuts in anchovy vinaigrette, or with the now-classic pairing of foie gras terrine and rhubarb, served with a lump of toasted sourdough. Main courses impress for their sensitively timed main ingredients, whether it be the 'wonderfully succulent and tender' venison that delighted a pre-Christmas visitor, or grilled sea bass that comes teamed with Orkney mussels, artichokes, monk's beard and bergamot. Desserts give enjoyable outings to some of the more traditional French gourmandises, such as floating islands with pink pralines, or William pear clafoutis, and there are cheeses from La Fromagerie. Apart from some of the very fancy stuff, most wines on the list may be taken by the bottle (from £14.50) or 250ml carafe (from £5).
Chef/s: Colin Kelly. **Open:** all week L 12 to 2.30 (3 Sun), D 5 to 11 (11.30 Fri and Sat, 10.30 Sun). **Closed:** 25 and 26 Dec, 1 Jan. **Meals:** alc (main courses £18 to £23). Set L £18.95. Set early D £22.95. Sun L £25.50. **Service:** 12.5% (optional). **Details:** Cards accepted. 60 seats. No music. Children allowed.

Wiltons

Blue-blooded British aristocrat
55 Jermyn Street, Mayfair, SW1Y 6LX
Tel no: (020) 7629 9955
www.wiltons.co.uk
⊖ Green Park, map 5
British | £100
Cooking score: 4

V

Like an impeccably groomed gentlemen's club, blue-blooded Wiltons looks right at home among the streets of St James's; it's swish, archaic, determinedly old school and one of the few restaurants in town where a 'jacket and tie' policy is still followed to the letter. This is the place to come if your fancy turns to lobster bisque, poached turbot, lamb cutlets, raspberry pavlova or a plateful of roast beef carved from the trolley. But Wiltons now has another side, thanks to the presence of 'tasting menu' specialist Andrew Turner in the kitchen. Who would have believed that this bastion of British conservatism would one day be serving up liquorice-marinated salmon with Cornish crab and tamarind cannelloni or cured foie gras and smoked duck with Parmesan marshmallows and fig purée? The patrician wine list is richly endowed with vintage clarets and Burgundies from the great years; eye-watering prices (from £38 skywards) are unlikely to trouble the old brigade in their bespoke Savile Row suits and Churchill shoes.

Chef/s: Andrew Turner. **Open:** Mon to Fri L 12 to 2.30, D 6 to 10.30. **Closed:** Sat, Sun. **Meals:** alc (main courses £20 to £45). Set L £45. Tasting D £80 (8 courses). **Service:** 12.5% (optional). **Details:** Cards accepted. 100 seats. No music. No mobile phones. Wheelchair access. Children allowed.

The Wolseley

All-dayer with piles of panache
160 Piccadilly, Mayfair, W1J 9EB
Tel no: (020) 7499 6996
www.thewolseley.com
⊖ Green Park, map 5
Modern European | £35
Cooking score: 2

V

Corbin and King's all-day Piccadilly brasserie recalls the grand old days of European dining. Get in whenever you can: the place is open for bowls of muesli and freshly pressed juices before work, through till the evening's last mouthful of truffled Coulommiers, offering a lively, upliftingly clattery ambience throughout. Breakfast dishes such as fishcake with poached egg are done with great panache, and the lunch and dinner specials like steak tartare, duck confit with ceps and ratte potatoes, or roast cod with colcannon in mustard sauce rarely disappoint. Roll back the culinary years with a heritage pudding such as pineapple upside-down cake. Wines open at £19 (£5.50 a glass). A sibling is due to open at 1 Kingsway, WC2 before the end of 2011.

Chef/s: Marc Benzimra. **Open:** all week L 12 to 3 (3.30 Sat and Sun), D 5.30 to 12 (11 Sun). **Closed:** 25 Dec, August bank hol. **Meals:** alc (main courses £11 to £30). **Service:** 12.5% (optional). **Details:** Cards accepted. 150 seats. Separate bar. No music. Wheelchair access. Children allowed.

ALSO RECOMMENDED

▲ Yalla Yalla

1 Green's Court, Piccadilly, W1F 0HA
Tel no: (020) 7287 7663
www.yalla-yalla.co.uk
⊖ Piccadilly Circus, map 5
Lebanese

Tucked down a Soho alleyway, this informal restaurant has a simple but stylish interior with pint-sized stools and tables making the most of its diminutive proportions. Lebanese and Middle Eastern cooking, particularly Beirut street food, is the theme here: maybe fattoush (£4.50), soujoc or falafel from the mezze menu, or mains such as moussaka (£9.50) or charcoal-grilled sea bass with citrus-scented rice and spicy tomato and coriander sauce (£12.50). Wines start at £18. Closed Sun. A sister restaurant is at 12 Winsley Street, W1W 8HQ; tel (020) 7637 4748.

Yauatcha

High-end dim sum and heady teas
15-17 Broadwick Street, Soho, W1F 0DL
Tel no: (020) 7494 8888
www.yauatcha.com
⊖ Tottenham Court Road, map 5
Chinese | £35
Cooking score: 3
V

Combining the attributes of a big-time dim sum joint, tea parlour and slinky restaurant, Yauatcha spreads itself across two floors on the fringes of Soho. If fun is required, pick the boisterous street-level space with its café tables, blue-frosted windows and super-slick staff; otherwise, descend to the exclusive basement, which has moody echoes of elder sibling Hakkasan (see entry). Either way, the kitchen knocks out high-end renditions of Chinatown staples (steamed har-gau dumplings, fluffy char siu buns) as well as upping the ante with more innovative, challenging platefuls: venison puffs, 'tea leaf' rolls, sea bass and lotus congee, spot-on halibut with red chilli and pickled cabbage or steamed chicken with wind-dried pork. For sheer occidental indulgence, finish with one of Yauatcha's exquisite desserts – perhaps chestnut and fig clafoutis with almond ice cream. To drink, heady teas and smoothies compete with glamorous cocktails and a list of trendy wines (from £26).

Open: all week 12 to 11.30 (12 to 10.30 Sun). **Closed:** 24 and 25 Dec. **Meals:** alc (£10 to £19). **Service:** 12.5% (optional). **Details:** Cards accepted. 185 seats. Separate bar. No mobile phones. Wheelchair access. Music. Children allowed.

Zafferano

Top Italian player
15 Lowndes Street, Belgravia, SW1X 9EY
Tel no: (020) 7235 5800
www.zafferanorestaurant.com
⊖ Knightsbridge, Hyde Park Corner, map 4
Italian | £45
Cooking score: 6

Zafferano has been a destination restaurant for modern Italian cooking since the mid-1990s. With its discreet frontage and elegant dining room, handsomely decorated in an effortlessly understated way, it fits its SW1 location to a T, and in Andy Needham it has a skilled interpreter of the cuisine, both in the imagination of his dishes and his sheer technique. The same passion for quality runs through every aspect, from a pre-meal 'nibble' of bruschetta brushed with garlic and topped with wild mushrooms to a veal cutlet with artichokes and potato purée – each owes everything to superb ingredients of unimpeachable quality. Pasta continues to be a strength, with reporters heaping praise on linguine with lobster, and a delicate ravioli of pheasant 'just tinged' with rosemary and served in a rich stock. Seafood is also pitch-perfect, perhaps roast Icelandic cod with chickpeas and a salsa verde ('second-to-none'), or shellfish and squid in a rich tomato and sweet chilli broth that 'calls for more bread to mop up every trace'; truffles have their seasonal place, too. An exemplary chocolate fondant with gianduia (hazelnut chocolate) ice cream is a good way to finish. Tuscany is a big player on the regional Italian wine list, which opens at £23.

Chef/s: Andy Needham. **Open:** all week L 12 to 2.30 (3 Sat and Sun), D 7 to 11 (10.30 Sun). **Closed:** 1 week Christmas. **Meals:** alc (main courses £12 to 26). Set L £21 (2 courses) to £26. Set D £34.50 (2 courses) to £49.50. **Service:** 13.5% (optional). **Details:** Cards accepted. 68 seats. Separate bar. No mobile phones. Wheelchair access. Music. Children allowed.

L'Absinthe

Good stuff at very keen prices
40 Chalcot Road, Primrose Hill, NW1 8LS
Tel no: (020) 7483 4848
www.labsinthe.co.uk
⊖ Chalk Farm, map 2
French | £21
Cooking score: 3

Neighbourly vibes and honestly crafted, bourgeois French food make an appealing package at Jean-Christophe Slowik's dressed-down bistro (think candles on bare tables), although readers suggest going in the evening if you're after some full-on Primrose Hill bonhomie. Either way, there is plenty of good stuff on offer at very keen prices: chicken liver parfait with port jelly, leeks in vinaigrette with poached egg, beef bourguignon and duck confit with braised Savoy cabbage have all been praised, although the kitchen can also rustle up textbook steak frites. To finish, it has to be absinthe-spiked crème brûlée, unless the boozy prospect of mango sorbet with rum appeals. L'Absinthe also runs its own wine shop, and almost everything on the all-French list is offered at retail price (with a standard £10 surcharge for drinking at the table). Vin de pays is £14.50.
Chef/s: Christophe Fabre. **Open:** Tue to Sun L 12 to 2.30 (4 Sat and Sun), D 6 to 10.30 (9.30 Sun). **Closed:** Mon, Aug, 1 week Christmas. **Meals:** alc (main courses £9 to £17). Set L Tue to Sat £9.95 (2 courses) to £12.95. Sun L £14.95 (2 courses) to £18.50. **Service:** 12.5% (optional). **Details:** Cards accepted. 60 seats. 14 seats outside. Separate bar. Music. Children allowed.

Symbols

Accommodation is available
Three courses for less than £30
V Separate vegetarian menu
£5-off voucher scheme
Notable wine list

The Albion

Stylish pub with hearty Brit grub
10 Thornhill Road, Islington, N1 1HW
Tel no: (020) 7607 7450
www.the-albion.co.uk
⊖ Angel, Highbury and Islington, map 2
British | £30
Cooking score: 2

£5 OFF

A 'real tardis of a place,' this wisteria-clad Georgian pub has a surprisingly light interior gussied up with pale heritage colours and candelabra-style fittings. Hearty British food is the order of the day: pork belly and black pudding terrine with chutney and toast is a typical starter, and there's a good selection from the grill (an 'above par' porterhouse steak impressed one reporter). Traditionally inspired mains run from Gloucester Old Spot sausages with mash and onion gravy to smoked haddock fishcake with spinach and poached egg, with sides such as buttered sprout tops or fennel, cannellini bean and sage salad. A modest selection of wines starts at £14.
Chef/s: David Johnson. **Open:** all week L 12 to 3 (4 Sat and Sun), D 6 to 10 (9 Sun). **Meals:** alc (main courses £10 to £20). Sun L £14 (2 courses) to £16.50. **Service:** 10% (optional). **Details:** Cards accepted. 105 seats. 120 seats outside. Separate bar. Wheelchair access. Music. Children allowed.

Almeida

Elegant Islington performer
30 Almeida Street, Islington, N1 1AD
Tel no: (020) 7354 4777
www.almeida-restaurant.co.uk
⊖ Angel, Highbury & Islington, map 2
Modern French | £34
Cooking score: 4

Like the adjacent theatre from which this restaurant takes its name, Almeida might not be a heavy-hitting tourist attraction or play home to stellar names, but it can always be relied upon for a classy and enjoyable performance. Alan Jones pulls the strings from an open-to-view kitchen, serving up an

elegant menu of modern French dishes. A signature main of slow-cooked belly of suckling pig with creamed Savoy cabbage and sauce aux épices scores highly with reporters, with perhaps a beef fillet tartare with Melba toast, and an orange and chocolate mousse coming either side. Some deft touches raise the standard of cooking above your run-of-the-mill Gallic restaurant, although one reporter notes that portions can be on the small side. A lengthy wine list leans heavily on the Old World, with the page of 'sommelier's picks' a useful addition. 'Brisk but friendly' service suits the bustling environment.
Chef/s: Alan Jones. **Open:** Tue to Sun L 12 to 2.30 (3.30 Sat and Sun), Mon to Sat D 5.30 to 10.30. **Meals:** alc (£14 to £19). Set L £15 (2 courses) to £20. Set D £28.50 (2 courses) to £33.50. Set theatre menu £15.95 (2 courses) to £18.95. Sun L £22.50 (2 courses) to £26.50. **Service:** 12.5% (optional). **Details:** Cards accepted. 88 seats. 10 seats outside. Separate bar. No music. Wheelchair access. Children allowed.

ALSO RECOMMENDED

▲ Il Bacio

178-184 Blackstock Road, Highbury, N5 1HA
Tel no: (020) 7226 3339
www.ilbaciohighbury.co.uk
⊖ Arsenal, map 2
Italian

For nigh on seven years Il Bacio has been a destination address for appreciative locals and the more discerning football fan heading for the Emirates Stadium. The décor is modern but simple, while service has the brisk efficiency of a well-oiled machine. There's skill in the kitchen too, with huge pizzas and mighty trattoria staples like melanzane alla parmigiana (£6), and vitello alla milanese (£13.50) backed up by Sardinian specialities, say fish stew or black tagliolini with langoustines and cuttlefish. Italian house wines are £11.50. Open all week D, also Sat and Sun L.

Bradleys

Appealing Gallic eatery
25 Winchester Road, Swiss Cottage, NW3 3NR
Tel no: (020) 7722 3457
www.bradleysnw3.co.uk
⊖ Swiss Cottage, map 2
French | £35
Cooking score: 3
£5 OFF

If you start with good raw materials and maintain balance and seasonality, you can hardly go wrong. Simon Bradley has been doing this in his appealing restaurant not far from the Hampstead Theatre in Swiss Cottage for 20 years. The French-orientated cooking has always been easy on the palate, mixing well-tried ideas with original but unforced marriages; perhaps grilled squid with porcini mushrooms and celery risotto ahead of a dish of rabbit – confit leg, mustard loin and pie – with Savoy cabbage and carrot purée. To finish, blood orange bavarois with Campari and orange sorbet hits the spot. The wine list is a model of its kind, arranged by style, with terse tasting notes, great producers and prices that are kept in check. House French is £16.95.
Chef/s: Simon Bradley. **Open:** Sun to Fri L 12 to 3, Mon to Sat D 6 to 11. **Closed:** bank hols. **Meals:** alc (main courses £16 to £19). Set L £13.50 (2 courses) to £17.50. Set D £24.50. Sun L £27. **Service:** 12.5% (optional). **Details:** Cards accepted. 60 seats. No music. No mobile phones. Children allowed.

The Bull & Last

Broad-shouldered Brit food and awesome ales
168 Highgate Road, Hampstead, NW5 1QS
Tel no: (020) 7267 3641
www.thebullandlast.co.uk
⊖ Tufnell Park, Kentish Town, map 2
Modern British | £30
Cooking score: 3

Famished walkers join the loyal congregation in search of sustenance at this ebullient boozer within striking distance of leafy Parliament Hill, and they are well rewarded with a tremendous line-up of real ales and plates of broad-shouldered, Brit-accented food. Crispy trotter won tons will take the edge off if you're camped in the bar, but head upstairs for some more filling treats. Skewered duck hearts are in tune with the zeitgeist, or you might start with a tartlet of Arbroath smokies and leeks with a poached egg. To follow, consider the gutsy merits of wild rabbit and beetroot pie, Welsh mutton broth or roast stone bass with parsnip purée and garlic potatoes, before signing off with buttermilk pudding or some 'sweeties' to nibble. Around 50 well-chosen wines start at £15.

Chef/s: Oliver Pudney. **Open:** all week L 12 to 3 (4 Sat, 12.30 to 4 Sun), D 6.30 to 10 (9 Sun). **Closed:** 24 and 25 Dec. **Meals:** alc (main courses £12 to £20). **Service:** not inc. **Details:** Cards accepted. 130 seats. 30 seats outside. Separate bar. Music. Children allowed. Car parking.

Café Japan

Outstanding sushi at ridiculously fair prices
626 Finchley Road, Golders Green, NW11 7RR
Tel no: (020) 8455 6854
⊖ Golders Green, map 1
Japanese | £18
Cooking score: 3

A pair who made the journey from east London and had no trouble parking on Finchley Road considered a visit here well worth the effort. It's an unabashed café, as the name announces, with a thriving takeaway trade that manages to produce sushi of outstanding quality at ridiculously fair prices. Enthusiastic praise is also forthcoming for bracing salads of seaweed, spinach, sesame and ginger, the freshest prawns or crunchy green beans in light tempura, and properly fatty grilled salmon in sharp but balanced teriyaki sauce. The chefs cope with the press of business without taking their collective eye off the ball, and the exemplary freshness of the seafood withstands comparison with the designer Japanese joints of Mayfair and Knightsbridge. Drink saké from £3 a glass, Japanese beer or house French at £12.50 a bottle.

Chef/s: Hideki Sato. **Open:** Tue to Sun L 12 to 2, D 6 to 10 (9.30 Sun). **Closed:** Mon, 25 and 26 Dec. **Meals:** alc (main courses £8 to £23). Set L £8.50 (2 courses) to £12. Set D £15 (2 courses) to £19. **Service:** not inc. **Details:** Cards accepted. 35 seats. Music. Children allowed.

ALSO RECOMMENDED

▲ Chilli Cool

15 Leigh Street, King's Cross, WC1H 9EW
Tel no: (020) 7383 3135
www.chillicool.com
⊖ Russell Square, King's Cross, map 2
Chinese £5 OFF

The name sums up the mood and the all-pervading gustatory tingle at this neighbourhood Szechuan canteen between Bloomsbury and King's Cross. Chilli heat meets tripe, intestines and other anatomical offcuts on a menu that never flinches or compromises: sliced pig's ears in sesame oil (£6.20), simmering tofu with minced meat and 'modern chop suey hotpot' (£12.80) are good calls, but also check out the 'poverty hot baby lobster'. Great value, fast turnaround. Wines from £11.90, although tea and beer are more efficient fire extinguishers for chilli-blitzed palates. Open all week.

The Drapers Arms

Bolt-hole that covers all the bases
44 Barnsbury Street, Islington, N1 1ER
Tel no: (020) 7619 0348
www.thedrapersarms.com
⊖ Highbury & Islington, Angel, map 2
British | £24
Cooking score: 2

Big parties in the upstairs dining room, dinner for two downstairs in the pub, family lunches in the garden – this Islington bolt-hole certainly has every eventuality covered. Drinkers are welcome, while eager diners are drawn by daily changing, seasonally-aware menus that deliver robust and uncomplicated combinations along the lines of potted crab on toast or plaice with brown shrimp, capers and parsley. The kitchen is also happy to apply on-trend touches here and there, perhaps duck heart, snail, dandelion and apple salad, yet is equally at home offering spotted dick and custard for dessert. Wines from £15.30.

Chef/s: James de Jong. **Open:** all week L 12 to 3 (4 Sun), D 6 to 10.30 (9.30 Sun). **Meals:** alc (main courses £10 to £15). **Service:** 12.5% (optional). **Details:** Cards accepted. 120 seats. 40 seats outside. Separate bar. Music. Children allowed.

500 Restaurant

Genuine neighbourhood Italian
782 Holloway Road, Archway, N19 3JH
Tel no: (020) 7272 3406
www.500restaurant.co.uk
⊖ Archway, map 2
Italian | £25
Cooking score: 2

The two guys behind this likeable Archway Italian have a soft spot for the dinky Fiat Cinquecento and decided to name their restaurant in its honour. It's a regulation neighbourhood haunt peddling sound renditions of regional food in the 'cucina povera' style – including well-reported pasta (perhaps ravioli with venison ragù or tagliatelle with langoustines, cherry tomatoes and air-dried bottarga). Other dishes ratchet up the earthiness, from a salad of raw artichokes with buffalo mozzarella to slow-cooked guinea fowl with prunes, white wine and thyme. After that, try coppa 500 (caramelised rhubarb with green apple sorbet). The wine list motors around Italy, bringing home some good regional stuff from £13.50.

Chef/s: Mario Magli. **Open:** Fri and Sat L 12 to 3, Mon to Sat D 6 to 10.30, Sun 12 to 9.30. **Closed:** 2 weeks Christmas, 2 weeks Aug. **Meals:** alc (main courses £11 to £16). **Service:** not inc. **Details:** Cards accepted. 35 seats. Wheelchair access. Music. Children allowed.

NEW ENTRY

The Gilbert Scott

Stunning surroundings and staunchly Brit food
St Pancras Renaissance Hotel, Euston Road, Euston, NW1 2AR
Tel no: (020) 7278 3888
www.thegilbertscott.co.uk
⊖ King's Cross St Pancras, map 2
British | £50
Cooking score: 2

George Gilbert Scott's grand hotel fell out of use decades ago, but a multi-million pound restoration, designed to emphasise its mid-Victorian splendours, looks like money well spent. 'We were blown away by the décor', has been a typical response of visitors to the restaurant. The staunchly British menu is taking longer to establish itself. While heritage tomato salad, nettle and watercress soup with egg yolk confit, snail and chicken pie, and Mrs Beeton's snow eggs have all been well executed, other dishes have found less favour. More polishing and finesse is required, especially when tightly packed tables, a £2 cover charge per person and sloppy service have been recurrent niggles. Wines from £25.

Chef/s: Marcus Wareing. **Open:** all week L 12 to 3, D 5.30 to 11. **Meals:** alc (main courses £16 to £28). Set early D £19 (2 courses) to £24. **Service:** 12.5% (optional). **Details:** Cards accepted. 110 seats. Separate bar. Wheelchair access. Children allowed.

NEW ENTRY

Homa

Groovy newcomer touting good ingredients
71-73 Stoke Newington Church Street, Stoke Newington, N16 0AS
Tel no: (020) 7254 2072
www.homalondon.co.uk
⊖ Arsenal, map 2
Modern European | £30
Cooking score: 2

With its designer good looks – marble counters, groovy tiles and Scandinavian furniture – newcomer Homa is a great fit in style-conscious Stokey. The simple Med-influenced cooking (pizza and small plates in the deli/wine bar at lunch; a full menu in the basement restaurant at dinner; brunch at weekends) is rather less statement-making. There are highs – such as perfectly fried squid and zucchini antipasti – and there are lows (a pizza's blackened base). However, good ingredients and appealing combinations such as locally produced N16 smoked salmon with burrata and pesto, and pappardelle with ragù largely keep such extremes in check. Sweet treats include tiramisu and Valrhona chocolate fondant. House wine is £14.50

Chef/s: Danilo Lubrano. **Open:** Tue to Sun L 10 to 3 (Sat 4, Sun 5), D 6 to 10.30 (10 Sun). **Closed:** Mon, 25 and 26 Dec. **Meals:** alc (main courses £13 to £19). **Service:** not inc. **Details:** Cards accepted. 80 seats. 25 seats outside. Separate bar. Music. Children allowed.

ALSO RECOMMENDED

▲ The Horseshoe

28 Heath Street, Hampstead, NW3 6TE
Tel no: (020) 7431 7206
⊖ Hampstead, map 2
Modern British

Home-brewed, Aussie-style beers are just one of the attractions at this laid-back but boisterous Hampstead boozer. Locals also reckon it's a 'solid option' for revved-up food, with 'doorstep' hunks of bread giving way to a daily menu of big-boned dishes ranging from pea soup with salt cod cakes (£6.50) to duck breast and leg with white beans and ham broth (£16.50) or whole plaice with samphire, garlic and lemon butter. For afters, follow the seasons with gooseberry fool or strawberries and cream. Snappy wines from £15.50. Open all week.

Also Recommended
Also recommended entries are not scored but we think they are worth a visit.

▲ Istanbul Iskembecisi

9 Stoke Newington Road, Stoke Newington, N16 8BH
Tel no: (020) 7254 7291
www.istanbuliskembecisi.co.uk
⊖ Dalston Kingsland, map 2
Turkish £5 OFF

Famous for serving Stoke Newington night owls until the wee small hours, this crowd-pulling, family-run stalwart deals in top-value Turkish food without frills. The signature 'iskembe' is a tripe soup pepped up with salt, vinegar and lemon juice; otherwise choose from terrific 'mezze' nibbles (£3 upwards) ranging from tamara and kisir (crushed wheat salad) to imam bayildi (stuffed aubergine) and grilled Turkish sausages. Mains (from £8.50) are mostly protein-heavy kebabs and grills, but also check out the Albanian-style liver with onion salad. House wine is £9.50. Open all week until 5am.

Jin Kichi

Sociable Tokyo-style hangout
73 Heath Street, Hampstead, NW3 6UG
Tel no: (020) 7794 6158
www.jinkichi.com
⊖ Hampstead, map 1
Japanese | £30
Cooking score: 1

It feels like a stripped-down hangout on a Tokyo backstreet, but this cute Japanese does the business in Hampstead, feeding the crowds with plates of sociable sushi and all manner of grilled yakitori skewers (from ox tongue with salt to pork and asparagus rolls). Nibble your way through small plates of salmon eggs with grated radish or sesame-dressed seaweed salad and progress to stewed belly pork, salmon teriyaki or a bowl of udon noodles topped with prawn tempura. Drink tea, saké or wine (from £3.20 a glass).

Chef/s: Atsushi Matsumoto. **Open:** Tue to Sun L 12.30 to 2, D 6 to 10.45 (10 Sun). **Closed:** Mon, 25 to 28 Dec, Tue after bank hols. **Meals:** alc (main courses £5 to £18). Set L £9.50 (2 courses) to £17.30. **Service:** 10% (optional). **Details:** Cards accepted. 40 seats. Music. Children allowed.

NEW ENTRY

Kentish Canteen

Conjuring up comfort classics
300 Kentish Town Road, Kentish Town, NW5 2TG
Tel no: (020) 7485 7331
www.kentishcanteen.co.uk
⊖ Kentish Town, map 2
British | £22
Cooking score: 2

Kentish Canteen has struck just the right chord with locals, offering bold, bright interiors, easy-going service, gentle pricing and a sure hand in the kitchen. Chefs John Cook and Clare Mitchell have good pedigrees and conjure up an appealing range of dishes, from pitch-perfect eggs Benedict at brunch to colourful 'Ottolenghi-style' salads. Evening meals favour comfort classics, perhaps a brilliant burger with the essential trimmings (cheese, bacon, chunky chips and coleslaw) or crab, lemon and chilli linguine – al dente, fresh and light. Puddings are good and a short wine list starts at £14.95.

Chef/s: John Cook and Clare Mitchell. **Open:** all week 12 to 10.30. **Closed:** 25 Dec. **Meals:** alc (main courses £8 to £15). **Service:** 12.5% (optional). **Details:** Cards accepted. 60 seats. 16 seats outside. Wheelchair access. Music. Children allowed.

NEW ENTRY

Made in Camden

Glorious global sharing plates
Roundhouse, Chalk Farm Road, Camden, NW1 8EH
Tel no: (020) 7424 8495
www.madeincamden.com
⊖ Chalk Farm, map 2
Fusion | £25
Cooking score: 3

The Roundhouse's former food offering was an average canteen serving sarnies and baked spuds, so its new incumbent Josh Katz didn't have too hard a job of raising the venue's gustatory game. In its first year Made in Camden has more than exceeded expectations – the space transformed into a slick, funky cantina with a talented team of Ottolenghi-trained chefs turning out arresting global sharing plates. Every bite bounds with fulsome flavours, whether pan-fried mackerel punchy with chermoula and smoked aïoli, sweet and salty miso-marinated chicken with pickled vegetables or melting belly pork lifted by fennel crumble and rhubarb relish. Finish with a 'divine' peanut parfait with salted butter caramel and don't miss knock-out brunches. Forgive the slightly muddled service – overall this is an impressive operation, extending to well-chosen wines from £17 a bottle (£4.20 a glass).

Chef/s: Josh Katz. **Open:** all week L 12 to 2.30 (10.30 to 3 Sat and Sun), D 6 to 10.30. **Closed:** 25 and 26 Dec. **Meals:** alc (main courses £12 to £16). **Service:** 12.5% (optional). **Details:** Cards accepted. 56 seats. Separate bar. Wheelchair access. Music. Children allowed.

ALSO RECOMMENDED

▲ Mangal 1 Ocakbasi

10 Arcola Street, Stoke Newington, E8 2DJ
Tel no: (020) 7275 8981
www.mangal1.com
⊖ Dalston Kingsland, map 2
Turkish

Cheap, noisy and regularly bursting at the seams, Mangal is Stoke Newington's archetypal ocakbasi – a no-frills Turkish canteen dealing in grills from the sizzling ocak, backed up by a few salads, pide and sac breads. Mezze (from £2) include hummus, cacik and lahmacun (a Turkish 'pizza' topped with minced meat), while the skewered offerings could include anything from lamb spare ribs to quail. House wine is £13, but you can BYO. Open all week. Note: no longer related to nearby Mangal 2 on Stoke Newington Road.

Market

Trendy eatery with no-nonsense Brit cooking
43 Parkway, Camden, NW1 7PN
Tel no: (020) 7267 9700
www.marketrestaurant.co.uk
⊖ **Camden Town, map 2**
Modern British | £27
Cooking score: 2

Market is the cosy neighbourhood eatery of choice for trendy Camden locals and those in search of boho shabby-chic décor and no-nonsense, seasonal British cooking. Bold and gutsy flavours prevail on a menu that shows a good understanding of letting well-sourced ingredients shine. Spicy devilled kidneys served on good sourdough, followed by perfectly cooked onglet steak with fries and aïoli impressed one reporter, who also praised the 'charming' service. Vegetarians may find it hard to find more than one choice per course. The accessible wine list starts at £16.40.
Chef/s: Charlie Bell and Davide del Gatto. **Open:** all week L 12 to 2.30 (1 to 3.30 Sun), Mon to Sat D 6 to 10.30. **Closed:** 24 Dec to 2 Jan, bank hols. **Meals:** alc (main courses £13 to £17). Set L £10 (2 courses). **Service:** 12.5% (optional). **Details:** Cards accepted. 50 seats. 4 seats outside. Music. Children allowed.

Morgan M

Fastidious French food
489 Liverpool Road, Islington, N7 8NS
Tel no: (020) 7609 3560
www.morganm.com
⊖ **Highbury & Islington, map 2**
Modern French | £43
Cooking score: 6

It may be uncomfortably close to the din of nearby Holloway Road, but all is serene and prosperous within Morgan Meunier's rather exclusive Islington restaurant. Half-hidden behind frosted glass windows, it's a model of understated, bijou elegance with burgundy tones, oak panelling and green-backed chairs grouped around heavily clothed tables. Morgan M's food is fastidious, sophisticated and unashamedly French – although his highly valued vegetarian menu goes against most deep-rooted Gallic prejudices: if meat is off limits, you should be thrilled by the prospect of an assiette of avocado and aubergine caviar with a thin tomato tuile and red pepper sorbet, or cannelloni of field mushrooms and tarragon with broad beans, diced cucumber and garlic soubise. Otherwise, enjoy the finely crafted, seasonal subtleties of seared red mullet with tomato and fennel purée, razor clams, saffron and lemon broth, La Vendée quail with couscous or a muscular dish of glazed belly pork 'aux épices' with seared fillet, apple purée and port jus. To start, Meunier's 'gorgeous' terrine of Les Landes foie gras with roasted pine nuts and cherry compote continues to draw rave reviews, while desserts have included a 'delightful' chocolate pudding as well as strawberry and rhubarb soufflé with rhubarb and Jurançon ice cream and strawberry coulis. The confident wine list has its heart and soul in Meunier's native land, but also accommodates a few émigrés from Spain and elsewhere. Bottles start at £19.50 (£6.50 a glass).
Chef/s: Morgan Meunier and Sylvain Soulard. **Open:** Wed to Fri and Sun L 12 to 1.30, Tue to Sat D 7 to 9. **Closed:** Mon, 24 to 30 Dec. **Meals:** Set L £24.50 (2 courses) to £28.50. Set D £43. Tasting menu £47 to £52. **Service:** 12.5% (optional). **Details:** Cards accepted. 50 seats. No mobile phones. Music. Children allowed. Car parking.

Odette's

Prowess, sparkle and inspired fish dishes
130 Regents Park Road, Primrose Hill, NW1 8XL
Tel no: (020) 7586 8569
www.odettesprimrosehill.com
⊖ **Chalk Farm, map 2**
Modern British | £35
Cooking score: 5

Since taking over control of this Primrose Hill evergreen, chef Bryn Williams has injected some new vim and vigour into the place.

Odette's swaggering, clubby interior chimes with the local arty crowd and the kitchen is on song, delivering food with unfailing prowess, sparkle and confidence. Fish steals most of the thunder, and Williams displays his talent with star turns such as hand-dived scallops with pork belly and apricot, salmon cooked in the style of coq au vin with leeks and Jerusalem artichokes and, of course, his inspired pairing of roasted turbot with oxtail, cockles and samphire – famously served at the Queen's 80th birthday celebrations. Game also receives up-to-the-minute treatment, as in roasted wood pigeon with foie gras, pickled cherries, chocolate and vanilla salt, and there are wholesome meat compositions too (braised pork cheek with chickpeas, chorizo and wild mushrooms, say). Desserts provide a showstopping finale as the kitchen sends out dreamy confections ranging from lemon curd Arctic roll with fig and pistachio to warm chocolate mousse with banana and passion-fruit sorbet. Otherwise, the chef shows his Welsh colours with a dish of Perl Wen cheese, confit walnuts and bara brith. Big names from France head up the thoughtfully assembled and authoritative wine list, closely followed by some gorgeously tasty numbers from Italy, Spain, South Africa and elsewhere. The 'sommelier's choice' offers an easy way in, with prices from £19 (£5 a glass).

Chef/s: Bryn Williams. **Open:** all week L 12 to 2.30 (3 Sat and Sun), D 6 to 10.30. **Closed:** 24 to 30 Dec. **Meals:** alc (main courses £16 to £23). Set L and D £16 (2 courses) to £20. Sun L £25. **Service:** 12.5% (optional). **Details:** Cards accepted. 60 seats. 35 seats outside. Separate bar. Music. Children allowed.

ALSO RECOMMENDED

▲ Ottolenghi

287 Upper Street, Islington, N1 2TZ
Tel no: (020) 7288 1454
www.ottolenghi.co.uk
⊖ Angel, Highbury & Islington, map 2
Mediterranean/Asian

Yotam Ottolenghi's original café/deli has all the trademarks of the burgeoning and fiercely fashionable chain – brilliant white décor, vibrant displays of salads and patisserie, and a dedication to bold, eclectic flavours. The Med waxes strongly, but Asia and the Middle East also have their say – witness baked baby artichokes with peas and barley (£9), coconut-crusted tiger prawns with green mango, cashews and coriander, or lemon and mascarpone tart (£5.50). Wines from £20. Open all week. Branches in Notting Hill, Kensington and Belgravia (see website for details); Yotam has also launched a full-on flagship restaurant, Nopi (see entry).

▲ El Parador

245 Eversholt Street, Camden, NW1 1BA
Tel no: (020) 7387 2789
www.elparadorlondon.com
⊖ Mornington Crescent, map 2
Tapas

Carlos Horrillo and Patrick Morcas have been running their small Spanish eatery for some 24 years, suggesting a rare level of reliability and consistency. It 'never fails to impress', not only for its imaginative tapas selection, but also for value for money. Noteworthy have been baby squid marinated with chilli, garlic, coriander and olive oil (£7.80), morcilla (Spanish blood sausage) with baby spinach, shallots, pine nuts and saffron oil, and setas (oyster mushrooms) with garlic, rosemary and black sesame seed dressing (£6). House Spanish is £15. Closed Sat and Sun L.

NEW ENTRY

Sardo Canale

Smart family-run Sardinian
42 Gloucester Avenue, Primrose Hill, NW1 8JD
Tel no: (020) 7722 2800
www.sardocanale.com
⊖ Camden Town, Chalk Farm, map 2
Sardinian | £30
Cooking score: 2

This family-run offshoot of Fitzrovia veteran Sardo is much-loved hereabouts. A listed building dressed in blasted brick walls, slate flooring and chi-chi furniture, with a pretty courtyard for summer eating provides the chic but homely backdrop for a menu that majors in the gutsiest of flavours. Homemade pasta is a guaranteed treat: crab and chilli linguine is enduringly popular and paves the way for the pearly simplicity of salt-baked sea bass or rich red-wine braised lamb shank. No complaints about the smooth service or the Sardinian wine list, which brims with little-known gems from £14.95 a bottle (£3.95 a glass).
Chef/s: Claudio Covino. **Open:** Thur and Fri L 12 to 3, Mon to Fri D 6 to 10.30. Sat and Sun 12 to 10.30. **Closed:** 25 and 26 Dec. **Meals:** alc (main courses £11 to £19). Sun L £23. **Service:** 12.5% (optional). **Details:** Cards accepted. 90 seats. 20 seats outside. Separate bar. Wheelchair access. Music. Children allowed.

Singapore Garden

Zesty oriental food with oomph
83 Fairfax Road, Swiss Cottage, NW6 4DY
Tel no: (020) 7328 5314
www.singaporegarden.co.uk
⊖ Swiss Cottage, map 2
Chinese/Malaysian | £30
Cooking score: 2

A Swiss Cottage hit since the 80s, the Singapore Garden comes exotically garbed with chinoiserie and luxuriant greenery – just right for its zesty oriental food. The kitchen wanders around China, hops over to Malaysia and beds down in Singapore for a menu of fragrant, emphatically spiced dishes with plenty of added oomph when needed. Take your pick from pork satay, dry-fried 'chiew yim' squid or intense beef rendang – but don't overlook seasonal specials such as 'grandma's braised pork belly', prawns and okra spiked with homemade dried shrimp 'blachan' or the iconic Singaporean crab with black pepper and butter. Drink Tiger beer or the house wine (£4.50 a glass).
Chef/s: Kok Sum Toh. **Open:** all week L 12 to 3 (5 Sun), D 6 to 11 (11.30 Fri and Sat). **Closed:** 4 days at Christmas. **Meals:** alc (main courses £8 to £30). Set L £20 (2 courses) to £25. Set D £35 (4 courses). **Service:** 12.5% (optional). **Details:** Cards accepted. 85 seats. 12 seats outside. Music. Children allowed.

Sushi-Say

Hospitable, personally run Japanese
33b Walm Lane, Willesden, NW2 5SH
Tel no: (020) 8459 7512
⊖ Willesden Green, map 1
Japanese | £25
Cooking score: 4

An honourable little Japanese oasis in the urban wastelands of Willesden Green sounds unlikely, but Katsuharu and Yuko Shimizu have been slicing sushi and battering tempura in this amicable neighbourhood eatery for more than 16 years. Despite a case of itchy feet a while back, they decided to stay put – much to the relief of their loyal fans. Top-grade sushi needs spanking fresh, top-grade raw materials and Mr Shimizu is a master of the art, pleasing his followers with supreme nigiri (fatty tuna, razor clams, sea urchin, eel, turbot…) as well as an array of glistening, perky sashimi. The kitchen also satisfies those who prefer other sensations, dishing up silky tofu dressed in soy, squid tentacles grilled with salt, beef teriyaki and delicate little bowls of ochazuke (rice in clear soup with adornments). All-inclusive set lunches are worth a go, and there are liquid refreshments aplenty; wines start at £18, but don't miss the fresh orange juice with agar-agar jelly.
Chef/s: Katsuharu Shimizu. **Open:** Sat and Sun L 12 to 3.30, Wed to Sun D 6.30 to 10 (10.30 Sat, 6 to 9.30 Sun). **Closed:** Mon, Tue, 25, 26 and 31 Dec, 1 and 2 Jan, 1 week Easter, 1 week Aug. **Meals:** alc

(main courses £10 to £26). Set L £12.50 to £19.50. Set D £24.50 to £41.50. **Service:** not inc. **Details:** Cards accepted. 41 seats. No music. Wheelchair access. Children allowed.

NEW ENTRY

Sushi of Shiori

Sparkling fresh sushi and sashimi
144 Drummond Street, Euston, NW1 2PA
Tel no: (020) 7388 9962
www.sushiofshiori.co.uk
⊖ Warren Street, Euston Square, map 2
Japanese | £25
Cooking score: 2

More Tokyo than London, Sushi of Shiori is one of those dinky places where customers need to overlook the confines of just one chef and eight counter-style seats and concentrate instead on the sparkling fresh nigiri sushi and glistening sashimi. Yellowtail, sea bass, turbot, flying-fish roe and more have passed the quality test, and the kitchen also sends out various maki rolls, miso soup and donburi (rice bowls topped with fish). Set menus help keep lunchtime bills low, while the selection of saké (300ml from £13.50) is well-considered and preferable to the token wine offerings from £28.

Chef/s: Takashi Takagi. **Open:** Tue to Sat L 11.30 to 2.30, D 5.30 to 10. **Closed:** Sun, Mon, 2 weeks Christmas and New Year, 1 week Aug, bank hols. **Meals:** alc (main course £9 to £16). Set L £12 (2 courses) to £15. Set D £20 (2 courses) to £30. **Service:** 10% (optional). **Details:** Cards accepted. 8 seats. Wheelchair access. Music. Children allowed.

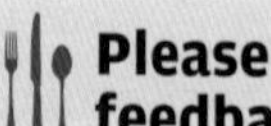

Please send us your feedback

To register your opinion about any restaurant listed in the Guide, or a new restaurant that you wish to bring to our attention, please visit the web address at the bottom of the page. Your feedback informs the content of the book and will be used to compile next year's reviews.

Trullo

Simple Italian with shining ingredients
300-302 St Paul's Road, Islington, N1 2LH
Tel no: (020) 7226 2733
www.trullorestaurant.com
⊖ Highbury and Islington, map 2
Italian | £30
Cooking score: 3

Alumni of Fifteen and the River Café (see entries) are the driving force behind this 'excellent' Italian tucked into a row of nondescript shops just off Highbury Corner. Bare boards, bistro chairs, paper tablecloths and a view of the kitchen set the tone for a simple, uncluttered style of cooking built on excellent ingredients. 'Very, very good' ravioli with homemade ricotta and tomato sauce kept one visitor happy, especially as it was followed by equally zesty braised rabbit with pancetta, Roseval potatoes and sprout tops. There's also a selection from the charcoal grill – lamb rump with smashed peas and wet garlic sauce, for example – followed by caramel pannacotta, all underpinned by 'very good and willing service'. Italian wines start at £17.

Chef/s: Tim Siadatan. **Open:** Sat and Sun L 12.30 to 2.15 (3 Sun), Mon to Sat D 6.30 to 10.15 (7 Sat). **Closed:** 24 Dec to 3 Jan, bank hols. **Meals:** alc (main courses £7 to £18). **Service:** not inc. **Details:** Cards accepted. 40 seats. Separate bar. Music. Children allowed.

ALSO RECOMMENDED

▲ XO

29 Belsize Lane, Belsize Park, NW3 5AS
Tel no: (020) 7433 0888
www.rickerrestaurants.com/xo
⊖ Belsize Park, map 2
Pan-Asian

The north London outpost of Will Ricker's pan-Asian empire, XO combines glossy metropolitan style and glamorous cocktails with dinky plates of food designed for grazing. Chef Tom Cajone is following the formula to the letter, delivering everything from black cod siu mai with pepper miso (£5.75) to Penang duck curry (£12.75), with sweet shrimp tempura, chilli tofu with wok-fried greens, and Peruvian-inspired beef fillet 'anticucho' in between. Desserts look west for the likes of banoffi pie. Eclectic wines from £15.50. Open all week. Takeaway next door.

The York & Albany

All-inclusive Ramsay package
127-129 Parkway, Camden, NW1 7PS
Tel no: (020) 7388 3344
www.gordonramsay.com
⊖ Camden Town, map 2
Modern European | £42
Cooking score: 4
V

Having taken over control of Murano as well as consulting at the Whitechapel Gallery Dining Room (see entries), Angela Hartnett closed the book on York & Albany at the end of 2010. Her long-term sidekick Colin Buchan remains at the stoves and he is capable of delivering some accomplished food – although Y&A's new incarnation seems more 'wobbly' than before, with 'disinterested service', long waits and 'stale' cheeses letting the side down. That said, the kitchen shows its mettle with a richly assertive assiette of smoked rabbit and a starry dish of pink-hued confit salmon with a pile of pickled mooli, capers and radish, although braised pig's cheeks with kohlrabi purée has been underwhelming. To conclude, cinnamon 'pot de crème' with port-infused pears, blue-cheese ice cream and walnuts is a bold concept that looks and tastes stunning. The wine list is a trademark Ramsay collection, with a tremendous range of global varietals, accommodating mark-ups and a terrific choice by the glass or carafe. Bottles start at £17.50.

Chef/s: Colin Buchan. **Open:** Mon to Sat L 12 to 3 (12.15 Sat), D 6 to 11. Sun 12 to 8.30. **Meals:** alc (main courses £17 to £22). Set L and early D £18 (2 courses) to £21. **Service:** 12.5% (optional). **Details:** Cards accepted. 120 seats. 35 seats outside. Separate bar. Wheelchair access. Music. Children allowed.

THE COCKTAIL HOUR

Pretty and potent, cocktails are enjoying a revival in the capital's hippest eateries. Exotic ingredients and elaborate recipes abound, with mixologists adding new twists to old favourites, resurrecting drinks from previous centuries, or simply letting their imagination run wild.

At Soho's **Hix**, try the 'historical curiosities', such as Punch à la Regent, a heady mix of sherry, rum, brandy, curaçao, pineapple syrup, lemon sherbet, citrus, green tea and Champagne. Travel back in time via the cocktail menu at **Hawksmoor**, with outlandish gems such as the Tobacco Old Fashioned - bourbon or rye with sugar and homemade tobacco bitters - harking back to the nineteenth century tradition of accompanying your cocktail with a cigar.

At **Pollen Street Social**, sample a Breakfast Martini of vodka, Grand Marnier, marmalade and toast, while at **Moti Mahal**, whet your appetite with a concoction of ginger-infused vodka, passion fruit, cumin and black pepper syrup and Champagne. And why not round it all off with a Melody AM: Granny Smith with honey, vodka, rosemary, Drambuie and peach bitter at **L'Atelier de Joël Robuchon**?

Albion

Café with bold-as-brass Brit food
2-4 Boundary Street, Shoreditch, E2 7DD
Tel no: (020) 7729 1051
www.albioncaff.co.uk
⊖ Old Street, Liverpool Street, map 2
British | £20
Cooking score: 2

Stake your claim at one of the closely packed tables and watch the goings-on in the open kitchen at this heroically British café, part of Sir Terence Conran's Boundary project (see entry, Boundary). Honest intent and bold-as-brass food is the deal and the menu lays down an emphatic marker with the likes of Welsh rarebit, devilled kidneys, and chicken and ham pie. Breakfast is served throughout the day, sandwiches or goodies from the in-house bakery tempt the coffee-and-chat punters, and you can expect to find kedgeree on the late-night menu. Pricing is friendly, there's free Wi-Fi and no bookings. Wines from £18.
Chef/s: Alex Umeh. **Open:** all week 8am to 11pm. **Meals:** alc (main courses £9 to £12). **Service:** 12.5% (optional). **Details:** Cards accepted. 60 seats. 18 seats outside. Wheelchair access. Music. Children allowed.

Amico Bio

Daring Italian vegetarian in the City
44 Cloth Fair, Barbican, EC1A 7JQ
Tel no: (020) 7600 7778
www.amicobio.co.uk
⊖ Barbican, map 5
Italian vegetarian | £18
Cooking score: 1

Pasquale Amico makes every effort to bring the essence of Italian cooking to this corner of London via his lively, informal restaurant. His is a meat-free vision realised with a confident performance, vibrant with colour, energy and style. Ravioli filled with ricotta, mushrooms and potato with a broccoli sauce, tempura of vegetables with a sweet-and-sour sauce or seitan (mock duck) and vegetable kebab with a red pepper dip are typical choices, while desserts include examples from the standard Italian repertoire, including good homemade sorbets. Wines from £13.50.
Chef/s: Pasquale Amico. **Open:** Mon to Fri 12 to 10.30, Sat 5 to 10.30. **Closed:** Sun, 25 and 26 Dec, bank hols, 1 week August. **Meals:** alc (main courses £7 to £8). **Service:** not inc. **Details:** Cards accepted. 40 seats. Separate bar. Music. Children allowed.

L'Anima

Confident, glossy Italian
1 Snowden Street, City, EC2A 2DQ
Tel no: (020) 7422 7000
www.lanima.co.uk
⊖ Liverpool Street, map 2
Italian | £47
Cooking score: 5

In a spectacularly conceived space a short walk from Liverpool Street Station, L'Anima puts on quite a show with its mix of glass, stone, marble and white leather. The interior may be dressed to impress, but the kitchen, tantalizingly glimpsed through small windows from the restaurant, keeps its head, avoiding frills and furbelows in favour of a straight-talking menu of regional Italian cooking. Francesco Mazzei knows his clients and ratchets up the components, the regional notes and imported ingredients, tempting the assembled crowd with the likes of mozzarella-stuffed deep-fried courgette flower or scallops and stoccafisso (dried cod) with anchovy sauce and (sustainable) Mottra Sterlet caviar. There's delicacy in a dish of silky linguine strewn with sweet white crabmeat and just a hint of chilli and lemon, while a robust signature dish of rabbit siciliana with its sweet-sour sauce shows an understanding of bold, deep flavours. Black Scotch beef steak (tagliata) with marrow bone, blue Pecorino cheese and wine sauce is a wonderful example of 'Italian regional cooking at its best.' Desserts are clever and innovative – liquorice zabaglione containing pistachio ice cream and nuggets of nut brittle was a complete winner at inspection. Excellent staff add a personable approach to

proceedings out front. Expect a tremendous bill, something the ultra-fine Italian wine list, opening at £19, will do little to alleviate.
Chef/s: Francesco Mazzei and Luca Terraneo. **Open:** Mon to Fri L 11.45 to 3, Mon to Sat D 5.30 to 10.30 (11 Sat). **Closed:** Sun. **Meals:** alc (main courses £12 to £35). Set L £24.50 (2 courses) to £28.50. **Service:** 12.5% (optional). **Details:** Cards accepted. 82 seats. Separate bar. Wheelchair access. Music. Children allowed.

NEW ENTRY

Bar Battu

Trendy bar with enticing natural wine
48 Gresham Street, City, EC2V 7AY
Tel no: (020) 7036 6100
www.barbattu.com
⊖ Bank, map 2
Modern European | £22
Cooking score: 2

If you hanker for a life beyond supermarket claret, then youthful, 'verging on trendy' Bar Battu might just do the trick. Organic and biodynamically produced 'natural wine' is the USP, and the place has an enticing list of mainly French names, which are offered by the glass, carafe or bottle (from £14.90). Sipping comes first, but it's also worth matching your chosen tipples with something from the range of small plates, excellent charcuterie and modern bistro dishes. A few minor glitches have been noted, but you can graze satisfyingly on smoked haddock and crab rémoulade, steak tartare with sourdough toast or boudin noir with mash, glazed apple and Calvados jus, before closing with chocolate marquise.
Chef/s: Sydney Aldridge. **Open:** Mon to Fri L 12 to 3, D 5 to 10. **Closed:** Sat, Sun, 25 and 26 Dec. **Meals:** alc (main courses £10 to £20). Set L and D £15 to £18. **Service:** 12.5% (optional). **Details:** Cards accepted. 110 seats. Separate bar. Music. Children allowed.

Bistro Bruno Loubet

Clever cooking and fabulous flavours
The Zetter, 86-88 Clerkenwell Road, Clerkenwell, EC1M 5RJ
Tel no: (020) 7324 4455
www.bistrotbrunoloubet.com
⊖ Farringdon, Barbican, map 5
Modern French | £35
Cooking score: 4

Following his return to the capital after an extended stint down under, once-fêted chef Bruno Loubet looks to be back on form – judging by glowing comments about his comfortably spacious restaurant in the Zetter Hotel. It may be billed as a modern French bistro, but the cooking is cleverer than that, drawing maximum flavour from even the simplest ingredients – excellent homemade boudin blanc, for instance, served with petits pois à la française or well-reported salmon tartare with radish and a pickled ginger/yuzu dressing. A smart, contemporary main course of rabbit tournedos with braised celery, carrot purée and lovage pesto is full of vibrancy and bold strokes, while a textbook thin apple tart with crème fraîche and cinnamon ice cream provides the perfect finish. Service is considered to be 'impeccable', and the well-spread wine list covers France particularly well, with prices kicking off at a very reasonable £15.50. Loubet also cooks for private dining events at sister hotel, the Zetter Townhouse.
Chef/s: Bruno Loubet. **Open:** all week L 12 to 2.30, D 6 to 10.30 (10 Sun). **Meals:** alc (main courses £14 to £22). **Service:** 12.5% (optional). **Details:** Cards accepted. 80 seats. 40 seats outside. Separate bar. Wheelchair access. Music. Children allowed.

Bonds

Banking on quality
Threadneedle Hotel, 5 Threadneedle Street, City, EC2R 8AY
Tel no: (020) 7657 8088
www.theetoncollection.co.uk
⊖ Bank, map 2
Modern European | £40
Cooking score: 5

£5 OFF

The designers have done a nifty job at converting an old marble-pillared temple to Mammon into a modern fine-dining venue with a light touch. A large, mirrored room with neatly aligned tables is full of convivial buzz, and there's a pleasingly informal tone to the operation. Barry Tonks brings modern European dynamics to the City with a menu that embraces British eclectic (Dorset crab with pea and pistachio mousse and pink grapefruit jelly) with French classique (foie gras terrine, quince purée and toasted brioche) – and adds a little Mediterranean sunshine too, perhaps in the form of a main course of sea bream cooked on a plancha and served with borlotti and basil minestrone and smoked bacon. Dual cooking techniques perfect the textures of ingredients such as Devonshire Red chicken, the breast poached and roasted, accompanied by morels, asparagus and gnocchi in mushroom cream sauce. French artisan cheeses are the savoury alternative to one of the relatively straightforward desserts (strawberry sherry trifle, crème brûlée, chocolate moelleux). Service has been known to let the side down badly with abrupt indifference. The wine list trades as extensively across the world as the nearby futures markets do, with Austria and Germany getting a look-in amid the French and southern hemisphere stars. Bottles open at £17 (£6 a glass).
Chef/s: Barry Tonks. **Open:** Mon to Fri L 12 to 2.30, D 6 to 10. **Closed:** Sat, Sun, 25 and 26 Dec, bank hols. **Meals:** alc (main courses £16 to £27). Set L £19.95. Set D £21.95. **Service:** 12.5% (optional). **Details:** Cards accepted. 80 seats. Separate bar. Wheelchair access. Music. Children allowed.

Boundary

Simple cooking that lets ingredients shine
2-4 Boundary Street, Shoreditch, E2 7DD
Tel no: (020) 7729 1051
www.theboundary.co.uk
⊖ Old Street, Liverpool Street, map 2
French | £45
Cooking score: 4

V

This transformation of a Victorian warehouse into a boutique hotel with various eating options comes with enormous swagger (what else would one expect from Sir Terence Conran?). Boundary is housed in the huge and humming basement – all bare brick and soaring ceilings – and hasn't wanted for custom since it opened in 2009. Trademark seafood plays a prominent role in the shape of oysters, crabs, lobsters or a shellfish gratin, helped along by a kitchen that reads from a largely French script – terrine de foie gras, bouillabaisse, carré d'agneau persillé – and recognises the appeal of familiar ideas. Menus show the confidence not to over-describe dishes, and the cooking is equally straightforward, with the focus on careful preparation. Seasonality dictates what's on offer, and the kitchen is not afraid to let good ingredients shine, hence the unexpected simplicity of a rotisserie chicken or shoulder of lamb. House French is £20.
Open: Wed to Fri and Sun L 12 to 3 (4 Sun), Mon to Sat D 6.30 to 10.30. **Meals:** alc (main courses £16 to £35). Set L £19.50 (2 courses) to £24.50. **Service:** 12.5% (optional). **Details:** Cards accepted. 140 seats. Separate bar. No mobile phones. Wheelchair access. Music. Children allowed.

Symbols

- Accommodation is available
- £30 Three courses for less than £30
- V Separate vegetarian menu
- £5 OFF £5-off voucher scheme
- Notable wine list

NEW ENTRY

Brawn

Unbuttoned neighbourhood eatery
49 Columbia Road, Shoreditch, E2 7RG
Tel no: (020) 7729 5692
www.brawn.co
⊖ Shoreditch, map 2
French | £25
Cooking score: 4

£30

It's hard to spot this unbuttoned neighbourhood eatery as signage is minimal; if it's Sunday and the flower market is in full swing, make sure you remember the street number. But once inside the former furniture warehouse you'll find it unpretentious, informal and welcoming. The kitchen deals in carefully sourced seasonal produce delivering a plain, unfussy, traditional style, its earthiness perfectly echoing the surroundings. Brawn (named after a dish of potted pig's head) has a broader European outlook than its sibling Terroirs (see entry), with menus short on adjectives but not on flavour. Charcuterie is impeccable – perhaps a chunk of rich, garlicky pork terrine or lardo di Colonnata. Elsewhere, the freshness of mackerel fillets is perfectly accented by fennel, anchovy and caper, and a pungent sauce ravigote accompanies a glorious tête de veau – the hit list goes on. For dessert, look no further than crêpes with salted caramel. The wine list is an illuminating tour through the mainly French and Italian world of serious modern drinking. Prices (from £14.50) are wallet-friendly, with plenty by the glass.

Chef/s: Ed Wilson and Owen Kenworthy. **Open:** all week L 12 to 3 (4 Sun), Mon to Sat D 6 to 11. **Closed:** 25 and 26 Dec, 1 Jan, bank hols. **Meals:** alc (main courses £12 to £15). Sun L £25. **Service:** 12.5% (optional). **Details:** Cards accepted. 70 seats. Wheelchair access. Music. Children allowed.

Also Recommended

Also recommended entries are not scored but we think they are worth a visit.

Buen Ayre

Top-notch, flame-licked steaks
50 Broadway Market, Hackney, E8 4QJ
Tel no: (020) 7275 9900
www.buenayre.co.uk
⊖ Bethnal Green, map 1
Argentinian | £40
Cooking score: 1

Standards may have slipped at this Argentinean stalwart, but on a good day the charcoal grill can still turn out top-notch, flame-licked steaks. The deluxe 'parrillada' – a mix of juicy, grass-fed ribeye and sirloin served with Argentinian sausages and Provolone cheese – continues to draw the crowds, although reports suggest that service isn't what it used to be. The patriotic wine list starts at £14.20 for a punchy Malbec, and it's worth saving space for the comforting dessert menu and, of course, a final espresso.

Chef/s: John Rattagan. **Open:** Fri to Sun 12 to 3.30 (3 Fri), all week D 6 to 10.30. **Closed:** 25 and 26 Dec, 1 Jan. **Meals:** alc (main courses £9 to £25). **Service:** 12.5% (optional). **Details:** Cards accepted. 37 seats. 24 seats outside. Music. Children allowed.

Café Spice Namasté

Exotic high-profile Indian
16 Prescot Street, Tower Hill, E1 8AZ
Tel no: (020) 7488 9242
www.cafespice.co.uk
⊖ Tower Hill, map 1
Indian | £32
Cooking score: 2

It is 16 years since Cyrus Todiwala's flagship restaurant opened in Whitechapel and it is still a firm favourite with readers, who praise the 'innovative' cooking. Pass the fluttering orange banners outside, and the colourful interior of this contemporary Indian exudes an exotic warmth. Although the Subcontinent remains the main influence of the kitchen, regional British produce is showcased, as is game when in season. Shredded, roasted mallard appears in a spicy chilli fry, whilst minced Herdwick mutton turns up in baked keema ghotala, both dishes sitting nicely beside the more traditional curries and tandooris. Wines from £17.95.

Chef/s: Angelo Collaco. **Open:** Mon to Fri L 12 to 3, Mon to Sat D 6.15 to 10.30 (6.30 Sat). **Closed:** Sun, 25 Dec to 1 Jan, bank hols. **Meals:** alc (main courses £14 to £20). Set L and D £25 (2 courses) to £30. **Service:** 12.5% (optional). **Details:** Cards accepted. 130 seats. Wheelchair access. Music. Children allowed.

ALSO RECOMMENDED

▲ Carnevale

135 Whitecross Street, Barbican, EC1Y 8JL
Tel no: (020) 7250 3452
www.carnevalerestaurant.co.uk
⊖ Barbican, map 5
Vegetarian

This pint-sized deli/restaurant is nothing out of the ordinary to look at, but it's the Med-inspired cooking that's the draw – vivid colours and flavours testify to the fact that vegetarian cooking need not be dull. Starters (£6.25) could include pumpkin gnocchi with spinach in roasted garlic cream, while mains (£12.50) might feature potato cakes with fennel, lemon and basil with Provençal vegetable casserole and mixed rocket salad. Raspberry vanilla crème brûlée is a typical dessert. House wine £15. Closed Sat L and Sun.

▲ Chinese Cricket Club

Crowne Plaza, 19 New Bridge Street, Blackfriars, EC4V 6DB
Tel no: (020) 7438 8051
www.chinesecricketclub.com
⊖ Temple, Mansion House, St Paul's, map 5
Chinese £5 OFF

China's first national cricket team hit the world stage in 2009, and this restaurant was named in their honour. As one of the Crowne Plaza hotel's in-house eateries, CCC can feel a tad corporate, but there's plenty to cheer when it comes to the food. Open your innings with assorted dim sum (from £4.50) or a small plate of 'hot and numbing chicken', before picking up something more substantial – perhaps twice-cooked pork or scallops with black beans (£14). House wine £19. Closed Sat L and Sun.

Cinnamon Kitchen

Ultra-cool City Indian
9 Devonshire Square, City, EC2M 4YL
Tel no: (020) 7626 5000
www.cinnamon-kitchen.com
⊖ Liverpool Street, map 2
Indian | £36
Cooking score: 4
£5 OFF

This sharp-suited City sibling of the patrician Cinnamon Club in Westminster (see entry) is a step up from your average street-food canteen, with the bonus of a standalone bar (Anise) and a courtyard terrace overlooking Devonshire Square. Cool shades of grey and mother-of-pearl with oriental motifs set the tone, while the kitchen delivers deftness and innovation in spades – no surprise, given that CC's executive chef Vivek Singh is behind the menu. Flavours punch well above their weight, whether it's a starter of pink-cooked duck with sesame and tamarind sauce or a sublimely rich guinea fowl curry. Ingredients are sourced with unusual diligence, and the results are up there with the best in town: meticulously timed partridge with a chilli and walnut glaze, lamb kebabs with smoky paprika raita, sea bass in a light sauce spiked with kokum fruit, and Hyderabadi 'haleem' (a dish of minced lamb and wheat) have all been heartily endorsed. Knowledgeably chosen wines start at £19.

Chef/s: Abdul Yaseen. **Open:** Mon to Fri L 12 to 3, Mon to Sat D 6 to 11. **Closed:** Sun, 25 and 26 Dec, 1 Jan, bank hols. **Meals:** alc (main courses £12 to £32). Set L £15 (2 courses) to £18. Set D £19 (2 courses) to £22. **Service:** 12.5% (optional). **Details:** Cards accepted. 130 seats. 60 seats outside. Separate bar. No music. No mobile phones. Wheelchair access. Children allowed.

Club Gascon

A seductive cavalcade of flavour-bombs
57 West Smithfield, City, EC1A 9DS
Tel no: (020) 7796 0600
www.clubgascon.com
⊖ Barbican, Farringdon, St Paul's, map 5
Modern French | £55
Cooking score: 6

£5 OFF 🍷 V

Once a Lyons tea house, this listed building is home to a jewel-like, faux marble-walled dining room emblazoned with floral displays and awash with radical grazing dishes – courtesy of chef-in-residence Pascal Aussignac, whose passionate quest for the culinary essence of southwest France continues to unravel its idiomatic flavours in revelatory detail. There are no conventional 'courses' here; instead diners are offered a cavalcade of concentrated, highly seductive flavour-bombs grouped under headings such as 'l'oceane' and 'les pâturages'. A signature plate of roasted frogs' legs with green quinoa and hare jus turns up under the heading 'la route du sel', while unctuous, velvety foie gras gets a section all to itself: it might be fashioned into a 'club burger' with guindilla chillies, served as carpaccio (in company with confit kumquat, Campari and lime) and even transmuted into 'popcorn'. Dip into the box of tricks and you'll also discover that Aussignac is no hide-bound, stay-at-home patriot either – witness incursions into the esoteric world of coconut-glazed black cod with white port and winkle risotto. After navigating your way through such a tantalising gastronomic tapestry you might hanker after something sweetly titillating: how about a croustillant of frosted almonds with candied citrus and brioche emulsion, or the complex sensory delights of a Roquefort and white chocolate doughnut with Armagnac jelly? The mighty wine list heads south in search of treasures from Tursan, Gaillac, Jurançon and more. Champagne and Bordeaux also receive plenty of attention, and there's a fine slate of 'vins au verre' from £6 a glass.

Chef/s: Pascal Aussignac. **Open:** Mon to Fri L 12 to 2, Mon to Sat D 7 to 10 (10.30 Fri and Sat). **Closed:** Sun, 24 Dec to 3 Jan, bank hols. **Meals:** alc (main courses £12 to £25). Set L £20 (2 courses) to £28. Tasting menu £55 (5 courses). **Service:** 12.5% (optional). **Details:** Cards accepted. 40 seats. Separate bar. Music. Children allowed.

The Coach & Horses

Dining pub with the right credentials
26-28 Ray Street, Clerkenwell, EC1R 3DJ
Tel no: (020) 7278 8990
www.thecoachandhorses.com
⊖ Farringdon, map 5
Modern British | £24
Cooking score: 3

£5 OFF £30

Despite outward appearances the Coach & Horses is no ordinary hostelry, and it has built up a reputation as 'one of the better pub dining rooms' in the capital. Cheerful, informative and relaxed staff contribute greatly to the atmosphere, while the menu is typically modern British, in that it blends old ideas with new. Chefs come and go, but food is simply prepared, say rabbit rillettes with piccalilli or ox tongue with pickles ('how nice to see this appear on a menu'). Fish and chips is a tried-and-tested main course, or you could opt for slow-roast lamb with kale and pearl barley, then buttermilk pudding with hazelnut and apple purée. Sunday lunch is well-reported, the beer is good, and wines (from £13.75) are fair value.

Chef/s: John Ring. **Open:** Sun to Fri L 12 to 3 (1 to 4 Sun), Mon to Sat D 6 to 10. **Closed:** 24 Dec to 3 Jan, Easter, bank hols. **Meals:** alc (main courses £10 to £16). Sun L £15 (2 courses) to £19. **Service:** 12.5% (optional). **Details:** Cards accepted. 70 seats. 36 seats outside. Separate bar. Music. Children allowed.

Comptoir Gascon

Gascon gastronomy
61-63 Charterhouse Street, Clerkenwell, EC1M 6HJ
Tel no: (020) 7608 0851
www.comptoirgascon.com
⊖ Farringdon, Barbican, map 5
French | £30
Cooking score: 4

Modish bare-brick walls, big blackboards and tightly-packed tables set the tone for Comptoir Gascon – the bustling bistro-style sibling of heavyweight French restaurant Club Gascon (see entry). But where Club dazzles with foie gras, frissons and flourishes, Comptoir instead goes for more simple, Gallic home-cooking to win over punters. Mains – split between 'végétal', 'mer' and 'terre' on the menu – might yield the likes of roast pigeon with sweet artichoke crush, or perhaps barbecued baby squid with braised celery and ink sauce. Most purists, however, will probably make a bee-line for the signature duck dishes – a tender duck confit with garbure béarnaise impressed on inspection – or the much-vaunted cassoulet 'Toulousain'. Desserts continue in a similarly hearty vein. A short but serious French wine list sees growers from South West France well represented, with bottles starting at £16. On the way home, drop in at Cellar Gascon – the wine bar member of the Gascon clan on the other side of Smithfield Market.

Chef/s: Stephan Mathenneau. **Open:** Tue to Sat L 12 to 2.30 (11 to 3 Sat), D 7 to 10 (11 Thur and Fri). **Closed:** Sun, Mon, 25 Dec to 5 Jan, Easter. **Meals:** alc (main courses £6 to £15). **Service:** 12.5% (optional). **Details:** Cards accepted. 44 seats. 8 seats outside. Wheelchair access. Music. Children allowed.

Visit us Online

To find out more about *The Good Food Guide*, please visit www.thegoodfoodguide.co.uk

NEW ENTRY

Coq d'Argent

Slick rooftop dining and lovely desserts
1 Poultry, City, EC2R 8EJ
Tel no: (020) 7395 5000
www.coqdargent.co.uk
⊖ Bank, map 2
French | £40
Cooking score: 2

Famed for its seductive, top-of-the-world terrace and views across the London skyline, this slick and sophisticated outfit is a magnet for City suits and those who like to linger over their gastronomic pleasures. Whether you are ensconced in the luxuriant garden bar/ brasserie or the smart, airy dining room, you can expect generous helpings of vigorous French bourgeois food. Recent hits have included mushroom parfait with jewel-like port jelly, comfortingly rich Camembert and leek fondue tart, and signature coq au vin served in its own pan. Desserts are 'simply lovely', especially an extravagant chocolate and caramel marquise with white chocolate. The huge wine list opens at £19.75.

Chef/s: Mickael Weiss. **Open:** Sun to Fri L 11.30 to 3 (12 Sun), Mon to Sat D 6 to 10 (6.30 Sat). **Closed:** bank hols. **Meals:** alc (main courses £16 to £25). Set L £28 (2 courses) to £32. Sun L £25 (2 courses) to £28. Tasting menu £46 (6 courses). **Service:** 12.5% (optional). **Details:** Cards accepted. 150 seats. Separate bar. No music. Wheelchair access. Children allowed.

The Don

Blue-chip wines and vibrant food
The Courtyard, 20 St Swithin's Lane, City, EC4N 8AD
Tel no: (020) 7626 2606
www.thedonrestaurant.co.uk
⊖ Bank, Cannon Street, map 2
Modern European | £35
Cooking score: 2

£5 OFF

Well-oiled ('the wine list deserves a good toot'), and well-established (in premises that were formerly the HQ of the Sandeman

fortified wine company), the Don is a popular venue for business lunches and City types. There are two parts to the operation: a basement bistro offering the likes of pork rillettes and spatchcock baby chicken with garlic and rosemary, and a ground-floor restaurant providing sophisticated modern European cooking. Foie gras crème brûlée with sorrel is a typical starter, while main courses take in roast rack of lamb or loin of venison. The wine list is one of the best in London, a global tour taking in everything from classic French bottles to fashionable modern producers, with roll calls of fortified wines adding depth. Prices start at £20.75.
Chef/s: Matthew Burns. **Open:** Mon to Fri L 12 to 3, D 6 to 10. **Closed:** Sat, Sun, 23 Dec to 4 Jan. **Meals:** alc (main courses £14 to £28). **Service:** not inc. **Details:** Cards accepted. 130 seats. No music. No mobile phones. Children allowed.

The Eagle

Still inspiring after all these years
159 Farringdon Road, Clerkenwell, EC1R 3AL
Tel no: (020) 7837 1353
⊖ Farringdon, map 5
Modern European | £20
Cooking score: 2

Two decades on, the Eagle still inspires. The pub set-up is basic: service is at the bar, the day's menu is chalked up behind the open kitchen, and 'yes, two more of you can fit round that rickety table'. The steak sandwich is a classic, but grilled quails with spelt salad and aïoli, bruschetta di caponata or octopus with paprika, lemon and potatoes are more interesting. For afters, there are Portuguese custard tarts or cheese. A neat list of a dozen wines, all under £20, follows the peregrinations of the cooking. On draught, there's Bombardier and, fittingly, Eagle IPA.
Chef/s: Ed Mottershaw. **Open:** all week L 12.30 to 3 (3.30 Sat and Sun), Mon to Sat D 6 to 10.30. **Closed:** 1 week Christmas, bank hols (except Good Fri D). **Meals:** alc (main courses £6 to £15). **Service:** not inc. **Details:** Cards accepted. 60 seats. 24 seats outside. Music. Children allowed.

Eyre Brothers

Exploring the flavours of Iberia
68-70 Leonard Street, Shoreditch, EC2A 4QX
Tel no: (020) 7613 5346
www.eyrebrothers.co.uk
⊖ Old Street, map 2
Spanish/Portuguese | £33
Cooking score: 2

A fixture in Shoreditch, this old favourite still draws crowds. It's decorated with an eye for quality and comfort, and is one of the few London venues where the kitchen gets its inspiration from the Iberian peninsula, so expect dishes like Portuguese seafood stew or blood sausage with fried turnip greens, garlic and black-eyed peas. Multi-ingredient main courses could follow, such as grilled black-leg chicken with Moorish spices, roast aubergine and red peppers, hazelnuts, coriander and yoghurt with ginger and lemon. Alternatively, there is aged T-bone steak à la plancha, and you could finish with tarta de Santiago (orange and almond cake). The all-Iberian wine list is packed with good bottles and stretches to some prestigious offerings. Prices start at £17.
Chef/s: David Eyre and João Cleto. **Open:** Mon to Fri L 12 to 3, Mon to Sat D 6 to 10 (7 Sat). **Closed:** Sun, Christmas to New Year. **Meals:** alc (main courses £11 to £25). **Service:** 12.5% (optional). **Details:** Cards accepted. 70 seats. Separate bar. Wheelchair access. Music. Children allowed.

Fifteen London

Jamie's trendy trattoria
15 Westland Place, Shoreditch, N1 7LP
Tel no: (020) 3375 1515
www.fifteen.net
⊖ Old Street, map 2
Italian | £46
Cooking score: 3

Bare filament bulbs and graffiti art give Fifteen's refurbished trattoria an urban edge that contrasts pleasingly with the Italian grub that's as rustic as ever (though there's pricier, prettier food in the restaurant downstairs). The apprentice chefs (trained as part of the charitable Jamie Oliver Foundation) are clearly paying attention in class: ravioli of friggitello peppers benefits from fine pasta and a well of luscious buttery sauce, while romanesco and anchovy risotto is nicely creamy. As for the excellent Label Anglais chicken with salsa piccante, the kitchen must share credit with the producer. Only a dried-out olive oil cake and the lingering memory of the reservation process (too bureaucratic for a trattoria) have ruined the mood. The brief wine list, overwhelmingly Italian, starts at £16.75.

Chef/s: Andrew Parkinson. **Open:** all week L 12 to 3, D 6 to 10. **Closed:** 25 Dec. **Meals:** alc (main courses £26 to £29). Set L £26 (2 courses) to £36. **Service:** 12.5% (optional). **Details:** Cards accepted. 65 seats. Separate bar. Wheelchair access. Music. Children allowed.

Galvin La Chapelle

Fine French cuisine and great service
35 Spital Square, Spitalfields, E1 6DY
Tel no: (020) 7299 0400
www.galvinrestaurants.com
⊖ Liverpool Street, map 2
Modern French | £45
Cooking score: 6

Kitchen meisters Jeff Galvin and Zac Whittle should be nervous – the front-of-house team gets even more praise than they do. Guests are made to feel not just welcome, but 'special' and reporters rave about 'impeccable service – attentive but not too interfering'. This, together with the grand, very romantic room in a former girls' school, lends a 'feeling of exclusivity'. Add 'faultless cooking' and the Galvins have a winning formula. The finely wrought French cuisine reveals new ways with classic pairings. A starter of Dorset crab lasagne is a Galvin mainstay, though highlights at inspection were a pair of intense and beautifully constructed terrines – one of Pyrenean lamb, another of guinea fowl, ham hock and foie gras. With Landaise chicken, leeks and truffled gnocchi, plus lamb shoulder, piperade and goats' cheese ravioli to follow, this pretty yet powerful cooking is not the for the lily-livered. Refreshing banana yoghurt ice cream with chilled chocolate fondant makes a welcome finish. Set menus including a 'family Sunday lunch' are a decent deal, leaving change for the predominantly French wine list that runs from £19 to £19,500 for a 1961 Hermitage La Chapelle.

Chef/s: Jeff Galvin and Zac Whittle. **Open:** all week L 12 to 2.30, D 6 to 10.30 (9.30 Sun). **Closed:** 25 and 26 Dec, 1 Jan. **Meals:** alc (main courses £17 to £33). Set L £25.50. Set D £29.50. Tasting menu £70 (7 courses). Sun L £25.50. **Service:** 12.5% (optional). **Details:** Cards accepted. 104 seats. 28 seats outside. Separate bar. No music. Wheelchair access. Children allowed.

Galvin's Café à Vin

Good-value Galvin offshoot
35 Spital Square, Spitalfields, E1 6DY
Tel no: (020) 7299 0404
www.galvinrestaurants.com
⊖ Liverpool Street, map 2
Modern European | £28
Cooking score: 4

Chris and Jeff Galvin's two-sided operation in Spital Square is 'exceptionally well-run', with the casual Café à Vin, in particular, proving a big hit. With its reasonable prices, flexible menu, well-timed service and informal atmosphere, it feels just right. There are some very good things to eat here: plates of charcuterie with celeriac rémoulade, steak tartare with sourdough toast, a 'fantastic' pizza from the wood oven, topped with purple fig, rosemary, honey, rocket and blue cheese, and wood-roast plaice with samphire, Puy lentils and brown shrimps. The set-lunch menu, described as 'faultless' by one who feasted on bresaola with beetroot, fine beans and mustard vinaigrette, followed by venison with prunes and chestnuts, is exceptional value, given the quality of the raw materials. Praise too, for baba au rhum with crème Chantilly. Next door is the upmarket La Chapelle (see entry). Wines from £18.

Chef/s: David Stafford. **Open:** all week 8am to 10.30pm (9am to 9.30pm Sun). **Closed:** 25 and 26 Dec, 1 Jan. **Meals:** alc (main courses £13 to £23). Set L and D £14.95 (2 courses). **Service:** 12.5% (optional). **Details:** Cards accepted. 47 seats. 60 seats outside. Separate bar. Wheelchair access. Music. Children allowed.

Great Eastern Dining Room

Hip pan-Asian stalwart
54-56 Great Eastern Street, Shoreditch, EC2A 3QR
Tel no: (020) 7613 4545
www.rickerrestaurants.com
⊖ Old Street, map 2
Pan-Asian | £35
Cooking score: 2

The duck, watermelon and cashew salad, chilli-salt squid and black cod one finds at all Will Ricker restaurants have become pan-Asian classics, and Londoners love them. They remain reliable picks from the neat collection of curries, tempura, salads, dim sum, sushi and (weirdly Western) puds on offer here, even if the flavours no longer have the power to surprise (unlike the clingfilm in our red pepper and cucumber uramaki). The trendy ground-floor bar and dining room still have a buzz, but for something more 'now' there's GloGlo's, the hip cocktail bar in the basement. Creative cocktailery and yakitori from the robata are the draws. Wines from £16.90.

Chef/s: Neil Witney. **Open:** Mon to Fri L 12 to 4, Mon to Sat D 6 to 10.30. **Closed:** Sun, bank hols. **Meals:** alc (main courses £8 to £28). Set L and early D £11 (2 courses). **Service:** 12.5% (optional). **Details:** Cards accepted. 70 seats. Separate bar. Music. Children allowed.

Symbols

- Accommodation is available
- £30 Three courses for less than £30
- V Separate vegetarian menu
- £5 OFF £5-off voucher scheme
- Notable wine list

The Gun

Popular Docklands eatery
27 Coldharbour, Canary Wharf, E14 9NS
Tel no: (020) 7515 5222
www.thegundocklands.com
⊖ Canary Wharf, map 1
British | £30
Cooking score: 2

Lazy weekend lunches are what the Gun was made for. With a prime spot on the river, opposite the O2, and a choice of dining areas including a lovely waterside terrace, it's easy to see why it's so popular. In summer, there's a separate alfresco restaurant, A Grelha, which serves up freshly grilled seafood, Portuguese style. Back inside the handsome pub dining room, white linen napery and uniformed waiters add an air of formality, and attract restaurant prices. The best dishes see British ingredients treated with minimal fuss, so expect rock oysters served on the shell, or slow-roast shoulder of Welsh lamb. The more cheffy dishes, such as braised beef and ox tongue soup with roast bone marrow, don't always hit the spot and portions can seem stingy. House wine £16.

Chef/s: Mark Fines. **Open:** all week L 12 to 3 (4 Sat and Sun), D 6 to 10.30 (6.30 to 9.30 Sun). **Closed:** 25 and 26 Dec. **Meals:** alc (main courses £13 to £27). Set L £15 (2 courses) to £18. **Service:** 12.5% (optional). **Details:** Cards accepted. 120 seats. 140 seats outside. Separate bar. Wheelchair access. Music. Children allowed.

ALSO RECOMMENDED

▲ The Hackney Pearl

11 Prince Edward Road, Hackney, E9 5LX
Tel no: (020) 8510 3605
www.thehackneypearl.com
⊖ Hackney Wick, map 1
Modern British £5 OFF

The hugely likeable Pearl is quite a local asset. It deliberately plays many roles, from coffee shop to casual drinkers' den and full-on restaurant. Vintage Formica tables and school chairs chime perfectly with cooking that makes a good fist of celebrating seasonal ingredients. Spiced potted beef with pea shoots and pickled walnuts (£5.60), onglet steak with Café de Paris butter and triple-cooked chips (£14.80) and good old Eton mess all star on the short menu, alongside weekend brunches and a brief but very good value wine list (from £15). Open all week.

Hawksmoor

'The best meat in London'
157 Commercial Street, City, E1 6BJ
Tel no: (020) 7247 7392
www.thehawksmoor.co.uk
⊖ Liverpool Street, Aldgate East, map 2
British | £60
Cooking score: 3

Reflecting the great British beef revival, Hawksmoor revitalises the steakhouse concept as a celebration of produce from these shores. Yorkshire-reared Longhorn beef aged 35 days by the Ginger Pig butchers is seared on the white-hot charcoal of a Josper grill to become what one reader dubs 'the best meat in London.' Cuts range from affordable but richly flavoured rump or ribeye, rising to the butter-soft luxury of chateaubriand and fillet, while supporting acts of braised pork ribs or scallops on colcannon almost threaten to upstage the intended stars. Round it all off with a chocolate ice cream sundae. A chop house-chic interior of stripped floors and solid tables, packed in almost bench-like, is hardly reflective of prices which, like the beef, are premium – although wines from £18 may soften the blow. There's a branch at 11 Langley Street, WC2H 9JG, tel: (020) 7856 2154, and a further outlet at 10-12 Basinghall Street, EC2V 5BQ.

Chef/s: Lewis Hannaford. **Open:** all week L 12 to 3 (11 to 4 Sat, 5 Sun), Mon to Sat D 6 to 10.30. **Closed:** 24 to 27 Jan. **Meals:** alc (main courses £12 to £30). **Service:** 12.5% (optional). **Details:** Cards accepted. 95 seats. Music. Children allowed.

Hix Oyster & Chop House

Plain British virtues
35-37 Greenhill Rents, Cowcross Street, Clerkenwell, EC1M 6BN
Tel no: (020) 7017 1930
www.hixoysterandchophouse.co.uk
⊖ Farringdon, map 5
British | £45
Cooking score: 4

The original of Mark Hix's growing chain of eateries consecrated to the virtues of British heritage cooking is near Smithfield meat market. Originally a sausage factory, it's a sleek, pared-down environment with tiled walls, uncovered floors and a marble oyster bar. The bivalves themselves are sourced from around the UK (Brownsea Island, Carlingford, West Mersea and so forth), and might appear in the bordelais fashion with spicy sausages from Sillfield Farm, Cumbria. As you might guess, provenance is everything, to the credit of both Hix and his chef Tom Hill. Lyme Bay sprats with caper mayonnaise, Looe Bay mackerel with tomato and fennel salad, and Torbay monkfish tail with rosemary are among the fish options, and there will be also be Blythburgh pork chops and rib steaks on the bone. Finish with a posset of sea buckthorn or strawberry and white chocolate cheesecake. Castilian house wines are £19.50 for white, £20 red.

Chef/s: Tom Hill. **Open:** Mon to Fri L 12 to 3, Mon to Sat D 5.30 to 11. Sun 12 to 9. **Closed:** 25 and 26 Dec, bank hols. **Meals:** alc (main courses £17 to £37). Set L and theatre menu £17.50 (2 courses) to £22.50. **Service:** 12.5% (optional). **Details:** Cards accepted. 76 seats. 8 seats outside. Music. Children allowed.

ALSO RECOMMENDED

▲ Kasturi

57 Aldgate High Street, Whitechapel, EC3N 1AL
Tel no: (020) 7480 7402
www.kasturi-restaurant.co.uk
⊖ Aldgate, map 2
Indian £5 OFF

With its striking Art Deco interiors and flashy design flourishes, Kasturi makes quite an impact amid the City's architectural monoliths, and the cooking is also a cut above the local curry house norm. The kitchen delivers Indian regional food with a degree of panache, whether you fancy a tandoori from the North West Frontier, spicy lamb cakes with coriander (£5.95) or Malabar prawns spiked with fennel and mustard seeds (£14.95). Jalfrezis and vindaloos satisfy the diehards, and there are keenly priced thalis too. Wines from £16.95. Closed Sun.

Lutyens

Style-conscious Conran classic
85 Fleet Street, City, EC4Y 1AE
Tel no: (020) 7583 8385
www.lutyens-restaurant.com
⊖ Chancery Lane, St Paul's, Temple, map 5
French | £36
Cooking score: 4

It seems rather fitting that Sir Terence Conran should pick a building designed by architectural grandee Sir Edwin Lutyens for this overtly style-conscious venture. What was a slab of patrician Edwardian grandeur has been transmuted into an all-encompassing bar/restaurant/members' club tailored to a rather conservative crowd who come for a taste of cross-Channel *bonne vie*. All the details are just so, and the animated dining room purrs contentedly. Conran's culinary DNA runs through the whole show, from glistening fruits de mer to rotisserie chickens: this is the world of steak tartare, soufflé suisse and côte de boeuf, although the kitchen also dallies with the likes of roast stuffed squid with romesco sauce, duck confit with coco beans and morteau sausage, and fillet of hake with steamed clams, pancetta and parsley. The results are confident, comforting and classy in equal measure – especially if you decide to finish with lemon tart or hot chocolate cake. The wine list is an illustrious, global big-hitter, with prices from £18.

Chef/s: David Burke. **Open:** Mon to Fri L 12 to 3, D 6 to 10. **Closed:** Sat, Sun, 24 Dec to 3 Jan, bank hols. **Meals:** alc (main courses £8 to £39). Set L (bar) £17.50 (2 courses). Set D £39.50. **Service:** 12.5% (optional). **Details:** Cards accepted. 120 seats. Separate bar. Wheelchair access. Music. Children allowed.

ALSO RECOMMENDED

▲ Medcalf

40 Exmouth Market, Clerkenwell, EC1R 4QE
Tel no: (020) 7833 3533
www.medcalfbar.co.uk
⊖ Farringdon, map 2
British

Competition is fierce in Exmouth Market, but this casual eatery is just about holding its own, valued for its starkly functional décor and honest, no-frills cooking. Hearty, uncomplicated flavours prevail: potted rabbit and prunes on toast (£6.95) to start, followed by venison and red wine sausages with mash and onion gravy or mussels with chilli and ginger and fries (£12.95). Apple charlotte and custard wraps meals up nicely, while a brief, globetrotting wine list kicks off at £16. Closed Sun D.

▲ Mehek

45 London Wall, Moorgate, EC2M 5TE
Tel no: (020) 7588 5043
www.mehek.co.uk
⊖ Moorgate, Liverpool Street, map 2
Indian £5 OFF

Mehek translates as 'fragrance' and this friendly pan-Indian restaurant on London Wall certainly lives up to its name when it comes to precise spicing and aromatic regional dishes. A starter of malai chops (£8.90) might be followed by a chef's special of jholsano mojadar squab (£13.50) – grilled squab marinated with tandoori masala sauce and garnished with fresh onion, coriander and peppers. The main carte is supplemented by a range of set menus. Wines from £15.95. Open Mon to Fri.

The Modern Pantry

Informal eatery with inspired flavour-juggling
47-48 St John's Square, Clerkenwell, EC1V 4JJ
Tel no: (020) 7553 9210
www.themodernpantry.co.uk
⊖ Farringdon, map 5
Fusion | £32
Cooking score: 3
£5 OFF

From the hard-working ground-floor café to the light, spacious upstairs dining rooms it's all rollickingly informal, with the Georgian town house lending itself elegantly to the simplicity of the whole operation. Anna Hansen's Antipodean-inspired cooking forms the nerve centre. Her juggling of contrasting flavours is inspired, so take your pick from tempura soft-shell crab served with a spicy brown crab sauce, shiitakes and pickled cucumber relish, or coconut and pandan duck leg curry with pak choi, harusame noodles, shimeji mushrooms and crispy shallots. That same level of complexity is maintained for desserts that might include an outstanding blood orange and sage pannacotta with basil and sesame praline filo. Breakfasts and Sunday brunch are held in justifiably high regard. The wine list (from £17.50) is a whistle-stop tour of old and new.
Chef/s: Anna Hansen. **Open:** Mon to Fri 12 to 11 (10pm Mon). Sat and Sun 9 to 4, 6 to 11. **Closed:** 24 to 26 Dec, bank hols. **Meals:** alc (main courses £15 to £23). Set L £18.50 (2 courses). Sun L £18.50. **Service:** 12.5% (optional). **Details:** Cards accepted. 100 seats. 30 seats outside. Wheelchair access. Music. Children allowed.

Also Recommended

Also recommended entries are not scored but we think they are worth a visit.

NEW ENTRY

Morito

Seriously good tapas
32 Exmouth Market, Clerkenwell, EC1R 4QL
Tel no: (020) 7278 7007
⊖ Farringdon, map 2
Tapas | £15
Cooking score: 4

A tiny slice of Spanish street life transported to Exmouth Market, Morito is the brainchild of Sam and Sam Clark, who run the legendary Moro next door. While the laid-back, no-frills space mirrors its sibling, the concept is tapas-only, with a no-booking policy to boot – expect to queue at busy times. Having elbowed your way to a bar stool or procured one of several small wooden tables, look forward to a menu bursting with bold Spanish flavours. Well-sourced produce and unfussy execution are typical of the Moro style, with deep-fried mussels and pine-nut tarator or fried chickpeas mixed with chopped tomato, chilli and coriander among seriously good things on offer. Elsewhere, there could be salt cod croquettes, octopus with potato and smoked paprika, and lamb chops with cumin and paprika. Spanish wines (from £16) are joined by a good selection of sherries.
Chef/s: Samuel and Samantha Clark. **Open:** Mon to Sat L 12 to 4, D 5 to 11. **Closed:** Sun, Christmas, New Year, bank hols. **Meals:** alc (tapas from £3 to £6.50). **Service:** 12.5% (optional). **Details:** Cards accepted. 36 seats. 6 seats outside. Separate bar. Wheelchair access. Music. Children allowed.

Moro

Sheer, palate-tingling excitement
34-36 Exmouth Market, Clerkenwell, EC1R 4QE
Tel no: (020) 7833 8336
www.moro.co.uk
⊖ Farringdon, map 2
Spanish/North African | £34
Cooking score: 4

There was a time when Moro, with its hard lines, impressive sourcing and resolutely simple cooking, stood out as a big, brash beacon of innovation. That it is now part of the scenery is testament to how far-reaching the revolution that it helped to start has been. The Spanish-North African food continues to strike an instant chord – 'we have never been able to get a table [even] with two to three days' notice; they have either shoehorned us in or we have sat outside,' says one reporter. The wood-fired oven and charcoal grill inspire many of the dishes. Warm crab on toast with a glass of Oloroso sherry is a good way to start, then char-grilled bream ('superb freshness and flavour') with a fresh cucumber salad, or wood-roasted chicken with saffron pilau, walnut and pomegranate sauce. Yoghurt cake with pistachios is a favourite dessert. Iberian peninsula wines start at £15.50.

Chef/s: Samuel and Samantha Clark. **Open:** Mon to Sat L 12.30 to 2.30, D 7 to 10.30. **Closed:** Sun, 24 Dec to 4 Jan, bank hols. **Meals:** alc (main courses £16 to £20). **Service:** 12.5% (optional). **Details:** Cards accepted. 106 seats. 18 seats outside. No music. Wheelchair access. Children allowed.

1 Lombard Street

Glossily exotic food in the City
1 Lombard Street, City, EC3V 9AA
Tel no: (020) 7929 6611
www.1lombardstreet.com
⊖ Bank, map 2
Modern European | £55
Cooking score: 6

A transfigured banking hall in the still-murmuring heart of the Square Mile, 1 Lombard Street makes the most of its spectacular Georgian interiors and oozes cultured poise – especially if you dine in the venue's exclusive inner sanctum. The flagship restaurant is home to some striking oil paintings, but most attention focuses on Herbert Berger's glossily exotic overtures into the world of contemporary cuisine. French themes are overlaid with a dash of wasabi here, a dot of green papaya there, and the results are seldom dull: seared foie gras might be teamed with sweet-and-sour chicory, spiced pears, bitter chocolate and balsamic vinaigrette, while sauté of native lobster and langoustines is bathed in a Sauternes and lime reduction. Dishes occasionally lack the 'sparkle' promised by all that visual showboating – rack of lamb with a ragoût of French beans and peas is a case in point – but thought-provoking desserts revitalise proceedings triumphantly. Classicism rules in a chocolate and passion-fruit macaroon, while a warm coffee sponge creatively paired with caramelised morels, parsnips and Jerusalem artichokes courts the current vogue for edgy savoury/sweet finales. Service treads carefully, although discreet detachment can sometimes descend into plain forgetfulness. By contrast, the adjoining bar/brasserie is a high-octane coven of bellowing suits who come here to guzzle fizz and nibble plates of Euro-Asian food. The full wine list puts France at the top of a very distinguished pile, but there are plenty of fine vintages from the global cellar too. Big spenders can delve into the Lombard Vault; others will find ample pickings from £20.

Chef/s: Herbert Berger. **Open:** Mon to Fri L 12 to 2.30, D 6 to 10.30. **Closed:** Sat, Sun, 25 and 26 Dec, 1 Jan, bank hols. **Meals:** alc (main courses £24 to £30). Set L £28 (2 courses) to £34. Set D £25. **Service:** 12.5% (optional). **Details:** Cards accepted. 180 seats. Separate bar. Wheelchair access. Music. Children allowed.

Pizza East

More than just excellent pizzas
56 Shoreditch High Street, Shoreditch, E1 6JJ
Tel no: (020) 7729 1888
www.pizzaeast.com
⊖ Liverpool Street, Old Street, map 2
Italian | £20
Cooking score: 2

Pizza East is big and canteen-like, with the kind of rough, industrial vibe you expect in Shoreditch. Basically Italian-American in style, with a strong backbone of good-quality Italian salumi (preserved meats) and cheeses – including brilliant speck, prosciutto, buffalo mozzarella, sheep's milk ricotta – there's more

to it than just excellent wood-fired pizzas. Lamb chops, beef lasagne, roast chicken, and meatballs as a starter (the veal version also appears on a deliciously robust pizza with prosciutto, sage and cream), have all been applauded. And puddings are absolutely worth leaving room for, especially a 'divine' salted chocolate caramel tart. Wines from £19.50. Pizza East Portobello is at 310 Portobello Road, W10; tel: (020) 7729 1888.
Chef/s: Jon Pollard. **Open:** all week L 12 to 5 (10am Sat and Sun), D 5 to 12 (1am Thur, 2am Fri and Sat). **Closed:** 25 and 26 Dec. **Meals:** alc (main courses £8 to £20). Set L and D (Tue) £15. **Service:** 12.5% (optional). **Details:** Cards accepted. 220 seats. Separate bar. Wheelchair access. Music. Children allowed.

Refettorio at the Crowne Plaza Hotel

Authentic Italian with vibrant food
19 New Bridge Street, City, EC4V 6DB
Tel no: (020) 7438 8052
www.refettorio.com
⊖ Blackfriars, map 5
Italian | £38
Cooking score: 2

Eight years on, the smart, refectory-style dining room still buzzes at lunch – evenings are quieter – and the approach to food remains consistent, namely vibrant Italian dishes based on fresh, seasonal ingredients, delivered by confident staff. The menus may read quite plainly – start, maybe, with thinly sliced cured neck of pork with rocket, balsamic onions and warm piadina bread for a forthright introductory salvo. Pasta is always well-considered (casarecci are served lightly sauced with fresh artichokes and pecorino), while main courses might deliver calf's liver with braised lentils and stewed red onion. Conclude with classic tiramisu. The all-Italian wine list opens at £18.50.
Chef/s: Alessandro Bay. **Open:** Mon to Fri L 12 to 2.30, Mon to Sat D 6 to 10.30 (10 Fri and Sat). **Closed:** Sun, 23 to 30 Dec. **Meals:** alc (main courses £7 to £23). Set D £23. **Service:** 12.5% (optional). **Details:** Cards accepted. 110 seats. Separate bar. Wheelchair access. Music. Children allowed. Car parking.

The Restaurant at St Paul's Cathedral

Chic eatery in a crypt
St Paul's Cathedral, St Paul's, EC4M 8AD
Tel no: (020) 7248 2469
www.restaurantatstpauls.co.uk
⊖ St Paul's, map 5
Modern British | £26
Cooking score: 2

Down in the crypt of St Paul's, away from the touristy hustle and bustle, this 'very welcoming and friendly' restaurant is the epitome of understated chic. Its painted stone walls, bare floors and vaulted ceiling create a clean, crisp backdrop for some indulgent and patriotic cooking. 'Deliciously creamy' chicken liver parfait with a very rich and fruity chutney delighted one diner, as did a 'really homely' pork neck fillet with cabbage and Puy lentils. Elderflower and rhubarb trifle is a typical pudding, but other sweet treats include the homemade jams and 'huge, fluffy scones' served at afternoon tea. Wine starts at £16.25.
Chef/s: Gavin Quinn. **Open:** all week 11.30 to 4.30 (3 Sun). **Meals:** Set L £21.50 (2 courses) to £25.95. **Service:** 10% (optional). **Details:** Cards accepted. 48 seats. No music. Wheelchair access. Children allowed.

Rhodes Twenty Four

Skyline vistas and eye-opening cooking
Tower 42, 25 Old Broad Street, City, EC2N 1HQ
Tel no: (020) 7877 7703
www.rhodes24.co.uk
⊖ Liverpool Street, map 2
British | £60
Cooking score: 4

The lofty reputation of this City eyrie isn't just down to the 'breathtaking' panoramic vistas – judicious service and slick interiors also make their mark. But the biggest eye-opener is head chef Adam Gray's cooking. He honours Gary

Rhodes' love affair with British food, delivering bold plates that rely on few frills to impress. Wood pigeon tart is a colourful construction of perfectly pink breast meat and ruby red beetroot perched on a buttery puff pastry disc. Crisp-skinned, delicately moist stone bass is bolstered with the late springtime gems of asparagus, Jersey Royals and summer truffle, while puds are nursery food elevated beyond all recognition – perhaps marmalade and chocolate Arctic roll. There's an enticing array of Champagnes, while the wine list (from £24 a bottle, £8 a glass) exhibits the French elite with highlights from around the world. 'Not cheap, but worth it'.
Chef/s: Adam Gray. **Open:** Mon to Fri L 12 to 2.30, D 6 to 9. **Closed:** Sat, Sun, bank hols, 25 Dec, 1 Jan. **Meals:** alc (main courses £17 to £31). **Service:** 12.5% (optional). **Details:** Cards accepted. 75 seats. Separate bar. Wheelchair access. Music. Children allowed.

Rivington Grill

A menu bursting with patriotic gems
28-30 Rivington Street, Shoreditch, EC2A 3DZ
Tel no: (020) 7729 7053
www.rivingtongrill.co.uk
⊖ Old Street, map 2
Modern British | £32
Cooking score: 2

The normality of this restaurant amid Shoreditch's surfeit of 'concept' eateries is a breath of fresh air. A sophisticated bistro promising 'the best of British cooking', its menu bulges with patriotic gems, from Manx kippers at breakfast through to Devonshire Red roast chicken carved at the table and served with sage, onion and liver stuffing and roast potatoes. A passion for this island's finest ingredients guarantees plenty of seafood, from potted shrimps or Dorset rock oysters to Anglesey sea bass with brown shrimps and caper butter. Finish with Bramley apple crumble and custard. Wines start at £17.25. There's a branch at 178 Greenwich High Road, SE10 8NN, tel: (020) 8293 9270.
Chef/s: Simon Wadham. **Open:** all week L 12 to 3 (11 to 4 Sat and Sun), D 6 to 11 (10 Sun). **Closed:** 25 Dec, 1 Jan. **Meals:** alc (main courses £14 to £30). **Service:** 12.5% (optional). **Details:** Cards accepted. 80 seats. Separate bar. No music. Wheelchair access. Children allowed.

Rochelle Canteen

No-frills East End hideaway
Rochelle School, Arnold Circus, E2 7ES
Tel no: (020) 7729 5677
www.arnoldandhenderson.com
⊖ Liverpool Street, map 2
British | £25
Cooking score: 2

This basic daytime eatery, carved out of a school bike shed and giving onto the school playground (now lawned and wonderful in summer), takes a dressed down, casual approach to things, with communal tables and no standing on ceremony. Margot Henderson's short menu trumpets tersely worded, no-frills seasonal dishes in the manner of her husband's restaurant St John (see entry). Modestly priced, straightforward dishes include cauliflower, leeks and butterbeans or asparagus and poached egg to start, with plaice and fennel or braised guinea fowl with broad beans and artichoke to follow, and strawberry ice cream for dessert. Unlicensed, but BYO with corkage £5.
Chef/s: Margot Henderson. **Open:** Mon to Fri 9.30am to 4.30pm. **Closed:** Sat, Sun, 25 Dec to 1 Jan, bank hols. **Meals:** alc (main courses £9 to £14). **Service:** not inc. **Details:** Cards accepted. 36 seats. 20 seats outside. No music. Wheelchair access. Children allowed.

Saf

Raw talent
152 Curtain Road, Shoreditch, EC2A 3AT
Tel no: (020) 7613 0007
www.safrestaurant.co.uk
⊖ Old Street, map 2
Vegetarian | £30
Cooking score: 4

£5 OFF **V**

'Consistently innovative, fresh and satisfying dishes served by knowledgeable staff in a relaxed, yet smart setting.' That's one verdict on this Shoreditch restaurant that has been peddling raw vegan food for four years – and is still up for the gig. Few items are heated beyond 48°C to preserve nutrients – so don't expect hot food. Do expect snappy global ideas and deep, precise flavours in dishes such as dolmades stuffed with cinnamon and raisin buckwheat pilaf and served with a cucumber and dill yoghurt. Meanwhile, mains could take in a pearl barley risotto of portobello and oyster mushrooms flavoured with caperberry and tarragon and served with a cashew truffle cream, or flax and pepper tacos with Mexican pâté, quacamole, and salsas of pineapple and tomato. Sweet things include a heaven-scented cranberry and rose soup.'Botanical' cocktails are an alternative to the specialist line-up of organic/biodynamic wines (from £25).

Chef/s: Faith Güuen. **Open:** Mon to Sat L 12 to 4, D 6 to 11. Sun 12 to 11. **Closed:** bank hols. **Meals:** alc (main courses £11 to £17). **Service:** not inc. **Details:** Cards accepted. 120 seats. 20 seats outside. Separate bar. Wheelchair access. Music. Children allowed.

Symbols

- Accommodation is available
- £30 Three courses for less than £30
- V Separate vegetarian menu
- £5 OFF £5-off voucher scheme
- Notable wine list

St John

Nose-to-tail pioneer
26 St John Street, Clerkenwell, EC1M 4AY
Tel no: (020) 3301 8069
www.stjohnrestaurant.com
⊖ Farringdon, map 5
British | £35
Cooking score: 5

Few chef/restaurateurs can fairly claim to have altered London's gastronomic landscape, but Fergus Henderson is one. In this cavernous, white-walled former smokehouse round the corner from Smithfield meat market, he began in the mid-1990s bringing back long-forgotten culinary values to a capital city sated with the often vapid luxuries of fine dining. St John's ethos has always been about the thrifty use of all those overlooked bits of meat, often paired with humble vegetation and wild pickings, and it remains a true original – despite the fact that its ground-breaking ideas have now become common currency. Back in the day you'd be hard pressed to find braised squid with alexanders or widgeon with lentils and chard anywhere else; now, any self-respecting pub or restaurant seeking to re-kindle the embers of folksy British gastronomy will be going down that route. Of course, the baldness and plain, uncompromising simplicity of St John's approach can sometimes be baffling – the focus is on is on the indisputable quality of the raw materials, not on what astonishing things might be done to them. Hence a daily menu that cuts straight to the chase: rabbit offal and pea purée; hake with fennel and green sauce; pigeon and radishes; roast lamb with turnip greens and anchovy, plus finishers including baked egg custard, Eccles with cake with Lancashire cheese or peach jelly and shortbread. The French wine list celebrates another kind of tradition, with prices from £20.65.

Chef/s: Chris Gillard. **Open:** Sun to Fri L 12 to 3 (1 to 3 Sun), Mon to Sat D 6 to 11. **Closed:** 1 week Christmas, Good Fri, Easter Mon. **Meals:** alc (main courses £7 to £24). **Service:** 12.5% (optional). **Details:** Cards accepted. 110 seats. No music. No mobile phones. Children allowed.

St John Bread & Wine

Quality no-frills cooking
94-96 Commercial Street, Spitalfields, E1 6LZ
Tel no: (020) 3301 8069
www.stjohnbreadandwine.com
⊖ Liverpool Street, map 1
British | £28
Cooking score: 3

Tucked away at the back of Spitalfields market, this buzzy Fergus Henderson eatery is the laid-back offshoot of St John (see entry), and it's run with the same conviction as its sibling. Breakfast and elevenses show off the output of the in-house bakery and the rest of the daily repertoire is dictated by the calendar, with much use of 'nose-to-tail' ingredients and gleanings from the regional British larder; dishes are often designed for sharing and the kitchen is reckoned to be 'utterly reliable', whether it is turning out 'velvety' butternut squash or 'perfectly cooked' plaice. Otherwise, the daily menu could yield pig's trotter and bacon on toast, or ox heart, watercress and pickled walnut. Follow up with nursery puds. The Francophile wine list moves gently up, from £20.65.

Chef/s: Lee Tiernan. **Open:** all week 9am to 11pm (10am Sat, 10.30pm Sun). **Closed:** 25 Dec to 1 Jan, Easter Mon. **Meals:** alc (main courses £14 to £27). **Service:** not inc. **Details:** Cards accepted. 60 seats. No music. Children allowed.

Searcy's

Flexible food for culture vultures
Level 2, Barbican Centre, Silk Street, Barbican, EC2Y 8DS
Tel no: (020) 7588 3008
www.searcys.co.uk/barbican-centre
⊖ Barbican, Moorgate, map 5
Modern European | £29
Cooking score: 3

The light, airy restaurant found on Level 2 of the Barbican looks on to St Giles Cripplegate Church and couldn't be handier for culture vultures. The appealing, cosmopolitan carte comes bolstered by fixed-price lunches, pre-theatre deals and small plates in the bar, and offers a commitment to good seasonal ingredients. In spring this means a salad of wood pigeon with asparagus, honey and sesame seeds, then roast sea trout with Jersey Royals, samphire and brown shrimp butter, or roast rump of lamb with chickpea and potato salad and piquillo pepper relish, with pannacota and English strawberries to finish. Wines are a well-chosen international mix, with bottles from £23.50.

Chef/s: Darren Archer. **Open:** Mon to Fri L 12 to 2.30, Mon to Sat D 5 to 10.30. **Closed:** Sun. **Meals:** Set L £18.50 (2 courses) to £22.50. Set D £24.50 (2 courses) to £29.50. **Service:** not inc. **Details:** Cards accepted. 72 seats. Separate bar. No mobile phones. Wheelchair access. Music. Children allowed. Car parking.

Soseki

An evocative slice of old Japan
20 Bury Street, City, EC3A 5AX
Tel no: (020) 7621 9211
www.soseki.co.uk
⊖ Liverpool Street, Bank, map 2
Japanese | £40
Cooking score: 3

Named after novelist Natsume Soseki, this stunning eatery evokes the sort of literary, Taishō-period teahouse the writer would have enjoyed. Book jackets line the walls of the bar, and the whole place is stuffed with covetable 1920s antiques, kimono tables, tatami mats and exotic screens. Soseki supports sustainable seafood and ethically sourced produce, which is used to telling effect in a series of ingredients-led 'kaiseki-kappo' banquets determined by the market: order 'omakase' ('it's up to you') style and let Kyoto star Shu Inagaki do the rest. A 'hanashi' feast, for example, will lead you through a sakizuke appetiser, wanmono clear soup, some seasonal sashimi and a steamed mushimono dish, before moving on to grilled, fried and vinegared specialities. Finally, the arrival of sushi, miso soup and pickles signals that proceedings are heading towards their conclusion. To drink, there are green teas, macha shots, sakés and organic wines (from £22).

Chef/s: Shu Inagaki. **Open:** Mon to Fri L 12 to 2.30, D 6 to 10. **Closed:** Sat, Sun, bank hols, Christmas to New Year. **Meals:** alc (main courses £14 to £45). Set L and D £21 (2 courses) to £25. Kaiseki menu £25 to £60. **Service:** 12.5% (optional). **Details:** Cards accepted. 60 seats. Separate bar. Music.

Tayyabs

Long-serving Punjabi canteen
89 Fieldgate Street, Whitechapel, E1 1JU
Tel no: (020) 7247 6400
www.tayyabs.co.uk
⊖ Whitechapel, Aldgate East, map 1
Pakistani | £20
Cooking score: 2

A local legend since 1972, Mohamed Tayyab's seminal Asian café has lost none of its edge and packs 'em in every night of the week. Despite some arty gentrification, the interior still feels cramped, queues are *de rigueur* and service runs at full stretch, but the kitchen delivers some of the best grilled meats in the East End (the minted lamb chops are wickedly good). However, there's much more to Tayyabs than hunks of animal protein: the tinda (pumpkin) curry is 'to die for' and orders for karahi fish, aloo meat or dhal gosht are always amply rewarded. Portions are big, prices are low and you can BYO booze, even though the place is unlicensed.

Chef/s: Wasim Tayyab. **Open:** all week L 12 to 5, D 6 to 11.30. **Meals:** alc (main courses £5 to £12). **Service:** not inc. **Details:** Cards accepted. 200 seats. Wheelchair access. Music. Children allowed.

Also Recommended

Also recommended entries are not scored but we think they are worth a visit.

ALSO RECOMMENDED

▲ Towpath Café

42 De Beauvoir Crescent, Dalston, N1 5SB
⊖ Old Street, map 2
Modern European

A basic café of sorts, the Towpath's canalside location is probably stumbled upon first time around, and it works best in fine weather – there's little space under cover. Food writer Lori de Mori and photographer Jason Lowe's quirky hole-in-the-wall (no phone number) delivers a daily changing menu that's geared for casual satisfaction: duck broth and smoked mackerel and potato salad sit alongside toasted Montgomery Cheddar with chillied quince jelly, and olive oil cake comes with citrus zest and blood orange juice. Prices range from £5 to £10; wines from £18. Open Tue to Sun L only. Cash only.

Les Trois Garçons

High-camp glamour and decent cooking
1 Club Row, Shoreditch, E1 6JX
Tel no: (020) 7613 1924
www.lestroisgarcons.com
⊖ Liverpool Street, map 1
French | £47
Cooking score: 2

Looking more like an antiques market than a restaurant, Les Trois Garçons is an Aladdin's cave dripping with shimmering chandeliers, strangely elegant taxidermy and vintage handbags. The cooking (classic French with endless creative flourishes) doesn't hit as many highs as the décor but produces winners, especially a never-off-the-menu rich, buttery home-cured foie gras in Sauternes. Elsewhere, there's Herdwick lamb with lemon thyme jus, and a choice of rich, indulgent desserts. Occasionally haughty service can raise eyebrows – as do bills, particularly with house wine at £24.50 a bottle.

Chef/s: Michael Chan. **Open:** Sun to Fri L 12 to 2.30, Mon to Sat D 6 to 9.30 (10 Wed and Thur, 10.30 Fri and Sat). **Closed:** 23 Dec to 4 Jan, bank hols. **Meals:** Set L £17.50 (2 courses) to £22. Set D £40.50

(2 courses) to £47. Sun L £35. Tasting menu £58.50. **Service:** 12.5% (optional). **Details:** Cards accepted. 60 seats. Music.

NEW ENTRY

28°-50°

Food that lets the wine shine
140 Fetter Lane, City, EC4A 1BT
Tel no: (020) 7242 8877
www.2850.co.uk
⊖ Chancery Lane, map 5
French | £28
Cooking score: 3

With belts tightened and boozy lunches now strictly verboten, this spacious City basement wine bar from the Texture team (see entry) has come at the right time. The food is 'well-cooked and unfussy', but the real highlight for at least one reporter is the fact that all wines are available by the glass in three sizes: 250ml, 125ml and – ideal for midday quaffing – 75ml. The food lets the wine shine: for example, onglet steak and triple-cooked chips with a 2005 Fumanelli Valpolicella; wild garlic risotto with a 2006 Brundlmayer Riesling. Starters such as 'excellent' duck rillettes or snails and bacon are generous – puds such as almond and cinnamon cake are mimsy by comparison. Service is 'efficient and friendly.' House wines are £19.50, but nothing on the 'interesting and fairly priced' regular list is over £45.
Chef/s: Paul Walsh. **Open:** Mon to Fri L 12 to 2.30, D 6 to 9.30. **Closed:** Sat, Sun, bank hols. **Meals:** alc (main courses £14.50 to £16.50). Set L £15.95. **Service:** 12.5% (optional). **Details:** Cards accepted. 60 seats. Separate bar. Wheelchair access. Music. Children allowed.

Average Price

The average price listed in main-entry reviews denotes the price of a three-course meal, without wine.

NEW ENTRY

Vanilla Black

Audacious veggie venture
17-18 Tooks Court, Farringdon, EC4A 1LB
Tel no: (020) 7242 2622
www.vanillablack.co.uk
⊖ Chancery Lane, map 5
Vegetarian | £33
Cooking score: 2

On first sight, Vanilla Black doesn't look much like a test-lab for veggie gastronomy – sensibly dressed with muted green walls and polished floorboards, the dining room sits perfectly with the well-heeled Chancery Lane clientele. Only with a glance at the menu does the penny drop – Brie ice cream, salt 'n' vinegar gel, Marmite-glazed almonds and even 'passion-fruit mayonnaise' are all among the concoctions coming from an audacious kitchen. Sage and shallot tarte Tatin with blue potatoes should win over the most ardent of carnivores, while staff trumpet the signature dish of poached egg and Ribblesdale cheese pudding. Desserts also follow the same pioneering spirit – try a rhubarb and vanilla milk shortbread with lavender ice cream. Wines from £16.
Chef/s: Andrew Dargue. **Open:** Mon to Fri L 12 to 2.30, Mon to Sat D 6 to 10. **Closed:** Sun, bank hols, 2 weeks Christmas. **Meals:** Set L £18.50 (2 courses) to £23.50. Set D £24.50 (2 courses) to £32.50. **Service:** 12.5% (optional). **Details:** Cards accepted. 45 seats. Music. Children allowed.

Viajante

A brilliantly eccentric restaurant
Patriot Square, Bethnal Green, E2 9NF
Tel no: (020) 7871 0461
www.viajante.co.uk
⊖ Bethnal Green, map 1
Modern European | £60
Cooking score: 5

Created by Nuno Mendes, who trained at El Bulli, Viajante continues to establish itself as one of London's most exciting restaurants.

Mendes' cooking is in what's now dubbed the 'modernist' vein and is technically astounding and original – though perhaps not always delicious. Viajante is found in a contemporary, Scandinavian-inspired dining room in edgy Bethnal Green's Town Hall Hotel. It rejects written menus and instead encourages guests to choose three (lunch only), six, nine or twelve courses (this last experience taking four hours). A Japanese-inspired dish of leek heart with lobster and leek consommé, raw squid, a frozen jus of its ink and pickled radishes, and a combo of cod and potatoes with gelatinous confit egg yolk and saffron were exceptional at inspection: balanced and thoughtful, not clever-clever. Bread with flavoured whipped butters and 'rather special' chocolate mushroom truffles are also excellent. Some 'trendy' combinations and obscure ingredients (leek 'ash' and milk skin) leave diners 'puzzled', however, as does the price they command. Lukewarm dishes – often a pitfall of cooking 'sous vide' – are another grumble. Some find the service muddled, others consider it generous and informed. The modern wine list (from £26) is hard to fathom without assistance. A more informal offshoot, The Corner Room, is in the same hotel, tel: (020) 7871 0460.

Chef/s: Nuno Mendes. **Open:** Wed to Sun L 12 to 2, all week D 6 to 9.30. **Closed:** 25 and 26 Dec. **Meals:** Set L £28 (3 courses), £50 (6 courses) or £70 (9 courses). Set D £65 (6 courses) or £90 (12 courses). **Service:** 12.5% (optional). **Details:** Cards accepted. 35 seats. Separate bar. No mobile phones. Wheelchair access. Music.

Please send us your feedback

To register your opinion about any restaurant listed in the Guide, or a new restaurant that you wish to bring to our attention, please visit the web address at the bottom of the page. Your feedback informs the content of the book and will be used to compile next year's reviews.

Viet Grill

Stunning vibes and street food
58 Kingsland Road, Shoreditch, E2 8DP
Tel no: (020) 7739 6686
www.vietnamesekitchen.co.uk
⊖ Old Street, map 2
Vietnamese | £16
Cooking score: 2

Amid the canteen-style restaurants on Kingsland Road's 'Pho Mile', Viet Grill is an altogether snazzier offering, its interior of dark wood furniture and bold leaf murals channelling a mix of French colonialism and urban cool. A good choice for anything from a date to a quick snack, it prides itself on offering 'what people really eat in today's Vietnam', from street food to showy specials. By day, snap up tasty, bargain dishes such as pho or charcoaled pork tenderloin. The evening menu offers everything from 'small eats' (maybe leafy meat dumplings) to 'campfire beef' or slow-cooked Mekong catfish. Wines, chosen by Malcom Gluck, start at £18.50.

Chef/s: Vinh Vu. **Open:** Mon to Sat L 12 to 3, D 5.30 to 11 (11.30 Fri and Sat). Sun 12 to 10.30. **Closed:** 23 Dec to 4 Jan. **Meals:** alc (main courses £7 to £25). Set L and D £21. Sat and Sun L £15. **Service:** 12.5% (optional). **Details:** Cards accepted. 120 seats. Separate bar. Music. Children allowed.

Vinoteca

Buzzing go-with-the-flow eatery
7 St John Street, Farringdon, EC1M 4AA
Tel no: (020) 7253 8786
www.vinoteca.co.uk
⊖ Farringdon, Barbican, map 5
Modern European | £25
Cooking score: 3

Thriving, buzzing and casual in the extreme, reporters love Vinoteca's atmosphere as much as its food and wine – it feels like a modest neighbourhood café, and the deal is to go with the flow. The menu has a grazing feel and modern European flavour: Jabugo cured meats or British cheeses to share, grilled razor clams with samphire, fennel and pickled radish or more substantial roasted guinea fowl breast with soft polenta, sun-dried tomato and pesto – all with their own wine matches. Reasonable pricing extends to the exemplary 275-bin global list, which puts quality above showiness or fanfares. The 25-strong, by-the-glass selection (from £3.75) is a good introduction, with bottles starting at £14.50. A second branch is now open in Marylebone (see entry).

Chef/s: John Murray. **Open:** Mon to Sat L 12 to 2.45 (4 Sat), D 5.45 to 10. **Closed:** Sun. **Meals:** alc (main courses £9 to £17). Set L £13.95 (2 courses) to £16.50. **Service:** 12.5% (optional). **Details:** Cards accepted. 30 seats. 8 seats outside. Separate bar. Music. Children allowed.

Wapping Food

Industrial-chic food arena
Wapping Hydraulic Power Station, Wapping, E1W 3SG
Tel no: (020) 7680 2080
www.thewappingproject.com
⊖ Wapping, map 1
Modern European | £32
Cooking score: 3

£5 OFF

This former power station in an oh-so-cool backwater of east London is a high-ceilinged temple to food and art. It combines a gallery space and restaurant where designer furniture sits comfortably against a backdrop of heavy machinery and bare brickwork. The menu reads like a list of the latest fashionable ingredients, so expect to find seasonal game alongside humble fish like sprats, skate and eel, while kohlrabi makes an appearance in a salad with sorrel and lemon. Bills can mount up (especially if you pile on the side dishes), but for a special occasion it's hard to beat the setting. The Mediterranean-tinged dishes find intriguing matches in an all-Australian wine list, with a decent selection by the glass. House wine is £19.

Chef/s: Dan Richards. **Open:** all week L 12 to 3 (1 to 3.30 Sat, 1 to 4 Sun), Mon to Sat D 6.30 to 11 (7 Sat). **Closed:** 24 Dec to 3 Jan, bank hols. **Meals:** alc (main courses £13 to £22). Set L and D £35.75 to £50. **Service:** 12.5% (optional). **Details:** Cards accepted. 150 seats. 50 seats outside. Separate bar. Wheelchair access. Music. Children allowed. Car parking.

Whitechapel Gallery Dining Room

Polished food with full-on flavours
77-82 Whitechapel High Street, Whitechapel, E1 7QX
Tel no: (020) 7522 7896
www.whitechapelgallery.org/dining-room
⊖ Aldgate East, map 1
Modern European | £25
Cooking score: 3

Murano's Angela Hartnett (see entry) has come on board as consultant here and her influence is immediately apparent in the menu's bold flavours and polished execution. The combinations are familiar, conservative even, yet appropriate in the hip gallery's surprisingly unhip panelled dining room. Like the restaurant, portions are small, although flavours are intense. 'The experience was more like a tasting than dinner', grumbled one reporter. Of the 'small plates' ('a very accurate description'), cauliflower soup with blue cheese beignets was rich to a fault, though a bigger plate of concentrated lamb, olive and lemon ragù with rigatoni was better judged. Pomegranate, pear and blood orange salad with candied olive makes a charming finish. Service is 'relaxed but attentive'. Wines start at £13.95.

Chef/s: Angela Hartnett and Emma Duggan. **Open:** Tue to Sun L 12 to 3 (4 Sun), Wed to Sat D 6 to 9.30. **Closed:** Mon, 25 Dec to 3 Jan. **Meals:** alc (main courses £11 to £17). **Service:** 12.5% (optional). **Details:** Cards accepted. 36 seats. No mobile phones. Wheelchair access. Music. Children allowed.

The Anchor & Hope

Gutsy victuals and good drinking
36 The Cut, South Bank, SE1 8LP
Tel no: (020) 7928 9898
⊖ Waterloo, Southwark, map 5
British | £25
Cooking score: 3

Anyone familiar with London's rollicking new pub scene will recognise the blueprint here: cramped, deliberately battered surroundings, dressed-down service, no bookings (Sundays excepted) and a daily menu stuffed with butcher's offcuts. Spanish-style tripe, duck hearts and deep-fried calf's brains with radishes and sauce gribiche are there for the taking, although first-timers have been heard 'giggling like excited schoolgirls' at the prospect of huge helpings of crab on toast, unctuous squid-ink risotto and duck poached in red wine with split peas, mint and aïoli. If two or three are gathered together, the seven-hour Swaledale lamb shoulder is also a must, and it would be sinful to quit without trying the 'absolutely amazing' flourless chocolate cake. A sharpener of quince and Prosecco fizz hits the spot, and there are quaffable wines aplenty from £13.50.

Chef/s: Jonathan Jones and Warren Fleet. **Open:** Tue to Sat L 12 to 2.30, Sun L at 2 (1 sitting), Mon to Sat D 6 to 10.30. **Closed:** Christmas, New Year, bank hols. **Meals:** alc (main courses £11 to £25). Sun L £30. **Service:** not inc. **Details:** Cards accepted. 45 seats. 20 seats outside. Separate bar. No music. Wheelchair access. Children allowed.

ALSO RECOMMENDED

▲ The Antelope

76 Mitcham Road, Tooting, SW17 9NG
Tel no: (020) 8672 3888
www.theantelopepub.com
⊖ Tooting Broadway, map 3
British

With décor that blends character with modern vogue, opening times pitched just right for the locale and food that is 'tasty', this solid Victorian pub hits all the right notes. The crowd-pleasing, fashionable menus offer plenty of interest at reasonable prices, from simple classics like pea and smoked ham soup (£4.50) and Lancashire hot pot (£24.50 for two) to lively versions of mussels with parsley, garlic, cream, shallots and chilli, or pork belly with morcilla (Spanish black pudding), haricot beans and tomato. Wines from £13.80. Open all week.

▲ L'Auberge

22 Upper Richmond Road, Putney, SW15 2RX
Tel no: (020) 8874 3593
www.ardillys.com
⊖ East Putney, map 3
French

Auberge by name, auberge by nature, Pascal Ardilly's Putney favourite delivers entente cordiale and provincial food in equally generous amounts, whether you're after entrecôte à la moelle or a big bowl of cassoulet. Alternatively, start with baked escargots in herb broth (£6.50) and proceed to pan-fried veal kidneys with sautéed apples (£14.95). Pascal is a trained patissier, so desserts such as dark chocolate moelleux are always worth a punt – you can even buy some to take home. House wine is £15.75. Open Tue to Sat D only.

Babur

Ethnic art meets culinary innovation
119 Brockley Rise, Forest Hill, SE23 1JP
Tel no: (020) 8291 2400
www.babur.info
map 1
Indian | £26
Cooking score: 2

Signs that Babur is different from your average high street Indian restaurant begin with the Bengal tiger perched on the roof of this slick, glass-fronted building, and continue inside with the bare brickwork and modish wood panelling. There's a contemporary slant to the menu, too, with a strong emphasis on seasonal game as well as fish dishes from southern India. East meets west in, say, gilthead bream with mustard and curry leaf mash or pot-

roasted rabbit with mustard and ginger, and there's plenty to delight vegetarians, such as a Punjabi paneer sandwich or a timbale of roasted aubergine masala. House wine is £16.75.
Chef/s: Praveen Kumar Gupta. **Open:** all week L 12 to 2.30 (4 Sun), D 6 to 11.30. **Closed:** 26 Dec. **Meals:** alc (main courses £11 to £16). Sun L buffet £11.95. **Service:** not inc. **Details:** Cards accepted. 72 seats. No mobile phones. Music. Children allowed. Car parking.

Baltic

Chilled out Eastern European
74 Blackfriars Road, Southwark, SE1 8HA
Tel no: (020) 7928 1111
www.balticrestaurant.co.uk
⊖ Southwark, map 5
Eastern European | £26
Cooking score: 2

There is a sense of expectation when you walk into this cavernous white room with its vaulted ceiling and modern art. Baltic draws an easy-going crowd, so chill out and soak up the vibes. A starter of moreish Siberian pelmeni (veal and pork dumplings with fresh chives), then hake, salmon and clams in a light broth with al dente vegetables, tomato and olives both hit the right spot. But filling and stodgy racuchy (apple fritters with crème fraîche) are more reminiscent of Eastern Europe back in the day. The good mood of the staff is a plus, however. Wines start at £16.50, and there are 70 different vodkas if you want to party.
Chef/s: Piotr Repinski. **Open:** all week L 12 to 3 (4.30 Sun), D 5.30 to 11.15 (10.30 Sun). **Closed:** 24 to 28 Dec. **Meals:** alc (main courses £13 to £19). Set L and D £14.50 (2 courses) to £17.50. Sun L £17.50 (2 courses) to £20.50. **Service:** 12.5% (optional). **Details:** Cards accepted. 120 seats. Separate bar. Wheelchair access. Music. Children allowed.

Brinkley's Kitchen

Affordable crowd-pleaser
35 Bellevue Road, Wandsworth, SW17 7EF
Tel no: (020) 8672 5888
www.brinkleys.com
⊖ Balham, map 3
Modern European | £28
Cooking score: 1

John Brinkley's cheery neighbourhood brasserie, with a patio for summer dining, keeps up appearances with a textbook, across-the-globe menu – it certainly appeals to Wandsworth residents. Take your pick from steamed chicken dim sum, seared teriyaki beef fillet or grilled lamb burger tweaked with tzatziki; otherwise choose to have either prawns or chicken in your Thai green curry. Desserts keep it closer to home with a hot toffee cake. The well-priced wine list opens at £12.50.
Chef/s: Paolo Zanca. **Open:** all week L 12 to 4 (11 to 4 Sat and Sun), Mon to Sat D 6 to 11. **Closed:** 24 to 28 Dec. **Meals:** alc (main courses £11 to £23). Set L £12 (2 courses) to £15. Sun L £14. **Service:** 12.5% (optional). **Details:** Cards accepted. 60 seats. 20 seats outside. Separate bar. Music. Children allowed.

NEW ENTRY
Cantinetta

Local Italian with inventive touches
162-164 Lower Richmond Road, Putney, SW15 1LY
Tel no: (020) 8780 3131
www.cantinetta.co.uk
⊖ Putney Bridge, map 1
Italian | £28
Cooking score: 3

With the Phoenix's fire growing dim, restaurateur Rebecca Mascarenhas has changed tack with the more Italian-focused Cantinetta (with a chef from the Giorgio Locatelli stable). At first glance the cooking explores familiar territory, but there are inventive touches worthy of a detour. For example, crispy deep-fried bone marrow and

Italian sausage are used to add a new dimension to a saffron risotto, and sea bream is paired with escarole and rounded off with a silky lemon sauce. Equally appealing, pear poached in red wine arrives with shavings of Diamante citron and a scoop of milk sorbet. Service is energetic. Wines, steeped in Italy, start from £14.50.

Chef/s: Federico Turri. **Open:** Tue to Sun L 12 to 2.30 (3 Sat and Sun), Mon to Sat D 6 to 10.30 (11 Fri and Sat). **Closed:** bank hols. **Meals:** alc (main courses £10 to £18). Set L and D £12.50 (2 courses) to £15.50. Sun L £18.50 (2 courses) to £21.50. **Service:** 12.5% (optional). **Details:** Cards accepted. 70 seats. 50 seats outside. Separate bar. Wheelchair access. Music. Children allowed.

Chapters All Day Dining

User-friendly brasserie
43-45 Montpelier Vale, Blackheath, SE3 0TJ
Tel no: (020) 8333 2666
www.chaptersrestaurants.com
map 1
Modern British | £30
Cooking score: 3

Make no mistake – Chapters does exactly what it says on the tin. Against an unfussy, modernist backdrop of clean lines, natural light and bare brickwork, it's in the business of delivering user-friendly food and drink right through the day. Helpful staff keep the mood upbeat, and the kitchen makes its mark with a raft of British and Euro-inspired dishes, particularly when it comes to steaks, burgers and lamb chops from the Josper charcoal oven. But there's something to suit most preferences, from Welsh cured meats or warm salt cod brandade to grilled haunch of Sika venison with braised red cabbage and damson sauce, or butternut squash and quinoa risotto. For afters, perhaps try an unusual pairing of coffee pannacotta with pear and walnut salad. Drinks cover all bases too, with house wines from £15.80.

Chef/s: Trevor Tobin. **Open:** all week 8am to 11pm (9am to 10pm Sun). **Closed:** 2 to 4 Jan. **Meals:** alc (main courses £10 to £28). **Service:** 12.5% (optional). **Details:** Cards accepted. 100 seats. 16 seats outside. Separate bar. Wheelchair access. Music. Children allowed.

ALSO RECOMMENDED

▲ Le Chardon

65 Lordship Lane, East Dulwich, SE22 8EP
Tel no: (020) 8299 1921
www.lechardon.co.uk
map 1
French £5 OFF

Housed in the shell of a Victorian grocer's, this Dulwich evergreen shows off its past with elaborate tiling and beautiful signage – although the food is unashamedly French in tone. Come here for moules marinière (£7.50), coq au vin or salmon with saffron and mussel sauce (£12.95); otherwise, gorge on fruits de mer before finishing sweetly with chocolate mousse. Locals also drop by for breakfast and Sunday lunch. International wines from £15.95. Open all week. There's a branch at 32 Abbeville Road, Clapham SW4 9NG; tel (020) 8673 9300.

Chez Bruce

Big-hitting neighbourhood star
2 Bellevue Road, Wandsworth, SW17 7EG
Tel no: (020) 8672 0114
www.chezbruce.co.uk
⊖ Balham, map 3
Modern British | £45
Cooking score: 6

The design tone of Bruce Poole's long-running Wandsworth venue has always been a masterpiece of understatement, but the new, larger dining room 'feels more comfortable, with tables less crammed than in the past'. On the dinner carte, the house style of assimilative European cooking is where the kitchen fully takes wing, mixing French, Spanish and Italian influences. A salad of carta di musica bread with ricotta, pata negra ham, Charentais melon and rosemary is like a fortissimo chord played by full orchestra, while a main course that delighted another reader offered Shetland salmon with Jerusalem artichoke purée, crisp greens, rich gnocchi, almonds and Parmesan foam – a triumph. The chicken ballottine with sweetcorn pancakes, trompettes and foie gras is another stunner, while dessert might be a passion-fruit meringue pie. It's all accompanied by an exemplary wine collection, in which every country is explored in due depth, even Germany. There are no notes, but there is an excellent sommelier. Prices open at £18.

Chef/s: Matt Christmas. **Open:** all week L 12 to 2.30 (3 Sat and Sun), D 6.30 to 10 (10.30 Fri and Sat, 7 to 9.30 Sun). **Closed:** 24 to 26 Dec. **Meals:** Set L Mon to Fri £21.50 (2 courses) to £27.50. Set L Sat and Sun £29.50 (2 courses) to £35. Set D £34.50 (2 courses) to £45. **Service:** 12.5% (optional). **Details:** Cards accepted. 100 seats. No music. No mobile phones. Wheelchair access. Children allowed.

Emile's

Long-serving Putney favourite
96-98 Felsham Road, Putney, SW15 1DQ
Tel no: (020) 8789 3323
www.emilesrestaurant.co.uk
⊖ Putney Bridge, map 3
Anglo-French | £29
Cooking score: 1

Former chef Sam Stafford has rejoined Andrew Sherlock in the kitchen, but little else has changed at this long-serving Putney favourite close to the river. Twenty-one years on, Emile's is still peddling a monthly menu of creditable Anglo-French dishes from wild mushroom and Stilton soufflé to ever-popular beef Wellington and grilled sea bass with roast snails, chervil mash and confit garlic. A new rare-breed supplier should enhance the meaty choice, while desserts are in the treacle tart/chocolate pot mould. House vin de pays is £13.90.

Chef/s: Andrew Sherlock and Sam Stafford. **Open:** Mon to Sat D only 7.30 to 11. **Closed:** Sun, 24 to 30 Dec, 2 Jan, Easter Sat, bank hols. **Meals:** Set D £25 (2 courses) to £28.50. **Service:** 10% (optional). **Details:** Cards accepted. 100 seats. No mobile phones. Music. Children allowed.

Enoteca Turi

Redoubtable Italian showpiece
28 Putney High Street, Putney, SW15 1SQ
Tel no: (020) 8785 4449
www.enotecaturi.com
⊖ Putney Bridge, map 3
Italian | £36
Cooking score: 3

Tuscan-toned red walls punctuated with period Italian photos help to summon up a genuine native mood in Giuseppe Turi's redoubtable Putney showpiece, and you can get a taste of things to come from the organic Delfico olive oil and bread that kick-start proceedings here. Directly imported provisions are touchstones for the kitchen's endeavours and Turi is well versed in his homeland's regional foodie heritage as well as its cultural roots. Strong seasonal flavours shine through, whether it's a Piedmontese salad of marinated rabbit with asparagus, chicory and zolfini beans or a 'secondo' of roast John Dory fillet with artichoke and tarragon risotto. Pasta is also a good shout – perhaps pappardelle with duck ragù or orecchiette with rapini (turnip broccoli), anchovy, chilli and toasted breadcrumbs. True to its name, Enoteca gives an outstanding account of the regional Italian wine scene across the board, and everything on the awe-inspiring, 300-bin list is thoughtfully annotated with fascinating tasting notes. Prices start at £17 (£6 a glass).

Chef/s: Massimo Tagliaferri. **Open:** Mon to Sat L 12 to 2.30, D 7 to 10.30 (11 Fri and Sat). **Closed:** Sun, 26 to 28 Dec, first week Jan. **Meals:** alc (main courses £13 to £24). Set L £16.50 (2 courses) to £19.50. Set D £26.50 (2 courses) to £30.50. **Service:** 12.5% (optional). **Details:** Cards accepted. 103 seats. No mobile phones. Wheelchair access. Music. Children allowed.

ALSO RECOMMENDED

▲ Entrée

2 Battersea Rise, Battersea, SW11 1ED
Tel no: (020) 7223 5147
www.entreebattersea.co.uk
⊖ Clapham Junction, map 3
Modern European

Well-heeled and sleek, Entrée mixes the noisy attributes of a lively ground-floor piano bar with some homely touches in the upstairs brasserie. Start with duck ballottine served with duck jelly and purple seed mustard, followed by a credible roast bream with crushed potatoes, green olives and watercress purée (£16.50). Save room for the sticky fig and ginger pudding with brandy caramel (£5). Wines start at £16.75. Open all week.

READERS RECOMMEND

four o nine

Modern European
409 Clapham Road, Clapham, SW9 9BT
Tel no: (020) 7737 0722
www.fouronine.co.uk
'The best octopus I've ever had in my life! I've gone time and time again and I've never been disappointed.'

NEW ENTRY

The Fox & Grapes

Bosi's born-again hostelry
9 Camp Road, Wimbledon, SW19 4UN
Tel no: (020) 8619 1300
www.foxandgrapeswimbledon.co.uk
⊖ Wimbledon, map 1
British | £30
Cooking score: 3

Lauded as the culinary baron of Mayfair (see Hibiscus), Claude Bosi also has a sneaking affection for the British pub, and his latest venture into this boozy world is a born-again hostelry in leafy SW19. The Fox & Grapes makes its point admirably and the menu doesn't overstay its welcome – moving easily from zingy crab on toast to crowd-pleasing steaks and burgers. Meanwhile, melting confit shoulder of lamb with fresh garlic and goats' cheese or pitch-perfect pollack with luxurious embellishments including a soft-cooked egg and mushroom vinaigrette won't disappoint those after a more adventurous hit. Puds pay homage to the WI and Mrs Beeton: excellent junket, trifle and crumbles all feature prominently. And, judging by the real ales and gluggable wines (from £18), this place is still proud to be a pub.

Chef/s: Patrick Leano. **Open:** all week L 12 to 3 (4 Sun), D 6 to 9.30. **Meals:** alc (main courses £13 to £27). **Service:** 12.5% (optional). **Details:** Cards accepted. 80 seats. No music. Wheelchair access. Children allowed.

ALSO RECOMMENDED

▲ Franco Manca

4 Market Row, Brixton, SW9 8LD
Tel no: (020) 7738 3021
www.francomanca.co.uk
⊖ Brixton, map 1
Italian

The wood-burning 'Tufae' oven was constructed on site by builders from Naples; it cooks pizzas in 40 seconds – although the chewy sourdough bases are rested for over 20 hours before baking. Toppings are limited to just six choices, but carefully sourced – organic tomatoes, perhaps teamed with mozzarella and organic chorizo or home-cured Gloucester Old Spot ham – and prices put high street chains to shame (£4.50 to £6.95). It's no wonder people queue round the block. Wines from £11.95. Open all week L and Thur to Sat D. Also at 144 Chiswick High Road, W4 1PU; tel (020) 8747 4822.

Readers Recommend

A 'readers recommend' review is a genuine quote from a report sent in by one of our readers. We intend to follow up these suggestions throughout the year to come.

Franklins

Trencherman helpings of true Brit food
157 Lordship Lane, East Dulwich, SE22 8HX
Tel no: (020) 8299 9598
www.franklinsrestaurant.com
map 1
British | £28
Cooking score: 2

With its stripped-back interior, paper cloths and utilitarian furnishings, Franklins is a happy-go-lucky amalgam of boisterous neighbourhood wine bar and ever-so-casual dining room. The owners clearly know a thing or two about local hospitality and keep the throngs amply fed with trencherman helpings of patriotic seasonal food. Forget foams and drizzles, this is the unvarnished world of chitterlings with curly kale and garlic, rabbit with cider and turnips, ox heart, and roast mallard with swede and bacon – all framed by plates of Colchester native oysters, lemon posset and savouries such as black pudding on toast. Drink London tap water or one of the easy-going wines (from £14.50). Don't miss the farm shop across the road.
Chef/s: Ralf Wittig. **Open:** all week 12 to 10.30 (12 to 10 Sun). **Closed:** 25 and 26 Dec, 1 Jan. **Meals:** alc (main courses £14 to £21). Set L £13.95 (2 courses) to £16.95. Set D £32.50. Sun L £ £14.50. **Service:** not inc. **Details:** Cards accepted. 95 seats. 12 seats outside. Separate bar. Wheelchair access. Music. Children allowed.

Harrison's

Buzzing local brasserie
15-19 Bedford Hill, Balham, SW12 9EX
Tel no: (020) 8675 6900
www.harrisonsbalham.co.uk
⊖ Balham, map 3
Modern British | £24
Cooking score: 1

Born out of Sam's Brasserie in Chiswick (see entry), Sam Harrison's Balham sibling outstrips most of its local neighbours, judging by the swarms buzzing around its pulsating bar and the equally popular, family-friendly dining room. Set deals, weekend brunch and Sunday jazz are crowd-pullers, and the regular menu also scores with brasserie staples such as moules marinière, shredded duck salad with toasted cashews, roast cod on Puy lentils and ribeye with fries. For afters, try Yorkshire rhubarb and apple crumble. Cocktails fuel the twentysomethings, while affordably priced global wines offer sound drinking from £15.
Chef/s: Nick Stones. **Open:** all week L 12 to 3 (4 Sat and Sun), D 6 to 10.30 (6.30 to 10.30 Sat, 6.30 to 10 Sun). **Closed:** 25 and 26 Dec. **Meals:** alc (main courses £11 to £20). Set L £13 (2 courses) to £16. Set D £15 (2 courses) to £18. Sun L £21. **Service:** 12.5% (optional). **Details:** Cards accepted. 90 seats. 12 seats outside. Separate bar. Wheelchair access. Music. Children allowed.

Inside

Stylish bistro with gutsy food
19 Greenwich South Street, Greenwich, SE10 8NW
Tel no: (020) 8265 5060
www.insiderestaurant.co.uk
map 1
Modern European | £27
Cooking score: 1

Minimalist restraint defines the interior of this smart neighbourhood bistro, but not the cooking, which majors in gutsy modern European dishes such as roasted butternut squash and sage risotto followed by baked brioche filled with chicken, mushroom, pancetta and leek with chive mash, garlic spinach and tarragon sauce. Desserts range from cosy apple and rhubarb crumble with vanilla custard through to warm ginger and pear pudding with mascarpone ice cream and toffee sauce. 'Prompt and cheerful' service also gets the thumbs-up. 'Decent quality and very reasonably priced' house wine starts at £16.30.
Chef/s: Guy Awford and Brian Sargeant. **Open:** Tue to Sun L 12 to 2.30 (3 Sat and Sun), Tue to Sat D 6.30 to 11. **Closed:** Mon, 24 to 26 Dec. **Meals:** alc (main courses £13 to £18). Set L £12.95 (2 courses) to £17.95. Set D and Sun L £17.95 (2 courses) to

£22.95. **Service:** not inc. **Details:** Cards accepted. 38 seats. No mobile phones. Wheelchair access. Music. Children allowed.

Lamberts

Good-natured gem of a restaurant
2 Station Parade, Balham, SW12 9AZ
Tel no: (020) 8675 2233
www.lambertsrestaurant.com
⊖ Balham, map 3
Modern British | £30
Cooking score: 2

£5 OFF

'Nice ambience, well laid-out, tables not too crowded, kindly lighting,' was how one visitor summed up Joe Lambert's good-natured gem of a restaurant. The unfussy mood is matched by competitive prices and sharp seasonal food – say soused mackerel set on four mini-potato pancakes with cucumber and spring onions, followed by roasted fallow deer or, perhaps, braised pig's cheek with crispy duck egg and apple, ahead of saddle of wild rabbit with roasted Jerusalem artichokes and green lentils. The uncluttered approach extends to desserts such as Seville orange pudding with poppy-seed custard. The nifty global wine list opens painlessly at £16.
Chef/s: Ryan Lowery. **Open:** Sat and Sun L 12 to 3 (5 Sun), Tue to Sat D 7 to 10.30. **Closed:** Mon. **Meals:** alc (main courses £15 to £18). Set L and D £17 (2 courses) to £20. Sun L £24. **Service:** 12.5% (optional). **Details:** Cards accepted. 59 seats. Music. Children allowed.

Light House

An alluring Wimbledon beacon
75-77 Ridgway, Wimbledon, SW19 4ST
Tel no: (020) 8944 6338
www.lighthousewimbledon.com
⊖ Wimbledon, map 3
Modern European | £30
Cooking score: 3

Hard-edged vibes and clamourous babbling may come with the territory in this capacious, light-filled restaurant, but there's no doubt it has been delighting the good folk of Wimbledon village for nigh on 13 years, and has lost none of its allure. The menu offers simple, clean-cut brasserie-style assemblies, blending no-nonsense home-grown classics like red-wine braised oxtail with champ and horseradish crème fraîche, or roast Middle White pork with baked swede, ruby chard and Bramley apple sauce with sunnier Med-influenced options such as salt cod fishcake with grilled chorizo and piquillo pepper relish or chicken breast stuffed with goats' cheese and tomato pesto. Desserts hit the pannacotta/vanilla cheesecake comfort zone, while some 18 wines come by the glass. Bottles from £15.50.
Chef/s: Chris Casey. **Open:** all week L 12 to 2.30 (3 Sun), Mon to Sat D 6 to 10.30. **Closed:** 25 to 28 Dec. **Meals:** alc (main courses £13 to £24). Set L £11.50 (2 courses) to £14.50. Early set D £14.50 (2 courses) to £18.50. Sun L £18.50 (2 courses). **Service:** 12.5% (optional). **Details:** Cards accepted. 80 seats. 15 seats outside. Wheelchair access. Music. Children allowed.

ALSO RECOMMENDED

▲ Lobster Pot

3 Kennington Lane, Elephant and Castle, SE11 4RG
Tel no: (020) 7582 5556
www.lobsterpotrestaurant.co.uk
⊖ Kennington, map 1
Seafood

For 21 years Hervé Regent has offered quality fish in a tiny room resembling a trawler cabin – you can delve into the large piscine repertoire by ordering a plateau de fruits de mer. The menu is predominantly old-fashioned French – whole grilled Dover sole with lemon butter sauce (£28.50), for instance – but expect to find sea bass with lemon grass, garlic, ginger, chilli and coriander sauce and pancakes stuffed with crème brûlée (£7), as well as a few token meat dishes. French wines from £17.50. Closed Sun and Mon. Brasserie Toulouse Lautrec, 140 Newington Butts, London SE11 4RN; tel (020) 7582 6800 is run by Hervé's sons.

Magdalen

Earthy flavours and astute cooking
152 Tooley Street, Southwark, SE1 2TU
Tel no: (020) 7403 1342
www.magdalenrestaurant.co.uk
⊖ London Bridge, map 1
Modern British | £30
Cooking score: 3
£5 OFF

Close to London Bridge, this buzzy, clutter-free restaurant is amply supplied with trendy native ingredients. The cooking is simple and precise, allowing earthy fare such as fried lamb's tongue (with dandelion and poached egg) or braised Hereford beef (served with parsnip, baby onions and bacon) to do the talking. There's a modern-classic feel to the interior and the food, but it doesn't get overly predictable; mussels, for instance, come with white wine, onions and sea lettuce. Elsewhere, confit rabbit is teamed with violet artichokes, fennel and olives, while slow-roast chicken comes with chard gratin, sage and roasting juices. Nostalgic puddings run from French toast with rhubarb and vanilla ice cream to prune and almond tart with crème fraîche. The international wine list starts at £20.
Chef/s: James Faulks and David Abbott. **Open:** Mon to Fri L 12 to 2.30, Mon to Sat D 6.30 to 10. **Closed:** Sun, 24 Dec to 3 Jan, 2 weeks Aug. **Meals:** alc (main courses £14 to £21). Set L £15.50 (2 courses) to £18.50. **Service:** 12.5% (optional). **Details:** Cards accepted. 90 seats. 4 seats outside. Separate bar. Wheelchair access. Music. Children allowed.

ALSO RECOMMENDED

▲ Platform

56-58 Tooley Street, Southwark, SE1 2SZ
Tel no: (020) 7403 6388
www.platformse1.co.uk
⊖ London Bridge, map 1
Modern British

Underneath the arches, with platform one of London Bridge Station right above, the two-tiered Platform boasts exposed brickwork, recycled furniture and an 'original, homey' atmosphere. It also offers bold-as-brass food with an eye for seasonality. Expect light bites and snacks such as potted cockles with pickled cucumber or fried pig's head with tartare sauce, as well as heartier portions of duck egg on toast with chorizo and English peas (£6.50) and smoked wood pigeon salad with pancetta, Jersey Royals and hazelnut oil (£13.50). House wine £18. Closed Sun.

Le Pont de la Tour

French favourite by the river
36d Shad Thames, Bermondsey, SE1 2YE
Tel no: (020) 7403 8403
www.lepontdelatour.com
⊖ Tower Hill, London Bridge, map 1
Modern French | £45
Cooking score: 3
£5 OFF

Spectacular location, awesome view of Tower Bridge, open-air dining in fine weather and a suave interior – this crowd-pleasing venue has a lot to offer. The broadly based French cooking comes with plenty of flexible options: oysters, caviar and crustacea are fixtures, but the kitchen also produces haunch of venison with game pithiviers and daube of beef. For something simpler, head to the grill for cod and salmon fishcakes or ribeye steak with sauce bordelaise. Poor service and misunderstandings have put some visitors off, especially as prices are stuck to the ceiling, but others contend that the food frequently rises some way to meet them. And for those on a City salary, the very fine wine list offers everything you could wish for, focusing on France but picking blue-chip names everywhere, and culminating in a long section of dessert wines. With precious little in the £25 to £30 bracket, those with smaller budgets should explore the good by-the-glass selection.
Chef/s: Lee Bennett. **Open:** all week L 12 to 3 (5 Sat, 4 Sun), D 6 to 11. **Meals:** Set L £26.50 (2 courses) to £31.50. Set D £44.50. Sun L £28.50. **Service:** not inc. **Details:** Cards accepted. 110 seats. 70 seats outside. Separate bar. Wheelchair access. Music. Children allowed.

Ransome's Dock

A world of culinary possibilities
35-37 Parkgate Road, Battersea, SW11 4NP
Tel no: (020) 7223 1611
www.ransomesdock.co.uk
map 3
Modern British | £34
Cooking score: 3

£5 OFF

On a south London riverside site near the Albert Bridge, a former ice factory has been home to the Lams' consistently appealing neighbourhood restaurant for nearly 20 years now. There is a world of culinary possibilities to choose from, in every sense, from the tapas dishes that have proved popular (Serrano ham, spinach and ricotta gnocchi, cheese and leek filo parcels) to the daily changing main menus, which describe a broad arc from crab cakes with mango salsa to navarin of lamb with Pink Fir Apple potatoes. Raw materials are conscientiously sourced, and this ensures that a sense of quality imbues every dish, all the way through to memorable desserts such as prune and Armagnac soufflé. Not the least glory of the place has always been the fantastic wine list, the work of a true devotee, which assiduously introduces drinkers to the likes of Roussette de Savoie, Thracian Pinot Noir and vintage-dated Madeira at prices that encourage experimentation. Bottles open at £15.50.

Chef/s: Martin and Vanessa Lam. **Open:** all week L 12 to 5 (3.30 Sun), Mon to Sat D 6 to 11. **Closed:** 24 to 27 Dec, Aug bank hol. **Meals:** alc (main courses £13 to £24). Set L £15.50 (2 courses). Sun L £22.50. **Service:** 12.5% (optional). **Details:** Cards accepted. 56 seats. 24 seats outside. Separate bar. Wheelchair access. Music. Children allowed.

Visit us Online

To find out more about *The Good Food Guide*, please visit www.thegoodfoodguide.co.uk

Rick's Café

Friendly Tooting treat
122 Mitcham Road, Tooting, SW17 9NH
Tel no: (020) 8767 5219
www.ricks-cafe.co.uk
⊖ Tooting Broadway, map 3
Modern European | £25
Cooking score: 1

Fans love the vibrant atmosphere and the welcoming staff at this veteran of the Tooting dining scene. It keeps up appearances with a free-wheeling menu full of global influences, so take your pick from crispy fried pigs' tails with sauce gribiche, then mains of Thai green chicken curry or wok-fried tiger prawns with chorizo, chickpeas and spinach, and for true Brits – steak and mushroom pie. Finish with chocolate brownie. House wine is £12.50.

Chef/s: Ricardo Gibbs. **Open:** Tue to Fri L 12 to 3, Mon to Fri D 6 to 10.30 (9 Mon). Sat and Sun 10am to 11pm. **Meals:** alc (main courses £8 to £16). Sun L £10. **Service:** 12.5% (optional). **Details:** Cards accepted. 40 seats. Wheelchair access. Music. Children allowed.

Roast

Promoting great British produce
Floral Hall, Stoney Street, Southwark, SE1 1TL
Tel no: (0845) 034 7300
www.roast-restaurant.com
⊖ London Bridge, map 1
British | £38
Cooking score: 2

A perfectly contemporary London eating place perched above the stalls of Borough Market – the UK's oldest market – and noted for its promotion of great British produce. So hang loose with menus that deal in the likes of pilchard fillets with Gentleman's Relish on toast or Lorne sausage Scotch egg with piccalilli. Then gather pace with braised feather blade of beef with caramelised onion and thyme dumpling or whole grilled bream with fennel, coriander and orange butter sauce. It's a place of fluctuating moods, veering from the frenzied hubbub of breakfast to more genteel intimacy at night. The wine list covers the whole spectrum of style, and prices start at £22.

Chef/s: Lawrence Keogh. **Open:** all week L 12 to 3 (12 to 5 Sat, 11.30 to 4 Sun), Mon to Sat D 6 to 11. **Closed:** 25 Dec. **Meals:** alc (main courses £12 to £30). Set L and D £22 (2 courses) to £25. Sun L £30. **Service:** 12.5%. **Details:** Cards accepted. 120 seats. Separate bar. Wheelchair access.

RSJ

Well-supported South Bank veteran
33 Coin Street, Southwark, SE1 9NR
Tel no: (020) 7928 4554
www.rsj.uk.com
⊖ Waterloo, Southwark, map 5
Modern British | £30
Cooking score: 3

£5 OFF **V**

A veteran of 31 editions of this Guide, RSJ continues to draw praise for 'good service' and reliable, good-value food. The nineteenth-century former stables was reinforced with rolled steel joists (RSJs) during the restaurant's construction – hence its name. A good-value fixed-price menu and snappy timing make it popular with theatre-goers, while a more leisurely meal from the carte could include spicy chorizo, red onion and potato salad followed by saddle of lamb with minted Jersey Royals and lamb jus. The British and European flavours continue at dessert, with plum and apple crumble with Calvados crème fraîche. 'The great joy in coming here is the list of Loire wines' adds one reader. There are some 250 treasures from the region, plus choice pickings from elsewhere. Prices start at £16.95.

Chef/s: Ian Stabler. **Open:** Mon to Fri L 12 to 2.30, Mon to Sat D 5.30 to 11. **Closed:** Sun, 24 to 26 Dec, Good Fri. **Meals:** alc (main courses £15 to £20). Set L and D £16.95 (2 courses) to £18.95. **Service:** 12.5% (optional). **Details:** Cards accepted. 90 seats. 12 seats outside. No music. Children allowed.

Skylon

Southbank spectacular
Southbank Centre, Belvedere Road, South Bank, SE1 8XX
Tel no: (020) 7654 7800
www.skylon-restaurant.co.uk
⊖ Waterloo, map 5
Modern European | £45
Cooking score: 2

V

Spread over Level 3 of the Royal Festival Hall, the sheer scale of Skylon is something to behold. This modish design homage to the 1950s throws in views of the Thames, with a full-dress, white-clothed restaurant as the culinary focus. Here diners can sample trendy Anglo-European dishes ranging from caramelised sweetbreads with broad beans, Granny Smith apple and Sauternes beurre blanc to steamed sea bass with fennel risotto, pickled mushrooms and carrot emulsion, with 'sweet sushi' to follow. The adjoining all-day grill deals in brasserie-style food (think roast cod with chickpea and chorizo ragoût), and there's also an absolutely fabulous bar for cocktails. Wines start at £21 (£5.50 a glass).

Chef/s: Helena Puolakka. **Open:** Restaurant: all week L 12 to 5, D 5.30 to 10.30. Grill: all week 12 to 11 (10.30pm Sun). **Closed:** 25 Dec. **Meals:** alc (main courses £12 to £24). Restaurant: set L £24.50 (2 courses) to £28.50; post-theatre D £26.75 (2 courses) to £30.75; set D £40 (2 courses) to £45; Sun L £24.50 (2 courses) to £28.50. Grill: set L £16 (2 courses) to £19; set D £19.50 (2 courses) to. **Service:** 12.5% (optional). **Details:** Cards accepted. 145 seats. Separate bar. No music. Wheelchair access. Children allowed.

Swan at the Globe

English classics with a contemporary edge
21 New Globe Walk, Bankside, SE1 9DT
Tel no: (020) 7928 9444
www.swanattheglobe.co.uk
⊖ Blackfriars, London Bridge, map 5
Modern British | £30
Cooking score: 4

Stunning views of St Paul's Cathedral across the river are a huge bonus at this high-decibel Bankside bar and brasserie attached to the Globe Theatre. The cooking is fashionably simple and mostly seasonal, and stands out from the legion of similar establishments nearby through the sheer quality of its ingredients and the high levels of skill in the kitchen. 'It's not cheap, but it is arguably fair value', reported one diner. Typical of the style are a starter of Brixham crab salad and red peppers dressing, and mains of lamb rump with Provençal vegetables and black olives or roast Atlantic cod with Shetland mussels and fennel broth. A slate of English cheeses and sweet things such as nougat parfait with Baileys sauce conclude things satisfyingly. Afternoon and high tea are worth noting, too. The enterprising wine list opens at £17.
Chef/s: Kieren Steinborn. **Open:** all week 12 to 10.15 (11 to 4.45 Sun). **Closed:** 25 Dec. **Meals:** alc (main courses £14 to £20). Sun L £19.50 (2 courses) to £22.50. **Service:** 12.5% (optional). **Details:** Cards accepted. 80 seats. Separate bar. Wheelchair access. Music. Children allowed.

Tapas Brindisa

Affordable, top-quality tapas
18-20 Southwark Street, Southwark, SE1 1TJ
Tel no: (020) 7357 8880
www.tapasbrindisa.com
⊖ London Bridge, map 1
Tapas | £20
Cooking score: 3

Just steps away from Borough Market, the Brindisa flagship trades on its stark functionality – concrete floors and tight-packed tables – and simple, affordable tapas with everything hanging on the sheer quality of the ingredients. There's nothing flashy about the presentation and no gimmicks either – just Ibérico de Bellota ham or air-cured tuna loin or a plate of padrón peppers. Deep-fried Monte Enebro cheese with orange blossom honey has become something of a signature dish. If you want something with a bit more pluck, try black rice with squid and allioli or smoked cured beef with goats' cheese. There's good drinking to be had on the all-Spanish list, with bottles from £19. Casa Brindisa and Tierra Brindisa are from the same stable (see entries).
Chef/s: Roberto Castro. **Open:** Mon to Sat L 12 to 3 (4 Fri and Sat), D 5.30 to 11. Sun 12 to 10. **Closed:** 25 and 26 Dec, 1 Jan. **Meals:** alc (tapas £5 to £22). **Service:** 12.5% (optional). **Details:** Cards accepted. 32 seats. 30 seats outside. Separate bar. Wheelchair access. Music. Children allowed.

Tentazioni

A tempting prospect
Lloyds Wharf, 2 Mill Street, Bermondsey, SE1 2BD
Tel no: (020) 7237 1100
www.tentazioni.co.uk
⊖ Bermondsey, London Bridge, map 1
Italian | £32
Cooking score: 3
£5 OFF **V**

Rich red walls, starry lighting, linen-swathed tables and the occasional addition of an opera singer make a suitably dramatic backdrop for Riccardo Giacomini's modern Italian cooking. The restaurant's name translates as 'temptation' and the monthly changing menu entices with speciality ingredients such as Castelluccio lentils with zampone di Modena (stuffed pig's trotter). A 'perfectly fried' fillet of lemon sole with wild mushrooms, truffle and a mustard sauce delighted one diner, as did the preceding 'light and summery' ravioli stuffed with artichoke purée and served with softened cherry tomatoes and mint. A separate pasta menu includes Tentazioni's signature dish of tagliatelle with butter and truffles. Finish with

classic tiramisu or a selection of Italian cheeses. An impressive selection of mostly Italian wines opens at £13.50.
Chef/s: Riccardo Giacomini. **Open:** Mon to Fri L 12 to 3, Mon to Sat D 6.30 to 10.45. **Closed:** Sun, 24 to 27 Dec, 1 and 2 Jan, bank hols. **Meals:** alc (main courses £15 to £21). Set L £15 (2 courses) to £18.50. Tasting menu £47.50 (7 courses). **Service:** 12.5% (optional). **Details:** Cards accepted. 50 seats. Wheelchair access. Music. Children allowed.

Tom Ilic

Big on gutsy meat cooking
123 Queenstown Road, Battersea, SW8 3RH
Tel no: (020) 7622 0555
www.tomilic.com
map 3
European | £34
Cooking score: 2

A much-needed revamp has done Tom Ilic's neighbourhood eatery a power of good, and his gutsy cooking now feels much more assured in its new setting. Broad-shouldered meat cookery is his forte, especially when it comes to all things porcine (try the 'dégustation' with pickled white cabbage and caramelised apple), but he can also deliver excellent braised oxtail raviolo with roasted sweetbreads or fillet of aged Kettyle beef with garlic beans and horseradish soufflé. If you would rather eat fish or vegetables, the kitchen can oblige with baked fillet of sea bass with squid and mussel broth or a fine lasagne of wild mushrooms, leeks and chestnuts. The wine list (from £19.50) covers all bases while keeping a lid on price.
Chef/s: Tom Ilic. **Open:** Wed to Sun L 12 to 2.30 (3.30 Sun), Tue to Sat D 6 to 10.30. **Closed:** Mon, 26 to 30 Dec, 1 week Aug, bank hols. **Meals:** alc (main courses £14 to £20). Set L £16.95 (2 courses) to £19.50. Set D £16.95 (2 courses) to £21.50. Sun L £21.50 (2 courses) to £25.50. **Service:** 12.5% (optional). **Details:** Cards accepted. 60 seats. Separate bar. Music. Children allowed.

Trinity

Neighbourhood high-achiever
4 The Polygon, Clapham, SW4 0JG
Tel no: (020) 7622 1199
www.trinityrestaurant.co.uk
⊖ Clapham Common, map 3
Modern European | £38
Cooking score: 5

Currently king of the hill in Clapham, this chic neighbourhood restaurant goes about its high-achieving business in the heart of the Old Town. Chef/proprietor Adam Byatt has flirted with test tubes and foams over the years, but his cooking now has a more orthodox bent, with the emphasis on exquisite presentation and imaginatively worked ingredients. Pig's trotter on sourdough with quails' eggs and crackling delivers a richly sweet collation tempered with intense sauce gribiche, although traditionalists may prefer the restrained thrills of a delicate-as-you-like vichyssoise served with fresh curd and just-cooked asparagus. Other winning dishes are 'warm' roast salmon complemented by a courgette flower stuffed with scallop mousse, bream with seaweed and burnt cucumber, and a fun-packed take on 'bagna cauda' involving slivers of lamb rump accompanied by a cannelloni of slow-cooked lamb, deep-fried sweetbreads, smoked anchovy and wild garlic purée. With groovy nibbles to start and generous portions to follow, puds can seem superfluous, but it's worth saving room for the lemon cake with limoncello, crème fraîche and fresh honeycomb, the amazingly light yoghurt mousse with lime and green tea jelly or some über-rich duck egg custard. The wine list matches the food for quality and value; prices start at £12 a carafe (£4.50 a glass).
Chef/s: Adam Byatt. **Open:** Tue to Sun L 12.30 to 2.30 (2 Sat, 4 Sun), Mon to Sat D 6.30 to 10. **Closed:** 25 to 30 Dec. **Meals:** alc (main courses £17 to £30). Set L £22 (2 courses) to £25. Sun L £28. Tasting menu £38. **Service:** 12.5% (optional). **Details:** Cards accepted. 63 seats. No music. Wheelchair access. Children allowed.

Tsunami

Fusion-tinged Japanese food
5-7 Voltaire Road, Clapham, SW4 6DQ
Tel no: (020) 7978 1610
www.tsunamirestaurant.co.uk
⊖ Clapham North, map 3
Japanese | £29
Cooking score: 3

Brown-hued, glass-ceilinged Tsunami can emanate a rather sultry vibe, although there's no lack of chatter or action as waiters rush around with trays of myriad little dishes. The huge menu encompasses traditional Japanese flavours including delicate agedashi tofu or nasu goma (grilled aubergine with sesame paste) as well as global fusion plates – perhaps punchy salt-and-chilli squid or beef tataki and baby leaf salad with a mustardy yuzu dressing. Fans of fashionable classics will delight in the wonderfully moist black cod marinated in sweet miso, and the kitchen also deals in top-class sushi and sashimi, including ultra-trendy eel and foie gras nigiri. To drink, there's an impressive choice of saké, although most people stick to cocktails or wine (from £16). A second branch is at 93 Charlotte Street, W1T 4PY; tel: (020) 7637 0050.

Chef/s: Ken Sam. **Open:** Sat and Sun L 12.30 to 4, all week D 6 to 10.30 (11 Fri, 5.30 to 11 Sat, 9.30 Sun). **Closed:** 25 and 26 Dec. **Meals:** alc (main courses £8 to £20). Set L £15. **Service:** 12.5% (optional). **Details:** Cards accepted. 75 seats. 20 seats outside. Separate bar. Wheelchair access. Music. Children allowed.

ALSO RECOMMENDED

▲ Village East

171-173 Bermondsey Street, Southwark, SE1 3UW
Tel no: (020) 7357 6082
www.villageeast.co.uk
⊖ London Bridge, map 1
Modern European

The warehouse conversion in which this collage of bars and dining rooms is housed is very twenty-first century, soft lights with textural surfaces making a good backdrop for some sharp modern cooking. Flexible menus offer spatchcock quail with pomegranate and mustard-seed vinaigrette (£8.60), then white miso skate wing with steamed rice, pak choi and pickled ginger (£17.30) or you could opt for just a simple beef burger or fish and chips. Wines from £16. Open all week.

Wright Brothers Oyster & Porter House

Bivalves and black stuff
11 Stoney Street, Southwark, SE1 9AD
Tel no: (020) 7403 9554
www.thewrightbrothers.co.uk
⊖ London Bridge, map 1
Seafood | £28
Cooking score: 2

Wright Brothers are synonymous with oysters, and their spit-and-sawdust eating house does the business just a shell's throw from Borough Market. Join the crowds huddled round barrels in the brick-walled bar, or wedge into one of the communal tables for some slurping and guzzling. Have your Duchy natives with a pint of Guinness, or sip fizz with a plate of 'speciales de Claire' and some sizzling hot chorizo; alternatively, fill up with dressed crab, moules marinière or fish pie. Those who don't fancy a pint of the 'black stuff' with their bivalves can order one of the easy-drinking wines (from £12.50 a carafe). There's a sibling at 13 Kingly Street, W1B 5PW, tel (020) 7434 3611, and Wright Brothers also run the Ferryboat Inn in Cornwall (see entry).

Chef/s: Phillip Coulter. **Open:** all week L 12 to 3 (4 Sat and Sun), D 6 to 10 (9 Sun). **Closed:** 25 and 26 Dec, bank hols. **Meals:** alc (main courses from £12 to £19). **Service:** not inc. **Details:** Cards accepted. 35 seats. No music. Wheelchair access. Children allowed.

Also recommended entries are not scored but we think they are worth a visit.

READERS RECOMMEND

Wuli Wuli

Chinese

15 Camberwell Church Street, Camberwell, SE5 8TR
Tel no: (020) 7708 5024

'Exceptional value. Standout dishes include fish fragrant aubergine with minced pork.'

Zucca

Vibrant Italian bursting with flavours

184 Bermondsey Street, Bermondsey, SE1 3TQ
Tel no: (020) 7378 6809
www.zuccalondon.com
⊖ London Bridge, Borough, map 1
Italian | £22
Cooking score: 3

In the hinterland around London Bridge, Zucca is a dependably busy, buzzy, open-plan place where the on-view kitchen is a hive of activity, producing appealing modern Italian food at surreally kind prices. Starters in particular are tremendous value for the likes of smoked eel bruschetta, San Daniele ham and fennel salami or sea bream carpaccio. Main course meats, perhaps a veal chop with spinach and lemon, are praised for their flavour and succulence, and there are always a couple of pasta dishes, such as fregola with mussels and chilli. An Amaretto tart gets the nod at dessert stage, although the tiramisu is perhaps more run-of-the-mill than it might be. Service is commendable too: 'staff look happy to be there'. A top-quality list of Italian wines, opening with glasses of Grechetto and Chianti from £4.50, allows you to explore the parameters of this still largely undiscovered wine country. The Piedmontese selections alone are a dream.

Chef/s: Sam Harris. **Open:** Tue to Sun L 12.30 to 3, Tue to Sat D 6.30 to 10. **Closed:** Mon, bank hols. **Meals:** alc (main courses £9 to £15). **Service:** not inc. **Details:** Cards accepted. 64 seats. Separate bar. No music. No mobile phones. Wheelchair access. Children allowed.

HIDDEN TEAS AND SECRET SUPPERS

Some of the the nation's hippest eateries are springing up in secret locations in our towns and cities, hidden even from the eagle eyes of *The Good Food Guide* inspectors.

These clandestine supper clubs, usually operating out of people's sitting rooms, emerged when the recession started, but diners are also drawn by the chance to meet new people and the desire to snoop around someone else's home.

The cooking varies from simple home-cooked fare - as at **The Spice Club** in Manchester - to the culinary wizardry of **The Loft Project** in east London where international guest chefs serve up menus at £120 a pop. On-trend afternoon tea also features: London's **Hidden Tea Room** and Edinburgh's **Queen of Tarts** appeal to sweet-toothed hipsters. There's even the chance of romance with regular singles dinners at Hackney's **Fernandez & Leluu.**

Expect to pay a suggested 'donation' of £25 to £35, and you can usually bring your own booze. Book early, as places such as Brixton's **Saltoun Supper Club** or Hari Covert's **Underground Restaurant** in Kent, fill up months in advance.

ALSO RECOMMENDED

▲ Adams Café

77 Askew Road, Shepherd's Bush, W12 9AH
Tel no: (020) 8743 0572
www.adamscafe.co.uk
⊖ Ravenscourt Park, Stamford Brook, map 1
North African £5 OFF

Refurbishment has given Frances and Abdel Boukraa's unusual café a fresh new look. Their menu is priced for one, two or three courses (£11.50, £14.50 and £16.95), and centres on Tunisian specialities, plus a few Mediterranean dishes for good measure. Couscous is the star of the show, but a tasty alternative is gargoulette – lamb casserole with fresh mint. Start with authentic brik with eggs and herbs; finish with Moroccan-style pancakes with honey sauce. Wines from £11.50 or BYO (corkage £3). Open Mon to Sat D only.

The Admiral Codrington

Jam-packed Chelsea bolt-hole
17 Mossop Street, Chelsea, SW3 2LY
Tel no: (020) 7581 0005
www.theadmiralcodrington.co.uk
⊖ South Kensington, map 3
Modern British | £28
Cooking score: 3

Bright and fresh after its refurb, the venerable and much-loved 'Cod' still manages to suck in hordes at the bar and regular overspill outside, but persevere through to the narrow, glass-roofed dining room at the back and you will be rewarded with aged Jack O'Shea steaks and a menu of capably rendered, freewheeling dishes including the legendary herb-crusted 'Admiral's cod'. Fish fans might also fancy yellowfin tuna tartare with crushed avocado or crab linguine with chilli, while the carnivorous contingent could veer towards grilled Ibérico pork chop with mustard sauce or honey-glazed confit duck with roasted nectarines, endive and walnut salad. After that, a triple chocolate brownie should suffice. There are real ales on tap, plus a succinct list of dependable wines from £15.50.

Chef/s: Fred Smith. **Open:** Mon to Sat L 12 to 2.30, D 6.30 to 11. Sun 12 to 9. **Closed:** 25 Dec. **Meals:** alc (main courses £14 to £28). **Service:** 12.5% (optional). **Details:** Cards accepted. 50 seats. 20 seats outside. Separate bar. Wheelchair access. Music. Children allowed.

Amaya

Sleek, slinky Indian
15 Halkin Arcade, Motcomb Street, Knightsbridge, SW1X 8JT
Tel no: (020) 7823 1166
www.realindianfood.com
⊖ Knightsbridge, map 4
Indian | £42
Cooking score: 3
V

Gustatory thrills and glamorous vibes go hand-in-hand at this captivating Belgravia Indian, although hedonism and high fashion ultimately play second fiddle to the theatrical goings-on in the open kitchen. Amaya's culinary trademark is tapas-style grazing, with much depending on output of the tandoor oven, sigri grill and tawa skillet. Little dishes arrive as they are ready – perhaps flash-grilled rock oysters with coconut and ginger, boned tandoori quail with apricots, or minced lamb kebabs smoked with cloves. Rich biryanis are the genuine article, akhrot gosht is slow-cooked with walnuts and star anise, and veggies can have a field day delving into plates of spinach and fig tikki, stir-fried fine beans or pan-roasted potatoes with sun-dried mango powder. The enterprising, spice-friendly wine list comes courtesy of expert Matthew Jukes; prices from £23.50.

Chef/s: Karunesh Khanna. **Open:** all week L 12.30 to 2.15 (2.45 Sun), D 6.30 to 11.30 (10.30 Sun). **Closed:** 25 Dec. **Meals:** alc (main courses £11 to £32). Set L £19.50. Tasting menu £38.50. Gourmet menu £70. **Service:** 12.5% (optional). **Details:** Cards accepted. 100 seats. Separate bar. Wheelchair access. Music. Children allowed.

Anglesea Arms

Punchy victuals and good drinking
35 Wingate Road, Shepherd's Bush, W6 0UR
Tel no: (020) 8749 1291
⊖ Ravenscourt Park, map 1
British | £35
Cooking score: 2

A blue-chip, pubby veteran in Shepherd's Bush, this foodie boozer continues to attract a boisterous crew with its promise of punchy victuals and good drinking. Vintage design and tightly packed tables provide the backdrop, while the menu touts Brit-inspired dishes with a few sunny Mediterranean nuances. Small plates of wolf fish goujons, shredded pork salad or smoked eel with a soft-boiled egg and watercress sit alongside hefty helpings of grilled lamb chops with polenta and purple sprouting broccoli or sea bass with braised fennel, lentils and gremolata. Tip-top real ales and gluggable wines from £16.50.
Chef/s: Matthew Cranston. **Open:** all week L 12.30 to 2.45 (3 Sat, 3.30 Sun), D 7 to 10.30 (10 Mon, 6.30 to 9.30 Sun). **Closed:** 25 to 27 Dec. **Meals:** alc (main courses £10 to £36). **Service:** 12.5% (optional). **Details:** Cards accepted. 85 seats. 25 seats outside. Separate bar. No music. Children allowed.

ALSO RECOMMENDED

▲ Ark

122 Palace Gardens Terrace, Notting Hill, W8 4RT
Tel no: (020) 7229 4024
www.ark-restaurant.com
⊖ Notting Hill Gate, map 4
Italian

The Ark is an enjoyable, unpretentious and popular Italian neighbourhood eatery noted for its summery terrace. The small dining room has simple décor and offers authentic, comforting cooking along the lines of melanzane alla parmigiana (£8.50), linguine with clams and white wine, and calf's liver with pancetta and mashed potato variety. There's also wild mushroom and black truffle tartlet, brown shrimp risotto with fennel and Pernod, and Champagne jelly with winter fruits. All-Italian wines from £17. Closed Sun and Mon L.

Assaggi

Fine-tuned rustic Italian food
39 Chepstow Place, Notting Hill, W2 4TS
Tel no: (020) 7792 5501
⊖ Notting Hill Gate, map 4
Italian | £50
Cooking score: 4
V

Italian rustic meets Notting Hill cool at Nino Sassu's modest dining room above a pub on smart Chepstow Place. Inside, Assaggi's vibrant minimalism and cheery vibes strike just the right note for fine-tuned, boldly flavoured food with a sunny disposition. Impeccably sourced ingredients are at the heart of things and the menu doesn't give much away when it comes to the details – although the kitchen's simple strokes are always guided by the seasons. Rustic Sardinian breads open the show, before disarmingly fresh antipasti – perhaps cuttlefish with artichokes and polenta, crab salad or a plate of exclusive Culatello di Zibello prosciutto. Pasta might include tagliolini with green herbs, while secondi offer veal cutlets, grilled sea bass and pancetta di maiale with the minimum of fuss or adornment. Desserts vary from day to day, but there's generally something seasonal and fruity as well as textbook tiramisu. The wine list canters through the Italian regions, offering plenty of interesting stuff from £22.95.
Chef/s: Nino Sassu. **Open:** Mon to Sat L 12.30 to 2.30 (1 to 2.30 Sat), D 7.30 to 11. **Closed:** Sun, 2 weeks from 24 Dec, bank hols. **Meals:** alc (main courses £20 to £28). **Service:** not inc. **Details:** Cards accepted. 35 seats. No music. Children allowed.

Awana

Malaysian high-flyer
85 Sloane Avenue, Chelsea, SW3 3DX
Tel no: (020) 7584 8880
www.awana.co.uk
⊖ South Kensington, map 3
Malaysian | £40
Cooking score: 1

£5 OFF **V**

The interior is smart, with swathes of polished teak, leather and glass, and a satay bar takes pride of place. It is the satay – meat or fish – that truly excels. Elsewhere, menus stick to the standard Malaysian repertoire, but high-quality ingredients shine through. Dry, coconut-based curries are recommended (say a curry kapitan with guinea fowl, made special with a dash of fragrant lemongrass), traditional beef rendang is rich and tender, and stir-fried aubergine with sambal has been praised. Wines from £19.

Chef/s: Verasamy Poliah. **Open:** all week L 12 to 3, D 6 to 11 (11.30 Thur to Sat, 10.30 Sun). **Closed:** 25 and 26 Dec, 1 Jan. **Meals:** alc (main courses £12 to £25). Set L £12.50 (2 courses) to £15. Set D £35 to £45 (5 courses). **Service:** 12.5% (optional). **Details:** Cards accepted. 90 seats. Separate bar. Music. Children allowed. Car parking.

Bar Boulud

French brasserie, New York style
Mandarin Oriental Hyde Park, 66 Knightsbridge, Knightsbridge, SW1X 7LA
Tel no: (020) 7201 3899
www.barboulud.com
⊖ Knightsbridge, map 4
French | £35
Cooking score: 4

'What a great place this is', sums up many readers' affection for Bar Boulud – in fact some are even happy to endure lengthy train rides for a taste of its friendly hospitality, reasonable prices and dependable French brasserie cooking. Of the London openings from international superstar chefs, this spin-off from New York's Daniel Boulud is the one that Londoners have taken to their hearts. The faithful flock to get their fill of excellent salade frisée lyonnaise, superb charcuterie and pâtés, soupe de poisson, coq au vin and steak frites. The piggie burger, however, is the star of the show – 'I have to say it's the best I've had' – served with 'delicious fries'. Desserts stay on track with the likes of coupe peppermint, a flourless sponge with hot chocolate sauce and mint/chocolate ice cream, and gâteau Basque with brandied cherries and vanilla anglaise. The wine list is extensive and expensive, but offers quality choices, with bottles from £22.50.

Chef/s: Dean Yasharian. **Open:** all week L 12 to 3, D 5.30 to 11 (10 Sun). **Meals:** alc (main courses £12 to £24). Set L £16 (2 courses) to £20. **Service:** 12.5% (optional). **Details:** Cards accepted. 165 seats. Separate bar. Wheelchair access. Music. Children allowed.

Bibendum

Icon with a magical mood
Michelin House, 81 Fulham Road, South Kensington, SW3 6RD
Tel no: (020) 7581 5817
www.bibendum.co.uk
⊖ South Kensington, map 3
French | £49
Cooking score: 4

V

Bibendum's brand of French cooking based on good seasonal produce has proved a winning formula here for 25 years. 'A really consistent, friendly neighbourhood restaurant', is how regulars view it, praising Matthew Harris's cooking as 'first-rate food'. The room hasn't changed either; the light-filled space on the first floor of Michelin House adds a timeless feel. Simplicity is evident in crab vinaigrette with herbs or grilled scallops with rosemary, fennel and blood orange salad, but all this indicates that attention is focused where it should be – raw materials are of good quality and techniques are sound. Successful main courses have included braised ox cheek ('melting and tender'), and confit of duck with braised celery heart and wild mushroom, while 'just brilliant' neatly sums up a dessert of tarte fine aux pommes. The wine list is a delight, shining brightest in France and with a healthy number of options under £30. Prices from £19.95.

Chef/s: Matthew Harris. **Open:** all week L 12 to 2.30 (12.30 to 3 Sat and Sun), D 7 to 11 (10.30 Sun). **Closed:** 25 and 26 Dec, 1 Jan. **Meals:** alc (main courses £18 to £34). Set L £26.50 (2 courses) to £30. Sun L and D £30. **Service:** 12.5% (optional). **Details:** Cards accepted. 90 seats. Separate bar. No music. No mobile phones. Children allowed.

Brompton Bar & Grill

Serving bistro classics with verve
243 Brompton Road, South Kensington, SW3 2EP
Tel no: (020) 7589 8005
www.bromptonbarandgrill.com
⊖ South Kensington, map 3
Anglo-French | £30
Cooking score: 2

Even well-heeled Knightsbridge needs a local bistro, a place with cartoons and French-style prints on the walls, windows opening up to the street and a chattery, fun-filled atmosphere – and this is it. The menu aims to cover two bases, taking in French standards (foie gras with brioche, snails à la bourguignonne, grilled halibut hollandaise), as well as modern British items. The latter might see you go from ham hock terrine with piccalilli or potted shrimps to smoked haddock and salmon fishcakes with curried mayonnaise and watercress. It's all brought off with reliable verve, and there's a short, well-chosen wine selection from £12.

Chef/s: Gary Durrant. **Open:** all week L 12 to 3 (3.30 Sat and Sun), D 6 to 10.30 (10 Sun). **Meals:** alc (main courses £13 to £24). Set L £15.50 (2 courses). Set D £18.50. Sun L £21.50. **Service:** 12.5% (optional). **Details:** Cards accepted. 60 seats. Separate bar. Music. Children allowed.

Le Café Anglais

Confident modern brasserie
8 Porchester Gardens, Notting Hill, W2 4DB
Tel no: (020) 7221 1415
www.lecafeanglais.co.uk
⊖ Bayswater, map 4
Anglo-French | £40
Cooking score: 4

Being located on the second floor of Whiteleys shopping centre hardly makes Le Café Anglais an instant choice as a destination restaurant, but Queensway is not well blessed with good places to eat and Rowley Leigh's modern brasserie is firmly settled into its stride – an all-day oyster bar and café at one end of the light, spacious room being the latest addition. The set-up continues to deliver well-rehearsed dishes in which prime ingredients (morels on toast, lobster with sauce béarnaise) produce seductive results. The classical French background also yields humbler items such as hors d'oeuvres of rabbit rillettes or a silky Parmesan custard with anchovy toast, and the kitchen can turn out some fine stuff – in particular the roast wood pigeon with braised peas and ham that was a notable hit at inspection. Queen of puddings is a perennial favourite, service is best described as 'plentiful but mechanical', and a classy wine list starts at £19.50.

Chef/s: Rowley Leigh and Colin Westal. **Open:** all week L 12 to 3.30, D 6.30 to 11 (11.30 Fri and Sat, 10.15 Sun). **Closed:** 25 and 26 Dec, 1 Jan. **Meals:** alc (main courses £9 to £30). Set L (Mon to Fri) £16.50 (2 courses) to £19.50. Set D £35. Sun L £24.50. **Service:** 12.5% (optional). **Details:** Cards accepted. 160 seats. Separate bar. No music. Wheelchair access. Children allowed. Car parking.

Cambio de Tercio

Inventive Spanish on top form
163 Old Brompton Road, Earl's Court, SW5 0LJ
Tel no: (020) 7244 8970
www.cambiodetercio.co.uk
⊖ Gloucester Road, map 3
Spanish | £40
Cooking score: 5
V

The cutting-edge Spanish cooking going on at this Earl's Court eatery is fittingly staged against a backdrop of throbbing colour – Rioja red, Serrano pink and Seville orange. Alberto Criado's cooking owes something to the nueva cocina of Spain's recent golden age, from the postmodernist tapas to the dynamic main-course combinations and comical desserts. A lollipop of fried Manchego is a good way to start proceedings, and there are some traditional tapas (grilled octopus with potato and paprika oil, perhaps), before the menu gets into overdrive. The famous deconstructed tortilla, inspired by superstar chef Ferran Adrià, consists of a barely cooked omelette medium-filled with caramelised onion and topped with paradoxically earthy potato foam. Sardines are marinated in sherry vinegar and come with Arbequina olives, baby gem and Martini Rosso jelly, while bomba (paella rice) might be garnished with Torta del Casar cheese and sea urchin caviar. Main courses see rabbit casseroled in sherry with poached quails' eggs, before the sweetly alarming prospect of cherry and Amaretto compote with chewing-gum ice cream arrives to finish you off. Seasonal tasting menus and vegetarian dishes help to ring the changes. The wine list begins by reminding us how good decent sherry is, before motoring on through the still barely known denominaciones of Spain's viticultural map. Old Reservas and fresh young fruit-bombs, Ribera del Duero and torrents of Rioja – it's all here, as well as wines by the glass from £5.50. New tapas/sherry bar sibling Capote y Toros is also worth seeking out at 157 Old Brompton Road, SW5 0LJ; tel (020) 7373 0567.

Chef/s: Alberto Criado. **Open:** all week L 12 to 3, D 6.30 to 11.30 (11 Sun). **Closed:** 25 Dec, last 2 weeks Aug. **Meals:** alc (main courses £18 to £23). Sat and Sun L £26. Tasting menu £37. **Service:** 12.5% (optional). **Details:** Cards accepted. 45 seats. 12 seats outside. Children allowed.

The Capital

Timeless, idiomatic haute cuisine
22 Basil Street, Knightsbridge, SW3 1AT
Tel no: (020) 7591 1202
www.capitalhotel.co.uk
⊖ Knightsbridge, map 4
French | £60
Cooking score: 6

It's difficult to reach the top – and even harder to stay there – but the Capital has been one of London's gastronomic grandees for decades, and it's still thriving. The sleek dining room has an air of sobriety and reverence that encourages restraint rather than vivacity; this is no glitterati playground, but a place for considered culinary appreciation and 'retro comfort' amid starched linen cloths, chandeliers and long drapes. Don't come here expecting gimmickry and experimentation; instead, the Capital champions French haute cuisine in all its timeless, idiomatic glory, complete with the proper filleting of fish, flambéing at the table, guéridon trolley service and other cherished skills. The kitchen also uses expensive, top-end ingredients with awe-inspiring technical acumen and assurance: salmon gravadlax is cut from the fattest part of the fish, with enough acidity in the dill sauce to offset the oily flesh; raviolo of foie gras is timed so that the filling retains its unctuous solidity while the wafer-thin pasta is just al dente amid a frothing cloud of leeks and truffle shavings. Elsewhere, a classic dish of barely cooked scallops with black pudding and crisped-up bacon can hardly be bettered. When it comes to dessert, all is artistry, poise and elegance – rhubarb compote with almond sorbet and yoghurt foam, for example. Needless to say, dinner is suitably topped and tailed with dainty canapés and petits fours. The

wine list embraces the French regions in loving detail, with peerless growers and prime vintages in abundance; there is also plenty of serious stuff from elsewhere. Prices start at £25 (£6 a glass), but mark-ups decrease as you ascend to the higher levels.
Chef/s: Jérôme Ponchelle. **Open:** all week L 12 to 2.30, D 6.45 to 11 (10.30 Sun). **Meals:** alc (main courses £24 to £38). Set L £29.50. Sun L £35. Tasting menu £70. **Service:** 12.5% (optional). **Details:** Cards accepted. 34 seats. Separate bar. Music. Children allowed. Car parking.

The Carpenter's Arms

Dressed-down bonhomie and please-all food
89-91 Black Lion Lane, Hammersmith, W6 9BG
Tel no: (020) 8741 8386
www.carpentersarmsw6.co.uk
⊖ Stamford Brook, Ravenscourt Park, map 1
Modern European | £25
Cooking score: 2

A happy, 'home-from-home gaff' staffed by an interested crew, the Carpenter's Arms reinforces its dressed-down local credentials with mismatched chairs, leatherette banquettes and a pretty garden for fine-weather carousing. The air of relaxed bonhomie also extends to a please-all menu of classic pub grub spiced up with some modish interlopers: fish pie and juicy homemade burgers might appear alongside cuttlefish ink risotto with grilled squid, roasted rabbit stuffed with wild rice and chorizo, or a toothsome dish of 'just rare' grilled yellowfin tuna topped with a dollop of tapenade. Real ales are in short supply, but the nifty wine list promises decent drinking from £16.50 (£4.30 a glass).
Chef/s: Nilton Campos. **Open:** all week L 12 to 3 (4 Sat and Sun), D 6 to 10 (9 Sun). **Meals:** alc (main courses from £10 to £17). **Service:** 12.5% (optional). **Details:** Cards accepted. 50 seats. 30 seats outside. Separate bar. Wheelchair access. Music. Children allowed.

Casa Brindisa

Homage to Iberian tapas
7-9 Exhibition Road, South Kensington, SW7 2HQ
Tel no: (020) 7590 0008
www.casabrindisa.com
⊖ South Kensington, map 3
Spanish | £25
Cooking score: 3

V 

With eating areas upstairs and down, this is the infectiously bustly South Kensington outpost of the burgeoning Brindisa group. Hung about with Spanish artefacts, from antique tinajas to farm implements, it won't leave you wanting for cultural orientation, especially when you set about the menu. Little tapas bites such as fine Ibérico and Trevélez ham with toasted broad beans lead on to platters of cured fish (smoked mackerel, anchovies, sardines and tuna), and dishes such as truffled revuelto (scrambled egg) with mushrooms and cheese, and baked sea bass with patatas 'a lo pobre' and pistachios. It's all as vivid and fresh as can be, and great fun into the bargain. Finish with Galician-style tarta di Santiago or crema catalana with pineapple. A comprehensive Spanish wine list opens with Macabeo and Garnacha house selections at £17.
Chef/s: Leonardo Rivera. **Open:** all week L 12 to 11 (10 Sun). **Closed:** 25 and 26 Dec. **Meals:** alc (tapas £5 to £22). **Service:** 12.5% (optional). **Details:** Cards accepted. 65 seats. 12 seats outside. Separate bar. Wheelchair access. Music. Children allowed.

NEW ENTRY
Cassis

An appealing French provincial package
232-236 Brompton Road, South Kensington, SW3 2BB
Tel no: (020) 7581 1101
www.cassisbistro.co.uk
⊖ South Kensington, map 3
French | £38
Cooking score: 4

Cassis manages to be formal and informal by turns: one is greeted as if entering a seriously swish restaurant, but then faced with 'a real

French brasserie feel', re-enforced by unclothed tables and floor-to-ceiling windows opening on to a line of tables on Brompton Road. This latest venture from Marlon Abela (of Greenhouse and Umu fame – see entries) is dedicated to the rustic cooking of south-west France, and chef David Escobar delivers an appealing package. Velvety, rich pumpkin soup with chestnut and Provençal goats' cheese, for example, silky pappardelle with slow-cooked wild boar ragù and chickpeas, and pitch-perfect herb-crusted rack of lamb, served with a smear of polenta, strips of very good chorizo, a few chestnuts, and a rich, sticky reduced sauce of cooking juices. For dessert, sweet Provençal fritters – oreillettes by any other name – are the real deal, served with outstanding homemade green tomato and orange jams. The extensive wine list is strong in France, but with top-class producers from around the world; bottles from £17.

Chef/s: David Escobar. **Open:** all week L 12 to 10.30. **Closed:** 25 and 26 Dec. **Meals:** alc (main courses £14 to £29). Set L £17 (2 courses) to £20. **Service:** 12.5% (optional). **Details:** Cards accepted. 90 seats. 10 seats outside. Separate bar. Wheelchair access. Music. Children allowed.

Le Cercle

Exquisite French food in miniature
1 Wilbraham Place, Belgravia, SW1X 9AE
Tel no: (020) 7901 9999
www.lecercle.co.uk
⊖ Sloane Square, map 3
Modern French | £45
Cooking score: 5

£5 OFF

A bijou eatery with a discreetly chic entrance, Le Cercle belies its basement setting with enormously high ceilings, rich fittings and ample elbowroom. Good-looking staff glide confidently around the tables, delivering a taste of south-west France to the assembled crowd. Portions are intentionally small – the idea is to graze your way through the menu, sharing along the way. Given the restaurant's obvious regional allegiance, there's surprisingly little foie gras on offer. That said, a crunchy 'bar' of duck liver with a chocolate 'moka' coating and a dish of wood pigeon 'royale' stuffed with the unctuous offal and rolled in Parma ham have been full of interest and beautifully presented. A lovely light broth of wild mushrooms served with a perfectly poached egg and a slice of Parmesan cake is also worth seeking out, likewise a fricassee of baby squid and pork belly with a sharp, fragrant, herby vinaigrette adding that extra frisson. The Tour de France wine list is priced to suit the location and its customers, pedalling all the way from Alsace to southern climes in search of vintage quality. Generous house recommendations start at £20 (£6 a glass).

Chef/s: Florent Fabulas. **Open:** Tue to Sat L 12 to 2, D 5.30 to 10.45. **Closed:** Sun, Mon, bank hols. **Meals:** alc (main courses £11 to £20). Set L £15. Tasting menu £35. **Service:** 12.5% (optional). **Details:** Cards accepted. 65 seats. Separate bar. Wheelchair access. Music. Children allowed.

NEW ENTRY

Chabrot Bistrot d'Amis

A Francophile's dream
9 Knightsbridge Green, Knightsbridge, SW1 X7QI
Tel no: (020) 7225 2238
www.chabrot.co.uk
⊖ Knightsbridge, map 4
French | £35
Cooking score: 5

This two-floored 'bistrot' is a diminutive patch of south-west France that could easily be overshadowed by the colossus of culinary names in the area. But it has its own culinary heritage, with some of London's most respected rising talents collaborating in the project. The menu reads like a Francophile's dream, liberally sprinkled with charcuterie, interesting salads, hearty fish and meat, great cheeses and tempting plats du jour. To start, an exceptionally unshowy dish of chilli-spiked, deep-fried baby squid vies for attention with an equally simple yet elegant salad of sweetly marinated beetroot overlaid with rich, perfectly ripe Rocamadour cheese. Mains tend

to be bourgeois in style: Savoy cabbage is stuffed with veal, ceps and chestnuts then poached in a light broth, while cod roasted with chorizo delivers a perfectly tender piece of fish enlivened by some punchy sausage. Also check out chef Thierry Laborde's signature dish of poulet farci au foie gras, presented in a stoneware pot for sharing. Service is very French, laid-back and full of character, although staff go about their business with charm and efficiency. They have also done everything to keep costs down in this high-value postcode; it would be hard to squeeze in another table or make the heavy-duty, pro-European wine list more financially welcoming. Prices start at £19.50 (£5 a glass).
Chef/s: Thierry Laborde. **Open:** Mon to Sat L 12 to 3.30, D 6.30 to 11. **Closed:** Sun. **Meals:** alc (main courses £16 to £32). Set L £12.50 (2 courses) to £17.50. **Service:** 12.5% (optional). **Details:** Cards accepted. 65 seats. Music. Children allowed.

Charlotte's Bistro

Slick neighbourhood eatery
6 Turnham Green Terrace, Chiswick, W4 1QP
Tel no: (020) 8742 3590
www.charlottes.co.uk
⊖ Turnham Green, map 1
Modern British | £29
Cooking score: 2

With its slick dark tones and upmarket bistro food, this sister site to Charlotte's Place in Ealing (see entry) has proved a hit since launching in early 2010. It's set over split levels, so either grab a stool at the open-fronted cocktail bar or head up to the restaurant for a modern bistro menu. A change of chef seems to have upped imagination in the kitchen, with the likes of langoustine bisque with smoked eel, apple and avocado mousse, or curried monkfish with pig's cheek and cauliflower now the norm. The early-bird menu (three courses and a cocktail) is popular, while house wines start at £18.
Chef/s: Wesley Smalley. **Open:** all week L 12 to 3, D 5.30 to 10 (9 Sun). **Meals:** alc (main courses £14 to £17). Set L £12 (2 courses) to £15. Early D (5.30 to 7) £26. Sun L £18.50 (2 courses) to £22.50. **Service:** 12.5% (optional). **Details:** Cards accepted. 60 seats. Separate bar. Music. Children allowed.

Charlotte's Place

Neighbourly generosity and keen prices
16 St Matthew's Road, Ealing, W5 3JT
Tel no: (020) 8567 7541
www.charlottes.co.uk
⊖ Ealing Broadway, Ealing Common, map 1
Modern European | £29
Cooking score: 4

Reckoned to be 'the best proper restaurant in Ealing by a long way', this elder sibling of Charlotte's Bistro (see entry) is a picture of cosy, neighbourly generosity spread over two floors. Informative, approachable staff keep the mood buoyant and the kitchen serves up 'wonderfully composed' seasonal food with a fair degree of aplomb. Star turns are many and varied: for some it's crispy pig's cheeks with braised pig's head and sauce gribiche, for others it's roast chicken suprême with leek ravioli, crispy wings and cep purée. Either way, interesting offbeat combos rub shoulders with sound ideas from the textbook – perhaps pea and ham hock soup, chateaubriand or lemon tart with Italian meringue and blackcurrant sorbet. Keen pricing extends to the well-spread global wine list, which opens at £16.
Chef/s: Greg Martin. **Open:** Mon to Sat L 12 to 3, D 6 to 9.30. Sun 12 to 9. **Closed:** 26 Dec to 4 Jan. **Meals:** alc (main courses £15 to £18). Set L £12 (2 courses) to £15. Early D (6 to 7) £26. Sun L £16.50 (2 courses) to £19.50. **Service:** 12.5% (optional). **Details:** Cards accepted. 52 seats. 10 seats outside. Music. Children allowed.

Chutney Mary

Glamorous contemporary Indian
535 King's Road, Fulham, SW10 0SZ
Tel no: (020) 7351 3113
www.realindianfood.com
⊖ Fulham Broadway, map 3
Indian | £32
Cooking score: 3
V

High-stepping Indian ladies with a penchant for flashy Westernised outfits and glossy 'lippy' were once nicknamed 'chutney Marys', so it's apt that this sumptuously revamped restaurant should come with a heavy dose of glamour. Spread over three opulent rooms (including a fabulous, cushion-strewn conservatory), it provides a sparkling backdrop to Siddharth Krishna's inventive, cross-cultural food. Vibrantly spiced Goan green chicken curry, Malabar biryani and tandoori lamb chops show the kitchen's orthodox side, while goose galouti (kebabs) with blueberry chutney, crispy marinated artichokes with 'tempered spinach' and a dish of slow-roasted lamb shank with red chilli and coriander mash suggest an appetite for the unexpected. Regulars who know the place have reported the occasional 'off night' of late; hopefully this is no more than a passing blip. The intelligent wine list is a harmonious match for the food, with prices from £23.
Chef/s: Siddharth Krishna. **Open:** Sat and Sun L 12.30 to 2.30 (3 Sun), all week D 6.30 to 11 (10.30 Sun). **Meals:** alc (main courses £15 to £23). Set L and D £22. **Service:** 12.5% (optional). **Details:** Cards accepted. 110 seats. No music. Wheelchair access. Children allowed.

Symbols

- Accommodation is available
- £30 Three courses for less than £30
- V Separate vegetarian menu
- £5 OFF £5-off voucher scheme
- Notable wine list

Clarke's

Sense-tingling seasonal flavours
124 Kensington Church Street, Notting Hill, W8 4BH
Tel no: (020) 7221 9225
www.sallyclarke.com
⊖ Notting Hill Gate, map 4
Modern British | £40
Cooking score: 4

When Sally Clarke brought char-grilling and sun-drenched Californian flavours to Notting Hill back in the 80s, it was hailed as revolutionary stuff bursting with new-age vitality. Some 27 years down the line, she is one of London's culinary icons with an MBE to her name, but she hasn't lost her appetite for direct, sense-tingling food. Seasonal clarity is her touchstone and the flavours hit you head-on – a salad of shaved purple artichokes and fennel with buffalo mozzarella and citrus dressing, for example. Although the Mediterranean influences are unmistakable, Sally has never watered down her commitment to native produce, serving Cornish squid with salsa verde, organic spelt and spiced cime di rape, enlivening home-smoked Aylesbury duck breast with blood oranges, and deploying Devon roe deer for a slow-cooked pie with winter truffles. British cheeses come with fig 'salame', and desserts might include Yorkshire rhubarb with Campari sorbet and brown sugar palmier ('an excellent combination of flavours and textures'). California dreamers will dote over the West Coast treats on the handpicked wine list (note the section devoted to Ridge Vineyards), but there are top names from France, Italy and the Antipodes too. Prices from £19.
Chef/s: Sally Clarke. **Open:** all week L 12.30 to 2 (12 Sat), Mon to Sat D 6.30 to 10. **Closed:** Christmas, New Year, bank hols. **Meals:** alc (main courses £19 to £36). Set D £40.50. **Service:** 12.5% (optional). **Details:** Cards accepted. 80 seats. No music. No mobile phones. Wheelchair access. Children allowed.

Le Colombier

French through and through
145 Dovehouse Street, Chelsea, SW3 6LB
Tel no: (020) 7351 1155
www.le-colombier-restaurant.co.uk
⊖ South Kensington, map 3
French | £50
Cooking score: 2

Didier Garnier's evergreen Chelsea restaurant is a local institution and ticks all the right boxes when it comes to the French bistro experience – a thoroughly *sympathique* atmosphere with bare floorboards, white-clad tables and a canopied terrace providing excellent alfresco opportunities. The kitchen continues to keep customers satisfied with the straightforward cooking of high-class comfort food. Foie gras terrine with fig jam or warm goats' cheese salad might be curtain-raisers to veal kidneys with mustard cream sauce or grilled monkfish with tomato and Vermouth sauce, while dessert could be something like tarte Tatin or crème brûlée. French wines from £17.50.

Chef/s: Philippe Tamet. **Open:** all week L 12 to 3 (3.30 Sun), D 6.30 to 10.30 (10 Sun). **Meals:** alc (main courses £18 to £31). Set L £19.50 (2 courses). Sun L £23. **Service:** 12.5% (optional). **Details:** Cards accepted. 50 seats. 20 seats outside. Separate bar. No music. Wheelchair access.

NEW ENTRY

Dinner by Heston Blumenthal

History in the making
Mandarin Oriental Hyde Park, 66 Knightsbridge, Knightsbridge, SW1X 7LA
Tel no: (020) 7201 3833
www.dinnerbyheston.com
⊖ Knightsbridge, map 4
British | £55
Cooking score: 7

It was a long time coming, but 2011's hottest opening has more than lived up to the hype. Dinner at Heston Blumenthal may be a world away from the Fat Duck (see entry), but it's still about showmanship – although the room itself is rather masculine and restrained, with unclothed tables and park views plus some jelly-mould wall lights signalling what is to come. In case you hadn't heard, Dinner is Blumenthal's interpretation of British food history – a blazing but meticulous assault on tired clichés and predictable conventions. Every dish comes date-stamped for authenticity, from 'rice and flesh' (accredited to the *Forme of Cury* cookbook c.1390) right up to 'cod in cider' (1940) – proof that this take on our gastronomic past isn't simply a glance backward into the dusty annals of *culinaria britannica*. The aforementioned medieval assemblage becomes a faultless saffron risotto suffused with red wine, calf's tail and red amaranth, while the wartime throwback is transformed into a wondrous fishy collation, all held together by a sublime buttery sauce. Meanwhile, another creation has already made it to the top of the charts: 'meat fruit' (c.1500). This may not have the instant tabloid appeal of snail porridge, but it's an icon in the making – a brilliant visual pun resembling a glossy 'mandarin' complete with bright green stalk and leaves; in fact it's a sphere of extraordinarily refined fruit jelly containing an unctuous chicken liver parfait. Other treats from this cornucopia of patriotic victuals have included a retread of that foppish Elizabethan conceit salmagundi and salt-cured 'powdered' duck (c.1670) served with smoked fennel and the richest, silkiest potato purée you could imagine. As a reinvention of our culinary heritage, Dinner convinces, startles and illuminates on every level: in the glass-walled kitchen, for example, there's a rotisserie spiked with pineapples, an essential component of the must-have 'tipsy cake' (a warm, sweet Georgian confection served in a cast-iron pot). It also sees Heston Blumenthal's trusted co-conspirator Ashley Palmer-Watts stepping out of the shadows, duly transmuting all that bookish research into top-end cooking that actually works for a savvy twenty-first century audience. It's a credit to his skill and logistical nous that the show runs as smoothly

as it does. A connoisseur's wine list is packed with star names and classy drinking (at a price); house recommendations start at £20.
Chef/s: Ashley Palmer-Watts. **Open:** all week L 12 to 2.30, D 6.30 to 10.30. **Meals:** alc (main courses £23 to £36). Set L £28. **Service:** 12.5% (optional). **Details:** Cards accepted. 104 seats. Separate bar. No music. Wheelchair access. Children allowed.

The Duke of Sussex

Atmospheric local with Spanish menus
75 South Parade, Chiswick, W4 5LF
Tel no: (020) 8742 8801
⊖ Chiswick Park, map 1
Spanish/British | £23
Cooking score: 2

This atmospheric, shabby-chic Victorian pub blends chandeliers and antique lampshades with cherub-adorned frescoes, and buzzes with locals enjoying a casual (if slightly incongruous) Spanish menu. Flashes of colourful red piquillo peppers enliven char-grilled squid, ham croquetas have the requisite dense texture and crunch, a heap of razor clams deftly balances the flavours of smoky chorizo, fresh chilli, lemon and parsley, and there are deeply satisfying rustic dishes such as fish stew with saffron potatoes and fennel alongside the odd Brit-inspired steaks and pies. It's all realistically priced and broadly successful. House wine is £15.
Chef/s: Chris Payne. **Open:** Tue to Sun 12 to 10.30 (9.30 Sun). Mon D only 5 to 10.30. **Meals:** alc (main courses £8 to £17). **Service:** not inc. **Details:** Cards accepted. 112 seats. 180 seats outside. Separate bar. Wheelchair access. Music. Children allowed.

To find out more about *The Good Food Guide*, please visit www.thegoodfoodguide.co.uk

e&o

Style, glamour and global flavours
14 Blenheim Crescent, Notting Hill, W11 1NN
Tel no: (020) 7229 5454
www.rickerrestaurants.com
⊖ Ladbroke Grove, map 4
Pan-Asian | £34
Cooking score: 3

As hip as ever, this pulsating Notting Hill honeypot still attracts buzzing hordes intent on serious socialising and intermittent grazing from an ever-dependable pan-Asian menu. As a long-serving member of Will Ricker's fusion empire, it ditches conventional courses in favour of fashionable 'eastern and oriental' mini-plates designed for sharing. The menu is sliced and diced into trendy categories, from soups, sushi and dim sum (crispy pork belly with black vinegar) to tempura, BBQs and salads (wing bean and green papaya with peanut brittle). Also expect curries, specials (rack of ribs with black pepper) and a hotchpotch of east-west desserts from gooey chocolate pud to black sesame mochi with aduki beans. Sexy cocktails suit the occasion, and the globetrotting wine list struts its stuff from £16 (£4 a glass).
Chef/s: Simon Treadway. **Open:** all week L 12.15 to 3 (12.30 to 4 Sat and Sun), D 6.15 to 11 (10.30 Sun). **Closed:** 25 and 26 Dec, 1 Jan, Aug bank hol. **Meals:** alc (main courses £10 to £28). Set L £19. **Service:** 12.5% (optional). **Details:** Cards accepted. 84 seats. 24 seats outside. Separate bar. Music. Children allowed.

The Ealing Park Tavern

Ramshackle charmer of a pub
222 South Ealing Road, Ealing, W5 4RL
Tel no: (020) 8758 1879
www.ealingparktavern.com
⊖ South Ealing, Northfields, map 1
Modern European | £27
Cooking score: 1

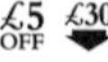

This ramshackle watering hole outstrips many of its boozy competitors, mainly because the kitchen continues to deliver simple, seasonal

and extremely reasonable food. Sit in the pared-down, panelled dining room and enjoy the likes of maiale tonnato (a porcine take on the old 'vitello' classic) or a zesty seasonal dish of leg of lamb (served pink) with spring vegetables and mint oil. To finish, lemongrass pannacotta with pineapple sorbet and strawberries is a delight. The pithy wine list starts at £15.50.

Chef/s: Aaron Craze. **Open:** Mon to Fri 12 to 3, D 6 to 10, Sat and Sun 12 to 10 (9 Sun). **Closed:** 25 and 26 Dec. **Meals:** alc (main courses £12 to £19). **Service:** 12.5% (optional). **Details:** Cards accepted. 70 seats. 80 seats outside. Separate bar. Wheelchair access. Music. Children allowed.

ALSO RECOMMENDED

▲ Ebury Restaurant & Wine Bar

139 Ebury Street, Belgravia, SW1W 9QU
Tel no: (020) 7730 5447
www.eburywinebar.co.uk
⊖ Victoria, map 3
Modern European £5 OFF

Established in 1959, this Belgravia bolt-hole still maintains its reputation with a menu that keeps pace in modern style with smoked haddock and quail 'Scotch egg' with Mediterranean vegetable compote (£7.95) and roast Barbary duck breast with confit duck pithiviers and mushroom duxelle (£17.50). To finish, there might be pineapple tarte Tatin with pineapple sorbet. A pedigree wine list helps to explain the enduring reputation; its thoroughbred selection (from £15.50) includes some 20 available by the glass (from £3). Open all week.

L'Etranger

A chic Franco-Japanese marriage
36 Gloucester Road, South Kensington, SW7 4QT
Tel no: (020) 7584 1118
www.etranger.co.uk
⊖ Gloucester Road, South Kensington, map 3
Modern French | £46
Cooking score: 4

£5 OFF

Pan-fried monkfish with razor clam, shichimi pepper and fennel carpaccio gives a clue to the Franco-Japanese culinary marriage on show at this chic, lilac-hued Kensington restaurant. Chef Jerome Tauvron's caramelised black cod with miso is on everyone's lips, but his oriental forays could also turn up grilled quail with rocket and soba rolls as well as scallop tartare with karasumi and black truffles. Steaks and sushi are comfortable bedfellows on the menu, although the beef is often 9th-grade Wagyu and the raw fish might include gold-standard maguro tuna. There are conventional modern Gallic outings too – perhaps cherry-smoked squab with foie gras sauce and celeriac, followed by Euro-accented desserts including a signature passion-fruit soufflé with blackcurrant jelly. It's overtly flashy stuff, with 'timely service' and the bonus of a staggeringly voluminous wine list offering a discounted selection at lunchtime. Full-on prices start at £22, but you'll need to invest considerably more for a taste of the pedigree Burgundies, Bordeaux, rare Sassicaias and grandees from the Napa Valley. Be warned: if you hear a strange voice in the toilets, it's probably a recording of Albert Camus reading from his novel *L'Etranger*!

Chef/s: Jerome Tauvron. **Open:** all week L 12 to 3, D 6 to 11 (11.30 Fri and Sat, 10 Sun). **Closed:** 26 and 27 Dec. **Meals:** alc (main courses £13 to £65). Set L £21 (2 courses) to £24. Sun L £24. **Service:** 12.5% (optional). **Details:** Cards accepted. 64 seats. Music. Children allowed.

Fifth Floor

Foodie heaven
Harvey Nichols, 109-125 Knightsbridge, Knightsbridge, SW1X 7RJ
Tel no: (020) 7235 5250
www.harveynichols.com
⊖ Knightsbridge, map 4
Modern European | £40
Cooking score: 3

The top-floor restaurant at Harvey Nicks has long been a draw for its successively elegant design schemes and brisk modern cooking. With the Foodmarket only yards away, it isn't surprising that the 'market menu' usually impresses, even in winter. Otherwise, the kitchen remit spreads over the modern European repertoire, to bring in pot-roasted smoked squab with celeriac and Granny Smith, perhaps followed by roasted halibut with buttered leeks, pistachios and raisins, with a wodge of chocolate truffle cake and clementine sorbet to finish. The encyclopaedic wine list reflects the quality of the wine shop on the same floor. Those on a budget might care to look no further than the house-brand selections, which include good crisp Bordeaux Sauvignon and Fiano from Campania, a Corbières rosé and Mendoza Malbec. Prices open at £22.50.

Chef/s: Jonas Karlsson. **Open:** all week L 12 to 3.30 (4 Fri to Sun), Mon to Sat D 6 to 11. **Closed:** 25 Dec. **Meals:** alc (main courses £17 to £27). Set L £19.50 (2 courses) to £24.50. Set D £24.50 (2 courses) to £29.50. Sun L £19.50 (2 courses) to £24.50. **Service:** 12.5% (optional). **Details:** Cards accepted. 80 seats. 26 seats outside. Separate bar. Wheelchair access. Music. Children allowed. Car parking.

Also Recommended

Also recommended entries are not scored but we think they are worth a visit.

ALSO RECOMMENDED

▲ First Floor

186 Portobello Road, Notting Hill, W11 1LA
Tel no: (020) 7243 0072
www.firstfloorportobello.co.uk
⊖ Ladbroke Grove, map 4
Modern European

The ground floor of this converted Victorian pub consists of a lived-in bar with easy chairs, while the First Floor aspires to more sophistication with its lavish décor and reasonably priced, Med-influenced cooking. Fixed-prices menus are good value, but look to the carte for wild mushroom fricassee on bruschetta (£8.75), roast pork belly with red cabbage and Calvados or fillet of sea bream on saffron mash with salsa (£19.50). For afters, perhaps dark and white chocolate mousse. Wines from £15. Closed Mon L.

The Gate

Vibrant veggie favourite
51 Queen Caroline Street, Hammersmith, W6 9QL
Tel no: (020) 8748 6932
www.thegaterestaurants.com
⊖ Hammersmith, map 1
Vegetarian | £25
Cooking score: 2

Originally a church and later a studio belonging to artist and engraver Sir Frank Brangwyn, these sparse, lofty premises have been home to the Gate since 1989. Veggie food is given a global shake-up here, with lots of Middle Eastern and Asian-nuanced flavours reflecting owner Michael Daniel's childhood memories – say aubergine pakoras with smoked chilli jam, char-grilled haloumi kebabs with chickpea salsa or winter vegetable tagine with dates and pickled lemon. The kitchen also looks to the Med for inspiration, knocking out generous plates of ricotta tortellini and carciofini (globe artichokes with polenta and sauce vierge). For afters, try the left-field pineapple and chilli crumble. House wine is £15.50, and organic wines are in plentiful supply.

Chef/s: Mariusz Wegrodzki. **Open:** Mon to Fri L 12 to 2.30, Mon to Sat D 6 to 10.30 (11 Sat). **Closed:** Sun, bank hols. **Meals:** alc (main courses £11 to £16). Set L £10 (2 courses). Set D £24. **Service:** 12.5% (optional). **Details:** Cards accepted. 60 seats. 30 seats outside. Music. Children allowed.

Geales

Much more than a chippy
2 Farmer Street, Notting Hill, W8 7SN
Tel no: (020) 7727 7528
www.geales.com
⊖ Notting Hill Gate, map 4
Seafood | £26
Cooking score: 1

Established in 1939, this legendary fish and chip shop was taken over by Mark Fuller in 2007 and he has recently opened a second outlet on Chelsea Green. The venerable original continues to satisfy the regulars, who hold court at tables covered with nostalgic black-and-white check cloths. Of course, there is much more on offer than 'posh' fish and chips, with classic fish pie and lobster spaghetti with tomato and basil appearing alongside steaks for non-fish eaters. Wines from £15.50.
Chef/s: Ollie Burges. **Open:** Tue to Sun L 12 to 2.30 (5 Sat and Sun), all week D 6 to 10.30 (5 to 10.30 Sat, 5 to 9.30 Sun). **Closed:** 25 to 27 Dec. **Meals:** alc (main courses £8 to £30). Set L £9.95 (2 courses). **Service:** 12.5% (optional). **Details:** Cards accepted. 75 seats. 16 seats outside. Music. Children allowed.

Gordon Ramsay

A world-class restaurant experience
68-69 Royal Hospital Road, Chelsea, SW3 4HP
Tel no: (020) 7352 4441
www.gordonramsay.com
⊖ Sloane Square, map 3
Modern French | £90
Cooking score: 9

'I now understand the difference between good food and sublime food', confessed one convert to the Gordon Ramsay way of doing things. Ramsay's Chelsea flagship has always prided itself on delivering breathtaking culinary excellence – even if the TV firebrand is rarely to be seen these days. Luckily he has a supreme lieutenant in the shape of head chef Clare Smyth, who can now do 'GR' better than the man himself, by all accounts. She certainly knows how to invoke the seasons: just consider a tiny consommé containing spring vegetables in an intense, Japanese-style broth, plus a nugget of velvety foie gras on toast to remind you exactly where you are; or a regal, buttery dish of sublime line-caught turbot wrapped in slivers of Welsh asparagus with meaty morels and all-pervasive notes of wild garlic; or even a gorgeous pre-dessert of sweet gariguette strawberries served as part of an elaborate Eton mess. There are other, more modish sensations too – from a picture-pretty, Asian-toned salad of Szechuan pork with tiger prawns and a mélange of char-grilled, pickled and marinated vegetables to three 'divine' scallops, each with a tiny topping (including a perfect, almost surreal quail's egg) on a 'swirl of molten green spring'. The Hospital Road kitchen also parades its big-statement dishes to rapturous applause: the ever-present ravioli of lobster, langoustine and salmon; the sautéed foie gras with roasted veal sweetbreads; the marinated pineapple 'ravioli' filled with mango and kiwi ('very fresh, very ripe, very delicate'). Many of these creations have become comfortingly familiar over the years, and even Ramsay's nod to weird gastro-science in the form of a dry-ice dazzler revealing white chocolate balls filled with strawberry ice cream is starting to look rather too obvious. And there's the rub: London's gastronomic landscape is changing fast and the pressure to keep ahead of the game is immense. What Ramsay delivers is undoubtedly a world-class restaurant experience, but its silky-smooth excellence can sometimes lack that extra gustatory edge and thrill factor. Mind you, it hardly seems to matter when the happy throngs are swept along by maître d' Jean-Claude Breton's gleefully persuasive tones and the attentions of his brilliantly orchestrated staff. They certainly know how to put on the style here, handling every detail with consummate panache. Needless to say, this full-on GR experience comes at 'special occasion' prices – especially if you commit to the awe-inspiring wine list in all its vintage glory. But ask for guidance and you won't be disappointed; there are enough treasures here to suit ample and penny-pinched wallets alike. House selections start at £24 (£6 a glass).

Chef/s: Clare Smyth. **Open:** Mon to Fri L 12 to 2.30, D 6.30 to 11. **Closed:** Sat, Sun. **Meals:** Set L £45. Set D £90. Tasting menu £120 (7 courses). **Service:** 12.5% (optional). **Details:** Cards accepted. 45 seats. Separate bar. No music. No mobile phones. Children allowed.

Haandi

Swish surrounds and exemplary food
136 Brompton Road, Knightsbridge, SW3 1HY
Tel no: (020) 7823 7373
www.haandi-restaurants.com
⊖ Knightsbridge, map 4
Indian | £30
Cooking score: 4
£5 OFF **V**

First of all, take note: this swanky Knightsbridge Indian has two separate entrances – one on Brompton Road, the other on nearby Cheval Place. Either way, the interior promises vibrant exoticism, with no stinting on the showy design gestures. You can also pick a ringside seat by the open kitchen and watch the chefs as they skewer tandoori meats, flip breads and stir the wide-bellied 'haandi' pots that give the place its name. This is a London outpost of the Nairobi-based restaurant group, although the menu parades exemplary dishes from the 'North Indian Frontier' – top-drawer grills and kebabs, chilli fish, saffron-hued chicken korma, rogan josh and a legendary egg curry. It's also worth taking a trek around the Subcontinent for dahi pakori and other Mumbai street snacks, textbook Goan vindaloo and Kashmiri dum aloo (baked potatoes with cashews, curd cheese and sultanas). To finish, choose rich carrot halwa or palate-cleansing mango kulfi. House wine is £18.50. There's a second branch at 301-303 Hale Lane, Edgware; tel (020) 8905 4433.

Chef/s: Ratan Singh. **Open:** all week L 12 to 3, D 5.30 to 11. **Closed:** 25 Dec. **Meals:** alc (main courses £7 to £16). Set L £11.95 (2 courses) to £14.95. **Service:** 12.5% (optional). **Details:** Cards accepted. 65 seats. Separate bar. Music. Children allowed.

The Harwood Arms

Remarkable British victuals
Walham Grove, Fulham, SW6 1QP
Tel no: (020) 7386 1847
www.harwoodarms.com
⊖ Fulham Broadway, map 3
British | £30
Cooking score: 5

The work of a dream team including Brett Graham from the Ledbury in Notting Hill and Mike Robinson of the Pot Kiln in Berkshire (see entries), the Harwood Arms' strapline is 'where the country comes to town'. Chef Barry Fitzgerald's cooking is true to that vision, offering plentiful rustic ingredients and traditional flavours without ever being predictable. Grilled salted ox tongue with a turnip and mustard croquette, 'bread and butter' pickles and dandelion, or 'sensational' poached salmon and cucumber sandwiches on rye and gin jelly are typical of the patriotic yet inventive style. Elsewhere a gut-busting dish of beef cheeks and Hereford snails braised in ale is served with smoked bone marrow on toast and parsley salad, while the coastal haul might yield brill with mussels and oatmeal fritters and seaweed butter. Readers also approve of 'good game in London' – perhaps packed into a pie alongside Somerset cider jelly, marinated prunes, raw celeriac and bitter leaves. Doughnuts are a popular finale – 'ridiculously good' cinnamon ones with lemon curd or the 'decadent' rhubarb variety with soured cream and ginger sugar. Drink Vaux ales or something from the serious wine list; bottles start at £15.50.

Chef/s: Barry Fitzgerald. **Open:** Tue to Sun L 12 to 3 (12.30 to 4 Sun), all week D 6.30 to 9.30 (7 to 9 Sun). **Closed:** 24 to 27 Dec, 1 Jan. **Meals:** alc (main courses £16 to £18). **Service:** 12.5% (optional). **Details:** Cards accepted. 40 seats. Separate bar. Music. Children allowed.

NEW ENTRY

The Havelock Tavern

Bona fide pub with appealing food
57 Masbro Road, Shepherd's Bush, W14 0LS
Tel no: (020) 7603 5374
www.havelocktavern.com
⊖ Shepherd's Bush, Olympia, map 1
Modern British | £25
Cooking score: 2

No bookings, no fuss, no tablecloths – the Havelock Tavern goes about its business as a bone fide pub, without the self-congratulatory posturing of some West London hostelries. Staff are 'super-helpful' and the kitchen keeps up as the crowds pour in, delivering a sharp daily menu of appealing dishes culled from the current 'gastro' repertoire. Bread is home-baked stuff and fish is always a good call – perhaps a slab of succulent organic salmon with piquant tapenade, sautéed ratte potatoes and juicy peperonata, or pollack fillet with pea purée and braised cherry tomatoes. Otherwise, expect anything from Thai pork meatballs to salt beef stovies with spring greens, fried egg and mustard sauce. Finish with cheeses or carrot cake and poached pears. Gluggable wines from £14.95.

Chef/s: James Howarth. **Open:** all week L 12.30 to 2.30 (3 Sun), D 7 to 10 (9.30 Sun). **Closed:** 25 and 26 Dec. **Meals:** alc (£9 to £14). Sun L £14. **Service:** not inc. **Details:** Cards accepted. 82 seats. 32 seats outside. No music. Wheelchair access. Children allowed.

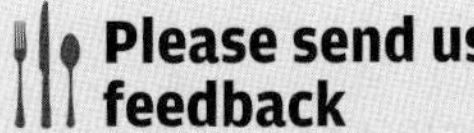

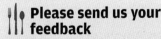

Please send us your feedback

To register your opinion about any restaurant listed in the Guide, or a new restaurant that you wish to bring to our attention, please visit the web address at the bottom of the page. Your feedback informs the content of the book and will be used to compile next year's reviews.

Hereford Road

Earthy British heritage cooking
3 Hereford Road, Notting Hill, W2 4AB
Tel no: (020) 7727 1144
www.herefordroad.org
⊖ Bayswater, map 4
British | £25
Cooking score: 4

The former Victorian butcher's shop with its simple black awning is now a sleek modern eatery with an open-plan kitchen and a positive, relaxed vibe. Westbourne Grove locals keep the place buzzing as the kitchen turns out a pretension-free version of earthy British heritage cooking in the St John mode (see entry). Start with a salad of lamb's sweetbreads and tongue with green beans and mint, or textbook potted crab, before pondering a main-course choice that takes in hake with cauliflower and capers, or a whole braised lamb shoulder with carrots and pearl barley, to feed three or even four. Marmalade and whisky ice cream or poached pear with meringue and cream should round things off satisfyingly. The short wine list opens at £18 (£3.50 a glass.)

Chef/s: Tom Pemberton. **Open:** all week L 12 to 3 (4 Sun), D 6 to 10.30 (10 Sun). **Closed:** 25 Dec to 2 Jan, 27 to 29 Aug. **Meals:** alc (main courses from £10 to £15). Set L £13 (2 courses) to £15.50. **Service:** not inc. **Details:** Cards accepted. 66 seats. 6 seats outside. No music. Wheelchair access. Children allowed.

Hunan

Chinese regional surprises
51 Pimlico Road, Chelsea, SW1W 8NE
Tel no: (020) 7730 5712
www.hunanlondon.com
⊖ Sloane Square, map 3
Chinese | £40
Cooking score: 3

The deal at this modestly appointed Pimlico Chinese is to go with the flow and put yourself in the hands of chef/proprietor Mr Peng and his son. There's no conventional menu; instead, the idea is to discuss your preferences, pitch your budget and wait to be surprised. What follows is a 'leave it to us' feast of up to 18 tapas-style dishes inspired by China's diverse regional cuisines, with minimal intervention from bulky noodles and rice. Expect bold flavours and contrasts, spice, intensity and all manner of culinary techniques deployed with dexterity. A little helping of steamed cod's roe with preserved vegetables is one possible palate sharpener, but the kitchen might also trundle out plates of marinated surf clam with moss hair, cold soy-braised duck or pickled bamboo with frogs' legs, plus herbal broths and some curious sweet finales. An impressive, well-informed wine and saké list kicks off at £16.

Chef/s: Michael Peng. **Open:** Mon to Sat L 12.30 to 2.30, D 6.30 to 11. **Closed:** Sun, 2 weeks from 24 Dec, bank hols. **Meals:** Set L £28.80. Set D £39.80. **Service:** 12.5% (optional). **Details:** Cards accepted. 48 seats. No music. Children allowed.

Il Convivio

Sleek Italian with first-class ingredients
143 Ebury Street, Chelsea, SW1W 9QN
Tel no: (020) 7730 4099
www.ilconvivio.co.uk
⊖ Victoria, Sloane Square, map 3
Italian | £39
Cooking score: 2

£5 OFF

Il Convivio continues to enjoy faithful support among the denizens of Belgravia for its blend of sleek modernity and vivid contemporary cooking. Starters such as beef carpaccio with celery and basil-infused virgin olive oil rely heavily on assemblies, but such a direct and easy appeal rests on first-class materials. The aim is a liaison between traditional and modern – so pasta dishes run to a stunning black spaghetti with lobster and spring onions, and mains deliver roasted rack of lamb with fine beans and a chestnut and stracchino cheese crêpe. Finish with white espresso ice cream. Italian wines from £14.

Chef/s: Jonathan Lees. **Open:** Mon to Sat L 12 to 3, D 7 to 10.30. **Closed:** Sun, 2 weeks from 25 Dec, bank hols. **Meals:** alc (main courses £13 to £29). Set L £17.50 (2 courses). Set D £23.50 (2 courses). **Service:** 12.5% (optional). **Details:** Cards accepted. 65 seats. Separate bar. Music. Children allowed.

Indian Zing

Cool venue, exciting food
236 King Street, Hammersmith, W6 0RF
Tel no: (020) 8748 5959
www.indianzing.co.uk
⊖ Ravenscourt Park, map 1
Indian | £27
Cooking score: 4

Indian cooking in Britain is on an exciting trajectory these days, leaving behind the old curry-house formula in favour of greater culinary integrity, regional definition and a range of less familiar ingredients. Thus Indian Zing, Manoj Vasaikar's neighbourhood venue in Hammersmith. The dining room is suave and relaxing, with smartly dressed tables and some Indian-themed pictures and artefacts, but it's what's on the menus that will make you sit up and take notice. Expect sharply delineated flavours and spices in dishes such as pea and potato pattie dressed in yoghurt, tamarind and sprouted beans, Khyber Pass lamb shank in poppy seeds, ginger and spices, and fish shirale (an assortment of seafood cooked in coconut milk with tomato and onion masala). Side dishes should not be missed, and there's gulab jamun with vanilla ice cream to finish. A carefully chosen wine list opens with house French from £16.

Chef/s: Manoj Vasaikar. **Open:** all week L 12 to 3 (1 to 4 Sun), D 6 to 11 (10 Sun). **Meals:** alc (main courses £9 to £19). Set L £12 (2 courses) to £15. **Service:** 12.5% (optional). **Details:** Cards accepted. 52 seats. 32 seats outside. No mobile phones. Wheelchair access. Music.

Kensington Place

Still rolling along
201-209 Kensington Church Street, Notting Hill, W8 7LX
Tel no: (020) 7727 3184
www.kensingtonplace-restaurant.co.uk
⊖ Notting Hill Gate, map 4
Modern British | £25
new chef

Back in the late 80s, this cavernous, glass-fronted big-hitter blazed a trail ahead of London's booming brasserie revolution, and it just keeps rolling along. Even Rowley Leigh's departure to Le Café Anglais (see entry) a few years back didn't knock it off course, although the kitchen now plots a less radical path through the gritty urban repertoire. There are still plenty of takers for old faithfuls such as chicken Caesar salad, Hereford flat-iron steak with triple-cooked chips, or rice pudding with Agen prunes, but going off-piste also pays generous dividends. New chef Daniel Loftin arrived just as we went to press, too late for us to receive any feedback, so reports are particularly welcome. Do note that the din in the echoey room can be deafening at peak times, but the serious-minded, cosmopolitan wine list should provide some alcoholic distraction. Choice is impeccable and mark-ups are very friendly, with prices starting at £18.95 (£4.95 a glass).
Chef/s: Daniel Loftin. **Open:** all week L 12 to 3, D 6.30 to 10.30. **Closed:** 26 Dec. **Meals:** alc (main courses £11 to £22). Set L and early D £16.50 (2 courses) to £19.50. **Service:** 12.5% (optional). **Details:** Cards accepted. 120 seats. Separate bar. Wheelchair access. Music. Children allowed.

Visit us Online
To find out more about *The Good Food Guide*, please visit www.thegoodfoodguide.co.uk

ALSO RECOMMENDED

▲ Kiraku

8 Station Parade, Uxbridge Road, Ealing, W5 3LD
Tel no: (020) 8992 2848
www.kiraku.co.uk
⊖ Ealing Common, map 1
Japanese

This terrific Japanese restaurant is opposite Ealing Common tube, which is a bonus. It's best to book as it is firmly on the Japanese community radar. One of many set lunch deals makes a good introduction, perhaps a trio of chef's sashimi – blisteringly fresh, thick slices of salmon, tuna, mackerel – with a generous serving of vegetable and prawn tempura ('oh-so-light batter'), a little salad, a miniature dish of green beans with peanut sauce, a bowl of fresh fruit, miso soup and rice, all for £17.50. Drink Kirin or Sapporo beer, £3.70. Closed Mon.

Kitchen W8

High-gloss, with full-on luxury food
11 Abingdon Road, Kensington, W8 6AH
Tel no: (020) 7937 0120
www.kitchenw8.com
⊖ High Street Kensington, map 4
Modern European | £36
Cooking score: 5

The cute name gives nothing away, but the fact that this glossy and eminently soothing Kensington destination is backed by the dream team of stellar chef Philip Howard and seasoned restaurateur Rebecca Mascarenhas almost guarantees a glitzy profile. Inside, it's predictably cool, chic, well-to-do and impeccably dressed – even if the surroundings are a tad stark, with lavish tablecloths and round mirrors interrupting the muted colour schemes. As for the food, full-on European luxury sets the tone, although the kitchen tempers any excesses with some fine-tuned seasonal Britishness – as in a signature starter of thinly sliced smoked eel with grilled mackerel, sweet mustard and 'ice lettuce' or a dish of crispy pork belly and slow-cooked cheek with crushed turnip and pickled cabbage. Elsewhere, a plump chicken and mushroom raviolo comes shrouded in a velouté of winter truffles with melted onions, while rump of veal might appear in company with caramelised cauliflower, roast salsify and Parmesan. Meals end impressively with a fine cheeseboard and niftily crafted desserts such as spiced financier with roasted pear, salt caramel and beurre noisette. Excellent sourdough bread is a bonus, set lunches are fine value (if a shade 'mean') and the attractive international wine list is a thoughtful match for the food; prices start at £15.95 (£4 a glass).

Chef/s: Mark Kempson. **Open:** all week L 12 to 2.30 (12.30 to 3 Sun), D 6 to 10.30 (6.30 to 9.30 Sun). **Closed:** 25 and 26 Dec, bank hols. **Meals:** alc (main courses £18 to £22). Set L £17.50 (2 courses) to £19.50. Set D £21.50 (2 courses) to £24.50. Sun L £25. **Service:** 12.5% (optional). **Details:** Cards accepted. 80 seats. No music. Wheelchair access. Children allowed.

NEW ENTRY

Koffmann's

The old master is back
The Berkeley, Wilton Place, Belgravia, SW1X 7RL
Tel no: (020) 7235 1010
www.the-berkeley.co.uk
⊖ Knightsbridge, Hyde Park Corner, map 4
French | £46
Cooking score: 5

'Welcome back, indeed, Monsieur Pierre', chimed a disciple, holding back the 'tears of joy' after a visit to Koffmann's. Having tested the water with a sell-out pop-up in Selfridges, the old master has returned with a vengeance, working his magic in the premises formerly occupied by the Boxwood Café. The man himself has talked a lot about returning to his Gascon roots and creating a mood of 'convivial bonhomie' here, although some have found the basement room a touch formal, with its muted lighting and low-key design. That said, there's nothing rarefied about the food, and Koffmann puts down a marker from the very start, with an amuse-bouche based on his fabled stuffed pig's trotter: its mix of crunchy skin, flaked meat and rémoulade is a 'masterclass in tastes and textures'. Other delights follow in measured succession: a sensational cassolette of snails and morels with parsley foam, wondrous soupe de poissons, Provençal rump of lamb with black olives ('never bettered') and show-stopping hare royale – fork-tender, braised meat with foie gras, dumplings and carrots in a deep, dark reduction. To conclude, oeufs à la neige was a rare treat for one who adores this classic dessert, although PK's intense pistachio soufflé with pistachio ice cream also has the power to thrill. Aside from the odd quibble about neglectful service, Koffmann's is a triumph of soothing generosity – especially as the experience is bolstered by a battalion of bold, earthy French regional wines (from £22).

Chef/s: Pierre Koffmann. **Open:** all week L 12 to 2.30 (3 Sat and Sun), D 6 to 10.30 (11 Thur to Sat). **Meals:** alc (main courses £20 to £39). Set L £21.50 (2 courses) to £25.50. Sun L £22.50 (2 courses) to £26. **Service:** 12.5% (optional). **Details:** Cards accepted. 120 seats. Separate bar. Music. Children allowed.

Launceston Place

Urbane contemporary cuisine
1a Launceston Place, South Kensington, W8 5RL
Tel no: (020) 7937 6912
www.launcestonplace-restaurant.co.uk
⊖ Gloucester Road, map 3
Modern British | £45
Cooking score: 4

One of the brighter stars in the D&D London constellation, Launceston Place is a classy customer, sleekly done out with charcoal-grey walls, moody lighting and inter-connected dining areas. Chef Tristan Welch sends out upscale, urbane renditions of contemporary British cuisine with an eye for dramatic detail, from roasted scallops with aromatic herbs presented on a wooden block surrounded by a ring of crushed shell, or pork cooked over 'cider wood' with hazelnut mash and shiny beads of cider jelly 'like golden caviar' to a dessert of baked egg custard with rhubarb and crumble emblazoned with a sweetshop bonanza of vibrant embellishments. The terrific set lunch also delivers the goods, judging by much-lauded standouts such as beef, beetroot and wild garlic risotto ('a riot of colour'). Meanwhile, those sampling the tasting menu in the 'chef's office' might be treated to sublime offerings including 'incredible' duck egg on toast with earthy Somerset truffle. Service is professional and gently paced, and the upper-crust wine list heads skywards from £20.

Chef/s: Tristan Welch. **Open:** all week L 12 to 2.30 (3 Sun), D 6 to 10 (6.30 to 9.30 Sun). **Closed:** 25 to 30 Dec, bank hols. **Meals:** Set L £22. Set D £45. Sun L £26. Tasting menu £60. **Service:** 12.5% (optional). **Details:** Cards accepted. 60 seats. Separate bar. Wheelchair access. Music. Children allowed.

The Ledbury

Astonishing food from an Aussie star
127 Ledbury Road, Notting Hill, W11 2AQ
Tel no: (020) 7792 9090
www.theledbury.com
⊖ Notting Hill Gate, Westbourne Park, map 4
Modern French | £75
Cooking score: 8
V

At first glance the Ledbury looks as suave and moneyed as the neighbourhood it serves, but there's more to this Notting Hill icon than icy, white-walled chic and leather chairs. Above all, the place exudes tangible domestic warmth and 'gracious hospitality', buoyed up by confident staff who know how do their job without drifting into servile automaton mode. It also sports a lovely city-meets-country terrace for those cherished fine days. By contrast, Brett Graham blazes away with vigour, authority and a fair degree of audacity in the kitchen, matching theatrical pizzazz and brio with comforting earthy ways, a fondness for baking and a seemingly inexhaustible supply of ideas. To start, a clutch of canapés (perhaps deep-fried quails' eggs with shaved truffle and chestnut purée) and a regularly replenished assortment of top-drawer breads set the mood before the serious work begins. Graham's red-hot signature dishes continue to thrill, although they are always in a state of flux: his flame-grilled mackerel with avocado, Celtic mustard and shiso could be re-cast with Tokyo turnips and herring roe, while a starry plate of Sika deer loin baked in Douglas Fir might appear with pumpkin purée, venison sausage, pickled walnuts, dried chicory and chanterelles, or with beetroot, smoked bone marrow and Pinot lees. 'Incredible flavours', textures, contrasts and high drama point up everything from a delectable starter of scallop ceviche, sliced kohlrabi and seaweed spiked with frozen horseradish to a show-stopping assemblage of succulent pigeon breast with Jerusalem artichoke purée, onion tart and a mysterious glass dome concealing the legs laid over smoking fennel twigs. When it comes to dessert, the sweet golden prettiness of a caramelised banana galette with salted caramel, passion fruit and peanut oil parfait is hard to trump, and the overall feelgood factor is sky-high: 'The cold outside could do nothing to dispel my utter contentment', noted one winter visitor. There is also plenty to content the soul and the palate when it comes to the wine list: a page of splendid tipples by the glass heralds a glorious assortment of bottles that goes way beyond snob-value clarets – check out the little-known German whites, fantastic Californian reds et al. Prices from £25.

Chef/s: Brett Graham. **Open:** Tue to Sun L 12 to 2.30, all week D 6.30 to 10.30 (7 to 10 Sun). **Closed:** 27 to 29 Aug, 24 to 27 Dec. **Meals:** alc (main courses £26 to £28). Set L £27.50 (2 courses) to £33.50. Set D £75. Tasting menu £95. Sun L £40. **Service:** 12.5% (optional). **Details:** Cards accepted. 62 seats. 24 seats outside. No music. No mobile phones. Wheelchair access. Children allowed.

ALSO RECOMMENDED

▲ Madsen

20 Old Brompton Road, South Kensington, SW7 3DL
Tel no: (020) 7225 2772
www.madsenrestaurant.com
⊖ South Kensington, map 3
Scandinavian

'The English in our group very much enjoyed the "exotic" Scandinavian food,' noted a Norwegian reporter, who was delighted to find pancakes with cloudberries that reminded him of home. This likeable South Kensington eatery fulfills everyone's expectations of a Nordic restaurant – 'clear design, warm welcome and tasty, simple food'. Lunchtime centres on 'smushi', small versions of the traditional Danish open sandwich, with various toppings (from £3.25), while dinner brings 'particularly good' gravlax and frikadeller – Danish pork meatballs (£12.95). Wine from £19.50. Closed Sun D.

The Mall Tavern

Buzzing foodie hot spot
71-73 Palace Gardens Terrace, Notting Hill, W8 4RU
Tel no: (020) 7229 3374
www.themalltavern.com
⊖ Notting Hill Gate, High Street Kensington, map 4
British | £25
Cooking score: 3

With its good-time mix of buzz, bonhomie and fairly priced sustenance, the Mall Tavern has become something of a foodie hot spot. Things are kept simple: close-packed tables, butcher-stripe napkins, bone cutlery, tumblers. And there's nothing incidental on the menu, no after-thoughts – everything is geared towards satisfaction and fun. The 'cow pie' is a star turn ('dense, juicy and meltingly good'), but other hits have included 'thick-cut and delicious' salmon, smoked on the premises, served with a warm, generous bun of soda bread, and char-grilled sea bass fillet on a bed of crunchy, peppery fennel with an English heritage tomato salad. Chicken Kiev and the Arctic roll selection for dessert (including After Eight and muscavado) also get the vote. The global wine list includes a terrific selection by the glass or carafe, with bottles from £17.

Chef/s: Jesse Dunford Wood. **Open:** all week 12 to 10. **Closed:** 1 week Dec. **Meals:** alc (main courses £10 to £30). **Service:** 12.5% (optional). **Details:** Cards accepted. 100 seats. 20 seats outside. Separate bar. Music. Children allowed.

Manson

Metropolitan vibes, reassuring food
676 Fulham Road, Fulham, SW6 5SA
Tel no: (020) 7384 9559
www.mansonrestaurant.co.uk
⊖ Parsons Green, map 3
British | £30
Cooking score: 4

With its expanse of wood flooring, bare tables and neutral tones, Manson achieves a stylish informality, projecting itself as a smart-casual sort of place – although the noise levels generated by the well-heeled diners can reach fever pitch at times. There is, however, something reassuring about the simple, well-prepared food with its penchant for strong British flavours and keen eye for the seasons. Starters range from a well-reported cream of celeriac soup to a beautifully presented quail's egg wrapped in trout with lime and mayo. Main courses are often kept simple (game hotpot), with classic flavour combinations, as in a confit of lamb shoulder teamed with bubble and squeak, or rump of Welsh Black beef with shallot marmalade. Desserts are equally comforting, perhaps poached pear with vanilla cream or a chocolate tart, while the global wine list opens at £17.

Chef/s: Alan Stewart. **Open:** Mon to Sat 12 to 3 (10 to 4 Sat), D 6 to 10.30. Sun 12 to 6. **Closed:** 25 and 26 Dec. **Meals:** alc (main courses £15 to £21). Set L £13.50 (2 courses) to £20. Set D (6 to 7 Mon to Fri) £16.95 (2 courses) to £18.95. **Service:** 12.5%

(optional). **Details:** Cards accepted. 62 seats. 6 seats outside. Separate bar. Music. Children allowed.

Marcus Wareing at the Berkeley

Stunning show from a culinary alchemist
The Berkeley, Wilton Place, Belgravia, SW1X 7RL
Tel no: (020) 7235 1200
www.marcus-wareing.com
⊖ Hyde Park Corner, Knightsbridge, map 4
Modern European | £80
Cooking score: 8
V

One could just about see Marcus Wareing's self-named dining room at the Berkeley Hotel as a restaurant *du quartier*, a Knightsbridge bolt-hole for moneyed shoppers, and an unexpectedly intimate place for a hotel dining concession, but that would be to ignore its claims as one of the capital's top food destinations. The air of assured professionalism with which the place is run adds a lot to the experience and more than makes up for any faint air of anonymity the viewless room has during the day. The David Collins dark-toned design gives a more clubby look than urban minimalism's ubiquitous 'greige'. It's the kind of place that can fill with chatter and still not feel shouty – and there is much to chatter about, in terms of both the quantity and the astonishment level of the food. Within the context of today's exploratory, speculative approach, Wareing is very much ploughing his own furrow. Good ideas abound, and the menus evolve at their own pace. At their best, the dishes have that alchemical quality that produces happy discoveries all over the place when ingredients are combined; an exemplary opening dish from the spring carte paired a generous chunk of warm Scottish lobster with celery-like wild alexanders, 'hen of the woods' (a wavy-capped wild mushroom), sea kale and wild garlic, adding further spark with slivers of cherry tangerine and a ground-note of lime. Main courses have included best end of Cornish lamb, tender as Turkish delight, with aubergine and roasted garlic, served with a side dish of mini-falafels sitting in pink peppercorn yoghurt. Or how about venison, farro, monk's beard, borage, liquorice and lychee? Reporters quite consistently resent the restricted choice on the set lunch menu (two at each stage), especially when not all goes well. A spring dish of Cornish pollack with orecchiette pasta and preserved lemon offered (surely not?) drily overcooked fish, while nobody appears to have liked the autumn main course of unyielding veal tongue in onion consommé. Such lapses are rare, though, and so much else, from the sesame Melba toasts with aubergine and cumin dip to the Manhattan pre-dessert with its cherry jelly and bourbon foam, and the chocolates with enjoyably crazy fillings (liquorice and fennel, orange and rosemary), is stunning. Desserts to conjure with have included a rich peanut parfait with Tanariva chocolate and pungently smoked caramel sauce. A thoroughgoing comprehensiveness brings quality German and Austrian wines, as well as oodles of posh French gear, on to a majestically sweeping list. Prices open at £24, and disappear into the clouds.

Chef/s: Marcus Wareing. **Open:** Mon to Fri L 12 to 2.30, Mon to Sat D 6 to 11. **Closed:** Sun, 1 Jan. **Meals:** Set L £38. Set D £80. Tasting menu £85 (6 courses) to £120. **Service:** 12.5% (optional). **Details:** Cards accepted. 65 seats. No music. No mobile phones. Wheelchair access. Children allowed.

Notting Hill Brasserie

Highly valued local destination
92 Kensington Park Road, Notting Hill, W11 2PN
Tel no: (020) 7229 4481
www.nottinghillbrasserie.com
⊖ Notting Hill Gate, map 4
Modern European | £42
Cooking score: 4

This chic brasserie was created from a row of three Edwardian town houses. Inside, all is affluent and dressed-up, and remodelling to create a cocktail bar area has splendidly enhanced the lure of the series of interlinked dining rooms. There's no doubt it's an appealing place, and for sheer indulgence there are the likes of rillettes of organic salmon with caviar and blinis, or wild mushroom risotto with pan-fried foie gras and crisp chicken wings – though both dishes signal that prices are high here. However, flavours and timings are notably good: a meaty piece of cod served with artichoke purée, wild mushrooms, salsify and red wine sauce, or roast loin of veal with honey-glazed root vegetables, cep purée and Madeira sauce, say. Elsewhere, the regular fixed-price lunch menu reads quite straightforwardly, teaming sausage rolls with butternut squash, brown shrimps and watercress with pollack, and cocoa bean crème brûlée with coffee ice cream. Wines from £18.50.

Chef/s: Karl Burdock. **Open:** all week L 12 to 3 (4 Sun), D 7 to 11 (10 Sun). **Closed:** 28 to 30 Dec, 28 and 29 Aug. **Meals:** alc (main courses £19 to £39). Set L £15.50 (2 courses) to £19.50. Sun L £29.50 (2 courses) to £36.50. **Service:** 12.5% (optional). **Details:** Cards accepted. 90 seats. Separate bar. Music. Children allowed.

One-O-One

Top-end seafood cookery
Sheraton Park Tower, 101 Knightsbridge, Knightsbridge, SW1X 7RN
Tel no: (020) 7290 7101
www.oneoonerestaurant.com
⊖ Knightsbridge, map 4
Seafood | £55
Cooking score: 6

V

A default destination for those who like their seafood with an extra helping of Knightsbridge glamour, One-O-One sits comfortably on the ground floor of the Sheraton Park Tower Hotel (but with its own entrance) and is a showcase for Breton chef Pascal Proyart's precision-tuned, high-end fish cookery. Signature 'petits plats' attract those who like a spot of exquisite piscine grazing – perhaps griddled mackerel fillet with saffron rouille, red pepper bruschetta and fennel salad – but the full menu is an equally stunning prospect. Proyart is a brand ambassador for the Norwegian Seafood Council, which is why red king crab from the Barents Sea and farmed halibut appear regularly – the latter starring in a regal main course atop cuttlefish tagliatelle with cocoa beans in a wild garlic velouté. The range of seafood is also generous enough to accommodate a voguish Japanese take on yellowfin tuna (with tempura-battered soft-shell crab, wasabi sorbet and seaweed salad) as well as whole sea bass baked under a crust of Breton sea salt, served with Champagne and shellfish sauce and a dollop of mash incorporating strands of sea lettuce. Meanwhile, meat-eaters are offered the likes of organic Derbyshire beef fillet lyonnaise with Burgundy sauce, cheeses promise a tip-top selection of Anglo-European specimens, and sweeter treats could feature a wickedly trendy combo of white chocolate mousse with juniper berries, lemon sorbet and gin-and-tonic jelly. A wine list grouped by grape variety contains much to entice, but at unforgiving prices; bottles start at £28.

Chef/s: Pascal Proyart. **Open:** all week L 12 to 2.30 (12.30 Sat and Sun), D 6.30 to 10. **Closed:** 25 Dec. **Meals:** alc (main courses £28 to £39). Set L £17 (2 courses) to £37. Tasting menu £45 (5 courses) to £55. **Service:** not inc. **Details:** Cards accepted. 51 seats. Separate bar. No music. No mobile phones. Wheelchair access. Children allowed. Car parking.

Pétrus

Impressive Knightsbridge revival
1 Kinnerton Street, Knightsbridge, SW1X 8EA
Tel no: (020) 7592 1609
www.gordonramsay.com
⊖ Knightsbridge, map 4
Modern French | £60
Cooking score: 5

V

The reincarnation of Gordon Ramsay's Pétrus, round a Knightsbridge corner from its original manifestation at the Berkeley Hotel, opts for the same relatively low-key interior styling. Café-crème tones are given depth with some Pomerol-red, and the central glass-fronted wine-store is a focal point. Sean Burbidge offers a not overly complex but impressively precise rendition of modern French-influenced cooking. The lunch menu is a particularly good deal, as was attested by the reporter who progressed from shellfish linguine in lobster and tomato bisque to braised pork cheeks with romanesco, turnips and spiced Madeira, then ended by disappearing down a white chocolate cylinder with coffee and mascarpone ice cream. Dishes are carefully constructed of elements that build to harmonious counterpoints rather than embattled face-offs, so a game main course might offer roasted Highland partridge with creamed cabbage, pancetta and a sauce of prunes, while lemon sole arrives with creamed celeriac and clams in five-spice. Vegetarian menus are equally well-considered, embracing baby artichokes in truffled mayonnaise and butternut cannelloni with wild mushrooms, pine nuts and sage sauce. The fabulous wine list reaches back into the nineteenth century (the 1899 Latour is a snip at £12,500), but has plenty to suit everyday tastes too. Prices, though, are brisk to rapacious. Glasses start at £5.80.

Chef/s: Sean Burbidge. **Open:** Mon to Sat L 12 to 2.30, D 6.30 to 10.30. **Closed:** Sun. **Meals:** Set L £30 to £60. Set D £60. Tasting menu £70 (7 courses). **Service:** 12.5% (optional). **Details:** Cards accepted. 58 seats. No music. Wheelchair access. Children allowed. Car parking.

El Pirata Detapas

Neighbourhood tapas bar
115 Westbourne Grove, Notting Hill, W2 4UP
Tel no: (020) 7727 5000
www.elpiratadetapas.co.uk
⊖ Notting Hill Gate, Bayswater, map 4
Spanish | £22
Cooking score: 3

A sleek, clean-lined contemporary venue in trend-conscious Westbourne Grove is the setting for the cutting-edge take on tapas offered by the Pirata, whose more traditional elder brother is to be found in Mayfair. The menu runs a gamut from dead-straight Spanish nibbles such as Padrón peppers and boquerones to more speculative dishes such as pigeon with fig purée and red cabbage in red wine, or seared scallops with a roulade of Iberian charcuterie and artichokes. It succeeds thanks to quality raw materials and the agreeably relaxed surroundings. Finish with cuajada (set milk-curd) and blackberries, or vanilla ice cream with treacle-dark Pedro Ximenez sherry poured over it. The wine list is your chance to explore the Spanish regions, starting with Castilian house at £14.50.

Chef/s: Fabio Da Silva. **Open:** Mon to Fri L 12 to 3, D 6 to 11, Sat and Sun 12 to 11. **Closed:** 25 to 26 Dec, 28 and 29 Aug. **Meals:** alc (tapas £2 to £18). Set L £9.95. Tasting menu £21. Chef's menu £25. **Service:** 12.5% (optional). **Details:** Cards accepted. 88 seats. Wheelchair access. Music. Children allowed.

Popeseye

A red-blooded steak-fest
108 Blythe Road, Olympia, W14 0HD
Tel no: (020) 7610 4578
⊖ Olympia, map 1
Steaks | £20
Cooking score: 1

Hardcore carnivores step up to the plate for a 'steak-fest' at Ian Hutchinson's unadulterated, red-blooded eatery. Just three cuts of peerless, properly aged Aberdeen Angus beef – sirloin, fillet and popeseye (aka rump) – are cooked on an open grill and served with chips plus optional salad; all you need to decide is the weight and the degree of sanguinity. That's it, apart from farmhouse cheeses and a few homemade puds. Beefy clarets and New World reds are the tipples of choice, with prices from £13.45. Also at 277 Upper Richmond Road, Putney SW15 6SP; tel (020) 8788 7733.

Chef/s: Ian Hutchinson. **Open:** Mon to Sat D only 6.45 to 10. **Closed:** Sun, Christmas, New Year, bank hols. **Meals:** alc (steaks £11 to £55). **Service:** 12.5% (optional). **Details:** Cash only. 34 seats. Music. Children allowed.

Portobello Ristorante Pizzeria

Eat-me pizza for sharing
7 Ladbroke Road, Notting Hill, W11 3PA
Tel no: (020) 7221 1373
www.portobellolondon.co.uk
⊖ Notting Hill Gate, map 4
Italian | £35
Cooking score: 1

A well-travelled reporter reckoned that, when it's on song, the food here can outdo what they've eaten in Italy. In an atmosphere of invigorating commotion, the place deals in straightforward ristorante cooking, from aubergine parmigiana to charcoal-grilled salsiccia sausage with chilli-hot sauce, via an eat-me list of pizza variations, to be ordered by the whole or half-metre and shared (the pescatora mixed seafood option will take some resisting). Finish with torta cioccolato, or rather, finish with good strong coffee and a limoncello. Sicilian house wines are £15.95.

Chef/s: Franco Ferro. **Open:** all week L 12 to 3.30 (4 Sat and Sun), D 6 to 10.30 (11.30 Fri and Sat). **Closed:** 25 and 26 Dec. **Meals:** alc (main courses £9 to £24). Set L £12. **Service:** 12.5% (optional). **Details:** Cards accepted. 85 seats. 40 seats outside. Wheelchair access. Music. Children allowed.

The Princess Victoria

Big-hearted food and tremendous wines
217 Uxbridge Road, Shepherd's Bush, W12 9DH
Tel no: (020) 8749 5886
www.princessvictoria.co.uk
⊖ Shepherd's Bush Market, map 1
British | £27
Cooking score: 3

Built as a dodgy 'dram shop' in 1828, before graduating to hardcore gin palace, the Princess Victoria is now the sort of foodie boozer everyone wants on their doorstep. The booming, cavernous interior is testament to the florid architectural prowess of 'supreme artiste' William Mortimer Brutton, but most people are easily distracted by the food and drink on offer. Eat in the noisy bar or the smart dining room from a menu that peddles generous plates of cured fish and charcuterie, steaks, pasta and a metropolitan lucky dip ranging from roast cod with Puy lentils, mustard and bordelaise sauce to homemade beef and pepper sausages with devilled jus. Former partner/sommelier Matt Wilkin bequeathed a tremendous 300-bin wine list before he left the business, with a brilliant selection by the glass or carafe and a global range at eminently friendly prices (from £14.90). The Princess also has its own wine shop, plus a fairylit back garden hidden from traffic-rammed Uxbridge Road.

Chef/s: Matt Reuther. **Open:** all week 12 to 10.30 (12 to 9.30 Sun). **Closed:** 24 to 27 Dec. **Meals:** alc (main courses £10 to £18). Set L £12.50 (2 courses) to £15. **Service:** not inc. **Details:** Cards accepted. 120 seats. 25 seats outside. Separate bar. Music. Children allowed. Car parking.

Racine

Flying the flag for French food
239 Brompton Road, Knightsbridge, SW3 2EP
Tel no: (020) 7584 4477
www.racine-restaurant.com
⊖ Knightsbridge, South Kensington, map 3
French | £35
Cooking score: 4

For 10 years Racine has been flying the flag for deep-rooted bourgeois French food and has long been treasured as a jewel among the French community of South Kensington. With its palette of dark browns, mirror-lined walls and white-clad, close-packed tables, the setting is spot-on – it perfectly fits Henry Harris's archetypal brasserie cuisine. An affordable fixed-price menu deals in the likes of ballottine of rabbit with beetroot and horseradish, rare onglet and persillade of braised beef with mustard sauce, and poached pear with vanilla ice cream and caramel sauce. The carte furnishes soupe de poissons, calf's brains with black butter and capers, skate with brown shrimps, confit of duck with lentils, and, of course, filet au poivre. Staff are good at their job and the wine list is dominated by France, with an opening price of £20.

Chef/s: Henry Harris. **Open:** all week L 12 to 3 (3.30 Sun), D 6 to 10.30 (10 Sun). **Closed:** 25 Dec. **Meals:** alc (main courses £16 to £30). Set L and early D £15.50 (2 courses) to £17.75. Sun L £18 (2 courses) to £20. **Service:** 14.5% (optional). **Details:** Cards accepted. 60 seats. 4 seats outside. No music. Children allowed.

Rasoi

Intimate, high-end Indian flagship
10 Lincoln Street, Chelsea, SW3 2TS
Tel no: (020) 7225 1881
www.rasoirestaurant.co.uk
⊖ Sloane Square, map 3
Indian | £59
Cooking score: 5
V

Diners visiting Rasoi would be forgiven for thinking they're entering someone's smart London home, not a fine-dining restaurant. But from the moment you ring the doorbell of the swanky Chelsea town house, through to the cosy, flock-wallpapered living-room-cum-restaurant, the intimacy of Vineet Bhatia's flagship Indian puts it in a different stratosphere from the hurly-burly of your normal balti house. All the hallmarks of top-end cuisine are present and correct, including amuse-bouches that range from classic Indian (poppadoms with a shot of sweet pineapple soup) to classic European (a pre-dessert of berry pannacotta). Cooking makes gentle use of spice and incorporates classical and South-East Asian elements to fine effect. Dishes such as grilled wasabi lobster with a gutsy lobster and lentil soup and coconut rice owe as much to France as India, while a main of prawns poached in a lemongrass and chilli sauce with a creamy khichdi comes with a distinct tang of Thailand. Desserts rely more on western tradition – memorably the indulgent 'chocolate craving', which is essentially five desserts in one blockbuster option. The wine list starts at £25 and leans heavily on the Old World to offer successful pairings with spicy food, including a good selection by the glass.

Chef/s: Vineet Bhatia. **Open:** Mon to Fri and Sun L 12 to 2.30, all week D 6 to 10.45 (11 Sat, 10 Sun). **Closed:** 25 and 26 Dec, 1 Jan. **Meals:** alc (main courses £29 to £40). Set L £21 (2 courses) to £27. Set D £49 (2 courses) to £59. Sun L £21. Tasting menu £85 (7 courses). **Service:** 12.5% (optional). **Details:** Cards accepted. 55 seats. No music. Children allowed.

Restaurant Michael Nadra

New look Chiswick favourite
6-8 Elliott Road, Chiswick, W4 1PE
Tel no: (020) 8742 0766
www.restaurant-michaelnadra.co.uk
⊖ Turnham Green, map 1
Modern European | £33
Cooking score: 4

Since revamping this Chiswick site (formerly Fish Hook), chef Michael Nadra has transformed it into a first-class neighbourhood eatery. Kitted out with dark banquettes and slate flooring, it's a suitably understated showroom for Nadra's simple and elegant cooking, where clean flavours and accomplished technique never give way to overblown ego or unnecessary frills. On inspection, an eastern-inspired dish of soft-shell crab tempura with seared tuna and sushi rice was expertly balanced – more than can be said for the one let-down: a muddled main of Cornish monkfish with candied beetroots, roasted peppers, brown shrimp and a truffle and balsamic dressing that would have benefited from far fewer big flavours. However, a deep, sticky and generous tarte Tatin more than made up for any inconsistencies. With superb value for money, a well-versed wine list starting at £16 and charming service, locals should feel chuffed at this site's upward trajectory.

Chef/s: Michael Nadra. **Open:** Tue to Sun L 12 to 2.30 (3.30 Sat and Sun), Tue to Sat D 6 to 10 (10.30 Fri and Sat). **Closed:** Mon, 25 and 26 Dec. **Meals:** Set L £19.50 (2 courses) to £24. Set D £27 (2 courses) to £33. Tasting menu £39 (6 courses) to £49. **Service:** 12.5% (optional). **Details:** Cards accepted. 48 seats. Music. Children allowed.

The River Café

Italian icon with winning ways
Thames Wharf, Rainville Road, Hammersmith, W6 9HA
Tel no: (020) 7386 4200
www.rivercafe.co.uk
⊖ Hammersmith, map 1
Italian | £60
Cooking score: 6

It's sometimes hard to believe that this Italian icon by the Thames started life as a refuelling point for Richard Rogers' architectural practice next door. Since then it has achieved stardom, outliving all those 'Tuscany in Fulham' clichés and remaining true to its cause – namely the pursuit of intuitive, vigorous cooking based on artisan ingredients and traditional techniques. Despite the sad death of co-founder Rose Gray in 2010, the River Café has kept the faith and continued its winning ways. Eating here doesn't come cheap, but you are paying for dedication and diligent sourcing, be it deliveries from Milan markets, line-caught fish from the English coast or gleanings from the Café's miraculous riverside garden. Fragrant green leaves and veggie adornments appear everywhere – cicoria shoots with anchovies and red wine vinegar, winter pickings strewn over prosciutto di Parma, sea kale and Swiss chard leavening a dish of seared scallops with fresh red chilli. Homemade pasta is a star turn, although a steel-chimneyed wood oven now dominates the chic, canteen-style dining room: its bounty might include a tranche of turbot with thinly sliced potatoes, trevise hearts and black olives or whole Anjou pigeon on Rosso di Montalcino bruschetta with carrots, fennel and celeriac al forno. To conclude, explore the regional delights of the cheese room or take the sweet route with pear and almond tart. Aside from Billecart-Salmon Champagne, the wine list is an Italian treasure trove bursting with big Barolos, Super Tuscans and goodies from Campania to Sicily. Prices start at £20 (£6.50 a glass).

Chef/s: Ruth Rogers. **Open:** all week L 12.30 to 2.15 (2.30 Sat, 12 to 3 Sun), Mon to Sat D 7 to 9.15. **Closed:** 23 Dec to 3 Jan, bank hols. **Meals:** alc (main courses £32 to £38). **Service:** 12.5% (optional). **Details:** Cards accepted. 110 seats. 85 seats outside. Separate bar. No music. Wheelchair access. Children allowed.

Roussillon

Polished Gallic jewel
16 St Barnabas Street, Chelsea, SW1W 8PE
Tel no: (020) 7730 5550
www.roussillon.co.uk
⊖ Sloane Square, map 3
Modern European | £65
Cooking score: 6

£5 OFF **V**

The instantly recognisable cream-coloured exterior with its wide bay window announces one of the glittering stars in well-heeled Chelsea's firmament. That its culinary helmsman Dan Gill should still be in his early twenties makes the level of attainment here all the more astonishing. It's a supremely relaxing, high-toned dining room, with crisp napery, quality glassware and flowers afloat in water on the tables, and there is also an elegant, gently lit private-dining area. One of the attractions has been seasonal vegetarian tasting menus (six courses at lunch, eight at dinner) of such gleaming creative opulence that many are tempted to forgo the foie gras for once in their lives. Start with broccoli velouté enriched with Cashel Blue and truffle, and don't look back. Otherwise, the menus deal in high-class proteins presented with acuity and style, from tuna ceviche with cucumber, pickled mooli and wasabi, through breast and leg of guinea fowl with a Lincolnshire Poacher croquette, creamed leeks and morels, to banana and cherry gâteau with peanut butter ice cream and sour cherry jam. This is cooking that is big on assertive, outstanding flavours which are melded into a state of soothing harmony on the palate. Service is top-drawer. The wines are, too, and even if you just stayed within the eponymous region of southern France, you'd be royally treated with aromatic vins de pays

and Collioure, but there are regiments of the classic and the classy from all over the globe. Prices open at £25 (£6.50 a glass).
Chef/s: Daniel Gill. **Open:** Mon to Fri L 12 to 2.30, Mon to Sat D 6.30 to 10. **Closed:** Sun, bank hols. **Meals:** Set L £37.50 (includes wine). Set D £58 (2 courses) to £65. Tasting menu £65 (vegetarian), £75 (non-vegetarian). **Service:** 12.5% (optional). **Details:** Cards accepted. 50 seats. No music. Wheelchair access. Children allowed.

Sam's Brasserie & Bar

Classic and modern flavours
11 Barley Mow Passage, Chiswick, W4 4PH
Tel no: (020) 8987 0555
www.samsbrasserie.co.uk
⊖ Chiswick Park, Turnham Green, map 1
Modern European | £25
Cooking score: 3

Tucked away off Chiswick High Road, this converted factory is brother to Harrison's in Balham (see entry). The décor is crisp, clean and modern, with natural light from large windows. The cooking is broadly European – a fair mix of classic and modern brasserie dishes running the gamut from chicken liver parfait with red onion marmalade via calf's liver with sage gnocchi, curly kale and white onion sauce to cod with crushed potatoes, wild garlic, shrimps and broad beans. The short fixed-price menus are reckoned to be excellent value, taking in seared chicken livers on toast with caper butter, plaice with lentils and salsa verde, and pomegranate parfait with gingerbread biscuits. The wine list is full of good ideas from all over the world. Bottles start at £15 and a decent number come by the glass.
Chef/s: Ian Leckie. **Open:** all week L 12 to 3 (4 Sat and Sun), D 6.30 to 10.30 (10 Sun). **Closed:** 25 and 26 Dec. **Meals:** alc (main courses £12 to £20). Set L £13 (2 courses) to £16. Early set D £15 (2 courses) to £18. Sun L £21. **Service:** 12.5% (optional). **Details:** Cards accepted. 100 seats. Separate bar. Wheelchair access. Music. Children allowed.

CLARE SMYTH
Restaurant Gordon Ramsay

What is the biggest myth about being a chef?
That we know how to cook everything. We are constantly learning new things and improving techniques.

Do you have a favourite local ingredient?
Honey. There are so many good honeys in London. We use one from the physic garden next door. They don't sell it in restaurants but we talked them into letting us have some.

What excites you most about the restaurant industry today?
That it is so diverse and there are so many different cuisines cooking at such a high level. As a customer you are spoilt for choice.

What's your favourite job in the kitchen?
Podding peas, prepping ceps, turning artichokes - all the jobs you didn't want to do when you were a commis!

What is your favourite food combination?
I don't have one. Combinations come from nature and are dependent upon everything that comes together in the same season. Nature dictates to us.

The Sands End

Pubby bonhomie and straightforward cooking
135-137 Stephendale Road, Fulham, SW6 2PR
Tel no: (020) 7731 7823
www.thesandsend.co.uk
⊖ Fulham Broadway, map 3
British | £28
Cooking score: 2

Residential Fulham's prized Sands End is a good-natured soul famed for its pubby bonhomie and a repertoire of food that mixes homespun cuisine with some sunny Mediterranean flourishes. The menu is a tribute to good British produce and the cooking is generally excellent in a straightforward way: pork rillette with celeriac and apple rémoulade or chicken livers on toast with marjoram and parsley could give way to the likes of roast cod with grilled, marinated aubergine and courgette salad or seared calf's liver with braised red cabbage, apple and hazelnut. Prices on the global wine list start at £15.50, with some 15 offered by the glass.

Chef/s: Tim Kensett. **Open:** all week L 12 to 3 (4 Sat and Sun), D 6 to 10 (9 Sun). **Closed:** 25 and 26 Dec. **Meals:** alc (main courses £14 to £20). Set L £13.50. **Service:** 12.5% (optional). **Details:** Cards accepted. 65 seats. 16 seats outside. Separate bar. Wheelchair access. Music. Children allowed.

The Thomas Cubitt

Dapper Belgravia public house
44 Elizabeth Street, Belgravia, SW1W 9PA
Tel no: (020) 7730 6060
www.thethomascubitt.co.uk
⊖ Victoria, map 3
British | £37
Cooking score: 3

The town house that Thomas Cubitt built may now be pressed into service as a pub, but it still manages to strike the perfect balance between Georgian elegance and comfort. Above the (fairly) boisterous bar is a first-floor restaurant in tasteful duck-egg and wood tones, with architectural prints, open fires and white menus as crisp as the linen. These are peppered with regional delights: lemon and thyme crusted chicken with Somerset rambler dumplings, for example, or roasted squash with Sussex Slipcote cheese. At inspection a rabbit, leek and mushroom pie with fragrant jus and morels was impeccably made – the quality of the dishes rarely falters, which is just as well given the rather high prices. Elsewhere, upkeep and standards remain high. Downstairs there's a more informal bar menu. House wine is £18.

Chef/s: Phillip Wilson. **Open:** all week L 12 to 3, D 6 to 9.30. **Meals:** alc (main courses £15 to £26). Set L £17.50 (2 courses) to £25. Set D £28 (2 courses) to £35. Sun L £15.50 (2 courses) to £19. Bar menu available. **Service:** 12.5% (optional). **Details:** Cards accepted. 130 seats. 20 seats outside. Separate bar. Music. Children allowed.

Timo

Affable local Italian
343 Kensington High Street, Kensington, W8 6NW
Tel no: (020) 7603 3888
www.timorestaurant.net
⊖ High Street Kensington, map 3
Italian | £38
Cooking score: 2

This small contemporary Italian remains ever popular, striking just the right note for a neighbourhood restaurant with its pleasant service and good-value lunch menu. Simple techniques define much of the output, from grilled squid with rocket, tomatoes and spicy dressing to wild venison bresaola with celeriac and horseradish salad. There's an inventive streak, too, seen in pasta dishes such as chestnut-flour pasta with wild duck ragù or smoked haddock with carrots, kohlrabi, leeks and crème fraîche with chives. Meals might end with nougat zuccotto (a combination of cake and ice cream) with pistachio sauce. Wines on the all-Italian list open at £17.

Chef/s: Stefano Gottardi. **Open:** Mon to Sat L 12 to 2.30, D 7 to 11. **Closed:** Sun. **Meals:** alc (main courses £7 to £25). Set L £13.90 (2 courses) to £16.

Service: not inc. **Details:** Cards accepted. 42 seats. 3 seats outside. Separate bar. Wheelchair access. Music. Children allowed.

NEW ENTRY

Tinello

Snappily dressed Locatelli spin-off
87 Pimlico Road, Pimlico, SW1W 8PH
Tel no: (020) 7730 3663
www.tinello.co.uk
⊖ Sloane Square, map 3
Italian | £38
Cooking score: 4

High-roller Giorgio Locatelli is the broker behind this snappily dressed Italian, but Tinello still manages to feel like a 'really lovely neighbourhood restaurant' rather than a big-city destination. Plenty of sharp service keeps things afloat, and the interior plays it low-key, with bare brick walls, oak floors and dangling lampshades. Frontmen Federico and Max Sali are Locatelli protégés, and it shows. Federico's cooking respects good ingredients and he delivers exact, restrained flavours across the board, opening the show with fashionable 'small eats' – perhaps tangy octopus 'agrodolce' – ahead of top-drawer mains. Char-grilled mackerel fillet comes with zesty rocket, pink grapefruit and radish salad, while loin of venison is given some seasonal oomph with pumpkin, watercress and hazelnuts. Desserts are less inspired, so opt for cheese – superb pecorino with medlar honey and fig mustard, say. Prices are perky for Pimlico, and sommelier Max Sali's wine list ticks all the boxes for serious intent, quality and value. Italy holds pole position, although top producers from elsewhere are not ignored. House selections start at £13 (£3.40 for a dinky 125ml glass).
Chef/s: Federico Sali. **Open:** Mon to Sat L 12 to 2.30, D 6.30 to 12. **Closed:** Sun, 24 Dec to 4 Jan, bank hols. **Meals:** alc (main courses £16 to £23). **Service:** not inc. **Details:** Cards accepted. 79 seats. No music. No mobile phones. Children allowed.

Tom Aikens

All change at Aikens flagship
43 Elystan Street, Chelsea, SW3 3NT
Tel no: (020) 7584 2003
www.tomaikens.co.uk
⊖ South Kensington, map 3
Modern French | £75
no score

V

The last three years have been worrying times for Tom Aikens and his Chelsea flagship, with administration bail-outs and lots of manoeuvring behind the scenes. In spring 2011 he announced that he had found a new backer in the shape of the Istanbul Doors Restaurant Group, then closed for a three-month refurbishment/revamp in July 2011. Details were sketchy as our deadline approached, hence no score, but the new set-up promises a completely new look, a more informal ambience and a series of new menus that will retain his signature style of cuisine. Those who dined at Elystan Street before the shutdown can confirm that Aikens is still a white-hot talent to be reckoned with – witness an 'absolutely beautiful' starter of roasted scallops with caramelised onions and bittersweet beetroot leaves, a seriously challenging gazpacho of ewes' milk cheese shot through with chervil, and a main course of John Dory with roasted cauliflower florets, smoked eel and myriad contrasting textures. Whether these, and many other heavenly dishes, will be consigned to the archives remains to be seen. Currently the wine list is a heavyweight, with a broad global spread, serious prices and house selections from £24 (£8 a glass). Note: some of the details and information given below may change once the revamped outfit is up and running from September 2011. Reports please.
Chef/s: Tom Aikens. **Open:** Mon to Fri L 12 to 2.30, Mon to Sat D 6.45 to 10.45. **Closed:** Sun, 25 to 28 Dec, bank hols. **Meals:** alc (main courses £30 to £40). Tasting menu L £55 (5 courses), D £85 (7 courses). **Service:** 12.5% (optional). **Details:** Cards accepted. 55 seats. Separate bar. Wheelchair access. Music. Children allowed.

Tom's Kitchen

Chic but pricey brasserie
27 Cale Street, Chelsea, SW3 3QP
Tel no: (020) 7349 0202
www.tomskitchen.co.uk
⊖ Sloane Square, South Kensington, map 3
Modern British | £60
Cooking score: 2

Not far from his flagship restaurant, Tom Aikens' British brasserie is 'a bit like a pub and fine for what it is'. The white-tiled interior is more chic than the comment suggests, though the preponderance of family favourites on offer (shepherd's pie and fish pie 'presented in a very workmanlike way') could certainly grace a boozer. Beetroot and feta salad, monkfish with saffron mash, and profiteroles with chocolate mousse have been declared good, but not 'special enough for the price' – particularly not with lattes at £3.75 and house wine from £20 adding to the damage. There's another branch at Somerset House on the Strand, and more in the offing.

Chef/s: Timothy Brindley. **Open:** all week L 12 to 3 (10 to 4 Sat and Sun), D 6 to 11. **Closed:** 25 and 26 Dec. **Meals:** alc (main courses £12 to £30). **Service:** 12.5% (optional). **Details:** Cards accepted. 72 seats. Separate bar. Wheelchair access. Music. Children allowed.

ALSO RECOMMENDED

▲ Tosa

332 King Street, Hammersmith, W6 0RR
Tel no: (020) 8748 0002
www.tosauk.com
⊖ Ravenscourt Park, Stamford Brook, map 1
Japanese £5 OFF

Don't be surprised to see a Croatian chef wielding the skewers at this jam-packed Japanese joint – a handy drop-in for those who enjoy the zingy flavours of char-grilled kushiyaki and yakitori. Try anything from ox tongue or chicken wing 'tips' to duck breast with spring onions, from around £2 a go; otherwise splash out with some sashimi, a bowl of udon noodles with assorted toppings (from £7.20) or deep-fried prawn tonkatsu. Drink Asahi beer, saké or the house wine at £13.50. Open all week. There's a branch at 152 High Road, East Finchley N1 9ED, tel (020) 8883 8850.

La Trompette

Culinary dazzlement and stunning wine
5-7 Devonshire Road, Chiswick, W4 2EU
Tel no: (020) 8747 1836
www.latrompette.co.uk
⊖ Turnham Green, map 1
Modern European | £40
Cooking score: 6

Here is another terrifically high-achieving neighbourhood restaurant that only makes a show of itself where it matters – on the plate. Behind the trim hedge is a fashionably muted interior, with a wood-panelled ceiling and bare wood floor, but smartly laid-up tables. It creates a restful backdrop for the culinary dazzlement to come, now in the hands of Anthony Boyd. The house style of creatively configured modern European dishes, drawing inspiration from southern France and the Mediterranean fringe, works to great effect in such deceptively simple dishes as scallops with squid, chorizo, garlic wafers and puréed white beans, or a pasta starter such as braised venison tagliatelle under a crust of buttery Beaufort cheese. Main courses use slow cooking for daube de boeuf bourguignonne, or Alsace-style pork belly and sausage with choucroute and leeks. Pastrywork passes muster when it comes to a vegetarian main course of potato and cep pithiviers with pickled cauliflower, and also the textbook tarte Tatin, in which the balance of tartness and caramelisation in the apple is flawlessly judged. Another dessert, pannacotta with beignets and summer fruits, 'produced gasps of delight' from its lucky recipient. To go along with these enticements is an equally alluring wine list, a stunner in fact, one that divides Italy and Germany into their regions before heading off into central Europe and the southern hemisphere. Prices are commendably restrained for the quality. Small glasses start at £3.50, bottles at £17.50.

Chef/s: Anthony Boyd. **Open:** all week L 12 to 2.30 (12.30 to 3 Sun), D 6.30 to 10.30 (7 to 10 Sun). **Closed:** 24 to 26 Dec. **Meals:** Set L £22 (2 courses) to £26. Early D £19.50. Set D £34.50 (2 courses) to £39.50. Sun L £32.50. **Service:** 12.5% (optional). **Details:** Cards accepted. 70 seats. 16 seats outside. No music. Wheelchair access. Children allowed.

Le Vacherin

Neighbourhood bistro with faithful fans
76-77 South Parade, Chiswick, W4 5LF
Tel no: (020) 8742 2121
www.levacherin.co.uk
⊖ Chiswick Park, map 1
French | £35
Cooking score: 4

This neighbourhood bistro, with its 'modern yet warm atmosphere', crisp white table linen, comfortable seating and straightforward cooking, keeps regulars coming back year after year. The cooking is deep-rooted bourgeois; Malcolm John knows his customers and doesn't seek to inflict shocks to their systems. Salmon rillettes, chicken liver and foie gras parfait or Burgundy snails and wild mushroom pie indicate the palette of flavours, followed, perhaps, by whole grilled lemon sole with tartare sauce, a 'faultless' 28-day aged chateaubriand for two, or confit of wild rabbit with Dijon mustard. There are no surprises, either, when it comes to desserts. Old faithful puddings take in petit pot au chocolat and profiteroles with coffee ice cream and caramel. Charming, friendly and relaxed service enhances the experience, which is completed by a wine list dominated by France (of course), with bottles from £17.95.
Chef/s: Malcolm John. **Open:** Tue to Sun L 12 to 3 (4 Sun), all week D 6 to 10.30 (11 Fri and Sat, 10 Sun). **Closed:** 25 and 26 Dec, bank hols. **Meals:** alc (main courses £19 to £26). Set L £20 (2 courses) to £25. Set D £28.50 (2 courses) to £35. Sun L £25. **Service:** 12.5% (optional). **Details:** Cards accepted. 72 seats. Separate bar. Music. Children allowed.

NEW ENTRY

Yashin Sushi

Innovative sushi newcomer
1A Argyll Road, Kensington, W8 7DB
Tel no: (020) 7938 1536
www.yashinsushi.com
⊖ High Street Kensington, map 4
Japanese | £50
Cooking score: 4

£5 OFF

They say good things come in small packages and it seems to be true with this tiny restaurant, which has dining areas spread over two floors. The place to sit is at the green tiled counter on the ground floor, rather than in the basement. Yashin Sushi is run by chefs from Nobu (see entry) and the menu revolves around omakase ('chef's selection'). Innovative sushi makes it a captivating experience – sea bream is paired with rice cracker and razor clam with shiso and fresh slices of yuzu, while some raw fish is lightly touched with a blowtorch just before serving to impair a little sweetness. Raw gems aside, hot and silky soya curd with a dip of fish stock jelly and wasabi is an octave lower, but equally interesting. End with white sesame ice cream served with fresh fruits and cubes of agar-agar. Service is cheery. Wines from £28, but ask for the shots of saké, which are served in test-tubes.
Chef/s: Yasuhiro Mineno and Shinya Ikeda. **Open:** all week L 12 to 3, D 6 to 10.30. **Closed:** 24 Dec to 4 Jan. **Meals:** alc D (dishes £6 to £14). Set L £13 to £60. **Service:** 12.5% (optional). **Details:** Cards accepted. 37 seats. 4 seats outside. Separate bar. Music. Children allowed.

Zaika

Adventurous Indian cooking
1 Kensington High Street, Kensington, W8 5NP
Tel no: (020) 7795 6533
www.zaika-restaurant.co.uk
⊖ High Street Kensington, map 4
Indian | £35
new chef

£5 OFF

Zaika's ornate carved stonework, mahogany panelling and moody lighting reminded one reporter of the set for a 'film noir', and there's no denying that this sleek, opulent Indian goes in for a great deal of high drama. Celeb chef Sanjay Dwivedi moved on in 2011 and his successor was still settling in as the Guide went to press – although the food is unlikely to change in concept or design. Expect a cavalcade of east-west crossovers along the lines of Goosnargh duck breast with parsnip mash and clove-infused jus or chilli-spiked lobster with sun-dried cauliflower, shellfish emulsion, sour spices and cocoa powder, plus some adventurous desserts such as tandoori pineapple with pineapple halva and cheesecake. High prices come with the territory, but 'sultry' service needs to be addressed. Wines start at £20.50. Send in your reports, please.

Chef/s: Jasbinder Singh. **Open:** Tue to Sun L 12 to 2.45, all week D 6 to 10.45 (9.45 Sun). **Closed:** 25 and 26 Dec, 1 and 2 Jan. **Meals:** alc (main courses £17 to £26). Set L £20 (2 courses) to £25. Tasting menu £45. **Service:** 12.5% (optional). **Details:** Cards accepted. 82 seats. Separate bar. Music. Children allowed.

Zuma

Supremely stylish jet setter
5 Raphael Street, Knightsbridge, SW7 1DL
Tel no: (020) 7584 1010
www.zumarestaurant.com
⊖ Knightsbridge, map 4
Japanese | £60
Cooking score: 5

Ultra-cool Zuma's mix of unyielding surfaces, marble pillars, rough-hewn wood, rock and steel can seem hard-edged (even primeval) but once night falls the moneyed hubbub overwhelms everything else – especially if you're among the guzzling crowds at the bar or getting a raw fix beside the sushi counter. Sit in the main dining room and you'll have a view of the open kitchen, where chefs fashion all manner of smart plates inspired by the ever-evolving world of Japanese cuisine. Dishes are designed for sharing and are brought to the table in waves as they are ready: spinach salad with ruby grapefruit and maple soy; chilled homemade tofu with condiments; sliced yellowtail with jalapeño relish, ponzu and pickled garlic; crispy langoustine tempura with red chilli dashi and onions. The robata grill also gets a serious workout, delivering anything from salt-grilled sea bass with burnt tomato and ginger relish to pork skewers with mustard miso, and it's worth watching for new arrivals on the menu (perhaps sweet popcorn tempura with yuzu salt). Predictably for SW7, such exquisite gastronomic pleasures come at truly 'mind-blowing' prices; drinkers also take a serious financial hit, although this is a saké-aficionado's paradise. Wines from £22.

Chef/s: Soon Le Ong. **Open:** all week L 12 to 2.30 (3 Fri, 12.30 to 3.30 Sat and Sun), D 6 to 11 (10.30 Sun). **Closed:** 25 Dec, 1 Jan. **Meals:** alc (main courses £5 to £95). Tasting menu £96. **Service:** 15% (optional). **Details:** Cards accepted. 130 seats. Separate bar. Wheelchair access. Music. Children allowed.

A Cena

Easy Italian with gutsy food
418 Richmond Road, Twickenham, TW1 2EB
Tel no: (020) 8288 0108
www.acena.co.uk
⊖ Richmond, map 1
Italian | £35
Cooking score: 2

Good for everyday dining as well as easy celebrations, A Cena offers an intelligent and gutsy take on modern Italian standards. Expect simple salads, perhaps winter greens with speck ham, dressed with ricotta and walnut, good homemade pasta, seabass 'in cartoccio' (wrapped in paper and baked), and pannacotta to finish. Friendly, reliable staff are a bonus, and the well-considered, patriotic wine list offers plenty of sound drinking from £16.50.

Chef/s: Nicola Parsons. **Open:** Tue to Sun L 12 to 2.30, Mon to Sat D 7 to 10.30. **Closed:** 24 to 27 Dec. **Meals:** alc (main courses £13 to £24). Sun L £21 (2 courses) £25. **Service:** not inc. **Details:** Cards accepted. 65 seats. Separate bar. No music. Children allowed.

The Bingham

Extraordinary, exceptional food by the river
61-63 Petersham Road, Richmond, TW10 6UT
Tel no: (020) 8940 0902
www.thebingham.co.uk
⊖ Richmond, map 1
Modern British | £55
Cooking score: 6

The Bingham's gold and silver-hued Georgian rooms and stunning Turner-esque views of Richmond Bridge would be reasons enough to visit, but its boutique dining room has also earned a big reputation among South London's culinary cognoscenti. Shay Cooper's extraordinary cooking may be too 'fussy' for some conservative palates, but the results are exceptional as he manipulates ingredients to suit his vision. A simple-sounding vegetable and goats' cheese salad with mushroom vinaigrette appears as an edible work of art, with shaved wild fungi interspersing whirls of mousse-like cheese, cleansing herbs and precisely arranged leaves, while a starter of barely cooked salmon is accompanied by frothed chanterelles and a generous chunk of roast foie gras for added grandeur. Main courses are no less eye-popping: rich red wine jus adds satisfying depth to a dish of poached brill with samphire, cep tortellini and salsify, while flavour-packed slow-cooked beef 'cap' with sweetbreads, Parmesan gnocchi and cauliflower is pulled together with a light polonaise dressing. Desserts follow a similar, intricately wrought path – a perfect strawberry parfait thrillingly enhanced with a sorbet, black olive caramel, Thai basil and meringue, for example. Service is dutifully professional, but it comes with a pleasing 'outer London' chattiness rather than severe, hierarchical posturing. The wine list is globally inclined with some thought-provoking numbers from Slovenia and Croatia tucked away among the elite Champagnes, grand Bordeaux, Italian patriarchs and trendy New World names. Prices start at £24 (£6 a glass).

Chef/s: Shay Cooper. **Open:** all week L 12 to 2.30 (12.30 to 4 Sun), Mon to Sat D 7 to 10 (6.30 to 10.30 Thur to Sat). **Meals:** Set L £22.50 (2 courses) to £26. Set D £55. Tasting menu £75. **Service:** 12.5% (optional). **Details:** Cards accepted. 38 seats. 14 seats outside. Separate bar. No music. No mobile phones. Wheelchair access. Children allowed. Car parking.

Brasserie Vacherin

A true all-day French brasserie
12 High Street, Sutton, SM1 1HN
Tel no: (020) 8722 0180
www.brasserievacherin.co.uk
map 1
French | £24
Cooking score: 2

The sibling of Le Vacherin, Le Cassoulet and Fish & Grill, Croydon (see entries), this place is a true all-day brasserie run along French lines. It will serve you breakfast, and won't close the door on you in that awkward hinterland between lunch and dinner. In surroundings of buttoned banquettes and tiled walls, it does the simple and classic things well. Leek and bacon tart, escargots de Bourgogne, and mains such as braised veal with carrots and mash, or whole roast sea bream in beurre noisette tick all the right boxes. And to finish, a slice of pear and almond tart with pistachio ice cream should fit the bill. Wines start at £15.50.

Chef/s: Matthew Stone. **Open:** all week 8am to 11pm (10.30 Sun). **Closed:** 25 Dec. **Meals:** alc (main courses £13 to £18). Set L and D £14 (2 courses) to £16.95. Sun L £16.95. **Service:** 12.5% (optional). **Details:** Cards accepted. 65 seats. 30 seats outside. Separate bar. Wheelchair access. Music. Children allowed.

Brilliant

Shining Punjabi star
72-76 Western Road, Southall, UB2 5DZ
Tel no: (020) 8574 1928
www.brilliantrestaurant.com
⊖ Hounslow West, map 1
Indian | £25
Cooking score: 3

£5 OFF £30

Undisputed king of the hill in West London's curry capital, the Anand brothers' flagship has grown from tiny beginnings back in the mid-70s to a well-oiled hospitality machine with famous fans and every facility from Bollywood films to outside catering – you can even get married here. But Brilliant's beating heart is still its vigorous, emphatically spiced Punjabi food, with some Kenyan nuances slotted in. It's so familar that hardcore fans often order without consulting the menu – butter chicken, tandoori lamb chops and karahi prawns, backed by exemplary roti breads and heaps of vegetable sides (aloo chollay, palak paneer etc). Groups share gut-busting bowls of keema peas or masaledar lamb, while those watching the calories look for the 'healthy options'. Traditional sweets such as rasmalai and falooda are worth a punt too. Drink lassi, beer or the house wine (£11).

Chef/s: Jasvinderjit Singh. **Open:** Tue to Fri L 12 to 3, Tue to Sun D 6 to 11.30 (12 Fri and Sat). **Closed:** Mon, 25 Dec. **Meals:** alc (main courses £5 to £13). **Service:** 10%. **Details:** Cards accepted. 225 seats. Music. Children allowed. Car parking.

ALSO RECOMMENDED

▲ The Brown Dog

28 Cross Street, Barnes, SW13 0AP
Tel no: (020) 8392 2200
www.thebrowndog.co.uk
map 1
Modern British

Set in the residential backstreets of Little Chelsea, this convivial canine-themed boozer finds room for a happy crowd of local drinkers and those with serious hunger pangs. Chef Ashley Hancill is carrying on where his predecessor left off, using home-grown and seasonal produce for a daily menu of Anglo-Mediterranean dishes along the lines of smoked duck breast with radishes, radicchio and horseradish (£7.75), broad bean and artichoke risotto, or black bream with samphire, new potatoes and sauce vierge (£15.75). Wines from £16.50. Open all week.

Brula

Congenial local with crunch-busting prices
43 Crown Road, St Margarets, Twickenham, TW1 3EJ
Tel no: (020) 8892 0602
www.brula.co.uk
⊖ Richmond, map 1
French | £30
Cooking score: 3

V

'I can go to the Tate for art, I go to Brula for food', observed one fan – referring to the refreshing, designer-free look of this one-time-butcher's shop. It may have lovely stained-glass windows, but what matters is the stuff on the plate, the crunch-busting prices and the air of congenial good humour. Little things mean a lot here, whether it's generously replenished bread or the offer of steak frites even if it's not on the menu. Reports of highly

enjoyable dishes abound: crab mayonnaise with beetroot-cured gravadlax; braised pork belly with caramelised apples and Madeira; Scotch onglet steak and oxtail croquette with dauphinoise potatoes, kale and wild mushrooms. To finish, frangipane and apple tart has gone down a treat and Brula's regional French wines (from £17) also get the nod.
Chef/s: Jamie Russel. **Open:** all week L 12 to 3, Mon to Sat D 6 to 10.30. **Closed:** 26 to 30 Dec. **Meals:** alc (main courses £14 to £25). Set L £13.75 (2 courses) to £18. Sun L £16.50. **Service:** 12.5% (optional). **Details:** Cards accepted. 40 seats. 8 seats outside. No music. Children allowed.

La Buvette

Charming, good-value bistro
6 Church Walk, Richmond, TW9 1SN
Tel no: (020) 8940 6264
www.labuvette.co.uk
⊖ Richmond, map 1
French | £22
Cooking score: 3

'Charming French bistro and good value for its location', is how one regular describes Bruce Duckett's smart restaurant, housed in the former rectory of the next-door St Mary Magdalene church. The resolutely Francophile menu may start with half a dozen escargots de Bourgogne or a mini croque-monsieur with frisée salad and cornichons, and move on to some old provincial favourites at main-course stage – pot-au-feu of beef brisket and ox tongue with chou farci and salsa verde, for example, or roast leg of rabbit with mustard sauce and a potato and bacon matafan (a thick crêpe). Desserts tend to have plenty of sweetness; witness banana clafoutis with caramel ice cream. Ten of the almost exclusively French wines on the single-page listing come by the glass or carafe; bottle prices from £14.
Chef/s: Buck Carter. **Open:** all week L 12 to 3, D 6 to 10. **Closed:** 25 and 26 Dec, Good Fri, Easter Sun. **Meals:** Set L £14.25 (2 courses) to £16.25. Set D £19 (2 courses) to £21.50. Sun L £19. **Service:** 12.5% (optional). **Details:** Cards accepted. 44 seats. 32 seats outside. No music. Children allowed.

Le Cassoulet

Food to make a Francophile purr
18 Selsdon Road, Croydon, CR2 6PA
Tel no: (020) 8633 1818
www.lecassoulet.co.uk
map 1
French | £30
Cooking score: 3

Bourgeois French cooking in South Croydon? *Zut alors!* Strange as it sounds, reporters can't get enough of Malcolm John's smart Gallic eatery, part of a mini-empire the restaurateur is building in unlikely south London locations. From the well-priced menu a dish of duck and pork cassoulet soaks up most of the praise, although whole roast sea bream with orange beurre blanc and Dorset crab mayonnaise also get a share of the plaudits. Desserts will have Francophiles purring: expect the likes of tarte Tatin, crème brûlée or a prune and Armagnac parfait, complete with suggested wine pairings. 'Welcoming and attentive' staff keep things moving, while a chunky wine list tours the length and breadth of France. Prices start at £16, with plenty available by the glass.
Chef/s: Jean Pierre Venturini. **Open:** all week L 12 to 3 (4 Sun), D 6 to 10.30 (11 Fri and Sat, 10 Sun). **Closed:** 25 and 26 Dec, 1 Jan. **Meals:** Set L £19. Set D £30. Sun L £22. **Service:** 12.5% (optional). **Details:** Cards accepted. 60 seats. Separate bar. Wheelchair access. Music. Children allowed.

Symbols

- Accommodation is available
- £30 Three courses for less than £30
- V Separate vegetarian menu
- £5 OFF £5-off voucher scheme
- Notable wine list

ALSO RECOMMENDED

▲ The Depot

Tideway Yard, Mortlake High Street, Barnes, SW14 8SN
Tel no: (020) 8878 9462
www.depotbrasserie.co.uk
map 1
Modern European

'One of south-west London's most enjoyable eating experiences in the summer', the Depot takes in river views from both the airy dining room and the terrace. There's a cheerful brasserie feel to the décor and a contemporary menu offering the likes of foie gras and chicken liver parfait with plum jam (£7.10), roast cod with celeriac purée, purple sprouting broccoli and morels or grilled bacon chop with mash, glazed apples and mustard cream (£12.95), and sticky fig and ginger pudding for dessert. Look for good lunch and dinner deals, too. House wine £16. Open all week.

▲ Eat17

28-30 Orford Road, Walthamstow, E17 9NJ
Tel no: (020) 8521 5279
www.eat17.co.uk
⊖ Walthamstow Central, map 1
British £5 OFF

Right in the heart of Walthamstow village, this relaxed and friendly restaurant caters for all-comers, from lunching mums to local professionals. No expense has been spared with the interior, which sports a winning mix of retro, vintage and modern touches. The menu takes in 'tidbits' such as Bath chaps and rosemary popcorn, as well as accessible dishes such as scallops with garlic butter and samphire (£6), beef and ale pie (£10) and curried chickpeas. Finish with chocolate brownie and ice cream. Wines from £13. Closed Sun D.

Also Recommended
Also recommended entries are not scored but we think they are worth a visit.

▲ The Exhibition Rooms

69-71 Westow Hill, Crystal Palace, SE19 1TX
Tel no: (020) 8761 1175
www.theexhibitionrooms.com
map 1
Modern European £5 OFF

David Massey and Geoff Ridgeon's appealing neighbourhood restaurant is an ever-reliable all-rounder, and a boon for this part of London. The kitchen plays it straight with the likes of double-baked cheese soufflé (£6) and beer-battered haddock, but also expect more upbeat ideas such as black bream with spiced aubergine, beetroot, black treacle dressing and pomegranate (£14). Sunday roasts and good-value themed evenings too (mussels and burgers on Monday, et al). House wine is £16. Open all week.

Fish & Grill

Reliable local eatery
48-50 South End, Croydon, CR0 1DP
Tel no: (020) 8774 4060
www.fishandgrill.co.uk
map 1
British | £25
Cooking score: 3

'Good, reliable local restaurant' just about sums up Malcom John's casual, unpretentious eatery – a sibling of Le Cassoulet and Le Vacherin (see entries). Seafood is treated simply, with mussels given the classic marinière treatment, Atlantic prawns served with garlic and chilli, and Dorset crab teamed with avocado mayonnaise and Avruga caviar. Elsewhere, the likes of whole megrim sole or sea bream are simply grilled and served with chips and tartare sauce – with beer-battered haddock for the traditionalists. Not in the mood for fish? Then look to the various steaks (from 28-day aged Aberdeen Angus beef), burgers, or leg of lamb – they all come highly rated. Finish with a good old-fashioned knickerbocker glory. House wines are £16.
Chef/s: Jason Nott. **Open:** all week L 12 to 3 (Sat and Sun 10 to 4), D 5 to 11 (Fri and Sat 4 to 11, Sun 4 to 10.30). **Closed:** 25 Dec. **Meals:** alc (main

courses £11 to £34). Set L and D £14.95 (2 courses) to £17.95. Sun L £17.95. **Service:** 12.5% (optional). **Details:** Cards accepted. 68 seats. 6 seats outside. Wheelchair access. Music. Children allowed.

The French Table

Ever popular neighbourhood veteran
85 Maple Road, Surbiton, KT6 4AW
Tel no: (020) 8399 2365
www.thefrenchtable.co.uk
map 1
French | £33
Cooking score: 4

Unwavering local support is a given at Eric and Sarah Guignard's heartily endorsed Surbiton eatery: 'I've been going since they opened and it just gets better and better', says one fan. Eating here dispels the dread of significant birthdays and puts the gloss on happy anniversaries, graduation bashes or business deals. The attention to detail is 'second to none', from the smart surrounds and effortlessly accommodating service to Eric's ever-skilful cooking. As a chef, he knows how to comfort his flock, but he's also ready to spring some surprises. A foie gras crème brûlée startled one reader, likewise a dish of salmon coated in crushed peanuts, but there are less challenging treats too: roast quail paired with celeriac rémoulade, crispy quails' eggs and pistachio purée, for instance, or the signature 'trilogy of pork'. To finish, gingerbread-and-butter pudding with poached pear is a standout. The lively global wine list opens at £16.50. Eric's passion for bread has come to fruition with the opening of his boulangerie next door.
Chef/s: Eric Guignard. **Open:** Tue to Sun L 12 to 2.30 (3 Sun), Tue to Sat D 7 to 10.30. **Closed:** Mon, 25 and 26 Dec. **Meals:** alc (main courses £12 to £20). Set weekday L £16.50 (2 courses) to £19.50. Sat L £22.50. Sun L £24.50. **Service:** 12.5% (optional). **Details:** Cards accepted. 48 seats. Music. Children allowed.

ALSO RECOMMENDED

▲ Frère Jacques

10-12 Riverside Walk, Kingston-upon-Thames, KT1 1QN
Tel no: (020) 8546 1332
www.frerejacques.co.uk
map 1
French

The riverside location ensures that this nicely appointed brasserie is a 'big-turnover place in summer', with the vagaries of the weather covered by a permanent awning and cheerful dining area inside. Gallic classics include sirloin minute steak and frites or salmon with béarnaise (£9.95 from the good-value 'rapide' menu). The carte furnishes more of the same in the shape of moules marinière (£6.50), confit duck, oxtail with mash and red wine jus (£15.50), and warm apple crêpes. Wines from £15.95. Open all week.

The Glasshouse

Sharp technique and deeply felt flavours
14 Station Parade, Kew, TW9 3PZ
Tel no: (020) 8940 6777
www.glasshouserestaurant.co.uk
⊖ Kew Gardens, map 1
Modern European | £40
Cooking score: 5

A long-serving destination of choice for foodies south of the river, the Glasshouse never flaunts its charms, although the revealing frontage is an alluring sight for anyone passing by. Out of the same stable as Chez Bruce and La Trompette (see entries), it offers reliable, modern classicism rather than experimental frivolities – an intelligent amalgam of sharp technique and deeply felt flavours. The menu is tweaked each session depending on the market and the weather, but it revels in strong natural tastes, contrasts and arty presentation: a giant pasta raviolo packed with clearly identifiable salmon and skate, for example, gets a welcome sweet/salt punch from some deftly arranged golden sultanas and capers. To follow, daube of beef, cooked long and slow, has all the unctuous richness that one could hope for, while roast silver mullet is given a luxury base of velvety smoked aubergine purée and a texture lift from crisp-fried baby squid. Puds such as warm ginger cake with rhubarb ice cream or chocolate fondant with white chocolate parfait will satisfy sweet-toothed punters, and the terrific cheeseboard should please the rest. The dining room is run by consummate professionals and the global list has enough treasures to distract a wine fan for days; in particular, look for the off-piste French regional selections, the German and Austrian gems and the Antipodean frontrunners. Prices from £18 (£4.50 a glass).

Chef/s: Daniel Mertl. **Open:** all week L 12 to 2.30 (3 Sun), D 6.30 to 10.30 (7 to 10 Sun). **Closed:** 24 to 26 Dec, 1 Jan. **Meals:** Set weekday L £21 (2 courses) to £26. Set D £34.50 (2 courses) to £39.50. Sat L £27.50. Sun L £32.50. **Service:** 12.5% (optional). **Details:** Cards accepted. 65 seats. No music. No mobile phones. Children allowed.

Incanto

Thrillingly creative Italian gem
41 High Street, Harrow-on-the-Hill, HA1 3HT
Tel no: (020) 8426 6767
www.incanto.co.uk
⊖ Harrow-on-the-Hill, map 1
Italian | £30
Cooking score: 4

'Right up to West End standards', trumpets a supporter of this little 'Harovian gem' – a sleek-looking, open-minded deli-cum-restaurant housed in a converted post office within shouting distance of the blue-blooded public school. Chef Marcus Chant continues to raise the bar here and his cooking is moving into thrilling new areas of creativity – how about a challenging risotto of bone marrow, n'duja (spicy Calabrian sausage), squid ink and crispy calamari, or a finely honed tripartite dish of Berkshire venison, comprising the loin with beetroot and balsamic purée, a Scotch egg with garlic aïoli, and splendid osso buco with celeriac and apple galette. A stunning starter of cured meats with balsamic jelly and irresistible 'crescentine' bread fritters has generated gasps of approval, and sassy desserts put a brave new spin on the classics – orange-blossom pannacotta alongside ginger bread pudding, lemongrass cannelloni with coconut sorbet or macadamia and praline semifreddo accompanied by roasted pear and Marsala jelly, for instance. Fascinating Italian regional wines dominate the enlightened list, with prices from £15.95.

Chef/s: Marcus Chant. **Open:** Tue to Sun L 12 to 2.30 (12.30 to 4 Sun), Tue to Sat D 6.30 to 10.30. **Closed:** Mon, 25 and 26 Dec, 1 Jan, bank hols. **Meals:** alc (main courses £14 to £23). Set L £18.95 (2 courses) to £21.95. Set D £19.95 (2 courses) to £23.95. **Service:** 12.5% (optional). **Details:** Cards accepted. 64 seats. Wheelchair access. Music. Children allowed.

NEW ENTRY

Indian Zilla

Impressive Indian with deeply satisfying dishes
2-3 Rocks Lane, Barnes, SW13 0DB
Tel no: (020) 8878 3989
www.indianzilla.co.uk
map 1
Indian | £24
Cooking score: 4

£5 OFF £30

Following the success of Indian Zing (see entry) and Indian Zest in Sunbury, Manoj Vasaikar has brought his trusted formula to SW13 and housed his latest restaurant in what was AWT's Barnes Grill. A plain, angular dining room focuses attention on the food, which impresses from the very outset: peppery poppadoms are soothed with a cooling coriander and mint dip; the Zilla 'kebab' is a banana leaf laden with juicy patties of minced asparagus, spinach and chicken with spicy onion chutney, while sides of smoked aubergine and sweetcorn or chickpeas with dried mango are typical of the kitchen's considered approach. Elsewhere, lamb rogan is slow-cooked and glossy, with a punch of knuckle juice and marrow. Dishes are deeply satisfying, but avoid gut-busting curry house excesses thanks to liberal scatterings of fresh

shoots and the occasional neat flourish (such as the addition of fresh tomato to a vivid bowl of yellow dhal. To drink, order a cold Cobra or a bottle of house wine (£16).
Chef/s: Manoj Vasaikar. **Open:** Mon to Fri L 12 to 3, D 6 to 11. Sat and Sun 12 to 11. **Closed:** 25 Dec. **Meals:** alc (main courses £9 to £22). Set L £12 (2 courses) to £15. **Service:** 12.5% (optional). **Details:** Cards accepted. 86 seats. 4 seats outside. Music. Children allowed.

ALSO RECOMMENDED

▲ Ma Cuisine

9 Station Approach, Kew, TW9 3QB
Tel no: (020) 8332 1923
www.macuisinebistrot.co.uk
⊖ Kew Gardens, map 1
French

With its close-packed tables, chequered floor and Toulouse-Lautrec posters, John McClements' eatery conjures up a traditional view of the French bistro, as does the menu. Brasserie old-stagers like Caesar salad and steak frites with peppercorn sauce share the spotlight with a mixed bag of dishes from boudin noir baked in pastry with Dijon mustard sauce (£6.50), monkfish wrapped in Parma ham with spinach and lobster cream (£17.50) to crêpes Suzette. Wines from £13.50. Open all week.

Madhu's

Chic, high-class Indian
39 South Road, Southall, UB1 1SW
Tel no: (020) 8574 1897
www.madhusonline.com
map 1
Indian | £22
Cooking score: 3

Madhu's dropped the suffix 'Brilliant' some years ago to avoid confusion with its sibling on Western Road (see entry), but it remains a testament to the Anand dynasty's culinary supremacy in Southall. The place looks pretty chic nowadays (shiny black surfaces, metal and mirrors abound), but the kitchen is still rooted in the domestic traditions of the Punjab – with a few nods to the family's time in East Africa. What it delivers is startlingly cheap, generous food shot through with thunderous, gleefully rich flavours and emphatic spicing. Aloo tikki, butter chicken, tandoori mixed grills and masala fish are all-time favourites; also try the deliciously named 'boozi bafu' (lamb chops simmered in a sumptuous tomato and onion sauce), and don't skimp on the excellent 'bread preparations'. House wine is £10, although lassi is a more soothing sip.
Chef/s: Rakesh Verma. **Open:** Mon and Wed to Fri L 12.30 to 3, Wed to Mon D 6 to 11.30. **Closed:** Tue. **Meals:** alc (main courses £5 to £10). Set L and D £20. **Service:** 10% (optional). **Details:** Cards accepted. 104 seats. Wheelchair access. Music. Children allowed.

Mandarin Palace

Knocking spots off Chinatown
559-561 Cranbrook Road, Gants Hill, IG2 6JZ
Tel no: (020) 8550 7661
⊖ Gants Hill, map 1
Chinese | £35
Cooking score: 2

V

A boon for dim sum diehards who don't want to trek into town for their daily fix, this ornate Chinese veteran off the Gants Hill roundabout continues to do a great job. Founded in 1974, it can still show Soho a thing or two with its fascinating range of skilfully fashioned dumplings, rolls and esoteric mouthfuls. Place your order by ticking the list: roasted pork buns, congee with grated scallop, crispy squid paste, 'drunken' chicken feet... take your pick. The full menu is a rewarding trawl through the core Cantonese repertoire, pulling out crispy duck with taro, baked king crab with chilli, sliced beef with garlic sauce and suchlike. Wines from £16.
Chef/s: Huorong Chen. **Open:** Mon to Sat L 12 to 4, D 6 to 11 (12 Fri and Sat). Sun 12 to 11. **Closed:** 25 Dec. **Meals:** alc (main courses £7 to £30). Set L £9.80. Set D £25. **Service:** 10%. **Details:** Cards accepted. 100 seats. Separate bar. Wheelchair access. Music. Children allowed. Car parking.

Mosaica @ The Factory

Funky flavour-fest
Chocolate Factory, Clarendon Road, Wood Green, N22 6XJ
Tel no: (020) 8889 2400
www.mosaicarestaurants.com
⊖ Wood Green, map 2
British | £30
Cooking score: 3
£5 OFF

Mosaica occupies the bare bones of an ex-chocolate factory, now reinvented as a New York-style loft space with lots of art, noise and atmosphere. The open kitchen adds to the buzz and gives a sense of theatre, pumping out a kaleidoscope of ingredients and flavours: seared foie gras with caramelised wild mushrooms and samphire, deep-fried sesame seed octopus with udon noodles, or venison haunch with truffled potatoes and roasted smoked garlic. Go for lunch and there's even gammon, egg and chips, plus some pasta dishes. Sweet things include a well-made dark chocolate and espresso fondant. Long-term owner Johnnie Mountain sold the business in December 2010, but head chef Steven Goode remains, ensuring continuity. The short, sharp wine list starts at £14.

Chef/s: Steven Goode. **Open:** Tue to Fri and Sun L 12 to 3 (1 to 4 Sun), Tue to Sat D 7 to 12 (1am Sat). **Closed:** Mon. **Meals:** alc (main courses £14 to £19). **Service:** 10% (optional). **Details:** Cards accepted. 80 seats. 20 seats outside. Wheelchair access. Music. Children allowed. Car parking.

Petersham Nurseries Café

Arcadian eatery with sunny food
Church Lane, off Petersham Road, Richmond, TW10 7AG
Tel no: (020) 8605 3627
www.petershamnurseries.com
⊖ Richmond, map 1
Modern British | £45
Cooking score: 4

Tucked at the back of a warehouse-sized, earth-floored greenhouse, this haphazard but oddly beautiful restaurant is a riot of plants and horticultural *objets d'art*, pots of herbs and reclaimed furniture. The eccentricity of the interior is matched by the quirkiness of Skye Gyngell's cooking, which blows first-timers away with its freshness, colour and vitality. Her short, weekly changing menu relies heavily on top-notch ingredients, with a leaning towards Italy. At times it is all about unctuous intensity (think cod's roe with mache lettuce, radishes and crème fraîche on crunchy bruschetta), although there is room for some seasonal clarity too: sea bass with asparagus and sauce vert is the embodiment of an English spring day, while guinea fowl with lentils, roasted tomatoes, aïoli and basil oil sings of the Med. Service is sweetly chaotic, bookings are like gold dust and the food is 'still heinously expensive'. Wines start at £19.

Chef/s: Skye Gyngell. **Open:** Wed to Sun L only 12 to 2.30 (12.30 Wed). **Closed:** Mon, Tue, 25 and 26 Dec, Easter Sun. **Meals:** alc (main courses £20 to £29). Set L Wed to Fri £26.50 (2 courses) to £29.50. **Service:** 12.5% (optional). **Details:** Cards accepted. 90 seats. No music. Wheelchair access. Children allowed.

The Restaurant at the Petersham

River views and stately dining
Nightingale Lane, Richmond, TW10 6UZ
Tel no: (020) 8940 7471
www.petershamhotel.co.uk
⊖ Richmond, map 1
Modern British | £45
Cooking score: 4
£5 OFF

Perched high on Richmond Hill, overlooking Petersham Meadows and one of the most famous stretches of the Thames, this florid Italian-Gothic edifice is stuffed with precious antiquity, from a lavish Portland stone staircase to portraits and sumptuous furnishings. The stately dining room is everything you might expect from such a grandiose venue (panoramic views included), and chef Alex Bentley panders to the mood by serving up plates of smoked salmon, fillet steak with béarnaise sauce and rum baba for

those who like their food with a heavy dose of familiarity. He also knows how to satisfy modern-day pleasure seekers – matching crispy rabbit leg with squid, turmeric couscous and black truffle bouillon, baking sea bass with a Parmesan crust, and serving roast venison with mushroom duxelle, walnuts, sweet potatoes and a chocolate/balsamic sauce. To finish, it's nostalgia all the way, although Bentley's take on trifle involves mango ganache, coconut tapioca and pineapple sorbet. The global wine list starts at £25.50.
Chef/s: Alex Bentley. **Open:** all week L 12.15 to 2.15 (12 to 3 Sun), D 7 to 9.45 (8.45 Sun). **Closed:** 24 to 26 Dec. **Meals:** alc (main courses £22 to £30). Set L £22 (2 courses) to £25.75. Set D £31.50 (2 courses) to £39. Sun L £33.50. **Service:** 10% (optional). **Details:** Cards accepted. 70 seats. Separate bar. No music. No mobile phones. Wheelchair access. Children allowed. Car parking.

★ READERS' RESTAURANT OF THE YEAR ★
LONDON

NEW ENTRY

Retro Bistrot

Flamboyant French bistro
114-116 High Street, Teddington, TW11 8JB
Tel no: (020) 8977 2239
www.retrobistrot.co.uk
map 1
French | £30
Cooking score: 3
£5 OFF **V**

A highly individual bistro, with friendly service and punchy French bourgeois cooking, Retro certainly stands out from the Teddington crowd. Inside, 'Parisian boudoir meets interior design shop' as the sassy, avant-garde décor flaunts its vibrant drapes, ritzy wallpaper and chandeliers; even the patron's suit has been tailored to match the colour scheme. By contrast, the menu stays firmly in the orthodox world of snails with garlic butter, terrines (perhaps duck à l'orange or foie gras with sweet wine jelly), moules provençale and Dover sole meunière. Sharing dishes such as chateaubriand also have their say, while the classic offensive continues with desserts ranging from vanilla crème brûlée to apricot soufflé. The results are unfussy, robust and accomplished, with strong Gallic back-up in the form of a well-spread wine list. Prices start at £14.90.
Chef/s: David Philpott. **Open:** Tue to Sun L 12 to 3.30, Tue to Sat D 6.30 to 11. **Closed:** Mon, 25 Dec, first 2 weeks Jan, first 2 weeks Aug, bank hols. **Meals:** alc (main courses £13 to £25). Set L £10.95 (2 courses) to £13.95. Set D £17.50 (2 courses) to 22.50. **Service:** 12.5% (optional). **Details:** Cards accepted. 110 seats. No mobile phones. Music. Children allowed.

ALSO RECOMMENDED

▲ Simply Thai

196 Kingston Road, Teddington, TW11 9JD
Tel no: (020) 8943 9747
www.simplythai-restaurant.co.uk
map 1
Thai

Patria Weerapan continues to impress after seven years at her compact restaurant, where the uncluttered modern dining room sets an appropriate tone for the vibrant Thai cooking. It's the quality of the ingredients that stands out, whether in starters such as fishcakes with cucumber relish or traditional hot-and-sour tom yum goong soup (£6.50). Main courses show the same commitment to good sourcing, from Barbary duck in a piquant curry to a speciality braised loin of lamb with aromatic herbs and spices (£13.95). House wine is £13.95. Open Tue to Sun D only.

Sonny's

Upmarket local eatery with lively cooking
94 Church Road, Barnes, SW13 0DQ
Tel no: (020) 8748 0393
www.sonnys.co.uk
map 1
Modern European | £30
Cooking score: 3
£5 OFF

A comfortably reassuring Barnes perennial, Sonny's was in danger of becoming slightly staid – but some new blood has perked it up no end and the whole place is humming once again. The kitchen deals in assertive Anglo-European flavours: goats' curd with marinated beetroot and polenta croûtons has a rustic simplicity, while a generous slice of halibut with a classic grenobloise sauce is a reminder of how effective bourgeois French cooking can be. Puds such as rum baba with mango cream, pineapple and passion fruit may seem a tad OTT for a neighbourhood eatery, but nobody with a sweet tooth is complaining. Service is accommodating, and the wine list offers plenty of stuff by the glass or pichet, with bottles from £14.50. Sonny's also has its own food shop.

Chef/s: Alex Marks. **Open:** all week L 12 to 4 (10am Sun), Mon to Sat D 7 to 10.30 (11 Fri and Sat). **Closed:** bank hols. **Meals:** alc (main courses £11 to £19). Set L £13.50 (2 courses) to £15.50. Set D £15.50 (2 courses) to £18.50. Sun L £20 (2 courses) to £24.50. **Service:** 12.5% (optional). **Details:** Cards accepted. 98 seats. 10 seats outside. Separate bar. Music. Children allowed.

Tangawizi

Classy local Indian
406 Richmond Road, Richmond, TW1 2EB
Tel no: (020) 8891 3737
www.tangawizi.co.uk
⊖ Richmond, map 1
Indian | £25
Cooking score: 2

'A real treat' for lovers of cut-above Indian food in the Richmond area, Tangawizi flaunts its presence with a lilac frontage and a multicoloured interior. The menu also looks good, promising specials such as lamb with chickpeas, 'home-style' chicken masaledar and a strange-sounding dish of marinated red snapper on Parmesan and Cheddar rice alongside vegetable samosas, rogan josh, prawn biryani and sag aloo. Sadly, glowing reports of classy tandoori prawns, finely spiced salmon tikka, punchy dhal makhani and impressive naans are tempered by niggles about 'artificial flavours' and overpowering three-pot sauces. Staff are welcoming, knowledgeable and enthusiastic. House wine is £13.95; otherwise drink lager or spicy masala Coke with mint.

Chef/s: Surat Singh Rana. **Open:** Sun L 12 to 2.30, all week D 6 to 11 (10.30 Sun). **Closed:** 25 and 26 Dec, 1 Jan. **Meals:** alc (main courses £7 to £16). **Service:** not inc. **Details:** Cards accepted. 60 seats. Music. Children allowed.

The Victoria

TV chef's popular all-rounder
10 West Temple Sheen, East Sheen, SW14 7RT
Tel no: (020) 8876 4238
www.thevictoria.net
⊖ Richmond, map 1
Modern British | £28
Cooking score: 3

A pretty pub with a romantic, purple-hued dining room, the Victoria has become a haven for locals hankering after grown-up food in sociable surroundings. It's home to TV chef Paul Merrett, who sources with care and cooks a raft of user-friendly dishes with a deft, professional touch. You might begin with baked crottin (goats' cheese) and Serrano ham on crostini with a heap of celeriac rémoulade, or a homemade Scotch egg with a punchy beetroot and bean salad, before sampling a 'perfectly tender' onglet steak with crispy onion rings and béarnaise. Otherwise, go global with steamed bass, wasabi-spiced pea purée and prawn toast. To finish, Merrett's chocolate pudding is 'devilishly good', by all accounts. Families descend on the place at weekends (there's a handy playground out back). The well-spread wine list starts at £16 (£3.95 a glass).

Chef/s: Paul Merrett. **Open:** all week L 12 to 2.30, D 6 to 10 (9 Sun). **Meals:** alc (main courses £13 to £18). Set L and early D £12.50 (2 courses). **Service:** 12.5% (optional). **Details:** Cards accepted. 80 seats. 60 seats outside. Separate bar. Wheelchair access. Music. Children allowed. Car parking.

ENGLAND

Bedfordshire, Berkshire,
Buckinghamshire, Cambridgeshire,
Cheshire, Cornwall, Cumbria, Derbyshire,
Devon, Dorset, Durham, Essex,
Gloucestershire & Bristol,
Greater Manchester,
Hampshire (inc. Isle of Wight),
Herefordshire, Hertfordshire, Kent,
Lancashire, Leicestershire and Rutland,
Lincolnshire, Merseyside, Norfolk,
Northamptonshire, Northumberland,
Nottinghamshire, Oxfordshire, Shropshire,
Somerset, Staffordshire, Suffolk, Surrey,
Sussex – East, Sussex – West,
Tyne & Wear, Warwickshire,
West Midlands, Wiltshire, Worcestershire,
Yorkshire

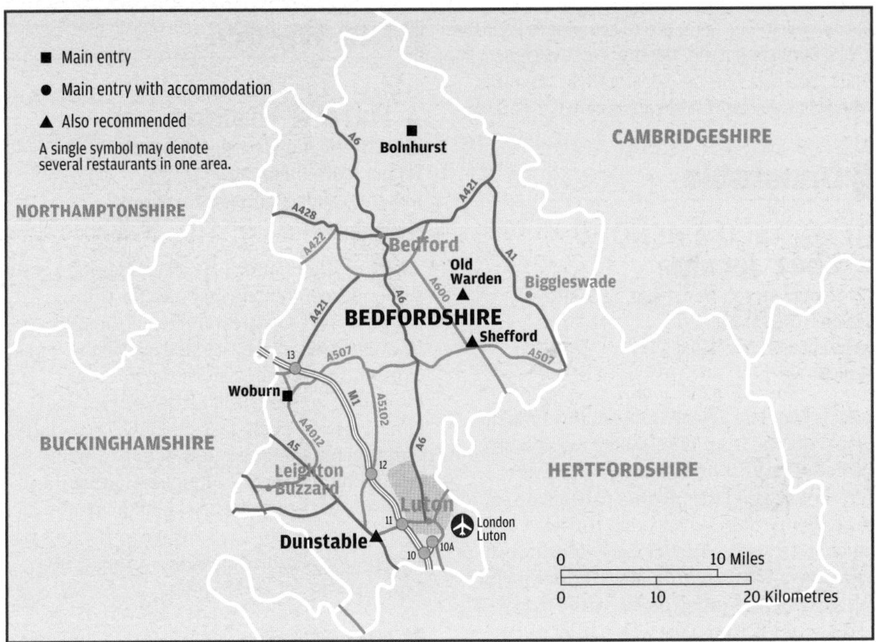

Bolnhurst

The Plough

Big-hearted food that sings
Kimbolton Road, Bolnhurst, MK44 2EX
Tel no: (01234) 376274
www.bolnhurst.com
Modern British | £35
Cooking score: 5

Head and shoulders above most restaurants in the region, the Plough shows exactly how to combine the gregarious virtues of country inn with the intelligence and culinary know-how of a serious-minded eatery. Owners Martin and Jayne Lee know their trade, but it wouldn't work without surefooted support from a brigade of bushy-tailed young staff. Appropriately, the kitchen is right behind the bar, giving the whole set-up a sense of cohesion. Big-hearted food with natural-born seasonal resonance is the name of the game; fine-dining affectations have no place here and the results sing on the plate. This may be Bedfordshire, but fish regularly gets top reviews, be it roast salmon with horseradish soufflé or fillet of brill fired up with an anchovy and chilli dressing. Otherwise, dry-aged Aberdeenshire steaks are a top shout, along with a peppy, Med-inspired dish of local free-range chicken with smashed cannellini beans and cavolo nero. To finish, don't miss the soufflés or the cheeses – three plates from three countries, with appropriate 'tracklements' (including confit de vin d'Alsace for the French). Meals begin with terrific fresh breads and a bottle of Sicilian olive oil, while coffee comes with 'the best mini-cookies around'. This is a working pub, so real ales are in good order – although most attention focuses on the cleverly conceived wine list. Numerous house recommendations from £15.70 (£4 a glass) precede a knowledgeable worldwide collection at highly competitive prices, plus some mouthwatering 'reserve' vintages for celebratory sipping.

Chef/s: Martin Lee. **Open:** Tue to Sun L 12 to 2, Tue to Sat D 6.30 to 9.30. **Closed:** Mon, first two weeks Jan. **Meals:** alc (main courses £16 to £27). Set L £15

(2 courses) to £19. Set D £16 (2 courses) to £20. Sun L £21. **Service:** not inc. **Details:** Cards accepted. 96 seats. 30 seats outside. Separate bar. No music. Wheelchair access. Children allowed. Car parking.

Dunstable

ALSO RECOMMENDED

▲ Chez Jerome

26 Church Street, Dunstable, LU5 4RU
Tel no: (01582) 603310
www.chezjerome.co.uk
French £5 OFF

Locals generate a lively buzz in this French bistro not far from Dunstable's town centre. Friendly service and decent cooking are watchwords and the menus are based on sound ingredients. Salmon and crab fishcakes and chicken fricassee with tarragon mushroom jus have been star turns on the set dinner menu (three courses from £19.95), while the à la carte could deliver a first-class fillet of beef with périgourdine sauce (£28.95) and crème brûlée (£4.75) pronounced 'the best I ever had'. House wine is £13.50. Open all week.

Luton

READERS RECOMMEND

Adam's Brasserie

Modern European
Luton Hoo Hotel, The Mansion House, Luton, LU1 3TQ
Tel no: (01582) 734437
www.lutonhoo.co.uk
'An eclectic brasserie housed in an old stable block. Expect rafters, chandeliers and vibrant flavours.'

Readers Recommend

A 'readers recommend' review is a genuine quote from a report sent in by one of our readers. We intend to follow up these suggestions throughout the year to come.

Old Warden

ALSO RECOMMENDED

▲ Hare & Hounds

High Street, Old Warden, SG18 9HQ
Tel no: (01767) 627225
www.hareandhoundsoldwarden.co.uk
Modern British

There's a slight air of Hansel and Gretel about this endearing village pub not far from Biggleswade. On the doorstep is the Old Warden Park vintage car and aeroplane exhibit, but the cooking at the Hare & Hounds is an attraction all of its own. Well-conceived, carefully presented dishes include tempura prawns and squid with soy-lime-chilli dip (£7), breast of pigeon with wild mushroom risotto dressed in white truffle oil (£16), and mango and kiwi pavlova (£6). Bar snacks are available too. Wines from £13. Open Tue to Sat and Sun L.

Shefford

ALSO RECOMMENDED

▲ The Black Horse

Ireland, Shefford, SG17 5QL
Tel no: (01462) 811398
www.blackhorseireland.com
Modern British

Open-plan modernity meets gnarled beams and cottage windows at this capably run inn way out in the breezy Bedfordshire sticks. Drinkers feel at home, but food comes first here and the kitchen sticks with a dependable repertoire, purveying the likes of brawn and confit duck terrine with sourdough crisps (£5.95), grilled fish and smoked Woburn venison with Puy lentils, figs and oranges (£17.95). 'Wickedly good' triple-cooked chips do the business and puds include Packham pear mousse with Calvados sauce. House wine is £15.50. No food Sun D. Accommodation.

Woburn

Paris House

Picture-perfect food in gorgeous surroundings
London Street, Woburn Park, Woburn, MK17 9QP
Tel no: (01525) 290692
www.parishouse.co.uk
Modern European | £67
Cooking score: 5

£5 OFF **V**

Drop-dead gorgeous on a summer's day, with muntjacs idling in the pastures of Woburn Park and the sun streaming in through mullioned windows, the black-and-white timbered Paris House is a dream. The dining room has its 'wicked side', with eye-catching red chandeliers and mischievous, Beryl Cook-style canvases on the walls. Equally jokey gastro-parodies got the kitchen noticed from day one, although most of these have been abandoned in favour of a more orthodox (some might say 'predictable') approach that yields 'fleshy' sea trout confit with marinated cucumber, guacamole and wasabi mayo, partridge with cep chutney and cauliflower purée, or pan-fried fillet of halibut with curried risotto and onion bhaji. Dishes look picture-perfect and technique is impeccable, although a touch more 'spirit and vigour' would be welcome. That said, the kitchen knows how to get the party swinging with some tongue-in-cheek desserts – a 'toffee apple' filled with astringent Granny Smith parfait or a twist on Black Forest gâteau involving sour-cherry marshmallow. Busy French service copes well with the demands of 'needlessly confusing' menus. The wine list offers rather conservative drinking from £20. Part of Alan Murchison's '10 in 8' stable – see L'Ortolan, La Bécasse and Angélique.

Chef/s: Phil Fanning. **Open:** Wed to Sun L 12 to 2, Tue to Sat D 7 to 9 (6.45 Sat). **Closed:** Mon, 24 Dec to 6 Jan. **Meals:** Set L £26 (2 courses) to £30. Set D £54 (2 courses) to £67. Sun L £30. Tasting menus L £36 (6 courses), D £71 (8 courses) to £95 (10 courses). **Service:** 12.5% (optional). **Details:** Cards accepted. 36 seats. Separate bar. No mobile phones. Music. Children allowed. Car parking.

SPARKLING SERVICE

Front-of-house staff are often the unsung heroes of the restaurant trade - while chefs bask in the glory and heat of the kitchen, the waiting staff keep things running smoothly, and ultimately ensure that people leave a restaurant happy and contented.

Raymond Blanc, of **Le Manoir aux Quat'Saisons**, is well aware that good service is as important as good food. One of his first jobs in catering was as a waiter, 'the biggest moment of my life,' he says. Blanc enjoyed giving pleasure and joy to people, 'it was a big revelation for a lad of 21.' This sentiment is echoed by Andrea Briccarello, the sommelier at **Galvin La Chapelle** and **Galvin's Café à Vin** in London. For him, one of the most rewarding aspects of his job is 'the happy smile on a guest leaving the restaurant: you know you've done good!'

Blanc firmly puts the emphasis on training staff properly. Yet even today he notes how often service is underestimated in this country. 'We must train better' is his message, one that is beginning to be heard as front-of-house becomes a serious career option for skilled people, and not simply a part-time job.

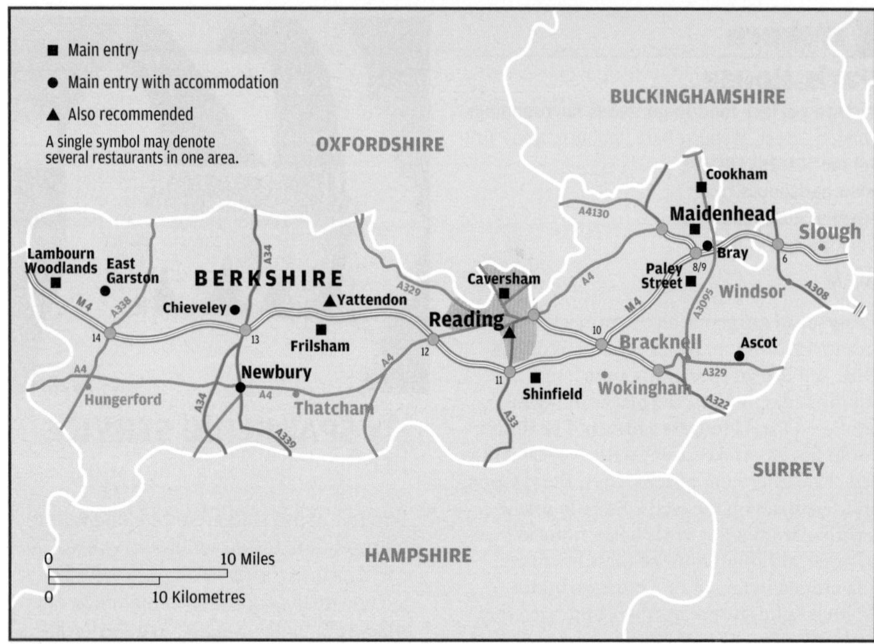

Ascot

NEW ENTRY

John Campbell at Coworth Park

Opulence and grand culinary ambitions

Coworth Park, London Road, Ascot, SL5 7SE

Tel no: (01344) 876600

www.coworthpark.com

Modern European | £60

Cooking score: 7

V

In 2010, the Sultan of Brunei funded a characteristically lavish revamp of this hulking country house set in expansive grounds adjoining Windsor Great Park; the result is a shiny, chic country cousin for his London flagship the Dorchester. It's a class act, combining a breezily relaxed vibe and sharp service with tasteful touches and plenty of ostentatious opulence. John Campbell, whose cerebral but soulful cuisine made the Vineyard at Stockcross a premier-league foodie destination for more than a decade (see entry), brings a fittingly grand culinary ambition to the mix. Dinner opens with a kaleidoscope of nibbles – perhaps ethereally textured hummus and unctuous anchovy foam with spiced crispbreads, satin-smooth mushroom soup and tiny arancini balls crowned with caviar. Campbell's cooking downplays transformational alchemy in favour of coaxing clean, deep flavours and intriguing textural contrasts from tersely described, familiar ingredients: 'scallop, chicken wing, turnip, walnut' translates as a deconstructed chicken wing (slow-cooked in a glossy jus of its own essence) pitched up alongside seared scallops, flash-fried ceps, cep purée and walnut foam on an earthy bed of confit turnip, crowned with a potent, chicken-flavoured tapioca crisp; 'crab' appears as a raviolo on sous-vide salsify, scattered with clams, topped with crisp artichoke shards and bathed in a shellfish sauce of symphonic intensity. By contrast, a main course of Royal Farm beef, polenta and beetroot has seemed rather pedestrian (despite a lip-smacking croquette of bone marrow).

Moving on, mango espuma with coconut cream and lime jelly in cucumber consommé is a hard act to follow, but exceptional cheeses and a dessert of molten 'hay chocolate' scattered with rose-flavoured marshmallows and foam, lychee sorbet, shards of blood orange and lashings of caramel should ensure a happy ending. Coworth Park's wine cellar is 'an oenophile's dream' and the list is a mightily impressive world tour from Argentina and Austria to the USA (even Lebanon gets an entire page to itself). Prices (from £28) are high, but so is the quality. Note: as our deadline approached, John Campbell announced that he was renouncing his executive role to focus on the restaurant, so changes may be in the air.

Chef/s: John Campbell and Olly Rouse. **Open:** all week L 12 to 2 (2.30 Sat and Sun), D 6.30 to 9.30. **Meals:** Set L and D £48 (2 courses) to £60. Sun L £17.50 (2 courses) to £22.50. Tasting menu £80. **Service:** 12.5%. **Details:** Cards accepted. 66 seats. Separate bar. No mobile phones. Wheelchair access. Music. Children allowed. Car parking.

Bray

The Fat Duck

The experience of a lifetime
1 High Street, Bray, SL6 2AQ
Tel no: (01628) 580333
www.thefatduck.co.uk
Modern British | £180
Cooking score: 10
V

You might be forgiven for thinking that the pressure of conceiving, orchestrating and delivering the hottest London launch of 2011 would impact on the genius behind the Fat Duck, but not even the razzmatazz surrounding Dinner by Heston Blumenthal (see entry) seems to have fazed the wizard of Bray. 'Just when you think it's all becoming a tad formulaic, he manages to inject new verve and enthusiasm into the place', observed one who has watched the Duck's relentless progress over the years. Eating here is the experience of a lifetime. Teasing out childhood memories and igniting fantastical fireworks may be Heston's stock in trade, but there is serious intent behind the sorcery: it's playful, desirable, electrifying stuff – never po-faced or vacuously experimental. Of course, gastro tourists and star-chasers still come in search of the iconic creations that have made HB a household name: the nitro-poached vodka and lime 'aperitif' is still offered (although it's been joined by a couple of alcoholic team mates) and the legendary snail porridge is back – as intensely grassy-green and buttery as ever, with the tenderest of gastropods lurking within its starchy mass. There's also a dish of salmon poached in liquorice, embroidered with tiny sequins of black truffle, asparagus, vanilla mayo and a salty shot of golden trout roe, as well as an 'haute' sensation involving roast foie gras, braised kombu seaweed and shards of carapace-like crab biscuit with some astringent barberry purée (replacing the rhubarb of old). And who can forget Heston's hallucinogenic homage to Alain Chapel – a fabulously indulgent conceit involving layers of quail jelly and crayfish cream topped with a film of chicken liver parfait, all cocooned within a forest-floor landscape of oak moss, earthy truffle 'toast' and swirling mist. So what's new? A witty, Ladurée-style beetroot and horseradish macaroon served as a palate-cleanser ('gone in a mouthful'); lollies that look sweet but taste savoury (tricolour 'Waldorf rocket'; 'salmon twister' mimicking the iconic ice lolly; unctuous, chocolatey 'foie gras feast'); also an eighteenth-century recipe for lamb with cubes of lightly cured cucumber and a bowl of meaty, gel-like consommé for slurping. Eventually, it's time to re-calibrate your taste buds with a draft of 'hot and iced' tea – two flavours and two completely different temperatures side-by-side in the same vessel. As the gustatory compass swings towards sweetness, out comes a dessert called 'BFG' – a zany reinvention of that 1970s cliché Black Forest gâteau which shows why the combination of cherries, chocolate, cream and Kirsch is still irresistibly sexy. There's also a day trip to the seaside in the shape of macerated strawberries with an olive oil biscuit swathed in a pink-icing 'picnic cloth', with camomile, crunchy roasted coriander and jelly – plus a dinky cone of strawberry ice cream. After that, some whisky wine gums ('I wish he made these commercially'), and finally a paper bag full of kids' sweet shop treats for you to nibble at table or save for later as you marvel at the wonder of it all. The whole shebang is delivered with good grace, enthusiasm and a terrific sense of fun by a team of 'sensational staff'. To enhance the vivid detailing even further, apply some judicious samplings from the fabulous wine list; otherwise dive headlong into its treasure chest of vinous pickings. Bottle prices (from £35) are painful – mind you, coming here was never about the money.

Chef/s: Heston Blumenthal. **Open:** Tue to Sun L 12 to 2 (3 Sun), Tue to Sat D 7 to 9.30. **Closed:** Mon, 2 weeks Christmas. **Meals:** Tasting menu L and D £180. **Service:** 12.5% (optional). **Details:** Cards accepted. 40 seats. No music. No mobile phones. Children allowed.

The Hinds Head

Ancient inn with revitalised food
High Street, Bray, SL6 2AB
Tel no: (01628) 626151
www.hindsheadbray.com
British | £40
Cooking score: 4

With reservations for the Fat Duck and Dinner (see entries) at a premium, Heston Blumenthal fans can still have recourse to the Hinds Head for a suitably pub-centric take on the great British boozer. It's a village inn that dates from Tudor times, complete with gnarled beams, low ceilings and warm wood panelling. Reporters may have found the period between chefs to be a rocky one, but at inspection Kevin Love appeared to have revitalised the kitchen and its aim of bringing refined technique to bear on robust classics. Tea-smoked salmon, pea and ham soup, venison and kidney pudding, steaks with bone marrow, the ubiquitous triple-cooked chips, even strawberry trifle, all deliver. Service is 'relaxed and efficient, laid-back and professional'. Expect ales from the Rebellion brewery in Marlow and wines from £18.75 – an indication that prices may exceed pubby expectations. The Crown, also on Bray's High Street, is the latest addition to the family. It's a relaxed alternative to the Hinds Head, offering a stock selection of British pub standards (tel: 01628 621936).

Chef/s: Kevin Love. **Open:** all week L 12 to 2.30 (4 Sun), Mon to Sat D 6.30 to 9.30. **Closed:** 25 and 26 Dec. **Meals:** alc (main courses £15 to £30). Set L and D £27.50. **Service:** 12.5% (optional). **Details:** Cards accepted. 90 seats. Separate bar. No music. Children allowed. Car parking.

The Waterside Inn

The old grand things done perfectly
Ferry Road, Bray, SL6 2AT
Tel no: (01628) 620691
www.waterside-inn.co.uk
French | £130
Cooking score: 7

To the gilded generation who were seduced by the seemingly effortless charm of the Waterside half an aeon ago, the place has never lost its magic. One lucky regular sums up its appeal as 'highly accomplished food with great service – and a setting in Paradise'. That last element counts for a lot, especially at a summer lunch when the room opens up to greet its stretch of the Thames and birdsong fills the air. If location were all, there would be little more to say, but the Waterside has always prided itself on offering the complete restaurant experience, founded on seamless professionalism, flawless courtesy and microscopic attention to detail. It's become *de rigueur* to comment on how defiantly traditional the cooking is, and it's true that nobody will spray you with liquid nitrogen, and the menus are loftily above the language of 'soil', 'dust' and 'air'. But that doesn't indicate any perverse disinclination to change and development. Today's menus might offer turbot roasted on the bone, accompanied by trompettes de mort, Tarbais beans and lardons in a richly robust sauce of Hermitage, or perhaps roast Challandais duck for two, served with soft polenta, chestnuts and poached

quince in a cider jus. There are old favourites, to be sure, such as quenelle de brochet (pike) with langoustine to start, or a puff-pastry cassolette of sautéed veal kidney in mustard, but the precision with which even these classics are rendered speaks of the fine-tuning expected of high-end cooking today. When dishes hit the right notes, their intensity lives long in the memory, as is avowed by a reader whose December dinner included superb venison with gently textured pumpkin subric, and closed with a high-octane date and cognac soufflé with coffee ice cream. The wine list too is a classic of the genre but, like the cooking, remains a work in progress, finding exciting new growers and outstanding vintages all the time, albeit mostly in France. Bring your plastic: wines by the glass start at £9.50.
Chef/s: Alain Roux. **Open:** Wed to Sun L 12 to 2 (2.30 Sun), D 7 to 10, also Tue D 1 Jun to 31 Aug. **Closed:** Mon, 26 Dec for five weeks. **Meals:** alc (main courses £50 to £70). Set L £42.50 (2 courses) to £58. Sun L £74. Tasting menu £147.50. **Service:** not inc. **Details:** Cards accepted. 70 seats. Separate bar. No music. No mobile phones. Car parking.

Caversham

Mya Lacarte

British produce; Gallic flavours
5 Prospect Street, Caversham, RG4 8JB
Tel no: (01189) 463400
www.myalacarte.co.uk
Anglo-French | £30
Cooking score: 2

Behind an unprepossessing frontage on a busy road in the heart of Caversham lies the somewhat unimaginatively named Mya Lacarte. French influences are evident everywhere, but there's also a healthy regard for British produce – from Fowey mussels and Hampshire beef, via the well-reported twice-baked butternut squash soufflé with organic Goring Heath leaves, to Ashampstead rabbit leg served with pommes boulangère, Basingstoke watercress and a gentle mustard cream sauce. Puddings often seem to come in trios of this and that (treacle tart, Jersey double cream, vanilla ice cream), while île flottante (with crème anglaise, caramel and shortbread) has been particularly noted. House wine is £13.95.
Chef/s: Loic Gautier. **Open:** all week L 12 to 3 (4 Sun), Mon to Sat D 5 to 10.30. **Closed:** 25 and 26 Dec, 1 Jan. **Meals:** alc (main courses £12.95 to £22). Set L and D (Mon to Wed only) £13.95 (2 courses) to £17.50. **Service:** not inc. **Details:** Cards accepted. 50 seats. Music. Children allowed.

Chieveley

The Crab at Chieveley

Skilful seafood and dazzling desserts
Wantage Road, Chieveley, RG20 8UE
Tel no: (01635) 247550
www.crabatchieveley.com
Seafood | £34
Cooking score: 3

£5 OFF ⊨ V

With its rural setting, thatched roof and dining room ceilings strewn with fishing nets, floats and shells, the Crab is rustic restaurant personified. Yet it is a lot more contemporary in attitude and operation than the décor suggests. Seafood plays a major role and there is general contentment when it comes to roast brill with fig and tarragon, dauphinoise potatoes and vanilla and celeriac purée, as well as cod with chorizo velouté, aubergine and red pepper concasse. A starter of Berkshire pork belly with smoked apple purée, Scotch egg and cider jus shows the menu is not just about fish, and desserts such as blood orange and white chocolate trifle with nougat ice cream are guaranteed to dazzle. Effusive comments, too, for 'brilliant service'. House wine is £20.
Chef/s: Nick Hope. **Open:** all week L 12 to 2.30 (3 Sun), D 6 to 10 (9.30 Sun). **Meals:** alc (main courses £18 to £35). Set L and D £15.95 (2 courses) to £19.95. Sun L £19.50 (2 courses) to £22.50. **Service:** 10% (optional). **Details:** Cards accepted. 100 seats. 50 seats outside. Separate bar. Wheelchair access. Music. Children allowed. Car parking.

Cookham

Maliks

Dynamic Indian with a starry clientele
High Street, Cookham, SL6 9SF
Tel no: (01628) 520085
www.maliks.co.uk
Indian | £30
Cooking score: 2

£5 OFF

The pastoral setting adds to the charm of Malik Ahmed's ivy-clad Indian restaurant, cunningly disguised as a country pub in the centre of Cookham, as its starry clientele doubtless attest. Take your place among the actors and sports luminaries for some dynamic, conscientiously presented Indian cooking that will suit both aficionados of the old favourites (sheek kebabs, biryanis and dhansaks), as well as those in the mood to branch out. Calamari stuffed with minced chicken and prawns, lamb with tamarind, and duck breast cooked in coconut milk add lustre to the operation. Firni (rice pudding seasoned with saffron and cardamom) is the signature dessert. Wines start at £15. Branches can be found in Buckinghamshire, at Gerrard's Cross, tel: (01753) 880888 and Marlow, tel: (01628) 482180.

Chef/s: Malik Ahmed and Shapon Miah. **Open:** all week L 12 to 2.30, D 6 to 11 (10.30 Sun). **Closed:** 25 and 26 Dec. **Meals:** alc (main courses £8 to £16). Set L £12 (2 courses) to £15. Set D £24 (2 courses) to £30. Sun L £10. **Service:** 10% (optional). **Details:** Cards accepted. 70 seats. No mobile phones. Wheelchair access. Music. Children allowed. Car parking.

Symbols

Accommodation is available

£30 Three courses for less than £30

V Separate vegetarian menu

£5 OFF £5-off voucher scheme

Notable wine list

East Garston

Queen's Arms Hotel

A safe bet for straightforward food
Newbury Road, East Garston, RG17 7ET
Tel no: (01488) 648757
www.queensarmshotel.co.uk
Modern British | £25
Cooking score: 2

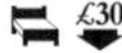

Country pursuits and horse racing are the main distractions in this lush corner of the Lambourn Valley, and the smartly gentrified Queen's Arms makes a congenial meeting point for chatting and checking the form (it's one of the few locations in the area where mobile phones actually work). The food is also a talking point, and the short menu makes a virtue of seasonality, offering vigorous, uncomplicated dishes such as stuffed slow-roast pork shoulder with pease pudding and apple sauce. Open your account with Ragstone goats' cheese and beetroot salad or pigeon breast with black pudding and lentils, before closing with jam roly-poly or dark chocolate brownie. House wine is £15.

Chef/s: Gary Burns. **Open:** all week L 12 to 2.30 (4 Sun), D 6.30 to 9.30 (7 to 9 Sun). **Closed:** 25 Dec. **Meals:** alc (main courses £11 to £18). Set L £21 (2 courses) to £25. Sun L £19 (2 courses) to £24. **Service:** not inc. **Details:** Cards accepted. 50 seats. 30 seats outside. Separate bar. Wheelchair access. Music. Children allowed. Car parking.

Frilsham

The Pot Kiln

Honest food's the game
Frilsham, RG18 0XX
Tel no: (01635) 201366
www.potkiln.org
British | £28
Cooking score: 1

'A great little pub serving totally honest food' was one reporter's verdict on this rural hostelry dating from 1700. It's a strongly rooted enterprise in which local suppliers dictate the repertoire (which includes venison shot by the owner, Mike Robinson). Given the local input, it's no surprise that the seasons are properly observed and you get what it says on the menu without distraction – say wild boar, venison and apple terrine, then mustard-crusted braised shoulder of lamb with pearl barley broth and winter chanterelles. Puddings include sinful treats like chocolate pecan tart with banana ice cream. House wine is £14.50.

Chef/s: Mike Robinson and Jonathan Taylor. **Open:** Wed to Mon L 12 to 2 (2.45 Sun), Wed to Sat and Mon D 7 to 9. **Closed:** Tue. **Meals:** alc (main courses £13 to £17). Set L £12.95 (2 courses) to £15.95. **Service:** 10% (optional). **Details:** Cards accepted. 48 seats. 100 seats outside. Separate bar. No music. Children allowed. Car parking.

Lambourn Woodlands

The Hare Restaurant

All-purpose venue with please-all food
Ermin Street, Lambourn Woodlands, RG17 7SD
Tel no: (01488) 71386
www.theharerestaurant.co.uk
Modern British | £35
Cooking score: 2

A Grade II-listed village inn turned open-plan restaurant-cum-bar, the revitalised Hare also sports a new Garden Room for private bashes – although its day-to-day business revolves around feeding and watering the Berkshire Downs set. Recent successes from the eclectic menu have included succulent scallops in pastry with hollandaise and Chinese greens, an oozing duck Scotch egg, and strips of beef with green peppercorn sauce and tarragon rice, but the kitchen can also dish up Thai crab cakes, grilled lemon sole with sauce vièrge and desserts such as whisky and sour cream cheesecake with ginger ice cream. An all-day lounge menu promises savoury muffins, salads, veggie mezze and the like. House wine is £17.

Chef/s: Paul Reed. **Open:** all week L 12 to 2 (2.30 Sun), D 7 to 9.30 (9 Sun). **Meals:** alc (main courses £13 to £23). Set L £21 (2 courses) to £27. Set D £20 (2 courses) to £35. Sun L £27. **Service:** not inc. **Details:** Cards accepted. 75 seats. 60 seats outside. Separate bar. Wheelchair access. Music. Children allowed. Car parking.

Maidenhead

Boulters Riverside Brasserie

Stylish brasserie with gorgeous views
Boulters Lock Island, Maidenhead, SL6 8PE
Tel no: (01628) 621291
www.boultersrestaurant.co.uk
Modern British | £30
Cooking score: 2

Following some gentle re-branding, Boulters now consists of the stylish Riverside Brasserie and a separate, self-contained Terrace Bar above – although you can still soak up gorgeous, uninterrupted views from this self-proclaimed 'jewel of the Thames' standing proud on its own little island. Choose the brasserie if you are after some carefully crafted modern food with a few European incursions – think slow-cooked neck of Berkshire venison with red cabbage, juniper jus and parsnip crisps. Breaded monkfish with saffron rouille and confit tomato makes a pleasing curtain-raiser, and you could close with something cheeky such as Black Forest gâteau soufflé with almond ice cream. House wine is £15.50.

Chef/s: Daniel Woodhouse. **Open:** Tue to Sun L 12 to 2.45, Tue to Sat D 6.30 to 9.30. **Closed:** Mon. **Meals:** alc (main courses £15 to £26). Set L £17.95 (2 courses) to £20.95. **Service:** 12.5% (optional). **Details:** Cards accepted. 100 seats. 20 seats outside. Separate bar. Wheelchair access. Music. Children allowed. Car parking.

Newbury

The Vineyard at Stockcross

Complex French cooking and brilliant wine
Newbury, RG20 8JU
Tel no: (01635) 528770
www.the-vineyard.co.uk
Modern French | £72
Cooking score: 6

£5 OFF V

Despite the name of Sir Peter Michael's hotel just outside Newbury, the vineyard he owns is actually in California. But the laid-back West Coast mood is certainly echoed in this extraordinary low-slung building, with its succession of large public rooms leading to a split-level dining room that looks like an artfully lit Hollywood film set by night. Daniel Galmiche took up the culinary reins in 2009, and guided the cooking in a more obviously contemporary French direction – and he has taken the Vineyard's regulars with him. One pre-Christmas couple enjoyed pumpkin velouté with Sainte-Maure goats' cheese foam, and duck and foie gras terrine with pear and orange jelly to start, before impeccably timed sole with potato and pancetta. A turkey dish, for all its fashionable slow cooking, didn't impress for either texture or flavour. Otherwise, the formidable level of technical complexity is what confers greatness on dishes such as pan-roasted scallops with chestnuts and ceps, rack and shin of veal with sweetbread, Swiss chard and smoked mash, and truffled Brillat-Savarin cheesecake with apple jelly and blackcurrant foam. A brilliant wine list offers as much enthusiasm in the various sub-regions of California as it does in the Médoc and the Côte d'Or. You'll need to hunt down the affordable listings, but there are decent bottles around the £18 mark.

Chef/s: Daniel Galmiche. **Open:** all week L 12 to 2, D 7 to 10. **Meals:** Set L £23 (2 courses) to £29. Set D £62 (2 courses) to £72. Sun L £39. L tasting menu £49. D tasting menu £99. **Service:** not inc. **Details:** Cards accepted. 90 seats. 50 seats outside. Separate bar. No mobile phones. Wheelchair access. Music. Children allowed. Car parking.

Paley Street

The Royal Oak

Inn with panache and fine food
Paley Street, SL6 3JN
Tel no: (01628) 620541
www.theroyaloakpaleystreet.com
British | £45
Cooking score: 6

The Parkinsons'country inn is extremely good at winning converts with its agreeable blend of rusticity and creature comforts, affluent vibes and terrific food. First-timers are instantly hooked, and when Sir Michael himself declares 'I eat there most of the days of the week, so it had better be good', the gauntlet has been duly thrown down. Fortunately, the Royal Oak has a chef who rises to the occasion with reliable panache, mixing an innovative streak with a flair for knowing his audience well. Readers love everything that's put in front of them, from a starter of pickled herring, creamed beetroot and horseradish to a glorious dish of peppered Denham venison haunch in sauce poivrade, served with superlative creamy mash in a copper pan. A feeling for British cookery's heritage ingredients also shows in, say, sea bass with cockles, mussels and samphire or brown hare and trotter pie, but dishes that require the lighter touch evince fine judgement too – witness a warm salad of smoked eel with bacon and frisée. Traditional desserts get good write-ups, whether for William pear tart with vanilla ice cream or bread-and-butter pudding, and there's also a roll call of pedigree English cheeses. The Parkinsons know their wines, and the list is a commendable mix of bullish southern hemisphere contenders alongside grandees from the classic French regions. Prices start at £17.50 (£12.50 for a 50cl carafe).

Chef/s: Dominic Chapman. **Open:** all week L 12 to 2.30 (3.30 Sun), Mon to Sat D 6.30 to 9.30 (10 Fri and Sat). **Meals:** alc (main courses £16 to £30). Set L £17.95 (2 courses) to £21. **Service:** 12.5%

(optional). **Details:** Cards accepted. 46 seats. 40 seats outside. Separate bar. Music. Children allowed. Car parking.

Reading

ALSO RECOMMENDED

▲ London Street Brasserie

2-4 London Street, Reading, RG1 4SE
Tel no: (01189) 505036
www.londonstbrasserie.co.uk
Modern European

Now more than a decade old, this brasserie in a former tollhouse sits snug to the river Kennet in the heart of Reading's town centre. A relaxed, informal restaurant with some alfresco seating, it offers a broad selection of dishes, from classic fish soup with rouille and croûtons (£7.20) to Moroccan spiced lamb with char-grilled vegetables and barley couscous (£18.90). Imaginative extras include roasted spiced pumpkin and butternut squash. Finish with baked Alaska. Wines from £18.50. Open all week.

Shinfield

L'Ortolan

Seductively classy destination
Church Lane, Shinfield, RG2 9BY
Tel no: (01189) 888500
www.lortolan.com
Modern French | £67
Cooking score: 6

£5 OFF ♦ V

On the outskirts of Reading, just a few minutes from the M4, and yet ensconced within its own little nest of seclusion, the creeper-clad L'Ortolan is dedicated wholeheartedly to the cause of fine dining. As well as a supremely gracious, handsomely appointed dining room, it offers the ubiquitous chef's table, where you're only a few feet from the action. Alan Murchison's cooking is a fantastically precise interpretation of all that is brightest and best about today's cutting-edge approach, weaving French technique and British ingredients together. Start with Cornish crab in wasabi yoghurt with coriander mayonnaise and lemongrass jelly, and follow up with veal loin and sweetbread with girolles and peas in a shatteringly intense truffled jus. Cheesecake for dessert could hardly be more in vogue just now, appearing here as a blackberry version with almond clafoutis, alongside a ginger beer and blackberry sorbet. Service is as impeccably detailed as the culinary skills, making for one of the classiest destinations in the Home Counties. A conscientiously compiled wine list opens with 11 by the glass (from £5), displays imagination and character all the way through, and there is decent choice under £30. Bottles start at £19.
Chef/s: Alan Murchison and Elliott Lidstone. **Open:** Tue to Sat L 12 to 2, D 7 to 9 (9.30 Fri and Sat). **Closed:** Sun, Mon, 24 Dec to 5 Jan. **Meals:** Set L £25 (2 courses) to £29.90. Set D £58 (2 courses) to £67. Gourmand menu £71. Chef's surprise menu £105 (10 courses). **Service:** 12.5% (optional). **Details:** Cards accepted. 64 seats. Separate bar. No mobile phones. Wheelchair access. Music. Children allowed. Car parking.

Yattendon

ALSO RECOMMENDED

▲ The Royal Oak

The Square, Yattendon, RG18 0UF
Tel no: (01635) 201325
www.royaloakyattendon.co.uk
Modern British

The hub of an affluent Berkshire village, this upper-crust, sixteenth-century inn still parades its history – although rug-strewn floors, drapes and contemporary design touches now set the tone in the smart bar and brasserie-style dining rooms. The food is also a mix of old and new, pitting oxtail soup, chicken Cordon Bleu, venison Wellington and profiteroles against tarragon crab cakes with caper relish (£7), goats' cheese and walnut risotto or braised shin of veal accompanied by orange gremolata and tagliatelle (£15). Wines from £16.85. Open all week. Accommodation.

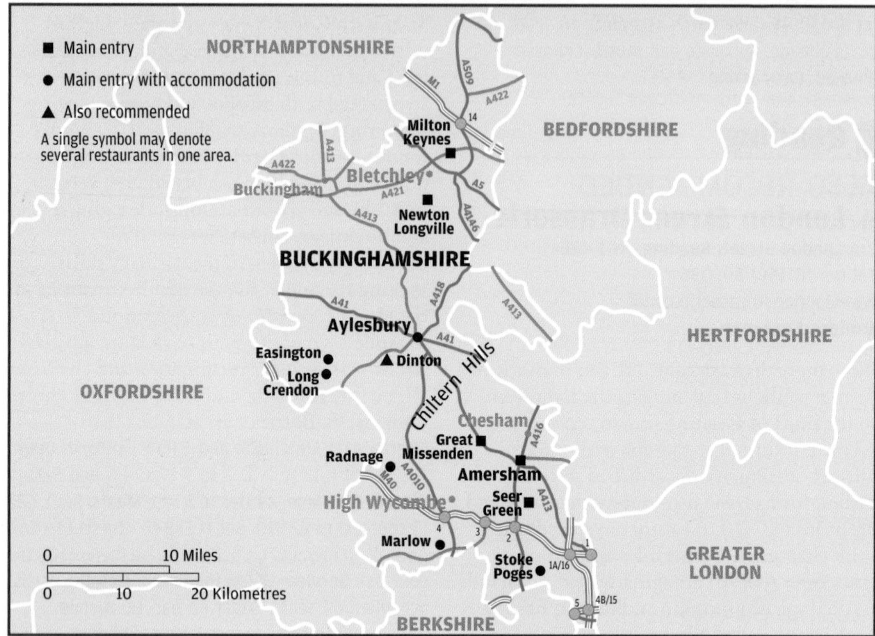

Amersham

Artichoke

Blossoming with new ideas
9 Market Square, Amersham, HP7 ODF
Tel no: (01494) 726611
www.artichokerestaurant.co.uk
Modern European | £44
Cooking score: 6

It's ironic that the fire which originally caused Laurie and Jacqueline Gear's restaurant to shut down has also proved to be its salvation. The Artichoke has now spread into the building next door and started afresh with the immediacy of an up-close open kitchen. The whole set-up bristles with confidence, liberating Laurie Gear's culinary sensibilities; his clear-sighted approach to seasonality has blossomed anew. Meals often begin with a shot of foam (perhaps a take on Waldorf salad with fresh apple tones singing through) and the natural world is never far away. Consider a springtime garland woven from cultivated and wild asparagus with piles of oh-so-fresh crab meat, perfectly runny quails' eggs and dinky crab 'marshmallows', all on a subtle, grassy-green herb emulsion. Or hazelnut-crusted pigeon breasts atop sticks of sweet/sharp pickled salsify: to one side, a swathe of earthy brown nuttiness studded with morels; to the other, a vivid green wild garlic purée. Challenging our preconceptions about ingredients is also a recurring theme; witness a dessert of malted pearl barley with poached peaches, a dollop of raspberry-beer ice cream and linseed tuile, finished with some blissful peach soup. All of this comes at gentle prices; the lunchtime tasting menu must be the best deal for miles around. A top-notch, knowledgeable wine list starts at £19.50.

Chef/s: Laurie Gear. **Open:** Tue to Sat L 12 to 2.30, D 6.30 to 11. **Closed:** Sun, Mon, 1 week Christmas, last week Aug, first week Sept, bank hols. **Meals:** alc (main courses £18 to £24). Set L £25. Set D £35 (2 courses) to £43.50. Tasting menu L £35 (5 courses), D £62 (7 courses). **Service:** 12.5% (optional). **Details:** Cards accepted. 34 seats. 2 seats outside. No mobile phones. Music. Children allowed.

ALSO RECOMMENDED

▲ The Crown Inn

16 High Street, Amersham, HP7 0DH
Tel no: (01494) 721541
www.thecrownamersham.com
British

A bullish, brick-fronted inn-with-rooms, the Crown chimes perfectly with the posh boutiques on Old Amersham's main drag. A new chef arrived just before the *Guide* went to press, but the menu still touts robust British seasonal dishes with a few Euro add-ons. Start with pigeon breast and St George's mushrooms (£6), move on to 'ris e bisi' (rice and peas) or duck leg with mash, black pudding and turnips (£13), and round off with lemon posset. Wines from £16.50 (£8.25 a carafe). No food Sun D. Reports please.

▲ Gilbey's

1 Market Square, Amersham, HP7 0DF
Tel no: (01494) 727242
www.gilbeygroup.com
Modern British

A colourful and ever-reliable all-rounder dispensing vivid bistro food in historic surroundings, complete with a pretty courtyard garden. The kitchen plays it straight, but be prepared for a few surprises: cod cheeks with warm pea and mint mousseline (£8.15), Jerusalem artichoke and parsley risotto with walnuts, and confit duck with turnips and beetroot tarte Tatin (£15.95) are typical, and there might be almond pannacotta with warm pear jelly to finish. There is afternoon tea, too. The Gilbey family's pedigree as wine importers guarantees sound drinking from £15.25. Open all week.

LAURIE GEAR
Artichoke

What did being awarded 'Best New Entry' in *The Good Food Guide 2011* mean to you?
We were very proud to be recognised by such a prestigious and well-read guide. It was a real boost to the whole team who worked so hard last year.

Who is your ideal diner?
Someone who is open minded, and has a real love of food and the provenance of the ingredients.

What do you eat when you're feeling lazy?
A sandwich of pastrami, mustard, mayonnaise and dill pickles. I try and have these ingredients in my fridge when I get home late at night.

What's your favourite job in the kitchen?
Preparing fish. It reminds me of my home town in Dorset.

What most excites you about the restaurant industry today?
The competition. It keeps you sharp, hungry and determined to satisfy your clients.

What kitchen gadget could you not live without?
My team. Gadgets I can live without.

Great Missenden

La Petite Auberge

Bastion of French virtues
107 High Street, Great Missenden, HP16 0BB
Tel no: (01494) 865370
www.lapetiteauberge.co.uk
French | £37
Cooking score: 3
£5 OFF

Gallic culinary virtues and family courtesy are alive and well at this 'petite' bastion of bourgeois gentility in a decidedly affluent Chiltern village – so expect to find a contented local crowd lapping up the gustatory pleasures of soupe de poissons, magret de canard and mousse au chocolat. There is nothing here to challenge, irritate or inflame the passions, but Hubert Martel is an assured chef who knows how to conjure up generous, satisfying dishes with all the right accents – whether it's a neatly contrived plate of snails 'en surprise' (served in tiny potato 'shells'), a pearly-white tranche of turbot with anchovies and caper sauce or textbook carré d'agneau with rosemary. Service is homely, personal and chatty. The succinct, all-French wine list starts at £17.50.
Chef/s: Hubert Martel. **Open:** Mon to Sat D only 7 to 10. **Closed:** Sun (except Mothering Sun L), 2 weeks Christmas, 3 weeks Easter, bank hols. **Meals:** alc (main courses £18 to £20). **Service:** not inc. **Details:** Cards accepted. 30 seats. No music. Wheelchair access. Children allowed.

Long Crendon

Angel Restaurant

Ever popular all-rounder
47 Bicester Road, Long Crendon, HP18 9EE
Tel no: (01844) 208268
www.angelrestaurant.co.uk
Modern European | £32
Cooking score: 2
£5 OFF

An engaging and perpetually popular all-rounder, this reinvented coaching inn now markets itself resolutely as a restaurant-with-rooms, although it still sports a bona fide bar with real ales, exposed beams and squashy sofas. Diners spread themselves across several eating areas (including a pretty conservatory), and the kitchen obliges them with ample helpings of twice-baked Oxford Blue cheese soufflé, a trio of Sandy Lane pork (fillet, belly and hock) and horseradish-crusted fillet of naturally reared beef with bourguignon sauce. Fish specials are also worth noting (perhaps grilled lemon sole with jasmine rice, pak choi and lemongrass butter) and the assiette of desserts keeps everyone happy. The global wine list offers terrific drinking by the glass or 50ml pichet (from £11.50), but there's also a cracking selection of style-led bottles featuring some lesser known grape varieties. Prices start at £15.50.
Chef/s: Trevor Bosch. **Open:** all week L 12 to 2.30, Mon to Sat D 7 to 9.30. **Closed:** 1 Jan. **Meals:** alc (main courses £16 to £36). Set L £14.95 (2 courses) to £19.95. Set D and Sun L £19.95 (2 courses) to £24.95. **Service:** not inc. **Details:** Cards accepted. 70 seats. 25 seats outside. Separate bar. Wheelchair access. Music. Children allowed. Car parking.

Marlow

Adam Simmonds at Danesfield House

Magnificent food, bursting with vitality
Henley Road, Marlow, SL7 2EY
Tel no: (01628) 891010
www.danesfieldhouse.co.uk
Modern European | £59
Cooking score: 8
£5 OFF V

An epically grandiose pile of castellated Gothic extravagance with Italianate overtones, Danesfield House looms impressively with 65 acres of formal gardens, some dramatic topiary and views of the Thames to get visitors in unbridled 'country house' mood. Inside, it's a riot of tapestries, antiques and paintings, although the flagship restaurant has a more contemporary and less intimidating feel, despite its whitewashed panelling, starched linen cloths and elegant tableware. Chef Adam

Simmonds now has full control of the food throughout the hotel, and this self-named dining room is his gastronomic mission statement. If you were in any doubt that he is now one of the top players on the UK restaurant scene, a couple of mouthfuls of his masterful sautéed veal sweetbreads with anchovy tortellini, girolles and cauliflower purée should seal the deal. It goes without saying that ingredients are sourced and deployed with consummate respect, care and intelligence; everything fits and resonates, whether it's a breathtaking starter of roasted Scottish scallops with three carrot-based accompaniments aligned on a classy slate, or a deeply autumnal assemblage of slow-cooked partridge breast with roasted ceps, pearl barley and nutmeg-tinged white onion purée. The detailing is exquisite: dried hazelnuts enlivening a dish of roasted chicken wings and white asparagus purée; wisps of yeast foam bringing some strange earthiness to poached fillet of brill with pied de mouton mushrooms – although these purposeful touches are much more than mere whimsical ancillaries. As for desserts, the kitchen lets rip, often focusing on specific ingredients and exploring their textures and contrasts in depth: William pear mousse with pear sorbet, walnut purée and roasted walnuts, for example, or an extraordinary construction of orange parfait and cardamom ice cream surmounted by pillars of orange and cardamom meringue. In fact, every painstaking detail and cleverly contrived little flourish is just so, from 'two very amusing bouches' to the beautiful mouthfuls of 'sweet happiness' that appear with coffee. This is food bursting with vitality, courtesy of a chef who has discovered real impetus and direction. The classy wine list is all about substance and nobility, with comprehensive regional coverage and sound judgement when it comes to food matching. Seasonal selections start at £23.50 (£6.50 a glass); also note the fine choice of sherries.
Chef/s: Adam Simmonds. **Open:** Thur to Sat L 12 to 3, Tue to Sat D 7 to 9.30. **Closed:** Sun, Mon, 16 Dec to 3 Jan, last 2 weeks Aug. **Meals:** Set L and D £47 (2 courses) to £59. Tasting menu £80. **Service:** 12.5% (optional). **Details:** Cards accepted. 20 seats. 60 seats outside. Separate bar. No music. No mobile phones. Wheelchair access. Car parking.

The Hand & Flowers

Endearing venue with alluring menus
126 West Street, Marlow, SL7 2BP
Tel no: (01628) 482277
www.thehandandflowers.co.uk
Modern British | £40
Cooking score: 6

Formed from a bundle of Georgian workers' cottages, the Kerridges' pub-cum-restaurant (with rooms a few yards away) is a highly endearing venue. Any sense of dining in cramped quarters is soon dispelled by the cheering ambience of low beams and flagged floors. Tom Kerridge is a confident, resourceful chef, and he uses the best of local supply lines and a little French technique to fashion modern British menus of great allure. A serving of veal sweetbread on butter-braised pearl barley with a lemon and caper fritter is a richly satisfying first course, or you might be seduced by the simple classicism of moules marinière simmered in stout. Dishes are precisely weighted and smartly presented, offering a slow-cooked duck breast with duck-fat chips and gravy as one main, or sea bream with pissaladière and chorizo mayonnaise for another. Reporters speak of depths of flavour that linger in the memory, and the pleasure of discovery, whether it's a finisher of unreconstructed crème brûlée or the less familiar likes of tonka bean pannacotta with rhubarb and ginger wine jelly. If the little cocktail list doesn't tempt you to let your hair down, the wines are quite inviting enough themselves, opening with a house selection from £22.20 for a good Mosel Riesling.
Chef/s: Tom Kerridge. **Open:** all week L 12 to 2.30 (3.30 Sun), Mon to Sat D 6.30 to 9.30. **Closed:** 24 to 26 Dec. **Meals:** alc (main courses £17 to £28). Set L Mon to Sat £12.50 (2 courses) to £16.50. **Service:** not inc. **Details:** Cards accepted. 50 seats. 20 seats outside. Music. Children allowed. Car parking.

Vanilla Pod

House of hidden delights
31 West Street, Marlow, SL7 2LS
Tel no: (01628) 898101
www.thevanillapod.co.uk
Modern European | £40
Cooking score: 5

 **V**

The perfect antidote to Marlow's culinary cacophony, according to one regular, the Vanilla Pod promises 'quiet grace' and soft-toned, neighbourly civility in what was TS Eliot's out-of-town bolt-hole. It's unstuffy, sociable, refined and an 'absolutely reliable' outpost of creative contemporary cooking. Michael Macdonald's approach is measured and doesn't puff itself up, but his dishes are never ordinary or ill-considered – witness a signature starter of seared scallops with vanilla-poached pears, red wine shallots and vanilla 'gastrique'. Daube of beef always gets good reviews, and there are seasonal forays into the countryside for roast grouse with buttery turnips, or well-hung venison bedded on choucroute and prunes. Fish comes through strongly too, in the shape of dainty warm-cured salmon with pickled fennel, or roast brill with Parmesan polenta, wild mushrooms and oxtail sauce. To finish, buttermilk pannacotta arrives with blueberries and two 'wobbling shards' of zingy lemon jelly, while the chocolate soup is 'to die for... even in Lent'. The brilliant-value set lunch may not appear with all the bells and whistles, but it still 'jingles and toots': intense pre-starter soups, butternut squash risotto with pickled shallots, megrim sole with lentils, and 'cakelets' of coffee frangipane with orange ice cream have left readers feeling thoroughly spoilt. Service is smart, knowledgeable and tactful, while the commendable French-led wine list provides classy drinking across the range. House recommendations start at £19.50 (£4.50 a glass).
Chef/s: Michael Macdonald. **Open:** Tue to Sat L 12 to 2, D 7 to 10. **Closed:** Sun, Mon, 24 Dec to 3 Jan. **Meals:** Set L £15.50 (2 courses) to £19.50. Set D £40. Gourmand menu £50 (7 courses). **Service:** not inc. **Details:** Cards accepted. 36 seats. 10 seats outside. Separate bar. No music. Children allowed.

Milton Keynes

NEW ENTRY

Taipan

The best dim sum for miles
5 Savoy Crescent, Milton Keynes, MK9 3PU
Tel no: (01908) 331883
www.taipan-mk.co.uk
Chinese
Cooking score: 3

Plumb in Milton Keynes' pedestrianised theatre district, Taipan outshines its rather corporate surroundings. Full-length windows allow plenty of light into the roomy, bright interior (both ground floor and mezzanine) – all the better to see the best dim sum for miles around. The kitchen excels at deep frying and produces exemplary yam paste croquettes (crisp coating, melting interior, savoury pork centre), and (from the pricey main menu) sublime crispy oysters – but marinated baby cuttlefish (just-so resilience), slithery cheung fun filled with plump prawns, and baked char siu pastries should also not be missed. At night, luxury seafood and hotpots such as braised beef belly with turnip hold the most allure. Drink tea, or something from the 40-strong wine list, which starts at £12.80. Chinese diners make special trips here. Enough said.
Chef/s: P M Lai. **Open:** all week L 12 to 3.30, D 5.30 to 11 (10 Sun). **Closed:** 24 to 26 Dec. **Meals:** alc (main courses £8 to £15). Set L and D £22 (6 courses) to £40. **Service:** 10% (optional). **Details:** Cards accepted. 120 seats. Wheelchair access. Music. Children allowed.

Newton Longville

The Crooked Billet

Home-produced food and breathtaking wine
2 Westbrook End, Newton Longville, MK17 0DF
Tel no: (01908) 373936
www.thebillet.co.uk
Modern British | £29
Cooking score: 2

£5 OFF 🍷 V £30

With its pristine thatched roof and well-to-do village location, the Billet looks every inch the country hostelry, but inside it's a different story. The Gilchrists have enlisted a battalion of local producers during their tenure here, and also make a virtue of industrious home-production – be it curing brisket or smoking bacon and duck sausages in the inglenook. Emma's cooking is ambitious, with lots of busy flavours jostling on the plate: just consider stone bass fillet with crushed charlotte potatoes, wilted spinach, roasted pepper salsa and anchovy beignet, or char-grilled pork ribeye with sage and apple salad, walnuts and truffled potato ravioli. Steaks receive plaudits, likewise the 'unforgettable' trolley loaded with ripe Anglo-French cheeses. Just about everything on the breathtaking, 200-bin wine list is available by the glass, and it's an endlessly fascinating world tour. Bottles start at £15.

Chef/s: Emma Gilchrist. **Open:** Tue to Sun L 12 to 2 (12.30 to 3.30 Sun), Mon to Sat D 7 to 9 (7 to 10 Fri, 6.30 to 10 Sat). **Closed:** 27 and 28 Dec. **Meals:** alc (main courses £11 to £27). Set L £16 (2 courses) to £19.50. Set D £19.50 (2 courses) to £23.50. Sun L £26. Tasting menu £65. **Service:** not inc. **Details:** Cards accepted. 60 seats. 50 seats outside. Separate bar. No music. Children allowed. Car parking.

Radnage

The Three Horseshoes

Charming inn with generous platefuls
Horseshoe Road, Bennett End, Radnage, HP14 4EB
Tel no: (01494) 483273
www.thethreehorseshoes.net
Modern British | £30
Cooking score: 3

Red kites circle above the garden of this charming country inn and restaurant-with-rooms set deep in the Chilterns. Expect lovely views and a smartly refurbished interior where original features sit comfortably with the pale, modern décor. Food is 'very good, but not complex' and comes in generous portions. Lunch brings simple sandwiches and burgers (homemade, with red onion compote and mature Cheddar cheese) and more substantial choices such as seared fillet of sea bream with pak choi, crispy potatoes and a chilli, garlic, ginger and peanut oil dressing. The snappy, international flavours continue at dinner, alongside traditional options such as char-grilled sirloin steak with green peppercorn sauce and all the trimmings. Finish with sticky toffee pudding. Wines start from £15.

Chef/s: James Norie. **Open:** Tue to Sun L 12 to 2.30 (3 Sun), Mon to Sat D 7 to 9.30. **Meals:** alc (main courses £16 to £20). Set L Tue to Sat £14.50 (2 courses) to £19. Set D £16 (2 courses) to £21. Sun L £27. **Service:** 10% (optional). **Details:** Cards accepted. 70 seats. 120 seats outside. Separate bar. Wheelchair access. Music. Children allowed. Car parking.

Seer Green

NEW ENTRY

The Jolly Cricketers

Real village local with lively food
24 Chalfont Road, Seer Green, HP9 2YG
Tel no: (01494) 676308
www.thejollycricketers.co.uk
Modern British | £28
Cooking score: 3

An accomplished spin on pub food may grace its tables, but landlady Amanda Baker has kept the Jolly Cricketers at the heart of Seer Green life. Locals sup from six real ales and enjoy jazz nights, book clubs and pub games in a stripped-down bar. Alongside, in homely contrast, is an intimate dining room done out in auction-room mahogany with cricket-themed bric-a-brac. A fine balance needs to be struck and the kitchen grasps it completely, offering mushroom soup with its own Scotch egg or cider-braised ham with crispy egg, chips and pineapple chutney, as well as rump steak and cottage pie. Look out for treats in sweet-shop jars and ice buckets brimming with bottles of wine from £15.10.

Chef/s: Gerd Greaves. **Open:** Tue to Sun L 12 to 2.30 (3.30 Sat and Sun), Tue to Sat D 6.30 to 9. **Closed:** 25 to 26 Dec, 2 weeks Jan. **Meals:** alc (main courses £12 to £19). **Service:** not inc. **Details:** Cards accepted. 36 seats. 40 seats outside. Separate bar. Music. Children allowed. Car parking.

Average Price

The average price listed in main-entry reviews denotes the price of a three-course meal, without wine.

Stoke Poges

Stoke Place, The Garden Room

Photo-shoot chic with thrilling food
Stoke Green, Stoke Poges, SL2 4HT
Tel no: (01753) 534790
www.stokeplace.co.uk
Modern British | £40
Cooking score: 4

Stoke Place may date from the seventeenth century, but at its heart is the Garden Room, a suitably cool, verdant backdrop for some thrilling contemporary food. Craig Van der Meer has refined his culinary vocabulary and is on a roll, delivering a succession of 'superbly executed', innovative dishes with precision and dramatic impact. A limpid lamb consommé with sweetbreads has impressed, likewise poached oysters brilliantly offset by vichyssoise jelly and oyster ice cream ('the very essence of shellfish'). Great timing and exemplary detailing have also lifted an unctuous dish of beef fillet and oxtail with cep risotto, as well as baked lobster and halibut with pak choi, salsify, lentils and a gently suffusing curried foam. Clever desserts put on a thoroughly modern show too – green tea brûlée with lapsang tea jelly and mascarpone ice cream, say. Seasonal cocktails supplement the ambitious global wine list; prices from £19.

Chef/s: Craig Van der Meer. **Open:** Mon to Sat L 12 to 2, all week D 7 to 10 (9.30 Sat and Sun). **Closed:** Sun, 24 Dec to 8 Jan. **Meals:** Set L £18 (2 courses) to £25. Set D £30 (2 courses) to £40. Tasting menu £65. **Service:** 12.5% (optional). **Details:** Cards accepted. 30 seats. Separate bar. No mobile phones. Wheelchair access. Music. Children allowed. Car parking.

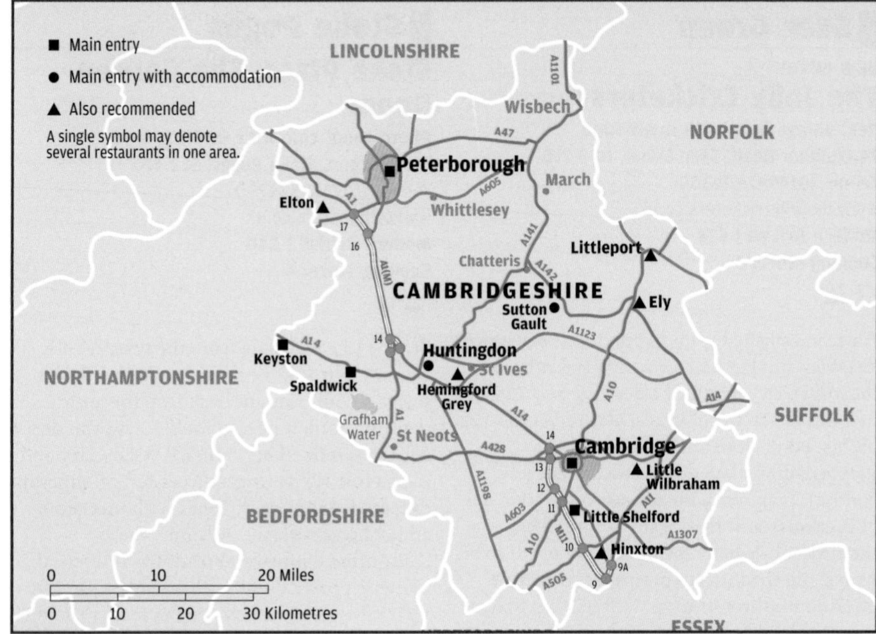

Cambridge

Cotto

Flavour-packed food and flexible menus
183 East Road, Cambridge, CB1 1BG
Tel no: (01223) 302010
www.cottocambridge.co.uk
Modern European | £40
Cooking score: 3

An ex-Victorian tramshed on one of the main approaches into the city centre, Cotto is a hive of activity. Students can drop in for a quick breakfast on the way to lectures, there are soups and sandwiches through the day, and a full dinner menu on three evenings. Hans Schweitzer's impressive cooking achieves depths of flavour from often quite straightforward ingredients, such as the much-lauded veal kidneys dijonnaise. One reporter sang the praises of the opulently sauced seafood cannelloni Nantua to start, followed by perfectly tender pancetta-wrapped guinea fowl stuffed with mushrooms and sage. Finish with caramelised pear frangipane tart with fleur de sel butterscotch sauce and double-cream ice. Wines start at £18, or £5 a glass.

Chef/s: Hans Schweitzer. **Open:** Tue to Fri L 9 to 3, Thur to Sat D 7 to 9. **Closed:** Sun, Mon, 25 Dec to 9 Jan, Aug. **Meals:** alc (main courses £5 to £20). Set L £20 (2 courses) to £25. Set D £40. **Service:** not inc. **Details:** Cards accepted. 45 seats. 10 seats outside. Music. Car parking.

Midsummer House

The loveliest restaurant in Cambridge
Midsummer Common, Cambridge, CB4 1HA
Tel no: (01223) 369299
www.midsummerhouse.co.uk
Modern British | £76
Cooking score: 7

Without question the loveliest restaurant in Cambridge, Daniel Clifford's converted Victorian villa stands squarely between the grassy reaches of Midsummer Common and the river Cam. Take a drink in the striking bar before drifting into the eminently soothing conservatory dining room overlooking the walled garden. A fine setting warrants fine service and the staff at Midsummer House are exemplary in every department, proffering advice and gauging the mood of each table to perfection: 'when did you last see a French maître d' helping a toddler with her drawing?' mused one reader. When he's on form, Clifford delivers a 'rich, delicate canvas of flavours', accented with beautifully judged notes: maple-caramelised sweetbreads with turnip, pistachio, ox tongue and maple jelly, for example, or a complex salad of artichokes, green olives, lemon and Parmesan emulsion to accompany oat-crusted red mullet. But he can sometimes over-egg ideas and go awry when it comes to composition (cubes of tasteless seaweed jelly and ready-shelled tiger prawns drowned in a divine 'essence of pea' velouté, for example). There's also a tendency to fall back on old tricks, such as the soda siphon of Champagne and grapefruit foam which dramatically opens proceedings. That said, prodigious technical skill is a given and desserts are bang on target, from a playful lemon posset with crunchy raspberry meringue 'pips' and bright raspberry jelly topped with ginger beer foam to an 'astounding' combination of orange, Hoegaarden beer sorbet, coriander and goats' cheese cake. On the downside, prices are reckoned to be 'rapacious' for what is offered, and the weighty wine list (from £23) offers little financial relief.

Chef/s: Daniel Clifford. **Open:** Wed to Sat L 12 to 1.45, Tue to Sat D 7 to 9.30. **Closed:** Sun, Mon, 2 week Dec to Jan. **Meals:** Set L £29.50 (2 courses) to £35. Set D £39.50 (4 courses). Tasting menus £76 (6 courses) to £95 (10 courses). **Service:** 12.5% (optional). **Details:** Cards accepted. 42 seats. Separate bar. No music. Children allowed.

Average Price

The average price listed in main-entry reviews denotes the price of a three-course meal, without wine.

Restaurant Alimentum

High-impact food in funky surrounds
152-154 Hills Road, Cambridge, CB2 8PB
Tel no: (01223) 413000
www.restaurantalimentum.co.uk
Modern European | £40
Cooking score: 6

£5 OFF

Currently the hottest ticket in Cambridge, Alimentum cuts quite a dash with its high-impact food, funky surrounds and urbane outlook. Designed by the team behind St Pancras Grand, it strips away the tired and stuffy conventions of 'fine dining' in favour of clubby black and red tones, smoked glass and a groovy soundtrack – plus glamorous cocktails at the bar and occasional live jazz. Chef/proprietor Mark Poynton is firing on all cylinders, delivering smart contemporary dishes full of vibrancy and bold strokes. Startling combinations include goats' curd with a texture of spring onion, stone bass with a salad of crab and turnip, radish and pistachio, and a trio of muntjac deer with cinnamon and chocolate. Even conventional beef bordelaise is taken to another level with braised shin and snails. Cheeses are ripeness personified and desserts are also guaranteed to dazzle, notably a brilliant juxtaposition of banana parfait, lime and Mojito sorbet – 'a perfect balance of sweetness and acidity'. Set lunches are no cop out, either – how about poached and roasted pigeon with boudin blanc, Savoy cabbage and a slick of broccoli purée? Effusive comments, too, for 'incredibly cheerful staff' and a tirelessly helpful young sommelier at the top of his game ('what an asset!'). The wine list is an illuminating tour through the world of serious modern drinking. Prices are wallet-friendly (from £18.50), and around 20 selections are offered by the glass or carafe.

Chef/s: Mark Poynton. **Open:** all week L 12 to 2.30 (4 Sun), Mon to Sat D 6 to 10. **Closed:** 24 to 30 Dec, bank hols. **Meals:** Set menu £30 (2 courses) to £40. Set L and early D £15.50 (2 courses) to £19.50. Tasting menu £60 (7 courses). **Service:** 12.5%

(optional). **Details:** Cards accepted. 60 seats. Separate bar. Wheelchair access. Music. Children allowed.

ALSO RECOMMENDED

▲ The Cambridge Chop House

1 Kings Parade, Cambridge, CB2 1SJ
Tel no: (01223) 359506
www.chophouses.co.uk
British

Pitched opposite King's College Chapel, this flag-waving eatery makes the most of its salubrious address by peddling beefy British flavours to the passing throngs. A meat-cleaver sign makes its intentions clear, and the menu rams home the point with mighty mixed grills, sausages and mash (£11) and cheekier numbers including potted squirrel and grilled cod cheeks (£6). Pud could be lemon posset (£5.50). Drink locally brewed Milton Ale from the cask or one of the Languedoc wines (from £17). Open all week. The St John's Chop House is at 21-24 Northampton Street; tel (01223) 353110.

Elton

ALSO RECOMMENDED

▲ The Crown Inn

8 Duck Street, Elton, PE8 6RQ
Tel no: (01832) 280232
www.thecrowninn.org
Modern British

Thatched, stone-built and overlooking the green, this village inn is big on atmosphere, with beams and real ales confirming warm pubby credentials. But the menu has a modern edge – a diverse list taking in anything from lunchtime sandwiches, burgers and fish and chips (£11.95) to the likes of ricotta and mint ravioli with pesto dressing (£5.50) and slow-cooked belly pork with an apple and pork samosa and cider sauce (£13.95) on the evening menu. House wine £15.95. No food Sun D and Mon L.

Ely

ALSO RECOMMENDED

▲ The Boathouse

5-5A Annesdale, Ely, CB7 4BN
Tel no: (01353) 664388
www.theboathouseely.co.uk
Modern British

A dreamy riverside location lures the crowds to this bright and breezy restaurant by the banks of the Ouse. Like its sibling the Cock at Hemingford Grey (see entry), the Boathouse does a good line in homemade sausages and fish specials, but the main menu has plenty to tempt too: think chicken and pigeon terrine with date chutney (£6.25), lamb chump with 'bashed peas' and fried potatoes (£18.50), and malted crème brûlée. Interesting regional bottled beers and promising wines (from £14); check the Languedoc specials. Open all week.

Hemingford Grey

ALSO RECOMMENDED

▲ The Cock

47 High Street, Hemingford Grey, PE28 9BJ
Tel no: (01480) 463609
www.thecockhemingford.co.uk
Modern British

A reconfigured village hostelry with two doors: the one marked 'pub' leads to a snug drinking den for fans of CAMRA-endorsed ales; the one labelled 'restaurant' conceals an open-plan room with scrubbed tables, chirpy staff and blackboards advertising homemade sausages and popular fish specials. Alternatively, dip into a lengthy menu that might promise duck parcels with sweet-and sour-cucumber (£7), braised pork cheeks with lamb's sweetbreads and parsnip purée (£15) or veggie toad-in-the-hole. Wines from £14 – note the Languedoc selection. Open all week.

Hinxton

ALSO RECOMMENDED

▲ The Red Lion Inn

32 High Street, Hinxton, CB10 1QY
Tel no: (01799) 530601
www.redlionhinxton.co.uk
Modern British

As village inns go, the sixteenth-century Red Lion has a distinct edge on quaintness, with its pink-washed timbered facade overlooked by a dovecot and the church. Inside it is full of promise and possibilities: a beamed and boarded bar offers pub classics, say steak and ale pudding (£13), while the restaurant delivers confit duck leg with saffron and fennel risotto (£8) ahead of sea bass and scallops with poached pear, pak choi, orange butter sauce and lemongrass foam (£18). House wine £14.20. Accommodation. Open all week.

Huntingdon

The Old Bridge Hotel

Seasonal food and smart-casual hospitality
1 High Street, Huntingdon, PE29 3TQ
Tel no: (01480) 424300
www.huntsbridge.com
Modern British | £33
Cooking score: 3

An 'ivy-clad heaven, with a riverside garden full of folk', this converted eighteenth-century bank has smart-casual hospitality down to a fine art – especially in the breezy, open spaces of the conservatory dining room. New chef James Claydon used to cook here back in the day, and he knows what is expected when it comes to matching meticulous produce with flavours from home and abroad. A perfectly pitched dish of meaty skate wing with samphire, sorrel, lemony crushed Jersey Royals and asparagus is the distillation of springtime in England, while pleasurable Mediterranean themes shine through in plates of tangy-sweet bresaola, chilli-spiked linguine with Dorset crab, or venison with confit garlic, cavolo nero and beetroot sauce. Neal's Yard cheeses are kept in peak condition and desserts such as Amaretto parfait gilded with threads of syrupy orange peel provide an effortless finish. Oenophile owner John Hoskins MW has put together a barnstorming global list that positively encourages adventurous sampling – thanks to 'flat' mark-ups, more than two-dozen brilliant selections by the glass and oodles of sub-£30 choice. Don't leave without browsing the wine shop.

Chef/s: James Claydon. **Open:** all week L 12 to 2.30, D 6.30 to 10. **Meals:** alc (main courses £14 to £25). Set L £15.50 (2 courses) to £19.50. Sun L £25. **Service:** not inc. **Details:** Cards accepted. 80 seats. 30 seats outside. Separate bar. No music. No mobile phones. Wheelchair access. Children allowed. Car parking.

Keyston

The Pheasant

A bullish foodie package
Loop Road, Keyston, PE28 0RE
Tel no: (01832) 710241
www.thepheasant-keyston.co.uk
Modern British | £30
Cooking score: 2

Once a struggling village drinking den, this dapper thatched inn is now a bullish foodie package sporting an in-house butchery, a weekend bakery, monthly supper clubs and more besides. Local game and meat ('from a 10-mile radius') are star turns on a daily menu that mixes and matches influences in unfussy modern style – so expect pigeon with fennel tarte Tatin or roast partridge with 'chocolate black pudding' and hollandaise in company with eggs Florentine, beef and oyster pie or crispy cod and brandade with warm potato salad and chorizo oil. Desserts such as rhubarb fool with lemon shortbread also have a seasonal ring. The innovative, easily accessed wine list is a big plus, with exciting modern names overshadowing the French classics and a healthy assortment of a dozen by the glass or carafe. Bottles start at £15.75.

Chef/s: Jay Scrimshaw and Theresa van Ruth. **Open:** all week L 12 to 2.30 (2 Sat), Mon to Sat D 7 to 9.30. **Meals:** alc (main courses £15 to £18). Set L and weekday D £14.95 (2 courses) to £19.95. **Service:** not inc. **Details:** Cards accepted. 80 seats. 111 seats outside. Separate bar. Music. Children allowed. Car parking.

Little Shelford

Sycamore House

Endearing home-from-home
1 Church Street, Little Shelford, CB22 5HG
Tel no: (01223) 843396
Modern British | £29
Cooking score: 2

For 19 years Michael and Susan Sharpe have run this endearing gem of a restaurant on the ground floor of their home with genuine enthusiasm. Reporters remain most contented with their visits, impressed by the honest effort and modest price of the four-course set menu. The kitchen deals in tried-and-trusted combinations: crab and red pepper tart, for example, ahead of braised leg of lamb with caper sauce or grilled cod and prawn thermidor, with sticky toffee pudding or William pear sorbet to finish. The wine list is a good example of the unpretentious approach, and opens at £15.

Chef/s: Michael Sharpe. **Open:** Wed to Sat D only 7.30 to 9. **Closed:** Sun, Mon, Tue, Christmas to New Year. **Meals:** Set D £28.50 (3 courses). **Service:** not inc. **Details:** Cards accepted. 24 seats. No music. No mobile phones. Children allowed. Car parking.

Little Wilbraham

ALSO RECOMMENDED

▲ The Hole in the Wall

2 High Street, Little Wilbraham, CB21 5JY
Tel no: (01223) 812282
www.the-holeinthewall.com
Anglo-European

With roses out front, hop-garlanded beams and a trophy list of real ales, this country pub is a classic. There's also no standing on ceremony when it comes to the food, which mixes local ideas with a touch of 'Elizabeth David provincial'. A salad of Bottisham smoked goose with red cabbage and orange (£5.95) could precede rabbit pie, roast cod with crayfish, sweetcorn and potato chowder (£16.75) or 12-hour duck leg with peas and pancetta. End with rhubarb and lemon fool. Wines from £15.50. No food Sun D or Mon.

Littleport

ALSO RECOMMENDED

▲ The Fen House

2 Lynn Road, Littleport, CB6 1QG
Tel no: (01353) 860645
Anglo-French

The enduring appeal of this treasured Fenland oasis is that very little seems to change. For 25 years the Georgian residence has served as the setting for David Warne's modern Anglo-French cooking and it's well worth seeking out for fixed-price menus (£39.50, plus complimentary cheese course) that take in homemade ravioli with a deeply savoury mushroom and sage filling, breast of duck with creamed leeks and ale gravy, and a rich chocolate and ginger mousse with gingered biscuits. Wines from £16.25. Note: open Fri and Sat D only.

Peterborough

NEW ENTRY

Jim's Bistro

Joie de vivre and honest cooking
52 Broadway, Peterborough, PE1 1SB
Tel no: (01733) 341122
www.jimsyard.biz
Modern European | £23
Cooking score: 2

An oasis in Peterborough's foodie wastelands, this immensely appealing, cosmopolitan bistro has joie de vivre written all over it. Set close to the town's famous Broadway Theatre, it pleases culture vultures with pre-show deals and satisfies everyone else with honest, direct

cooking. Like its sibling Jim's Yard (see entry, Lincolnshire), it takes care with the details – fine soft bread, butter 'rustique' in dinky domed dishes, gorgeous blue-handled Laguiole cutlery, terrines wrapped in virgin-white lard, heart-pumping coffee. Smoked haddock and salmon risotto is a rich version, crisp-skinned sea bream is served on sautéed new potatoes with pokey chorizo, lamb is cooked 'osso buco' and there's textbook crème brûlée to finish. Affable service comes with a sweet French accent. Wines start at £14.25.
Chef/s: John Needham. **Open:** Tue to Sat L 12 to 2.30, D 5.30 to 9.30. **Closed:** Sun, Mon, 2 weeks from 24 Dec, last week Jul, first week Aug. **Meals:** alc (main courses £9 to £17). Pre-theatre D £12 (2 courses) to £15. **Service:** not inc. **Details:** Cards accepted. 40 seats. Wheelchair access. Music. Children allowed.

Spaldwick

The George of Spaldwick

Cracking modern pub food
5-7 High Street, Spaldwick, PE28 0TD
Tel no: (01480) 890293
www.georgeofspaldwick.co.uk
Modern British | £16
Cooking score: 2

Hungry A14/A1 travellers desperate for a decent pit-stop west of Huntingdon should look no further than the sixteenth-century George, a cracking country pub overlooking Spaldwick's quaint village green. Wonky walls, old timber, boarded floors and inglenook fireplaces blend effortlessly with bold fabrics, leather sofas and contemporary artwork throughout the bar, dining areas and vaulted restaurant. Food, too, is bang up-to-date; the eclectic modern pub menu takes in pork terrine with spiced apple chutney, butternut squash risotto and vanilla crème brûlée. Everything is made in-house, from the classic burger and stone-baked pizzas to the breads and tomato ketchup. Wines from £14.
Chef/s: Darrell Haylett. **Open:** Tue to Sun L 12 to 2.30 (5 Sun), Mon to Sat D 6 to 9.30 (9 Mon). **Closed:** 1 Jan. **Meals:** alc (main courses £10 to £11). Set L and D £12.95 (2 courses) to £15.95. Sun L £10. **Service:** not inc. **Details:** Cards accepted. 105 seats. 40 seats outside. Separate bar. Wheelchair access. Music. Children allowed. Car parking.

Sutton Gault

The Anchor Inn

Snug inn with lots to love
Bury Lane, Sutton Gault, CB6 2BD
Tel no: (01353) 778537
www.anchor-inn-restaurant.co.uk
Modern British | £27
Cooking score: 2

'I've known this place over the years and still love it, love it, love it!' enthuses one Guide workhorse of this snug inn with magnificent Fenland views. It's an opinion backed up by other warm and contented accounts of welcoming fires, 'friendly, unpretentious' service and good food. The kitchen is a champion of local produce, though it looks across Europe for culinary inspiration, coming up with smoked salmon blinis, ballottine of pheasant and Parma ham served with Savoy cabbage, cannellini beans and bacon in a creamy cider sauce, and cappuccino crème brûlée. House wine is £14.60.
Chef/s: Adam Pickup and Majiec Bilewski. **Open:** all week L 12 to 2 (Sun 2.30), D 7 to 9, (6.30 to 9.30 Sat, 6.30 to 8.30 Sun). **Meals:** alc (main courses £11 to £22). Set L £13.95 (2 courses) to £17.95. **Service:** not inc. **Details:** Cards accepted. 65 seats. 20 seats outside. No music. No mobile phones. Children allowed. Car parking.

Please send us your feedback

To register your opinion about any restaurant listed in the Guide, or a new restaurant that you wish to bring to our attention, please visit the web address at the bottom of the page. Your feedback informs the content of the book and will be used to compile next year's reviews.

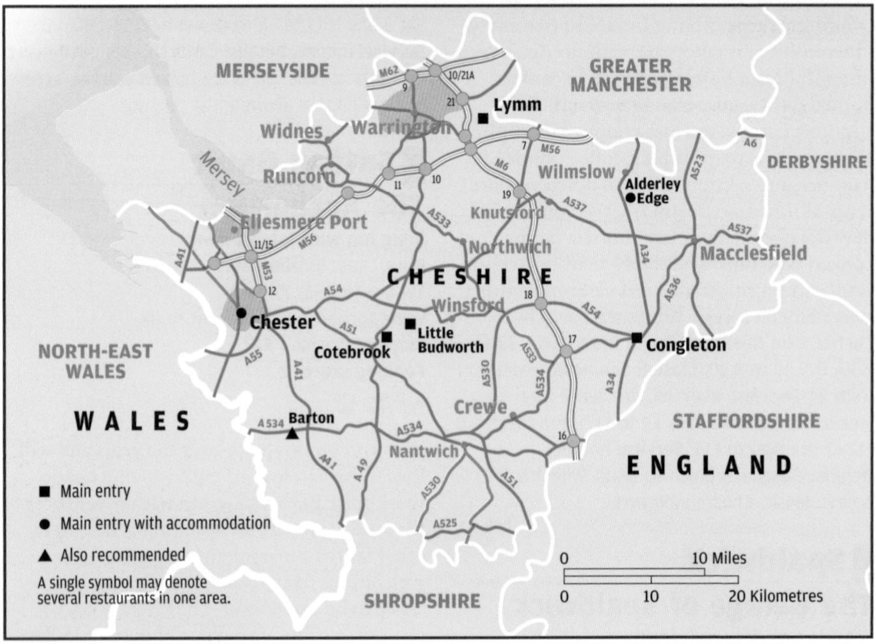
MERSEYSIDE
GREATER MANCHESTER
DERBYSHIRE
Lymm
Widnes
Warrington
Runcorn
Mersey
Wilmslow
Alderley Edge
Knutsford
Ellesmere Port
Northwich
Macclesfield
CHESHIRE
Winsford
Chester
Little Budworth
Cotebrook
Congleton
NORTH-EAST WALES
WALES
Crewe
STAFFORDSHIRE
Barton
Nantwich
ENGLAND
SHROPSHIRE
M62
M56
M6
M53
A6
A523
A537
A533
A34
A536
A54
A51
A41
A55
A530
A534
A49
A525
■ Main entry
● Main entry with accommodation
▲ Also recommended
A single symbol may denote several restaurants in one area.
0 10 Miles
0 10 20 Kilometres

Alderley Edge

Alderley Edge Hotel

Chef with his finger on the pulse
Macclesfield Road, Alderley Edge, SK9 7BJ
Tel no: (01625) 583033
www.alderleyedgehotel.com
Modern British | £44
Cooking score: 3

V

'Every need is catered for' at this locally renowned, conservatory-style restaurant behind the Elizabethan-Gothic façade of the Alderley Edge Hotel, where exceptionally helpful staff are on hand to guide visitors through some conspicuously ambitious food. The airy dining room feels refreshingly unstuffy, and chef Chris Holland has his finger on the pulse – gilding his elaborately worked dishes with 'tomato bubbles', 'verjus capsules', textures and other modish embellishments. He also likes 'sous-vide', applying the technique to everything from venison loin with pickled rhubarb and granola to 'luscious' Gressingham duck with confit, cassoulet and smoked foie gras. To start, readers have relished the 'great summer feel' of roasted tuna with watermelon and cucumber, while a happy marriage of mint custard, chocolate sorbet and banana sponge has concluded proceedings with 'wows' of delight. A big international wine list opens with house recommendations from £17.95.

Chef/s: Chris Holland. **Open:** all week L 12 to 2 (4 Sun), Mon to Sat D 7 to 10. **Meals:** alc (main courses £24). Set L £19.95 (2 courses) to £23.95. Set D £33.95. Sun L £23.95. Tasting menu £58.50 (6 courses). **Service:** not inc. **Details:** Cards accepted. 80 seats. 26 seats outside. Separate bar. Wheelchair access. Music. Children allowed. Car parking.

Aylesbury

Hartwell House

Imposing country house with traditional food
Oxford Road, Aylesbury, HP17 8NR
Tel no: (01296) 747444
www.hartwell-house.com
Modern European | £47
Cooking score: 3

£5 OFF

Few can suppress a sense of awe at Hartwell House's imposing Jacobean frontage, with its ashlar-cast parapets and double-height bays, or its 900 acres of pristine grounds. Once inside, a warren of towering ceilings, endless Greco-Romanisms and ornate architraves add their charms to the unabashedly elegant country house experience. In the restaurant, staff and tables are stiffly dressed, matching the classicism of lamb rump with boulangère potato, carrot ribbons and lamb noisettes. There are more adventurous ideas such as fillet of sea bass with herb crushed potatoes, globe artichokes and fennel froth, but most diners will find watercress soup or calf's livers, bacon and creamed potatoes blending seamlessly with their staunchly traditional expectations. Wines follow suit – French-led (from £22.50) with some global acknowledgements and surprisingly broad choice under £50.
Chef/s: Daniel Richardson. **Open:** all week L 12.30 to 1.45, D 7.30 to 9.45. **Meals:** alc (main courses £26 to £30). Set L £23.50 (2 courses) to £30.95. Set D £39. Sun L £33.95. **Service:** not inc. **Details:** Cards accepted. 60 seats. Separate bar. No music. No mobile phones. Wheelchair access. Car parking.

Dinton

ALSO RECOMMENDED

▲ La Chouette

High Street, Dinton, HP17 8UW
Tel no: (01296) 747422
www.lachouette.co.uk
Belgian

There's something oddly captivating and decidedly unorthodox about this time-warp Belgian 'auberge' filled with chef/patron Frédéric Desmette's paintings of chouettes (owls) – although some readers find the man himself too irascible and opinionated for comfort. The menu is set firmly in archaic gastronomic aspic – think chicken liver salad (£9.70), salmon fillet in boozy 'bière blanche' (wheat beer) sauce (£16.80) and well-reported crêpes Normande – so give thanks for the crusty, oven-fresh breads, Belgian beers and superlative French wines from £15.50. Closed Sat L and Sun.

Easington

NEW ENTRY

The Mole & Chicken

Attractive inn with true pubby dishes
Easington, nr Long Crendon, Easington, HP18 9EY
Tel no: (01844) 208387
www.themoleandchicken.co.uk
Modern British | £30
Cooking score: 1

This highly attractive country pub makes a good impression right from the start. Traditional touches like dark, low beams are nicely offset by stripped pale wood, overstuffed sofas, cushions and candles. It's a welcoming place serving straight and true pubby dishes such as chilli-fried squid with garlic, lemon and olive oil, river Exe mussels with cider, cream, parsley and crusty bread, and braised ham hock and white onion pudding with mustard and parsley sauce. Pud could be caramelised apple tart with cinnamon ice cream. Wines from £16.95.
Chef/s: Steve Bush. **Open:** all week L 12 to 2.30 (3.30 Sun), D 6.30 to 9.30 (6 to 9 Sun). **Closed:** 25 Dec. **Meals:** alc (main courses £13 to £24). Set L and D £12.95 (2 courses) to £16.95. **Service:** not inc. **Details:** Cards accepted. 60 seats. 50 seats outside. Wheelchair access. Music. Children allowed. Car parking.

Barton

ALSO RECOMMENDED

▲ The Cock O' Barton

Barton Road, Barton, SY14 7HU
Tel no: (01829) 782277
www.thecockobarton.co.uk
Modern European £5 OFF

The vast acreage of dining areas in this sprawling roadhouse could be off-putting, but any initial sense of chill is mitigated by the warmth of the welcome. Terrine of wild rabbit with apricot mousse, watercress and date loaf is a wholesome plateful and a snip at £6.95, while mains include pan-fried pork cutlet, chorizo, garlic roast potatoes, spinach and smoked paprika sauce (£14.95). Puddings are irresistible, especially the warm spiced apple crumble with crème anglaise and vanilla ice cream. House wines £14.15. Closed Mon.

Chester

1539 Restaurant & Bar

Racing certainty for big flavours
Watergate Square, Chester, CH1 2LY
Tel no: (01244) 304611
www.restaurant1539.co.uk
Modern British | £27
Cooking score: 1

Spectacular racecourse views and an open kitchen provide plenty of distractions at this sleek modern restaurant and bar. With so much to watch, the décor is minimalist but there's nothing understated about the cooking; it brings in big flavours from around the world, from 'fantastic' Moroccan spiced chicken breast with roasted root vegetables, sultana and chilli couscous to roast chump of Conwy Valley lamb with garlic mashed potatoes, confit tomato and black olives. To finish, maybe iced rhubarb parfait. Wines start at £14.75.
Chef/s: Robert Brittain. **Open:** Mon to Fri L 12 to 3, D 6 to 9.30. Sat 12 to 9.30, Sun 12 to 5. **Closed:** 1 and 2 Jan. **Meals:** alc (main courses £11 to £28). Set L £10 (2 courses) to £13.95. Sun L £12.50. **Service:** not inc. **Details:** Cards accepted. 200 seats. 50 seats outside. Separate bar. No mobile phones. Wheelchair access. Music. Children allowed. Car parking.

NEW ENTRY

Joseph Benjamin

Relaxed dining in the heart of the city
140 North Gate Street, Chester, CH1 2HT
Tel no: (01244) 344295
www.josephbenjamin.co.uk
Modern European | £25
Cooking score: 2

Named after owners Joe and Ben Wright, this all-purpose deli/eatery close to the city centre gets a lot of footfall, with shoppers dropping by for coffee and sandwiches as well as full meals. The kitchen mixes regional produce with ideas from faraway lands in lively, eclectic style: Cheshire asparagus is served with Berwick Edge cheese and Wirral watercress mayo, wild black bream appears with a crab, octopus and samphire paella, and local belly pork meets Toulouse sausage in a gutsy cassoulet. Desserts jump from the homely (spiced apple cake) to the exotic (pineapple pavlova), and wine buffs have a field day sampling by the glass (from £3.75).
Chef/s: Joe Wright. **Open:** Tue to Sun L 12 to 3 (4 Sun), Thur to Sat D 6 to 9.30. **Closed:** Mon, 25 Dec to 1 Jan. **Meals:** alc (main courses £9 to £18). Sun L £12.75 (2 courses) to £19.95. **Service:** not inc. **Details:** Cards accepted. 40 seats. 14 seats outside. Separate bar. Wheelchair access. Music. Children allowed.

Symbols

- Accommodation is available
- £30 Three courses for less than £30
- V Separate vegetarian menu
- £5 OFF £5-off voucher scheme
- Notable wine list

NEW ENTRY

Michael Caines at ABode Chester

New Chester high flyer
Grosvenor Road, Chester, CH1 2DJ
Tel no: (01244) 347000
www.michaelcaines.com
Modern British | £45
Cooking score: 4

V

'High level' is the name of the game at Michael Caines' hallmark restaurant within the latest branch of the ABode chain. Set on the fifth floor of the hotel, the smart bar and dining room overlook Chester racecourse and the city's historic court buildings. There's also lofty ambition when it comes to the food, whether you are grazing or plunging into the tasting menu – although chef Stuart Collins is applying his own considerable skills to Caines' fine-tuned formula. A signature dish of sublime spinach and Parmesan tortellini with pea purée, braised celery and mint foam is an exciting way to start, before mains bring fascination in the form of pan-fried mackerel with sautéed squid, Kalamata olive and tapenade linguine, or herb-crusted Herdwick lamb rump with wild garlic, caramelised aubergine and cumin sauce. The thrills continue right to the end, with a trio of chocolate or 'unctuous' macerated Morello cherries and vanilla cream. Service is unstuffy and knowledgeable, and the wine list is full of interesting possibilities. House selections start at £24.50 (£5.75 a glass).

Chef/s: Stuart Collins. **Open:** Mon to Sat L 12 to 2.30, D 6 to 9.45. **Closed:** Sun. **Meals:** alc (main courses £17 to £27). Set L £13.50. Set early D £16.95 (2 courses) to £24. Tasting menu £68. **Service:** 12% (optional). **Details:** Cards accepted. 70 seats. 10 seats outside. Separate bar. No mobile phones. Wheelchair access. Music. Children allowed. Car parking.

Simon Radley at the Chester Grosvenor

High-end food with a sense of fun
Eastgate, Chester, CH1 1LT
Tel no: (01244) 324024
www.chestergrosvenor.com
Modern European | £69
Cooking score: 6

V

The majestic Chester Grosvenor's hot-shot restaurant is a sight to behold – a luxury-strewn, pillared room with a veritable battalion of dutiful waiters poised to glide into action. 'It's like watching a ballet', quipped one reporter. Service is impeccable, but this is definitely an 'expensive hit'. Simon Radley's food is precise, assured and consistent, although visitors have struggled to find the 'wow factor' – despite clever juxtapositions and abundant high-end technique. That said, a sense of fun is evident right from the start: order 'pond life' and you can expect watercress whip with crayfish tails, garlic snails and a frog's leg bonbon. Readers have also been impressed by a tricksy combo of hand-dived scallop with ham knuckle, 'sticky feet' (aka pig's trotter) and Alsace beer, as well as some highly intricate meat cookery: cep-dusted beef fillet served with a plateful of Burgundian indulgence (bone marrow, a snail and sticky beef cheek) reminded one recipient of 'suppers in the wine region'. To conclude, desserts conjure up a starburst of 'multitudinous flavours', with special cheers for 'Arabica' (chilled mascarpone and iced latte with Amaretto jelly and cocoa nib brittle). Then there are the extras – a mind-boggling bread selection, an immense cheese trolley and a tongue-tingling assortment of dinky petits fours. The awesome 60-page wine list is quite a read, but a top sommelier is on hand to navigate you through the legions of French aristocrats, Italian whites, Aussie reds and more besides, starting at £15.95.

Chef/s: Simon Radley. **Open:** Tue to Sat D only 6.30 to 9. **Closed:** Sun, Mon, 25 and 26 Dec. **Meals:** Set D £69, Tasting menu £90 (8 courses). **Service:** 12.5%

(optional). **Details:** Cards accepted. 40 seats. 40 seats outside. Separate bar. No music. No mobile phones. Wheelchair access. Car parking.

Congleton

L'Endroit

A warm welcome and lip-smacking food
70-72 Lawton Street, Congleton, CW12 1RS
Tel no: (01260) 299548
www.lendroit.co.uk
French | £30
Cooking score: 3

All is joyfully warm and welcoming inside L'Endroit – thanks in part to enthusiastic staff and ever-present Belgian chef/patron Eli Leconte. He regularly plunders the Cheshire countryside for game and fungi, although his cooking speaks with a strong French accent and readers have found much to enjoy. Hot goats' cheese drizzled with L'Endroit's own honey gets votes aplenty, likewise homemade black pudding salad with raisins and apples, vanilla-marinated gravlax, and seared scallops with beurre blanc and spinach – not forgetting 'best-ever' grilled rib of local beef for two and a superlative dish of lip-smacking cassoulet packed with gamey sausages. As for dessert, seasonal fruit tarts go down well. Cheeses are English, but the wine list offers sound drinking possibilities from France and beyond; prices start at £13.25.
Chef/s: Eli Leconte. **Open:** Tue to Fri L 12 to 2, D 6 to 10 (10.30 Sat). Sun L 12 to 2 (May to Sept). **Closed:** Mon, last 2 weeks Feb, 1 week Jun, 1 week Sept. **Meals:** alc (main courses £13 to £18). Set L £11.95 (2 courses). **Service:** not inc. **Details:** Cards accepted. 36 seats. 12 seats outside. Wheelchair access. Music. Children allowed. Car parking.

GARRY CLARK
Simon Radley at the Chester Grosvenor

What is the most difficult aspect of your job?
Going to a big tasting where I will try so many wonderful wines and knowing that there are some I'll have to reject. There's a limit to how big your wine list can be, and knowing when to stop can be hard.

What's your favourite tipple when not drinking wine?
I'm not a really big drinker but I do like a nice cold beer every now and then. My desert island drink would be Irn Bru!

Which product, person or innovation has been the most influential in your field of expertise?
Product: the internet. As a source of information it is invaluable. Person: Gerard Basset. The man is a legend. Innovation: smartphones. The number of wine-related apps is stunning.

Have you noticed any wine trends over the last few years?
When the recession first hit, people weren't drinking wine at all. We noticed then that we had a huge gap missing in our list. We had only three wines under £25. We went out and sourced nearly two dozen more and saw a big increase.

Cotebrook

Fox & Barrel

Friendly pub with inspired food
Foxbank, Cotebrook, CW6 9DZ
Tel no: (01829) 760529
www.foxandbarrel.co.uk
Modern British | £24
Cooking score: 2

£5 OFF £30

The whitewashed pub in a village north of Tarporley gets its name from a former landlord's act of kindness when he saved a fox from the local hunt by hiding it in a barrel. A vast open fireplace and low-hanging ceiling beams make a suitable backdrop for the inspired modern pub cooking, which is ordered at the bar. Full-throated praise comes from a reader who proceeded from twice-baked cheese soufflé to duck breast with honey-glazed pears and parsnips, and found nothing wanting. Fish dishes may include sea bass with crab and chorizo linguine, and Eton mess is a good finale. Wines start at £14.45.

Chef/s: Richard Cotterill and Aaron Totty. **Open:** all week 12 to 9.30 (9 Sun). **Meals:** alc (main courses £9 to £18). **Service:** not inc. **Details:** Cards accepted. 100 seats. 60 seats outside. Separate bar. No music. Children allowed. Car parking.

Little Budworth

Cabbage Hall

Roadside eatery with lots of choice
Forest Road, Little Budworth, CW6 9ES
Tel no: (01829) 760292
www.cabbagehallrestaurant.com
Modern British | £30
Cooking score: 2

'Cabbages' are offcuts of material, we are informed, and as this was once a tailor's home we may be sure the name has nothing to do with brassicas. Robert Kisby's homely roadside eatery offers a variety of dining options, from themed lunch platters to an enjoyable hodgepodge of global cuisine. Reporters have singled out the lobster risotto and game terrine en croûte starters, after which it's on to herb-crusted rack of lamb in Madeira or cod with chorizo and tomato, finishing with West Country-style apple 'dappy' pudding with blackcurrant sorbet. Wines start at £15.95.

Chef/s: Robert Kisby. **Open:** Wed to Mon L 12 to 6, Wed to Sat and Mon D 6 to 10. **Closed:** Tue, 24 and 25 Dec, 2 to 13 Jan. **Meals:** alc (main courses £14 to £22). Set L and D £16.95 (2 courses) to £21.95. Sun L £12.95. **Service:** not inc. **Details:** Cards accepted. 72 seats. 50 seats outside. Separate bar. No mobile phones. Wheelchair access. Music. Children allowed. Car parking.

Lymm

The Church Green

Great pub grub and an ambitious restaurant
Higher Lane, Lymm, WA13 0AP
Tel no: (01925) 752068
www.thechurchgreen.co.uk
Modern British | £45
Cooking score: 2

£5 OFF V

The identity of the Church Green's chef-proprietor is no secret – Aiden Byrne has filled his pleasant pub and restaurant with the books, china and olive oil that bear his name. What that stands for is more confused. On the pub side, doorstep burgers and flawless pies are great for Lymm to have around. Ambitious restaurant dishes aren't always so capably balanced; foie gras with hazelnut risotto and a quenelle of palm sugar ice cream is knocked sideways by too much Parmesan, while the Gruyère crust on a piece of cod hides a tangle of undercooked onions. There's technical skill in the accompanying gnocchi and much more besides, but the heart of each dish needs attention. House wine is £15.

Chef/s: Aiden Byrne. **Open:** all week L 12 to 3 (3.30 Sun), D 6 to 10 (10.30 Fri and Sat). **Closed:** 25 Dec. **Meals:** Set L £17.50 (2 courses) to £22.50. Set D £28.50 (2 courses) to £37.50. Sun L £22.50. Tasting menu £68 (7 courses). Bar menu available. **Service:** not inc. **Details:** Cards accepted. 60 seats. 40 seats outside. Separate bar. Wheelchair access. Music. Children allowed. Car parking.

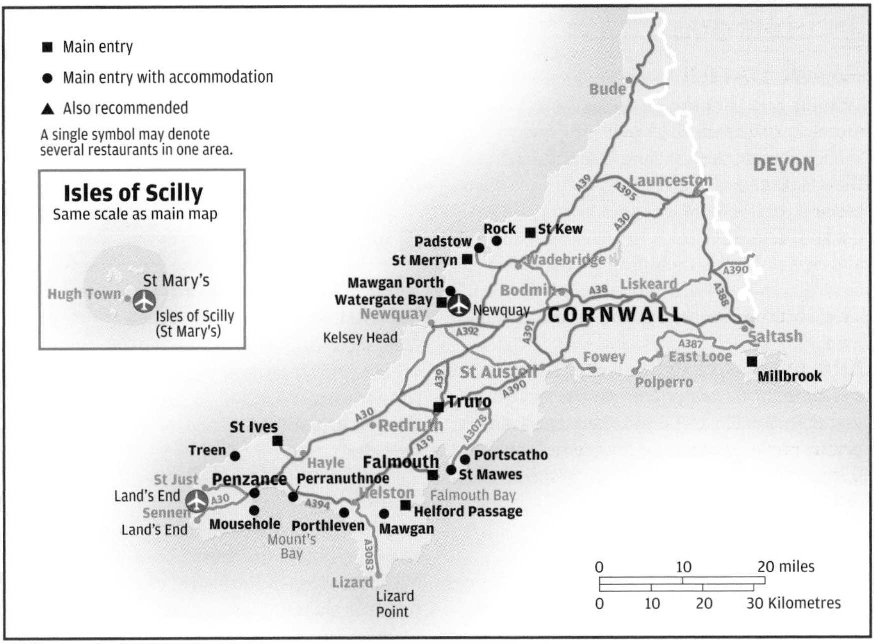

Falmouth

NEW ENTRY

Rick Stein's Seafood Bar

Seafood tapas from a master

Events Square, Discovery Quay, Falmouth, TR11 3XA

Tel no: (01841) 532700

www.rickstein.com

Seafood | £30

Cooking score: 3

Rick Stein's new Seafood Bar sits above his bustling fish and chip shop on Falmouth's waterfront. Chef Paul Ripley was one of Stein's lieutenants back in the day and has returned to the fold for this livewire venture, proving his worth with a menu built around 'seafood tapas'. Just about everything appeals, but highlights have included Spanish-style octopus salad, gremolata prawns, stir-fried squid with red chilli and spring onion, and 'exceptionally fresh' grilled scallops topped with guindillo peppers, chorizo and crisp breadcrumbs – not forgetting crema catalana for an authentic tapas finish. Local beers and ciders are complemented by a wine list starting at £17.50.

Chef/s: Paul Ripley. **Open:** Tue to Sat L 12 to 2.30, Mon to Sat D 5 to 9. **Closed:** Sun, 25 and 26 Dec, 1 May. **Meals:** alc (main courses £6 to £33). **Service:** not inc. **Details:** Cards accepted. 35 seats. Separate bar. Wheelchair access. Music. Children allowed.

Helford Passage

NEW ENTRY

Ferryboat Inn

Bivalves and brilliant views

Helford Passage, TR11 5LB

Tel no: (01326) 250625

www.ferryboatinnhelford.com

Seafood | £23

Cooking score: 2

Perched at the bottom of a steep wooded glade on the Helford estuary, this 300-year-old nautical watering hole has been given an on-trend refit by oyster specialists the Wright Brothers (see entry, London). Plump bivalves from WB's Duchy 'farm' on the Helford River are a star turn, but the kitchen also serves up home-smoked salmon, bowls of Fowey mussels in cider, meaty line-caught mackerel fillets with tangy rhubarb chutney and crisp-skinned roast hake with caper butter and brown shrimps. Otherwise drop by for well-rendered pub grub including cottage pie and macaroni cheese, with chocolate tart or vanilla pannacotta and summer fruit to finish. Wines from £16.50.

Chef/s: Ben Lightfoot. **Open:** all week L 12 to 3, D 6 to 9. **Closed:** Mon winter only. **Meals:** alc (main courses £8 to £15). Sun L £9.95. Bar menu available. **Service:** not inc. **Details:** Cards accepted. 80 seats. 50 seats outside. Separate bar. Wheelchair access. Music. Children allowed.

Mawgan

New Yard Restaurant

First-rate food, with highlight puds
Trelowarren Estate, Mawgan, TR12 6AF
Tel no: (01326) 221595
www.trelowarren.com
Modern British | £31
Cooking score: 3

£5 OFF

This former coach house on the Trelowarren Estate capitalises on its idyllic location by sourcing over 90 per cent of its ingredients from within a 15-mile radius. The clean and restrained look of the restaurant is enhanced by a blazing log fire, but the alfresco tables are where most diners head for in summer. Reports this year have been full of praise for the 'welcoming atmosphere', 'attention to detail' and Olly Jackson's food, with readers applauding the 'cooked to perfection' gnocchi with goats' cheese sauce and the spot-on duck with parsnip purée. Desserts have been a particular highlight for many, with the burnt honey cream, pistachios and brandy oranges garnering as much acclaim as the all-Cornish cheese selection. Wines from £19.

Chef/s: Olly Jackson. **Open:** all week L 12 to 2 (2.30 Sun), Mon to Sat D 7 to 9. **Closed:** Mon and Tue from Oct to Mar, Mon from Mar to Whitsun. **Meals:** alc (main courses £15 to £22). Set L £17. Set D £27. Sun L £21. **Service:** not inc. **Details:** Cards accepted. 50 seats. 12 seats outside. Wheelchair access. Music. Children allowed. Car parking.

Mawgan Porth

The Scarlet Hotel

Eco-hotel with spectacular views
Tredragon Road, Mawgan Porth, TR8 4DQ
Tel no: (01637) 861800
www.scarlethotel.co.uk
Modern British | £43
new chef

£5 OFF

A modern eco-hotel on the clifftop at Mawgan Porth, the Scarlet commands fantastic views of the beach, bay and headland, but nonetheless manages a level of intimacy suited to its village location. We learned of Ben Tunnicliffe's departure as our deadline approached, and as the new chef, Jeremy Medley, had not yet taken up his position, we are unable to comment on menus or style. Tunnicliffe's team was, however, remaining in place and we are certain the hotel's commitment to local suppliers will continue as before. The exemplary, user-friendly wine list has imaginative, broadly based selections that are grouped by style, and with nearly everything by the bottle, half-litre or glass (from £19.50, £14.50 and £5.25 respectively) – a hugely commendable approach.

Chef/s: Jeremy Medley. **Open:** all week L 12 to 2, D 7 to 9.30. **Closed:** 5 weeks Jan/Feb. **Meals:** Set L £16 (2 courses) to £19.50. Set D £34 (2 courses) to £42.50. **Service:** not inc. **Details:** Cards accepted. 80 seats. 30 seats outside. Separate bar. No mobile phones. Wheelchair access. Music. Car parking.

Millbrook

The View

Outstanding clifftop package
Treninnow Cliff Road, Millbrook, PL10 1JY
Tel no: (01752) 822345
www.theview-restaurant.co.uk
Modern British | £30
Cooking score: 2

Perched above the cliffs at Whitsand Bay and fully living up to its name, this popular, well-run restaurant attracts locals and visitors with the quality and worth of its fresh seafood. Plenty of flavours are mobilised, as in a starter of red mullet with lemon grass velouté or a salad of mint, watermelon and feta (a 'delicious combination'), and a main course of 'cooked to perfection' monkfish accompanied by a pea and broad bean purée. There's choice for meat eaters, too, with best end of lamb served with fennel sauté and a pomegranate reduction. For a resonant finale, try the excellent vanilla pannacotta. Wines from £16.50.

Chef/s: Matt Corner. **Open:** Wed to Sun L 12 to 2, D 7 to 9. **Closed:** Mon, Tue, Feb. **Meals:** alc (main courses £15 to £23). **Service:** not inc. **Details:** Cards accepted. 45 seats. 20 seats outside. Wheelchair access. Music. Children allowed. Car parking.

Mousehole

2 Fore Street

Straight-talking piscine delights
2 Fore Street, Mousehole, TR19 6PF
Tel no: (01736) 731164
www.2forestreet.co.uk
Seafood | £30
Cooking score: 2

With the harbour out front, it's no wonder thoughts turn to flappingly fresh fish at this prettily designed local restaurant. Straight-talking piscine delights from the Cornish boats are indeed Fore Street's forte. Chummy chef/owner Joe Wardell 'really cares about his food', whether he is dishing up bowls of plump Exe mussels with hunks of home-baked bread, sea bass fillets with braised fennel, tiger prawns and sweet tomato dressing or roasted skate with capers, cornichons and paprika croûtons. Crab cakes and burgers might feature on the light lunch menu, while desserts could yield steamed marmalade pudding or almond meringue with lemon mousse. Wines from £14.50.

Chef/s: Joe Wardell. **Open:** all week L 12 to 3, D 6 to 9.30. **Closed:** 3 Jan to 10 Feb. **Meals:** alc (main courses £13 to £16). **Service:** not inc. **Details:** Cards accepted. 36 seats. 20 seats outside. Music. Children allowed.

Padstow

Paul Ainsworth at No. 6

Cosy retreat with accomplished cooking
6 Middle Street, Padstow, PL28 8AP
Tel no: (01841) 532093
www.number6inpadstow.co.uk
Modern British | £34
Cooking score: 6

£5 OFF

Amid the surging bustle and overflowing car parks of this once tranquil Cornish harbour town, Paul Ainsworth's restaurant feels like a cosy retreat. A warren of rooms on both levels is pleasantly decorated with black-and-white tiled floors, glass ornaments and impeccably Sunday-best table settings. The bargain lunch deal, with its two choices at each course, is a canny way of siphoning off at least some of the throng outside, while the carte uncoils expansively into a repertoire of dishes that have the crystal ring of modern British authenticity. How else to style a starter of flaked smoked haddock piled onto a stack of green leek and grainy black pudding, encircled by creamily moreish vichyssoise (spoon provided)? To follow, perhaps a startling pairing of braised ox cheek and raw shredded rump, with glass noodles, chilli and pak choi in beef consommé or a large, astonishingly flavourful veal chop glazed in its gravy, served with asparagus, a little pan of tarragon-spiked egg mayonnaise and a heap of hefty, flawlessly textured dripping-fried chips, all served on a bread board. Desserts aim for

lightness (pear with praline custard and pear sorbet), but might miss balance (witness a vanilla pannacotta and poached rhubarb that came topped with a rock-hard gingery biscuit, under which it subsided into a helpless splodge). Staff are pin-sharp and ready with advice – not least with the exclusive, hand-picked wine list, which opens with 14 juicy selections by the glass (from £4). Otherwise, expect a colourfully annotated selection of top numbers from across the globe ('elegant, glamorous, feisty and downright dangerous', according to the blurb). Bottles start at £15.
Chef/s: Paul Ainsworth. **Open:** Tue to Sat L 12 to 2, D 6 to 10. **Closed:** Sun (Nov to Apr), Mon (exc bank hols), 24 to 26 Dec, 8 Jan to 1 Feb. **Meals:** alc (main courses £15 to £21). Set L £15 (2 courses) to £20. **Service:** not inc. **Details:** Cards accepted. 45 seats. 6 seats outside. No mobile phones. Music. Children allowed.

Rick Stein's Café

Feel-good crowd-pleaser
10 Middle Street, Padstow, PL28 8AP
Tel no: (01841) 532700
www.rickstein.com
Seafood | £25
Cooking score: 1

Holidaying families and Padstein tourists happily rub shoulders (literally) in this informal outpost of Rick Stein's empire. Breakfast starts the day, otherwise order from a menu that promises plenty of seafood (grilled sardines, moules marinière, goujons of plaice with salsa verde) alongside a mixed bag of crowd-pleasers (aubergine curry, chicken satay, ribeye steak with chips, and a 'light, tangy' orange tart). It might be a 'weensy bit overpriced', but everyone seems to enjoy the experience. Wines from £18.
Chef/s: Ross Geach. **Open:** all week L 12 to 3, D 6.30 to 9.30. **Closed:** 25 and 26 Dec, 1 May. **Meals:** alc (main courses £11 to £17). Set D £22. **Service:** not inc. **Details:** Cards accepted. 36 seats. 14 seats outside. Wheelchair access. Music. Children allowed.

St Petroc's Bistro

Cheerful Rick Stein eatery
New Street, Padstow, PL28 8EL
Tel no: (01841) 532700
www.rickstein.com
Modern European | £34
Cooking score: 2

This cheerful bistro was set up as a budget alternative to the Seafood Restaurant (see entry), but over the years it has become a destination in its own right. Despite the Rick Stein association, seafood doesn't steal the limelight – although you will find modern ideas like fried squid with smoked pimentón and garlic mayonnaise or grilled fillet of cod with beer, bacon and Savoy cabbage. Back on land, the range extends to chicken breast with Muscat wine and black pudding, plus a choice of 28-day aged Aberdeen Angus and Charolais-cross steaks. Bringing up the rear are appealing desserts such as lemon posset with berry compote. Wines from £18.35.
Chef/s: Paul Harwood and David Sharland. **Open:** all week L 12 to 2, D 6.30 to 9.30. **Closed:** 25 and 26 Dec, 1 May. **Meals:** alc (main courses £14 to £24). Set L (winter only) £17.85. **Service:** not inc. **Details:** Cards accepted. 56 seats. 36 seats outside. Separate bar. Wheelchair access. Music. Children allowed.

The Seafood Restaurant

Rick Stein's seafood beacon
Riverside, Padstow, PL28 8BY
Tel no: (01841) 532700
www.rickstein.com
Seafood | £64
Cooking score: 3

Just across the harbour from where the fishing boats are moored each day, Rick Stein's original Padstow address still draws fish lovers from far and wide. They come in search of the freshest seafood, and are treated to the sight of it being prepared at the great circular bar in the centre of the room. Sign up for the tasting menu to appreciate this bounty: lobster salad with lemon and chive dressing, half-shell queenies, sea bass with roasted fennel seeds and sauce vierge, and red mullet with girolles and sun-dried tomatoes were enough cumulatively to send one reporter away in a state of bliss. The prices continue to excite comment (over £30 for a small grilled sole), and service sometimes seems cheerfully amateurish, but the place remains one of the southwest's reference venues. Wines from £19.60.

Chef/s: Stephane Delourme and David Sharland. **Open:** all week L 12 to 2.30, D 7 to 10. **Closed:** 25 and 26 Dec, 1 May. **Meals:** alc (main courses £18 to £47). Winter set L £29.50. Tasting menu £67 (6 courses). **Service:** not inc. **Details:** Cards accepted. 90 seats. Separate bar. No music. Wheelchair access.

Penzance

NEW ENTRY

The Bakehouse

Cornwall meets the Med

Old Bakehouse Lane, Chapel Street, Penzance, TR18 4AE

Tel no: (01736) 331331

www.bakehouserestaurant.co.uk

Modern European | £26

Cooking score: 3

'Bakehouse and steakhouse' is the full strapline at Andy and Rachel Carr's funky little venue set in a palm-filled courtyard. Spread over two floors (complete with the original bread oven and exhibits by local artists), it deals in locally reared Angus beef and seafood from the Newlyn boats supplemented by a few wild clifftop pickings. Steaks come with a variety of sauces, 'rubs' and butters, but look to the coast for the most lively offerings: crab florentine is subtly enhanced with five-spice and waxy sea beet, while Falmouth scallops are served with caper, lemon and sage butter; elsewhere, a stew of hake with mussels, olives and fennel reminded one reader of a Catalan zarzuela. For dessert, try zingy lemon tart or rich chocolate truffle torte with clotted cream. Wines from £13.95.

Chef/s: Andy Carr. **Open:** all week D only 6.15 to 9. **Closed:** 24 to 27 Dec, Sun (Nov to Mar). **Meals:** alc (main courses £10 to £20). Set D £13.95 (2 courses before 7.15). **Service:** not inc. **Details:** Cards accepted. 56 seats. Music. Children allowed.

The Bay

Art, views and Cornish flavours

Hotel Penzance, Britons Hill, Penzance, TR18 3AE

Tel no: (01736) 366890

www.bay-penzance.co.uk

Modern British | £32

Cooking score: 3

£5 OFF V

This light and contemporary restaurant is as well-known for its local art exhibitions as for its breathtaking rooftop views of Mount's Bay. Both are matched by the food, which is creative, seasonal and dedicated to showcasing local produce, some of it from Cornwall's smallest suppliers. Everything is made on the premises, from the bread to the ice cream, and there's even a special vegan menu with three choices per course. Locally landed seafood naturally takes take the lead, with lobster and shellfish getting their own menu. On the carte, a starter of smoked trout with saffron-braised leeks, lightly poached egg and paprika oat biscuit might make way for halibut with red wine-braised oxtail, salsify and oyster mushrooms. Wrap things up with banana and passion fruit pavlova. Wines from £16.75.

Chef/s: Ben Reeve. **Open:** Sun to Fri 7am to 11pm, Sat B 7.15 to 9.30, D 6.15 to 9. **Closed:** first 2 weeks Jan. **Meals:** Set L £12.50 (2 courses) to £17.50. Set D £25 (2 courses) to £32. Sun L £18.50. **Service:** not inc. **Details:** Cards accepted. 40 seats. 10 seats outside. Separate bar. No mobile phones. Music. Children allowed. Car parking.

Average Price

The average price listed in main-entry reviews denotes the price of a three-course meal, without wine.

Harris's

Cooking that pleases the palate
46 New Street, Penzance, TR18 2LZ
Tel no: (01736) 364408
www.harrissrestaurant.co.uk
Modern European | £32
Cooking score: 2

£5 OFF

Roger and Anne Harris moved into this side-street address in 1972. Now in their fourth decade, they still work hard and run their popular restaurant to a well-tried formula: they understand their customers and offer sound cooking that pleases the palate. The kitchen takes full advantage of the abundant Cornish seafood, serving scallops with a fresh herb dressing and partnering John Dory, roasted on the bone, with a red pepper sauce. Elsewhere, meat fans can expect noisettes of local spring lamb or medallions of venison. To finish, West Country cheeses are an alternative to desserts such as little chocolate pots. Wines from £15.95.

Chef/s: Roger Harris. **Open:** Tue to Sat L 12 to 2, Mon to Sat D 7 to 9. **Closed:** Sun, Mon (winter only), 3 weeks winter. **Meals:** alc (main courses £17 to £33). **Service:** 10%. **Details:** Cards accepted. 20 seats. Separate bar. No mobile phones. Music. Children allowed.

Perranuthnoe

Victoria Inn

Historic inn with a foodie outlook
Perranuthnoe, TR20 9NP
Tel no: (01736) 710309
www.victoriainn-penzance.co.uk
Modern British | £27
Cooking score: 2

£5 OFF £30

Nicknamed 'the pink pub', this venerable village inn has some 200 years of history etched into its walls – although it strikes a more contemporary pose when it comes to food. Cornish produce is used to good effect in a repertoire of dishes ranging from refreshingly simple Newlyn crab with wild garlic, new potato and herb salad to a dish of pan-fried plaice with cherry tomatoes ignited by the salty, sweet tones of anchovy butter. Chef/landlord Stewart Eddy's belly pork is 'to die for', likewise his risottos, while dessert might bring vanilla pannacotta and basil syrup with local strawberries and lemon ice cream. Wines from £14.50.

Chef/s: Stewart Eddy. **Open:** all week L 12 to 2 (3 Sun), Mon to Sat D 6.30 to 9. **Closed:** Mon (Oct to Easter), 25 and 26 Dec, 1 Jan. **Meals:** alc (main courses £10 to £17). **Service:** not inc. **Details:** Cards accepted. 60 seats. 28 seats outside. Separate bar. Music. Children allowed. Car parking.

Porthleven

Kota

Racy fusion cooking
Harbour Head, Porthleven, TR13 9JA
Tel no: (01326) 562407
www.kotarestaurant.co.uk
Fusion/Modern European | £27
Cooking score: 2

£5 OFF £30

Kota's chef/co-owner Jude Kereama has Maori blood in his veins, but don't expect any tongue-waggling 'haka' challenges at this 300-year-old cornmill by Porthleven harbour. Instead, he raises the temperature with some racy fusion cooking based around Cornish ingredients, especially seafood ('kota' is the Maori word for fish). Crispy salt-and-pepper squid comes with mango and green papaya salad, tempura Falmouth Bay oysters are tweaked with wasabi tartare sauce, and there are bonito flakes in the chowder. But it's not all crossover: pigeon with black pudding, roast garlic and watercress stunned one reader, while desserts keep it close to home with top-drawer chocolate fondant and plum crème brûlée. House wine is £13.95.

Chef/s: Jude Kereama. **Open:** Fri and Sat L 12 to 2, Mon to Sat D 5.30 to 9. **Closed:** Sun (exc bank hols and Mother's Day), 1 Jan to 7 Feb. **Meals:** alc (main courses £12 to £19). Set L and early D £15 (2 courses) to £19.50. **Service:** not inc. **Details:** Cards accepted. 40 seats. Separate bar. Wheelchair access. Music. Children allowed.

Portscatho

Driftwood

Clifftop hotel with standout cooking
Rosevine, Portscatho, TR2 5EW
Tel no: (01872) 580644
www.driftwoodhotel.co.uk
Modern European | £44
Cooking score: 5

High on the clifftop looking over Gerrans Bay, this boutique hotel is perfectly positioned to capitalise on the sunny Cornish maritime vista. Plenty of that luminous glow finds its way into the dining room too, which is decked out in nautical hues of sunshine and sea, with crisply dressed tables. It takes a lot to stand out among the competition in Cornwall these days, but Chris Eden manages it with cooking that ranges far and wide for culinary influence, but stays close to home for supplies, particularly of exemplary seafood. The journey might embark with citrus-glazed mackerel, pickled ginger, heritage carrots, cucumber and fennel in a seaweed cream dressing. That might lead to local Old Spot pork with pickled apple purée, chanterelles and sweetcorn or perhaps roast turbot with crushed Jerusalem artichokes, hazelnuts, salsify, prawns and Parma ham – multi-dimensional dishes that are reported favourably. To finish, locally sourced lemon verbena arrives in the guise of a sorbet with white chocolate and vanilla garnishes. Cornish and other English cheeses are top-drawer. Wines start at £18.

Chef/s: Chris Eden. **Open:** all week D only 7 to 9.30. **Closed:** 4 Sept to 3 Feb. **Meals:** Set D £38 (2 courses) to £44. **Service:** not inc. **Details:** Cards accepted. 34 seats. Separate bar. No mobile phones. Music. Car parking.

Rock

Nathan Outlaw Seafood & Grill

Impeccably sourced Cornish seafood
St Enodoc Hotel, Rock Road, Rock, PL27 6LA
Tel no: (01208) 863394
www.nathan-outlaw.com
Seafood | £35
Cooking score: 4

This relaxed seafood grill is the more informal of Nathan Outlaw's two restaurants located in the St Enodoc Hotel (see Restaurant Nathan Outlaw). The split-level dining room and terrace boasts splendid views of the Camel Estuary, and the kitchen makes good use of the best fish and seafood available from local markets. Peter Biggs keeps dishes as simple as possible, ensuring the impeccable ingredients are perfectly displayed in dishes such as a signature starter of Cornish fish stew comprising scallops, squid and Porthilly mussels. This might be followed by stuffed lemon sole on the bone with parsley butter and dumplings, pan-fried pollack with brown shrimps, or char-grilled pork chop. Uneven cooking marred a meal for one reporter, who thought prices a little high for the 'small' portions; although another found 'everything cooked to perfection'. All wines on the 40-strong list are available by the glass and carafe, and bottles start at £19.

Chef/s: Peter Biggs. **Open:** all week L 12 to 3, D 6 to 9.30. **Meals:** alc (main courses £14 to £24). Set L and D £15 (2 courses) to £18. Sun L £23 (2 courses) to £27. **Service:** 10% (optional). **Details:** Cards accepted. 50 seats. 25 seats outside. Separate bar. No mobile phones. Wheelchair access. Music. Children allowed. Car parking.

Restaurant Nathan Outlaw

Awe-inspiring food from a top talent
St Enodoc Hotel, Rock Road, Rock, PL27 6LA
Tel no: (01208) 863394
www.nathan-outlaw.com
Modern British/Seafood | £75
Cooking score: 8

V

Not the least interesting aspect of Nathan Outlaw's career to date is his unwavering commitment to his adopted Cornwall. You might have put money on him jumping ship and heading to London, or some other urban cauldron, when his name burst out of the small print and into the writing over the door some years ago, but you'd have been wrong. He has gone defiantly – and hearteningly – native. There is an unbroken line of commitment that leads from the Cornish day-boats to the kitchens at Rock, an elongated village settlement on the Camel estuary. In a dining room that combines elegance with an atmosphere of studious intensity, one of the finest dining experiences in the south-west (or anywhere) is going on. The drill centres on a six-course dinner menu, four of which are fish-based, with a brace of sweet treats to follow. Certain dishes appear to have earned the status of stalwarts of the repertoire, such as the sublime opener that sees a piece of John Dory teamed with tiny brown shrimps and diced cucumber, along with a deep-fried breaded oyster, its flesh rendered to a sensuous melting tenderness inside the crunchy coating. A piece of pine nut-crusted cod on a sauce combining BLT components is a witty and successful exercise, while the money dish at inspection this time was a crisp-skinned piece of black bream with saffron-stained squid in a sauce full of richly aromatic Provençal notes – green olive, red pepper and, hauntingly, sweet orange. The less than convincing note occurs with the final fish course, when a meaty element (perhaps juicily succulent shredded ham hock) is inveigled, but runs the risk of knocking the piece of fish it accompanies – in this case, turbot – into touch. Variations tipped by readers have included memorably scented rosemary-cured cod or smoked bream with a sauce based on the ingredients of piccalilli, and nobody minds at all the fact that the whole show typically takes nigh on three hours to reach its conclusion. Desserts may not be quite up to the level of the foregoing. A square of lime tart with elderflower syrup was a welcome light finish in May – its accompanying mint-crammed yoghurt sorbet destroyed the otherwise perfect choice of partnering wine, a South African fortified Muscat. The sommelier, himself South African, is a credit to the whole operation, advising knowledgeably and unpatronisingly on the choices with each course (should you sign up for the combined food-and-wine deal), and the list itself is full of seriously sexy gear. Mark-ups will make many south-westerners gasp, but there is class throughout. Start with a glass of Camel Valley Brut, made just up the road, at £14.50. Otherwise bottles start at £28.

Chef/s: Nathan Outlaw. **Open:** Tue to Sat D only 7 to 9. **Closed:** Sun, Mon, 20 Dec to early Feb. **Meals:** Tasting menu £75 (7 courses). **Service:** 12.5% (optional). **Details:** Cards accepted. 24 seats. No mobile phones. Wheelchair access. Music. Car parking.

St Ives

Alba

Thrilling harbour views and vibrant food
Old Lifeboat House, Wharf Road, St Ives, TR26 1LF
Tel no: (01736) 797222
www.thealbarestaurant.com
Modern European | £29
Cooking score: 3

The old lifeboat house on St Ives' waterfront has become a talking point over the years, not simply because of its contemporary vibes, thrilling views and fine canvases but also because it parades some of Cornwall's best produce. Chefs are visible behind a glass screen, fashioning vibrant, eclectic dishes from locally sourced ingredients – perhaps a seafood 'tasting plate' comprising an unusual combo of crab with shiitake mushrooms, a couple of succulent scallops enhanced by a fine star-anise velouté, prawn and sesame balls in beurre blanc, and delicate tempura of seasonal mackerel. Those with other culinary preferences might prefer free-range chicken saltimbocca with crisp polenta, and desserts are right on the money – witness a clean-tasting assiette of strawberries involving Eton mess, a tart and 'gazpacho'. Wines from £12.50.

Chef/s: Grant Nethercott. **Open:** all week L 12 to 2.30, D 5.30 to 10. **Closed:** 25 and 26 Dec. **Meals:** alc (main courses £11 to £20). Set L and D £14.25 (2 courses) to £17.25. **Service:** not inc. **Details:** Cards accepted. 65 seats. Wheelchair access. Music. Children allowed.

Alfresco

Vibrant harbourfront venue
The Wharf, St Ives, TR26 1LF
Tel no: (01736) 793737
www.alfrescocafebar.co.uk
Modern British | £27
Cooking score: 2

Buoyed by its cracking harbour views and animated vibes, open-fronted Alfresco does a good line in ozone-fresh local seafood – perhaps excellent scallops on pea purée with pancetta 'crackle', big-flavoured smoked haddock, hake and mussel chowder or delicately cooked wild sea bass with a crab cake, roasted salsify and coriander velouté. If meat is on your mind, you might veer towards venison carpaccio with beetroot and watercress before considering crispy belly pork on cabbage and hog's pudding with mead jus. Cheeses are artisan West Country heroes, while desserts might feature chocolate fondant with saffron clotted cream or rhubarb frangipane with stem ginger ice cream. Terrific set menus offer the best value, according to readers. House wines from £12.95.

Chef/s: Jamie Phillips. **Open:** all week L 12 to 3, D 6 to 10. **Closed:** 4 Jan to 8 Feb. **Meals:** alc (main courses £13 to £19). Set L and D £15.95 (2 courses) to £21.90. **Service:** not inc. **Details:** Cards accepted. 26 seats. 12 seats outside. Music. Children allowed.

NEW ENTRY

The Black Rock

Arty, discreet local eatery
Market Place, St Ives, TR26 1RZ
Tel no: (01736) 791911
www.theblackrockstives.co.uk
Modern European | £25
Cooking score: 2

A cool new arrival on the crowded local scene, David Symons' converted hardware shop is discreetly ensconced just a stone's throw from the harbour. Works by St Ives artists line the walls of the monochrome dining room, and the open kitchen delivers some intelligent flavours and imaginative ideas, from organic gravadlax with apple crème fraîche and beetroot to a memorable dark chocolate and star anise truffle cake with fennel ice cream. In between, poached turbot might arrive with a harmonious assortment of celeriac, crab bonbons, crispy Parmesan gnocchi and asparagus, wild Cornish venison is given the 'bolognese' treatment and belly pork is served the old way, with crackling, apples and parsnips. Quaffable house wine is £15.50.

Chef/s: David Symons. **Open:** Mon to Sat D only 6 to 10. **Closed:** Sun, Nov, Jan. **Meals:** alc (main courses £13 to £17). Set D £15.50 (2 courses) to £17.95. **Service:** 10% (optional). **Details:** Cards accepted. 36 seats. Separate bar. Music. Children allowed.

Blas Burgerworks

Laid-back eco-friendly burger bar
The Warren, St Ives, TR26 2EA
Tel no: (01736) 797272
www.blasburgerworks.co.uk
Burgers | £15
Cooking score: 1

Squirreled away down a narrow street behind the harbour, this granite storehouse is now a laid-back, eco-friendly burger bar with a contemporary utilitarian design. The tables are fashioned out of reclaimed wood and local produce is the mantra in the kitchen. Burgers cooked on the char-grill are made from Cornish meat and free-range chicken, with day-boat fish often arriving from the bay outside. Tuck into a cheeseburger topped with Cornish Blue and wash it down with local ale or cider. Tempting puds include chocolate brownie with ice cream, and a bottle of house wine is £14.50 (£3.40 a glass).

Chef/s: Sally Cuckson, Marie Dixon and Sarah Newark. **Open:** Tue to Sun D only 6 to 10 (all week 5 to 10 during school hols). **Closed:** Mon, 1 Nov to 15 Dec, 8 Jan to mid Feb, first week May. **Meals:** alc (main courses £8 to £11). **Service:** not inc. **Details:** Cards accepted. 34 seats. Music. Children allowed.

Porthminster Beach Café

Funky beach hangout
Porthminster Beach, St Ives, TR26 2EB
Tel no: (01736) 795352
www.porthminstercafe.co.uk
Seafood | £35
Cooking score: 4

Sheltering below the steep rise of Porthminster Point, this hangout really does sit right on the beach. Reliably popular in summer, it's also a magnificent setting in blustery November ('a gale blowing', hollered one intrepid soul, 'waves crashing just outside the windows, brilliant!'). The bill of fare is seafood cooked every which way the global cookbook comes up with. One successful lunch began with superb fried cuttlefish in citrus miso, and went on to baked hake with white bean purée, and what are confidently declared the best fish and chips to be found anywhere (beer-battered haddock with homemade tartare, and chips cooked with whole cloves of garlic and sprinkled with crisp-fried rosemary spikes). At dinner, things go up a gear, perhaps for braised pork cheeks with parsnip purée in Cornish cider or baked pollack with spinach and a truffled egg-yolk parcel. Dessert could be caramelised banana with pistachio ice cream and honeycomb. Wines are grouped by style, including 'elegant' and 'serious', starting at £14.95.

Chef/s: Mick Smith. **Open:** all week L 12 to 3, D 6 to 9.30. **Closed:** Jan. **Meals:** alc (main courses £15 to £24). **Service:** not inc. **Details:** Cards accepted. 60 seats. 70 seats outside. No mobile phones. Music. Children allowed.

St Andrew's Street Bistro

Relaxed, tucked-away bistro
16 St Andrew's Street, St Ives, TR26 1AH
Tel no: (01736) 797074
www.bistrostives.co.uk
Modern European | £25
Cooking score: 1

Down a narrow street behind the harbour, this former pilchard works has a new owner and a new chef since the last edition of the Guide, and is now open for lunch as well as dinner. The lofty space is lighter, local art adorns the walls and the cooking is now Italian-influenced, with seasonal menus. Homemade basil bread with white bean and garlic purée, a generous portion of Fowey mussels with chorizo, peppers, garlic and tomato, and belly pork with creamed mash have all been praised. Warm almond and rhubarb tart with homemade vanilla ice cream is a good pud. Wines from £13.50.

Chef/s: Aaron Bailey. **Open:** all week L 12 to 2, D 6 to 10. **Closed:** 8 Jan to 14 Feb, 2 weeks Nov. **Meals:** alc (main courses £12 to £19). **Service:** not inc. **Details:** Cards accepted. 60 seats. Separate bar. No mobile phones. Music. Children allowed.

St Kew

St Kew Inn

Pubby vibes and flavourful food
St Kew, PL30 3HB
Tel no: (01208) 841259
www.stkewinn.co.uk
Modern British | £27
new chef

A fifteenth-century stone hostelry not far from Wadebridge, the St Kew Inn was once home to the masons who built the nearby St James's church. It makes a wonderful spot for an outdoor meal on a summer's day, with the hanging baskets in full bloom, and in the darker months there'll be a roaring fire inside. David Tranier, promoted from sous chef, maintains the style of modern pub food. Potted shrimps on sourdough toast or a plate of spicy sausages, are good ways to start, and could be followed by crispy belly pork in mustard sauce or pan-roasted cod with spiced chickpea stew. Round things off with rhubarb fool and shortbread. Order your drinks at the bar, with wines from £3.55 a glass. Early reports suggest the kitchen is taking time to adjust to the changes. Reports please.

Chef/s: David Tranier. **Open:** all week L 12 to 2, D 6.30 to 9. **Closed:** 25 Dec. **Meals:** alc (main courses £10 to £20). Sun L £10.50. **Service:** not inc. **Details:** Cards accepted. 60 seats. 50 seats outside. Separate bar. No music. No mobile phones. Children allowed. Car parking.

St Mawes

Hotel Tresanton

Seductive seaside bolt-hole
27 Lower Castle Road, St Mawes, TR2 5DR
Tel no: (01326) 270055
www.tresanton.com
Modern European | £40
Cooking score: 4

Overlooking the Fal estuary, Olga Polizzi's seaside bolt-hole for jaded townies has more than a touch of the Med about it – just the ticket for Cornwall. It scores high in the atmosphere stakes, with a seductive terrace and breezily elegant dining room that reflects the refined style of the cooking. Local and seasonal produce are naturally the lynchpins of the fixed-price menus, which offer four choices per course. Starters might feature foie gras and chicken liver parfait with damson chutney, and seafood is a strong suit – from Cornish oysters to hand-dived scallops with asparagus, beetroot and shallot crisp. Sea bass has come served with crab cake, squid, steamed clams, leeks and carrots, but meat dishes are handled well too, perhaps best end of lamb teamed with gratin potatoes, red onion marmalade and parsnips. Satisfying desserts have included a version of Tunisian orange cake with yoghurt sorbet. House wines from £18.

Chef/s: Paul Wadham. **Open:** all week L 12.30 to 2.30, D 7 to 9.30. **Closed:** 2 weeks Jan. **Meals:** alc (main courses £16 to £22). Set L £26.50 (2 courses) to £35. Set D £31 (2 courses) to £43. Sun L £35. **Service:** not inc. **Details:** Cards accepted. 55 seats. 100 seats outside. Separate bar. No music. No mobile phones. Car parking.

St Merryn

Rosel & Co

Easy-going eatery with appealing food
The Dog House, St Merryn, PL28 8NF
Tel no: (01841) 521289
www.roselandco.co.uk
Modern British | £35
Cooking score: 4

A mix of chunky wood tables, local art and a partial view of the kitchen create a mood of easy reassurance in this dining room next door to the Dog House Bar. Zane Rosel is an accomplished cook with a raft of appealing ideas up his sleeve: pear salad, served with blue cheese pannacotta and watercress, for example, or chicken and leek terrine teamed with bacon, Parmesan and anchovy mayonnaise. Everything is underpinned by first-class raw materials, mostly from the region, which are showcased on a short, to-the-point menu. Top marks for well-timed hake with mussel risotto, sorrel and chives, likewise the quality of a pork chop and belly served with swede gratin and pickled cabbage, and for a blood orange terrine with star anise parfait and almond bread. It all comes with a decent, affordable wine list, which opens at £16.

Chef/s: Zane Rosel. **Open:** Tue to Sat D only 7 to 9. **Closed:** Sun, Mon, Jan, Feb. **Meals:** Set D £29.50 (2 courses) to £34.50. **Service:** not inc. **Details:** Cards accepted. 20 seats. No mobile phones. Music.

READERS RECOMMEND

The Cornish Arms

British
Churchtown, St Merryn, PL28 8ND
Tel no: (01841) 520288
www.rickstein.com
'Good addition to the Rick Stein empire...a first-class pub lunch.'

Treen

The Gurnard's Head

Going from strength to strength
Treen, TR26 3DE
Tel no: (01736) 796928
www.gurnardshead.co.uk
Modern British | £28
Cooking score: 3

A spectacular, remote location overlooking the sea is home for this rambling old inn on the winding coast road from St Ives. It's full of character, with a bright, yet relaxed modern look to the comfortable bar area and spacious ('but still quite informal') dining area. What powers the kitchen is local materials – with a particular slant on fish – which are woven into an ever-changing menu. Marinated squid and wild leaf salad, and hake with purple sprouting broccoli, potato gnocchi and vierge dressing are typical of the kitchen's 'plain-speaking' style. Meat dishes can include confit belly pork or braised lamb shoulder, while desserts such as rhubarb mousse with white chocolate ice cream are spot-on. The global wine list has lots of interesting choices from £15.50.

Chef/s: Bruce Rennie. **Open:** all week L 12.30 to 2.30 (12 Sun), D 6.30 to 9.30. **Closed:** 24 and 25 Dec, 5 days Jan. **Meals:** alc (main courses £14 to £17). Set L £14.50 (2 courses) to £16.75. **Service:** not inc. **Details:** Cards accepted. 50 seats. 50 seats outside. Separate bar. No music. No mobile phones. Children allowed. Car parking.

Truro

Tabb's

A beguiling favourite
85 Kenwyn Street, Truro, TR1 3BZ
Tel no: (01872) 262110
www.tabbs.co.uk
Modern British | £35
Cooking score: 4

£5 OFF

Sitting pretty in what was a run-down boozer, Tabb's wins over the Truro crowd with its beguiling intimacy, soft lilac hues and sharply crafted food. All the familiar trademarks are still present and correct, from a daily selection of home-baked breads to the signature chocolates that sign off every meal. Nigel Tabb cooks with style and sensitivity, matching pan-fried scallops with chorizo, snow peas and tagliatelle nero, perking up pressed confit of duck with homemade piccalilli, and invigorating loin of wild venison with mushroom and onion goulash and some vibrant red pepper jus. He also respects ingredients, be it skilfully filleted neck of lamb or breast of Terras Farm duck. Locals will be delighted to learn that Tabb's is open for lunch once again, delivering satisfaction in the shape of, say, Provençal fish soup with chilli relish followed by triumphant calf's liver with a demi-tasse of 'unctuous' casseroled beef shin. Around 40 commendable wines kick off at £14.95 (£4 a glass).

Chef/s: Nigel Tabb. **Open:** Tue to Fri L 12 to 2, Tue to Sat D 6.30 to 9. **Closed:** Sun, Mon, 1 week Jan. **Meals:** alc (main courses £15 to £20). Set L £18.50

(2 courses) to £25. **Service:** not inc. **Details:** Cards accepted. 30 seats. Separate bar. No mobile phones. Music. Children allowed.

Watergate Bay

Fifteen Cornwall

Pukka chic on the beach
On the beach, Watergate Bay, TR8 4AA
Tel no: (01637) 861000
www.fifteencornwall.co.uk
Italian | £27
Cooking score: 4

The Cornish outpost of the Jamie Oliver Foundation (JO's now-legendary training programme for disadvantaged youngsters) is pitched right by the beach overlooking the West Country's grooviest surfing destination – complete with perfect waves, photogenic sandscapes and jaw-dropping sunsets. Breakfast is a breezy wake-up call, and the place buzzes as lunchtime approaches. Top shouts from recent, typically perky meals have included a risotto of Jerusalem artichokes and spinach, gorgeously sticky slow-cooked ox cheek, and a dish of roast pollack 'saltimbocca' with borlotti beans, Swiss chard and crispy sage. After that, try vanilla and grappa pannacotta with 'boozy prunes' and ricciarelli biscuits. Dinner is a fixed-price, five-course deal with similar 'funky rustic' dishes and an extra helping of pukka chic (expect the likes of crispy John Dory fillet with cianfotta, purple sprouting broccoli and balsamic salsa). The global wine list is as hip as everything else here, with trendy producers, a few oddballs and good drinking across the range. Prices start at £19.50 (£5 a glass).
Chef/s: Andy Appleton. **Open:** all week L 12 to 2.30, D 6.15 to 9.15. **Meals:** alc (main courses £18 to £23). Set L £27. Set D £58 (5 courses). **Service:** not inc. **Details:** Cards accepted. 100 seats. Wheelchair access. Music. Children allowed. Car parking.

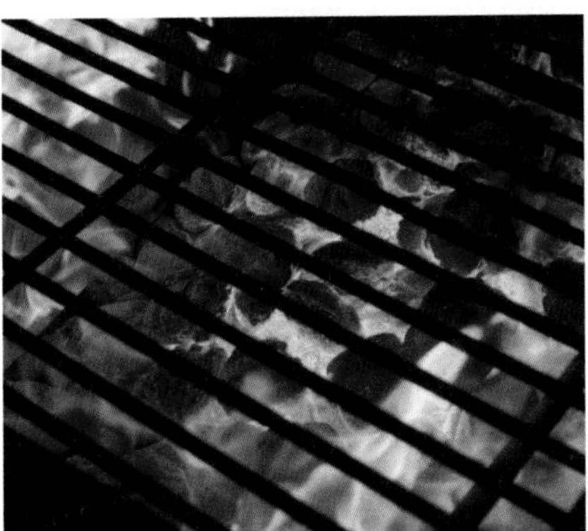

THE PRICE OF FLAME

When it comes to grilling, there's only one name on the lips of the nation's finest chefs: Josper. This Spanish import enables cooking over charcoal in an enclosed cast alloy 'oven'. The combination of direct and radiant heat instantly seals the ingredients, locking in moisture and, of course, flavour. 'We use the Josper for all steaks over two inches thick,' says Richard Turner of **Hawksmoor**, 'the all-encompassing heat gives a delicious crust while the interior remains juicy.'

'I bought a Josper oven for **Fish & Chips** in Falmouth after lunch at Mitch Tonks' **Seahorse** restaurant in Dartmouth,' says Rick Stein. 'It gets to temperatures normally only found in a tandoor which means that fillets of fish like John Dory can be roasted so quickly that the skin is crisp while the centre is still succulent with a slight aroma of charcoal.' At £10k to £18k, a Josper is a serious investment but it's a price worth paying for chefs such as Jason Atherton who has installed one at **Pollen Street Social**. 'They're great for vegetables too,' says Josper's UK development chef Michael Eyre, who suggests blasting blanched asparagus in the Josper for 40 seconds. Anyone for Josper carrots?

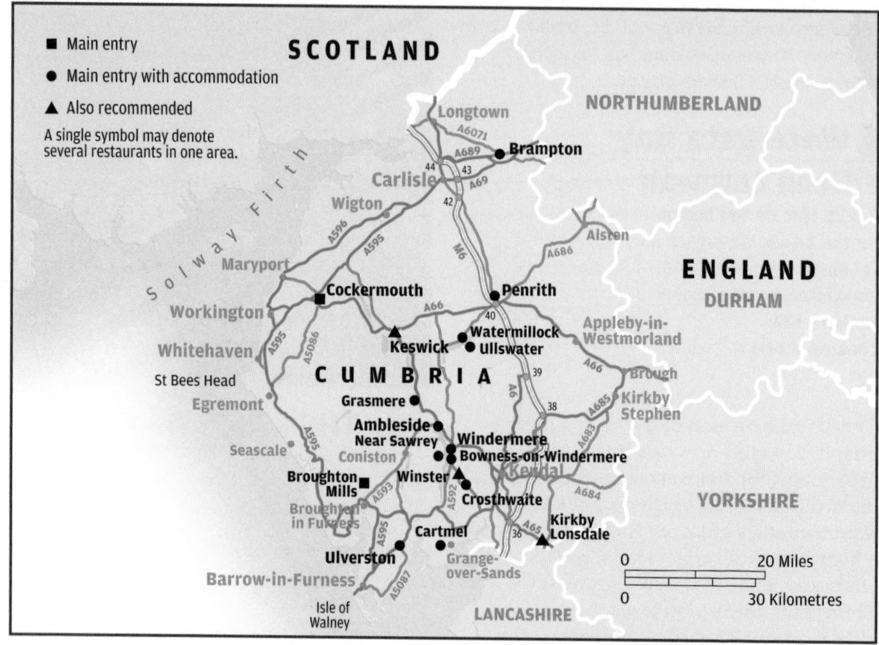

Ambleside

The Drunken Duck Inn

Handsome all-rounder
Barngates, Ambleside, LA22 0NG
Tel no: (015394) 36347
www.drunkenduckinn.co.uk
Modern British | £30
Cooking score: 2
V

This fine old Cumbrian pub has fantastic views, fetching beams, wood fires and an on-site brewery. The fashionable menus are driven by seasonal produce, with simple pub classics offered at lunch – Cheddar and goats' cheese ploughman's or pork, chicken and stuffing pie with air-dried ham and piccalilli. The full menu offers a mix of English domestic and Mediterranean ways, with ham hock ravioli served with garlic and saffron mayonnaise, and wild mushrooms alongside the likes of duck cottage pie. Conclude with cranachan or sticky toffee pudding. An impressive, carefully annotated wine list starts at £22.50.

Chef/s: Jonny Watson. **Open:** all week L 12 to 4, D 6 to 9.30. **Closed:** 25 Dec. **Meals:** alc (main courses £13 to £26). **Service:** not inc. **Details:** Cards accepted. 60 seats. 40 seats outside. Separate bar. No music. No mobile phones. Wheelchair access. Children allowed. Car parking.

Bowness-on-Windermere

Linthwaite House

Joyful views and confident modern cooking
Crook Road, Bowness-on-Windermere, LA23 3JA
Tel no: (015394) 88600
www.linthwaite.com
Modern British | £52
Cooking score: 5
£5 OFF V

The hilltop setting overlooking Lake Windermere and the fells is a joy in itself, but is further enhanced by the 14 acres of well-kept grounds in which this elegant white mansion house stands. A triptych of images that refer to the surrounding landscape adorns the smart, neutral-hued dining room, where a vigorous version of the modern British style is Richard Kearsley's undoubted forte. Confident combining brings on mackerel escabèche with a crab beignet and sardine and red pepper dressing, or ballottine of salmon with beetroot-cured gravadlax and saffron-pickled fennel, to start. Reporters feel that things really get into their stride at main-course stage: medium-rare loin of Cartmel venison is accompanied by a perfectly crisp tartlet of caramelised red onion and damson purée in a chocolate-enriched port jus, or there may be beef two ways – pink-cooked fillet and braised short rib – served with an intriguing little dish of smoked mash. Successful desserts have included a baked egg custard with poached rhubarb and ginger ice cream, as well as pistachio cake with honey ice cream and a grilled fig – 'almost the eastern Mediterranean on a plate'. A comprehensive, quality-conscious wine list is arranged by grape variety and style, with helpful notes including the alcohol content in each case. Prices open at £18.

Chef/s: Richard Kearsley. **Open:** all week L 12.30 to 2, D 6.30 to 9. **Meals:** Set L £14.95 (2 courses) to £19.95. Set D £52 (4 courses). Sun L £24.95. **Service:** not inc. **Details:** Cards accepted. 60 seats. 40 seats outside. Separate bar. No mobile phones. Wheelchair access. Music. Children allowed. Car parking.

Brampton

Farlam Hall

Lakeland retreat with lots to love

Brampton, CA8 2NG

Tel no: (016977) 46234

www.farlamhall.co.uk

Modern British | £44

Cooking score: 3

Lauded as 'the epitome of Victorian comfort', the Quinion family's Lakeland retreat has been chugging along personably for more than three decades, and visitors love everything about the place – from its dreamy landscaped gardens to dinner at eight in the thoroughly traditional restaurant. Daily fixed-price menus follow the old custom, with a sorbet dropped in before the main course, and there's nothing here to offend or challenge: grilled Thornby Moor goats' cheese with stir-fried vegetables is one way to start, with centrepieces offering anything from wild salmon fillet on smoked salmon risotto to excellent boned quail stuffed with chicken mousse on herb mash with Madeira jus. Cheeses come next, before raspberry bavarois or a confection of hazelnut marshmallow with bananas conclude proceedings with an old-world flourish. Wines start at £19.75 (£5.25 a glass).

Chef/s: Barry Quinion. **Open:** all week D only 8 to 8.30. **Closed:** 25 to 30 Dec. **Meals:** Set D £44 (4 courses) to £46 (5 courses). **Service:** not inc. **Details:** Cards accepted. 45 seats. No music. No mobile phones. Wheelchair access. Children allowed. Car parking.

Broughton Mills

Blacksmiths Arms

Quaint inn with gutsy, traditional food

Broughton Mills, LA20 6AX

Tel no: (01229) 716824

www.theblacksmithsarms.com

Modern British | £22

Cooking score: 2

As country restaurants go, the Blacksmiths Arms has a distinct edge on quaintness, with its idyllic (some say 'very isolated') setting and ancient, unspoilt interior – 'quite an experience', thought one reporter. It's perfect for those who've built up an appetite while walking or those looking for gutsy, traditional food. Menus deliver natural smoked haddock fishcakes with minted pea purée, crispy pancetta, poached egg and tartare sauce alongside slow-braised shoulder of minted lamb Henry and whole spatchcock partridge. Reports suggest service comes with 'attitude'. House wine is £12.55.

Chef/s: Paul McKnight. **Open:** Tue to Sun L 12 to 2, D 6 to 9. **Closed:** Mon, 25 and 26 Dec. **Meals:** alc (main courses £11 to £17). **Service:** not inc. **Details:** Cards accepted. 38 seats. 24 seats outside. Separate bar. No music. Children allowed. Car parking.

Cartmel

L'Enclume

Nature meets the avant-garde
Cavendish Street, Cartmel, LA11 6PZ
Tel no: (015395) 36362
www.lenclume.co.uk
Modern British | £69
Cooking score: 9
£5 OFF V

Few restaurants can match food and setting more harmoniously than Simon Rogan's L'Enclume. This hewn-out stone smithy deep in the Cumbrian Peninsula breathes 'nature', from eerie fungal sculptures, plants entwined in glass globes and piles of pebbles on each table to an enchanting garden by a stream. It's an achingly romantic prospect – especially if you stay over. Rogan isn't a native Lakelander, but he has mainlined the region's larder since arriving here, amassing some 200 suppliers, setting up his own farm and dispatching his chefs on regular forays for 'free food'. The accumulated bounty finds its way on to three menus (8 or 12 courses, plus a veggie spread), and the results speak for themselves: 'utterly engrossing', 'mesmerising', 'performance art at its best'... the superlatives go on and on. Over the years he has pruned back his style, abandoning high-wire culinary acrobatics in favour of crystal-clear innovation. If the menu says 'Herdwick hogget, turnips, cider and chenopodiums', that's exactly what you get: an unbelievably flavoursome nugget of juicy flesh alongside a milky lamb's sweetbread on a blob of silky purée, with primeval leaves and crunchy turnips sliced into tiny discs, plus a few spoonfuls of potent, lip-sticking jus laced with local cider – just to prove that the kitchen can also do orthodox haute cuisine. Picking star turns is like singling out tunes from a hit musical, but consider a disc of smoked egg yolk 'with the texture of lemon curd', coated in mushroom dust and surrounded by some choice fungal specimens and deftly arranged rock samphire (unrelated to the ubiquitous marsh plant) or cod tongues aligned with skinned broad beans, sprigs of aromatic marjoram, sea aster leaves and a stunning lemony dressing. What impresses is Rogan's ability to extract pure essence from base ingredients and also his revelatory way with herby 'wildings': fronds of pineapple weed (aka wild camomile) in a limpid springtime broth with artichoke dumplings and skinned sun-blush tomatoes, strips of lovage stalk dehydrated into crazy anise-scented twirls, sea buckthorn adding its briny tang to liquorice cream. The mood ebbs and flows, and just when you think it is all becoming a tad gentle, the kitchen launches a blaze of colour or white-hot intensity: perhaps a vertical construction of carrots tangled with nasturtium flowers or cylinders of salt-baked kohlrabi wrapped in kale leaves with a serving of supercharged chicken offal bolognese and drops of thyme oil so intense they taste like undiluted aromatherapy. Before things move towards their sweet finale, you can slip in an extra course from the cheese trolley. Then it's on to desserts proper, but don't expect razzle-dazzle or a sugar rush: instead, the kitchen works wonders of a different kind – perhaps a heady confection of sticky gingerbread and buttermilk with chervil granita in a lidded ceramic pot. From the first nibble of smoked eel croquette to the last sip of celery milkshake, this is a gastronomic trip like no other. L'Enclume is all about nudging boundaries and opening up culinary perceptions; it's also about the sheer pleasure of fine food in all its diversity – a light-hearted, conversational place where no one feels out of their depth, thanks to superb management and confident staff who know how to demystify the details without losing their sense of humour. The wine list announces its serious intentions with a stellar choice of fizz, before scouring the globe in search of quality. Mark-ups are friendly, and a dozen house selections start at £23 (£4 a glass). Note: Simon Rogan now has a foothold

in London with the arrival of Roganic – a two-year venture at 19 Blandford Street, W1U 3DH; tel (020) 7486 0380.
Chef/s: Simon Rogan. **Open:** Wed to Sun L 12 to 1.30, all week D 6.45 to 9.30. **Meals:** Set L £25 (3 courses). Set menu £69 (8 courses) to £89 (12 courses). **Service:** not inc. **Details:** Cards accepted. 50 seats. No music. No mobile phones. Wheelchair access. Car parking.

Rogan & Company

Heartwarming brasserie
The Square, Cartmel, LA11 6QD
Tel no: (015395) 35917
www.roganandcompany.co.uk
Modern British | £25
Cooking score: 4

Simon Rogan's second Cartmel venture, just round the corner from L'Enclume (see entry) has settled into a rhythm in recent months, the flexible menu as popular with casual diners on the ground floor as it is with those looking for something a bit fancier in the handsome upstairs room. The kitchen does a good line in cost-conscious modern British brasserie dishes – no whizzes or foams, but seasonal British ingredients that taste the way they came into this world. It's happy to celebrate the humbler things of life: a plate of farm-grown peas in the pod to nibble, moules marinière with crusty bread, a burger made with beef fillet, a bowl of fresh cherries for dessert. But there's also duck and foie gras terrine with rhubarb chutney, pan-fried sea trout with sautéed broccoli, almonds and hollandaise, and a bitter chocolate tart with raspberry ice cream. Service gets the thumbs-up, too. Wines from £13.40.
Chef/s: Louie Lawrence. **Open:** Mon to Sun L 12 to 2.30, D 6.30 to 9. **Closed:** Mon (Nov to Mar). **Meals:** alc (main courses £11 to £25). Set Sun L £19.95. **Service:** not inc. **Details:** Cards accepted. 80 seats. 8 seats outside. Separate bar. Wheelchair access. Music. Children allowed.

Cockermouth

Quince & Medlar

Veteran Lakeland veggie
13 Castlegate, Cockermouth, CA13 9EU
Tel no: (01900) 823579
www.quinceandmedlar.co.uk
Vegetarian | £27
Cooking score: 4

V 

'Superb food at very moderate prices with a range of good wines, all organic, at a fraction of the prices at most restaurants.' So notes one diner, neatly summing up the reasons to visit this veteran vegetarian restaurant, which has been quietly doing its own thing for 23 years. It occupies the owners' home and the comfortable Victorian setting sets the tone for a style of cooking that echoes the trends without being enslaved by them. A wholesome rusticity runs through starters such as a 'superb' salad of roasted beetroot with horseradish on a blini or potted peperonata with cheese shortbreads, followed, perhaps, by leek and butternut cassoulet with a rich tomato, cider, marjoram and paprika sauce and cheesy herb dumplings. Most dishes can also be served vegan. Finish with a classic dessert such as sticky toffee pudding. Organic wines do indeed come at very reasonable prices, kicking off at £14.10.
Chef/s: Colin Le Voi. **Open:** Tue to Sat D only 6.30 to 9.30. **Closed:** Sun, Mon, 24 to 26 Dec. **Meals:** alc (main courses £14). **Service:** not inc. **Details:** Cards accepted. 26 seats. No mobile phones. Music.

Crosthwaite

The Punch Bowl

Stylish village pub with excellent food
Lyth Valley, Crosthwaite, LA8 8HR
Tel no: (015395) 68237
www.the-punchbowl.co.uk
Modern British | £30
Cooking score: 3

Overlooking the Lyth Valley and next to St Mary's Church, the Punch Bowl is still very much a free house, dispensing local real ales and genuine hospitality, but it also successfully bridges that hard-to-achieve divide between village pub and stylish restaurant-with-rooms. The kitchen is not trying to reinvent the culinary wheel, but the carefully sourced produce is precisely cooked and thoughtfully presented. One reporter commended the 'relaxed atmosphere and helpful service', while another praised the 'excellent' food, which ranges from a starter of glazed Lancashire cheese soufflé with tomato chutney to a main of stuffed pork tenderloin with black pudding, pancetta, confit potatoes, spinach and roasted shallots. A 'heavenly' chocolate fondant with mandarin sorbet is one of the impressive desserts. Wines start at £16.50.

Chef/s: Euan Davidson. **Open:** all week 12 to 9. **Meals:** alc (main courses £10 to £20). **Service:** not inc. **Details:** Cards accepted. 95 seats. 60 seats outside. Separate bar. Wheelchair access. Music. Children allowed. Car parking.

Please send us your feedback

To register your opinion about any restaurant listed in the Guide, or a new restaurant that you wish to bring to our attention, please visit the web address at the bottom of the page. Your feedback informs the content of the book and will be used to compile next year's reviews.

Grasmere

The Jumble Room

Riffling through the global cookbook
Langdale Road, Grasmere, LA22 9SU
Tel no: (015394) 35188
www.thejumbleroom.co.uk
Global | £40
Cooking score: 2

£5 OFF

Gigantic pictures of farmyard creatures peer down at you from the oxblood-coloured walls of this idiosyncratic restaurant-with-rooms, which sets out to prove that not all Lakeland venues are about floral chintz. The kitchen riffles through the global cookbook to produce menus that run from starters of Provençal fish soup and duck crostini with Puy lentils to mains of Hyderabad chicken and Thai seafood curry or beer-battered haddock and chips. Reorientate yourself at dessert stage with a serving of bread-and-butter pudding or Yorkshire rhubarb pavlova with ginger ice cream. A short, enthusiastically written wine list opens at £13.95 for a Chilean Sauvignon.

Chef/s: Trudy and David Clay. **Open:** Sat and Sun L 12 to 3.30, Wed to Sun D 5.30 to 9.30. **Closed:** Mon, Tue, 11 to 26 Dec, weekdays Jan and early Feb. **Meals:** alc (main courses £14 to £26). **Service:** not inc. **Details:** Cards accepted. 48 seats. 8 seats outside. Music. Children allowed.

Keswick

ALSO RECOMMENDED

▲ Swinside Lodge

Grange Road, Newlands, Keswick, CA12 5UE
Tel no: (017687) 72948
www.swinsidelodge-hotel.co.uk
Modern British £5 OFF

Built as a private residence in 1745, Swinside Lodge is the epitome of Lakeland tranquillity, with peaceful gardens and views out towards Windermere. Four-course dinners (£45) offer archetypal 'country house' cooking with a nod to the region's larder – think slow-cooked crispy pork with red cabbage, onion and thyme soup with home-baked bread and mains of sea bass fillet wrapped in air-dried ham with fennel, celeriac and garlicky prawns. After that, perhaps choose dark chocolate and walnut brownie with Kirsch cherries. House wine is £18.50. Open all week D only.

Kirkby Lonsdale

ALSO RECOMMENDED

▲ The Sun Inn

6 Market Street, Kirkby Lonsdale, LA6 2AU
Tel no: (015242) 71965
www.sun-inn.info
British

Mark and Lucy Fuller have worked wonders with this seventeenth-century inn overlooking the church, upgrading, revamping and reinvigorating the place. Carefully sourced produce is the starting point for food that fizzes with fashionable flourishes, whether nibbles from the all-day menu – potted shrimps, salt beef or whitebait, say – or dinner of creamed goats' cheese and marinated beetroot and walnut dressing (£5.95) followed by confit leg and cured breast of duck with watercress and orange salad (£15.95). Desserts include the likes of rhubarb crumble tart with ginger custard and ginger syrup or dark chocolate fondant with pistachio cream and praline. House wine is £13.25. No food Mon L.

Near Sawrey

Ees Wyke

Beatrix Potter bolt-hole
Near Sawrey, LA22 0JZ
Tel no: (015394) 36393
www.eeswyke.co.uk
Modern British | £35
Cooking score: 2

Ees Wyke is a Georgian house on just the right scale for a small hotel and insulated from the hurry and scurry of the world by meadows, Esthwaite Water and sheep grazing on fells. Evenings run to a classic country house format, starting with drinks in the lounge before heading to the dining room for Richard Lee's five-course, set-price dinner. His execution is careful and his recipes well-tried – witness dishes such as wild mushrooms on toasted croûton with chervil and tarragon cream, duck breast with Chinese five-spice and star anise, and crème caramel with orange and Grand Marnier. House wine is £19.50.

Chef/s: Richard Lee. **Open:** all week D only 7.30 (1 sitting). **Meals:** Set D £35 (5 courses). **Service:** not inc. **Details:** Cards accepted. 16 seats. No music. No mobile phones. Car parking.

Penrith

George & Dragon

Estate pub with a landmark restaurant
Clifton, Penrith, CA10 2ER
Tel no: (01768) 865381
www.georgeanddragonclifton.co.uk
Modern British | £24
Cooking score: 3

£5 OFF £30

Restored by local craftsmen using stone, slate and other materials in character with its Georgian beginnings, this whitewashed inn belongs to the Lowther Estate and has a rewarding foodie relationship with the estate's pastures, woods and wild acres. The family rear their own rare-breed porkers, venison is a seasonal highlight and there's plenty of greenery from the garden – all of which add local colour to Paul McKinnon's food. His cooking avoids pyrotechnics, but even the simplest dishes show high levels of culinary achievement: twice-baked cheese soufflé is a signature starter, pan-fried pig's liver is served with wild mushrooms and pea fricassee, and salmon comes with Jersey Royals and salsa verde. For pud, opt for a comforting chocolate pot or rhubarb and apple crumble. The short wine list opens at £14.

Chef/s: Paul McKinnon. **Open:** all week L 12 to 2.30, D 6 to 9. **Closed:** 26 Dec. **Meals:** alc (main courses £11 to £20). Sun L £10.95. **Service:** not inc. **Details:** Cards accepted. 84 seats. 45 seats outside. Separate bar. Wheelchair access. Music. Children allowed. Car parking.

Ullswater

Sharrow Bay

Grande dame of country house hotels
Ullswater, CA10 2LZ
Tel no: (01768) 486301
www.sharrowbay.co.uk
Modern British | £75
Cooking score: 5
V

Alarm bells have been ringing over the quality of the cooking at this long-established Guide grandee; recent reports have been rather uneven, but the balance is still tilted in Sharrow Bay's favour. Some quibbles relate to the prices and the service – hardly sharp enough, and not what many people would expect from the *grande dame* of the country house hotel scene. But, on the day, Colin Akrigg's cooking has a soundness to it – classically founded, slick and professional. Memorable results have included scallops on thyme fondant with roasted shallot purée and Noilly Prat sauce; a fine salad of smoked duck breast with spiced poached pear, Cashel Blue cheese and walnut dressing; a Suissesse soufflé of spinach, Stilton and roasted onion; and noisette of local venison, served with braised sherry lentils, butternut squash purée and brandy and port sauce. Desserts might take in a perfectly executed and intensely flavoured vanilla and blackcurrant soufflé or a trio of strawberry desserts. The wine list does not seek to overawe, although the cellar has the bottles for it, choosing to open quietly with the Sharrow Selection of some 15 or so good-value wines by the glass or bottle (from £20.50). The depth of the list emerges through page after page of pricier fine French vintages, complemented by interesting bottles from the rest of Europe and the New World.
Chef/s: Colin Akrigg and Mark Teasedale. **Open:** all week L at 1, D 8 to 10. **Meals:** Set L £35 and £45 (5 courses). Set D £75 (6 courses). Sun L £45. **Service:** not inc. **Details:** Cards accepted. 50 seats. No music. No mobile phones. Wheelchair access. Car parking.

Ulverston

The Bay Horse

Romantic charmer with breathtaking views
Canal Foot, Ulverston, LA12 9EL
Tel no: (01229) 583972
www.thebayhorsehotel.co.uk
Modern British | £36
Cooking score: 3
V

Persevere through Ulverston's industrial hinterland to find this civilised old coaching inn on the shore of the Leven Estuary. Glorious views, romantic sunsets and, for the past 23 years, the hospitality of chef-patron Robert Lyons continue to draw visitors to this waterside retreat. The intimate conservatory restaurant makes the most of the stunning views across Morecambe Bay – a fine setting for the monthly changing evening carte, which is served promptly at 8pm. The confident kitchen team produces skilfully cooked dishes that typically take in chicken liver pâté with cranberry and ginger purée, followed by rack of Lakeland lamb with garlic and rosemary, and dark chocolate mascarpone cheesecake. Lunchtime bar food and an afternoon 'light bites' menu are also available. Service is unobtrusive, from friendly and professional staff. Fans of South African wines have plenty to shout about when it comes to the wine list. Prices start at £16.50.
Chef/s: Robert Lyons and Kris Hogan. **Open:** all week L 12 to 3 (2 Mon, 4 Sun), D 7.30 for 8 (1 sitting). **Meals:** alc (main courses £22 to £27). Set D £25 (2 courses) to £31. **Service:** not inc. **Details:** Cards accepted. 50 seats. 20 seats outside. Separate bar. No mobile phones. Wheelchair access. Music. Car parking.

Watermillock

Rampsbeck Country House Hotel

Seductively situated lakeside mansion
Watermillock, CA11 OLP
Tel no: (017684) 86442
www.rampsbeck.co.uk
Modern British | £50
Cooking score: 4

Don't be daunted by the manicured lawns or grand country house demeanour of this Victorian mansion overlooking Ullswater – it puts on a friendly face and the mood in the large dining room is far from stuffy, despite the glittering chandeliers. Warm, affectionate staff contribute to the relaxed mood and the kitchen shows considerable flair in its interpretations of the Anglo-French repertoire. A starter of pan-fried skate wing with lemon and caper dressing is handled with real subtlety, while roast lamb loin with twice-cooked leg, confit shallots and vine-ripened cherry tomatoes is a pitch-perfect blend of flavours and textures. The kitchen also has a few clever tricks up its sleeve, serving roast hare with beetroot purée and chanterelles, matching turbot with langoustine tortellini, and accompanying roast monkfish with chorizo and char-grilled spring onions. Finally, Szechuan pepper adds some extra spice to a dessert of poached apple with gingerbread ice cream. Breads and other homemade extras are impressively good, and the exceptional wine list also deserves plaudits. Selections from France, Italy and Australia are particularly noteworthy, with prices starting at £16.95.

Chef/s: Andrew McGeorge. **Open:** all week L 12 to 1.30, D 7 to 9. **Meals:** Set L £26 (2 courses) to £32. Set D £49.50 to £55 (4 courses). Sun L £32. **Service:** not inc. **Details:** Cards accepted. 40 seats. Separate bar. No mobile phones. Wheelchair access. Music. Children allowed. Car parking.

Windermere

Gilpin Hotel & Lake House

Family-run retreat with serious food
Crook Road, Windermere, LA23 3NE
Tel no: (015394) 88818
www.gilpinlodge.co.uk
Modern British | £53
Cooking score: 5

V

Most people still think of this serene Lakeland retreat as Gilpin Lodge, although the emphasis is now firmly on the hotel and the place seems to have lost some of its cherished charm as a result. It can feel rather 'anonymous', with 'disjointed' service in the four candlelit dining rooms, although Russell Plowman's food is no poor relation in the hospitality stakes. Lunches play it safe with ham hock terrine or guinea fowl with wild mushrooms as the kitchen saves its creative shots for dinner. If you're in the mood for something 'classic', consider twice-baked Cumbrian rarebit soufflé or tenderloin, cheek and belly of pork with sage dumplings; otherwise, move up a notch for Russell's richly flavoured 'signature' dishes. To start, Loch Duart organic salmon might be paired with 'seaweed' and cauliflower and horseradish purée; mains could take in anything from loin of rose veal with crispy ravioli of braised loin, soubise cream and Madeira sauce, to roast Goosnargh duckling with turnip roots and leaves, grain mustard and roasting juices. Meals are peppered with fashionable extras, while desserts could yield milk chocolate mousse with maple-roasted pecans and orange sorbet. Each dish comes with a suggestion from the mighty contingent of top-drawer French wines and illustrious international numbers, starting at £25 (£6.50 a glass).

Chef/s: Russell Plowman. **Open:** all week L 12 to 2, D 6.30 to 9.15. **Meals:** Set L Mon to Sat £27. Set D £52.50 (5 courses). Sun L £30. **Service:** not inc. **Details:** Cards accepted. 60 seats. 30 seats outside. Separate bar. No music. No mobile phones. Wheelchair access. Car parking.

STEFAN LYDKA
Holbeck Ghyll

When did you first know you wanted to be a sommelier?
I was always fascinated with the skill behind pairing food and wine. Being a sommelier +would give me the opportunity to taste many different wines with all sorts of delicious foods!

What is the most difficult aspect of your job?
Keeping up with price changes. For example, the fluctuations in currency exchanges and the rise and fall of VAT.

Name three qualities needed to be a successful sommelier.
To be humble, not arrogant, well-presented and not intimidating.

Have you noticed any wine trends over the last few years?
Grape varieties tend to change with fashion. Ten to fifteen years ago it was all Chardonnay but now it's Pinot Grigio or Viognier.

What is the most rewarding aspect of your job?
Knowing a guest has had a fantastic wine experience that was down to me and the advice I gave them.

Holbeck Ghyll

Majestic views and fabulous wines
Holbeck Lane, Windermere, LA23 1LU
Tel no: (015394) 32375
www.holbeckghyll.com
Modern British | £60
Cooking score: 5

Built in Victorian times as a hunting lodge for Lord Lonsdale of boxing fame, Holbeck Ghyll pulls no punches when it comes to majestic views and fabulous wines. You can enjoy uninterrupted vistas across Windermere to the Langdale Fells from the terrace or the grandly traditional, oak-panelled dining room, where David McLaughlin's food also sets out to impress. Lakeland ingredients and French imports are given slick, country house treatment with no stinting on luxurious accoutrements: roast Périgord quail appears with seared foie gras, boudin blanc and truffle jus, poulet de Bresse might be partnered by cep purée and creamed baby leeks, while roast loin of venison brings some earthy rusticity to the table in company with pumpkin purée, braised red cabbage and herb gnocchi. Cumbrian lamb is given a decent outing too (perhaps with black olives, confit peppers and aubergine). Desserts involve much time-consuming artifice in the form of lemon assiettes, chocolate plates and the likes of vanilla-poached pineapple with coconut sorbet, passion fruit jelly and banana beignets. The cheese trolley is a winner, but the real *pièce de résistance* is Holbeck Ghyll's lavish and constantly evolving wine list. France receives top billing, but don't ignore serious vintages from fine producers in Italy, Chile, California and beyond. 'Personal house selections' start at £29 (£7.90 a glass).

Chef/s: David McLaughlin. **Open:** all week L 12.30 to 2, D 7 to 9.30. **Meals:** Set L £24 (2 courses) to £30. Set D £60. Gourmet menu £78 (7 courses). **Service:** not inc. **Details:** Cards accepted. 50 seats. No music. No mobile phones. Wheelchair access. Car parking.

Jerichos at the Waverley

Clever flavours from a dynamic duo
College Road, Windermere, LA23 1BX
Tel no: (015394) 42522
www.jerichos.co.uk
Modern British | £32
Cooking score: 5

This rather magisterial property with its expansive rooms was built in the Victorian era as a temperance hotel, but you won't be pressured to sign the pledge here these days. The restaurant opts for a stripped-down look, with board floors and undressed tables offset by crimson drapes, and Messrs Blaydes and Dalzell cook in vigorous modern British style, with multi-faceted dishes that can be quite filling at first-course stage, but are full of cleverly harmonised flavours. A pressed terrine of ham knuckle and confit duck with pea and ham sauce and a vinaigrette is typical of the starter approach. The restrained scope of the menus (four choices at each stage) allows for pin-sharp focus on each dish, seen perhaps in fried skate with toasted almonds, capers and shrimps, served with potato rösti and beetroot fondant, while one reporter was full of praise for the pink-cooked local venison, accompanied by shredded cabbage and bacon in a reduction of red wine. Gird your loins for rich desserts, such as chocolate and salted peanut tart with dark chocolate sorbet and caramel sauce. The wine list is a model of concision, presenting its inspired selections according to what food categories they will match. Bottles from £16, glasses from £5.

Chef/s: Chris Blaydes and Tim Dalzell. **Open:** Fri to Wed D only 7 to 9. **Closed:** Thur, 24 to 26 Dec, 1 Jan, last week Nov, first week Dec, last 3 weeks Jan. **Meals:** alc (main courses £16 to £25). **Service:** not inc. **Details:** Cards accepted. 28 seats. Music. Car parking.

The Samling

Comforting tradition and modern style
Ambleside Road, Windermere, LA23 1LR
Tel no: (015394) 31922
www.thesamlinghotel.co.uk
Modern British | £60
new chef

The Samling resides in a 67-acre estate near Lake Windermere, where Wordsworth once came to pay his rent. The elegant villa exudes comforting tradition and stylish modernism in equal measure, something that also applies to the food on the plate – the kitchen makes a virtue of finding new things to do with some unimpeachable regional produce. We learned of chef Daniel Grigg's arrival just as we were going to press, too late for us to receive any feedback on performance, so reports are particularly welcome. The wine list starts at £25.

Chef/s: Daniel Grigg. **Open:** all week L 12 to 1.30, D 7 to 9.30. **Meals:** Set L £35. Set D £60. Tasting menu £70. **Service:** not inc. **Details:** Cards accepted. 22 seats. 20 seats outside. Wheelchair access. Music. Children allowed. Car parking.

Winster

ALSO RECOMMENDED

▲ The Brown Horse Inn

Winster, LA23 3NR
Tel no: (015394) 43443
www.thebrownhorseinn.co.uk
Modern British

There's no shortage of stunningly converted inns in beautiful locations, but this one piles on the style with a microbrewery and a flourishing smallholding. The appealing menu of good-value pub and bistro classics includes chicken liver parfait (£5.95) or fish and chips (£12.50). Wrap things up with strawberry crème brûlée and coconut ice cream. Wines from £13.95. Accommodation. Open all week.

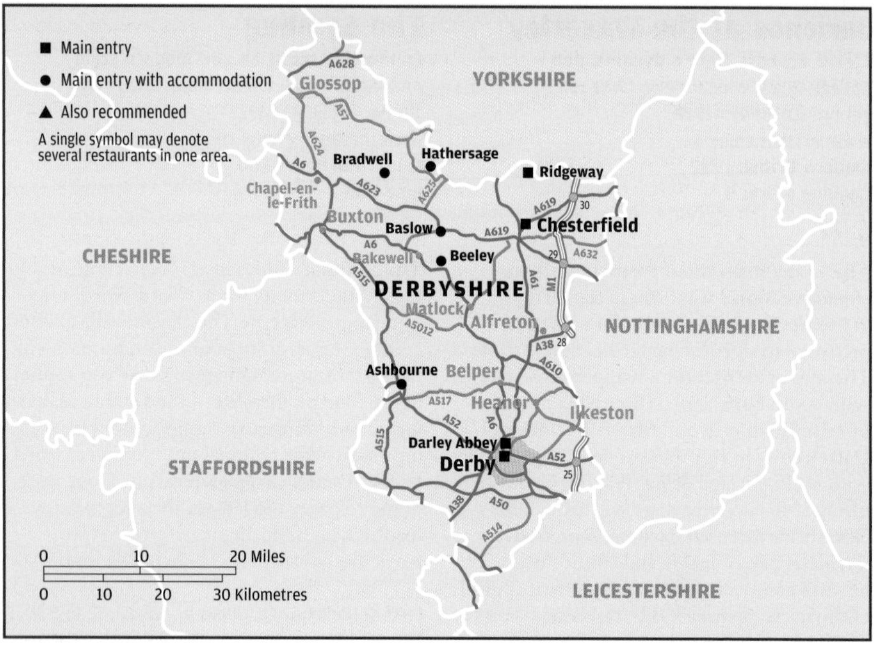

■ Main entry
● Main entry with accommodation
▲ Also recommended
A single symbol may denote several restaurants in one area.

0 10 20 Miles
0 10 20 30 Kilometres

Ashbourne

Callow Hall

Elegant country house hotel
Mappleton Road, Ashbourne, DE6 2AA
Tel no: (01335) 300900
www.callowhall.co.uk
Modern British | £45
Cooking score: 2

An elegant, comfortable country house hotel isn't the first place you'd look for on-trend ingredients, but in among the palate-cleansing sorbets and turned vegetables chef Anthony Spencer conceals unusual greens and Spanish-style charcuterie. Callow Hall is on the edge of the Peaks and looks and feels as traditonal as can be, with a series of intimate dining rooms. Food has integrity, along with the occasional wobble. Start with white asparagus served with cured pork loin and a poached egg, then move on to venison, butchered on-site, with rich accompaniments. Desserts are often fruity affairs. House wine, from a relatively short list, is £20.

Chef/s: Anthony Spencer. **Open:** all week L 12.30 to 1.30, D 7.30 to 8.30. **Meals:** alc (main courses £20 to £24). Set L £20 (2 courses) to £25. Set D £45 (4 courses). Sun L £28.50. **Service:** not inc.
Details: Cards accepted. 70 seats. 10 seats outside. Separate bar. Wheelchair access. Music. Children allowed. Car parking.

The Dining Room

An intimate dining odyssey
33 St John Street, Ashbourne, DE6 1GP
Tel no: (01335) 300666
www.thediningroomashbourne.co.uk
Modern European | £40
Cooking score: 4

The Dales' characterful restaurant is housed in an early seventeenth-century beamed house. By the time we go to press, there should be a self-catering apartment next to it, although you could be forgiven for not wanting to self-cater when Peter Dale is on hand. The drill is a

single sitting for dinner, for which all the curing, smoking, preserving, butchery and baking is done in-house. A huge succession of courses produced single-handedly delivers one astonishment after another. One moment you're in Japan for pork with damson, umeboshi plum, kombu (kelp) and sesame, the next you're reorientated in old England with black pudding, apple and mustard. Smoked salmon with Russian salad, black bread and avruga takes an eastern turn, but where chicken liver parfait with foie gras snow, quince, celeriac and pomegranate comes from is anybody's guess. The hit-rate is remarkably high, given the diversity, all the way to a hot and cold serving of treacle tart with flavours of lime leaf, citrus and vanilla. Choose from a stylistically arranged wine list that starts at £22.
Chef/s: Peter Dale. **Open:** Tue to Sat D only 7 (1 sitting). **Closed:** Sun, Mon, 1 week over Shrove Tue, 1 week Sept, last 2 weeks Dec. **Meals:** Set weekday D £40 (8 courses). Sat D £48 (16 courses). **Service:** not inc. **Details:** Cards accepted. 16 seats. No mobile phones. Wheelchair access. Music.

Baslow

Cavendish Hotel, Gallery Restaurant

Ducal dinner destination
Church Lane, Baslow, DE45 1SP
Tel no: (01246) 582311
www.cavendish-hotel.net
Modern British | £41
Cooking score: 2

The jury's out on the recent refurbishment at the Gallery Restaurant. Contemporary duck-egg blue and white paintwork strikes a faintly discordant note amid the gilded landscape paintings and aristocratic ambience of the Duke of Devonshire's country inn. Luckily, there are still views of the gently rolling Derbyshire countryside to complement the modern British menu. At inspection a worthy starter of smoked ham hock and pastrami terrine was followed by a generous helping of roast pork with duck-fat roast potatoes and caramelised apple sauce. However, reader reports have flagged up the occasional misfiring dish, and also indicate that service may be on the slide. The substantial wine list starts at £16.50.
Chef/s: Wayne Rogers. **Open:** all week L 12 to 2.30, D 6.30 to 10. **Meals:** Set L and D £30.90 (2 courses) to £50. **Service:** 5%. **Details:** Cards accepted. 50 seats. Separate bar. No mobile phones. Wheelchair access. Music. Children allowed. Car parking.

Fischer's Baslow Hall

Sensational food in a stellar retreat
Calver Road, Baslow, DE45 1RR
Tel no: (01246) 583259
www.fischers-baslowhall.co.uk
Modern European | £72
Cooking score: 7
V

'A Peak District institution', Max and Susan Fischer's fondly regarded restaurant-with-rooms comes nattily attired in full baronial garb – although this is no archaic architectural showpiece. Baslow Hall was built in 1907 at the behest of a vicar with a penchant for the past, and in the Fischers' hands it cleverly sidesteps the pomp, circumstance and lordly posturing that can plague some grand country houses. From the moment you are greeted at the door, the whole place feels as warm as a family home – albeit one with the trappings of prosperity. Service is dutifully observant, 'no detail is overlooked' and plaudits roll in for Rupert Rowley's sensational food. Here is a kitchen that satisfies the old guard with the most succulent and tender Derbyshire lamb (crusted with mint from the garden), as well as delivering sensory blitzkriegs for those with a taste for adventure – how about a theatrical dish of cod smoked over Lapsang Souchong tea with beetroot and horseradish bubbles, crispy capers and garlands of micro-herbs. Menus are many and varied, but everything is driven by impeccable sourcing, stunning technique, invention and an abundance of rich, deep flavours. Lunch has yielded some splendid stuff, notably a fine plateful of

Goosnargh duck breast and braised leg with honey and orange glaze, mandarins and boulangère potatoes, as well as a host of highly intricate desserts including roasted almond pannacotta with baked apple granita, sugared doughnut and malt ice cream. But the real showstopper is Rowley's extravagant 'gourmet' menu, a must-have if your wallet can take it. A warm Stilton and celeriac mousse mischievously embellished with Stilton 'snow', hazelnut powder, quince purée and apple jelly deploys the chef's armoury to the full, likewise a pavé of dry-aged sirloin cooked for 12 hours in Ardbeg whisky and presented with pickled and candied baby beets and smoked onion pannacotta. Also expect some big-city globalism (wasabi ice cream in a dish of pomegranate-glazed monkfish) and a few party tricks to lighten the mood (a marshmallow and caramel 'Scotch egg', for example). The top-drawer wine list oozes class on every page, from high-rolling vintage Burgundies to enticing Aussies at egalitarian prices. House selections start at £22 (£5.50 a glass).

Chef/s: Rupert Rowley. **Open:** all week L 12 to 1.30, D 7 to 8.30. **Closed:** 25, 26 and 31 Dec. **Meals:** Set L £28.50 (2 courses) to £33.50. Set D £42 (2 courses) to £48. Gourmet D £72. Sun L £42. Tasting menu £68. **Service:** not inc. **Details:** Cards accepted. 50 seats. Separate bar. No music. No mobile phones. Car parking.

Rowley's

Lively brasserie with comfort food
Church Lane, Baslow, DE45 1RY
Tel no: (01246) 583880
www.rowleysrestaurant.co.uk
Modern British | £27
Cooking score: 1

Rupert Rowley, in partnership with Max and Susan Fischer (see entry, Fischer's Baslow Hall), continues to win over tourists and locals with his casual restaurant in a strikingly converted pub. The straightforward British cooking produces some engaging results, and main courses have been particularly praised by reporters, who ate fillet of sea bass with shellfish linguine and smoked salmon bisque, and peppered, thick-cut rump steak with fries, green salad and pink peppercorn sauce. To start, there may be beetroot risotto, with vanilla crème brûlée to finish. House wine is £18.25.

Chef/s: Thomas Samworth. **Open:** all week L 12 to 2.30 (3 Sun), Mon to Sat D 6 to 9 (10 Fri and Sat). **Meals:** alc (main courses £15 to £19). Set L £21 (2 courses plus 1 drink) to £24. Sun L £24. **Service:** not inc. **Details:** Cards accepted. 64 seats. 12 seats outside. Separate bar. Wheelchair access. Music. Car parking.

Beeley

The Devonshire Arms

Well-to-do country inn
Devonshire Square, Beeley, DE4 2NR
Tel no: (01629) 733259
www.devonshirebeeley.co.uk
Modern British | £25
Cooking score: 2

A stone-built inn on the Chatsworth Estate, the Devonshire Arms combines the pastoral charm of a village hostelry with an up-to-date approach to wining and dining. Thus the log fires and old beams that come as standard are offset with some daringly multicoloured, stripy decor in the brasserie. Here, dishes such as squid and mussel sausage with smoked bacon and apple in lemongrass-chilli-lime dressing, and shoulder and leg of lamb korma with roasted parsnips and spiced rice spin the culinary compass-needle. Bar snacks offer the likes of beef topside sandwich or home-smoked mackerel pâté on toast with orange marmalade. There's a plethora of cakes for afternoon tea, or brasserie desserts such as Bakewell tart with matching ice cream. A well-chosen modern wine list starts at £15.50.

Chef/s: Alan Hill. **Open:** all week L 12 to 3 (4 Sun), D 6 to 9.30. **Meals:** alc (main courses £10 to £24). Sun L £13.95. **Service:** not inc. **Details:** Cards accepted. 60 seats. 20 seats outside. Wheelchair access. Music. Children allowed. Car parking.

Bradwell

The Samuel Fox Inn

Country pub favourite
Stretfield Road, Bradwell, S33 9JT
Tel no: (01433) 621562
www.samuelfox.co.uk
Modern British | £25
Cooking score: 1

The Samuel Fox may feel more contemporary than rustic, but it has the kind of atmosphere you can only get in a country pub. It scores with capable service and it's also prepared to invest in decent raw materials. There's little doubt that the kitchen can deliver unfussy dishes: to start you might choose belly pork and black pudding terrine with apple chutney, then slow-braised shoulder of lamb with creamed Savoy cabbage and mashed potato, and then warm parkin and caramel apple for dessert. Wines from £16.

Chef/s: Charles Curran. **Open:** all week L 12 to 2 (5 Sat and Sun), D 6 to 9 (9.30 Fri and Sat). **Meals:** alc (main courses £11 to £17). Set L £12.50 (2 courses) to £15.50. Set D £15 (2 courses) to £18. **Service:** not inc. **Details:** Cards accepted. 48 seats. 20 seats outside. Music. Children allowed. Car parking.

Chesterfield

Non Solo Vino

A real find in Chesterfield
417 Chatsworth Road, Brampton, Chesterfield, S40 3AD
Tel no: (01246) 276760
www.nonsolovino.co.uk
Italian | £30
Cooking score: 3

It is three years since Peter Gately and Andrea Sgaravatto added a restaurant to their wine shop. The gamble has paid off; it has become so popular with locals that they have added an alfresco terrace with extra seating. Although the menu can be limited when the kitchen isn't fully staffed, there have been no complaints about the consistency of the cooking. An appealing repertoire of modern Italian dishes might include a 'light and creamy' starter of Gorgonzola and Parmesan risotto, followed by a precisely cooked loin of Derbyshire lamb, dauphinoise potatoes, shallot purée, and red wine and golden raisin sauce. The all-Italian wine list offers 20 by the glass.

Chef/s: Matt Bennison. **Open:** Tue to Sun L 12 to 2.30 (3 Sun), Tue to Sat D 7 to 11. **Closed:** Mon, 25 to 26 Dec, 1 Jan, bank hols. **Meals:** alc (main courses from £12 to £25). Set L £15.95 (2 courses) to £19.95. **Service:** not inc. **Details:** Cards accepted. 58 seats. Separate bar. Music. Children allowed. Car parking.

ALSO RECOMMENDED

▲ The Old Post

43 Holywell Street, Chesterfield, S41 7SH
Tel no: (01246) 279479
www.theoldpostrestaurant.co.uk
Modern European 

This Grade II-listed Elizabethan building has been home to Hugh and Mary Cocker's intimate, friendly restaurant for the past decade. The fixed-price lunch (£13.95 for two courses) may include roast belly pork glazed in crab apple jelly with parsnip champ, and apple and pear crumble with vanilla custard. Reporters have praised the 'first-class' Sunday lunch. House wine is £15.50. Open Wed to Fri and Sun L, Tue to Sat D. No credit cards.

Darley Abbey

Darleys

Tourist hot spot with lively food
Darley Abbey Mills, Haslams Lane, Darley Abbey, DE22 1DZ
Tel no: (01332) 364987
www.darleys.com
Modern British | £35
Cooking score: 3

V

Part of a much bigger World Heritage Site stretching across the Derwent Valley, this converted cotton mill by the river is a surefire crowd-puller. However, Darleys' touristy appeal can put pressure on the kitchen, judging by a regular trickle of reports citing inconsistencies and overcooking 'to the point of destruction'. But there are success stories too, especially at lunchtime: potted ham in a Kilner jar with piccalilli, cannon of beef (cooked pink as requested) and sticky toffee pudding with rum and raisin ice cream have all gone down nicely. In the evening, visitors can expect a smattering of modish partnerships – goats' curd pannacotta with peppered Bloody Mary, cumin-coated monkfish with candied carrots and curry foam, or saffron French toast with baked figs and crème fraîche. The all-purpose wine list starts at £15.50.

Chef/s: Jonathan Hobson and Mark Hadfield. **Open:** all week L 12 to 2 (2.30 Sun), Mon to Sat D 7 to 9.30. **Closed:** 2 weeks from 25 Dec, bank hols. **Meals:** alc (main courses £19 to £22). Set L £17.95 (2 courses) to £20. Sun L £22.50. **Service:** not inc. **Details:** Cards accepted. 60 seats. Separate bar. Music. Children allowed. Car parking.

Derby

Zest

Pretension-free neighbourhood eatery
16d George Street, Derby, DE1 1EH
Tel no: (01332) 381101
www.restaurantzest.co.uk
Modern British | £25
Cooking score: 1

Housed in a handsome stable building that once stored hay, Zest has since turned its attention to feeding two-legged customers with sturdy modern British fare. The cheery crimson dining room is an agreeable place to graze on dishes such as pan-fried sea bass with herb and lemon potatoes and butter sauce, or a hearty herb-roasted pork steak with mustard mash and onion gravy; end with apple and cinnamon crumble. A good-value set lunch menu is a wise move, and wines start at £14 a bottle.

Chef/s: Chris Bailey. **Open:** Mon to Sat L 12 to 3, D 5.30 to 10. **Closed:** Sun. **Meals:** alc (main courses £14 to £19). Set L £9.95 (2 courses) to £11.95. Set D £15.95 (2 courses) to £17.95. **Service:** not inc. **Details:** Cards accepted. 60 seats. Wheelchair access. Music. Children allowed.

READERS RECOMMEND

Masa

Modern European
The Old Wesleyan Chapel, Brook Street, Derby, DE1 3PF
Tel no: (01332) 203345
www.masarestaurantwinebar.com
'Serious food and great service in an amazing Wesleyan chapel.'

Mumbai Chilli

Indian
28 Stenson Road, Derby, DE23 1JB
Tel no: (01332) 767090
www.mumbaichilliderby.co.uk
'Wonderful...true regional Indian dishes cooked to authentic perfection.'

Hathersage

The George Hotel

Rugged Peak District getaway
Main Road, Hathersage, S32 1BB
Tel no: (01433) 650436
www.george-hotel.net
Modern British | £37
Cooking score: 2

Born as a coaching inn some five centuries ago, the George looks every inch the Peak District getaway, although its rugged stone walls now conceal a clean-lined, contemporary interior. Likewise, the contrast between the hotel's oak-beamed heritage and the food served in the George's restaurant couldn't be more telling, especially when the kitchen sends out elaborate plates of seared scallops with pumpkin and cumin purée, Moroccan spiced caramel and apple dressing, or roast loin of venison with vanilla-poached pear, truffled potatoes and elderberry sauce. Despite high aspirations, some have found the food poorly executed and 'uninspiring', and

service has its ups and downs, but the wine list comes good with plenty of well-chosen bottles at fair prices (from £14.95).
Chef/s: Helen Heywood. **Open:** all week L 12 to 2.30, D 6.30 to 10 (7 to 10 Sat and Sun). **Meals:** Set L and D £29.25 (2 courses) to £36.50. Early set D £19.30. Sun L £20.50. **Service:** not inc.
Details: Cards accepted. 50 seats. Separate bar. No mobile phones. Wheelchair access. Music. Children allowed. Car parking.

Ridgeway

The Old Vicarage

Emblematic food, enchanting surroundings
Ridgeway Moor, Ridgeway, S12 3XW
Tel no: (0114) 2475814
www.theoldvicarage.co.uk
Modern British | £65
Cooking score: 7
£5 OFF

With its woodland walks, wild-flower meadows, copses and productive gardens laid out by a Victorian horticulturist, this enchanting converted vicarage could be a world away from Sheffield's urban sprawl, yet it's barely eight miles from the old 'steel city'. Here is a top-end destination that puts personal comfort above grand gestures, while maintaining its stature as one of England's most emblematic country restaurants. Since the late 80s, Tessa Bramley has been taking culinary inspiration from the world outside, pacing her efforts with the calendar and treading confidently through the convoluted byways of contemporary British cuisine. Faultless ingredients are the key, and everything connects. A dish of roast lamb fillet served on a confit shoulder with sweetbreads, spiced plums and cauliflower purée feels right and natural on the plate, likewise pan-fried Whitby cod allied with buttered parsnips, purple sprouting broccoli, chive mash and a surprising rhubarb and star anise sauce. Elsewhere, earthy themes give way to free-flowing eclecticism: a heady whiff of the sun-scorched Middle East wafts through nutmeg-spiced sea bass fillet with pickled lemon, pistachio couscous and lemongrass sauce, while the scent of Périgord black truffles suffuses a dish of local Charolais beef fillet with thyme-roasted beetroot. Tessa also has a sneaking affection for the old English ways when it comes to dessert, serving baked chocolate pudding with chocolate fudge sauce and custard, partnering new season's rhubarb with lemon sponge, and fashioning a flummery from passion fruit. Meals drift pleasurably towards their conclusion as guests consider the merits of unpasteurised cheeses from the UK's top producers, and the final flourish comes with exotically spiced chocolate 'thins' made from 'single-origin' organic cocoa beans. The Old Vicarage also has its own wine-importing business, with personal links to some of the world's most illustrious producers; the result is a mighty list with classics from iconic Old World estates alongside boutique names from the Americas and the Antipodes. 'Special recommendations' offer top value; otherwise, you can order a bottle of vin de pays for around £28. Also note the splendid choice of Anglo-European bottled beers.
Chef/s: Tessa Bramley and Nathan Smith. **Open:** Tue to Fri L 12.30 to 2, Tue to Sat D 6.30 to 9.30 (6 Sat). **Closed:** Sun, Mon, 26 Dec to 5 Jan, first 2 weeks Aug, bank hols. **Meals:** Set L £30 (2 courses) to £40. Set D £65 (4 courses). Tasting menu £70.
Service: not inc. **Details:** Cards accepted. 40 seats. 16 seats outside. Separate bar. No music. No mobile phones. Wheelchair access. Children allowed. Car parking.

Readers Recommend
A 'readers recommend' review is a genuine quote from a report sent in by one of our readers. We intend to follow up these suggestions throughout the year to come.

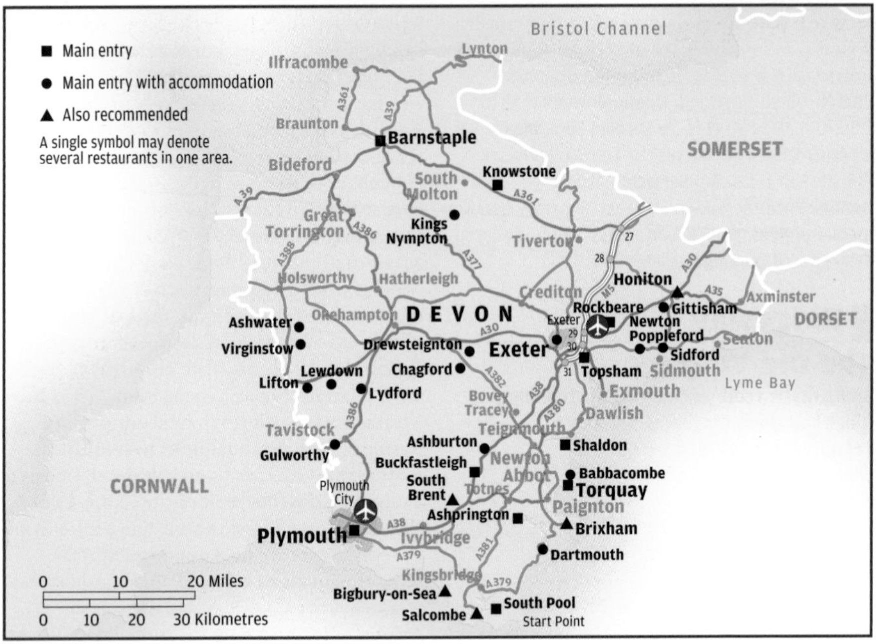

Ashburton

Agaric

Heartfelt natural cooking
30 North Street, Ashburton, TQ13 7QD
Tel no: (01364) 654478
www.agaricrestaurant.co.uk
Modern British | £35
Cooking score: 4

Shelves lined with homemade comestibles testify to the industrious foodie spirit behind Nick and Sophie Coiley's crusading local restaurant. There's not a trace of stuffy formality here, but bags of good humour, local loyalty and a real dedication to the virtues of heartfelt natural cooking. West Country produce shines on the concise menu, from bowls of fish soup with rouille, croûtons and Montgomery's Danegeld cheese to herb-crusted best end of lamb with spinach mousse and a boozy vinous gravy. The unadorned approach is also applied to organically reared duck in various forms: the breast might be roasted and served with Swiss chard and a beetroot and blackcurrant compote, while the leg could be braised in red wine with oranges and green olives. Esoteric 'country cheeses' with titles such as No Name and Bakesy Meadow are alternatives to calendar-friendly puds including poached new season's rhubarb with vanilla syrup and custard tart. The 30-bin wine list does its job, with prices pitched from £17.95.

Chef/s: Nick Coiley. **Open:** Wed to Fri L 12 to 2, Wed to Sat D 7 to 9.30. **Closed:** Sun to Tue, 25 Dec to 2 Jan, 2 weeks Aug. **Meals:** alc (main courses £16 to £22). Set L £14.95 (2 courses). **Service:** not inc. **Details:** Cards accepted. 28 seats. 16 seats outside. Separate bar. No music. No mobile phones. Wheelchair access. Children allowed.

Average Price

The average price listed in main-entry reviews denotes the price of a three-course meal, without wine.

Ashprington

★ ALFRESCO RESTAURANT OF THE YEAR ★

The Vineyard Café

Quirky alfresco café
Sharpham Estate, Ashprington, TQ9 7UT
Tel no: (01803) 732178
www.thevineyardcafe.co.uk
Modern British | £25
Cooking score: 1

'Superb location, though requires effort to find', noted a reporter about Rosie Weston's gem of a seasonal café on the Sharpham Estate. The setting is 'idiosyncratic' (seating is alfresco, with every climatic eventuality covered), and the kitchen is uncompromising in its local sourcing and unbranded enterprise. English asparagus with a soft poached egg, English spring lamb and platters of Sharpham cheese are crowd-pullers, and the menu also scores with crab cakes, confit duck leg, and rhubarb and almond tart. Readers 'can't say enough about this place'. Sharpham vineyard wines from £9.95.

Chef/s: Rosie Weston. **Open:** all week 10 to 5, L 12 to 2 (2.30 Sat and Sun). **Closed:** Oct to Easter. **Meals:** alc (main courses £9 to £17). **Service:** not inc. **Details:** Cards accepted. 50 seats outside. Wheelchair access. Children allowed. Car parking.

Ashwater

Blagdon Manor

Hospitable West Country treasure
Ashwater, EX21 5DF
Tel no: (01409) 211224
www.blagdon.com
Modern British | £38
Cooking score: 2

Tucked away down lanes winding through the glorious countryside of the Cornish/Devon border, Steve and Liz Morey's seventeenth-century farmhouse is a treasure from the moment you step over the threshold and wander through the stone-flagged library and inviting lounges. Homely and comfortable rather than grand and pretentious, this intimate country house hotel offers views extending to Dartmoor from the conservatory dining room, alongside honest modern British cooking. Fixed-price menus brim with seasonal produce and a typical dinner may open with pan-fried mackerel with beetroot, horseradish and tarragon, followed by 'Welsh rarebit'-glazed beef fillet with cottage pie, braised onions and confit garlic. Leave room for hot chocolate soufflé with praline ice cream. Wines start at £15.

Chef/s: Steve Morey. **Open:** Fri to Sun L 12 to 1.30 (2 Sun), Wed to Sun D 7 to 9. **Closed:** Mon, Tue, Jan. **Meals:** Set L £17 (2 courses) to £20. Set D £33 (2 courses) to £38. Sun L £25. **Service:** not inc. **Details:** Cards accepted. 28 seats. Separate bar. No music. No mobile phones. Wheelchair access. Car parking.

Babbacombe

The Cary Arms

Beachside inn with big-hearted food
Beach Road, Babbacombe, TQ1 3LX
Tel no: (01803) 327110
www.caryarms.co.uk
Modern British | £28
Cooking score: 2

Billed as 'the inn on the beach', Lana de Savary's reinvented Devon boozer feels rather swanky these days, with its boutique bedrooms and gorgeous terraces overlooking the briny aquatic action. Even so, the place stays true to its roots with real ales in the rough-hewn bar. Expect a big-hearted line-up of generous dishes with more than a nod to the regional larder – perhaps warm Cornish goats' cheese with beetroot salad, roasted Creedy Carver duck on sweet potato mash, Brixham crab salad and puds such as treacle tart with clotted cream. Wines from £14.50.

Chef/s: Ben Kingdon. **Open:** all week L 12 to 3, D 6.30 to 9. **Meals:** alc (main courses £10 to £19). **Service:** not inc. **Details:** Cards accepted. 60 seats. 100 seats outside. Music. Children allowed. Car parking.

Barnstaple

James Duckett at the Old Custom House

A godsend for the neighbourhood
9 The Strand, Barnstaple, EX31 1EU
Tel no: (01271) 370123
www.jamesduckett.co.uk
Modern European | £33
Cooking score: 2
V

James Duckett's good-natured 'gem' in Barnstaple's historic custom house is run with genuine enthusiasm for the fine things in life. Wine tastings and a cookery school make it a godsend for the neighbourhood, but Duckett's real passion is Devon produce, which is given a serious workout on his lively menu. He drops skate knobs into split-pea soup, serves hog's pudding with slow-roast pork belly, and partners perfectly crisped-up confit duck with summer beets and blood orange. Fish sparkles – brill fillet on salt cod colcannon with mustard sauce, say – and readers have drooled over his liquorice ice cream parfait. Wines start at £14.50.
Chef/s: James Duckett. **Open:** Tue to Sat L 12 to 2.30, D 7 to 10. **Closed:** Sun, Mon, 26 Dec, first 2 weeks Jan. **Meals:** alc D (main courses £15 to £19). Set L £14 (2 courses) to £17. Midweek set D £23 to £28. Tasting menu £65. **Service:** not inc.
Details: Cards accepted. 50 seats. 16 seats outside. No mobile phones. Wheelchair access. Music. Children allowed.

Bigbury-on-Sea

ALSO RECOMMENDED

▲ The Oyster Shack

Milburn Orchard Farm, Stakes Hill, Bigbury-on-Sea, TQ7 4BE
Tel no: (01548) 810876
www.oystershack.co.uk
Seafood

Sit under the giant sail on deck or by a log fire in the shack itself, and enjoy 'simply wonderful food and great service in a stunning location'. Oysters are, unsurprisingly, the thing here, either *au naturel* (£8.75 for 6) or in a variety of styles including baked with lime, peppers, bacon, Worcestershire sauce and Tabasco. Crabs, lobsters, mussels and the likes of hake with basil cream sauce (£18) flesh out the menu, which might finish with lemon posset. House wine £19.50. Open all week.

Brixham

ALSO RECOMMENDED

▲ The Brixham Deli

68a Fore Street, Brixham, TQ5 8EF
Tel no: (01803) 859585
www.thebrixhamdeli.co.uk
Modern British

There are just four tables filling the available floorspace in this classy deli tucked off one end of Brixham quay, but they can be reserved. Ensconced amid shelves of jams and chutneys, surveying the cheese and charcuterie counters, it's a more-than-pleasant stopover. Light bites through the day are supplemented by a lunch menu that takes in baked goats' cheese and beetroot in a balsamic-dressed salad (£5.95), steak burgers with mozzarella and bacon, chicken Caesar (£8.95), and cheesecake of the day. House wine is £3.10 a glass. Open Mon to Sat.

Buckfastleigh

Riverford Field Kitchen

Organic farm where vegetables shine
Wash Barn, Buckfastleigh, TQ11 0JU
Tel no: (01803) 762074
www.riverford.co.uk
British | £27
Cooking score: 4

'It is the only place I have been where the vegetables totally outshone the meat', enthused a visitor to this modern refectory-style farm restaurant at Riverford Organic. There's one sitting for lunch and dinner and, unless you are a large group, you share a table 'and take pot luck with your neighbours'. There's no menu either, but good cooking is at the heart of Jane Baxter's kitchen. She uses whatever is available on the farm that day to create quantities of vibrant vegetable dishes, and bowls are placed on the table for everyone to share. They can be anything from beetroot gratin and spring greens with red pepper dressing to roast saffron potatoes with almonds and bay leaves. There's also one meat dish, possibly chicken, rump steak or leg of lamb on a bed of parsnip purée with leeks. Expect the likes of lemon and orange tart for dessert, and arrive early for a guided tour of the farm. House wine is £15.50.

Chef/s: Jane Baxter. **Open:** all week L 1 (1 sitting), D 7.30 (1 sitting). **Closed:** 24 Dec to 15 Jan. **Meals:** Set L £19.90 (2 courses). Set D £26.50 (3 courses). **Service:** not inc. **Details:** Cards accepted. 64 seats. No music. Wheelchair access. Children allowed. Car parking.

Chagford

Gidleigh Park

Country house thoroughbred
Chagford, TQ13 8HH
Tel no: (01647) 432367
www.gidleigh.com
Modern European | £99
Cooking score: 7

£5 OFF V

Negotiating the twisting single-track lane leading to Gidleigh Park is guaranteed to get your pulse racing even before you catch sight of the mansion's lauded vistas. This prime piece of Devon real estate comes with all the expected baggage – a tennis court, a gurgling stream, landscaped gardens and Dartmoor views. Inside, be prepared for hushed corporate whispers and ever-so-formal, metronomic service – some 'lightening up' and hands-on personality would work wonders out front. There's also a feeling that chef/proprietor Michael Caines is doing Gidleigh a disservice by not cooking here full-time, although his deputy Ian Webber is a fine interpreter of the style, and the food is never less than exquisite. This is the thoroughbred world of contemporary European cuisine, but it's overlaid with lightness, precisely considered flavours and balance, from fabulous langoustine cannelloni with braised fennel, sauce vierge and shellfish bisque to a renowned combo of pearly turbot and diced scallops with tiny wild mushrooms, leeks and silky chive sauce. Caines' talent for finding extra levels of depth and comfort without descending into cloying overkill is legendary and he is equally at home updating the classics (a terrine of foie gras with Sauternes jelly, quince and sultana purée) or fashioning startling ideas from the global front line – a stunning combo of Cornish sea bass with Thai purée and lemongrass foam, for example. If Gidleigh has an Achilles' heel, it's at the sweet end of proceedings: reporters have been disappointed by a poorly timed pistachio soufflé with pistachio sauce and pistachio ice cream, while petits fours can seem more like rather prosaic 'mini desserts'. The wine list is awesome in its scope and authority, with expense-account French grandees in pole position, but plenty for those on smaller budgets. Prices start at £25 (£8.50 a glass).

Chef/s: Michael Caines and Ian Webber. **Open:** all week L 12 to 2.30, D 7 to 9.30. **Meals:** Set L £37 (2 courses) to £47.50. Set D £99. Tasting menu £55 (5 courses) to £120 (8 courses). **Service:** not inc. **Details:** Cards accepted. 50 seats. Separate bar. No music. No mobile phones. Wheelchair access. Car parking.

Please send us your feedback

To register your opinion about any restaurant listed in the Guide, or a new restaurant that you wish to bring to our attention, please visit the web address at the bottom of the page. Your feedback informs the content of the book and will be used to compile next year's reviews.

NEW ENTRY
22 Mill Street

Elegant eatery with enjoyable food
22 Mill Street, Chagford, TQ13 8AW
Tel no: (01647) 432244
www.22millst.com
Modern British | £42
Cooking score: 4
V

Chagford is an utterly charming Dartmoor community, one of the old tin-mining towns cunningly disguised as a village. Just off the square is this elegant restaurant-with-rooms. Its interior décor is a clever mix of ancient stone walls and modern wood-toned understatement, and the generously sized tables are nicely spaced. Ashley Wright offers a style of clean-lined, unpretentious food, whether a simple assemblage consisting of a sliver of duck foie gras on a piece of pan-fried salmon, the two united by a vivid green pea purée, or local lamb – with an earthy slew of lentils for one reporter, creamed violet potato and char-grilled courgette for another. Alternatively, a generous tranche of Cornish hake with melty-textured sweetcorn beignets might appeal. Deconstructed desserts are enjoyable, say a vanilla cheesecake that has lost its raspberry purée top to one side, its shortbread-crumb base scattered in two drifts, one topped with honey ice cream. Wines from a short list are cannily chosen, especially the house selections, which start at £19.50.
Chef/s: Ashley Wright. **Open:** Tue to Sat L 12 to 2, D 7 to 10. **Closed:** Sun, Mon. **Meals:** Set L £16.95 (2 courses) to £21.95. Set D £36 (2 courses) to £42. Tasting menu £59. **Service:** not inc. **Details:** Cards accepted. 26 seats. 6 seats outside. Separate bar. Music. Children allowed.

Dartmouth

NEW ENTRY
Angélique

Enticing, mightily effective food
2 South Embankment, Dartmouth, TQ6 9BH
Tel no: (01803) 839425
www.angeliquedartmouth.co.uk
Anglo-French | £56
Cooking score: 4
£5 OFF V

Now part of Alan Murchison's reach-for-the-stars Fine Dining Group (see entries for La Bécasse, Ludlow; L'Ortolan, Shinfield; Paris House, Woburn), Angélique has gone through a few manifestations over the years, having once been the legendary Carved Angel. Darren Brown takes up the culinary reins to produce an enticing modern menu with some original touches. Dishes can be mightily effective, as in a starter of lightly toasted scallops with cauliflower beignets, air-dried ham and slices of artichoke, the flavours all pulling together into a harmonious whole. Lamb rump at a lunch inspection was impressively tender, served with Parmesan gnocchi, carrot purée and fried sage in a rich, winey jus. Other dishes can feel less well attended to – salmon tartare with avocado and cucumber and a rather pallid wasabi mayonnaise isn't quite more than the sum of its parts. But desserts will make you feel indulged (if the pre-dessert hasn't already done so), perhaps with a parade of chocolate tart, walnut semifreddo and white chocolate ice cream. The wine list covers all the main bases briskly and efficiently, if not altogether thrillingly. Glasses start at £5.50, bottles £20.
Chef/s: Darren Brown. **Open:** Wed to Sun L 12 to 2, D Tue to Sat D 6.30 to 9 (9.30 Fri and Sat). **Closed:** Mon. **Meals:** Set L £25 (2 courses) to £29. Set D £47 (2 courses) to £56. Tasting menu £60.
Service: 12.5% (optional). **Details:** Cards accepted. 60 seats. Separate bar. Music. Children allowed.

The Seahorse

Lively eatery with wonderful fish
5 South Embankment, Dartmouth, TQ6 9BH
Tel no: (01803) 835147
www.seahorserestaurant.co.uk
Seafood | £32
Cooking score: 4

The Dartmouth quayside is suddenly looking a tastier proposition than when it was all ice creams and tea. Mitch Tonks and Mat Prowse opened here in 2008, bringing quality seafood to the town in a stylish venue with comfortable banquette seating, antique mirrors and wine stacks. Reporters are single-minded in their appraisal, giving the thumbs-up to the warm friendliness with which the place is imbued, and the fresh-as-a-daisy fish and shellfish. A copious main course of fritto misto is a revelation, from monkfish to squid via six other items, with properly gloopy aïoli for dipping, while John Dory benefits from well-timed roasting on the bone. Prior to that, you might consider cuttlefish in ink with polenta, or something as straightforward as shrimps on toast, and there's rice pudding or cheesecake to finish. A couple of meat dishes are offered too. Those wine shelves are worth exploring, with a host of imaginatively chosen bottles from £17 for an all-purpose Loire Sauvignon.

Chef/s: Mitch Tonks and Mat Prowse. **Open:** Wed to Sun L 12 to 2.30 (12.30 Sun), Tue to Sat D 6 to 10. **Closed:** Mon, 25 and 26 Dec, 1 Jan. **Meals:** alc (main courses £17 to £28). Set L £15 (2 courses) to £20. **Service:** not inc. **Details:** Cards accepted. 40 seats. 4 seats outside. Wheelchair access. Music. Children allowed.

Drewsteignton

NEW ENTRY

The Old Inn

Renovated hostelry with tip-top food
Drewsteignton, EX6 6QR
Tel no: (01647) 281276
www.old-inn.co.uk
Modern European | £40
Cooking score: 3

The Old Inn is a sensitively renovated village hostelry turned restaurant-with-rooms, with big old sofas facing the fire and a pair of low-ceilinged rooms for dining. Duncan Walker arrived here from 22 Mill Street, Chagford (see entry), and brings a lively sense of modernist ambition to menus that offer four choices per course. Openers at inspection were tip-top: a piece of seared foie gras with chunks of apple caramelised in honey and Calvados, and a fabulous piece of red mullet in crystal-clear fish consommé full of ginger and coriander. Mains were more obviously pubby – a tiny serving of spring lamb with a potato and olive cake in scythingly salty jus, and a rather better guinea fowl in the form of braised breast and a leg roll, with ceps and stem broccoli. A plate of raspberry variations in April seems a bit out of place; look instead to the sublime shopping list that is 'chocolate, coffee, cardamom, orange and brandy'. The short wine list opens at £17.

Chef/s: Duncan Walker. **Open:** Wed to Sat D only 7 to 8.45. **Closed:** Sun to Tue. **Meals:** Set D £39.50. **Service:** not inc. **Details:** Cards accepted. 16 seats. No music. No mobile phones. Wheelchair access. Children allowed.

Exeter

Michael Caines at ABode Exeter

Grown-up chic and full-flavoured food
Royal Clarence Hotel, Cathedral Yard, Exeter, EX1 1HD
Tel no: (01392) 223638
www.michaelcaines.com
Modern European | £45
Cooking score: 4

The Exeter branch of Michael Caines' ABode operation must be on the best site of the lot, occupying the front of the Royal Clarence Hotel, right by the city's fine cathedral. A large, brasserie-style room, it is dominated by bare dark-wood tables, bright, food-themed pictures, and mirrors. The smartly drilled service is a couple of shades more formal than you might expect. Certain dishes have become repertoire favourites – a starter of duck liver with orange-braised chicory, candied walnuts and Gewürztraminer raisins, the roast loin and confit shoulder of lamb with fennel purée and tapenade sauce – and they deliver big, punchy flavours. Elsewhere, the early-evening menu can bring impressive smoked salmon cannelloni in saffron pasta with cucumber foam, and good braised pork loin. Finish with salted caramel fondant or pistachio nougat glacé topped with cocoa-nib mousse. An extensive wine list offers some of its wares by the 50cl carafe. Glass prices start at £5.90.
Chef/s: Craig Dunn. **Open:** Mon to Sat L 12 to 2.30, D 6 to 10. **Closed:** Sun. **Meals:** alc (main courses £22 to £25). Set L £13.50. Tasting menu £58. **Service:** 12.5% (optional). **Details:** Cards accepted. 64 seats. Separate bar. No mobile phones. Wheelchair access. Music. Children allowed.

Also Recommended

Also recommended entries are not scored but we think they are worth a visit.

Gittisham

Combe House

Seductive, self-sufficient foodie hotel
Gittisham, EX14 3AD
Tel no: (01404) 540400
www.combehousedevon.com
Modern British | £49
Cooking score: 5
£5 OFF V

Part aristocratic Arcadia, part self-sufficient foodie hotel, Combe House is an immediately enthralling prospect, with Arabian horses frolicking in the grounds, pheasants strutting their stuff and a lovely summerhouse beside the increasingly productive vegetable garden. The owners of this Grade I-listed Elizabethan manor have also turned the old kitchen into a bakery and started to rear chickens, pigs and sheep as part of their dedicated enterprise. It's seductively beguiling and guaranteed to summon up whimsical musings about the good life. Chef Hadleigh Barrett is well up to the task, taking his cue from the land and exploiting as many local resources as possible. A modern sensibility is at work here, pairing rabbit confit with pickled carrots and cumin-roasted hazelnuts, matching roast loin of lamb with a braised neck suet pudding, fondant potato and crushed home-grown swede, and getting the best out of prime line-caught sea bass (perhaps with wild mushrooms, soured cabbage and Gewürztraminer velouté). There's also no dumbing-down at lunchtime, judging by effusive reports of brill with chard, baby fennel and lobster sauce, quail ravioli and a whisky-spiked pannacotta with raspberry jelly, honeycomb crackle and oatmeal crisp. The subterranean cellars are tailor-made for nurturing a tremendous assortment of inspired global wines, helpfully laid out for food matching. Seasonal house selections start at £20 (£5.50 a glass).
Chef/s: Hadleigh Barrett. **Open:** all week L 12 to 2.30, D 7 to 9.30. **Closed:** 2 to 12 Jan. **Meals:** Set L £28 (2 courses) to £33. Set D £49. Sun L £36. **Service:** not inc. **Details:** Cards accepted. 75 seats. Separate bar. No mobile phones. Wheelchair access. Music. Children allowed. Car parking.

Gulworthy

The Horn of Plenty

Ravishing views and high-flying food
Gulworthy, PL19 8JD
Tel no: (01822) 832528
www.thehornofplenty.co.uk
Modern European | £50
new chef

'From the canapés to coffee – an experience not to be missed' commented one satisfied visitor who enjoyed dinner at this creeper-clad Georgian manor house set in five acres of gardens with wide-ranging views down the wooded Tamar Valley. The ravishing vistas through huge windows in the dining room add to the thrill of it all, but then we learned of the departure of Stuart Downie too late to respond with an inspection or receive any feedback. New chef Scott Paton was previously at The Jack in the Green for nine years (see entry, Rockbeare, Devon) and was just about to take up his position as we went to press. No menus were available, but Paton is a strong supporter of local suppliers and known for his avoidance of trendy flimflam. In the past the fixed-price lunch menu has been exceptional value and a showcase for the kitchen's ability and meticulous technique. The wine list opens at £21.50. Reports please.
Chef/s: Scott Paton. **Open:** all week L 12 to 2, D 7 to 9. **Meals:** Set L £19.50 (2 courses) to £24.50. Set D £49.50. **Service:** not inc. **Details:** Cards accepted. 40 seats. 30 seats outside. Separate bar. No mobile phones. Wheelchair access. Music. Children allowed. Car parking.

Symbols

Accommodation is available
Three courses for less than £30
V Separate vegetarian menu
£5-off voucher scheme
Notable wine list

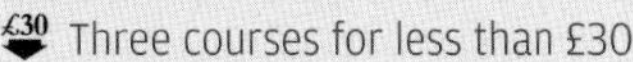

Honiton

ALSO RECOMMENDED

▲ The Holt

178 High Street, Honiton, EX14 1LA
Tel no: (01404) 47707
www.theholt-honiton.com
Modern British

Home-smoked provisions are the star turns at this thriving pub/restaurant opposite Honiton's Art Deco cinema, and you can even buy them to take away. Otherwise, the regularly changing menus offer doughty British fodder along the lines of mutton faggot with confit leeks and anchovies (£6.50), grilled sea bass with a shrimp fritter or braised duck leg with pork cheek, parsnip purée and roasted garlic mash (£15.50). To finish, consider chocolate orange mousse cake with chocolate sauce. House wines from £14. Closed Sun and Mon.

Kings Nympton

The Grove Inn

Exemplary thatched hostelry
Kings Nympton, EX37 9ST
Tel no: (01769) 580406
www.thegroveinn.co.uk
British | £22
Cooking score: 2

It is everything you would want from a thatched country inn. Beamed ceilings, winter fires, locals mingling at the bar, drinking great real ales while everyone in the open-plan dining area tucks into food with an admirable commitment to local produce. The formula is simple. Menus deal in well-wrought dishes that are fresh and flavourful. A hearty portion of rustic chicken liver pâté, perhaps, or beetroot and apple soup, followed by skate with a brown butter and caper sauce or a 'perfect' individual beef Wellington, and thick, gooey treacle tart with a ball of rich local cream to finish. Wines from £14.50.

Chef/s: Deborah Smallbone. **Open:** Tue to Sun L 12 to 2 (2.30 Sun), Tue to Sat D 7 to 9.30. **Closed:** Mon. **Meals:** alc (main courses £10 to £17). **Service:** not inc. **Details:** Cards accepted. 28 seats. 12 seats outside. Separate bar. No music. No mobile phones. Wheelchair access. Children allowed.

Knowstone

The Masons Arms

Dreamy pub with impeccable food
Knowstone, EX36 4RY
Tel no: (01398) 341231
www.masonsarmsdevon.co.uk
Modern British | £43
Cooking score: 6

It may be squirrelled away in a remote Exmoor backwater, but that doesn't deter visitors from trekking out to Mark and Sarah Dodson's picture-perfect, thirteenth-century thatched pub. You can still sup ale and warm your cockles by the open fire, but this place is really about Mark's sure-footed modern cooking – all those years in the rarefied world of haute cuisine have paid dividends here, although there's nothing prissy about a dish of, say, Devon beef fillet with rich oxtail, parsnip purée and red wine jus. Of course there is pin-sharp accuracy on the plate, but there's a huge helping of generosity too – especially when it comes to deploying regional raw materials. The litany of top dishes says it all: wild mushroom risotto with Parmesan and a poached egg; a duo of hare loin and 'flaked' braised leg with Brussels sprouts and red wine jus; and a pairing of red mullet and halibut with crushed new potatoes, samphire and a saffron-infused bouillon have all been loudly endorsed. Desserts are also a 'picture to behold', whether it's passion fruit and ginger parfait with warm winter fruits or pannacotta with roasted pineapple and a brandy-snap biscuit. At lunchtime, people often drop by for a starter or two – perhaps tomato and black olive tart with rocket sorbet, or smoked scallops with lime and star anise. Sarah is a treasure out front, welcoming everyone with genuine warmth and good humour. The unfussy wine list yo-yos between the Old and New Worlds, with plenty of sound drinking at easy prices from £14.50 (£5 a glass).

Chef/s: Mark Dodson. **Open:** Tue to Sun L 12 to 2, Tue to Sat D 7 to 9. **Closed:** Mon, first week Jan, first week Sept. **Meals:** alc (main courses £18 to £23). Sun L £34.50. **Service:** not inc. **Details:** Cards accepted. 30 seats. 16 seats outside. Separate bar. No mobile phones. Music. Children allowed. Car parking.

Lewdown

Lewtrenchard Manor

Vibrant seasonal cooking
Lewdown, EX20 4PN
Tel no: (01566) 783222
www.lewtrenchard.co.uk
Modern British | £55
Cooking score: 6

£5 OFF **V**

A Jacobean manor peeping out from its own little hollow to the northwest of Dartmoor, Lewtrenchard has seen it all. The colourful Gould family and its various scions – adventurers, Oriental traders, roustabouts, hymn composers – have come and gone, while its ornate interiors and extensive gardens remain beautifully preserved against the generations. It's no surprise that it offers the full-dress dining experience, with crisp table linen, gleaming glassware and posies, nor that there is a chef's table option (though perhaps a little startling that they've called it the Purple Carrot). John Hooker heads up the kitchen (Jason Hornbuckle is now general manager), but continues to source from the bounty of the West Country, as well as from the kitchen garden, for a style of classically based cooking that isn't afraid to try out some modern flourishes. A truffled goats' cheese mousse comes with pain d'épices, pickled beetroot and balsamic jelly for an array of stimulating flavours, before a tranche of bream turns up with braised fennel and vanilla foam. Meats are more mainstream, offering potato gratin, roast shallots and red wine with ribeye, or ratatouille with rump and shoulder of lamb. The fairground flavours of contemporary desserts crop up in options such as dark chocolate délice with peanut mousse and banana ice cream. Nine house wines from £22 (£5 a glass) are the foundation of a list that extends democratic coverage outside France and keeps prices restrained.

Chef/s: John Hooker. **Open:** all week L 12 to 2, D 7 to 9. **Meals:** Set L £15 (2 courses) to £19. Set D £55. **Service:** not inc. **Details:** Cards accepted. 50 seats. Separate bar. No mobile phones. Wheelchair access. Music. Car parking.

ALSO RECOMMENDED

▲ The Harris Arms

Portgate, Lewdown, EX20 4PZ
Tel no: (01566) 783331
www.theharrisarms.co.uk
Modern British £5 OFF

Carefully nurtured regional supply lines keep the kitchen well endowed at this family-run pub on the Devon/Cornwall border. Artisan cheeses, day-boat fish and free-range meats take their turn on a lively menu that might promise pork cheeks with sweet potato and mushroom hash (£5.95) ahead of sautéed Creedy Carver chicken on tagliatelle or confit duck with haricot bean and chorizo ragoût (£14.95). There are plentiful 'pub classics' too, plus familiar puds such as warm treacle sponge. Knowledgeably chosen wines from £15. No food Sun D and Mon.

Lifton

The Arundell Arms

Civilised sporting retreat
Fore Street, Lifton, PL16 0AA
Tel no: (01566) 784666
www.arundellarms.com
Modern British | £43
Cooking score: 4
£5 OFF 🛏

This stone-built former coaching inn is an unabashed magnet for hunters, shooters and fishers, situated not far from Dartmoor, and run by the same family since the early 60s. Choose from a brace of bar/restaurants or the smarter primrose-walled main dining room. Fixed-price menus (including a five-course tasting option) offer a wealth of regional produce cooked in modern English fashion. Grey mullet with creamed lentils, tomato and chives might open a meal, followed by pork tenderloin with black pudding, Savoy cabbage, glazed parsnips and peppercorn sauce, or a fish casserole in white wine with leeks and saffron potatoes. Finish delicately with passion fruit délice, served with a pink Champagne and lemon sorbet, or else a platter of English farmhouse cheeses with oatcakes and cranberry chutney. The wine list zips niftily through the main regions but is unerring in its selections, which include Pinson Chablis, Neil Ellis South African Sauvignon and Mount Edward Pinot Noir from New Zealand. Glasses start at £4.80, bottles £17.50.

Chef/s: Steven Pidgeon. **Open:** all week L 12 to 2, D 7 to 10. **Meals:** Set L £19.50 (2 courses) to £24.50. Set D £42.50. Sun L £26. Tasting menu £47.50. **Service:** not inc. **Details:** Cards accepted. 80 seats. 20 seats outside. Separate bar. Wheelchair access. Music. Children allowed. Car parking.

Lydford

The Dartmoor Inn

Pub that's a cut above
Moorside, Lydford, EX20 4AY
Tel no: (01822) 820221
www.dartmoorinn.com
Modern British | £30
Cooking score: 3
£5 OFF 🛏 V

Found on the western edge of Dartmoor National Park, the Burgess family's sixteenth-century pub-with-rooms is a cut above your average hiker-geared watering hole. A cosy bar area, complete with a roaring log fire and upmarket pub-grub menu, may cater for walkers fresh from the tors, but it's in the patchwork of quaint dining rooms that the kitchen really shows its ambition. Local produce stars in dishes such as Cornish crab bisque, belly pork with black pudding and scallops or a medium-rare sirloin of beef with

'excellent' slow-cooked oxtail. There's praise for the 'best-prepared and cooked grouse we had ever eaten', but gripes relating to bland vegetables and very slow service. A separate vegetarian menu is a nice touch and house wines start at £14.95.
Chef/s: Andrew Honey and Philip Burgess. **Open:** Tue to Sun L 12 to 2.30 (3 Sat and Sun), Mon to Sat D 6 to 10. **Meals:** alc (main courses £14 to £24). Set L and D £16.50 (2 courses) to £20.50. Sun L £19.75 (2 courses) to £25.75. **Service:** not inc. **Details:** Cards accepted. 65 seats. 25 seats outside. Separate bar. No music. No mobile phones. Children allowed. Car parking.

Newton Poppleford

Moores'

Ticking all the right boxes
6 Greenbank, High Street, Newton Poppleford, EX10 OEB
Tel no: (01395) 568100
www.mooresrestaurant.co.uk
Modern British | £23
Cooking score: 1

Jonathan and Kate Moore's warmly welcoming restaurant-with-rooms used to be Newton Poppleford's village shop, and it still has an endearing, homespun feel. The food also ticks all the right boxes for honest endeavour, whether you are sampling seared local venison carpaccio followed by 'superbly fresh' fillet of Brixham brill with spinach, fennel and baby baked potatoes or tackling a rack of Devon lamb with leek mash, sautéed Savoy cabbage and pine nuts, ahead of some splendid West Country cheeses. House wine is £13.95.
Chef/s: Jonathan Moore. **Open:** Tue to Sun L 12 to 1.30 (1 Sat), Tue to Sat D 7 to 9.30. **Closed:** Mon, first 2 weeks Jan. **Meals:** Set L £15 (2 courses) to £19.95. Set D £17.50 (2 courses) to £22.45 (Sat £27.50). Sun L £15. **Service:** not inc. **Details:** Cards accepted. 32 seats. 12 seats outside. No mobile phones. Wheelchair access. Music. Children allowed.

Plymouth

Tanners

A winning formula
Prysten House, Finewell Street, Plymouth, PL1 2AE
Tel no: (01752) 252001
www.tannersrestaurant.com
Modern British | £34
Cooking score: 3

'Characterful', remarked a visitor to the Tanner brothers' restaurant, which is housed in the oldest domestic building in Plymouth. Five centuries of history – beamed ceilings, stone walls and tapestries – create a fine atmosphere, and the kitchen impresses. The brothers' formula has served customers well for 13 years; they use excellent quality raw materials to perk up interest, although menus play a fairly safe modern British tune. Reporters have emerged full of praise for a warm sweet onion tart with flaked salmon and Creedy Carver duck breast served with beets, confit garlic and squash. Other ingredients are equally well handled – roast cod is fashionably teamed with linguine, spinach, chorizo and crab butter sauce, while glazed passion fruit tart with a dark chocolate sorbet makes an indulgent finish. Wines from £14.95.
Chef/s: Martin Compton, Chris and James Tanner. **Open:** Tue to Sat L 12 to 2.30, D 7 to 9.30. **Closed:** Sun, Mon, 24 to 31 Dec, first week Jan. **Meals:** alc (main courses £14 to £28). Set L £14 (2 courses) to £18. Set D £20 (Tue to Thur). **Service:** not inc. **Details:** Cards accepted. 60 seats. 40 seats outside. No mobile phones. Wheelchair access. Music. Children allowed.

Chef/s: Matthew Mason. **Open:** all week L 12 to 2 (12 to 9 Sun), D 6 to 9 (9.30 Fri and Sat). **Closed:** 25 Dec to 5 Jan. **Meals:** alc (main courses £17 to £25). Set L and D £19.95 (2 courses) to £25. Sun L £19.95. Tasting menu £42.50. **Service:** not inc. **Details:** Cards accepted. 120 seats. 80 seats outside. Separate bar. Wheelchair access. Music. Children allowed. Car parking.

ALSO RECOMMENDED

▲ Lemon Tree Café & Bistro

2 Haye Road South, Elburton, Plymouth, PL9 8HJ
Tel no: (01752) 481117
www.lemontreecafe.co.uk
Modern European £5 OFF

Not far from Plymouth and the rolling acres of the South Hams, the Lemon Tree is a vividly decorated country bistro with a breath of Marrakech. Winter mezze evenings (£24.95) are a popular draw. Otherwise, look to the blackboards for some highly capable rustic cookery, along the lines of smoked haddock chowder (£4.25), pork loin with roasted pumpkin and apple vinaigrette (£6.95), and highly praised plum and orange crumble with clotted cream. Wines from £12.95. Open Tue to Sat L and Fri D.

Rockbeare

The Jack in the Green

Village charmer with something for everyone
London Road, Rockbeare, EX5 2EE
Tel no: (01404) 822240
www.jackinthegreen.uk.com
Modern British | £30
Cooking score: 3
£5 OFF **V**

Paul Parnell's aim is to provide something for everyone at this charming village inn. The industrious kitchen can do you a plate of fish and chips or a braised faggot, but there's also a range of fixed-price menus of accomplished modern British dishes, starring excellent produce from local suppliers. A first course of sea bass with chorizo and pickled pineapple might be followed by roasted loin and braised shoulder of Exmoor venison with parsnip purée and red cabbage, or Parmesan-crusted halibut with curried cauliflower and an emulsified lime sauce. Desserts can be just as racy, especially when olive oil cake, served with mandarin sorbet and passion fruit posset, is in the offing. Eight wines by the glass at £3.95 (bottles from £15.50) head up a well-annotated list.

Salcombe

ALSO RECOMMENDED

▲ South Sands Beachside Restaurant

Bolt Head, Salcombe, TQ8 8LL
Tel no: (01548) 859000
www.southsands.com
Seafood £5 OFF

You (or the SatNav) will have fun finding the South Sands, a brand-new boutique hotel shoehorned in by a little inlet of the same name, not far from Salcombe. Tables on a decked terrace overlook the bucket-and-spade wielders, and the indoor restaurant seating is pleasant too, in a big wide-windowed room, all blond wood with bevies of uniformly gliding waiters. The cooking, under the aegis of Mitch Tonks, offers his trademark simple seafood: breadcrumbed cod cheeks with delicate garlic mayonnaise, monkfish with tomato, olives and capers (£16.50) and properly made vanilla pannacotta to finish. Wines start at £4.10 by the glass. Open all week.

Please send us your feedback

To register your opinion about any restaurant listed in the Guide, or a new restaurant that you wish to bring to our attention, please visit the web address at the bottom of the page. Your feedback informs the content of the book and will be used to compile next year's reviews.

Shaldon

Ode

Creative organic champion
21 Fore Street, Shaldon, TQ14 0DE
Tel no: (01626) 873977
www.odetruefood.co.uk
Modern British | £35
Cooking score: 5

£5 OFF

Naming a restaurant after its postcode and illuminating the dining room with soy candles might seem left field, but there's serious intent here and Ode has a full-on commitment to accredited organic food as part of its exemplary green credentials. Tim and Clare Bouget have fitted out their three-storey Georgian town house according to strict eco principles (even their flowers are picked locally), and the kitchen puts its money on Devon produce, ethically reared meat and sustainable fish. The result is intensely seasonal cooking that sings with creativity and flavour. To start, confit of pressed Crediton duck and Savoy cabbage is enlivened with medlar syrup, while chilli-glazed Lyme Bay mackerel might be invigorated with pickled vegetables, coconut milk and turmeric. Influences from Tim's gastronaut travels are also spread sensitively across main courses (steamed John Dory with cumin crust, smoked aubergine, tabbouleh and tahini sauce, say), although more comforting, homespun flavours get an airing too: roast salt marsh lamb with minted hollandaise and spring vegetables has been enthusiastically received. To conclude, West Country cheeses vie for attention with Montezuma chocolate tart, cocoa caramel and mulled-wine ice cream. Service is sweet, prices are not prohibitive and the all-organic/biodynamic wine list is full of treasures. Bottles start at £16.50.

Chef/s: Tim Bouget. **Open:** Thur and Fri L 12 to 1.30, Wed to Sat D 7 to 9.30. **Closed:** Sun to Tue, 3 weeks Oct, 25 and 26 Dec, bank hols. **Meals:** alc (main courses £17 to £23). Set L £17.50 (2 courses) to £22.50. **Service:** not inc. **Details:** Cards accepted. 24 seats. No mobile phones. Wheelchair access. Music. Children allowed.

Sidford

The Salty Monk

Homemade food to be proud of
Church Street, Sidford, EX10 9QP
Tel no: (01395) 513174
www.saltymonk.co.uk
Modern British | £43
Cooking score: 4

£5 OFF **V**

Hospitality is a plus at this Sidford fixture, thanks to the warmth of the Witheridges, who create a refreshingly welcoming feel. Cooking is honest and the menus aim to comfort rather than challenge. The repertoire ranges from warm salmon mousse wrapped in smoked salmon with a lemon butter sauce, via perfectly timed brill fillets with saffron gnocchi and baby spinach, to wild boar steak served with champ potatoes, and the kitchen's own wild boar and apple sausages plus crab apple jelly. Indeed everything, from the bread to the petits fours, is made in-house. Results on the plate may lack a 'wow' factor, but fine local and seasonal ingredients are handled carefully to produce clear, well-balanced flavours. There's good choice for vegetarians, and puddings please too, including warm Devon apple sponge with butterscotch sauce. The wine list is cosmopolitan and prices are fair, with house selections from £14.95.

Chef/s: Andy Witheridge. **Open:** Thur to Sun L 12 to 2, all week D 6 to 9. **Closed:** 2 weeks Nov, Jan. **Meals:** Set L £25 (2 courses) to £29.50. Set D £39.50 (2 courses) to £42.50. Sun L £29.50. **Service:** not inc. **Details:** Cards accepted. 36 seats. 14 seats outside. Separate bar. Wheelchair access. Music. Children allowed. Car parking.

Also Recommended

Also recommended entries are not scored but we think they are worth a visit.

South Brent

ALSO RECOMMENDED

▲ The Turtley Corn Mill

Avonwick, South Brent, TQ10 9ES
Tel no: (01364) 646100
www.turtleycornmill.com
British £5 OFF

This ivy-smothered former mill-with-waterwheel in the sumptuous South Hams, not far from Plymouth, makes a characterful country hotel, kitted out in light, airy, modern fashion. It offers a brasserie-style menu taking in the likes of goats' cheese and red onion tart with salad (£5.90), followed by haddock in real ale batter with chips and minted mushy peas (£13.25), as well as lighter dishes such as moules marinière. Wines from £17.30. Open all week.

South Pool

The Millbrook Inn

Proper village pub with top-notch food
South Pool, TQ7 2RW
Tel no: (01548) 531581
www.millbrookinnsouthpool.co.uk
Modern European | £30
Cooking score: 2
£5 OFF

From the locally brewed ale to the spot-on service, high standards are obvious at this very proper old-fashioned village pub. There's plenty of local support, but the surge of visitors who negotiate the narrow lanes or come up with the tide from Salcombe are drawn by well-sourced, seasonal raw materials cooked with enthusiasm and honest effort. Ample supplies of fish, meat and game are transformed into uncluttered dishes: potted crab; whole lemon sole with chive, lemon and caper butter sauce; and braised shoulder of lamb with spiced couscous; plus pheasant casserole from the good-value bar menu. Finish with sticky toffee pudding or pineapple parfait with strawberry and clotted-cream ice cream. Wines from £14.50.

Chef/s: Jean-Philippe Bidart. **Open:** all week L 12 to 2 (2.30 Sun), D 7 to 9. **Meals:** alc (main courses L £10 to £15, D £16 to £18). Sun L £15. **Service:** 10% (optional). **Details:** Cards accepted. 38 seats. 48 seats outside. No music. Children allowed.

Topsham

La Petite Maison

Cute restaurant with accomplished food
35 Fore Street, Topsham, EX3 0HR
Tel no: (01392) 873660
www.lapetitemaison.co.uk
Modern European | £37
Cooking score: 4
£5 OFF

The bijou name says it all; genuine personable intimacy is the key to Douglas and Elizabeth Pestell's cute little restaurant. Occupying a centuries-old, bow-windowed building in trendy Topsham by the river Exe, its homely appeal is matched by delightfully friendly service and accomplished food with strong Gallic undertones – although West Country ingredients are the kitchen's primary building blocks. Herb-crusted Somerset pork loin with slow-roasted belly, black pudding, leeks and cider jus is typical of the style, and spot-on Lyme Bay crab risotto is a seasonal treat. Regulars have also applauded goats' cheese soufflé with tomato and pesto dressing, 'exceptional lamb', and medallions of venison with a venison croquette, braised red cabbage and red wine jus. Desserts garner gushing reviews, too – 'amazing' pear tarte Tatin or chocolate and griottine cherry clafoutis with chocolate ice cream, for instance. Regional French names stand out on the well-spread, 60-bin wine list; house recommendations start at £17.75 (£4.40 a glass).

Chef/s: Douglas Pestell and Sarah Bright. **Open:** Tue to Sat L 12.30 to 2 (bookings only), D 7 to 10. **Closed:** Sun, Mon, 26 to 31 Dec, 2 weeks Jun. **Meals:** Set L and D £30.75 (2 courses) to £36.95. **Service:** not inc. **Details:** Cards accepted. 26 seats. No mobile phones. Music. Children allowed.

Torquay

The Elephant

Sleek, imaginative cooking
3-4 Beacon Terrace, Torquay, TQ1 2BH
Tel no: (01803) 200044
www.elephantrestaurant.co.uk
Modern British | £45
Cooking score: 5

£5 OFF

Down on the harbour front, with appealing sunset views over the marina and the bay, Torbay's classiest operation maintains an impressive level of consistency. Split clearly over two levels (a spacious, brisk, ground-floor brasserie and a more formal first-floor room on spring/summer evenings only), it's run with an adept combination of well-oiled efficiency and bonhomie. Simon Hulstone's cooking uses some superb south-western produce – Torbay scallops, Paignton crab, Cornish lamb, Crediton duck, Vulscombe goats' cheese – in a highly burnished style of modern British that's brimful of good ideas. Those scallops might appear on a serving of risotto with strips of Savoy cabbage, all lit up with the intensity of preserved lemon, or there could be seared squab to start, with mushroom carpaccio and a salad of pickled onion and hazelnuts. Main courses appear copiously yet neatly garnished, as with the walnut-crusted duck breast that comes with pak choi, celeriac purée, tiny mushrooms, a honeyed jus textured with crumbled pain d'épices, and – the touch of genius – a side dish of battered duck tongues on a salad with caramelised pear and walnut. A pairing of Scotch beef fillet and cuttlefish is another bold but successful exercise, and dessert might offer a winning combination of crunchy chocolate ganache with salted caramel ice cream and puréed banana. A decent wine list includes the aptly named Gosset Brut Excellence as house Champagne. House wines are £15.50.

Chef/s: Simon Hulstone. **Open:** Brasserie: Tue to Sat L 12 to 2, D 6.30 to 9. Restaurant: Tue to Sat D only 7 to 9. **Closed:** Brasserie: Sun, Mon, first 2 weeks Jan. Restaurant: Sun, Mon, Oct to Apr. **Meals:** Brasserie: Set L £17.50 (2 courses) to £21.50. Set D £21 (2 courses) to £25. Restaurant: Tasting menu £55. **Service:** 10% (optional). **Details:** Cards accepted. 74 seats. Separate bar. No mobile phones. Music. Children allowed.

Virginstow

Percy's

Food doesn't get more local than this
Coombeshead Estate, Virginstow, EX21 5EA
Tel no: (01409) 211236
www.percys.co.uk
Modern British | £40
Cooking score: 4

£5 OFF 🛏 V

'The wonderful freshness of the raw materials, bred or grown on their own estate, and the enterprising cooking make this an exceptional place', enthused a reader who had visited this remarkable country estate and hotel for the first time. For 16 years the Bricknell-Webbs have held their own in this corner of Devon, using fresh and local supplies, much of it from their 130-acre organic farm, and producing extremely successful food. It's a small-scale operation, built around a limited-choice dinner of modern country cooking prepared with stately authority by Tina Bricknell-Webb. As a first course, wild mushroom and pork liver parfait with sage toast, marrow, bean and onion chutney manages to combine richness and simplicity in one dish. Mains could offer the choice between fillet of cod with tarragon and spring onion butter or pink roast loin of lamb. White chocolate and cardamom pannacotta makes a fitting finale. Wines from £20.

Chef/s: Tina Bricknell-Webb. **Open:** all week D only 6.30 to 9. **Meals:** Set D £40. **Service:** not inc. **Details:** Cards accepted. 24 seats. Separate bar. No mobile phones. Wheelchair access. Music. Car parking.

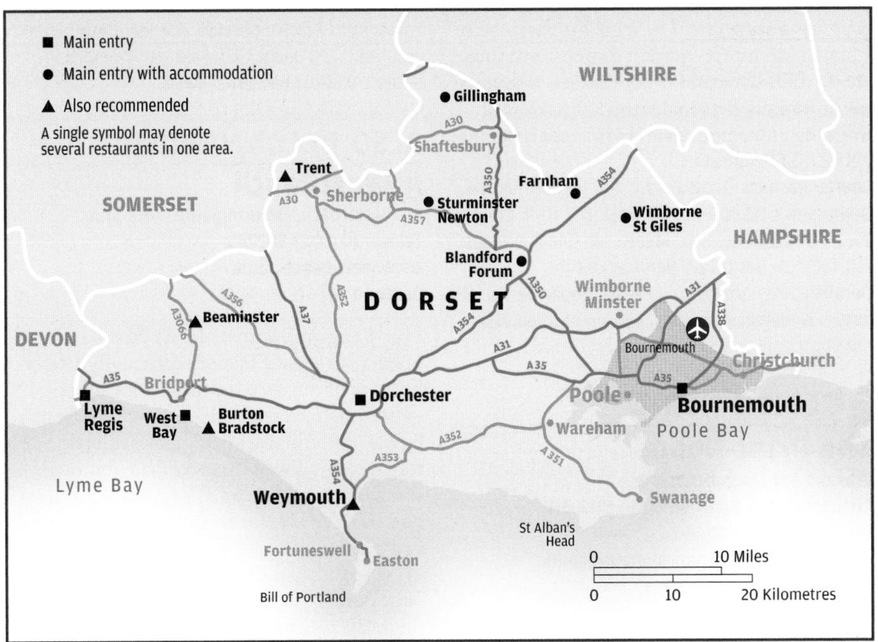

Beaminster

ALSO RECOMMENDED

▲ The Wild Garlic

4 The Square, Beaminster, DT8 3AS
Tel no: (01308) 861446
www.thewildgarlic.co.uk
British £5 OFF

In a former life this centuries-old building was a tollhouse, but nowadays it fulfils its function as a contemporary eating house – 'a perfect blend of modern rusticity and stylish warmth'. Direct, earthy, heart-on-sleeve dishes make up the short-choice menus, fuelled by a dedication to well-sourced seasonal produce: pigeon breast with a pear purée and black pudding (£8), rack of lamb teamed with wild garlic pesto and seaweed (£16), and pear sponge served with Somerset apple-brandy ice cream. Wines from £14. Closed Sun, Mon and Tue.

Blandford Forum

Castleman Hotel

Delightful Dorset hideaway
Chettle, Blandford Forum, DT11 8DB
Tel no: (01258) 830096
www.castlemanhotel.co.uk
Modern British | £25
Cooking score: 2

£5 OFF £30

More of a neighbourly restaurant-with-rooms than an overbearing country hotel, this personable retreat has been in safe hands since 1996 and is still a delightful Dorset hideaway. Occupying a remodelled dower house in an 'estate village', it's a genteel, eye-catching prospect with the promise of sound, regionally sourced food to boot. Game terrine with celeriac rémoulade could lead on to boozy daube of lamb with thyme and garlic on parsnip mash or medallions of local venison with port sauce. Fish is shipped in from the coast (perhaps pan-fried brill with shrimp, dill and lemon butter), while desserts could bring

pear frangipane tart. The wine list packs quite a punch, despite its modest dimensions; there are no duds here, and every bottle is testament to the owners' personal knowledge, careful sourcing and enthusiasm. House selections are £14 (£3.50 a glass).
Chef/s: Barbara Garnsworthy and Richard Morris. **Open:** Sun L 12.30 to 2, all week D 7 to 9. **Closed:** 25, 26 and 31 Dec, Feb. **Meals:** alc (main courses £10 to £20). Set L £22. **Service:** not inc. **Details:** Cards accepted. 45 seats. Separate bar. No music. Wheelchair access. Children allowed. Car parking.

Bournemouth

The Print Room

Vibrant Art Deco brasserie
Richmond Hill, Bournemouth, BH2 6HH
Tel no: (01202) 789669
www.theprintroom-bournemouth.co.uk
Modern European | £25
Cooking score: 2
£30

As big Art Deco spaces go, this recently refurbished conversion of the old *Bournemouth Echo* print room is an absolute stunner (imagine a vast zinc bar, giant mirrors and chandeliers). The food takes in flavours from across the globe, but the emphasis is on indigenous ingredients delivered in upmarket 'Manhattan style'. Ham hock cake with crushed peas is a colourful combo on a black slate, silky calf's liver comes with creamy mash and a first-rate red onion and marmalade jus, and fish fans might be tempted by five-spice salmon with sesame fettuccine and pak choi. For afters, the well-balanced assiette of rhubarb (fool, cheesecake and sorbet) is a winner. There's weekend breakfast and afternoon tea, too. The wine list is a drinker-friendly collection of well-annotated tipples from good sources. Bottles start at £15.95 and there's ample choice by the glass.
Chef/s: Ian Gibbs. **Open:** all week L 12 to 3, Mon to Sat D 6 to 10.15. **Meals:** alc (main courses £8 to £25). Set L £10 (2 courses) to £15. Sun L £15 (2 courses) to £18.50. **Service:** not inc. **Details:** Cards accepted. 120 seats. Separate bar. Wheelchair access. Music. Children allowed.

ALSO RECOMMENDED

▲ WestBeach

Pier Approach, Bournemouth, BH2 5AA
Tel no: (01202) 587785
www.west-beach.co.uk
Seafood £5 OFF

Slap-bang on Bournemouth's West Beach, this open-plan seaside favourite naturally attracts its share of punters, the main draw being spanking-fresh seafood – everything from bowls of bouillabaisse to 'grand fruits de mer' for two. In between, expect a trawl though smoked haddock kedgeree (£7.50), mussels with fries or hazelnut-crusted brill with pork belly and cauliflower purée (£16.95). WestBeach's fish and chips are good enough to satisfy quizzical northerners, while meat eaters might be swayed by herb-crusted rack of lamb or roast beef. House wine is £16.75. Open all week.

Burton Bradstock

ALSO RECOMMENDED

▲ Hive Beach Café

Beach Road, Burton Bradstock, DT6 4RF
Tel no: (01308) 897070
www.hivebeachcafe.co.uk
Seafood

An archetypal seaside café, perched on a headland close to the beach, this cracking venue takes full advantage of the catch from the local boats. Order at the counter and wait for your tempura-battered cod, whole 'undressed' brown crab with sweet chilli and paprika mayo, salad and chips (£15.50) or grilled mackerel fillets with salsa verde and samphire. Wines from £14.05. Open all week for breakfast and lunch, plus afternoon snacks and occasional suppers (Fri and Sat only) – weather permitting.

Dorchester

Sienna

Mighty impressive little restaurant
36 High West Street, Dorchester, DT1 1UP
Tel no: (01305) 250022
www.siennarestaurant.co.uk
Modern British | £43
Cooking score: 4

Russell Brown cooks while his wife Elena serves and together they have carved out a very personal, unassuming restaurant, one that runs in its own way and at its own speed. Cooking is technically assured and instinctively true, with local and seasonal raw materials the mainstay of the short, set-price menus. Reporters have emerged full of praise for the simplicity of 'beautifully fresh' brill in a beurre blanc sauce, noting the kitchen's commitment to excellence without reaching for outré combinations to sustain interest. Cold roast peppered venison loin, for example, comes teamed with celeriac rémoulade, rocket and shaved pecorino, while a main course might feature twice-cooked pork belly in happy partnership with sage, onion and cider sauce. The execution impresses mightily, and the effort is maintained all the way to desserts, which might include a warm treacle tart with spiced date purée, chestnut and apple salsa and vanilla ice cream. An affordable, wide-ranging wine list opens at £17.50.
Chef/s: Russell Brown. **Open:** Tue to Sat L 12 to 2, D 7 to 9. **Closed:** Sun, Mon, 2 weeks spring and autumn. **Meals:** Set L £25.50 (2 courses) to £28.50. Set D £36.50 (2 courses) to £43. Tasting menu £55 (6 courses). **Service:** not inc. **Details:** Cards accepted. 15 seats. No mobile phones. Music.

Farnham

The Museum Inn

Several notches above your average pub
Farnham, DT11 8DE
Tel no: (01725) 516261
www.museuminn.co.uk
Modern British | £32
Cooking score: 3

There's plenty of praise for the 'sumptuous', 'outstanding' and 'amazing' food on offer at this handsome country inn. Portions are generous and there's a roast on Sundays, but it's several notches above your average pub. Décor in the restaurant is refined and the cooking follows suit, showing a flair for invention that belies the country setting. Gressingham duck three ways (foie gras parfait, smoked breast and seared liver with brioche and Seville orange marmalade) is a typical starter, while mains such as baked hare pie with venison sausage, roasted venison loin, celeriac, roasted beets and cocoa and juniper jus reveal serious intent. The same goes for desserts such as bitter chocolate fondant with coffee mousse and raspberry and vodka sorbet. The substantial, French-dominated wine list kicks off at £18.50.
Chef/s: Ricky Ford. **Open:** all week L 12 to 2.30 (3 Sun), D 7 to 9.30. **Closed:** 25 Dec. **Meals:** alc (main courses £15 to £20). Bar menu available. **Service:** 10% (optional). **Details:** Cards accepted. 96 seats. 24 seats outside. Separate bar. No music. No mobile phones. Wheelchair access. Children allowed. Car parking.

Gillingham

Restaurant Stock Hill

Masterful, deeply felt European cookery
Stock Hill House, Stock Hill, Gillingham, SP8 5NR
Tel no: (01747) 823626
www.stockhillhouse.co.uk
European | £40
Cooking score: 5

V

From the original Osbert Lancaster cartoon hanging in the breakfast room to the William Morris wallpaper and fondly accumulated curios, Stock Hill has quite a tale to tell – in fact, Austrian-born Peter Hauser and his English wife Nita celebrated 25 years as custodians of their beloved Victorian abode during 2010. Meals always begin with puff pastry canapés in the lounge, before guests pass through to the elegantly appointed dining room. At table, the first salvo is a palate-sharpening amuse-bouche (perhaps a little lovage soup) before Peter shows the full breadth of his masterful, deeply felt European cookery. Recipes from his homeland point up the day's menu, although he's happy to cross borders in search of flavour. His marinated herrings with fennel and red onion cream continues to wow readers, and a starter of marinated venison in Merlot has also pleased. After that, expect richness and subtlety in the form of, say, veal paupiettes with Noilly Prat sauce or calf's liver with a ham and sage stuffing, cranberry sauce and assorted vegetables. The Viennese tradition has its way when it comes to luscious desserts: a meringue 'baiser', Yuletide muskatzimerle, kaffecremtorte, fürst pückler... the list of creamy, 'picture-perfect' creations goes on and on. Some unusual Austrian names figure on the wine list, with house selections from £24.95.

Chef/s: Peter Hauser. **Open:** Tue to Sun L 12.15 to 1.45 (12.30 to 1.30 Sat), all week D 7.15 to 8.45 (7.30 to 8.30 Mon, 7 to 8 Sun). **Meals:** Set L £17.50 (2 courses) to £22.50. Set D £40. Sun L from £26.50. **Service:** not inc. **Details:** Cards accepted. 24 seats. 8 seats outside. No music. No mobile phones. Car parking.

Lyme Regis

Hix Oyster & Fish House

Seafood that speaks for itself
Cobb Road, Lyme Regis, DT7 3JP
Tel no: (01297) 446910
www.hixoysterandfishhouse.co.uk
Seafood | £38
Cooking score: 3

Another in Mark Hix's elastically expanding empire of seafood restaurants, this one sits high up overlooking the Cobb, with sweeping views of Dorset's Jurassic coast. The unbuttoned informality means no coverings on either tables or floor and that unfussy approach extends to the cooking, which is content to let the super-fresh fish and shellfish speak for themselves. Reports have been mixed of late, but successful meals have taken in a generous serving of Morecambe Bay potted shrimps, home-cured Cobb smoked salmon with soda bread, and main courses such as whole roast red gurnard with Poole cockles and alexanders or well-timed fillet of hake. Sea buckthorn is the apt addition to a berry posset, or there's more mainstream apple crumble and custard. Wines start at £17.

Chef/s: Phil Eagle. **Open:** Wed to Sun L 12 to 3, D 6 to 10. **Closed:** Mon, Tue, 25 and 26 Dec. **Meals:** alc (main courses £14 to £24). Set L and early D £15.50 (2 courses) to £19.50. **Service:** 12.5% (optional). **Details:** Cards accepted. 45 seats. Music. Children allowed.

★ READERS' RESTAURANT OF THE YEAR ★ SOUTH WEST

The Mill Tea & Dining Room

Adorable riverside bolt-hole
Mill Lane, Lyme Regis, DT7 3PU
Tel no: (01297) 445757
www.teaanddiningroom.com
British | £30
Cooking score: 2

£5 OFF

Anthony McNamara's team 'put their heart and soul into the Mill', according to followers of this adorable riverside bolt-hole, a lovingly eccentric riot of etchings, antique Union Jacks and vintage teacups. Hand-bound menus promise a goodly assortment of proud British dishes, whether you're after a hot Scotch egg with piccalilli at lunchtime or six gargantuan oysters presented 'on beach pebbles', followed by slow-cooked duck with pickled red cabbage come evening. Beef tea with a shortcrust pastry 'lid' is unmissable, whole local plaice might appear with cockles and bacon, and you could close with vanilla ice cream and warm salted caramel. Drink homemade bramble and damson cordial or one of the unusual French wines (from £13.50).

Chef/s: Anthony McNamara. **Open:** Tue to Sun L 12 to 4.30 (5 Sun), Tue to Sat D 6.30 to 10. **Closed:** Mon (exc bank hols), 2 Jan to 1 Feb. **Meals:** alc (main courses £14 to £23). Set L £15 (2 courses) to £18. **Service:** not inc. **Details:** Cards accepted. 20 seats. 20 seats outside. No mobile phones. Music. Children allowed.

Sturminster Newton

Plumber Manor

Comfort, solace and familiarity
Sturminster Newton, DT10 2AF
Tel no: (01258) 472507
www.plumbermanor.com
Anglo-French | £35
Cooking score: 2

Like a vintage Bentley, or even your favourite great aunt, blue-blooded Plumber Manor deserves that caring touch and, as home to the Prideaux-Brune family for four centuries, it's never short of TLC. An unchanging stronghold of English propriety, it seldom gets troubled by fickle fashion; eating here is all about comfort, solace and familiarity, from canapés in the lounge to the calorific excesses of the sweet trolley. In between, Brian Prideaux-Brune feeds his jolly, doting flock with quiet confidence. There are no puffed-up fripperies, just sound renditions of smoked salmon paupiettes, chicken suprême with lemon and tarragon or brill with orange and chives, not forgetting chateaubriand to share. House wines from £16.50.

Chef/s: Brian Prideaux-Brune. **Open:** Sun L 12.30 to 1.30, all week D 7 to 9.30. **Closed:** 24 Jan to 3 Mar. **Meals:** Set D £28 (2 courses) to £35. Sun L £25. **Service:** not inc. **Details:** Cards accepted. 65 seats. Separate bar. No music. No mobile phones. Wheelchair access. Children allowed. Car parking.

Trent

ALSO RECOMMENDED

▲ The Rose & Crown

Trent, DT9 4SL
Tel no: (01935) 850776
www.roseandcrowntrent.co.uk
Modern British

For centuries the Rose & Crown has been the focal point of this unmarred Dorset village and has everything you could want from a local – open fires, a warm welcome and a kitchen that takes the spirit of pub food and gives it a polish. Tuna, duck egg, green bean and tomato salad (£5.95), and venison steak with sauté potatoes, braised red cabbage, baby onion and pancetta sauce (£16.95) are typical choices, with Dorset apple cake to finish. Wines from £12.95. No food Sun D and Mon.

West Bay

Riverside Restaurant

Ever-popular seafood veteran
West Bay, DT6 4EZ
Tel no: (01308) 422011
www.thefishrestaurant-westbay.co.uk
Seafood | £35
Cooking score: 3

The Watsons have now lost count of how long their abidingly popular coastal restaurant, not far from Bridport, has been in the *Guide*, which is testimony to the formidable levels of consistency they have set. Chefs may come and go, but the commitment to fresh fish from sustainable sources never wavers. Looking out over the Jurassic coastline, one pair of diners enjoyed fried prawns in a Thai-style broth of coconut milk, coriander and chilli, grilled mackerel fillets with baked asparagus and apple purée, and the star main course – a selection of the day's best fish and shellfish cooked en bourride, served with salad. Whole fish grilled on the bone with sea salt and lemon are also a big draw. Finish with baked cheesecake and rhubarb compote. House French is £17.50 a litre.

Chef/s: Ben Streak. **Open:** Tue to Sun L 11.45 to 2.15, Tue to Sat D 6.30 to 8.45. **Closed:** Mon, 4 Dec to 11 Feb. **Meals:** alc (main courses £13 to £40). Set L £18.25 (2 courses) to £24. **Service:** not inc. **Details:** Cards accepted. 80 seats. 25 seats outside. Separate bar. No music. No mobile phones. Wheelchair access. Children allowed.

Weymouth

ALSO RECOMMENDED

▲ Crab House Café

Ferryman's Way, Portland Road, Weymouth, DT4 9YU
Tel no: (01305) 788867
www.crabhousecafe.co.uk
Seafood

A seafood shack on a Dorset beach, overlooking the Portland coastline, the Crab House could barely be better positioned to take advantage of the sea's bounty. Sit under a pink parasol on fine days for the full experience. Menus change fast enough to make your head spin, but the day's haul might yield a half-pint of Portland shrimps (£5.50), and roast bream stuffed with sardines, sun-dried tomatoes and spinach (£15.50), plus the all-important crabs and oysters. Wines from £14.20. Open Wed to Sat, and Sun L.

Wimborne St Giles

The Bull Inn

Buffed-up village hostelry
Coach Road, Wimborne St Giles, BH21 5NF
Tel no: (01725) 517300
www.bullinnwsg.com
Modern British | £27
Cooking score: 2

£5 OFF £30

The estate that surrounds the Bull is the family seat of the Ashley-Coopers, Earls of Shaftesbury, a line that has furnished England with one noted philosopher and a chamberful of parliamentarians down the generations. The inn itself is a modernised village hostelry with a buffed-up look, and a menu of well-rendered modern British dishes. Breaded cod cheeks with smoked bacon, cabbage and lentils in mustard cream is a good opener, ahead of char-grilled rump steak in garlic butter or gurnard with parsnip purée and wild mushrooms. Finish with Seville orange steamed sponge pudding and custard. House Spanish is £16.95.

Chef/s: Ian Craddock. **Open:** all week L 12 to 2.30 (4 Sun), D 6 to 9.30 (7 to 9 Sun). **Meals:** alc (main courses £13 to £24). Set L £15 (2 courses). **Service:** 10% (optional). **Details:** Cards accepted. 50 seats. 40 seats outside. No music. Wheelchair access. Children allowed. Car parking.

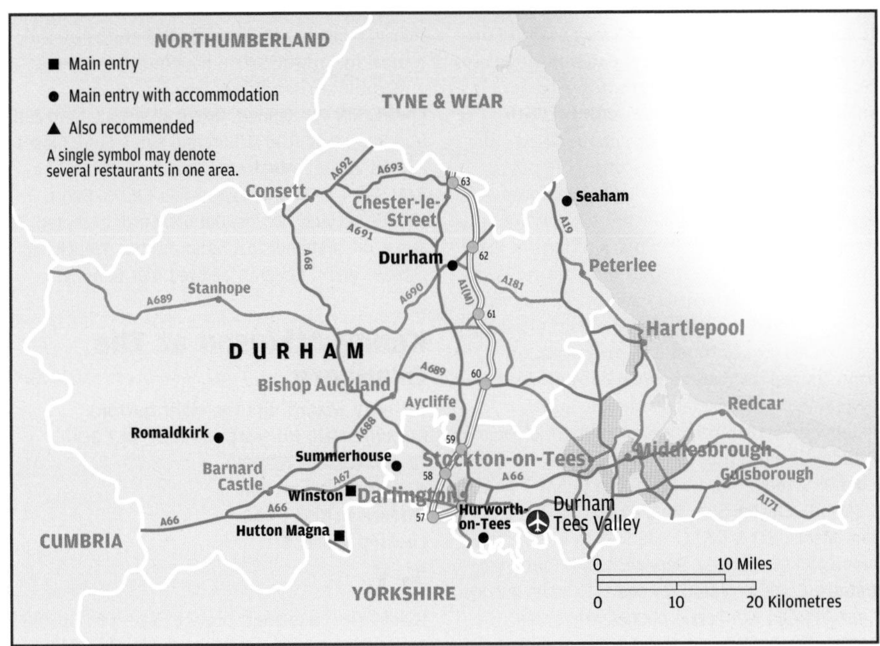

Durham

Bistro 21

Friendly bistro with sturdy comfort food
Aykley Heads House, Aykley Heads, Durham, DH1 5TS
Tel no: (0191) 3844354
www.bistrotwentyone.co.uk
Modern British | £33
Cooking score: 2

V

'Interesting menu, food always exceptional, pleasant atmosphere and good service', was one enthusiastic response to Terry Laybourne's relaxed and unpretentious bistro. Menus of a sensible length focus on showing off good raw materials and manage to push most of the right buttons. Sturdy comfort food could bring Cheddar cheese and spinach soufflé, ahead of confit beef featherblade with pearl barley, roast shallots and red wine sauce. Desserts come with appropriate ice cream garnishes: rhubarb and custard tart with vanilla; warm chocolate pudding with pistachio. House wine is £16.95.

Chef/s: Gareth Lambert. **Open:** Mon to Sat L 12 to 2.30, D 7 to 10.30. **Closed:** Sun, bank hols. **Meals:** alc (main courses £15 to £22). Set L and D £15.50 (2 courses) to £18. **Service:** 10% (optional). **Details:** Cards accepted. 60 seats. 20 seats outside. Separate bar. Wheelchair access. Music. Children allowed. Car parking.

Gourmet Spot

Adventurous restaurant with big ideas
The Avenue, Durham, DH1 4DX
Tel no: (0191) 3846655
www.gourmet-spot.co.uk
Modern European | £38
Cooking score: 4

£5 OFF

Tagged onto a hotel, but clearly no afterthought, the Gourmet Spot showcases ambitious modern cooking in a self-consciously 'modern' dining room (black furniture, black-and-red artwork). While the décor won't suit all tastes, the menu showcases sensible combinations, right down to details such as an amuse of mi-cuit salmon with cherry tomatoes, coriander and a jellied cube of salmon and saffron consommé. Peppery watercress velouté with sautéed marjoram gnocchi, beetroot and beetroot ice cream is an engaging starter, while a main of lemon sole en papillote with pickled grape, caramelised onion and confit potato salad impresses with subtly layered flavours. After a bright-tasting palate cleanser of blueberry and tarragon espuma, a dessert of rhubarb compote, set ginger custard, pistachio mousse and honeycomb brings things to a showy close. An international wine list opens at £15.

Chef/s: Stephen Hardy. **Open:** Tue to Sat D only 5.30 to 9. **Closed:** Sun, Mon, 25 and 26 Dec, 1 week Jan. **Meals:** Set D £20 (2 courses) to £38. Tasting menu £55 (8 courses). **Service:** 12.5% (optional). **Details:** Cards accepted. 24 seats. 12 seats outside. Separate bar. No mobile phones. Wheelchair access. Music. Children allowed. Car parking.

Hurworth-on-Tees

NEW ENTRY

The Bay Horse

Village pub of substance
45 The Green, Hurworth-on-Tees, DL2 2AA
Tel no: (01325) 720663
www.thebayhorsehurworth.com
Modern British | £32
Cooking score: 2

V

Here's an updated village pub of substance, complete with a fire-warmed bar and a civilised dining room. Service is smiley and warm and there's an air of relaxed unpretentiousness, with light lunches pleasing the locals and a carte that mixes standards with more contemporary ideas. Potted Whitby crab, beef casserole with parsley dumplings, and rabbit suet pudding share the honours with, say, pressed belly pork with swede and maple syrup relish, pig's cheek croquette, onion and thyme purée, roasted swede cubes and braised Toulouse sausage. Bringing up the rear is a cast list of desserts that might include lemon meringue tart with blueberry purée and apple sorbet. Wines from £16.95.

Chef/s: Marcus Bennett. **Open:** all week L 12 to 2.30 (4 Sun), D 6 to 9.30 (10 Fri and Sat, 9 Sun). **Closed:** 25 and 26 Dec. **Meals:** alc (main courses £13 to £24). Set L £12.95 (2 courses) to £15.95. Sun L £20.95. **Service:** not inc. **Details:** Cards accepted. 78 seats. 64 seats outside. Separate bar. Wheelchair access. Music. Children allowed. Car parking.

Kenny Atkinson at The Orangery

Culinary wizard hits the right buttons
Rockliffe Hall, Hurworth-on-Tees, DL2 2DU
Tel no: (01325) 729999
www.rockliffehall.com
Modern British | £48
Cooking score: 5

V

Rockliffe has everything we expect to find in a country retreat these days, from a sprawling golf course, hydrotherapy pool and dance studio to a top-end restaurant occupying the Victorian orangery. Even if you're not here to play a few rounds or shed a few pounds, the setting itself is majestic. It all happens (apart from the golf) in a redbrick, mostly eighteenth-century house on the banks of the Tees, where the surrounding countryside is balm enough. With windows all around and above, and light from soft lanterns in the evenings, the Orangery is a dining room with a difference, and its presiding culinary wizard knows how to hit the right buttons. Dishes are complex but effective, combining duck confit, ham hock and Savoy cabbage in a rolled terrine, accompanied by celeriac, pickled apple and a sliver of sautéed liver, for example. A main course of turbot with clams and spinach in a coriander-spiked curry sauce elicited gasps of amazement from one reporter, as did the Grand Reserve main course of loin and shoulder of local lamb with artichokes, leeks and girolles. Finish with excellent dark chocolate fondant with banana ice cream and butterscotch sauce. Service has been worryingly extemporaneous on occasion

– room for improvement. An extensive, fine wine-list offers plenty by the glass, from £5.50.

Chef/s: Kenny Atkinson. **Open:** Tue to Sat D only 6 to 9.30. **Closed:** Sun, Mon. **Meals:** Set D £37.50 (2 courses) to £47.50. Tasting menu £67.50. **Service:** not inc. **Details:** Cards accepted. 60 seats. Separate bar. No mobile phones. Wheelchair access. Music. Car parking.

Hutton Magna

The Oak Tree Inn

Remarkably well-crafted dishes
Hutton Magna, DL11 7HH
Tel no: (01833) 627371
Modern British | £32
Cooking score: 3

This little whitewashed pub has divided its single room into part comfy village bar/part grown-up restaurant under the caring tenure of Alastair and Claire Ross. They produce some remarkably well-crafted dishes. A salad of fig, beetroot and blue cheese with a honey truffle dressing was exceptional. Hand-rolled linguine with smoked haddock, mussels and curry butter sauce was another triumph. From half-a-dozen mains, sea bass with chorizo and mussels was well received, so was fillet steak atop crushed potatoes and bacon, though the menu might also stretch to silver hake with crab and spinach cannelloni, John Dory with scallops, and duck breast with belly pork. An original dessert menu, select beers and whiskies, and a modest wine list (from £12.50) complete a commendable operation.

Chef/s: Alastair Ross. **Open:** Tue to Sun D only 6 to 11 (5.30 to 10.30 Sun). **Closed:** Mon, 24 to 27 and 31 Dec, 1 Jan. **Meals:** alc (main courses £18 to £20). **Service:** not inc. **Details:** Cards accepted. 20 seats. Separate bar. No mobile phones. Music. Car parking.

Average Price

The average price listed in main-entry reviews denotes the price of a three-course meal, without wine.

Romaldkirk

The Rose & Crown

Old-world village charmer
Romaldkirk, DL12 9EB
Tel no: (01833) 650213
www.rose-and-crown.co.uk
Modern British | £35
Cooking score: 3

£5 OFF

Romaldkirk remains essentially unchanged since Georgian times, and so, externally, does this old coaching inn sited snugly on the green. Run by Alison and Christopher Davy for the past 23 years, it's an archetypal country pub inside, with a traditional bar/brasserie and real ales, a log fire and a please-all menu serving the likes of smoked haddock soufflé and braised oxtail. In the oak-panelled dining room, a repertoire of modern British cooking could open with sea bass, roasted fennel and Pernod cream, before pink breasts of wood pigeon with potato rösti, sweet onion confit and juniper berry sauce. Finish with baked egg custard. House wine is £16.95.

Chef/s: Christopher Davy and Andrew Lee. **Open:** Sun L 12 to 1.45, all week D 7.30 to 9. **Closed:** 24 to 26 Dec. **Meals:** Set L £18.50. Set D £35 (4 courses). Bar menu available. **Service:** not inc. **Details:** Cards accepted. 24 seats. 24 seats outside. Separate bar. No music. No mobile phones. Wheelchair access. Children allowed. Car parking.

Seaham

Seaham Hall, The White Room

Boutique clifftop hotel with ambitious cooking
Lord Byron's Walk, Seaham, SR7 7AG
Tel no: (0191) 5161400
www.seaham-hall.co.uk
Modern British | £55
Cooking score: 4

Seaham Hall is now a luxury boutique hotel with its own spa and a flagship restaurant housed in two pale-hued dining rooms. Chef

Ian Swainson was formerly at La Bécasse in Ludlow (see entry), and his menus suggest a stronger regional accent than before – as well as a sense of fun. Locally landed fish could include halibut with toasted rice royale, burnt onion purée, salt and vinegar 'rice crispies' and liquorice, while Northumberland heritage beef might be partnered by horseradish, oyster, parsley porridge and red wine. Desserts also push the boat out – fruit-infused chocolate sorbet with lime leaf mousse, sweet basil jelly and chocolate sherbet, for example. Seaham's huge international wine list is packed with judiciously sourced growers and an excellent choice of vintages. Abundant halves and some 20 selections by the glass encourage exploration; bottles from £24.

Chef/s: Ian Swainson. **Open:** Fri to Sun L 12 to 2, all week D 7 to 10. **Meals:** Set L £32. Set D £30 (3 courses) to £55. Tasting menu £65. Sun L £32. **Service:** not inc. **Details:** Cards accepted. 40 seats. Separate bar. No mobile phones. Wheelchair access. Music. Children allowed. Car parking.

Summerhouse

NEW ENTRY

The Raby Hunt

Personally run restaurant-with-rooms
Summerhouse, DL2 3UD
Tel no: (01325) 374237
www.rabyhuntrestaurant.co.uk
Modern British | £34
Cooking score: 3

£5 OFF

This 'delightful family-run restaurant' may look like a pub, but inside it's smart and sassy, with simple modern furnishings, bare floorboards and striking artwork. Charming staff give 'very personal' service and chef/proprietor James Close's cooking is 'bursting with good ideas' such as a generous, balanced warm morteau sausage salad with poached egg or belly pork (nicely crisped) with pork tenderloin, dauphinoise potato, ranch dressing and – surprisingly but not unsuccessfully – Little Gem lettuce topped with barbecue sauce. Despite the occasional eyebrow-raiser this is satisfying, imaginative cooking, and a dessert of rice pudding with strawberry jam and cinnamon ice cream hits all the right notes. Wines come from small independent producers worldwide, and include some good organic and biodynamic options. Bottles start at £14.95.

Chef/s: James Close. **Open:** Thur to Sun L 12 to 2, Wed to Sat D 6.30 to 9. **Closed:** Mon, Tue, 25 and 25 Dec, 1 Jan. **Meals:** alc (main courses £13 to £25). Set L £14.75 (2 courses) to £17.75. Sun L £16.50. **Service:** not inc. **Details:** Cards accepted. 30 seats. 6 seats outside. Separate bar. Wheelchair access. Music. Children allowed. Car parking.

Winston

NEW ENTRY

The Bridgewater Arms

Character, warmth and excellent ingredients
Winston, DL2 3RN
Tel no: (01325) 730302
www.thebridgewaterarms.com
Modern European | £32
Cooking score: 1

On the edge of a pretty village, this one-time schoolhouse is decorated with photographs of its former life. Tall leaded windows, bookshelves and a large fireplace make for a characterful bar that draws locals and diners alike. The restaurant is smart and cosy, with polished wood floors and linen-clad tables. Excellent ingredients and generous portions define dishes such as duck, mango and pancetta salad or pan-fried sea bass and king scallops on greens with sweet chilli sauce and lime crème fraîche. Creamy rice pudding with a punchy raspberry compote makes a satisfying dessert. A short wine list opens at £15.

Chef/s: Paul Grundy and Richard Vart. **Open:** Tue to Sat L 12 to 2, D 6 to 9. **Closed:** Sun, Mon, 25 to 27 Dec. **Meals:** alc (main courses £14 to £26). **Service:** not inc. **Details:** Cards accepted. 50 seats. Separate bar. Music. Children allowed. Car parking.

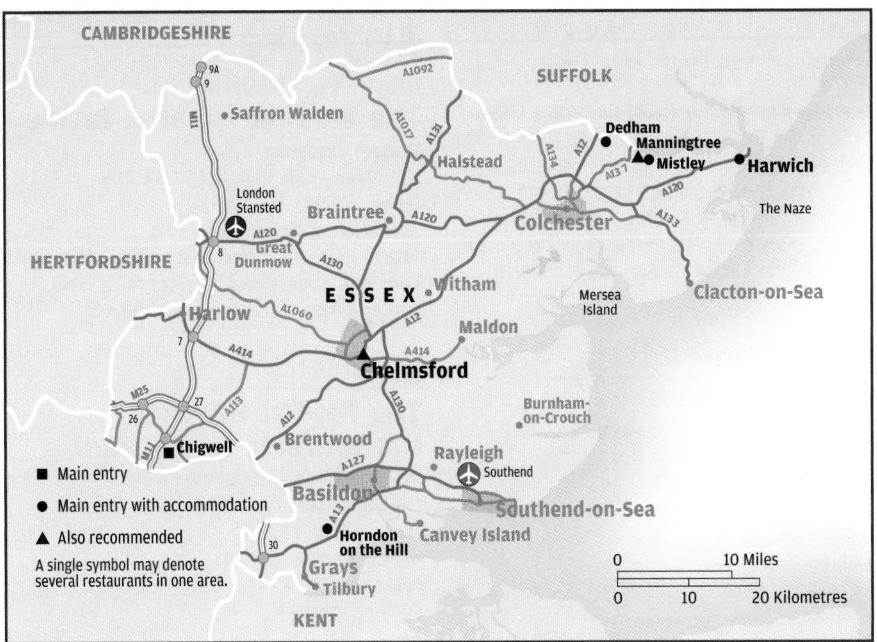

Chelmsford

ALSO RECOMMENDED

▲ Barda

30-32 Broomfield Road, Chelmsford, CM1 1SW
Tel no: (01245) 357799
www.barda-restaurant.com
Modern European £5 OFF

With its smartly chic interior and decked patio outside, Barda looks good in any weather. Set in Chelmsford's West End, its serious intent is signalled by a lively list of Med/Asian dishes ranging from tempura vegetables with sweet chilli and coriander dipping sauce (£6) to homely slow-cooked pork belly with creamed leeks and bacon, crispy crackling and thyme jus (£16.95). Rib-sticking desserts include sticky toffee pudding and vanilla and mixed berry cheesecake. Wines start at £14.95. Closed Sun and Mon.

Chigwell

The Bluebell

A great local asset
117 High Road, Chigwell, IG7 6QQ
Tel no: (020) 8500 6282
www.thebluebellrestaurant.co.uk
Modern European | £40
Cooking score: 1

Sedate as you enter, but with a 'loud, brash' dining room at the back, the Bluebell continues to be a great local asset. There's a new owner, but the chef remains and his all-embracing menu offers everything from starters of spiced smoked haddock and yellow pepper chowder or twice-baked goats' cheese soufflé to main courses such as spiced monkfish tail and minted mushy peas with chips and curry sauce, or roast loin and braised haunch of venison alongside poached pear and Parma ham boulangère potatoes. There are plainer dishes too, such as steaks and mixed grills. Desserts could include dark chocolate fondant or crème brûlée. House wine is £16.50.

Chef/s: Gavin Maguire. **Open:** Tue to Sun L 12 to 2 (4 Sun), Tue to Sat D 6.45 to 9.30 (6.30 to 10.30 Sat). **Closed:** Mon. **Meals:** alc (main courses £18 to £29). Set L £17.95 (2 courses) to £21.95. Set D £20.95 (2 courses) to £25.95, Sun L £25.95. Tasting menu £45.95. **Service:** not inc. **Details:** Cards accepted. 100 seats. No mobile phones. Music. Children allowed.

Dedham

The Sun Inn

Fine old inn with Med flavours
High Street, Dedham, CO7 6DF
Tel no: (01206) 323351
www.thesuninndedham.com
Mediterranean | £26
Cooking score: 3

This fine old inn in the heart of Dedham has been cleverly reworked without losing any of its rustic charm. Low-key and comfortable, it offers a robustly seasonal menu built around fresh, carefully sourced ingredients with the food more than living up to expectations in every detail, from 'delicious fresh mackerel' to 'wonderful' local and regional cheeses. Linguine with clams, Prosecco, orange zest and parsley sets the Med-influenced tone, and flavour is built up robustly in main courses – perhaps roast mallard teamed with curly kale gratin, potatoes and Suffolk Blue cheese. There are more homely dishes too, such as Red Poll beef and ale pie. Desserts, like the rest of the menu, vary with the seasons and could include pannacotta with baked Yorkshire rhubarb. Wines from £13.50.

Chef/s: Ugo Simonelli. **Open:** all week L 12 to 2.30 (3 Sat and Sun), D 6.30 to 9.30 (10 Sat). **Closed:** 25 and 26 Dec. **Meals:** alc (main courses £9 to £18). Set L and D £12 (2 courses) to £15. **Service:** not inc. **Details:** Cards accepted. 75 seats. 75 seats outside. Separate bar. Music. Children allowed. Car parking.

Fryerning

READERS RECOMMEND

The Woolpack Bar & Bistro

Modern European
Mill Green Road, Fryerning, CM4 0HS
Tel no: (01277) 352189
www.woolpackfryerning.com
'Warm welcome, classic tasty menu and relaxed grown-up atmosphere. Perfect for a meal for two or with a small group of friends.'

Harwich

The Pier at Harwich, Harbourside Restaurant

Prime seafood and fine views
The Quay, Harwich, CO12 3HH
Tel no: (01255) 241212
www.milsomhotels.com
Seafood | £37
Cooking score: 2

Pitched slap-bang on Harwich quayside, this long-serving hotel dining room scores with its nautical vibes, fine views and old-school seafood cookery. Prime piscine pickings are delivered to the door each morning, and the kitchen pleases just about everyone with its egalitarian menu. Harwich lobsters 'any way you like' are a speciality, but the choice might extend to skate with caper butter, walnut and thyme-crusted cod with parsnip cream or the 'ultimate' fish and chips (monkfish goujons in tempura batter). Dedham Vale steaks satisfy the red-meat contingent, while puds could yield dark chocolate and rum torte. House wine is £17.25. Little sister the Ha'penny Pier serves bistro food downstairs.

Chef/s: Chris Oakley. **Open:** all week L 12 to 2, D 6 to 9.30. **Meals:** alc (main courses £16 to £39). Set L £20 (2 courses) to £25.50. Sun L £24 (2 courses) to £29. **Service:** 10%. **Details:** Cards accepted. 80 seats. Separate bar. No mobile phones. Music. Children allowed. Car parking.

Horndon on the Hill

The Bell Inn

Medieval pub with comforting, classy food
High Road, Horndon on the Hill, SS17 8LD
Tel no: (01375) 642463
www.bell-inn.co.uk
Modern European | £30
Cooking score: 2

Run by the Vereker family for some 70 years, this medieval inn is renowned in these parts for its culinary ambition. Nevertheless, beams, flagstone floors and panelled walls contribute to the pubby ambience, as do an informal atmosphere and microbrewery ales. Stuart Fay's modern European food combines comfort and class, and his daily menus reflect an understanding of contemporary ideas. Take sea bass escabèche with gremolata, pickled fennel and tomato consommé jelly, venison fillet and confit shoulder with haggis ravioli and caramelised cauliflower, or vanilla pannacotta with rhubarb and ginger ice cream. House wines from £13.95.

Chef/s: Stuart Fay. **Open:** all week L 12 to 1.45 (2.30 Sun), D 6.30 to 9.45 (7 Sun). **Closed:** 25 and 26 Dec, bank hols. **Meals:** alc (main courses £12 to £23). Bar menu available. **Service:** not inc. **Details:** Cards accepted. 80 seats. 36 seats outside. Separate bar. No music. Wheelchair access. Children allowed. Car parking.

Manningtree

ALSO RECOMMENDED

▲ Lucca Enoteca

39-43 High Street, Manningtree, CO11 1AH
Tel no: (01206) 390044
www.luccafoods.co.uk
Italian

Manningtree locals generate a lively buzz at this rustically designed Italian restaurant, a spin-off from the Mistley Thorn (see entry). Wood-fired pizzas form the backbone of the menu, from classics such as napolitana (£6.45) and quattro formaggi to upper-crust toppings such as goats' cheese, fior di latte mozzarella, roasted peppers, garlic and pancetta. Alternatively, you might consider papardelle with wild boar sausage (£8.75), lasagne or a salad. Wood-fired roasts are offered on Saturday and Sunday. Italian wines from £13.95. Open all week.

Mistley

The Mistley Thorn

Upbeat eatery with starry seafood
High Street, Mistley, CO11 1HE
Tel no: (01206) 392821
www.mistleythorn.com
Modern European | £25
Cooking score: 2

This gently upgraded pub-with-rooms makes an informal stage for Sherri Singleton's Mediterranean-inspired cooking. The interior is light and modern, and the menu is built around decidedly local ingredients. Seafood plays a leading role: Mersea oysters, silver mullet (with chickpeas, roast tomato, spinach and tapenade), and day-boat squid (with chilli, garlic, lemon oil and herbs). Meat options include seared pigeon breast salad, venison steak with béarnaise and very good burgers. Finish with elderflower-berry jelly with vanilla ice cream. House wine is £14.95.

Chef/s: Sherri Singleton. **Open:** all week L 12 to 2.30 (5 Sat and Sun), D 6.30 to 9.30 (10 Sat). **Meals:** alc (main courses £11 to £17). Set L £10.95 (2 courses) to £13.95. Sun L £12.95 (2 courses) to £15.95. **Service:** not inc. **Details:** Cards accepted. 70 seats. 12 seats outside. Music. Children allowed. Car parking.

Readers Recommend

A 'readers recommend' review is a genuine quote from a report sent in by one of our readers. We intend to follow up these suggestions throughout the year to come.

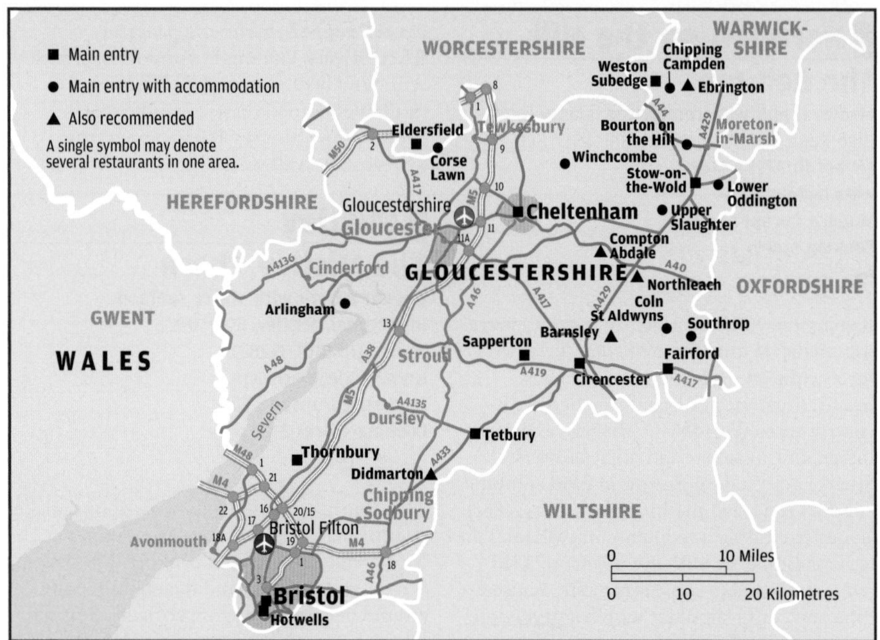

Arlingham

The Old Passage

Confident seafood cookery
Passage Road, Arlingham, GL2 7JR
Tel no: (01452) 740547
www.theoldpassage.com
Seafood | £32
Cooking score: 3

£5 OFF

An isolated Georgian farmhouse with views across the river Severn to the Forest of Dean, this is about as tranquil as restaurants get. Seafood is the speciality, served against a backdrop of work by local artists (all for sale). Feast on fruits de mer or the shellfish tasting menu, or go à la carte with Fowey mussels in cider cream sauce, followed by roast skate wing with spring greens, crushed new potatoes and caper butter sauce. Alternatively, try seared breast of pigeon with celeriac gratin, ahead of sirloin of beef with hand-cut chips and béarnaise sauce. To finish, maybe chocolate brownie and clotted-cream ice cream. A varied international wine list kicks off at £18.50.

Chef/s: Mark Redwood. **Open:** Tue to Sun L 12 to 2 (2.30 Sun), Tue to Sat D 7 to 9 (9.30 Sat). **Closed:** Mon, 25 and 26 Dec. **Meals:** alc (main courses £18 to £45). Set L £15 (2 courses) to £20. **Service:** not inc. **Details:** Cards accepted. 40 seats. 20 seats outside. Wheelchair access. Music. Children allowed. Car parking.

Barnsley

ALSO RECOMMENDED

▲ The Village Pub

Barnsley, GL7 5EF
Tel no: (01285) 740421
www.thevillagepub.co.uk
Modern British

In the heart of the Cotswolds, this pretty village pub ticks all the boxes when it comes to honey-coloured stone, open fires and flagstones. Refurbished in 2010, the luxurious fabrics and shiny new bar add a modern touch, and the food is a contemporary twist on British cooking. Start with potted brown shrimps with lemon and granary toast (£6.95) move on to Badminton venison with roast apple, red cabbage and Anna potatoes (£14) and finish with vanilla crème brûlée (£6). Wines from £16.75. Open all week.

Bourton on the Hill

Horse & Groom

Restored inn with satisfying food
Bourton on the Hill, GL56 9AQ
Tel no: (01386) 700413
www.horseandgroom.info
Modern British | £25
Cooking score: 2

A proudly restored country inn of Cotswold stone sitting on a hill, master of all it surveys, the Horse & Groom is credit to Tom and Will Greenstock and their contribution to the local hospitality scene. Will cooks, offering a menu of carefully conceived modern British dishes founded on quality raw materials. Griddled ox tongue with Puy lentils and salsa verde sets things rolling satisfyingly. A reader who enjoyed a main-course chicken breast accompanied by Savoy cabbage, bacon and pine nuts appreciated the obvious care taken with timing and presentation. Fish could be roasted cod with mussel and saffron stew, while pudding might be pear and almond tart with Jersey cream. Wines start at £13.85.
Chef/s: Will Greenstock. **Open:** all week L 12 to 2 (2.30 Sun), Mon to Sat D 7 to 9 (9.30 Fri and Sat). **Closed:** 25 Dec, 31 Dec, 1 week Jan. **Meals:** alc (main courses £11 to £19). **Service:** not inc. **Details:** Cards accepted. 70 seats. 56 seats outside. Separate bar. No music. Children allowed. Car parking.

Bristol

The Albion

Seasonal cooking and impeccable ingredients
Boyces Avenue, Clifton, Bristol, BS8 4AA
Tel no: (0117) 9733522
www.thealbionclifton.co.uk
British | £31
Cooking score: 3

This upmarket pub and dining room is now into its seventh year and although reporters have noted that the heritage colours and wooden floors of the seventeenth-century inn may be starting to look a little scuffed around the edges, there are certainly no such complaints about the food. Clarke Oldfield's cooking is fiercely seasonal, and impeccably sourced produce is a high priority – from Dorset crab, dry-aged rump steak and seasonal game to British artisan cheeses and Yorkshire rhubarb. A spring inspection meal opened with an intensely flavoured Cornish red mullet soup, went on to expertly handled smoked trout and crab fishcake with samphire and hollandaise, and finished with a refreshing set yoghurt pudding with blood oranges and caramel. House wines start from £16.
Chef/s: Clarke Oldfield. **Open:** Tue to Sun L 12 to 3, Tue to Sat D 7 to 10. **Closed:** 25 and 26 Dec. **Meals:** alc (main courses £10 to £24). Set L £11.50 (2 courses) to £15. Set D £26 (2 courses) to £31. Sun L £14.95. **Service:** 10% (optional). **Details:** Cards accepted. 110 seats. 44 seats outside. Separate bar. Wheelchair access. Music. Children allowed.

Bell's Diner

Surprising flavours and sound cooking
1-3 York Road, Montpelier, Bristol, BS6 5QB
Tel no: (0117) 9240357
www.bellsdiner.co.uk
Modern British | £38
Cooking score: 4

£5 OFF

The modest shop frontage of this neighbourhood bistro in Bristol's bohemian quarter doesn't quite prepare you for the refined interior, or the innovative modern

cooking. Although Chris Wicks still has a firm hand on the tiller in the kitchen, he has allowed Alex Collins and the young, ambitious team to have more input when it comes to the menu. The result is food that depends less on kitchen wizardry and more on seasonality and local sourcing. Flavour combinations continue to surprise, but they are underpinned by solid techniques. A well-balanced starter of pork belly, apple, crayfish, peas and broccoli may seem quite straight-forward compared to more ambitious halibut with a 'lasagne' of oxtail, salsify, turnip and chervil. Classy desserts include rhubarb and hibiscus soufflé with rhubarb sorbet and vanilla ice cream. A carefully sourced wine list starts at £18, and 10 are now available by the carafe as well as the glass.
Chef/s: Christopher Wicks and Alex Collins. **Open:** Tue to Fri L 12 to 2.30, Mon to Sat D 7 to 10. **Closed:** Sun, 24 to 30 Dec, bank hols. **Meals:** Set L and D £31 (2 courses) to £37.50. Tasting menu £47.50. **Service:** 10% (optional). **Details:** Cards accepted. 50 seats. Music. Children allowed.

Bordeaux Quay

Versatile harbourside landmark
V-Shed, Canons Way, Bristol, BS1 5UH
Tel no: (0117) 9431200
www.bordeaux-quay.co.uk
Modern European | £33
Cooking score: 2

£5 OFF

After a period of management changes and the arrival of a new head chef, things have settled down at this former docks warehouse on Bristol's harbourside. The buzzy downstairs brasserie is still the place to enjoy informal meals and weekend brunches, but there is an increased Italian influence upstairs, where seasonality is the cornerstone of the more formal restaurant menu. The cooking is rustic and unpretentious – seared duck livers with pomegranate seeds and caramelised red onion might be followed by pan-fried fillet of John Dory with crab arancini, salsify and bisque dressing. An interesting, Italian-dominant wine list starts at £17.
Chef/s: Alex Murray. **Open:** Sun L 12 to 3, Tue to Sat D 6 to 10. **Closed:** Mon, 24 to 26 Dec, 1 Jan. **Meals:** alc (main courses £11 to £22). **Service:** 10% (optional). **Details:** Cards accepted. 160 seats. Separate bar. Wheelchair access. Music. Children allowed.

Café Maitreya

Vibrant veggie favourite
89 St Mark's Road, Easton, Bristol, BS5 6HY
Tel no: (0117) 9510100
www.cafemaitreya.co.uk
Vegetarian | £23
Cooking score: 4

£5 OFF **V** £30

Originally a Victorian bakery, this upbeat and contemporary vegetarian hangout has long been an integral part of this colourful street packed with multicultural restaurants, cafés and world food shops. There is some serious innovation in the open kitchen and chef Mark Evans creates tantalising flavour combinations from organic and foraged local ingredients. He pushes each dish to the max, using spices and numerous techniques to keep things interesting, and the food often brings a smile to the face of diners. A relatively simple-sounding starter described as a 'sizzling fajita' turns out to be Jerusalem artichoke, roast red pepper and baby carrot in a chilli and paprika marinade served with guacamole, tomato salsa and sour cream with a buckwheat tortilla. It might be followed by crisp potato rösti with leek and pistachio in a light dill and cider sauce, served with marinated celeriac, apple and hazelnut. Tequila sunrise trifle ends things exotically. House wine £13.30.
Chef/s: Mark Evans. **Open:** Tue to Sat D only 6.30 to 9.45. **Closed:** Sun, Mon, 24 to 27 Dec, 1 Jan. **Meals:** Set D £19.95 (2 courses) to £22.95. **Service:** not inc. **Details:** Cards accepted. 55 seats. Separate bar. Wheelchair access. Music. Children allowed.

Casamia

Much culinary derring-do
38 High Street, Westbury on Trym, Bristol, BS9 3DZ
Tel no: (0117) 9592884
www.casamiarestaurant.co.uk
Italian | £45
Cooking score: 5

The domestic moniker, terracotta tiles and pretty courtyard might suggest a 'sole mio' trattoria, but siblings Jonray and Peter Sanchez-Iglesias have no truck with spag bol or lasagne. Casamia's tersely worded tasting menus conceal much culinary derring-do and some clever avant-garde conceits – notably a fascinating blend of scrambled duck egg with 'cured pig' and an exquisitely delicate piece of salmon with bulgur wheat. Meats tend to receive more purposeful, robust treatment, from a witty dish of beef cheek with roast potatoes, pickled onion, horseradish and puffed corn (shades of a pub lunch!) to saddle of lamb with 'melting' kidney, carrots and parsley. Given the brothers' voracious appetite for new tricks, the occasional ill-met marriage is almost inevitable: one reader found a Nordic-inspired amalgam of beetroot, barley, iced yoghurt and pickled fennel 'revolting'. Luckily, the kitchen saves its best till last, wheeling out the liquid nitrogen for a dessert involving Cox's apple and winter spices, serving a kettle-corn soup with lemon sorbet, and presenting deconstructed tiramisu in a foil container. While the food is full of surprises, any gustatory drama can be flattened by 'chaotic and uncaring service', not to mention unacceptably long waits (partly the result of the kitchen delivering dishes 'in batches' for the whole restaurant). The wine list offers a package tour of the vinous world, with prices from £20.50.
Chef/s: Jonray and Peter Sanchez-Iglesias. **Open:** Sat L 12 to 2.30, Tue to Sat D 7 to 10. **Closed:** Sun, Mon, bank hols. **Meals:** Tasting menu £45 (6 courses) to £68. **Service:** not inc. **Details:** Cards accepted. 40 seats. Separate bar. No mobile phones. Wheelchair access. Music. Children allowed.

Culinaria

Bristol's culinary royals
1 Chandos Road, Redland, Bristol, BS6 6PG
Tel no: (0117) 9737999
www.culinariabristol.co.uk
Modern British | £34
Cooking score: 4

Having ruled Bristol's restaurant scene for more than three decades, Stephen and Judy Markwick are starting to think about retirement, and it seems likely that they will be calling it a day sometime in 2012. But, for now, it's business as usual at their much-loved restaurant in the city's Redland district. Stephen has always been noted for his exact fish cookery (perhaps fillet of sea bass with samphire and crab sauce), but his lively Anglo-Mediterranean menu might also promise straightforward ideas ranging from braised shoulder of mutton with pearl barley to a colourfully exotic dish of spiced duck breast with blood orange, pomegranate and star anise. To start, you might try ham hock terrine with piccalilli, while desserts could promise satisfaction in the guise of rhubarb and frangipane tart or warm rice pudding with a Muscat-poached pear. Stephen is also highly regarded as a champion when it comes to wine, and his concise list is a model of its kind – thoughtfully assembled, affordable and packed with terrific drinking from unusual sources. Prices start at £17 (£4.50 a glass).
Chef/s: Stephen Markwick. **Open:** Thur to Sat L 12 to 2, D 6.30 to 9. **Closed:** Sun to Wed, 2 weeks Christmas/New Year, 1 week spring, 2 weeks summer, 1 week autumn. **Meals:** alc (main courses £14 to £19). Set L £15.50 (2 courses) to £20. **Service:** not inc. **Details:** Cards accepted. 30 seats. 6 seats outside. No music. Wheelchair access. Children allowed.

Flinty Red

Live-wire local restaurant
34 Cotham Hill, Bristol, BS6 6LA
Tel no: (0117) 9238755
www.flintyred.co.uk
European | £25
Cooking score: 3

Friendly service from tireless staff, a well-priced, regularly changing list of interesting wines by the glass and a daily changing menu of 'tapas-style portions giving the opportunity to share and to mix dishes' is making this live-wire local restaurant a real draw. Ingredients are impeccably sourced, with praise for a platter of 'wonderful' morcilla de Bourgos with chorizo and deep-fried panisse (puréed chickpeas), as well as ricotta ravioli with sage butter, a dish of cuttlefish and monkfish with red peppers, and grilled quail with cavolo nero and porcini bread sauce. Forced rhubarb with Seville orange curd and meringue has been pronounced 'the best we had ever tasted'. Wines from £16.

Chef/s: Matthew Williamson. **Open:** Tue to Sat L 12 to 3, Mon to Sat D 6.30 to 10. **Closed:** Sun, first two weeks Jan, last week Aug. **Meals:** alc (main courses from £12 to £16). **Service:** not inc. **Details:** Cards accepted. 36 seats. Separate bar. Wheelchair access. Music. Children allowed.

Greens' Dining Room

Delightful, good-value bistro
25 Zetland Road, Bristol, BS6 7AH
Tel no: (0117) 9246437
www.greensdiningroom.com
Modern European | £30
Cooking score: 3

Hidden away in a leafy side street off the main drag, Greens' is the quintessential family-run neighbourhood bistro. Brother chefs Simon and Andrew Green stick to their seasonal style of cooking, with daily changing menus that pay homage to influences such as Elizabeth David, Jane Grigson and Claudia Roden. Despite the closely packed tables, one reporter praised the 'very relaxed setting', whilst another hailed the set menus as 'excellent value'. There is a degree of confidence in the simplicity of the cooking – for example a starter of fish soup and rouille followed by a tenderloin of pork, semolina gnocchi and thyme. Finish with fig and almond tart or hot chocolate fondant. The single-page wine list includes 18 by the glass and bottles start at an appealing £14.50. At the time of going to press we were notified Greens' was up for sale, so please check before visiting.

Chef/s: Andrew and Simon Green. **Open:** Tue to Sat L 12.30 to 2.30, D 6.30 to 10. **Closed:** Sun, Mon, 1 week Dec, last 2 weeks Aug. **Meals:** alc (main courses £9 to £12). Set L £10 (2 courses) to £21. Set D £15 (2 courses) to £29.50. **Service:** not inc. **Details:** Cards accepted. 38 seats. 16 seats outside. No mobile phones. Music. Children allowed.

Lido

Gloriously bracing setting with sunny food
Oakfield Place, Clifton, Bristol, BS8 2BJ
Tel no: (0117) 9339533
www.lidobristol.com
Mediterranean | £28
Cooking score: 3

What has to be one of the singular dining experiences of the region sees a vibrant modern glass-walled restaurant overlooking the pool of a Victorian lido and spa complex. It's as gloriously bracing a setting as it sounds, and the food is full of the piquancy and freshness of sunnier climes than Bristol can generally lay claim to. Salt cod and spinach fritters with aïoli are one way to begin, before bass with blood orange and a fennel and potato salad, or wood-roasted suckling pig with olives and rosemary. One pair of satisfied customers reported that 'the hearty and warming wheatberry soup with cime di rapa (turnip tops) tasted as good as it felt wholesome, while the wet rice dish was better than anything you might find in Barcelona'. House Spanish is £16.50.

Chef/s: Freddy Bird. **Open:** all week L 12 to 3, Mon to Sat D 6.30 to 10. **Meals:** alc (main courses £15 to £18). Set L and D £15 (2 courses) to £20. **Service:** not inc. **Details:** Cards accepted. 90 seats. 60 seats outside. Separate bar. No mobile phones. Wheelchair access. Music. Children allowed.

NEW ENTRY

The Muset by Ronnie

Stylish restaurant with appealing food
12-16 Clifton Road, Bristol, BS8 1AF
Tel no: (0117) 9737248
www.ronnies-restaurant.co.uk/muset
Modern European | £30
Cooking score: 4

£5 OFF

Four years after opening Ronnies in Thornbury (see entry), Ron Faulkner has taken over the former Muset restaurant, a Clifton fixture for more than 30 years. But Muset by Ronnie couldn't be more different to its predecessor: cream leather banquettes, exposed brick walls and dark wood make the split-level restaurant feel lighter and more spacious. Closed-circuit TV feeds live footage of the kitchen to diners at the chef's table – the only table where you can also bring your own wine (a nod to the original Muset's reputation as Bristol's first BYO). The menu is concise but appealing – a starter of seared Lyme Bay scallops with garlic purée, pancetta and sage, for example, might make way for Ibérico pork chop, Hispi cabbage, celeriac coleslaw and mustard, while desserts garner praise – notably a pistachio cake with poached rhubarb, rose and yoghurt. House wines from £15.75.

Chef/s: David Underwood. **Open:** Tue to Sun L 12 to 2.30, Tue to Sat D 6 to 10 (11 Fri and Sat). **Closed:** Mon, 25 to 27 Dec, 1 to 3 Jan. **Meals:** alc (main courses £16 to £23). Set L £9.75 (2 courses) to £12.75. Set D £12.75 (2 courses) to £15.75. Sun L £16 (2 courses) to £19. **Service:** 12.5% (optional). **Details:** Cards accepted. 72 seats. Separate bar. Wheelchair access. Music. Children allowed.

riverstation

Big, sunny flavours by the harbour
The Grove, Bristol, BS1 4RB
Tel no: (0117) 9144434
www.riverstation.co.uk
Modern European | £30
Cooking score: 3

£5 OFF

A 1950s river-police station provides the minimalist setting for this evergreen bar and kitchen on Bristol's harbourside. Wood, steel and glass feature heavily in both the downstairs bar and the upstairs restaurant, and both levels have terraces with harbour views. In the restaurant, the partially open kitchen turns out Mediterranean-inspired food such as ravioli of slow-cooked hare with lentil broth and caramelised salsify, followed by rack of Wiltshire lamb with persillade, flageolet bean 'hummus' and ratatouille. The big flavours may not be to everyone's taste; one diner felt a nice piece of grey mullet was overpowered by its herb crust, but a 'delicious' dessert of vanilla and almond tart with fruit coulis and clotted cream put that meal back on course. The international wine list includes some good half-bottles. Bottles start at £14.95.

Chef/s: Peter Taylor. **Open:** all week L 12 to 2.30 (3 Sun), Mon to Sat D 6 to 10 (10.30 Wed and Thur, 11 Fri and Sat). **Closed:** 25 and 26 Dec. **Meals:** alc (main courses £13 to £22). Set L £12.75 (2 courses) to £15.50. Set D £14.75 (2 courses) to £18.50. Sun L £19.50. **Service:** not inc. **Details:** Cards accepted. 120 seats. 20 seats outside. Separate bar. No music. Children allowed.

Rockfish Grill

Star-spangled seafood and more
128-130 Whiteladies Road, Bristol, BS8 2RS
Tel no: (0117) 9737384
www.rockfishgrill.co.uk
Seafood | £33
Cooking score: 4

One of Mitch Tonks' latest ventures (see also the Seahorse, Dartmouth), the Rockfish is the restoration and rejuvenation of a former FishWorks site. Star-spangled seafood –

delivered daily from Brixham – continues to be the attraction and the menu promises top-drawer renditions of the classics (fish soup, whole Devon crab with mayonnaise, fried cod with chips), plus a sprinkling of the unusual: devilled monkfish livers is a simple but unusual starter and worth ordering if it's on, or there could be cuttlefish cooked in ink with fried polenta. Main course fish (and a couple of far-from-token meat dishes) are often simply cooked over the charcoal fire, perhaps wild black bream roasted on the bone with herbs and garlic, or ribeye of local beef with béarnaise sauce. La Fromagerie keeps the cheese lobby happy, or try date pudding with clotted cream. Wines from £17. A further branch is at 8 South Embankment, Dartmouth, Devon; tel: (01803) 832800.
Chef/s: Jake Platt. **Open:** Tue to Sun L 12 to 2.30, Tue to Sat D 6 to 10. **Closed:** Mon, 25 and 26 Dec, 1 Jan. **Meals:** alc (main courses £12 to £26). Set L and early D £12.50 (2 courses) to £15. **Service:** not inc. **Details:** Cards accepted. 52 seats. Music. Children allowed.

Cheltenham

Le Champignon Sauvage

Thrilling tastes from a high-achiever
24-26 Suffolk Road, Cheltenham, GL50 2AQ
Tel no: (01242) 573449
www.lechampignonsauvage.co.uk
Modern French | £59
Cooking score: 8

Fast approaching their quarter-century in Cheltenham, David and Helen Everitt-Matthias have steadily forged a commanding reputation in the West Country and beyond. The old 'mushroom' retains something of the feel that upscale neighbourhood restaurants had in the late 80s – bright, spacious surroundings, abstract art and a midnight-blue colour scheme, with tables clothed in full-length napery; a contrast to the white walls, bare floorboards and absence of linen that are today's norm. David's cooking has accrued confidence and panache through the years – so that although some dishes may have become finely crafted stalwarts of the regionally based menus, they can still dazzle. Glowing reports come in for the starter of scallops with pumpkin in chestnut velouté, garnished with chestnut and white balsamic caramel, and the main-course fillet of zander with razor clams, tuber and chervil purée and verjus syrup – dishes that exhibit a sophisticated culinary intelligence. Local game might turn up in the form of red-legged partridge with a purée of boletus mushrooms and stuffed cavolo nero. Flavours such as liquorice, fennel and bergamot confer a very grown-up aura on the desserts: the fabled chocolate and olive tart with fennel ice cream still elicits rave reviews. Even more memorable has been a coconut macaroon served with iced coconut milk and lotus-seed ice cream. Reporters are increasingly perturbed by the straightjacketed approach to service. Breads are fabulous, but take a long while to arrive; all the more exasperating when the first course follows almost immediately, and the overall pace is exceedingly sedate. It's worth lingering over the wine list, which is an admirable, user-friendly document, teeming with good growers at mark-ups that are by no means frightening. House selections start at £15, and there are plenty of half-bottles.
Chef/s: David Everitt-Matthias. **Open:** Tue to Sat L 12.30 to 1.15, D 7.30 to 8.30. **Closed:** Sun, Mon, 10 days Christmas, 3 weeks Jun. **Meals:** Set L and Tues to Fri D £26 (2 courses) to £32. Sat D £48 (2 courses) to £59. **Service:** not inc. **Details:** Cards accepted. 40 seats. Separate bar. No music. No mobile phones. Children allowed.

Please send us your feedback

To register your opinion about any restaurant listed in the Guide, or a new restaurant that you wish to bring to our attention, please visit the web address at the bottom of the page. Your feedback informs the content of the book and will be used to compile next year's reviews.

Lumière

Cutting-edge cooking
Clarence Parade, Cheltenham, GL50 3PA
Tel no: (01242) 222200
www.lumiere.cc
Modern British | £44
Cooking score: 4

 **V**

The unassuming frontage on a busy road close to Cheltenham's central bus station certainly hasn't hindered the progress of Jon Howe and Helen Aubrey's intimate and cutting-edge restaurant since they took over in 2009. Service here is 'calm and understated', with Helen and her small team skilfully avoiding cliché or stuffiness. The purple hues and leather banquettes add an elegance to the relaxed contemporary room, which forms a contrasting backdrop to Jon's bold and innovative cooking. An 'ingenious' starter of foie gras teamed with fig purée, honeycomb, Amaretto jelly and gingerbread was 'exciting, surprising and sublime', according to one contented recipient, while others have praised a 'delicious' main course of local Butts Farm hogget cooked three ways and served with a rich lamb jus. A 'beautifully presented' poached rhubarb, hibiscus sorbet, caramelised filo, ginger and yoghurt pannacotta is typical of the noteworthy desserts. The serious wine list starts at £19.

Chef/s: Jon Howe. **Open:** Wed to Sat L 12 to 1.45, Tue to Sat D 7 to 9. **Closed:** Sun, Mon, 2 weeks Jan, 2 weeks summer. **Meals:** Set L £20 (2 courses) to £24. Set D £38 (2 courses). Tasting menu L £44, D £55. **Service:** not inc. **Details:** Cards accepted. 28 seats. No mobile phones. Music.

Symbols

- Accommodation is available
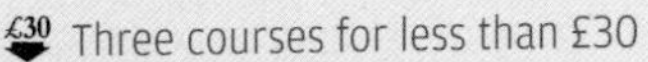
- Three courses for less than £30
- V Separate vegetarian menu
- £5-off voucher scheme
- Notable wine list

The Royal Well Tavern

Tucked-away bistro with seasonal food
5 Royal Well Place, Cheltenham, GL50 3DN
Tel no: (01242) 221212
www.theroyalwelltavern.com
Modern British | £26
Cooking score: 4

The restaurant is housed in a former pub, tucked away close to the town's central bus station and a short walk from the Promenade. With its partially open kitchen, highly polished dark wood and curving banquettes, the look and feel is that of 'smart pub meets French brasserie'. Since stepping up to the role of head chef a few years ago, Andrew Martin has stamped his authority on the menu, which majors in gutsy bistro-style dishes delivered with the minimum of fuss. Start with confit duck, chorizo and chickpea salad or half a pint of North Atlantic prawns, before moving on to hake, roast fennel, broad beans and brown shrimps. To finish, blueberry clafoutis arrives with crème Chantilly, or you could choose raspberry and almond tart. The attractively priced set deal is a popular lunchtime and early-evening choice. The concise and well-chosen French wine list starts at £16.

Chef/s: Andrew Martin. **Open:** Mon to Fri L 12 to 3, D 5 to 9.30 (10.30 Fri), Sat 12 to 10.30. Sun 10 to 4. **Meals:** alc (main courses £10 to £18). Set L and early D £10 (2 courses) to £12.50. Sun L £14 (2 courses) to £16. **Service:** 10% (optional). **Details:** Cards accepted. 50 seats. Separate bar. Wheelchair access. Music. Children allowed.

ALSO RECOMMENDED

▲ Brosh

8 Suffolk Parade, Cheltenham, GL50 2AB
Tel no: (01242) 227277
www.broshrestaurant.co.uk
Eastern Mediterranean £5 OFF

Former Moro chef Raviv Hadad's chilled-out restaurant remains a Cheltenham favourite, thanks to its original take on Mediterranean, North African and Middle Eastern cooking. The extensive selection of mezze dishes are popular options, as are standout carte choices of chicken liver with sherry and honey, garlic sourdough bruschetta (£6.75) and roast Gressingham duck breast, ginger basmati pilaf, pistachio and pomegranate (£18.95). Fragrant desserts include almond and rum tart with fig compote. Wines from £13.95. Open Wed to Sat D.

READERS RECOMMEND

The Daffodil

Modern British

18-20 Suffolk Parade, Cheltenham, GL50 2AE
Tel no: (01242) 700055
www.thedaffodil.com

'A lovely, Art Deco style 1920s venue. The service was second to none – the waiters and waitresses were attentive and their timing was superb.'

Chipping Campden

ALSO RECOMMENDED

▲ Eight Bells Inn

Church Street, Chipping Campden, GL55 6JG
Tel no: (01386) 840371
www.eightbellsinn.co.uk
Modern British

A buzzing honeypot hostelry in the heart of Chipping Campden, the fourteenth-century Eight Bells scores with its flagstone floors, mighty stone walls, winter fires and summer terraced garden. Honest pub cooking at reasonable prices is the deal, featuring traditional fish and chips, deep-filled chicken and leek pie (£13.50), medallions of pork with caramelised apples, lyonnaise potatoes and a grain mustard jus, and good old sticky toffee pudding (£6) among desserts. Wines from £14.50. Accommodation. Open all week.

Readers Recommend

A 'readers recommend' review is a genuine quote from a report sent in by one of our readers. We intend to follow up these suggestions throughout the year to come.

Cirencester

Made by Bob

Buzzing Italian eatery/deli

The Corn Hall, Unit 6, 26 Market Place, Cirencester, GL7 2NY
Tel no: (01285) 641818
www.foodmadebybob.com
Mediterranean | £25
Cooking score: 3

£5 OFF £30

After working in respected London restaurants such as Bibendum (see entry), chef Bob Parkinson has settled in the Cotswolds, where his modern Italian cooking has proved a big hit with locals. They are drawn by the precise, uncluttered cooking, which has now expanded into dinner on selected evenings. 'The place buzzes', noted one reporter although such popularity has resulted in long waits for tables and some haphazard service. From the daily changing menu, a bold, satisfying starter of fish soup with rouille, Gruyère and croûtons may be followed by squid, lemon, caper and parsley risotto. Many dishes are also available to take home from the deli. A short, accessible wine list starts at £16.

Chef/s: Bob Parkinson. **Open:** Mon to Sat L 12 to 3, Thur and Fri D 7 to 9.30. **Closed:** Sun, 25 and 26 Dec. **Meals:** alc (main courses £11 to £17). **Service:** not inc. **Details:** Cards accepted. 42 seats. Wheelchair access. Music. Children allowed.

Coln St Aldwyns

The New Inn

Wide-ranging pub food
Main Street, Coln St Aldwyns, GL7 5AN
Tel no: (01285) 750651
www.new-inn.co.uk
Modern British | £30
Cooking score: 2

£5 OFF

This traditional sixteenth-century coaching inn plays host to tourists, walkers and locals in equal measure and looks every inch the old-fashioned English country pub, with its creeper-clad frontage, rambling interior, beams and flagstone floors. The menu is wide-ranging, with deli boards of charcuterie, seafood or cheese, pub favourites like fish and chips or sausage, mash and onion gravy, and more imaginative offerings of, say, pressed pigeon and confit rabbit terrine ahead of gilthead bream fillet with capers, new potatoes and tomato and spring onion salsa. For afters, perhaps orange-scented pannacotta. House wine is £8.50.

Chef/s: Darren Bartlett. **Open:** all week L 12.30 to 2.30 (3 Sun), D 7 to 9 (9.30 Fri and Sat). **Meals:** alc (main courses £12 to £19). **Service:** not inc. **Details:** Cards accepted. 54 seats. 80 seats outside. Separate bar. Music. Children allowed. Car parking.

Compton Abdale

ALSO RECOMMENDED

▲ The Puesdown Inn

Compton Abdale, GL54 4DN
Tel no: (01451) 860262
www.puesdown.cotswoldinns.com
Modern British £5 OFF

This Cotswold stone inn with period features aplenty now plies its trade as a smart pub/restaurant. Light lunch dishes and pizzas give way to seasonal evening menus with a strong Mediterranean influence, where tried-and-tested ideas like warm salad of chicken livers with raspberry vinegar dressing (£5.50), roast cod in a light curry sauce or rump of lamb with dauphinoise potatoes and a tian of courgette and aubergine (£16.50) are typical choices. Finish with glazed lemon tart. House wine £13.50. No food Sun.

Corse Lawn

Corse Lawn House Hotel

A bastion of quiet excellence
Corse Lawn, GL19 4LZ
Tel no: (01452) 780771
www.corselawn.com
Anglo-French | £35
Cooking score: 3

V

Where other restaurants might draw attention to themselves by leaping on and off bandwagons, the Corse Lawn ploughs a less dramatic furrow – 'the menu hasn't changed much in decades, but who cares?' observes one fan. Consistent low-key excellence marks them out. Simplicity and precision keep the cooking finely balanced, delivering exemplary chicken liver parfait, whole roast flounder on the bone with tartare sauce, as well as 'fantastic roast lamb carved off the bone' and a 'wonderful' vanilla pannacotta with poached plums for Sunday lunch. Whether in the bistro or restaurant, you always get efficient, but not intrusive, service. Choice and price in both are much the same, but there is more flexibility in the bistro, with the possibility of light snacks. And then there's the wine list, with its in-depth coverage of aristocratic French regions, and a fair selection from further afield. It's all excellent value, starting at £18.

Chef/s: Andrew Poole and Martin Kinahan. **Open:** all week L 12 to 2, D 7 to 9.30. **Closed:** 24 to 26 Dec. **Meals:** alc (main courses £13 to £23). Set L £22.95 (2 courses) to £25.95. Set D £33.50. Sun L 25.95. Set bistro L and D £15 (2 courses) to £20. **Service:** not inc. **Details:** Cards accepted. 45 seats. 45 seats outside. Separate bar. No music. Wheelchair access. Children allowed. Car parking.

Didmarton

ALSO RECOMMENDED

▲ The Kings Arms

The Street, Didmarton, GL9 1DT
Tel no: (01454) 238245
www.kingsarmsdidmarton.co.uk
British £5 OFF

The bar dispenses real ale and drinkers are made welcome, but value-for-money cooking is the thing at this seventeenth-century Cotswold inn, and people come from miles around to eat here. The straightforward menu focuses on the seasonal and the hearty, illustrated by rustic dishes such as devilled kidneys (£7.25) and confit of duck leg (£12.95), alongside plenty of local game – possibly pigeon with black pudding and apple chutney, and venison casserole with 100 per cent chocolate. House wine £14.95. Open all week.

Ebrington

ALSO RECOMMENDED

▲ The Ebrington Arms

Ebrington, GL55 6NH
Tel no: (01386) 593223
www.theebringtonarms.co.uk
Modern British £5 OFF

A gem of a seventeenth-century inn found in a pretty, off-the-beaten-track village, yet only two miles from Chipping Campden and the gardens at Hidcote Manor. Menus boast a few old pub favourites like steak, Guinness and mushroom pie, but the kitchen likes to up the tempo, serving a rich crab bisque with twice-baked soufflé of smoked haddock and Cheddar (£6) ahead of grilled cutlet, braised shoulder and roasted rump of Cotswold lamb (£15.50), before finishing with sherry and red berry trifle. House wine £16.50. Accommodation. Open all week.

Eldersfield

The Butchers Arms

Fiercely seasonal cooking
Lime Street, Eldersfield, GL19 4NX
Tel no: (01452) 840381
www.thebutchersarms.net
Modern British | £37
Cooking score: 4

Picture the scene: a tidy little two-room boozer in a bucolic Gloucestershire backwater, with wooden settles around a wood-burning stove and real ales tapped direct from the cask. The setting may be rose-garlanded rustic, but James Winter's food bristles with class and modern-day resolve. Local sourcing is at the heart of his commendably short, fiercely seasonal menu, whether it's Huntsham Farm pig's cheek with black pudding and Bramley apples, precisely timed loin of roe deer with celeriac purée, beetroot relish and potato galette, or gloriously tender mallard with braised red cabbage, confit goose and parsnip purée. Fish from the Cornish day-boats also shows up strongly – as in meaty monkfish wrapped in Ibérico ham alongside a sensitive pairing of scallops and lentils. This is 'extremely accomplished and assured cooking', notes an avid fan. There's also no dipping when it comes to desserts such as rich chocolate torte with toffee ice cream. The pin-sharp, 40-bin wine list opens with 10 house selections from £16 (£3.95).

Chef/s: James Winter. **Open:** Wed to Sun L 12 to 1 (bookings only) , Tue to Sat D 6 to 9. **Closed:** Mon, first week Jan, 10 days end Aug. **Meals:** alc (main courses £18 to £24). **Service:** not inc. **Details:** Cards accepted. 26 seats. Separate bar. No mobile phones. Music. Car parking.

Fairford

Allium

Inventive cooking, informed service
1 London Street, Fairford, GL7 4AH
Tel no: (01285) 712200
www.alliumfood.co.uk
Modern British | £44
Cooking score: 6
£5 OFF

'Naturally extraordinary food' is how one reader describes Allium's modernist use of keenly sourced Cotswolds produce. The dining room matches, with generously spaced mahogany tables and softening pale blues – smart, modern and bright in contrast to a traditional Cotswold stone frontage. James Graham's kitchen is inventive, yet never without reason; for instance putting local rabbit back in the field – poached loins and confit leg are served with a 'soil' of oatmeal and mushrooms from which baby carrots protrude; or slow-braised blade of beef with purple potato, enoki mushrooms, snails and crusty shards of oxtail as a vivid, edible, depiction of a stone wall. Visual memories are frequently triggered – soused sardines sitting in a roll-back tin or sticky toffee pudding moistened by a milk and Weetabix sphere. But successful dishes aren't all concept-driven; chocolate mousse, orange parfait and yogurt ice cream appeals solely on grounds of deliciousness. Such adventurous cooking requires approachable and informed service, and Erica Graham's brigade do not disappoint; their delivery of a centrepiece cheeseboard, and guidance through a wine list starting at £23 (as well researched as it is priced), come in for particular praise.

Chef/s: James Graham. **Open:** Wed to Sun L 12 to 2, Tue to Sat D 7 to 9. **Closed:** Mon, 2 weeks Jan. **Meals:** Set L £23 (2 courses) to £25.50. Set D £23 (2 courses) to £43.50. Sun L £25.50. Tasting menu £65. **Service:** not inc. **Details:** Cards accepted. 34 seats. Separate bar. No mobile phones. Music. Children allowed.

JAMES GRAHAM
Allium

What would you cook Great Britain's Olympic team?
Whatever they want if they've won gold!

Do you have a favourite local recipe or ingredient?
The local venison that I shoot myself.

What's your favourite tipple?
Peaty single malt scotch.

What do you eat when you're feeling lazy?
A sausage sandwich.

What's the best training for a chef?
Working in the best kitchen you can talk yourself into.

What's been the worst culinary trend of recent years?
Whoopie pies.

...And the best?
A return to locally sourced produce.

What's your favourite job in the kitchen?
Butchery.

What is your favourite food combination?
Chicken and thyme.

Hotwells

NEW ENTRY

The Pump House

Flawless flavours from a foraging champ
Merchants Road, Hotwells, BS8 4PZ
Tel no: (0117) 9272229
www.the-pumphouse.com
Modern British | £30
Cooking score: 3

This former Victorian pumping station is perched on the waterfront where Bristol's city docks meet the river Avon. Toby Gritten concentrates on bold, well-defined seasonal flavours and is also a keen forager, as can be seen from the jars of pickles on the wooden dresser next to the bar. Grab one of the scrubbed pine tables or relax on squishy sofas with bar snacks such as Butcombe beer and Barkham Blue rarebit. Alternatively, get to grips with the carte, which might kick off with a well-composed dish of hot-cured mackerel with pickled Yorkshire rhubarb, Serrano ham and watercress purée, followed by a precisely cooked butter-roast John Dory with black pudding and palourde clams. Desserts include sticky toffee pudding and warm bitter chocolate fondant. Wines start at £17.

Chef/s: Toby Gritten and Tony Casey. **Open:** all week L 12 to 3, D 7 to 9.30. **Closed:** 25 Dec. **Meals:** alc (main courses £15 to £19). **Service:** 10% (optional). **Details:** Cards accepted. 70 seats. 70 seats outside. Separate bar. No mobile phones. Wheelchair access. Music. Car parking.

Please send us your feedback

To register your opinion about any restaurant listed in the Guide, or a new restaurant that you wish to bring to our attention, please visit the web address at the bottom of the page. Your feedback informs the content of the book and will be used to compile next year's reviews.

Lower Oddington

The Fox Inn

Sturdily agreeable pub food
Lower Oddington, GL56 0UR
Tel no: (01451) 870555
www.foxinn.net
British | £26
Cooking score: 1

£5 OFF V £30

The Fox is as traditionally English as it gets – warm and welcoming, with beams, open fires and stone-flagged floors. Despite a change at the stoves the sourcing of good raw materials remains a priority and the kitchen distinguishes itself with honest effort. Tarragon potted shrimps makes a good start, then, perhaps, braised oxtail with cannellini beans in a rich red wine sauce or pancetta-wrapped baked hake served with a parsley sauce. Desserts are along the lines of sticky toffee pudding and crème brûlée. Wines from £18.

Chef/s: Phil Carter. **Open:** all week L 12 to 2.30 (3.30 Sun), D 6.30 to 10 (7 to 9.30 Sun). **Closed:** 25 Dec. **Meals:** alc (main courses £11 to £18). **Service:** not inc. **Details:** Cards accepted. 85 seats. 100 seats outside. Separate bar. No music. Children allowed. Car parking.

Northleach

ALSO RECOMMENDED

▲ The Wheatsheaf Inn

West End, Northleach, GL54 3EZ
Tel no: (01451) 860244
www.cotswoldswheatsheaf.com
Modern British

Run by the team behind the Royal Well Tavern in Cheltenham (see entry), this seventeenth-century coaching inn is situated on the edge of Northleach's pretty market square. Although it still attracts the locals for a pint of ale by the open fire, foodies flock here for the modern British grub. Typical dishes include wild mushrooms and snails on toast (£5) and Butts Farm faggots with mashed potatoes, chutney and red wine (£10). End, perhaps, with lemon tart. House wine is £16. Open all week.

Sapperton

The Bell at Sapperton

Well-groomed dining destination
Sapperton, GL7 6LE
Tel no: (01285) 760298
www.foodatthebell.co.uk
Modern British | £30
Cooking score: 3

This well-groomed stone-built Cotswold village pub was taken over by Paul Davidson and Pat LeJeune in 1999 and it has remained a well-patronised dining destination ever since. Christopher Lee took over at the stoves just after last year's Guide went to press and reports suggest that he has quickly stamped his authority in the kitchen. He has also extended the pub's commitment to the careful sourcing of prime ingredients, from rare-breed beef and pork to olive oil produced by a local family at their Greek olive groves. Starters include Belted Galloway beef carpaccio with baby capers, shallots and shaved Parmesan, while mains could feature the likes of fillet of Loch Duart salmon with saffron butter sauce and braised fennel. Wines start at £17.50.
Chef/s: Christopher Lee. **Open:** all week L 12 to 2.15 (2.30 Sat, 3 Sun), D 7 to 9.30 (9 Sun). **Closed:** 25 Dec. **Meals:** alc (main courses £12 to £24). **Service:** not inc. **Details:** Cards accepted. 65 seats. 65 seats outside. No music. No mobile phones. Wheelchair access. Car parking.

Southrop

The Swan at Southrop

Stand-out-from-the-crowd cooking
Southrop, GL7 3NU
Tel no: (01367) 850205
www.theswanatsouthrop.co.uk
Modern British | £28
Cooking score: 4

'When I'm away I look forward to coming back and going to the Swan, I like it that much', enthused one local; another noted 'we eat there a lot despite having moved slightly out of the area'. The lure is a rambling interior kitted out with style and flair, plus open fires, 'superb service with friendly smiles' and Sebastian Snow's cooking, which stands out from the crowd not least because he starts with high-quality, often local, raw materials. His style is at once classical yet contemporary, embracing potted haddock and Melba toast alongside a less usual partnership of skillet-roast foie gras with fried duck egg, balsamic vinegar and brioche. Lamb, pearl barley and leek pudding or sea trout with pea and bacon compote might follow, then a well-kept selection of unpasteurised British cheeses, and desserts such as blood orange and Campari jelly with Jersey clotted cream and candied peel. House wine is £14.
Chef/s: Sebastian Snow. **Open:** all week L 12 to 3, Mon to Sat D 6 to 10. **Closed:** 25 Dec, bank hols. **Meals:** alc (main courses £13 to £19). Set L and D (Mon to Fri) £13.50 (2 courses) to £17.50. **Service:** not inc. **Details:** Cards accepted. 75 seats. 24 seats outside. Separate bar. No mobile phones. Children allowed.

Stow-on-the-Wold

The Old Butcher's

Straight-talking big flavours
7 Park Street, Stow-on-the-Wold, GL54 1AQ
Tel no: (01451) 831700
www.theoldbutchers.com
Anglo-European | £25
Cooking score: 3

Apart from the name itself, there are few reminders of the building's previous life; inside all is sleek and contemporary, with unbuttoned vibes, swathes of glass and smart furnishings. Peter Robinson is a straight-talking chef who deals in big, beefy flavours, sometimes pulling ideas from the British tradition, sometimes looking abroad for ideas. His soups are a hit (Jerusalem artichoke adorned with foie gras, say), and he keeps the home crowd happy with brawn on toast, slip sole with chips or Old Spot pork chop with fennel, garlic and parsley. Those with a taste for Landaise salad, venison pappardelle or brandade of cod with poached egg also come away replete, while sweet-toothed diners can pick anything from baked Alaska to apple and Calvados crumble. House Duboeuf is £15.

Chef/s: Peter Robinson. **Open:** all week L 12 to 2.30, D 6 to 9.30 (10 Sat, 7 to 9 Sun). **Closed:** 1 week May, 1 week Oct. **Meals:** alc (main courses £14 to £19). **Service:** not inc. **Details:** Cards accepted. 45 seats. 12 seats outside. Wheelchair access. Music. Children allowed.

Tetbury

The Chef's Table

Terrific French-inspired deli/bistro
49 Long Street, Tetbury, GL8 8AA
Tel no: (01666) 504466
www.thechefstable.co.uk
French | £33
Cooking score: 4

Spread over two floors of a one-time antiques emporium, Michael Bedford's terrific deli-cum-bistro brings some culinary savoir-faire to the streets of Tetbury. Perch beside the counter and watch the goings-on in the open kitchen, or stake your claim at one of the pine tables. Rustic French food without compromise is the deal, and the menu lays down an emphatic marker with bowls of Marseilles-style bouillabaisse, onion tarte Tatin and plates of charcuterie with baked Brie. A generous streak also runs through mains of grilled ribeye with fries and béarnaise, genuine chicken Kiev and slow-braised oxtail with dauphinoise potatoes and buttered Savoy cabbage. Fish varies with the market – perhaps line-caught Cornish ling with grilled leeks, garlic mash and warm hazelnut dressing – and the uncluttered approach extends to desserts such as blood orange jelly with chocolate ganache. Don't miss the cracking array of European cheeses with pickled grapes either. House 'plonk' is £16.50.

Chef/s: Michael Bedford. **Open:** Mon to Sat L 12 to 2.30, Wed to Sat D 7 to 9.30. **Closed:** Sun, 25 and 26 Dec, 1 Jan. **Meals:** alc (main courses £16 to £22). **Service:** not inc. **Details:** Cards accepted. 55 seats. Music. Children allowed.

Thornbury

Ronnies

Low-key gem
11 St Mary Street, Thornbury, BS35 2AB
Tel no: (01454) 411137
www.ronnies-restaurant.co.uk
Modern European | £35
Cooking score: 3

Bare stone walls, warm lighting and modern artwork make for a relaxed, stylish setting in this popular restaurant tucked away in a shopping precinct. Owner Ronnie Faulkner 'always makes himself known and is on hand to make sound recommendations regarding the wine', while well-drilled staff provide 'excellent' service. The please-all menu offers everything from roast cannon of lamb with a herbed crust, creamed leeks and rosemary jus, through to Moroccan spiced nut roast with honey-roasted parsnips, salsify and butternut squash purée. A starter of 'fall-apart' roasted belly pork delighted one diner, as did the 'superb flavours and presentation' of a sea bass main course. Desserts centre on favourites such as apple, rhubarb and ginger crumble. A nicely annotated wine list starts at £15.

Chef/s: George Kostka. **Open:** Tue to Sun L 10 to 3, Tue to Sat D 6.30 to 11. **Closed:** Mon. **Meals:** alc (main courses £13 to £22). Set L £9.75 (2 courses) to £12.75. Set D £16 (2 courses) to £19. **Service:** not inc. **Details:** Cards accepted. 72 seats. 30 seats outside. Wheelchair access. Music. Children allowed.

Upper Slaughter

Lords of the Manor

Blissful bolt-hole with dynamic dishes
Upper Slaughter, GL54 2JD
Tel no: (01451) 820243
www.lordsofthemanor.com
Modern French | £65
Cooking score: 6

£5 OFF

If, stuck in traffic, you dreamed up an escape to a country house retreat of honeyed stone somewhere in the Cotswolds, it would look pretty much exactly like this seventeenth-century rectory with its walled gardens, stretching parkland and lake. The dining room, in muted buffs and beiges, is restful, but it's the scene for some dynamic culinary action from Matt Weedon. A fixed-price menu of around half-a-dozen choices per course is now the centrepiece, although the six-course tasting menu continues. There is an enjoyable sense of intricacy in compositions such as smoked wood pigeon breast with braised pork pastilla, salt-baked beetroot, apple and onion crackling dressed in sherry vinegar, or scallops with butternut squash, pancetta, truffled gnocchi and Parmesan – dishes that do their job of creating a sense of anticipation about what's to come. That might be sea bass with hand-rolled macaroni and a langoustine in a shellfish essence with truffle foam, or perhaps loin of venison from a local estate, served with a portion of the liver, in a sauce energised with spiced Valrhona chocolate and port. Desserts keep up the pace with kalamansi soufflé, accompanied by lime tea mousse and piña colada ice cream. An exemplary wine list uncoils over the globe with breathtaking generosity of coverage, taking in England's best sparklers, regional Italian specialities and plenty of classic claret. Bottles start at £18, small glasses at £5.50.

Chef/s: Matt Weedon. **Open:** all week L 12 to 2, D 7 to 9.30. **Meals:** Set D £65. Sun L £40. Tasting menu £75 (7 courses) to £99 (10 courses). **Service:** 10% (optional). **Details:** Cards accepted. 50 seats. Separate bar. No music. No mobile phones. Children allowed. Car parking.

Weston Subedge

NEW ENTRY

The Seagrave Arms

Stylish inn with confident local food
Friday Street, Weston Subedge, GL55 6QH
Tel no: (01386) 840192
www.seagravearms.co.uk
Modern British | £25
Cooking score: 3

£5 OFF £30

Rescued from closure and spruced up in style during 2010, this listed Georgian coaching inn stands on the edge of the Cotswolds not far from Chipping Campden. Inside it puts on a classy show, with leather armchairs in the bar and candles on old dining tables. The kitchen buys wisely from farms and producers in the region for a repertoire of confident modern dishes, so expect the likes of partridge and polenta terrine with confit garlic, braised rabbit with Dijon mustard or Lighthorne lamb's sweetbreads with smoked chorizo, lemon salad and almond pesto on the well-balanced menu. Fish specials are listed on a board, and desserts might promise hot chocolate and hazelnut fritters. Drinkers have local ales to sup, as well as some decent wines (from £15.50).

Chef/s: Kevin Harris. **Open:** Tue to Fri L 12 to 3, D 6 to 9.30. Sat and Sun 12 to 9.30. **Closed:** Mon, second week Jan. **Meals:** alc (main courses £12 to £18). **Service:** not inc. **Details:** Cards accepted. 36 seats. 20 seats outside. Separate bar. No music. Wheelchair access. Children allowed. Car parking.

Winchcombe

5 North Street

Pint-sized eatery with stellar food
5 North Street, Winchcombe, GL54 5LH
Tel no: (01242) 604566
www.5northstreetrestaurant.co.uk
Modern European | £60
Cooking score: 6

V

The Ashenfords' comfortingly homely but high-achieving place commands great loyalty. 'It's about a 40-minute drive for me, but I consider myself extremely fortunate to have such a superb restaurant so close', says one fan. The restaurant is a 400-year-old timbered building, all low beams, with a tiled fireplace and lobster-coloured walls. It's run with great warmth out front by Kate, while Marcus is in charge of the foodie fireworks. His style is a dynamic mix of influences, as in an opening dish that combines roast monkfish with a parsnip purée seasoned with ras el hanout, alongside pak choi and pickled pineapple in a dressing of curry and vanilla oil. That might lead on to a presentation of local game with chestnut choucroute, caramelised pumpkin, crisp kale and a reduction of port and juniper, although beef fillet – as is usually the way – is treated more classically than anything else, with wild mushrooms, baby onions and mash in truffle essence. A trio of chocolate desserts delivers up a slice of marquise with a 'seriously intense chocolate hit', a tiny cup of fluffy 'cappuccino' and a scoop of sorbet, all united by a boozy, prune-based sauce. The wine list confines itself to a few choices from each of the main regions, with prices from £21.

Chef/s: Marcus Ashenford. **Open:** Wed to Sun L 12.30 to 1.30, Tue to Sat D 7 to 9. **Closed:** Mon, 2 weeks Jan, 1 week Aug. **Meals:** alc (main courses £20 to £23). Set L £22 (2 courses) to £26. Set D £38 (3 courses) to £48. Sun L £32. **Service:** not inc. **Details:** Cards accepted. 26 seats. Music. Children allowed.

Wesley House

Lively, confident British cooking
High Street, Winchcombe, GL54 5LJ
Tel no: (01242) 602366
www.wesleyhouse.co.uk
Modern European | £38
Cooking score: 3

Medieval to the core, this cherished town-centre hotel was built as a merchant's house in 1435. The building may breathe antiquity, but the food has a modern accent, with the cooking picking up a trend here and there but always allowing ingredients to dictate proceedings. Readers relish everything they are offered, from a goats' cheese fondue enlivened by a blood orange, chicory, French bean and hazelnut salad, and tender fillet of beef served with celeriac, potato purée, forest mushrooms and Madeira sauce, to sticky toffee pudding with toffee sauce and vanilla ice cream. A simpler menu is available in the next-door bar and grill, say sharing platters of charcuterie or cheese, plus fishcakes, duck confit et al. Wines from £16.

Chef/s: Martin Dunn. **Open:** all week L 12 to 2, Mon to Sat D 7 to 9.30 (10 Fri and Sat). **Meals:** alc (main courses £17 to £27). Set L £12.95 (2 courses) to £15.95. Set D £19.95 (2 courses) to £24.95. Sun L £20. **Service:** not inc. **Details:** Cards accepted. 70 seats. Separate bar. No mobile phones. Music. Children allowed.

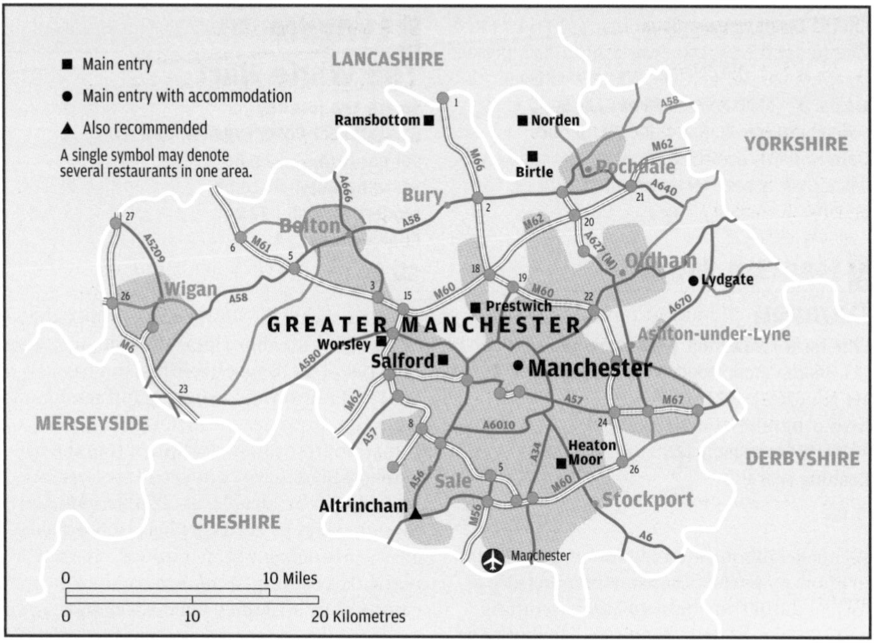

■ Main entry
● Main entry with accommodation
▲ Also recommended
A single symbol may denote several restaurants in one area.

Altrincham

ALSO RECOMMENDED

▲ Dilli

60 Stamford New Road, Altrincham, WA14 1EE
Tel no: (0161) 9297484
www.dilli.co.uk
Indian

Many consider Dilli to be south Manchester's best Indian by far, because its kitchen is devoted to faithfully recreating traditional regional cooking. Here are street snacks from Delhi, Mumbai and Kolkata – perhaps jhaal moori (spicy puffed rice, roasted peanut and channa dhal mix) served with spicy chutneys (£4.95), ginger-marinated lamb chops baked in the tandoor, a slow-cooked lamb dish from Kashmir (£9.99) and seafood infused with coconut milk and spices. Service is 'friendly but a bit haphazard'. Wines from £12.95. Open all week.

Birtle

The Waggon at Birtle

Hearty grub in a one-time pub
131 Bury and Rochdale Old Road, Birtle, BL9 6UE
Tel no: (01706) 622955
www.thewaggonatbirtle.co.uk
Modern British | £25
Cooking score: 2

It was once a no-nonsense roadside boozer, but the Waggon's pubby exterior now hides a crisp, clean-lined restaurant dealing in gutsy Brit-influenced dishes. Local ingredients and hearty flavours show up well, from steak sandwiches and shepherd's pie at lunchtime to a terrine of 'Pugh's piglets' with chorizo and quince chutney or loin of rabbit wrapped in Parma ham with spring onion mash for dinner. Fish also gets a good airing (perhaps a salad of crab with fennel, samphire and citrus oil), while seasonal puds could feature peach and apricot pavlova or raspberry shortbread with elderflower cream. Wines start at £13.80.

Chef/s: David Watson. **Open:** Thur and Fri L 12 to 2, Wed to Sat D 6 to 9.30, Sun 12.30 to 7.30. **Closed:** Mon, Tue, 26 Dec to 3 Jan, 2 weeks summer. **Meals:** alc (main courses £9 to £22). Set D £14.95 (2 courses) to £16.95. Sun L £10.50. **Service:** not inc. **Details:** Cards accepted. 50 seats. Separate bar. Wheelchair access. Music. Children allowed. Car parking.

Heaton Moor

Damson

Chic local restaurant with imaginative food
113 Heaton Moor Road, Heaton Moor, SK4 4HY
Tel no: (0161) 4324666
www.damsonrestaurant.co.uk
Modern European | £28
Cooking score: 2

A chic neighbourhood restaurant decked out in plummy purple, Damson offers 'suburban formal dining' in a 'relaxed and welcoming environment'. The 'unfailingly delicious' food has a modern European bent, with influences running all the way from Scandinavia (gravadlax) to France (roast rump of lamb with flageolet beans, pancetta and vegetable hash) and occasionally reaching farther east, as in a main course of pan-fried halibut with wilted Asian greens, Bombay potatoes, aubergine chutney and red lentil dressing. Caramelised pain perdu with roasted pear, honeycomb, Earl Grey jelly and honey and yoghurt ice cream typifies the imaginative desserts. A 'superb, elegantly described' wine list offers a broad selection of trophy winners and exclusive names at very fair prices – look for the Champagne Lallier and Valenciso Rioja Reserva by the glass. Bottles start at £13.95.

Chef/s: Simon Stanley. **Open:** all week L 12 to 3 (7.30 Sun), Mon to Sat D 5.30 to 9.30 (10 Fri and Sat). **Closed:** 25 and 26 Dec, 1 Jan. **Meals:** alc (main courses £11 to £30). Set L and D £13.95 (2 courses) to £16.95. **Service:** not inc. **Details:** Cards accepted. 80 seats. 20 seats outside. Separate bar. Music. Children allowed.

Lydgate

The White Hart

Worth the journey
51 Stockport Road, Lydgate, OL4 4JJ
Tel no: (01457) 872566
www.thewhitehart.co.uk
Modern British | £28
Cooking score: 4

High up where the mist meets the hills, the White Hart sits above local rivals in more ways than one. This long-established inn has accommodation and a slightly stiff restaurant added on, but since the menu is the same throughout, the best place to eat is in the bar-cum-brasserie. Two comfortable rooms are looked after by capable, unfazeable staff, and though the pub classics are here, some dishes are surprisingly global in outlook. Starters are particularly strong; a smoked haddock Scotch egg comes with a spicy square of chorizo and a well-matched sweet red pepper sauce, while poached ballottine of salmon, flecked with herbs, has hot, crisp crayfish fritters and light parsley mayonnaise. Mains might be plaice with brown shrimp butter or a roast rump of lamb with a powerful broth and slippery rosemary dumplings. Desserts take in traditional toffee pud or fragrant mango soufflé. A friendly, well-annotated wine list starts at £15.50, but drinkers should note that beer is well kept, too.

Chef/s: Paul Cookson. **Open:** Mon to Sat L 12 to 2.30, D 6 to 9.30. Sun 12.30 to 8. **Closed:** 26 Dec, 1 Jan. **Meals:** alc (main courses £14 to £25). Set L £14.50. Sun L £19.95. **Service:** not inc. **Details:** Cards accepted. 44 seats. 40 seats outside. Separate bar. Wheelchair access. Music. Children allowed. Car parking.

Manchester

NEW ENTRY

Australasia

Cool Pan-Asian proposition
1 The Avenue, Spinningfields, Manchester, M3 3AP
Tel no: (0161) 8310288
www.australasia.uk.com
Pan-Asian | £37
Cooking score: 2

Occupying one of the most successful basement locations known to Manchester, Australasia is a pan-Asian proposition with a laid-back attitude. Be-denimed staff serve a long, cool, light room full of attractive beach house-style booths. Drinkers cluster at the bar (there's a DJ), while the other end is dominated by a glassed-in kitchen. At inspection, early shine had dulled a little, leaving the greasiness of a tempura soft-shell crab and the chlorophyll flavours of barramundi with Japanese parsley exposed. Sushi is good, though, and a mango soufflé pudding wonderfully theatrical. The wine list, brought to the table on an iPad, isn't restricted to the New World and starts at £17.
Chef/s: Carl Ryder. **Open:** Mon to Thur L 12 to 3, D 5 to 10.30. Fri to Sun 12 to 10.45. **Meals:** alc (main courses £14 to £45). **Service:** not inc. **Details:** Cards accepted. 150 seats. Separate bar. Wheelchair access. Music. Children allowed. Car parking.

The French at the Midland Hotel

Decades of ritual and splendour
16 Peter Street, Manchester, M60 2DS
Tel no: (0161) 2363333
www.qhotels.co.uk
Anglo-French | £47
Cooking score: 2

This is where Manchester people go for an occasion – the chandeliered, gloriously old-fashioned dining room is an opulent bubble stuffed with polished glassware and endless silver. Some find it oppressive, especially the level of formality during service, which 'isn't to everybody's modern taste'. Paul Beckley cooks some fancy-pants dishes – organic salmon tartare with cucumber jelly, quail's egg and caviar; lemon sole with crab linguine and shellfish cream – although not all of it musters enthusiasm. But for fans it's a 'real experience', a 'fantastic venue, which should be sampled at least once'. The wine list opens at £23.50.
Chef/s: Paul Beckley. **Open:** Tue to Sat D only 7 to 10.30. **Closed:** Sun, Mon, bank hols. **Meals:** alc (main courses £23 to £38). **Service:** not inc. **Details:** Cards accepted. 40 seats. Separate bar. Wheelchair access. Music. Children allowed.

The Gallery Café

An unusually good café
Whitworth Art Gallery, Oxford Road, Manchester, M15 6ER
Tel no: (0161) 2757497
www.themoderncaterer.co.uk
Modern British | £12
Cooking score: 2

£5 OFF £30

Dubbed the 'Tate of the North', the Whitworth Art Gallery is renowned for its collection of British watercolours, but also draws visitors with its unusually good café, owned by local foodie champion Peter Booth. The simple, snappy menu opens with breakfast, then progresses to lively international dishes such as Turkish-style meatballs with plum tomatoes and roast potatoes, aloo gobi with cucumber raita and chapati, or char-grilled chicken salad with spinach, guacamole, crispy bacon and lemon. There's also a selection of sandwiches and wraps, plus an imaginative children's menu. Wines are priced from £12 a bottle.
Chef/s: Volkan Alkur. **Open:** Mon to Sat L 11.30 to 3.30, Sun 12 to 2.30. **Closed:** 23 Dec to 2 Jan. **Meals:** alc (main courses £8 to £9). **Service:** not inc. **Details:** Cards accepted. 38 seats. 24 seats outside. No music. No mobile phones. Wheelchair access. Children allowed. Car parking.

Greens

Adventurous, well-loved veggie
43 Lapwing Lane, West Didsbury, Manchester, M20 2NT
Tel no: (0161) 4344259
www.greensdidsbury.co.uk
Vegetarian | £24
Cooking score: 2

Simon Rimmer records 22 years of supporting the vegetarian cause in 2012, and the fact that his restaurant has stood the test is cause for celebration. 'I love Greens, I am not vegetarian but I love going there, you never feel like you are missing out on meat', is a typical comment from reporters who appreciate startling combinations such as rice noodle salad with peanuts, radish, beansprouts and pickled ginger with hot Vietnamese nuoc cham dressing and gentler interpretations like leek, thyme and roasted squash cannelloni with cream and white wine sauce. Chips, chocolate pots and service also get the thumbs up. House wine is £13.75.

Chef/s: Simon Rimmer. **Open:** Tue to Sun L 12 to 2 (3 Sat, 12.30 to 3.30 Sun), all week D 5.30 to 10.30. **Closed:** bank hols. **Meals:** alc (main courses £11 to £13). Set L £10.50 (2 courses). Set D £17.50. Sun L £17.50. **Service:** not inc. **Details:** Cards accepted. 80 seats. Music. Children allowed.

The Lime Tree

Long-running Didsbury trouper
8 Lapwing Lane, West Didsbury, Manchester, M20 2WS
Tel no: (0161) 4451217
www.thelimetreerestaurant.co.uk
Modern British | £29
Cooking score: 3

Many of the Lime Tree's hardcore supporters have been coming to this Didsbury trouper for more than 20 years, lured by its sunny disposition, open-minded menus and easy prices. Most agree that it still delivers the goods, although occasional references to 'sloppy food' and 'mediocre service' suggest it may struggle at peak times. A host of dishes have been recommended, from plump moules marinière and goats' cheese tart with balsamic onion confit to a three-part combo involving pigeon breast, black pudding (an earthy slice of Lancashire's finest) and a nugget of belly pork as fine as anything in Chinatown. To follow, seared sea bass with a salmon fishcake, asparagus, tomato and basil sauce has been more convincing than rather ersatz coq au vin, while iced rum-and-raisin parfait should satisfy any sweet cravings. The clued-up, contemporary wine list has been assembled with quality and value in mind. House selections start at £13.95 (£4.75 a glass) and 'wines of the month' are a terrific bonus.

Chef/s: Jason Parker. **Open:** Tue to Fri and Sun L 12 to 2.30, all week D 5.30 to 10 (10.30 Fri and Sat, 9 Sun). **Closed:** 25 and 26 Dec, 1 Jan. **Meals:** alc (main courses £12 to £22). Set L and early D £13.95 (2 courses) to £15.95. Sun L £17.95. **Service:** not inc. **Details:** Cards accepted. 75 seats. 20 seats outside. Music. Children allowed.

Michael Caines at ABode Manchester

Smooth city-centre dining
107 Piccadilly, Manchester, M1 2DB
Tel no: (0161) 2005678
www.michaelcaines.com
Modern European | £44
Cooking score: 4

£5 OFF V

Reporters have been quick to spot the change of chef at Michael Caines' hallmark restaurant and to praise the 'fantastic food' and 'really splendid dining experience'. But then Mark Rossi is no stranger to ABode hotels – he cooked at the Canterbury branch (see entry) for a number of years, and now brings his considerable skills to the Manchester kitchen. He starts with sound ingredients and balances their flavours with judgement, thanks in part to some tried-and-tested Caines signature dishes, from duck liver teamed with pickled rhubarb and lemongrass jelly to best end of Cheshire lamb with a lamb brochette, spring vegetables, fondant potato and roasting juices.

But there's also warm salad of quail with celeriac, apple, hazelnut, smoked bacon and fried quail's egg, and wild sea bass with razor clam, lemon purée, samphire, baby fennel and herb oil, alongside 'perfect' glazed lemon tart and a host of popular fixed-price deals. Wines from £23.

Chef/s: Mark Rossi. **Open:** Mon to Sat L 12 to 3, D 6 to 10. **Closed:** Sun, 26 to 30 Dec. **Meals:** alc (main courses £23 to £26). Set L £13.50. Set D £16.95 (2 courses) to £24. **Service:** 12% (optional). **Details:** Cards accepted. 74 seats. Separate bar. No mobile phones. Wheelchair access. Music. Children allowed.

Second Floor

Modish food and voguish wine
Harvey Nichols, 21 New Cathedral Street, Manchester, M1 1AD
Tel no: (0161) 8288898
www.harveynichols.com
Modern European | £40
Cooking score: 4

'A great way to relieve the stresses of shopping', quipped one reporter who found himself among the ladies who lunch, deal-brokering suits and fashionistas at this sleek dining room on the second floor of Harvey Nicks, where plate-glass windows look out towards Exchange Square and Manchester's very own Wheel. Chef Stuart Thomson deals in complex, 'competition-style' food with lots of modish touches, but the results are sharp and satisfying. The drill is to assemble your own fixed-price menu from a pool of on-trend combos that might include rabbit ravioli with black pudding, carrot and rabbit foam ahead of slow-cooked venison with beetroot purée and choucroute, or rainbow trout with parsley risotto and smoked macadamia nuts. Meanwhile, arty desserts such as chocolate 'four ways' or Earl Grey pannacotta with orange sabayon chime perfectly with the aspirational surroundings. The pulse-quickening, cosmopolitan wine list is voguish enough for any Mancunian oenophile, but also puts its weight behind gilt-edged Champagnes and pedigree names from the classic regions. Harvey Nicks' own-label house selections start at £19, and prices are fair across the board – you can even nip over to the nearby shop 'to check the mark-ups'.

Chef/s: Stuart Thomson. **Open:** all week L 12 to 3 (4 Sun), Tue to Sat D 6 to 9.30. **Closed:** 25 Dec, 1 Jan, Easter Sun. **Meals:** Set L and D £30 (2 courses) to £40. **Service:** 10% (optional). **Details:** Cards accepted. 60 seats. Separate bar. Wheelchair access. Music. Children allowed.

READERS RECOMMEND

Tandoori Flame

Indian
483 Barlow Moor Road, Chorlton, M21 8AG, Manchester
'Run by a local Sikh family...the food is absolutely fantastic, in particular a long list of Punjabi specials and amazing breads.'

The Marble Arch

British
73 Rochdale Road, Manchester, M4 4HY
Tel no: (0161) 8325914
'What a great place...lovely pub, the food was very good.'

Norden

Nutters

Menus with a sense of adventure
Edenfield Road, Norden, OL12 7TT
Tel no: (01706) 650167
www.nuttersrestaurant.co.uk
Modern British | £34
Cooking score: 3

A Georgian manor house in over six acres of parkland, overlooking Ashworth Moor, is home to Andrew Nutter's highly individual venue. On a clear day, please note, you can see Jodrell Bank. It's run with friendliness and enthusiasm, and there is a sense of adventure about the menus. As one loyal regular summed it up, 'much of the food is locally sourced and there is real passion in the cooking and combination of ingredients'. An inventive approach to fish might see brill dressed in lemon and cashew pesto, and served with pearl barley and smoked haddock cream sauce, while slow-braised pork belly might be accompanied by rumbledethumps (crisp-cooked cabbage, potato and onion) in a red wine reduction. Finish with raspberry cheesecake. An enterprising list opens with Gascon house wines at £14.65.

Chef/s: Andrew Nutter. **Open:** Tue to Sun L 12 to 2 (4 Sun), D 6.30 to 9.30 (8 Sun). **Closed:** Mon, 1 or 2 days after Christmas and New Year. **Meals:** alc (main courses £17 to £23). Set L £13.95 (2 courses) to £16.95. Gourmet D £40 (6 courses). Sun L £22.50. **Service:** not inc. **Details:** Cards accepted. 146 seats. Separate bar. No mobile phones. Wheelchair access. Music. Children allowed. Car parking.

Prestwich

Aumbry

Upmarket cooking in cottagey surroundings
2 Church Lane, Prestwich, M25 1AJ
Tel no: (0161) 7985841
www.aumbryrestaurant.co.uk
British | £34
Cooking score: 4

 **V**

'Unforgettable' and 'amazing' Aumbry defies its unassuming setting ('a rather run-down area of Prestwich') to deliver upmarket cooking in smart cottagey surroundings. Co-owner and chef Mary-Ellen McTague has stints at the Fat Duck and local big-hitter ramsons (see entries) under her belt, but resists anything fancy here in favour of patriotic dishes done with precision and charm. Game casserole with a rosemary scone kicks off a winter tasting menu, while an 'excellent value' lunch opens with black pudding Scotch egg with mushroom relish and tomato ketchup. Wild Cumbrian venison with parsnip purée, roast beets and thyme and juniper dumplings is a typically comforting main, and a dessert of treacle tart with lemon jelly and Earl Grey ice cream sums up the nostalgic, classy approach perfectly. With just 26 seats it's a pint-sized gem, but there are plans to expand the kitchen and then the menu. A balanced, international selection of 70-plus wines opens at £15.

Chef/s: Mary-Ellen McTague and Laurence Tottingham. **Open:** Wed to Sun L 12 to 2.30 (4 Sun), Wed to Sat D 7 to 9.30. **Closed:** Mon, Tue, 25 and 26 Dec, first 2 weeks Jan. **Meals:** alc (main courses £15 to £22). Sun L £17.50 (2 courses) to £21.50. Sun L £20.50 (2 courses) to £25.50. Tasting menu £55. **Service:** 10% (optional). **Details:** Cards accepted. 26 seats. No mobile phones. Wheelchair access. Music. Children allowed.

Ramsbottom

Hideaway

A little beauty
16-18 Market Place, Ramsbottom, BL0 9HT
Tel no: (01706) 822005
www.ramsons-restaurant.com
Italian | £23
Cooking score: 1

Louise Varley's cellar Hideaway is just that: a self-styled 'enoteca con cucina' tucked snugly beneath ramsons (see entry). There is nothing unduly ostentatious about the operation; simplicity is evident in a no-choice menu that begins with a sharing plate of 'wonderful' antipasti (fish, meat and cheese) and extends to soups (minestrone or broccoli and Stilton), then the likes of slow-cooked shoulder of lamb with rosemary potatoes and mixed green vegetables, before the option of 'wonderfully creamy' pannacotta or Italian cheeses – or both. Drinking is courtesy of ramsons' glorious wine cellar, with bottles from £21.

Chef/s: Louise Varley. **Open:** Tue to Thur D 7 to 8.30, Fri and Sat 8 (1 sitting). **Closed:** Sun and Mon, 25 and 26 Dec, 1 Jan. **Meals:** Set midweek D £15 (2 courses) to £18. Set D £23 (4 courses) to £26 (5 courses). **Service:** not inc. **Details:** Cards accepted. 20 seats. Music. Children allowed.

★ WINE LIST OF THE YEAR ★

ramsons

Dazzling Italian fine dining
16-18 Market Place, Ramsbottom, BL0 9HT
Tel no: (01706) 825070
www.ramsons-restaurant.com
Italian | £38
Cooking score: 6

£5 OFF

Chris Johnson has been wowing Ramsbottom since the mid-1980s. His restaurant may have undergone several transmutations since that era, but he has always ploughed an idiosyncratic furrow, carrying the torch for quality produce and the fine art of food and wine matching. The present incarnation of ramsons is its most successful to date, an exploration of Italian fine dining dazzlingly rendered by chef Abdulla Naseem. Highlights for one reporter included a wonderfully earthy wild mushroom soup with truffle infusion ('I would have been content eating that for the next two hours'), and a trio of full-flavoured lamb cuts – loin, belly and kidney – with silky dauphinoise. Great panache is brought to the Italian staples, such as a prawn and squid risotto with grilled monkfish in parsley sauce, or the pumpkin purée and intense Marsala sauce that accompany roast veal. Choose your allegiance at cheese stage with either an artisan Piedmontese or seasonal British selection, before subsiding into textbook pannacotta with raspberry coulis or, more unusually, treacle tart with Earl Grey ice cream. To match the food, Chris Johnson has accrued a peerless cellar of handpicked wines from Italy's regional vineyards. His knowledge, passion and sheer commitment show in every bottle, with pithy summaries and illuminating descriptions offering guidance for novices and experts alike; his personal recommendations are also beyond reproach. Prices start at £21.
Chef/s: Abdulla Naseem. **Open:** Wed to Sun L 12 to 2.30 (1 to 3.30 Sun), Tue to Sat D 7 to 9. **Closed:** Mon, 26 Dec, 1 Jan. **Meals:** Set L £10 (1 course) to £32. Set D £32 (2 courses) to £40. Sun L £31. **Service:** not inc. **Details:** Cards accepted. 34 seats. No mobile phones. Music. Children allowed.

Sanmini's

Authentic South Indian flavours
Carrbank Lodge, Ramsbottom Lane, Ramsbottom, BL0 9DJ
Tel no: (01706) 821831
www.sanminis.com
Indian | £30
Cooking score: 3

£5 OFF **V**

'We have two of the best restaurants in the north-west, right here in Ramsbottom', noted a proud local, referring not only to Dr Mini Sankar's South Indian restaurant, but also to nearby ramsons (see entry). Housed in a nineteenth-century gatehouse, Sanmini's is by no means a curry house. The cooking is authentic and the menu reads well; half is vegetarian and there's prowess in every department, from the poppadoms and vibrant chutneys that crank up the palate, via 'tiffin' specialities, including idli (rice cakes) with thick lentil sambar and fresh masala dosa with spicy potato filling, to distinctive versions of prawn masala and mutton Madras. There are plans to introduce Indian wine, otherwise house Australian is £13.95.
Chef/s: Sundara Moorthy and Mr Sathyanand. **Open:** Tue to Sun L 12 to 2.30, D 6.30 to 9.30 (10.30 Fri to Sun). **Closed:** Mon, 2 weeks Jan. **Meals:** alc (main courses £8 to £14). Sun L £17.50. Theme menu £29.50. **Service:** not inc. **Details:** Cards accepted. 40 seats. Separate bar. No mobile phones. Wheelchair access. Music. Children allowed.

Please send us your feedback

To register your opinion about any restaurant listed in the Guide, or a new restaurant that you wish to bring to our attention, please visit the web address at the bottom of the page. Your feedback informs the content of the book and will be used to compile next year's reviews.

Salford

The Mark Addy

Comfort food by the river
Stanley Street, Salford, M3 5EJ
Tel no: (0161) 8324080
www.markaddy.co.uk
British | £24
Cooking score: 2

Billed as Manchester's original riverside pub (but found across the border in Salford), this Victorian hostelry remains robustly unsusceptible to fashion. Robert Owen Brown's menu fits the bill, listing the kind of comfort food everybody likes to eat: devilled kidneys on toast, beef and oyster suet pudding, pork belly, ribeye steak with duck-fat chips. Black pudding potato cake (with a soft poached egg) has been described as 'nicely-conceived and executed, a bit like a Lancashire twist on corned beef hash', and the regional theme continues at dessert with Eccles cake served with Lancashire cheese. Good value extends to the wine list, where bottles start at £13.50.

Chef/s: Robert Owen Brown. **Open:** all week L 12 to 3, D 5 to 10. **Closed:** 26 Dec to 2 Jan. **Meals:** alc (main courses £9 to £14.50). Set L and D £18 (2 courses) to £22.50. Sun L £10.50. **Service:** not inc. **Details:** Cards accepted. 80 seats. 40 seats outside. Music. Children allowed. Car parking.

Worsley

Grenache

Popular laid-back local bistro
15 Bridgewater Road, Walkden, Worsley, M28 3JE
Tel no: (0161) 7998181
www.grenacherestaurant.co.uk
Modern British | £27
Cooking score: 2

An intimate neighbourhood venue, Grenache (named after a French wine grape) remains abidingly popular with locals. It's run with a distinctly laid-back air – slightly too much so for one or two reporters – and catches the modern bistro ambience with bare tables, gentle lighting and some well-wrought, up-to-date food. Accurately timed scallops on little discs of black pudding with sharp apple purée is a modern-day classic, as is a main course of pork fillet with wilted spinach, moreish fondant potato and a sweet berry sauce. Return to the playground for concept desserts such as bubblegum pannacotta with lime coulis and a 'jammy dodger'. House French blends, including both shades of the Grenache grape, are £12.45.

Chef/s: Ken Calder. **Open:** Sun L 1 to 6, Wed to Sat D 5.30 to 9 (9.30 Fri and Sat). **Closed:** Mon, Tue, first week Jan. **Meals:** alc (main courses £10 to £22). Set D £13.95 (2 courses) to £16.95. Sun L £9.95. **Service:** not inc. **Details:** Cards accepted. 34 seats. Separate bar. Wheelchair access. Music.

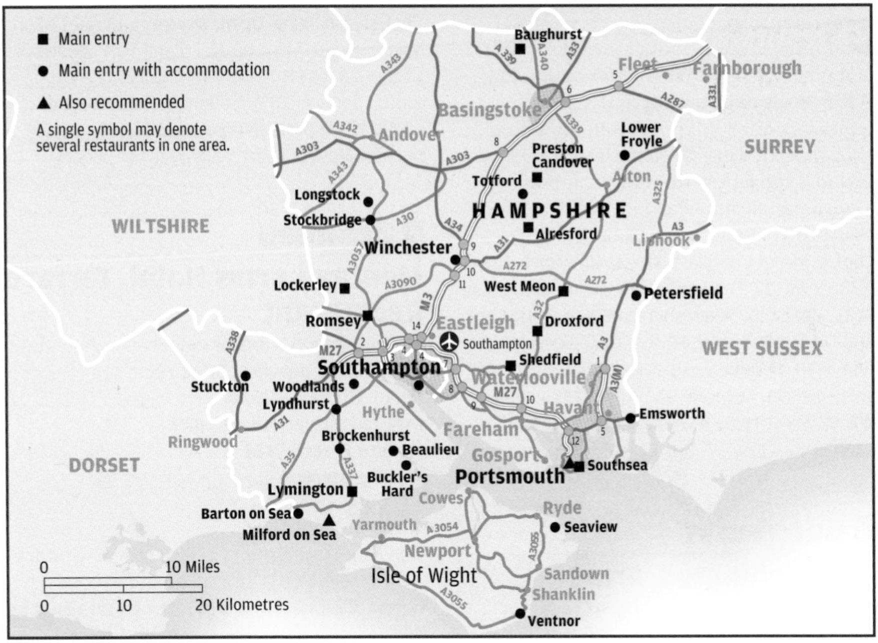

■ Main entry
● Main entry with accommodation
▲ Also recommended
A single symbol may denote several restaurants in one area.

Alresford

Caracoli

Deli/café that's a real treat
15 Broad Street, Alresford, SO24 9AR
Tel no: (01962) 738730
www.caracoli.co.uk
Modern British | £16
Cooking score: 1

Visitors enthuse about the unpretentious informality of this contemporary deli/café as much as they do about the cooking, noting that it's 'a sophisticated treat for this otherwise sleepy Hampshire market town'. Coffee and homemade cakes are a draw – one regular confesses to driving miles for a weekly fix of fruit muffins – but lunch pulls the crowds with hearty soups, twice-baked goats' cheese and watercress soufflé or smoked haddock and leek fishcakes with beurre blanc. And Sunday brunch with the morning papers is just 'perfect'. Wines from £13.50. There is a branch at 168 High Street, Guildford.

Chef/s: Alex Thomelin. **Open:** all week 8.30am to 5pm (10 to 5 Sun). **Closed:** 25 and 26 Dec. **Meals:** alc (main courses £5 to £8). **Service:** not inc. **Details:** Cards accepted. 37 seats. 30 seats outside. Wheelchair access. Music. Children allowed.

Barton on Sea

Pebble Beach

Glorious clifftop eatery
Marine Drive, Barton on Sea, BH25 7DZ
Tel no: (01425) 627777
www.pebblebeach-uk.com
French | £32
Cooking score: 3

 **V**

A sleek modern restaurant and café bar with classy accommodation to boot, Pebble Beach serves everything from morning pastries and lunchtime sandwiches through to a full à la carte. The breathtaking clifftop location, with views of the Needles, sets the tone for a menu rich in seafood. There's a strong French accent to offerings such as Breton-style fish soup or lamb rump with boulangère potatoes and ratatouille. Simpler choices include a selection from the char-grill and 'lighter options' like Asian crispy duck salad. Finish with the familiar comforts of sticky toffee pudding or chocolate fondant. The lengthy wine list includes specialities from the Campillo vineyard in Spain, where Pebble Beach has its own cellar. House wines from £16.55.

Chef/s: Pierre Chevillard. **Open:** all week L 11 to 2.30 (3 Sat, 12 to 3 Sun), D 6 to 11 (6.30 to 10.30 Sun). **Meals:** alc (main courses £13 to £44). Set L and D £24.50 (2 courses) to £31.50. **Service:** 10% (optional). **Details:** Cards accepted. 90 seats. 40 seats outside. Separate bar. No mobile phones. Wheelchair access. Music. Children allowed. Car parking.

Baughurst

The Wellington Arms

Mellow vibes and seriously good food
Baughurst Road, Baughurst, RG26 5LP
Tel no: (0118) 9820110
www.thewellingtonarms.com
Modern British | £25
Cooking score: 4

There's a sense of true dedication about Jason King and Simon Page's bucolic pub-with-rooms, which is noted for its mellow vibes and seriously good food. An industrious kitchen produces daily menus packed with sharp, seasonal dishes built around local ingredients (from home-grown pumpkin flowers to Hampshire Downs lamb) – although Med flavours give the food its real kick, as in a summery starter of gazpacho of home-grown tomatoes, cucumbers and red peppers with extra virgin olive oil. The quality also shows in homespun dishes such as 'perfect' mushrooms on toast, dab with caper butter sauce or home-reared roast rack of pork with crackling, crushed potatoes and apple sauce. To finish, reporters have praised apple and honey sponge in a home-made custard. Service is simply 'fantastic' and the short, wide-ranging wine list starts at £22.

Chef/s: Jason King. **Open:** all week L 12 to 2 (4 Sun), Mon to Sat D 7 to 9.30 (6 Fri and Sat). **Meals:** alc (main courses £11 to £19). Set L £15.75 (2 courses) to £18.75. **Service:** 10% (optional). **Details:** Cards accepted. 22 seats. 20 seats outside. No mobile phones. Music. Children allowed. Car parking.

Beaulieu

Montagu Arms Hotel, Terrace Restaurant

Intriguing food worth a detour
Palace Lane, Beaulieu, SO42 7ZL
Tel no: (01590) 612324
www.montaguarmshotel.co.uk
Modern French | £55
Cooking score: 6

£5 OFF V

The Montagu Arms is a seventeenth-century red-brick inn that lurks deep in the New Forest National Park. In a setting that could be the backdrop for a Midsomer Murder or three, the Terrace dining room is all wood panelling, layers of chintz and flounce, ornately framed mirrors and gorgeous table appointments. Matthew Tomkinson rises to the stately occasion with menus founded on game and pork from the New Forest, fish from the south coast, and vegetables and herbs from the hotel's kitchen garden. It's cooking that comes with a high degree of technical gloss and immaculate presentational skills, seen in dishes like a starter of slow-cooked oxtail and celeriac 'lasagne' with buttered spinach and horseradish cream, followed perhaps by grilled sea bass with braised onions, Jerusalem artichoke purée, sauté potatoes and smoked bacon sauce. Neat detailing includes the guinea fowl Kiev that comes with its roast breast, alongside curly kale and a mushroom purée. Attractive dessert combinations take in dark chocolate délice with praline, lavender ice cream and burnt orange syrup. A French-led wine list aims for value, with bottles from £23 (£5.75 a glass).

Chef/s: Matthew Tomkinson. **Open:** Wed to Sun L 12 to 2.30, Tue to Sun D 7 to 9.30. **Closed:** Mon. **Meals:** alc (main courses £32 to £35). Set L £19 (2 courses) to £25. Sun L £29.50. Tasting menu £75. **Service:** not inc. **Details:** Cards accepted. 50 seats. 30 seats outside. Separate bar. No mobile phones. Wheelchair access. Music. Car parking.

Brockenhurst

The Pig

Kitchen garden pickings
Beaulieu Road, Brockenhurst, SO42 7QL
Tel no: (01590) 622354
www.thepighotel.co.uk
Modern British | £30
no score

As we went to press, the Pig, formerly the Simply at Whitley Ridge, was taken over by Robin Hutson (co-founder of the original Hotel du Vin group). It represents the first in a proposed collection of mid-market, boutique country hotels where the emphasis will be on food produced by the hotel's kitchen garden, supplemented by local supplies and foraged pickings. James Golding remains as chef and it is expected that his unadorned brasserie style of cooking will continue. Reports please.
Chef/s: James Golding. **Open:** all week L 12 to 2.30 (3 Sun), D 6.30 to 9.30 (10 Fri and Sat). **Meals:** alc (main courses £14 to £22). Set L £12.50 (2 courses) to £19.50. Set D £15 (2 courses) to £30. Sun L £25. **Service:** 12.5% (optional). **Details:** Cards accepted. 70 seats. 60 seats outside. Separate bar. No mobile phones. Wheelchair access. Children allowed. Car parking.

Buckler's Hard

The Master Builder's

Versatile venture with river views
Buckler's Hard, SO42 7XB
Tel no: (01590) 616253
www.themasterbuilders.co.uk
Modern British | £30
Cooking score: 2

Grab a window table if you fancy taking full advantage of the views over the river Beaulieu from this revitalised eighteenth-century residence, once home to shipbuilder extraordinaire Henry Adams. Part of Lord Montagu's Estate, it attracts legions of boating types and tourists who come to quaff ales in the bar, feast on summertime BBQs or partake of some sound seasonal food. The menu may be short, but it finds room for game specials and masses of local fish – anything from bestselling Lymington crab salad to roast brill with New Forest mushrooms and artichoke purée. Start with a salad of Dorset Blue Vinny and pears; finish with rhubarb mille-feuille and custard. House wine is £14.50.
Chef/s: Neil Dowson. **Open:** all week L 12 to 2.30 (3 Sat and Sun), D 7 to 9. **Meals:** alc (main courses £13 to £19). Sun L £20. **Service:** not inc. **Details:** Cards accepted. 60 seats. 20 seats outside. Separate bar. Music. Children allowed. Car parking.

Droxford

The Bakers Arms

Deeply agreeable village inn
High Street, Droxford, SO32 3PA
Tel no: (01489) 877533
www.thebakersarmsdroxford.com
Modern British | £27
Cooking score: 3

Droxford lies in the Meon Valley, within the South Downs National Park. It's a picture-postcard location for the Corderys' deeply agreeable whitewashed village inn, with its exposed brickwork, tiled floor, plain wood tables and blackboard menus. Chef Richard Harrison mixes robust tradition (a bowl of onion soup, perhaps, followed by a chicken and mushroom pie with mash and gravy) with techniques from further afield. So you could start with smoked salmon pappardelle with garlic and Parmesan butter, and go on with slow-cooked crispy duck leg with polenta and damson sauce. Then treat yourself with chocolate and fudge brownie and butterscotch ice cream, or take a punt on the regional cheese selection. House wines are £14.95.
Chef/s: Richard Harrison. **Open:** Tue to Sun L 12 to 2, Tue to Sat D 7 to 9. **Closed:** Mon. **Meals:** alc (main courses £13 to £18). Set L and D £13. Sun L £14.95.

Service: not inc. **Details:** Cards accepted. 40 seats. 20 seats outside. No music. Children allowed. Car parking.

Emsworth

Fat Olives

Delightful restaurant with sunny food
30 South Street, Emsworth, PO10 7EH
Tel no: (01243) 377914
www.fatolives.co.uk
Modern British | £33
Cooking score: 3

Fat, juicy olives naturally set the ball rolling at Lawrence and Julia Murphy's delightful little restaurant in a converted fisherman's cottage, and they taste all the better with a few hunks of home-baked bread. Lawrence's cooking runs with the seasons and takes full advantage of the local catch for some forthright, Med-inspired dishes: seared scallops with butternut squash purée and pickled raisins sounds intriguing, but you might also find grilled lemon sole with brown shrimp, caper and lemon risotto on offer. Meat fans could pick a salad of roast pigeon, duck gizzard and watercress before rabbit pie with roasted loin and mustard sauce, while those with a sweet tooth get ample pleasure from, say, fig and almond terrine or dramatic feats of spun sugar and fancy saucing. Around 50 global wines start at £13.95.
Chef/s: Lawrence Murphy. **Open:** Tue to Sat L 12 to 1.45, D 7 to 9.15. **Closed:** Sun, Mon, 1 week Christmas, 1 week Feb, 2 weeks Jun. **Meals:** alc (main courses £15 to £23). Set L £17.50 (2 courses) to £19.50. **Service:** not inc. **Details:** Cards accepted. 24 seats. 10 seats outside. Wheelchair access. Music. Children allowed.

36 On The Quay

Alluring restaurant-with-rooms
47 South Street, Emsworth, PO10 7EG
Tel no: (01243) 375592
www.36onthequay.co.uk
Modern French | £52
Cooking score: 6

Pitched right by Emsworth's cobbled quayside, Ramon and Karen Farthing's alluring restaurant-with-rooms sits happily within the confines of a seventeenth-century cottage overlooking the water. Given the location, it's no surprise that fish plays a starring role on the succinct menu: scallops are regularly endorsed (perhaps served on caponata with roasted red peppers, Parmesan crisps and a smooth potato cream), while a piece of roasted turbot might appear in company with steamed pork 'échine', shimeji mushrooms and baby leeks. By contrast, meat is given more robustly traditional treatment – as in beef fillet with gently braised shin, caramelised baby onions, thyme-spiked mushrooms and red wine sauce. Ramon's trademark technical prowess and intricate, labour-intensive approach resurface at the end, with fruity assemblages including a much admired 'lemon selection' involving creamy mousse, a hot soufflé and warm tart with contrasting garnishes. But for all its charm and intimacy, issues of deadly slow service are seldom far from reporters' minds: 'I nearly froze to death waiting for food in my cold corner of the dining room', confessed one poor soul. Luckily, the wine list should help distract the palate if time is dragging: it's a terrific read, with a host of interesting names, offbeat producers and fine vintages from around the world. The style-driven layout encourages astute food matching, and prices are commendable across the range. Seasonal selections start at £17.95 (£4.95 a glass).
Chef/s: Ramon Farthing. **Open:** Tue to Sat L 12 to 1.45, D 6.45 to 9.30 (6.30 Fri and Sat). **Closed:** Sun, Mon, 24 to 26 Dec, first 2 weeks Jan, last week May, last week Oct. **Meals:** Set L £21.95 (2 courses) to £26.95. Set D £40 (2 courses) to £52. **Service:** not

inc. **Details:** Cards accepted. 50 seats. Separate bar. No music. No mobile phones. Wheelchair access. Children allowed.

Isle of Wight

NEW ENTRY

The Pond Café

Lovely little Anglo-Italian

Bonchurch Village Road, Bonchurch, Isle of Wight, PO38 1RG

Tel no: (01983) 855666

www.robert-thompson.com

Mediterranean | £30

Cooking score: 3

This intimate, informal offshoot of the Hambrough in nearby Ventnor (see entry) occupies a cute, slate-roofed stone cottage in a gorgeous location, overlooking a beautifully landscaped duck pond with the lofty, leafy escarpment of St Boniface Down providing an impressive backdrop. The kitchen puts a fashionable spin of seasonal, local and foraged ingredients with some simple Italian cooking along the lines of wild garlic ribollita (Tuscan soup), pork chop dressed with capers and parsley, and pannacotta of grappa, rhubarb and mint. A spring Sunday lunch impressed with a succession of simple dishes cooked with care and attention, notably sardine fillets on roast cherry plum tomatoes dressed with black olives, basil and rocket and a plump, bouncy-fresh slab of cod perched on a gently zesty pile of braised borlotti beans. The wine list opens at £18.

Chef/s: James Newnham. **Open:** all week L 12 to 2.30, D 6 to 9.30. **Closed:** 27 Dec to 27 Jan, 1 to 17 Nov. **Meals:** alc (main courses £11 to £24). Set L £18. Sun L £22 (2 courses) to £26. **Service:** not inc. **Details:** Cards accepted. 24 seats. 24 seats outside. Separate bar. Music. Children allowed.

Average Price

The average price listed in main-entry reviews denotes the price of a three-course meal, without wine.

Robert Thompson at the Hambrough

Astonishing food from a true artist

Hambrough Road, Ventnor, Isle of Wight, PO38 1SQ

Tel no: (01983) 856333

www.robert-thompson.com

Modern French | £55

Cooking score: 7

£5 OFF V

In a relatively short space of time Robert Thompson has reversed the fortunes of the Hambrough hotel, and turned the seaside resort of Ventnor into a premier league foodie destination. The small, smart but unfussy dining room exudes an easy, informal ambience and commands a fine view over the English Channel, while service strikes precisely the right balance: attentive and professional. Thompson's food is by turns inventive and orthodox, with a razor-sharp focus on quality. The evergreen terrine of smoked eel, foie gras, belly pork and Granny Smith apple seems a permanent fixture, but the menu evolves gradually and reflects current culinary trends in a pragmatic, often subtle, way. Dishes are enlivened with wild ingredients and showcase the best island produce, as well as fine foodstuffs from further afield. One of the highlights at inspection was a superb piece of rose veal fillet on a lip-smacking slick of bone marrow purée with lashings of rich, thyme-scented Madeira gravy alongside fat, buttery spears of white asparagus sandwiched between crunchy tuiles and spread with a tangy paste of piquillo peppers. Seafood dishes are equally enticing: gilthead bream with lasagne of crab, chilli and spring onion in a lemongrass bisque was 'the star of the night' for one reporter, while another was enraptured by a pairing of red mullet and seared scallops on a lightly dressed bed of courgette linguine with a foamy smoked garlic velouté and dollops of purple basil pesto. Desserts tend to be subtle twists on familiar themes: perhaps a classic rum baba with caramelised banana and rum-and-raisin ice cream or a magnificent tarte Tatin, paired

with an intensely aromatic cassia bark ice cream and sauced with subtly salted caramel. The mighty wine list cherry-picks top names, terroirs and varietals from across the globe, and there's real sensitivity to food matching. Selections by the glass (from £4.50) are truly eye-opening, with bottles starting at £24.
Chef/s: Robert Thompson. **Open:** Tue to Sat L 12 to 1.30, D 7 to 9.30. **Closed:** Sun, Mon, 27 Dec to 27 Jan, 18 days Nov, 11 days May. **Meals:** Set L £24 (2 courses) to £28. Set D £48 (2 courses) to £55. Tasting menu £70. **Service:** not inc. **Details:** Cards accepted. 45 seats. No mobile phones. Music. Children allowed.

NEW ENTRY

The Royal Hotel

Refined dining in an elegant setting
Belgrave Road, Ventnor, Isle of Wight, PO38 1JJ
Tel no: (01983) 852186
www.royalhoteliow.co.uk
Modern British | £40
Cooking score: 3

A regal Regency edifice of local limestone, set in attractive gardens, the Royal Hotel harks back to the *belle époque* glory days of Ventnor and retains a breezy, retro panache. Lunch in the conservatory could bring a well-executed soufflé made with the local Gallybagger cheese, a textbook lobster thermidor of generous proportions, and a creamy casserole of locally caught whiting, prawns and assorted molluscs with a dollop of butter-rich mashed potato. Dinner, a more formal affair in the cavernous Appuldurcombe Restaurant, might start with smoked breast of wood pigeon, poached rhubarb and blood orange purée, go on to best end of lamb with a dinky shepherd's pie and Savoy cabbage, and finish with a modish tasting plate riffing on chocolate. Wines from £18.
Chef/s: Alan Staley. **Open:** all week L 12 to 1.45, D 6.30 to 9.30. **Closed:** 5 to 19 Jan. **Meals:** alc (main courses £12 to £19). Sun L £29. **Service:** not inc. **Details:** Cards accepted. 120 seats. 30 seats outside. Separate bar. No music. Wheelchair access. Car parking.

The Seaview Hotel

Stylish seaside hotel with island food
High Street, Seaview, Isle of Wight, PO34 5EX
Tel no: (01983) 612711
www.seaviewhotel.co.uk
Modern British | £28
Cooking score: 2

Most readers seem to enjoy themselves at this sharply styled, vaguely nautically themed hotel just up the street from the sea. Menus lean towards seafood and brasserie favourites such as crab ramekin with baked garlic bread or pan-fried pigeon breast with a fried quail's egg, mixed garden leaves and balsamic dressing, and the kitchen favours good, seasonal produce. Poached fillet of herb-crusted cod with a spiced tomato and courgette chutney and white wine sauce is a typical main course, while spotted dick with rich custard is a comforting, old-fashioned dessert. House wine is £15.50.
Chef/s: Colby Meredith. **Open:** all week L 12 to 2.30 (3 Sat and Sun), D 6.30 to 9.30 (9.45 Fri and Sat). **Closed:** 21 to 26 Dec. **Meals:** alc (main courses £13 to £17). Sun L £19.95. **Service:** not inc. **Details:** Cards accepted. 80 seats. 30 seats outside. Separate bar. Wheelchair access. Music. Children allowed. Car parking.

Lockerley

NEW ENTRY

The Kings Arms

A cracking village local
Romsey Road, Lockerley, SO51 0JF
Tel no: (01794) 340332
www.kingsarmsatlockerley.co.uk
British | £25
Cooking score: 2

Thriving again after a period locked up and unloved, the eighteenth-century Kings Arms is now a cracking village local with an impressive new look. There's a civilised feel in the bar and adjoining dining room, with crackling winter fires, fat candles on old

dining tables, and walls plastered with local artwork setting the scene for Tim Futter's appealing modern British menus. Food is unpretentious but well-executed and draws on carefully garnered produce – asparagus with champ and local Winchester cheese, hake with niçoise salad and aïoli, and warm rice pudding with raspberry sauce are typical choices from the menu. Wine starts at £14.95.
Chef/s: Tim Futter. **Open:** all week L 12 to 2 (3 Sun), D 7 to 9. **Closed:** 25 Dec. **Meals:** alc (main courses £11 to £19). **Service:** not inc. **Details:** Cards accepted. 45 seats. 14 seats outside. Separate bar. Wheelchair access. Music. Children allowed. Car parking.

Longstock

The Peat Spade Inn

Charming, food-focused country inn
Village Street, Longstock, SO20 6DR
Tel no: (01264) 810612
www.peatspadeinn.co.uk
Modern British | £28
Cooking score: 2

An agreeable feeling of pastoral prosperity characterises this charming pub-with-rooms. It's found in Longstock, a thatched estate-village in the Test Valley, home to one of the more expensive fly-fishing 'beats' in the country, so it's no surprise that angling folk are the target audience. But the place is also food-focused and, combined with personable hospitality, it's an attractive prospect for day-trippers, too. Good pub classics such as steak and kidney pie appear at lunch, while dinner brings slow-roasted belly pork with apple purée and black pudding, and assiette of lamb (shepherd's pie, rack, sweetbreads) with parsnip purée, spring greens and young carrots. Eton mess ends things agreeably. Wines from £15.25.
Chef/s: Andy Rolfe. **Open:** all week L 12 to 2 (2.30 Sat, 3.30 Sun), D 7 to 9 (9.30 Fri and Sat). **Closed:** 25 Dec. **Meals:** alc (main courses £9 to £21). Set L Mon to Thur £19.50 (2 courses). Sun L £25. **Service:** not inc. **Details:** Cards accepted. 50 seats. 30 seats outside. Wheelchair access. Music. Children allowed. Car parking.

Lower Froyle

The Anchor Inn

Hampshire hostelry with county-brewed ales
Lower Froyle, GU34 4NA
Tel no: (01420) 23261
www.anchorinnatlowerfroyle.co.uk
Modern British | £28
Cooking score: 2

One of a trio of southern counties' pubs under the Millers Collection banner, this gussied-up Hampshire hostelry espouses 'green and pleasant' English virtues with a nod to country pursuits and the outdoor life. The kitchen looks to the locality for ingredients, but also mixes up influences in true modern British style: pork rillettes with piccalilli and watercress rubs shoulders with bruschetta of Cornish squid, while Saxon Splendour sausages line up alongside sea bass fillet with warm potato salad. Chorizo adds some spice to free-range chicken Kiev, Laverstoke mozzarella gets a good outing, and desserts might produce caramelised 'apple crumble' cheesecake. To drink, there are Hampshire-brewed ales and 50 creditable wines from £16.50.
Chef/s: Kevin Chandler. **Open:** all week L 12 to 2.30 (3 Sat, 4 Sun), D 6.30 to 9.30 (10 Fri and Sat, 7 to 9 Sun). **Closed:** 25 Dec. **Meals:** alc (main courses £12 to £22). **Service:** 10% (optional). **Details:** Cards accepted. 75 seats. 40 seats outside. Separate bar. Music. Children allowed. Car parking.

To find out more about *The Good Food Guide*, please visit www.thegoodfoodguide.co.uk

Lymington

Egan's

Unpretentious family restaurant
24 Gosport Street, Lymington, SO41 9BE
Tel no: (01590) 676165
Modern British | £30
Cooking score: 2
V

A bastion of the Lymington scene, John and Deborah Egan's unpretentious eatery is housed in a late-Victorian building that once did duty as the town's police station. Nothing disturbs the peace these days as the kitchen turns out commendable food based on carefully assembled ingredients. Menus change daily, and the style is comforting rather than assertive. Pan-fried veal sweetbreads appear atop a butternut squash risotto, monkfish and tiger prawns come dressed in a mustard sauce, and a trio of Dorset lamb is served with creamed swede, rosemary and redcurrant reduction. As for desserts, think warm pistachio tart or chocolate fondant with kumquat compote. Wines from £16.55.
Chef/s: John Egan. **Open:** Tue to Sat L 12 to 2, D 6.30 to 10. **Closed:** Sun, Mon, 2 weeks from 25 Dec. **Meals:** alc (main courses £15 to £22). Set L £14.95 (2 courses) to £17.45. **Service:** not inc. **Details:** Cards accepted. 50 seats. 20 seats outside. Separate bar. No music. Wheelchair access. Children allowed.

Lyndhurst

Lime Wood, The Dining Room

Invigorating food in a top-end destination
Beaulieu Road, Lyndhurst, SO43 7FZ
Tel no: (023) 80287167
www.limewood.co.uk
Modern British | £50
Cooking score: 6
V

Now firmly established as a boutique New Forest destination of the first order, Lime Wood comes with trademark David Collins design, a spa and two different restaurants. Top billing goes to the Dining Room – a spectacular construction of ash panelling, intricate chandeliers, leather seating and exclusive napery, with jaw-dropping views of the landscaped Italianate garden. Welcoming, knowledgeable and efficient staff do their best to leaven the mood with courteous good humour, and chef Luke Holder's stylish cooking delivers some brilliant ideas based around the produce of the region. Flavours are pure and clean, textures and flavours are true and there's proper respect for the calendar. From the very start this is invigorating stuff, as the kitchen tinges crab linguine with lemon verbena and assembles Poole Bay crab with Sopley Farm asparagus, candied apple and coriander. To follow, a seafood nage of precisely timed salmon, monkfish and turbot might vie for attention with mischievous 'Iron Aged pork' (belly and cheek with foie gras and apple) or a Med-inspired dish of rabbit with veal sweetbreads, lardo di colonnata and polenta cake. For dessert, chocolate fondant and raspberry sorbet are models of their kind, while sublime, finely judged lavender pannacotta is lifted by 'real honeycomb'. The top-end international wine list has a wealthy contingent of fancy fizz and French varietals as well as cherry-picked goodies from around the globe. Prices start at £17.50.
Chef/s: Luke Holder. **Open:** Tue to Sun L 12 to 2.30, D 7 to 10. **Closed:** Mon. **Meals:** Set L £18.50 (2 courses) to £22.50. Set D £40 (2 courses) to £50. Sun L £37.50. **Service:** 12.5% (optional). **Details:** Cards accepted. 66 seats. Separate bar. Wheelchair access. Music. Children allowed. Car parking.

Milford on Sea

ALSO RECOMMENDED

▲ The Marine

Hurst Road, Milford on Sea, SO41 0PY
Tel no: (01590) 644369
www.themarinerestaurant.co.uk
Modern British £5 OFF

A stunning new Art Deco-styled venue on the Milford seafront, the Marine has quickly nailed its populist colours to the mast. Local boy Sam Hughes moved here from the Sir Charles Napier in Oxfordshire (see entry) and

bar, although most people favour the adjoining mirrored dining rooms. Spanish chef Andres Alemany offers a colourful assortment of tapas nibbles alongside his broadly European menu, and sourcing is at a premium – whether it's Pata Negra ham from Salamanca or watercress from Alresford. Foie gras and chicken liver parfait is exemplary, fish soup is deeply flavoured, and rack of lamb is timed to perfection. The kitchen also shows its precision and flair by elevating grilled plaice with warm crab and potato salad and adorning pot-roast quails with apricots, prunes and pine nuts. For dessert, try crema Catalana or tangy lemon tart. Wines start at £14.

Chef/s: Andres Alemany. **Open:** Tue to Sun L 12 to 3 (4 Sun), Tue to Sat D 6 to 10. **Closed:** Mon, 25 and 26 Dec, bank hols excluding 1 Jan. **Meals:** alc (main courses £10 to £24). **Service:** not inc. **Details:** Cards accepted. 50 seats. 60 seats outside. Separate bar. No mobile phones. Music. Children allowed. Car parking.

Romsey

NEW ENTRY

The Three Tuns

Upbeat neighbourhood local
58 Middlebridge Street, Romsey, SO51 8HL
Tel no: (01794) 512639
www.the3tunsromsey.co.uk
British | £18
Cooking score: 2

The team behind the Chesil Rectory in Winchester (see entry) have taken on this ancient pub set snugly amid the old cottages of Middlebridge Street. They've stayed true to its pubby roots, and the open fires, dark beams and timbers are matched by simple, hearty cooking. Potted duck arrives in a Kilner jar, beef burgers on wooden boards, while specials up the ante with the likes of saddle of rabbit with black pudding, raisin purée and honey and rosemary jus. Pricing is very reasonable, portions are hearty, ingredients are good quality and the experience is totally unpretentious, as the high-tempo buzz from the bar testifies. Well-selected global wines from £15.95.

Chef/s: James Wills. **Open:** all week L 12 to 2.30 (3 Fri and Sat, 4 Sun), Mon to Sat D 6 to 9 (9.30 Fri and Sat). **Closed:** 25 Dec. **Meals:** alc (main courses £9 to £15). Sun L £12. **Service:** not inc. **Details:** Cards accepted. 60 seats. 40 seats outside. Separate bar. Wheelchair access. Music. Children allowed. Car parking.

Shedfield

Vatika

Viticulture meets the Indian new wave
Wickham Vineyard, Botley Road, Shedfield, SO32 2HL
Tel no: (01329) 830405
www.vatikarestaurant.com
Indian | £40
Cooking score: 5

Once you have recovered from the culture shock of finding a radical Indian restaurant in the verdant surroundings of a Hampshire vineyard, Vatika will begin to cast its spell. Set up by pioneering chef Atul Kochhar of Benares fame (see entry, London), it's a style-conscious and decidedly posh set-up with eye-watering prices, glorious views over the fruitful acres from the clean-lined, grey-toned dining room, and a battalion of smart staff poised for action. Forget the rather clichéd PR puffs about 'modern British food with a unique Indian twist'; instead, marvel at the chef's ability to transform, re-invent and subvert traditional flavours with prodigious culinary technique and a sensitivity to native ingredients. If you were in any doubt about the kitchen's lofty intentions, a little dish of tempura-battered prawns with lentil jelly and purée or smoked quail kebabs with stir-fried asparagus and tomato jam should set the record straight. Other ideas such as spice-cured salmon with puffed rice and cucumber cress soup, or shoulder of Laverstoke lamb with spinach gnocchi and mint yoghurt are a world away from Mumbai or Kolkata, and there's no sign of kulfi or gulab jamun when it comes to dessert: hibiscus jelly with raspberry sorbet and brûlée, anyone? Each dish is also flagged with a suggested tipple from the invigorating, ever-evolving global wine list, including an assortment of home-grown representatives from Wickham itself. Prices start at £18.

Chef/s: Jitin Joshi. **Open:** Fri to Sun L 12 to 2.15, Wed to Sat D 6 to 9.15. **Closed:** Mon, Tue, 1 Nov to 5 Feb. **Meals:** Set L and D £35 (2 courses) to £40. Tasting menu £50 (6 courses) to £75. **Service:** 12.5% (optional). **Details:** Cards accepted. 52 seats. 35 seats outside. Wheelchair access. Music. Children allowed. Car parking.

Southampton

Namaste Kerala

Affordable, vibrant South Indian food
4a Civic Centre Road, Southampton, SO14 7FL
Tel no: (023) 80224422
www.namaste-kerala.co.uk
Indian | £15
Cooking score: 1

A modest upstairs restaurant, convivial Namaste is a good bet for vibrantly flavoured South Indian cooking. There's a fascinating vegetarian selection – maybe parippu vada (crunchy lentil patties) followed by vendakka (tamarind-spike okra) or pineapple pachadi – plus a strong selection of Keralan seafood: try the 'home-style' king fish with green mango or koonthal ulathiyathu (baby squid with ginger, tomato and roasted coconut). Kormas and dhansaks please the curry-house brigade, and the handmade breads are good, too. Wines from £12.95.

Chef/s: Abdul Muneer. **Open:** all week L 12 to 2.30, D 6 to 11. **Closed:** 25 and 26 Dec. **Meals:** alc (main courses £7 to £12). Set L buffet £7.95. **Service:** not inc. **Details:** Cards accepted. 65 seats. No mobile phones. Music. Children allowed.

The White Star Tavern

Lively urban bar with on-trend dining
28 Oxford Street, Southampton, SO14 3DJ
Tel no: (023) 80821990
www.whitestartavern.co.uk
Modern British | £25
Cooking score: 2

Once a hotel for ocean-going passengers, the White Star has been creatively revamped as a self-styled 'boutique inn' with a fashionable, young-at-heart outlook, chill-out lounges and alfresco opportunities on the pavement. Leather chesterfields and retro chairs emphasise the informal all-day ethos, while the kitchen's 'on-cue' brasserie-style output ticks all the boxes. In-vogue 'small plates' are ideal for grazing or sharing (perhaps deep-fried Laverstoke Park mozzarella served with watercress pesto), while larger offerings might take in free-range Hampshire belly pork with champ cake and cider gravy, or whole Dover sole with purslane butter, foraged sea beet and fat chips. Conclude with lavender crème brûlée and shortbread. The compact global wine list sets sail with house selections at £14.50.

Chef/s: Jim Hayward. **Open:** all week L 12 to 2.30 (3 Fri, 4 Sat and Sun), D 6 to 9.30 (10 Fri and Sat, 9 Sun). **Closed:** 25 Dec. **Meals:** alc (main courses £12 to £18). **Service:** not inc. **Details:** Cards accepted. 64 seats. 26 seats outside. Wheelchair access. Music. Children allowed.

Southsea

Montparnasse

Much-loved bistro with inventive touches
103 Palmerston Road, Southsea, PO5 3PS
Tel no: (023) 92816754
www.bistromontparnasse.co.uk
Modern European | £34
Cooking score: 4

There is a genuine feeling of affection radiating from the many readers' reports we receive for this sparely but smartly decorated modern European bistro. Special occasions always seem to go with a swing, and people appreciate the inventive touches with which Nikolas Facey elevates his cooking above the standard bill of fare. Velvety soups, perhaps field mushroom with bacon and herb dumplings, come in for consistent praise, as does the belly pork, which spends 24 hours in a very gentle oven to emerge as the last word in melting tenderness, in company with butternut squash and rosemary terrine. Fish might be roasted turbot with fennel, beetroot and orange, while desserts try out ingenious compositions such as key lime parfait with lime curd and tequila jelly. Wines start at £17.50.

Chef/s: Nikolas Facey. **Open:** Tue to Sat L 12 to 1.30, D 7 to 9.30. **Closed:** Sun, Mon. **Meals:** Set L and D £31.50 (2 courses) to £36.50. **Service:** not inc. **Details:** Cards accepted. 30 seats. Music. Children allowed.

Restaurant 27

High-definition French food to rave about
27a South Parade, Southsea, PO5 2JF
Tel no: (023) 92876272
www.restaurant27.com
Modern French | £40
Cooking score: 5

The simple white building was once a chapel, which confers a certain austerity on the interior. Its plain white ambience of bare tables, high-blinded windows and muted spot-lighting is occasionally found a little underwhelming in readers' otherwise rave reviews. In former times it has attracted the Beatles while being sufficiently august for Sir Winston Churchill, but in Kevin Bingham's hands it has become a fine destination restaurant offering a high-definition version of modern French food. Fish dishes avoid lapsing into blandness with pin-sharp treatments: marinated seared tuna is accompanied by pickled vegetables, sea bass by a salt cod beignet, sweetcorn and pea velouté. There may not be much French about a serving of Hampshire lamb with bubble and squeak and black pudding, other than the finely honed proficiency of its execution, but the juxtaposition of roasted chervil roots, prunes and liquorice with the famous 30-hour belly of pork could only have been inspired from across the Channel. A reporter who was persuaded to try a nip of the Valpolicella Recioto before ordering found it an impeccable match for the chocolate brownie and cherry sauce as promised. In all, the wine list is a good little number, opening with house French blends at £19.

Chef/s: Kevin Bingham. **Open:** Sun L 12 to 2.30, Wed to Sat D 7 to 9.30. **Closed:** Mon, Tue, 25 Dec. **Meals:** Set D £40. Sun L £27. **Service:** not inc. **Details:** Cards accepted. 34 seats. Separate bar. Wheelchair access. Music. Children allowed.

Stockbridge

The Greyhound Inn

Good looks and comforting food
31 High Street, Stockbridge, SO20 6EY
Tel no: (01264) 810833
www.thegreyhound.info
Modern British | £30
new chef

This elegant fifteenth-century inn next to the river Test is set in the heart of world-famous fishing country, as the angling paraphernalia in the bar suggests. These days, the old pub is more a smart restaurant-with-rooms, despite the abundance of low beams, open fires and scrubbed-wood tables. Its relaxed style is the perfect backdrop for the comforting, uncomplicated modern brasserie food that is the Greyhound's trademark. Alan Haughie, formerly head chef at Hotel TerraVina (see entry), was due to take over the kitchen after we went to press, but it seems the compact menu complemented by blackboard specials looks set to continue – in the past pressed confit rabbit and roasted pear terrine and free-range pork loin with pork and fennel rillette have been typical offerings. There's good drinking to be had, whether it's a pint of real ale or a glass of something from the well-considered wine list, which starts at £16.

Chef/s: Alan Haughie. **Open:** all week L 12 to 2 (2.30 Fri to Sun), Mon to Sat D 7 to 9 (9.30 Fri and Sat). **Closed:** 24 to 26 Dec, 1 Jan. **Meals:** alc (main courses £12 to £21). Bar menu available. **Service:** not inc. **Details:** Cards accepted. 40 seats. 20 seats outside. Separate bar. Music. Children allowed. Car parking.

Stuckton

The Three Lions

Old-fashioned English auberge
Stuckton, SP6 2HF
Tel no: (01425) 652489
www.thethreelionsrestaurant.co.uk
Anglo-French | £40
Cooking score: 5

£5 OFF

The Three Lions was already a bastion of New Forest hospitality long before Mike and Jayne Womersley arrived in the mid 90s, and nothing much changes at this lovely old farmhouse surrounded by sylvan acres – especially when it comes to food. Chef Mike still puts his faith in the old ways, serving up goats' cheese with tomato relish or a galette of smoked haddock to start, before teasing his customers with coq au vin 'in reverse', loin of lamb 'with crispy bits' or wild turbot gilded with garlic 'scales'. Elsewhere, local game gets a seasonal airing (roe deer with chanterelles) and desserts play to a similar, well-thumbed score – hazelnut parfait with cherries and pistachio tuile is about as challenging as it gets. The food is undoubtedly of a high order, with peerless ingredients and bold flavours to the fore, but reports keep coming of ungracious, 'amateurish' service and seriously outmoded décor (think salmon-pink woodchip walls and patterned carpets). Thankfully the high-class wine list wins over doubters with its laudable selection of top-drawer stuff from elite independent producers worldwide. Prices are very fair, with plenty of fine drinking from £14.75 and masses of vintage stuff for big spenders.

Chef/s: Mike Womersley. **Open:** Tue to Sun L 12 to 2, Tue to Sat D 7 to 9 (9.30 Sat). **Closed:** Mon, last 2 weeks Feb. **Meals:** alc (main courses £18 to £25). Set L £21.50. Set D £24.50. **Service:** not inc. **Details:** Cards accepted. 60 seats. 10 seats outside. Separate bar. No mobile phones. Wheelchair access. Music. Children allowed. Car parking.

Totford

The Woolpack Inn

Stylish inn with hearty pub staples
Totford, SO24 9TJ
Tel no: (0845) 2938066
www.thewoolpackinn.co.uk
Modern British | £30
Cooking score: 2

Brian Ahearn runs this stylishly refurbished inn, restaurant and B&B with his wife Jarina. It sits on an old droving route, and the bar menu stays true to its pubby roots with a clutch of hearty staples – maybe ham, duck egg and chips, or Heineken-battered fish and chips with mushy peas and tartare sauce. In the smart, pale-walled dining room things are more refined: caramelised foie gras with Bramley apples and brioche might be followed by Candover Park partridge with sprouts, new potatoes, roasted chestnuts and bacon. Finish with vanilla rice pudding. Wines from £15.

Chef/s: Brian Ahearn. **Open:** all week L 12 to 2.30 (3 Sat and Sun), D 6.30 to 8.30 (9 Fri and Sat). **Meals:** alc (main courses £11 to £19). Set L £11.50 (2 courses) to £14.95. **Service:** 10% (optional). **Details:** Cards accepted. 76 seats. 40 seats outside. Separate bar. Music. Children allowed. Car parking.

West Meon

The Thomas Lord

Rustic charm and appealing food
High Street, West Meon, GU32 1LN
Tel no: (01730) 829244
www.thethomaslord.co.uk
British | £30
Cooking score: 2

This rural local is named after the founder of Lord's Cricket Ground, who is buried in the churchyard. It is everything a village pub should be, oozing rustic charm with beams, open fires and a laid-back vibe that draws in drinkers, dogs and walkers, while delivering a concise and appealing menu bristling with local produce. Herbs, salads and vegetables come from the garden, while meat, game and other materials are sourced from farms and artisan producers across Hampshire and southern England. This translates as potted squirrel with carrot chutney, River Test eel, leek and bacon pie with chive mash, and Cardsmill Farm lamb loin with swede purée and red wine sauce. Wines from Berry Bros & Rudd start at £15.75.

Chef/s: Gareth Longhurst. **Open:** Tue to Fri L 12 to 3, D 6 to 11, Sat and Sun 12 to 11. **Closed:** Mon, 25 Dec. **Meals:** alc (main courses £12 to £19). **Service:** 10% (optional). **Details:** Cards accepted. 70 seats. 40 seats outside. Separate bar. No music. Wheelchair access. Children allowed. Car parking.

Winchester

The Black Rat

Quirky ex-pub with accomplished cooking
88 Chesil Street, Winchester, SO23 0HX
Tel no: (01962) 844465
www.theblackrat.co.uk
Modern British | £35
Cooking score: 5

It may look like an unremarkable town boozer, but the Black Rat's interior tells a different story: every inch of the place is stuffed full of heritage and quirky eclecticism, from an inglenook and head-cracking beams to anatomical prints and shelves of legal tomes. Large oak tables add to the homely atmosphere and ease visitors gently into Chris Bailey's accomplished culinary world. Here is a chef who fills his larder with seasonal ingredients and works them up into precisely timed, imaginative dishes packed with accessible flavours. He also likes to surprise: how about a brilliant starter of wild garlic velouté with a brioche 'toastie' of Hereford snails and cep butter, or Secretts Farm asparagus with caper and sardine rillettes? Mains might include unctuous, slow-cooked daube of ox cheek, or braised pig's cheeks with morteau sausage, although one reader got his thrills from an unreformed plate of venison heart. Bailey also knows a thing or two about fish cookery – witness lemon sole with crisp polenta and shrimp velouté or 'hand-speared' plaice with Portland crab, fennel and sauce vierge. To finish, cherry blossom jelly with coconut sorbet and 'fizzy' grapes is a model of exact flavours and vivid textures. Service is youthfully efficient, and the 80-bin wine list has some appetising global pickings from £20 (£6 a glass).

Chef/s: Chris Bailey. **Open:** Sat and Sun L 12 to 2.15, all week D 7 to 9.30. **Closed:** 2 weeks Christmas, 2 weeks Easter, 1 week end of summer. **Meals:** alc (main courses £19 to £25). Set L £19.50 (2 courses) to £23.50. **Service:** not inc. **Details:** Cards accepted. 50 seats. 20 seats outside. Separate bar. Music. Children allowed.

The Chesil Rectory

Modern food and half-timbered heritage
1 Chesil Street, Winchester, SO23 0HU
Tel no: (01962) 851555
www.chesilrectory.co.uk
Modern British | £28
Cooking score: 4

Damian Brown and his team have bedded in comfortably since taking over this venerable fifteenth-century dwelling just off Winchester's main drag. The restaurant's crooked, half-timbered frontage still drips heritage, but new banquettes, vintage chandeliers and curios now lend some zest to the antiquated beamed interior. Service has upped its game of late, and the cooking has also received a shot in the arm with the recent arrival of Neil Thornley – who formerly worked for Marco Pierre White. He was still settling in as the Guide went to press, but an early meal yielded clear, crisp flavours, bags of refinement and 'well-dressed plates' including soft-boiled Hampshire quails' eggs with hollandaise and mushroom duxelle, as well as venison from nearby Blackmoor Estate with fondant potato, creamed cabbage and bacon. For dessert, hot raspberry soufflé with raspberry sauce was a classic star turn, with plenty of 'wow'. A state-of-the-art preservation system guarantees faultless wines by the glass, with bottles kicking off at around £20.

Chef/s: Neil Thornley. **Open:** all week L 12 to 2.30 (3 Sun), D 6 to 9.30 (10 Fri and Sat, 9 Sun). **Closed:** 25 and 26 Dec, 1 Jan, bank hols. **Meals:** alc (main courses £13 to £20). Set L and D £15.95 (2 courses) to £19.95. **Service:** not inc. **Details:** Cards accepted. 72 seats. Separate bar. Music. Children allowed.

Hotel du Vin & Bistro

Celebrated wines and sunny food
14 Southgate Street, Winchester, SO23 9EF
Tel no: (01962) 841414
www.hotelduvin.com
Modern European | £35
Cooking score: 3

The original branch of the nationwide HDV chain occupies a Georgian house in the centre of Winchester and has been decked out in style, with bare floorboards, polished tables, leather-upholstered period chairs and hallmark wine-related regalia. Chefs may come and go here, but the cooking's sunny style remains assured: the light, all-round approach accommodates bistro classics as well as more modish ideas, from dry-aged Donald Russell ribeye steak with pommes frites and béarnaise to a fillet of halibut elegantly teamed with wild asparagus, white crab meat and samphire. Desserts are re-runs of old faithfuls such as pain perdu or crème brûlée. They do 'vin' extremely well here, and the celebrated wine list's starry names are supported by a host of more accessible tipples (from £19), a commendable choice of half-bottles and plenty of carefully chosen options by the glass. Ask the sommeliers for advice if in doubt.

Chef/s: Adam Fargin. **Open:** all week L 12 to 1.45 (12.30 to 2.15 Sun), D 7 to 9.45 (10.15 Sat and Sun). **Meals:** alc (main courses £14 to £29). **Service:** 10% (optional). **Details:** Cards accepted. 70 seats. 30 seats outside. Separate bar. No music. Wheelchair access. Children allowed. Car parking.

Woodlands

Hotel TerraVina

Laid-back, wine-lover's delight
174 Woodlands Road, Woodlands, SO40 7GL
Tel no: (023) 80293784
www.hotelterravina.co.uk
Modern European | £40
Cooking score: 4

A tiny village on the edge of the New Forest may not be the first place you'd think of looking for a California-style boutique hotel, but Gérard and Nina Basset have conjured just such a creation out of an attractive Victorian house. Light and air fill the informal dining room, which opens out on to a terrace for summer meals. Bare tables and pale wood tones establish the breezy, laid-back mood, and the cooking follows through with sound renditions of modern British fare. Neil Cooper, previously sous chef, now heads up the kitchen. Expect to start with something like pressed trout, lemon sole and leek terrine, and go on to roast loin of locally sourced pork with puréed carrot and pak choi, or organic salmon with crushed potatoes in chervil butter. Simple but tempting desserts include pecan pie with amaretti ice cream. Gérard Basset is one of the UK's leading wine evangelists, and his list is a finely honed roll call of pedigree worldwide producers, arranged by style with prices that don't feel as though they're straining at the leash. Start at £15.75 for a very drinkable Merlot/Grenache blend from the Languedoc.

Chef/s: Neil Cooper. **Open:** all week L 12 to 2, D 7 to 9.45. **Meals:** alc (main courses £16 to £25). Set L £20.50 (2 courses) to £27. Sun L £21.50 (2 courses) to £28.50. **Service:** not inc. **Details:** Cards accepted. 56 seats. 26 seats outside. Separate bar. No music. Wheelchair access. Children allowed. Car parking.

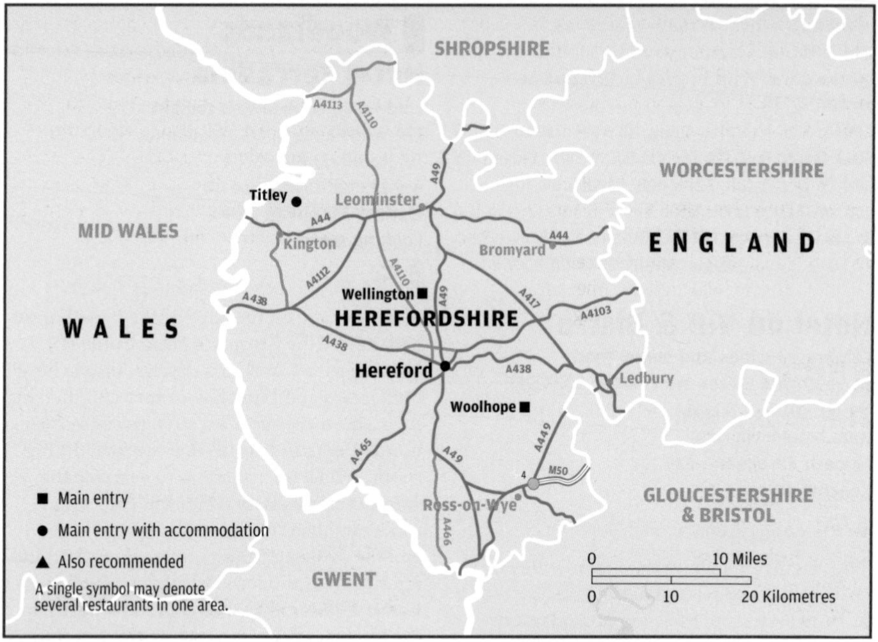

■ Main entry
● Main entry with accommodation
▲ Also recommended
A single symbol may denote several restaurants in one area.

Hay-on-Wye

READERS RECOMMEND

Richard Booth's Bookshop Café

Modern British
44 Lion Street, Hay-on-Wye, HR3 5AA
Tel no: (01497) 820322
www.boothbooks.co.uk
'Innovative, fresh delicious food. Great service, friendly staff. A real gem of a restaurant.'

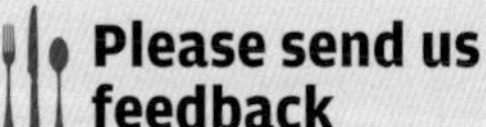

Please send us your feedback

To register your opinion about any restaurant listed in the Guide, or a new restaurant that you wish to bring to our attention, please visit the web address at the bottom of the page. Your feedback informs the content of the book and will be used to compile next year's reviews.

Hereford

Castle House

Swish food in a swanky setting
Castle Street, Hereford, HR1 2NW
Tel no: (01432) 356321
www.castlehse.co.uk
Modern British | £35
Cooking score: 4
£5 OFF

Tucked down a quiet street in the heart of Hereford, Castle House is a gracious building sporting a fresh interior that combines modern and classical themes to good effect. On fine days, begin your visit on the terrace overlooking the river – there are also glimpses from the smart, airy dining room. Here, Claire Nicholls' cooking shows a sound grasp of classical techniques, but efforts to add a touch of modern pizzazz sometimes go awry, as in a starter of crab tian with apples, celeriac and – less convincingly – paprika cinder toffee. A main course of pan-fried sea bass with shiitake mushrooms, fine beans,

cauliflower purée, cauliflower tempura, caper and lemon oil is on safer ground, likewise a homely dessert of sticky banana and date pudding with butterscotch sauce, roast bananas and vanilla ice cream. A substantial wine list, divided by style, opens at £15.
Chef/s: Claire Nicholls. **Open:** all week L 12 to 2, D 6.30 to 9.30 (9 Sun). **Meals:** alc (main courses £13 to £24). Sun L £24. Tasting menu £50 (7 courses). **Service:** not inc. **Details:** Cards accepted. 36 seats. 24 seats outside. Separate bar. Wheelchair access. Music. Children allowed. Car parking.

Titley

The Stagg Inn

Foodie pub star
Titley, HR5 3RL
Tel no: (01544) 230221
www.thestagg.co.uk
Modern British | £33
Cooking score: 5

V

It's a tribute to Steve and Nicola Reynolds' tenacity and dedication that they have managed to preserve the Stagg as an honest-to-goodness country hostelry while taking it into the foodie big time. Their old drovers' inn still feels just right, with an infectiously happy atmosphere and 'lots of smiles' from well-organised, obliging staff. The whole set-up also hums with self-sufficient 'cottage economy', although there's nothing folksy about Steve's straight-talking food: good culinary sense and natural flair define every dish, whether it's homemade black pudding with belly pork and onion purée, Credenhill snails mingled with mushrooms, chestnuts and bacon, or saddle of Marches venison in honest company with caramelised shallots, rösti and root vegetables. Regally rendered fillet steak with crispy home-cut chips and 'precise' béarnaise also gets rave reviews, so it's surprising that some readers have found Steve's Sunday roasts disappointingly 'chewy and bland'. Meals always end strongly with a mighty trolley loaded with ripe specimens from the region's cheesemakers, while desserts promise crafty creations such as zingy lemon tart or a rich feast of chocolate (mousse, sorbet and ice cream). Tidy presentation steers clear of Jackson Pollock daubs and splashes, and the ancillaries are all present and correct: hugely enjoyable home-baked bread, excellent coffee with macaroons, Herefordshire ciders, and a wine list that shows knowledge and intelligence about its station. Expect a broad sweep of grape varieties and reputable growers, stress-free prices and abundant half-bottles. House selections start at £14.50 (£3.65 a glass).
Chef/s: Steve Reynolds. **Open:** Tue to Sun L 12 to 2 (2.15 Sun), Tue to Sat D 6.30 to 9 (9.30 Sat). **Closed:** Mon, 25 to 27 Dec, 2 weeks Jan/Feb, first 2 weeks Nov. **Meals:** alc (main courses £16 to £22). Sun L £19.30. **Service:** not inc. **Details:** Cards accepted. 70 seats. 16 seats outside. Separate bar. No music. No mobile phones. Children allowed. Car parking.

Wellington

The Wellington

Good value, heart-on-sleeve cooking
Wellington, HR4 8AT
Tel no: (01432) 830367
www.wellingtonpub.co.uk
Modern British | £27
Cooking score: 2

It has been 10 years since Ross Williams breathed new life and vigour into this country pub, and his enthusiasm remains undimmed. Local ales keep the drinkers happy, while gutsy, straight-talking food draws folk from further afield. Regional produce is sourced with a vengeance, be it pedigree Hereford beef, Lay and Robson's oak-smoked salmon, or duck from Madgett's Farm. The result is seasonal menus bursting with sharply executed ideas: a warm salad of wild mushrooms served with smoked pancetta, poached bantam egg and polenta croûtons, or a rack of Marches lamb with a mini-shepherd's pie, sage mash, spring cabbage and redcurrant sauce. House wine is £13.50.
Chef/s: Ross Williams. **Open:** Tue to Sun L 12 to 2 (12.30 Sun), Mon to Sat D 7 to 9. **Closed:** 25 and 26 Dec. **Meals:** alc (main courses £12 to £18). Sun L

£17.50. **Service:** not inc. **Details:** Cards accepted. 70 seats. 20 seats outside. Separate bar. Music. Children allowed. Car parking.

Woolhope

NEW ENTRY

The Butchers Arms

Rustic pub with fresh flavours
Woolhope, HR1 4RF
Tel no: (01432) 860281
www.butchersarmswoolhope.com
Modern European | £23
Cooking score: 2

The latest venture from Guide veteran Stephen Bull finds him at the helm of this unreformed country boozer surrounded by rolling Herefordshire fields. Catch some rays outside by a trickling stream or park yourself in the bar, where farming implements on rough walls set the bucolic tone. Fresh flavours and seasonality drive the kitchen and the cooking has a splendidly rustic, unrefined edge, from the excellent home-baked rolls and fish soup with garlic croûtes to wholesome baked muscovado custard with candied orange peel. In between, anchovy-crumbed gilthead bream is served appealingly with warm potato salad, while crispy breast of Chepstow duck is perked up with lime compote. Wines start at £14.50.

Chef/s: Stephen Bull. **Open:** Tue to Sun L 12 to 2, Tue to Sat D 6.30 to 9. **Closed:** Mon, 25 Dec. **Meals:** alc (main courses £11 to £15). **Service:** not inc. **Details:** Cards accepted. 60 seats. 20 seats outside. No music. Wheelchair access. Children allowed. Car parking.

MY SHERRY AMOUR

If you can't remember the last time you had sherry, now could be the time to rediscover it. The drier styles, Fino and Manzanilla in particular, are superb with the strongly flavoured nibbles - cured hams, aged cheeses, salted anchovies - that are not kind to more delicate white wines.

A tot of dry or medium-dry sherry was once the British default aperitif when dining out, with good reason. It has a powerfully stimulating effect on the appetite - its savoury flavour prepares the palate for the first taste of food. As fashions turned in the 80s towards drinking something fizzy to set the ball rolling, sherry got rather forgotten.

It didn't help that many restaurants and pubs didn't (and sometimes still don't) know how to store it. Pale dry sherry should be drunk within a week and served well-chilled. Kept for longer, it starts to taste stale. Spanish restaurants and tapas bars are the best bets for well-kept sherry and often have dedicated sherry listings. The drier styles can be drunk with a range of mains and tapas, while the sweetest and darkest, Oloroso Dulce or PX, can accompany the richest desserts and cheeses, or make fine digestifs.

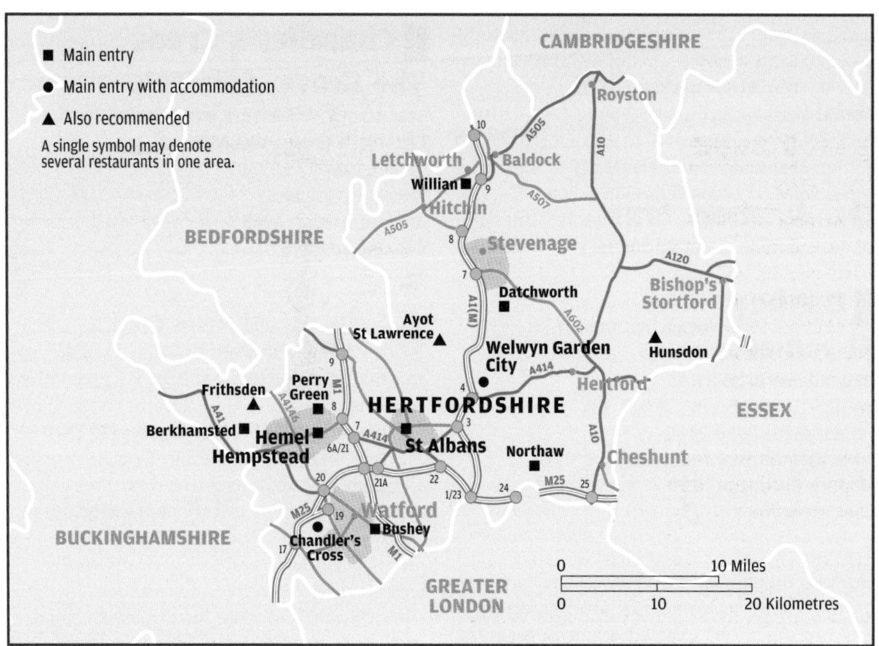

Ayot St Lawrence

ALSO RECOMMENDED

▲ The Brocket Arms

Ayot St Lawrence, AL6 9BT
Tel no: (01438) 820250
www.brocketarms.com
Modern British £5 OFF

George Bernard Shaw's house (National Trust) is just a stroll from this fourteenth-century inn – hence the throng of famished tourists and wannabe literati in the minuscule bar and opened-up dining room. The kitchen celebrates humble cuts and plunders the pub-grub back catalogue for the likes of moules marinière with cider and broad beans, beef shin and mushroom pie or veal rump with triple-cooked chips, before puds such as chocolate soup with vanilla ice cream. Two courses £12.95 at lunch (£19.95 dinner). Tip-top real ales and everyday wines (from £13.80). No food Sun D. Accommodation.

Berkhamsted

The Gatsby

Deco decadence and pretty food
Rex Cinema, 97 High Street, Berkhamsted, HP4 2DG
Tel no: (01442) 870403
www.thegatsby.net
Modern European | £35
Cooking score: 2

Knock back funky cocktails in the Gatsby's pulsating bar or mingle with movie buffs waiting for the show at this dazzlingly opulent Art Deco cinema-cum-foodie destination – think ornate mirrored columns, lofty sculpted ceilings and glittering chandeliers. Matthew Salt cooks in the modern vein, fashioning pretty dishes from the European mainstream – perhaps a tart of Chiltern pigeon with mushroom duxelle and chestnuts or roast rump and braised shoulder of lamb with garlicky creamed potatoes and spinach. He also jazzes up Dover sole meunière with lime

and coriander salsa, as well as assuaging sweet-toothed longings with, say, pineapple pannacotta. Wines start at £15.95.
Chef/s: Matthew Salt. **Open:** Mon to Sat L 12 to 2.30, D 5.30 to 10.30. Sun 12 to 9.30. **Closed:** 25 and 26 Dec. **Meals:** alc (main courses £15 to £26). Set L and D £13.95 (2 courses) to £18.90. Sun L £14.95. **Service:** not inc. **Details:** Cards accepted. 100 seats. 30 seats outside. Separate bar. Music. Car parking.

Bushey

St James

Dependable local asset
30 High Street, Bushey, WD23 3HL
Tel no: (020) 8950 2480
www.stjamesrestaurant.co.uk
Modern European | £30
Cooking score: 1

The view across to St James's church hasn't changed much since this Bushey asset opened its doors almost 15 years ago, and neither has the cooking. Don't expect fireworks, foams or frippery here; do expect time-honoured comforts in the shape of smoked salmon and avocado salad, rump of lamb with ratatouille, and braised chicken breast with mushrooms and tarragon. Come for lunch and you'll probably find bangers and mash, while desserts could add an extra dollop of easy satisfaction in the shape of Toblerone cheesecake with black cherries. House wine is £15.95.
Chef/s: Matt Cook. **Open:** all week L 12 to 2.30, Mon to Sat D 6.30 to 10. **Closed:** 25 and 26 Dec, bank hols. **Meals:** alc (main courses £14 to £22). Set L £14.95 (2 courses). Set D £16.95 (2 courses). Sun L £19.95 (2 courses) to £24.50. **Service:** 12.5% (optional). **Details:** Cards accepted. 100 seats. 20 seats outside. Separate bar. No mobile phones. Wheelchair access. Music. Children allowed. Car parking.

Chandler's Cross

The Grove, Colette's

Star-struck venue with eye-popping food
Chandler's Cross, WD3 4TG
Tel no: (01923) 807807
www.thegrove.co.uk
Modern British | £65
Cooking score: 5

These days, the sleek, glossy Grove is synonymous with a certain sort of stardom, and there may be gasps of 'OMG!' given the celebrity count here – it's a home-from-home for football's moneyed aristocracy, after all. As the hotel's flagship restaurant, Colette's puts on a suitably ostentatious show, with a 'sexy' bar area, huge canvases and abstract sculptures in the dining room. Prices are pitched at premiership WAGs rather than fans on the terraces, and the supremely confident kitchen aims to dazzle. To start, soft, fleshy Brixham crab contrasts with a squid ink-blackened langoustine, avocado and droplets of tomato and cucumber coulis, while scallops might be paired with peanut purée, radish and lime. After that, Lincolnshire pork is subjected to similarly creative treatment – the belly meat laid over a slice of pickled pineapple, and its lusty cheek arriving separately atop a ragoût of Cornish lobster with borlotti beans and sweet cicely. As for dessert, Yorkshire rhubarb perked up with Amalfi lemon cream and meringues hits the mark – or you might fancy a clever chocolate confection in a glass. Jokes abound, from the bread rolls delivered in a canvas bag to the kooky 'sweet shop' petits fours. The astonishing cheese trolley gets rave reviews, service goes the extra mile, and the wine list promises good drinking from the lesser-known regions; prices start at £27.
Chef/s: Russell Bateman. **Open:** Tue to Sat D 7 to 9.30. **Closed:** Sun and Mon. **Meals:** Set D £65. Tasting menu £80 (7 courses). **Service:** not inc. **Details:** Cards accepted. 40 seats. Separate bar. No mobile phones. Wheelchair access. Music. Car parking.

Datchworth

The Tilbury

Full-blooded food from a local champion
Watton Road, Datchworth, SG3 6TB
Tel no: (01438) 815550
www.thetilbury.co.uk
Modern British | £27
Cooking score: 3

'Village pub' proclaims a sign on the wall of this foursquare red-brick inn, which still acts the part with real ales on tap and basic, 'take-it-or-leave-it' service. Otherwise, the Tilbury's smart open-plan interior, convivial vibes and enterprising cooking are firmly in tune with the modern pub zeitgeist. Local food champion Paul Bloxham runs this place as his flagship, matching his menus to the calendar and peddling full-blooded dishes such as deep-fried duck egg with house-cured bacon and dandelion, or rose veal and ham pie with chunky celeriac chips. His larder also accommodates everything from Herdwick lamb to South Devon steak, and he scours the markets for fish – perhaps butter-poached Shetland lobster and brill with sweetcorn and basil pappardelle. Flavours are true and portions large, but the end results can often seem rather rich and rough-hewn. The short global wine list starts at £11 a carafe. A sibling, the Blue Anchor, can found in St Albans (see entry).

Chef/s: Paul Bloxham and Ben Crick. **Open:** all week L 12 to 3 (5 Sun), Mon to Sat D 6 to 11. **Meals:** alc (main courses £10 to £23). Set L and D £12 (2 courses) to £16. Sun L £16. **Service:** not inc. **Details:** Cards accepted. 70 seats. 40 seats outside. Separate bar. No mobile phones. Wheelchair access. Music. Children allowed. Car parking.

Also Recommended

Also recommended entries are not scored but we think they are worth a visit.

Frithsden

ALSO RECOMMENDED

▲ The Alford Arms

Frithsden, HP1 3DD
Tel no: (01442) 864480
www.alfordarmsfrithsden.co.uk
Modern British

The founder member of a five-strong Home Counties' mini-chain known for its gussied-up food, Country Living interiors and desirable locations, the Alford Arms is set deep in National Trust territory close to Ashridge. The kitchen follows the house style, offering seasonal 'small plates' and 'main meals' ranging from warm soused mackerel with beetroot purée (£6.50) to lamb's liver and devilled kidneys with soft polenta and sweet paprika sauce (£13.25). After that, perhaps blood orange and buttermilk pannacotta. All-European wines from £14.50 (£3.70 a glass). Open all week.

Hemel Hempstead

Restaurant 65

Admirable local eatery with capable cooking
65 High Street, Old Town, Hemel Hempstead, HP1 3AF
Tel no: (01442) 239010
www.restaurant65.com
Modern British | £28
Cooking score: 2

Grant Young and his team are gaining in confidence at this admirable neighbourhood restaurant opposite Hemel Hempstead's Old Town Hall and Arts Centre. This is a 'little guy' set-up of the best sort, challenging the town's junk-food reputation with hard graft, honest intent and capable cooking. Ideas make sense, whether it's a herby risotto with a separate pot of roasted vegetables, seared mackerel fillet with beetroot, carrot and celeriac coleslaw or a plate of slow-roast belly pork with bubble and squeak, apple purée and

is settling into his new role with a menu of accessible brasserie food: expect the likes of seared scallops with sauce vierge (£8.50) and slow-roast pork tenderloin with red cabbage and mustard mash (£15.50) followed by Eton mess with cookies. House wine is £14. Closed Mon and Tue. Reports please.

Petersfield

JSW

Clarity and pure panache
20 Dragon Street, Petersfield, GU31 4JJ
Tel no: (01730) 262030
www.jswrestaurant.com
Modern British | £48
Cooking score: 6

£5 OFF V

Chef/proprietor Jake Saul Watkins went for considered understatement when naming his restaurant, and there's something decidedly personal about this converted seventeenth-century inn off Petersfield's main drag. He has filled the discreetly lit, pale-walled dining room with arty prints by his sister and imbued the whole place with a quietly subdued feeling of provincial class. His short menu doesn't give much away, either – although prosaic descriptions such as fillet of local sea bass with tiger prawn ravioli and asparagus or loin and cheek of veal with cauliflower purée conceal all manner of tricksy devices and elaboration. Clarity is the key and JSW never takes his eye off the ball when it comes to respecting the seasons – a dish involving 'three textures' of lamb is enhanced with summer vegetables and fragrantly perfumed with bergamot, for example, while salmon might be served 'warm' with watercress risotto and horseradish velouté. There is also a great deal to marvel at when it comes to desserts such as an exquisitely simple vanilla cheesecake with strawberry sorbet or a voguish bittersweet/savoury combo of dark chocolate and chicory délice with chicory ice cream. JSW's wine list is a passionately assembled, 700-bin giant that never takes liberties when it comes to mark-ups. The list is evenly split between the Old and New Worlds, with much depending on 'terroir'. The range of half-bottles is matchless, sub-£30 choice is brilliant and there are 14 selections by the glass (from £6).

Chef/s: Jake Saul Watkins. **Open:** Tue to Sat L 12 to 1.30, D 7 to 9.30. **Closed:** Sun, Mon. **Meals:** Set L £19.50 (2 courses) to £25. Set D £39.50 (2 courses) to £48. Tasting L £42.50 (5 courses). Tasting D £52.50 (5 courses). **Service:** not inc. **Details:** Cards accepted. 45 seats. 35 seats outside. No music. No mobile phones. Wheelchair access. Children allowed. Car parking.

Portsmouth

ALSO RECOMMENDED

▲ Abarbistro

58 White Hart Road, Portsmouth, PO1 2JA
Tel no: (023) 92811585
www.abarbistro.co.uk
Modern British

This light, airy dockside bar/restaurant makes pleasing first impressions. The relaxed atmosphere and stylish setting carry over onto the menu, which cherry-picks bistro classics such as belly pork, apple mash and mustard cabbage (£13) and the odd global favourite – falafels, tzatziki and chilli jam (£8), say – and offers them alongside fresh seafood. Beer-battered fish and chips with pea purée is considered 'the best', service is friendly, and £13.50 for house wine reflects reasonable prices across the board. Open all week.

Preston Candover

NEW ENTRY

Purefoy Arms

Village hostelry firing on all cylinders
Alresford Road, Preston Candover, RG25 2EJ
Tel no: (01256) 389777
www.thepurefoyarms.co.uk
Modern European | £35
Cooking score: 3

Deep in the north Hampshire countryside, this Victorian village hostelry is firing on all cylinders following a recent takeover and makeover. There's still space for drinking at the

sage jus. To finish, try chocolate and hazelnut parfait or cardamom-infused egg custard 'brûlée'. House French is £14.

Chef/s: Grant Young. **Open:** Tue to Fri and Sun L 12 to 2 (3 Sun), Tue to Sat D 6.30 to 10. **Closed:** Mon, 26 to 30 Dec. **Meals:** alc (main courses £13 to £18). Set L £13.50 (2 courses) to £16.50. **Service:** not inc. **Details:** Cards accepted. 30 seats. No mobile phones. Music. Children allowed. Car parking.

ALSO RECOMMENDED

▲ Pepper Hut

61 High Street, Old Town, Hemel Hempstead, HP1 3AF
Tel no: (01442) 233777
www.pepperhut.co.uk
Indian £5 OFF

The bright new incarnation of Cochin Cuisine comes with sunny yellow walls, a confident outlook and a menu that has been fleshed out with more seafood and vegetarian dishes from the coastal province of Kerala. Crispy nibbles and zingy pickles set the tone, before authentically spiced starters such as kathrikka (deep-fried aubergine with tomato chutney) or mussels 'molly' (£3.75). To follow, try one of the dosas, the special crab curry or erachi olathiyathu (a punchy lamb stir-fry with turmeric, black pepper and sliced coconut, £7.25). Wines from £9.95. Open all week.

Hunsdon

ALSO RECOMMENDED

▲ Fox & Hounds

2 High Street, Hunsdon, SG12 8NH
Tel no: (01279) 843999
www.foxandhounds-hunsdon.co.uk
Modern European

A cream-fronted pub in an attractive little village not far out of London, the Fox & Hounds goes for a fairly relaxed look in the bar, with a smart, chandeliered dining room and a terrace for summer dining. A menu of straightforward bistro dishes combines European influences for Normandy black pudding with a fried duck egg (£7), whole grilled mackerel with a warm salad of brown shrimps, cockles and fennel (£10), and pannacotta with rhubarb. Wines from £14.50. No food Sun D and Mon.

Northaw

The Sun at Northaw

Terrific inn packed with regional delights
1 Judges Hill, Northaw, EN6 4NL
Tel no: (01707) 655507
www.thesunatnorthaw.co.uk
British | £25
Cooking score: 3

'Absolutely terrific! Restored my faith in proper British regional food', was the comment of one who was more than happy to find this well-heeled, whitewashed village inn that has been opened up, freshened up and generally given a fashionably folksy look. Oliver Smith buys locally and sets great store by the provenance of his raw materials, and his menu abounds with regional delights: wild Brancaster mussels are teamed with Suffolk cider and local leeks; Herefordshire rose veal appears alongside whipped rosemary potatoes and roasted Jerusalem artichokes; duck egg custard tart is paired with poached rhubarb; while from a bargain lunch menu comes ham hock terrine, piccalilli and crumpets, followed by pollack fillet with beetroot, sprouting broccoli and capers. It's all backed up by real ales and wines from £17.

Chef/s: Oliver Smith. **Open:** Tue to Sun L 12 to 3 (4 Sat, 5 Sun), Tue to Sat D 6 to 10. **Closed:** Mon. **Meals:** alc (main courses £13 to £19). Set L £13.50 (2 courses) to £17.50. Sun L £26.50 (2 courses) to £32.50. **Service:** not inc. **Details:** Cards accepted. 80 seats. 60 seats outside. Separate bar. Wheelchair access. Music. Children allowed. Car parking.

Perry Green

NEW ENTRY

The Hoops Inn

Homespun enterprise and honest food
Perry Green, SG10 6EF
Tel no: (01279) 843568
www.hoops-inn.co.uk
British | £20
Cooking score: 1

Sculpture vultures visiting the nearby Henry Moore Foundation pack the rustic, open-plan interior and ample outdoor spaces at this revamped village boozer – a well-organised outfit that was once the artist's local (his house is across the road). The kitchen keeps it homespun, baking soda bread, curing salmon and serving spiky piccalilli with boards of carefully sourced British charcuterie. Daily fish deliveries might yield hake fillet with roasted beetroot pesto, juicy Suffolk pork T-bone is served with fennel and caper coleslaw, and puds are faithful servants such as creamy lemon posset. House wine is £14.95.

Chef/s: Mark Williams. **Open:** Tue to Sun L 12 to 2.30 (5 Sun), D 6 to 9.30. **Closed:** Mon. **Meals:** alc (main courses £8 to £15). Sun L £12.95. **Service:** 12.5% (optional). **Details:** Cards accepted. 45 seats. 70 seats outside. Separate bar. Wheelchair access. Music. Children allowed. Car parking.

St Albans

The Blue Anchor

Revamped local food champ
145 Fishpool Street, St Albans, AL3 4RY
Tel no: (01727) 855038
www.theblueanchorstalbans.co.uk
Modern British | £25
Cooking score: 2

There's no mistaking the family likeness at this offshoot of Paul Bloxham's pub the Tilbury (see entry). Like its big brother, this classily refurbished boozer opposite Verulamium Park is essentially about championing regional produce. This one deals in a mix of traditional and contemporary ideas, from ham and black pudding hash with deep-fried duck egg and homemade brown sauce to curried quail with coconut rice, onion and green pepper. Elsewhere, stuffed pig's trotter is teamed with potato and artichoke purée, and Seville orange marmalade adds zest to duck breast served atop clapshot, kale, lentils and shallots. Wines from £15.95.

Chef/s: Paul Bloxham, Mark Thurlow and Brian Smith. **Open:** Tue to Fri L 12 to 3, D 6 to 10, Sat 12 to 10, Sun 12 to 5. **Closed:** Mon. **Meals:** alc (main courses £10 to £23). Set L and D £12 (2 courses). **Service:** not inc. **Details:** Cards accepted. 50 seats. 40 seats outside. Separate bar. No mobile phones. Wheelchair access. Music. Children allowed. Car parking.

Darcy's

Hip vibes and racy food
2 Hatfield Road, St Albans, AL1 3RP
Tel no: (01727) 730777
www.darcysrestaurant.co.uk
Modern European | £32
Cooking score: 2

Ladies who lunch and the local smart set make a beeline for this former blacksmith's just off St Albans' main drag, drawn by its hip vibes and racily eclectic food. Since founder Kate d'Arcy's sad death in 2010, long-serving Aussie chef Ruth Hurren has taken sole charge of the place and shored up its reputation as the top ticket in town. Big hits from the Pacific Rim rub shoulders with Euro-accented dishes, so be prepared for sticky hoisin quail or 'deconstructed sashimi tuna ramen' alongside smoked chicken and butternut squash linguine or Parmesan-crusted cod with red pesto. For afters, chocolate and peanut butter cheesecake hits the right note. Flavours are bright, presentation is dramatic and prices are easy. Wines favour the New World, with bottles from £13.90.

Chef/s: Ruth Hurren and Jonathan Harding. **Open:** all week L 12 to 3, D 6 to 9.30 (10 Fri and Sat, 9 Sun). **Closed:** 26 to 28 Dec, 1 to 3 Jan. **Meals:** alc (main courses £12 to £24). Set L and D £12 (2 courses) to £15. Sun L £16.90 (2 courses) to £19.90.

Service: 12.5% (optional). **Details:** Cards accepted. 90 seats. 20 seats outside. Separate bar. Wheelchair access. Music. Children allowed.

Lussmanns

Smart eatery with something for everyone
Waxhouse Gate, off High Street, St Albans, AL3 4EW
Tel no: (01727) 851941
www.lussmanns.com
Modern European | £24
Cooking score: 1

Lussmanns is a refreshing and likeable antidote to most high-street eateries – smart and comfortable with a robust attitude to provenance and seasonality. Reporters approve of the 'buzzy atmosphere' and attention to detail – 'my rare tuna steak was (unusually for most places) correctly cooked'. There's something for everyone on the menu; warmed chicory salad with Stilton, pear and walnuts, fish pie, crab linguine and a cheese burger all come in for praise. Chocolate and walnut brownie is popular, too. House wine is £14.60. Branches in Hertford and Bishop's Stortford.

Chef/s: Nick McGowan. **Open:** all week 12 to 10 (10.30 Fri and Sat, 9 Sun). **Meals:** alc (main courses £8 to £23). Set L and D £10.95 (2 courses) to £13.95. Sun L £10.95. **Service:** not inc. **Details:** Cards accepted. 100 seats. 10 seats outside. Wheelchair access. Music. Children allowed.

Please send us your feedback

To register your opinion about any restaurant listed in the Guide, or a new restaurant that you wish to bring to our attention, please visit the web address at the bottom of the page. Your feedback informs the content of the book and will be used to compile next year's reviews.

Welwyn Garden City

Auberge du Lac

Drop-dead gorgeous, with food to match
Brocket Hall, Brocket Road, Welwyn Garden City, AL8 7XG
Tel no: (01707) 368888
www.aubergedulac.co.uk
Modern French | £55
Cooking score: 6

V

Part of aristocratic Brocket Hall's corporate hospitality and leisure package, but a destination in its own right, Auberge du Lac looks like something out of a fairy tale – a drop-dead gorgeous converted hunting lodge beside an ornamental lake with all the velvety gloss and plutocratic class of a purring Aston Martin. Chef Phil Thompson remains in confident control of the kitchen, delivering precise contemporary food designed to thrill and satisfy in equal measure. French technique is at the heart of things, although the cooking is never slavishly Gallic – witness a starter of octopus braised in red wine with marinated artichokes, chorizo, wasabi and grain mustard. However, any freewheeling global overtures are tempered by stellar specialities from the cross-Channel mainstream – hay-baked Pyrenean milk-fed lamb with goats' cheese, spiced couscous and an anchovy and sweetbread pithiviers, for example. To conclude, expect prettily adorned flavour bombs such as poached baby pineapple with passion-fruit meringue, char-grilled pineapple and coconut. Dinner doesn't come cheap, but the set lunch (with two glasses of superior wine included) is a prime deal for the likes of roast quail breast with chicken liver parfait and pear jelly followed by pan-roasted halibut with creamed leeks, trompettes de mort and herb croquettes. There's a 'sommelier's table' in the cellars, and the 750-bin wine list is a patrician blockbuster that pays full homage to the glories of regional French winemaking, as well as lifting treasures from Italy, Spain, Australia and beyond. Prices start at £22.

Chef/s: Phil Thompson. **Open:** Tue to Sat L 12 to 2, D 7 to 9.30. **Closed:** Sun, Mon, 27 Dec to 13 Jan. **Meals:** Set L £32.50. Set D £45 (2 courses) to £55. Tasting menu £65. **Service:** 10% (optional). **Details:** Cards accepted. 60 seats. 40 seats outside. No mobile phones. Wheelchair access. Music. Children allowed. Car parking.

Willian

The Fox

Popular pub with quality grub
Willian, SG6 2AE
Tel no: (01462) 480233
www.foxatwillian.co.uk
Modern British | £25
Cooking score: 2

Beside the village green and pond, this popular pub boasts fresh contemporary décor, a relaxed and friendly atmosphere, regularly changing modern menus, real ales (some from the owner's Brancaster Brewery) and a decent wine list. Oh, and a shop selling fresh fish from Norfolk round the back – the Nyes also own the White Horse in Brancaster Staithe (see entry, Norfolk). Cooking is unfussy, as befits the pub setting, but you can still expect quality ingredients such as tempura oysters with sweet chilli sauce, locally made pork sausages with mash and onion gravy, loin of venison with red cabbage, and iced lemon soufflé. House wine is £15.50.

Chef/s: Chris Jones. **Open:** all week L 12 to 2 (2.45 Sun), Mon to Sat D 6.45 to 9 (6.30 to 9.15 Fri and Sat). **Meals:** alc (main courses £12 to £19). Bar menu available. **Service:** 10% (optional). **Details:** Cards accepted. 70 seats. 16 seats outside. Separate bar. No mobile phones. Wheelchair access. Music. Children allowed. Car parking.

THE OLD IS NEW

From wild herbs to purple potatoes, there are many reasons to try something new (but actually rather ancient) this year. Retro dishes such as ox cheeks may now be old hat, but an air of austerity and nostalgia continues to drive innovations.

Dinner by Heston Blumenthal revisits historical dishes such as turkey pudding with mushrooms, cockscomb and bone marrow, while menus across the country brim with foraged ingredients and retro ideas: springtime nettle soup at **ramsons** in Ramsbottom; millet pudding with spelt and Blackstick blue, burnt pear and alexanders at **L'Enclume** in Cartmel; and slip sole in seaweed butter at **The Sportsman** in Seasalter to name but a few. Heritage ingredients are being resurrected: at **Llys Meddyg** in Pembrokeshire, violet potatoes are made into vividly coloured dumplings, while back at **L'Enclume** you'll find rare breed pork with salsify, onions and hedge garlic.

Wherever your stomach leads you, you're likely to encounter a clear focus on the countryside and what it can provide. Amusingly, most of what currently seems clever and new has been around for years; we simply forgot about it.

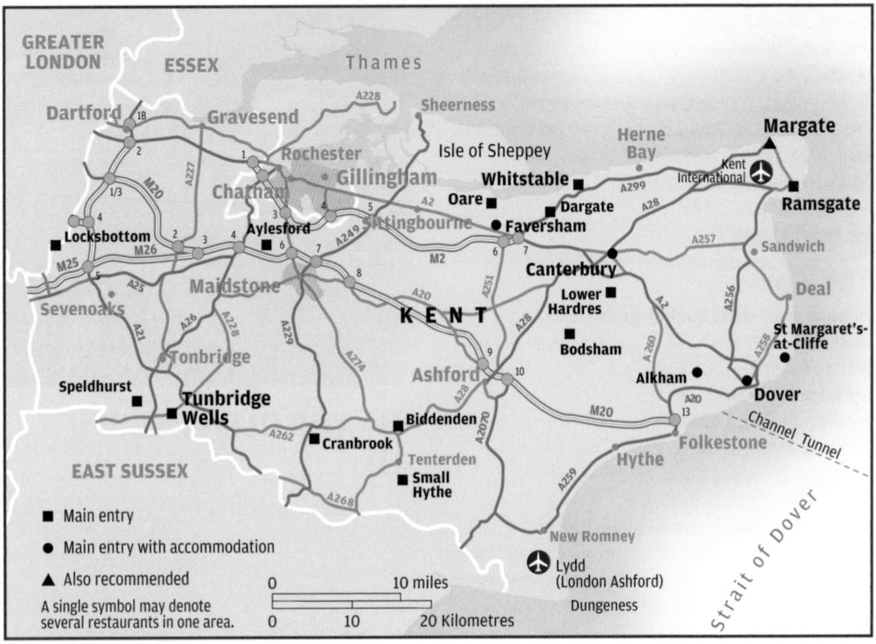
GREATER LONDON
ESSEX
Thames
Dartford
Gravesend
Sheerness
Isle of Sheppey
Rochester
Gillingham
Chatham
Herne Bay
Margate
Kent International
Whitstable
Oare
Dargate
Faversham
Ramsgate
Sittingbourne
Aylesford
Locksbottom
Sandwich
Canterbury
Maidstone
Sevenoaks
Lower Hardres
Deal
KENT
Bodsham
St Margaret's-at-Cliffe
Tonbridge
Ashford
Alkham
Dover
Speldhurst
Tunbridge Wells
Biddenden
Cranbrook
Tenterden
Small Hythe
Folkestone
Channel Tunnel
Hythe
EAST SUSSEX
New Romney
Lydd (London Ashford)
Dungeness
Strait of Dover
M25
M26
M20
M2
A2
A20
A21
A26
A28
A227
A228
A229
A249
A251
A256
A257
A258
A259
A260
A262
A268
A274
A299
A2070
■ Main entry
● Main entry with accommodation
▲ Also recommended
A single symbol may denote several restaurants in one area.
0 10 miles
0 10 20 Kilometres

Alkham

The Marquis at Alkham

Food with flair and care

Alkham Valley Road, Alkham, CT15 7DF

Tel no: (01304) 873410

www.themarquisatalkham.co.uk

Modern British | £43

Cooking score: 4

£5 OFF

With its polished wood surfaces and well-upholstered feel, the transformation of this former country pub may be swish rather than personal, but chef Charlie Lakin has set the kitchen off to a rollicking good start. He makes his mark with attention to detail and the sourcing of raw materials (especially local). Fine-tuned flavours come through strongly, whether it's organic salmon marinated in beetroot juice and teamed with soused baby beetroot and a set cauliflower cream, or smoked guinea fowl breast with a rich galantine of the leg and foie gras. Elsewhere, fillet of Dexter beef is accompanied by 'heart-stoppingly rich' sarladaise potatoes, perfectly cut by a watercress and shallot purée. To finish, banana soufflé with tonka bean ice cream is a winner. The kitchen's efforts can be let down by 'very slow' service, a recurring theme in reports. Kentish ales and ciders supplement the extensive wine list, which opens at £14.50, and aims to suit all palates and budgets.

Chef/s: Charles Lakin. **Open:** Tue to Sun L 12 to 2.30 (3 Sun), Mon to Sat D 6.30 to 9.30. **Meals:** Set L £17.50 (2 courses) to £22.50. Set D £42.50. Sun L £22.50. Sun D £17.50 (2 courses). Tasting menu £50 (6 courses). **Service:** not inc. **Details:** Cards accepted. 60 seats. 30 seats outside. Separate bar. No music. No mobile phones. Wheelchair access. Car parking.

Aylesford

Hengist

Flavour-packed food with a deft touch
7-9 High Street, Aylesford, ME20 7AX
Tel no: (01622) 719273
www.hengistrestaurant.co.uk
Modern French | £38
Cooking score: 3
£5 OFF **V**

Part of Richard Phillips' group of Kent eateries, Hengist is set in a sixteenth-century building. Ancient beams and brick blend effortlessly with contemporary touches, creating an elegant and intimate dining space in which to sample new chef Jon Baldock's modern French cooking. Top-notch ingredients and a deft touch combine to produce some creative, full-flavoured dishes. From the seasonal carte, perhaps a starter of scallops with apple and winter truffle salad, celeriac purée and balsamic dressing could precede 32-day aged beef fillet is served with braised ox cheek and bordelaise jus. To finish, try the bread-and-butter pudding with caramelised banana and whisky ice cream. The Tuesday and Friday evening 'market menu' is great value. House wine from £14.95.
Chef/s: Jon Baldock. **Open:** Tue to Sun L 12 to 2.30, Tue to Sat D 6.30 to 10. **Closed:** Mon. **Meals:** alc (main courses £17 to £22). Set L £12.95 (2 courses) to £14.95. Set D £25.50 (3 courses). Sun L £18.50. Tasting menu £48 (6 courses). **Service:** 12.5% (optional). **Details:** Cards accepted. 60 seats. Separate bar. Music. Children allowed. Car parking.

Biddenden

The West House

Clever food without any flimflam
28 High Street, Biddenden, TN27 8AH
Tel no: (01580) 291341
www.thewesthouserestaurant.co.uk
Modern European | £38
Cooking score: 5

Graham and Jackie Garrett have carved out a very personal niche at their converted weaver's cottage smack in the middle of pretty Biddenden. They have honed the business of cooking and courteous hospitality over the years – although some have found the resulting experience rather flat. Graham's short menu makes deceptive reading, with dish descriptions concealing a great deal of technical accomplishment and culinary intelligence – this is clever, high-end cooking without flimflam. A 'truly sensational' take on a pub classic involving a dinky ham hock with a superbly innovative Scotch egg fashioned from black pudding blew one reader away. But the underlying instinct for true tastes and contrasts also yields more complex results – perhaps warm smoked haddock carpaccio with bacon dressing, pickled rock samphire and pea shoots or a dish of gurnard fillet with braised spiced lentils and a carrot and onion bhaji on the side. Desserts offer tricks and treats based on the flavours of the past, so expect a 'trifle' made from sherry jelly, Catalan custard and mascarpone or a sweet-shop 'Crunchie' of white honeycomb parfait with dark chocolate sorbet. The kindly priced global wine list opens with tasty house selections from £11.50 a 500ml carafe (£4.75 a glass).
Chef/s: Graham Garrett. **Open:** Tue to Fri and Sun L 12 to 2 (3 Sun), Tue to Sat D 7 to 9.30. **Closed:** Mon, 2 weeks from Christmas, 2 weeks Aug. **Meals:** Set L £25. Set D £38. Sun L £35 (2 courses) to £38. Tasting menu £50. **Service:** 12.5% (optional). **Details:** Cards accepted. 32 seats. Wheelchair access. Music. Children allowed. Car parking.

ALSO RECOMMENDED

▲ The Three Chimneys

Hareplain Road, Biddenden, TN27 8LW
Tel no: (01580) 291472
www.thethreechimneys.co.uk
Modern British

Set back from the main road on the fringes of the village, the Three Chimneys looks like every tourist's dream of a real country pub, with almost six centuries of history under its belt. The kitchen is capable of delivering seriously good dishes along the lines of potted shrimps (£8.95), duck leg confit (£17.95) or a beautifully presented, pink roast rump of lamb with Mediterranean vegetables. House wine is £16.50. Open all week.

Bodsham

Froggies at the Timber Batts

Traditional pub, classic French food
School Lane, Bodsham, TN25 5JQ
Tel no: (01233) 750237
www.thetimberbatts.co.uk
French | £35
Cooking score: 1

£5 OFF

The deeply rural Timber Batts is a well-patronised fifteenth-century inn with magnificent views. Inside it really looks the part of an old-world country inn, matched by the serving of excellent ham, egg and chips in the simple beamed bar. But there's also croque-monsieur, and a restaurant menu of fish soup with rouille, chicken suprême basquaise and duck leg confit; Joël Gross runs an English pub for eternal Francophiles, with cheerful young staff and house wines (£18.50) from a cousin's vineyard in the Loire.
Chef/s: Joël Gross. **Open:** Tue to Sun L 12 to 2 (2.30 Sat, 12.30 to 2.30 Sun), Tue to Sat D 7 to 9 (9.30 Fri and Sat). **Closed:** Mon, 25 to 31 Dec, Tue after bank hols. **Meals:** alc (main courses £16 to £25). Set L £16 (2 courses) to £20. Sun L £20.50 (2 courses) to £25.65. **Service:** not inc. **Details:** Cards accepted. 50 seats. 50 seats outside. Separate bar. Music. Children allowed. Car parking.

Canterbury

The Goods Shed

Good food from the market
Station Road West, Canterbury, CT2 8AN
Tel no: (01227) 459153
www.thegoodsshed.net
Modern British | £28
Cooking score: 2

It is 10 years since the Goods Shed opened as the only daily farmers' market in the UK. This is a thoroughly distinctive enterprise with its own butcher, baker, fishmonger, grocery and vegetable stalls, and a simply styled, rustic restaurant overlooking it all. Rafael Lopez's cooking takes what it can from the market, fashioning the harvest into plain-speaking, unshowy dishes. Expect generous plates of asparagus with a soft-boiled egg and Isle of Mull cheddar or white onion soup with herb pesto, well-timed hake with crab, fennel and tarragon, and Kentish boar sausages with rhubarb compote. Young staff are 'enthusiastic'. Well-priced wines from £14.
Chef/s: Rafael Lopez. **Open:** Tue to Sun L 12 to 2.30 (3 Sat and Sun), Tue to Sat D 6 to 9.30. **Closed:** Mon, 25 and 26 Dec, 1 Jan. **Meals:** alc (main courses £11 to £20). **Service:** not inc. **Details:** Cards accepted. 75 seats. No music. Children allowed. Car parking.

Michael Caines at ABode Canterbury

Good ideas presented with flair
High Street, Canterbury, CT1 2RX
Tel no: (01227) 826684
www.michaelcaines.com
Modern European | £45
Cooking score: 5

£5 OFF V

Sitting snugly on the medieval high street, the Canterbury branch of the ABode hotel group offers a large, light room with a bare-board floor and crisply clothed tables as the setting for the Michael Caines dining experience, in the capable hands of Jean-Marc Zanetti. Rather than going down the route of brasserie standards, the group opts for distinctly more ambitious cooking, full of good ideas presented with flair. Start with veal sweetbreads, fried off and served with a mushroom tortellino and spinach in scented Gewürztraminer sauce. Main courses display the same understanding of counterpointed flavours in the likes of roasted mallard with stewed blackberries and celeriac tart, or monkfish modishly wrapped in Parma ham, served with creamed leeks, tomato fondue and mussels in saffron velouté, with each element bringing its own depth of flavour to the whole. To finish, it's worth waiting for a

Bramley apple and ginger soufflé, with Granny Smith sorbet and cider coulis. Wines by the glass from £5.20 (£21.75 a bottle) head up a broadly based list that is arranged by grape variety as far as possible.

Chef/s: Jean-Marc Zanetti. **Open:** all week L 12 to 2.30, Mon to Sat D 6 to 10. **Meals:** alc (main courses £19 to £24). Set L £13.50. Set D £21 (2 courses) to £26. Sun L £14.95. **Service:** 12% (optional). **Details:** Cards accepted. 75 seats. No mobile phones. Wheelchair access. Music. Children allowed. Car parking.

Cranbrook

Apicius

Artistry and big-statement cooking
23 Stone Street, Cranbrook, TN17 3HF
Tel no: (01580) 714666
www.restaurant-apicius.co.uk
Modern European | £32
Cooking score: 6

Tim Johnson and Faith Hawkins' converted shop in a fifteenth-century Flemish weaver's dwelling in the centre of Cranbrook is a little gem – unstuffily informal, good-humoured and dedicated to the principles of real food. Tim injects vivid flavours and some bold combinations into his innovative modern cooking. Diners kick off, perhaps, with an inspired marriage of smoked duck breast with red-wine pears, orange jelly and walnut and chicory salad, or an equally impressive ham hock ballottine, served with spring pea velouté and foie gras mousse. Main courses get straight to the point, plundering the region for slow-roast shoulder of Kentish pork and its accompanying creamed potato, baby spinach and caramelised apple purée, and for sparkling-fresh fillet of halibut with ceps, Pink Fir Apple potatoes, leeks and baby artichokes. The kitchen is equally confident at dessert stage, sending out some dazzling treats, notably a brilliant juxtaposition of iced apricot mousse, candied almonds, amaretti-dusted coconut jelly and almond cream. Small details such as bread and petits fours have been praised, and prices are very reasonable for the quality of the food and the cooking. The wallet-friendly modern wine list (from £18) includes a good selection of half-bottles and some 11 by the glass.

Chef/s: Timothy Johnson. **Open:** Wed to Fri and Sun L 12 to 2, Wed to Sat D 6 to 9. **Closed:** Mon, Tue. **Meals:** Set L £26 (2 courses) to £30. Set D £31 (2 courses) to £36. Sun L £26 (2 courses) to £30. **Service:** 12.5% (optional). **Details:** Cards accepted. 30 seats. No music. No mobile phones. Wheelchair access.

Dargate

The Dove Inn

Pub with high-class comfort food
Plum Pudding Lane, Dargate, ME13 9HB
Tel no: (01227) 751360
www.thedoveinndargate.co.uk
Modern British | £26
Cooking score: 2

Little changes at this simple uncluttered country pub: winter visitors are still welcomed with a crackling log fire, a few drinkers line the bar, and diners come for high-class comfort food that is in keeping with the tone. Potted brown shrimps, and breast of corn-fed chicken with black pudding and dripping chips give a solid British dimension to the modern cooking, but there's a Mediterranean feel, too, with the likes of wild mushroom risotto or confit shoulder of marsh lamb with Parmesan polenta. Lunchtime burgers, fishcakes and hearty filled baguettes are good value. Shepherd Neame supply the beer, and wines start at £15.

Chef/s: Phillip MacGregor. **Open:** Tue to Sun L 12 to 2, Tue to Sat D 7 to 9. **Closed:** Mon, one week Feb. **Meals:** alc (main courses £13 to £18). **Service:** not inc. **Details:** Cards accepted. 25 seats. 25 seats outside. Separate bar. No mobile phones. Wheelchair access. Music. Children allowed. Car parking.

Dover

The Allotment

Mightily satisfying urban bistro
9 High Street, Dover, CT16 1DP
Tel no: (01304) 214467
www.theallotmentdover.com
Modern British | £23
Cooking score: 3

'Dover is not somewhere you would expect to find a high standard of cooking', observed a ferry-bound visitor, happily adding that Dave Flynn's small but expansively welcoming restaurant 'contradicts that idea most thoroughly'. Reports applaud the simplicity that plays a strong part in dishes such as exquisite Spanish Trevélez ham served with celeriac, or the popular garlic and chilli prawns. This is not daring cooking, but it is freshly prepared from quality raw materials, as seen in 'melt-in-the-mouth' braised pork in cider, a rich Moroccan-style lamb served with couscous, and a show-stealing blueberry cheesecake. House wine is £15; the rest of the short, global list is offered at a uniform £19.

Chef/s: David Flynn. **Open:** Tue to Sat 8.30am to 11pm. **Closed:** Sun, Mon, 24 Dec to 16 Jan. **Meals:** alc (main courses £8 to £16). **Service:** not inc. **Details:** Cards accepted. 26 seats. 26 seats outside. Wheelchair access. Music. Children allowed.

Faversham

Read's

Long-serving gastronomic grandee
Macknade Manor, Canterbury Road, Faversham, ME13 8XE
Tel no: (01795) 535344
www.reads.com
Modern British | £56
Cooking score: 6

£5 OFF

David and Rona Pitchford have established Read's as a grandee on the Kent restaurant scene. Devotion to their customers is matched by loyalty to their home turf, and any home-grown endeavours are now fuelled by foodie activity across the county – from the Brogdale fruit trials to rare-breed meats reared on pastures owned by the local Wildlife Trust. The result is a repertoire of finely honed, seasonal dishes with influences from France and the Med grafted on to its British backbone. Roast loin of lamb is served on Savoy cabbage with celeriac fondant, sablé potatoes and rosemary jus, while breast of duck appears atop orange-braised chicory with kumquat purée and almond potatoes. Given the restaurant's reputation for 'enriching lives', wacky quotes beside each dish seem like genuinely affectionate frivolities rather than naff gimmickry: consider Brecht's credo 'grub first, then ethics', while sampling your fillet of locally smoked eel on new potato salad with tapenade and crispy bacon, but ignore Gerald Ford's dictum 'eating and sleeping are a waste of time' when ordering dessert – perhaps dark chocolate and salted caramel délice with hazelnut praline and milk ice cream. Back in the late 70s, Read's was one of the first serious restaurants in the UK to offer a totally British cheeseboard, and it remains a highlight of any meal here. Similarly, David Pitchford's passionately accumulated, 300-bin wine list has become a trademark over the years. Sixty cannily chosen 'best buys' (from £20) provide an unmissable introduction to the treasures on offer; also check out the fascinating flights of dessert tipples.

Chef/s: David Pitchford. **Open:** Tue to Sat L 12 to 2, D 7 to 9. **Closed:** Sun, Mon, 25 and 26 Dec, first week Jan, 2 weeks early Sept. **Meals:** Set L £25. Set D £56. **Service:** not inc. **Details:** Cards accepted. 55 seats. 24 seats outside. Separate bar. No music. No mobile phones. Wheelchair access. Children allowed. Car parking.

Average Price

The average price listed in main-entry reviews denotes the price of a three-course meal, without wine.

Folkestone

READERS RECOMMEND

Rocksalt

Seafood

4-5 Fishmarket Road, Folkestone, CT19 6AA

Tel no: (01303) 884633

www.rocksaltfolkestone.co.uk

'Overlooks Folkestone harbour...great spot for lunch. The quality of the ingredients is high, prices reasonable.'

Locksbottom

Chapter One

Big-city cooking at affordable prices

Farnborough Common, Locksbottom, BR6 8NF

Tel no: (01689) 854848

www.chaptersrestaurants.com

Modern European | £45

Cooking score: 5

Occupying a mock-Tudor building in Kent's own 'metroland', Chapter One has become a landmark for local foodies. The surroundings may please, but the main attraction is Andrew McLeish's supremely confident and technically assured cooking; commuters (and others) weaned on the gastronomic ways of the metropolis will recognise the culinary footprint, although prices are a world away from W1 overkill. Regionally sourced ingredients are the building blocks for a menu that might pair braised Kentish snails with smoked potato purée and poached cod cheeks, or combine pan-fried hake with lobster, gnocchi, oyster leaf and cockle butter. The Josper grill is deployed for everything from mackerel rillettes to prime ribeye steaks. The kitchen also dips into the exotic flavour box for the likes of roast Loch Duart salmon with aubergine purée, braised chickpeas and rose-petal harissa. To finish, white chocolate pannacotta with lime sorbet and pistachio espuma is suitably on-trend. At lunchtime (Sundays excepted) you can eat even more affordably in the brasserie, where the menu promises deep-fried fishcakes, tagliatelle with pork ragù and suchlike. France takes pole position on the pedigree wine list, although auspicious global varietals also figure prominently. Prices start at £16 (£4.75 a glass).

Chef/s: Andrew McLeish. **Open:** all week L 12 to 2.30 (3 Sun), D 6 to 11 (12 Fri and Sat, 10.30 Sun). **Closed:** first week Jan. **Meals:** alc (main courses £15 to £19). Set L £18.95. Sun L £20.50. **Service:** 12.5% (optional). **Details:** Cards accepted. 110 seats. 20 seats outside. Separate bar. Wheelchair access. Music. Children allowed. Car parking.

Lower Hardres

The Granville

Generous, uncluttered satisfaction

Street End, Lower Hardres, CT4 7AL

Tel no: (01227) 700402

www.thegranvillecanterbury.com

Modern European | £29

Cooking score: 4

More approachable and easier to book than its big brother The Sportsman in Whitstable (see entry), this is everything a solid roadside pub should be. Drinkers have ample space for supping pints of Shepherd Neame at the bar, while hungry souls can spread themselves around the rustically attired dining room. True to form, spot-on sourcing, big flavours and generous, uncluttered satisfaction are the kitchen's hallmarks, with lots of appetising ideas on the blackboard. Some dishes are fixtures (crispy duck with smoked chilli salsa, roast belly pork with crackling and apple sauce), but it's an ever-evolving feast. Recent hits have included a smoked salmon and wild garlic tart, carefully timed pollack with tartare sauce, and a nifty dessert of apple sorbet and jelly with burnt cream. The focaccia is always excellent and you can expect most main dishes to arrive with roast potatoes and a heap of greens. Service is 'sweet but slow' and the keenly priced, 40-bin wine list offers sound imbibing from £14.50 (£3.60 a glass).

Chef/s: Jim Shave. **Open:** Tue to Sun L 12 to 2 (2.30 Sun), Tue to Sat D 7 to 9. **Closed:** Mon, 26 Dec, 1 Jan. **Meals:** alc (main courses £15 to £19). **Service:** not inc. **Details:** Cards accepted. 55 seats. 30 seats outside. Separate bar. Wheelchair access. Music. Children allowed. Car parking.

Margate

ALSO RECOMMENDED

▲ The Ambrette

44 King Street, Margate, CT9 1QE
Tel no: (01843) 231504
www.theambrette.co.uk
Indian £5 OFF

Culinary expectations are not high when you get to Margate, yet people report well of the Ambrette. Try to turn a blind eye to the run-down building, for the food is a pleasant surprise. Dev Biswal's modern Indian cooking trumpets sound regional ingredients – Godmersham wood pigeon with ginger, aromatic spices, a game-mince patty, shallot and coriander raita (£5.25), brochettes of leg of Kentish lamb, slow-cooked with Kashmiri spices (£14.95) – and rounds it off with brilliant desserts. Service lacks polish, though. House wine £12.95. Closed Mon.

Oare

The Three Mariners

Popular pub where everything's done well
2 Church Road, Oare, ME13 0QA
Tel no: (01795) 533633
www.thethreemarinersoare.co.uk
Modern British | £25
Cooking score: 3

Something about The Three Mariners hits exactly the right spot, and year in, year out it remains one of the area's most popular pubs. Chef John O'Riordan now runs the place, continuing the excellent-value set lunch and the general buzzy atmosphere. There are a pair of dining rooms, a fine-weather terrace and a roomy bar for those with just a liquid appetite. The locally sourced food has no airs and graces: choice ranges from skate cheeks with lemon, garlic and parsley, via homely slow-braised ox cheek with red wine and porcini sauce to silky vanilla crème brûlée. It is all very well done, though reporters have noted that service could be more welcoming. House wine is £13.

Chef/s: John O'Riordan. **Open:** Tue to Sun L 12 to 2.30 (3.30 Sat, 4 Sun), Tue to Sat D 6.30 to 9 (9.30 Fri and Sat). **Closed:** Mon. **Meals:** alc (main courses £11 to £18). Set L £11.50 (2 courses) to £16.50. **Service:** not inc. **Details:** Cards accepted. 50 seats. 30 seats outside. Separate bar. No music. No mobile phones. Music. Children allowed. Car parking.

Ramsgate

Age & Sons

Terrific café/restaurant
Charlotte Court, Ramsgate, CT11 8HE
Tel no: (01843) 851515
www.ageandsons.co.uk
Modern British | £24
Cooking score: 3

Spread over three floors, in a 'nice conversion of an old warehouse near the harbour', Toby Leigh's terrific café/restaurant brings some culinary savoir-faire to Ramsgate. What sets this place apart is its uncompromising local sourcing, and readers applaud the kitchen's efforts. A starter of gnocchi with braised ox tongue has gone down well, but also look for venison if it is on the menu, fresh fish such as sea bass with spinach, salsify and brown shrimps, and pork belly with mashed potato, red cabbage and cider sauce. Otherwise, investigate the day's cheeses, kept at just the right temperature, and desserts such as pumpkin cake with sloe syrup. Enthusiastic staff ensure a warm welcome, and there are plenty of decent wines from £15.

Chef/s: Toby Leigh. **Open:** Wed to Sun L 12 to 3.30 (12.30 Sun), Wed to Sat D 6.30 to 9.30. **Closed:** Mon, Tue, 2 to 25 January. **Meals:** alc (main courses £10 to £22). Set L & D £9.50 (2 courses) to £12.50, not Sat D. Sun L £9.50. **Service:** not inc. **Details:** Cards accepted. 42 seats. 40 seats outside. Separate bar. Music. Children allowed.

ALSO RECOMMENDED

▲ Eddie Gilbert's

32 King Street, Ramsgate, CT11 8NT
Tel no: (01843) 852123
www.eddiegilberts.com
Seafood £5 OFF

You get 'good-quality food, attentive service and a good variation on the traditional fish and chips' at this Ramsgate combo – fishmonger and chippy downstairs, restaurant upstairs. The simple things are the best: 'very plump' cockles in lemon juice, mussels in Kent cider with cream and parsley, lightly boiled duck egg with eel soldiers, and 'damn good' haddock and chips (£9.50). There's also fritto misto, yoghurt and masala-marinated mackerel, and hot chocolate fondant (£5). Wines from £12.50. Closed Sun D.

St Margaret's-at-Cliffe

The Bay Restaurant

Cheery seaside vibes and cosmopolitan ideas
The White Cliffs Hotel, High Street, St Margaret's-at-Cliffe, CT15 6AT
Tel no: (01304) 852229
www.thewhitecliffs.com
Modern British | £25
Cooking score: 2

£5 OFF £30

Gavin Oakley, owner of nearby Wallett's Court (see entry), took over this prettily situated, weatherboarded inn in 2008, sprucing it up to create a fresh contemporary feel and a clutch of stylish rooms. It gives off a cheery seaside vibe (the beach is a mile away) and the food is just the ticket too, with keen prices, cosmopolitan ideas and plenty of locally landed seafood. Whether you fancy fish and chips or braised belly pork, the kitchen can oblige. It also rings the changes with roasted haunch of venison with forest mushrooms and winter greens, and desserts such as Black Forest chocolate brownie with black cherry ice cream. Wines from £15.50.

Chef/s: Andrew Butcher. **Open:** all week L 12 to 2, D 7 to 9. **Meals:** alc (main courses £14 to £20). Sun L £10 (1 course). **Service:** not inc. **Details:** Cards accepted. 50 seats. 50 seats outside. Separate bar. Wheelchair access. Music. Children allowed. Car parking.

Wallett's Court

Manor house with attention-grabbing food
Westcliffe, St Margaret's-at-Cliffe, CT15 6EW
Tel no: (01304) 852424
www.wallettscourt.com
Modern British | £40
Cooking score: 1

£5 OFF

The period features of this venerable manor house provide plenty to catch the eye. The food, too, deserves attention, and the repertoire celebrates regional producers and the seasons. A goats' cheese and shallot tart starter with poached pear and hazelnut salad could be followed by slow-braised pig's cheek with turnip and white onion broth, with a forced rhubarb crumble soufflé to finish. It comes with a wine list that certainly hits the spot, long on quality, short on pretension, with reasonable prices (from £16.95) to boot.

Chef/s: Ryan Tasker. **Open:** Sun L 12 to 2.30, all week D 7 to 9. **Meals:** Set D £40 (2 courses) to £45. Sun L £14.95 (2 courses) to £19.95. **Service:** not inc. **Details:** Cards accepted. 80 seats. Separate bar. Music. Children allowed. Car parking.

Small Hythe

Richard Phillips at Chapel Down

Convincing seasonal cooking and local wine
Chapel Down Vineyard, Small Hythe, TN30 7NG
Tel no: (01580) 761616
www.richardphillipsatchapeldown.co.uk
Modern British | £33
Cooking score: 3

V

The setting, above Chapel Down Vineyard's winery, is robustly rural, so this cool and contemporary restaurant is a surprise; it makes a strong visual statement that emphasises the kitchen's contemporary credentials. There's an acute seasonal edge to the cooking, mixed with a few Mediterranean touches and highly worked presentation, whether it's a heap of Cornish crab and crayfish tangled with roasted red peppers, avocado, baby watercress leaves and a light gazpacho dressing, or pork (slow-cooked belly, roast loin, braised cheek) teamed with creamed cabbage, black pudding and grain mustard sauce. The set lunch is equally convincing: potted salt beef with horseradish mayonnaise, sea bream with garlic and herb gnocchi and watercress purée, and poached pear with amaretti crumble. Service is willing but can lack polish. Chapel Down wines head a list that opens at £16.95.

Chef/s: Richard Phillips and Craig Wales. **Open:** Tue to Sun L 12 to 3.30 (6 Sun), Thur to Sat D 6.30 to 10.30. **Closed:** Mon. **Meals:** alc (main courses £15 to £19). Set L £12.95 (2 courses) to £14.95. Set D Thur only £25.50. Sun L £13.95. **Service:** not inc. **Details:** Cards accepted. 54 seats. 24 seats outside. Separate bar. Music. Children allowed. Car parking.

Speldhurst

George & Dragon

Historic pub with crowd-pulling cooking
Speldhurst Hill, Speldhurst, TN3 0NN
Tel no: (01892) 863125
www.speldhurst.com
Modern British | £25
Cooking score: 3

The George & Dragon is one of England's oldest pubs – a magnificent early thirteenth-century timbered building filled with inglenooks, vast flagstones, carved beams and ancient panelling. Bang-up-to-date cooking pulls in the crowds, however. The confident kitchen draws on excellent seasonal and organic ingredients sourced within a 30-mile radius. Dishes such as Rye Bay fish and chips show respect for pub tradition, but there are more ambitious choices too, perhaps Brede wild boar loin, sausage and pie with polenta cake and creamed cabbage, or sea bream with Jersey Royals, samphire and lemon and clam butter. Start with ham hock terrine and finish with a first-class sticky toffee pudding with vanilla ice cream. House wines from £14.90.

Chef/s: Michelle Porter. **Open:** all week L 12 to 2.30 (3.30 Sun), Mon to Sat D 7 to 9.30 (6.30 Sat). **Closed:** 1 Jan. **Meals:** alc (main courses £11 to £20). **Service:** 12.5% (optional). **Details:** Cards accepted. 110 seats. 120 seats outside. Separate bar. Wheelchair access. Music. Children allowed. Car parking.

Tunbridge Wells

Thackeray's

Refined modern French food
85 London Road, Tunbridge Wells, TN1 1EA
Tel no: (01892) 511921
www.thackerays-restaurant.co.uk
Modern French | £45
Cooking score: 4

V

Kent native Richard Phillips is now into his second decade as culinary custodian of William Makepeace Thackeray's old house – although the satirical Victorian wordsmith wouldn't recognise the place these days. Subtle elegance and up-to-the-minute design flourishes define the low-ceilinged dining room, where refined modern French cuisine is the order of the day. Phillips has a feel for his home turf, deploying ingredients with finesse and dexterity: a terrine of Dover sole and lime crème fraîche appears with four companions, including an oyster beignet and Wealden smoked eel; a duo of roast loin and braised shoulder of venison is embellished with cep purée; and line-caught sea bass might appear with roast violet artichokes and a butter bean and truffle fricassee. Desserts are also modishly intricate; witness a warm pistachio cake paired with black olive sorbet, orange blossom gel and carrot purée. Staff are totally professional but never 'starchy', and the wine list is packed with serious possibilities. House selections start at £14.

Chef/s: Christopher Bower. **Open:** Tue to Sun L 12 to 2.30, Tue to Sat D 6.30 to 10.30. **Closed:** Mon. **Meals:** alc (main courses £23 to £28). Set L £16.95 (2 courses) to £18.95. Set D £24.50 (2 courses) to

£26.50. Sun L £28.50. Tasting menu £65. **Service:** 12.5% (optional). **Details:** Cards accepted. 72 seats. 30 seats outside. Separate bar. Music. Children allowed.

ALSO RECOMMENDED

▲ The Black Pig

18 Grove Hill Road, Tunbridge Wells, TN1 1RZ
Tel no: (01892) 523030
www.theblackpig.net
Modern British £5 OFF

Cocktails and home-baked bread are part of a deliberately trendy package at this Tunbridge local with a foodie dining room attached. Deli-style ham boards are a feature, although the menu yo-yos between pub-grub staples (burgers, beer-battered cod) and more fashionable dishes – anything from goats' cheese salad with pickled beetroot (£5) to seared sea bass with mussel and saffron broth or slow-braised oxtail and wild mushroom pappardelle (£12.50). Pud could be lemon tart with raspberry sorbet. House wine is £15. Food all week.

Whitstable

JoJo's

Tapas star gets it right
2 Herne Bay Road, Whitstable, CT5 2LQ
Tel no: (01227) 274591
www.jojosrestaurant.co.uk
Tapas | £25
Cooking score: 4

Now settled into their new premises, Nikki Billington and her team are clearly getting it right, having created a genuinely unaffected eatery that draws appreciative folk from way beyond east Kent. The imaginatively converted former supermarket overlooking the North Sea deals well with light and space – a perfect backdrop for matchless seasonal ingredients that come with a generous Mediterranean input and a refreshingly direct approach to flavour. Every plate speaks for itself. From the specials board comes tender venison loin, slow-cooked pig's cheek with the crispiest of crackling atop a salad of leaves, walnuts and strips of raw celeriac and apple, or char-grilled squid, which might appear in company with chorizo, red pepper, garlic and haricot beans. The printed menu remains static, a port of call for regulars returning for impeccable charcuterie, mutton and feta koftas or Billington's famed deep-fried calamari. The popular BYO policy remains (corkage £2).

Chef/s: Nikki Billington, Adam Taylor and Rosemary Dawkins. **Open:** Wed to Sun L 12.30 to 2.30 (3.30 Sun), Tue to Sat D 6.30 to 9. **Closed:** Mon. **Meals:** alc (tapas £5 to £13). **Service:** not inc. **Details:** Cash only. 60 seats. No mobile phones. Wheelchair access. Music. Children allowed.

The Sportsman

Astonishing food in a dressed-down pub
Faversham Road, Seasalter, Whitstable, CT5 4BP
Tel no: (01227) 273370
www.thesportsmanseasalter.co.uk
Modern British | £32
Cooking score: 6

As you make the pilgrimage from Whitstable across windswept marshes, it's worth remembering that this area once fed the kitchens of Canterbury Cathedral. These days, however, it's an unofficial harvesting ground for The Sportsman – a gently buzzing, weather-beaten pub serving some of the most astonishing food of its kind in the UK. The landscape sets the mood – especially if the moon is full, or shimmering seaside light is streaming through the windows – and the whole place has a very special charge. Forget the poncey posturing of 'fine dining' and relish fine food as it should be, with paper napkins and dressed-down service. Stephen and Philip Harris have masterminded proceedings here since 1999, and have accrued sackfuls of self-sufficient cred along the way – baking 'fantastic' breads, churning their own butter, making sea salt, dry-curing hams, foraging 'free food' and supporting the locality's producers. The result is a chalked-up, daily menu full of delights – extraordinarily intense chicken liver pâté with mushroom carpaccio, deeply flavoured beetroot soup and unctuous pork belly with the 'most perfect crackling and mash you could ever find' are just some of its seasonal joys. As for fish, the mussel and bacon chowder garnished with ground bacon and chives is a bowl of pure potency, red mullet comes with a barnstorming bouillabaisse sauce, and brill fillets are simply laid on a heap of cabbage with a richly resonant vin jaune sauce. Meanwhile, desserts are from 'pudding heaven', especially the cherry and almond tart with cream-cheese ice cream. Philip Harris is happy to proffer shrewd advice when it comes to choosing from the tidy, affordable wine list. Bottles start at £15.95.

Chef/s: Stephen Harris and Dan Flavell. **Open:** Tue to Sun L 12 to 2 (2.30 Sun), Tue to Sat D 7 to 9. **Closed:** Mon, 25 and 26 Dec. **Meals:** alc (main courses £17 to £22). Tasting menu £55. **Service:** not inc. **Details:** Cards accepted. 55 seats. No mobile phones. Music. Children allowed. Car parking.

Wheelers Oyster Bar

One-off seaside gem
8 High Street, Whitstable, CT5 1BQ
Tel no: (01227) 273311
Seafood | £34
Cooking score: 4

'It's odd, a bit eccentric...but the food is damn good', is one verdict on this long-standing oyster bar and restaurant. With just four counter stools in the front and four tables in the small, old-fashioned back parlour it may be tiny, but it is beautifully astute at delivering cooking that is simultaneously skilled, sensitive and robust. Indeed, there is a hardcore following for Mark Stubbs' imaginative modern fish dishes: perhaps a generous, brilliantly cohesive starter of citrus-crumbed dab fillets served atop lobster and panzanella (bread and tomato) salad, the plate dotted with puréed wild garlic and fennel mayonnaise. To follow, a top-drawer dish of blanquette of lemon sole, cooked on the bone and presented with a pile of Kentish sea kale, crab ravioli, wild garlic and vongole sauce, then a delicate vanilla pannacotta with rhubarb. Bread is now made on the premises, service ambles along in a well-meaning way, and there's no licence, so BYO.

Chef/s: Mark Stubbs. **Open:** Thur to Tue 1 to 7.30 (7 Sun). **Closed:** Wed, 8 to 24 Jan. **Meals:** alc (main courses £19 to £22). **Service:** not inc. **Details:** Cash only. 16 seats. No music. Children allowed.

Williams & Brown Tapas

A taste of Spain
48 Harbour Street, Whitstable, CT5 1AQ
Tel no: (01227) 273373
www.thetapas.co.uk
Tapas | £25
Cooking score: 2

The enduring attraction of Whitstable's long-standing tapas bar is Christopher Williams' real understanding of the Spanish way of cooking. Décor is low-key, with a few cramped tables and bar stools at marble counters running the length of the windows. The menu includes 'simple, delicious' roasted cherry tomatoes on garlic toast, char-grilled lamb gigot with butter beans and aïoli, boquerones with guindilla peppers, and paella, all delivered quickly from the open kitchen. Your bill will soon add up, though Spanish house is a reasonable £14.95.

Chef/s: Christopher Williams, Andy Cozens and Antonio Julio. **Open:** all week L 12 to 2 (2.45 Sat and Sun), D 6 to 9 (9.30 Fri, 9.45 Sat). **Closed:** Tue and Wed from Nov to end Mar. **Meals:** alc (main courses £5 to £16). **Service:** 10% (optional). **Details:** Cards accepted. 32 seats. 6 seats outside. No mobile phones. Music. Children allowed.

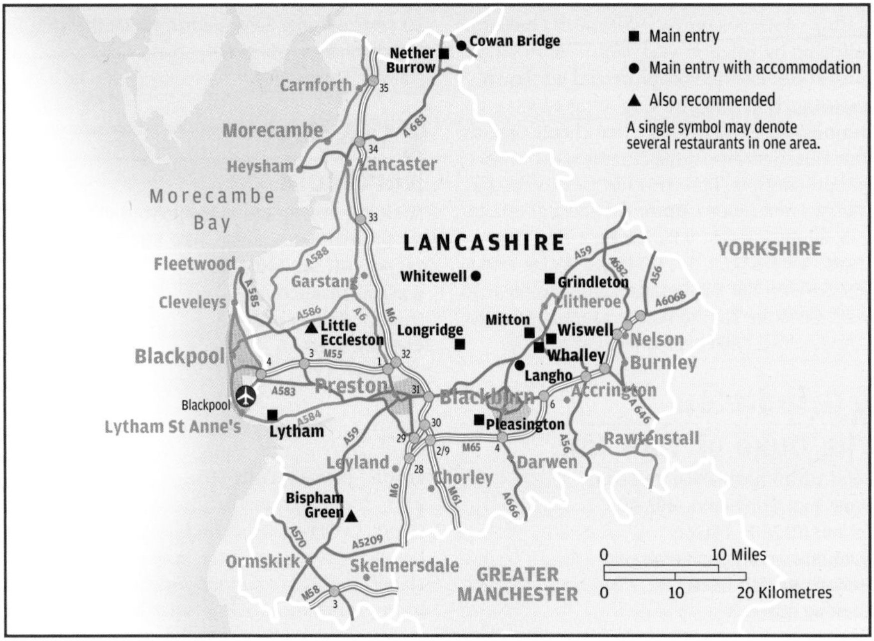

Bispham Green

ALSO RECOMMENDED

▲ The Eagle & Child

Malt Kiln Lane, Bispham Green, L40 3SG
Tel no: (01257) 462297
www.eagleandchildbispham.co.uk
British £5 OFF

Still resolutely a village hostelry, complete with a drinkers' bar, this enterprising eighteenth-century country pub and farm shop a few miles from the M6 also serves as a busy venue for generous food with a North Country accent. Plenty of local connections show up in the likes of wood pigeon with Madeira and mushroom sauce (£13) and Belted Galloway organic steak Rossini (£20) and there are Lancashire cheeses, locally made ice cream or good old apple crumble and custard to finish. Wines from £13.50. Open all week.

Cowan Bridge

Hipping Hall

Assured cooking in a lovely setting
Cowan Bridge, LA6 2JJ
Tel no: (01524) 271187
www.hippinghall.com
Modern British | £50
Cooking score: 4

This distinguished seventeenth-century house is in a 'beautiful setting' and its star turn is the fifteenth-century dining room where a minstrels' gallery, beamed ceiling and tapestry-covered walls lay on the period style without seeming fusty. Brent Hulena heads up the kitchen and he has built a reputation for simple but artful dishes that surf the seasons with ease. 'Faultless' and 'superbly executed' choices have included 'luscious' pork belly with crispy skin, accompanied by pickled shaved vegetables to cut through the richness, and beautifully tender ox cheek with a 'delicate but wonderfully rich sauce'. Elsewhere,

scallops with pea purée and pancetta might be followed by fillet of wild halibut with wild mushroom risotto, samphire and nettles. A 'melting chocolate pudding' wins a big thumbs-up, as do the excellent cheeses and the 'fun and inventive' canapés, amuse-bouche and pre-dessert. The wine list kicks off at £20.
Chef/s: Brent Hulena. **Open:** Sat and Sun L 12 to 1.45, all week D 7 to 9.15. **Closed:** 1 week Jan. **Meals:** Set L £29.50. Set D £49.50. Tasting menu £65. **Service:** not inc. **Details:** Cards accepted. 30 seats. Separate bar. No mobile phones. Wheelchair access. Music. Children allowed. Car parking.

Grindleton

The Duke of York Inn

Food with imagination and skill
Brow Top, Grindleton, BB7 4QR
Tel no: (01200) 441266
www.dukeofyorkgrindleton.com
Modern British | £28
Cooking score: 3
£5 OFF £30

'A wonderful dining experience', pronounced one reader, and such praise is echoed in many other reports for Michael Heathcote's splendid Ribble Valley pub. Reporters have particularly liked the pub's relaxed feel and 'reasonable' prices, as well as the chef's commitment to local produce. The menu shows a thorough understanding of ingredients, flavours and textures, as displayed in starters such as Lancashire cheese soufflé with walnut and beetroot salad. Meat and fish get equal billing on the main courses – roast fillet of cod with ginger-scented pak choi, king prawn tortellini and langoustine beurre blanc jostling for attention alongside Goosnargh chicken breast and Kiev with local greens, cauliflower mousse and dauphinoise potato. Desserts are of the comforting rhubarb trifle variety. The accessible wine list starts at £14.75.
Chef/s: Michael Heathcote. **Open:** Tue to Sun L 12 to 2, D 6 to 9 (5 to 8 Sun). **Closed:** Mon, 25 Dec. **Meals:** alc (main courses £13 to £26). Set L £11.99 (2 courses) to £13.99. Set D £12.99 (2 courses) to £14.99. Sun L £14.50 (2 courses) to £17.50. **Service:** not inc. **Details:** Cards accepted. 70 seats. 30 seats outside. Separate bar. No music. No mobile phones. Wheelchair access. Children allowed. Car parking.

Langho

Northcote

Mixing it among the metropolitan elite
Northcote Road, Langho, BB6 8BE
Tel no: (01254) 240555
www.northcote.com
Modern British | £50
Cooking score: 6
£5 OFF V

Northcote is a late Victorian manor house originally built for a single lady, who rattled around in it for a mere five years before selling it on. Not far from Blackburn, it enjoys a serene Lancashire spot and has recently benefited from a revamp. A space-age chandelier adds a contemporary note to the light dining room with its garden view, and there are seascapes and such by local artists. Nigel Haworth has been one of the handful of northern chefs who have enabled regions such as Lancashire to mix it among the metropolitan elite. The kitchen works with fine local materials to produce inspired combinations such as black pudding with pink trout in mustard and nettle sauce or Herdwick mutton as another starter, dressed in capers, honey and mint, with puréed Jerusalem artichoke. Reporters love being introduced to the unexpected, as in a main course of Cockerham goat encased in crisp puff pastry, served with salt-baked celeriac and watercress, or the roast halibut that comes with bacon and tempura-battered cauliflower in a fondue of Lancashire cheese. Eccles cakes and Manchester tart (the latter accompanied by a banana fritter) are highlights among desserts, and the vegetarian menus are full of invention too. There is also an excellent wine list with glass prices starting at £4.20.
Chef/s: Nigel Haworth and Lisa Allen. **Open:** all week L 12 to 1.30 (2 Sun), D 7 (6.30 Sat) to 9.30 (10 Sat, 9 Sun). **Closed:** 25 Dec. **Meals:** alc (main courses £23 to £34). Set L £25.50. Set D £56.50 (5 courses). Sun L £36 (4 courses). Tasting menu £82

(7 courses). **Service:** 10% (optional). **Details:** Cards accepted. 60 seats. Separate bar. No mobile phones. Wheelchair access. Music. Children allowed. Car parking.

Little Eccleston

ALSO RECOMMENDED

▲ The Cartford Inn

Cartford Lane, Little Eccleston, PR3 0YP
Tel no: (01995) 670166
www.thecartfordinn.co.uk
Modern European £5 OFF

Expect to find a new kitchen, riverside restaurant and eight extra bedrooms at this handsome seventeenth-century inn on the banks of the river Wyre – which underlines its success since Patrick and Julie Beaume took the helm. The vibe and style are bold and contemporary and the brasserie-style food draws on locally sourced ingredients, from scallops and cauliflower gratin (£7.25) to main course favourites like Pilling Marsh lamb hotpot (£9.95). Dessert could be glazed lemon tart with raspberry sorbet. House wine is £14.95. No food Mon L.

Longridge

Longridge Restaurant

Paul Heathcote's Lancashire flagship
104-106 Higher Road, Longridge, PR3 3SY
Tel no: (01772) 784969
www.longridgerestaurant.co.uk
British | £40
new chef

 **V**

Paul Heathcote may have sold off some of his culinary assets in the region, but his slick flagship restaurant in a whitewashed cottage continues to fly the flag and deliver lashings of generous hospitality. New chef Hywel Griffith arrived from Ynyshir Hall in Wales (see entry) as the Guide was going to press, but it seems likely he will continue Longridge's esteemed reputation as a champion of re-invented British regional food with occasional cutting-edge add-ons. Dished such as grilled black pudding with a 62°C duck egg, hash browns and mustard hollandaise or roast Goosnargh duck breast and confit leg with beetroot, thyme and orange have become standards over the years and will hopefully continue to thrill as the kitchen re-groups. The lively wine lists starts at £16.50 (£4 a glass).

Chef/s: Hywel Griffith. **Open:** Wed to Sun L 12 to 2.30 (8 Sun), Wed to Sat D 7 to 9.30 (10 Fri, 6 to 10 Sat). **Closed:** Mon, Tue. **Meals:** alc (main courses £20 to £28). Set L £14.50 (2 courses) to £19.50. Sun L £25. Gourmet menu £45. **Service:** not inc. **Details:** Cards accepted. 60 seats. Separate bar. Music. Children allowed. Car parking.

Lytham

Hastings Eating & Drinking House

All-purpose regional eatery
26 Hastings Place, Lytham, FY8 5LZ
Tel no: (01253) 732400
www.hastingslytham.com
British | £25
Cooking score: 3

Local man Warrick Dodds returned to his roots in 2009 to bring this all-purpose eatery to the Fylde coast, not far from Blackpool. Regionally sourced produce is rounded up and presented either in a light-bite, bar food format or as more formal dishes in the split-level restaurant, where striking contemporary artworks add vibrancy and the cooking does the rest. Start with shrimp, duck egg and mace salad with tarragon mayonnaise, marsh samphire and a crumpet to orientate yourself, before Goosnargh duck breast with prunes and duck-fat chips, or hickory-smoked salmon with fennel in saffron and coriander dressing. The bread-and-butter pudding comes gussied up with chocolate and Baileys. Sunday brunch is a popular occasion and the short wine list opens at £14.99 for house wines from southwest France, with eight available by the glass.

Chef/s: Warrick Dodds. **Open:** Tue to Sun 11 to 2.30 (5 Sun), Tue to Sat D 5 to 10. **Closed:** Mon. **Meals:** alc (main courses £9 to £19). Set L £9.95 (2 courses) to £13.95. Set D £12.95 (2 courses) to £17.95. Sun L £13.99. **Service:** not inc. **Details:** Cards accepted. 120 seats. 40 seats outside. Separate bar. Music. Children allowed.

Mitton

The Three Fishes

A beacon of Lancashire quality
Mitton Road, Mitton, BB7 9PQ
Tel no: (01254) 826888
www.thethreefishes.com
British | £23
Cooking score: 2

It may be squirreled away in the Forest of Bowland, but that doesn't stop visitors trekking out to Nigel Haworth's original Ribble Valley Inn (see entries for the Highwayman, and Clog & Billycock). You can still sup real ales and warm your cockles by open fires, but this place is really about food. All the Haworth trademarks are here – matchless local and seasonal ingredients, and a refreshingly direct approach to flavour. Battered haddock and chips cooked in dripping is 'difficult to ignore', but there's serious competition from liver and crispy bacon or rack of lamb with haricot beans in tomato sauce. Knickerbocker Glory is a nicely nostalgic pud. House wine is £14.50. Note, bookings are now taken.

Chef/s: Simon Bower. **Open:** Mon to Sat L 12 to 2, D 6 to 9 (5.30 to 9 Sat). Sun 12 to 8.30. **Closed:** 25 Dec. **Meals:** alc (main courses £9 to £20). Sun L £15 (2 courses) to £19.50. **Service:** not inc. **Details:** Cards accepted. 120 seats. 40 seats outside. Separate bar. No music. Wheelchair access. Children allowed. Car parking.

Nether Burrow

The Highwayman

Twenty-first century local
Burrow Road, Nether Burrow, LA6 2RJ
Tel no: (01524) 273338
www.highwaymaninn.co.uk
British | £20
Cooking score: 2

This country pub is upbeat and modishly rustic in a twenty-first century fashion; winter fires crackle and a jaunty, smiling welcome greets newcomers and regulars alike. Success lies in its strong North Country identity, with cooking that makes a good fist of celebrating scrupulously sourced regional ingredients. Every dish speaks for itself, whether a lunchtime snack of Sandhams cheese on toast, a North Sea fish pie or Herdwick mutton pudding with forager's mash, black peas and capers. Desserts such as lemon meringue pie are equally convincing in their own way. House wine is £14.50. Note: like other Ribble Valley Inns (The Three Fishes, Clog & Billycock, see entries), The Highwayman now takes bookings.

Chef/s: Colin McKevitt. **Open:** Mon to Sat L 12 to 2, D 6 to 9 (5.30 Sat). Sun 12 to 8.30. **Closed:** 25 Dec. **Meals:** alc (main courses £9 to £20). **Service:** not inc. **Details:** Cards accepted. 120 seats. 40 seats outside. Separate bar. No music. Wheelchair access. Children allowed. Car parking.

Pleasington

The Clog & Billycock

Pulling out all the stops
Billinge End Road, Pleasington, BB2 6QB
Tel no: (01254) 201163
www.theclogandbillycock.com
British | £20
Cooking score: 2

This third link in Nigel Haworth's Ribble Valley Inns chain comfortably straddles the divide between pub and restaurant, dispensing a marvellous range of Daniel Thwaites beers, but elsewhere pulling out all the stops for customers in search of food. Loyal regulars return enthusiastically for cooking that draws on a strong regional identity – for one visitor, Lancashire hot pot 'really did embrace all that is good about local produce and traditional cooking'. Cheese and onion pie, platters of local seafood, char-grilled Goosnargh chicken, and jam roly-poly and custard are all comfortingly familiar, 'nothing flash'. Wines from £14.50. Note, all Ribble Valley Inns now take bookings (see entries for the Highwayman and the Three Fishes).

Chef/s: James Harper. **Open:** Mon to Sat L 12 to 2, D 6 to 9 (5.30 Sat), Sun 12 to 8.30. **Closed:** 25 Dec. **Meals:** alc (main courses £9 to £20). **Service:** not inc. **Details:** Cards accepted. 136 seats. 50 seats outside. Separate bar. Wheelchair access. Children allowed. Car parking.

Whalley

Food by Breda Murphy

Popular deli/restaurant with excellent food

Abbots Court, 41 Station Road, Whalley, BB7 9RH
Tel no: (01254) 823446
www.foodbybredamurphy.com
Modern British | £24
Cooking score: 2

This popular deli/restaurant has attracted reams of praise for its smiling, efficient staff and 'continually changing' selection of 'excellent' food, all of which is cooked on the premises. It's a daytime-only venue with fortnightly themed evenings on Fridays and Saturdays, and it's worth booking ahead, whether calling in for lunch or a 'true English afternoon tea'. Expect sprightly, flavoursome dishes such as warm salad of Goosnargh chicken livers with honey-glazed chipolatas and sautéed mushrooms followed by Breda's fish pie with champ or char-grilled steak with carrot and beansprout salad and Thai dressing. Puds include treats like chocolate fondant cake and saffron rice pudding. Wines start at £12.95.

Chef/s: Gareth Bevan. **Open:** Tue to Sat L 10 to 6, Fri and Sat D 7 to 9.30. **Closed:** Sun, Mon, 24 Dec to 4 Jan. **Meals:** alc (main courses £7 to £16). Set D £42.50 (5 courses). **Service:** not inc. **Details:** Cards accepted. 50 seats. 20 seats outside. Wheelchair access. Music. Children allowed. Car parking.

Whitewell

The Inn at Whitewell

A grand inn for all seasons

Whitewell, BB7 3AT
Tel no: (01200) 448222
www.innatwhitewell.com
British | £32
Cooking score: 3

Comfort and seemingly effortless vintage chic is what this centuries-old inn is all about. It's a handsome, rambling place set high on the banks of the river Hodder, with long-ranging views towards the Trough of Bowland. Food is a key part of the operation and a flexible approach means plenty of choice on where to eat (the bar gets the thumbs-up from readers). The cooking is underpinned by well-sourced ingredients and a sound knowledge of the classics, as in a starter of smoked Goosnargh chicken with a beetroot and horseradish relish and garlic cream. Mains could include roast fillet of pancetta-wrapped pork served with grain mustard mash, red onion marmalade, Bramley apple purée and cider roasting juices. The wine list features a few interesting bottles and value is fair throughout (prices start at £13.50).

Chef/s: Jamie Cadman. **Open:** all week L 12 to 2, D 7.30 to 9.30. **Meals:** alc (main courses £15 to £26). **Service:** not inc. **Details:** Cards accepted. 150 seats. 30 seats outside. Separate bar. No music. No mobile phones. Wheelchair access. Children allowed. Car parking.

DINING AT SOURCE

Reconnecting with the countryside has made restaurants proud of their suppliers, citing them on menus and striving to source the finest ingredients locally. Many restaurants even offer dining at source. At **The Parrot Inn** in Surrey and **The Black Sheep** in Pembrokeshire, ingredients come from the owners' nearby farms. Venture into the grounds of many restaurants and you'll find rows of beanpoles, heritage tomatoes, carrots and herbs. **The Bell at Skenfrith**, the **Felin Fach Griffin** near Brecon and even **Pied-à-Terre** in Fitzrovia are among many that nurture kitchen gardens, while **The Pot Kiln** in Berkshire offers game shot by the owners.

Foraged food is flourishing, from samphire with wild sea trout at **The Foxhunter** in Monmouthshire to wood sorrel with vintage potatoes at **L'Enclume**. Restaurants such as **Fins** in Ayrshire offer locally caught fish; it also boasts a smokehouse and farm shop. Other restaurants with produce for sale include **Food by Breda Murphy** in Lancashire and **The Goods Shed** in Canterbury Farmers' Market, where everything comes directly from producers' stalls. Food doesn't get more traceable than that.

Wiswell

NEW ENTRY

Freemasons Country Inn

Gussied-up boozer with foodie aspirations
8 Vicarage Fold, Wiswell, BB7 9DF
Tel no: (01254) 822218
www.freemasonswiswell.co.uk
Modern British | £30
Cooking score: 4

Local spies reckon that the Ribble Valley is quietly morphing into a foodie destination – witness the return of chef Steven Smith, who was brought up in these parts before hitting the big time. Now he's at the helm of the Freemasons, a gussied-up country inn with lofty gastronomic aspirations and an underwritten mood of classy informality. 'Waking up the taste buds' is his business, and he proves the point with a tricksy starter of tandoori monkfish, pork nuggets and scratchings with sweet potato and cumin, or a cocktail of Muncaster crab, apple, radish and shaved fennel. Mains provide real interest too; crispy breast of lamb with wild garlic, bacon risotto and morel sauce, or butter-poached haddock with leeks, mussels and local cider, plus chips served in a dinky metal basket ('a nice touch'). Clever desserts also earn top marks for flavour and presentation; lemon meringue pie with Walnut Whips and salted walnut ice cream, for example. The 250-strong wine list offers a goodly assortment by the glass, with bottles from £14.50.

Chef/s: Steven Smith. **Open:** Tue to Sat L 12 to 2.30, D 5.30 to 9 (6 to 9.30 Fri and Sat). Sun 12 to 8. **Closed:** Mon, 3 to 19 Jan. **Meals:** alc (main courses £15 to £24). Set L and D £12.95 (2 courses) to £15.95. Sun L £22.95. **Service:** not inc. **Details:** Cards accepted. 75 seats. No mobile phones. Music. Children allowed.

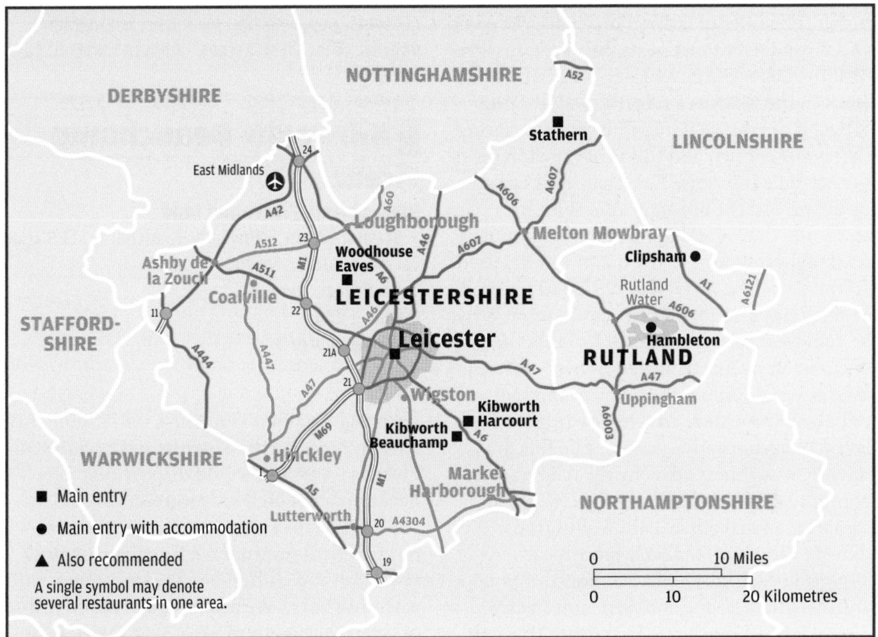

Clipsham

The Olive Branch

Pretty village inn with top ingredients
Main Street, Clipsham, LE15 7SH
Tel no: (01780) 410355
www.theolivebranchpub.com
British | £31
Cooking score: 3

A glance at the suppliers' map on the back of the menu should tell you that regional sourcing is the mantra behind this impressive foodie inn – although it also has the seasons covered with its log fires and pretty summertime garden. Warm pumpkin-seed bread, juicy sausages, locally reared meats and artisan cheeses are some of the building blocks for a daily line-up of dishes ranging from pub classics (smoked haddock fishcakes) to more adventurous plates – say rabbit, hazelnut and pickled carrot salad or baked sea bass with chickpea and chorizo caponata. Puddings are a draw, as is the 'first-class' drinks selection: real ales share the limelight with a terrific list of imaginatively chosen wines from £16.50.

Chef/s: Sean Hope. **Open:** all week L 12 to 2 (3 Sun), D 7 to 9.30 (9 Sun). **Meals:** alc (main courses £13 to £25). Set L £16.95 (2 courses) to £19.95. Set D £26.50. Sun L £24.95. **Service:** not inc. **Details:** Cards accepted. 48 seats. 30 seats outside. Separate bar. Wheelchair access. Music. Children allowed. Car parking.

Hambleton

Hambleton Hall

An outstanding country house hotel
Ketton Road, Hambleton, LE15 8TH
Tel no: (01572) 756991
www.hambletonhall.com
Modern British | £70
Cooking score: 7
V

Tim and Stefa Hart are into their fourth decade at the helm of Hambleton, one of central England's outstanding country house

hotels. The tides of fashion may have ebbed and flowed over those years, but a certain level of stylish panache never goes out of vogue. Built in the 1880s as a rather grand hunting lodge, it overlooks Rutland Water in a setting that is all serenity, and this is reflected in the immaculate interiors. The décor is light and uplifting and the dining room, with its terracotta drapes and upholstery, is supremely relaxing. Now turn to the menu and the food. Aaron Patterson arrived in 1992, and his is one of the longest residencies in the country. What he achieves is astonishing, all brought off without an overbearing ego or over-written menus – if anything the descriptions almost undersell the dishes, which are composed of layers of authoritative flavour. The foie gras terrine, its richness offset by the tang of cherry compote, delighted one reporter, while the signature main course, hare Wellington, delivers eloquent, tenderly juicy meat alongside cabbage and bacon, fondant potato and a brilliant prune and Armagnac sauce. That note of French classicism runs through many dishes, but there are also more recognisably modern British forays, such as the wasabi and sesame pannacotta that comes with steak tartare and bresaola, or the caramelised endive and puréed kumquat that accompany a roast breast and confit leg of Goosnargh duck. A nice pause is allowed before desserts, which only heightens their impact when they arrive. Lemon tart lives up sharply to the second half of its name, an orange jelly is full of 'exploding sprinkles', or you might opt for the uncomplicated luxury of a passion fruit soufflé, served with passion fruit and banana sorbet. Accompanying the opulent cooking is an equally glitzy wine list, but one that hunts down small producers as carefully as the famous names. Look for Vrignaud's Chablis, Vajra's Langhe Nebbiolo and The Ruins Syrah, from an organic vineyard in South Africa's Robertson Valley, among much else. Prices start around £20.
Chef/s: Aaron Patterson. **Open:** all week L 12 to 1.30, D 7 to 9.30. **Meals:** alc (main courses £33 to £39). Set L £22 (2 courses) to £36.50. Set D £38.50 (3 courses) to £47.50. Sun L £43. Tasting menu £67. **Service:** 12.5% (optional). **Details:** Cards accepted. 60 seats. Separate bar. No music. No mobile phones. Wheelchair access. Children allowed. Car parking.

Kibworth Beauchamp

Firenze

Pitch-perfect Florentine food
9 Station Street, Kibworth Beauchamp, LE8 0LN
Tel no: (0116) 2796260
www.firenze.co.uk
Italian | £35
Cooking score: 3

£5 OFF

Lino and Sarah Poli's mission is to imbue this ancient Leicestershire hamlet with echoes of Florence, and few would dispute that they have delivered on their promise. Lino's cooking is true to the seasons, pleasing the punters with summer truffle risotto or pasta with crab and chilli when the sun shines, and warming hearts with helpings of bollito misto or celeriac cannelloni with confit pork and lentils come winter. Readers have also endorsed the merits of pitch-perfect fillet steak with pesto and halibut poached in red wine, as well as the legendary rosewater pannacotta layered with Turkish delight. Also don't miss the tremendous array of artisan cheeses with chestnut honey and 'mustard fruits'. Service is quietly attentive; Sarah Poli is lauded as an 'amazing hostess'. The wine list parades Italian viticulture in all its vinous glory, from baronial Tuscans to Sicilian wild cards. Top names abound, but check the Firenze selection for bargains from £17.50; otherwise take an extended tour by the glass.
Chef/s: Lino Poli and Max Faulkner. **Open:** Tue to Sat L 12 to 3, D 7 to 11. **Closed:** Sun, Mon, bank hols, 25 and 26 Dec, 1 Jan. **Meals:** alc (main courses £17 to £25). Set L and D (Mon to Thur) £17.50 (2 courses) to £22.50. **Service:** not inc. **Details:** Cards accepted. 60 seats. Wheelchair access. Music. Children allowed.

Kibworth Harcourt

NEW ENTRY

Boboli

Italian surprise package
88 Main Street, Kibworth Harcourt, LE8 0NQ
Tel no: (0116) 2793303
www.bobolirestaurant.co.uk
Italian | £25
Cooking score: 1

In the next village to sibling Firenze (see entry), Boboli is a cheery surprise package with all the artisan attributes of its *fratello maggiore*, plus an Italianate piazza out back. Drop by at any time for a pizza or a plate of carefully wrought rustic pasta. Otherwise, try a bowl of cockle-warming ribollita (Tuscan soup) ahead of 'mamma's lasagne', richly gooey belly pork with roast fennel, or fillet of mackerel with lentils and pancetta. Regional Italian cheeses are served with 'mustard fruits', and the tasty little wine list (from £14.75) is packed with choice pickings from the Firenze cellar.

Chef/s: Lino Poli and Tom Wilde. **Open:** all week 10am to 9.30pm (4pm Sun). **Closed:** 25 and 26 Dec, 1 Jan, bank hols. **Meals:** alc (main courses £8 to £17). Set L £13.50 (2 courses) to £16.50. Sun L £14.50 (2 courses) to £22.50 (4 courses). **Service:** not inc. **Details:** Cards accepted. 90 seats. 28 seats outside. Separate bar. Music. Children allowed. Car parking.

Leicester

Entropy

Crowd-pulling all-dayer
42 Hinckley Road, Leicester, LE3 0RB
Tel no: (0116) 2259650
www.entropylife.com
Modern British | £30
Cooking score: 4

Don't be fooled by the simple appearance of this all-day restaurant and bar in a less-than-attractive suburb to the west of Leicester's city centre. Although the blackboard menus feature toasted panini and a range of easy options, the printed daily menu, served at lunch and dinner, hints at skill and knowledge in the kitchen. Goats' cheese beignets add a distinctly cheffy note to a peppery watercress soup, as do the well-judged wild mushroom tortelloni that accompany a deliciously gamey roast pheasant. Simpler dishes such as sausage and mash or steak and chips demonstrate the restaurant's commitment to sourcing quality ingredients. Desserts are more showy; pannacotta comes with a Muscadel jelly, while chocolate fondant is pepped up with bergamot and served with homemade pistachio ice cream. Given the flashes of occasional brilliance in the kitchen, it's no surprise that the breakfasts also draw a crowd. House wine is £15.50.

Chef/s: Tom Cockerill. **Open:** all week 10.30am to 10pm (9.30 to 6 Sun). **Closed:** 25 and 26 Dec, 1 Jan. **Meals:** alc (main courses £11 to £19). Sun L £10. **Service:** not inc. **Details:** Cards accepted. 40 seats. 10 seats outside. Separate bar. Wheelchair access. Music. Children allowed.

ALSO RECOMMENDED

▲ Bobby's

154-156 Belgrave Road, Leicester, LE4 5AT
Tel no: (0116) 2660106
www.eatatbobbys.com
Indian vegetarian £5 OFF

Family-run Bobby's (named after a Bollywood blockbuster) is a vegetarian guru among Belgrave Road's sweet centres and sari shops. It's come a long way since its café/takeaway days back in the 70s, although Gujarati food in all its subtle, spicy glory is still the kitchen's strength, from brilliant kachori, patra, dhokla and other farsan snacks (from £3.50) to sizzling mogo (cassava) kebabs, numerous takes on paneer, assorted veggie specials, say creamy peas with fenugreek (£4.95), and even some Indo-Chinese specialities. House wine is £8.95, but regulars drink lassi. Open all week.

▲ Maiyango

13-21 St Nicholas Place, Leicester, LE1 4LD
Tel no: (0116) 2518898
www.maiyango.com
Modern European £5 OFF

Tricked out like a funky ethnic nightspot, this good-time venue attached to Hotel Maiyango is a riot of wooden beach-shack cladding, silky drapes, cushions and tribal artefacts. Brain-teasing cocktails and clubby sounds add to the groove, although the kitchen takes its work seriously, plundering the city's excellent fish market and local suppliers for upbeat dishes ranging from seared scallops with Thai mussels and cauliflower purée to roast rump and shoulder of Moroccan-spiced lamb with apricots and walnuts. To finish, try luscious date parfait. Three courses £29 (£19.50 at lunchtime). Wines from £16.75. Closed Sun L.

Stathern

Red Lion Inn

Hospitable pub with good local grub
2 Red Lion Street, Stathern, LE14 4HS
Tel no: (01949) 860868
www.theredlioninn.co.uk
British | £20
Cooking score: 2

This pretty red-roofed inn in the Vale of Belvoir is all about warming hospitality. 'They didn't know it was a special occasion, but the way we were looked after, they didn't need to', was one reader's heartening eulogy. Hanging kitchen utensils and crooked beams make a homely backdrop for some assured pub cooking along the lines of deep-fried whitebait, proper fish pie and the highly praised beef brisket with rösti potato and cabbage. Lincolnshire sausages come from the village butcher. Finish with chocolate tart and pistachio ice cream. The short wine list opens with house French at £13.75, £3.50 a glass.
Chef/s: Sean Hope. **Open:** all week L 12 to 2 (3 Sun), Mon to Sat D 6.30 to 9 (7 to 9.30 Sat). **Meals:** alc (main courses £9 to £17). Set L £12.50 (2 courses) to £15.50. Sun L £19.50. **Service:** not inc. **Details:** Cards accepted. 60 seats. 60 seats outside. Separate bar. Wheelchair access. Music. Children allowed. Car parking.

Woodhouse Eaves

NEW ENTRY

Paul Leary at The Woodhouse

Village restaurant with big ideas
43 Maplewell Road, Woodhouse Eaves, LE12 8RG
Tel no: (01509) 890318
www.thewoodhouse.co.uk
Modern British | £35
Cooking score: 3

£5 OFF **V**

Chef Paul Leary has his thumb in several Leicester pies, but this loyally supported village destination remains his top priority. Nestled cheek-by-jowl with its cottage neighbours, the Woodhouse is famed for its big ideas and grandstanding approach to regional produce. Low lights and pastel hues set the mood, while Leary adorns his pretty plates with all manner of flavours, textures and embellishments – although these can get in the way of the essentials. Wild pickings also have their say and the kitchen stays with the programme: witness rare-breed belly pork with peanut milk, halibut paired with sticky nuggets of oxtail and crisped-up buckthorn, or an elaborate dish of aged local beef with purple nettle risotto, parsley root and scurvy grass hollandaise. Meals are fleshed out with trendy extras, from a shot of chilled tomato consommé to a green apple sorbet perfumed with Parma violet 'fragments'. House wine is £20.
Chef/s: Paul Leary. **Open:** Tue to Fri and Sun L 12 to 2.30 (4 Sun), Tue to Sat D 6.30 to 10 (7 Sat). **Closed:** Mon, 26 and 31 Dec, 1 Jan. **Meals:** Set L £11.50 (2 courses) to £14. Set D £15.95 (2 courses) to £35. Sun L £21.95. Tasting menu £55 (9 courses). **Service:** not inc. **Details:** Cards accepted. 50 seats. Separate bar. Music. Children allowed. Car parking.

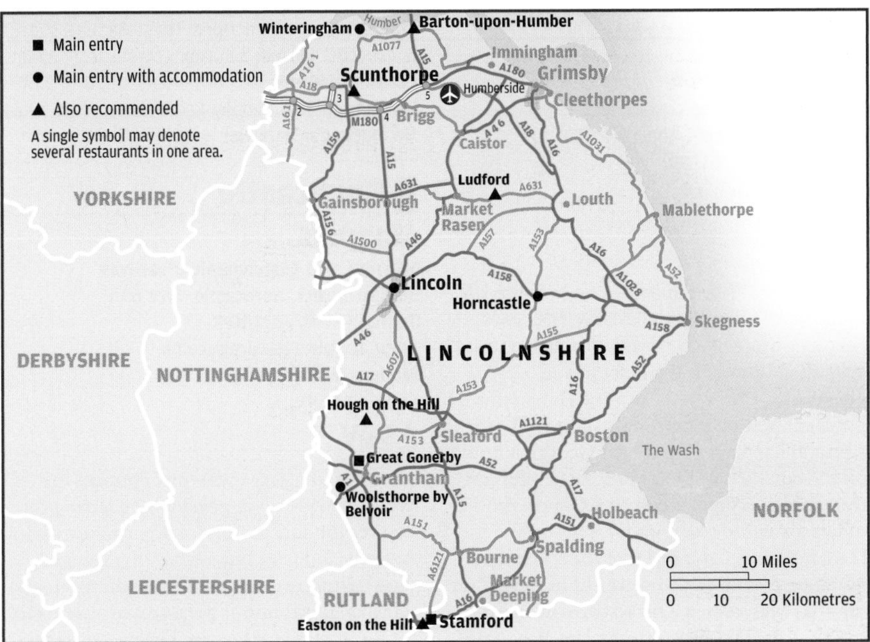

Barton-upon-Humber

ALSO RECOMMENDED

▲ Elio's

11 Market Place, Barton-upon-Humber, DN18 5DA
Tel no: (01652) 635147
www.elios-restaurant.co.uk
Italian

After almost 30 years at his trattoria-with-rooms, Elio Grossi can consider himself an old hand at the restaurant game. But despite his longevity he remains as enthusiastic as ever, thanks to a loyal following drawn by a menu that's as Italian as Puccini. The culinary magnum opus embraces antipasti (from £5.50), pastas, pizzas and high-protein main courses such as bistecca alla pizzaiola or osso buco alla milanese (£16.50). Set menus are good value. Italian house wine is £18.50. Accommodation. Open Mon to Sat D only.

Easton on the Hill

ALSO RECOMMENDED

▲ The Exeter Arms

21 Stamford Road, Easton on the Hill, PE9 3NS
Tel no: (01780) 756321
www.theexeterarms.net
Modern British £5 OFF

The refurbishment of this roadside inn not far from the A1 has created an upbeat country retreat that oozes relaxed, unbuttoned charm and character. A crowd-pleasing menu of straightforward modern British food hits all the right notes, whether it's a simple dish of macaroni cheese made with Lincolnshire Poacher (£10) or confit duck leg with chorizo, butter beans and spinach (£13.50). Desserts such as vanilla pod pannacotta with raspberry broth have a high comfort factor, too. House wine is £13.95. Accommodation. No food Sun D.

Great Gonerby

Harry's Place

A rare treasure
17 High Street, Great Gonerby, NG31 8JS
Tel no: (01476) 561780
Modern French | £60
Cooking score: 7

£5 OFF

In a world of 'latest openings' and chefs with their own TV shows, a place like Harry's becomes more of a treasure with each passing year. Well into their third decade of operations, Harry and Caroline Hallam have pursued their own personal trajectory with admirable tenacity. In a listed Georgian house on the outskirts of Grantham, they offer just three tables, a short menu and a whole world of heartwarming hospitality. This is the Hallams' home, and one that they welcome you into as though you were old friends. One reporter was offered a lift to the station by Harry as the taxi was running late. When not chauffeuring, he is a dab hand in the kitchen too. The menus are built around carefully chosen ingredients of impeccable quality, and the culinary approach is classically based French, with deeply rich, wine-based sauces a strong point. A bowl of garlicky mushroom soup with truffle oil is an earthy delight on a cold day; its alternative, perhaps, escalopes of Scottish salmon in a sauce combining Sauternes and Noilly Prat. Main course proteins are out of the top drawer: poulet de Bresse, black Gascon pork, local Longhorn beef, fantastic seasonal game such as grouse and woodcock. Pork loin is teamed with duck foie gras and prunes, its sauce combining Vouvray and Calvados as well as fresh sage and tarragon for huge savoury impact. Sea bass is lightly sautéed and served with black lentils in a sauce of red wine, basil and coriander. A disinclination to gild the lily sees desserts such as apricot soufflé or cherry brandy jelly with peppered yoghurt favoured over anything more elaborate. It's accompanied by an almost provocatively short wine list that opens with Riojas at £5 a glass for white, but is otherwise mostly classic French.

Chef/s: Harry Hallam. **Open:** Tue to Sat L 12.30 to 2, D 7 to 8.30. **Closed:** Sun, Mon, 1 week from 25 Dec, bank hols. **Meals:** alc (main courses £38 to £39). **Service:** not inc. **Details:** Cards accepted. 10 seats. No music. Car parking.

Horncastle

Magpies

Warmth and gastronomic pleasures
73 East Street, Horncastle, LN9 6AA
Tel no: (01507) 527004
www.magpiesrestaurant.co.uk
Modern British | £42
Cooking score: 5

V

A terrace of black-and-white cottages in a Wolds market town provides the setting for this very model of a personally run restaurant. Andrew and Caroline Gilbert manage the show with great warmth and dedication, and there are gastronomic pleasures in abundance for those making the trip. The mood is easy, and Andrew's cooking takes full account of Lincolnshire's larder, respecting the seasons and celebrating the good things of the region with some highly accomplished, modern food full of clear tastes and contrasts. A trio of Lincoln Red beef (rolled ribeye, steak and kidney sausage, braised tongue with caramelised shallots) is one telling signature dish, and he looks to Grimsby for fish – perhaps roasted sea bass in partnership with Thai crab cakes, mooli and pomegranate salad. There's smoked eel too, as well as a generous helping of local game – witness boned and roasted partridge deliciously embellished with potato and pancetta terrine, candied garlic and maple-glazed parsnips. The sight of a mischievous 'sweet shop terrine' with Turkish delight sorbet or Liquorice Allsorts ice cream might set you reminiscing, but the kitchen also assembles some very grown-up desserts (orange and passion-fruit soufflé with lime yoghurt sorbet, say). The wine list is pure delight for aficionados, with top-flight French names and a contingent of serious, wallet-

friendly goodies from the Americas and the Antipodes. Around 20 Corney & Barrow house recommendations start at £16.05.
Chef/s: Andrew Gilbert. **Open:** Wed to Fri and Sun L 12 to 2, Wed to Sun D 7 to 9.30. **Closed:** Mon, Tue, 27 Dec to mid Jan. **Meals:** alc L only (main courses £16.95). Set D £42. **Service:** not inc. **Details:** Cards accepted. 34 seats. 8 seats outside. No mobile phones. Wheelchair access. Music. Children allowed.

Hough on the Hill

ALSO RECOMMENDED

▲ The Brownlow Arms

Grantham Road, Hough on the Hill, NG32 2AZ
Tel no: (01400) 250234
www.thebrownlowarms.com
British

There's always a 'warm and welcoming atmosphere' at this intimate country inn and restaurant-with-rooms. Dinner is the main event, driven by quality local, seasonal produce, and the kitchen's accomplished traditional approach is given a modern spin. Oak-smoked salmon with beetroot mousse and salad (£7.50) might be followed by herb-crusted shoulder of lamb with crushed root vegetables and rosemary jus (£15.95). Desserts have included steamed rhubarb and stem ginger pudding with rhubarb and custard ice cream. House wine is £15.95. Open Mon to Sat D and Sun L.

Lincoln

The Old Bakery

Charming restaurant with great ingredients
26-28 Burton Road, Lincoln, LN1 3LB
Tel no: (01522) 576057
www.theold-bakery.co.uk
Modern European | £30
Cooking score: 2

This 'very friendly' restaurant occupies a charming old building and modern conservatory in the heart of Lincoln near the cathedral and castle. Local ingredients and international influences combine in inventive dishes such as pan-fried Lincolnshire partridge breast with pear carpaccio, pearl barley, butternut squash and mustard risotto, followed by hay and herb-roasted Gloucester Old Spot baby pig with red cabbage, potato purée and Armagnac sautéed plums, or slow-braised beef brisket with a horseradish potato cake, sherry-braised red onion and thyme sauce. A lengthy international wine list, divided by style, kicks off at £14.95.
Chef/s: Ivano de Serio. **Open:** Tue to Sun L 12 to 2, Tue to Sat D 7 to 9. **Closed:** Mon, 26 Dec, 1 Jan. **Meals:** alc (main courses £14 to £25). Set L £12.50 (2 courses) to £16.50. Sun L £17 (3 courses). **Service:** not inc. **Details:** Cards accepted. 75 seats. Wheelchair access. Music. Children allowed.

ALSO RECOMMENDED

▲ No 14 Bistro

14 Bailgate, Lincoln, LN1 3AE
Tel no: (01522) 576556
www.no14bistro.co.uk
French £5 OFF

Formerly Fourteen, this Lincoln fixture has been recast as an unreformed bistro of the coq au vin/cassoulet/steak frites variety. Inside, the mood is welcoming and there's obvious attention to detail in the kitchen. Open with baked Camembert or a soufflé of the day (£6.25), move on to hot venison and foie gras pie or a bowl of fish-packed bouillabaisse (£15.95) and finish with crêpes Suzette. House wine £12.50. Open all week.

Ludford

ALSO RECOMMENDED

▲ The Black Horse Inn

Magna Mile, Ludford, LN8 6AJ
Tel no: (01507) 313645
www.blackhorseludford.co.uk
Modern British £5 OFF

Once part of a smallholding on the Louth/Market Rasen Road, this family-run boozer is now bang on the money when it comes to serving stripped-down rustic food with a strong British accent. Oxtail terrine (£4.95), roast goose breast with date sauce, and mutton casserole with pearl barley (£12.50) plead the patriotic cause, while salt cod brandade, hake en papillote and veal chop with apples and Calvados wave the continental flag. Finish with steamed orange pudding or prune and Armagnac tart. Wines from £13.45. No food Sun D or Mon.

Scunthorpe

ALSO RECOMMENDED

▲ San Pietro

11 High Street East, Scunthorpe, DN15 6UH
Tel no: (01724) 277774
www.sanpietro.uk.com
Modern European

Housed in a Grade II-listed windmill with courtyard gardens, the Catalano family's restaurant looks to Italy for much of its inspiration, although the kitchen happily accommodates Yorkshire beef fillet, slow-cooked belly pork and home-smoked duck breast. Pan-fried scallops with pea tortellini and pea sorbet, or potted rabbit with foie gras (£8.95) might precede a duo of chicken with Parmesan, sweet potato and red pesto cream (£18.95) or sea trout on lobster and truffle risotto. To finish, perhaps a hot chocolate pyramid. House wine is £17.50. Closed Mon L and Sun.

Stamford

NEW ENTRY

Assiette Dameon Clarke

Confident newcomer with assured food
8-9 St Paul's Street, Stamford, PE9 2BE
Tel no: (01780) 489071
www.assietterestaurant.co.uk
Modern British | £35
Cooking score: 3

Occupying a wonky old terraced house within hooraying distance of Stamford's public school, Assiette's low-beamed dining room sits quaintly below street level, with oblong mirrors adding depth and some 'gaudy' modern art enhancing the chatty, unbuttoned mood. This is the first solo venture from seasoned chef Dameon Clarke and his assured food comes with considerable attention to the finer details – despite the odd flirtation with deep-fried garlic butter and suchlike. A dish of roasted lamb loin with two confit 'Scotch eggs', milky sweetbreads, tiny white turnips and fresh peas shows maturity and confidence, while John Dory with white asparagus and artichoke barigoule or pan-fried turbot with buttered spinach, heirloom carrots and cauliflower purée suggest a feel for fish. To finish, don't miss the deconstructed lemon meringue pie with towers of wobbly, aromatic basil jelly and zesty lemon ice. The 50-bin wine list does its job; prices from £15.95.

Chef/s: Dameon Clarke. **Open:** Tue to Sun L 12 to 3, Tue to Sat D 6 to 9.30. **Closed:** Mon. **Meals:** alc (main courses £19 to £23). Set L £15.50 (2 courses) to £20.50. Set D £17.50 (2 courses) to £22.50. Sun L £16.95 (2 courses) to £21.95. **Service:** not inc. **Details:** Cards accepted. 60 seats. 20 seats outside. Music. Children allowed.

Jim's Yard

Terrific neighbourhood eatery
3 Ironmonger Street, Stamford, PE9 1PL
Tel no: (01780) 756080
www.jimsyard.biz
Modern European | £26
Cooking score: 2

There's much to praise about the Trevors' low-key neighbourhood eatery: the setting in converted seventeenth-century cottages, the pretty courtyard, the robustly seasonal menus, the charming service. The cooking more than lives up to expectations in every detail – 'no nonsense, no messing, but pitched exactly right', whether it's flavourful chicken liver and garlic pâté, potato gnocchi with rocket, Cornish Yarg and marinated artichokes or rump of lamb with chorizo, rosemary cassoulet and roast new potatoes. Among straightforward posh comfort desserts, a wonderful warm egg custard tart with

poached rhubarb stands out. Wines from £14.25. Related to Jim's Bistro, Peterborough, see entry.
Chef/s: James Ramsay. **Open:** Tue to Sat L 12 to 2.30, D 6 to 9.30. **Closed:** Sun, Mon, 2 weeks from 25 Dec, last week Jul, first week Aug. **Meals:** alc (main courses £12 to £18). Set L 13.50 (2 courses) to £16.50. **Service:** not inc. **Details:** Cards accepted. 50 seats. 24 seats outside. Separate bar. Wheelchair access. Music. Children allowed.

Winteringham

Winteringham Fields

Something rather special
1 Silver Street, Winteringham, DN15 9ND
Tel no: (01724) 733096
www.winteringhamfields.co.uk
Modern European | £75
Cooking score: 5

For some it's '*la crème de la crème*', for others it's simply an adorable, special-occasion hideaway, but everyone concurs that Winteringham Fields is North Lincolnshire's finest. This renovated farmhouse out in the flatlands may not look much from the outside, but the ordinary frontage hides something rather special, from the moment you are personally greeted by chef/proprietor Colin McGurran and his superbly trained, ever-attentive staff. Inside, all is sumptuous furnishings and open fires, but it's the food that really captures the imagination. Lunch continues to get top reviews, although similar dishes are also the cornerstones of the carte and tasting menus. What follows can be truly dazzling: an 'incredibly potent' Parmesan pannacotta to alert the palate, silky celeriac velouté enriched with a 62oC poached egg, salt-crusted quail with escabèche, pressed vegetable terrine and toasted bread espuma... the procession of luxurious, finesse-laden successes goes on and on. The kitchen can also play tricks, wrapping up smoked haddock risotto in a potato 'cannelloni' and serving it with a quail's egg baguette, for example. Fanciful, multi-layered desserts also deliver a barrage of big hits – think chocolate and pistachio feuillantine with confit orange zest and sensational, 'lingering' pistachio ice cream. Take time out (or stay over) if you want to get the full measure of the distinguished wine list: pages of glorious Burgundies and other French treasures give way to beefy Sassicaias, trendy Tasmanians, luscious 'stickies' and more besides. Prices start at £28 (£7.50 a glass).
Chef/s: Colin McGurran. **Open:** Tue to Sat L 12 to 3, D 7 to 10. **Closed:** Sun, Mon, 2 weeks Dec/Jan, 3 weeks Aug. **Meals:** Set L £35 (2 courses) to £39.95. Set D £65 (2 courses) to £75. Tasting menu £79. **Service:** not inc. **Details:** Cards accepted. 80 seats. Separate bar. No music. No mobile phones. Children allowed. Car parking.

Woolsthorpe by Belvoir

Chequers Inn

Honest country boozer
Main Street, Woolsthorpe by Belvoir, NG32 1LU
Tel no: (01476) 870701
www.chequersinn.net
Modern British | £26
Cooking score: 1

£5 OFF £30

'What a treat', exclaimed a winter visitor to this traditional country pub, much taken by the blazing fires and the large, traditional-looking bar ('all beams and big kitchen tables'). Reporters have been delighted with the honest food and homespun English die-hards (sausage, mash and onion gravy) as much as classic European ideas such as ham hock terrine with white bean purée or fillet of cod with chorizo, potato and vegetable cassoulet. Good fixed-price deals, too. House wine £14.
Chef/s: Mark Nesbit. **Open:** all week L 12 to 2.30 (4 Sun), D 6 to 9.30 (8.30 Sun). **Meals:** alc (main courses £10 to £18). Set L £11.50 (2 courses) to £15. Set D £13.50 (2 courses) to £16.50. Sun L £11.95 (2 courses). **Service:** not inc. **Details:** Cards accepted. 90 seats. 60 seats outside. Separate bar. Wheelchair access. Music. Children allowed. Car parking.

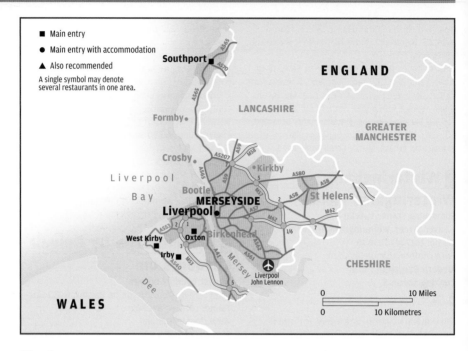

Irby

Da Piero

From Sicily with love
5 Mill Hill Road, Irby, CH61 4UB
Tel no: (0151) 6487373
www.dapiero.co.uk
Italian | £30
Cooking score: 5

It's been a busy year for Piero and Dawn Di Bella. They have not only trained up their son to work in the kitchen, but have also expanded into the premises next door – which should alleviate the rather 'cramped' conditions and 'cliquey intimacy' experienced by some visitors. Otherwise, it's business as usual at this warmly affectionate little restaurant in the far-flung reaches of the Wirral. Da Piero stands or falls by its ingredients and the main man provides an object lesson in diligent sourcing, whether he is procuring provisions from his native Catania or the Merseyside markets. The result is cooking of extraordinary clarity, with rustic detailing and a profusion of natural, sun-drenched flavours. Sicily is the principal gastronomic marker, defining everything from silky-soft caponata with sweet/vinegary undertones to canni cunzata (marinated char-grilled beef rump served with grilled tomatoes on the vine) – an 'absolute belter', according to one devotee. Others have rhapsodised over perfectly al dente linguine with a 'clingy' lemon dressing, meaty Sicilian sausages with stewed Umbrian lentils, penne with a ragù of hand-minced rose veal, and meatballs with tomato and pea sauce. Desserts also win hearts and minds, if glowing reports of a rich cannolo with Piero's special candied orange peel are anything to go by. The all-Italian wine list offers a whistle-stop tour of the regions, with prices from £10.90 a carafe.

Chef/s: Piero Di Bella. **Open:** Tue to Sat D only 6 to 11. **Closed:** Sun, Mon, 25 and 26 Dec, 1 and 2 Jan, 2 weeks Aug. **Meals:** alc (main courses £14 to £23). **Service:** not inc. **Details:** Cards accepted. 32 seats. Music. Children allowed.

Liverpool

Delifonseca

Full-on flavours above a deli
12 Stanley Street, Liverpool, L1 6AF
Tel no: (0151) 2550808
www.delifonseca.co.uk
Modern European | £20
Cooking score: 2

'Won't eat anywhere else', declares one fan of this informal restaurant tucked above a delicatessen of the same name. Downstairs there's 'the best produce from local farmers' markets and more', while upstairs much of that same produce comes as sharing platters or fillings in sandwiches (New Orleans po' boy; falafel wrap). The daily changing blackboard menu include soups such as cock-a-leekie or hot-and-sour beef, and full-flavoured mains ranging from wholesome root vegetable cottage pie with horseradish mash to mutton, date and tamarind curry with basmati rice and chickpea dhal. Hazelnut cake with vanilla ice cream comes highly recommended. Wines start at £13.35. A second restaurant, Delifonseca Dockside, has opened on Brunswick Quay, Sefton Street, Liverpool L3 4BN, tel: (0151) 2550808.

Chef/s: Saul O'Reilly. **Open:** Mon to Sat 12 to 9 (9.30 Fri and Sat). **Closed:** Sun, 25 Dec to 1 Jan, bank hols. **Meals:** alc (main courses £8 to £14). **Service:** not inc. **Details:** Cards accepted. 55 seats. Music. Children allowed.

NEW ENTRY

Host

More than high-street noodles
31 Hope Street, Liverpool, L1 9HX
Tel no: (0151) 7085831
www.ho-st.co.uk
Pan-Asian | £20
Cooking score: 1

It's a canteen that serves noodles, but not quite as you know them. From the team behind 60 Hope Street (see entry), Host takes the pan-Asian quickfire model and gives it a 50s fillip, with retro décor and a menu that's more restaurant than noodle shop. Service can vary as dishes such as sweetcorn fritters with tamarind caramel or a creamy-hot yellow seafood curry are brought to the long tables. Flavours are true, if not complex. House wine is £15, though you may prefer a beer.

Chef/s: Dave Fitzsimmons. **Open:** all week 11am to 11pm (10.30pm Sun). **Closed:** 25 and 26 Dec, 1 Jan. **Meals:** alc (main courses £9 to £13). **Service:** 10% (optional). **Details:** Cards accepted. 150 seats. 20 seats outside. Separate bar. Wheelchair access. Music. Children allowed.

The London Carriage Works

Satisfying menus, thick with local produce
Hope Street Hotel, 40 Hope Street, Liverpool, L1 9DA
Tel no: (0151) 7052222
www.thelondoncarriageworks.co.uk
Modern European | £40
Cooking score: 3

The London Carriage Works is one of Liverpool's best-known restaurants and is co-owned by leading local chef Paul Askew, a champion of local ingredients. So expect a menu packed with the best the area can offer, from pan-seared king scallops with slow-cooked belly pork to breast of pheasant with confit leg, curly kale, parsnip purée, quince and natural jus. Even desserts such as Cheshire apple and gingerbread crème brûlée give regional flavours a look-in. Named after the original owners' sign was uncovered during renovations, the building is a 'relaxed, chic' setting for afternoon tea as well as lunch and dinner. The wine list is as wide-ranging as the menu, with prices starting at £16.

Chef/s: Paul Askew. **Open:** all week L 12 to 3, D 5 to 10. **Meals:** alc (main courses £14 to £29). Set L and D £15 (2 courses) to £20. **Service:** not inc. **Details:** Cards accepted. 70 seats. Separate bar. Wheelchair access. Music. Children allowed.

NEW ENTRY

Lunya

Catalan cooking with a Liverpudlian twist
18-20 College Lane, Liverpool One, Liverpool, L1 3DS
Tel no: (0151) 7069770
www.lunya.co.uk
Spanish | £15
Cooking score: 2

Long-cherished dreams have a habit of disappointing, but ex-businessman Peter Kinsella's deli and tapas restaurant has charmed many readers since it opened in Liverpool's funky shopping district in 2010. 'Quality is the watchword,' observes one reader, and high standards apply to ingredients throughout. The brick-lined dining room has a relaxed air and the extensive menu speaks of Kinsella's Liverpudlian childhood as well as his Spanish travels. Try tender tortilla de hash – with corned beef and baked beans – or Catalan scouse made with morcilla and chorizo. Despite the odd inconsistency, classics like patatas bravas are well-rendered, and dessert might show off turrón in a classy sundae with sherry-soaked raisins. House wine from an all-Spanish list is £13.95.

Chef/s: Eirian Lunt. **Open:** all week 12 to 10pm (10.30pm Wed and Thur, 11pm Fri and Sat, 9.30pm Sun). **Closed:** 25 Dec. **Meals:** alc (£4 to £16). Set weekday L £7.95 (2 courses) to £9.95. **Service:** not inc. **Details:** Cards accepted. 150 seats. 30 seats outside. Wheelchair access. Music. Children allowed. Car parking.

The Side Door

Welcoming, good-value little bistro
29a Hope Street, Liverpool, L1 9BQ
Tel no: (0151) 7077888
www.thesidedoor.co.uk
Modern European | £30
Cooking score: 2

Handy for the universities and popular with theatre-goers, this 'excellent' bistro is a relaxed and economical alternative to Hope Street's grander eateries. A handsome Georgian building furnished with reclaimed tables and chairs, its clean, uncluttered air is enhanced by bare wood floors and white walls. The menus offer familiar flavours from around the world: maybe pan-fried chicken livers with harissa and pea couscous, ahead of roast duck breast with chorizo, Puy lentils and mash, with pear and almond tart and ice cream for dessert. The lunchtime Caesar salad is 'always a winner'. Wines start at £13.95.

Chef/s: Sean Millar and Michael Robinson. **Open:** Mon to Sat L 12 to 2.30 (2 Sat), D 6 to 10. **Closed:** Sun, 25 to 27 Dec, 1 Jan, bank hols. **Meals:** alc (main courses £12 to £18). Set L £12.95 (2 courses) to £14.95. Set D £13.95 (2 courses) to £25.95. Theatre menu £16.95 (2 courses) to £18.95. **Service:** 10% (optional). **Details:** Cards accepted. 52 seats. Music. Children allowed.

60 Hope Street

A smart Liverpool address
60 Hope Street, Liverpool, L1 9BZ
Tel no: (0151) 7076060
www.60hopestreet.com
Modern British | £40
Cooking score: 1

V

The Georgian frontage is traditional, the interior deliberately plain, but 60 Hope Street remains one of the smartest addresses in town. Here, the Manning brothers built a reputation for refined brasserie cooking with a Scouse inflection; with a new chef on board, could there be a reliance on past glories? At inspection Stilton soufflé, rich and light, would have been improved by more cheese and better chutney; good panko-crumbed pollack needed braised, not scorched, leeks. Desserts, such as smoked chocolate fondant, can be inventive and service is, in the main, attentive and considerate. Readers still rate the place, recommending 'great offers' at lunchtime. If it's not being thrown in as part of a deal, house wine is £16.95; otherwise, the full list abounds with tantalising possibilities from across the winemaking world.

Chef/s: Damien Flynn. **Open:** Mon to Fri L 12 to 2.30, Mon to Sat D 5 to 10.30. Sun 12 to 8. **Closed:** bank hols, 1 Jan, 26 Dec. **Meals:** alc (main courses £17 to £30). Set L and D £20 (2 courses) to £25. **Service:** not inc. **Details:** Cards accepted. 150 seats. 12 seats outside. Separate bar. Music. Children allowed.

★ READERS' RESTAURANT OF THE YEAR ★ NORTH WEST

Spire

A top Liverpool performer
1 Church Road, Liverpool, L15 9EA
Tel no: (0151) 7345040
www.spirerestaurant.co.uk
Modern European | £28
Cooking score: 4

Currently a top performer in the city, thanks to its competitive prices, warm vibes and sharp seasonal food, Spire is just a stroll from iconic Penny Lane and looks tickety-boo with its exposed brickwork, abstract art and wrought-iron staircase. The kitchen is openly eclectic, soaking up influences from near and far, but always taking due care with ingredients and presentation. Crispy confit duck served with Moroccan potato salad is a runaway success, although supporters have also cheered the foie gras parfait with sour cherries and the fillet of Red Poll beef with braised oxtail and horseradish cream. Mainstream European ideas receive plenty of attention too, whether it's grilled fillets of lemon sole with poached potatoes, red pepper and caper butter or a classic pairing of Goosnargh chicken breast and braised thigh with baby leeks and red wine sauce. To finish, hot chocolate fondant is a winner, with peach Melba pannacotta a close second. The wine list also casts its net wide, with decent drinking from £13.95.

Chef/s: Matt Locke. **Open:** Tue to Fri L 12 to 2.30, Mon to Sat D 6 to 9.30. **Closed:** Sun, 1 to 14 Jan. **Meals:** alc (main courses £14 to £20). Set L £9.95 (2 courses) to £12.95. Set D £13.95 (2 courses) to £16.95. **Service:** not inc. **Details:** Cards accepted. 70 seats. No mobile phones. Music. Children allowed.

Oxton

Fraiche

High drama and startling innovation
11 Rose Mount, Oxton, CH43 5SG
Tel no: (0151) 6522914
www.restaurantfraiche.com
Modern French | £45
Cooking score: 7

A mercurial one-man band on Merseyside, Marc Wilkinson runs diminutive Fraiche according to his own rules – commissioning suede chairs and freaky glass artworks to point up his tiny brown and cream-toned dining room, tutoring staff to his own standards of culinary knowledge and playing with flavours on the very fringes of gastronomic experimentation. Quite a feat for a modest 14-cover restaurant in a leafy conservation village not far from the urban expanses of Liverpool. Having adopted high-end, contemporary French cuisine as his framework, he looks to France for much of his produce but also manages to buy locally when it's up to scratch (unsalted butter is from a farm near Malpas, for example). The result is three different menus – 'elements', 'signature' and 'bespoke' (a surprise package spotlighting some of Marc's boldest creations), plus a separate 'concept' version featuring new ideas on Sundays. Dish descriptions are terse in the extreme – 'artichoke, hen's egg, smoked nut', 'wild sea bass, hazelnut quinoa, leeks', but the epigrammatic names conceal high drama and startling innovation on the plate, as well as an extraordinary amount of skill, artistry and sheer hard work. A 'signature' trip, for example, might take you all the way from a lead-off appetiser of rich cauliflower velouté and mussels dotted with crunchy passion-fruit seeds to apple soup, lemongrass pannacotta or cheeses 'with contrasting textures', via a bonbon of sweetbreads with smoked olive and apple textures, sea bass fillet with aubergine yoghurt and verjus, and (in more orthodox territory) loin of Herdwick lamb with fondant potato and chervil cream. The barnstorming, 300-bin wine list plunders the

world's vineyards for fascinating flavours, and mark-ups are friendly – even the heavyweight contingent of 'fine' vintages (mostly French grandees) won't necessarily break the bank. House wines start at £19.50 (£4.50 a glass); also note the excellent choice of sherries.
Chef/s: Marc Wilkinson. **Open:** Fri and Sat L 12 to 1.30, Wed to Sun D 7 to 9 (6 to 7 Sun). **Closed:** Mon, Tue, 25 Dec, first 2 weeks Jan, 2 weeks Aug. **Meals:** Set L £20 (2 courses) to £26.50. Set D £45 (3 courses). Bespoke menu £65. **Service:** not inc. **Details:** Cards accepted. 14 seats. 8 seats outside. Separate bar. No mobile phones. Wheelchair access. Music. Children allowed.

Southport

Bistrot Vérité

Good-humoured neighbourhood eatery
7 Liverpool Road, Birkdale, Southport, PR8 4AR
Tel no: (01704) 564199
French | £25
Cooking score: 3

A bastion of robust Gallic food in Southport's satellite village of Birkdale, Marc Vérité's self-named 'bistrot' is all you could wish for in a casual, good-humoured neighbourhood eatery. Check out the daily blackboard menu for a slice of boldly flavoured 'Provincial' cooking à la Elizabeth David – think crispy boudin noir with goats' cheese and apples, slow-braised pork cheeks with Armagnac and prunes, or sautéed calf's liver and kidney dijonnaise. Fish also has its say in classic soupe de poissons, a Brittany-style casserole with white wine and leeks or a combo of grilled sea bass fillet and seared scallops with celeriac purée and beurre rouge. For dessert, look no further than warm apple tart, rum baba or chocolate and orange marquise with crème anglaise. A short international wine list opens with vins de pays at £15.95 (£9.50 a carafe).
Chef/s: Marc Vérité. **Open:** Tue to Sat L 12 to 1.30, D 5.30 to 9.30. **Closed:** Sun, Mon, 25 and 26 Dec, 1 Jan, 1 week Feb, 1 week Aug. **Meals:** alc (main courses £9 to £25). **Service:** not inc. **Details:** Cards accepted. 45 seats. 14 seats outside. Music. Children allowed.

West Kirby

NEW ENTRY

The Collingwood

A second home for Aiden Byrne
Black Horse Hill, West Kirby, CH48 6DS
Tel no: (0151) 6254525
www.thecollingwood.co.uk
Modern British | £35
Cooking score: 3

£5 OFF **V**

Aiden Byrne has chosen a capacious Wirral pub – plain on the outside, tasteful on the inside – as the home for his second solo venture after the Church Green, Lynn (see entry). There's a pleasing flexibility about the menus; well-rendered pub food is offered alongside considerably more involved (and ambitiously priced) 'restaurant' dishes. Dinner might be a nutty salad of tender, rare sirloin with little truffle-topped potatoes and curls of watercress, followed by a macho bowl of crisp Fleetwood scampi with huge beef-dripping chips, though, sadly, no peas. Olive oil-poached salmon is a more refined fish dish, dressed with vibrant, silky pumpkin purée and sweet-sour pumpkin gnocchi. There's good stuff here, though not everything gels; at inspection a dessert of confit rhubarb with custard pannacotta was a travesty, and service was still finding a level. Wines from a brief list start at a pleasing £15 (£3 by the glass).
Chef/s: Aiden and Louis Byrne. **Open:** 12 to 9 (10 Fri and Sat, 5 Sun). **Closed:** 25 Dec. **Meals:** alc (main courses £23 to £28). Set D £29 (2 courses) to £35. Sun L £12.50. **Service:** not inc. **Details:** Cards accepted. 145 seats. 150 seats outside. Separate bar. Wheelchair access. Music. Children allowed. Car parking.

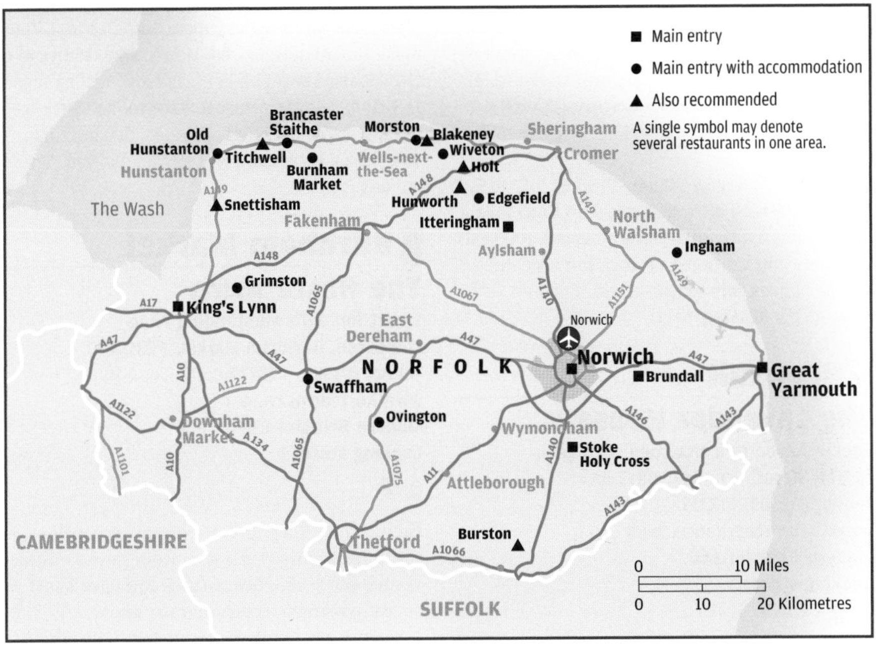

■ Main entry
● Main entry with accommodation
▲ Also recommended
A single symbol may denote several restaurants in one area.

Blakeney

ALSO RECOMMENDED

▲ The Moorings

High Street, Blakeney, NR25 7NA
Tel no: (01263) 740054
www.blakeney-moorings.co.uk
Modern British

Menus proudly trumpet locally landed seafood and seasonal game at this bistro-style café just a few yards from Blakeney's quay and miles of salt marsh. A platter of locally smoked fish with dill and mustard sauce (£8.50) is a good way to start, while simple, accurate cooking allows key flavours to shine through in dishes such as halibut with wilted spinach and fennel cream (£17.95) or lamb's kidneys sautéed with pancetta and rosemary with white bean ragoût (£16.50). Finish with rhubarb, honey and saffron tart. House wine is £14. Open all week for L, Tue to Sat D.

Brancaster Staithe

The White Horse

Thoroughbred with fabulous views
Brancaster Staithe, PE31 8BY
Tel no: (01485) 210262
www.whitehorsebrancaster.co.uk
Modern British | £26
Cooking score: 3

Spacious and pleasing though they are, the White Horse's multi-functional premises (pub, restaurant, hotel) might struggle to compete with the stupendous views of dinghy-strewn salt marshes from the dining room and conservatory. In summer, front and back patios also come into play. Fortunately, the food doesn't detract from the vista. The menu majors in marine life, so after a starter of creamy white bean soup there could be monkfish, accurately cooked and well-paired with cream and cider sauce. Or you might choose tapas, perhaps sweet escabèche of mackerel. Local food is a highlight, be it springtime asparagus or oysters. To finish, the sharing assiette (including sublime lemon tart) is recommended. Polite, prompt staff and an appealing global wine list (from £15.50) further distinguish this well-groomed thoroughbred.

Chef/s: Avrum Frankel. **Open:** all week L 12 to 2, D 6.30 to 9. **Meals:** alc (main courses £10 to £18). **Service:** not inc. **Details:** Cards accepted. 100 seats. 130 seats outside. Separate bar. No music. No mobile phones. Wheelchair access. Children allowed. Car parking.

Brundall

The Lavender House

Foodie haven in a thatched cottage
39 The Street, Brundall, NR13 5AA
Tel no: (01603) 712215
www.thelavenderhouse.co.uk
Modern British | £40
Cooking score: 3

V

Restaurateur Richard Hughes has fingers in several Norfolk pies, but this lovely thatched cottage a few miles from Norwich remains his first love: he runs a cookery school here and recently returned to the kitchen full time. East Anglian flavours sing out proudly on his dinner menus, from a little salad of three Norfolk cheeses with pickled pear to Lowestoft cod fillet with Brancaster mussels, leek and saffron chowder or Middle Eastern-themed breast of Breckland duck with parsnip purée, medjool dates and couscous. His smoked potato mash is legendary, while desserts might promise iced peanut butter parfait, caramel, chocolate mousse and salted peanuts – a Snickers bar, anyone? Sunday lunch is served in the Willi Opitz Room (homage to the legendary Austrian winemaker) and a Duval Leroy Champagne bar accentuates the restaurant's oenophile credentials. Dessert tipples are a star turn on the auspicious wine list, but there are classy names wherever you look. Prices start at £18.95 (£4.75 a glass).

Chef/s: Richard Hughes. **Open:** Sun L 12 to 2, Thur to Sat D 6.30 to 11. **Closed:** Mon to Wed, 26 Dec to 6 Jan. **Meals:** Set D £39.95 (5 courses). Tasting menu £58. Sun L £25 (4 courses). **Service:** not inc. **Details:** Cards accepted. 46 seats. Separate bar. Wheelchair access. Music. Children allowed. Car parking.

Burnham Market

The Hoste Arms

Smart inn with outstanding wine
The Green, Burnham Market, PE31 8HD
Tel no: (01328) 738777
www.hostearms.co.uk
Modern British | £30
Cooking score: 2

Facing the village green, the seventeenth-century coaching-inn is a rather grand edifice as such places go, beautifully converted and encompassing a traditional bar and conservatory extension as well as convivial dining rooms. A boldly ambitious menu of modern brasserie dishes offers plenty to choose from: start with truffled chicken liver parfait, or soft-shell crab tempura with mango/chilli/mint salsa, before setting about a well-marbled, 21-day-aged rib steak with beer-battered onion rings or lamb curry with all the trimmings. As well as desserts like apple bavarois with caramel sauce and apple sorbet, there are good English cheeses. A thoroughly commendable job has been done in the wine department, with assiduous notes to describe the outstanding global range, from glasses of house wine at £3.90 to the lush Austrian dessert tipples of Willi Opitz.

Chef/s: Aaron Smith. **Open:** all week L 12 to 2, D 6 to 9. **Meals:** alc (main courses £11 to £20). **Service:** not inc. **Details:** Cards accepted. 140 seats. 100 seats outside. Separate bar. No music. No mobile phones. Wheelchair access. Children allowed. Car parking.

Burston

ALSO RECOMMENDED

▲ The Crown

Mill Road, Burston, IP22 5TW
Tel no: (01379) 741257
www.burstoncrown.com
Modern European £5 OFF

'It's like dropping by to see an old friend', chimes a fan of this admirably chirpy, timber-framed Norfolk boozer, which parades its charms with a huge inglenook fireplace, ales from East Anglian microbreweries, live gigs and some thoroughly commendable food. Stay with the blackboard for the most interesting dishes – perhaps home-smoked duck with pickled courgettes (£5), mille-feuille of pork and artichokes with crab apple jelly (£14) or olive-crusted cod with bubble and squeak. House wine is £14. No food Sun D.

Edgefield

The Pigs

Boozer with bold-as-brass food
Norwich Road, Edgefield, NR24 2RL
Tel no: (01263) 587634
www.thepigs.org.uk
British | £23
Cooking score: 1

 £30

Honest intent, good drinking and bold-as-brass food are prime assets at this boozer deep in the Norfolk countryside. Tim Abbott scours the county and beyond for seasonal produce and puts it to proper use on a menu packed with juicy flavours. Tapas-style 'iffits' open proceedings (mutton pasties, beef dripping toast, smoked eel with beetroot relish), while mains could offer venison burgers or mighty helpings of 'Perfick' pork belly with 'smoky bacon' beans and black pudding. Beers are from Norfolk's brewing heroes, wines are from Adnams (prices start at £15.50).

Chef/s: Tim Abbott. **Open:** Mon to Sat L 11 to 3, D 6 to 9. Sun 12 to 9. **Meals:** alc (main courses £10 to £15). **Service:** not inc. **Details:** Cards accepted. 80 seats. 40 seats outside. Separate bar. No music. Wheelchair access. Children allowed. Car parking.

Great Yarmouth

Seafood Restaurant

Quality seafood and a warm welcome
85 North Quay, Great Yarmouth, NR30 1JF
Tel no: (01493) 856009
www.seafoodrestaurant-greatyarmouth.co.uk
Seafood | £35
Cooking score: 2

£5 OFF

'I have been eating here for over 25 years and the quality and service never falters', noted one visitor to this welcoming seafood restaurant, which is now well into its third decade. Miriam and Christopher Kikis are 'delightful hosts', according to another, all of which suggests a high level of consistency both front-of-house and in the kitchen, where the best seasonal fish is treated simply and without frills. Grilled prawns in garlic butter or native oysters might be followed by wild sea bass with chilli, garlic and soy sauce, or Dover sole with Dijon mustard and smoked ham. House wine from £14.50.

Chef/s: Christopher Kikis. **Open:** Mon to Fri L 12 to 1.45, Mon to Sat D 6.30 to 10.30. **Closed:** Sun, 2 weeks Christmas, last 2 weeks May, bank hols. **Meals:** alc (main courses £12 to £33). Set L £17 (2 courses) to £22. **Service:** not inc. **Details:** Cards accepted. 42 seats. Separate bar. Music. Car parking.

Visit us Online

To find out more about *The Good Food Guide*, please visit www.thegoodfoodguide.co.uk

Grimston

Congham Hall, The Orangery

Modern country house cooking
Lynn Road, Grimston, PE32 1AH
Tel no: (01485) 600250
www.conghamhallhotel.co.uk
Modern British | £40
Cooking score: 3

V

A fine Georgian manor house in a 'lovely setting', Congham Hall is what most people would expect a country house to be. It exudes comforting tradition and stylish modernism in equal measure – something that also applies to the food on the plate. Dishes are a refined version of modern British cooking and though reports have been mixed, at its best the kitchen exudes a quiet confidence. Local and seasonal produce remain the mainstay of the menu, from soused mackerel (with goats' cheese, watercress and hazelnut dressing) to cannon of lamb with a cannelloni of braised shoulder, spring greens and sauce antiboise, or skate wing with poached ratte potatoes and spring vegetables in a garden herb-infused nage. House wine is £22.

Chef/s: David Hammond. **Open:** all week L 12 to 1.45, D 7 to 9.15. **Meals:** alc (main courses £21 to £26). Set L £17.25 (2 courses) to £21.50. Sun L £25. Gourmand Menu £71.50. **Service:** not inc. **Details:** Cards accepted. 60 seats. 20 seats outside. No music. No mobile phones. Wheelchair access. Car parking.

Holt

ALSO RECOMMENDED

▲ Byfords

1 Shirehall Plain, Holt, NR25 6BG
Tel no: (01263) 711400
www.byfords.org.uk
Modern European

Self-styled as a 'continental-style café, store and posh B&B', Byfords is the sort of informal eatery all small towns should have. Set in a series of rambling beamed rooms, it buzzes through the day, serving breakfast and brunch, afternoon tea, all-day deli boards and 'posh' pizzas (from £6.95). There are also grazing dishes like chilli and lemon crab cakes or crispy beef with soy and chilli dip, and more substantial lunch and evening dishes, perhaps confit duck leg with horseradish mash and port jus (£14.95). Wines start at £15.50. Open all week.

Hunworth

ALSO RECOMMENDED

▲ The Hunny Bell

The Green, Hunworth, NR24 2AA
Tel no: (01263) 712300
www.thehunnybell.co.uk
Modern British

A refuelling point for walkers and cyclists, the Hunny Bell is out of the same menagerie as the Wildebeest Arms and Mackintosh's Canteen (see entries). Trading on its lovely setting, delightful beer garden and Victorian lineage, it serves up Norfolk ales and honest local food ranging from proper ploughman's right up to slow-braised venison. In between, expect twice-baked Norfolk Dapple cheese soufflé (£5.95), wild duck breast with Savoy cabbage and roasted celeriac (£12.95) and puds such as lavender pannacotta. House wine is £15. Open all week.

Ingham

The Ingham Swan

Ancient inn with thoroughly modern food
Sea Palling Road, Ingham, NR12 9AB
Tel no: (01692) 581099
www.theinghamswan.co.uk
Modern European | £36
Cooking score: 2

Moored on the outer fringes of the Norfolk Broads, this born-again thatched inn is now the setting for chef/proprietor Daniel Smith's culinary endeavours. Centuries-old timbers testify to the age of the building, but the cooking strikes a thoroughly modern note. Expect a good showing of Norfolk produce

(from Brancaster mussels to local lamb) and plenty of free-ranging, eclectic combos such as goats' cheese and sweet onion tartlets with Serrano ham and avocado purée or honey and ginger-roast guinea fowl with Savoy cabbage and orange jus. Real ales are from nearby Woodforde's Brewery, and the carefully chosen wine list includes 10 house selections at £18.50 (£4.95 a glass).
Chef/s: Daniel Smith. **Open:** Tue to Sun L 12 to 2 (3 Sun), Tue to Sat D 7 to 9. **Closed:** Mon, 25 and 26 Dec, 2 weeks Jan. **Meals:** alc (main courses £13 to £25). Set L £14.95 (2 courses) to £17.95. Set D £17.95 (2 courses) to £21.50. Sun L £17.95. **Service:** not inc. **Details:** Cards accepted. 52 seats. 20 seats outside. Music. Children allowed. Car parking.

Itteringham

The Walpole Arms

Inviting and well-run foodie hostelry
The Common, Itteringham, NR11 7AR
Tel no: (01263) 587258
www.thewalpolearms.co.uk
Modern British | £25
Cooking score: 2

Originally owned by Lord Walpole, this brick-built hostelry has become an inviting foodie haunt in the mid-Norfolk backwoods. You can slurp oysters or nibble lamb 'scrumpets' at the oak-beamed bar, but it pays to upgrade to the restaurant if you fancy sampling Jamie Guy's robust cooking to the full. His daily repertoire ranges from ham hock and split-pea salad to sprouting broccoli tempura, taking in calf's liver with crispy onions and thyme jus or mushroom and wild garlic risotto along the way. Fish from the coast could include witch sole with caper and lemon butter, and there might be salt caramel cheesecake to finish. Wines from £13.95.
Chef/s: Jamie Guy. **Open:** all week L 12 to 3 (4 Sun), Mon to Sat D 6 to 11. **Meals:** alc (main courses £8 to £18). Set L £12 (2 courses) to £15. Set D and Sun L £15 (2 courses) to £20. **Service:** not inc. **Details:** Cards accepted. 80 seats. 70 seats outside. Separate bar. Children allowed. Car parking.

Kings Lynn

NEW ENTRY

Market Bistro

Quaint eatery with quality local food
11 Saturday Market Place, Kings Lynn, PE30 5DQ
Tel no: (01553) 771483
www.marketbistro.co.uk
Modern British | £23
Cooking score: 2

Opposite a church in Lynn's oldest quarter, Market Bistro occupies quaint little premises (front lounge, fashionably grey back restaurant, upstairs roof terrace and private dining room) that have seen several restaurants come and go. Readers certainly hope it stays, judging from comments like 'lovely atmosphere' and 'fantastic locally sourced produce'. Sourcing and home production is indeed important on a menu offering own-smoked salmon or pigeon breast matched with watercress and pickled mushrooms, followed by roast lamb with a ramekin of flavoursome lamb stew. Finish with exemplary Norfolk strawberry cheesecake. The 26-strong wine list starts at £13.40.
Chef/s: Richard Golding. **Open:** Mon to Sat L 12 to 2, D 5 to 9. **Closed:** Sun, 25 and 26 Dec. **Meals:** alc (main courses £10 to £24). **Service:** not inc. **Details:** Cards accepted. 35 seats. 12 seats outside. Separate bar. Wheelchair access. Children allowed.

Morston

Morston Hall

Class act by the coast
The Street, Morston, NR25 7AA
Tel no: (01263) 741041
www.morstonhall.com
Modern British | £60
Cooking score: 5

V

Morston Hall sells itself with trim gardens, a certain brick-and-flint sturdiness and bags of culinary know-how. The house may be grandly Jacobean, but owners Galton and Tracy Blackiston try to keep things grounded with no-choice daily menus brimming with local flavours and acute seasonal detailing – be it baked line-caught cod with wild garlic sauce and braised salsify, or roast saddle of Norfolk lamb accompanied by beetroot purée, a cassoulet of haricot beans and home-cured bacon. Visitors have also raved over poached breast of teal with damson cheese and a dish of grilled black bream with locally foraged mushrooms and a lordly Champagne and caviar sauce, while treacle tart with custard ice cream and lemon purée is a brilliant conceit if you fancy finishing on a sweet note. For many, Morston Hall is 'an oasis of calm and professionalism', although some reports suggest that not everything is hunky-dory here: sloppy housekeeping, ill-trained staff 'trying to be posh' and a general lack of finesse can take the sheen off Galton's exceptional food. However, nothing dents the sense of occasion when it comes to perusing the leather-bound wine list. A page of house selections offers the chance to sample pure class by the glass (a Trimbach Pinot Gris, for example), with bottles starting at £25.

Chef/s: Galton Blackiston and Richard Bainbridge. **Open:** Sun L 12.30 for 1 (1 sitting), all week D 7.30 for 8 (1 sitting). **Closed:** 24 to 26 Dec, first 3 weeks Jan. **Meals:** Set D £60 (5 courses). Sun L £35. **Service:** not inc. **Details:** Cards accepted. 50 seats. Separate bar. No music. No mobile phones. Wheelchair access. Children allowed. Car parking.

Norwich

★ READERS' RESTAURANT OF THE YEAR ★
EAST ENGLAND

Roger Hickman's

Clean-cut seasonal flavours
79 Upper St Giles Street, Norwich, NR2 1AB
Tel no: (01603) 633522
www.rogerhickmansrestaurant.com
Modern British | £38
Cooking score: 5

£5 OFF

Roger Hickman's return to Norwich has been heralded as a triumph, and readers agree that he has lightened the mood considerably at his old stamping ground (formerly Adlard's). The dining room now feels cordial and chatty as well as affably civilised, and many of the old regulars are returning to reclaim their favourite tables in the sought-after, moodily lit area towards the rear of the restaurant. Hickman's cooking relies on clean-cut seasonal flavours, with fresh-faced presentation. A starter of wild duck breast with plum purée and an absolutely perfect deep-fried egg is given added richness with foie gras mousse, while roast scallops might appear in company with pork belly and shallot purée. Main courses tend to offer something equally robust (braised lamb with roast loin, aubergine caviar, wilted spinach and 'silky mash', for example) and desserts highlight the kitchen's fastidious touch – witness a flawless chocolate tart with tonka bean cream and 'superbly textured' hazelnut ice cream. Dinner also comes dressed up to the nines with some enticing extras including a palate-sharpening amuse-bouche (perhaps an intense butternut squash and coconut soup) as well as Hickman's outrageously mischievous, trompe l'oeil passion-fruit 'egg yolk'. The clear, thoughtful wine list parades top names such as Charles Melton Nine Popes and Avondale Muscat Rouge at extremely manageable prices. Bottles start at £17 and there are 14 tip-top selections from £4.50 a glass.

Chef/s: Roger Hickman. **Open:** Tue to Sat L 12 to 2.30, D 7 to 10. **Closed:** Sun, Mon, first week Jan, last week Aug, bank hols. **Meals:** Set L £16 (2 courses) to £19. Set D £30 (2 courses) to £38. Tasting menu £50. **Service:** not inc. **Details:** Cards accepted. 40 seats. Music. Children allowed.

ALSO RECOMMENDED

▲ The Assembly House

Theatre Street, Norwich, NR2 1RQ
Tel no: (01603) 626402
www.assemblyhousenorwich.co.uk
Modern British

Norwich's most stately and aristocratic eatery, the magnificent Georgian Assembly House is also a social hub and hotbed of artistic endeavours. Breakfast/brunch brings Cley

Smokehouse kippers, eggs Benedict and club sandwiches, while lunch promises everything from fishcakes with smoked paprika aïoli (£6) or goats' cheese and Waldorf salad to Norfolk bangers or seared salmon with tagliatelle, caper and olive dressing (£11.50). Genteel afternoon tea is an unmissable, must-book treat; also check out the bespoke sweet 'shop'/ cake counter in the lofty, pillared hall. Kir Royal is £6.50 a glass. Open all week.

▲ Mackintosh's Canteen

Unit 410, Chapelfield Plain, Norwich, NR2 1SZ
Tel no: (01603) 305280
www.mackintoshscanteen.co.uk
British

This sleek modern 'canteen' offers salads, sandwiches and light meals downstairs and 'honest British food' upstairs – although choices such as moules marinière (£6.95) or wild mushroom risotto suggest a slightly broader scope. True British options include macaroni cheese and toad-in-the-hole. The homemade beef burgers (from £8.95) come highly recommended. Desserts range from crème brûlée to bread-and-butter pudding. Staff 'are knowledgeable and make you feel special'. The international wine list starts at £16.25. Open all week.

▲ Shiki

6 Tombland, Norwich, NR3 1HE
Tel no: (01603) 619262
www.shikirestaurant.co.uk
Japanese

A leafy alfresco space scores bonus points at this terrific little Japanese canteen opposite Norwich Cathedral. Shiki rocks, as customers slurp noodles and spoon up bowls of nourishingly rich donburi (from £4.50) while energetic, T-shirted staff whizz around with dishes from the open kitchen. This is street food rather than high art – honest sushi and thick-cut sashimi (from £8.50), succulent yakitori skewers, teppanyaki, textbook tempura and other staples are all on target. Drink green tea, Japanese beer or saké (from £4 a shot), and pay as you leave. Closed Sun.

Old Hunstanton

The Neptune

Seriously good food
85 Old Hunstanton Road, Old Hunstanton, PE36 6HZ
Tel no: (01485) 532122
www.theneptune.co.uk
Modern British | £47
Cooking score: 5

Kevin and Jacki Mangeolles' perfectly chilled restaurant-with-rooms close to the breezy expanses of the Norfolk coast is a former coaching inn that has been given a mellow makeover, with muted colours, candles and original fireplaces creating just the right mood. Kevin is capable of delivering some seriously good stuff, including a best-selling starter of lobster tortellini with roast pork and a dish of halibut with caviar sauce that has been 'cooked to perfection'. He is known for tapping into the local network, hence smoked haddock ravioli with Brancaster mussels or brill fillet pointed up with Thornham oyster mayo, but he is also starting to elaborate: consider a dish of pan-fried ribeye with braised Aberdeen Angus, accompanied by beef tea, twice-cooked 'macaire' potato and mushroom purée. To finish, there are simple strokes (sticky toffee pudding with poached pear), as well as flashes of tongue-in-cheek artifice (yoghurt and honey sorbet partnered by toasted porridge, gooseberry sauce and brioche croûtons). Occasionally, the cooking goes awry and you would think you were in a different restaurant, especially those reporters who have complained of 'miserly and unadorned' portions; the line between small helpings and parsimony might be too fine for some. The wine list, however, is admirable, with eleven house recommendations starting at £18.50.

Chef/s: Kevin Mangeolles. **Open:** Sun L 12 to 1.30, Tue to Sun D 7 to 9. **Closed:** Mon, 2 weeks Nov, 3 weeks Jan. **Meals:** alc (main courses £25 to £27). Sun L £28.50. **Service:** not inc. **Details:** Cards accepted. 24 seats. No mobile phones. Music. Car parking.

Ovington

The Café at Brovey Lair

Fusion fish... and more
Carbrooke Road, Ovington, IP25 6SD
Tel no: (01953) 882706
www.broveylair.com
Pan-Asian/Seafood | £53
Cooking score: 6

£5 OFF V

'Not so much a restaurant as a dinner party thrown by a brilliant chef', is one view of Tina and Mike Pemberton's idiosyncratic 'café' in their own home. When the couple set up Brovey Lair it was a refreshingly new way of doing things, long before the concept became the stuff of reality TV. While the dinner party approach isn't for everyone, many have been left marvelling at the results: at her best, Tina produces 'imaginative dishes of delightfully complex tastes and lightness'. Brovey is a global seafood specialist, and some would like to see more variety, both in the species and the now familiar run through of salads and soups, teppanyaki grills, stir-fries and global desserts (perhaps Moroccan almond and orange cake with roasted figs). But when everything clicks, the results can be thrilling, blisteringly sharp and full of vivid contrasts: Chinese sesame coated scallops with chilli bean shoot and coriander salad, with lime, ginger and spring onion vinaigrette, crab and polenta cakes with chilli, coriander and ribbons of sweet-and-sour cucumber, fillet of wild sea bass baked in a Thai marinade with Nanjing black rice, and Cajun-spiced swordfish with vine tomato and sweet chilli marinade have all drawn rave reviews. Wines start at £17.95.
Chef/s: Tina Pemberton. **Open:** all week L by special arrangement, D 7.45 (1 sitting, prior bookings only). **Closed:** 25 and 26 Dec. **Meals:** Set L and D £52.50 (4 courses). **Service:** 10%.
Details: Cards accepted. 20 seats. 20 seats outside. No mobile phones. Wheelchair access. Music. Car parking.

TINA PEMBERTON
The Café at Brovey Lair

What is the biggest myth about being a chef?
That they don't enjoy their friends' cooking. Result is I'm hardly ever invited over to dinner, but when I am I love being out of the kitchen for a few precious hours, no matter what the food's like.

What's your favourite tipple?
Champagne - you can always find something to celebrate.

What's the worst culinary trend of recent years?
The belief that foams, jus and spirals of flavourless coulis add excitement to the dish. Once, on being presented with such a decorated plate, American comedian Jackie Mason asked the waiter 'Do I eat it or hang it on the wall?'

...And the best?
The availability in the retail sector of many exotic ingredients formerly only found in restaurants, enabling domestic cooks to create meals once unheard of in an average household.

What is your favourite food combination?
East meets West in a fusion of tastes, spices and colours.

Sheringham

READERS RECOMMEND

Marmalade's Bistro

British
5 Church Street, Sheringham, NR26 8QR
Tel no: (01263) 822830
www.marmaladesbistro.com
'Little eatery with honest, seasonal, intelligent stuff.'

Snettisham

ALSO RECOMMENDED

▲ The Rose & Crown

Old Church Road, Snettisham, PE31 7LX
Tel no: (01485) 541382
www.roseandcrownsnettisham.co.uk
Modern British £5 OFF

Open log fires, twisting passageways, red-tiled floors and oak-beamed rooms make for a quintessentially English setting right in the heart of a charming Norfolk village. The food straddles traditional pub offerings and more adventurous options; try Brancaster mussels marinière to start (£5.95) and then Holkham bangers and mash with onion gravy or seared wood pigeon breast with Brie dauphinoise, cavolo nero and jus (£13.50). To finish, maybe caramel and walnut mousse with orange shortbread. Wines from £14. Open all week.

Stoke Holy Cross

The Wildebeest Arms

Sound cooking and excellent wines
82-86 Norwich Road, Stoke Holy Cross, NR14 8QJ
Tel no: (01508) 492497
www.thewildebeest.co.uk
British | £28
Cooking score: 2

£30

Look out for a blazing yellow edifice amid the little brick cottages of Stoke Holy Cross and expect more blazing yellow walls within, festooned with Africana. As for the food, bits of it may lack subtlety and some is far too complicated, but the basic cooking of most items is fair; perhaps Brancaster mussels marinière or grilled fillet of mackerel, as well as pheasant breast served with cocotte potatoes, Savoy cabbage, bacon and caraway, crispy pork rillette, celeriac and beetroot jus. Puddings are fruity, creamy and enjoyable. Wine's the thing here – in racks, chill cabinets, arranged on the bar. The excellent global list is printed in a weighty bound volume, with prices from £16.

Chef/s: Eden Derrick. **Open:** all week L 12 to 2 (12.30 to 2.30 Sun), D 7 to 9. **Closed:** 25 and 26 Dec. **Meals:** alc (main courses £9 to £22). Set L £14.95 (2 courses) to £18.95. Set D £19.50 (2 courses) to £21.50. Sun L £21.50. **Service:** not inc. **Details:** Cards accepted. 80 seats. 40 seats outside. Separate bar. Wheelchair access. Music. Children allowed. Car parking.

Swaffham

Strattons

Flamboyant eco champ
4 Ash Close, Swaffham, PE37 7NH
Tel no: (01760) 723845
www.strattonshotel.com
Modern British | £30
Cooking score: 3

The basement restaurant at this unusual Queen Anne villa in the centre of town is run on sound eco-conscious lines, using lots of organic produce, supporting local growers and catering for an array of dietary requirements. Current chef Sam Bryant is maintaining the house style of simple dishes that are big on natural flavour. Rabbit and pork rillettes in a jar with piccalilli and toast, beer-battered hake or muntjac and smoked Dapple cheese burger with thrice-fried chips have all garnered good reports, along with fine side dishes of chorizo, broad bean and mint salad and griddled asparagus. Finish with an apple and stout fritter with spiced sugar and brown bread ice cream. Wines start at £20.

Chef/s: Sam Bryant. **Open:** Sun L 12 to 2.30, all week D 6.30 to 9. **Closed:** 1 week Christmas. **Meals:** alc (main courses £12 to £17). **Service:** not inc. **Details:** Cards accepted. 28 seats. 8 seats outside. No mobile phones. Music. Children allowed. Car parking.

Titchwell

ALSO RECOMMENDED

▲ Titchwell Manor

Titchwell, PE31 8BB
Tel no: (01485) 210221
www.titchwellmanor.com
Modern European £5 OFF

Over the last two decades Titchwell Manor has fared well under the stewardship of Margaret and Ian Snaith, who have transformed it from a stuffy gentlemen's club into a sleek boutique hotel. Son Eric runs the kitchen, which turns out an ambitious seven-course menu (£40) for the conservatory restaurant: expect highly worked dishes along the lines of 'foie gras terrine, chocolate, spiced bread, smoke and orange', halibut with artichokes, whelks and mushrooms or rhubarb consommé with ginger tapioca. Simpler, brasserie-style food is offered in the bar-cum-'eating rooms'. Wines from £15.50. Open all week.

Wiveton

Wiveton Bell

Pure north Norfolk inn with extras
Blakeney Road, Wiveton, NR25 7TL
Tel no: (01263) 740101
www.wivetonbell.com
Modern British | £25
Cooking score: 2

Pitched by Wiveton village green and the church – just a stroll from the salt marshes – the 300-year-old Bell is pure north Norfolk, although its seriously gussied-up interior (polished plank floors, chunky tables et al) feels like a home-from-home for the seasonal influx of migrating city escapees. Occasionally the place misfires, but most readers agree that the kitchen makes a good fist of things – especially when it comes to handling local fish and game. Bowls of Morston mussels, pigeon breast with celeriac rémoulade and slow-cooked Briston belly pork with black pudding mash have gone down well, likewise top-notch beer-battered haddock with chips. For afters, perhaps try summer pudding or toffee cheesecake. Wines start at £15.50, and there are Norfolk ales too.

Chef/s: Jamie Murch. **Open:** all week L 12 to 2.15 (2.30 Sun), D 6 to 9. **Closed:** 25 Dec. **Meals:** alc (main courses £11 to £20), Sun L £13.45. **Service:** not inc. **Details:** Cards accepted. 62 seats. 60 seats outside. No music. Children allowed. Car parking.

ALSO RECOMMENDED

▲ Wiveton Farm Café

Wiveton Hall, Wiveton, NR25 7TE
Tel no: (01263) 740515
www.wivetonhall.co.uk/cafe.htm
Modern British

A spin-off from Wiveton Hall and its fruit-filled acres (PYO in season), this colourful café is a quirky little Norfolk diamond. 'Farm to table' is Alison Yetman's mantra and she proves the point with lunch menus ranging from asparagus, pea and mint soup (£5.95) or spinach and Gruyère tart to pan-fried pigeon breast with a warm ham hock, roasted beetroot and Puy lentil salad (£10.50). Breakfast and afternoon tea, too. Wines from £12.50; beers from Yetman's microbrewery in Holt. Open all week Easter to end Nov (tapas Thur to Sat D).

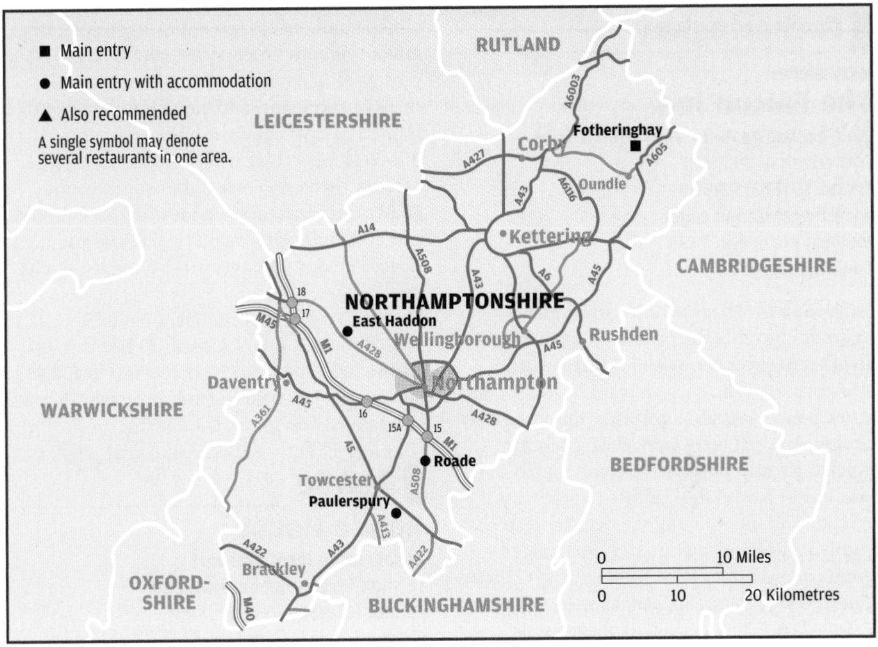

■ Main entry
● Main entry with accommodation
▲ Also recommended
A single symbol may denote several restaurants in one area.

East Haddon

NEW ENTRY

The Red Lion

Re-born country inn with snazzy food
Main Street, East Haddon, NN6 8BU
Tel no: (01604) 770223
www.redlioneasthaddon.co.uk
Modern British | £23
Cooking score: 3

Back in the day, this substantial stone hostelry was the golden-hued benchmark for auspicious country inns hereabouts, and it has taken on a confident new foodie persona of late – thanks to the intervention of local boy Adam Gray (chef at Rhodes Twenty Four, see entry). With protégé Anthony Horn heading up the kitchen, the result is a menu of snazzily reinvented Brit food in true Gary R style: battered pollack, soused mackerel and mutton shepherd's pie please the lunch crowd, but it pays to pick more adventurously from the daily line-up. A cleverly deconstructed pigeon and mushroom tart with celeriac purée shows real acumen, while more robust flavours burst through in a dish of pearly roast hake on butter bean and tomato stew. There's also a touch of urbane style and finesse about a cylinder of iced toffee mousse served alongside a 'spot' of intense toffee sauce and a boozy sultana compote. Wines from £15.25.

Chef/s: Adam Gray and Anthony Horn. **Open:** all week L 12 to 2.30 (4 Sun), Mon to Sat D 6 to 10. **Meals:** alc (main courses £10 to £19). **Service:** not inc. **Details:** Cards accepted. 80 seats. 50 seats outside. Wheelchair access. Music. Children allowed. Car parking.

Symbols

- Accommodation is available
- £30 Three courses for less than £30
- V Separate vegetarian menu
- £5 OFF £5-off voucher scheme
- Notable wine list

Fotheringhay

NEW ENTRY

The Falcon Inn

Well-heeled hostelry with robust food
Fotheringhay, PE8 5HZ
Tel no: (01832) 226254
www.thefalcon-inn.co.uk
Modern European | £35
Cooking score: 2

Nestled in the shadow of Fotheringhay's majestic church is the proud-looking Falcon – an affluent stone inn with a courtyard and conservatory. The current team is doing good work here – witness a robustly rendered dish of slow-braised belly pork with garlicky greens, parsnip purée and thyme jus. To start, you might fancy smoked duck with baby spinach and blood oranges, while desserts have yielded a luscious mango tart with Greek yoghurt and honey. Bottles start at £12.95.
Chef/s: Danny Marshall. **Open:** all week L 12 to 2.15 (3 Sun), D 6.15 to 9.15 (8.30 Sun). **Meals:** alc (main courses £12 to £22). Set L £12.95 (2 courses) to £15.50. **Service:** not inc. **Details:** Cards accepted. 75 seats. 60 seats outside. Separate bar. No music. Wheelchair access. Children allowed. Car parking.

Paulerspury

The Vine House

Blissful restaurant-with-rooms
100 High Street, Paulerspury, NN12 7NA
Tel no: (01327) 811267
www.vinehousehotel.com
Modern British | £31
Cooking score: 4
£5 OFF

'Sheer bliss' from the moment you meander past the japonicas, this bewitching restaurant-with-rooms in a lovely old farmhouse testifies to years of hands-on dedication. Owner Julie Springett is always there, out front; husband Marcus seldom strays from the kitchen. Their intensely seasonal food has grown in confidence of late, with everything in its rightful place on the short daily menu. Springtime might herald a delicate 'jelly' of salt cod and sea bass on a slick of sweet garlic purée tinged with curry oil, ahead of an outstanding combo of Jacob's lamb (thick slices of succulent saddle on chunky pea purée framed by two curved rib bones with unbelievably crispy meat – 'a masterstroke'). Later in the year, you might order a 'divine' salad of marinated beetroot and goats' cheese, and conclude with warm treacle tart and clotted cream. The accessible wine list opens at £16.95.
Chef/s: Marcus Springett. **Open:** Tue to Sat L 12 to 1.45, all week D 6 to 9. **Closed:** 25 Dec to 3 Jan. **Meals:** Set L and D £27.50 (2 courses) to £30.95. **Service:** not inc. **Details:** Cards accepted. 28 seats. Separate bar. No music. Car parking.

Roade

Roade House

Respectable local stalwart
16 High Street, Roade, NN7 2NW
Tel no: (01604) 863372
www.roadehousehotel.co.uk
Modern British | £32
Cooking score: 3
£5 OFF

Witness Middle England at its most tweedily respectable, with well-spaced tables and an inoffensive décor of creams, browns and pale bamboo. The food is equally unshowy, giving ingredients a gentle European treatment. Smoked haddock fishcake comes with pancetta, poached egg and beurre blanc, while breast of guinea fowl is stuffed with chicken and herb mousseline and served with mushroom sauce. Some reports indicate that flavours, technique and service may not thrill quite as much as they did, but the kitchen still turns out some fine dishes, such as an excellent warm goats' cheese and leek tart. House wine is £16.
Chef/s: Chris Kewley. **Open:** Mon to Fri and Sun L 12 to 2, Mon to Sat D 7 to 9.30. **Closed:** 26 to 30 Dec, bank hols. **Meals:** alc (main courses £16 to £24). Set L £20 (2 courses) to £23. Sun L £23. **Service:** not inc. **Details:** Cards accepted. 50 seats. Separate bar. No music. Wheelchair access. Children allowed. Car parking.

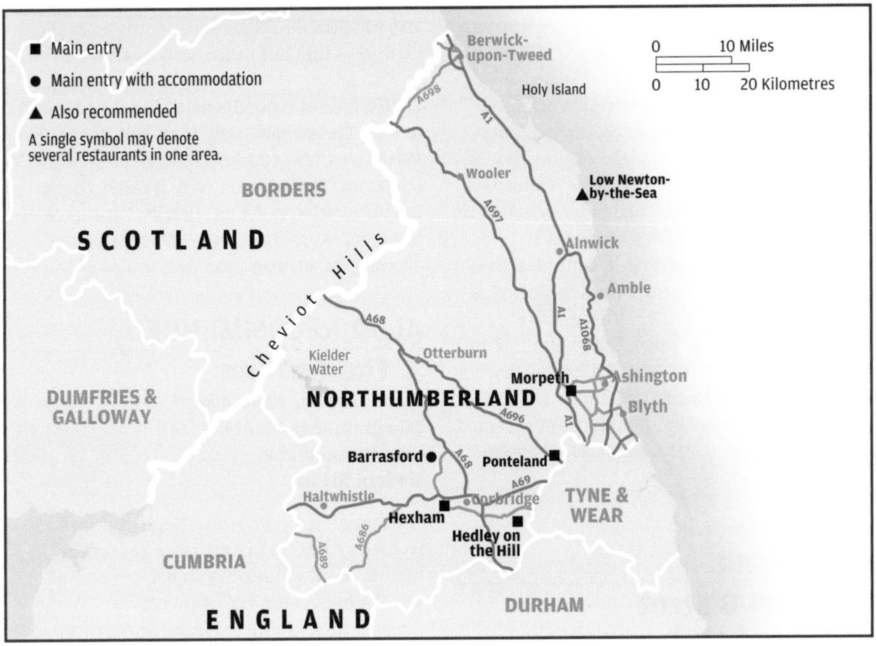

■ Main entry
● Main entry with accommodation
▲ Also recommended
A single symbol may denote several restaurants in one area.

0 10 Miles
0 10 20 Kilometres

Berwick-upon-Tweed
Holy Island
A698
A1
Wooler
Low Newton-by-the-Sea
BORDERS
SCOTLAND
A697
Alnwick
Cheviot Hills
Amble
A68
A1
A1068
Kielder Water
Otterburn
Morpeth
Ashington
DUMFRIES & GALLOWAY
NORTHUMBERLAND
Blyth
A696
A1
Barrasford
A68
Ponteland
A69
Haltwhistle
Corbridge
TYNE & WEAR
Hexham
A686
A689
Hedley on the Hill
CUMBRIA
DURHAM
ENGLAND

Barrasford

The Barrasford Arms

A good line in comforting fare
Barrasford, NE48 4AA
Tel no: (01434) 681237
www.barrasfordarms.co.uk
Modern British | £24
Cooking score: 2

Overlooking Haughton Castle, this smartly renovated eighteenth-century coaching inn does a good line in comforting, traditional fare – maybe pressed Northumbrian ham hock terrine with pease pudding and toasted country bread, followed by slow-cooked shank of lamb in rosemary, garlic and red wine with champ mash. There are occasional European touches too; one reporter was very impressed by the halibut on crab risotto, while grilled grey mullet might come with roasted bell peppers, chorizo and tomato and saffron broth. Finish with local cheeses or hearty desserts such as warm chocolate brownie or sticky toffee pudding. Wines from £13.50.

Chef/s: Tony Binks. **Open:** Tue to Sun L 12 to 2 (2.30 Sun), Mon to Sat D 6.30 to 9. **Closed:** bank hols. **Meals:** alc (main courses £10 to £17). Set L £11.50 (2 courses) to £14.50. Sun L £14 (2 courses) to £16.50. **Service:** not inc. **Details:** Cards accepted. 70 seats. 12 seats outside. Separate bar. Music. Children allowed. Car parking.

Hedley on the Hill

The Feathers Inn

Drovers' inn with real oomph
Hedley on the Hill, NE43 7SW
Tel no: (01661) 843607
www.thefeathers.net
British | £23
Cooking score: 2

Local hero and foodie crusader Rhian Cradock has injected some real oomph into this 200-year-old drovers' inn high above the

Tyne Valley without sacrificing its open fires, tankards or traditional pub games. His homemade black pudding is a star turn (perhaps served with Northumbrian bacon and a poached egg), and he works wonders with artisan produce from the region. Try ox cheek braised in stout, a risotto of Vallum Farm beetroot with Allerdale goats' cheese, or saddle of venison in pastry with wild mushrooms. Check the handpumps for the current line-up of North Country ales; check the blackboards for wine (from £13).

Chef/s: Rhian Cradock. **Open:** Tue to Sun L 12 to 2 (2.30 Sun), Tue to Sat D 6 to 8.30. **Closed:** Mon, first 2 weeks Jan. **Meals:** alc (main courses £10 to £14). Sun L £18. **Service:** not inc. **Details:** Cards accepted. 42 seats. 20 seats outside. No music. Children allowed. Car parking.

Hexham

Bouchon Bistrot

Excellent, good-value French classics
4-6 Gilesgate, Hexham, NE46 3NJ
Tel no: (01434) 609943
www.bouchonbistrot.co.uk
French | £24
Cooking score: 4

£5 OFF £30

Inside this 'sober-fronted stone town house' is a bustling version of a French bistro, offering 'excellent eating at very reasonable cost'. The building is Grade II-listed and its elegant interior – which extends over three floors – showcases original beams, exposed brickwork and open stone fireplaces. French country cooking is the mainstay of the menu, so expect classics like French onion soup with garlic croûtons, snails with garlic butter, coq au vin, and crispy confit duck with lyonnaise potatoes, bacon and Savoy cabbage. Colonial traditions inform rack of lamb stuffed with dried fruits, served with couscous and spiced tomato compote, while braised pork cheeks on fresh tagliatelle and ginger and orange sauce adds a touch of invention. Desserts dwell on the unreconstructed comfort of apple tarte Tatin with vanilla ice cream, cherry clafoutis, and profiteroles. Wines are mostly French – Georges Duboeuf house selections start at £13.25.

Chef/s: Nicolas Duhil. **Open:** Tue to Sat L 12 to 2, D 6 to 9.30. **Closed:** Sun, Mon, bank hols, 1 week Feb. **Meals:** alc (main courses £12 to £20). Set L £10.50 (2 courses) to £12.95. Set early D £12.95 (2 courses) to £14.95. **Service:** not inc. **Details:** Cards accepted. 150 seats. Wheelchair access. Music. Children allowed. Car parking.

ALSO RECOMMENDED

▲ The Rat Inn

Anick, Hexham, NE46 4LN
Tel no: (01434) 602814
www.theratinn.com
Modern British

A homely inn with stone-flagged floors and real fires, the Rat's name is a mystery but its history as an alehouse goes back over 200 years. One visitor was 'blown away' by the 'simple, locally sourced' food and strong, up-front flavours. Terrine of local game with fig chutney (£6.50) gets the thumbs-up; after that, maybe pan haggerty (£10.95) then chocolate brownie with fudge ice cream. Wines are priced from £12.95 a bottle. No food Sun D and Mon.

Low Newton-by-the-Sea

ALSO RECOMMENDED

▲ The Ship Inn

Newton Square, Low Newton-by-the-Sea, NE66 3EL
Tel no: (01665) 576262
www.shipinnnewton.co.uk
Modern British £5 OFF

One of a cluster of fishermen's cottages just yards from a beautiful beach, this cosy whitewashed inn has a lot going for it – including its own microbrewery. Food options combine local and international themes, from grilled haloumi with roasted red peppers, tomato and basil (£4.95) to Northumberland spring lamb cutlets with new potatoes and Yorkshire asparagus

(£12.50). Local hand-picked crab is a speciality. Finish with chocolate brownies and ice cream. Wines start at £14.45. Open all week (check for seasonal variations).

Morpeth

Bridge Street Inn & Restaurant

Revamped town-centre venue
59 Bridge Street, Morpeth, NE61 1PQ
Tel no: (01670) 516200
www.bridgestreetinn.co.uk
Modern British
Cooking score: 2

No expense has been spared on the interior of this town-centre pub (formerly Black Door Bar & Dining Rooms), where exposed stonework, leather sofas and chandeliers create a classy but laid-back vibe, with the bar very much at the heart of the operation. Choose to eat here or in the smart upstairs dining room, where an à la carte menu offers classics such as smoked haddock chowder or black bream with fennel, onion confit and tapenade. In the bar, try hearty ham hock terrine with homemade chutney, followed by coley with crushed potato and French-style peas, then sticky toffee pudding. Wines start at £12.95 in the restaurant (prices are cheaper downstairs).
Chef/s: Andrew Laurie and Stephen Birkett. **Open:** all week L 12 to 2.30 (3 Sun), Mon to Sat D 5.30 to 9.30. Restaurant Sun L 12 to 3, Thur to Sat D 5.30 to 9.30. **Meals:** alc (main courses £8 to £19). Sun L £12.95 (2 courses) to £14.95. **Service:** not inc. **Details:** Cards accepted. 100 seats. Separate bar. Wheelchair access. Music. Children allowed.

Ponteland

Café Lowrey

Setting the bar for neighbourhood eateries
33-35 The Broadway, Darras Hall, Ponteland, NE20 9PW
Tel no: (01661) 820357
www.cafelowrey.co.uk
Modern British | £28
Cooking score: 3

A friendly, unpretentious restaurant offering accessible, accomplished cooking, Café Lowrey sets the bar for neighbourhood restaurants everywhere. Set in an unassuming parade of shops, it makes like a French bistro with a tiled floor, simple white and grey décor, a blackboard menu and white napery. The bistro vibe extends to the cooking, with fresh baguette and a starter of grilled black pudding and chorizo salad setting a simple, uncluttered tone. Excellent ingredients shone through in a main of pan-fried sea bass with lemon and thyme, crushed potato and sauce vierge, while a generous dessert of treacle tart with cream combined a sticky, rustic filling with beautifully fine and crisp pastry. Like everything else, the wine list is straightforward, offering a modest international selection that starts at £15.95.
Chef/s: Ian Lowrey. **Open:** Sat and Sun L 12 to 2 (3 Sun), Tue to Sat D 5.30 to 10 (6 Sat). **Closed:** Mon, bank hols. **Meals:** alc (main courses £14 to £24). Set L and early D £14.95 (2 courses) to £17.95. **Service:** not inc. **Details:** Cards accepted. 70 seats. Wheelchair access. Music. Children allowed. Car parking.

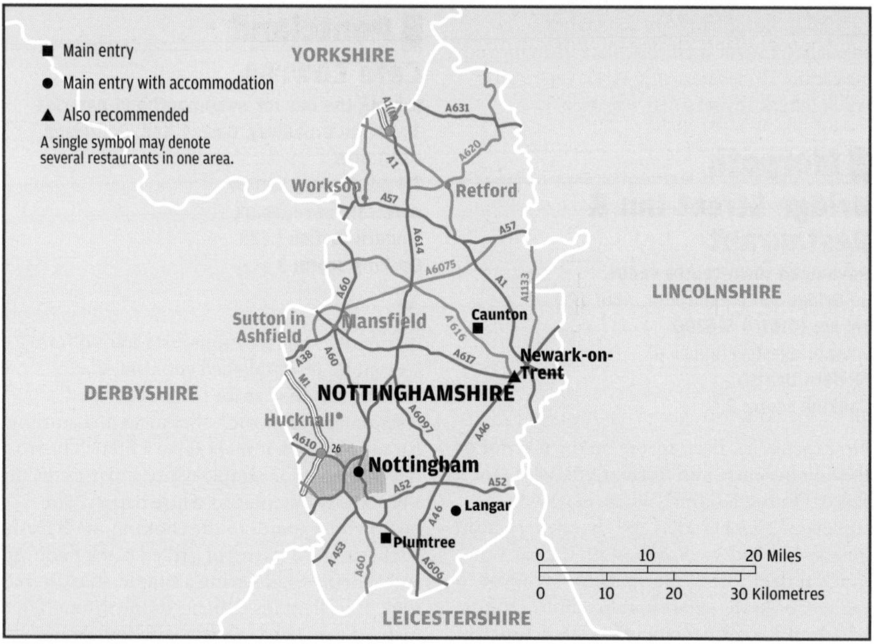

Caunton

Caunton Beck

All-day crowd puller
Main Street, Caunton, NG23 6AB
Tel no: (01636) 636793
www.wigandmitre.com
Modern British | £27
Cooking score: 2

Good old-fashioned hospitality is the order of the day at this pub/restaurant in a sixteenth-century cottage, where food and drink are served all the way from hearty breakfasts to 'last orders at the bar'. The kitchen draws on good local ingredients and the flexible menu evolves throughout the day, from sandwiches to twice-baked ham hock 'rarebit' soufflé, pan-seared escalope of salmon with caper and chive hollandaise or pot-roast spring chicken breast with mozzarella and smoked bacon. Finish with rhubarb and custard iced parfait. Service is 'friendly and cheerful', according to one reporter, and the interesting, well-considered wine list starts at £14.25.

Chef/s: Valerie Hope and Andy Pickstock. **Open:** all week 8am to 10pm. **Closed:** 25 and 26 Dec, 2 weeks Aug, bank hols. **Meals:** alc (main courses £13 to £20). Set L and D £12.75 (2 courses) to £15.25. **Service:** not inc. **Details:** Cards accepted. 84 seats. 32 seats outside. Separate bar. No music. Wheelchair access. Children allowed. Car parking.

Langar

Langar Hall

A very personal English idyll
Church Lane, Langar, NG13 9HG
Tel no: (01949) 860559
www.langarhall.co.uk
Modern British | £35
Cooking score: 4

Imogen Skirving has been cosseting visitors to Langar Hall for more than 25 years, but still finds time to meet and greet – a personal detail that is much appreciated by all who arrive at this country mansion. The quintessentially English idyll begins as you head up the long drive and continues amid crystal chandeliers, statues and marble pillars – although this is no stiff-collared country pile. Pickings from the garden find their way into the kitchen, along with bountiful regional produce and ever-popular home-reared lamb. There's also game from Belvoir Estate – perhaps char-grilled fallow deer with cauliflower and caramelised chicory. Fish is given more modish treatment, as in seared scallops with roast chicken wing, Jerusalem artichokes, chestnuts and Brussels sprouts, while desserts could usher in poached autumn fruits with gingerbread crumb and star anise ice cream. Take note of Imogen's personal recommendations on the well-spread wine list. Prices start at £18.

Chef/s: Gary Booth. **Open:** all week L 12 to 2, D 7 to 9.30 (7 to 10 Fri, 6 to 10 Sat, 6 to 8.30 Sun). **Meals:** alc (main courses £13 to £25). Set L £16.50 (2 courses) to £21.50. Set D £23.50 (2 courses) to £28.50. Sun L £28. **Service:** 10% (optional). **Details:** Cards accepted. 70 seats. 35 seats outside. Separate bar. No music. Wheelchair access. Children allowed. Car parking.

Newark-on-Trent

ALSO RECOMMENDED

▲ Café Bleu

14 Castle Gate, Newark-on-Trent, NG24 1BG
Tel no: (01636) 610141
www.cafebleu.co.uk
Modern European £5 OFF

'A very lively outfit', begins one commentary on this riverside bistro close to the ruins of Newark Castle. It's been going a long time – everyone gets to know it, they like the vibrant art, live music evenings, winter log fires, the walled courtyard garden and they return. The cooking is Anglo-European without fireworks, a typical meal progressing through smoked haddock and leek risotto (£7.95) via braised blade of beef with truffled mash (£16.95) to mascarpone crème brûlée (£6.95). House Australian is £14.25. Closed Sun D.

Nottingham

Hart's

Understated Nottingham landmark
Standard Court, Park Row, Nottingham, NG1 6GN
Tel no: (0115) 9110666
www.hartsnottingham.co.uk
Modern British | £40
Cooking score: 5

V

Tim Hart's generously welcoming restaurant (with rooms in the adjoining hotel) has been a faithful servant in Nottingham since the late 90s, becoming something of a local landmark in the process. Occupying part of the old General Hospital building, it generates a mood of understated elegance and down-to-earth bonhomie where everyone feels at home (especially when live entertainment is on the menu). There's no standing on ceremony and no false posturing – what you see is what you get when it comes to service and food. To start, Hart's house salad is 'a must', according to fans, although the kitchen might up the ante with a dish of pan-fried monkfish with smoked duck, spiced lentil and mint yoghurt. Mains look to the enlightened brasserie repertoire for the likes of sea bass with sweetcorn and clam chowder, roast Whissendale veal loin with braised shoulder and a tarragon faggot, or a jazzy dish of poached and roast chicken with chorizo, piquillo peppers, artichokes and pak choi. To finish, pineapple tarte Tatin sent one reporter into raptures, but the choice might also run to a swanky metropolitan combo of apple terrine with prune and honey cake and a cinnamon shot. The style-led wine list is even-handed and egalitarian in its scope, with respected growers and fine vintages scattered liberally among its pages. Prices (from £18.50) are very fair.

Chef/s: Tom Earle. **Open:** all week L 12 to 2, D 6 to 10.30 (9 Sun). **Closed:** 1 Jan. **Meals:** alc (main courses £15 to £24). Set L £14.95 (2 courses) to £17.95. Set D £20 (2 courses) to £26. Sun L £25. **Service:** 12% (optional). **Details:** Cards accepted. 80 seats. Separate bar. No music. No mobile phones. Wheelchair access. Children allowed. Car parking.

The Larder on Goosegate

Vintage charm and gutsy dishes
1st Floor, 16-22 Goosegate, Hockley, Nottingham, NG1 1FE
Tel no: (0115) 9500111
www.thelarderongoosegate.co.uk
British | £25
Cooking score: 2

The first Boots the Chemist occupied this Victorian building, and its stylish interior (heritage colours, bare floorboards, chandelier lighting) oozes vintage charm. Chef-proprietor Ewan McFarlane trained under Antonio Carluccio back in the day, and an unmistakable Italian influence surfaces in dishes such as Swiss chard and ricotta agnolotti. Butchery is done in-house, so expect lesser-known cuts of steak (picanha, hanger), and unusual local game including hare, rook and squirrel. Seared ox heart with Stilton dressing and rocket could be followed by equally gutsy mains such as megrim sole with wild garlic and cockle sauce. Wines on a substantial, international list start at just £12.50.

Chef/s: Ewan McFarlane. **Open:** Sat and Sun L 12 to 2.30, Tue to Sat D 6 to 10. **Closed:** Mon. **Meals:** alc (main courses £10 to £19). Set L and D £13.95 (2 courses) to £16.95. **Service:** not inc. **Details:** Cards accepted. 60 seats. Music. Children allowed.

Restaurant 1877

British grub, old and new
128 Derby Road, Canning Circus, Nottingham, NG1 5FB
Tel no: (0115) 9588008
www.restaurant1877.com
British | £25
Cooking score: 2

Built by Nottingham-based giant Boots as one of its original sites in 1877, this spectacular edifice is now a self-proclaimed 'traditional English restaurant', and the kitchen rams home its unvarnished John Bull credentials by dishing up 'Midland rarebit', Derbyshire hotpot and Cambridge burnt cream. However, it's not completely rooted in the past: delve among the pies and roasts and you might also find home-cured salmon with pickled fennel, pan-fried belly pork and scallops with apple purée, or duck breast with celeriac, cranberries and red cabbage. The wine list is organised by grape variety and has handy food-matching notes; prices from £16.

Chef/s: Antony Baxter. **Open:** Fri to Sun L 12 to 3, Tue to Sat D 5 to 10 (10.30 Fri and Sat). **Closed:** Mon, 24 to 26 Dec. **Meals:** alc (main courses £10 to £19). Set L and theatre D £9.95. Sun L £13.50 (2 courses) to £16.95. **Service:** 10% (optional). **Details:** Cards accepted. 80 seats. Separate bar. Wheelchair access. Music. Children allowed.

Restaurant Sat Bains

Jaw-dropping brilliance from a superstar
Lenton Lane, Nottingham, NG7 2SA
Tel no: (0115) 9866566
www.restaurantsatbains.com
Modern British | £75
Cooking score: 9

V

Stumbling upon Sat Bains' remarkable restaurant-with-rooms holed up in Nottingham's industrial wastelands can be a culture shock, but persevere, because this cleverly fashioned barn conversion is home to one of the UK's most astonishing culinary talents. Once inside, the classy, stone-floored dining room will win you over immediately with its trendy glass artwork and desirable hangings. Only the unflattering lighting and sterile reception area have caused momentary murmurings – otherwise, this is a rare treat and 'as perfect an experience as you are likely to want'. Meals revolve around two tasting menus, laid out laterally with coloured dots signifying the dominant tastes (sweet, sour, umami, etc); there's also a 'chef's table' version that can be booked in advance for lunch, plus a 'unique' online format where diners tick their selections from a choice of 20 seasonal boxes: sweetcorn, elderflower, oxtail, Goosnargh duck . . . and the enigmatically titled NG7 2SA (a hotchpotch of wild pickings from the restaurant's postcode area, perhaps enlivened with a starry horseradish pannacotta). Whatever you choose, don't miss Bains' celebrated 'perfect 10' from *Great British Menu*; everyone orders it, and no wonder – it's a mind-expanding, ethereal creation involving a duck egg cooked for hours at 60°C, accompanied by a gentle pea sorbet, some strong-tasting ham and a flourish of pea shoots. Seafood and vegetables tend to shine early in proceedings, be it a combo of salty, sweet scallops with a slice of soft, fatty belly pork, cubes of apple purée and crushed cornflakes (pure texture, pure contrast), or salt-baked celeriac and truffles transformed by a heavenly chicken jus. After that, 'superstar dishes' abound: mutton cooked two ways with shallots, herbs and a spectacular sauce takes this once-humble meat to a new level ('quite simply the finest main course I have ever eaten', enthused one reader), while shreds of unctuous braised Wagyu beef might be served atop crunchy shards of asparagus and alexanders ('inspired cooking'). Elsewhere, a cheeky parody of Asian BBQs brings together a slice of daringly rare roe deer loin, a tiny venison kofta, braised Little Gem, a beetroot crisp, some cucumber and yoghurt. Then comes a 'crossover' for re-setting the palate, before sweetness takes over as the prevailing sensation: it might be a tiny 'postage stamp' of toast between a layer of pungent Stilton and sweet pineapple, or a similar riff involving feta and vanilla. Bains' desserts often play wicked tricks with convention – perhaps a sweet 'curry' involving a thick sauce, spicy yoghurt pannacotta and mango sorbet with a scattering of crunchy coconut ('clever, very clever', observed one reporter) or a quenelle of ultra-rich chocolate ganache topped with crystallised violet flowers and an olive oil 'pastille'. Extraordinary innovation, acute detailing and jaw-dropping levels of complexity, plus diaphanous textures, earthy regionality and visual spectacle – it's all here, and readers adore every moment of the superlative, palate-challenging show. Of course, your wallet may 'take a battering', but it's hard to protest with such brilliance on display – especially as all diners are 'treated like royalty' and the sommelier is a fount of vinous knowledge. Following a revamp, the 200-bin wine list is now more sensitively tailored to the food, with excellent matching possibilities across the range, a cleaner, more informative layout and a greater emphasis on exciting new names. Prices start at £22.

Chef/s: Sat Bains. **Open:** Tue to Sat L 12.30 (1 sitting), D 7 to 9. **Closed:** Sun, Mon, 2 weeks Dec/ Jan, 3 weeks Aug. **Meals:** Tasting menu £75 (7 courses) to £89 (10 courses). **Service:** 12.5% (optional). **Details:** Cards accepted. 36 seats. Separate bar. No mobile phones. Wheelchair access. Music. Car parking.

World Service

Ultra-cool global hot spot
Newdigate House, Castle Gate, Nottingham, NG1 6AF
Tel no: (0115) 8475587
www.worldservicerestaurant.com
Modern British | £35
Cooking score: 3

£5 OFF

The designers obviously had a field day at this ultra-cool venue, creating a Japanese-style pebble garden out front and filling the interior with ethnic artefacts from Indonesian vases and batik drapes to prancing wooden horses and oriental statuary. World music tinkles in the background and the kitchen melds global ideas with gusto – but also a sense of purpose. A starter of cured beef is embellished with pickled shimeji mushrooms, plum confiture, Manchego cheese and mooli, while sea bass might keep company with chickpea purée, brandade croquette, chilli salsa and pak choi. Other dishes have a more grounded, orthodox feel (butter-poached chicken on garlic and parsley risotto, say), and desserts stay close to home for banoffi cheesecake or egg custard tart with nutmeg ice cream. A page of sherries opens the comprehensive wine list, which includes house selections from £16.

Chef/s: Garry Hewitt. **Open:** all week L 12 to 2.15 (3.30 Sun), Mon to Sat D 7 to 10 (6.30 Sat). **Closed:** 25 and 26 Dec, first week Jan. **Meals:** alc (main courses £14 to £25). Set L £14 (2 courses) to £19.

Sun L £19.50. **Service:** 10% (optional).
Details: Cards accepted. 80 seats. 30 seats outside. Separate bar. Music.

ALSO RECOMMENDED

▲ Delilah

15 Middle Pavement, Nottingham, NG1 7DX
Tel no: (0115) 9484461
www.delilahfinefoods.co.uk
Modern European

With more than 200 cheeses and an extensive range of charcuterie, this charming deli has no shortage of ingredients for its tapas-style menu. Perch at the nine-stool food bar for anything from breakfast to an early-evening bite with a glass of wine. Hot choices range from 'green' eggs and ham (£5.95) in the morning to a seafood and fish crostini selection later in the day. Cold food includes luxurious salads and a European charcuterie platter (£14.95). A 150-strong wine list starts at £12.99. Open all week.

▲ Iberico World Tapas

Shire Hall, High Pavement, Nottingham, NG1 1HN
Tel no: (0115) 9410410
www.ibericotapas.com
Spanish/Tapas

The elaborately tiled, vaulted basement beneath the old courthouse can get jam-packed with happily noshing groups (hence the two evening sittings), although an easy-going, laid-back atmosphere prevails. Well-priced tapas of chorizo in red wine, potato and onion tortilla (£4) and ample charcuterie and cheese selections keep the traditionalists happy, while more contemporary ideas, say black cod with spicy miso or inside-out chicken wings with yuzu sweet chilli dressing (£6), add more variety. Wines from £15. Closed Sun.

Plumtree

Perkins

Revamped family favourite
Station House, Station Road, Plumtree, NG12 5NA
Tel no: (0115) 9373695
www.perkinsrestaurant.co.uk
Modern European | £29
Cooking score: 2

Chugging along contentedly after its 2010 revamp, Perkins still has what it takes as a convivial, family-friendly eatery with interesting add-ons. Old-stagers might not recognise the converted Victorian railway station these days, what with its clean-lined, contemporary interior and chef's table, but readers continue to applaud the kitchen's efforts. A 'tureen' of melting beef blade with mustard sauce has gone down well, but also look for home-smoked specialities, 'light bites' (pigeon breast with pea and mint purée) and decent puds such as blueberry cheesecake. House wine is £16. The Perkins mini-empire now includes Escabeche, a tapas restaurant/bar at 27 Bridgford Road, West Bridgford, NG2 6AU, tel: (0115) 9817010 – reports please.
Chef/s: Sarah Newham. **Open:** all week L 12 to 2 (3.30 Sun), Mon to Sat D 6 to 10. **Meals:** alc (main courses £10 to £19). Set L and D £12.50 (2 courses) to £15.50. Sun L £15.50 (2 courses) to £18.95. **Service:** not inc. **Details:** Cards accepted. 76 seats. 20 seats outside. Separate bar. No mobile phones. Wheelchair access. Music. Children allowed. Car parking.

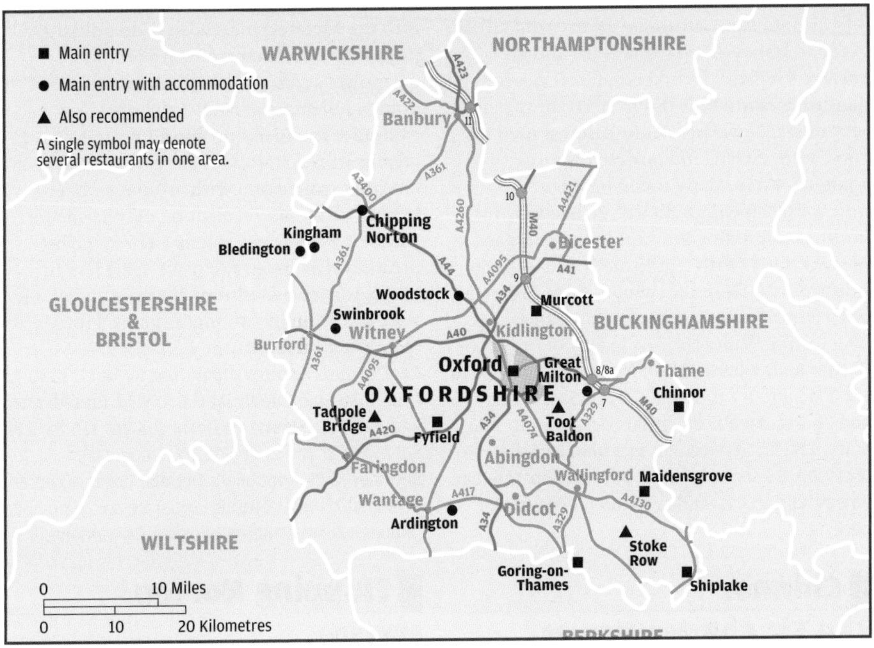

■ Main entry
● Main entry with accommodation
▲ Also recommended
A single symbol may denote several restaurants in one area.

0 10 Miles
0 10 20 Kilometres

Ardington

The Boar's Head

Pretty timber-framed all-rounder
Church Street, Ardington, OX12 8QA
Tel no: (01235) 833254
www.boarsheadardington.co.uk
Modern British | £30
Cooking score: 3

An ever-so-English pretty estate village creates just the right impression for visitors to this well-groomed timbered pub. Cheerful décor and open fires reinforce the mood and, in keeping with the rustic-chic surrounds, the cooking is British done in a modern style, tapping into a network of local producers. Bruce Buchan's food appeals for well-executed straightforwardness: smoked haddock chowder with poached egg, tempura scallops with chilli jam, or roast woodcock with pheasant croustade and wild mushrooms. Exotic and imaginative dishes, like assiette of suckling pig with squid chips and sweet-and-sour fondant potato, are similarly sure-footed. To finish, there may be date and walnut pudding. Wines from £19.50.
Chef/s: Bruce Buchan. **Open:** all week L 12 to 2 (2.30 Sun), D 7 to 9.30 (8.30 Sun). **Meals:** alc (main courses £17 to £25). Set L £12.50 (2 courses) to £15.50. Sun L £25. Tasting menu £39.50 (6 courses). **Service:** not inc. **Details:** Cards accepted. 40 seats. 24 seats outside. Separate bar. Wheelchair access. Music. Children allowed. Car parking.

Bledington

The Kings Head Inn

Textbook village hostelry
The Green, Bledington, OX7 6XQ
Tel no: (01608) 658365
www.thekingsheadinn.net
Modern British | £24
Cooking score: 2

Owned by Archie and Nicola Orr-Ewing from the Swan Inn at Swinbrook (see entry) this sixteenth-century inn seems to have it all

– from a sublime setting on a Cotswold village green to honey-hued stone walls and an ancient fireplace. Drinkers sup real ales in the flagstoned bar, while diners head for the airy restaurant. New chef Andy Kilburn used to cook at the Swan, and he delivers a straightforward daily menu based on unimpeachable ingredients: grilled Cornish sardines might be followed by flavour-packed blade of beef (with truffle mash and wild mushrooms) from the owners' farm in Fifield, with lemon posset producing a creamy conclusion. Wines from £15.50.

Chef/s: Andy Kilburn. **Open:** all week L 12 to 2 (2.30 Sat and Sun), D 7 to 9 (9.30 Fri and Sat). **Closed:** 25 and 26 Dec. **Meals:** alc (main courses £5 to £25). Sun L £14.50. **Service:** not inc. **Details:** Cards accepted. 65 seats. 50 seats outside. Separate bar. Wheelchair access. Music. Children allowed. Car parking.

Chinnor

The Sir Charles Napier

Surreal, cockle-warming Chiltern retreat
Sprigg's Alley, Chinnor, OX39 4BX
Tel no: (01494) 483011
www.sircharlesnapier.co.uk
Modern British | £37
Cooking score: 4

As seasonally dependable and firmly rooted as a beech tree up on Bledlow Ridge, this charmer weaves its magic with surreal sculptures and horticultural bounty stitched into the fabric of a cockle-warming Chiltern retreat. Ever-present Julie Griffiths has been its heart and soul since the 70s and has nurtured some talented chefs along the way. Sam Hughes departed in 2010, but new incumbent Chris Godfrey has the house style in his blood: how about a blissful springtime dish of red mullet, sea bass and sweet clams in a saffron-hued bouillabaisse broth with a pile of sea spinach and samphire? As ever, 'food for free' and game play a telling role in the kitchen – perhaps wild garlic risotto with morels or even a barnstorming venison and beetroot pie for the lunchtime crowd. The kitchen's incursions into the Mediterranean also yield gold dust: juicy veal cutlet smeared with lemony gremolata and served with diamonds of golden polenta and baby artichokes, for example. To finish, intriguing 'dessert' ice creams (treacle tart, say) are hard to resist, lavender pannacotta with aromatic ras-el-hanout purée is a revelation, and the cheese tray brings treasures aplenty. The wine list breathes class, from exclusive 'sparklers' to luscious 'stickies', with noble Burgundies and sexy Californians among its gems. House recommendations from £15.95.

Chef/s: Chris Godfrey. **Open:** Tue to Sun L 11.30 to 2.30 (3.30 Sun), Tue to Sat D 6 to 9.30. **Closed:** Mon, 24 to 27 Dec. **Meals:** alc (main courses £16 to £29). Set L and D Tue to Fri £15.50 (2 courses). **Service:** 12.5% (optional). **Details:** Cards accepted. 70 seats. 70 seats outside. Separate bar. No mobile phones. Music. Children allowed. Car parking.

Chipping Norton

NEW ENTRY

Wild Thyme

Unpretentious vibes, open-minded cooking
10 New Street, Chipping Norton, OX7 5LJ
Tel no: (01608) 645060
www.wildthymerestaurant.co.uk
Modern British | £35
Cooking score: 3

'This is seriously good cooking – Nick and Sally are definitely going places', enthused one reporter of this small, unpretentious restaurant-with-rooms. The menu plays to seasonal strengths; the kitchen chooses ingredients with care and takes an open-minded approach to things gastronomic. Double-baked goats' cheese soufflé with roasted beetroot, red onion marmalade and toasted hazelnuts is a typical starter, which might line up alongside 'superb' local smoked venison and winter salad dressed with blackberry vinaigrette. Meaty game faggots or pheasant breast en crépinette served atop a heap of braised pearl barley, Savoy cabbage and bacon lardons make notable main courses, while Mediterranean fish stew is simply 'sublime' (ditto the dark chocolate fondant with salted caramel centre). Good bread, and wines from £14.

Chef/s: Nicholas Pullen. **Open:** Tue to Sat L 12 to 2, D 7 to 9. **Closed:** Sun, Mon, 1 Jan for 2 weeks, 1 week May. **Meals:** alc (main courses from £12 to £22). **Service:** not inc. **Details:** Cards accepted. 35 seats. 10 seats outside. Music. Children allowed.

Fyfield

The White Hart

Unspoilt pub with impressive food
Main Road, Fyfield, OX13 5LW
Tel no: (01865) 390585
www.whitehart-fyfield.com
Modern British | £30
Cooking score: 3

Renowned for its food among Oxford's cognoscenti, this largely unspoilt fifteenth-century pub in picturesque Fyfield continues to impress. Heavy beams, exposed stonework and tiled flooring characterise both the bar (plentiful local ales) and the adjacent restaurant (almost ecclesiastical, with its high ceilings). 'Seasonal' and 'local' have true meaning on a menu where, in May, tasty fried Farmoor trout fillet on herb-speckled celeriac rémoulade could be followed by an exquisite spring dish of tender rack of lamb with sweetbreads, tongue, samphire and little broad beans from the White Hart's sizeable vegetable patch, then full-flavoured strawberries sandwiched between shortcake biscuits with vanilla cream. Service, from cheery precision-drilled staff, ran smoothly at inspection, though readers' experiences have occasionally differed. Wines from an appealing list start at £16.50.

Chef/s: Mark Chandler. **Open:** Tue to Sun L 12 to 2.30 (4 Sun), Tue to Sat D 7 to 9.30. **Closed:** Mon (exc bank hols). **Meals:** alc (main courses £13 to £19). Set L £16 (2 courses) to £19. Sun L £20 (2 courses) to £23. **Service:** not inc. **Details:** Cards accepted. 66 seats. 50 seats outside. Separate bar. Music. Children allowed. Car parking.

Goring-on-Thames

Leatherne Bottel

Delightful riverside dining
The Bridleway, Goring-on-Thames, RG8 0HS
Tel no: (01491) 872667
www.leathernebottel.co.uk
Modern European | £40
Cooking score: 3

The white-fronted Bottel, formerly a row of cottages, has a head-start location on a riverbank in the upper reaches of the Thames. Outdoor tables under parasols are a particular draw in summer. Its stock-in-trade is a gently daring version of modern European cooking, built around bold, high-impact flavours. Portland crab with melon and dill, accompanied by cucumber sorbet is a well-conceived starter that could be followed by venison with celeriac cream and chestnuts, or the steamed sea bream that left one reporter impressed by its bed of saffron-scented pea risotto, but slightly agnostic about its sweet chilli jam dressing. Desserts might include frozen white chocolate mousse with figs in port and pistachio praline. The wine list is particularly rich in fine Burgundies, but is good throughout, with house wines from £21 – though prices get a bit 'oo-er' as the quality ladder is climbed.

Chef/s: Julia Abbey. **Open:** all week L 12 to 2.15 (2.30 Sun), Mon to Sat D 7 to 9. **Meals:** alc (main courses £16 to £25). Set L £15.95 (2 courses) to £19.50. Set D £19.95 (2 courses) to £ 25.50. Sun L £31. Tasting menu L £47.50. Tasting menu D £68. **Service:** 10%. **Details:** Cards accepted. 38 seats. 60 seats outside. Separate bar. No music. No mobile phones. Wheelchair access. Children allowed. Car parking.

Great Milton

Le Manoir aux Quat'Saisons

'Close to heaven'
Church Road, Great Milton, OX44 7PD
Tel no: (01844) 278881
www.manoir.com
Modern French | £96
Cooking score: 8
V

Few can claim to have influenced the cooking of an entire generation of British chefs and home cooks, but Raymond Blanc, who received The Good Food Guide Lifetime Achievement Award in 2011, is undoubtedly one of them. The cookbooks and TV shows continue to come and go, bearing eloquent testimony to the fact that the years haven't seen any diminuendo in his passion for cooking and its possibilities. However, it is here, in this Oxfordshire fastness of honey-coloured stone, that the centre of gravity has remained. From its charming gardens, where glasshouses and polytunnels are incubating next season's (or tomorrow's) dinner, to the gracious house itself, with its air of refined calm and its conservatory dining room, it's the complete package, and all the more remarkable for the fact that things have not stood still where it matters – in the kitchen. Blanc and his head chef Gary Jones continue to devise menus that use the best the British Isles and the Manoir gardens have to offer, in a style of presentation that isn't afraid to court complexity for its impact, but is also content to let ingredients speak naturally for themselves. The 'menu classique' is where nostalgics will head: a first course of salmon fondant with cucumber in a wasabi and mooli vinaigrette looks like a gently tweaked version of a dish that was in Blanc's first cookbook. It could be followed by the sublime, earthy opulence of the truffle-creamed wild mushroom risotto. The carte is the leading suit, however, with its procession of surprising and extraordinary dishes: tuna and scallop ceviche with shaved fennel and oscietre, dressed in lime; Gressingham duck breast with braised endive and yuzu confit in a sauce of jasmine tea and raisins. Desserts supply the final flourish, perhaps in the form of a deconstructed tiramisu or rhubarb and gariguette strawberry crumble with fromage blanc ice cream. The trolley of fabulous, carefully kept, mature cheeses will prove hard to ignore, as will the exemplary wine list, which devotes tireless effort these days to sourcing biodynamic and organic tipples wherever they are made. Traditionalists will appreciate the honour-guards of Bordeaux and Burgundy, but there are also fine Portuguese and South American bottles, great English sparklers and pedigree German Rieslings. What a pity that the economics of the place mean that mark-ups are inevitably hefty. There are plenty of wines by the glass, but even they are mostly in double figures and the glass is of the smallest size. Bottles start at around £32.

Chef/s: Raymond Blanc and Gary Jones. **Open:** all week L 12 to 2.30, D 7 to 10. **Meals:** alc (main courses £46 to £48). Set L £57.50 (3 courses). Set L and D £105 (5 courses). Tasting menu £130 (9 courses). **Service:** not inc. **Details:** Cards accepted. 90 seats. Separate bar. No mobile phones. Wheelchair access. Music. Children allowed. Car parking.

Kingham

The Kingham Plough

A townie's rural dream
The Green, Kingham, OX7 6YD
Tel no: (01608) 658327
www.thekinghamplough.co.uk
Modern British | £26
Cooking score: 3

The Kingham Plough is a genuine pub with a proper bar – its Cotswold village setting the kind of rural picture that townies dream about. But this is no rural backwater; rather, it's a strongly rooted enterprise, noted for food, in which local supplies are sourced from the immediate locality. The bar offers an upbeat take on pub grub (sausage rolls, Scotch eggs, snails and mushrooms on toast), but upgrade to the dining room for intensely seasonal dishes, which in winter could mean pressed terrine of locally shot pheasant and ham hock (with celeriac salad and damson cheese on toast), Evenlode lamb pudding and halibut with leek, langoustine and shellfish stew. Meals end with a mighty selection of nine local cheeses, otherwise there's Clementine cheesecake and a matching sorbet. Wines from £15.

Chef/s: Emily Watkins and Gareth Fulford. **Open:** all week L 12 to 2 (2.30 Sat and Sun), Mon to Sat D 7 to 8.45. **Closed:** 25 Dec. **Meals:** alc (main courses £12 to £27). **Service:** not inc. **Details:** Cards accepted. 74 seats. 28 seats outside. Separate bar. No music. No mobile phones. Wheelchair access. Children allowed. Car parking.

Maidensgrove

NEW ENTRY

The Five Horseshoes

Hidden gem with cut-above pub grub

Maidensgrove, RG9 6EX

Tel no: (01491) 641282

www.thefivehorseshoes.co.uk

Modern British | £25

Cooking score: 1

It's way out in the sticks, but once you have tracked down the Five Horseshoes on its remote hillside perch, you can soak up those rolling Chiltern views before venturing inside. Park yourself beneath the bar's low-beamed ceilings, sup a pint of real ale and look forward to some upgraded pub food with a seasonal flavour. Open with seared scallops, mussels and local crayfish, move on to slow-braised belly pork with dauphinoise, apple purée and cider sauce, and conclude with lemon tart and raspberry sorbet. Wines from £16.

Chef/s: Sean Le Roux. **Open:** all week L 12 to 3 (4 Sun), Tue to Sun D 6 to 10 (9 Sun). **Closed:** 2 weeks Jan. **Meals:** alc (main courses £11 to £25). Set L and D £11.95 (2 courses) to £14.95. **Service:** not inc. **Details:** Cards accepted. 90 seats. 230 seats outside. Separate bar. No music. Wheelchair access. Children allowed. Car parking.

Murcott

The Nut Tree Inn

Pubby vitality and fine-tuned flavours

Main Street, Murcott, OX5 2RE

Tel no: (01865) 331253

www.nuttreeinn.co.uk

Modern British | £38

Cooking score: 5

The Norths run this reinvented thatched pub as a family affair: Michael and his sister manage the kitchen, while wife Imogen takes care of business out front. They smoke their own salmon, buy beef from a nearby farm and have porkers rooting around in the garden, but their food is a world away from anything on *River Cottage*. There's an acute seasonal edge to the cooking and fine-tuned flavours come through strongly, whether it's crispy calves' sweetbreads with celeriac rémoulade or a pan-fried terrine of pig's head and black pudding teamed with sauerkraut, piccalilli dressing and fried quails' eggs. Elsewhere, braised shoulder of Oxfordshire lamb is turned into a torte with potatoes and some creamed spinach on the side, while Scottish halibut is poached in olive oil before appearing with a green herb risotto and young fennel hollandaise. There's also no diffidence about offering fishcakes or open veggie lasagne, but things turn serious again when it comes to dessert: dark chocolate fondant appears with cardamom ice cream and orange jelly; sticky toffee pudding is gussied up with a caramelised apple tart and praline ice cream. Guest ales, bar snacks and low beams emphasise the Nut Tree's pubby vitality, and the fairly priced wine list trades in well-chosen bottles from £15.95.

Chef/s: Michael and Mary North. **Open:** Tue to Sun L 12 to 2.30 (3 Sun), Tue to Sat D 7 to 9. **Closed:** Mon. **Meals:** alc (main courses £17 to £27). Set L and D £18 (2 courses) to £22. **Service:** not inc. **Details:** Cards accepted. 70 seats. 40 seats outside. Separate bar. Music. Children allowed. Car parking.

Oxford

The Anchor

Pub credentials and foodie aspirations
2 Hayfield Road, Oxford, OX2 6TT
Tel no: (01865) 510282
www.theanchoroxford.com
Modern British | £25
Cooking score: 2

Real ales, roaring fires, pub games and a book club reinforce the Anchor's credentials as a neighbourhood boozer, although chef/ landlord Jamie King has upped its profile on the food front. Despite the odd gripe about 'stodginess', the kitchen generally delivers: sweet little Fowey mussels in cream sauce with bread for mopping up, attractively presented chicken ballottine on celeriac mash with red cabbage, and a big helping of sticky toffee pud have all been applauded. The Anchor's broad culinary remit also extends to lightly cured duck with poached duck egg and chicory salad, venison sausages with beetroot mash and lemon posset with Yorkshire rhubarb. Wines from £14.55.

Chef/s: Jamie King. **Open:** all week L 12 to 2.30 (3 Sun), D 6 to 9.30 (6.30 to 8.30 Sun). **Closed:** 25 and 26 Dec. **Meals:** alc (main courses £12 to £16). **Service:** not inc. **Details:** Cards accepted. 70 seats. 35 seats outside. Separate bar. Wheelchair access. Music. Children allowed. Car parking.

Ashmolean Dining Room

Versatile rooftop restaurant
Beaumont Street, Oxford, OX1 2PH
Tel no: (01865) 553823
www.ashmoleandiningroom.com
Mediterranean | £27
Cooking score: 2

This remodelled, glassy space at the top of the Ashmolean Museum holds a special place in the social mores of academic Oxford. It's quite a set-up. The spacious refectory-style room is awash with natural light and the fair-weather terrace sports fine rooftop views. The flexible menu sends out a zesty assortment of mainly Euro-inspired dishes such as plates of Spanish and Italian charcuterie or English cheeses, Sicilian vegetable salad, a Greek dish of lamb chops with dried oregano, chilli beans, char-grilled peppers and anchovies, and vanilla, honey and grappa pannacotta. There's afternoon tea, too. Wines from £15.

Chef/s: Arun Manickam. **Open:** Tue to Sun 12 to 8.45 (10 to 6 Sun). **Closed:** Mon. **Meals:** alc (main courses £11 to £18). Set L and D £20 (2 courses) to £25. **Service:** not inc. **Details:** Cards accepted. 100 seats. 100 seats outside. Wheelchair access. Music. Children allowed. Car parking.

Branca

Lively all-day Italian
111 Walton Street, Oxford, OX2 6AJ
Tel no: (01865) 556111
www.branca-restaurants.com
Italian | £23
Cooking score: 1

It would be 'hard to think of a better neighbourhood restaurant', reckoned one reporter, extolling the virtues of this lively old-stager on the eastern edge of Oxford's Jericho district. There's lots of light and space, and the all-day menu proudly displays its Italian lineage with slow-roasted piedmontese pepper with buffalo mozzarella, risottos, pasta and a short choice of stone-baked pizzas. Organic salmon and smoked haddock fishcakes and crème brûlée broaden the appeal. Good meal deals, too. A short Italian wine list opens at £14.95.

Chef/s: Michael MacQuire. **Open:** all week 11am to 11pm (10am Sat and Sun). **Meals:** alc (main courses £9 to £17). Set L and D £10.95 (2 courses). Sun L £12.95. **Service:** not inc. **Details:** Cards accepted. 100 seats. 60 seats outside. Separate bar. Wheelchair access. Music. Children allowed.

Also recommended entries are not scored but we think they are worth a visit.

Cherwell Boathouse

An idyllic institution
50 Bardwell Road, Oxford, OX2 6ST
Tel no: (01865) 552746
www.cherwellboathouse.co.uk
Modern British | £32
Cooking score: 1

£5 OFF 🍷 V

The Verdin family's working Victorian boathouse is an Oxford institution, much loved for its 'great hospitality', prestigious wine list and idyllic Englishness – you can even hire a punt and go for a paddle on the Cherwell. There's also no shortage of decent seasonal food on offer, and the short menu is packed with good things: potted wild rabbit and grilled marinated duck leg with pickled cabbage in winter; crab meat and dandelion salad followed by rack of lamb with carrot purée, peas and courgettes come summer. France dominates as regards wine, but also look for Spanish treasures and some compelling New World names. Otherwise, dip into the 'shortlist' for cracking house selections from £14 (£3.75 a glass).
Chef/s: Carson Hill. **Open:** all week L 12 to 2 (2.30 Sat and Sun), D 6 to 9.30. **Closed:** 24 to 30 Dec. **Meals:** alc (main courses £14 to £18). Set midweek L £12.50 (2 courses). Set D £19.50 (2 courses) to £26. Sun L £24. **Service:** 10% (optional). **Details:** Cards accepted. 70 seats. 40 seats outside. Separate bar. No music. No mobile phones. Wheelchair access. Children allowed. Car parking.

Gee's

Oxford landmark with comforting food
61 Banbury Road, Oxford, OX2 6PE
Tel no: (01865) 553540
www.gees-restaurant.co.uk
Modern British | £33
Cooking score: 2

'What more could you want?' asked one fan of this Victorian conservatory restaurant, delighted with the food, the 'well-chosen' wines and the 'very enjoyable' jazz evenings. It's an Oxford landmark and Gee's menu aims to comfort rather than challenge, the repertoire of unfussy modern British brasserie-style dishes ranging from roasted veal loin with shank ravioli and buttered spinach to whole plaice with roasted salsify, lemon and shrimp butter. Results on the plate may lack the 'wow' factor, but ingredients are handled carefully to produce well-balanced flavours in, say, crab pancake with butternut squash or a simple main of venison pudding with winter greens. Wines from £16.95.
Chef/s: Simon Cottrell. **Open:** all week L 12 to 3 (3.30 Sat and Sun), D 5.45 to 11 (11.30 Fri and Sat, 10.30 Sun). **Closed:** 25 and 26 Dec. **Meals:** alc (main courses £14 to £24). Set L £15.95 (2 courses) to £19.95. Sun L £22.95 (2 courses) to £25.95. Sun D £23.95 (2 courses) to £26.95. **Service:** 12.5% (optional). **Details:** Cards accepted. 85 seats. 20 seats outside. Separate bar. Music. Children allowed.

ALSO RECOMMENDED

▲ Chiang Mai

130a High Street, Oxford, OX1 4DH
Tel no: (01865) 202233
www.chiangmaikitchen.co.uk
Thai

Tucked down a narrow alleyway, this popular restaurant is housed in a rickety timber-framed building that dates from the seventeenth-century. It may look like a quaint old tea shop, but the ornate wood carvings are a reminder that this place delivers authentic Thai cooking. The lengthy menu offers plenty of choice, with one reporter praising the 'excellent' khanom jeep dumplings (£6.60) and 'subtly spiced' venison curry (£9.90). Service is 'efficient, friendly and helpful'. Wines from £13.85. Open all week.

▲ Edamamé

15 Holywell Street, Oxford, OX1 3SA
Tel no: (01865) 246916
www.edamame.co.uk
Japanese

Catering amiably for students, tourists and academics alike, this tiny Japanese eatery is a busy, economical and enjoyable place. Here a single luncher can grab pork tonkatsu or chicken miso ramen (£9), while friends get together in the evening to share the likes of stir-fried strips of pork loin marinated in soy and ginger or salmon fillets marinated and poached in teriyaki sauce (£8). Go on Thursday evenings for the sushi menu. Saké from £4; wine from £13. Open Wed to Sun L, Thur to Sat D.

▲ The Magdalen Arms

243 Iffley Road, Oxford, OX4 1SJ
Tel no: (01865) 243159
www.magdalenarms.com
British

Set up by alumni from the Anchor & Hope in London (see entry), this re-born boozer is a 'fantastic asset' for those living in Oxford's suburban quarter. The kitchen takes its cue from the Waterloo original, turning out unreformed Brit grub including salt lamb and barley broth (£5), braised Hereford beef shin with horseradish cream (£13.60) and a comforting autumnal dish of slow-cooked oxtail pie. Also expect some rustic European detours for the likes of Provençal fish stew. Wines from £12.50. No food Mon, Tue L, Sun D.

▲ Shanghai 30s

82 St Aldates, Oxford, OX1 1RA
Tel no: (01865) 242230
www.shanghai30s.com
Chinese £5 OFF

This slinky first-floor venue has a good reputation for imaginative Chinese food and lunchtime dim sum. It occupies two distinguished wood-panelled rooms, where piano music and smartly dressed staff add to the nostalgic charm. The food straddles the familiar and the new; you could try the Qi family's almond chicken (minced breast coated with almonds, crisp-fried, with lemon sauce) and then Tsingtao beer duckling (£8.80) or crispy pork in a lychee glaze (£7.95). International wines start at £12.50. Open all week.

RYAN SIMPSON
Orwells

What does winning *The Good Food Guide 2012* Readers' Restaurant of the Year mean to you?
It gave me a great sense of achievement, and demonstrated that you must listen to your customers.

What would you cook Great Britain's Olympic team?
Seared scallops with broad beans and verjus sauce, followed by rump of venison, monk's beard and layered vegetable cake, followed by lemon and blueberry tart and cream cheese sorbet.

What's been the best culinary trend of recent years?
Foraging for local delights and eating from the land.

What is your favourite food combination?
Surf and turf, or sweet and sour.

What most excites you about the restaurant industry today?
The customer's perception of a quality establishment; there is no need for stuffiness, enjoying food should be a relaxing experience in relaxing surroundings.

Shiplake

★ READERS' RESTAURANT OF THE YEAR ★
NATIONAL WINNER

Orwells

A handsome and well-bred eatery
Shiplake Row, Shiplake, RG9 4DP
Tel no: (01189) 403673
www.orwellsatshiplake.co.uk
Modern British | £45
Cooking score: 5

Whizz kids Ryan Simpson and Liam Trotman renamed this upper-crust Oxfordshire hostelry after George Orwell, who grew up in Shiplake – although their approach to things gastronomic is definitely more twenty-first century than 1984. Orwells is a well-bred and handsome eatery on every level, with lots of pubby attributes but also a serious side. Brakspear's ales and ancient beams set the tone in the bar, where the menu takes pub grub to a new level: how about quail escabèche, rabbit Scotch eggs, or drooling over muntjac and hazelnut burgers with 'historic' triple-cooked chips? Meanwhile, things move up a gear in The Room, a dinky, dinner-only destination serving incisive dishes with bags of technical know-how and clear, clean flavours. A starter of Chiltern roe deer carpaccio with hazelnuts, lobster bonbons and hibiscus confirms the kitchen's seasonal intentions, likewise pan-seared Brixham brill with rosemary dumplings, mussel broth, fennel and orange, although readers are also quick to applaud 'truly stunning' veggie creations including caramelised kohlrabi with glazed onions, root vegetable layer cake and chanterelles. 'Presentation is prissy, and all the better for it', observed one insightful correspondent, doubtless referring to delectable desserts such as orange, Champagne and grapefruit terrine with blood orange and rosemary sorbet. Staff are attentive but never intrusive, and the wine list promises sound drinking from £14.95.

Chef/s: Ryan Simpson and Liam Trotman. **Open:** Tue to Sun L 11.30 to 3 (3.30 Sun), Tue to Sat D 6.30 to 9.30. The Room: Tue to Sat D only 7 to 9.30. **Closed:** Mon, first 2 weeks Jan, 1 week mid-Apr, first 2 weeks Sept. **Meals:** alc (main courses £18 to £28). Set L £10 (2 courses) to £15.50. Sun L £19.95 (2 courses). **Service:** not inc. **Details:** Cards accepted. 50 seats. 40 seats outside. Separate bar. No mobile phones. Wheelchair access. Music. Children allowed. Car parking.

Stoke Row

ALSO RECOMMENDED

▲ The Crooked Billet

Newlands Lane, Stoke Row, RG9 5PU
Tel no: (01491) 681048
www.thecrookedbillet.co.uk
Modern European

A country pub original to the extent that there is no bar counter, the Billet is an endearingly lopsided, beamed and flagged village hostelry, where Paul Clerehugh has had the pleasure of serving a number of celebrity chefs and even (pop fans, please note) Kylie! Extensive menus encompass chilli mussels with coconut and coriander (£8.10), hare braised in red wine and juniper wth turnip and prune gratin (£17.95) and Bakewell tart with custard. Wines from £19.55. Open all week.

Swinbrook

The Swan Inn

Idyllic stone pub
Swinbrook, OX18 4DY
Tel no: (01993) 823339
www.theswanswinbrook.co.uk
Modern British | £30
Cooking score: 2

This lovely, creeper-covered stone pub beside the Windrush River has taken on a new lease of life under the accomplished duo Nicola and Archie Orr-Ewing, who also run the Kings Head Inn at nearby Bledington (see entry). It's an idyllic prospect, with bantams in the garden, heavy beams and roaring winter fires within, but the main attraction is what comes out of the kitchen. Devilled duck hearts on toast, whole grilled lemon sole served with new potatoes, broccoli and white crab butter

with lemon, and elderflower pannacotta define the uncluttered approach and impeccable sourcing. Wines from £15.
Chef/s: Richard Burkert. **Open:** all week L 12 to 2 (2.30 Fri to Sun), D 7 to 9 (9.30 Fri and Sat). **Closed:** 25 and 26 Dec. **Meals:** alc (main courses £13 to £17). **Service:** not inc. **Details:** Cards accepted. 65 seats. 65 seats outside. Separate bar. Wheelchair access. Music. Children allowed. Car parking.

Tadpole Bridge

ALSO RECOMMENDED
▲ The Trout at Tadpole Bridge

Tadpole Bridge, SN7 8RF
Tel no: (01367) 870382
www.troutinn.co.uk
British

Standing proud beside a humpback bridge spanning the river Thames, the stone-built Trout feels reassuringly English to a T. Food takes due account of seasonal and regional produce, with a please-all menu that in winter could deliver warm salad of wood pigeon (£7.95) and roast partridge with chestnut and thyme stuffing (£15.95), as well as bowls of mussels, fish and chips, and steamed beef and ale pie. Raspberry and strawberry crème brûlée ends things nicely. Wines from £14. Open all week. Accommodation.

Toot Baldon

ALSO RECOMMENDED
▲ The Mole Inn

Toot Baldon, OX44 9NG
Tel no: (01865) 340001
www.themoleinn.com
Modern European

This reconfigured country pub may still attract drinkers, but it's also a destination for people who care about food. A bright, modern feel is tempered by touches such as exposed stone, beams and standing timbers. The kitchen mixes and matches influences in unfussy modern style, so expect shredded duck, chilli, beanshoots, lime and coriander (£6.95) or sesame-seared sea bass with spicy rice noodles, alongside bangers and mash or crispy confit duck leg with Puy lentils and pommes mousseline (£15.95). Wines from £18.50. Open all week.

Woodstock

The Feathers

New-look old-school charmer
Market Street, Woodstock, OX20 1SX
Tel no: (01993) 812291
www.feathers.co.uk
Modern British | £50
Cooking score: 4

£5 OFF

An adventurous makeover has left this venerable hotel restaurant a brighter, more modern space. Wood-panelled walls in the front section (there are white walls to the rear) temper the effect of vibrant modern art and a startlingly colourful carpet. Likewise, Marc Hardiman's regularly changing fixed-price carte (there's also a tasting menu) pushes many modish buttons, and incorporates several add-ons (a pre-starter of creamy celeriac soup, perhaps) that partially explain the modest portions. Luxury ingredients, complex combinations, expert presentation and precise cooking were evident in a texturally adroit, yet rich, starter of buttery foie gras matched with ginger beer jelly, smoked duck, apple compote and crisp bread, also in a main of turbot, confit chicken wing, wild mushrooms and bitter lemon pith, and a pudding of chocolate délice (filled with very salty caramel, served with porridge ice cream). Balance may sometimes need addressing, and service – impeccable at inspection – hasn't always impressed readers, but a lengthy and accessible wine list (from £20) adds appeal.
Chef/s: Marc Hardiman. **Open:** Tue to Sun L 12 to 2.30 (3 Sun), Mon to Sat D 7 to 9 (9.30 Fri and Sat). **Meals:** Set L and D £39.50 (2 courses) to £49.95. Sun L £24.50. **Service:** 10% (optional).
Details: Cards accepted. 40 seats. 20 seats outside. Separate bar. No music. No mobile phones. Children allowed.

■ Main entry
● Main entry accommodation
▲ Also recommended
A single symbol may denote several restaurants in one area.

NORTH-EAST WALES
CHESHIRE
Whitchurch
Ellesmere
Market Drayton
Oswestry
STAFFORDSHIRE
Newport
Shrewsbury
Telford
ENGLAND
WALES
Minsterley
Marton
SHROPSHIRE
MID WALES
Church Stretton
Bridgnorth
WEST MIDLANDS
Munslow
Wistanstow
Craven Arms
Llanfair Waterdine
Ludlow
WORCESTERSHIRE
HEREFORDSHIRE
0 10 20 Miles
0 10 20 30 Kilometres

Llanfair Waterdine

The Waterdine

A serious restaurant in pub clothing
Llanfair Waterdine, LD7 1TU
Tel no: (01547) 528214
www.waterdine.com
Modern British | £33
Cooking score: 4

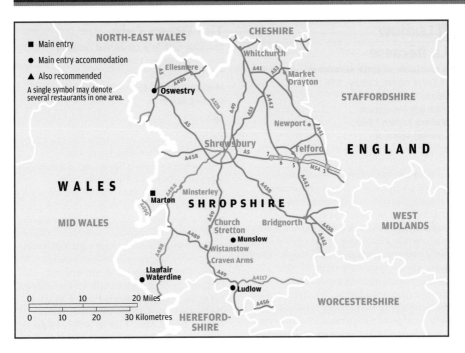

On the face of it there is little to distinguish Ken and Isabel Adams' off-the-beaten-track Welsh longhouse from any other sixteenth-century drovers' inn hereabouts. While it may feel olde-worlde – there's a wood burner in the inglenook and money is not lavished on the décor – the Waterdine is a restaurant in pub clothing. Fixed-price menus at lunch and dinner (booking is essential), offering five choices per course, are where the effort is concentrated. Ideas are not usually controversial (simple seasonal soups like a winter roast parsnip with walnut pesto, say, and old-fashioned pork terrine with beetroot chutney) and supplies tend to be local (Mortimer Forest roe deer saddle, for example, with mushrooms and celeriac). The garden also plays a big part in the kitchen's output. Not all reporters find such simplicity of style to their taste, but the overwhelming majority view is of consistently good food and friendly, welcoming service. Wines from £18.50.

Chef/s: Ken Adams. **Open:** Thur to Sun L 12 to 3, Tue to Sat D 7 to 10. **Closed:** Mon, 1 week spring, 1 week autumn. **Meals:** Set L £22.50. Set D £32.50. **Service:** not inc. **Details:** Cards accepted. 24 seats. Separate bar. No music. No mobile phones. Car parking.

Average Price

The average price listed in main-entry reviews denotes the price of a three-course meal, without wine.

Ludlow

La Bécasse

A cavalcade of taste sensations
17 Corve Street, Ludlow, SY8 1DA
Tel no: (01584) 872325
www.labecasse.co.uk
Modern French | £60
Cooking score: 6

£5 OFF **V**

La Bécasse – part of Alan Murchison's growing empire of top-end restaurants – occupies the fabric of a seventeenth-century coaching inn. It makes the most of the building's historic oak panelling and stone walls, while a Champagne bar upstairs adds some contemporary metropolitan pizzazz to proceedings. 'Incredibly talented' Will Holland heads up the kitchen, and his full-strength 'gourmand menu' has delivered a cavalcade of 'absolute taste sensations', from Ragstone goats' cheese mousse with beetroot and plum purée, liquorice and balsamic jelly to a winning dish of pan-fried halibut with morteau sausage, cauliflower, curried lime emulsion and honeycomb. Desserts also show clever modern thinking and artistry: a 'Cointreau crumble' soufflé with blood orange carpaccio, olive oil jelly and brown bread ice cream, for example. There's no denying that the kitchen knows how to impress, although 'it doesn't always deliver a great deal of joy'; flavours can be muted and all that 'mind-boggling intricacy' can result in too many distractions on the plate. Some readers have also been troubled by 'arrogant, dismissive and cursory service', although staff are helpful and knowledgeable when it comes to advising on the carefully considered, 160-bin wine list where bottles start at £19.

Chef/s: Will Holland. **Open:** Wed to Sun L 12 to 2, Tue to Sat D 7 to 9 (9.30 Fri and Sat). **Closed:** Mon, 2 weeks Christmas and New Year. **Meals:** Set L £26 (2 courses) to £30. Set D £54 (2 courses) to £60. Sun L £30. Gourmand menu £65 (7 courses). **Service:** 12.5% (optional). **Details:** Cards accepted. 35 seats. Separate bar. No mobile phones. Music. Children allowed. Car parking.

The Green Café

Cracking café in a converted cornmill
Mill on the Green, Ludlow, SY8 1EG
Tel no: (01584) 879872
Modern British | £19
Cooking score: 1

Modest, honest and generous, this cracking café occupies a converted cornmill overlooking the river Teme, and matches splendid views with 'invariably fresh', seasonally attuned food. Coffee and cakes keep the passing crowds replenished, but the place peaks at lunchtime, when the kitchen shows off its green credentials. Come here for silky gnocchi with Italian sausage ragù, rich confit duck and mutton cassoulet, or a bowl of smoked haddock chowder. Cheery staff will even provide hot-water bottles if it's chilly on the terrace. Organic wines from £16.50.

Chef/s: Clive Davis. **Open:** Tue to Sun 10am to 4.30pm. **Closed:** Mon, 3 Jan to 14 Feb. **Meals:** alc (main courses £7 to £12). **Service:** not inc. **Details:** Cash only. 30 seats. 25 seats outside. No music. Wheelchair access. Children allowed.

Mr Underhill's

Seductive hideaway with hands-on excellence
Dinham Weir, Ludlow, SY8 1EH
Tel no: (01584) 874431
www.mr-underhills.co.uk
Modern European | £60
Cooking score: 6

V

Chris and Judy Bradley's seductive hideaway beneath the ramparts of Ludlow Castle holds a special place in the town's gastronomic annals. For three decades, Mr Underhill's has epitomised independent, hands-on excellence. While not everyone buys into the intensely personal style, guests still expect to see their names inscribed at the top of each bespoke menu, safe in the knowledge that dinner will consist of eight little courses. They also know that everything will gel – even if there's no choice until the galaxy of desserts comes into view. The culinary themes are as comfortingly familiar as the waters tumbling over nearby Dinham Weir; trusted ideas are perpetually re-worked as new ones are fashioned in their image (Bradley's renowned duck liver custard was served with quince confit in 2008; three years later, it appeared with sweetcorn cream and lemongrass glaze). There's always something dainty at the top of the order (maybe a vodka sponge with green tea ice cream), before soup, fish and meaty creations are brought out. On a typical night, you might find halibut with a fennel and pollen crust on leek purée, followed by slow-roast 'magret de canard' with Savoy cabbage, duck confit and coffee vinaigrette. Then Chris slips in a mini-dessert (lychee sponge, say), before a cornucopia of sweet delights and Anglo-French cheeses bring the curtain down. Judy Bradley's presence out front is a joy, and she is also the brains behind the lovingly assembled wine list. A new 'pod bar' allows more wines to be offered by the glass, and the full works opens with 20 high-value 'special selections' from £21.

Chef/s: Chris Bradley. **Open:** Wed to Sun D only 7.30 (1 sitting). **Closed:** Mon, Tue, 25 and 26 Dec, 1 Jan, 1 week June, 1 week end Oct/early Nov. **Meals:** Set D £59.50 (8 courses). **Service:** not inc. **Details:** Cards accepted. 30 seats. 30 seats outside. No music. No mobile phones. Children allowed. Car parking.

Marton

Gartells at the Sun Inn

Pubby hospitality, real ales, honest food
Marton, SY21 8JP
Tel no: (01938) 561211
www.suninn.org.uk
Modern British | £21
Cooking score: 1

The Gartell family have stamped their mark on this historic stone hostelry close to the Welsh border since moving in some six years ago. As well as dispensing real ales and honest pub grub in the Sun's hospitable bar, they have also established a cordial restaurant where customers can partake of roast venison with braised red cabbage, medallions of pork and black pudding with mustard and apple sauce or steamed brill with fennel and mushrooms (a typical special from the fish menu). To finish, perhaps iced strawberry parfait. House wine is £13.95.

Chef/s: Peter Gartell. **Open:** Wed to Sun L 12 to 2, Tue to Sat D 7 to 9.30. **Closed:** Mon. **Meals:** alc (main courses £10 to £16). Sun L £14.95 (2 courses) to £17.95. **Service:** not inc. **Details:** Cards accepted. 60 seats. 20 seats outside. Separate bar. No music. Wheelchair access. Children allowed. Car parking.

Munslow

The Crown Country Inn

Historic inn with posh comfort food
Corvedale Road, Munslow, SY7 9ET
Tel no: (01584) 841205
www.crowncountryinn.co.uk
Modern British | £28
Cooking score: 3

'Richard and Jane Arnold have created something very special here', remarked one reader, musing about the Crown's curious mix of pub, restaurant and 'hideaway rooms'. Once a 'hundred house' where local justice was seen to be done, the Grade-II listed building is now highly valued for its food. Eat in the flagstoned bar or upstairs restaurant from a menu that has delivered a parfait of chicken livers with Bramley apple chutney and 'sumptuous' home-baked bread, ahead of braised lamb shoulder with mustard-creamed cabbage and caper and tarragon sauce. The British cheeseboard is a winner, and desserts might offer cinnamon pannacotta with warm spiced gingerbread, poached pear and butterscotch sauce. Wines start at £14.95.

Chef/s: Richard Arnold. **Open:** Tue to Sun L 12 to 2, Tue to Sat D 6.45 to 8.45. **Closed:** Mon, 24 to 27 Dec, 1 to 4 Jan. **Meals:** alc (main courses £14 to £18). Set L and D £13.50 (2 courses) to £18.50. Sun L £19.50. **Service:** not inc. **Details:** Cards accepted. 65 seats. 20 seats outside. Separate bar. No mobile phones. Music. Children allowed. Car parking.

CUTTING-EDGE KITCHENS

As technology moves on and boundaries shift, high-end chefs are more able than ever to indulge their inner geek.

At **Fraiche**, Marc Wilkinson would like an ultra-sonic machine, 'for the extraction of the aromatic and flavourful components of vegetables, flowers and herbs. This allows you to achieve a freshness of taste that would normally be lost during the cooking process, and without losing natural colours.'

Simon Rogan of **L'Enclume** is always on the lookout for innovations. 'My latest technological find is my new ThermoGlo heat lamps,' he says. 'Keeping food warm at the pass without giving off large amounts of heat has been a problem, but they apply infra-red energy at a specific micron wavelength. Food absorbs this energy, transferring it into heat more efficiently, and the gentle nature of the heat pattern allows food to be held longer whilst maintaining quality.'

At **Restaurant Sat Bains**, induction units allow food to be placed directly on the heat source. Bains says, 'Induction cooks food evenly, quickly and cleanly. The first evening we cooked on induction we went from using 80 pots a night to three!'

Oswestry

Sebastians

Affordable haute cuisine
45 Willow Street, Oswestry, SY11 1AQ
Tel no: (01691) 655444
www.sebastians-hotel.co.uk
French | £40
Cooking score: 3
V

With its beams, crooked floors and chintz, this sixteenth-century dwelling looks like a devoutly English teashop, but first impressions can be deceptive: since 1989, Michelle and Mark Sebastian Fisher have been running this place as a cordial little hotel and restaurant with an unmistakable Gallic accent. Dinner menus are written in French (with English descriptions) and the monthly fixed-price deal runs to five courses, including a 'petit appetiser' and a sorbet. The result is a convincing and affordable version of haute cuisine that might yield anything from pheasant breast wrapped in sweet-cured bacon with date purée and goats' cheese emulsion to roast monkfish with pumpkin purée and toasted pearl barley sauce. French cheeses are served with a warm Welsh rarebit and grape chutney, while desserts could include a slice of iced white chocolate and banana crêpe. House wines start at £16.95.

Chef/s: Mark Sebastian Fisher and Richard Jones. **Open:** Tue to Sat D only 6.30 to 9.30. **Closed:** Sun, Mon, 25 and 26 Dec, bank hols. **Meals:** Set D £19.95 (3 courses) to £39.50 (5 courses). **Service:** not inc. **Details:** Cards accepted. 40 seats. 20 seats outside. Separate bar. No mobile phones. Music. Children allowed. Car parking.

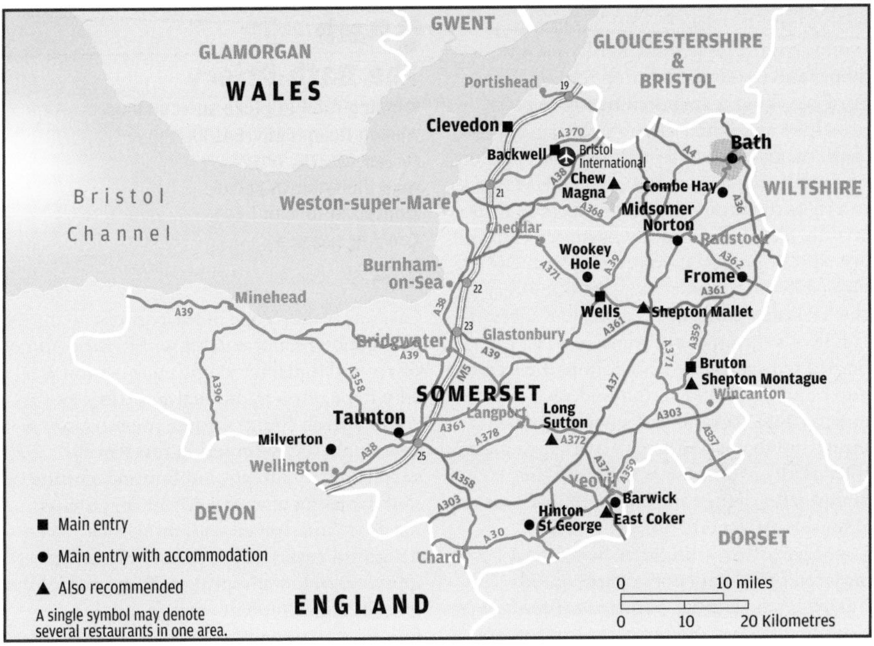

Backwell

The New Inn

Smart pub with high standards
86 West Town Road, Backwell, BS48 3BE
Tel no: (01275) 462199
www.newinn-backwell.co.uk
Modern European | £25
Cooking score: 3

This extended roadside hostelry is still a pub that attracts the locals, but it has also become a destination restaurant. Inside, the pubby appeal blends with heritage colours, trendy wallpaper and stone walls. Nathan Muir's cooking demonstrates sound talent and a commendable commitment to top-class raw materials. Chunky partridge and wild rabbit terrine arrives with beetroot compote and celery, while fish comes in the shape of roast fillet of pollack on Puy lentils. Desserts have included bitter chocolate tart with beetroot and marshmallow parfait. Wines from £14.50.

Chef/s: Nathan Muir. **Open:** all week L 12 to 2.30 (4 Sun), Mon to Sat D 6 to 9.30 (6.30 to 10 Fri, 7 to 10 Sat). **Closed:** 25 and 26 Dec. **Meals:** alc (main courses £10 to £20). Set L £11.50 (2 courses) to £15. Set D Fri and Sat £19.50 (2 courses) to £25. Sun L £16.50 (2 courses) to £19.50. Bar menu available. **Service:** not inc. **Details:** Cards accepted. 45 seats. 25 seats outside. Separate bar. Music. Children allowed. Car parking.

Barwick

Little Barwick House

Polished restaurant-with-rooms
Rexes Hollow Lane, Barwick, BA22 9TD
Tel no: (01935) 423902
www.littlebarwickhouse.co.uk
Modern British | £44
Cooking score: 5

The timelessness of this beautifully situated Georgian dower house lends meals here both informality and a sense of occasion. The atmosphere is relaxed and unhurried, the feeling 'middle-class English': cosy sitting rooms, comfortable sofas, family photos, drapes and two linked dining rooms. Tim Ford's cooking is anchored firmly to basic principles and while there are few ambitious leaps, menus are based on the simple handling of good (often regional) ingredients. He sticks to a tight repertoire that might include a silky raviolo, plump with 'nicely flavoured crab and just a hit of ginger', a dollop of julienne of vegetables on top and 'lovely, rich, buttery' chervil sauce. 'Pink and very tender' slices of saddle of venison could come next, set on braised red cabbage with a dollop of beetroot purée and 'a rather superfluous deep-fried potato rösti'. Portions are generous, which means indulgent puddings – perhaps a glass filled with citrus desserts (lemon posset, orange jelly, orange and lemon mousse) served alongside an almond florentine and a raspberry sorbet – might be best shared between two. Incidentals charm: good canapés in the lounge, homemade breads, West Country cheeses, and the care of customers. And there is no questioning the quality and commitment of the wine list. It's arranged by style, deftly mixing Old World and New, offering a good selection of half-bottles. Bottle prices from £18.95.

Chef/s: Tim Ford. **Open:** Wed to Sun L 12 to 2, Tue to Sat D 7 to 9.30. **Closed:** Mon, 2 weeks Jan, 1 week end Aug. **Meals:** Set L £23.95 (2 courses) to £27.95. Set D £37.95 (2 courses) to £43.95. Sun L £29.95. **Service:** not inc. **Details:** Cards accepted. 40 seats. 12 seats outside. Separate bar. No music. Car parking.

Please send us your feedback

To register your opinion about any restaurant listed in the Guide, or a new restaurant that you wish to bring to our attention, please visit the web address at the bottom of the page. Your feedback informs the content of the book and will be used to compile next year's reviews.

Bath

The Bath Priory

Winning food in plush surroundings
Weston Road, Bath, BA1 2XT
Tel no: (01225) 331922
www.thebathpriory.co.uk
Modern European | £69
Cooking score: 5
V

Given that this is one of the region's destination restaurants, set within the confines of a grand hotel, it's tempting to assume that all will be ultra-traditional at the Priory. Of course, plush country house trappings are *de rigueur*, but any whispering reverence is supplanted by a happy hubbub and smiling staff. Come here with a decent appetite, as meals are interleaved with numerous delightful extras. A beautifully presented lobster raviolo with spring cabbage and lobster bisque sounds modest enough, but it's followed by two sets of amuse-bouches before the main course appears. Michael Caines' lieutenant Sam Moody shows his prowess with a winning dish of slow-cooked, anise-crusted duck breast offset by a superbly rich orange purée and bitter chicory, although he might also press the luxury button for Brixham turbot poached in truffle butter with braised beef cheek and cep sauce. Desserts are many and tempting (praline soufflé with praline ice cream, for example), but brace yourself for a two-pronged cavalcade of petits fours. The 500-strong wine list has been constructed with care, and advice is proffered sensitively. France leads the way, but it's worth considering top-drawer stuff from Italy, California and Australia too. Prices start at £27.

Chef/s: Michael Caines and Sam Moody. **Open:** all week L 12 to 2.30, D 6 to 9.30 (9.45 Fri and Sat). **Meals:** Set L £25.50 (2 courses) to £32. Set D £57 (2 courses) to £68.50. Sun L £40. Tasting menu £84 (8 courses) to £90. **Service:** not inc. **Details:** Cards accepted. 80 seats. 40 seats outside. No music. Wheelchair access. Car parking.

Casanis

French to its fingertips
4 Saville Row, Bath, BA1 2QP
Tel no: (01225) 780055
www.casanis.co.uk
French | £30
Cooking score: 1

Hard by the Assembly Rooms in Georgian Bath, here is a restaurant that's French to its fingertips. Extending over two floors, with an alluring courtyard garden for fine-weather dining, it offers the kind of honest-to-goodness bistro cuisine you thought was an endangered species. Fish soup à la provençale with all the trimmings, carré d'agneau with French beans, dauphinoise and a jus enriched with black olives and thyme, and tarte au chocolat are the kinds of crowd-pleasers to expect. The concise French list opens with Languedoc house wines at £17.95.

Chef/s: Laurent Couvreur. **Open:** Tue to Sat L 12 to 2, D 6 to 10. **Closed:** Sun, Mon, 25 to 28 Dec, 1 to 10 Jan, 1 week Aug. **Meals:** alc (main courses £14 to £25). Set L £14.75 (2 courses) to £18.75. Set D £18.50 (2 courses) to £22.50. **Service:** not inc. **Details:** Cards accepted. 50 seats. 16 seats outside. Separate bar. Music. Children allowed.

King William

No-nonsense nose-to-tail eating
36 Thomas Street, Bath, BA1 5NN
Tel no: (01225) 428096
British | £26
Cooking score: 2

'Nicely decorated in a rustic manner that feels like a pair of comfy slippers,' is how one visitor viewed this tiny Georgian pub not far from the city centre. Noted for gutsy, nose-to-tail eating, the dishes may sometimes struggle to make their expected impact, but among successes have been beef skirt on toast with horseradish cream, roast pork belly, and a Sunday roast chicken 'very well cooked and very succulent' with good roast vegetables. Desserts run to mulled wine-poached plums with vanilla cream, and cranberry and apple sponge pudding with ginger custard. Staff are friendly, if occasionally forgetful, and the wine list opens at £14.

Chef/s: Chris Holton. **Open:** Wed to Sun L 12 to 3, all week D 6 to 10 (9 Sun). **Closed:** 25 and 26 Dec. **Meals:** alc (main courses £11 to £19). **Service:** 10% (optional). **Details:** Cards accepted. 50 seats. Separate bar. Music. Children allowed.

The Marlborough Tavern

Sophisticated food pub
35 Marlborough Buildings, Bath, BA1 2LY
Tel no: (01225) 423731
www.marlborough-tavern.com
British | £27
Cooking score: 3

A short stroll from the Royal Crescent, this sophisticated food pub is now well-established as a local favourite. Drinkers are still attracted to the central bar of the airy, high-ceilinged room, but Richard Knighting's modern British cooking draws foodies with its unfussy, seasonal style. Tip-top local ingredients are the cornerstone of the menu, which has a roll call of suppliers on the back. The daily changing line-up might start with beignets of Devon crab and soft herbs, served with a piquant pineapple salsa and sweet pickled cucumber. Pan-fried lamb's liver with sage-buttered mash, cabbage, mustard and roast onion gravy is a typical main course, which might be followed by spiced rice pudding with plum and ginger compote. House wine is £15.50.

Chef/s: Richard Knighting. **Open:** all week L 12.30 to 2.30 (3 Sat, 4 Sun), D 6 to 9.30 (10 Fri and Sat). **Closed:** 25 Dec. **Meals:** alc (main courses £11 to £22). Set L £12 (2 courses) to £15. **Service:** not inc. **Details:** Cards accepted. 70 seats. 60 seats outside. Wheelchair access. Music. Children allowed.

The Queensberry Hotel, Olive Tree Restaurant

Comfort, quirks and clever cooking
4-7 Russel Street, Bath, BA1 2QF
Tel no: (01225) 447928
www.thequeensberry.co.uk
Modern British | £45
Cooking score: 4

It may be at the heart of patrician Bath, but there's something 'almost anti-establishment' about this elegant town house hotel. A lively sense of humour pervades the place and the good vibrations filter down to the Olive Tree, where amiable staff, warm lighting and whitewashed walls all help to brighten up the basement dining room. The kitchen tips a tentative hat to fusion – crab risotto (a little dry on inspection) is brought to life by crisp, soft-shell crab tempura, while British vegetables and shoots are enhanced by savoury-sweet miso and orange – but also knows when to shun it. Duck appears as a combo of roasted breast, seared liver and spring roll confit in a Jackson Pollock-like presentation with butternut squash purée, while desserts might see caramel mousse matched with peanut-butter ice cream. The wine list also puts on an upbeat, populist show: out go elitist verbiage, hefty mark-ups and bottle-only exclusivity, and in come 43 by-the-glass options and common-sense classifications of 'green, tangy and dry' or 'warm and spicy' applied to an imaginative and pedigree line-up starting at £17.
Chef/s: Nick Brodie. **Open:** Tue to Sun L 12 to 2 (12.30 to 2.30 Sun), all week D 7 to 10. **Meals:** alc (main courses £17 to £29). Set L £16.50 (2 courses) to £19.50. Sun L £18.50 (2 courses) to £22.50. **Service:** 10% (optional). **Details:** Cards accepted. 60 seats. Separate bar. Music. Children allowed.

Also Recommended

Also recommended entries are not scored but we think they are worth a visit.

The White Hart Inn

Unbuttoned food from a Bath veteran
Widcombe Hill, Widcombe, Bath, BA2 6AA
Tel no: (01225) 338053
www.whitehartbath.co.uk
Modern British | £26
Cooking score: 2

Just a two-minute walk from Bath's railway station, the White Hart is reckoned to be one of the city's oldest watering holes and also doubles up as a backpackers' hostel. Popular with rugby fans who fill the bar on match days, this busy place has a strong local following and the well-tended walled garden makes for excellent alfresco dining. Veteran Bath chef Rupert Pitt and his team have built a reputation for consistent and well-priced food. The unbuttoned European dishes are seasonal and plenty of local producers are name-checked on the concise menu. A starter of warm butterbean and caramelised onion tart with spicy sausage might be followed by Neston Park ribeye steak with garlic and herb butter and French fries. Wines from £13.90.
Chef/s: Rupert Pitt, Jason Horn, Rachel Milsom and Luke Gibson. **Open:** all week L 12 to 2, Mon to Sat D 6 to 10 (9 Mon and Tue). **Closed:** 25 Dec, bank hols. **Meals:** alc (main courses £12 to £17). Set L £12.50 (2 courses). Sun L £18.50 (2 courses) to £22. **Service:** not inc. **Details:** Cards accepted. 50 seats. 50 seats outside. Wheelchair access. Music. Children allowed.

ALSO RECOMMENDED

▲ The Garrick's Head

7-8 St Johns Place, Bath, BA1 1ET
Tel no: (01225) 318368
www.garricksheadpub.com
British £5 OFF

Smack next door to Bath's famous Theatre Royal and in the same family as the city's King William pub (see entry), Charlie Digney's eighteenth-century watering hole is a civilised spot for pre-or post-performance suppers. Choose either the laid-back bar, decked out with comfortable sofas, or the swish dining room, then check out the microbrewery ales and the cracking modern British menu, which offers the likes of smoked haddock and mussel chowder (£7.45), Wiltshire venison with beetroot and port sauce (£16.95) and lemon tart with Chantilly cream. Wines from £14. Open all week.

▲ Yak Yeti Yak

12 Pierrepont Street, Bath, BA1 1LA
Tel no: (01225) 442299
www.yakyetiyak.co.uk
Nepalese

Nepalese home cooking is the deal at this multi-roomed restaurant in the basement of an eighteenth-century town house. The kitchen conjures up flavours that are subtle and light, vegetarians are well catered for (cauliflower pakora and various dhal dishes stand out), and there's more besides: say, steamed spiced pork dumplings with fresh hemp-seed chutney (£5.50) or slow-cooked lamb with bamboo shoots, blackeye peas, potato, tomato and coriander (£7.90). Creamed saffron yoghurt is a good way to finish. House wine is £13.20. Open all week.

Bilbrook

READERS RECOMMEND

Dragon House Hotel

Modern British
Bilbrook, TA24 6HQ
Tel no: (01984) 640215
www.dragonhouse.co.uk
'Excellent service, very good value, top quality food; but don't tell anyone, it's our secret.'

Readers Recommend

A 'readers recommend' review is a genuine quote from a report sent in by one of our readers. We intend to follow up these suggestions throughout the year to come.

Bruton

At the Chapel

Seasonal food meets ecclesiastical chic
High Street, Bruton, BA10 0AE
Tel no: (01749) 814070
www.atthechapel.co.uk
Modern British | £28
Cooking score: 2

A seventeenth-century Congregational chapel is the oddly fascinating setting for this unusual venture – an open-minded eatery with a bakery, food store and wine shop attached. High arched windows and smart refectory tables suggest ecclesiastical chic, and the kitchen feeds the faithful with everything from breakfast porridge and bacon sarnies to wood-fired pizzas, char-grilled chicken salad or Barnsley chop with peas, broad beans and Jersey Royals. Starters such as Dorset crab and saffron mayonnaise or asparagus with a fried duck egg keep it seasonal, and you can say 'amen' with lemon posset or chocolate torte with clotted cream. House wine is £13 (£3.25 a glass); also note the organic bottles.

Chef/s: Steven Horrell. **Open:** Tue to Sun L 12 to 3, Tue to Sat D 6 to 9.30. **Closed:** Mon. **Meals:** alc (main courses £11 to £19). **Service:** not inc. **Details:** Cards accepted. 70 seats. Separate bar. No music. Wheelchair access. Children allowed.

Chew Magna

ALSO RECOMMENDED

▲ The Pony & Trap

Knowle Hill, Chew Magna, BS40 8TQ
Tel no: (01275) 332627
www.theponyandtrap.co.uk
Modern British £5 OFF

A 200-year-old cottage pub within easy reach of Bristol's urban sprawl, this high-profile foodie set-up takes its sourcing seriously. Char-grilled Coombe Farm ribeye with chunky chips (£16.95) is a bestseller, but the kitchen's prime local pickings might also yield a duo of pork with celeriac purée, or pressed lamb breast with crispy sweetbreads, liver and aubergine salad. Seared Cornish scallops with black pudding (£6.95), plates of tapas and 'amazing' wild mushroom risotto cater for less carnivorous palates. Pud could be orange and cardamom crème brûlée. Wines from £11.95. Closed Sun eve and Mon in winter.

Clevedon

Murrays

Italian goodies for foodies
87-93 Hill Road, Clevedon, BS21 7PN
Tel no: (01275) 341555
www.murraysofclevedon.co.uk
Italian | £26
Cooking score: 4

The Murrays have consolidated their business over the past year by moving the next-door deli into the restaurant to create a more relaxed café feel. The restaurant is now tucked away at the back and feels much cosier than before. The food is simpler, but the kitchen shows the same serious commitment to seasonality and top-drawer produce. There is still a pronounced Italian accent to the menu, which also includes a range of excellent sandwiches and authentic stone-baked pizzas. In late spring, a starter of Cornish crab, leek and saffron tart with mixed leaves might be followed by Parma ham and wild mushroom lasagne, or poached shoulder of rose veal with peas, broad beans, asparagus, new potatoes and mint. Desserts include affogato and Amalfi lemon cheesecake. House wine from £11, but you can also pluck a fine Italian bottle from the shop and pay £6 corkage.
Chef/s: Reuben Murray. **Open:** Mon to Sat 8am to 5pm (10 to 4 Mon, 8 to 8 Thur and Fri). **Closed:** Sun, 25 and 26 Dec. **Meals:** alc (main courses £8 to £19). **Service:** not inc. **Details:** Cards accepted. 40 seats. Separate bar. No mobile phones. Music. Children allowed.

Combe Hay

The Wheatsheaf

Popular inn with sophisticated food
Combe Hay, BA2 7EG
Tel no: (01225) 833504
www.wheatsheafcombehay.com
Modern British | £30
Cooking score: 4

Just 15 minutes from Bath, this impressive sixteenth-century pub is located in idyllic countryside overlooking a lush valley. Tables in the three-tiered garden are especially popular in summer and the adjoining vegetable plot supplies the kitchen. There have been significant changes at the stove, with Edward Raines stepping up to his first head chef role. He has quickly stamped his identity on the menu and his dishes offer bold, well-defined flavours. A starter of Dorset scallops might arrive with a silky hazelnut purée, samphire and Frangelico dressing, while herb-crusted cannon of spring lamb could be served with a punchy niçoise garnish and potato fondant. To finish, a rich mille-feuille of dark and white chocolate is balanced with a refreshing mascarpone sorbet. Service has improved of late, but portion sizes are still considered on the small side for the high prices charged. The 150-strong, European-only wine list starts at £16.95.
Chef/s: Edward Raines. **Open:** Tue to Sun L 12 to 2 (2.30 Sat, 3 Sun), Tue to Sat D 6.30 to 9.30 (10 Sat). **Closed:** Mon, 25 to 27 Dec, first week Jan. **Meals:** alc (main courses £13 to £20). Sun L £24.50. **Service:** 10% (optional). **Details:** Cards accepted. 60 seats. 80 seats outside. Separate bar. Music. Children allowed. Car parking.

East Coker

ALSO RECOMMENDED

▲ Helyar Arms

Moor Lane, East Coker, BA22 9JR
Tel no: (01935) 862332
www.helyar-arms.co.uk
British

There's much to praise about this modest fifteenth-century village inn, not least Mathieu Eke's straightforward approach to cooking and the fact that he cares about the provenance of his supplies. A rich game terrine (£5.95), a comforting toad-in-the-hole with bubble and squeak (£9.75) or a 'huge, meaty faggot and a healthy dose of mash topped with peas' are lessons in content over style, while desserts such as individual lemon meringue pie bring things to a reassuringly old-school finish. Wines from £14.95. Accommodation. Open all week.

Frome

READERS RECOMMEND

The Archangel

Modern European
1 King Street, Frome, BA11 1BH
Tel no: (01373) 456111
www.archangelfrome.com
'A lovely boutique hotel and restaurant, with original stone walls, beams and even a medieval alley.'

Hambridge

READERS RECOMMEND

Brown & Forrest

Modern British
Bowdens Farm, Hambridge, TA10 0BP
Tel no: (01458) 250875
www.smokedeel.co.uk
'Attached to a smokery – simple, but fresh and delicious and excellent value.'

Hinton St George

The Lord Poulett Arms

Elegant inn with flavourful food
High Street, Hinton St George, TA17 8SE
Tel no: (01460) 73149
www.lordpoulettarms.com
Modern British | £25
Cooking score: 3

At the heart of a tiny village full of thatched cottages, this elegant seventeenth-century inn has been given a new lease of life by Steve Hill and Michelle Paynton. Visitors are instantly charmed by the rural chic of the sleek interior with its rug-strewn flagged floors and open log fires, although one reporter noted that there were 'few smiles and a lack of a warm welcome' from staff. Gary Coughlan's menu offers bold flavours and a strong commitment to local ingredients, and the likes of traditional fish and chips attract as much praise as pan-roasted corn-fed chicken suprême with smoked bacon, sour cream, chive mash and red wine sauce. Desserts include a classic Valrhona chocolate fondant with vanilla ice cream. Wines from £14.

Chef/s: Gary Coughlan. **Open:** all week 12 to 9.15. **Closed:** 26 Dec. **Meals:** alc (main courses £9 to £22). **Service:** not inc. **Details:** Cards accepted. 70 seats. 100 seats outside. Separate bar. No music. Wheelchair access. Children allowed. Car parking.

Long Sutton

ALSO RECOMMENDED

▲ The Devonshire Arms

Cross Lane, Long Sutton, TA10 9LP
Tel no: (01458) 241271
www.thedevonshirearms.com
British

Inspired, inventive and realistically priced cooking emanates from the kitchen at this rather grand inn overlooking Long Sutton's village green. Reporters have praised the 'delicious' homemade bread, Dorset crab brûlée (£7.95), wood pigeon and baby spinach salad with roasted hazelnuts, and duck confit with roasted vegetables and creamy mash (£13.95). For afters, try the pear and almond clafoutis with marmalade ice cream or the West Country cheeseboard. Wines from £15.70. Accommodation. Open all week.

Midsomer Norton

The Moody Goose at the Old Priory

Creative cooking with flair
Church Square, Midsomer Norton, BA3 2HX
Tel no: (01761) 416784
www.theoldpriory.co.uk
Modern British | £40
Cooking score: 4
V

In a particularly tranquil corner of Somerset, the Shores' ancient stone-built hotel is a welcoming retreat from the madding crowd. Antique furniture and light colour schemes make for a nice mix of old and new. This could also be said of Stephen Shore's cooking, which draws from local sources, including the Priory's own kitchen garden. A pair of winter lunchers had nothing but eulogies for their starters of game terrine with beetroot and celeriac, and ham hock with lentils, both based on 'carefully sourced and beautifully presented ingredients'. Mains run to sea bass with chorizo and roasted cherry tomatoes, as well as braised blade and fried fillet of beef with horseradish mousseline. The combinations work well, bringing out the best in their respective components; this is equally true of a dessert of apple and raisin clafoutis, accompanied by sharply flavoured apple sorbet. Wines start at £18.50 (£4.85 a glass).
Chef/s: Stephen Shore. **Open:** Mon to Sat L 12 to 1.30, D 7 to 9.15 (7.30 Mon). **Closed:** Sun, 25 Dec, 1 Jan. **Meals:** Set L and D £32.50 (2 courses) to £39.50. **Service:** not inc. **Details:** Cards accepted. 34 seats. Wheelchair access. Music. Children allowed. Car parking.

Milverton

The Globe

Locally minded village inn
Fore Street, Milverton, TA4 1JX
Tel no: (01823) 400534
www.theglobemilverton.co.uk
Modern British | £25
Cooking score: 2
£5 OFF £30

Despite exhibiting something of an identity crisis when it comes to interior design, this 'stripped-out' Georgian pub is a real godsend for Milverton. Since arriving in 2006, current incumbents Mark and Adele Tarry have made the Globe a hub for the local community, and their sterling efforts have been rewarded by an appreciative crowd. Their commitment to the area extends from real ales and ciders to regionally sourced menus taking in the likes of pan-roasted partridge breast with parsnip purée, char-grilled ribeye in peppercorn sauce, and smoked haddock with leeks and a poached egg. Finish with richly fortifying rice pudding and clotted cream. Gascon house wines at £11.80 head up a short but serviceable list.
Chef/s: Mark Tarry and Kaan Atasoy. **Open:** Tue to Sun L 12 to 2, Mon to Sat D 7 to 9. **Closed:** Bank hol evenings, 2 days Jan. **Meals:** alc (main courses £11 to £ 18). Sun L £8.50 (1 course). **Service:** not inc. **Details:** Cards accepted. 50 seats. 20 seats outside. Separate bar. No mobile phones. Wheelchair access. Music. Children allowed. Car parking.

Shepton Mallet

ALSO RECOMMENDED

▲ Blostin's

29-33 Waterloo Road, Shepton Mallet, BA4 5HH
Tel no: (01749) 343648
www.blostins.co.uk
Modern British

Nick and Lynne Reed have been running the show for some 27 years, and their small restaurant's reputation is founded on a congenial atmosphere, quality cooking and a resolute focus on value. Fixed-price dinners

(£21 for three courses) stick to a well-tried formula of generous Anglo-French food: salmon fishcakes with dill mustard sauce, before breast of duck with poached pears and cassis, then chocolate brownie, chocolate sauce and vanilla ice cream to finish. House wine is £14.25. Open Tue to Sat D only.

Shepton Montague

ALSO RECOMMENDED

▲ The Montague Inn

Shepton Montague, BA9 8JW
Tel no: (01749) 813213
www.themontagueinn.co.uk
Modern European £5 OFF

Known affectionately as the Monty, the O'Callaghans' 200-year-old Somerset boozer is famed for its stupendous views and sound culinary endeavours. Food is of the free-range, home-cooked variety, with a few eclectic influences brought to bear in dishes such as seared scallops with chorizo, chicken breast wrapped in Serrano ham with sweet potato purée (£14.50) and chocolate marquise with mango sorbet. Rabbit terrine, butternut squash soup (£4.95) and saddle of venison have also pleased those with homespun appetites. House wine £14.50. No food Sun D.

Somerton

READERS RECOMMEND

Market Bar and Bistro

Modern British
28 Market Place, Somerton, TA11 7NB
Tel no: (01458) 272468
www.marketbar.co.uk
'Relaxed atmosphere, friendly welcome, efficient service but no rush. We would definitely go there again.'

Taunton

The Castle, Brazz

From bastion to cheerful brasserie
Castle Green, Taunton, TA1 1NF
Tel no: (01823) 272671
www.the-castle-hotel.com
British | £46
Cooking score: 4
V

Changes are afoot at this old stager. Its principal dining room is now used only for breakfasts for hotel residents, and the focus of the culinary action has moved to Brazz, the informal café-style venue with its own entrance to one side. A big, white room extends back from the bar area, the rear half under a domed ceiling with night-sky spot-lighting around a little skylight. It's run with cheerful efficiency, offering a menu of carefully wrought brasserie favourites. Start with a warm smoked haddock and leek tartlet or dressed crab, and proceed to a top-drawer steak, simply grilled fish or a confit leg of Creedy Carver duck on a stack of Savoy and pancetta with apple balls, celeriac purée and aromatic five-spice jus. A few specials supplement the main action, including, perhaps, in early summer a fine version of Eton mess with spearmint syrup and strawberry sorbet. A wine list of good-value drinking is supplemented by some of the old treasures the Castle has always kept, and is headed up by a slate of glass selections from £4.40, with bottles from £19.

Chef/s: Jamie Raftery. **Open:** all week L 12.30 to 2, Mon to Sat D 7 to 9.30. **Meals:** alc (main courses £24 to £26). Set L and D £18.95 (2 courses) to £23.95. **Service:** 12.5% (optional). **Details:** Cards accepted. 70 seats. 30 seats outside. Separate bar. No mobile phones. Wheelchair access. Music. Children allowed. Car parking.

The Willow Tree

Top ingredients and big-impact dishes
3 Tower Lane, Taunton, TA1 4AR
Tel no: (01823) 352835
www.thewillowtreerestaurant.com
Modern British | £34
Cooking score: 6

The Willow Tree takes a little finding in the centre of town, but head for the water's edge and look for the whitewashed seventeenth-century moathouse. Inside it's as pleasantly rustic as a country pub, with venerable low beams and an inglenook fireplace, and there are a few outdoor tables on the canalside terrace. Darren Sherlock trained with the Roux brothers, but over the past decade has honed his own style here for dynamic cooking that uses a plethora of local meat and game, Creedy Carver poultry and Newlyn fish. The front-of-house approach of Rita Rambellas, who pitches things perfectly between friendliness and discretion, is duly noted by a regular who offers his own awards from the menu stalwarts. 'Best starter: the Montgomery Cheddar soufflé with walnut and celery cream sauce. Best dessert: the bread-and-butter pudding with vanilla ice cream. Best main? They're all wonderful.' That last category might take in seared fillets of gilthead bream with new potato salad, asparagus, green olives and pomodorino tomtaoes in pine-nut and basil dressing, as well as roast best end of local lamb with bubble and squeak, green beans and pea purée. Half-a-dozen wines by the glass at £5.75 lead off a list that looks for value everywhere from Argentina to Bordeaux. Bottles start at £18.95.

Chef/s: Darren Sherlock. **Open:** Tue, Wed, Fri and Sat D only 6.30 to 9. **Closed:** Mon, Thur, Sun, Jan, Aug. **Meals:** Set D Tue and Wed £27.95, Fri and Sat £33.95. **Service:** 10% (optional). **Details:** Cards accepted. 25 seats. 10 seats outside. Separate bar. No mobile phones. Music. Children allowed.

Wells

Goodfellows

A chef who understands seafood cookery
5 Sadler Street, Wells, BA5 2RR
Tel no: (01749) 673866
www.goodfellowswells.co.uk
Modern British | £37
Cooking score: 5

In the heart of England's smallest cathedral city, close to the cathedral itself, Goodfellows is comprised of a French patisserie and café for croissants, pastries and tarts, as well as a pleasingly laid-back restaurant with seating around an open kitchen on the ground floor, and a more up-close-and-personal room under an atrium roof upstairs. Seafood is the specialist subject, but those not so inclined can quite easily have a bowl of truffled Jerusalem artichoke velouté and parsnip crisps, followed by duck confit with foie gras and mushroom sauce, and emerge quite as happy as their piscophile companions. The latter, however, will have had the benefit of Adam Fellows' seasoned understanding of fish cookery. Choose from starters such as smoked haddock with pancetta, pea shoots and quail's egg in a mildly curried sauce, and mains like sea bream on spelt 'risotto' with saffron and star-anise; otherwise sign up for the six-course tasting menus, on which only the dessert won't feature something from the sea. A fondness for pastrywork makes tarts of one sort or another the favoured finales, perhaps a pineapple Tatin with mango and lime mousse and coconut sorbet. House wines are £13.50.

Chef/s: Adam Fellows. **Open:** Tue to Sat L 12 to 2, Wed to Sat D 6.30 to 9.30. **Closed:** Sun, Mon, bank hols (exc Good Friday). **Meals:** alc (main courses £12 to £23). Set L £19.50 (2 courses) to £21.50. Set D £37. Tasting menu £55. **Service:** not inc. **Details:** Cards accepted. 30 seats. Music. Children allowed.

The Old Spot

Expertly run neighbourhood favourite
12 Sadler Street, Wells, BA5 2SE
Tel no: (01749) 689099
www.theoldspot.co.uk
Modern European | £29
Cooking score: 4

Views across the green to Wells Cathedral are just one of the assets at this expertly run eatery – a congenial labour of love from Ian and Clare Bates, who have kitted out their Spot with bare tables, bare floorboards, painted panelling and framed menus referencing Ian's culinary background. The unfussy mood is matched by a short, sharp menu peppered with clear, natural and uncluttered flavours. Starters of wood pigeon crépinettes with celeriac and caramelised apples, or a disarmingly simple dish of leeks vinaigrette with goats' cheese, beetroot and walnuts could give way to grilled hanger steak with girolles, braised shoulder of lamb with onion purée, or a Med-inspired pairing of roast grey mullet with sautéed squid, saffron couscous and ratatouille. Desserts such as warm almond cake with passion-fruit curd and mango are equally convincing in their own way. A dozen wines by the glass open the nifty global list. Bottle prices start painlessly at £15.95.

Chef/s: Ian Bates. **Open:** Wed to Sun L 12.30 to 2.30, Tue to Sat D 7 to 10.30. **Closed:** Mon, 1 week Christmas. **Meals:** Set L £13.50 (2 courses) to £15.50. Set D £23.50 (2 courses) to £28.50. Sun L £23.50. **Service:** not inc. **Details:** Cards accepted. 50 seats. No music. Children allowed.

Wookey Hole

The Wookey Hole Inn

Zany village pub
High Street, Wookey Hole, BA5 1BP
Tel no: (01749) 676677
www.wookeyholeinn.com
Modern British | £30
Cooking score: 1

This bustling inn with its mad, art-filled interior and wacky sculpture garden still has more razzmatazz than anywhere else in town. And quite a way outside, for that matter. It's noted for honest intent, good drinking and menus packed with juicy flavours. Dishes range from wild boar burger with smoked apple-wood cheese and caramelised apple, via smoked haddock and salmon fishcakes, to roast chicken breast stuffed with chilli and ginger, served with jasmine rice and coconut sauce. Strawberry pavlova makes a nice finish. House wine is £14.50.

Chef/s: Adam Kennington. **Open:** all week L 12 to 2.30 (3 Sun), Mon to Sat D 7 to 9.30. **Closed:** 25 and 26 Dec. **Meals:** alc (main courses £14 to £24). Sun L £16.95 (2 courses) to £19.95. **Service:** not inc. **Details:** Cards accepted. 70 seats. 100 seats outside. Separate bar. Music. Children allowed. Car parking.

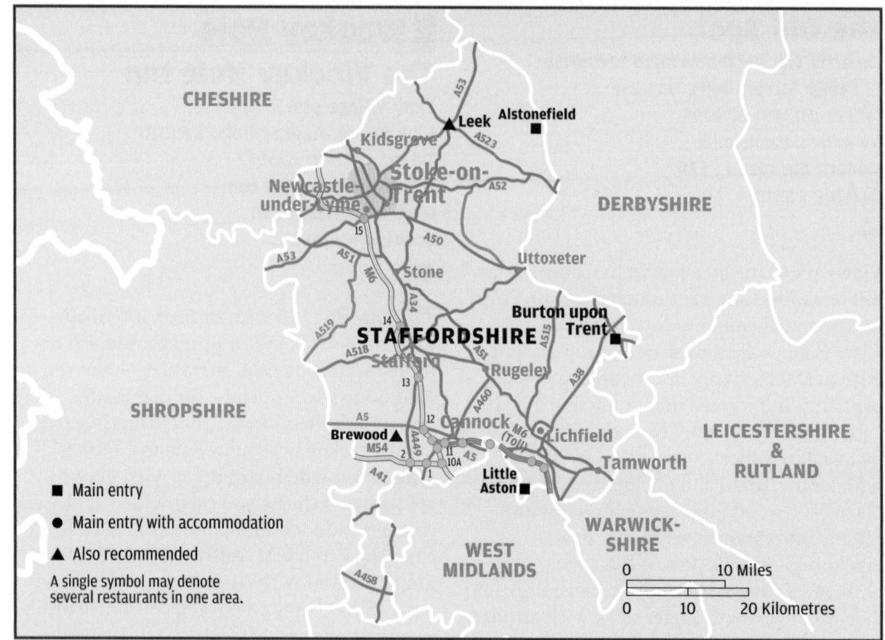

Alstonefield

The George

Village local with comfort food
Alstonefield, DE6 2FX
Tel no: (01335) 310205
www.thegeorgeatalstonefield.com
Modern British | £30
Cooking score: 2

At the heart of the Peak District, this unspoilt eighteenth-century inn can be described as a true village local. The cooking is confidently unfussy, as in a lunch dish of shin of beef, red wine and root vegetable casserole served with mashed potato and crusty bread – simple but tasty comfort food. Ingredients are as local as possible, including the pub's own vegetable patch, and the kitchen lets natural flavours shine through in dishes such as loin of lamb served with a pudding of the braised shoulder, buttered greens and homemade sloe gin jus, and lemon and rosemary posset with mulled berries. House wine is £15.

Chef/s: Chris Rooney. **Open:** all week L 12 to 2.30, D 7 to 9 (6.30 to 8 Sun). **Closed:** 25 Dec. **Meals:** alc (main courses £10 to £23). **Service:** not inc. **Details:** Cards accepted. 40 seats. 40 seats outside. Separate bar. No music. No mobile phones. Children allowed. Car parking.

Brewood

ALSO RECOMMENDED

▲ The Mess

3 Market Place, Brewood, ST19 9BS
Tel no: (01902) 851694
www.the-mess.co.uk
Modern European £5 OFF

By day, the Mess feeds shoppers, walkers and crews from narrowboats on the nearby Shropshire Union Canal; by night, this laudable local asset morphs into a chandelier-lit bistro full of honest intent, with a short menu of satisfying dishes at knockdown prices. Good shouts have included beetroot and carrot crostini with five-spice dressing (£3.85), chicken breast with creamy broad beans and bacon (£12.25), and sea bass with lyonnaise potatoes and tomato butter. For afters, try bread-and-butter pudding. 'Lazy' jazz brunch on Sundays. House wine is £11.95. Closed Sun to Thur D.

Burton upon Trent

99 Station Street

A cheery local asset

99 Station Street, Burton upon Trent, DE14 1BT
Tel no: (01283) 516859
www.99stationstreet.com
Modern British | £30
Cooking score: 1

Ross and Susan Boardman's old-town bistro close to Burton's breweries is a local asset, and the owners recently broadened their appeal with an online shop selling home-cooked produce. Homemade sausages on bubble and squeak are a speciality, but the menu might also take in roast rack of local lamb, twice-cooked pork belly in cider with wholegrain mustard sauce, or spinach and leek tart with three Staffordshire cheeses. Finish with caramelised Cambridge cream. House wine is £11.95, or try a Burton Bridge beer.
Chef/s: Daniel Pilkington. **Open:** Wed to Sun L 11.30 to 2.30 (12 to 2.30 Sun), Wed to Sat D 6 onwards. **Closed:** Mon, Tue, 25 to 30 Dec, 1 Jan, bank hols. **Meals:** alc (main courses £13 to £22). Set L £9.75 (2 courses) to £10.95. Sun L £16.95. **Service:** not inc. **Details:** Cards accepted. 40 seats. Music. Children allowed.

Leek

ALSO RECOMMENDED

▲ Qarma

Cross Mill, Cross Street, Leek, ST13 6BL
Tel no: (01538) 387788
www.the-qarma.com
Indian £5 OFF

Housed in a converted mill, this highly popular Staffordshire Indian gets an emphatic thumbs-up for its 'royal welcome', opulent interiors, brilliant service and admirable use of local and free-range produce. The kitchen turns out the usual time-honoured staples, but also springs some vibrant surprises in the shape of tandoori scallops with grape dressing (£4.95), beetroot and coconut samosas, spiced 'fangash' fish with coriander (£9.45), marinated steak masala and superb Bangladeshi crab. Lemon and ginger naan is a change from the norm, too. House wine is £12.95. Closed Mon to Sat L.

Little Aston

NEW ENTRY

Mint

Bushy-tailed brasserie with big flavours

52 Thornhill Road, Streetly, Little Aston, B74 3EN
Tel no: (0121) 3530488
www.mint-restaurant.com
Modern British | £37
Cooking score: 3
£5 OFF

Mint strikes quite a pose in this gastronomically challenged area, with its black-and-white frontage overlooking Sutton Park. Spread over two floors, with lots of contemporary design flourishes, its bushy-tailed, brasserie-style menu is peppered with regional produce. Tamworth goats' cheese comes with a zesty combo of pineapple carpaccio, fresh mint and pea shoots, Great Wyrley beef is given the 'presse' treatment with truffle mash and pied bleu mushrooms, and Cannock venison is tricked out with Shenstone parsnips, baby fennel, chicory and chocolate. Flavours are emphatic, presentation dramatic and there is on-trend sweetness in the shape of, say, carrot cake with nutmeg jelly and Parmesan ice cream. Cocktails shore up Mint's bar credentials and the wine list offers cosmopolitan drinking from £15.
Chef/s: Myles Matthews. **Open:** Wed to Sat D 6.30 to 9.30 (9.45 Fri and Sat), Sun 10am to 7pm. **Closed:** Mon, Tue, 1 week Easter, last week Aug, first week Sept. **Meals:** Set D £29.50 (2 courses) to £36.50. Sun L £17.95 (2 courses) to £19.95. **Service:** 10% (optional). **Details:** Cards accepted. 40 seats. 20 seats outside. Separate bar. No mobile phones. Wheelchair access. Music. Children allowed. Car parking.

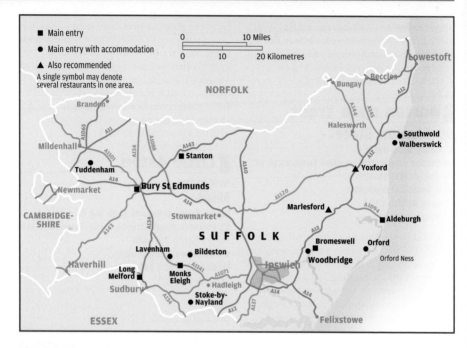

■ Main entry
● Main entry with accommodation
▲ Also recommended
A single symbol may denote several restaurants in one area.

0 10 Miles
0 10 20 Kilometres

NORFOLK, SUFFOLK, CAMBRIDGESHIRE, ESSEX

Lowestoft, Beccles, Bungay, Brandon, Halesworth, Southwold, Walberswick, Mildenhall, Stanton, Tuddenham, Yoxford, Newmarket, Bury St Edmunds, Marlesford, Stowmarket, Aldeburgh, Bromeswell, Orford, Lavenham, Bildeston, Woodbridge, Orford Ness, Haverhill, Long Melford, Monks Eleigh, Ipswich, Hadleigh, Sudbury, Stoke-by-Nayland, Felixstowe

Aldeburgh

The Lighthouse

Aldeburgh's top performer
77 High Street, Aldeburgh, IP15 5AU
Tel no: (01728) 453377
www.lighthouserestaurant.co.uk
Modern British | £25
Cooking score: 2

A beacon on the High Street since 1994, Aldeburgh's foodie supremo still beams as brightly as ever. The Lighthouse is more casual these days, with a bare-tabled café space out front, but its culinary focus has never waned. Fish from the local boats remains its trump card – anything from Dover sole dressed with herb oil to sea bass fillet on spinach and roasted peppers – but the kitchen also satisfies shoppers, festival-goers and holidaymakers with chicken liver and bacon salad, feta and courgette cakes, char-grilled steaks and other hardy perennials. Fishcakes are a bestseller, while puds could run to quince frangipane with zabaglione ice cream. Knowledgeably chosen, modestly priced wines from £15.95.
Chef/s: Guy Welsh and Sara Fox. **Open:** all week L 12 to 2 (2.30 Sat and Sun), D 6.30 to 10. **Meals:** alc (main courses £11 to £17). **Service:** not inc. **Details:** Cards accepted. 100 seats. 15 seats outside. No music. No mobile phones. Wheelchair access. Children allowed.

152 Restaurant

Unbuttoned neighbourhood eatery
152 High Street, Aldeburgh, IP15 5AX
Tel no: (01728) 454594
www.152aldeburgh.com
Modern European | £23
Cooking score: 1

'Reliable and unpretentious' 152 is tucked down an alleyway between beach and High Street. Its relaxed atmosphere is helped along by 'friendly, attentive' service from owner Andrew Lister. A gently rustic, uncluttered

interior provides a fitting backdrop for simple dishes along the lines of battered cod with chips and homemade tartare sauce or 'meltingly tender' belly pork with mash and green beans. Local ingredients are to the fore, as in an 'excellently cooked' skate wing with caper butter, sautéed potatoes and samphire. Wines start at £15.50.

Chef/s: Chris Selby. **Open:** all week L 12 to 3, D 6 to 10. **Meals:** alc (main courses £11 to £18). Set L and D £12.95. Sun L £13.95. **Service:** not inc. **Details:** Cards accepted. 52 seats. 28 seats outside. Wheelchair access. Music. Children allowed.

Regatta

Breezy seaside brasserie
171 High Street, Aldeburgh, IP15 5AN
Tel no: (01728) 452011
www.regattaaldeburgh.com
Modern British | £25
Cooking score: 1

Celebrating 20 years in 2012, this old campaigner continues to draw the Aldeburgh crowds, being 'family-friendly, useful as an all-day drop-in, and very seaside'. Robert Mabey works to a basic printed menu that rarely changes – perhaps home-smoked salmon with pickled samphire or locally caught sprats, followed by slow-cooked duck leg with pan-fried foie gras – supplemented by blackboard specials of mostly local fish. In high summer, when the whole frontage is thrown open, 'it feels like being in France'. Wines from £14.

Chef/s: Robert Mabey. **Open:** all week L 12 to 2, D 6 to 10. **Closed:** 24 to 26 and 31 Dec, 1 Jan. **Meals:** alc (main courses £11 to £19). **Service:** not inc. **Details:** Cards accepted. 90 seats. No music. No mobile phones. Children allowed.

ALSO RECOMMENDED

▲ The Aldeburgh Market Café

170-172 High Street, Aldeburgh, IP15 5EY
Tel no: (01728) 452520
www.thealdeburghmarket.co.uk
Modern British £5 OFF

A boon to the Aldeburgh scene, this local foodie enterprise was set up by Sara Fox – the brains behind the Lighthouse restaurant (see entry). Sitting cheek by jowl with a fishmonger's, greengrocer's and deli, the perky café deals in eclectic all-day fodder: breakfast on kippers or kedgeree (£6.75), move on to Singapore noodles at lunchtime, and get your sweet kicks from a slab of warm Greek orange cake with yoghurt and honey (£4.25). Eco-friendly drinks too, with wine from £3.25 a glass. Open all week (seasonal suppers Thur to Sat).

Bildeston

The Bildeston Crown

Slick mix of ancient and modern
High Street, Bildeston, IP7 7EB
Tel no: (01449) 740510
www.thebildestoncrown.com
Modern British | £45
Cooking score: 4

'Absolutely perfect in every category' enthused one reporter, who went on to praise the 'inventive, faultlessly cooked food' at this refurbished fifteenth-century timber-framed inn on Bildeston's main street. The heavy beams and original fabric of the former coaching inn are complemented by contemporary trappings, and it's an appropriate setting for Chris Lee's modern cooking. Presentation ensures that dishes look the part and local, seasonal produce features prominently in both the simple 'Crown Classics' menu and the carte. Traditional British favourites such as fish stew or char-grilled rib of Suffolk beef for two to share make the Classics menu appeal to all-comers.

A more innovative and ambitious streak is displayed in dishes such as duck breast, confit gizzard, liver and parsnip, or breast of chicken with lobster, gnocchi and fennel. Service is 'attentive but discreet', according to one reporter. House wines from £16 (£3.25 a glass).
Chef/s: Chris Lee. **Open:** all week L 12 to 3, D 7 to 10 (9.30 Sun). **Meals:** alc (main courses £14 to £25). Set L £20 (2 courses) to £24. Sun L £25. **Service:** not inc. **Details:** Cards accepted. 80 seats. 40 seats outside. Separate bar. No music. Wheelchair access. Children allowed. Car parking.

Bromeswell

NEW ENTRY

The British Larder

Big-hearted regional food foray
Orford Road, Bromeswell, IP12 2PU
Tel no: (01394) 460310
www.britishlardersuffolk.co.uk
British | £30
Cooking score: 3

£5 OFF

Conceived as the 'living embodiment' of their online recipe hub, The British Larder is Ross Pike and Madalene Bonvini-Hamel's big-hearted foray into the world of regional food, with Suffolk leading by example: Butley oysters, Kelsale turnips, Bramfield beef, Sutton Hoo chicken... the list goes on and on. In the main it's generous, full-flavoured stuff, from buttery hake with cockles, samphire and sea aster leaves to braised belly pork with colcannon and rhubarb compote, with smoked fish, cured meats, farmhouse cheeses and desserts such as plum Eton mess keeping the whole show firmly rooted. The setting, a revitalised roadside pub with acres of open space out back, is a folksy, 'Sunday supplement' mix of corn dollies, herbs in flowerpots, old-fashioned grocer's scales and shelves of homemade provisions. The snappy wine list starts at £16.50.
Chef/s: Ross Pike. **Open:** all week L 12 to 3, D 6 to 9 (9.30 Fri and Sat). **Meals:** alc (main courses £14 to £21). Sun L £22.50 (2 courses) to £27.50. **Service:** not inc. **Details:** Cards accepted. 65 seats. 80 seats outside. Separate bar. Wheelchair access. Music. Children allowed. Car parking.

Bury St Edmunds

Maison Bleue

A bastion of racy French seafood
30-31 Churchgate Street, Bury St Edmunds, IP33 1RG
Tel no: (01284) 760623
www.maisonbleue.co.uk
Seafood | £33
Cooking score: 4

'Unshowy but serious' neatly sums up Regis Crépy's much-loved Maison Bleue – a bastion of French seafood in the heartlands of Suffolk. Contemporary artworks and designer flourishes chime neatly with the light, modern tone of the cooking, which brings some racy ideas to the table. Salmon mi-cuit comes with fennel emulsion, marinated halibut is invigorated with grapefruit and star anise sauce, and carpaccio of gilthead bream with soy, wasabi and flat parsley dressing has been deemed 'miraculous'. The kitchen can also do classic (think Mediterranean fish soup or roast monkfish with cider sauce), and meat is more than a sideline – witness melting pork tenderloin with honey and cardamom sauce, or 'perfectly pink' roast duck with hazelnuts. Desserts also get a good press, particularly lemon verbena crème brûlée and a trio of coffee confections. Service is as keen as moutarde, and the wine list is a predominantly Gallic affair, with fish-friendly whites grabbing most of the limelight. Prices start at £14.95 (£3.95 a glass).
Chef/s: Pascal Canevet. **Open:** Tue to Sat L 12 to 2, D 7 to 9.30. **Closed:** Sun, Mon, Jan, 2 weeks summer. **Meals:** alc (main courses £15 to £24). Set L £16.95 (2 courses) to £19.95. Set D £29.95. **Service:** not inc. **Details:** Cards accepted. 65 seats. No mobile phones. Music. Children allowed.

Pea Porridge

Something quite special
28-29 Cannon Street, Bury St Edmunds, IP33 1JR
Tel no: (01284) 700200
www.peaporridge.co.uk
Modern British | £28
Cooking score: 3

'What a find', was one reporter's verdict after dining at this quirkily named neighbourhood restaurant. Housed in a former nineteenth-century cottage bakery, Pea Porridge is basic and unpretentious in style, but beyond the wooden floors and exposed brick is something quite special. 'First-class service' is efficient and welcoming, whilst Justin Sharp's modern European cooking is deceptively simple, and packed with gutsy, bold flavours. From a menu described by one reader as 'well-priced and very exciting', a starter of lightly curried sweetbreads with young spinach was hailed 'different, interesting and delicious'. This might be followed by grilled ox tongue served with dauphinoise, black pudding and wild mushrooms, ahead of tarte Tatin or poached quince, honey yoghurt and shortbread. Wine starts at £13.95.

Chef/s: Justin Sharp. **Open:** Tue to Sat L 12 to 2, D 6.30 to 9.30. **Closed:** Sun, Mon, 2 weeks Christmas, 2 weeks Sept. **Meals:** alc (main courses £13 to £19). Set L and D £11.95 (2 courses) to £15.95. **Service:** not inc. **Details:** Cards accepted. 46 seats. 12 seats outside. Music.

Buxhall

READERS RECOMMEND

The Buxhall Crown

British
Mill Road, Buxhall, IP14 3DW
Tel no: (01449) 736521
www.thebuxhallcrown.co.uk

'Sound reputation locally and a thumbs-up for food. Probably one of the better foodie pubs in the area.'

Lavenham

The Great House

Revitalised French favourite
Market Place, Lavenham, CO10 9QZ
Tel no: (01787) 247431
www.greathouse.co.uk
Modern French | £40
Cooking score: 4

V

Overlooking the old market square in this magnificent medieval town, Regis Crépy's elegant restaurant-with-rooms continues to elicit high praise from visitors. 'The great triumph of the Great House is that it never disappoints' is a typical comment. Since the refurbishment of 2008, the food here has excelled, the more contemporary twist on Gallic classics currying favour with regulars. An 'exquisite' starter of sashimi tuna poached in olive oil and served with a niçoise-style vinaigrette and a 'lovely and pink' main course of roasted rack of English lamb with rosemary sauce have both been singled out by reporters. A cocktail glass of verrine (black cherry, vanilla cream and a crumble topping with white balsamic and vanilla sorbet) is one of the more notable desserts, although the French and local cheeses are 'always a joy to behold'. The extensive wine list offers a number of bargains and starts at £16.40.

Chef/s: Regis Crépy. **Open:** Wed to Sun L 12 to 2.30, Tue to Sat D 7 to 9 (9.30 Fri and Sat). **Closed:** Mon, 3 weeks Jan, 2 weeks summer. **Meals:** alc (main courses £20 to £24). Set L £17.50 (2 courses) to £21. Set D £31.95 (3 courses). Sun L £31.95. **Service:** not inc. **Details:** Cards accepted. 50 seats. 24 seats outside. No mobile phones. Music. Children allowed. Car parking.

Long Melford

Scutchers

Hall house with flavour-packed cooking
Westgate Street, Long Melford, CO10 9DP
Tel no: (01787) 310200
www.scutchers.com
Modern British | £43
Cooking score: 2

Nick and Di Barrett took over this fifteenth-century hall house way back in 1991, and they have made the very best of the setting. It has been comfortably refurbished in recent years and the knocked-through rooms (with standing timbers intact) create a relaxed atmosphere. Nick Barrett's short menus are simply conceived but deliver plenty of flavour, as in sautéed veal kidneys served in a puff pastry case with a tarragon and Dijon cream sauce, or main courses like turbot with a herby Parmesan and prawn risotto and lime butter sauce. Apple and blackberry nutty crumble with real custard is an old-fashioned pud. House wines from £17.

Chef/s: Nicholas Barrett. **Open:** Tue to Sat L 12 to 2, D 7 to 9.30. **Closed:** Sun, Mon, 24 to 28 Dec. **Meals:** alc (main courses £18 to £28). Set L and D £22 (2 courses) to £28. **Service:** not inc. **Details:** Cards accepted. 65 seats. 20 seats outside. No music. Wheelchair access. Children allowed. Car parking.

Marlesford

ALSO RECOMMENDED

▲ Farmcafé & Foodmarket

Main Road (A12), Marlesford, IP13 0AG
Tel no: (01728) 747717
www.farmcafe.co.uk
Modern British

Breakfast is the top deal at this cracking pitstop beside the A12: pull in for a full Suffolk (from £6.40), Orford kippers or smoked salmon and scrambled eggs. Come lunchtime, the emphasis shifts to colourful salads, herby fishcakes, double-crust steak and mushroom pie (£9.40) and specials such as skate with capers. What sets this place apart is its uncompromising local sourcing and unbranded enterprise, with foodie shopping and takeaways adding to the allure. Drinks range from yoghurt smoothies and Fairtrade teas to Suffolk beers and a few wines (£11.90). Open all week.

Monks Eleigh

The Swan Inn

A proper local and a foodie destination
The Street, Monks Eleigh, IP7 7AU
Tel no: (01449) 741391
www.monkseleigh.com
Modern British | £25
Cooking score: 3

The Swan is a thatched pub with a pleasantly updated interior in a sleepy Suffolk village. It is testament to Nigel and Carol Ramsbottom's assiduous professionalism that the place is at once a proper local and a foodie destination. Look to the blackboard menus for evidence of Nigel's finely honed culinary skills, which make some memorable dishes of carefully bought supplies. Queen scallops with herb breadcrumbs and olive oil, followed by ricotta and spinach pancakes with a creamy Parmesan sauce delighted one reporter, while others have recommended spicy Thai pork with chilli, local venison casserole and vincigrassi lasagne, made with Parma ham and porcini mushrooms. Banana crème brûlée and marmalade pudding divide opinion as to which is the best. Service has been described as 'impeccable, not intrusive but very attentive'. Wines start at £13.50.

Chef/s: Nigel Ramsbottom. **Open:** Tue to Sun L 12 to 2 (1.30 winter), Tue to Sat D 7 to 9 (8.30 winter). **Closed:** Mon, 25 and 26 Dec, 2 weeks school summer hols. **Meals:** alc (main courses £10 to £20). Set L and D £15.75 (2 courses) to £19.75. **Service:** not inc. **Details:** Cards accepted. 40 seats. 16 seats outside. No music. Children allowed. Car parking.

Orford

The Trinity, Crown & Castle

Warm vibes and big local flavours
Orford, IP12 2LJ
Tel no: (01394) 450205
www.crownandcastle.co.uk
Modern British | £29
Cooking score: 4

Thirteen years on, there's a lot to be said for the Crown & Castle under its owners Ruth and David Watson. The warm vibe of their country hotel and its genuinely unaffected eatery still has city folk jumping in their cars at the first chance of a break. Pub-style lunches take in ham, fried egg and chips or steak and kidney pie, but elsewhere there's a breezy, modern feel to menus where local flavours loom large and inspiration comes from near and far: Gressingham duck breast accompanied by spiced butternut and apricot tagine and yoghurt or osso buco with risotto alla milanese and gremolata sit happily beside homespun English die-hards such as potted shrimps and fish pie. Desserts are a suitably varied bunch, taking in anything from blackcurrant and cassis jelly to New York-style baked cheesecake. The wine list is categorised by style; 13 are offered by the glass, and prices move gently upwards from £16.50.

Chef/s: Nick Thacker and Ruth Watson. **Open:** all week L 12.15 to 2.15, D 6.45 to 9.15. **Meals:** alc (main courses £14 to £22). **Service:** not inc. **Details:** Cards accepted. 50 seats. Separate bar. No music. No mobile phones. Car parking.

Southwold

The Crown Hotel

Big-city flavours and showcase wine
90 High Street, Southwold, IP18 6DP
Tel no: (01502) 722275
www.adnams.co.uk
Modern British | £35
Cooking score: 2

Blanket media coverage has put Southwold firmly on the metropolitan lifestyle map, and a rash of trendy boutiques now provide distraction for the town's incomers when they're not carousing in the Crown. It's 'first come, first served' in the rumbustious Parlour, where the 'hard' seats are like gold dust and the kitchen deploys ingredients from Suffolk's larder for a menu that bristles with big-city flavours. Sustainable fish is a good call (cod with roasted leeks, celeriac and wild mushrooms, say), but you might also find a trio of wild rabbit, Dingley Dell pork belly cooked in hay, or fried duck egg with crispy capers and dandelion leaves. As the flagship of wine fashionista Adnams, the Crown is also a showcase for one of the UK's sexiest lists. Oddball gems and classic beauties abound, with 20 mouthwatering selections offered by the glass. Bottles start at £17.95.

Open: all week L 12 to 2.30 (3 Sun), D 6.30 to 9 (6 to 9 Sat). **Meals:** alc (main courses £12 to £19). Sun L £19.95. **Service:** not inc. **Details:** Cards accepted. 90 seats. 32 seats outside. Separate bar. No music. No mobile phones. Wheelchair access. Children allowed. Car parking.

Sutherland House

High style, low food miles
56 High Street, Southwold, IP18 6DN
Tel no: (01502) 724544
www.sutherlandhouse.co.uk
Modern British | £25
Cooking score: 2
£5 OFF · £30

This venerable, fifteenth-century restaurant-with-rooms occupies the oldest house in Southwold. The kitchen is zealous about using local, seasonal ingredients, and makes sure that most of its raw materials don't have to travel far to reach it – cod (one mile), steak (10 miles). What exceptions there are, such as scallops (Scotland), clearly earn their place. Simplicity is paramount, with grilled mackerel, beetroot and pesto, then pork belly with bacon-wrapped fillet, black pudding, apple fondant and cabbage sparkling on a menu that concludes with a spot-on chocolate brownie. Mixed reports on service. Wines from £17.50.
Chef/s: Jed Tejada. **Open:** all week L 12 to 3, D 7 to 9. **Closed:** 25 Dec, 2 weeks Jan. **Meals:** alc (main courses £11 to £19). Set L £15 (2 courses) to £18. Sun L £18. **Service:** not inc. **Details:** Cards accepted. 40 seats. 30 seats outside. Separate bar. No mobile phones. Wheelchair access. Music. Children allowed. Car parking.

Stanton

The Leaping Hare

Vineyard eatery with fine local produce
Wyken Vineyards, Stanton, IP31 2DW
Tel no: (01359) 250287
www.wykenvineyards.co.uk
Modern British | £29
Cooking score: 2
£5 OFF £30

A 'hotbed of defiant utopianism', Wyken Hall promotes viticulture while sporting dreamy knot gardens, orchards, ancient woodland, a crafts complex, farmers' markets and an eatery specialising in fiercely local produce. Set in a 400-year-old barn, the Leaping Hare serves 'unrivalled' eggs Benedict, top-drawer cakes and 'properly silky' ice creams, plus lunch dishes ranging from Gressingham duck breast pan-smoked over vine prunings to rump of home-reared lamb, or wild venison with celeriac gratin, red cabbage and Puy lentils. One visitor reckons the lemon verbena pannacotta is 'the best ever'. Occasional evening meals are in a similar vein, and unmissable Wyken wines start at £15 – also try the home-brewed Good Dog Ale.
Chef/s: Jon Ellis. **Open:** all week L 12 to 2.30, Fri and Sat D 7 to 9. **Closed:** 25 Dec to 6 Jan. **Meals:** alc (main courses £13 to £20). Set L £16.95 (2 courses) to £18.95. **Service:** not inc. **Details:** Cards accepted. 55 seats. 25 seats outside. No music. No mobile phones. Wheelchair access. Children allowed. Car parking.

Stoke-by-Nayland

The Crown

Invigorated village inn with enterprising food
Park Street, Stoke-by-Nayland, CO6 4SE
Tel no: (01206) 262001
www.crowninn.net
Modern British | £26
Cooking score: 2
£30

'Brilliant food, fantastic service and great value for money', enthused one first-time visitor, obviously smitten by this invigorated village inn. The kitchen shows enterprise and ambition, combining a sharp eye for local detail with a generally cosmopolitan outlook. The result is a repertoire that ranges from Blythburgh pork terrine with piccalilli to roast chicken with watercress, duck-fat chips and aïoli or orecchiette with new season's broccoli, chilli, lemon, garlic and Parmesan. It also takes in fresh East Coast fish and simple desserts like hot apple pie with whipped cream. Wines from £14.50.
Chef/s: Mark Blake and Dan Hibble. **Open:** Mon to Sat L 12 to 2.30, D 6 to 9.30 (10 Fri and Sat). Sun 12 to 9. **Closed:** 25 and 26 Dec. **Meals:** alc (main courses £9 to £18). **Service:** not inc. **Details:** Cards accepted. 120 seats. 100 seats outside. Separate bar. No music. Wheelchair access. Children allowed. Car parking.

Tuddenham

★ UP-AND-COMING CHEF OF THE YEAR ★
PAUL FOSTER

Tuddenham Mill

Culinary daring and attention-grabbing ideas
High Street, Tuddenham, IP28 6SQ
Tel no: (01638) 713552
www.tuddenhammill.co.uk
Modern British | £40
Cooking score: 5

This eighteenth-century watermill has been brought up to date with more than just a lick of paint and it now provides an ideal setting for the contemporary cooking that is Paul Foster's forte. There is a vigorous streak of culinary daring running through his menus, with plenty of attention-grabbing ideas among the choices offered – as in a starter of corn-fed chicken wings partnered with brown shrimp, local baby cucumber and chicory purée – plus a nose for sharp seasonal partnerships, perhaps roasted watermelon, Bosworth Ash goats' cheese, nettle juice and sea aster. The focus, however, is on sound culinary principles backed up by well-sourced materials: salted hake served atop a vibrantly green watercress tapioca, the flavour pointed up by clams and confit garlic, or lamb rump and shoulder teamed with feta, smoked potato and red onion fondue. Even conventional Denham Estate fallow deer is taken to another level with coconut. Desserts dazzle, especially when a perfect balance of sweetness and acidity is achieved in a brilliant juxtaposition of whipped sea buckthorn, soft meringue, raspberries and crispy rice. An international wine list has pricey peaks, but house selections start at £19.95.

Chef/s: Paul Foster. **Open:** all week L 12 to 2, D 6.30 to 10. **Meals:** alc (main courses £18 to £26). Sun L £20 (2 courses) to £24. Tasting menu £65. **Service:** not inc. **Details:** Cards accepted. 54 seats. 35 seats outside. Separate bar. Music. Children allowed. Car parking.

Walberswick

The Anchor

Dream team in a Suffolk getaway
Main Street, Walberswick, IP18 6UA
Tel no: (01502) 722112
www.anchoratwalberswick.com
Modern British | £24
Cooking score: 2

Sophie and Mark Dorber have exactly the right credentials for fashion-conscious, chilled-out Walberswick and they suit this revitalised Arts and Crafts property down to the ground. She is an enthusiastic and open-minded disciple of the local/seasonal school of country cooking who happily jogs her way from Asian duck broth via roast cod with gnocchi and pig's cheek to cherry beer pannacotta with coconut ice cream. He is a guru from the drinks trade – hence the boozy recommendations beside each dish on the menu: a bottle of Brooklyn lager or a glass of Spanish Gaba do Xil with a tapas platter, for example. Nifty wines from Adnams of Southwold start at £16.25.

Chef/s: Sophie Dorber. **Open:** all week L 12 to 3, D 6 to 9. **Closed:** 25 Dec. **Meals:** alc (main courses £13 to £23). **Service:** not inc. **Details:** Cards accepted. 94 seats. 100 seats outside. Separate bar. No music. Wheelchair access. Children allowed. Car parking.

Woodbridge

The Crown at Woodbridge

Quirky, charming bolt-hole with wow factor
Thoroughfare, Woodbridge, IP12 1AD
Tel no: (01394) 384242
www.thecrownatwoodbridge.co.uk
Modern European | £27
Cooking score: 3

The designers really went to town when they revamped this fine old seventeenth-century inn, throwing just about every trick in the book at the interior and filling it with fashion-mag glitz. 'Funky boutique' is the style and the place simply buzzes with success. True to form, the cooking has a cosmopolitan edge and the menu sets out to please the locals, Woodbridge's sailing set and swarms of seasonal evacuees from the big city. The kitchen can do rustic (ham, duck egg and thrice-fried chips, Barnsley chop et al) as well as delivering fully paid-up, modern-day concoctions ranging from cockle and curried cauliflower fritters with pickled cucumber and sherry caramel to sea bass with squid ink gnocchi, Jerusalem artichokes, spinach and salsa verde. The pin-sharp wine list starts at £15.

Chef/s: Stephen David and Luke Bailey. **Open:** all week L 12 to 2.15, D 6.15 to 9. **Closed:** 25 Dec. **Meals:** alc (main courses £13 to £23). Set L & D £16 (2 courses) to £20. **Service:** not inc. **Details:** Cards accepted. 70 seats. 24 seats outside. Separate bar. Wheelchair access. Music. Children allowed. Car parking.

The Riverside

Meals and movies by the river
Quayside, Woodbridge, IP12 1BH
Tel no: (01394) 382587
www.theriverside.co.uk
Modern British | £26
Cooking score: 1

£5 OFF £30

A popular and reliable restaurant with plenty of alfresco seating, The Riverside is part of a cinema-bar-restaurant complex that's now well into its third decade. There are good-value film and meal deals most days, including 'fish 'n' flicks' and lunchtime tapas offers. The main menu has a modern British flavour: smoked haddock chowder and poached egg followed by roast rack of lamb with dauphinoise potatoes and red wine sauce are typical offerings, possibly followed by pecan pie with honey and ginger ice cream. Wines start at £15.

Chef/s: Chris Lynch. **Open:** all week L 12 to 2.15 (12.30 to 2.30 Sun), Mon to Sat D 6 to 9.30 (10 Fri and Sat). **Closed:** 25 and 26 Dec, 1 Jan. **Meals:** alc (main courses £10 to £28). Set D with film £30. **Service:** not inc. **Details:** Cards accepted. 55 seats. 30 seats outside. Separate bar. No mobile phones. Wheelchair access. Music. Children allowed.

Yoxford

ALSO RECOMMENDED

▲ Main's Restaurant

High Street, Yoxford, IP17 3EU
Tel no: (01728) 668882
www.mainsrestaurant.co.uk
Modern British

A 'clever balance of arty informality' typifies this well-supported local restaurant, where Nancy Main bakes bread and keeps the mood upbeat while husband Jason works like a 'dynamo' in the kitchen. His genuine approach to Suffolk produce might yield carpaccio of roe deer with egg mimosa (£6.50), 'simply sublime' Dover sole with roasted peppers, oregano and sherry vinegar (£15) or slow-roast ox cheek with pickled red cabbage. After that, a trio of fennel, beetroot and orange ice creams makes an intriguingly refreshing finale. Wines from £13.50. Open Tue to Sat D only.

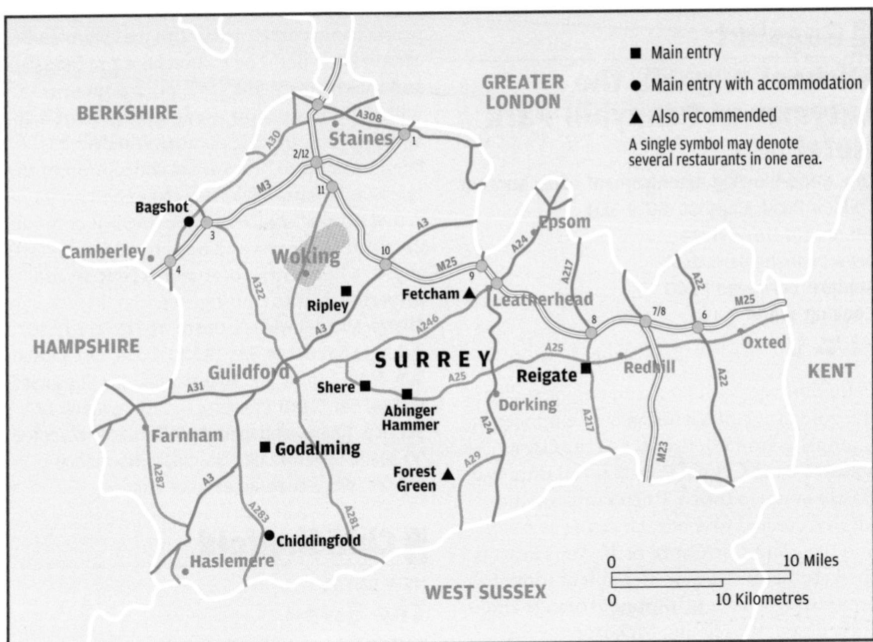

Abinger Hammer

Drakes on the Pond

High-class village restaurant
Dorking Road, Abinger Hammer, RH5 6SA
Tel no: (01306) 731174
www.drakesonthepond.com
Modern British | £47
Cooking score: 4

A Surrey stalwart set in gentle commuter-belt countryside by the A25, Drakes on the Pond has always promised a great deal, and chef/proprietor John Morris certainly understands the nuances of French-inspired contemporary cuisine – 'nouvelle' portions on huge white plates, pretty flourishes and 'deeply satisfying' demi-glace sauces are his trademarks. The low-ceilinged dining room can feel a tad dated with its burgundy carpets and peach walls, but there's nothing outmoded about tempura scallops with pan-fried squid and chorizo, breast of quail with crispy leg, cardamom-spiked carrot purée and cep sauce or a dessert of zesty lemon posset with lemon meringue ice cream. Sadly, Drakes has let itself down badly at lunchtime, when the pared-back menu has offered 'underwhelming' plates of chicken liver parfait, confit duck and slow-cooked belly pork without much finesse or attention to detail. Service would also benefit from a few more smiles. House wine is £17.95.

Chef/s: John Morris. **Open:** Tue to Sat L 12 to 1.30, D 7 to 9.30. **Closed:** Sun, Mon, 1 week Christmas. **Meals:** alc (main courses £24 to £30). Set L £22.50 (2 courses) to £25.95. **Service:** not inc. **Details:** Cards accepted. 32 seats. No music. No mobile phones. Wheelchair access. Children allowed. Car parking.

Readers Recommend

A 'readers recommend' review is a genuine quote from a report sent in by one of our readers. We intend to follow up these suggestions throughout the year to come.

Bagshot

Michael Wignall, the Latymer at Pennyhill Park Hotel

One mind-blowing astonishment after another
London Road, Bagshot, GU19 5EU
Tel no: (01276) 471774
www.pennyhillpark.co.uk
Modern European | £60
Cooking score: 7

£5 OFF V

Pennyhill was built by a civil engineer during the golden age of Victorian civil engineering. Completed in 1851, the year of the Great Exhibition at Crystal Palace, it's an impressive stately home in over 120 acres of parkland, ideally situated for both the racing at Ascot and the golfing at Wentworth. At its heart is the Latymer restaurant, an opulent room in contrasting shades of autumnal orange and leafy green. It's a fitting backdrop for the pyrotechnical cooking of its signature chef, the formidably talented Michael Wignall. He is in the vanguard of British contemporary cooking, absorbing techniques from the European modern masters and forging them into an intensely personal style of challenging but always exciting food. Reporters are usually left breathless: 'So much to take in, but all absolutely mind-blowing,' gasps one. 'One of the courses was a cassoulet of clam and squid with a puffed squid-ink tapioca wafer set in a small eggcup-shaped "coquette" bowl.' Of course it was. The tasting menus, in vegetarian, fish or meat versions, reliably deliver one astonishment after another: marinated rainbow trout with slow-cooked octopus and chervil mousseline in seaweed tea; loin of Lakeland hare with calf's sweetbreads and a fricassee of Hereford snails; poached breast of Anjou pigeon with bread and bay purée, pain perdu and jasmine jus. Even the cheese serving, perhaps of Fourme d'Ambert and Beaufort, comes with a smoked paprika crisp and Pedro Ximénez jelly. After that, one dessert may be all about carrot, while the other offers pedigree dark chocolate with a prune pannacotta, cardamom ice cream and caramel powder. The recherché ingredients and treatments – 'ink lace', pork popcorn, white chocolate snow – add to the fun of it all, and bear witness that as much intellect has been brought to bear on the conception of the menu as labours have been expended on its actual production. Wines are fine but come at uncomfortable prices. The glass selection starts at £9, while bottles of mature claret ascend imperiously into four figures.

Chef/s: Michael Wignall. **Open:** Wed to Fri L 12.30 to 2, Tue to Sat D 7 to 9.15 (9.30 Fri and Sat). **Closed:** Sun, Mon, 1 to 14 Jan. **Meals:** Set L £26 (2 courses) to £34. Set D £60 (3 courses). Tasting menu £82. **Service:** 12.5% (optional). **Details:** Cards accepted. 50 seats. Separate bar. No music. No mobile phones. Wheelchair access. Car parking.

Chiddingfold

NEW ENTRY

The Swan

Delightful inn with sunny food
Petworth Road, Chiddingfold, GU8 4TY
Tel no: (01428) 684688
www.theswaninnchiddingfold.com
Modern European | £28
Cooking score: 2

£5 OFF £30

This historic inn in a picture-postcard village on the West Sussex borders has been given a modern makeover by Anneiara and Stuart Davies, who re-launched the Swan in June 2010 to local delight. Inside, the white-walled dining areas are dotted with French prints and stylish black-and-white photographs, and a pretty terraced garden makes the perfect spot when the weather is kind. A salad of smoked duck with balsamic onions or fillet of sea bass with crushed potatoes and asparagus are typical of the simple, Mediterranean-influenced menu, while good kitchen skills are demonstrated by well-executed sauces such as a chive beurre blanc or tarragon-flecked béarnaise. There's praise, too, for Sunday roasts. House wine is £15.95.

Chef/s: Spencer Ralph. **Open:** all week L 12 to 3, D 6.30 to 10 (9 Sun). **Meals:** alc (main courses £12 to £20). Set L £20 (3 courses) to £22. Set D £35 (3 courses) to £38. Sun L £14 to £15. **Service:** not inc. **Details:** Cards accepted. 90 seats. 60 seats outside. Separate bar. Wheelchair access. Music. Children allowed. Car parking.

Fetcham

ALSO RECOMMENDED

▲ The Bell

Bell Lane, Fetcham, KT22 9ND
Tel no: (01372) 372624
www.bellfetcham.com
British £5 OFF

There's lots of outdoor seating at this handsome whitewashed pub on the outskirts of Leatherhead. Inside, choose between the smart rear dining room, or the comfy bar area. By day, expect decent renditions of classic pub grub including award-winning pies, fish and chips and proper burgers (all £10.95). In the evening, these are joined by more ambitious dishes such as potted duck confit, or herb-crusted grey mullet (£12.95). Despite the roadside location, the terraced garden is a pleasant spot for lunch alfresco. House wine £15.90. Open all week.

Forest Green

ALSO RECOMMENDED

▲ The Parrot Inn

Forest Green, RH5 5RZ
Tel no: (01306) 621339
www.theparrot.co.uk
Modern British

Overlooking the village green, the Parrot looks every inch the old-fashioned country pub with its rambling interior, log fire, flagstones and beams – it all adds up to a pleasant ambience. The menu is a showcase for what's in season (meat comes from the owner's farm), illustrated by rustic dishes such as roasted Jerusalem artichokes, Sussex Slipcote cheese and hazelnut salad (£5.50), and home-cured salted Middle White belly pork with lentils (£12.75). Ginger syrup cheesecake (£5.60) is a sweet hit. House wine £15. No food Sun D.

Godalming

La Luna

Bona fide Italian gastronomy
10-14 Wharf Street, Godalming, GU7 1NN
Tel no: (01483) 414155
www.lalunarestaurant.co.uk
Italian | £27
Cooking score: 4
£5 OFF £30

The pride of Godalming for more than a decade, Daniele Drago's loyally supported neighbourhood restaurant brings more than a touch of la dolce vita to the Surrey commuter belt. It also raises the stakes when it comes to provincial Italian food in the region. Instead of lasagne and other trattoria clichés, La Luna tantalises its customers with bowls of Tuscan ribollita, tomato essence and a swish of Fontodi olive oil, or gnocchi swathed in a pork and fennel sausage ragù with Scamorza cheese. To begin, there are stuzzichini nibbles alongside the likes of seared king prawns with Sicilian orange and char-grilled onion salad, while 'secondi' promise bona fide plates of baked sea bass with steamed sprouting broccoli, pickled caperberries and salsa verde, or free-range quail involtini with smoked ham and a Jerusalem artichoke foam. To conclude, look beyond tiramisu to Prosecco-poached pear with Muscat and dried fruit 'risotto' pudding. The food is supported by a blisteringly good list of Italian regional wines that roams from Lombardy and Liguria to Sicily and Sardinia, picking up treasures along the way. A pared-down, easy-drinking selection starts at £13.

Chef/s: Valentino Gentile. **Open:** Tue to Sat L 12 to 2, D 7 to 10 (6.30 Sat). **Closed:** Sun, Mon, 25 and 26 Jan, 1 Jan, 1 week Aug. **Meals:** alc (main courses £10 to £20). Set L £11.95 (2 courses) to £14.50. **Service:** not inc. **Details:** Cards accepted. 58 seats. No mobile phones. Music. Children allowed.

Reigate

The Westerly

Bistro that runs on charm and integrity
2-4 London Road, Reigate, RH2 9AN
Tel no: (01737) 222733
www.thewesterly.co.uk
Modern British | £31
Cooking score: 4
£5 OFF

This compact restaurant consisting of two dining rooms with big windows looking out on to the street runs on dedication, charm and integrity. The short menus seem to evolve slowly, but Jon Coomb never veers from his philosophy of combining high-quality raw materials with spot-on timing to produce accomplished modern country cooking. Home in on salt cod brandade with braised octopus and chorizo or ham hock, pigeon and foie gras terrine, or mains of wood pigeon Wellington with Parmentier potatoes. Classical techniques and European flavours are the foundation, often given an individual identity: in, for example, a dessert of burnt Sauternes custard with rhubarb jelly. A three-page wine list has been imaginatively chosen and, even more imaginatively, some dozen are offered by the glass, 375ml or 500ml pot Lyonnais, prices starting at £15.45.

Chef/s: Jon Coomb. **Open:** Wed to Fri L 12.30 to 3, Tue to Sat D 7 to 10. **Closed:** Sun, Mon, 25 Dec until first Tue in Jan. **Meals:** alc (main courses £17 to £22). Set L £19.50 (two courses) to £21.50. **Service:** not inc. **Details:** Cards accepted. 44 seats. No music. Children allowed.

ALSO RECOMMENDED

▲ Tony Tobin @ The Dining Room

59a High Street, Reigate, RH2 9AE
Tel no: (01737) 226650
www.tonytobinrestaurants.co.uk
Modern European £5 OFF

Reliable hands in the kitchen continue to draw Reigate locals and incomers to this well-run first-floor restaurant. Warm leek and Gruyère tart and fillet steak meatballs are typical of the weekday special set menu (three courses £21), while the carte (two courses £29.50) mixes classics like chicken liver parfait and Madeira jelly with crispy aromatic duck, butternut squash purée and sweet curry cream. House wine is £16.95. Closed Sat L and Sun D.

Ripley

Drake's Restaurant

Cutting-edge, big-attitude food
The Clock House, High Street, Ripley, GU23 6AQ
Tel no: (01483) 224777
www.drakesrestaurant.co.uk
Modern British | £55
Cooking score: 6
£5 OFF **V**

Behind the trim Georgian façade of the Clock House lies Steve Drake's elegant neighbourhood restaurant, which comes with a panelled private-dining room, a walled garden for balmy days, and a vista of widely spaced tables and striking local artworks. Drake works at the sharp end of the modern British spectrum, constantly pushing boundaries and experimenting, rather than falling back as many do on the tried-and-tested dishes of a decade ago. Combinations are nothing if not daring, the more so since the menu specifications confine themselves mostly to simply listing the ingredients. Scallop, black garlic, gremolata, truffle meringue and sweetcorn provides food for thought before the food itself turns up. Likewise, langoustine, compressed pineapple, crispy pig's ears, cabbage and bacon. The high-wire act derives from the fact that most of the components are assertively flavoured ingredients that might be thought hard to combine, as in a main course of roast and braised duck with grilled melon, potato and liquorice. The trend for marine flora is celebrated in a halibut dish that comes with sea purslane, oyster cream and a sauce based on seawater. Dessert might be banana with warm pistachio cake and black olive and banana parfait. Complaints of long waits perhaps

reflect the patience that such intricate cuisine mandates. Wines by the glass from £5.50 lead a comprehensive list, with bottles from £22.
Chef/s: Steve Drake. **Open:** Wed to Sat L 12 to 1.30 (summer only Wed), Tue to Sat D 7 to 9.30. **Closed:** Sun, Mon, 2 weeks Jan. **Meals:** Set L £22 (2 courses) to £28. Set D £45 (2 courses) to £55. Tasting menu £70 (6 courses). **Service:** not inc. **Details:** Cards accepted. 46 seats. No mobile phones. Music. Children allowed.

Shere

Kinghams

Hands-on country restaurant
Gomshall Lane, Shere, GU5 9HE
Tel no: (01483) 202168
www.kinghams-restaurant.co.uk
Modern British | £38
Cooking score: 2

A seventeenth-century house with a delightful garden and low, beamed interiors has been home to Paul Baker's hands-on country restaurant since 1993. Go for the gazebo table if you can during the summer. Sourcing locally and following the seasons, he presents a wide-ranging menu of contemporary British cooking that tries out some bold and inspired ideas. A meal might take in spiced scallops on pease pudding in a lentil and shallot dressing, redcurrant-glazed duck breast with a parfait of the liver in brown bread and walnut sauce, and lemon meringue pie. Wines from £16.95.
Chef/s: Paul Baker. **Open:** Tue to Sun L 12 to 2 (4 Sun), Tue to Sat D 7 to 11. **Closed:** Mon, 25 Dec to 5 Jan. **Meals:** alc (main courses £15 to £20). Set L and D £16.95 (2 courses) to £22.90. Sun L £23.95. **Service:** not inc. **Details:** Cards accepted. 47 seats. 20 seats outside. Wheelchair access. Music. Children allowed. Car parking.

HOTEL DINING

After years in the dining doldrums, hotel restaurants have never been so stylish.

Dinner – The Mandarin Oriental: Heston Blumenthal reinvents historical dishes with typical panache at this stunning venue. Meat fruit and tipsy cake star.

Gordon Ramsay – The Savoy Grill: The Grill serves up appealing dishes such as charcoal-grilled chateaubriand with pommes soufflées in Art Deco surrounds.

Koffmann's – The Berkeley: Savour Pierre Koffmann's signature dishes – scallops with squid ink, braised pig's trotter with morels – in a chic setting.

Marcus Wareing at The Berkeley: Canapés, amuse-bouches and pre-desserts ensure diners leave fully sated, while the menu's northern notes provide extra interest at this exemplary fine-dining spot.

Kenny Atkinson at The Orangery – Rockliffe Hall: Atkinson's seasonal menu with ingredients sourced from local suppliers is a hit.

Marcus Wareing – The Gilbert Scott @ St Pancras Renaissance: In this iconic building, Wareing pays homage to British classics such as tweed kettle and water tart.

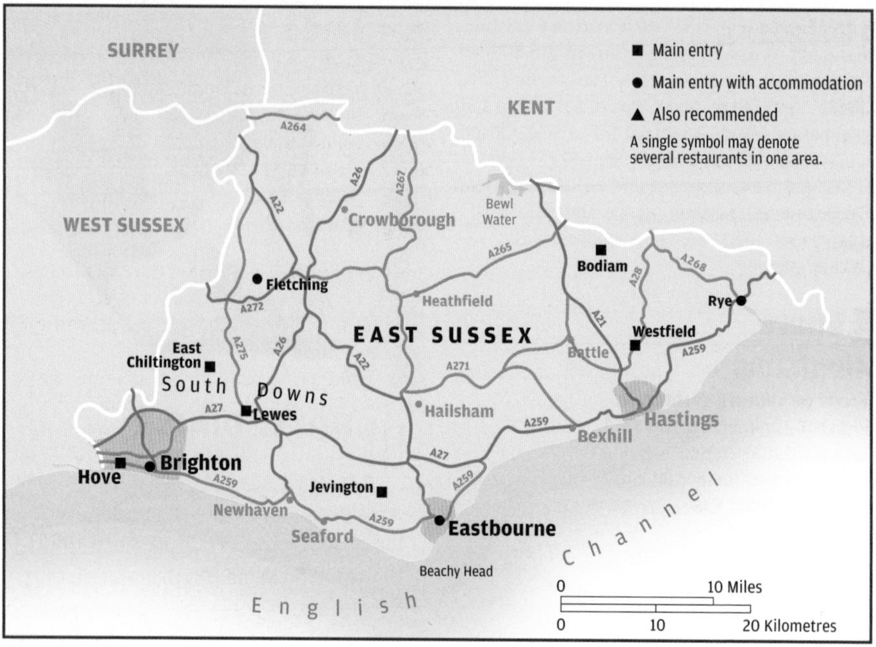

Bodiam

The Curlew

Seriously good stuff
Junction Road, Bodiam, TN32 5UY
Tel no: (01580) 861394
www.thecurlewrestaurant.co.uk
Modern British | £30
Cooking score: 4

The white-painted clapboard façade is all that remains of this former seventeenth-century coaching inn; inside is a bullish, metropolitan-style restaurant, but with enough charm of its own to keep you lingering, mainly in the form of Neil McCue's sharp-toned cooking. He buys diligently from a network of local suppliers and transforms the haul into a bright, vibrant modern British menu with an acute seasonal edge. Fine-tuned flavours come through strongly, whether it's asparagus with a soft-poached egg and hollandaise or a slow-cooked Jacob's ladder chop ('that fell off the bone and oozed good taste') with beef-dripping potatoes. Elsewhere, there's some seriously good stuff in the form of sweetly timed whole lemon sole with a heap of buttery brown shrimps and capers, 'delicious' Pink Fir Apple potatoes served on the side, bread-and-butter pudding that 'despite its girth was very light', and 'perfect' homemade bread. A good, carefully assembled wine list covers a lot of ground. Prices from £16.

Chef/s: Neil McCue. **Open:** Wed to Sun L 12 to 2.30 D 6 to 9.30 (9 Sun). **Closed:** Mon, Tue, two weeks Jan, one week Jun, one week Nov. **Meals:** alc (main courses £16 to £18). Set L £16 (2 courses) to £20. **Service:** not inc. **Details:** Cards accepted. 64 seats. 30 seats outside. Music. Children allowed. Car parking.

Average Price

The average price listed in main-entry reviews denotes the price of a three-course meal, without wine.

Brighton

NEW ENTRY

Chilli Pickle

Idiosyncratic modern Indian
17 Jubilee Street, Brighton, BN1 1GE
Tel no: (01273) 900383
www.thechillipicklebistro.co.uk
Indian | £22
Cooking score: 3

The move from Meeting House Lane to spacious new premises within Myhotel seems to have done Alun and Dawn Sperring's idiosyncratic Indian a power of good, and its glass, steel and contemporary design touches now provide a suitably chic backdrop for some terrific regionally inspired cooking. Plates of tapas-style street food are the main event at lunchtime (think kathi kebabs rolled in naan bread, dosas and all-inclusive thalis), while dinner brings a thrilling subcontinental tour taking in everything from Punjabi tandoori platters to fiery mutton laal mans from Rajasthan or finely balanced seafood machar jhol (a Bengali specialty). Extras such as crispy nibbles, vegan aubergine 'crush' and sweet pineapple pickle add to the excitement, and it's worth trying the multicoloured barfi (Indian sweetmeats) for a genuine finish. Wines from £14.50.

Chef/s: Alun Sperring. **Open:** Wed to Mon L 12 to 3, D 6 to 10.30. **Closed:** Tue, 25 Dec. **Meals:** alc (main courses £9 to £19). **Service:** not inc. **Details:** Cards accepted. 115 seats. 30 seats outside. Wheelchair access. Music.

Symbols

- Accommodation is available
- Three courses for less than £30
- V Separate vegetarian menu
- £5-off voucher scheme
- Notable wine list

Due South

Magical seafront eatery
139 Kings Road Arches, Brighton, BN1 2FN
Tel no: (01273) 821218
www.duesouth.co.uk
Modern European | £28
Cooking score: 2

Converted fishing premises under the arches on Brighton beach make this a magical location. Watch the sea lapping on the shingle as you set about Michael Bremner's enterprising and locally based, pan-European cooking. A reporter writes of a memorable lunch that took in beetroot with gingerbread and horseradish crème fraîche to start, moved on to grilled flounder on smoky crushed potatoes mixed with crabmeat, and finished up with rhubarb pannacotta. Taste of Sussex menus wear their regional commitment proudly on the sleeve, and may feature South Brockwells Farm venison with pappardelle pasta. The short wine list opens at £15 (£4.50 a glass).

Chef/s: Michael Bremner. **Open:** all week L 12 to 3.30, D 6 to 9.45. **Closed:** 25 and 26 Dec. **Meals:** alc (main courses £12 to £24). Set L £10 (2 courses) to £15. Set D £20 (2 courses) to £25. Sun L £15. **Service:** 10% (optional). **Details:** Cards accepted. 56 seats. 40 seats outside. Wheelchair access. Music. Children allowed.

NEW ENTRY

Food For Friends

Return of a veggie legend
17-18 Prince Albert Street, The Lanes, Brighton, BN1 1HF
Tel no: (01273) 202310
www.foodforfriends.com
Vegetarian | £24
Cooking score: 1

A Guide favourite way back in the 80s, Brighton's veggie legend is making a comeback, thanks to a cute makeover and some fine-tuned eclectic cooking. Once an archetypal slice of left-field hippiedom, it's now in tune with the town's 'urban chic' zeitgeist – dispensing global flavours in bright, contemporary surrounds. Influences are garnered from all over as the kitchen jogs its way from broad bean risotto fritters, sumac-spiced aubergine rolls and Mexican rösti to Thai sharing platters, tofu 'pockets' and teriyaki-glazed soba noodles. To finish, try Portuguese custard tart. Great-value express lunches. Wines from £19.95.

Chef/s: Lisa Walker. **Open:** all week 12 to 10. **Closed:** 25 Dec. **Meals:** alc (main courses £11 to £13). Set L £11.95 (2 courses) to £14.95. Set D £21.95. Sun L £9.95. **Service:** not inc. **Details:** Cards accepted. 70 seats. 20 seats outside. No mobile phones. Music. Children allowed.

The Ginger Dog

Banging the drum for top-quality produce
12-13 College Place, Brighton, BN2 1HN
Tel no: (01273) 620990
www.gingermanrestaurants.com
Modern British | £25
Cooking score: 3

The latest addition to the Gingerman group (see also Gingerman and Ginger Pig in Brighton, and Ginger Fox in West Sussex) is a small Kemptown pub that bangs the same drum as its siblings for top-quality produce and diverse flavours. Scallops, for example, are teamed with sweetcorn, chorizo and pea shoots, while brill might be served with a devilled crab croquette and spinach and curry cream. You might also find a pie of rabbit with chanterelle mushrooms and Madeira or butter-roast fillet of pork with potato and celeriac dauphinoise. Desserts yo-yo from tradition – Seville orange marmalade sponge with bay leaf custard, say – to contrasting ideas like passion-fruit pannacotta with passion-fruit jelly, millionaire's shortbread and toasted coconut. House wine is £15.

Chef/s: Ben McKellar and Robin Boerhorst. **Open:** all week L 12 to 2 (12.30 to 3 Sat, 12.30 to 4 Sun), D 6 to 10. **Closed:** 25 Dec. **Meals:** alc (main courses £10 to £18). Set L £10 (2 courses). **Service:** not inc. **Details:** Cards accepted. 30 seats. Separate bar. Music. Children allowed.

The Ginger Pig

Welcoming pub with a skilful kitchen
3 Hove Street, Brighton, BN3 2TR
Tel no: (01273) 736123
www.gingermanrestaurants.com
Modern British | £25
Cooking score: 4

'Gingerman' Ben McKellar's 'busy and welcoming' pub scores with a pleasingly contemporary décor and capable service, and it's also prepared to invest in decent raw materials. There's little doubt that the kitchen can deliver unfussy dishes with skill and dexterity. Regulars have praised 'superb calf's liver, first-class partridge, super desserts'. Spiced mackerel and mackerel tartare with pickled cucumber, apple and horseradish makes a punchy start, while sea bass with crispy king prawn, stir-fried vegetables and a fragrant mussel and coconut broth lines up alongside game pie with spiced red cabbage and creamed mash among main courses. Anchovy toast with watercress or British and Irish cheeses are alternatives to the sweet hit of blood orange pannacotta with Muscat jelly or brown sugar tart with Greek yoghurt sorbet. An international line-up of wines at fair prices hits just the right note, with bottles starting at £15.

Chef/s: Dave Metterill and Ben McKellar. **Open:** all week L 12 to 2 (3 Fri, 12.30 to 4 Sat and Sun), D to 10. **Closed:** 25 Dec. **Meals:** alc (main courses £11 to £18). Set L £10 (2 courses). **Service:** not inc. **Details:** Cards accepted. 60 seats. 35 seats outside. Separate bar. Wheelchair access. Music. Children allowed.

Gingerman

Hot spot for the foodie swarms
21A Norfolk Square, Brighton, BN1 2PD
Tel no: (01273) 326688
www.gingermanrestaurants.com
Modern European | £32
Cooking score: 3

Now well into its second decade, the founding member of Ben McKellar's Brighton-based 'Ginger' empire remains a cool hot spot for the town's foodie swarms. Done out in muted tones, its intimate, high-ceilinged dining room provides the backdrop for some assured, fashion-conscious cooking that sometimes seems more West End than South Coast – haunch of venison marinated in fresh liquorice, for example. A starter of seared Rye Bay scallops with pumpkin purée, sage beurre noisette and pumpkin crisps ticks all the boxes, but there's also room for more classically inclined compositions such as rack of Sussex lamb with fondant potato, roasted Jerusalem artichokes and Madeira. To finish, sticky date pudding and a lemon drizzle bun with poached quince dust off some well-tried British themes. The sharp, eclectic wine list starts at £15 (£3.75 a glass).

Chef/s: Simon Neville-Jones and Ben McKellar. **Open:** Tue to Sun L 12.30 to 2, D 7 to 10. **Closed:** Mon, 25 Dec, 2 weeks winter. **Meals:** Set L £15 (2 courses) to £18. Set D £28 (2 courses) to £32. Sun L £20. **Service:** not inc. **Details:** Cards accepted. 32 seats. Music. Children allowed.

The Restaurant at Drakes

Sheer culinary impact
43-44 Marine Parade, Brighton, BN2 1PE
Tel no: (01273) 696934
www.therestaurantatdrakes.co.uk
Modern British | £40
Cooking score: 6

£5 OFF

A water feature fashioned from a jagged lump of granite announces Drakes, a modern town-house hotel not far from the pier. Inside, it sports a lounge bar and a cool basement dining room, reached down what feels like a secret staircase. Andrew MacKenzie has been cooking here since 2004, and has established the place as Brighton's first stop for ambitious contemporary fine dining. It isn't the most ostentatious style of cuisine and it doesn't subscribe to the 'krazy kombinations' school of thought, but the cooking shows real flair and sensitivity when it comes to ingredients and a feel for their impact on the palate. There's also a fondness for earthier flavours rather than vapid luxuries, witness one reader's account of a rapturous meal that progressed from pressed calf's tongue terrine with piccalilli to roast skate on potato galette with brown shrimps in tomato and caper butter. Elsewhere, the kitchen proves the point with a trio of pork (braised cheek, confit belly and tenderloin) and rump of lamb with grilled kidney and artichoke barigoule, while desserts such as poached rhubarb with Champagne sorbet show classy intent. Wines start at £18 (£5 a glass).

Chef/s: Andrew MacKenzie. **Open:** all week L 12.30 to 1.45, D 7 to 9.30. **Meals:** Set L and D £29.95 (2 courses) to £39.95. Sun L £25 (2 courses) to £30. Tasting menu £55 (5 courses). **Service:** 12.5% (optional). **Details:** Cards accepted. 46 seats. Separate bar. No mobile phones. Music. Children allowed.

NEW ENTRY
Sam's of Seven Dials

Reinvented Brighton favourite
1 Buckingham Place, Brighton, BN1 3TD
Tel no: (01273) 885555
www.sevendialsrestaurant.co.uk
British | £26
Cooking score: 2

Sam Metcalfe has revived and recast his old Sevendials restaurant on Buckingham Place as a more casual, all-inclusive eatery, complete with attractive contemporary design and alfresco opportunities. A lively buzz pervades the dining room, where customers can enjoy a mixed bag of die-hard and innovative dishes fashioned from seasonal ingredients – think asparagus with poached duck egg and wild garlic butter, well-executed saddle of rabbit stuffed with boudin noir, or roast cod with saffron potatoes, samphire and capers. Steaks are cooked as requested, chips are the real thing and desserts might take in staples such as lemon posset. House wines from £14. Sam's of Brighton is at 1 Paston Place; tel: (01273) 676222.

Chef/s: Sam Metcalfe. **Open:** Mon to Sat L 12 to 3, D 6 to 10. Sun 12 to 8. **Closed:** 25 and 26 Dec. **Meals:** alc (main courses £10 to £18). Set L £10. **Service:** not inc. **Details:** Cards accepted. 55 seats. 40 seats outside. Wheelchair access. Music. Children allowed. Car parking.

Terre à Terre

Veggie maverick with funky global cooking
71 East Street, Brighton, BN1 1HQ
Tel no: (01273) 729051
www.terreaterre.co.uk
Vegetarian | £29
Cooking score: 3

V 

Since 1993, this maverick veggie has been putting on the style in Brighton's wacky foodie scene with its extrovert vibes and funky global cooking – although the kitchen has toned down some of its freewheeling forays of late. Terre à Terre was spouting 'pukka speak' long before Jamie O, and the menu still rolls off the tongue: 'baby batters' are pieces of buttermilk-soaked haloumi dipped in chip-shop batter and served with a mini Bloody Mary, while 'pimped potsticker' comprises a fried savoury dumpling served on a bonanza of Szechuan stir-fried vegetables with edamame, cashew and yuzu pesto plus a tamari/mirin/chilli dressing. Among the 'sweeties', expect 'tipsy coconut cakelets' and 'frisky alco-affogato'. Regular promotions and 'terre à verre' set deals are also worth investigating, and the organically inclined drinks list runs from ultra-cool beers and nectars to cocktails and wines (from £17.50).

Chef/s: Dino Pavledis. **Open:** all week 12 to 10.30 (11 Sat). **Closed:** 25 and 26 Dec. **Meals:** alc (main courses £13 to £15). **Service:** not inc. **Details:** Cards accepted. 100 seats. 15 seats outside. Wheelchair access. Music. Children allowed.

READERS RECOMMEND

Planet India

Indian
4-5 Richmond Parade, Brighton, BN2 9PH
Tel no: (01273) 818149
'Authentic, affordable Indian home cooking. Friendly service in laid-back, colourful surroundings. Exceptional dahi bhel puri.'

East Chiltington

The Jolly Sportsman

Carefully composed bistro dishes
Chapel Lane, East Chiltington, BN7 3BA
Tel no: (01273) 890400
www.thejollysportsman.com
Modern British | £28
Cooking score: 2

V 

The Jolly Sportsman is to be found in a perfectly serene hamlet not far north of Brighton. You can choose to eat in the snug bar or in one of the dedicated dining rooms (including a garden room), and the cheery rural atmosphere will fill you with contentment. The British bistro-style dishes are carefully composed and based on sound local ingredients. Spiced scallops with grape salad, venison loin in chocolate-spiked sauce with a mini-cottage pie, and an oat-crumbled rhubarb and custard tart added up to a satisfying evening for one winter diner. The fixed-price lunch is a bargain. Wines start at £15.50.

Chef/s: Alistair Doyle. **Open:** all week L 12 to 2.30 (3.30 Sun), D 6.30 to 9.30 (10 Fri and Sat, 9 Sun). **Closed:** 25 and 26 Dec. **Meals:** alc (main courses £10 to £19). Set L £12.50 (2 courses) to £15.75. Set D £16.50. Sun L £18.50. **Service:** not inc. **Details:** Cards accepted. 100 seats. 40 seats outside. Separate bar. No music. Wheelchair access. Children allowed. Car parking.

Eastbourne

The Grand Hotel, Mirabelle

Bygone-era charms and precision-tuned food
King Edward's Parade, Eastbourne, BN21 4EQ
Tel no: (01323) 412345
www.grandeastbourne.com
Modern European | £40
Cooking score: 5

£5 OFF

An epic architectural 'wedding cake', this self-proclaimed 'White Palace' overlooking Eastbourne promenade is a *grande dame* among English seaside hotels and still flaunts its blue-blooded, bygone-era charms to a mature, civilised crowd. The BBC Palm Court Orchestra used to broadcast here, and whispers of the 'good old days' still waft through the pale-pink Mirabelle restaurant – a ballroom-like space patrolled by dapper waiters 'who seem to have been in place for years'. There is much trolley-wheeling and dome-lifting here, although Gerald Röser's precision-tuned food is shot through with purposeful modern aspirations and seasonal awareness. Of course, some luxurious flamboyance is to be expected, but it's tempered with a gentle touch and a feel for clarity on the plate. The succinct menu is also bolstered by a raft of 'seasonal classics' promising the likes of roast wild sea bass with spiced butter beans, aubergine caviar and chorizo oil dressing or magret of duck with star anise, salsify tarte Tatin and cavolo nero, followed by blackcurrant-poached pears with Champagne syllabub. Lunch also gets the nod from readers, who have singled out duck liver parfait and roast salmon with tomato tart and fennel purée – not forgetting heady lavender ice cream and a slate of impressive cheeses. The wine list is a suitably grand affair that brings together the good, the great and the exceedingly rare from across the vinous globe, although one reader reckoned that prices (from £22.75) weren't 'grounded in the real world'.
Chef/s: Gerald Röser. **Open:** Tue to Sat L 12.30 to 2, D 7 to 10. **Closed:** Sun, Mon, first 2 weeks Jan. **Meals:** Set L £20 (2 courses) to £24. Set D £40. Tasting menu £8.50. **Service:** not inc. **Details:** Cards accepted. 50 seats. Separate bar. No mobile phones. Wheelchair access. Music. Car parking.

Fletching

The Griffin Inn

Recipe for a quality day out
Fletching, TN22 3SS
Tel no: (01825) 722890
www.thegriffininn.co.uk
Modern European | £30
Cooking score: 3

Relaxed and relaxing, this Sussex stalwart has lots of local support. The ancient pub is full of old beams, open fires and unforced charm, and with its wonderful views from the garden over the Ouse Valley it's most people's idea of a quality day out. Beer-battered cod and wild boar sausages with mash give a good solid British dimension to modern cooking with its feet on the ground, but there's a Mediterranean feel too, with well-reported dishes such as steamed razor clams with chilli, garlic and white wine, or smoked haddock with a potato rösti, poached egg, cavolo nero and hollandaise. Underpinning the food is a well-constructed, well-annotated wine list, with house selections from £14.90 and plenty by the glass.
Chef/s: Matthew Sandells. **Open:** all week L 12 to 2.30 (3 Sat and Sun), Mon to Sat D 7 to 9.30. **Closed:** 25 Dec. **Meals:** alc (main courses £12 to £25). Sun L £30. **Service:** 10% (optional).

Please send us your feedback

To register your opinion about any restaurant listed in the Guide, or a new restaurant that you wish to bring to our attention, please visit the web address at the bottom of the page. Your feedback informs the content of the book and will be used to compile next year's reviews.

Details: Cards accepted. 65 seats. 35 seats outside. Separate bar. No music. No mobile phones. Wheelchair access. Children allowed. Car parking.

Hove

The Foragers

Foodie pub that celebrates local ingredients
3 Stirling Place, Hove, BN3 3YU
Tel no: (01273) 733134
www.theforagerspub.co.uk
Modern British | £20
Cooking score: 2

As the voguish name suggests, this likeable rustic pub follows the 'Brighton goes native' trend right down to its local organic bread and Sussex butter. Mismatched tables chime perfectly with cooking that speaks its mind and makes a good fist of celebrating regional ingredients. Wild rabbit suet pudding comes with truffled mash and kale, ham hock and parsley risotto is topped with a poached egg, and there's always some fish from the coast – perhaps served with sun-dried tomato and white bean stew. For afters, try an assortment of Nut Knowle goats' cheeses or take the sweet route with toffee and walnut tart. House wine is £14. The owners also run the King's Head in Lewes (see entry).

Open: all week L 12 to 3 (4 Sat, 5 Sun), Mon to Sat D 6 to 10. **Meals:** alc (main courses £9 to £15). **Service:** not inc. **Details:** Cards accepted. 90 seats. 90 seats outside. Separate bar. Wheelchair access. Music. Children allowed.

Graze Restaurant

Popular eatery with tasting menus
42 Western Road, Hove, BN3 1JD
Tel no: (01273) 823707
www.graze-restaurant.co.uk
Modern British | £30
Cooking score: 4

'Smallish, narrow premises (ground floor and basement with salon privé area), décor a bit mix-and-match and front windows which open up on fine days', is how one visitor summed up Kate Alleston's popular restaurant. The food is modern British, the menu format a not-quite-wholehearted embrace of grazing dining; while the seven-course tasting menus are where the main energy seems to be invested, you can order pretty much the same dishes from a conventional, fixed-price carte. They might be as simple as beetroot risotto or pork fillet and braised pork cheek with creamed parsley root, while interesting-sounding marriages (scallops with a pig's trotter croquette and tamarind velouté) have demonstrated assured technical expertise. Sadly flavours can be less intense than desired – occassionally a dish will fail to hang together or will seem underwhelming. Desserts such as chilled pear and saffron soup, however, are properly flavoured. Wines from £15.

Chef/s: Gethin Russell-Jones. **Open:** all week L 12 to 2 (3.30 Sun), D 6.30 to 9.30 (9 Sun). **Closed:** 10 days early Jan. **Meals:** Set L £14 (2 courses) to £18. Set D £24 (2 courses) to £30. Sun L £16. Tasting menu £40 (7 courses). **Service:** 12% (optional). **Details:** Cards accepted. 50 seats. 4 seats outside. Separate bar. Music. Children allowed.

NEW ENTRY

The Hove Kitchen

A new hub for Hove
102-105 Western Road, Hove, BN3 1FA
Tel no: (01273) 725495
www.thehovekitchen.com
Modern European | £20
Cooking score: 2

Hove Kitchen's canopied glass frontage, with alfresco tables and well-spaced, comfortable seating inside, makes it an attractive addition to Western Road's social scene – especially as breakfast and brunch are part of the package. A satisfied buzz testifies to efficient service and precise, no-nonsense cooking, be it spot-on asparagus accompanied by a rich, fried duck egg and pecorino, or flavoursome rump of Sussex lamb married with peas, pancetta and garlic confit. Fish also shows a sure touch,

judging by a deft octopus and potato terrine with guindilla chillies, char-grilled mackerel fillets or roast plaice with samphire. For dessert, try the terrific apricot and almond tart. House wines from £13.50.
Chef/s: Steve Beadle. **Open:** all week L 12 to 3 (4 Sat, 5 Sun), Tue to Sat D 5.30 to 10 (9 Tue). **Closed:** 25 and 26 Dec. **Meals:** alc (main courses £9 to £15). Set L and early D £10. Sun L £12.50. **Service:** not inc. **Details:** Cards accepted. 80 seats. 50 seats outside. Separate bar. Wheelchair access. Music. Children allowed.

NEW ENTRY

The Meadow

Fervent local champion
64 Western Road, Hove, BN3 2JQ
Tel no: (01273) 721182
www.themeadowrestaurant.co.uk
British | £26
Cooking score: 2

More stylish than some of its neighbours leading Brighton's foodie charge, this bright, high-ceilinged restaurant in a converted banking hall owes much to the zealous enthusiasm of local champion William Murgatroyd. His seasonal menu highlights regional ingredients ranging from Arun Valley beef (the star of a Sunday lunch) to sensitively handled fish from the South Coast boats: roast Rye Bay plaice might appear with chickpeas and capers, 'tongue sole' is dressed with dandelion and claytonia (winter purslane) leaves, and smoked prawns turn up alongside parsley-crusted hake. To start, grilled asparagus with poached duck egg and hollandaise is exemplary in every department, while carefully crafted desserts might include honeycomb cheesecake with basil sugar. House wines from £16. The Meadow now has its own farm shop/traiteur (don't miss the home-churned butter).
Chef/s: William Murgatroyd. **Open:** Tue to Sun L 12 to 2.30 (3 Sun), Tue to Sat D 6.30 to 9 (10 Fri and Sat). **Closed:** Mon, 24 to 30 Dec. **Meals:** alc (main courses £11 to £20). Set L and D £10 (2 courses). Sun L £19.75. **Service:** 10% (optional). **Details:** Cards accepted. 55 seats. No mobile phones. Wheelchair access. Music. Children allowed.

Jevington

The Hungry Monk

Endearing eatery with resourceful cooking
Jevington Road, Jevington, BN26 5QF
Tel no: (01323) 482178
www.hungrymonk.co.uk
Modern European | £35
Cooking score: 2

In the hinterland between Brighton and Eastbourne, the Mackenzies' long-running restaurant is an endearingly rustic, stone-built place, all wonky beams and jumbled furniture inside. It's run with a sense of warm hospitality that is appreciated by readers, who are also impressed by the accomplished and resourceful cooking. A squid and mussel stew might be the tempting prelude to a carefully constructed main course such as roast rabbit wrapped in prosciutto, stuffed with ham and leeks and served with mustard sauce. To finish, there is always the famous banoffi pie (invented here) or perhaps macadamia and caramel cheesecake. Four French house wines are £17.95.
Chef/s: Gary Fisher. **Open:** Wed to Sun L 12 to 2 (2.30 Sun), Tue to Sun D 6.45 to 9.30 (9 Sun). **Closed:** Mon. **Meals:** alc (main courses £17 to £21). Set D £35.50 (3 courses). Sun L £30.95. **Service:** 12.5% (optional). **Details:** Cards accepted. 38 seats. No music. No mobile phones. Wheelchair access. Children allowed. Car parking.

Lewes

NEW ENTRY

The Kings Head

Foodie pub where pure flavours shine
9 Southover High Street, Lewes, BN7 1HS
Tel no: (01273) 474628
Modern British | £26
Cooking score: 2

The team behind The Foragers in Hove (see entry) have refashioned this green-gabled boozer close to the ruins of Lewes Priory as a youthful foodie pub with local affiliations. Traditional wooden floors and low ceilings belie a thoroughly modern culinary approach that does full justice to free-range, seasonal and sustainable produce. Pure flavours are allowed to shine in starters of wild rabbit rillettes or asparagus with hot butter and almonds, while mains might usher in unctuous pot-roasted belly pork, succulent skirt steak with hand-cut chips or delicate pan-fried wild black bream. For afters, exemplary hazelnut tart should do the trick. Wines from £13.85 (£3.65 a glass).

Chef/s: John Aldridge. **Open:** all week L 12 to 3 (4 Sat and Sun), Mon to Sat D 6 to 10. **Meals:** alc (main courses £12 to £17). Bar menu available. **Service:** not inc. **Details:** Cards accepted. 40 seats. 70 seats outside. Separate bar. Wheelchair access. Music. Children allowed.

Rye

The George Grill

Well-to-do inn with good ingredients
98 High Street, Rye, TN31 7JT
Tel no: (01797) 222114
www.thegeorgeinrye.com
Modern European | £26
Cooking score: 2

Extensive renovation has ensured that the sixteenth-century George now takes pride of place on Rye's pretty high street. There's a wonderful mix of the old – expect ancient timbers and a blazing winter fire in the lively George Tap, and a buzzy, informal atmosphere and open-to-view kitchen in the stylishly extended restaurant. Andrew Billings oversees an all-day, Mediterranean grill-style menu of simple modern dishes that make the most of Rye Bay fish and top-drawer local and seasonal produce. The monthly changing menu offers the likes of beef carpaccio with celeriac rémoulade or potted shrimps with fennel salad, ahead of 'superb' Romney Marsh lamb chop with roast samphire, toasted hazelnuts and salsa verde, or whole grilled lobster with garlic, chilli and parsley. Comforting desserts include sticky toffee pudding. House wines from £18.

Chef/s: Andrew Billings. **Open:** all week 12 to 10. **Meals:** alc (main courses £12 to £25). **Service:** not inc. **Details:** Cards accepted. 75 seats. 30 seats outside. Separate bar. Music. Children allowed.

Landgate Bistro

Landmark venue with fine local food
5-6 Landgate, Rye, TN31 7LH
Tel no: (01797) 222829
www.landgatebistro.co.uk
Modern British | £27
Cooking score: 3

Snuggled into a pair of conjoined cottages behind elegant Regency shopfronts, the long-running Landgate is a landmark venue on one of the prettier stretches of Sussex coast. Martin Peacock has some fine local produce to call on, not least the famous Rye Bay scallops, which may appear wrapped in bacon and sauced with sherry and shallots. Meats from the vicinity might appear as a main course of local boar spiked with cumin and chilli, served with lemon couscous and Greek yoghurt, although lamb shank in red wine and balsamic with creamy mash may prove equally hard to resist. Zingy lemon tart with matching sorbet ends things well. Sussex ales are on hand to supplement the short wine list, with house French at £14.60.

Chef/s: Martin Peacock. **Open:** Sat and Sun L 12 to 2.15, Tues to Sat D 7 to 9 (9.15 Sat), Sun (bank hol weekends only) D 7 to 9. **Closed:** Mon, 24, 26 and 31

Dec, bank hols. **Meals:** alc (main courses £11 to £19). Set L £12.90 (2 courses) to £15.90. Set D (Wed and Thur only) £15.90 (2 courses) to £18.90. **Service:** not inc. **Details:** Cards accepted. 32 seats. Separate bar. No mobile phones. Music. Children allowed.

Webbe's at the Fish Café

Easy-going seafood eatery
17 Tower Street, Rye, TN31 7AT
Tel no: (01797) 222226
www.webbesrestaurants.co.uk
Seafood | £24
Cooking score: 2

This rather stark, red-brick building on one of the main roads through Rye attracts its share of punters, the main draw being the spanking fresh seafood served in the open-plan ground floor café. Rye Bay scallops, locally smoked haddock and mackerel, and beer-battered cod are staples, although the kitchen's eclectic haul might also yield char-grilled squid with pak choi and spring onion stir-fry with sweet soy and tamarind sauce, or monkfish and tiger prawn Thai green curry. Desserts include crème caramel, perhaps with blood oranges, but a plate of English cheeses makes a tempting alternative. House wine is £14.95.
Chef/s: Matthew Drinkwater. **Open:** all week L 12 to 2.30, D 6 to 9.30. **Closed:** 2 weeks Jan. **Meals:** alc (main courses £10 to £17). **Service:** not inc. **Details:** Cards accepted. 90 seats. No mobile phones. Wheelchair access. Music. Children allowed.

READERS RECOMMEND

Hayden's

British
108 High Street, Rye, TN31 7JE
Tel no: (01797) 224501
www.haydensinrye.co.uk
'The food is hearty and straightforward and portions are very generous.'

Westfield

The Wild Mushroom

Discreet, pleasing country restaurant
Woodgate House, Westfield Lane, Westfield, TN35 4SB
Tel no: (01424) 751137
www.wildmushroom.co.uk
Modern British | £28
Cooking score: 3

Set in a converted Victorian farmhouse, the Wild Mushroom has been pleasing the locals for years, but seems to have stepped up a gear of late. Inside, the mood is discreetly classy, with knowledgeable staff on hand to meet, greet and advise. Details such as home-baked breads and canapés suggest the kitchen is on fine form, and there is much to applaud elsewhere. Fish is mostly from the South Coast boats – perhaps delicate tartare of mackerel or wild sea bass with pak choi – and there's also local game in season (roast breast and confit mallard with port and orange sauce, say). Generous, slow-cooked meat dishes such as ox cheek in Shiraz sauce are recommended too, and desserts show exemplary attention to detail: try the iced peanut parfait with salted praline and strawberry jam. House wine is £16.95.
Chef/s: Chris Weddle and Paul Webbe. **Open:** Tue to Sun L 12 to 2 (2.30 Sun), Tue to Sat D 7 to 9.30. **Closed:** Mon, 25 Dec, 15 to 22 Aug, 24 to 31 Oct. **Meals:** alc (main courses £12 to £19). Set L £16.95 (2 courses) to £19.95. Sun L £23. Tasting menu £32. **Service:** not inc. **Details:** Cards accepted. 40 seats. Separate bar. No mobile phones. Wheelchair access. Music. Children allowed. Car parking.

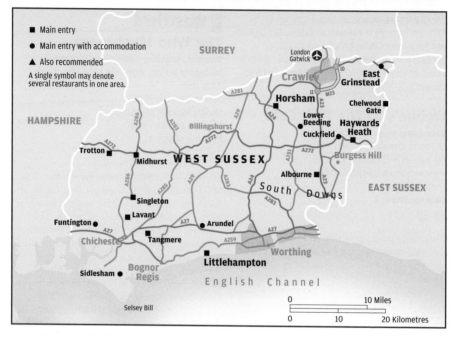

■ Main entry
● Main entry with accommodation
▲ Also recommended
A single symbol may denote several restaurants in one area.

Albourne

The Ginger Fox

Convivial country pub star
Muddleswood Road, Albourne, BN6 9EA
Tel no: (01273) 857888
www.gingermanrestaurants.com
Modern British | £25
Cooking score: 4

Sitting handsomely at the junction of two roads, this reassuringly solid thatched pub consists of a series of dining areas – and some space for drinking and sitting – with stone and wood floors, an open fire and a rustic look that's straight out of the pages of *Country Living*. The kitchen sets its sights on the abundant Sussex larder for some terrific ideas. Good ingredients, like Redlands Farm ribeye, are given what has become standard modern treatment: grounded in tradition but spiced up with Eastern promise and flavours of the Mediterranean. Venison kofta accompanied neatly by fennel and blood orange salad and tzatziki or spicy pheasant spring rolls with ketjap manis (a syrupy Indonesian version of soy sauce) sit alongside sound classics like beef, mushroom and ale pie or slow-braised lamb shoulder. Desserts find their voice with chocolate bavarois, blood orange jelly and orange chocolate-chip ice cream. House wine is £15. (West Sussex outpost of Ben McKellar's mini empire – see Gingerman, Ginger Dog and Ginger Pig in Brighton).
Chef/s: Caye Nunez and Ben McKellar. **Open:** all week L 12 to 2 (12.30 to 3 Sat, 12.30 to 4 Sun), D 6 to 10. **Closed:** 25 Dec. **Meals:** alc (main courses £11.50 to £17.50). Set L £10 (2 courses). **Service:** not inc. **Details:** Cards accepted. 60 seats. 90 seats outside. Separate bar. Wheelchair access. Music. Children allowed. Car parking.

Average Price

The average price listed in main-entry reviews denotes the price of a three-course meal, without wine.

Arundel

Arundel House

Spot-on restaurant-with-rooms
11 High Street, Arundel, BN18 9AD
Tel no: (01903) 882136
www.arundelhouseonline.com
Modern European | £30
Cooking score: 2

The very model of a reinvigorated, prosperous restaurant-with-rooms, Arundel House goes about its business diligently. Uncomplicated cooking of mostly local ingredients is the kitchen's forte, and set-price menus offer a generous choice of six items per course, with a supplement here and there for, perhaps, a starter of scallops fashionably paired with black pudding, crispy pancetta and sweet chilli dressing. Move on to rabbit loin and pigeon breast, flash-fried and teamed with parsnip purée and roasted new potatoes, and finish with pear parfait with hot glazed poached pear. It is all supported by an impressive, reasonably priced wine list, strong on French classics but offering fine bottles from all quarters too. Prices start at £18, and there is an admirable choice by the half-bottle.
Chef/s: Luke Hackman. **Open:** Tue to Sat L 12 to 2, D 7 to 9.30. **Closed:** Sun, Mon, 24 to 28 Dec, 1 week Apr, 1 week Oct. **Meals:** Set L £18 (2 courses) to £24. Set D £24 (2 courses) to £30. **Service:** 10% (optional). **Details:** Cards accepted. 32 seats. Music.

ALSO RECOMMENDED

▲ The Town House

65 High Street, Arundel, BN18 9AJ
Tel no: (01903) 883847
www.thetownhouse.co.uk
Modern British

Reporters love the 'first-class food, very good service and splendid décor' of this restaurant-with-rooms opposite the castle. A special feature is the magnificent, sixteenth-century gilded ceiling, transported in its entirety from Italy by a previous owner. The food impresses with its serious intentions. The set-price menu (lunch £19.50, dinner £29 for three courses) might offer scallops with pea purée, then glazed belly pork with spiced white cabbage and fondant potatoes, and burnt lemon cream for dessert. House wine is £13.95. Closed Sun and Mon.

Chelwood Gate

NEW ENTRY

Red Lion

Inviting pub with fine food
Lewes Road, Chelwood Gate, RH17 7DE
Tel no: (01825) 740265
www.raffansredlion.co.uk
Modern British | £24
Cooking score: 4

Regular readers will remember Mark Raffan as chef and co-proprietor of Gravetye Manor (see entry). He has now taken on this beautifully located Shepherd Neame pub a few miles down the road. It looks inviting. Beyond the bar is a classy open-plan dining area, which leads out onto a vast expanse of garden (a work in progress) with the Ashdown Forest beyond. The menu is perfectly pitched to suit both locals and visitors from further afield with an appetite for big-city food: simple ideas like fish and chips or steak and mushroom pie line up alongside 'very fine' seared Rye Bay scallops with creamed leeks, tomato salsa and pea shoots – which one reporter devoured with 'gusto'. Other well-reported dishes have included fillet of baby sea bass with spring onion potato, leeks, prawns, capers and lemon-herb butter, and a memorable dessert of vanilla pannacotta with poached Yorkshire rhubarb. Wines from £16.
Chef/s: Mark Raffan. **Open:** Tue to Fri and Sun L 12 to 3 (5 Sun), D 5 to 11. Sat 12 to 11. **Closed:** Mon. **Meals:** alc (main courses £11 to £17). **Service:** not inc. **Details:** Cards accepted. 90 seats. 90 seats outside. Separate bar. Wheelchair access. Music. Car parking.

Cuckfield

Ockenden Manor

Top-end cooking with panache
Ockenden Lane, Cuckfield, RH17 5LD
Tel no: (01444) 416111
www.hshotels.co.uk
Modern French | £53
Cooking score: 5

£5 OFF

Ockenden Manor is a small country house in an extended seventeenth-century building, quite away from it all in its nine acres of grounds, but hardly out of the town centre. It is grand and humble at the same time – not as personalised as some, nor as anaesthetised as others, though by the time you read this the spa and extra bedrooms may have opened. Prize draw, though, must be Stephen Crane's dazzling culinary talent. He uses plenty of upmarket materials – Carlingford oysters, for example, served au naturel, as a beignet and in a fricassee with cucumber and horseradish, or sauté foie gras with apple, grapes and verjus – but such ingredients often share the stage with relatively humble ones: witness a dish of bresaola, brisket, tongue and bone marrow of Longhorn beef, or ox cheek with parsnip gratin and bourguignon sauce. The fixed-price lunch menu is good value; perhaps scallop with delicate gnocchi and silky wild mushroom ragù, then smoked haddock with mashed potato, French beans and a perfect poached egg, and a pleasantly citrusy caramelised lemon tart with a restrained blackcurrant sauce for dessert. Extras may not be in quite the same league, but good bread comes in different varieties. The wine list is a high-class heavyweight, with prices to match. Ten house selections at £23 offer the best value.

Chef/s: Stephen Crane. **Open:** all week L 12 to 2, D 6.30 to 9. **Meals:** Set L £16.50 (2 courses) to £23.45. Set D £53 (3 courses). **Service:** not inc.
Details: Cards accepted. 70 seats. Separate bar. No music. No mobile phones. Wheelchair access. Children allowed. Car parking.

READERS RECOMMEND

Cuckoo Restaurant

Modern European
1 Broad Street, Cuckfield, RH17 5LJ
Tel no: (01444) 414184
www.cuckoorestaurant.co.uk
'We knew we were in for a treat before we had even walked through the door.'

East Grinstead

Gravetye Manor

Enchanting Elizabethan charmer
Vowels Lane, East Grinstead, RH19 4LJ
Tel no: (01342) 810567
www.gravetyemanor.co.uk
Modern British | £50
Cooking score: 4

As you motor along the mile-long wooded drive expect to be wowed. Set in a peaceful valley and surrounded by the natural garden created by famed Victorian horticulturalist William Robinson, this enchanting Elizabethan house has a timeless quality. Following a period of uncertainty, both hotel and restaurant are back on song, with a gently refurbished interior, polished, unstuffy service, and accomplished cooking from a confident kitchen brigade headed by Rupert Gleadow. He draws on locally sourced organic ingredients and seasonal produce from the walled kitchen garden: plump seared scallops with cauliflower purée, curry foam and coriander shoots, a perfectly cooked turbot fillet served with brown crab mousse, asparagus and tomatoes and chervil vinaigrette, and apple pannacotta with poached rhubarb and rhubarb sorbet. The majestic wine list promises good drinking from £23.

Chef/s: Rupert Gleadow. **Open:** all week L 12 to 2, D 6.30 to 9.30. **Meals:** alc (main courses £17 to £28). Set L £20 (2 courses) to £25. Set D £30 (2 courses) to £37. Sun L £35. **Service:** 12.5% (optional).
Details: Cards accepted. 45 seats. 20 seats outside. Separate bar. No music. No mobile phones. Wheelchair access. Car parking.

East Wittering

READERS RECOMMEND

Samphire

Modern British
57 Shore Road, East Wittering, PO20 8DY
Tel no: (01243) 672754
www.samphireeastwittering.co.uk
'Absolutely fantastic! Delicious Dover sole and heavenly puddings too.'

Funtington

Hallidays

Village restaurant with notable food
Watery Lane, Funtington, PO18 9LF
Tel no: (01243) 575331
www.hallidays.info
Modern British | £35
Cooking score: 2

The thatched, flint-built cottages from which Halliday's has been hewn date back to the fourteenth century, and are a thoroughly atmospheric pastoral setting for seasonally based cooking that makes good use of local supply lines. Andrew Stephenson rings the changes weekly on menus that might take in home-cured gravadlax with a potato pancake, beetroot relish and crème fraîche, followed by daube of venison in red wine with herbed mash or roast skate in classic array, with capers, parsley and lemon. Dessert might be a buttermilk mousse flavoured with Seville orange, served with poached rhubarb. Wines start at £16.50.
Chef/s: Andrew Stephenson. **Open:** Wed to Fri and Sun L 12 to 3. Wed to Sat D 6 to 9. **Closed:** Mon, Tue, 1 week Mar, 2 weeks Aug. **Meals:** alc (main courses £17 to £19). Set L £14.50 (2 courses) to £19.50. Set D £21 (2 courses) to £26. Sun L £22. **Service:** not inc. **Details:** Cards accepted. 26 seats. Separate bar. No music. Wheelchair access. Children allowed. Car parking.

Haywards Heath

Jeremy's Restaurant

Enchanting venue where ingredients rule
Borde Hill Garden, Balcombe Road, Haywards Heath, RH16 1XP
Tel no: (01444) 441102
www.jeremysrestaurant.com
Modern European | £35
Cooking score: 4

£5 OFF

'An unpretentious restaurant full of smiling people', observed one reader who was bowled over by this enchanting venue among the verdant delights of Borde Hill Garden – eating alfresco is a must when the weather's kind. Guide followers will be familiar with Jeremy Ashpool's earlier ventures and fans will also know that his cooking goes with the flow, picking up a trend here and there but always allowing ingredients to dictate proceedings. He enlivens tea-smoked Barbary duck with carrot purée and blood orange dressing, serves the ubiquitous roast belly pork with crackling and lightly steamed kale, and offers South Coast brill with clams, buttered spinach and crushed Pink Fir Apple potatoes. Creative dishes such as grilled polenta with portobello mushrooms and braised fennel show empathy with the veggie cause, while desserts promise seasonal goodies including buttermilk and thyme pannacotta with roasted rhubarb. A neat global wine list starts at £16.50.
Chef/s: Jeremy Ashpool and Richard Cook. **Open:** Tue to Sun L 12.30 to 2.30 (3 Sun), Tue to Sat D 7 to 9.30. **Closed:** Mon, first 2 weeks Jan. **Meals:** alc (main courses £15 to £24). Set L and D £15 (2 courses) to £18. Sun L £25 (2 courses) to £29.50. **Service:** not inc. **Details:** Cards accepted. 60 seats. 40 seats outside. Separate bar. No mobile phones. Wheelchair access. Music. Children allowed. Car parking.

Horsham

Restaurant Tristan

Cracking quality and bright ideas
3 Stans Way, Horsham, RH12 1HU
Tel no: (01403) 255688
www.restauranttristan.co.uk
Modern European | £38
Cooking score: 5

Since opening in 2008, Tristan Mason has created quite a stir in Horsham's old town, for the sort of cooking you might normally expect to have to head to the city lights to find. The first-floor room in a beamed sixteenth-century house has been kitted out in spare contemporary style, with small multi-coloured abstracts and unclothed black tables. It's a fitting context for a cooking style that mixes modern British thinking with French techniques, on menus that use random capitalisations to add to the thought-provoking nature of the dishes. Combinations sound risky, but arrive on the plate (or slate) in fine fettle, as when lobster ravioli and rabbit terrine appear hand-in-hand with some blackened leek and the scent of truffle. A quail's egg in kataifi (shredded filo) is accompanied by a venison burger in a velouté of this year's must-have, the wild herb alexanders. Unusual ingredients crop up in mains too, when a little oca (a yam-like tuber) makes a garnish for lamb saddle, pastilla and aubergine – or there might just be a positively mainstream partnership of lemon sole and crab, alongside wild mushrooms and Jerusalem artichoke. Tristan's take on tiramisu is worth a punt, as is the banana tarte Tatin with walnut and parsley ice cream. The well-written wine list continues to develop in the right direction. Prices open at £19.

Chef/s: Tristan Mason. **Open:** Tue to Sat L 12 to 2.30, D 6.30 to 9.30. **Closed:** Sun, Mon, 25 to 31 Dec. **Meals:** Set L £14 (2 courses) to £18. Set D £14 (2 courses) to £38. Tasting menu £50. **Service:** 12.5% (optional). **Details:** Cards accepted. 38 seats. No mobile phones. Wheelchair access. Music. Children allowed.

Lavant

The Earl of March

Historic inn with upbeat modern food
Lavant Road, Lavant, PO18 0BQ
Tel no: (01243) 533993
www.theearlofmarch.com
Modern British | £30
Cooking score: 4
£5 OFF

Records confirm that William Blake penned *Jerusalem* while gazing across the South Downs from this 200-year-old coaching inn, and the views out to Goodwood are still truly inspirational. But 'green and pleasant' vistas now have to compete with some upbeat modern food – thanks to Giles Thompson and his team. Pub lunches are served in the bar, but it pays to upgrade to the restaurant for generous dishes such as 'meltingly tender' venison prettily presented on chive mash with red cabbage, curly kale and roasted root vegetables. Local flavours loom large, whether it's butternut squash soup with Sussex Blue cheese, rack of Southdown lamb with aubergine caviar or vanilla pannacotta with spiced mulled plums. Fans of slate get their fill of the stuff here – it turns up on the floor of the light-filled dining room and is used for plating up all manner of different dishes. 'Mini gastronauts' have their own menu and wine drinkers can expect sound drinking from £15.80.

Chef/s: Giles Thompson and Ben Eve. **Open:** all week L 12 to 2.30 (4 Sun), D 5.30 to 9.30 (12 to 9.30 Apr to Oct). **Meals:** alc (main courses £14 to £18). Pre-theatre D £18.50 (2 courses) to £22.50. **Service:** not inc. **Details:** Cards accepted. 70 seats. 60 seats outside. Separate bar. Wheelchair access. Music. Children allowed. Car parking.

Littlehampton

East Beach Café

Eye-popping seaside drop-in
Sea Road, Littlehampton, BN17 5GB
Tel no: (01903) 731903
www.eastbeachcafe.co.uk
Modern British | £23
Cooking score: 2

A beach café and seaside kiosk like no other, this radical piece of architectural 'driftwood' (courtesy of Thomas Heatherwick) is guaranteed to get tongues wagging with its extraordinary weatherbeaten design and refreshingly honest, family-friendly food. Presentation can seem rough-hewn and prices are on the high side, but the kitchen's heart is in the right place: sustainable seafood and local ingredients crop up in everything from weekend breakfasts to lunches and seasonal suppers. Kick off with ham hock salad or crab and leek tart, move on to fish stew, pumpkin spring rolls or a bespoke East Beach burger, and conclude with steamed pear pudding. Wines from £13.95.

Chef/s: David Whiteside. **Open:** all week L 12 to 3 (3.30 Sun), D 6.30 to 8.30 (D Thur to Sat only from Oct to Jun). **Closed:** 21 to 26 Dec. **Meals:** alc (main courses £9 to £17). **Service:** not inc. **Details:** Cards accepted. 60 seats. Wheelchair access. Music. Children allowed. Car parking.

Lower Beeding

The Pass

Dazzling fireworks from a formidable chef
South Lodge Hotel, Brighton Road, Lower Beeding, RH13 6PS
Tel no: (01403) 891711
www.southlodgehotel.co.uk
Modern British | £35
Cooking score: 7

Not the least achievement of the chef's-table trend of recent years has been a distinct improvement in the working atmosphere in restaurant kitchens. All the 'effing and blinding' that so horrified TV viewers has now given way to the gentler manners that befit polite company. The South Lodge Hotel just outside Horsham has made a virtue of the spectator principle by installing not just one table but a whole small restaurant in the kitchen pass, complete with video monitors for those with their backs to the action. Here, the phenomenon is in total harmony with the level of proficiency, as Matt Gillan is a formidably talented chef with a host of good ideas and the skills to bring them to dazzling fruition. Choose the number of courses you feel you can get through, and then settle back for the firework display. Dishes explore the full range of taste categories, textures and temperatures: an early course might be beetroot tartare and horseradish ice cream with orange and watercress, followed perhaps by a serving of salmon confit with celeriac, cucumber and passion fruit. Presentations are, as one reader attests, 'imaginative and delicate', even for something like Middle White pork with cabbage and cassoulet, while desserts are the best kind of naughty, adding popcorn and soy sauce to pannacotta. With standard glasses starting at £9.25, wine prices reflect the five-star surroundings.

Chef/s: Matt Gillan. **Open:** Wed to Sun L 12 to 2, D 7 to 9. **Closed:** Mon, Tue, 2 weeks Jan. **Meals:** alc (main courses £14 to £19). Set D £35 (5 courses). Sun L £35. Tasting menu £45 (6 courses) to £70. **Service:** 10% (optional). **Details:** Cards accepted. 22 seats. Separate bar. No music. No mobile phones. Children allowed. Car parking.

Please send us your feedback

To register your opinion about any restaurant listed in the Guide, or a new restaurant that you wish to bring to our attention, please visit the web address at the bottom of the page. Your feedback informs the content of the book and will be used to compile next year's reviews.

Midhurst

★ PUB OF THE YEAR ★

The Duke of Cumberland Arms

Breathtaking pub with hearty Brit food
Henley, Midhurst, GU27 3HQ
Tel no: (01428) 652280
www.dukeofcumberland.com
Modern British | £32
Cooking score: 3

Infectiously welcoming, this renovated country pub makes the most of its centuries-old building and amazing setting on a hillside in the middle of the Sussex countryside. Local ales tapped straight from the cask and ancient beams set the tone in the bar, where hearty Brit food – cottage pie, fish and chips – please the lunchtime crowd. The same menu is offered in the contemporary dining room, but it pays to plan an evening visit, when Simon Goodman's cooking has a more cosmopolitan edge and an acute seasonal feel: samphire with prawns in lemon and garlic butter, and scallops with pea purée, crispy bacon and asparagus velouté opened one May meal. Elsewhere, confit belly pork with apple and Calvados glaze, creamed Savoy cabbage and thyme and port jus displays fine-tuned flavours, and dessert can be the lightest of sticky toffee puddings. Alfresco opportunities are many, service is superb and house wine is £13.

Chef/s: Simon Goodman. **Open:** all week L 12 to 2, Tue to Sat D 7 to 9. **Meals:** alc (main courses £16 to £22). **Service:** not inc. **Details:** Cards accepted. 56 seats. 80 seats outside. Separate bar. Music. Children allowed. Car parking.

To find out more about *The Good Food Guide*, please visit www.thegoodfoodguide.co.uk

Sidlesham

The Crab & Lobster

Bang-up-to-date Brit cooking
Mill Lane, Sidlesham, PO20 7NB
Tel no: (01243) 641233
www.crab-lobster.co.uk
Modern European | £34
Cooking score: 3

Situated down a small Sussex lane near Pagham Harbour nature reserve, this chic restaurant-with-rooms has come a long way since it was transformed from a tired boozer into a stylish food destination. It may still look like a pub with its fireplaces and flagstone floors, but the cooking is bang-up-to-date and the food is driven by well-sourced local produce. Reporters have praised the seafood dishes – perhaps Selsey crab and king prawn cocktail, or a main course of sea bass on champ with clam and smoked-bacon fish cream. Meatier main courses might take in slow-braised belly pork with garden pea purée, black pudding and Madeira jus. One reader praised the 'wonderful and very friendly' service. Bottles start at £15.85.

Chef/s: Macolm Goble. **Open:** Mon to Fri L 12 to 2.30, D 6 to 9.30 (10 Fri), Sat and Sun 12 to 10 (9 Sun). **Meals:** alc (main courses £15 to £28). Set L £18.50 (2 courses) to £21.50. **Service:** not inc. **Details:** Cards accepted. 48 seats. 50 seats outside. Wheelchair access. Music. Children allowed. Car parking.

Singleton

The Partridge Inn

Pub favourites and plenty of choice
Singleton, PO18 0EY
Tel no: (01243) 811251
www.thepartridgeinn.co.uk
British | £25
Cooking score: 1

Two years on and this younger sibling of the Earl of March in nearby Lavant (see entry) has worn in and warmed up very nicely. It dates

from the sixteenth century and there's period feel by the pint (expect locally brewed ales on tap), though food is a key part of the operation. A flexible approach means plenty of choice – with an array of starters, sandwiches and light bites, plus plates of pub favourites including sausage and mash or beer-battered cod fillet and chips, backed up by blackboard specials. House wine is £14.95.

Chef/s: Achim Klein. **Open:** all week L 12 to 2 (3 Sat and Sun), D 6 to 9 (9.30 Fri and Sat). **Meals:** alc (main courses £11 to £20). **Service:** not inc. **Details:** Cards accepted. 70 seats. 80 seats outside. Separate bar. Wheelchair access. Music. Children allowed. Car parking.

Tangmere

Cassons

Good food near Goodwood
Arundel Road, Tangmere, PO18 0DU
Tel no: (01243) 773294
www.cassonsrestaurant.co.uk
Modern British | £39
Cooking score: 2

'A treat in all ways', just about sums up this endearing restaurant, which runs along happily with Vivian and Cass Casson at the helm. It occupies two nineteenth-century farm workers' cottages and pleases visitors with a distinct brand of modern British cooking. Scallops with fresh herb purée and smoked salmon crisps, 'rich and perfectly tender' venison fillet, and loin, belly and confit leg of suckling pig (with crackling, potato mille-feuille, parsnip velouté, wilted greens and cider reduction) have been well received. Praise, too, for dark chocolate cylinder with chocolate mousse, passion fruit and passion fruit sorbet. Wines from £20.

Chef/s: Vivian Casson. **Open:** Wed to Sun L 12 to 2 (2.30 Sun), Tue to Sat D 7 to 10. **Closed:** Mon, 26 to 30 Dec, 1 Jan. **Meals:** Set L £15 (2 courses) to £20. Set D weekdays £24 (2 courses) to £31. Set D weekends £31 (2 courses) to £39. Sun L £22.50 (2 courses) to £28. **Service:** not inc. **Details:** Cards accepted. 36 seats. 16 seats outside. Separate bar. No mobile phones. Wheelchair access. Music. Children allowed. Car parking.

Tillington

READERS RECOMMEND

The Horse Guards Inn

Modern British
Upper Road, Tillington, GU28 9AF
Tel no: (01798) 342332
www.thehorseguardsinn.co.uk
'Pretty old inn that rambles out into a lovely garden; food is taken seriously here.'

Trotton

The Keepers Arms

Dyed-in-the-wool Sussex pub
Terwick Lane, Trotton, GU31 5ER
Tel no: (01730) 813724
www.keepersarms.co.uk
Modern British | £26
Cooking score: 1

The Keepers Arms is an ancient country pub tweaked for the twenty-first century. Beams, standing timbers, polished tables and a pair of open fires keep the interior somewhere between hostelry and restaurant. The food is a promising mix of pub classics (fish and chips or burgers) and brasserie favourites jazzed up with a few voguish flourishes, say mushroom duxelle tart with a poached egg and hollandaise followed by fillet of turbot with asparagus, wild garlic pesto and broad bean tagliatelle. Wines from £15.

Chef/s: Charlotte Piper-Hodgson. **Open:** all week L 12 to 2 (2.30 Sun), D 6.30 to 9.30 (7 to 9 Sun). **Closed:** 25 and 26 Dec. **Meals:** alc (main courses £13 to £22). **Service:** not inc. **Details:** Cards accepted. 50 seats. 26 seats outside. Separate bar. Wheelchair access. Music. Children allowed. Car parking.

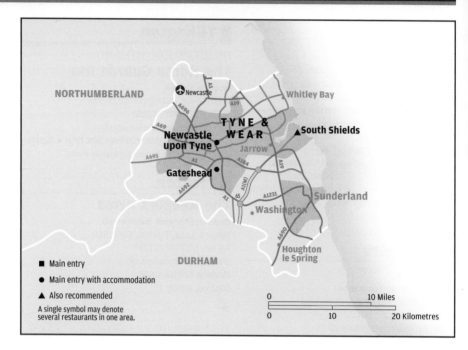

NORTHUMBERLAND
Newcastle
Whitley Bay
TYNE & WEAR
South Shields
Newcastle upon Tyne
Jarrow
Gateshead
Sunderland
Washington
Houghton le Spring
DURHAM
A1
A19
A696
A69
A695
A184
A1(M)
A692
A1231
A690
65

■ Main entry
● Main entry with accommodation
▲ Also recommended
A single symbol may denote several restaurants in one area.

0 10 Miles
0 10 20 Kilometres

Gateshead

Eslington Villa

Satisfying dishes in a civilised setting
8 Station Road, Low Fell, Gateshead, NE9 6DR
Tel no: (0191) 4876017
www.eslingtonvilla.co.uk
Modern British | £25
new chef

Built around 1880 for a local industrialist who fancied a bolt hole away from the region's mining and railways, Eslington Villa stands in two acres of landscaped grounds overlooking a leafy valley. We were notified of the arrival of chef Jamie Walsh too late to respond with an inspection, but the hotel has built a reputation on offering dependable cooking and we feel that this will not change. Eight house selections (from £16.95) open the 60-bin wine list. Reports please.

Chef/s: Jamie Walsh. **Open:** Sun to Fri L 12 to 2 (3 Sun), Mon to Sat D 5.30 to 10 (7 to 10 Sat). **Closed:** 25 and 26 Dec, bank hols. **Meals:** Set L £13.95 (2 courses) to £16.95. Set D £20.95 (2 courses) to £24.95. Sun L £19.50. **Service:** not inc. **Details:** Cards accepted. 80 seats. 20 seats outside. Separate bar. Wheelchair access. Music. Children allowed. Car parking.

Newcastle upon Tyne

Blackfriars Restaurant

Britain's oldest eating house?
Friars Street, Newcastle upon Tyne, NE1 4XN
Tel no: (0191) 2615945
www.blackfriarsrestaurant.co.uk
British | £25
Cooking score: 3

Originally a refectory for Dominican 'blackfriars', this adjunct to the medieval priory (circa 1239) lays claim to being Britain's 'oldest eating house' and revels in its antiquity. Bawdy, ale-swilling bonanzas are staged in the restaurant and the new banqueting hall, or you can soak up the history with a picnic in the grassy courtyard. The kitchen skilfully deploys

a full quota of regional ingredients in its quest for unadulterated Britishness, from potted Northumberland beef with rye bread to traditional 'singing hinnies' (fruity griddle cakes) with hedgerow bramble jam. In between, belly pork with apple and celeriac dumplings or a plate of heritage ribeye with bone-marrow butter should keep the old patriots happy, while smart dishes such as halibut with spelt risotto, sautéed artichokes and smoked chicken wing catapult diners back to the present. Wines start at £15 (£4 a glass).
Chef/s: Troy Terrington. **Open:** all week L 12 to 2.30 (4 Sun), Mon to Sat D 6 to 12. **Closed:** 25 and 26 Dec, 1 Jan, bank hols. **Meals:** alc (main courses £9 to £20). Set L and D £12 (2 courses) to £15. Sun L £11. **Service:** 10% (optional). **Details:** Cards accepted. 72 seats. 50 seats outside. Separate bar. Music. Children allowed.

Café 21

Buzzy, stylish quayside brasserie
Trinity Gardens, Quayside, Newcastle upon Tyne, NE1 2HH
Tel no: (0191) 2220755
www.cafetwentyone.co.uk
Modern British | £38
Cooking score: 3
V

Terry Laybourne's buzzy, stylish quayside brasserie is now into its third decade and remains a well-patronised dining and drinking venue for locals. 'You can relax in a safe pair of hands here', noted one reporter who also praised the 'well-crafted classics cooked with care'. Staff achieve the 'right balance between friendliness and professionalism' and the modern British brasserie food isn't afraid to plunder influences from further afield. Starters may feature an Asian salad with gingered seafood or steak tartare on hot toast, whilst mains take on a more European flavour in the form of coq au vin or grilled lobster with garlic butter, new potatoes and green salad. Finish with an Eton mess or a classic treacle tart. A well-considered wine list starts at £16.95.
Chef/s: Chris Dobson. **Open:** all week L 12 to 2.30, D 5.30 to 10.30. **Closed:** 25 and 26 Dec, 1 Jan, Easter Mon. **Meals:** alc (main courses £14 to £30). Set L and D £16.50 (2 courses) to £20. **Service:** 10% (optional). **Details:** Cards accepted. 100 seats. Separate bar. Wheelchair access. Music. Children allowed.

David Kennedy's Food Social

Relaxed venue with prime food
Biscuit Factory, Stoddart Street, Newcastle upon Tyne, NE2 1AN
Tel no: (0191) 2605411
www.foodsocial.co.uk
Modern British | £26
Cooking score: 3

David Kennedy has transformed his restaurant, previously Brasserie Black Door, by renaming it – the change marks an amicable parting of the ways with co-owner David Ladd. The roomy, bare-boards space continues to blend seamlessly with the art emporium that is the Biscuit Factory (the UK's largest commercial art gallery) and early reports note that the kitchen remains on song. Various menus promise generosity and value in the shape of social bites (tapas-style dishes), well-priced set lunch and early-evening deals, and a carte that could open with North Sea fish soup, go on to rabbit, fennel and tarragon pudding, and finish with hot chocolate fondant with blood orange sorbet. A short, modern wine list 'hits the spot', with bottles starting at £13.50. More reports please.
Chef/s: David Kennedy. **Open:** all week L 12 to 2 (3 Sat and Sun), Mon to Sat D 5.30 to 9 (10 Sat). **Closed:** 25 and 26 Dec, 1 and 2 Jan. **Meals:** alc (main courses £11 to £16). Set L and early D £12.95 (2 courses) to £15.95. Sun L £13.95 (2 courses) to £17.95. **Service:** 10% (optional). **Details:** Cards accepted. 56 seats. Separate bar. Wheelchair access. Music. Children allowed. Car parking.

Fisherman's Lodge

A hidden surprise on Tyneside
Jesmond Dene, Jesmond, Newcastle upon Tyne, NE7 7BQ
Tel no: (0191) 2813281
www.fishermanslodge.co.uk
Modern British | £35
new chef

Built as a retreat for Victorian industrialist and innovator Lord William Armstrong, Fisherman's Lodge nestles within the leafy, secluded expanses of Jesmond Dene – just a short drive from the humming heart of Newcastle. This country idyll on Tyneside is a charmer, although it has had a rather shaky time since changing hands in 2009. Another new chef is now heading up the kitchen and the food still has a modern impetus – plus a few archaic echoes for the traditionalists (think pheasant ballottine or lobster thermidor). Typically you might begin with a fricassee of artichokes with a deep-fried egg, move on to fillet of beef with truffled pomme purée and foie gras casserole, and conclude with pear tarte Tatin or Kahlua soufflé with coffee 'soil' and white chocolate ice cream. House wine is £16.

Chef/s: Daniel Jolley. **Open:** all week L 12 to 2, Mon to Sat D 6 to 9.30. **Closed:** 25 Dec, 1 Jan. **Meals:** alc (main courses £15 to £33). Set L and D £19.95 (2 courses) to £23.95. Sun L £18. **Service:** 10% (optional). **Details:** Cards accepted. 60 seats. 24 seats outside. Separate bar. Wheelchair access. Music. Children allowed. Car parking.

Symbols

Accommodation is available
Three courses for less than £30
V Separate vegetarian menu
£5-off voucher scheme
Notable wine list

Jesmond Dene House

Kitchen full of craft and care
Jesmond Dene Road, Newcastle upon Tyne, NE2 2EY
Tel no: (0191) 2123000
www.jesmonddenehouse.co.uk
Modern European | £50
Cooking score: 5

This stunning Arts and Crafts house set among leafy gardens feels a world away from the bustle of Newcastle but is actually within striking distance of the city centre. Old and new are comfortably combined in the grand public rooms, where sombre wood panelling and gracious stonework are cheered by simple modern furnishings. The dining area spills out into a bold modern conservatory with garden views. Here, impeccable staff do justice to chef Michael Penaluna's precise but sometimes playful cooking: a 'to-die-for and very clever' chocolate sphere which melts as hot chocolate sauce is poured over it to reveal an ice cream, shortbread and caramel filling is a case in point. An inspection visit got off to a swimming start with an amuse of tomato and pepper gazpacho with cucumber jelly and Mozzarella, followed by simple but sophisticated venison carpaccio with pickled plums, beetroot and horseradish cream. This is pretty food, with much use of flowers and wild herbs – as in a main of roasted halibut with sesame seeds, garden carrots, carrot and lavender purée, celeriac and cow parsley. The ample international wine list makes interesting reading, and kicks off at a reasonable £16.

Chef/s: Michael Penaluna. **Open:** all week L 12 to 2 (12.30 to 2.30 Sat, 12.30 to 3.15 Sun), D 7 to 9.30 (10 Sat). **Meals:** alc (main courses £19 to £39). Set L £16.50 (2 courses) to £22.50. Set D and Sun L £23 (2 courses) to £26. Tasting menu £55. Bar menu available. **Service:** 10% (optional). **Details:** Cards accepted. 70 seats. 28 seats outside. Separate bar. Wheelchair access. Music. Children allowed. Car parking.

NEW ENTRY

Pan Haggerty

Suave city eatery with ambitious food

21 Queen Street, Newcastle upon Tyne, NE1 3UG

Tel no: (0191) 2210904

www.panhaggerty.com

Modern British | £30

Cooking score: 2

£5 OFF

In the heart of Newcastle's lively Quayside area, this suave metropolitan eatery is decked out in muted earthy shades and simple modern furnishings. The menu promises 'rustic British food' but the reality is more ambitious, as in a starter of herby pea and ham consommé with ham hock and a spring onion dumpling or a main of pan-seared fillet of sea bream with king scallops, leeks and crab bisque. The 'rustic' element is reserved for desserts such as caramelised banana bread-and-butter pudding. A snappy list of international wines starts at £14.50.

Chef/s: Simon Wood. **Open:** all week L 12 to 2.30 (4 Sun), Mon to Sat D 5.30 to 9.30 (5 to 10 Sat). **Closed:** 25 to 27 and 31 Dec, 1 Jan, bank hols. **Meals:** alc (main courses £14 to £20). Set L £12.95 (2 courses) to £15.95. Set early D £14.95 (2 courses) to £17.95. Sun L £12.95 (2 courses) £15.95. **Service:** 10% (optional). **Details:** Cards accepted. 60 seats. Music. Children allowed.

ALSO RECOMMENDED

▲ Caffè Vivo

29 Broad Chare, Newcastle upon Tyne, NE1 3DQ

Tel no: (0191) 2321331

www.caffevivo.co.uk

Italian

Newcastle supremo Terry Laybourne's latest venture comes with an Italian accent; the bustling, glass-fronted café is dedicated to the freshest and most straightforward kind of Italian cooking. The flexible, easy-eating menus stay mainly with popular choices – antipasti boards to share (£7.50 per person) and pasta dishes such as pappardelle with rustic Italian vegetables (£5.60) are generally enjoyable, as are some of the regional main dishes such as Tuscan-braised venison with mascarpone, Parmesan polenta and wild mushrooms. Wines from £15.40. Closed Sun and Mon.

▲ Sky Apple Café

182 Heaton Road, Heaton, Newcastle upon Tyne, NE6 5HP

Tel no: (0191) 2092571

www.skyapple.co.uk

Vegetarian

'Newcastle's favourite left-field veggie', notes a visitor who took a shine to this long-standing shabby chic café, with its 'cosy, homely feel'. Café by day, occasional restaurant by night, hearty breakfasts give way to snacks and more substantial dishes such as battered haloumi and chips, or spinach and cream cheese lasagne (£6.50). The evening menu moves up a gear: hiyashi chukka (a Japanese-style summer salad, £4.80) and chocolate and geranium tart. BYO (licence applied for as we went to press). Cash only. Closed Sun.

South Shields

ALSO RECOMMENDED

▲ Colmans

182-186 Ocean Road, South Shields, NE33 2JQ

Tel no: (0191) 4561202

www.colmansfishandchips.com

Seafood

'Famous for fish and chips since 1926', trumpets this evergreen family business, and many readers agree, considering Colmans to be one of the few outstanding eateries of its kind left in the UK. Unpretentious, no-nonsense, good-quality fish and properly fried chips is what they do, whether it's whiting (£7.50), 'the best haddock, chips and mushy peas', or lemon sole (£13.95). Battered scampi are of an 'unbelievable quality', and staff are 'super-friendly and so helpful'. Wines from £13.95. Open all week.

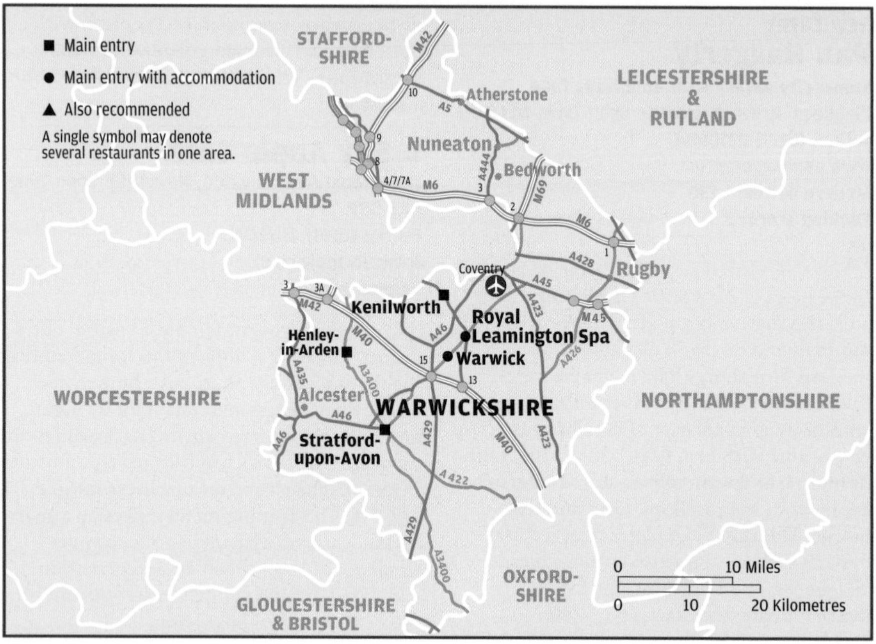

Henley-in-Arden

The Bluebell

Hospitable foodie inn
93 High Street, Henley-in-Arden, B95 5AT
Tel no: (01564) 793049
www.bluebellhenley.co.uk
Modern European | £27
Cooking score: 3

An archetypal half-timbered Tudor inn with top real ales and a good line in local hospitality, the Bluebell is also a serious foodie contender in these parts. Home-grown and carefully sourced ingredients take precedence in the kitchen, and new chef Saleem Ahmed is already winning over the crowds with his skilful modern cooking. Recent hits have included warm pigeon and beetroot salad with a port reduction, steak and local ale pie, and a terrific dish of sticky braised pork belly and cheek with crackling and truffled potatoes. Rustic breads and antipasti boards also get the vote, and meals end in style with noteworthy puddings. Tables by the log fire are like gold dust in winter, and afternoon tea on the terrace is a tempting summertime prospect. The short wine list includes 16 by the glass, with bottles from £15.15.

Chef/s: Saleem Ahmed. **Open:** Tue to Sun L 12 to 2.30 (3.30 Sun), Tue to Sat D 6 to 9.30. **Closed:** Mon. **Meals:** alc (main courses £11 to £27). Set L and D £17.50 (2 courses) to £19.95. **Service:** not inc. **Details:** Cards accepted. 45 seats. 38 seats outside. Separate bar. Music. Children allowed. Car parking.

Kenilworth

Restaurant Bosquet

A slice of provincial France
97a Warwick Road, Kenilworth, CV8 1HP
Tel no: (01926) 852463
www.restaurantbosquet.co.uk
French | £40
Cooking score: 3

Stepping into Bernard and Jane Lignier's beguiling restaurant is like coming upon a devotedly cared-for *pension de famille* in a

French provincial backwater, rather than a busy Kenilworth thoroughfare. Inside, it breathes benevolence, warmth and personality, with a loving collection of pretty prints, antiques and silk drapes all around. Yes, Bosquet may seem set in its Gallic ways (staples ranging from foie gras terrine with truffle dressing to blueberry and almond tart have been around for years), but the kitchen also accommodates more modern thinking – consider veal sweetbreads glazed with pomegranate molasses. Bernard Lignier's breads are of the highest order, and his sure touch shows in a vivid dish of sweetly timed scallops with burnished saffron sauce. But bistro-style presentation can let the side down, and heavy-handed petits fours look 'decidedly amateurish'. French regional wines start at £17.50.

Chef/s: Bernard Lignier. **Open:** Tue to Fri L 12 to 1.15 (bookings only), Tue to Sat D 7 to 9.30. **Closed:** Sun, Mon, 1 week Christmas, 2 weeks July/Aug. **Meals:** alc (main courses £20 to £23). Set L and D Tue to Fri £32.50. **Service:** not inc. **Details:** Cards accepted. 26 seats. No music. No mobile phones. Children allowed.

Leamington Spa

Mallory Court, Main House Dining Room

Gracious country house dining
Harbury Lane, Leamington Spa, CV33 9QB
Tel no: (01926) 330214
www.mallory.co.uk
Modern British | £60
Cooking score: 5

£5 OFF

Just outside Leamington Spa, Mallory Court is an ivy-covered vision of the gracious living of a century ago. That atmosphere has been painstakingly established inside, with sofas to sink into, as well as an oak-panelled dining room in the main house, where the high-backed chairs and elegant table settings create a feeling of effortless refinement. Simon Haigh draws inspiration from the contemporary British and French repertoires to construct a series of fixed-price menus with plenty to mull over. Stuffed quail is poached, then roasted, and comes with celeriac mousse and hazelnuts for an intricately worked opener, while accompaniments based on fine pasta are favoured – perhaps for smoked bacon cannelloni with roasted scallops and butternut squash. Interesting main-course combinations have included red mullet with chicken 'nougat' and Little Gem, but also dishes from the more classical end of the spectrum, such as roast beef fillet with braised oxtail and morels in Madeira sauce. And imaginative labours are brought to bear on desserts, too – a caramelised poached pear might come with eucalyptus mousse and chicory ice cream, or roasted black figs with warm gingerbread and spiced ice. Four wines from the nearby Welcombe Hills vineyard head up a global list that starts at £20.

Chef/s: Simon Haigh. **Open:** Sun to Fri L 12 to 1.30, all week D 6.30 to 8.30 (9 Fri and Sat). **Meals:** Set L £25.50 (2 courses) to £32.50. Set D £45. Sun L £39. **Service:** not inc. **Details:** Cards accepted. 50 seats. 20 seats outside. Separate bar. No mobile phones. Wheelchair access. Music. Children allowed. Car parking.

NEW ENTRY

Restaurant 23

Satisfaction in every mouthful
23 Dormer Place, Leamington Spa, CV32 5AA
Tel no: (01926) 422422
www.restaurant23.co.uk
Modern European | £39
Cooking score: 5

£5 OFF

The first thing you notice on entering this converted Regency town house is the open kitchen. Peter Knibb is happy to show off his work, in fact the whole place has an air of self-assured authority. The dining room is discreet, cosmopolitan and understated, with muted colours, mirrored alcoves and a soundtrack that banishes all thoughts of pompous solemnity. The kitchen delivers hugely enjoyable modern food with razor-sharp technique – not surprising given that Knibb honed his skills alongside Jun Tanaka at Pearl in London (see entry). Everything is fastidiously conceived, but there are bright ideas too. A starter of milky roasted rabbit loin with confit croquettes and tiny morsels of just-bloody liver is lifted with date purée and fragments of crunchy, bitter chicory, while a slab of sea bass is presented on a bundle of shredded leeks with a limpid broth, some palate-rousing chorizo, cocoa beans and charred squid. The kitchen can also handle big, beefy flavours (dry-aged beef fillet with a mound of smoked potato purée and a forceful bordelaise sauce enriched with bone marrow), but it applies a gentler touch to desserts such as Cox's apple terrine with crisp filo, blackberry sorbet and orange purée. Service is accurately judged, all the incidentals are just-so, and the 150-bin wine list is a winner: exceptional selections from Alsace and the Loire head up a strong regional French presence, but also look for idiosyncratic numbers from elsewhere. Bottles start at £18.50.

Chef/s: Peter Knibb. **Open:** Tue to Sat L 12.15 to 2.30, D 6.15 to 9.45. **Closed:** Sun, Mon, 25 and 26 Dec, first 2 weeks Jan, last 2 weeks Aug. **Meals:** alc (main courses £19 to £26). Set L £17 (2 courses) to £19.50. Set D £22 (2 courses) to £25. Tasting menu £55. **Service:** not inc. **Details:** Cards accepted. 24 seats. No mobile phones. Music. Children allowed.

Shipston-on-Stour

READERS RECOMMEND

Ashley James Restaurant

Modern British

Old Mill Hotel, Mill Street, Shipston-on-Stour, CV36 4AW

Tel no: (01608) 661421

www.theoldmillshipston.com

'They are trying very hard, have extremely pleasant staff and dishes are very well presented.'

Stratford-upon-Avon

NEW ENTRY

No 9 Church St

A dandy local drop-in

9 Church Street, Stratford-upon-Avon, CV37 6HB

Tel no: (01789) 415522

www.no9churchst.com

Modern British | £28

Cooking score: 1

£5 OFF £30

On a wide street in Stratford's 'old town', this 400-year-old listed building is now a dandy local drop-in, thanks to culinary buddies Wayne Thomson and Dan Robinson. Shoppers, culture vultures and tourists pack the amiable first-floor dining room for satisfying, no-frills food at eminently 'non-greedy' prices: lunch is a top deal (try a creamy leek risotto with plump mussels followed by braised merguez sausages with smoked paprika, or grilled ling with a poached egg and hollandaise). Evening brings some more ambitious ideas, such as Jimmy Butler's pork 'three ways'. Wines from £14.50.

Chef/s: Wayne Thomson. **Open:** all week L 12 to 2.30 (4 Sun), Mon to Sat D 5.30 to 9.30. **Closed:** 1 week Christmas. **Meals:** alc (main courses £12 to £19). Set L and pre-theatre D £11.50 (2 courses) to £15. Sun L £18. **Service:** not inc. **Details:** Cards accepted. 40 seats. Separate bar. Music. Children allowed.

NEW ENTRY

The Rooftop Restaurant

A feast fit for Falstaff

The Royal Shakespeare Theatre, Waterside, Stratford-upon-Avon, CV37 6BE

Tel no: (01789) 403449

www.rsc.org.uk

British | £25

Cooking score: 2

Quinces, oysters, wild thyme... the appetising menu reads like something from one of the Bard's plays, although this dramatic wraparound eatery/bar above the Royal

Shakespeare Theatre offers much more than 'cakes and ale'. Well-coached, funky staff never miss a cue in the lofty dining room, which has brilliant views of narrowboats and swans on the Avon. The kitchen doffs its hat to St George, and arty presentation celebrates the new culinary Albion – note the juicy, warm potted beef in a Kilner jar sitting beside a piece of 'bone' packed with tarragon butter. Open with roast artichokes, salsify and chard, proceed to a Falstaffian dish of lamb's liver with white pudding mash and curly kale, and bow out with a cheeky take on Eton mess involving those quinces and frangipane tart. Snappy wines from £15.50 (£4 a glass).

Chef/s: Nick Funnell. **Open:** all week 11am to 11pm (12 to 6 Sun). **Closed:** 24 to 26 Dec. **Meals:** alc (main courses £12 to £19). Set L and early D £15.50 (2 courses) to £18.50. **Service:** 10% (optional). **Details:** Cards accepted. 152 seats. 20 seats outside. Separate bar. No music. Wheelchair access. Children allowed.

Warwick

Rose & Crown

Crowd-pulling, down-to-earth pub
30 Market Place, Warwick, CV34 4SH
Tel no: (01926) 411117
www.roseandcrownwarwick.co.uk
British | £30
Cooking score: 1

This straightforward pub scores with a pleasingly simple décor and capable service. It buzzes all day, thanks to its market square location and the fact that it's prepared to invest in decent raw materials. There's little doubt the kitchen can deliver unfussy dishes, from snacky options – deli boards of cheese, charcuterie or fish – to more hearty offerings of, say, bangers and mash or sustainable fishcake with watercress salad and tartare sauce. Warm orange and almond cake is a typical pud. Wines from £14.25.

Chef/s: Simon Malin. **Open:** all week 8am to 10pm (11 Fri and Sat). **Closed:** 25 Dec. **Meals:** alc (main courses £11 to £18). **Service:** 12.5% (optional). **Details:** Cards accepted. 52 seats. 36 seats outside. Separate bar. Music. Children allowed.

Tailors

Creative cuisine from a dynamic duo
22 Market Place, Warwick, CV34 4SL
Tel no: (01926) 410590
www.tailorsrestaurant.co.uk
Modern British | £35
Cooking score: 3

Wedged in among the market square's busy throng, this pint-sized restaurant really was a tailor's, although it's now in the business of delivering high-end cuisine to a gregarious local crowd. Inside it can seem like a 'hotbed of social intercourse', but the young lady of the house controls the show with a diamond mix of chattiness and savoir-faire. Meanwhile, the kitchen's dynamic duo sends out a succession of elaborately worked, challenging ideas on wacky plates. Ingredients are top-notch and presentation is fiercely à la mode – huge, sweetly timed scallops on discs of confit ham hock with apple purée and pungent pickled blackberries, for example, or rump of Lighthorne lamb cooked 'aggressively' pink with a moreish shepherd's pie 'rissole', crushed swede and bubbles of concentrated carrot essence encased in agar 'skin'. Tailors also gets plus points for its bargain-priced set lunch and creative vegetarian menu. House wines start at £15.50.

Chef/s: Dan Cavell and Mark Fry. **Open:** Tue to Sat L 12 to 2, D 6.30 to 9.30. **Closed:** Sun, Mon, 24 to 31 Dec. **Meals:** Set L £12 (2 courses) to £15.95. Early-evening menu £17 (2 courses) to £22. Set D £29.50 (2 courses) to £34.50. **Service:** not inc. **Details:** Cards accepted. 28 seats. Music. Children allowed.

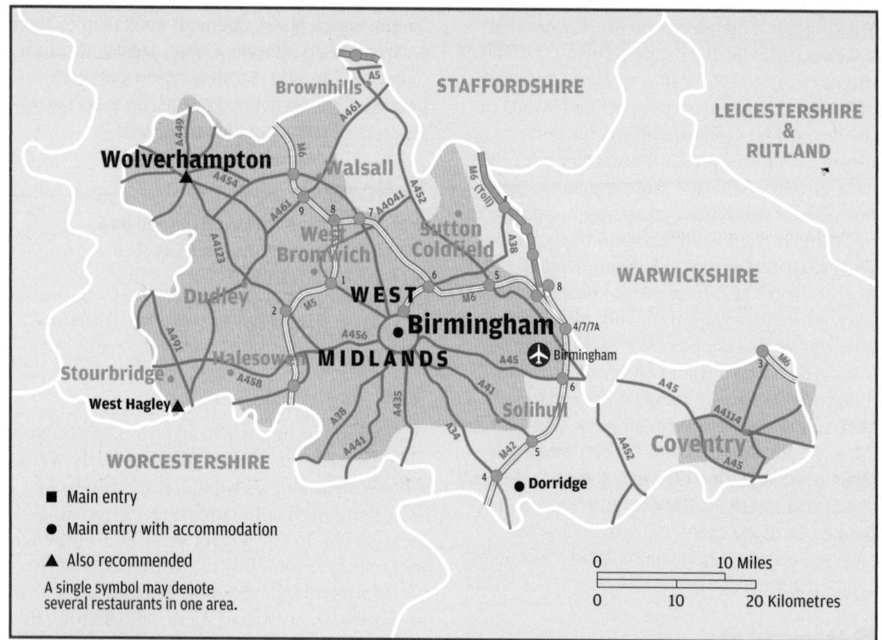

Birmingham

★ READERS' RESTAURANT OF THE YEAR ★
MIDLANDS

Edmunds

Cooking to take your breath away
6 Central Square, Brindleyplace, Birmingham, B1 2JB
Tel no: (0121) 6334944
www.edmundsrestaurant.co.uk
Modern European | £43
Cooking score: 6
£5 OFF 🍷 **V**

There's no shortage of vocal support for Andy Waters' intimate, lovingly maintained restaurant – and rightly so. Set amid the upbeat surroundings of the Brindleyplace canalside development, Edmunds is one of the city's top culinary performers, with a subdued, classy feel enhanced by long drapes, striking modern sculptures on the window sills and gentle light emanating from stainless steel lamps. Urbane civility reigns. Waters is a highly talented chef with classical technique in his blood and a nose for sharp seasonal partnerships – perhaps sea trout and Cornish crab with deep-fried scallop, quail's egg, lemon and poppy seeds; a superb starter of rabbit and wild mushroom lasagne with seared duck liver and rosemary velouté; or pan-seared zander with deep-fried sprats, freshwater crayfish and lime cream sauce. He can also play it straight and true, offering flawless plates of roast Cornish lobster or Jimmy Butler's free-range belly pork embellished with nothing more than apples and Calvados, as well as fashioning all manner of precision-tuned treats ranging from a miniature mozzarella salad served on a silver spoon to Valrhona chocolate délice with a tasting of rhubarb and rosewater syrup. Ultimately, readers adore Waters' smart, 'incredibly flavoursome' cooking for its clarity, attention to detail and all-round excellence: 'whether it's an amuse-bouche, a suckling pig or an unsurpassed fondant, there's always something to take your breath away', commented one fan. Meanwhile, Beverley

Waters and her front-of-house team ensure that regulars and 'fresh faces' are treated with equal courtesy, charm and genuine warmth. Sommelier Nuno Martins' meticulously chosen wine list matches the food at every turn, with top-class producers, no excess baggage and excellent recommendations from £21.50 (£4 a 125ml glass).

Chef/s: Andy Waters. **Open:** Tue to Fri L 12 to 2, Tue to Sat D 7 to 10 (5.30 Fri and Sat). **Closed:** Sun, Mon, 25 and 26 Dec, 1 week Jan, 1 week Apr, 1 week Aug, 1 week Oct. **Meals:** Set L £18 (2 courses) to £20. Set D £39.50 (2 courses) to £42.50. Tasting menu £63.95. **Service:** 10%. **Details:** Cards accepted. 40 seats. 12 seats outside. Wheelchair access. Music.

Hotel du Vin & Bistro

Spectacular bistro with cosmopolitan wine
25 Church Street, Birmingham, B3 2NR
Tel no: (0121) 2000600
www.hotelduvin.com
European | £40
Cooking score: 2

The red-brick magnificence of the building makes this one of the HDV chain's more spectacular architectural gems. Once the Eye Hospital, it sits in the midst of Birmingham's jewellery quarter and is kitted out in the group's chic, faintly retro style. Modern bistro dishes form the menu's backbone, so you could start with scallops in Pernod butter, and motor on with confit duck leg with sticky red cabbage and port jus, while the even more trad plats du jour take in the likes of steak frites and coq au vin. The vast cosmopolitan wine list remains a strong draw, served perhaps as a three-glass flight (from £16) to see you through a meal. Bottles start at £16.50.

Chef/s: Nick Turner. **Open:** all week L 12 to 2 (12. 30 to 2.30 Sat and Sun), D 6 to 10 (10.30 Thur to Sat, 7 to 10 Sun). **Meals:** alc (main courses £12 to £21). Sun L £24. **Service:** 10% (optional). **Details:** Cards accepted. 90 seats. Separate bar. Wheelchair access. Music. Children allowed.

Jyoti's Vegetarian

Zingy treats and rock-bottom prices
1045 Stratford Road, Hall Green, Birmingham, B28 8AS
Tel no: (0121) 7785501
www.jyotis.co.uk
Indian vegetarian | £15
Cooking score: 1

This family-run restaurant serves memorable Indian vegetarian food in a neighbourhood overrun with touristy balti houses. Beyond the colourful sweetmeat counter, the brightly lit canteen serves up authentic plates at bargain-basement prices. The menu offers a vast choice, so dip into the array of street snacks (perhaps peppers stuffed with spicy masala) before exploring the cracking range of punchy curries – anything from spinach with lentils to potatoes spiked with fenugreek. Unlicensed, but you can BYO wine.

Chef/s: Harsha and Bhavna Joshi. **Open:** all week 12.30 to 10 (8 Sun). **Closed:** 25 and 26 Dec, 1 to 5 Jan. **Meals:** alc (main courses £6 to £13). Set L and D £13. **Service:** not inc. **Details:** Cards accepted. 40 seats. Wheelchair access. Music. Children allowed.

Lasan

Chic, award-winning Indian eatery
3-4 Dakota Buildings, James Street, St Paul's Square, Birmingham, B3 1SD
Tel no: (0121) 2123664
www.lasan.co.uk
Indian | £30
Cooking score: 3

Having received an award on Gordon Ramsay's *F-Word*, Lasan is understandably full of pride. It's a chic contemporary Indian eatery with light modern décor and a menu of unimpeachably fresh, precisely seasoned dishes that push the boundaries of what Midlanders have traditionally expected from subcontinental cooking. Nadan mathi are sardines roasted in Keralan spices and soured with kokum juice, or you could start with lemon sole Goan-style, marinated in yoghurt

and mint. Thengapal duck is seared strips of the breast in a sauce of caramelised onions, peppers and ground fennel seeds, while layers of powerful flavour are coaxed out of the slow-cooked lamb dish gosht kaliya, its sauce crackling with crushed black pepper. Finish with ras malai and pistachio cream. House Australian is £15.75 (£3.95 a glass).
Chef/s: Aktar Islam. **Open:** Sun to Fri L 11 to 2.30, all week D 6 to 11. **Closed:** 25 Dec. **Meals:** alc (main courses £13 to £19). **Service:** not inc. **Details:** Cards accepted. 64 seats. Separate bar. Wheelchair access. Music. Children allowed.

Loves Restaurant

Intimate vibes and intricate food
Browning Street, Canal Square, Birmingham, B16 8FL
Tel no: (0121) 4545151
www.loves-restaurant.co.uk
Modern British | £40
Cooking score: 4
£5 OFF **V**

Birmingham's rejuvenated canal basin is now one of the city's style icons, and there are satisfying views of its waterfront bustle from this congenial restaurant. Steve Love cooks while wife Claire runs front-of-house, with help from occasionally 'nervy' young staff. The contemporary interior can seem too darkly serious for some, although smoked glass and chocolate-toned wallpaper provide the perfect backdrop for intimate assignations and thoughtful foodie musings. Steve's cooking is intricate, carefully judged and 'palette-style' pretty, although he also keeps an eye on the calendar. A signature starter of seared tuna with variations on the beetroot theme is a guaranteed 'winner', likewise a decidedly complex dish of Herefordshire ribeye rolled in carrot 'ash' and served with crispy tongue, ox cheek, celeriac choucroute and smoked potato mash. There are some savvy oriental fusions too – 'surprisingly delicious' chicken satay partnered by raw and pickled cauliflower, mung bean dhal, chilli syrup and peanut brittle is regularly applauded, and desserts show a mischievous streak (coconut and pineapple porridge with gingerbread ice cream, say). The wine list is a spot-on, cherry-picked selection from some of the world's most exciting and reputable producers, with fair mark-ups across the board. Prices start at £19.50 (£5 a glass).
Chef/s: Steve Love. **Open:** Tue to Sat L 12 to 1.45, D 7 to 9.30. **Closed:** Sun, Mon, 2 weeks Christmas, last 2 weeks Aug, 5 days Easter. **Meals:** Set L and midweek D £20 (2 courses) to £25. Set D £35 (2 courses) to £39.50. Tasting menu £65. **Service:** 10% (optional). **Details:** Cards accepted. 44 seats. Separate bar. No mobile phones. Wheelchair access. Music. Children allowed.

Metro Bar & Grill

Bullish Brummie contender
73 Cornwall Street, Birmingham, B3 2DF
Tel no: (0121) 2001911
www.metrobarandgrill.co.uk
Modern European | £25
Cooking score: 2

Metro was part of the first wave as resurgent Birmingham brushed up its foodie credentials during the late 90s – in fact it's the very model of a cool modern eatery, slap bang in the city's financial quarter. Suits come and go at the bar; others linger in the lofty, atrium-lit restaurant where char-grilled steaks and seafood are the main attractions (check the fish board for specials). Alternatively, consider squid and chorizo salad, lobster ravioli, monkfish and oxtail hotpot or duck breast with black pudding hash from a compendium of bullish contemporary dishes. House wine is £14.95. A second branch is at 680-684 Warwick Road, Solihull, B91 3DX, tel: (0121) 7059495.
Chef/s: Mike Smith. **Open:** Mon to Fri L 12 to 2.30, Mon to Sat D 6 to 10. **Closed:** Sun, 24 Dec to 3 Jan, Easter, bank hols. **Meals:** alc (main courses £12 to £23). Set L and D £14.95 (2 courses) to £17.95. **Service:** 10% (optional). **Details:** Cards accepted. 80 seats. Separate bar. Wheelchair access. Music.

Opus

Buzzy big-city brasserie
54 Cornwall Street, Birmingham, B3 2DE
Tel no: (0121) 2002323
www.opusrestaurant.co.uk
Modern British | £36
Cooking score: 2
£5 OFF

Floor-to-ceiling windows, skylights and swathes of wine racking crank up the metropolitan buzz in this cool, upscale Brummie brasserie, and the kitchen's fondness for provenance shows in its regular 'dinner series' – special events highlighting British food heroes. The evidence is also plain to see on the daily market-led menu: twice-baked Kidderton Ash goats' cheese soufflé could be followed by loin of Balmoral venison with turnip gratin and prune purée, or steamed brill with Lyme Bay scallops and chanterelles. They also do 'some of the best steaks in town', while seasonal desserts such as a trio of Yorkshire rhubarb show the same devotion to duty. Wines start at £15 (£5 a glass).
Chef/s: David Colcombe. **Open:** Mon to Fri L 12 to 2, Mon to Sat D 6 to 10 (7 to 10 Sat). **Closed:** Sun, 24 Dec to 4 Jan, bank hols. **Meals:** alc (main courses £16 to £27). Set L and D £19. Market menu (Tue to Fri D) £28. **Service:** 12.5% (optional). **Details:** Cards accepted. 80 seats. Separate bar. No music. Wheelchair access. Children allowed.

Purnell's

Witty, dynamic dishes from a TV chef
55 Cornwall Street, Birmingham, B3 2DH
Tel no: (0121) 2129799
www.purnellsrestaurant.com
Modern British | £46
Cooking score: 6

Tricked out in fashionable 'art gallery' style with clean lines, bare tables and plenty of natural light, this converted Victorian building in Birmingham's financial district is still à la mode in the city – no doubt bolstered by Glynn Purnell's TV profile. He's clearly a chef with bags of personality and his cooking is a witty, even playful, take on the free-wheeling modern British style – although some feel that he has the scope and talent for much more. Lamb's sweetbreads with sweetcorn purée alongside carrots cooked in toffee, passion fruit, cumin and coriander sets the bar high with its exciting textures and contrasts, but a dish of poached duck egg yolk with black pudding can seem prosaic and 'mushy' by comparison. Purnell's penchant for Indian flavours is much enjoyed (brill simmered in coconut milk with spiced Puy lentils, peas and 'coconut crunch' has gone down well) and he also knows how to spin the classics – witness melt-in-the-mouth daube of beef perked up with leek and crème fraîche fondue. Desserts are equally dynamic ideas ranging from egg custard embellished with crystallised tarragon, black-peppered honeycomb and strawberries to high-octane chocolate tart pitted against a tangily refreshing pineapple sorbet. If you fancy some serious fun, book a seat for Purnell's eight-course roller-coaster ride – although there are signs that the place is starting to take itself a shade too seriously, with smiles and good humour in short supply out front. A classically orientated wine list opens with costly French vintages, but there are plenty of less aristocratic offerings from £22.95 (£5.95 a glass).
Chef/s: Glynn Purnell. **Open:** Tue to Fri L 12 to 1.30, Tue to Sat D 7 to 9.30. **Closed:** Sun, Mon, 1 week Christmas and New Year, 1 week Easter, 2 weeks Aug. **Meals:** Set L £22 (2 courses) to £26. Set D £38 (2 courses) to £46. Tasting menu £75 (8 courses). **Service:** 12.5% (optional). **Details:** Cards accepted. 45 seats. Separate bar. No mobile phones. Wheelchair access. Music.

Please send us your feedback

To register your opinion about any restaurant listed in the Guide, or a new restaurant that you wish to bring to our attention, please visit the web address at the bottom of the page. Your feedback informs the content of the book and will be used to compile next year's reviews.

Saffron

Cut-above, glitzy Indian
909 Wolverhampton Road, Oldbury, Birmingham, B69 4RR
Tel no: (0121) 5521752
www.saffron-online.co.uk
Indian | £19
Cooking score: 2

'A great little Indian with bags of style and sophistication', Saffron curries favour with its sleek, glitzy décor and innovative, cleverly presented food. Dishes such as spiced red mullet with a chickpea and spinach 'gateau', cumin and coriander-scented beurre blanc are a world away from gut-busting Brummie baltis, and the kitchen's east-west love affair also yields 'tronconettes' of Scottish lobster, Highland venison with a rustic potato cake, and a dish of grilled scallops, cod and prawns on crisp spinach with garlicky spiced mash. Tandooris and kormas please the die-hards, and vegetables are a cut above the norm. Impeccable service and keen prices too, with wines from £10.50.

Chef/s: Sudha Shankar Saha and Avijit Mondal. **Open:** all week L 12 to 2.30, D 5.30 to 11. **Meals:** alc (main courses £8 to £20). Set L £6.95 (2 courses). **Service:** not inc. **Details:** Cards accepted. 96 seats. Wheelchair access. Music. Children allowed. Car parking.

Simpsons

A class act
20 Highfield Road, Edgbaston, Birmingham, B15 3DU
Tel no: (0121) 4543434
www.simpsonsrestaurant.co.uk
Modern French | £45
Cooking score: 6

V

'Very welcoming' is a fair description of this classically proportioned Georgian villa set in the leafy Edgbaston suburbs. Chef Luke Tipping's determination is impressive and so is his consistency. His cooking may not be carving out any new territory, but it is inventive and carefully controlled for flavour and texture. Scallops, for example, are presented unshowily, on a bed of orzo pasta with tiny pieces of squid and chorizo, while a flawless breast of roasted Gressingham duck is pleasingly offset by swede fondant, baby beetroot, caramelised pear and a silky chocolate sauce. This is modern French cooking backed up by a proper grounding in the old ways. Desserts are clever – a ball of dark Manjari chocolate decked out with gold leaf encasing an orange parfait and served with a warm orange sauce, poured over by the staff, was a complete winner at inspection. Compliments, too, for the black olive bread from the 'terrific' selection and the 'anticipative service'. For one reporter, a visit after a two-year gap 'really represented a return to form for a place that was once one of my favourite restaurants'. The 300-strong wine list, like the food, is a class act. Prices start from £20, with plenty of choice in the £30 bracket, before rising quickly to premier league.

Chef/s: Luke Tipping. **Open:** all week L 12 to 2 (2.30 Sat and Sun), Mon to Sat D 7 to 9.30 (10 Fri and Sat). **Closed:** 25 Dec, bank hols. **Meals:** alc (main courses £25 to £28). Set L £35. Set D £37.50. Tasting menu £77. **Service:** 12.5% (optional). **Details:** Cards accepted. 70 seats. 20 seats outside. No music. No mobile phones. Children allowed. Car parking.

Turners

Thrilling food and terrific value
69 High Street, Harborne, Birmingham, B17 9NS
Tel no: (0121) 4264440
www.turnersofharborne.com
Modern European | £50
Cooking score: 6

'Great food in a totally unexpected suburban setting', notes one reader who joins the chorus of approval for this modest-looking restaurant in leafy Harborne. Turners may be small, but it's beautifully informed when it comes to delivering 'terrific value and extremely accomplished cooking' – no wonder it's among Birmingham's culinary elite. The remarkable set-lunch menu gets everyone excited, especially as it includes an amuse-bouche and petits fours in the price. There's no dumbing down on the plate either, judging by reports: starters of sliced Gressingham duck breast with an inventive fig and hazelnut dressing, or marinated salmon accompanied by a plum relish, coriander and redcurrants are brilliantly cohesive and 'more than the sum of their parts'. To follow, Richard Turner might dazzle the assembled company with a top-drawer dish of tender, rare partridge breast presented with a delicate tortellini of confit leg, a pile of Puy lentils and buttered cabbage. Desserts pull some clever strokes – a 'truly wonderful' Agen prune soufflé with a sliver of Earl Grey sorbet eased into its heart, for example. The full carte also shows Turner's ability to compose thrillingly intricate ideas from all manner of components: how about organic salmon with pomegranate, black olive, pistachio, goats' cheese and radish, or Cornish brill with chicken wings, squash, white asparagus and gnocchi? Service is capable, easy-paced and entirely professional, and the wine list includes some fine stuff from Austria as well as a notable choice by the glass (from £6.50).

Chef/s: Richard Turner. **Open:** Tue to Fri L 12 to 2, Tue to Sat D 6.45 to 9.30. **Closed:** Sun, Mon. **Meals:** Set L £22.50 (2 courses) to £25. Set D £40 (2 courses) to £50. **Service:** 12.5% (optional). **Details:** Cards accepted. 26 seats. Wheelchair access. Music. Children allowed. Car parking.

ALSO RECOMMENDED

▲ Bank

4 Brindleyplace, Birmingham, B1 2JB
Tel no: (0121) 6334466
www.bankrestaurants.com
Modern British £5 OFF

An up-to-the-minute contemporary brasserie in the Brindleyplace development, the Birmingham outpost of Westminster's Bank (see entry, London), combines a bright, expansive interior with covetable outdoor tables for warm days. A menu of brasserie favourites encompasses Thai prawn cakes with sweet chilli dip (£7.25), smoked haddock and leek risotto with a poached egg as starter or main, a range of steak options and slow-cooked lamb shank with roast roots (£16.75). Finish with New York cheesecake and berry coulis. Wines from £15.60. Open all week.

Dorridge

The Forest

First-class food and service
25 Station Approach, Dorridge, B93 8JA
Tel no: (01564) 772120
www.forest-hotel.com
Modern European | £25
Cooking score: 3

£5 OFF £30

The Forest has come a long way from its days as a railway hotel, although it's still an all-comers' destination with chintzy echoes and a reputation for accessible food. Lately the kitchen has turned up the heat, and visitors have welcomed its confident new approach. Chef Dean Grubb now inhabits the world of crispy frogs' legs with scallops and earthy Jerusalem artichoke purée ('a runaway triumph'), baked cod with wild garlic risotto, and rabbit with Madeira and crushed peas. Elsewhere, a full-on cassoulet/paella hybrid involving monkfish, squid, chorizo, pesto butter beans and boned chicken wings has gone down a storm, while raspberry and thyme Arctic roll has impressed with its clean, exact flavours. Assured cooking is matched by punctilious service, and the wide-ranging wine list offers tremendous value from £13.95 (£3.75 a glass).

Chef/s: Dean Grubb. **Open:** all week L 12 to 2.30 (3 Sun), Mon to Sat D 6.30 to 10. **Closed:** 25 Dec. **Meals:** alc (main courses £10 to £17). Set L and D £13.45 (2 courses) to £17.90. Sun L £14.95 (2 courses) to £17.95. **Service:** 10% (optional). **Details:** Cards accepted. 70 seats. 50 seats outside. Separate bar. Wheelchair access. Music. Children allowed. Car parking.

West Hagley

ALSO RECOMMENDED

▲ West One

159 Worcester Road, West Hagley, DY9 0NW
Tel no: (01562) 885328
www.westonehagley.co.uk
Modern British £5 OFF

Agreeably spacious West One adds an extra culinary dimension to eating out on the West Midlands/Worcestershire border. Typical dishes from a lively menu might include haddock beignets (aka fishcakes) on caper aïoli (£6) and slow-roast belly of Bromsgrove lamb with tomato chutney and a rather succulent potato slice (£19), while crème brûlée with pineapple sorbet could close proceedings on a balanced note. Fixed-price lunch and dinner menus offer great value. Wines from £12.95. Closed Mon.

Wolverhampton

ALSO RECOMMENDED

▲ Bilash

2 Cheapside, Wolverhampton, WV1 1TU
Tel no: (01902) 427762
www.thebilash.co.uk
Indian

Bilash is a cheery family-run business that's been a hit with locals since 1982, and its menu is dotted with dishes that have won awards in local curry competitions. Typical choices from the inventive repertoire include kakuri sheek kebab (£7.95), spicy lamb tikka hasina (£14.50) and the Bilash Super, the restaurant's own invention comprising grilled chicken tikka in a spicy tomato sauce. Good vegetarian options might run to paneer moiley. Wines from £18.90. Closed Sun.

VEGETARIAN DINING

We are always on the lookout for restaurants that make a genuine effort to cater well for vegetarians. This year our 'V' symbol has only been awarded to establishments offering a separate vegetarian menu. Here are some of our top picks.

La Bécasse, Ludlow - offers a vegetarian *gourmand* menu at lunch and dinner

Blue Sky Café, Bangor - serves a plentiful selection of local, seasonal vegetarian options

David Bann, Edinburgh - a sleek set-up, with a menu that offers exciting vegetarian combinations

The Gate, London - generous portions and a global style, set in a former church

Jyoti's Vegetarian, Birmingham - a wide choice of authentic vegetarian fare, with a BYO option and bargain prices

Northcote, Langho - vegetarian versions of all four of its menus are on hand

Quince & Medlar, Cockermouth - good value, creative dishes and an organic wine list from a veteran vegetarian

Terre à Terre, Brighton - a veggie maverick, serving global food since 1993

Berwick St James

The Boot Inn

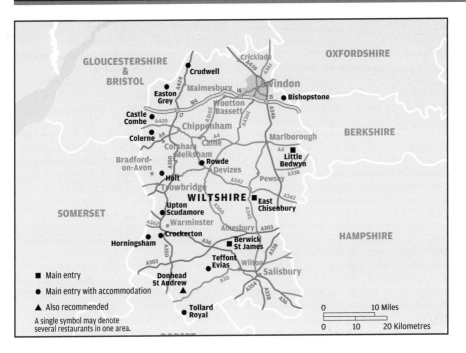

Little treasure of a pub
High Street, Berwick St James, SP3 4TN
Tel no: (01722) 790243
www.bootatberwick.co.uk
British | £24
Cooking score: 1

A favourite stop-off for Stonehenge pilgrims and West Country holidaymakers, this 'little treasure of a pub' offers top value, warm neighbourly vibes and some unfussy home cooking. Britannia rules on a daily blackboard menu that keeps it seasonal with the likes of rabbit and cider casserole, peppered skate with creamed leeks or Shropshire fidget pie – they even toss pancakes on Shrove Tuesday. Recent hits have also included a salad of Welsh cockles with laverbread, 'well-filled' steak and kidney pud, and confit duck on caramelised oranges. Wadworth ales; wines from £13.50.

Chef/s: Giles Dickinson. **Open:** Tue to Sun L 12 to 2.15 (2.30 Sun), Tue to Sat D 6.30 to 9.15 (9.30 Sat). **Closed:** Mon, 25 Dec, first 2 weeks Feb. **Meals:** alc (main courses £10 to £16). Sun L 12.50 (2 courses) to 16.50. **Service:** not inc. **Details:** Cards accepted. 35 seats. 24 seats outside. Wheelchair access. Music. Children allowed. Car parking.

Bishopstone

Helen Browning at the Royal Oak

Country pub with organic cred
Cues Lane, Bishopstone, SN6 8PP
Tel no: (01793) 790481
www.royaloakbishopstone.co.uk
British | £28
Cooking score: 3

£5 OFF £30

It's a rare sort of place that exhorts customers to barter their home-grown fruit and veg for meals and drinks, but Helen Browning's disarmingly friendly village pub does just

that, as a back-up to produce from her own Eastbrook Farm. Chef Barny Haughton brings equally serious eco-culinary cred to the table – a pioneer of seasonal, local and organic ingredients, he ran the much-loved Quartier Vert restaurant in Bristol for two decades. Here he keeps things simple; his daily changing menus run the gutsy gamut from rustic Italian via country French to hearty British favourites: a 'proper Tuscan bread salad', say, or a meaty slab of duck terrine, not to mention an 'uncommonly unctuous' macaroni cheese, a magnificent pork fillet accompanied by excellent potato gratin, carrots, chard and 'perfect' gravy, and a textbook cherry clafoutis. There's a decent choice of wines by the glass (from £4).
Chef/s: Barny Haughton. **Open:** all week L 12 to 2.30 (3 Sat, 12.30 to 3.30 Sun), D 6 to 9.30 (6.30 to 8.30 Sun). **Meals:** alc (main courses £10 to £25). **Service:** not inc. **Details:** Cards accepted. 45 seats. 25 seats outside. Music. Children allowed. Car parking.

Castle Combe

The Manor House Hotel, Bybrook Restaurant

Eye-catching culinary highs
Castle Combe, SN14 7HR
Tel no: (01249) 782206
www.manorhouse.co.uk
Modern British | £60
Cooking score: 5
V

Nothing says 'grand' quite like a slow approach by car through landscaped grounds, especially when there's a fourteenth-century manor house awaiting you. The building itself is magnificent, full of sculpted stonework and fine stained glass, and its big-ticket restaurant, the Bybrook (named after the river that runs through the estate) makes a gracious setting from which to enjoy those sylvan views. Richard Davies is achieving some eye-catching culinary highs here, with a style of food that doesn't stint on the good stuff, but is still replete with inventive zest. A truffled risotto with oyster beignet makes a fabulous opening statement, but is neatly counterpointed by the simple earthiness of parsley purée; otherwise try a tian of Salcombe Bay crab with guacamole in a gazpacho of tomatoes and peppers. Mains maintain that brisk pace in multi-layered dishes that manage to avoid undue complication, witness slow-cooked rose veal with a portion of the sweetbread, alongside braised red cabbage and Jerusalem artichoke in a rich Madeira jus. Desserts can offer all the fondants, mousses and ice creams of chocolate or toffee you can handle, but may well tempt with something along the offbeat lines of pumpkin custard and ginger cake in spicy syrup. A formidable list of fine wines starts at £24.50.
Chef/s: Richard Davies. **Open:** Sun to Fri L 12.30 to 2, all week D 7 to 9 (9.30 Fri). **Meals:** Set L £25 (2 courses) to £30. Set D £60. Sun L £31. Tasting menu £72. **Service:** 12.5% (optional). **Details:** Cards accepted. 70 seats. Separate bar. No music. No mobile phones. Wheelchair access. Children allowed. Car parking.

Colerne

Lucknam Park

Elevated contemporary cooking
Colerne, SN14 8AZ
Tel no: (01225) 742777
www.lucknampark.co.uk
Modern British | £70
Cooking score: 6
V

A measure of how seductive the whole Lucknam Park experience can be was typified by the reporter whose party of eight (including small grandchild) rolled up in teeming rain for a celebration, had their cars valet-parked, and were then 'superbly looked after' throughout their lunch. The mile-long drive lined with linden trees creates a sense of expectation that the grand old pile, not far from Bath, does nothing to disappoint. The dining room is easy on the eye, with sparkling chandeliers, layers of table linen and coffee-coloured drapes adding to the sense of refinement. Hywel Jones offers a range of fixed-price menus that deal in an elevated version of contemporary British food, full of interesting supporting elements and superb main ingredients. A 'crisp compression' sounds bracing, and denotes a terrine of local pork, teamed with roast langoustine, creamed potato and sauce gribiche. That might be the prelude to braised brill with Cornish crab, buttered iceberg, baby artichokes and macaroni in truffle butter, or perhaps a serving of local venison with an oxtail and squash fritter in damson sauce, while dessert brings a tart of Valrhona milk chocolate alongside pistachio parfait and mandarin mousse. The Brasserie is a more informal space, with a menu that embraces tip-top steaks and burgers, even a salami pizza starter. A cosmopolitan wine list offers a vast wealth of choice, and not necessarily all for crazy money. Prices open just above £20.

Chef/s: Hywel Jones. **Open:** Tue to Sat D only 6.30 to 10.30. **Closed:** Sun, Mon. **Meals:** Set D £70 to £90. **Service:** not inc. **Details:** Cards accepted. 64 seats. No music. No mobile phones. Wheelchair access. Children allowed. Car parking.

Crockerton

The Bath Arms

Prosperous foodie pub
Clay Street, Crockerton, BA12 8AJ
Tel no: (01985) 212262
www.batharmscrockerton.co.uk
Modern British | £25
Cooking score: 3

£5 OFF £30

You can expect to be handsomely looked after at this traditionally attired, prosperous coaching inn surrounded by open country close to Longleat. The kitchen plays it straight, feeding locals, families and tourists with plates of fishcakes and buttered broad beans, braised lamb with saffron potatoes and more offbeat ideas such as fillet of black bream with shrimp, butternut squash and spinach salsa – not forgetting side orders of 'wonderful champ'. There are baguettes and burgers too, plus well-reported daily specials (chicken breast with parsnip mash, smoked bacon and roasted onions, or Chinese pork with glass noodle salad, say) and a line-up of familiar puds such as apple crumble or blueberry pavlova. House wine is £16.50. A new 60-seater restaurant is in the pipeline.

Chef/s: Dean Carr. **Open:** all week L 12 to 2, D 6.30 to 9. **Meals:** alc (main courses £11 to £16). Sun L £10.95. **Service:** not inc. **Details:** Cards accepted. 80 seats. 50 seats outside. Separate bar. Music. Children allowed. Car parking.

Crudwell

The Rectory Hotel

Hospitality and quality
Crudwell, SN16 9EP
Tel no: (01666) 577194
www.therectoryhotel.com
British | £29
Cooking score: 3

The handsome Georgian rectory, set in three acres of formal walled gardens, has a cool, loosely defined period style within. It's a well-managed operation, offering just the sort of hospitality that both travellers and locals appreciate – nothing is posh or grand. The oak-panelled restaurant is open only at dinner, when the kitchen makes a virtue of simplicity and shows a laudable commitment to top-class, seasonal raw materials. The creditable, fixed-price menu may start with Cornish crab risotto with a herb and fish cream sauce, go on to roast Old Spot tenderloin with celeriac purée and chou farci, and finish with chilled vanilla rice pudding with blood orange jelly. The manageable wine list is a decent global selection, with house selections from £15.50.

Chef/s: Peter Fairclough. **Open:** all week D only 7 to 9 (9.30 Fri and Sat). **Meals:** Set D £25 (2 courses) to £29. **Service:** not inc. **Details:** Cards accepted. 24 seats. 20 seats outside. Separate bar. Wheelchair access. Music. Children allowed. Car parking.

ALSO RECOMMENDED

▲ The Potting Shed

The Street, Crudwell, SN16 9EW
Tel no: (01666) 577833
www.thepottingshedpub.com
British £5 OFF

This roadside hostelry looks every inch the old-fashioned country pub, with its rambling interior, beams and open fires. The cooking, more modern than you would expect from the traditional surroundings, responds to the seasons and sourcing is a strength – from home-cured Wye Valley salmon (£6.95), via pan-roast Bath lamb chump to halibut with savoury mussel broth (£18.95). But pub favourites are not ignored – expect beef burgers, steaks and fish and chips, too. Wines from £14.70. Open all week.

Donhead St Andrew

ALSO RECOMMENDED

▲ The Forester

Lower Street, Donhead St Andrew, SP7 9EE
Tel no: (01747) 828038
www.theforesterdonheadstandrew.co.uk
Modern European £5 OFF

A thatched, stone-built village inn not far from Shaftesbury, with low ceilings and a comforting country atmosphere, makes a lovely setting for modern pub cooking that looks far and wide for influences. Menus might take in Cornish crab soup with pecorino toast (£6.50), roast breast of Creedy Carver duck with chicory tart and braised red cabbage in garlic jus (£17.50), and classic rice pudding with quince purée. Fixed-price lunch menus are good value. Wines from £13.95. No food Sun D.

Also Recommended

Also recommended entries are not scored but we think they are worth a visit.

East Chisenbury

Red Lion

Infectiously welcoming foodie hot spot
East Chisenbury, SN9 6AQ
Tel no: (01980) 671124
www.redlionfreehouse.com
Modern British | £28
Cooking score: 5
£5 OFF £30

Guy and Brittany Manning worked their passage through some of the world's top kitchens before bedding down in the wilds of Wiltshire, and have transformed this infectiously welcoming country pub into something of a foodie hot spot – but without a speck of pretence or pomposity. This is an industrious set-up, with the dynamic duo producing everything from generous focaccia bread to punchy chorizo, which might be used as a stuffing for chicken or as an embellishment for confit duck with tomato-braised spelt and salsa verde. There's a disarming simplicity about some dishes on the terse daily menu (caramelised onion and Montgomery Cheddar tart, say), but there's intricacy and precision too – witness a big-city combo of roast cod with olive oil mash, roast fennel, piquillo pepper relish and gremolata. To finish, baked passion-fruit Alaska has induced 'groans of delight', but the kitchen also tosses in a few more frivolous ideas – coconut moelleux with marinated pineapple, toasted coconut and lemon sherbet, for example. Otherwise investigate the day's cheeses, kept at just the right temperature and presented with oaty crackers and a strip of homemade quince paste. Real ales from Wiltshire microbreweries are on tap, and the style-driven, 40-bin wine list has plenty of worthwhile drinking from £14.50 (£5 a glass). Note: B&B facilities are in the pipeline.

Chef/s: Guy Manning. **Open:** Tue to Sun L 12.30 to 2 (3 Sun), Tue to Sat D 6.30 to 9. **Closed:** Mon, 2 weeks Jan. **Meals:** alc (main courses £13 to £20). **Service:** 12.5% (optional). **Details:** Cards accepted. 45 seats. 20 seats outside. Music. Children allowed. Car parking.

Easton Grey

Whatley Manor, The Dining Room

Scintillating food and sensual triumphs
Easton Grey, SN16 0RB
Tel no: (01666) 822888
www.whatleymanor.com
Modern French | £73
Cooking score: 8
£5 OFF

Even by blue-chip, out-of-town standards, Whatley Manor is quite a package. Set deep in the Wiltshire countryside, it began as a 1920s hunting lodge, before reinventing itself as a full-on country house experience complete with a spa, velvety lawns and lavender-scented gardens tended by a team of horticulturists (the hotel even has its own florist). From the moment you pass through its fortress-like oak gates, this is opulent stuff, although the interior may suggest Lucerne rather than Old Albion (Whatley's owners hail from Switzerland). Thankfully, the showpiece Dining Room is free from Glühwein glugging – this is chef Martin Burge's domain and it provides a fittingly eclectic backdrop to his devastatingly attractive food. Polished wood floors, Japanese screens, square black mirrors and Italian silks set the tone, service seldom puts a foot wrong and the thrills come in gentle but unexpected waves – Burge likes to keep his customers on their toes, every sensory fibre suitably charged and ready for the next surprise. It begins with a carnival of miraculous amuse-bouches, perhaps a poached quail's egg with tiny leeks and kipper espuma. Having raised the bar sky high, the kitchen proves its point with some scintillating starters: braised snails set in cassonade, topped with red wine sauce infused with veal kidney, or a tasting of duck accompanied by cured foie gras, pistachio purée, baby beets and young shoots – exquisitely fashioned on the plate, blisteringly good on the palate. After that, Burge might turn his attention to a robust old-school dish of roast venison loin dressed with its own sausage, 100 per cent grated bitter chocolate and a rich Shiraz reduction, or uncover challenging possibilities in the shape of pan-fried halibut with a smoke-glazed scallop, pickled clams and almond purée. Aside from a near-legendary sweet/savoury crossover of black truffle ice cream with creamed Roquefort and deep-fried goats' cheese, he also fashions a mousse from chicory and layers it wittily with bitter coffee and mascarpone cream (homage to bottles of Camp 'coffee', perhaps?) It is all achieved with supreme confidence, ambition and a sense of high style, but with a merciful absence of mawkish pomp. The wine list is formidable in its scope, quality is never in doubt and mark-ups won't intimidate. Desirable house selections start at £19.50 (£5 a glass).

Chef/s: Martin Burge. **Open:** Wed to Sun D only 7 to 10. **Closed:** Mon, Tue. **Meals:** Set D £73. Tasting menu £96 (7 courses). **Service:** 10% (optional). **Details:** Cards accepted. 40 seats. Separate bar. Wheelchair access. Music. Car parking.

Holt

The Tollgate Inn

Farm produce and careful sourcing
Ham Green, Holt, BA14 6PX
Tel no: (01225) 782326
www.tollgateholt.co.uk
Modern British | £26
Cooking score: 2
£5 OFF £30

Set in two acres of farmland with an ever-burgeoning menagerie of livestock (including Exmoor sheep), the sixteenth-century Tollgate has come a long way since its days as a schoolhouse, weaving shed and Baptist chapel. Carefully sourced ingredients are now the building blocks for a repertoire of British dishes that might run from local mushroom risotto with a free-range poached egg to Cornish pollack on tomato fondue with creamy mustard sauce. Open with confit duck on Savoy cabbage with orange and marmalade sauce, finish with Bramley apple crumble or lemon and lime posset. House wine is £13.50. Don't miss the new food shop in the pub's converted barn.

Chef/s: Alexander Venables. **Open:** Tue to Sun L 12 to 2, Tue to Sat D 7 to 9. **Closed:** Mon, 25 Dec, 1 Jan. **Meals:** alc (main courses £13 to £19). Set L £15.50 (2 courses) to £17.95. Set D £16.50 (2 courses) £19.95. **Service:** not inc. **Details:** Cards accepted. 60 seats. 40 seats outside. Separate bar. No mobile phones. Wheelchair access. Music. Children allowed. Car parking.

Horningsham

The Bath Arms

Stylishly revamped inn
Longleat Estate, Horningsham, BA12 7LY
Tel no: (01985) 844308
www.batharms.co.uk
Modern British | £30
Cooking score: 2

V

The interior of this seventeenth-century, ivy-clad coaching inn close to the gates of Longleat House has been revamped with style: floorboards in the bar and Indian furnishings elsewhere create a look that is appealing without being flamboyant. Straightforward bar meals take in sandwiches, salads and the likes of fishcakes with tartare sauce, while dinner in the restaurant brings the full works. You could start with Creedy Carver duck liver parfait with smoked duck and sherry vinegar jelly, go on to a nage of Brixham seafood with spring vegetables, and finish with pecan pie and butternut ice cream. Wines from £15.75.

Chef/s: Chris Gregory. **Open:** all week L 12 to 2.30, D 7 to 9 (9.30 Fri and Sat). **Meals:** Set L £12.50 (2 courses) to £15. Set D £24.50 (2 courses) to £29.50. Sun L £15 (2 courses) to £18. Bar menu available. **Service:** not inc. **Details:** Cards accepted. 40 seats. 60 seats outside. Separate bar. Wheelchair access. Music. Children allowed. Car parking.

Little Bedwyn

The Harrow at Little Bedwyn

Stunning food with wines to match
Little Bedwyn, SN8 3JP
Tel no: (01672) 870871
www.theharrowatlittlebedwyn.co.uk
Modern British | £48
Cooking score: 6

V

The tag 'inn' was dropped years ago, when Roger and Sue Jones set about re-fashioning this red-brick, Wiltshire watering hole as a top-flight country restaurant with interconnecting rooms and an alfresco terrace. 'We believe in "real" farming and "real" food', insist the owners, and their commitment shows in just about everything from Pembrokeshire lobsters and Scottish langoustines to pork from Gloucestershire or grouse and venison from the Yorkshire moors; they even indulge in a bit of truffle hunting themselves. The results on the plate are inspired, sensitive and intelligent, whether it involves pairing line-caught turbot with chicken and foie gras torte and a morel and chicken broth, or spicing up Llanllwni Hillside duck with sweet potato, aubergine pancake and yoghurt. As an opener, sashimi of diver-caught scallops with a little salad of Torbay crab and micro leaves shows enviable restraint and clarity, while effortlessly harmonious desserts such as chocolate délice with pistachio ice cream never flatter to deceive. 'Stunning food and wine matching at its best', chimed one reporter excitedly – no doubt bowled over by the terrific recommendations listed beside each dish on the menu. The full list is also testament to the owners' passion, knowledge and enthusiasm for the subject: they were among the first to pour Krug Champagne, Penfolds Grange and premier cru clarets by the glass, and their cellar is a treasure trove of pedigree names ranging from R. López de Heredia's Spanish barnstormers to Pinot Noirs courtesy of Sir Peter Michael's Californian winery. Bottles start at £21.

Chef/s: Roger Jones and John Brown. **Open:** Wed to Sat L 12 to 3, D 6 to 11. **Closed:** Sun to Tue, 25 Dec to 6 Jan, last 2 weeks Aug. **Meals:** alc (main courses £25 to £28). Set L £30. Set D £50 (5 courses). Tasting menu £70. **Service:** not inc. **Details:** Cards accepted. 34 seats. 28 seats outside. Separate bar. No mobile phones. Wheelchair access. Music. Children allowed.

Oaksey

READERS RECOMMEND

The Wheatsheaf at Oaksey

Modern British
Wheatsheaf Lane, Oaksey, SN16 9TB
Tel no: (01666) 577348
www.thewheatsheafatoaksey.co.uk
'We shared probably the best chocolate fondant I have ever had. Service was very friendly and the open fire was great.'

Rowde

The George & Dragon

Pleasing pub with serious seafood
High Street, Rowde, SN10 2PN
Tel no: (01380) 723053
www.thegeorgeanddragonrowde.co.uk
Modern British | £30
Cooking score: 4

£5 OFF

'My favourite place for a quick, delicious midweek dinner or a special celebratory dinner,' notes one happy punter, succinctly summing up the George & Dragon's broad appeal. A sixteenth-century coaching inn, replete with exposed beams, bare floorboards, antique rugs and open fireplaces, it reputedly sits on a cavernous tunnel that runs all the way to Salisbury. Fish and seafood dominate the menu, even creeping into 'superb' meat options such as char-grilled ribeye steak with crayfish and tomato hollandaise, or roast chicken breast with Caesar salad and fresh anchovies. Wholly fishy options range from 'huge, succulent and sweet' dressed crab, maybe with rocket and crispy toast, to roast monkfish with green peppercorn cream sauce. Homemade puddings crank up the comfort factor with favourites such as sticky toffee or chocolate and orange bread-and-butter. A short international wine list kicks off at £12.50.

Chef/s: Christopher Day. **Open:** all week L 12 to 3 (4 Sat and Sun), Mon to Sat D 6.30 to 10 (11 Sat and Sun). **Meals:** alc (main courses £14 to £28). Set L and D £15.50 (2 courses) to £18.50. Sun L £18.50. **Service:** 10% (optional). **Details:** Cards accepted. 42 seats. 60 seats outside. Separate bar. Music. Children allowed. Car parking.

Teffont Evias

Howard's House Hotel

Country comforts and quietly confident food
Teffont Evias, SP3 5RJ
Tel no: (01722) 716392
www.howardshousehotel.co.uk
Modern European | £45
Cooking score: 3

£5 OFF

Cocooned in 'deeply sleepy Wiltshire', this bewitching seventeenth-century dower house is a rhapsodic slice of 'Lark Ascending' English pastoral, complete with a bubbling stream and enchanting gardens. Country comforts mean a lot here, as does the ability to produce meticulously crafted food. Chef Nick Wentworth has a sharp eye for local detail, serving loin of venison with red cabbage, quinces and chestnut jus as well as assembling a trio of pork (braised cheek, confit belly and fillet) with a sage potato cake and shallot purée. This may be landlocked Wiltshire, but fresh fish also turns up in the guise of, say, halibut fillet with braised lentils, confit garlic and Madeira jus, while desserts could promise chocolate délice with peanut butter mousse and caramel milkshake. Old and New World wines (from £21) co-exist happily.

Chef/s: Nick Wentworth. **Open:** all week L 12.30 to 2, D 7 to 9. **Closed:** 1 week Christmas. **Meals:** Set L £24 (2 courses) to £28.50. Set D £36 (2 courses) to £45. Tasting menu £55. **Service:** not inc. **Details:** Cards accepted. 26 seats. 20 seats outside. No mobile phones. Music. Children allowed. Car parking.

Tollard Royal

The King John Inn

Welcoming inn with focus on food
Tollard Royal, SP5 5PS
Tel no: (01725) 516207
www.kingjohninn.co.uk
Modern British | £30
Cooking score: 3

A few years ago this was a derelict pub in fine countryside. Alex and Gretchen Boon transformed it into a warmly welcoming inn, and also shifted the emphasis firmly to the food. Served amid log fires on undressed wooden tables, dishes are rich and sustaining, with an acute seasonal edge. Local game brings whole roast teal served with pommes Anna and Calvados jus, or pheasant wrapped in bacon and teamed with woodland mushrooms, and there are interesting ways with fish, as in apple-smoked sardines (with potato cake and lemon butter) or squid in lemonade batter with clams and chorizo. There's simplicity, too, in a rose veal chop teamed with chips, salad and béarnaise, while for dessert dark chocolate and orange terrine with chilli syrup beckons. House wine is £15.95.

Chef/s: Simon Trepass. **Open:** all week L 12 to 2.30 (3 Sun), D 7 to 9.30. **Closed:** 31 Dec. **Meals:** alc (main courss £13 to £20). **Service:** not inc. **Details:** Cards accepted. 70 seats. 40 seats outside. Separate bar. No mobile phones. Wheelchair access. Car parking.

Upton Scudamore

The Angel Inn

Immensely likeable village hostelry
Upton Scudamore, BA12 0AG
Tel no: (01985) 213225
www.theangelinn.co.uk
Modern British | £29
Cooking score: 2

Carol and Tom Coates have clocked up a decade at this immensely likeable seventeenth-century hostelry in the heart of a pretty Wiltshire village. The sheltered, south-facing terrace is a huge draw. Inside, the whole place is done out in the style of a country inn, with bare tables, polished boards and walls covered with local art for sale. Fish gets top billing on the daily specials blackboard, but there's also braised lamb shank and confit duck leg. Starters include game terrine with piccalilli, while desserts have included winter-berry baked cheesecake with strawberry sorbet. House wine is £13.95.

Chef/s: Peter Laurenson. **Open:** all week L 12 to 2, D 6.30 to 9.30. **Closed:** 26 Dec, 1 Jan. **Meals:** alc (main courses £14 to £18). Set L £18. Set D £25. **Service:** not inc. **Details:** Cards accepted. 60 seats. 40 seats outside. Separate bar. Music. Children allowed. Car parking.

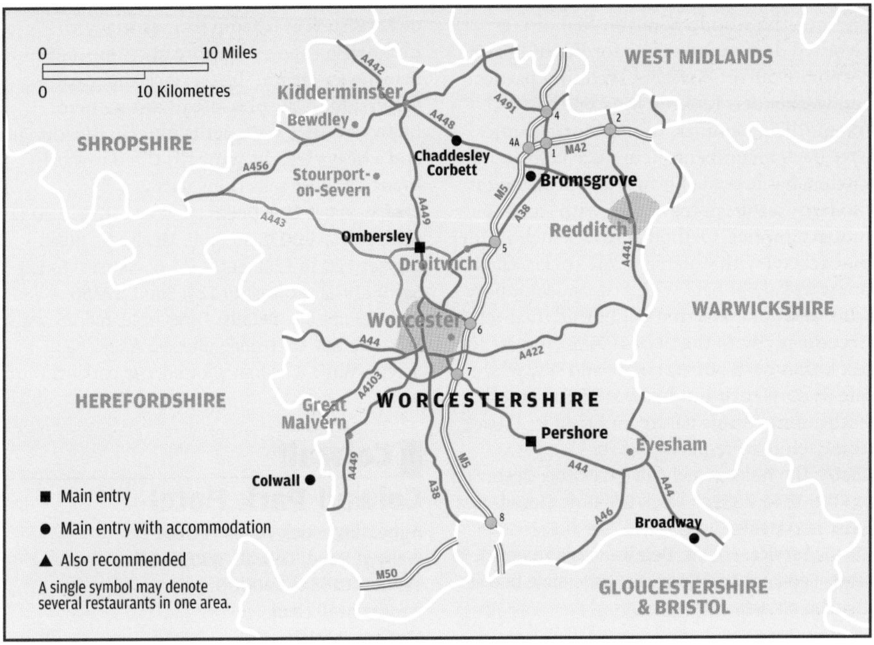

0 10 Miles
0 10 Kilometres

■ Main entry
● Main entry with accommodation
▲ Also recommended
A single symbol may denote several restaurants in one area.

Broadway

Russell's

Boutique brasserie with panache
20 High Street, Broadway, WR12 7DT
Tel no: (01386) 853555
www.russellsofbroadway.co.uk
Modern British | £30
new chef

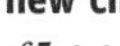

Named after iconic furniture designer Gordon Russell, who once had his headquarters in this honey-coloured Georgian building, this is a boutique restaurant-with-rooms, where a stylish bar and L-shaped dining room open on to a tranquil courtyard. Damian Clisby arrived just as the Guide went to press, too late for us to receive any feedback. Initial plans, however, seemed to involve no great change of style, with the kitchen spanning everything from tapas plates to modern brasserie-style dishes of mussels in cider, cream and parsley sauce or herb-crusted lamb cutlet with a shepherd's pie of the shoulder. The concise international wine list starts at £19. The adjoining building has been transformed into the Workshop (tel: 01386 858435), an informal venue serving hearty British dishes. Reports please.

Chef/s: Damian Clisby. **Open:** all week L 12 to 2.30, Mon to Sat D 6 to 9.30. **Meals:** alc (main courses £11 to £23). Set L and D £12.95 (2 courses) to £15.95. Sun L £23.45. **Service:** not inc. **Details:** Cards accepted. 60 seats. 30 seats outside. Wheelchair access. Music. Children allowed. Car parking.

Bromsgrove

Grafton Manor

Stately pile with spiced-up menus
Grafton Lane, Bromsgrove, B61 7HA
Tel no: (01527) 579007
www.graftonmanorhotel.co.uk
Modern British | £22
Cooking score: 3

Extensive refurbishment is under way at this auspicious Midlands getaway, but the stately pile still clings on to its sixteenth-century lineage – no wonder Grafton Manor is a favoured destination venue for Birmingham's corporate out-of-towners, wedding parties and weekenders looking for some pastoral tranquillity. Members of the Morris family have been incumbents here since 1945 and the kitchen has become known for sprinkling its modern European repertoire with some spicy Indian tempters. Orthodox dishes such as fillet of mackerel with watercress and rocket salad or braised blade of beef with Stilton leeks, port sauce and potato terrine might find themselves in company with the likes of lamb and cashew nut koftas with pomegranate and sev, while safe desserts such as whisky steamed pudding with confit orange ice cream bring it all back home. House French is £13.95

Chef/s: Tim Waldron and Adam Harrison. **Open:** Sun to Fri L 12 to 2.30, all week D 7 to 9. **Closed:** first week Jan. **Meals:** Set L £14.95. Set D £22. Sun L £16.95. **Service:** not inc. **Details:** Cards accepted. 55 seats. Separate bar. No music. No mobile phones. Children allowed. Car parking.

Chaddesley Corbett

Brockencote Hall

Inventive food with a modern outlook
Chaddesley Corbett, DY10 4PY
Tel no: (01562) 777876
www.brockencotehall.com
Modern French | £40
Cooking score: 4

£5 OFF V

'Back on form' is the consensus when it comes to Brockencote Hall – a rather imposing country seat by a lake in 70 acres of parkland well away from the Midlands' industrial sprawl. James Day has settled confidently into his role, and is now dishing up bold, inventive French food with an increasingly modern outlook, from a demi-tasse of carrot and orange soup ('gloriously rich and creamy, one of the most memorable soups I have ever had') to slow-cooked belly of Jimmy Butler's pork, teamed with cabbage and bacon, spiced apple and Pommery mustard jus – a dish of 'superbly balanced flavours'. Skill, rigour and eye-popping presentation also define artful desserts such as parsnip pannacotta with caramelised apple, shortbread crumb and brioche ice cream. 'Top service and great views' add to the pleasure of dining here, likewise coffee with petits fours in the lounge and a heavyweight wine list tilted towards France. House selections start at £18.

Chef/s: James Day. **Open:** all week L 12 to 1.30 (2 Sun), D 7 to 9.30 (8.30 Sun). **Meals:** alc (main courses £20 to £28). Set L £17 (2 courses) to £22. Set D £19 (2 courses) to £24. Sun L £27.50. **Service:** not inc. **Details:** Cards accepted. 75 seats. Separate bar. No mobile phones. Wheelchair access. Music. Children allowed. Car parking.

Colwall

Colwall Park Hotel

Appealing mock-Tudor retreat
Walwyn Road, Colwall, WR13 6QG
Tel no: (01684) 540000
www.colwall.co.uk
Modern British | £30
Cooking score: 3

£5 OFF

With the Malvern Hills as an ever-so-English backdrop, this substantial mock-Tudor hotel aims for broad appeal – especially when it comes to hospitality and nourishment. The oak-panelled Seasons Restaurant satisfies traditionally-minded guests and special-occasion foodies alike with its 'brasserie favourites' and 'gourmet specials' – a broad swathe of dishes embracing everything from tagliatelle with pesto or char-grilled ribeye to roast chump of Longdon Marsh lamb with thyme mash and braised lentils, or crisp sea bass fillets with Mediterranean vegetables and red pepper coulis. Kick off with beetroot-marinated gravadlax or spiced pork terrine, and conclude with plum pannacotta or apricot-glazed bread-and-butter pudding. Occasional disappointments (especially around Christmastime) have marred the picture of late, but hopefully these seasonal blips have been corrected. A fistful of wines by the 500ml carafe (£11.50) stand out on the workmanlike international list.

Chef/s: James Garth. **Open:** all week L 12 to 2 (2.30 Sun), D 7 to 9. **Meals:** alc (main courses £12 to £22). Set L £16.95 (2 courses) to £19.95. **Service:** not inc. **Details:** Cards accepted. 40 seats. Separate bar. No mobile phones. Wheelchair access. Music. Children allowed. Car parking.

Ombersley

The Venture In

Cracking food in a crooked house
High Street, Ombersley, WR9 0EW
Tel no: (01905) 620552
Anglo-French | £37
Cooking score: 3

Take one look at the Venture In's blackened beams, wonky floors, exposed stonework and mighty inglenook and you'll understand why this crooked, half-timbered house is reckoned to be the oldest dwelling in Ombersley. Dating from 1430, it also comes with a resident ghost – although there's nothing scary about chef/proprietor Toby Fletcher's culinary box of tricks. He serves slices of lightly fried ham hock and black pudding terrine with a poached egg, hollandaise and Madeira jus, partners beef fillet with a bourguignon garnish and wholegrain mustard mash, and dresses up roast pork loin with sautéed girolles and a port jus. Fish specials depend on the market, while desserts could range from dark chocolate mousse with orange ice cream to iced banana parfait with a pineapple and banana crumble. Seven house wines (from £16) kick off the carefully assembled list.
Chef/s: Toby Fletcher. **Open:** Tue to Sun L 12 to 2, Tue to Sat D 7 to 9.30. **Closed:** Mon, 1 week Christmas, 1 week Feb, 1 week May, 2 weeks Aug. **Meals:** Set L £23 (2 courses) to £27. Set D £37. Sun L £27. **Service:** not inc. **Details:** Cards accepted. 32 seats. Music. Car parking.

Pershore

Belle House

Purveyor of lively, big-flavoured food
5 Bridge Street, Pershore, WR10 1AJ
Tel no: (01386) 555055
www.belle-house.co.uk
Modern British | £31
Cooking score: 3

Big arched windows are a reminder that this Georgian-fronted building once did duty as Pershore's fire station, but it now plays another role in local life as a purveyor of lively food – you can even stock up at their traiteur if you fancying eating *chez vous*. Those who book a table in the restaurant can expect plenty of smart ideas and emphatic flavours, from smoked chicken and spinach risotto or escabèche of sea bass with confit potatoes and ratatouille to iced apple parfait with an apple 'shot' and Calvados caramel. In between, the kitchen dishes up the likes of braised and roasted pork fillet with black pudding and celeriac or monkfish and scallops on fettuccine with fish cream. The bright global wine list promises decent drinking and fair value from £15.95 (£3.95 a glass).
Chef/s: Steve Waites and Sue Ellis. **Open:** Tue to Sat L 12 to 2, D 7 to 9.30. **Closed:** Sun, Mon. **Meals:** Set L £14 (2 courses) to £21. Set D £24.50 (2 courses) to £31. **Service:** not inc. **Details:** Cards accepted. 80 seats. Separate bar. Wheelchair access. Music. Children allowed.

Shatterford

READERS RECOMMEND

Dominique's

Modern French
Bellmans Cross Inn, Bridgnorth Road, Shatterford, DY12 1RN
Tel no: (01299) 861322
'Truly very good. I hadn't been to Dominique's for some years, but Dominique himself brought my food out. He'd remembered me. Oysters and lobster are excellent.'

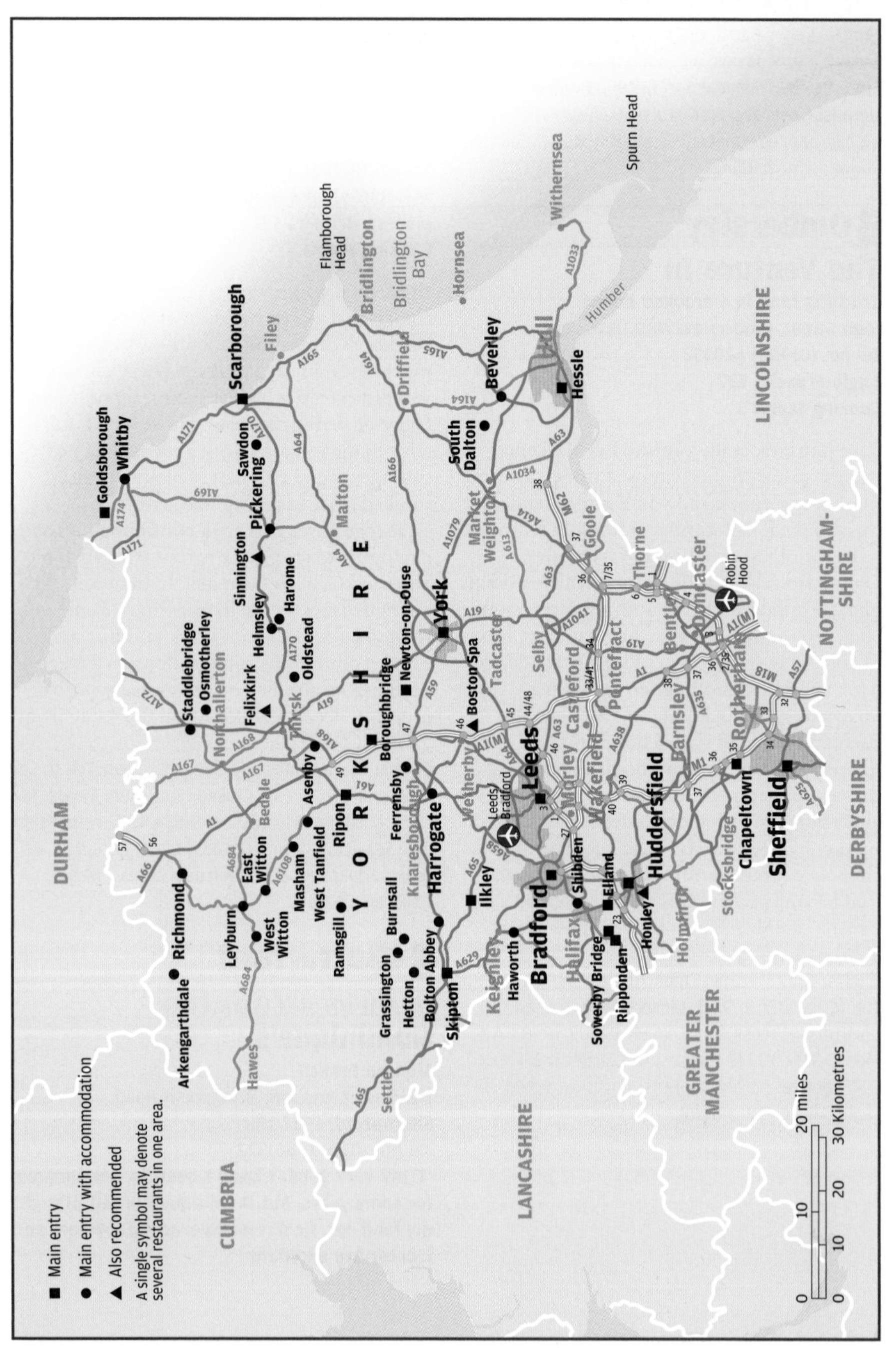
■ Main entry
● Main entry with accommodation
▲ Also recommended
A single symbol may denote several restaurants in one area.
DURHAM
CUMBRIA
LANCASHIRE
GREATER MANCHESTER
DERBYSHIRE
NOTTINGHAMSHIRE
LINCOLNSHIRE
YORKSHIRE
Goldsborough
Whitby
Scarborough
Filey
Flamborough Head
Bridlington
Bridlington Bay
Hornsea
Withernsea
Spurn Head
Humber
Hull
Hessle
Beverley
South Dalton
Driffield
Market Weighton
Malton
Sawdon
Pickering
Sinnington
Helmsley
Harome
Oldstead
Staddlebridge
Osmotherley
Northallerton
Felixkirk
Thirsk
Asenby
Boroughbridge
Newton-on-Ouse
York
Boston Spa
Tadcaster
Selby
Goole
Thorne
Doncaster
Robin Hood
Bentley
Rotherham
Sheffield
Chapeltown
Barnsley
Pontefract
Castleford
Wakefield
Morley
Leeds
Leeds/Bradford
Wetherby
Harrogate
Knaresborough
Ferrensby
Ripon
Bedale
Richmond
Arkengarthdale
Leyburn
East Witton
West Witton
Masham
West Tanfield
Ramsgill
Burnsall
Grassington
Hetton
Bolton Abbey
Skipton
Ilkley
Keighley
Haworth
Bradford
Shibden
Halifax
Sowerby Bridge
Ripponden
Elland
Huddersfield
Honley
Holmfirth
Stocksbridge
Hawes
Settle
0 10 20 miles
0 10 20 30 Kilometres

Arkengarthdale

The Charles Bathurst Inn

Unpretentious Dales pub
Langthwaite, Arkengarthdale, DL11 6EN
Tel no: (01748) 884567
www.cbinn.co.uk
British | £23
Cooking score: 1

'Never a bad meal in nine years' reports one regular, who rates the steak at this unpretentious pub as 'the best I ever tasted'. Exposed beams and a real fire make for a 'cosy, comfortable' setting. The day's offerings are listed on an imposing mirror at the end of the bar; maybe local pheasant and pistachio terrine with pear chutney, ahead of smoked haddock fillet with leek and Cheddar torte, poached egg and hollandaise sauce, with apple crumble for dessert. Wines start at £15.95.

Chef/s: Gareth Bottomley. **Open:** all week L 12 to 2, D 6.30 to 9. **Closed:** 25 Dec. **Meals:** alc (main courses £12 to £20). Sun L £13. **Service:** not inc. **Details:** Cards accepted. 100 seats. Separate bar. Wheelchair access. Music. Children allowed. Car parking.

Asenby

Crab & Lobster

Quirky pub with forthright fish dishes
Dishforth Road, Asenby, YO7 3QL
Tel no: (01845) 577286
www.crabandlobster.co.uk
Modern British | £35
Cooking score: 2

One enamoured reporter writes of the Crab & Lobster: 'I love the place so much I am getting married there in the summer'. This represents pretty well visitors' deep pleasure in this quirky thatched pub. 'Amusing' maritime bric-a-brac sets the scene, giving notice that the long menu focuses heavily on fishy things. Dishes are treated in simple, forthright fashion, with everything from beer-battered local haddock and chips to roast monkfish tail with fricassee of lentils, smoked bacon and potatoes with a Burgundy and brown shrimp sauce. Meaty offerings come in the form of good steaks, assiette of pork and loin of venison, while sticky date pudding is a good way to finish. House wine is £24.

Chef/s: Stephen Dean. **Open:** all week L 12 to 2.30, D 7 to 9.30. **Meals:** alc (main courses £17 to £40). Set L £15.95 (2 courses) to £18.95. **Service:** not inc. **Details:** Cards accepted. 110 seats. 30 seats outside. Separate bar. Wheelchair access. Music. Children allowed. Car parking.

Beverley

Whites Restaurant

Lovingly run eatery with imaginative food
12-12a North Bar Without, Beverley, HU17 7AB
Tel no: (01482) 866121
www.whitesrestaurant.co.uk
Modern British | £31
Cooking score: 2

A down-to-earth restaurant offering 'an excellent all-round experience', Whites is lovingly run by chef/proprietor John Robinson, whose cooking, notes one regular, has shown 'a consistent improvement in the levels of both ambition and realisation' over the past three years. Your table is yours for the night, which gives plenty of time to enjoy imaginative but sensible combinations such as cannelloni of chicken with feta, kale and tomato and chilli salsa, followed by wild halibut with satay sauce and pickled cucumber. Then maybe cashew and date slice with toffee sauce and anise syrup for dessert. Service is 'excellent – attentive without being too obtrusive'. Wines start at £16.

Chef/s: John Robinson. **Open:** Tue to Sat L 12 to 2, D 6.30 to 9. **Closed:** Sun, Mon, 25 Dec to early Jan, 1 week Aug. **Meals:** alc (main courses £18 to £20). Set L £15 (2 courses) to £17.95. Set D £18 (2 courses) to £22.50. Tasting menu £50. **Service:** not inc. **Details:** Cards accepted. 30 seats. No mobile phones. Wheelchair access. Music. Children allowed.

Bolton Abbey

The Devonshire Arms, Burlington Restaurant

Plush antiquity and rarefied dining
Bolton Abbey, BD23 6AJ
Tel no: (01756) 710441
www.burlingtonrestaurant.co.uk
Modern French | £65
Cooking score: 6

V

The Burlington is Yorkshire's prime spot for special occasions. From the first amuse to the final petits fours (by way of espumas, smoke-filled cloches, pre-desserts, fine wines and a substantial bill) this is full-on rarefied dining – 'The best meal I've ever eaten', chimed one reader. Steve Smith's deceptively simple dish-headings – 'lamb', 'venison', 'halibut' – don't give much away, especially when it comes to the highly complex techniques required to deliver each pitch-perfect plate. 'Sweetcorn', for example, involves a textbook velouté poured over morels, 'chicken nuggets' and a scoop of heady truffle ice cream, while another beautiful summer starter sees lightly cured salmon paired with white crab meat, cucumber, avocado and oyster cream. Lamb rump is served 'winningly sweet and tender', and a dish of sea bass with cauliflower purée, wilted sea kale and a heap of shrimps in brown butter has also impressed. To finish, mango cheesecake is matched with an intense mango sorbet and delicate coconut foam. If dabs, dots and good looks occasionally win over substance, as in an under-flavoured amuse of white asparagus espuma, it is forgivable in the face of Smith's undoubted dazzle. The wine list is a legend of epic proportions – some 2,000 bins including the great, the good and the exceedingly rare from across the winemaking globe. Around 20 brilliant house selections come by the glass, with bottles from £17.

Chef/s: Steve Smith. **Open:** Sun L 12 to 2.30. Tue to Sun D 7 to 9.30. **Closed:** Mon. **Meals:** Set D £65. Sun L £35. Tasting menu £72. Prestige menu £80. **Service:** 12.5% (optional). **Details:** Cards accepted. 60 seats. Separate bar. No music. No mobile phones. Wheelchair access. Car parking.

The Devonshire Brasserie

Colourful eatery on a Duke's estate
Bolton Abbey, BD23 6AJ
Tel no: (01756) 710710
www.devonshirebrasserie.co.uk
Modern British | £30
Cooking score: 2

A restaurant in a country house hotel situated in the middle of the Duke of Devonshire's 30,000-acre estate may sound a little intimidating, but the Brasserie offers a riotously colourful room run with cheering informality, as well as tables in the Yorkshire sunshine, when it obliges. Choose from a menu of proper brasserie dishes: smoked mackerel and new potato terrine with horseradish, followed by venison Wellington or char-grilled sea bass stuffed with wild rice, and then chocolate fondant and vanilla ice cream to finish. Wines start at £16.95.

Chef/s: Daniel Field. **Open:** all week L 12 to 2.30 (4 Sun), D 6 to 9 (6.30 to 10 Fri and Sat, 6.30 to 9 Sun). **Meals:** alc (main courses £13 to £20). **Service:** not inc. **Details:** Cards accepted. 70 seats. 40 seats outside. Wheelchair access. Music. Children allowed. Car parking.

Boroughbridge

The Dining Room

Professional cooking with a sure touch
20 St James Square, Boroughbridge, YO51 9AR
Tel no: (01423) 326426
www.thediningroomonline.co.uk
Modern British | £30
Cooking score: 4

£5 OFF

All is reassuring, congenial and comfortingly domesticated at Chris and Lisa Astley's green-painted Queen Anne house overlooking Boroughbridge's market square. Guests assemble for drinks in the lounge, before being led downstairs to the low-key dining room, where the real business of the evening begins. Chris Astley's cooking isn't about to scare the horses, but he has a sure touch and a professional way of doing things. A starter of confit duck with caramelised shallots and a smoky Jack Daniels sauce might be followed by an intermediate dish of smoked haddock, saffron and chive risotto. Then it's on to the main courses – perhaps fillet of sea bass with a vermouth and tarragon butter sauce, or local free-range belly pork on creamed potatoes with apple compote and cider sauce – before desserts such as prune and Armagnac frangipane tart bring proceedings to a satisfying conclusion. The carefully assembled, 100-bin wine list opens with house recommendations from £22 (£4.95 a glass).

Chef/s: Chris Astley. **Open:** Sun L 12 to 2, Tue to Sat D 7 to 9.15. **Closed:** Mon, 26 Dec, 1 Jan, bank hols. **Meals:** alc (main courses £19). Set L £20.95 (2 courses) to £26.90. Set D £25.80 (2 courses) to £29.95. **Service:** not inc. **Details:** Cards accepted. 32 seats. 22 seats outside. Separate bar. No mobile phones. Music. Children allowed.

ALSO RECOMMENDED

▲ The Crown Inn

Roecliffe, Boroughbridge, YO51 9LY
Tel no: (01423) 322300
www.crowninnroecliffe.com
Modern British

Five years on, there's a lot to be said for this venerable beamed inn under its proprietors Karl and Amanda Mainey. Excellent supply lines and an industrious kitchen define the food, with Colchester oysters, Whitby crab (perhaps in a soup with a fresh crab fritter, £6.95), homemade goats' cheese and own-smoked haddock all appearing on seasonal menus alongside steak and mushroom pie (£12.95), confit duck leg, and apple and almond crumble. House wine is £15.95. Open all week. Accommodation.

Boston Spa

ALSO RECOMMENDED

▲ The Fish House

174 High Street, Boston Spa, LS23 6BW
Tel no: (01937) 845625
www.fishhouseboston.com
Seafood

'Everything that came out was perfect', begins one fairly typical report on this 'nice little three-room restaurant' just off the High Street. It flies the flag for good eating hereabouts, beginning with a warm welcome and delivering a gentle interpretation of very fresh seafood, taking in chunky fish soup and aïoli (£7.50), 'lovely' fish pie and 'excellent' tempura of local bream and king prawns (£16). Desserts have included an enjoyable sticky toffee pudding. Wines start at £14.50. Closed Sun D and Mon.

Bradford

Prashad

Top-notch Indian veggie
86 Horton Grange Road, Bradford, BD7 2DW
Tel no: (01274) 575893
www.prashad.co.uk
Indian Vegetarian | £18
Cooking score: 3

Kaushy Patel started cooking at this unprepossessing site on a windy Bradford corner 20 years ago, when it was little more than a streetwise takeaway. Prashad has evolved since then, and with daughter-in-law Minal now heading up the kitchen, the place is going from strength to strength. Pethis (spiced coconut deep-fried in a fluffy potato coating) and dhal kachori (ground lentil balls rolled in chapati flour) have real depth of flavour, while masala dosas are reckoned to be masterpieces, filled with spiced potato and onions and served with lentil sambar and yoghurt dip. Meanwhile, exquisite puris are just perfect for scooping up tamarind-sharp chaat. This is 'fabulous Gujarati vegetarian food', according to one fan, and it's served by

cheerful waiters who are happy to give advice about specific dishes. Unlicensed, but drink lassi or fruit juice.
Chef/s: Minal Patel. **Open:** Tue to Sun L 11 to 3 (5 Sat and Sun), D 6 to 10.30 (5 Sat and Sun). **Closed:** Mon, 25 and 26 Dec. **Meals:** alc (main courses £8 to £15). **Service:** not inc. **Details:** Cards accepted. 40 seats. Music. Children allowed.

Burnsall

Devonshire Fell

Unbeatable location with panoramic views
Burnsall, BD23 6BT
Tel no: (01756) 729000
www.devonshirefell.co.uk
Modern British | £32
new chef

It's hard to beat the Fell for a classic Dales location – a commanding stone house perched high above the Wharfe as it meanders beneath Burnsall's three-arched bridge. As we went to press we learned there had been changes in the kitchen. It was too late to send an inspector or receive any feedback, but in the past the formula has been to serve steak and chips, burgers, sticky toffee pudding and such like, with more ambitious dishes appearing at dinner. Wines start at £16.50, and there's a private cellar for the more adventurous. Reports please.
Chef/s: Oliver Adams. **Open:** all week L 12 to 2 (3 Sun), D 7 to 9. **Meals:** alc (main courses £14 to £19). **Service:** 12.5% (optional). **Details:** Cards accepted. 35 seats. 20 seats outside. Separate bar. Wheelchair access. Music. Children allowed. Car parking.

Symbols

- Accommodation is available
- £30 Three courses for less than £30
- V Separate vegetarian menu
- £5 OFF £5-off voucher scheme
- Notable wine list

Chapeltown

Greenhead House

Tucked-away cottage with alluring menus
84 Burncross Road, Chapeltown, S35 1SF
Tel no: (0114) 2469004
www.greenheadhouse.com
Modern European | £42
Cooking score: 2

Greenhead is a seventeenth-century stone cottage in a leafy suburb of Sheffield, a world away from city bustle inside its walled garden. Neil Allen's stock-in-trade is a resourceful exploration of some of classic European dishes, perhaps beginning with tartiflette made with potato, bacon and Reblochon cheese. A soup or sorbet provides a transition into mains such as halibut on griddled courgettes dressed in garlic, chilli and basil oil, or peppered beef fillet in creamy grain-mustard sauce. Finish with chocolate mocha pudding with chocolate sauce and vanilla ice cream. House wines are £19.50.
Chef/s: Neil Allen. **Open:** Fri L 12 to 1, Wed to Sat D 7 to 8.30. **Closed:** Sun to Tue, 23 Dec to 4 Jan, 2 weeks Jun, 2 weeks Aug to Sept. **Meals:** Set D £43 to £46.50 (4 courses). Light lunch menu available. **Service:** not inc. **Details:** Cards accepted. 32 seats. No music. No mobile phones. Wheelchair access. Children allowed. Car parking.

East Witton

The Blue Lion

Friendly inn that's a real find
East Witton, DL8 4SN
Tel no: (01969) 624273
www.thebluelion.co.uk
Modern British | £32
Cooking score: 4

V

'We considered this pub to be the find of our holiday', enthused one couple of Paul Klein's Georgian coaching inn. They found it in a pretty Dales village near Leyburn, and enjoyed the warm-hearted welcome, unspoiled country atmosphere, and John Dalby's resourceful, superior cooking. There's plenty to choose from on menus that might offer a robust starter of braised pig cheek with black pudding and apple and parsnip purée sauced with red wine, followed by fillets of black bream with mussels, fennel and spring onion mash, or locally shot game such as pheasant, the breast wrapped in bacon and served in thyme butter sauce with a risotto. Desserts can be as light as raspberry sorbet with orange salad, or as get-stuck-in as sticky toffee pudding with butterscotch sauce and banana ice cream. A concisely annotated wine list furnishes good drinking with imaginative, fairly priced choices throughout. The house selection starts at £17.65.

Chef/s: John Dalby. **Open:** all week L 12 to 2, D 7 to 9 (9.15 Fri and Sat). **Meals:** alc (main courses £12 to £24). **Service:** not inc. **Details:** Cards accepted. 80 seats. 20 seats outside. Separate bar. No music. Wheelchair access. Children allowed. Car parking.

Elland

La Cachette

Cheery hideaway with bistro classics
31 Huddersfield Road, Elland, HX5 9AW
Tel no: (01422) 378833
www.lacachette-elland.com
Modern European | £25
Cooking score: 2

The 'hiding place' (to translate) is, in fact, a mere three minutes or so off the M62 and is a cheery bar/restaurant with well-spaced tables and some eye-catching décor, including a wall-mounted stag's head. A menu of Anglo-French bistro dishes takes in classic eggs Benedict or seafood cocktail to start, with perhaps duck breast on rösti with sticky red cabbage and orange sauce to follow. Good English cheeses are the alternative to homely puddings like sticky toffee with vanilla ice cream. Reports suggest the place is a little more reliable on weekdays than at the busier weekends. House wines start at £14.95.

Chef/s: Jonathan Nichols. **Open:** Mon to Sat L 12 to 2.30, D 6 to 9.30 (10 Fri and Sat). **Closed:** Sun, 2 weeks Aug, 2 weeks Jan, bank hols (exc 25 and 26 Dec). **Meals:** alc (main courses £11 to £24). Set L £12.95 (2 courses). Set D £21.95. **Service:** not inc. **Details:** Cards accepted. 90 seats. Separate bar. Music. Car parking.

Felixkirk

ALSO RECOMMENDED

▲ The Carpenters Arms

Felixkirk, YO7 2DP
Tel no: (01845) 537369
www.thecarpentersarmsfelixkirk.com
Modern British

Real ales and roaring fires reinforce the Carpenters Arms credentials as a country pub, although it has upped its profile on the food front. Carefully sourced local and regional ingredients are the building blocks for a tried-and-tested menu of modern British cooking. Despite the odd gripe about stodginess, the kitchen generally delivers: ham hock terrine with tomato chutney (£5.95), peppered loin of venison with dauphinoise potatoes and redcurrant sauce (£17.95) and baked vanilla cheesecake. House wine is £13.95. Open all week.

Ferrensby

The General Tarleton

High-profile foodie beacon
Boroughbridge Road, Ferrensby, HG5 0PZ
Tel no: (01423) 340284
www.generaltarleton.co.uk
Modern British | £30
Cooking score: 4

A serious foodie beacon just off the A1, the General Tarleton has made the quantum leap from bucolic Yorkshire hostelry to high-profile bar/brasserie and restaurant – thanks to tireless chef/proprietor John Topham. Hatched from the equally prestigious Angel at Hetton (see entry), it takes a similar approach to hospitality, with the emphasis on flexible menus and much talk of 'traceability and seasonality'. The food may have 'North Country roots', but dishes often come with big-city airs and graces – just consider a signature 'tasting of rabbit' composed of roast loin and best end, herb-stuffed leg and a minty pie alongside celeriac purée, girolles, broad beans and truffle jus. Grilled homemade black pudding with spiced rhubarb pickle and seared foie gras is a favourite starter, while desserts tout the likes of vanilla pannacotta with spiced plums. The wine list has plenty of invigorating drinking at unscary prices; house recommendations start at £15.90 (£3.20 a glass).

Chef/s: John Topham. **Open:** all week L 12 to 2, D 5.30 to 9.15 (8.30 Sun). **Meals:** alc (main courses £13 to £20). Set L £12 (2 courses) to £15. Sun L £15 (2 courses) to £18.50. **Service:** not inc. **Details:** Cards accepted. 150 seats. 80 seats outside. No music. Wheelchair access. Children allowed. Car parking.

Goldsborough

NEW ENTRY

The Fox & Hounds

Serious food in a Yorkshire hideaway
Goldsborough, YO21 3RX
Tel no: (01947) 893372
www.foxandhoundsgoldsborough.co.uk
Modern European | £32
Cooking score: 5

Missing from the last edition of the Guide because of some uncertainty as to whether or not Jason and Sue Davies would continue (which has now been happily resolved), the Fox & Hounds is going from strength to strength, judging by reports. Considered quite unique, as well as being 'devilish hard to find on a dark night', this former country boozer has been given a mellow makeover – 'a mixture of mismatched antiquities and modern furniture, with a touch of Cath Kidston'. There is little choice on the menu, but Jason is a conjuror of good ingredients and a precise cook capable of delivering some seriously good stuff, including a starter of 'exceptional quality' buffalo mozzarella, baby red beetroot and Sicilian Merinda tomatoes, and a brill fillet 'cooked to perfection' and pointed up with a pea, spring onion and asparagus braise and Bonnotte potatoes. Elsewhere, a 'superb' carpaccio of venison (tossed in a pan, sliced thin, and lightly doused with olive oil and a touch of balsamic), hare-stuffed ravioli in sage and butter, and halibut on a bed of garlic and herb crushed potatoes with an anchovy drizzle have all been applauded. To finish there are more simple strokes, with a dark chocolate truffle cake topped with espresso mascarpone cream described as 'basic but compelling'. Sue takes charge of courtesies out front and oversees the clear, thoughtful wine list, which opens at £14.

Chef/s: Jason Davies. **Open:** Wed to Sat D only 6.30 to 8.30. **Closed:** Sun to Tue, 24 to 28 Dec, 2 weeks Jan. **Meals:** alc (main courses £16 to £24). **Service:** not inc. **Details:** Cards accepted. 28 seats. No mobile phones. Music. Children allowed.

Grassington

Grassington House Hotel

Impressive field-to-fork food
5 The Square, Grassington, BD23 5AQ
Tel no: (01756) 752406
www.grassingtonhousehotel.co.uk
Modern British | £29
Cooking score: 3

£5 OFF £30

Now in its fourth year under John and Sue Rudden, the Grassington House Hotel continues to impress visitors. 'An excellent food experience', noted one reporter, with another particularly enjoying the fact that John's 'field to fork' commitment to local produce even extends to rearing his own rare-breed pigs. There is a strong regional accent to the cooking, especially if you begin with Yorkshire venison carpaccio with sweetcorn and juniper blinis. Raw ingredients are impeccably sourced for main courses such as roast Goosnargh duck breast with duck spring roll and orange honey jus, or slow-cooked belly pork with black pudding, Alsace cabbage, sage fritter and creamed potato. Recommended desserts include cherry parfait with roast figs and cream. House wine from £15.

Chef/s: John Rudden. **Open:** Mon to Fri L 12 to 2.30, D 6 to 9.30, L and D 12 to 9.30 Sat, 12 to 8.30 Sun. **Meals:** alc (main courses £24 to £35). Set L and D £13 (2 courses) to £16.50. Sun L £14.50. Tasting menu £40 (6 courses). **Service:** not inc. **Details:** Cards accepted. 50 seats. 36 seats outside. Separate bar. Music. Children allowed. Car parking.

Harome

The Pheasant Hotel

Impressive inn with highly personal food
Mill Street, Harome, YO62 5JG
Tel no: (01439) 771241
www.thepheasanthotel.com
Modern British | £40
Cooking score: 5

V

With the Star (see entry) and the Pheasant virtually next door to each other, Harome is a village unusually blessed. The connection is Peter Neville, who co-owns the Pheasant with the Star's proprietors Jacquie and Andrew Pern. To his great credit the kitchen has established its own identity; this is no overflow option. In contrast with the more high-powered dishes at the Star, Neville's imprint is lighter, more delicate, with an increasing emphasis on herbs, flowers and foraged foods. Whether you eat in the dining room, conservatory or the wisteria-decked terrace overlooking the village duck pond, the menu offers 10 dishes to be taken as starters or mains. Lobster with sweetcorn, artichoke fritters, wood sorrel and cobnuts is a typical autumn offering. Poached salmon in brown butter comes with squash, baby leeks, sea buckthorn and purslane. Desserts follow a similar theme with pannacotta and damsons or a tart of caramelised salsify. A wide-ranging wine list starts at £17 (£5 a glass).

Chef/s: Peter Neville. **Open:** all week L 12 to 2, D 7 to 9. **Meals:** alc (main courses £7 to £22). Set L £23.50 (2 courses) to £28.50. Set D £36. Sun L £28.50. Tasting menu £55. **Service:** not inc. **Details:** Cards accepted. 40 seats. 12 seats outside. Separate bar. No mobile phones. Wheelchair access. Music. Children allowed. Car parking.

The Star Inn

Delightful hostelry full of foodie ambition
High Street, Harome, YO62 5JE
Tel no: (01439) 770397
www.thestaratharome.co.uk
Modern British | £45
Cooking score: 5

This is a curate's egg of a place: parts of it are very good and other parts... The shell, as it were, is a delight: an appealing ancient thatched pub with its corresponding no-booking bar, comfortable country restaurant and twenty-first century extension, where foodie ambition is centred on the formal dining room. In the last edition of this Guide we wondered whether Andrew and Jacquie Pern's empire had become overstretched with expansion, high aspirations and prices (and it certainly is pricey). Reports continue to be mixed: Dexter beef carpaccio teamed with Lowna Dairy goats' cheese and a relish of golden beetroot and grated horseradish; Whitby crab with Pickering watercress and a delicate, herb mayonnaise; and wood pigeon Rossini that was 'so much lighter than the more traditional beef fillet' are warmly approved. Yet a game of roulette seems to operate with some dishes: pressed corned beef terrine topped by 'very bitter' brown ale jelly; a lamb suet pudding that came with a leathery crust but 'excellent' Jerusalem artichoke purée and garlic, caper and rosemary cream. An inspector also lost out with undercooked calf's liver and an 'underwhelming' spiced bread-and-butter pudding. The wine list, however, keeps pace with changing times and remains good value. More than a dozen selections come by the glass, with bottles starting at £17.95.

Chef/s: Andrew Pern. **Open:** Tue to Sun L 11.30 to 2 (12 to 6 Sun), Mon to Sat D 6.30 to 9.30. **Closed:** 26 Dec, 1 Jan. **Meals:** alc (main courses £18 to £26). **Service:** not inc. **Details:** Cards accepted. 70 seats. 30 seats outside. Separate bar. Wheelchair access. Music. Children allowed. Car parking.

Harrogate

Orchid Restaurant

Authentic pan-Asian eatery
Studley Hotel, 28 Swan Road, Harrogate, HG1 2SE
Tel no: (01423) 560425
www.orchidrestaurant.co.uk
Pan-Asian | £30
Cooking score: 2

Not many Northern hotel dining rooms offer pan-Asian cuisine, least of all in sedate Harrogate. But the Orchid, a contemporary restaurant in the Eastern-inspired basement of the Studley Hotel, subverts familiar hotel fare with a menu that reaches out to China, Indonesia, Japan, Korea, Malaysia, the Philippines, Thailand and Vietnam. Chef Kenneth Poon and his team please omnivores with calabasha prawns – tiger prawns, butternut squash, green beans and coconut milk – or strips of Cantonese sizzling sirloin with peppercorns and lemongrass. Meanwhile Thai mixed vegetable curry with shredded lime leaves, or Korean steamed stuffed dumplings with black vinegar and spring onion dip should keep vegetarians happy. Tuesday means sushi and Sunday hosts the ever-popular lunchtime buffet. A short wine list (from £16.90) features a selection from the Trimbach Estate in Alsace to pair off with the commendable spicy cuisine.

Chef/s: Kenneth Poon. **Open:** Mon to Fri and Sun L 12 to 2, all week D 6 to 10. **Meals:** alc (main courses £8 to £21). Set L £9.95 (2 courses) to £12.95. Sun L £15.70. **Service:** 10% (optional). **Details:** Cards accepted. 75 seats. 24 seats outside. Separate bar. Music. Children allowed. Car parking.

Sasso

Consistently excellent pasta
8-10 Princes Square, Harrogate, HG1 1LX
Tel no: (01423) 508838
www.sassorestaurant.co.uk
Italian | £38
Cooking score: 3

Readers have been divided about this rambling basement restaurant, with reports ranging from 'memorable' to 'disappointing'. After we downgraded Sasso last year we were happy to enjoy a better, less elaborate meal. A 'Sasso' salad of bacon, chicken, black olives and tomato, and another of goats' cheese, bresaola and fresh pear, were both good. Pasta dishes have been consistently excellent and a tomato and wild boar ragù didn't disappoint. Sea bass fillet stuffed with spinach and prawn mousse was accurately cooked and nicely matched with a plate of green beans, grilled mushroom, roast potato and an excellent tempura carrot. Good bread rolls, salty focaccia, whipped butter and attentive service rounded off a reassuring return. The strong Italian wine list has plenty of decent drinking around the £25 mark, although more by-the-glass options would be welcome. A fruity Lacryma was the pick. (Some information may be out of date as no details were provided by the restaurant.)

Chef/s: Stefano Lancellotti. **Open:** Mon to Sat L 12 to 2, D 5.45 to 10 (10.30 Fri and Sat). **Meals:** alc (main courses £14 to £22). Set L £8.95 (2 courses). **Service:** 10% (optional). **Details:** Cards accepted. 60 seats. 16 seats outside. Music. Children allowed.

NEW ENTRY

Van Zeller

Urban-cool food
8 Montpellier Street, Harrogate, HG1 2TQ
Tel no: (01432) 508762
www.vanzellerrestaurants.co.uk
Modern British | £40
Cooking score: 3
£5 OFF

Tom Van Zeller's smart Harrogate restaurant has a strong local following – a spate of nominations praise his inventive cooking. From a menu that offers just five choices per course a riot of ingredients and tastes burst forth, notably winter truffle and glazed baby turnips with hazelnut sablé, grapefruit and lapsang souchong espuma – 'an absolute triumph of perfectly balanced flavours, scents and textures'. But, considering the prices, execution is not as clear as it should be: brill with Puy lentils, celery, shallots 'en papillote' and a sticky, but comfortingly sweet red wine jus, was 'a dish that wouldn't be out of place in a good pub for a lot less'. Yet there's no quibbling with the quality of ingredients; cheeses are in prime condition and a slab of parkin, sweet and sticky, served with new season's Yorkshire rhubarb was a fitting finale for the good value, no-choice set lunch. Wines from £15.50.

Chef/s: Tom Van Zeller. **Open:** Tue to Sun L 12 to 2 (3 Sun), Tue to Sat D 6 to 9. **Closed:** Mon. **Meals:** alc (main courses £18 to £30). Set L and D £15.50 (2 courses) to £20.50. Sun L £20. **Service:** not inc. **Details:** Cards accepted. 32 seats. Music. Children allowed.

ALSO RECOMMENDED

▲ Hotel du Vin & Bistro

Prospect Place, Harrogate, HG1 1LB
Tel no: (01423) 856800
www.hotelduvin.com
Modern European £5 OFF

The Harrogate branch of the HDV follows the group's successful formula, offering a loosely themed, French-style bistro that gives a nod to the style of food served. Expect crowd-pleasers like French onion soup (£5.50) and rump steak, frites and béarnaise (£17.95) alongside more cosmopolitan ideas like harissa-brushed sardines, wild Whitby sea bass with confit fennel and sauce vierge (£13.95) and braised lamb shoulder with lamb cutlet and garlic mash (£16.95). The wine list delves deep into France, but offers equally impressive choices from elsewhere; prices from £16.50.

READERS RECOMMEND

The Claret

Modern British
5-7 Montpellier Parade, Harrogate, HG1 2TJ
Tel no: (01423) 562468
www.theclaret.co.uk
'Small menu, but well constructed, with daily specials; very reasonably priced along with a well chosen wine list.'

Haworth

Weavers

Amiable Brontë stop-off
15 West Lane, Haworth, BD22 8DU
Tel no: (01535) 643822
www.weaversmallhotel.co.uk
Modern British | £27
Cooking score: 3
£5 OFF 🛏 V £30

A Guide fixture since the late 80s and a veteran of the Brontë tourist trail, Weavers offers shelter from the wuthering storms while nourishing its flock with oodles of family hospitality and thoughtfully rendered food. Forget heritage tearoom clichés, this is cannily reinvented Yorkshire cooking with a nod to the region's multicultural complexion. Rösti fishcakes are given a spicy masala drizzle, winter squash and cobnut risotto is sprinkled with cep 'dust', and confit Goosnargh duck is accompanied by an apple brandy and toffee-apple sauce. But it's back to the roots for bangers and colcannnon with 'proud to be gravy', meaty pies with buttery shortcrust pastry or slow-cooked Pennine lamb 'shrugged from the bone' with hotpot potatoes. For afters, try a steamed pud or some artisan Yorkshire cheese. Commendable wines from £15.

Chef/s: Colin and Jane Rushworth. **Open:** Wed to Fri L 12 to 2, Tue to Sat D 6.30 to 9. **Closed:** Sun, Mon, 2 weeks Christmas. **Meals:** alc (main courses £13 to £20). Set L and D £15 (2 courses) to £17.50. **Service:** not inc. **Details:** Cards accepted. 65 seats. Separate bar. No mobile phones. Music. Children allowed.

Helmsley

Feversham Arms Hotel

Slick country hotel with smart food
High Street, Helmsley, YO62 5AG
Tel no: (01439) 770766
www.fevershamarmshotel.com
Modern European | £45
Cooking score: 4

Horticulturally extravagant poolside gardens, a sleek cocktail bar and a bespoke spa are just some of the worldly assets at this grandly extended Yorkshire coaching inn – and that's before you consider the restaurant. There have been subtle changes, but Simon Kelly continues to send out fresh, light seasonal dishes. These might typically include a delicate blue cheese mousse, a simple beetroot salad with feta cheese and walnuts, or an exceptional guinea fowl and pearl barley risotto. Peanut parfait and Tunisian orange cake are among a strong dessert selection, though the odd inconsistency has been reported in the creation and execution of some. An extensive wine list and expert service round off a thoroughly professional operation. Wine from £23.

Chef/s: Chris Staines and Simon Kelly. **Open:** all week L 12 to 2 (12.30 to 2.30 Sun), D 6.30 to 9.30. **Meals:** alc (main courses £18 to £24). Set L £27.50 (2 courses) to £32.50. Set D £45 (3 courses). Tasting menu £45. **Service:** not inc. **Details:** Cards accepted. 80 seats. 40 seats outside. Separate bar. No mobile phones. Wheelchair access. Music. Car parking.

Hessle

Artisan

Gimmick-free Humberside treasure
22 The Weir, Hessle, HU13 0RU
Tel no: (01482) 644906
www.artisanrestaurant.com
Modern European | £42
Cooking score: 5

'The restaurant is now also our home' say Richard and Lindsey Johns, devoted owners of this hugely likeable Georgian town house hard by the Humber Bridge. Refurbishment has allowed them the chance to become domesticated here, but it hasn't affected the sincere welcome or top-notch food served in their 16-cover dining room. The menu may be short but it never fails to set pulses racing, judging by reports of crisp-skinned wild sea bass on a rich, creamy risotto or seared fillet of venison with spinach and Madeira sauce. On Fridays and Saturdays visitors can explore the full breadth of Richard's cooking with a tasting menu that always kicks off with hunks of home-baked bread and a little appetiser (perhaps an espresso cup of powerful celeriac soup). After that, there's generally something clean-cut such as a juicy salad of heritage tomatoes or Scottish scallops with bacon, poached apple and scallop bisque. Highfalutin gestures and fine-dining conceits have no place here, but every dish is a class act, delivered with natural skill and perspicacity – as in roast best end of Nidderdale lamb with braised shoulder, crushed potato, carrot purée and red wine sauce. To conclude, choose dessert (Belgian chocolate pot with orange-curd ice cream, say) or artisan cheeses with tomato chutney. Two dozen wines start at £22.

Chef/s: Richard Johns. **Open:** Fri and last Sun of every month L 1 to 2, Wed to Sat D from 7.15. **Closed:** Mon, Tue, 2 weeks Jan, 1 week Easter. **Meals:** Set D £42. Sun L £20 (2 courses) to £25. Tasting menu £50 (6 courses). **Service:** not inc. **Details:** Cards accepted. 16 seats. No mobile phones. Music. Children allowed. Car parking.

Hetton

The Angel Inn

Culinary delight in the Dales
Hetton, BD23 6LT
Tel no: (01756) 730263
www.angelhetton.co.uk
Modern British | £27
Cooking score: 3
£5 OFF 🍷 🛏 V £30

This ever-popular and pioneering Dales inn has been a Guide stalwart for over 25 years. Dine on Angel classics of Provençal fish soup, or little 'moneybags' of seafood with lobster sauce and follow with ribeye steak – all dishes that have been on the menu from day one. The Angel's enduring virtues are intact, but on inspection it seemed the kitchen was in danger of treading water – illustrated by a dull, dry starter of black pudding, deep-fried bacon and egg in breadcrumbs and chutney. The fish specials perk up, though, with the likes of hake with prawn butter sauce or smoked haddock rarebit. Readers report 'such a good experience' and also praise the vegetarian choices. For all the Angel's long love affair with wine, our waiter admitted the list confused him; it could also benefit from more sub-£25 bottles. Wine drinkers should home in on France and Italy when it comes to considering the lovingly compiled, world-class list, although there is ample choice from around the globe – note the admirable and lesser-known bottles from small estates. House recommendations start at £15.75.
Chef/s: Mark Taft and Bruce Elsworth. **Open:** Mon to Sat L 12 to 3, D 6 to 9 (9.45 Fri, 10 Sat), Sun 12 to 8.30. **Closed:** 3 days Jan. **Meals:** alc (main courses £12 to £20). Set L and D £11.50 (2 courses) to £14.95. Sun L £11.50. **Service:** not inc.
Details: Cards accepted. 80 seats. 30 seats outside. Separate bar. No music. No mobile phones. Wheelchair access. Children allowed. Car parking.

Honley

ALSO RECOMMENDED

▲ Mustard and Punch

6 Westgate, Honley, HD9 6AA
Tel no: (01484) 662066
www.mustardandpunch.co.uk
British

Reporters continue to applaud this local favourite in the centre of Honley, singling out the excellent value for money of the two/three course set dinner (£19.50/£22.95), which includes a half-bottle of house wine. The kitchen is fuelled by a dedication to well-sourced local and seasonal produce – perhaps pickled mackerel with bubble and squeak and mustard-seed onion sauce, followed by rabbit, leek and bacon pie, then pannacotta with mulled black cherries and honeycomb. Wines from £14.50. Open Mon to Sat D only.

Huddersfield

Bradley's Restaurant

Good-value eclectic food
84 Fitzwilliam Street, Huddersfield, HD1 5BB
Tel no: (01484) 516773
www.bradleysrestaurant.co.uk
Modern European | £30
Cooking score: 2

Despite its location in a big old industrial warehouse, Bradley's is surprisingly intimate and there's generally an appealing buzz in the split-level brasserie. Andrew Bradley knows a thing or two about the restaurant business, and his 'prime time' menu with a half-bottle of wine is a guaranteed hit with the locals. A galette of feta cheese, peppers and green olives makes a colourful, sure-footed starter, and you could follow with well-judged sea bass fillet with creamed leeks and piquant balsamic dressing. Finish in North Country style with a hunk of parkin doused in butterscotch sauce or live it up with liquorice ice cream. House wines start at £14.95. There's a branch at 46-50 Highgate, Heaton, Bradford; tel (01274) 499890.

Chef/s: Jamie Rowans. **Open:** Mon to Fri L 12 to 2, Mon to Sat D 6 to 10 (5.30 Fri and Sat). **Closed:** Sun, bank hols. **Meals:** alc (main courses £10 to £20). Set L £6.25 (2 courses) to £8.25. Set D £15.95 (2 courses) to £19.95. **Service:** not inc. **Details:** Cards accepted. 120 seats. Separate bar. Wheelchair access. Music. Children allowed. Car parking.

Ilkley

The Box Tree

Delivering marvels on the plate
35-37 Church Street, Ilkley, LS29 9DR
Tel no: (01943) 608484
www.theboxtree.co.uk
Anglo-French | £55
Cooking score: 6

When it was announced last year that Marco Pierre White was returning to his 'spiritual home' the Box Tree, and going into partnership with owner Simon Gueller, there was a collective holding of breath. Would White muscle in and upset the apple cart? The legendary restaurant has been through trying times down the years. Only since Gueller took over in 2004 has stability returned. Happily, White and Gueller are old mates and any changes are subtle indeed. Judging by an inspection meal, Gueller is resolutely in command and on song and his French-based menu retains such favourites as roast scallops, creamed celeriac and white truffle, papillotte of pigeon, and hot apricot soufflé. Vegetables are another strong suit: a pomme mousseline was superb, while an assortment of perfectly timed spring pickings served with braised lamb shank were sublime. Desserts, as in a nougatine glacée with a sprightly passion-fruit and grapefruit salad, were also very commendable. Service is expert, attentive without being overbearing. Wines, as you might imagine, are outstanding, and the expansive list has great vintages like a 1982 Cheval Blanc at £1,400 alongside plenty of more accessible £25 bottles.
Chef/s: Simon Gueller. **Open:** Fri to Sun L 12 to 2, Tue to Sat D 7 to 9.30. **Closed:** Mon, 27 to 30 Dec, 1 to 6 Jan. **Meals:** Set L £25. Set D £35. Sun L £30. **Service:** not inc. **Details:** Cards accepted. 50 seats. Separate bar. No mobile phones. Wheelchair access. Music. Children allowed.

Farsyde

Great-value town brasserie
1-3 New Brook Street, Ilkley, LS29 8DQ
Tel no: (01943) 602030
www.thefarsyde.co.uk
Modern British | £25
Cooking score: 3

Friendly staff and friendly prices help to keep this long-running Ilkley restaurant ticking over, and the informality of chef/proprietor Gavin Beedham's approach is much appreciated by the local crowd. Pitched behind a bold glass frontage, it plays the contemporary game with striking colour schemes, plenty of bright brasserie ideas on the menu and a freewheeling approach to flavour – as in salmon, cod and prawn 'boudin' atop spinach and caramelised apples, or Gressingham duck breast on curly kale with plum compote and a duck and quail's egg tartlet. Readers have also applauded rare rump of beef with pancetta, mushroom and rocket salad, 'sublime' lemon tart and a trio of rhubarb (including a 'crumble sorbet'). Set lunches and early-evening deals are a snip, and the well-considered wine list provides affordable back-up, with bottles from £14.25.
Chef/s: Gavin Beedham. **Open:** Tue to Sat L 11.30 to 2, D 6 to 10. **Closed:** Sun, Mon, 25 and 26 Dec, 1 and 2 Jan. **Meals:** alc (main courses £14 to £20). Set L £15.65. Early-evening set D £16.45 (2 courses). **Service:** not inc. **Details:** Cards accepted. 82 seats. Separate bar. Wheelchair access. Music. Children allowed.

Ilkley Moor Vaults

Pleasing pub with seriously good puds
Stockeld Road, Ilkley, LS29 9HD
Tel no: (01943) 607012
www.ilkleymoorvaults.co.uk
Modern British | £20
Cooking score: 2

A crowd-pleasing formula of reliable food coupled with a relaxed atmosphere proves a winning combination at Joe McDermott's 'cared-for' pub. The sourdough bread – made daily – is 'wonderful' and meats from the pub's own smokehouse might feature in a charcuterie plate, alongside starters of garlic prawns or winter vegetable soup. As a main course, slow-roast belly pork may be served with mash, spinach and apple sauce, or there could be smoked haddock with mustard sauce. Seriously good puddings include chocolate and hazelnut truffle cake and sticky toffee pudding. A laconic wine list has been compiled with an eye for value. House French is £13.90.

Chef/s: Sabi Janak. **Open:** all week L 12 to 2.30 (3 Sun), Mon to Sat D 6 to 9. **Meals:** alc (main courses £9 to £18). **Service:** not inc. **Details:** Cards accepted. 60 seats. 50 seats outside. No music. Wheelchair access. Children allowed. Car parking.

Leeds

Anthony's Restaurant

Fizzing culinary escapades
19 Boar Lane, Leeds, LS1 6EA
Tel no: (0113) 2455922
www.anthonysrestaurant.co.uk
Modern European | £45
Cooking score: 6

Eight years ago Anthony Flinn roared onto the Leeds dining scene. Since then he has opened Piazza by Anthony in the Corn Exchange (see entry) and Anthony's Patisserie in the Victoria Quarter, but his talent remains firmly rooted in the kitchen at Anthony's. A high degree of technical competence suffuses everything, and although there is plenty of daring juxtaposition – teaming crab with braised chicken hearts and a lemon and basil sorbet, for instance – they are not outlandish. To begin, diners get palate-teasing potions: a sealed bottle with a straw containing a velouté, perhaps celeriac or even garlic and almond; it's 'an intriguing way to start'. Then a 'simple but effective' loaf of bread to share is followed by starters of scallop with tomato jelly and chorizo cream, or braised pig cheek with baby squid, orzo and squid cracker. After that, venison loin and carpaccio comes with cocoa jelly and, unusually, prawns. Desserts can astonish too, whether chilled mandarin soup with cardamom ice cream and pistachio sponge – 'my personal highlight' – or pumpkin cake with warm cinnamon espuma and treacle ice cream. The audacity pays off, thanks to excellent raw materials and clean, pure flavours. Several reporters are not convinced by each and every flavour combination, but others are impressed by the good-value lunch. All agree that service could be more relaxed. On the drinks front, the beer menu is well worth exploring. Vinous tipples start at £15.70.

Chef/s: Anthony James Flinn. **Open:** Tue to Sat L 12 to 2, D 7 to 9.30 (10 Sat). **Closed:** Sun, Mon, Christmas to New Year. **Meals:** Set L £21 (2 courses) to £24. Set D £36 (2 courses) to £45. Tasting menu £65. **Service:** not inc. **Details:** Cards accepted. 40 seats. Separate bar. No mobile phones. Wheelchair access. Music. Children allowed.

Brasserie Forty 4

Converted mill with on-the-money food
44 The Calls, Leeds, LS2 7EW
Tel no: (0113) 2343232
www.brasserie44.com
Modern European | £29
Cooking score: 3

If the kitchen in this waterside brasserie – a converted mill – offers the over-familiar standards of belly pork, calf's liver and sirloin steak, at least it does them well. Add a contemporary room of rustic brick/industrial architecture and a small balcony for sunny days, and you have the recipe for a pleasing venue. At inspection, tempura vegetables with chilli sauce were fairy-light and crisp, a grey mullet special was nicely matched with comforting dauphinoise, duck confit was textbook, but an overgenerous hand with the double cream in the chicken pie and an insubstantial pastry topping misfired. Puddings are of the homely variety, including crumbles, tarts, cheesecake and brownies. The fizzing 200-bin wine list promises invigorating drinking at every turn, whether you are after a French classic or a New World young blood. Prices start at £16 (£3.95 a glass).

Chef/s: Roy Dickinson. **Open:** Mon to Sat L 12 to 2 (1 to 3 Sat), D 6 to 10 (5 Sun). **Closed:** Sun, bank hols (excl Good Friday), 25 and 26 Dec. **Meals:** alc (main courses £12 to £19). Early bird Set D £22.95 (3 courses). **Service:** 10% (optional). **Details:** Cards accepted. 120 seats. 18 seats outside. Separate bar. Music.

Fourth Floor

And shopping too...

Harvey Nichols, 107-111 Briggate, Leeds, LS1 6AZ
Tel no: (0113) 2048000
www.harveynichols.com
Modern British | £30
Cooking score: 2

The Leeds branch of Harvey Nichols strikes a casually contemporary pose with its long bar, open kitchen and rooftop views. The kitchen deals in seasonal produce and modern flavours, and its formula is based on a flexible aim to please, with dishes ranging from seasonal specials to broadly familiar brasserie dishes. While inspection found the output to be not always entirely consistent, prudent selection from the carte can still deliver the goods, say grilled mackerel with escabèche vegetables and confit lemon dressing, followed by Yorkshire venison loin with shallot tarte Tatin, carrot purée and liquorice sauce, and pannacotta with raspberry coulis. The wine list offers a truly cosmopolitan choice from around the globe, with big-hitting names and easy-drinking tipples all making a contribution. Own-label house selections start at £19.50.

Chef/s: Richard Harley. **Open:** all week L 12 to 3 (4 Sun), Tue to Sat D 5.30 to 10. **Closed:** 25 Dec, 1 Jan, Easter Sun. **Meals:** alc (main courses £13 to £23). Set L and D £17 (2 courses) to £20. **Service:** 10% (optional). **Details:** Cards accepted. 80 seats. 20 seats outside. Separate bar. Wheelchair access. Music. Children allowed.

The Olive Tree

Fun-loving taverna

Oaklands, 55 Rodley Lane, Leeds, LS13 1NG
Tel no: (0113) 2569283
www.olivetreegreekrestaurant.co.uk
Greek | £25
Cooking score: 1

For more than 20 years, George Psarias' cheerful Greek taverna has been entertaining loyal fans with its family atmosphere, friendly, efficient service and excellent-value cooking. Magnificent plates of mezze are a popular choice, as are meatballs, chicken dishes, maybe kota hydra (pan-fried chicken with white wine and cream), and simple char-grilled salmon. Other classics include moussaka, kofte and spanakopita. Desserts such as baklava and cheesecake are all homemade. International wines start at £13.95. There are two sister restaurants of the same name in Headingley and Chapel Allerton.

Chef/s: Andreas Jacouvu and George Psarias. **Open:** Mon to Sat L 12 to 2, D 6 to 10, Sun 12 to 10. **Closed:** 25 and 26 Dec, 1 Jan. **Meals:** alc (main courses £11 to £21). Set L £9.95 (2 courses) to £12.95. Set D £14.95 (3 courses). Sun L £9.95. **Service:** 10% (optional). **Details:** Cards accepted. 140 seats. Separate bar. Music. Children allowed. Car parking.

Average Price

The average price listed in main-entry reviews denotes the price of a three-course meal, without wine.

Piazza by Anthony

All-day eatery in a stunning space
The Corn Exchange, Call Lane, Leeds, LS1 7BR
Tel no: (0113) 2470995
www.anthonysrestaurant.co.uk
Modern European | £28
Cooking score: 3

Piazza is proof, if proof were needed, that Anthony Flinn is one of the safest pairs of hands on the Leeds restaurant scene. After setting high standards with his nearby Anthony's (see entry), this operation in the magnificently refurbished Corn Exchange shows an equal capability with a more commercial concept. Various Flinn-owned foodie shops surround the all-day restaurant, which offers the sort of stuff you want to eat every day. Prices are realistic, with dishes such as stew and dumplings offered for two or more to share, while salads (chicken Caesar, say), pasta or rice combos come as starters or mains. Chicken Kiev, plump with garlicky herb butter, and lightly battered haddock with mushy peas, chips and tartare sauce neatly encapsulate the Piazza experience, as do the very good breakfasts. House wine from £13.95.

Chef/s: Ben Sharp. **Open:** all week 10am to 10pm (10.30pm Fri and Sat, 9pm Sun). **Closed:** 25 and 26 Dec, 1 Jan. **Meals:** alc (main courses £8.50 to £21). **Service:** 10% (optional). **Details:** Cards accepted. 118 seats. Separate bar. Wheelchair access. Music. Children allowed.

Please send us your feedback

To register your opinion about any restaurant listed in the Guide, or a new restaurant that you wish to bring to our attention, please visit the web address at the bottom of the page. Your feedback informs the content of the book and will be used to compile next year's reviews.

★ READER'S RESTAURANT OF THE YEAR ★
NORTH EAST

Salvo's

Pizzas and pasta worth queueing for
115 Otley Road, Headingley, Leeds, LS6 3PX
Tel no: (0113) 2755017
www.salvos.co.uk
Italian | £28
Cooking score: 2

'Food quality, atmosphere and service are so consistently excellent that everyone accepts the wait for a table (bookings only taken for Sunday)', noted one regular; 'brilliant place, family feel, great vibes all round', enthused another. People travel for miles to eat at this Leeds landmark, where the Dammone family continue to prove that a pizza, done well, is a thing of wonder. The rest of the menu is a zesty assortment of Italian classics – antipasti, seafood linguine, braised lamb shoulder and grilled chop with dauphinoise potatoes – backed up by excellent service and well-priced Italian wines (from £15.95). The family also run the café/deli Salumeria at 109 Otley Road.

Chef/s: Gip Dammone and Giuseppe Schirripa. **Open:** Mon to Sat L 12 to 2, D 6 to 10.30 (5.30 to 11 Fri and Sat). Sun 12 to 9. **Closed:** 25 and 26 Dec, 1 Jan. **Meals:** alc (main courses £8 to £19). Set L £10.50 (2 courses). Early set D £13.50 (2 courses) to £16.50. **Service:** not inc. **Details:** Cards accepted. 88 seats. Separate bar. Wheelchair access. Music. Children allowed.

ALSO RECOMMENDED

▲ Hansa's

72-74 North Street, Leeds, LS2 7PN
Tel no: (0113) 2444408
www.hansasrestaurant.com
Indian vegetarian £5 OFF

A beacon of Gujarati vegetarian food in Leeds, Hansa's celebrated its 25th anniversary 2011. This ethnic favourite is also famed as an all-woman set-up, with Mrs Hansa Dabhi still very much in control of proceedings. Expect draped ceilings, an Indian vocal soundtrack, family photos and some fine-tuned home cooking – kachori, dhokla and other 'sharuaat' starters (from £3.95), assorted dosas, chaats and uthappam, plus bowls of vadhu (mung beans and chickpeas with yoghurt), masala-stuffed aubergines and special dry curries involving gheloda (mini-cucumbers). All-in thalis from £11.50; organic wines from £13.95. Open Sun L and Mon to Sat D.

▲ Kendells Bistro

St Peters Square, Leeds, LS9 8AH
Tel no: (0113) 2436553
www.kendellsbistro.co.uk
French £5 OFF

Strong on atmosphere and with an extensive blackboard menu (those furthest away will appreciate the binoculars placed on each table), Kendells is the place to come for French cooking of old, from onion soup to île flottante. In between there could be oeufs au meurette (eggs poached in red wine, £6.90), a black pudding tart with onions, belly pork with potatoes, rosemary and garlic (£13.90) and 'absolutely wonderful' stuffed quail with foie gras and French-style peas. House wine is £16.90. Open Tue to Sat D only.

▲ Sukhothai

8 Regent Street, Chapel Allerton, Leeds, LS7 4PE
Tel no: (0113) 2370141
www.sukhothai.co.uk
Thai

Ten years on, Sukhothai remains the pride of Chapel Allerton – a much-loved Thai restaurant. Visitors continue to plunder the 150-dish menu for well-balanced tom yum soup (£4.95), mixed starters (including spring rolls, fishcake, prawn toast and vegetables in batter), roast duck red curry with coconut milk, tomato and pineapple (£8.95), steamed sea bass and anything with noodles. There's a full selection of vegetarian dishes, and wines from £12.95. Closed Mon to Wed L. Branches in nearby Headingley and Harrogate.

READERS RECOMMEND

Dough Bistro

Modern British
293-295 Spen Lane, West Park, Leeds, LS16 5BD
Tel no: (0113) 2787255
www.doughbistro.co.uk
'All dishes presented exceptionally; without doubt a rare find.'

Leyburn

The Sandpiper Inn

Restored hostelry with gutsy dishes
Market Place, Leyburn, DL8 5AT
Tel no: (01969) 622206
www.sandpiperinn.co.uk
Modern British | £29
Cooking score: 3

Jonathan and Janine Harrison's seventeenth-century inn in the centre of Leyburn is not a place for showy gestures, but it scores heavily with its pleasingly relaxed attitude. The cooking is a canny mix of robust English with a dollop of Gallic richness, and a few spicy forays further afield; it is even possible to get upmarket sandwiches at lunchtime, alongside omelette Arnold Bennett and sausage, mash and onion gravy. Dinner heralds a few more ambitious items and gives a genuine nod to local suppliers: wood pigeon, blood orange and walnut salad; Moroccan-spiced Nidderdale chicken with lemon and coriander couscous; and pressed Dales lamb with creamed leeks and garlic. To finish, sticky toffee pudding with butterscotch sauce has been spot-on. Wines from £13.95.

Chef/s: Jonathan Harrison. **Open:** Tue to Sun L 12 to 2.30, D 6.30 to 9 (9.30 Fri and Sat). **Closed:** Mon, Tue in winter. **Meals:** alc (main courses £11 to £18). **Service:** not inc. **Details:** Cards accepted. 40 seats. 20 seats outside. Separate bar. Music. Children allowed.

Masham

Samuel's at Swinton Park

Exhilarating cooking and Gothic grandeur
Swinton Park, Masham, HG4 4JH
Tel no: (01765) 680900
www.swintonpark.com
Modern British | £45
Cooking score: 5

The Cunliffe-Lister family's ancestral home is quite a joint, a sprawling battlemented pile set in 200 acres of parkland in the Yorkshire Dales. It's the kind of place in which it's easy to feel a little overawed, as one reporter noted: 'the dining room with its high ceiling and Victorian portraits seems to invite low voices and hushed tones'. Once acclimatised, though, the focus is very much on Simon Crannage's exhilarating version of modern British cooking, which draws on the neighbouring estate for game, and on the four-acre walled garden for much of the fresh produce. A signature tasting menu of seven courses is the showcase: expect a thrilling journey that might take you from oak-smoked eel with artichokes and apple textures via barbecued pork belly with a scallop and smoked orange, a dish of Swinton venison with pear and chestnuts in red wine, and much else besides, before alighting at a serving of Yorkshire parkin with banana and ginger. Some report the simplest things – an earthy wild mushroom risotto, a summery strawberry sorbet – as the most memorable. The wine list looks for original flavours to complement it all, from Oregon Viognier to South African Syrah. Prices open at £18.50.

Chef/s: Simon Crannage. **Open:** Tue to Sun L 12.30 to 2, all week D 7 to 9.30 (10 Fri and Sat). **Meals:** Set L £21.50 (2 courses) to £25. Set D £48. Sun L £28. Tasting menu £60 (7 courses) to £70 (10 courses). **Service:** not inc. **Details:** Cards accepted. 60 seats. 20 seats outside. Separate bar. No mobile phones. Wheelchair access. Music. Children allowed. Car parking.

Vennell's

Top cooking, top value
7 Silver Street, Masham, HG4 4DX
Tel no: (01765) 689000
www.vennellsrestaurant.co.uk
Modern British | £28
Cooking score: 5

Regular appearances by chef Jon Vennell and his family add to the personal appeal of this chintzy, purple-fronted restaurant off Masham's market square. Inside it feels very 'Sunday best', but without the stiff-collared formality: pretty landscapes hang on the creamy walls, the tables are smartly laid and service runs along unobtrusively. Jon Vennell's cooking doesn't puff itself up either, but delivers real class at prices nobody can sniff at. Yorkshire produce shows up strongly on his succinct dinner menus, from a gut-busting oxtail and mushroom suet pudding with a mini ribeye steak, root vegetables and rich jus to a more complex, creamily sauced assemblage involving pork confit topped with crackling in company with chickpeas, carrot vermicelli and pak choi. Fish from the East Coast ports also finds favour – perhaps a stunning starter of seared scallops with artichokes and cress or pan-fried sea bream with confit chicken wings, pea purée and velouté. Finally, there's always a plate of fine Yorkshire cheeses to bring the curtain down, along with cleanly presented desserts such as an assiette of lemon (a posset, an iced mousse with pine nuts, a sponge and a dollop of lemon curd). Sunday lunch gets the nod from regulars, likewise the choice of 'distinguished' house wines at £15.95 (£4.50 a glass).

Chef/s: Jon Vennell. **Open:** Sun L 12 to 4, Tue to Sun D 7.15 to 11. **Closed:** Mon, 2 weeks Jan. **Meals:** Set D £23.50 (2 courses) to £27.90. Sun L £19.95. **Service:** not inc. **Details:** Cards accepted. 30 seats. Separate bar. No mobile phones. Music. Children allowed.

Newton-on-Ouse

The Dawnay Arms

Brit cooking with verve and gusto
Newton-on-Ouse, YO30 2BR
Tel no: (01347) 848345
www.thedawnayatnewton.co.uk
British | £25
Cooking score: 4

A whitewashed riverside pub (with its own pontoon) in a pretty village north of York, where you can eat in the stone-flagged bar or the light-filled dining room at chunky wooden tables. Soup, sandwiches, risotto, pies and fish and chips are in place at lunchtime, extending to the likes of pheasant in air-dried ham, honeyed duck breast, and steamed pork and cider pudding in the evening. There have been mixed reports since last year's Guide, but an inspection meal of leek and potato soup, queen scallops with melted cheese, and halibut with mushroom risotto found all on solid form. One gripe was for a beef pie which would have benefited from longer, slower cooking, but the quality of pastry, gravy and a miniature pan of chips rescued it. Puddings follow the same unpretentious model, offering sticky toffee pudding, pear and almond tart, crème brûlèe and hot chocolate fondant. Good service and good bread complete an all-round smooth operation. House wines £14.50.

Chef/s: Martel Smith. **Open:** Tue to Sun L 12 to 2.30 (6 Sun), Tue to Sat D 6 to 9. **Closed:** 1 to 4 Jan. **Meals:** alc (main courses £12 to £21). Set L £11.95 (2 courses) to £14.95. Set D £12.95 (2 courses) to £15.95. Sun L £14.95 (2 courses) to £17.95. **Service:** not inc. **Details:** Cards accepted. 60 seats. 40 seats outside. Separate bar. Wheelchair access. Music. Children allowed. Car parking.

Oldstead

The Black Swan

Highly capable restaurant with ambitions
Oldstead, YO61 4BL
Tel no: (01347) 868387
www.blackswanoldstead.co.uk
Modern British | £40
Cooking score: 3

V

Since the Banks family traded up from village pub to full blown restaurant-with-rooms they've enjoyed growing accolades. The Black Swan is tucked away in a pretty corner of north Yorkshire; the sandwiches and ploughmans in the pubby downstairs bar belie greater sophistication upstairs. Chef Adam Jackson offers a six-course tasting menu and carte, whose values are shown in steak tartare with beetroot pickle, wild sea bass with extras of celeriac purée, confit celery and fondant potatoes, or a saddle of venison with onion risotto. Local produce is the not-too-dogmatic mainstay of the menus, and proceedings conclude with a wide-ranging cheeseboard and pleasing desserts. The wine list is solid, with a helpful 'recommended' section and plenty of options by the glass and bottle (from £15.95). Service is sharp to formal, but this doesn't harm the relaxed feel amid flowers, antiques and candlelight.

Chef/s: Adam Jackson. **Open:** Thur to Sun L 12 to 2 (2.30 Sun), all week D 6 to 9. **Closed:** 2 weeks Jan. **Meals:** alc (main courses £18 to £25). Set L £20 (2 courses) to £25. Sun L £28. **Service:** not inc. **Details:** Cards accepted. 30 seats. 24 seats outside. Separate bar. No mobile phones. Music. Children allowed. Car parking.

Osmotherley

Golden Lion

No fads, just confident, accomplished food
6 West End, Osmotherley, DL6 3AA
Tel no: (01609) 883526
www.goldenlionosmotherley.co.uk
Anglo-French | £24
Cooking score: 3

This eighteenth-century inn overlooking the market square still has the air of a true village local, and indeed there's a good buzz about the place. The food takes in the spirit of pub grub and gives it the occasional modern polish – well-reported deep-fried squid with tartare sauce, perhaps, or goats' cheese, chorizo and red pepper salad with harissa dressing – but on the whole there's a resoundingly reassuring, retro feel to tried-and-trusted dishes such as chicken Kiev with home-made chips, and steak and kidney pie with a suet crust and rich gravy (as well as honest mash and red cabbage). Good old ginger sponge with stewed plums and custard is one way to finish. House wine is £15.95.

Chef/s: Chris and Judy Wright and Sam Hind. **Open:** Wed to Sun L 12 to 2.30 (3 Sun), all week D 6 to 9. **Closed:** 25 Dec. **Meals:** alc (main courses £9 to £19). **Service:** not inc. **Details:** Cards accepted. 75 seats. 20 seats outside. No mobile phones. Music. Children allowed.

Pickering

The White Swan Inn

Oozing big-hearted Yorkshire hospitality
Market Place, Pickering, YO18 7AA
Tel no: (01751) 472288
www.white-swan.co.uk
Modern British | £35
Cooking score: 3

Once a refuelling point for stagecoaches running between York and Whitby, this centuries-old inn has been in the hands of the Buchanan family for more than 30 years. Big-hearted Yorkshire hospitality oozes from the place, and the kitchen knows how to feed its guests (even if it occasionally 'overcooks' some dishes). Find a cosy alcove in the drinkers' bar or head for the traditionally appointed dining room if you fancy home-smoked venison, fish pie or mustard-glazed Tamworth belly pork (courtesy of ace butchers the Ginger Pig). Other star turns might range from potted Whitby crab with celeriac rémoulade and grilled Rowley Round goats' cheese with thyme-roasted beetroot to char-grilled Longhorn ribeye with oven-dried tomatoes and chunky chips. Desserts could feature spiced apple crumble made with fruit from Ampleforth Abbey. The top-drawer wine list stands out by virtue of its commitment to lesser-known producers (a Pinot Gris from Cristom Vineyard in Oregon, say). Prices start at £14.30 (£3.60 a glass), although the owners' illustrious St Emilion collection is worth some serious investment.

Chef/s: Darren Clemmit. **Open:** all week L 12 to 2, D 6.45 to 9. **Meals:** alc (main courses £13 to £22). Sun L £16.50 (2 courses) to £22.50. **Service:** not inc. **Details:** Cards accepted. 55 seats. 20 seats outside. Separate bar. No music. Wheelchair access. Children allowed. Car parking.

Ramsgill

The Yorke Arms

A chef with stellar talents
Ramsgill, HG3 5RL
Tel no: (01423) 755243
www.yorke-arms.co.uk
Modern British | £60
Cooking score: 6

Not far from Harrogate, by Ramsgill village green, the Atkins' creeper-clad former coaching-inn and shooting lodge is worth seeking out, not least for the soul-refreshing location. Like the best modern country inns, it's smart and elegant but not in the least stuffy. The dining room has the feel of a private house, with bare, simply laid tables, the better to focus on the stellar talents of Frances Atkins. 'We are always trying to find excuses to eat lunch here', one reporter confides. But who needs an excuse when the cooking is reason enough? Locally sourced meats are a particular strength, with signature dishes such as loin of lamb with mutton fricassee and sweetbreads in sauce soubise, or the now-famous beef fillet with wild mushrooms and foie gras in a truffled jus. Seasonal game is a reliable delight, especially the grouse. Frances Atkins' philosophy is to build on the tried-and-true, adding personal touches as she goes: witness a first course of Wensleydale soufflé with a scallop, emitting hints of vanilla and tomato; or a parkin dessert that comes with mango, carrot and cream cheese, with prune and Armagnac ice cream. To cap it all, an extravagantly fine wine list is on hand, offering superlative selections from the classic French regions as well as good shorter choices from further south. House selections start at £18.

Chef/s: Frances Atkins. **Open:** all week L 12 to 2, D 7 to 9 (8 Sun). **Meals:** alc (main courses £24 to £40). Set L £35. Sun L £40. Tasting menu £85. **Service:** not inc. **Details:** Cards accepted. 50 seats. 20 seats outside. Separate bar. Music. Children allowed. Car parking.

Richmond

The Punch Bowl Inn

Hearty portions of spot-on food
Low Row, Richmond, DL11 6PF
Tel no: (01748) 886233
www.pbinn.co.uk
Modern British | £23
Cooking score: 1

This comfortable seventeenth-century inn in the beautiful Swaledale valley continues to impress reporters, who comment on the 'friendly atmosphere' and 'spot-on' food. The unfussy cooking is based on local ingredients and portions are hearty: pan-fried pigeon breast with smoked bacon, black pudding and pickled beetroot salad might be followed by braised beef, bacon and red wine casserole. Chocolate sponge with custard is one of the comforting desserts, although cheese lovers will make a beeline for the regional selection. Wine from £15.95.

Chef/s: Andrew Short. **Open:** all week L 12 to 2, D 6.30 to 9. **Closed:** 25 Dec. **Meals:** alc (main courses £12 to £20). **Service:** not inc. **Details:** Cards accepted. 60 seats. Music. Children allowed. Car parking.

Ripon

Lockwoods

All-dayer that aims to please
83 North Street, Ripon, HG4 1DP
Tel no: (01765) 607555
www.lockwoodsrestaurant.co.uk
Modern British | £27
Cooking score: 1

The dedication to local, regional and seasonal produce is refreshing at this all-day restaurant. There is nothing cluttered or fancy about the food, which aims to please with a mix of bistro favourites (duck confit, fishcakes) and more elaborately worked restaurant dishes such as sea bass teamed with prawn, pea and saffron risotto, spiced crab cake and shellfish cream. Lunchtime sandwiches broaden the appeal, there's an all-Yorkshire cheeseboard, and baked ginger parkin for dessert. The short global wine list opens at £14.40.

Chef/s: Ronayut Grimshaw. **Open:** Tue to Sat L 12 to 2.30, D 6 to 9.30 (10 Fri and Sat). **Closed:** Sun, Mon, 25 and 26 Dec. **Meals:** alc (main courses £12 to £20). Set D £17.50 (2 courses) to £19.95. **Service:** not inc. **Details:** Cards accepted. 60 seats. Wheelchair access. Music. Children allowed.

ALSO RECOMMENDED

▲ The Old Deanery

Minster Road, Ripon, HG4 1QS
Tel no: (01765) 600003
www.theolddeanery.co.uk
Modern British £5 OFF

Linda Whitehouse is 'welcoming, enthusiastic, chatty and helpful', and clearly enjoys running her lovely old hotel opposite Ripon's cathedral. Understated modern styling works well with period features and the kitchen aims for a recognisable contemporary style, providing everything from fixed-price lunches to distinctive dishes like crispy goats' cheese with sweet and sour beetroot (£7) and wild sea bass with butternut squash, crab croquette and coconut bisque (£17). Reports have praised service this year. Wines from £15.75. Closed Sun D.

Ripponden

El Gato Negro Tapas

Spain reigns in the Pennines
1 Oldham Road, Ripponden, HX6 4DN
Tel no: (01422) 823070
www.elgatonegrotapas.com
Spanish | £25
Cooking score: 5

Simon Shaw's neighbourhood tapas joint has spread a blanket of joy across Ripponden, and residents have been packing the place since it opened six years ago. Others 'make the schlep along the M62' and reckon it is 'well worth the trip'. The menu fits the casual style of the place – a paper placemat where you tick what you want and give it to the server – and many of the dishes are 'classics of the tapas genre'. Others are on good nodding acquaintance with Spanish cuisine; a few seem to have more tenuous links. Here are light and delicate jamón croquetas; 'bang-on for rich flavour' black ink rice, avocado and squid; 'absolutely delicious' lamb skewers with spiced chickpea purée, harissa and yoghurt dressing, and a 'cheffy presentation' of belly pork, roasted scallop and morcilla 'with a couple of blobs of sauce and a foam', plus a selection of regional Spanish cheese served with bread, quince paste and pressed fig and almond wheel. Good ingredients all, well executed, and with 'not a single duff dish amongst the lot'. Inedit beer, developed by Ferran Adrià and Catalan brewer Damm, is an interesting alternative to an intelligently composed list of Spanish, Argentinian and Chilean wines, with prices from £14.95.

Chef/s: Simon Shaw. **Open:** Sat and Sun L 12 to 2 (3 to 8 Sun), Wed to Sat D 6 to 9.30 (10 Fri and Sat). **Closed:** Mon, Tue, 25 Dec to 6 Jan, 13 to 28 Jun. **Meals:** alc (tapas £8 to £13). Set D £35 for 2 (inc wine). **Service:** not inc. **Details:** Cards accepted. 50 seats. No mobile phones. Wheelchair access. Music. Children allowed.

Sawdon

The Anvil Inn

Village pub forges ahead
Main Street, Sawdon, YO13 9DY
Tel no: (01723) 859896
www.theanvilinnsawdon.co.uk
Modern European | £25
Cooking score: 2

The stone furnace and tools remain in this eighteenth-century smithy, which now functions as a village pub and restaurant-with-rooms. The bar has a steep pitched roof, wood-burning stove and iron candle chandeliers while the restaurant is cosy and intimate, with an adjoining coffee lounge for pre-and post-dinner fireside drinks. In between, take your pick from a menu that spans traditional and international influences – say, aromatic crispy duck followed by braised mini brisket joint with shallot and red-wine cooking liquor and mash. Finish with gingerbread cake, homemade ice cream and toffee sauce. Wines start at £14.95.

Chef/s: Mark Wilson. **Open:** Wed to Sun L 12 to 2 (2.30 Sun), D 6.30 to 9 (6 to 8 Sun). **Closed:** Mon, Tue, 25 and 26 Dec, 1 Jan. **Meals:** alc (main courses £12 to £16). **Service:** not inc. **Details:** Cards accepted. 36 seats. Separate bar. No mobile phones. Music. Children allowed. Car parking.

Also recommended entries are not scored but we think they are worth a visit.

Scarborough

Lanterna

Much-loved Italian charmer
33 Queen Street, Scarborough, YO11 1HQ
Tel no: (01723) 363616
www.lanterna-ristorante.co.uk
Italian | £40
Cooking score: 3

Regulars won't hear a word said against this charming Italian restaurant, which has become as much a part of the local landscape as Boyes department store. Dining goes on in a pair of small rooms, and is concerned to do the traditional Italian things well. Fish and seafood dishes – perhaps spaghetti with velvet crab – reliably come in for high praise, and the chicken coronata is another local favourite. Well-made carnaroli risottos with porcini offer plenty of earthy savour, the winter truffle menus even more. Old-fashioned richnesses such as beef fillet sauced with Taleggio, cream and grappa, and the all-important, properly glutinous zabaglione, are good reference points too. The place is run with much-appreciated warmth and there is a carefully constructed list of good Italian wines, starting at £13.95.

Chef/s: Giorgio Alessio. **Open:** Mon to Sat D only 7 to 9.30. **Closed:** Sun, 25 and 26 Dec, Oct, Nov. **Meals:** alc (main courses £14 to £45). **Service:** not inc. **Details:** Cards accepted. 35 seats. Music. Children allowed.

Sheffield

Artisan

Sharp neighbourhood bistro
32-34 Sandygate Road, Crosspool, Sheffield, S10 5RY
Tel no: (0114) 2666096
www.relaxeatanddrink.co.uk
Modern British | £28
Cooking score: 3

£5 OFF £30

Crosspool local boy Richard Smith has been nurturing this sharp neighbourhood bistro for more than 15 years and admits that Artisan is now 'part of my soul'. Culinary trends may come and go, but he has stayed true to his roots and his egalitarian ethos by concentrating on what he calls 'honest classical cookery'. 'Full Monty' breakfast salads, potted rabbit and 'plates of pig' are pure Yorkshire, although continental accents take over when it comes to truffled mushroom and spinach tart with hollandaise, cassoulet or crisp-skinned sea bass with saffron mash, tapenade and roast tomato sauce. Beef from Thornbridge Estate gets its own menu and Artisan now has a bespoke cheese trolley. Cheery staff bustle around in smart new uniforms, and the wine list has also been given a revamp, with plenty of good drinking from £15.

Chef/s: Dan Gower. **Open:** all week L 12 to 3 (4 Sun), D 5 to 9.30. **Closed:** 1 Jan. **Meals:** alc (main courses £12 to £28). Set L £12 (2 courses) to £15. Set D £22 (2 courses) to £28. Sun L £22. **Service:** not inc. **Details:** Cards accepted. 70 seats. 8 seats outside. Separate bar. Wheelchair access. Music. Children allowed.

★ BEST VALUE FOR MONEY ★

NEW ENTRY

Kitchen

Terrific-value, eclectic bistro food
762 Ecclesall Road, Sheffield, S11 8TB
Tel no: (0114) 2671351
www.sheffieldkitchen.com
Modern European | £23
Cooking score: 3

Bustling, noisy and a 'great hit' with the locals, this energetic, down-home bistro is nestled in a shopping parade on ever-busy Ecclesall Road. Inside, all is light and airy, with wooden floors, functional furniture and a pared-down menu that delivers unfussy food at highly attractive prices. At lunchtime, a 'feed the people' cheeseburger is terrific value, and in the evening chef John Parsons lets his creative juices flow – especially when it comes to seafood. Cod with ham, pea purée, Parmesan and garlic jelly is typical of his snappy, eclectic style, although he might also turn his hand to duck breast with sour plums and balsamic dressing, or lamb rump with salsa verde. Pud could be crème brûlée. Wines also come at knockdown prices, from £12.75.

Chef/s: John Parsons. **Open:** Wed to Sat L 12 to 3, D 6 to 9. **Closed:** Sun to Tue, 25 and 26 Dec, 1 Jan, Easter. **Meals:** alc (main courses £8 to £22). Sun L £15. **Service:** not inc. **Details:** Cards accepted. 42 seats. Wheelchair access. Music. Children allowed.

The Milestone

Characterful corner pub on the up
84 Green Lane, Sheffield, S3 8SE
Tel no: (0114) 2728327
www.the-milestone.co.uk
British | £30
Cooking score: 2

Matt Bigland and Marc Sheldon have certainly imbued their laid-back pub with bags of feel-good personality. In the kitchen things are equally upbeat, with big-hearted flavours stuffed into a lively menu that might jump from pigeon breast with gin-and-tonic jelly and spiced red cabbage to flank of rare beef with horseradish mash, purple sprouting broccoli and Wentworth ale gravy, or fillet of plaice with sea vegetables, baby new potatoes, cockles and nut butter sauce. Prices are keen, especially if you arrive in time for the early-bird menu and its offer of two courses plus a pint or glass of wine. The worldwide wine list is equally affordable, with bottles from £13.50. Wig & Pen by The Milestone is part of the same stable (see entry).

Chef/s: James Wallis. **Open:** Mon to Fri 12 to 4, 5 to 10. Sat 12 to 11. Sun 12 to 9. **Closed:** 25 and 26 Dec, 1 Jan. **Meals:** alc (main courses £13 to £17). Set L and early D £14 (2 courses). **Service:** not inc. **Details:** Cards accepted. 100 seats. Separate bar. Wheelchair access. Music.

Moran's Restaurant

Suburban gem with knockout food
289b Abbeydale Road South, Dore, Sheffield, S17 3LB
Tel no: (0114) 2350101
www.moranssheffield.co.uk
Modern European | £32
Cooking score: 4

The sight of a converted showroom in a bland shopping precinct won't ignite your passions, but don't be discouraged: Bryan and Sarah Moran's modest neighbourhood restaurant aims high. They have tarted up this rather boxy 'shack' with good taste and an eye for detail, but it's the menu that really defies suburban preconceptions: consider home-smoked duck breast on a pear, orange and pickled walnut salad with sweet 'sherry tea' dressing, or goats' cheese fondant with beetroot mousse, broad beans and balsamic reduction. Bryan's food may be moving relentlessly towards the world of micro leaves, but he still finds time to re-work some cloth-capped, North Country staples – perhaps fillet steak with mash and a dinky steak and kidney pud, or roast rack of lamb on buttered Savoy cabbage with a little Lancashire hotpot and some haggis bonbons on the side. After that, expect iced pistachio parfait with warm pistachio cake and cherry sorbet, rather than fruit cake with cheese. Carefully chosen wines yo-yo between Europe and the southern hemisphere, with house selections from £12.95.

Chef/s: Bryan Moran. **Open:** Wed to Sun L 12 to 2 (3 Sun), Tue to Sat D 7 to 9. **Closed:** Mon, first 2 weeks Jan. **Meals:** alc (main courses £13 to £21). Sun L £20.95. **Service:** not inc. **Details:** Cards accepted. 65 seats. 20 seats outside. Separate bar. Wheelchair access. Music. Children allowed. Car parking.

NEW ENTRY

Wig & Pen by The Milestone

Über-cool pub with gutsy food
44 Campo Lane, Sheffield, S1 2EG
Tel no: (0114) 2722150
www.the-wigandpen.co.uk
British | £28
Cooking score: 2

A new venture from the team behind the Milestone (see entry), this venerable city pub started life as a murky drinking den for Sheffield lawyers; these days it's an über-cool bar/restaurant with wooden walls and booths for discreet assignations rather than legal wrangling. Printed on brown paper, the menu promises robust brasserie-style dishes running from crab ballottine with smoked pepper and tomato velouté to roast rump of lamb with crushed Jersey Royals, confit tomatoes and tarragon dressing, or pan-fried mackerel fillets with fennel, tapenade and rosemary oil. To finish, raspberry and Prosecco jelly with black pepper shortbread, basil granita and basil syrup is an exquisite treat. House wines from £13.50.

Chef/s: Simon Ayres. **Open:** Mon to Fri L 12 to 4, D 5 to 10. Sat 12 to 11. Sun 12 to 5. **Closed:** 25 and 26 Dec. **Meals:** alc (main courses £14 to £20). **Service:** 10% (optional). **Details:** Cards accepted. 120 seats. 20 seats outside. Separate bar. Music. Children allowed.

ALSO RECOMMENDED

▲ Lokanta

478-480 Glossop Road, Sheffield, S10 2QA
Tel no: (0114) 2666444
www.lokanta.co.uk
Turkish

'The food is good, the service friendly and the atmosphere buzzing', noted a visitor to the Günays' smart Turkish restaurant. Mezze (£3.95 to £6.45) can constitute an entire meal, but a couple of reporters shared just three: minty feta cheese rolls, simply grilled haloumi and lightly battered calamari with a creamy walnut sauce, before going on to a 'generous' mixed grill of lamb and chicken kebabs, meatballs and spicy beef sausage (£13.95) and finishing with baklava 'unctuous with honey'. Homemade Turkish bread is 'fabulous'. Turkish wines from £12.95. Closed Mon.

▲ Rafters

220 Oakbrook Road, Nether Green, Sheffield, S11 7ED
Tel no: (0114) 2304819
www.raftersrestaurant.co.uk
Modern British

Beams, brickwork and rafters (of course) add some rough-hewn chic to this neighbourhood favourite in a leafy Sheffield suburb. Look for the discreet entrance and head upstairs for a taste of chef/proprietor Marcus Lane's ambitious cooking. His fixed-price dinner menus (£36 for three courses) have delivered roast pigeon on barley risotto and spiced crab with shellfish fritters ahead of perfectly pink Round Green venison with balsamic beetroot, and few readers can resist his bread-and-butter pudding with butterscotch sauce. House wine is £15.50. Open Mon and Wed to Sat D only.

READERS RECOMMEND

Silversmiths Restaurant & Bar

Modern British
111 Arundel Street, Sheffield, S1 2NT
Tel no: (0114) 270 6160
www.silversmiths-restaurant.com
'Food, atmosphere and service were all brilliant.'

Readers Recommend

A 'readers recommend' review is a genuine quote from a report sent in by one of our readers. We intend to follow up these suggestions throughout the year to come.

Shibden

Shibden Mill Inn

A near-perfect country pub
Shibden Fold, Shibden, HX3 7UL
Tel no: (01422) 365840
www.shibdenmillinn.com
Modern British | £27
Cooking score: 3

'If you had to invent a perfect country pub, the Shibden would come close', observed one traveller – referring to this beguiling seventeenth-century inn, folded away in a verdant valley close to Halifax. Originally a working mill, it comes complete with a bubbling stream, a succession of tiny rooms and bags of heritage appeal. The kitchen delivers seriously hearty food with plenty of clever, modern touches and regional overtones: a risotto of moorland partridge breast, pearl barley and confit duck might be followed by roast loin of lamb, served appealingly with a pine-nut and mint crumble. Alternatively, look to the coast for, say, sea bream with roast scallops, smoked eel fishcake and brown shrimp butter, before concluding with a modish vanilla and white chocolate rice pudding. The wine list is a deliberately cosmopolitan compilation, with prices from £14.75.

Chef/s: Darren Parkinson. **Open:** Mon to Sat L 12 to 2, D 6 to 9.30. Sun 12 to 7.30. **Closed:** 26 Dec. **Meals:** alc (main courses £10 to £23). **Service:** not inc. **Details:** Cards accepted. 140 seats. 40 seats outside. Separate bar. Music. Children allowed. Car parking.

Please send us your feedback

To register your opinion about any restaurant listed in the Guide, or a new restaurant that you wish to bring to our attention, please visit the web address at the bottom of the page. Your feedback informs the content of the book and will be used to compile next year's reviews.

Sinnington

ALSO RECOMMENDED

▲ Fox & Hounds

Main Street, Sinnington, YO62 6SQ
Tel no: (01751) 431577
www.thefoxandhoundsinn.co.uk
Modern British £5 OFF

'A very pleasant experience which makes you want to book up again before you leave', exclaimed a visitor about this eighteenth-century coaching inn on the edge of the North York Moors. Honest intent and lashings of good local produce deliver soups such as a 'heartening and spicy' parsnip (£4.95), mains of Yorkshire rabbit casserole with dumplings or a platter of fish pie, tiger prawns, smoked haddock rarebit and mini-fish and chips (£17.50). End with lemon posset. House wine is £13.95. Open all week. Accommodation.

Skipton

Le Caveau

Atmospheric subterranean dining
86 High Street, Skipton, BD23 1JJ
Tel no: (01756) 794274
www.lecaveau.co.uk
Anglo-French | £30
Cooking score: 2

Secreted in a sixteenth-century, barrel-vaulted basement beneath Skipton's award-winning High Street, Le Caveau certainly lives up to its subterranean moniker. Mighty beams, candlelight and rugged stone walls create a moody backdrop, while Richard Barker's unshowy Anglo-French cooking stays well within its comfort zone. Blackboard specials add variety to a seasonal menu that might promise ham hock, black pudding and apple terrine, rack of Wharfedale spring lamb with a Dijon mustard crust, or Yorkshire sirloin steak with horseradish mash. Adventurous souls might order yellowfin tuna served on noodles with soy and lemongrass dressing, while desserts such as Eton mess close proceedings on a familiar note. Georges Duboeuf house French is £14.95.

Chef/s: Richard Barker. **Open:** Tue to Fri L 12 to 2, Tue to Sat D 7 to 9.30 (5 to 10 Sat). **Closed:** Sun, Mon, first week Jan, first week Jun, 2 weeks Sept. **Meals:** alc (main courses £14 to £23). Set L £10.95 (2 courses) to £14.95. Set D £15.95 (2 courses) to £20. **Service:** not inc. **Details:** Cards accepted. 26 seats. Separate bar. Music. Children allowed.

South Dalton

The Pipe & Glass Inn

Pubby virtues and fine food
West End, South Dalton, HU17 7PN
Tel no: (01430) 810246
www.pipeandglass.co.uk
Modern British | £33
Cooking score: 5

V

Since pitching camp at the Pipe & Glass in 2006, James and Kate Mackenzie have turned this whitewashed Wolds hostelry into a little marvel of good humour, pubby virtues and fine food. The spirit of 'beer and skittles' is alive and well here, despite sky-high culinary aspirations: you can sup pints of ale and gorge on beef suet pudding as the fire crackles and the music plays, or partake of some more auspicious sustenance in the thickly carpeted, conservatory-style extension. The food hits you with big, assertive flavours, the seasons have their say and the confidence is palpable: consider baked hare in a juniper-spiked pasty with a collation of pickled girolles and air-dried ham, or fillet of John Dory in company with curly kale colcannon, cockle stew and a monkfish fritter. James is also happy to give pub-grub throwbacks a shake-up, applying some canny on-trend touches here and there: Gloucester Old Spot potted pork comes in a jar with sticky apple and crackling, while fish pie is invigorated with pickled fennel salad. Each dish feels newly minted, and meals end strongly with spirit-lifting desserts such as warm treacle tart with egg-nog ice cream and nutmeg custard. The gently priced wine list does its job without putting on airs; bottles start at £14 and 20 selections are offered by the glass.

Chef/s: James Mackenzie. **Open:** Tue to Sun L 12 to 2 (4 Sun), Tue to Sat D 6 to 9.30. **Closed:** Mon (exc bank hols), 2 weeks Jan. **Meals:** alc (main courses £10 to £23). **Service:** not inc. **Details:** Cards accepted. 90 seats. 60 seats outside. Separate bar. No mobile phones. Wheelchair access. Music. Children allowed. Car parking.

Sowerby Bridge

NEW ENTRY

Gimbals

Cheerful eatery with upbeat food
76 Wharf Street, Sowerby Bridge, HX6 2AF
Tel no: (01422) 839329
www.gimbals.co.uk
Modern European | £28
Cooking score: 2

Set in a row of terraced houses, Simon and Janet Baker's cheerful restaurant cuts quite a dash from the off, with its Rococo mirrors, dramatic light fittings and metallic sculptures. Their attractively presented, rustic food also pleases: start with something 'cold' or 'warm' (perhaps 'sticky' goats' cheese with strawberries and balsamic, or squid and chorizo on butter beans with basil oil), before sampling garlicky slow-cooked leg of lamb in paper with lemon and thyme, chickpea purée and mint – 'Greece on a plate', bursting with sunny, fragrant undertones. To finish, consider St Clements posset with sugared raspberries. House wines from £14.90.

Chef/s: Mark Ferrier. **Open:** Mon to Sat D only 6.30 to 9.15. **Closed:** Sun, 25 and 26 Dec. **Meals:** alc (main courses £13 to £19). Set D £15.90 (2 courses) to £18.90. **Service:** not inc. **Details:** Cards accepted. 50 seats. Wheelchair access. Music. Children allowed.

Staddlebridge

McCoys at the Tontine

A delightfully oddball destination
Staddlebridge, DL6 3JB
Tel no: (01609) 882671
www.mccoystontine.co.uk
Modern British | £41
Cooking score: 3

Longevity is a virtue at the McCoy brothers' delightfully oddball destination just off the A19, and one devout regular who has been frequenting the Tontine since it opened back in the 70s confirms that the place has 'stood the test of time'. The bistro-style restaurant still exudes a heady whiff of eccentricity and the menu looks determinedly to the past, taking punters on a retro trip from moules marinière and prawn cocktail to featherlight crêpes San Lorenzo filled with Chantilly cream. Roast foie gras with grapes and brioche is 'the daddy of all starters', while enduring mains include 'mouthwatering' Grassington duck with confit sausage and onion tarte Tatin. House wine is £18.75.

Chef/s: Simon Whalley. **Open:** all week L 12 to 2, D 6.30 to 9 (9.45 Fri and Sat, 8.30 Sun). **Closed:** 25 and 26 Dec, 1 to 3 Jan. **Meals:** alc (main courses £22 to £29). Set L £15.95 (2 courses) to £17.95. Sun L £22.50. **Service:** not inc. **Details:** Cards accepted. 90 seats. Music. Children allowed. Car parking.

West Tanfield

NEW ENTRY

The Bruce Arms

Fine food for this pretty part of Yorkshire
Main Street, West Tanfield, HG4 5JJ
Tel no: (01677) 470325
www.brucearms.co.uk
Modern British | £26
Cooking score: 3

'It really does show when chef and proprietor are one and the same', writes one reporter of this stone-built, eighteenth-century roadside inn. Inside, the flag-floored bar and two dining areas are interlinked, with beams, log fires, polished tables and sporting paraphernalia mixed with some lively contemporary paintings. The unfussy mood is matched by Hugh Carruthers' short, sharp menu peppered with clear, natural and uncluttered flavours. Sweet mussels in cream sauce with good bread for mopping up, precisely timed turbot with Jersey Royals, asparagus and broad beans, or gloriously tender calf's liver on mash and excellent spring greens have all been applauded, while a textbook chocolate fondant proves there's no dipping when it comes to desserts. House wine is £13.95.

Chef/s: Hugh Carruthers. **Open:** Tue to Sun L 12 to 2.30 (3 Sun), Tue to Sat D 5.30 to 9.30. **Closed:** Mon, 2 weeks Feb. **Meals:** alc (main courses £13 to £20). Set L £12.50 (2 courses). **Service:** not inc. **Details:** Cards accepted. 40 seats. 30 seats outside. Wheelchair access. Music. Children allowed. Car parking.

West Witton

The Wensleydale Heifer

Big-city seafood in the country
Main Street, West Witton, DL8 4LS
Tel no: (01969) 622322
www.wensleydaleheifer.co.uk
Seafood | £35
Cooking score: 3

The Heifer continues to win over tourists and locals with its beguiling mix of log-fired pub, smart dining rooms and dedication to seafood. Spanking fresh fish has been given an emphatic thumbs-up on eager-to-please menus. Keep it simple with a generous plate of fish and chips, or a seafood pie; otherwise explore one of the more exotic options – perhaps a starter of scallops with cauliflower and Indian-spiced curry, or a main course of whole roast sweet-chilli sea bass with crab and prawn stuffing. There are also several meat options, ranging from a straightforward ribeye steak (with rocket and Parmesan salad, frites, Madeira jus and truffle) to a spicy

Moroccan shoulder of lamb with couscous. Baked Alaska and knickerbocker glory are nicely retro puds. House wine is £17.50.
Chef/s: David Moss. **Open:** all week L 12 to 2.30, D 6 to 9.30. **Meals:** alc (main courses £15 to £23). Set L and D £17.50 (2 courses) to £19.50. Sun L £18.50. **Service:** 10% (optional). **Details:** Cards accepted. 75 seats. 40 seats outside. Separate bar. Wheelchair access. Music. Children allowed. Car parking.

Whitby

Green's

Clued-up seafood champion
13 Bridge Street, Whitby, YO22 4BG
Tel no: (01947) 600284
www.greensofwhitby.com
Seafood | £30
Cooking score: 3
V

Whitby may be addicted to fish and chips, but Rob Green's livewire set-up takes seafood to another level in the town. This is a clued-up, two-tiered operation with a buzzy bistro on the ground floor and a swish dining room upstairs (think low lights and intimate booths). One accessible menu now fits all, although fish from name-checked Whitby trawlers remains the main attraction – fillet of turbot with a vegetable nage and poached shellfish, say. Otherwise, expect an eclectic bonanza taking in grilled scallops with Parmesan and pesto, bouillabaisse and Thai seafood curry as well as fish pie, moules frites and oysters every which way. Alternatively, shun seafood in favour of a Yorkshire-reared rump steak or a grilled pork chop with black pudding. Wines start at £15.25. Note: the Greens recently added two 'boutique apartments' to their accommodation in the town.
Chef/s: Rob Green and Ryan Osbourne. **Open:** Mon to Fri L 12 to 2, D 6.30 to 9.30 (10 Fri). Sat and Sun 12 to 10. **Closed:** 25 and 26 Dec, 1 Jan. **Meals:** alc (main courses £11 to £22). **Service:** not inc. **Details:** Cards accepted. 56 seats. Separate bar. No mobile phones. Wheelchair access. Music. Children allowed.

Magpie Café

King of the fish and chip cafés
14 Pier Road, Whitby, YO21 3PU
Tel no: (01947) 602058
www.magpiecafe.co.uk
Seafood | £25
Cooking score: 2

A Whitby resident since the 1940s (and a Guide fixture for more than three decades), the Magpie certainly has longevity on its side. Pitched right by the quay, it's become the doyen of fish and chip cafés, buying from boats that trawl well-managed fishing grounds and casting its net beyond cod and haddock to include species such as ling, coley and pollack. Families dote on the place, lured by 'best-ever' examples of the fryer's art, plus more flashy piscine offerings such as bouillabaisse ('timed to perfection'). Be sure to leave room for one of the Magpie's famous puds – perhaps boozy sherry trifle or Yorkshire fruitcake with a hunk of Hawes Wensleydale cheese. There are meat dishes for those who must and wine from £13.95.
Chef/s: Ian Robson and Paul Gildroy. **Open:** all week 11.30 to 9. **Closed:** 25 and 26 Dec, 4 to 27 Jan. **Meals:** alc (main courses £7 to £23). **Service:** not inc. **Details:** Cards accepted. 120 seats. Wheelchair access. Music. Children allowed.

York

NEW ENTRY

de'Clare Café

Exciting newcomer with all-round quality
1 Peter Lane, York, YO1 8SW
Tel no: (01904) 652920
www.declaredeli.co.uk
Spanish | £18
Cooking score: 2

Tucked down a side street, this is an informal newcomer to watch. Big, round tables and Verner Panton chairs offset a menu of Spanish-inspired dishes such as a gorgeous plate of grilled Monte Enebro cheese with orange blossom honey dressing. Elsewhere on the menu expect meat and cheese platters, hot chorizo salad or braised chicken breast with raisins, pine nuts and saffron. Desserts scored highly, with fresh dates soaked in coffee and cardamom syrup, or a turrón mousse with sherry-marinated raisins. Teatime indulgences run from decadent chocolate and Guinness cake, to quince and almond tart. Good coffee and a bright Spanish wine list confirm an all-round quality ethic.

Chef/s: Sally Duncan. **Open:** all week 8am to 6pm (10 to 8 Thur to Sat, 10 to 4 Sun). **Closed:** 25 and 26 Dec, bank hols. **Meals:** alc (main courses £8 to £14). **Service:** not inc. **Details:** Cards accepted. 36 seats. Wheelchair access. Music. Children allowed.

J. Baker's Bistro Moderne

Affordable fine dining and fun

7 Fossgate, York, YO1 9TA
Tel no: (01904) 622688
www.jbakers.co.uk
Modern British | £30
Cooking score: 5

£5 OFF

Jeff's Baker's self-proclaimed 'bistro moderne' ranks among York's finest, not least because its fun, thrills and gastro treats are dealt out at prices everyone can afford. Also, his short and playful menu is always a one-off – how about Whitby crab with seaweed and sesame biscuits, followed by Goosnargh duck with 'leftover Christmas pudding', blood orange and parsnip, or perhaps rabbit pie and mash with Agen prunes and 'in-house lardons'. Very occasionally it all goes wrong in the kitchen and out front, but most readers are unreservedly positive – especially when it comes to cheeky desserts such as 'lemon tops' (a rich concoction of lemon-curd ice cream, meringue and lemon thyme custard) or maybe apple crumble sundae with a touch of curry. If you fancy the full works, order the seven-course tasting menu – an unpredictable adventure that depends on whatever Baker fancies cooking. Meanwhile, the upstairs 'chocolate lounge' has its own special temptations for fans of the cocoa bean, while lunchtime callers can sample Baker's inventive wares in the form of 'grazing plates'. Good value extends to the wine list, which opens at £15.50.

Chef/s: Jeff Baker. **Open:** Tue to Sat L 12 to 3.30, D 6 to 10. **Closed:** first week Jan. **Meals:** Set L £9 (2 courses) to £12. Set D £25 (2 courses) to £29.50. Tasting menu £37.50. **Service:** 10% (optional). **Details:** Cards accepted. 56 seats. Separate bar. Wheelchair access. Music. Children allowed.

Le Langhe

Foodie heaven

The Old Coach House, Peasholme Green, York, YO1 7PW
Tel no: (01904) 622584
www.lelanghe.co.uk
Italian | £35
Cooking score: 4

Since the move to bigger premises, Le Langhe has established itself as a stellar Italian restaurant, not just for York but Yorkshire itself. Behind the well-stocked Italian deli is an airy mezzanine, a dining terrace and, upstairs, a beamed room for a superior evening meal. While the cooking appears relaxed and effortless, what arrives is frequently exceptional. At its simplest, it is a wooden board bearing impeccably sourced Italian cured meats or cheeses with olives and bread. Elsewhere there might be wild rabbit terrine or a fish broth, delicate pared-back pasta dishes such as ravioli of roasted pumpkin and goats' cheese, and mains of roast quail with porcini and herb oil. To finish, a chocolate and hazelnut torte with pistachio ice cream is the star of a starry firmament of cakes and tarts. A fabulous Italian wine list reflects proprietor Ottavio Bocca's intense commitment with plenty of big names by the glass. Prices run from £14.50 for a bottle of Gavi to £114.50 for a 2007 Kurni.

Chef/s: Ottavio Bocca. **Open:** Mon to Sat L 12 to 3, Fri and Sat D 7 to 9. **Closed:** Sun, 1 to 20 Jan. **Meals:** alc (main courses £17 to £22). Set L £12.50 (2 courses) to £22.50. Tasting menu £35 (6 courses).

Service: not inc. **Details:** Cards accepted. 50 seats. 20 seats outside. No mobile phones. Music. Children allowed.

Melton's

Impressively good stuff
7 Scarcroft Road, York, YO23 1ND
Tel no: (01904) 634341
www.meltonsrestaurant.co.uk
British | £30
Cooking score: 5

£5 OFF

Readers continue to offer unstinting praise for this consistent neighbourhood restaurant just south of the city walls. 'A real gem' notes one, while another comments: 'very good food in pleasant surroundings, served by pleasant people'. The pleasant people in question are husband and wife team Michael and Lucy Hjort, who opened in 1990 and have been Guide stalwarts ever since. Lucy operates front-of-house while Michael heads the kitchen. Melton's style is accomplished but unpretentious, allowing top-class Yorkshire produce to take centre stage. Their beef comes from Highland cattle reared on the limestone pastures of the Yorkshire Dales, and the pheasant from the North York Moors is served with Ampleforth Abbey's cider apple brandy. There are Whitby crab cakes with organic leeks; Yorkshire rhubarb and two custards with iced rhubarb sticks, and, to finish, a plate of well-chosen native cheeses. Over and above a knowledgeable wine list with nothing topping £26 and plenty of half-bottles, Lucy Hjort offers wine suggestions for every dish. The bill is restrained for food of this calibre, and coffee and water are complimentary. Good-value 'first Saturday' (and Monday) lunches and early-bird dinners ensure Melton's retains its strong local following.
Chef/s: Michael Hjort. **Open:** Tue to Sat L 12 to 2, D 5.30 to 9.30 (10 Sun). **Closed:** Sun, Mon, 3 weeks Christmas, 1 week Aug. **Meals:** alc (main courses £15 to £19). Set L £20.50 (2 courses) to £24. Tasting menu £35. **Service:** not inc. **Details:** Cards accepted. 42 seats. Music. Children allowed.

Melton's Too

Boisterous bistro for all-comers
25 Walmgate, York, YO1 9TX
Tel no: (01904) 629222
www.meltonstoo.co.uk
Modern European | £20
Cooking score: 2

Melton's Too is Melton's other half (see entry), a busy, buzzy bistro with benches, bucket chairs and the daily papers downstairs, while upstairs it's rough old floorboards and exposed brick with blow-ups of the York Food Festival – a reminder of owner Michael Hjort's role as Director. Workshops and tastings run through the year, as do dinners highlighting regional produce. Simple and gutsy food characterises a menu that might offer buttery baked mushrooms with melted Swaledale cheese or a pleasing 'Lebanese' plate with hummus, filo parcel and crisp and tender falafel. Mains could be coq au vin or smoked haddock with poached egg and mustard sauce, followed by a selection of homely puddings. Good-value express lunches and early-evening dinners are a regular feature. Wines start at £14.50.
Chef/s: Michael Hjort. **Open:** all week 10.30am to 10.30pm (9.30pm Sun). **Closed:** 25 and 26 Dec, 1 Jan. **Meals:** alc (main courses £9 to £13). Set L and early D £12.50 (2 courses). **Service:** 10% (optional). **Details:** Cards accepted. 120 seats. Separate bar. Wheelchair access. Music. Children allowed.

SCOTLAND

Borders, Dumfries & Galloway,
Lothians (inc. Edinburgh),
Strathclyde (inc. Glasgow), Central, Fife,
Tayside, Grampian, Highlands & Islands

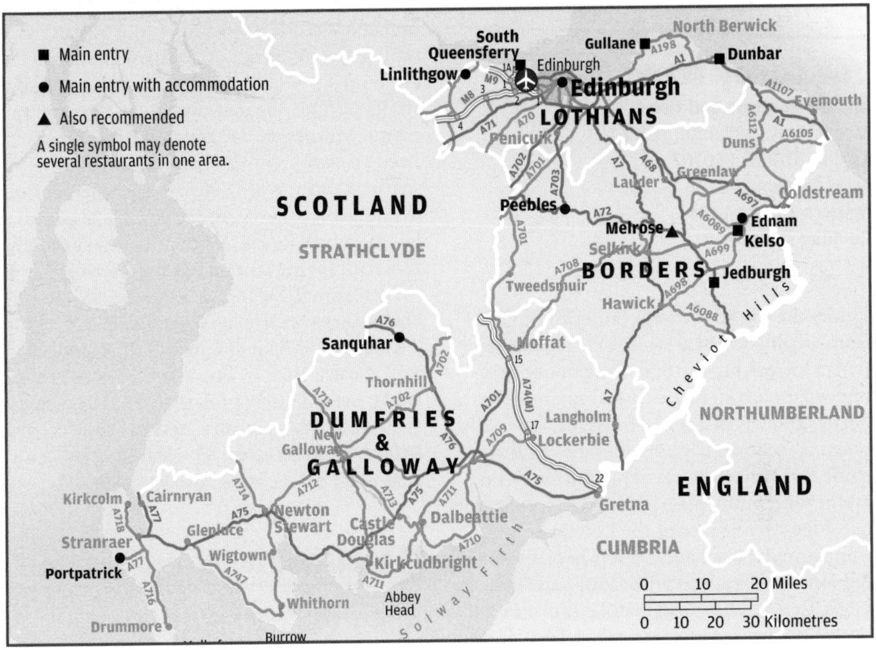

■ Main entry
● Main entry with accommodation
▲ Also recommended
A single symbol may denote several restaurants in one area.

Edenwater House

Edenwater House

Tranquil retreat with rewarding cooking
Ednam, TD5 7QL
Tel no: (01573) 224070
www.edenwaterhouse.co.uk
Modern British | £36
Cooking score: 4

The former Ednam Manse is a tranquil country hotel, steeped in history and overlooking Eden Water and the surrounding countryside. If residents haven't bagged all the tables, you may just get a dinner booking and be rewarded with a three-course menu of well-wrought country house cooking. A typical meal might progress from sautéed Eyemouth langoustines with seafood croquettes and mango and cucumber salsa, through a show-stopping main course such as guinea fowl breast stuffed with morel mousseline and wrapped in Parma ham, served with celeriac and kale purée and shallot Tatin, to the alluring indulgence of chestnut cheesecake with a compote of fig, plum, pear and pomegranate. House Languedoc at £16 heads up a carefully annotated list of classy wines that takes in Slovenia and Lebanon, as well as the headline French regions.

Chef/s: Jacqui Kelly. **Open:** Tue to Sat D only 8 (1 sitting). **Closed:** Sun, Mon, 1 Dec to 1 Mar. **Meals:** Set D £28 (2 courses) to £36. **Service:** not inc. **Details:** Cards accepted. 16 seats. No music. No mobile phones. Car parking.

Symbols

- Accommodation is available
- £30 Three courses for less than £30
- V Separate vegetarian menu
- £5 OFF £5-off voucher scheme
- Notable wine list

Jedburgh

The Caddy Mann

Mecca for game and fish
Mounthooly, Jedburgh, TD8 6TJ
Tel no: (01835) 850787
www.caddymann.com
Modern British | £29
Cooking score: 2

Ignore the slightly 'wonky' interiors and far-from-sophisticated service – chef/proprietor Ross Horrocks is 'the best thing' about this idiosyncratic restaurant. Spending five years at Gleneagles has sharpened his skills, especially when it comes to cooking his beloved Borders game and fish: a terrine of pigeon and wild rabbit with plum sauce and a duck spring roll combines the essence of the Lowlands with some oriental brio, and readers have also liked his combo of scallops with slow-cooked belly pork. To follow, sea bass with lemon and dill risotto has been perfectly judged, likewise local lamb three ways. Finely executed desserts such as a cheeky 'Jaffa cake' with cinder toffee go down a storm, the cheeseboard is 'sensational' and wines start at £12.95.

Chef/s: Ross Horrocks. **Open:** all week L 12 to 2, Fri and Sat D 7 to 9. **Closed:** 25 and 26 Dec, 1 and 2 Jan. **Meals:** alc (main courses £9 to £19). **Service:** not inc. **Details:** Cards accepted. 50 seats. 12 seats outside. No mobile phones. Wheelchair access. Children allowed. Car parking.

Kelso

NEW ENTRY

The Cobbles Inn

Local beer and victuals
7 Bowmont Street, Kelso, TD5 7JH
Tel no: (01573) 223548
www.thecobblesinn.co.uk
Modern European | £25
Cooking score: 1

Chef Gavin Meiklejohn has become a local hero in Kelso, setting up the Tempest microbrewery as well as re-energising this updated Victorian coaching inn. You can sample the full range of Tempest ales here, although the Cobbles is also attracting plaudits for its eclectic pub grub and serious restaurant menu. Mushroom rarebit cooked in 'black beer' on crispy sourdough is full of sweet, sharp nuances, while a dish of melting venison Wellington comes generously enriched with a boozy chocolate sauce. For afters, baked apple tart with thyme custard has hit the target. Wines from £13.50.

Chef/s: Gavin Meiklejohn. **Open:** Tue to Sun L 12 to 2 (2.30 Sat and Sun), D 6 to 9 (9.30 Fri and Sat, 8 Sun). **Closed:** Mon, 26 Dec, 1 Jan, 2 weeks Jan. **Meals:** Set D £20.95 (2 courses) to £24.95. Sun L £18.95. Bar menu available. **Service:** not inc. **Details:** Cards accepted. 65 seats. Separate bar. Wheelchair access. Music. Children allowed.

Melrose

ALSO RECOMMENDED

▲ Burt's Hotel

Market Square, Melrose, TD6 9PL
Tel no: (01896) 822285
www.burtshotel.co.uk
Modern British

The Henderson family's small hotel successfully combines the roles of inn and restaurant. The dining room is done in loosely defined period style, with busily patterned fabrics and impeccably laid tables, but the bar retains its polished wood furniture and casual feel – the setting for informal lunches or suppers. Formal restaurant dinners (three courses £36) offer chicken, pheasant and smoked bacon terrine, then pork fillet, belly and cheek with Savoy cabbage, apple purée and Calvados sauce, and an assiette of chocolate to finish. Wines from £15.35. Open all week.

Also Recommended

Also recommended entries are not scored but we think they are worth a visit.

Peebles

Cringletie House

Bold style in a baronial pile
Edinburgh Road, Peebles, EH45 8PL
Tel no: (01721) 725750
www.cringletie.com
Modern British | £30
Cooking score: 4

£5 OFF 🍷 🛏 V

Set in 25 acres of sculpted Borders real estate, Cringletie House has the high baronial style down to a T, with turrets and gables, a vintage dovecote and a thriving seventeenth-century walled garden. Inside, the elegant Sutherland Room piles on the classicism with a carved oak fireplace and a delightful trompe l'oeil mural on the ceiling, à la Sistine Chapel. Craig Gibb's cooking also has a classical backbone, whether he is fashioning a subtly sweet 'fresh as air' starter of langoustine with cauliflower purée, serving Jerusalem artichoke velouté with foie gras ice cream and bacon cakes, or plucking apples from the garden for a dessert involving a textbook soufflé, sorbet and rum-soaked compote. In between, boned squab with morels and broad beans is a perfect gamey take on cassoulet with a piquant jus, while turbot fillet might be paired with Eyemouth crab, shallot purée and tomato and basil dressing. Cringletie's owners have travelled the globe in search of fine wines from elite, independent producers, and the list is a tribute to their knowledge and enthusiasm. Prices start at £18.50.

Chef/s: Craig Gibb. **Open:** all week L 12.30 to 2.30, D 6.30 to 9. **Closed:** 8 to 27 Jan. **Meals:** Set L £10 (2 courses) to £15. Set D £25 (2 courses) to £30. Sun L £10 (2 courses) to £22.50. Tasting menu £59. **Service:** not inc. **Details:** Cards accepted. 50 seats. Separate bar. No mobile phones. Wheelchair access. Music. Children allowed. Car parking.

NEW ENTRY

Osso

Tearoom by day; restaurant by night
Innerleithen Road, Peebles, EH45 8AB
Tel no: (01721) 724477
www.ossorestaurant.com
Modern British | £29
Cooking score: 3

As day turns to night, buzzy Osso morphs effortlessly from populist cake shop into serious-minded restaurant, and its functional modern interior copes well with these schizophrenic demands. Once the buggy-pushing mums have departed, the place puts on its glad rags and a splendid eatery emerges from the crumbs and toys. The kitchen turns out a succession of precise up-to-date dishes, ranging from zingily fresh sweet potato and ginger soup or seared scallops with foie gras, cauliflower and apple, to espresso-spiked affogato with thick, gloopy black cherries. For main course, delicate truffle-stuffed ballottine of chicken leg might be served on a capably executed leek and herb risotto, while halibut fillet could be matched with curried split peas. Set menus are terrific value and the brief wine list includes some thoughtful offerings from £13.50.

Chef/s: Ally McGrath. **Open:** all week L 11 to 4.30, Tue to Sat D 6 to 9. **Closed:** 25 Dec, 1 Jan. **Meals:** alc (main courses £13 to £21). Set D £18.50 (2 courses) to £24. **Service:** not inc. **Details:** Cards accepted. 37 seats. 4 seats outside. Wheelchair access. Music. Children allowed.

Portpatrick

Knockinaam Lodge

Splendid isolation, splendid food
Portpatrick, DG9 9AD
Tel no: (01776) 810471
www.knockinaamlodge.com
Modern British | £58
Cooking score: 5

£5 OFF

With wooded glens and rugged cliffs all around, it's easy to imagine some high drama being played out in the shadow of this Victorian hunting lodge – no wonder the area inspired John Buchan's thriller *The 39 Steps*. Knockinaam revels in its isolation, with 30 acres of lavish gardens running down to a private beach overlooking the Irish Sea. As for the food, long-serving chef Tony Pierce produces a refined version of Scottish country house cooking for guests assembled in the sedate, quietly intimate dining room. Native ingredients are treated with due respect, although France is the main culinary influence on the daily changing, four-course dinner menu. There's no choice until it comes to 'cheese or dessert', but poise, finesse and fully rounded satisfaction are guaranteed. On a February night you might begin with grilled fillet of Luce Bay sea bass with pesto and green olive tapenade before sipping a bowl of leek, potato and truffle soup. The centrepiece is generally meat – perhaps slow-roast fillet of Speyside beef served with shallot purée, spiced lentils, seared duck foie gras and a port and thyme reduction. Finally, those of a sweet-toothed persuasion might be swayed by the prospect of an individual pear tarte Tatin with vanilla ice cream and Calvados caramel. Owner David Ibbotson has assembled a loving and authoritative collection of top-drawer bottles from every corner of the winemaking world. Growers and vintages are impeccable, with house selections opening at £22.

Chef/s: Tony Pierce. **Open:** all week L 12 to 2, D 7 to 9. **Meals:** Set L £40 (4 courses). Set D £58 (5 courses). Sun L £30 (4 courses). **Service:** not inc. **Details:** Cards accepted. 22 seats. Separate bar. No mobile phones. Wheelchair access. Music. Car parking.

Sanquhar

Blackaddie House Hotel

Food to set the pulse racing
Blackaddie Road, Sanquhar, DG4 6JJ
Tel no: (01659) 50270
www.blackaddiehotel.co.uk
Modern British | £45
Cooking score: 4

£5 OFF

Guide veteran Ian McAndrew is back on form, cooking up a storm at this sixteenth-century stone house with gardens bordered by the river Nith. Blackaddie's dining room makes a rather sedate setting for what one reader called 'an explosion of flavours' based on locally sourced produce: free-range meat comes from nearby Sunnyside Farm and McAndrew scours the region for everything else. The result is precise food with lots of detailing and highly worked presentation – witness a dish involving slow-braised Dexter beef shin with a coconut crust, served with beetroot and garlic purées, foraged girolles and shallot pannacotta. Elsewhere, reporters have endorsed halibut fillet on kedgeree 'risotto' with soft-boiled quails' eggs and a salad of confit chicken, as well as Gloucester Old Spot pork 'three ways' with carrot purée and mille-feuille potatoes. Desserts also set the pulse racing – perhaps iced damson parfait, a 'study in cinnamon' or peach brûlée. A well-considered wine list puts the emphasis firmly on food-friendly tipples from £19.95.

Chef/s: Ian McAndrew and Gordon Graham. **Open:** all week L 12 to 2, D 6.30 to 9.30. **Closed:** 27 to 30 Dec. **Meals:** alc (main courses £16 to £29). Set L £18.50 (2 courses) to £24. **Service:** not inc. **Details:** Cards accepted. 22 seats. Separate bar. No mobile phones. Wheelchair access. Music. Children allowed. Car parking.

Dunbar

The Creel

Fashionable round-the-world food
25 Lamer Street, Dunbar, EH42 1HJ
Tel no: (01368) 863279
www.creelrestaurant.co.uk
Modern British | £25
Cooking score: 3

Logan Thorburn is a food crusader, a champion of East Lothian's native produce with aims that are more ethical than commercial. Menus are sensibly compact and appealing, and the result is genuine, unaffected natural cooking – a perfect match for the unpretentious bistro setting. A crisp tempura of squid with a sesame and soy dipping sauce is typical of Logan's fashionable round-the-world treatments, while grilled collops of monkfish with patatas bravas and a light aïoli dressing is all about great flavours. Desserts highlight the virtues of simplicity with light cinnamon beignet soufflés, rich chocolate sauce and pouring cream. The short wine list does its job, with decent choice and, like the rest of the menu, fair prices. House recommendations from £15.50.

Chef/s: Logan Thorburn. **Open:** Wed to Sun L 12 to 2, Thur to Sat D 6.30 to 9. **Closed:** Mon, Tue. **Meals:** Set L £14.25 (2 courses) to £18.25. Set D £19.50 (2 courses) to £25. **Service:** not inc. **Details:** Cards accepted. 36 seats. No mobile phones. Wheelchair access. Music. Children allowed.

Symbols

Accommodation is available
Three courses for less than £30
V Separate vegetarian menu
£5-off voucher scheme
Notable wine list

Edinburgh

NEW ENTRY

Angels with Bagpipes

Old Town meets the 21st century
343 High Street, Royal Mile, Edinburgh, EH1 1PW
Tel no: (0131) 2201111
www.angelswithbagpipes.co.uk
Modern European | £35
Cooking score: 3

AWB is a great addition to the Edinburgh food scene. The latest from Marina Crolla of the Valvona & Crolla dynasty (see entry), it's an antidote to the touristy tack on the upper Royal Mile. Surprisingly modern and spacious given the cramped, ancient locale, this is where suits and Morningside mink (vintage, of course) commingle to the popping of Prosecco corks. Reporters are unanimous in their praise for sweet and smoky pigeon breast served with pearl barley and parsnip purée, while slow-cooked beef shin on buttery mash with crispy cavolo nero and a precise veal jus dissolves sweetly on impact, elevating a simple lunch into something refined and satisfying. Desserts are lightly executed big-hitters: mousse, brownie, sponge, parfait. House wine is £17.90.

Chef/s: Paul Whitecross. **Open:** all week 12 to 10. **Closed:** 24 to 26 Dec. **Meals:** alc (main courses £13 to £21). Set L £14.80 (2 courses) to £18.80. **Service:** not inc. **Details:** Cards accepted. 70 seats. 24 seats outside. No mobile phones. Wheelchair access. Music. Children allowed.

The Balmoral, Number One

Star restaurant at a princely address
1 Princes Street, Edinburgh, EH2 2EQ
Tel no: (0131) 5576727
www.restaurantnumberone.com
Modern European | £62
new chef

V

Sitting like a grand bastion at one end of Princes Street, the Balmoral continues to confound expectations in the best ways. Despite its clock tower and soaring lobby, there is no sense of hauteur about the place – especially in the comfortable dining room, which has been the scene for some short-circuiting of preconceptions in the past. New chef Paul Burns moved here from Airds Hotel, Port Appin (see entry) as the Guide was going to press, but comes with a reputation for cooking immaculately fresh seafood, robust meat dishes and affectionate, old-school desserts. However, his arrival shouldn't impact on the quality of the Balmoral's superb cheese trolley or indeed its satisfyingly encyclopaedic wine list – a fine collection of big names from across the major countries, with some notably good Italians standing out. Prices start at £25 (£8 a glass). Reports please.

Chef/s: Paul Burns. **Open:** all week D only 6.30 to 10. **Closed:** first 2 weeks Jan. **Meals:** Set D £62. Tasting menu £69. **Service:** not inc. **Details:** Cards accepted. 55 seats. Separate bar. No mobile phones. Wheelchair access. Music. Children allowed.

The Bonham

Smart hotel with stimulating menus
35 Drumsheugh Gardens, Edinburgh, EH3 7RN
Tel no: (0131) 2266050
www.thebonham.com
Modern French | £40
Cooking score: 4

The personification of boutique Edinburgh chic, this sleekly refashioned Victorian town house goes about its business as an über-cool hospitality destination with a 'good, solid restaurant' attached. Gigantic mirrors and contemporary artwork catch the eye in the snazzily attired dining room, although most attention focuses on the stimulating food emanating from Michel Bouyer's kitchen. Born in Brittany, he fuses influences from his home patch and beyond with top-drawer Scottish produce and assorted global flavours. Seared scallops with a pig's trotter croquette impressed one reader, although the bivalves have also been paired with Achiltibuie kipper brandade, pannacotta and curry sauce. Elsewhere, indigenous meat and game are deployed with dexterity and fine French technique – a duo of lamb with sunny, seasonal companions in the shape of aubergine and ricotta cannelloni, Kalamata olives, green asparagus tartare and wild garlic pesto, for example. As a finale, you might consider hot vanilla soufflé with 'apple pie' ice cream. The wide-ranging, 50-bin wine list opens at £17.50.

Chef/s: Michel Bouyer. **Open:** all week L 12 to 2.30, D 6.30 to 10. **Meals:** alc (main courses £20 to £60). Set L and D £16.50 (2 courses) to £20. Sun L £20. **Service:** not inc. **Details:** Cards accepted. 60 seats. Wheelchair access. Music. Children allowed. Car parking.

Café St Honoré

Like being in Paris
34 North West Thistle Street Lane, Edinburgh, EH2 1EA
Tel no: (0131) 2262211
www.cafesthonore.com
French | £34
Cooking score: 3

£5 OFF

More old-school Parisian than Edinburgh's New Town, this characteristic French brasserie has close-set tables, bentwood chairs, a checkerboard floor and pleasant staff. The friendly and relaxed setting perfectly fits the archetypal brasserie menu of unpretentious cuisine and top-quality seasonal ingredients. Classics such as confit duck leg with braised lentils, or organic coq au vin rub shoulders with more native influences, perhaps a starter of smoked haddock Cullen skink or mains of Perthshire venison haunch wth dauphinoise potato, shallots, local beetroot, red cabbage and haggis bonbon. Honey and oat parfait with cinnamon porridge keeps up the Scottish theme, but dark chocolate pithiviers with crème fraîche sorbet brings you back to France. House wine is £17.90.

Chef/s: Ben Radford and Neil Forbes. **Open:** all week L 12 to 2, D 5.15 to 10 (6 Sat and Sun). **Closed:** 24 to 26 Dec, 1 to 2 Jan. **Meals:** alc (main courses £17 to £24). Set L £15.50 (2 courses) to £19.50. D £18

(2 courses) to £22.50. Sun L £15.50 (2 courses). **Service:** 10% (optional). **Details:** Cards accepted. 48 seats. Music. Children allowed.

NEW ENTRY

Castle Terrace

Superlative cooking, sensational food
33-35 Castle Terrace, Edinburgh, EH1 2EL
Tel no: (0131) 2291222
www.castleterracerestaurant.com
Modern British | £45
Cooking score: 5

V

Chef Dominic Jack has hit Edinburgh with a fully sharpened set of Sabatiers. His tutelage at two of Paris's most vaunted institutions (L'Arpège and Taillevent) is to Edinburgh's gain. Working in partnership with Tom Kitchin (see entry, The Kitchin), he has created a serious addition to the capital's increasingly impressive culinary scene. The restaurant's warm, sumptuous, autumnal colours are matched by superlative cooking – 'the food was sensational', raved one reporter. 'The entire experience just underpinned perfection, from the outstanding level of customer service to each and every dish', noted another. The details are fascinating: at inspection, halibut ceviche, served sushi-style with a wasabi-heaped sliver of baked lemon, punched well above its weight; tenderly crunchy breadcrumbed veal kidney in a Pommery mustard veal jus, cornered by turrets of fondant potato and framed by tender strips of braised celery, made for an arty interpretation of a bourgeois French classic, and vanilla pannacotta and rosemary jelly sensationally offset some early rhubarb. Elsewhere, cromesquis of pig's trotters, hare royale and steamed orange pudding have displayed 'superb attention to detail'. The wine list has a core of French classics with a good selection from other Old World and New World vineyards and plenty by the glass. Bottles start at £20.
Chef/s: Dominic Jack. **Open:** Tue to Sat L 12 to 2, D 6.30 to 10. **Closed:** 24 Dec to 17 Jan. **Meals:** alc (main courses £19 to £29). Set L £20. Tasting menu £60 (6 courses). **Service:** 10% (optional). **Details:** Cards accepted. 55 seats. Separate bar. Wheelchair access. Music. Children allowed.

Centotre

Buzzing all-day Italian cafè
103 George Street, Edinburgh, EH2 3ES
Tel no: (0131) 2251550
www.centotre.com
Italian | £23
Cooking score: 2

You can have anything from morning coffee to a three-course dinner at Victor and Carina Contini's buzzing all-day café. As members of the celebrated family that established Valvona & Crolla (see entry), you can expect a genuine enthusiasm for straightforward Italian cooking built around top quality British and Italian ingredients ('the best balsamic vinegar we have tasted'). Pizza and pasta form the bulk of the menu, but there's also antipasti including great prosciutto di Parma, rose veal Milanese-style (fried in egg and breadcrumbs), fresh mackerel roasted with thyme and lemon, and chocolate mousse with amaretti biscuits for dessert. A decent choice of Italian wines starts at £14.95.
Chef/s: Carina Contini. **Open:** all week L 12 to 5, D 5 to 10 (10.30 Thurs, 11 Fri and Sat, 9 Sun). **Closed:** 25 and 26 Dec. **Meals:** alc (main courses £9 to £21). Set L £16.95 (2 courses) to £19.95. **Service:** not inc. **Details:** Cards accepted. 146 seats. 40 seats outside. Separate bar. Wheelchair access. Music. Children allowed.

David Bann

Veggie with vivid global flavours
56-58 St Mary's Street, Edinburgh, EH1 1SX
Tel no: (0131) 5565888
www.davidbann.co.uk
Vegetarian | £22
Cooking score: 2

V 

David Bann's veggie hot spot instantly dispels any myths about rainbow T-shirts and lentil burgers, thanks to sexy lighting, high-gloss décor and vivid global flavours.The exuberant menu reads like a foodie shopping list, so brace yourself before considering home-smoked tofu served on organic udon noodles with pak choi, shiitake mushrooms and a sauce of roasted red pepper, ginger, chilli, mirin and coriander, or Dunsyre Blue cheese, beetroot and apple soufflé with assorted additions. Thankfully, things get sleeker when it comes to desserts such as hot pear and passion fruit tart. Weekend brunches promise a frisky take on the full English, and wine buffs have plenty of sound drinking from £13.75.

Chef/s: David Bann. **Open:** all week 12 to 10 (10.30 Fri, 11 to 10.30 Sat, 11 to 10 Sun). **Closed:** 25 and 26 Dec, 1 Jan. **Meals:** alc (main courses £10 to £13). Set L and D £16.50 (2 courses) to £21.50. **Service:** not inc. **Details:** Cards accepted. 80 seats. No music. Children allowed.

The Dogs

Food with plenty of bite
110 Hanover Street, Edinburgh, EH2 1DR
Tel no: (0131) 2201208
www.thedogsonline.co.uk
Modern British | £19
Cooking score: 3

This high-ceilinged and refreshingly informal Georgian town house buzzes with conversation, clatter and general excitement – no doubt generated by the prospect of 'blood and guts' gastronomy at knockdown prices. The Dogs has mastered the nose-to-tail concept, and shows its dedication to the cause by serving pig's cheeks, devilled ox liver and slow-braised lamb's heart stuffed with prunes and bacon, as well as faggots with home-pickled beetroot, livid green garlic mayo and pickled shallots (a pièce de résistance, according to one reader). There are also plates of home-smoked salmon with piccalilli and hake fillet with mustard sauce, while raspberry cranachan with whisky jelly ends proceedings on a patriotic high. The wine list provides sound back-up from £14.20. Italian-themed sibling Amore Dogs is at 104 Hanover Street; tel (0131) 2205155, and fish-friendly Seadogs is at 43 Rose Street; tel (0131) 2258028.

Chef/s: James Scott. **Open:** all week L 12 to 4, D 5 to 10. **Closed:** 25 Dec, 1 Jan. **Meals:** alc (main courses £8 to £20). **Service:** not inc. **Details:** Cards accepted. 60 seats. No music. Children allowed.

Forth Floor

Splendid views and stylish food
Harvey Nichols, 30-34 St Andrews Square, Edinburgh, EH2 2AD
Tel no: (0131) 5248350
www.harveynichols.co.uk
Modern European | £34
Cooking score: 3

With the Forth estuary in sight in one direction from the panoramic windows, the punning name can be forgiven. In the other direction, the city is laid out in all its splendour, best enjoyed from one of the alfresco tables perched on the edge. The place exudes Harvey Nicks style, from the creative cocktails to the menus of well-wrought brasserie dishes. Proceed from seared scallops with carrot and aniseed purée and coconut air, via braised Scottish beef shin with roast Provençal vegetables, spiced puréed aubergine and garlic confit, towards saffron-poached pear with honey cream and lemon pastry – and emerge duly satisfied. The house-branded wines alone are impressive, ranging from Sicilian Fiano to Marlborough Pinot Noir, but the main list is a masterpiece, full of classy growers and choice vintages. Prices start at £19.

Chef/s: Stuart Muir. **Open:** all week L 12 to 2.45 (3.30 Sat and Sun), Tue to Sat D 6 to 10. **Closed:** 25 Dec, 1 Jan. **Meals:** alc (main courses £16 to £22). Set L £22.50 (2 courses) to £27.50. Sun L £29.50 (2 courses) to £34.50. **Service:** 10% (optional). **Details:** Cards accepted. 65 seats. 12 seats outside. Separate bar. Wheelchair access. Music. Children allowed. Car parking.

La Garrigue

A taste of Languedoc
31 Jeffrey Street, Edinburgh, EH1 1DH
Tel no: (0131) 5573032
www.lagarrigue.co.uk
French | £30
Cooking score: 3

£5 OFF

Named after the scrubby vegetation of his native Languedoc, Jean-Michel Gauffre's restaurant brings a taste of the south to Auld Reekie. Sharpen your appetite with a shot of pastis or a Muscat-based aperitif while considering the short-and-sweet menu: saffron-hued fish soup is a 'heady bowl of delight' bolstered by unashamedly bold garlic bread, and cassoulet is among the most potent you'll taste this side of the Med, according to reports. Other tempters might include gutsy rabbit rillettes with chicory and pomegranate salad or pan-fried halibut with spicy Camargue rice, squid sausage and fennel stew. Lavender crème brûlée sings with pure Languedoc fragrance, or you could finish with nougat ice stuffed with crystallised fruit. The wine list naturally focuses on little-known treasures from warm southerly vineyards, with prices from £14.50. A second branch, La Garrigue in the New Town, is now open at 14 Eyre Place, EH3 5EP, tel (0131) 5581608. Reports please.

Chef/s: Jean-Michel Gauffre. **Open:** Mon to Sat L 12 to 2.30, D 6.30 to 9.30. **Closed:** Sun, 26 and 27 Dec, 1 to 3 Jan. **Meals:** Set L £13.50 (2 courses) to £15.50. Set D £24.50 (2 courses) to £30. Sun L £15.50. **Service:** 10% (optional). **Details:** Cards accepted. 45 seats. No music. Wheelchair access. Children allowed.

NEW ENTRY

Guchhi Indian Seafood & Bar

Vivacious modern Indian cuisine
9-10 Commercial Street, Edinburgh, EH6 6JA
Tel no: (0131) 5555604
www.guchhi.com
Indian | £22
Cooking score: 2

'Guchhi is the work of a clearly passionate chef', enthused one happy visitor to this snazzy Leith venue. While the menu takes in meaty Indian classics including biryanis, rogan josh and jalfrezi, the emphasis is on seafood, offered tapas-style, but with the option of larger dishes in the evening. It's a winning formula, not least because the vivacity of the cooking makes such a powerful case. Recent highlights have included a well-executed tandoori-smoked mackerel, a whole tandoori crab ('messy to eat, but worthwhile') and tapas of cumin-spiced haddock, chilli-butter scallops, and oysters with curry crumbs. A compact, seafood-friendly wine list starts at £13.50.

Chef/s: Sachin Dhanola. **Open:** all week L 11 to 3, D 6 to 11 (11.30 Fri and Sat). **Meals:** alc (main courses £7 to £29). Set L and D £8.95 (2 courses) to £10.95. **Service:** not inc. **Details:** Cards accepted. 48 seats. 20 seats outside. Separate bar. Wheelchair access. Music. Children allowed.

Kalpna

Benchmark Indian veggie
2-3 St Patrick Square, Edinburgh, EH8 9EZ
Tel no: (0131) 6679890
www.kalpnarestaurant.com
Indian Vegetarian | £19
Cooking score: 2

A veteran of the Edinburgh scene, Ajay Bhartdwaj's likeable restaurant remains a benchmark for Indian veggie food in the city. The menu has been tweaked of late, although it still offers a spicy cocktail of dishes drawn from Gujarat, Rajasthan and beyond. Shaam savera (spinach leaves stuffed with homemade

paneer, saffron, vegetables and nuts) is a perennial favourite, but the kitchen also sends out a mixed bag of traditional and esoteric ideas ranging from pakoras and masala dosas to baked, stuffed potato 'barrels' served with two contrasting sauces. Lunch is a buffet and there are all-inclusive thalis in the evening. Drink lassi, beer or house wine (£12.50).
Chef/s: Hukam Singh Dhanni. **Open:** Mon to Sat L 12 to 2, D 5.30 to 10.30 (11 Sat). **Closed:** Sun (exc Edinburgh Festival), 25 and 26 Dec. **Meals:** alc (main courses £6 to £10). Set L £7 (buffet). Set D from £13.50. **Service:** 10%. **Details:** Cards accepted. 50 seats. Music. Children allowed.

The Kitchin

Thrilling waterfront star
78 Commercial Quay, Leith, Edinburgh, EH6 6LX
Tel no: (0131) 5551755
www.thekitchin.com
Modern European | £60
Cooking score: 6
V

A moodily-lit former whisky distillery along the waterfront at Leith, Tom Kitchin's restaurant is one of the more thrilling destinations in the Scottish capital. Despite the urban location, Kitchin is one of those chefs who likes to get out when he can into the real world, to the harbours and game estates, in order to keep tabs on the impeccable seasonal produce with which his suppliers furnish him. The menu may evolve at a fairly stately pace, but that does minimise the number of less-than-successful experiments a constantly changing approach can risk. Thus the rolled pig's head, crispy ear and roast langoustine starter remains as stunning as when it was first conceived. Fish dishes for sharing are a rarity these days, but the whole roasted John Dory from Shetland reminds us what a delight they can be; cooked on the bone, it comes with fennel and squid and (somewhat unyielding) fondant potato. A trolley of superb Scottish and French cheeses will give you due pause, but it's hard to miss desserts such as the fine apple mille-feuille with chestnut parfait and elderberry sorbet. Service can be oddly breakneck, perhaps reflecting the adrenaline rush the kitchen is on. Wine is taken seriously, with a plethora of exciting producers and an imaginative, seasonally changing, by-the-glass selection from around £9.50. Bottles start at £26.
Chef/s: Tom Kitchin. **Open:** Tue to Sat L 12.15 to 2.30, D 6.30 to 10.30. **Closed:** Sun, Mon, 24 Dec to 24 Jan. **Meals:** alc (main courses £30 to £33). Set L £25. Tasting menu £70 (6 courses). **Service:** not inc. **Details:** Cards accepted. 50 seats. 30 seats outside. Separate bar. No mobile phones. Wheelchair access. Music. Children allowed. Car parking.

NEW ENTRY

Mark Greenaway at Hawke & Hunter

One-stop shop for the vibesters
12 Picardy Place, Edinburgh, EH1 3JT
Tel no: (0131) 5570952
www.no12picardyplace.com
Modern British | £40
Cooking score: 3

The arrival of chef Mark Greenaway completed this one-stop shop for the city's vibesters, adding accomplished cooking to an increasingly trendy urban enclave. Spread over five floors of a Georgian town house, this former gentlemen's club has moved seamlessly into the twenty-first century: there are bedrooms, bars and even a discreet nightclub. The dining room's bare stone walls, vast astragalled windows and enormous brass lampshades create a curiously warm setting for dishes such as confit of duck leg with beetroot carpaccio, 'well-executed and beautifully presented' rolled skate wing sous-vide with crispy squid and olive mash, and 'so refreshing' Bramley apple served six ways. House wine £18.
Chef/s: Mark Greenaway. **Open:** Tue to Sat L 12 to 3, D 5.30 to 10. **Closed:** Sun, Mon, 2 to 14 Jan. **Meals:** alc (main courses £16 to £28). Set L and D £16.50 (2 courses) to £20. **Service:** 10% (optional). **Details:** Cards accepted. 70 seats. Separate bar. Music. Children allowed.

★ READERS' RESTAURANT OF THE YEAR ★
SCOTLAND

Ondine

Sleek metropolitan seafood restaurant
2 George IV Bridge, Edinburgh, EH1 1AD
Tel no: (0131) 2261888
www.ondinerestaurant.co.uk
Seafood | £45
Cooking score: 4

A huge hit with reporters, stylish seafood specialist Ondine is perched above the Royal Mile, with panoramic windows providing views over George IV Bridge. Its telling mix of suave vibes, classy service and informality extends to the cooking, which promises sophistication as well as fish and chips. The kitchen's commitment to sustainability also offers balm to the conscience, and dishes really sing on the plate. Readers have praised scallops with chorizo, 'the best lobster thermidor ever' and 'sublime' fish curry, but Roy Brett's team can also deliver perfectly seasoned squid tempura, Shetland mussels 'mouclade' with a subtle garam masala broth, and 'beautifully cooked' Dover sole on the bone with hand-cut chips. To finish, chocolate and banana pot with pecan shortbread has almost been outgunned by a 'great' chocolate truffle served with home-blended coffee. Like everything else in this terrific venue, the wine list is assured and to the point. Prices start at £16.50 (£3.90 a glass).
Chef/s: Roy Brett. **Open:** all week L 12 to 3, D 5.30 to 10. **Closed:** 24 to 26 Dec, 1 to 10 Jan. **Meals:** alc (main courses £11 to £38). Set L and D £15.95 (2 courses) to £18.95. **Service:** not inc. **Details:** Cards accepted. 74 seats. Wheelchair access. Music. Children allowed.

Plumed Horse

Strong, clear flavours and skilled techniques
50-54 Henderson Street, Edinburgh, EH6 6DE
Tel no: (0131) 5545556
www.plumedhorse.co.uk
Modern European | £55
Cooking score: 5

It's four years since Tony Borthwick moved the Plumed Horse from out-of-the-way Crossmichael to its current stable in the gritty environs of Leith's waterside development, and he recently decided to apply some refurbishment to the place. The dining room now has a lighter, more contemporary feel and he is planning to add an 'accessible' wine cellar downstairs. Otherwise, it's business as usual in the kitchen. Tony's cooking is all about strong, clear flavours and he is fond of harnessing different cooking techniques on the plate – foie gras soufflé with a cromesquis-style foie gras 'nugget' and Gewürztraminer jelly is a signature dish, and similar leitmotifs run through everything from a starter of hot and cold wood pigeon with plum and fig jam to a casserole of free-range rose veal with sautéed kidney and sweetbread, shallot purée and roast celeriac. Fish from the Scottish ports is given an enlightened workout, too – perhaps sautéed sea bream fillet paired with oyster and smoked salmon or roast monkfish with a hand-dived scallop, smoked eel, sauce vierge and 'green' ham sauce. To conclude, it's worth sharing the Laphroaig whisky and honeycomb baked Alaska with honey ice cream and candied nuts if it's on. France takes a starring role on the well-spread wine list, with prices from £20.
Chef/s: Tony Borthwick. **Open:** Tue to Sat L 12.30 to 1.30, D 7 to 9. **Closed:** Sun, Mon. **Meals:** Set L £26. Set D £55. Tasting menu £65 (8 courses). **Service:** not inc. **Details:** Cards accepted. 40 seats. No mobile phones. Wheelchair access. Music.

Restaurant Martin Wishart

The jewel in Edinburgh's crown
54 The Shore, Leith, Edinburgh, EH6 6RA
Tel no: (0131) 5533557
www.martin-wishart.co.uk
Modern French | £65
Cooking score: 8
V

'Excellence personified' trumpeted one convert after an ecstatic visit to Martin Wishart's emblematic restaurant overlooking Leith's upwardly mobile waterfront. The dining room doesn't give much away – mirrored pillars, pastel blue shades and measured understatement – but everything hinges on the truly awe-inspiring dishes conjured up by this supreme Scottish kitchen. Wishart is the most exacting and intelligent chef currently working north of the border, and his brilliantly executed food manages to steer a course between suave opulence and fashionable fireworks without ever seeming forced or mannered. Little details mean a great deal here, whether it's 'masterly bread', a slate of amuse-bouches or a cascade of petits fours including a mini Opéra gâteau, lemon blancmange, a white chocolate and passion-fruit sandwich, myriad macaroons and more besides. In between, the Caledonian star allows his imagination to let rip, creating an exotic ceviche of halibut with mango and passion fruit, pulling off a surprisingly delicate combo of lemon sole with veal kidney, and teasing the traditionalists with a dish of braised beef cheek, pumpkin seed brittle, caramelised endive and red wine sauce. He is also sure-footed and endlessly inventive when it comes to transmuting native ingredients: Kilbrannan langoustine with parsnip, white chocolate and melted smoked butter, for example, or roast loin and civet of mountain hare with Puy lentils, apple, beetroot and black pudding sauce. Desserts are nothing short of miraculous as Wishart plays with the sensual possibilities of, say, rhubarb or pulls out an haute cuisine masterstroke in the shape of Valrhona chocolate délice with salted praline and Sacher sponge – plus some peanut and milk foam to bring it bang up to date. Dinner requires a serious financial outlay, but come for lunch and you can sample top cooking at knockdown prices (think red mullet with smoked haddock and potato mousseline followed by dark chocolate crémeux with almond sablé and griottine cherries). Despite one or two minor blips, service generally maintains its cool composure – although staff are not immune to the 'occasional giggle'. An 'extremely knowledgeable' sommelier is also on hand to guide diners through the intricacies of the wine list: expect big names but also a fabulous assortment of rare gems from artisan regional growers. Prices start at £27, half-bottles are numerous and you can sip by the glass from around £5.50. Martin Wishart has also put his name to the flagship restaurant at the Cameron House Hotel by Loch Lomond, tel (01389) 755565.

Chef/s: Martin Wishart. **Open:** Tue to Sat L 12 to 2 (1.30 Sat), D 6.30 to 9.30. **Closed:** Sun, Mon, 24 to 26 and 31 Dec, 2 weeks Jan. **Meals:** Set L £28.50. Set D £65. Tasting menu £70 (6 courses). **Service:** not inc. **Details:** Cards accepted. 50 seats. Wheelchair access. Music. Children allowed.

Rhubarb at Prestonfield

Unrestrained opulence and elaborate food
Prestonfield House, Priestfield Road, Edinburgh, EH16 5UT
Tel no: (0131) 2251333
www.prestonfield.com
Modern European | £50
Cooking score: 4

Built in 1687 for the city's Lord Provost, Prestonfield has been sky-rocketed into the twenty-first century and now does duty as a drippingly romantic destination overlaid with lush design features and modern sensibilities. Rhubarb is suitably dramatic in its own right – two opulent Regency dining rooms boasting thick drapes, dusky fabrics and exotic colour schemes, plus parkland views and a menu of elaborately worked contemporary dishes. Scottish flavours shine forth, from a

starter of Mull crab with honey-roast ham ribs and hazelnuts to roast loin of Strathspey roe deer with liver farci, white carrot purée, pickled carrots and walnut butter. Elsewhere, wild leeks from Prestonfield's grounds grace a dish of line-caught cod with spring cabbage, cockles and chorizo croquettes, while chateaubriand and sauced sirloin steak are a sop to the traditionalists. As expected, desserts put rhubarb at the top of the heap (perhaps served with vanilla brioche and hibiscus custard). The wine list is an oenophile's gazetteer of epic proportions, with house selections from £22 (£5.50 a glass).
Chef/s: John McMahon. **Open:** all week L 12 to 2 (3 Sat and Sun), D 6 to 10 (11 Fri and Sat). **Meals:** alc (main courses £18 to £34). Set L £16.95 (2 courses) to £30. Set D £30. **Service:** not inc. **Details:** Cards accepted. 90 seats. 20 seats outside. Separate bar. No mobile phones. Wheelchair access. Music. Children allowed. Car parking.

21212

Kooky food from a serious-minded madcap
3 Royal Terrace, Edinburgh, EH7 5AB
Tel no: (0131) 5231030
www.21212restaurant.co.uk
Modern French | £67
Cooking score: 5

Renegade chef Paul Kitching has spent the last year or two winning over the burghers of Auld Reekie, but he is still courting controversy at this high-ceilinged Georgian town house. The moniker 2-1-2-1-2 isn't the latest formation for Hearts football team, but a mannered reference to the restaurant's menu (two dishes, then one, then two . . .). Confused? That's the way Kitching likes it. He's an unreformed madcap prone to zany experimentation and kooky deconstructions, with the odd playful, post-ironic reference thrown in for good measure – just consider 'pulsating lamb with smoked bacon crisps' (a 13-component bonanza involving everything from pease pudding and barley to sweet potato, Gordal olives and spicy melon). Elsewhere, his take on curry with merguez sausage offers an 'undistinguished' gustatory tour in a breakfast bowl, while 'Chinese-style' sea bass leads him into the far-from-oriental world of saffron pancakes and chorizo. Some have found this rollercoaster ride truly revelatory ('each plate was a discussion topic in itself' mused one convert); others have dismissed it as an 'unmemorable muddle of flavours'. That said, cheeses are excellent and a dish of 'classical trifle' ends proceedings on an upbeat note. 21212 might be fun, but Kitching isn't joking when it comes to menu prices or mark-ups on the serious wine list. Bottles start at £22.
Chef/s: Paul Kitching. **Open:** Tue to Sat L 12 to 1.45, D 6.45 to 9.30. **Closed:** Sun and Mon. **Meals:** Set L £26 (2 courses) to £46. Set D £67 (5 courses). **Service:** not inc. **Details:** Cards accepted. 36 seats. Separate bar.

Valvona & Crolla Caffè Bar

Lively all-day landmark
19 Elm Row, Edinburgh, EH7 4AA
Tel no: (0131) 5566066
www.valvonacrolla.co.uk
Italian | £24
Cooking score: 3

£5 OFF £30

Founded in 1934, the Contini family's remarkable foodie pioneer has progressed 'from market stall to dot.com and is now a noisy, all-day landmark at the heart of Edinburgh's social life. Shopping and grazing go hand in hand here, although everything revolves around tip-top Italian provisions and gleanings from Scotland's big-name producers. The action begins with breakfast (don't miss the bombolone doughnuts), but you can call in at any time for plates of antipasti, toasted panetelli or some stuzzichini nibbles. Later on, pizzas and handmade pasta put in an appearance, alongside big bowls of zuppa di pesce, green veggie frittata and cotechino sausage with lentils and mustard fruits – not forgetting heaven-sent Milanese ice creams. The Continis are also Italian wine merchants par excellence, and their cellar is second to none in Scotland. Sample any bottle from the shelves at retail price (plus £6 corkage) or drink adventurously by the glass, thanks to a Cruvinet preservation system. Sibling venue the VinCaffè is in Multrees Walk shopping centre, tel (0131) 5570088.

Chef/s: Mary Contini. **Open:** Mon to Sat 8.30am to 5.30pm (8am to 6pm Fri and Sat), Sun 10 to 3.30. **Closed:** 25 and 26 Dec, 1 and 2 Jan. **Meals:** alc (main courses £10 to £15). Set L £12.95 (2 courses) to £15.95. **Service:** not inc. **Details:** Cards accepted. 60 seats. Music. Children allowed.

The Vintners Rooms

Historic surrounds and confident cooking
The Vaults, 87 Giles Street, Leith, Edinburgh, EH6 6BZ
Tel no: (0131) 5546767
www.vintnersrooms.com
Italian | £50
Cooking score: 4

Not far from the Leith waterfront is the oldest commercial building in Scotland. In the ornate, sixteenth-century candlelit dining room, the food maintains the Mediterranean drift that has infused the place of late, offering scallops with prawns and pancetta to start, followed by a textbook risotto with carnaroli rice, radicchio and gooey Taleggio, herb-crusted red mullet with spinach and mash, or duck with balsamic shallots. Finish with poached pear and tarragon ice cream. One couple weren't happy to find themselves plonked in the bar when the dining room was unexpectedly occupied by a party, but there is at least a range of 1,300 malt whiskies with which to console oneself. Wines are a magisteral listing of classics, with plenty of great names in France and Italy, but shorter shrift is shown to the southern hemisphere. Prices open at £21.50.

Chef/s: Francesco Guarini. **Open:** Tue to Sat L 12 to 2, D 7 to 10. **Closed:** Sun, Mon, 25 and 26 Dec, 1 and 2 Jan. **Meals:** alc (main courses £19 to £27). Set L £19.50 (2 courses) to £23.50. **Service:** not inc. **Details:** Cards accepted. 35 seats. Separate bar. Wheelchair access. Music. Children allowed. Car parking.

The Witchery by the Castle

Gothic theatricality and romance
Castlehill, Royal Mile, Edinburgh, EH1 2NF
Tel no: (0131) 2255613
www.thewitchery.com
Modern British | £40
Cooking score: 2

Look for the gilded heraldic sign if you want to unearth this evocative slice of Gothic theatricality hard by Edinburgh's tourist-trap castle. Choose the lavish oak-panelled Witchery itself (a grand sixteenth-century hall draped in tapestries) or eat in the droolingly romantic Secret Garden, reached via a stone staircase. Either way, expect Scottish produce in abundance, from dressed Isle of Mull crab and diver-caught scallops with pancetta to loin of Cairngorm venison with squash purée, red cabbage and chocolate oil, or 'three little pigs' (a well reported dish of slow-braised belly pork, roast tenderloin and grilled shoulder bacon). The Witchery's mammoth wine list is a truly encyclopaedic tome, with exhaustive global coverage, fair prices and a huge selection of half-bottles to boot. A dozen house recommendations start at £19.50 (£4.95 a glass).

Chef/s: Douglas Roberts. **Open:** all week L 12 to 4, D 5.30 to 11.30. **Closed:** 25 and 26 Dec. **Meals:** alc (main courses £16 to £39). Set L and pre-theatre D £14.95 (2 courses) to £30. **Service:** not inc. **Details:** Cards accepted. 110 seats. 18 seats outside. Music. Children allowed.

ALSO RECOMMENDED

▲ Fishers Bistro

1 The Shore, Leith, Edinburgh, EH6 6QW
Tel no: (0131) 5545666
www.fishersbistros.co.uk
Seafood

Proceedings in this colourful bistro on the harbourfront at Leith are overseen by a beatifically smiling mermaid. It's a buzzy, well-run place (sibling to Fishers in the City, Thistle Street) with a seafood-led menu where freshness is all. Start with grilled sardines persillade (£6.50), and proceed to Shetland halibut with tomato and pepper confit and lobster rouille, or Isle of Gigha salmon with Szechuan-spiced aubergine and lime crème fraîche (£14.95). Pudding could be chocolate praline brownie. Wines from £13.95. Open all week.

▲ John Hope Gateway Restaurant

Royal Botanic Garden, Arboretum Place, Edinburgh, EH3 5LR
Tel no: (0131) 5522674
www.gatewayrestaurant.net
Modern European £5 OFF

Housed in the landmark Gateway building (Edinburgh's answer to the Eden Project), this eatery offers snappy daytime nourishment for droves of eco-minded visitors. Lunch is the main event and the kitchen tosses eclectic flavours aplenty into the Scottish pot: Loch Duart smoked salmon is tweaked with wasabi crème fraîche, seared Ayrshire pork loin is given the spicy Szechuan treatment and grilled mackerel appears with a chunky Greek salad (£10.50). To finish, apricot rice pudding (£4.60) has been 'a triumph'. House wine £15.95. Open all week.

Gullane

La Potinière

An immensely pleasurable dining trip
34 Main Street, Gullane, EH31 2AA
Tel no: (01620) 843214
www.la-potiniere.co.uk
Modern British | £40
Cooking score: 6
V

Mary Runciman and Keith Marley are the highly convincing double act behind this affable restaurant housed in a rather singular-looking grey-stone building. They are celebrating 10 years in residence in 2012, and during that time they have cemented La Potinière's status as one of Scotland's top country restaurants – a reputation that hinges on diligent sourcing and culinary wisdom. These days, tags such as 'seasonal' and 'local' are bandied about willy-nilly as PR-speak, but listing suppliers beside the day's menu seems perfectly natural here, not a gimmick. Cooking duties are shared and the results on the plate can be spectacular, a gently paced procession of fastidiously executed and beautifully balanced dishes from start to finish. Choice is limited – especially at lunchtime – but it's an easy and immensely pleasurable trip from, say, cheese mille-feuille with plum compote and pine-nut salad through to chocolate bavarois with coffee and Pedro Ximénez granita, orange salad and a chocolate snap. In between, you might find a soothing soup of smoked salmon with crème fraîche ahead of a dish of seared beef fillet (courtesy of AK Stoddart, according to the menu) with a brioche and horseradish crust, turnip fondant, some cep mash and a deep Madeira sauce. Tradition dictates that dinner ends with a plate of fabulous cheeses, followed by coffee with petits fours. The evolving wine list is helpfully split into two price tiers, with plenty of serious drinking below £30.

Chef/s: Mary Runciman and Keith Marley. **Open:** Wed to Sun L 12 to 1.30, D 7 to 8.30. **Closed:** Mon, Tue, 3 weeks Jan, 1 week Oct, bank hols. **Meals:** Set L £18.50 (2 courses) to £22.50. Set D £40 (5 courses). Sun L £22.50. **Service:** not inc. **Details:** Cards accepted. 24 seats. No music. No mobile phones. Wheelchair access. Children allowed. Car parking.

Linlithgow

Champany Inn

Aberdeen Angus reigns
Champany Corner, Linlithgow, EH49 7LU
Tel no: (01506) 834532
www.champany.com
Scottish | £70
Cooking score: 3

When Clive and Anne Davidson moved into this collection of sixteenth-century farm buildings back in 1983, they could never have imagined that they would still be peddling prime Aberdeen Angus steak almost three decades later. But Champany remains synonymous with some of the best beef in the land – reared on home turf, aged for three weeks in an ionised chill room and cooked on specially designed stoves. Simply choose your cut from the chilled counter (sirloin, porterhouse, T-bone or a whole rib for carving at the table), then decide what sauce you require. Champany also tops up its offering with Loch Gruinart oysters, char-grilled Dornoch lamb, butter-poached lobster and even plates of organic cod and chips – plus Stilton 'from the truckle'. Good beef needs a good tipple, and the awesome, 1,000-bin list has treasures in abundance, covering every region imaginable. France, Spain and South Africa are the standouts, with six own-label Cape selections starting at £20.50 (£5.15 a glass). For something more affordable, try the adjoining Chop & Ale House.

Chef/s: David Gibson, Clive Davidson and Richie Gilfillan. **Open:** Mon to Fri L 12.30 to 2, Mon to Sat D 6.30 to 10. **Closed:** Sun, 25 and 26 Dec, 1 and 2 Jan. **Meals:** alc (main courses £29 to £49). Set L £22.95 (2 courses) to £31.90. Set D £42.50. **Service:** 10%. **Details:** Cards accepted. 50 seats. 16 seats outside. Separate bar. No music. No mobile phones. Wheelchair access. Car parking.

South Queensferry

The Boat House

Scottish seafood by the Forth
22 High Street, South Queensferry, EH30 9PP
Tel no: (0131) 3315429
www.theboathouse-sq.co.uk
Seafood | £28
Cooking score: 2

Views of the two Forth Bridges almost steal the show at this all-purpose eatery by the river. Pick the street-level deli/bistro if you're after a daytime fill-up – think wraps, sandwiches, fish and chips or a special such as twice-cooked belly pork on sweet potato mash. Alternatively, descend to the white-walled restaurant (evenings only), where the menu majors in accessible seafood cookery. No-frills starters such as tempura soft-shell crabs or smoked haddock fishcakes could give way to grilled whole John Dory dressed with caper and lemon butter, or roast cod fillet served on a cream chowder. Meat fans might be offered steak or duck breast with braised red cabbage, while those wanting a sweet finish could order sticky toffee pudding or pannacotta. Corney & Barrow house wines are £13.95 (£3.95 a glass).

Chef/s: Paul Steward. **Open:** all week 12 to 9.30 (12.30 to 9 Sun). **Closed:** 2 days Christmas, 2 days New Year. **Meals:** alc (main courses £16 to £24). Set L £15.95 (2 courses). Set D £17.95 (2 courses). **Service:** not inc. **Details:** Cards accepted. 50 seats. 40 seats outside. Separate bar. Wheelchair access. Music. Children allowed.

ALSO RECOMMENDED

▲ The Grill at Dakota

Dakota Hotel Forth Bridge, Ferrymuir Road, South Queensferry, EH30 9QZ
Tel no: (0131) 3193690
www.dakotahotels.co.uk
Modern European

A black glass-plated monolith in the shadow of the Forth Bridge, the Dakota Hotel is also home to a modish restaurant offering a menu of please-all international food. Grilled steaks and luxury crustacea are centrepieces of the menu (a fully embellished 7oz sirloin will set you back £20.95), with global back-up from venison ragù, saffron risotto, monkfish curry and suchlike. Kick off with Cullen skink or crispy goats' cheese with kohlrabi and walnuts (£6.95), and close with iced honeycomb parfait. House wine is £15.95. Open all week.

Annbank

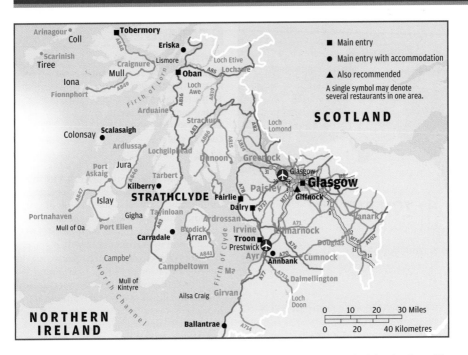

Browne's at Enterkine House

Enchanting views and personal charm
Enterkine Estate, Annbank, KA6 5AL
Tel no: (01292) 520580
www.enterkine.com
Modern European | £35
Cooking score: 4

Country house splendour plus a generous dollop of informality and personal charm is the theme at this sparkling 1930s residence with enchanting views over the river Ayr. Originally built for a P&O shipping magnate, Enterkine stands at the heart of a 310-acre estate with lovely walks and plenty of opportunities for some Scottish-style R&R. Chef Paul Moffat does the place proud with a bright modern menu that fuses native raw materials with influences from France and beyond. Smoked trout and Mull Cheddar soufflé might be revved up with perky chorizo jam, spinach soubise, smoked almond and chicory salad; rump of Blackface lamb could be served with kidney, a vegetable tian, goats' cheese and smoked anchovy beignet; and John Dory is given a rustic Mediterranean slant with fregula sarda and borlotti beans – plus some sea purslane for local effect. Considered elaboration and artifice continue all the way to desserts such as pineapple tarte Tatin with tarragon milk sorbet and star anise sauce. House wines start at £21.95 (£5.35 a glass).

Chef/s: Paul Moffat. **Open:** all week L 12 to 2, D 7 to 9. **Meals:** alc (main courses £11 to £25). Set L £16.50 (2 courses) to £18.50. Set D £35 (2 courses) to £40. Sun L £16.50 (2 courses) to £18.50. **Service:** not inc. **Details:** Cards accepted. 40 seats. Separate bar. Music. Children allowed. Car parking.

Average Price

The average price listed in main-entry reviews denotes the price of a three-course meal, without wine.

TOM KITCHIN
The Kitchin

What do you eat when you're feeling lazy?
Contrary to some chefs I love cooking when I'm off.

What's been the worst culinary trend of recent years?
Undoubtedly the current trend for eating food straight out of a packet, heated in the microwave. Fresh food doesn't need to be time consuming to prepare. It tastes so much better and is much healthier.

...And the best?
I'm fanatical about cooking 'à la minute', something I was taught during my time working with Alain Ducasse, and I try and implement this as much as I can at The Kitchin. It's very much in keeping with our 'From Nature to Plate' philosophy where everything is as fresh as possible.

What's your favourite job in the kitchen?
A true highlight for me each year is the arrival of the first grouse on the Glorious Twelfth. I enjoy the entire process of collecting, plucking and preparing the birds.

What is your favourite food combination?
Spring lamb with broad beans and peas, or wild salmon with Scottish asparagus.

Ballantrae

Glenapp Castle

Dazzling cooking at a top-notch hotel
Ballantrae, KA26 0NZ
Tel no: (01465) 831212
www.glenappcastle.com
Modern British | £60
Cooking score: 6

£5 OFF

The Castle is a spectacular piece of Victorian medieval pastiche, soaring with turrets and battlements on its rise, amid 36 acres of splendid grounds. It overlooks the wild and windswept Ayrshire coast, with views of the Isle of Arran in the distance, and there can be few more captivating prospects than to see the sun go down from one of the two dining rooms. Adam Stokes reliably delivers the final piece of the jigsaw with contemporary cooking that is full of imagination and a high degree of finish in every dish. A reporter who took the six-course dinner menu, on which choice is only necessary for main-course meat and dessert, was all praise. Starting with seared peppered yellowfin tuna, black olives and crisp shallots, it progressed through smoked ham hock and foie gras terrine with hazelnut dressing, and roasted scallops sprinkled with crushed pork crackling, to loin of local lamb with celery, pomegranate and wild garlic bread. After a pause to nibble at some Scottish cheeses with white truffle honey, dessert may be cranachan soufflé with oatmeal and whisky. The wine list lingers over Bordeaux and Burgundy in some detail, before nipping briskly round the rest of the world. Prices open at £28.

Chef/s: Adam Stokes. **Open:** all week L 12.30 to 2, D 7 to 10. **Closed:** Christmas week, 2 Jan to late Mar. **Meals:** Set L £37.50. Set D £60 (6 courses). **Service:** not inc. **Details:** Cards accepted. 34 seats. No music. No mobile phones. Wheelchair access. Children allowed. Car parking.

Carradale

Dunvalanree

Enchanting home-from-home
Port Righ, Carradale, PA28 6SE
Tel no: (01583) 431226
www.dunvalanree.com
Modern British | £28
Cooking score: 2

£5 OFF £30

This enchanting restaurant-with-rooms is in a lovely spot, perched on a cliff above Port Righ Bay with magnificent views of Arran. There is a sense of true dedication, too. It is a very personal operation, with attentive service from Alan Milstead, while his wife's food appeals for its well-executed integrity. Her three-course dinner menus make excellent use of regional produce: Kilbrannan scallops appear on a mooli rémoulade, Kintyre sea bass fillets come stuffed with coriander butter and wrapped in bacon, while rack of Saddell lamb is teamed with wilted pea shoots and served with minted gravy. Finish with crème brûlée. Wines from £14.50.

Chef/s: Alyson Milstead. **Open:** all week D only 7 to 9 (1 sitting). **Closed:** 1 week Dec, 2 weeks Oct. **Meals:** Set D £22.50 (2 courses) to £27. **Service:** not inc. **Details:** Cards accepted. 18 seats. No mobile phones. Wheelchair access. Music. Children allowed. Car parking.

Dalry

Braidwoods

Precision-tuned cooking and incisive flavours
Drumastle Mill Cottage, Dalry, KA24 4LN
Tel no: (01294) 833544
www.braidwoods.co.uk
Modern British | £43
Cooking score: 6

'Utterly memorable!' exclaimed one correspondent after lunching in style at Keith and Nicola Braidwood's rugged country restaurant fashioned from two whitewashed mill cottages. Unobtrusive, courteous and thoughtful service is spot-on for a modest dining room that fuses rough-hewn rusticity with flashes of contemporary style, and Keith's food still displays a natural-born affinity with the seasons – albeit with some sharp, incisive flavours all of his own. At lunchtime, his 'impeccable creations' could include confit of Gressingham duck with warm beetroot salad and pine nuts, followed by grilled fillet of halibut with asparagus risotto, but he ups the ante for seriously good dinners. To start, seared, hand-dived Wester Ross scallops are piled intriguingly on finely shredded, sauté Brussels sprouts with just a smidgen of perky ginger and chilli, before diners are offered soup – perhaps cream of celeriac tinged with truffle oil and fleshed out with slivers of smoked chicken. Top-notch Scottish ingredients also have their emphatic say when it comes to deeply flavoured, precision-tuned main courses – fillet of Auchengree Farm beef or loin of Highland roe deer on baby spinach, cauliflower purée and thyme essence, for instance. Flawless desserts, meanwhile, look to the classic vocabulary for rhubarb crème brûlée or iced Agen prune and Armagnac parfait with caramelised orange sauce. The wine list is a neatly balanced, elite collection garnered from top growers across the globe, with some particularly fine white Burgundies, Aussie reds and a serious contingent of half-bottles. House selections start at £22.95 (£5.75 a glass).

Chef/s: Keith Braidwood. **Open:** Wed to Sun L 12 to 1.30, Tue to Sat D 7 to 9. **Closed:** Mon, 25 Dec to 20 Jan, first 2 weeks Sept. **Meals:** Set L £23 (2 courses) to £27. Set D £43. Sun L £30. **Service:** not inc. **Details:** Cards accepted. 24 seats. No music. No mobile phones. Children allowed. Car parking.

Please send us your feedback

To register your opinion about any restaurant listed in the Guide, or a new restaurant that you wish to bring to our attention, please visit the web address at the bottom of the page. Your feedback informs the content of the book and will be used to compile next year's reviews.

Fairlie

Fins

Flavour-packed fish favourites
Fencefoot Farm, Fairlie, KA29 0EG
Tel no: (01475) 568989
www.fencebay.co.uk
Seafood | £35
Cooking score: 2

Jill and Bernard Thain's airy wood-floored restaurant opened in 1994 and has built its reputation on a fail-safe formula of fresh fish landed by the couple's boat, prepared and cooked with care, and served by courteous, helpful staff. This 'thoroughly enjoyable experience' is topped off by a cook/craft shop, smokehouse and self-catering accommodation nearby. On the plate, expect classics with clear flavours – maybe moules marinière or oysters on ice ahead of 'beautifully grilled' halibut with squat lobsters and langoustines in Chardonnay sauce. For purists there are hot or cold seafood platters offering a seasonally changing catch. Wines start at £14.70.

Chef/s: Jane Burns. **Open:** Tue to Sun L 12 to 2.30, Tue to Sat D 7 to 9. **Closed:** Mon, 25 and 26 Dec, 1 and 2 Jan. **Meals:** alc (main courses £10 to £31). **Service:** not inc. **Details:** Cards accepted. 50 seats. No mobile phones. Wheelchair access. Music. Car parking.

Giffnock

ALSO RECOMMENDED

▲ The Giffnock Ivy

219 Fenwick Road, Giffnock, G46 6JD
Tel no: (0141) 6201003
www.giffnockivy.co.uk
Modern European

No relation to the Covent Garden icon, The Giffnock Ivy is unexpectedly smart and stylish for a suburban Glasgow eatery – thanks to muted colours and hand-carved panelling. The kitchen deals in straightforward, honest cooking along the lines of grilled Stornoway black pudding with poached egg (£6.25), rump of lamb with herb fondant potato, sautéed spinach and Puy lentil jus or succulent, crisp-skinned sea bream with fine beans and chive beurre blanc (£13.95). For pud, try lemon posset with raspberries. Wines from £13.95. Closed Mon.

Glasgow

Brian Maule at Chardon d'Or

Gallic sensibility and Scottish produce
176 West Regent Street, Glasgow, G2 4RL
Tel no: (0141) 2483801
www.brianmaule.com
French | £45
Cooking score: 4

'I've been on several occasions and have never been disappointed' is a typical comment about this elegant, split-level restaurant set in a genteel Victorian town house. Beyond the porticoed entrance is a relaxed and light dining room with starched napery and highly polished glassware. Brian Maule is Scottish, but once worked as head chef at Le Gavroche (see entry, London) and it's this classical French training that explains the deep-rooted Gallic sensibility and commitment to top-drawer ingredients. Maule's hands-on approach can be spotted in an intricate starter of mille-feuille of smoked haddock, asparagus tips and chive cream, which might be followed by braised beef cheek with creamed mashed potatoes and red wine sauce. To finish, a classic apple tarte Tatin with vanilla ice cream and butterscotch sauce might share the billing with a more contemporary warm soft chocolate cake with Cointreau cream, orange reduction and pistachio powder. The drinker-friendly wine list offers a spread of bottles from Europe and the southern hemisphere, with due consideration given to pedigree growers and top vintages. Check out the 'wines for the season', which offer excellent value from £19 (£4.50 a glass).

Chef/s: Brian Maule. **Open:** Mon to Fri L 12 to 2.30, Mon to Sat D 5 to 9 (10 Fri and Sat). **Closed:** Sun, bank hols. **Meals:** alc (main courses £23 to £28). Set L and D £17.50 (2 courses) to £20.50. Tasting menu

£58 (6 courses). **Service:** not inc. **Details:** Cards accepted. 140 seats. Separate bar. Music. Children allowed.

Gamba

Glasgow seafood stalwart
225a West George Street, Glasgow, G2 2ND
Tel no: (0141) 5720899
www.gamba.co.uk
Seafood | £40
Cooking score: 3

Modern, comfortable and relaxing, Derek Marshall's long-standing basement restaurant continues to draw the crowds. Cosmopolitan seafood is the kitchen's business, from seared red mullet on Caesar salad or yellowfin tuna sashimi with wasabi, soy and pickled ginger to seared hand-dived scallops with chorizo peperonata, via popular classics such as lobster thermidor, goujons of haddock with chips or a plate of langoustines with garlic and herb butter. Alternatively, assuage any cravings for red meat with a peppered fillet steak or duck confit, before rounding off with chocolate tart and honeycomb ice cream or passion fruit and mango crème brûlée. Prices are on the high side, so set lunch and evening deals are much appreciated by the regulars. Wines from £18.95.
Chef/s: Derek Marshall. **Open:** Mon to Sat L 12 to 2.30 (2.15 Sat), all week D 5 to 10 (9 Sun). **Closed:** 25 and 26 Dec, 1 and 2 Jan. **Meals:** alc (main courses £14 to £39). Set L and D £16.95 (2 courses) to £19.95. **Service:** not inc. **Details:** Cards accepted. 62 seats. Separate bar. Music. Children allowed.

Stravaigin

Inventive, good-value food
28 Gibson Street, Glasgow, G12 8NX
Tel no: (0141) 3342665
www.stravaigin.com
Modern European | £30
Cooking score: 2

V

Sassy Stravaigin is a 'laid-back and casual' café/bar and restaurant in Glasgow's vibrant West End. The name means 'to wander' and the menu does just that, channelling worldwide influences while championing Scottish ingredients. Steamed West Coast mussels might come with sweet chilli and coriander, while homely haggis is served the traditional way with neeps and tatties. Next, maybe 'simple but delicious' roasted chicken breast with mash, roasted vine tomatoes and jus, or a 'very good' curry from a changing selection. Finish with white chocolate and truffle délice with fig jelly and Riesling sorbet. International wines start at £14.95. A sister restaurant, Stravaigin 2 at 8 Ruthven Lane, tel: (0141) 3347165, is receiving good feedback.
Chef/s: Douglas Lindsay. **Open:** all week L 11 to 5, D 5 to 1. **Closed:** 25 and 26 Dec, 1 Jan. **Meals:** alc (main courses £9 to £23). Set L £10 (2 courses) to £14.95. Set pre-theatre D £13.95 (2 courses) to £15.95. **Service:** not inc. **Details:** Cards accepted. 100 seats. 20 seats outside. Separate bar. Music. Children allowed.

Ubiquitous Chip

Glasgow icon
12 Ashton Lane, Glasgow, G12 8SJ
Tel no: (0141) 3345007
www.ubiquitouschip.co.uk
Modern British | £40
Cooking score: 4

A national treasure and a pioneer of provenance, this Glasgow evergreen celebrated 40 years as a Scottish champion in 2011. The Chip has evolved organically since the 70s without slavishly courting fashion, and some of its groundbreaking dishes are still around: the legendary venison haggis with 'champit tatties' (mashed potatoes), the Garvellach scallops partnered by a rösti, garlic compote and Chambery coral sauce, and the roast Perthshire wood pigeon (served with mushroom and pearl barley risotto these days). Chips are still off the menu (geddit?) but changes are in the air: two state-of-the-art tanks are now populated with live crustacea, and some new blood is gently filtering through in the shape of, say, grilled monkfish with haricot beans, pea-shoot tempura and a

fennel and almond sauce. To finish, roll back the years with the renowned Herbridean 'snow egg', a jellied confection involving carrageen moss and a shot of Grand Marnier. Overall, this place is a real leviathan, with four different dining zones (including a showpiece restaurant built around an amazing glass-roofed courtyard) and a truly majestic compendium of top-drawer Burgundies and Bordeaux matched by vinous treasures from Italy, Austria, California and elsewhere. House selections start at £18.35 (£4.60 a glass), and there are bargains aplenty in the bar/brasserie.
Chef/s: Andy Mitchell. **Open:** all week L 12 to 2.30 (12.30 to 2.45 Sun), D 5.30 to 11. **Closed:** 25 Dec, 1 Jan. **Meals:** Set L £24.95 (2 courses) to £29.95. Set D £34.95 (2 courses) to £39.95. Sun L £19.95. **Service:** not inc. **Details:** Cards accepted. 100 seats. Separate bar. No music. Children allowed.

La Vallée Blanche

Cared-for neighbourhood bistro
360 Byres Road, Glasgow, G12 8AY
Tel no: (0141) 3343333
www.lavalleeblanche.com
French | £32
Cooking score: 3

Decked out in the style of an Alpine chalet, with rustic wood-panelled walls and warm lighting, this French eatery is a far cry from the busy Byres Road outside. There are menus to suit most circumstances, including weekend brunch (eggs Benedict, croque-monsieur) and pre-theatre bargains: potted chicken with lemon, thyme and parsley, cornichons, shallots and onion bread, followed by fillet of Scrabster hake with white bean, spring onion and peat-smoked haddock cassoulet, for example. Evening brings classics such as braised pig's cheeks with carrot purée and salad of pickled carrots and fennel, ahead of braised shoulder of mutton pot-au-feu. Sweet soufflés (maybe apple with chestnut ice cream) are a speciality. French wines start at £16.95
Chef/s: Simon Brown. **Open:** Tue to Sun L 12 to 2.15 (3.30 Sat and Sun), D 5.30 to 10. **Closed:** Mon, 25 Dec, 1 Jan. **Meals:** alc (main courses £13 to £25). Set L and pre-theatre D £13.95 (2 courses) to £16.95. **Service:** not inc. **Details:** Cards accepted. 74 seats. Music. Children allowed.

ALSO RECOMMENDED

▲ Crabshakk

1114 Argyle Street, Glasgow, G3 8TD
Tel no: (0141) 3346127
www.crabshakk.com
Seafood

Owned and designed by Glasgow architect John McLeod, Crabshakk is a tight, intimate, all-day galley kitchen with a scattering of rough-hewn tables, an industrial steel staircase and a glass-clad bar. Cram in for some elbow-to-elbow seafood – oysters, tempura squid (£6.95), a 'wee fish supper' or half a dozen little crab cakes on a plate. Otherwise, go for broke and share a mighty seafood platter (£60). Steak, veggie risotto and chocolate cake complete a hot little package. House wine from £16.95. Closed Sun D and Mon.

▲ Kember & Jones

134 Byres Road, Glasgow, G12 8TD
Tel no: (0141) 3373851
www.kemberandjones.co.uk
International

An upmarket deli/café in the Hillhead district near the university, Phil Kember and Claire Jones's fine-food emporium is also a kitchenware and cookery book shop. The café is open all day, from breakfast bites such as Wiltshire ham and Gruyère croissant (£4.95), through lunchtime sandwiches and salads (perhaps chorizo, Manchego, paprika-roast potato and olive) to hearty platters of French, Italian or Spanish charcuterie (£12.95) or cheeses. Blackboards list the day's specials and there is a profusion of tempting patisserie. Wines start at £13.95. Open all week.

▲ Red Onion

257 West Campbell Street, Glasgow, G2 4TT
Tel no: (0141) 2216000
www.red-onion.co.uk
Global £5 OFF

John Quigley earned his stripes at Andrew Edmunds (see entry, London) before becoming personal chef to Tina Turner, Bryan Adams and other rock gods. Now he's the driving force behind this high-profile Glasgow eatery, where you can sample unfussy globetrotting food ranging from seared scallops with chorizo, haggis cakes or duck spring rolls with chilli vinegar (£6.50) to Moroccan-spiced rump of lamb with harissa, quesadillas or roast monkfish with prawn and pea korma (£15). Caramel shortcake is a top dessert and three-dozen eclectic wines start at £14.95. Open all week.

READERS RECOMMEND

Number Sixteen

Modern British
16 Byres Road, Glasgow, G11 5JY
Tel no: (0141) 3392544
www.number16.co.uk
'Our experience here left us full, contented and excited to return for another amazing meal'

Isle of Colonsay

The Colonsay

Classy island getaway with star fish
Scalasaig, Isle of Colonsay, PA61 7YP
Tel no: (01951) 200316
www.colonsayestate.co.uk
Modern British | £22
Cooking score: 2

Pristine sandy beaches, a rich variety of wildlife, archaeological remains and eighteenth-century inns are pretty impressive sights individually, but when grouped together on the remote, sparsely populated Isle of Colonsay the result can be breathtaking. The Colonsay's bar operates as the island's hub – the place for light lunches, island-brewed beer and unfussy comfort. Evening meals, served in the bar or contemporary restaurant, are built around first-class local and home-grown produce. Colonsay crab on toast, then halibut with courgettes, parsley and chive butter, or rump of lamb with pea purée and mint oil, followed by rhubarb crumble are typical choices. Prices on the short, modern wine list start at £12.50.

Chef/s: Darren McGuigan. **Open:** all week L 12 to 3, D 6 to 9.30 (5.30 Fri and Sun). **Closed:** Jan to Mar, Nov to Christmas. **Meals:** alc (main courses £11 to £20). **Service:** not inc. **Details:** Cards accepted. 40 seats. 20 seats outside. Separate bar. No mobile phones. Wheelchair access. Music. Children allowed. Car parking.

Isle of Eriska

Isle of Eriska Hotel

Elegant food on a private island
Ledaig, Isle of Eriska, PA37 1SD
Tel no: (01631) 720371
www.eriska-hotel.co.uk
Modern British | £44
new chef

Readers are quick to reach for the superlatives when applauding the Buchanan-Smiths' palatial Victorian mansion, which stands proud on its own private island. This 'unique' prospect is reached via a bridge you drive over, but once across you can wallow in the sheer remote pleasure of it all; everything runs at a gentle pace, and 'polite, correct' service adds to the overall mood. Long-serving chef Robert MacPherson has moved on, to Airds Hotel at Port Appin (see entry), and Simon McKenzie (ex Vineyard at Stockcross, Limewood) arrived just as we went to press. In the past the hotel has been known for its fine country house cooking, with everything made in-house (from home-baked rolls to the fudge with coffee) and superbly sourced raw materials creating an immediate impact. The mighty 'chariot de fromages' is a spectacular sight, and the well-spread wine list caters for all tastes; prices (from £12.50) are a steal. Reports please.

Chef/s: Simon McKenzie. **Open:** all week D only 7.30 to 9. **Closed:** Jan. **Meals:** Set D £44 (4 courses). **Service:** not inc. **Details:** Cards accepted. 60 seats. Separate bar. No music. No mobile phones. Wheelchair access. Car parking.

Isle of Mull

★ FISH RESTAURANT OF THE YEAR ★

Café Fish

Simple, fresh and fabulous seafood
The Pier, Main Street, Tobermory, Isle of Mull, PA75 6NU
Tel no: (01688) 301253
www.thecafefish.com
Seafood | £27
Cooking score: 3

'First-rate in every way' is the verdict of one reporter who has been dining at Café Fish since it first opened five years ago. Occupying a former ticket office on the pier at Tobermory, this relaxed eatery has great views of the bay and Calve Island. Climb the external stairs to the whitewashed terrace or the bright and breezy café itself, where you might even glimpse the day's catch arriving in the open-plan kitchen – shellfish from the restaurant's own boat or monkfish, Dover sole, cod and squid from local boats – all showcased on the concise menu and specials board. Top shouts from recent meals have included langoustine Caesar salad, queen scallops sautéed with smoked bacon, Tuscan fish stew ('packed with scallops, mussels, salmon and myriad others'), and peat-smoked haddock stuffed with squat lobsters baked in cream. A 'splendid berry meringue' makes a memorable finish. Wines from £14.90.

Chef/s: Liz McGougan. **Open:** all week L 12 to 3, D 6 to 9. **Closed:** Nov, Jan, Feb. **Meals:** alc (main courses £10 to £20). **Service:** not inc. **Details:** Cards accepted. 34 seats. 36 seats outside. Music. Children allowed.

Kilberry

The Kilberry Inn

Dream destination with satisfying seafood
Kilberry Road, Kilberry, PA29 6YD
Tel no: (01880) 770223
www.kilberryinn.com
Modern British | £29
Cooking score: 3

You'll need to drive 15 miles down a single-track road to discover the windswept Kilberry Inn, but this rose-clad stone cottage is something of a dream destination with its gorgeous views out to the Hebrides. It is run with all the hospitable warmth one hopes for in somewhere remote, and also pleases visitors with its refreshingly simple approach to local food. Seafood is the big draw, and readers have waxed lyrical about everything from the home-smoked mackerel and chorizo-crusted cod to roast monkfish with leeks in romesco sauce. Meanwhile, meat eaters should be satisfied by slabs or Ormsary beef or herb-crusted rack of lamb, while sweet-toothed guests have spoken highly of the Tunisian orange and almond cake. Wines are arranged by style, from £15.

Chef/s: Clare Johnson. **Open:** Tue to Sun L 12.15 to 2.15, D 6.30 onwards. **Closed:** Mon, Jan to mid Mar. **Meals:** alc (main courses £13 to 20). **Service:** not inc. **Details:** Cards accepted. 30 seats. 10 seats outside. No mobile phones. Music. Car parking.

Oban

Ee-Usk

Straightforward seafood cookery
North Pier, Oban, PA34 5QD
Tel no: (01631) 565666
www.eeusk.com
Seafood | £30
Cooking score: 1

This pitched-roofed, glassed-in restaurant sits on the harbourfront at Oban, making the most of maritime views along the Argyll coast towards Mull and Lismore. Reporters enjoy the laid-back, light-filled atmosphere, and the

menu of straightforwardly presented fresh seafood. Start with crab claws or smoked haddock chowder, and proceed to baked halibut with creamed leeks, or salmon and prawns in Mornay sauce. Lemon torte with cream makes a satisfying finale. House Spanish is £14.95 (£3.80 a glass).
Chef/s: Jane Scott. **Open:** all week L 12 to 3, D 6 to 9. **Closed:** 25 and 26 Dec, 1 Jan, 2 weeks Jan. **Meals:** alc (main courses £9 to £20). Set L £11.95 (2 courses) to £13.95. Set D £15.95 (2 courses) to £17.95. **Service:** not inc. **Details:** Cards accepted. 100 seats. 24 seats outside. Wheelchair access. Music. Car parking.

Waterfront

Sparkling-fresh seafood
1 Railway Pier, Oban, PA34 4LW
Tel no: (01631) 563110
www.waterfrontoban.co.uk
Seafood | £25
Cooking score: 1

Their motto is 'from the pier to the pan as soon as we can', and there is no denying the freshness of the seafood at this first-floor restaurant near the ferry terminal. It has a fashionable vibe, with specials appearing on a screen. Try the classic lobster bisque, Thai prawn curry with coriander rice or something from the 'unique' lobster menu, and round off with, perhaps, homemade lemon meringue tartlets and coconut ice cream. Wines on a short list start at £15.50. A second branch has opened close to the harbour at Tobermory, tel: (01688) 302365.
Chef/s: Roy Stalker. **Open:** all week L 12 to 2.15, D 5.30 to 9.30. **Closed:** 25 Dec. **Meals:** alc (main courses £10 to £25). Set L and D £12.50 (2 courses). **Service:** 10% (optional). **Details:** Cards accepted. 80 seats. 20 seats outside. Separate bar. Music. Children allowed. Car parking.

Troon

MacCallums Oyster Bar

Top-drawer Scottish fish
The Harbour, Troon, KA10 6DH
Tel no: (01292) 319339
Seafood | £25
Cooking score: 2

Overlooking the harbour, a fair way out of the town centre if you're walking it, John MacCallum's seafood restaurant surveys a timeless scene, where seals and guillemots disport themselves. It offers a nice mix of classic and modern dishes, with perhaps salt-and-chilli squid and Thai-spiced dip to get things going, before the main business might be roast pollack wrapped in ham with garlic mash, or grilled halibut with green beans and toasted pine nuts in tomato and caper dressing. Finish with well-made pineapple Tatin and coconut ice cream. House wines at £14.95 look to Chile, Australia and Argentina for the three colours.
Chef/s: Phillip Burgess. **Open:** Tue to Sun L 12 to 2.30 (3.30 Sun), Tue to Sat D 6.30 to 9.30. **Closed:** Mon, 3 weeks Dec to Jan. **Meals:** alc (main courses £11 to £28). **Service:** 10%. **Details:** Cards accepted. 43 seats. Music. Children allowed. Car parking.

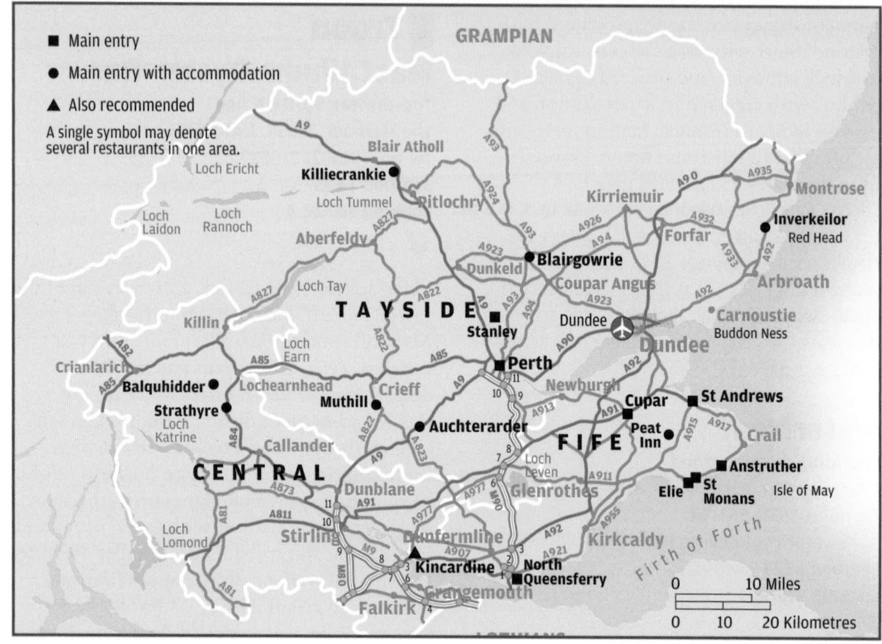

Balquhidder

Monachyle Mhor

Hidden gem with generous hospitality
Balquhidder, FK19 8PQ
Tel no: (01877) 384622
www.mhor.net
Modern British | £47
Cooking score: 5
V

Hidden away at the end of a tortuous track that meanders along the shores of Loch Voil, the Lewis family's flagship hotel is enveloped by the 2000-acre Trossachs National Park – a wild region forever linked with Rob Roy MacGregor. Over the years, they have built up a thriving foodie enterprise in these parts – although Monachyle and its livestock pastures are their main focus. Spending time here is like 'one of those private house parties you dream about', mused one reader who was particularly taken by the all-embracing spirit of gracious hospitality and genial bonhomie. Tom Lewis knows his own backyard and his food always rings true, whether he is cooking venison from the estate ('like butter') or fashioning a dish of monkfish with its liver, braised chicory, fennel, vanilla and orange. At dinner, an amuse-bouche of Tongue oyster mousse with cucumber salad creates a tingle on the palate, before starters add to the sensory thrills with, say, a candied beetroot and apple salad or hand-dived Orkney scallop with confit chicken wing, buttered leeks and prune. Lightness and modernity prevail – even desserts such as marmalade steamed pudding with ginger biscuit and 'proper custard' avoid cloying heaviness. The wine list is a highly personal selection of family favourites from all corners of the globe, with some irresistible 'oddballs' among the gilt-edged vintages. Prices start at £22 (£5.50 a glass).

Chef/s: Tom Lewis and Michael Hobbins. **Open:** all week L 12 to 2, D 7 to 9.30. **Closed:** 5 to 31 Jan. **Meals:** alc (main courses £16 to £27). Set D £46 (5 courses). Sun L £32. **Service:** not inc. **Details:** Cards accepted. 44 seats. 20 seats outside. Separate bar. No mobile phones. Wheelchair access. Music. Children allowed. Car parking.

Memus

READERS RECOMMEND

The Drovers

Modern British
Memus, DD8 3TY
Tel no: (01307) 860322
www.the-drovers.com
'A gem of a place, welcoming and pleasant.'

Strathyre

Creagan House

Dreamy farmhouse with stand-out food
Strathyre, FK18 8ND
Tel no: (01877) 384638
www.creaganhouse.co.uk
French | £32
Cooking score: 4

'Always been a great place to eat and stay, with wonderful breakfasts as well as dinners', says one of many happy customers who regularly beat a retreat to this lovely seventeenth-century farmhouse set deep amid the splendour of the Highlands. An imposing stone fireplace, 'medieval' tapestries, candlelight and a vaulted ceiling deliver baronial grandeur by the bucketload, but it's also a relaxed and intimate setting. Cherry Gunn handles front-of-house affairs in a gentle and low-key manner and is a 'veritable encyclopaedia of information about food, wine, location, books'. Gordon Gunn demonstrates equal expertise in the kitchen, delivering French classics with occasional Scottish overtones – maybe roast monkfish tail in pancetta with Jerusalem artichoke purée and orange and vermouth sauce followed by local lamb chops with a lamb and anchovy pie and tomato-laced gravy. A French-biased wine list opens at £16.45.

Chef/s: Gordon Gunn. **Open:** Fri to Tue D only 7.30 for 8 (1 sitting). **Closed:** Wed, Thur, 24 to 26 Dec, 18 Jan to 8 Mar, 7 to 22 Nov. **Meals:** Set D £31.50. **Service:** not inc. **Details:** Cards accepted. 14 seats. Separate bar. No music. No mobile phones. Wheelchair access. Car parking.

JEAN-CHRISTOPHE FROGÉ
Restaurant Martin Wishart

When did you first know you wanted to be a sommelier?
I trained as a waiter at first. The person taking care of me was a sommelier. He introduced me to the world of wines and the service that goes with it.

What's your favourite tipple when not drinking wine?
Dark, older rums are very interesting and are great to pair with food as well.

Which person has been most influential in your field of expertise?
It would have to be Robert Parker. Most of the top end Bordeaux are now made to get the highest rating possible from him as their prices will depend on it.

Have you noticed any wine trends over the last few years?
Rosé wines are currently very popular.

Do you have any advice for selecting a wine from the wine list?
The most expensive is not always the best. Look for the vintage; sometimes you will find that the medium vintages are not too expensive and they are usually drunk in their earlier years.

Anstruther

The Cellar

Major-league player with glorious seafood
24 East Green, Anstruther, KY10 3AA
Tel no: (01333) 310378
www.cellaranstruther.co.uk
Seafood | £40
Cooking score: 6

The fourth decade beckons for Peter and Susan Jukes, and long may they roll. This gem of a restaurant behind the Fisheries Museum, just off the harbour front, has long been one of Scotland's major-league players, and yet the achievement is worn with a refreshing absence of self-aggrandisement or undue flash. The cosy, beamed interior was once a cooperage and smokery for the herring industry. Meals begin with an appetiser of marinated herring in acknowledgement of the heritage, and then it's on to a seafood-centred menu that makes a virtue of its uncomplicated approach to quality prime materials. Crayfish bisque with a swirl of cream and a little Gruyère, or dressed crab with lemon mayonnaise, might open proceedings in gloriously traditional style. Then come mains such as a warm salad of monkfish, scallops and mussels in herb and garlic butter with tomato and chilli, or a piece of grilled North Sea halibut with greens, pine nuts, smoked bacon and hollandaise – the kind of signature dish that has regulars coming back for more. Have a fillet steak if you're not marine-minded, before finishing with date and ginger pudding, vanilla ice cream and butterscotch sauce. House wines at £18.50 from Spain, France and Chile hint at the expansive embrace of a list that takes in many reference growers. Most of the clarets need a bit more time – but with so much good seafood on offer, who needs claret?

Chef/s: Peter Jukes. **Open:** Fri and Sat L from 12.30, Tue to Sat D 6.30 to 9. **Closed:** Sun, Mon, 24 to 26 Dec. **Meals:** Set L £19.95 (2 courses) to £24.95. Set D £34.95 (2 courses) to £39.95. **Service:** not inc. **Details:** Cards accepted. 40 seats. Separate bar. No music. No mobile phones. Children allowed.

Cupar

Ostlers Close

Well-honed foodie gem
25 Bonnygate, Cupar, KY15 4BU
Tel no: (01334) 655574
www.ostlersclose.co.uk
Modern British | £40
Cooking score: 5

The years drift by, but nothing dims Jimmy and Amanda Graham's enthusiasm or devotion to duty in this modest cottage restaurant down a 'close' alley off Cupar's main street. They celebrated three decades in the business during 2011 and an air of carefully nurtured domesticity still wafts through their well-honed set-up. The mood may be cosy, but this is also a slick operation attuned to current thinking when it comes to scrupulous local sourcing and seasonality. Jimmy is an old hand at teasing out the best from top-drawer ingredients and he handles them brilliantly, matching seared hand-dived scallops with roasted Glamis asparagus and wild garlic pesto, or pepping up hake fillet with a stir-fry of pine nuts, sultanas and crispy Serrano ham. He also knows a thing or two about meat and game: roast saddle of roe deer with skirlie (Scottish savoury oatmeal) and shallots in red wine sauce has gone down a storm, but he might also serve pot-roast pigeon breast on a potato scone with pork belly confit or give beef the old-fashioned treatment with Yorkshire pudding, braised oxtail and horseradish sauce. As for desserts, readers swear by the pannacotta (perhaps served with poached garden rhubarb, Earl Grey syrup and rhubarb sorbet). The handwritten wine list reads well, with some interesting names and prices from £18.

Chef/s: Jimmy Graham. **Open:** Sat L 12.15 to 1.30, Tue to Sat D 7 to 9.30 (6.30 Sat). **Closed:** Sun, Mon, 25 and 26 Dec, 1 and 2 Jan, 2 weeks school hols (Apr and Oct). **Meals:** alc (main courses £19 to £23). **Service:** not inc. **Details:** Cards accepted. 28 seats. No music. No mobile phones. Children allowed.

Elie

Sangster's

Small restaurant with big ideas
51 High Street, Elie, KY9 1BZ
Tel no: (01333) 331001
www.sangsters.co.uk
Modern British | £40
Cooking score: 5

It may not look much from the outside, but step inside Bruce and Jacqueline Sangster's engaging town house conversion and you'll discover a neat, comfortable and homely dining room full of warmth and geniality. It may be small, but the kitchen is full of big ideas when it comes to transforming home-grown and local ingredients. Hand-dived scallops from Ross-shire might be jazzed up with a chilli, galangal and coriander dressing, while crispy-crusted quails' eggs could appear as a starter with cauliflower, truffle oil and a black pudding crumble. To follow, there might be venison from Glen Isla, chicken from Gartmorn Farm (perhaps served with Savoy cabbage, salsify, date purée and foie gras) or some fish from the coast – perhaps seared fillet of John Dory accompanied by butterbean and tomato stew with a red pepper essence. Refined simplicity, pitch-perfect technique and pretty presentation and are the kitchen's trademarks, and there's also plenty of skill when its comes to finely crafted desserts such as a light and fragrant passion fruit and vanilla posset with roast pineapple and coconut sorbet. The carefully annotated, 100-bin wine list casts its net wide for top drinking from independent growers and prestigious estates across the globe. Choice is impeccable and mark-ups are gentle, with house selections starting at £18.50.

Chef/s: Bruce Sangster. **Open:** Sun L 12.30 to 1.30, Tue to Sat D 7 to 8.30. **Closed:** Mon, 25 and 26 Dec, Jan, first 2 weeks Nov. **Meals:** alc (main courses £18 to £25). Sun L £27.50. **Service:** not inc. **Details:** Cards accepted. 28 seats. No music. No mobile phones.

Kincardine

ALSO RECOMMENDED

▲ The Unicorn

15 Excise Street, Kincardine, FK10 4LN
Tel no: (01259) 739129
www.theunicorn.co.uk
Modern British £5 OFF

Sir James Dewar, inventor of the vacuum flask, was born in this seventeenth-century coaching inn in the heart of historic Kincardine. These days it cuts a dash with simple modern décor, particularly in the brasserie, where pale walls and clean lines let the food do the talking. Expect familiar dishes prepared with 'attention to detail' – maybe black pudding with poached egg and pancetta salad (£5.75) then 'outstanding' lamb shank with garlic mash and rosemary sauce (£16.95), with sticky toffee pudding for dessert. Wines from £14.95. Brasserie closed Sun D and Mon.

North Queensferry

The Wee Restaurant

A diamond under the Forth bridge
17 Main Street, North Queensferry, KY11 1JG
Tel no: (01383) 616263
www.theweerestaurant.co.uk
Modern European | £32
Cooking score: 3

It has been a post office, jail, ironmonger's and more besides, but this 100-year-old building is now a 'wee' culinary diamond under the Forth Bridge. Since arriving in 2006, Craig and Vikki Wood have stamped their mark on the place and turned it into one of the 'best local restaurants' in Fife, noted for its assertive modern cooking, cordial atmosphere and agreeable prices. A creamy dish of Shetland mussels with spring onions and bacon has impressed, likewise a cracking plateful of 'melt-in-the-mouth' beef brisket, but the kitchen also absorbs in-vogue European themes – from fried calf's tongue with crispy fennel salad and salsa verde or pancetta-wrapped megrim fillet with caponata and Puy

lentil vinaigrette to vanilla pannacotta with rhubarb and Prosecco jelly. Well-chosen wines start at £15.75 (£5 a glass).
Chef/s: Craig Wood. **Open:** all week L 12 to 2, D 6.30 to 9 (6 to 9 Fri). **Closed:** 25 and 26 Dec, 1 and 2 Jan. **Meals:** Set L £16.50 (2 courses) to £20. Set D £26 (2 courses) to £32. **Service:** not inc. **Details:** Cards accepted. 36 seats. Music. Children allowed.

Peat Inn

The Peat Inn

Graceful, satisfying food
Peat Inn, KY15 5LH
Tel no: (01334) 840206
www.thepeatinn.co.uk
Modern European | £55
Cooking score: 6

Six miles from St Andrews, the Peat Inn still manages to feel gorgeously remote. A Georgian inn transformed into a stylish contemporary hotel, it has a character all its own as a result of the Smeddles' tireless attention to detail in every aspect. Dining takes place in a series of three interlinked rooms, done out in muted coffee tones. Geoffrey Smeddle calls upon pedigree local ingredients and the culinary techniques of modern Europe to craft a style that is graceful and satisfying. He allows an array of components to build up to an emphatic statement – a pairing of spiced monkfish and curried mussels, supported by the sharpnesses of radish, puréed parsley and pickled ginger, or a main course that presents the roasted loin and braised shoulder of hare, offsetting its richness with quince compote and parsnip purée. The six-course tasting menus offer a grand opportunity to experience the range, taking in a soup course such as mushroom consommé with ricotta gnocchi, chorizo and poached quail egg, as well as the obligatory pair of desserts, including lychee parfait with mango and lemongrass sorbet and white chocolate and lime mousse. The French-led wine list encompasses many fine growers and mature vintages at fairly pneumatic prices. Bottles start at £20.
Chef/s: Geoffrey Smeddle. **Open:** Tue to Sat L 12.30 to 1.30, D 7 to 9. **Closed:** Sun, Mon, 25 and 26 Dec, 1 week Nov, 2 weeks Jan. **Meals:** alc (main courses £21 to £26). Set L £18. Set D £35. Tasting menu £60 (6 courses). **Service:** not inc. **Details:** Cards accepted. 40 seats. Separate bar. No music. No mobile phones. Wheelchair access. Children allowed. Car parking.

St Andrews

The Seafood Restaurant

Good looks and spanking fresh fish
The Scores, Bruce Embankment, St Andrews, KY16 9AB
Tel no: (01334) 479475
www.theseafoodrestaurant.com
Seafood | £45
Cooking score: 4

Quite a sight by the famous West Sands, this modish cube-like construction of glass and metal stands out like a beacon – especially when it's lit up. The combination of trendy good looks and sustainable seafood seldom fails, although a new bar area and a downstairs kitchen add to the restaurant's all-round pulling power. Also new is an extravagant seafood platter. Otherwise, imaginative flavours and dinky portions are the order of the day when it comes to hake with potato terrine, oyster mushrooms and carrot purée, or sea bass paired with chorizo risotto and crispy leeks. Creel-caught Pittenweem crab and Loch Duart salmon are bestsellers, with Lancashire-bred quail or Perthshire venison and pearl barley for those of other persuasions. The kitchen seldom falters, although the smell of detergent and the sight of staff cleaning down tables before the end of service ruined it for one party. The comprehensive, high-rolling wine list swaggers its way through Europe and the New World. House recommendations start at £22 (£5.50 a glass) and there's a decent choice of half-bottles.
Chef/s: Debbie Robson. **Open:** all week L 12 to 2.30 (3 Sun), D 6.30 to 10. **Closed:** 25 and 26 Dec, 1 Jan. **Meals:** Set L £22 (2 courses) to £26. Set D £40 (2

courses) to £45. **Service:** not inc. **Details:** Cards accepted. 60 seats. 20 seats outside. No music. No mobile phones. Wheelchair access.

ALSO RECOMMENDED

▲ The Doll's House

3 Church Square, St Andrews, KY16 9NN
Tel no: (01334) 477422
www.houserestaurants.com
Modern European

One of a four-strong mini-chain of casual eateries, the Doll's House promises easy-going vibes and special-occasion fizz at user-friendly prices – the set lunch (£6.95 for two courses) is tremendous value. Otherwise dip into the zingy modern carte for the likes of avocado and pea pannacotta with chilli oil, smoked pheasant breast with bacon risotto and walnut vinaigrette, or sea bass with lime and crayfish sauce (£14.50), before rounding things off with blackberry cheesecake and bramble compote. House wine is £14.95. Open all week.

▲ The Vine Leaf

131 South Street, St Andrews, KY16 9UN
Tel no: (01334) 477497
www.vineleafstandrews.co.uk
Modern British £5 OFF

Ian and Morag Hamilton have been at the helm of their eye-catching restaurant for 26 years, and the format of a fixed-price, dinner-only menu (£26.50/£29.95 for two/three courses) is tried and tested. There's ample choice, with fish a speciality, vegetarians well catered for and meat dishes not neglected. Caramelised red onion and Gruyère tart, then lemon sole with prawns and garlic-herb butter or braised ox cheek, followed by blueberry meringue pie are typical choices. Wines from £15.90. Open Tue to Sat D only.

St Monans

Craig Millar @ 16 West End

Re-branded seafood specialist
16 West End, St Monans, KY10 2BX
Tel no: (01333) 730327
www.16westend.com
Seafood | £40
Cooking score: 5

Chef Craig Millar is now the sole owner of St Monans' much-lauded Seafood Restaurant. He has re-branded the place to mark the beginning of a new era, but it seems that this estimable fish specialist will stay firmly on course. One thing is certain: the venue itself – created from a 400-year-old fisherman's cottage overlooking St Monans harbour – boasts some of the most breathtaking views around. Sustainable seafood is Millar's passion and he treats it with striking contemporary élan: a superb pairing of halibut with cauliflower and truffle risotto; diver-caught scallops with gnocchi, Jerusalem artichoke mousse and lemon and thyme jelly; or cod with crushed potatoes, kale, oyster mushrooms and soy dressing, for example. Veggies and meat eaters fare well, too (Jarlsberg tart with red onion confit and a cassoulet of lamb, pork and smoked bacon spring to mind), and Millar is already dreaming up some new desserts including fruit ravioli with Kaffir lime leaves and coconut sorbet. The on-trend wine list bristles with young guns and prestige names from top producers – with a strong bias towards fish-friendly whites. House selections start at £18 (£4 a glass). Note: ring in advance for seasonal opening times from November to March. Reports please.

Chef/s: Craig Millar. **Open:** Wed to Sun L 12.30 to 2, D 6.30 to 9. **Closed:** Mon, Tue, 25 and 26 Dec, 1 Jan. **Meals:** Set L £22 (2 courses) to £26. Set D £35 (2 courses) to £45. **Service:** not inc. **Details:** Cards accepted. 44 seats. 30 seats outside. Separate bar. No music. No mobile phones. Wheelchair access. Children allowed. Car parking.

Auchterarder

Andrew Fairlie at Gleneagles

Meticulously polished cooking
Auchterarder, PH3 1NF
Tel no: (01764) 694267
www.andrewfairlie.co.uk
Modern French | £85
Cooking score: 7

V

The Gleneagles name guarantees exclusivity and suggests corporate wealth as well as multi-national flag-waving – whether it's for golf or political deal-brokering. More than 800 acres of landscaped grounds surround the hotel, but once you have done the necessary marvelling at the lavishness of it all, it's time to focus on matters gastronomic. Andrew Fairlie's self-named restaurant operates as an autonomous business within the hotel – and there's no doubting that this is an ego-driven set-up: the letters AF are entwined on a lectern at the entrance and there are two portraits of Fairlie himself, looking shattered after a hard service. The evening begins with 'unmemorable' nibbles at the bar while decisions are made regarding the menu. Then you are ushered through heavy curtains into a womb-like, windowless dining room with black walls, dim lights and immaculately laid tables. Fairlie's signature dish of home-smoked Scottish lobster dressed with warm lime and herb butter is seldom off the menu and it remains one of the less exacting items on offer. Fashionable detailing, hints of deconstruction and a globally inclined approach to modern French cuisine are the prevailing themes: you can see them at work in a refreshing starter of hand-dived scallops with sea vegetables and yuzu purée on the side, or roast fillet of sea bass accompanied by poached langoustine, lomo ham and a drizzle of warm vinaigrette. Fish is certainly a forte, but there are other arcane creations to marvel at (even if the 'wow' factor is sometimes rather muted): a brilliantly executed seasonal plate of Highland roe deer with beetroot and sloe gin has been applauded, likewise slow-cooked sirloin and beef cheek tinged with dark soy and balsamic jus. An extra cheese course might yield an extraordinary combination of farmhouse Morbier with young Hispi cabbage, verjus and cumin, while a fabulous confection of lime curd, coconut sablé and pineapple sorbet has closed proceedings on a high. Expect to pay handsomely for the food and be prepared to dig even deeper if you want something serious from the wine list; prices shoot skywards from around £30.

Chef/s: Andrew Fairlie. **Open:** Mon to Sat D only 6.30 to 10. **Closed:** Sun, 24 and 25 Dec, 3 weeks Jan. **Meals:** Set D £85 (3 courses) to £125 (6 courses). **Service:** not inc. **Details:** Cards accepted. 54 seats. No mobile phones. Wheelchair access. Music. Car parking.

Blairgowrie

Kinloch House Hotel

A showcase for grand Scottish hospitality
Dunkeld Road, Blairgowrie, PH10 6SG
Tel no: (01250) 884237
www.kinlochhouse.com
Modern British | £53
Cooking score: 5

Erected in 1840 for a 'nouveau riche' family in the jute trade, Kinloch House is a dignified, creeper-clothed showcase for traditional Scottish hospitality in the grand manner – complete with impressive panelled rooms, fabulous antique furniture, a portrait gallery and a walled garden amid its 25 acres of lush grounds. You almost expect a tartaned piper to appear as formal meals are played out in the pleasantly airy, chandeliered dining room. Chef Steve MacCallum knows his way around the national larder and his cooking is pitched firmly in the familiar middle ground of chicken liver terrine with date chutney, herb-crusted loin of lamb with Madeira sauce, and baked apple with caramel ice cream – although there's no shortage of natural élan or technical know-how about the results on the plate. Occasionally he adds an extra flourish or two, serving Gressingham duck breast with wild mushrooms, candied beetroot and broad beans or matching orange pannacotta with poached rhubarb, but nothing seems to upset this very steady ship. Reporters have also enjoyed the assorted Scottish and Irish cheeses that bring culinary events to a safe conclusion, while those who veer towards the wine list are in for a real treat. Bottles from top Chilean producer Vina Veñtisquero are given special prominence (with prices from £26), but there's also a heavy Burgundian presence alongside a sprinkling of goodies from Italy and the Antipodes.

Chef/s: Steve MacCallum. **Open:** all week L 12.30 to 1.45, D 7 to 8.30. **Closed:** 14 to 29 Dec. **Meals:** Set L £19.50 (2 courses) to £25.50. Set D £53. Sun L £30. **Service:** not inc. **Details:** Cards accepted. 34 seats. Separate bar. No music. No mobile phones. Wheelchair access. Car parking.

Inverkeilor

Gordon's

Dazzling dinners and charming hosts

Main Street, Inverkeilor, DD11 5RN

Tel no: (01241) 830364

www.gordonsrestaurant.co.uk

Modern British | £47

Cooking score: 5

'The Watson family are the most charming hosts imaginable', is a characteristically enthusiastic comment about this long-established and enduringly popular family-run restaurant-with-rooms found in a tiny hamlet between Arbroath and Montrose. The wooden-beamed dining room is an intimate setting with sandstone walls and stained glass windows, the domain of Maria Watson, who is the epitome of a 'very welcoming hostess'. In the kitchen, her husband Gordon and son Garry continue to dazzle with their bold, confident and complex cooking. A dinner from the short menu could start with boneless quail stuffed with Stornoway black pudding and presented on a bed of Puy lentils – 'a wonderful combination of flavours and a most memorable dish', or an 'exquisitely light' double-baked Isle of Mull Cheddar soufflé. A main course loin of Scotch venison with Pinot Noir jus, creamed greens and celeriac has been 'cooked to perfection and the best I have ever tasted'. To finish, an impressive mango iced parfait with a pineapple compote, lychee sorbet and coconut tuile demonstrates a good skills set in the desserts section, although reports have noted 'disappointing' coffee with the petits fours. A wine list helpfully arranged by grape variety starts at £16.50.

Chef/s: Gordon and Garry Watson. **Open:** Wed to Fri and Sun L 12.30 to 1.30, Tue to Sun D 7 to 8.30 (6.30 Sun). **Closed:** Mon, 2 weeks Jan. **Meals:** Set L £27 (3 courses). Set D £47.50 (4 courses). **Service:** not inc. **Details:** Cards accepted. 24 seats. No music. No mobile phones. Wheelchair access. Children allowed. Car parking.

Killiecrankie

Killiecrankie House

Sympathetically run hotel in a lovely setting

Killiecrankie, PH16 5LG

Tel no: (01796) 473220

www.killiecrankiehotel.co.uk

Modern British | £38

Cooking score: 3

 **V**

Built as a residence for a Victorian vicar with a penchant for views, this sympathetically run hotel stands in wooded grounds overlooking the Pass of Killiecrankie. Owner Henrietta Fergusson and long-serving chef Mark Easton make 'a wonderful team', and visitors are full of praise for their very personal approach and attention to detail. Dinner puts the emphasis on Scottish produce, and the results are delicate as well as skilful: a salad of home-smoked brown trout with horseradish and tomato dressing could precede roast grouse with sautéed curly kale, carrot purée and wild mushrooms or grilled cod fillet with seared scallops and saffron sauce. To finish, iced rhubarb and ginger mousse might fit the bill. House wines are £18.

Chef/s: Mark Easton. **Open:** all week D only 6.30 to 8.30. **Closed:** 3 Jan to mid Mar. **Meals:** Set D £38 (4 courses). **Service:** not inc. **Details:** Cards accepted. 35 seats. Separate bar. No music. No mobile phones. Wheelchair access. Children allowed. Car parking.

Muthill

Barley Bree

New life for an old inn
6 Willoughby Street, Muthill, PH5 2AB
Tel no: (01764) 681451
www.barleybree.com
Modern British | £30
Cooking score: 3

Warmth, personality and skilfully crafted food make for a winning formula at Fabrice and Alison Bouteloup's popular restaurant-with-rooms. Set in the heart of Muthill, the former eighteenth-century coaching inn delivers a cosy and traditional atmosphere, wooden floors, open fires and a genuine welcome. Fabrice's short, French-inspired lunch and dinner menus change weekly and make sound use of quality ingredients, perhaps confit duck leg and chanterelle terrine with pear chutney or seared South Uist scallops with aubergine and cumin caviar, then wild halibut with saffron, fennel and pepper stew, or spiced belly pork with lentils and smoked bacon and a classic apple tarte Tatin with vanilla ice cream to finish. House wine is £15.

Chef/s: Fabrice Bouteloup. **Open:** Wed to Sat L 12 to 2, D 6 to 9. Sun 12 to 7.30. **Closed:** Mon, Tue, 25 to 27 Dec, 2 weeks Feb, 2 weeks Oct. **Meals:** alc (main courses £17 to £23). **Service:** not inc. **Details:** Cards accepted. 32 seats. No music. Children allowed. Car parking.

Perth

Deans @ Let's Eat

Elaborate food in classic surrounds
77-79 Kinnoull Street, Perth, PH1 5EZ
Tel no: (01738) 643377
www.letseatperth.co.uk
Modern British | £28
Cooking score: 3

Willie and Margo Deans' stylishly spacious dining room should set you at your ease, although you should be prepared for plenty of action when it comes to the food. Willie is a confident chef with a penchant for robust flavours and powerful combinations heaped high on the plate, but his dishes have a tendency to overwhelm – just consider a twice-baked cheese and cauliflower soufflé with black pudding and a sauce of caramelised red onion marmalade. That said, succulent, sweet scallops with slow-cooked pork ribs, soy and ginger is a happy marriage, and pink medallions of beef sit contentedly in a big-hitting veal jus with mushroom ketchup, caraway-roasted carrots, garlic and tarragon cream. After that, a triumphant gingerbread pudding with caramel, vanilla and rum ice cream may stop you in your tracks. Wines from £18.

Chef/s: Willie Deans. **Open:** Tue to Sat L 12 to 2.30, D 6 to 9.30. **Closed:** Sun, Mon. **Meals:** alc (main courses £13 to £20). Set L £13.95 (2 courses) to £15.95. Set D £18.95 (2 courses) to £22.95. **Service:** not inc. **Details:** Cards accepted. 60 seats. No mobile phones. Wheelchair access. Music. Children allowed.

NEW ENTRY

The North Port Restaurant

New player next to the Concert Hall
8 North Port, Perth, PH1 5LU
Tel no: (01738) 580867
www.thenorthport.co.uk
Modern British | £25
Cooking score: 2

With its sombre wood panelling and cramped conditions, North Port – found just a step from Perth's Concert Hall – can feel a bit like dining in Nelson's quarters aboard HMS *Victory*, but thankfully the food is from a different world. Given the maritime moniker, fish is always a good call – anything from subtle smoked haddock ravioli with pea shoots and Parmesan to grilled sea bass ('as fresh as an easterly') with pink Champagne and chive sauce. The kitchen also turns its hand to whipped goats' cheese mousse with beetroot carpaccio or seared pork fillet with broad beans and black pudding, while desserts such as the sinful pot au chocolat are devoured with alacrity. Wines from £13.95.

Chef/s: Kevin Joubert. **Open:** Tue to Sat L 12 to 2.30, D 5 to 9.30. **Closed:** Sun, Mon, first week Jan, 3 to 7 Jul. **Meals:** alc (main courses £11 to £18). Set L £8.95 (2 courses). Pre-theatre D £13.95 (2 courses) to £16.95. **Service:** not inc. **Details:** Cards accepted. 55 seats. Separate bar. Music. Children allowed.

63 Tay Street

Smart local with throught-provoking food
63 Tay Street, Perth, PH2 8NN
Tel no: (01738) 441451
www.63taystreet.co.uk
Modern British | £35
Cooking score: 3

 **V**

Graeme Pallister's smart modern restaurant, done in relaxing tones of beige and blue, looks out over the Tay towards Kinnoull Hill; a restful prospect for a city venue. A willingness to experiment without pitching headlong into undue complication has delivered some effective dishes, such as Mull scallops with ham, lentils and a chilli galette, followed perhaps by local lamb served with Parmesan-laced dauphinoise and vegetables braised in Madeira. Even the lunch menu has offered the thought-provoking likes of roast quail with pear Kiev, bittersweet cabbage and foie gras sauce. Scottish and French cheeses are the alternative to spiced vanilla parfait. Pedigree German wines feature on a list that zips around the globe in search of excellence. Prices open at £20.

Chef/s: Graeme Pallister. **Open:** Tue to Sat L 12 to 2, D 6.30 to 9. **Closed:** Sun, Mon. **Meals:** Set L £22. Set D £35 (5 courses). **Service:** not inc. **Details:** Cards accepted. 32 seats. No mobile phones. Music. Children allowed. Car parking.

Stanley

The Apron Stage

Small is beautiful
5 King Street, Stanley, PH1 4ND
Tel no: (01738) 828888
www.apronstagerestaurant.co.uk
Modern British | £27
Cooking score: 3

'This is what all small restaurants should aspire to be like', noted one visitor to Shona Drysdale and Jane Nicoll's quirky 18-seater restaurant, which occupies one room of a terrace house. It feels surprisingly spacious thanks to a mix of trompe l'oeil mirrors and pale colours, while the food is fiercely seasonal and the blackboard menu refreshingly short and unpretentious. It offers, perhaps, twice-baked crab and Gruyère soufflé with nectarine salsa as a starter, before moving on to medallion of Angus beef fillet with slow-braised shin, spinach potato cake and port jus. Finish with sloe gin jelly with crystallised blueberries. The well-considered, 20-bin wine list starts at £15.

Chef/s: Shona Drysdale. **Open:** Fri L 12 to 2, Wed to Sat D 6.30 to 9.30. **Closed:** Sun to Tue, 1 week Sept, 1 week Christmas. **Meals:** alc (main courses £14 to £18). Set L £13.75 (2 courses) to £16.75. **Service:** not inc. **Details:** Cards accepted. 18 seats. No mobile phones. Wheelchair access. Music.

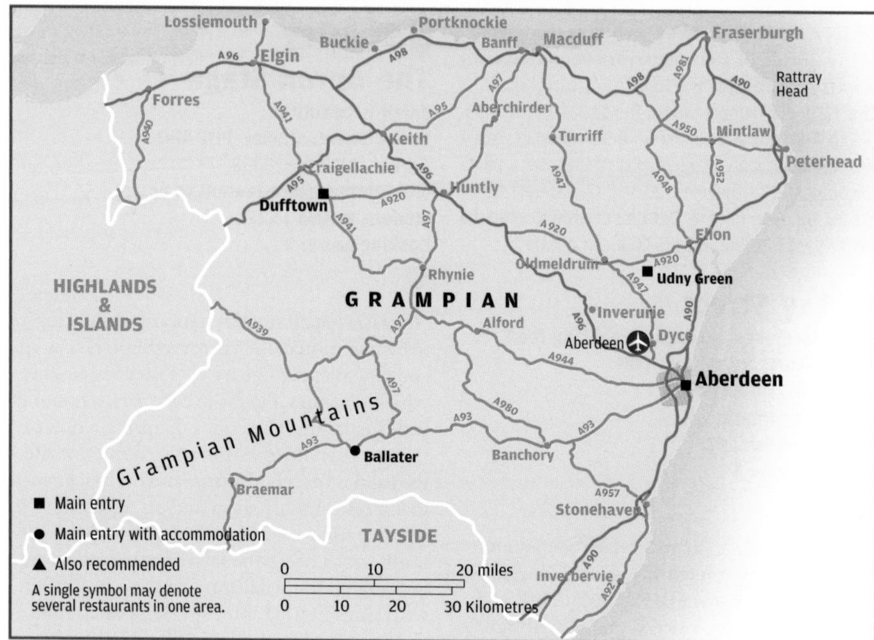

Aberdeen

Silver Darling

Fish-loving harbourside heavyweight
Pocra Quay, North Pier, Aberdeen, AB11 5DQ
Tel no: (01224) 576229
www.thesilverdarling.co.uk
Seafood | £43
Cooking score: 6

Perched high above the harbour entrance in Aberdeen, Didier Dejean's long-running seafood-led restaurant is perfectly poised to take in the breathtaking views along Scotland's north-east coast. Floor-to-ceiling windows offer all the visual diversion needed, so that the interior décor of pale walls hung with small pictures hardly needs to compete. It's also, of course, a prime location for the bracingly fresh fish and shellfish that the menu majors in. The culinary style draws on Dejean's homeland, but blends in some strategic modern eclecticism as the mood takes him: squid may be paired with belly pork cooked on a plancha and served with pak choi and shiitake mushrooms, or there could be scallops on curried butternut squash purée, dressed in pesto and raisins. After that, main courses deliver the classical likes of cheese-crusted fillet of halibut in green sauce, or a more obviously Spanish monkfish with chorizo and pipérade. Meat eaters might opt for local beef sirloin, dry-aged for 21 days and served with sweet potato terrine, tomatoes and garlic and rosemary jus. Chocolate fondant with pistachio ice cream and a matching sauce is one way of indulging yourself at dessert stage. Wines open at £23.50.

Chef/s: Didier Dejean. **Open:** Sun to Fri L 12 to 1.45 (3 Sun), Mon to Sat D 6.30 to 9.30. **Closed:** 2 weeks Christmas and New Year. **Meals:** alc (main courses £15 to £26). Set L £17.50 (2 courses) to £21.50. **Service:** 10%. **Details:** Cards accepted. 50 seats. No mobile phones. Music. Children allowed.

READERS RECOMMEND

Fusion Bar & Bistro

Modern British
10 North Silver Street, Aberdeen, AB10 1RL
Tel no: (01224) 652959
www.fusionbarbistro.com
'Extremely pleasant young staff and an excellent Sunday lunch. Generous helpings of meat from a renowned local butcher with local grazing.'

Ballater

Darroch Learg

Bastion of Scottish family hospitality
Braemar Road, Ballater, AB35 5UX
Tel no: (013397) 55443
www.darrochlearg.co.uk
Modern British | £45
Cooking score: 5

A landmark anniversary was celebrated in the hills around Ballater in 2011, when the Franks family clocked up a half-century, through successive generations, at the helm of this sublimely situated Victorian country house hotel. Gazing out over the Dee towards Lochnagar – with some golf in the interim view – it has a dining room that opens into a conservatory, the better to drink in the scenery. David Mutter cooks a well-practised menu of modern British dishes, using many fine regional ingredients in a style that emphasises their pedigree. Smoked haddock ravioli in sauce vierge might start a dinner, while, in a meeting of the islands, Skye scallops are paired with Orkney black pudding on parsnip purée with five-spice sauce. Venison from a Deeside estate appears as a cut of loin alongside smoked haunch, with Puy lentils, turnip confit, fine beans, goats' cheese and morels in a compendious main course, or there could be prime Scotch beef with horseradish relish in red wine and oxtail sauce. A two-tone chocolate cake, served warm with crème fraîche, makes a signature finisher, and there are illustrious Scottish cheeses too. A classical wine list leads off with some majestic French gear, with shorter but well-chosen selections from elsewhere. Prices open at £23 (£6.50 a glass).
Chef/s: David Mutter. **Open:** Sun L 12.30 to 2, all week D 7 to 9. **Closed:** 1 week Christmas, last 3 weeks Jan. **Meals:** Set D £45 (3 courses). Sun L £24 (3 courses). Tasting menu £55. **Service:** not inc. **Details:** Cards accepted. 48 seats. No music. No mobile phones. Wheelchair access. Children allowed. Car parking.

The Green Inn

Generous hospitality and expert food
9 Victoria Road, Ballater, AB35 5QQ
Tel no: (013397) 55701
www.green-inn.com
Modern European | £41
Cooking score: 3
V

The building was once a temperance hotel, but abstinence and pious sobriety have no place in its current incarnation as a family-run restaurant-with-rooms. Generous hospitality is the order of the day in the conservatory and red-hued dining room, where visitors can sample Chris O'Halloran's carefully crafted food. He serves a salad of West Coast crab with jellied crab essence and lovage vichyssoise, partners seared saddle of roe deer with creamed celeriac, wild mushrooms and sweet peppercorn sauce, and brightens up home-salted cod with chickpeas, piquillo peppers, samphire and anchovy dressing. Desserts come with a '20-minute wait', which is understandable if you fancy a trademark soufflé (passion fruit or rhubarb and ginger, say), but seems hardly justified for a dish of ice cream. The well-spread global wine list kicks off with eight house recommendations from £20.95.
Chef/s: Chris O'Halloran. **Open:** Wed to Mon D only 7 to 9. **Closed:** Tue, 2 weeks Dec, 2 weeks Jan. **Meals:** Set D £34 (2 courses) to £42. **Service:** not inc. **Details:** Cards accepted. 28 seats. Separate bar. No mobile phones. Music. Children allowed.

Banchory

READERS RECOMMEND

Cow Shed Restaurant

Modern British

Raemoir Road, Banchory, AB31 5QB

Tel no: (01330) 820813

www.cowshedrestaurantbanchory.co.uk

'The tasting menu was sublime, shin of beef was melting and the halibut was perfect.'

Dufftown

La Faisanderie

Crowd-pleasing French cooking

2 Balvenie Street, Dufftown, AB55 4AD

Tel no: (01340) 821273

French | £32

Cooking score: 3

On a corner site near the clock tower on Dufftown's main square, La Faisanderie is a small, relaxed restaurant with, according to one reader, more than a hint of French bistro about it, which perhaps goes some way to explaining the name. Eric Obry cooks in a largely Gallic style, taking a quality-first approach to sourcing and cooking – he grows 40 per cent of all herbs and vegetables used in the restaurant, and shoots and butchers the venison himself. Hot-smoked lamb fillet with poached pear, honey and Pommery mustard dressing makes an opulent starter, while among main courses pot-au-feu teal comes stuffed with a black truffle farci and is served with foie gras velouté. Desserts are favourites, such as plum clafoutis with whisky ice cream and passion-fruit syrup. House wine is £13.90.

Chef/s: Eric Obry. **Open:** all week L 12 to 1.30, D 6 to 8.30. **Closed:** Tue and Wed (Nov to Mar), Jan. **Meals:** alc (main courses £18 to £21). Set L £15.20 (2 courses) to £18.50. Set D £32. **Service:** not inc. **Details:** Cards accepted. 30 seats. No mobile phones. Wheelchair access. Music. Children allowed.

Glenkindie

READERS RECOMMEND

Glenkindie Arms

Modern British

Glenkindie, AB33 8SX

Tel no: (01975) 641288

www.theglenkindiearms.com

'The welcome was warm, the ambience relaxed, the chef-patron talked us through the locally sourced menu.'

Udny Green

Eat on the Green

Meals with a sense of occasion

Udny Green, AB41 7RS

Tel no: (01651) 842337

www.eatonthegreen.co.uk

Modern European | £37

Cooking score: 2

A stone-built Scottish inn 20 minutes' drive from Aberdeen, facing the village green and the church, Craig Wilson's place is noted for the friendliness of the welcome and the sense of occasion that all reporters find when they eat here. Unimpeachable regional ingredients find their way into dishes that keep an eye on current trends. Expect tempura langoustine with saffron mayonnaise, caper salsa and fennel, followed by marinated venison loin with pear purée and Puy lentils, and then perhaps a taster dessert plate that includes lemon rice pudding, mango pavlova and more. A well-written wine list opens at £18.70 (£4.65 a glass).

Chef/s: Craig Wilson. **Open:** Wed to Fri and Sun L 12 to 1.45, Wed to Sun D 6.30 to 8.45 (6 to 9 Fri and Sat). **Closed:** Mon and Tue. **Meals:** alc (main courses £19 to £25). Set L £21.95 (2 courses) to £24.95. Sat D £49 (4 courses). Sun L £24.95 (2 courses) to £29.95. **Service:** not inc. **Details:** Cards accepted. 70 seats. No mobile phones. Wheelchair access. Music. Children allowed. Car parking.

■ Main entry

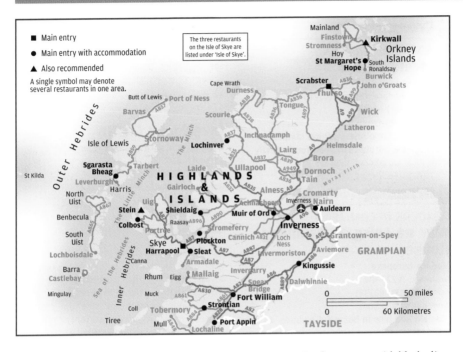

● Main entry with accommodation

▲ Also recommended

A single symbol may denote several restaurants in one area.

The three restaurants on the Isle of Skye are listed under 'Isle of Skye'.

Auldearn

Boath House

Distinguished country house with chic cooking
Auldearn, IV12 5TE
Tel no: (01667) 454896
www.boath-house.com
Modern European | £70
Cooking score: 5

Enveloped by 20 acres of manicured grounds complete with an ornamental lake and a walled garden, Boath House has been dubbed 'the most beautiful Regency residence in Scotland'. And, following years of dutiful and tireless restoration by its current custodians Don and Wendy Matheson, it fully deserves that accolade once again. Long-serving chef Charlie Lockley has also played his part, shoring up Boath's culinary reputation with his six-course dinner menus. After aperitifs in the lounge, guests are treated to a precise display of chic modern cooking inspired by home-grown and regional ingredients. First comes a soup (perhaps carrot with black olive crumbs); then a little palate-charging dish of, say, pig's trotters with snails and wild garlic might give way to a serving of scallops, leeks and hazelnuts embellished with chickweed. The fourth course generally makes a more substantial statement – say ruby veal breast with lingot beans and celeriac or halibut with langoustine and celery. Then it's on to cheese (Corra Linn with silverskin onions and crispbreads), before dessert brings the curtain down. Lunch is a much simpler repast, pared back to two or three courses in similar vein. The wine list reads well, with plenty of sound vintages from the Old and New Worlds; house recommendations start at £21 (£7.50 a glass).

Chef/s: Charlie Lockley. **Open:** all week L 12.30 to 1.15, D 7 (1 sitting). **Meals:** Set L £24 (2 courses) to £30. Set D £70 (6 courses). **Service:** not inc. **Details:** Cards accepted. 28 seats. No music. No mobile phones. Children allowed. Car parking.

Cromarty

READERS RECOMMEND

Crofters Bistro

Seafood

11 Marine Terrace, Cromarty, IV10 8UL
Tel no: (01381) 620844
www.croftersbistro.co.uk

'A little beachside bistro...fairly simple and sometimes a bit old-fashioned food, mostly from local suppliers.'

Drumbeg

READERS RECOMMEND

Blar na Leisg at Drumbeg House

Modern European

Drumbeg, IV27 4NW
Tel no: (01571) 833325
www.blarnaleisg.com

'The old and new in beautiful balance. An arty, intimate hotel showcasing local Scottish produce.'

Fort William

Crannog

Pier restaurant with top-quality seafood

Town Pier, Fort William, PH33 6DB
Tel no: (01397) 705589
www.crannog.net

Seafood | £30

Cooking score: 2

This simple seafood restaurant on the pier in windswept Fort William knows what it's about. 'Fish this good does not need to be buried in sauce', declared a reader, glad to find that indeed it wasn't. Stunning lochside views add to the allure of menus that deal in the likes of Scrabster hake with Puy lentils, halibut with chorizo ratatouille, and baked cod with crab and spinach risotto. Exemplary freshness is the watchword. Meat eaters might be lured by a dual serving of Argyll venison – loin and haunch – with spiced red cabbage and butternut purée. Finish with plum tart and mulled wine sorbet. Wines go from £15.75.

Chef/s: Stewart MacLachlan. **Open:** all week L 12 to 2.30, D 6 to 9. **Closed:** 25 Dec, 1 Jan. **Meals:** alc (main courses £15 to £20). Set L £11.95 (2 courses). **Service:** not inc. **Details:** Cards accepted. 60 seats. Wheelchair access. Music. Children allowed. Car parking.

Inverlochy Castle

Baronial pile with turbo-charged food

Torlundy, Fort William, PH33 6SN
Tel no: (01397) 702177
www.inverlochycastlehotel.co.uk

Modern British | £67

Cooking score: 6

Nestled snugly in the foothills of Ben Nevis close to its thirteenth-century namesake, Inverlochy is a mighty baronial pile that parades its glories for all to appreciate: 'I never saw a lovelier or more romantic spot', wrote Queen Victoria in her diary after spending a week cocooned within its castellated splendour. Wide staircases, galleried halls, chandeliers and portrait-lined walls are some of its finer points, and there are pieces of antique furniture 'to take your breath away'. Service is perfectly correct and formality reigns – so 'jacket-and-tie, please'. In the kitchen, Philip Carnegie is capable of delivering a turbo-charged version of high-end contemporary cuisine, applying subtlety and invention to all manner of ideas and locally inspired partnerships. Isle of Skye crab is dressed with a green apple salad, sorbet and crisps, saddle of rabbit is teamed up with roast Loch Linnhe prawns and a bisque-style sauce, and loin of venison is poached in gin before ending up on the plate with braised Little Gem and caramelised figs. Lunch also delivers, judging by a luxurious starter of roasted veal sweetbreads with celeriac and foie gras, followed by pork fillet wrapped in Serrano ham alongside its own braised cheek and a cabbage and black pudding roulade. To finish, the kitchen unleashes some pretty pyrotechnics in the shape of a superbly light passion fruit bavarois with coconut parfait and mango, or caramel-poached pear with toffee

mousse. The swanky wine list covers France in detail before jetting off worldwide. 'Recommended' bottles start around £35, but you can drink more affordably if you delve.
Chef/s: Philip Carnegie. **Open:** all week L 12.30 to 1.45, D 6 to 10. **Meals:** Set L £28 (2 courses) to £38. Set D £67. **Service:** not inc. **Details:** Cards accepted. 45 seats. Separate bar. No mobile phones. Wheelchair access. Music. Car parking.

NEW ENTRY

The Lime Tree

Ambitious food in arty surroundings
The Old Manse, Achintore Road, Fort William, PH33 6RQ
Tel no: (01397) 701806
www.limetreefortwilliam.co.uk
Modern European | £30
Cooking score: 4

Painter David Wilson set up The Lime Tree as a showpiece Highland art gallery, but tacked on this restaurant-with-rooms as an extra crowd-puller. Set in a converted Victorian manse, the place comes with terrific views of Loch Linnhe and the mountains beyond, although much attention is now focused on the high-impact food. 'We had angels dancing on our taste buds', wrote one reporter ecstatically after sampling an impeccable dish of langoustines with air-dried ham, crab apple jelly and pickled quince purée, followed by roast halibut and scallops with celeriac rémoulade, toasted salsify and hazelnut emulsion. An excellent 'tasting of beef' and slow-cooked Ayrshire belly pork with black pudding fritters, pear and star anise purée show that the kitchen is equally at home with Scottish-reared meat, while desserts such as honey parfait with tamarind jam and cardamom apples highlight its finesse in the sweet department. Wines start at £17.
Chef/s: John Wilson. **Open:** all week D only 6.30 to 9. **Closed:** 24 to 26 Dec. **Meals:** Set D £29.95. **Service:** not inc. **Details:** Cards accepted. 32 seats. No mobile phones. Wheelchair access. Music. Children allowed. Car parking.

ALSO RECOMMENDED

▲ Lochleven Seafood Café

Onich, Fort William, PH33 6SA
Tel no: (01855) 821048
www.lochlevenseafoodcafe.co.uk
Seafood £5 OFF

Off the beaten track on the shores of Loch Leven, this buzzy café and shop is a showcase for local seafood. Fine raw ingredients are handled with care and simplicity – surf clams cooked with ham and sherry (£7.95) or whole brown crab served with mayonnaise, say. For meat fans, there's pan-roasted venison saddle with braised red cabbage, roasted chestnuts and root vegetables (£18.95). End with tiramisu. House wine is £14.55. Open all week in summer, check winter opening.

Inverness

Abstract at Glenmoriston Town House

Swanky dining with bells and whistles
20 Ness Bank, Inverness, IV2 4SF
Tel no: (01463) 223777
www.abstractrestaurant.com
Modern French | £50
Cooking score: 5

In a salubrious stretch of riverside hotels and eateries, Abstract stands out as the slickest option, its interior sporting modern artwork, polished wood and retro touches. An outdoor seating area with river views makes the most of sunny days, and there's a piano bar for after-dinner mingling. Well-drilled French staff add to the air of cool sophistication, and Bruce Morrison's cooking lives up to all that promise with an arty approach backed by great ingredients and a firm understanding of the basics. It's a deeply satisfying combination that manages to balance a 'wow' factor with comfort-zone eating. A starter of sautéed asparagus and morels with celeriac cream and slowly cooked duck egg yolk is a case in point, while braised pig's head with sweet potato purée, crispy pig's ear loaf, mascarpone pannacotta, glazed vegetables and honey and five-spice sauce does its bit for nose-to-tail eating. Vanilla and blueberry ripple ice cream with whisky jelly, warm honey and blueberry madeleines offers a similar balance of nostalgia and invention. For a lengthier indulgence, the seven-course 'Taste of Abstract' menu is good value. A decent but not overly long wine list offers plenty from France and a smattering of international finds, starting at £15.

Chef/s: Bruce Morrisson. **Open:** Tue to Sat D only 6 to 10. **Closed:** Sun, Mon, 8 and 9 Jan. **Meals:** alc (main courses £22 to £28). Tasting menu £55 (8 courses). **Service:** not inc. **Details:** Cards accepted. 30 seats. 35 seats outside. Separate bar. No mobile phones. Wheelchair access. Music. Children allowed. Car parking.

Rocpool

Fizzy riverside brasserie
1 Ness Walk, Inverness, IV3 5NE
Tel no: (01463) 717274
www.rocpoolrestaurant.com
Modern European | £31
Cooking score: 2

£5 OFF

A buzzy modern brasserie on the banks of the river Ness, Rocpool's dark leather seats, bare tables and 1930s-style lighting lend it a slick metropolitan edge. Popular, relaxed and merry, it offers good service and imaginative, continent-crossing food. 'Outstanding bread' opens things nicely, and a starter of mushroom soup has proved to be 'excellent – smooth, unctuous and properly mushroomy'. Lunchtime cauliflower pakora might come with 'delightful, light-touch use of classic curry house accompaniments', while traditional tastes are sated by loin of venison with Parma ham, black pudding creamed parsnips, wild mushrooms and crisp-fried potato. Classic desserts include lemon meringue pie. Wines start at £16.50.

Chef/s: Steven Devlin. **Open:** Mon to Sat L 12 to 2.30, all week D 5.45 to 10. **Closed:** Sun (Oct to Jun only), 25 and 26 Dec, 1 to 3 Jan. **Meals:** alc (main courses £12 to £23). Set L £11.95 (2 courses). Early set D £13.95 (2 courses). **Service:** not inc. **Details:** Cards accepted. 60 seats. Music. Children allowed.

Isle of Harris

Scarista House

Island bounty in a converted manse
Sgarasta Bheag, Isle of Harris, HS3 3HX
Tel no: (01859) 550238
www.scaristahouse.com
Modern British | £43
Cooking score: 2

V

An air of relaxed country house chic pervades this handsome old manse overlooking golden sands on the Isle of Harris, so book a window seat and watch the sun set over the Atlantic. Tim and Patricia Martin make intelligent use of whatever comes their way, be it local game, meat or seafood: if the boat's come in you might be offered a plate of simply cooked langoustines, or Stornoway halibut with Champagne and chive sauce. Starters keep it simple (Black Ale blinis with peat-smoked salmon and pink grapefruit vinaigrette) and desserts are the comforting, homemade kind: steamed date pudding with toffee sauce and ginger ice cream is a winner. House wine is £17.

Chef/s: Tim and Patricia Martin. **Open:** all week D only 8 (1 sitting). **Meals:** Set D £43 (3 courses) to £50. **Service:** not inc. **Details:** Cards accepted. 24 seats. No music. Wheelchair access. Children allowed. Car parking.

Symbols

- Accommodation is available
- £30 Three courses for less than £30
- V Separate vegetarian menu
- £5 OFF £5-off voucher scheme
- Notable wine list

Isle of Skye

NEW ENTRY

Creelers of Skye

Accomplished cooking in 'a fish shed'
Harrapool, Broadford, Isle of Skye, IV49 9AQ
Tel no: (01471) 822281
www.skye-seafood-restaurant.co.uk
French | £24
Cooking score: 2

One reader described this tiny seafood restaurant as a 'shed' but was impressed by the cooking. The paper tablecoths and napkins are a deliberate understatement, but there is no denying David Wilson's passion for seafood. His cooking is authentically French, with some Cajun twists. Bouillabaisse is made to a traditional Marseillaise recipe and costs £62 for two people, but for a more modest bill, pan-browned local hand-dived king scallops would be a good choice, followed by braised local monkfish tail in a soy and Pernod cream reduction. Finish with lime cheesecake and red pepper sauce. Wines from £14.50.
Chef/s: David Wilson. **Open:** Mon to Sat L 12 to 5, D 5 to 10. **Closed:** Sun, 1 Nov to 1 Mar. **Meals:** alc (main courses £8 to £17). **Service:** not inc. **Details:** Cards accepted. 28 seats. Wheelchair access. Music. Children allowed. Car parking.

Kinloch Lodge

Creative cooking and dreamy views
Sleat, Isle of Skye, IV43 8QY
Tel no: (01471) 833333
www.kinloch-lodge.co.uk
Modern British | £60
Cooking score: 5

£5 OFF V

Beneath Kinloch Hill on the shores of Loch na Dal, this isolated country house is as romantic as they come. The family seat of the Macdonald clan, it has been run as a luxury hotel by Lord and Lady Macdonald for nearly four decades. Ancestral portraits, blazing log fires and a warm welcome are to be taken for granted – along with exemplary cooking by Brazilian chef Marcello Tully. He impresses with his creativity, precision and flair – from an opening 'soupçon' of parsnip and Pernod or celeriac and blue cheese to a series of dishes showcasing local treats such as Mallaig monkfish (roasted and served with Moray pork cheeks and caramelised passion fruit jus) or wild Isle of Muck duck with fondant potato, braised red cabbage, lardons, mushrooms and a rich game jus. Tully's cooking is sure-footed; diners have praised its 'consistent quality from beginning to end'. Unexpected extras such as delicate fishy nibbles and a frothy lightly spiced pea soup add up to an 'amazing bargain'. Finish with classic bread-and-butter pudding. The wine list is a mighty collection of knowledgably chosen bottles with plenty of depth in the French regions, but impressive drinking across the board. Mark-ups (especially on 'fine and interesting vintages') are exceedingly fair; prices start at £24 (£6 a glass). Also check out the fascinating beer and whisky 'flights'.
Chef/s: Marcello Tully. **Open:** all week L 12 to 2.30, D 6.30 to 9. **Closed:** 24 to 26 Dec. **Meals:** Set L £26.99 (2 courses) to £29.99. Set D £55 (2 courses) to £60. **Service:** not inc. **Details:** Cards accepted. 40 seats. Separate bar. No mobile phones. Wheelchair access. Music. Children allowed. Car parking.

The Three Chimneys

A memorable prospect
Colbost, Isle of Skye, IV55 8ZT
Tel no: (01470) 511258
www.threechimneys.co.uk
Modern British | £60
Cooking score: 5

V

'From the minute we opened the door to the moment they bid us a fond farewell, The Three Chimneys was first class. This is Scotland at its finest'. So runs a typical eulogy for Shirley and Eddie Spear's converted crofter's cottage down a single-track road by the shores of Loch Dunvegan. Remoteness is a virtue here and the whole place is imbued with a sense of enduring domesticity, from the thick stone walls and built-to-last furniture to the smell of bread wafting through the house. But this is no bonnie nostalgia trip: the Spears have sympathetically upgraded the facilities (note the new chef's table in the extended kitchen) and Michael Smith delivers polished contemporary food inspired by matchless produce from the region. Menus change daily, with dinner as the showcase and seafood topping the bill – think pan-fried monkfish cheeks with fennel confit, pickled winkles and a claret reduction, or grilled halibut and scallop with braised rhubarb, curly kale and vanilla velouté. If something meatier is required, look for Blackface lamb haggis with neeps, or roast Lochalsh red deer with tattie scones, Ayrshire bacon, celeriac and beetroot gravy. Lunch also receives plaudits, from a 'divine' seafood platter to chocolate délice with blaeberries and the 'world-famous' hot marmalade pudding with Drambuie custard. The Spears have accumulated a prestigious collection of wines over the years, with France in the ascendancy but New World pickings also making an impact. Prices start at £18.50, half-bottles are a strength and there's a great choice by the glass.

Chef/s: Michael Smith. **Open:** Mon to Sat L 12.15 to 1.45, all week D 6.15 to 9.45. **Closed:** 6 to 21 Jan. **Meals:** Set L £28.50 (2 courses) to £37. Set D £60. Tasting menu £85 (7 courses). **Service:** not inc. **Details:** Cards accepted. 42 seats. 8 seats outside. Separate bar. No music. No mobile phones. Wheelchair access. Car parking.

ALSO RECOMMENDED

▲ Loch Bay

1-2 Macleod Terrace, Stein, Isle of Skye, IV55 8GA
Tel no: (01470) 592235
www.lochbay-seafood-restaurant.co.uk
Seafood £5 OFF

Yards from the pier in the fishing village of Stein, this 'relaxed, unpretentious' little restaurant serves spanking fresh fish and seafood. Aptly enough, it used to be a fisherman's cottage. Today's catch might become hearty fish soup, crab and lobster risotto (£7.25) or something simple such as fillet of halibut with white wine sauce (£16). The ultimate indulgence is a shared shellfish platter (£72.50), but leave room for hot cranberry, white chocolate and orange pudding. Wines start at £16.50. Closed Sun and Mon.

Kingussie

The Cross

Old mill with great food and wine
Ardbroilach Road, Kingussie, PH21 1LB
Tel no: (01540) 661166
www.thecross.co.uk
Modern British | £50
Cooking score: 5

£5 OFF

The remote location, north of the Grampians, in an old mill by the river Gynack, is a tonic for the weary townie if ever there was one. David and Katie Young run The Cross with that soul-nurturing mission very much in mind, and the solid beams and exposed stone walls speak of the venerability of the place. The format is a four-course dinner menu kept nice and simple, with a pair of alternatives at every stage bar the first. The dishes are informed by a network of pedigree Highland growers and producers, including game from local estates and shellfish from Lochalsh. A summer dinner kicked off Indian-style with a fish pakora served with cucumber raita, before progressing to either lobster and langoustine tian with avocado and lovage 'vichyssoise' or seared rabbit with Ragstone goats' cheese and passion fruit, and then herb-crusted salmon in ginger velouté or haunch and osso buco of venison with soured cabbage. Dessert might offer bitter chocolate and cherry tart with white chocolate ice cream, or a plate of variations on a theme of Amalfi lemon. A painstakingly annotated list of quality wines is arranged by grape, with suggestions for food matches, and includes dozens of fine producers in both hemispheres in exhilarating array. Bottles start at £26.

Chef/s: David Young and Becca Henderson. **Open:** Tue to Sat D only 7 to 8.30. **Closed:** Sun, Mon, 1 week Christmas, Jan. **Meals:** Set D £50. **Service:** not inc. **Details:** Cards accepted. 24 seats. No music. No mobile phones. Car parking.

Lochinver

Albannach

Highland retreat with sensitive cooking
Baddidarroch, Lochinver, IV27 4LP
Tel no: (01571) 844407
www.thealbannach.co.uk
Modern British | £55
Cooking score: 6

Almost camouflaged on a wooded rise above the harbour, Albannach gathers its Scottish remoteness about it like a morning mist. It'll take you about two hours from the airport at Inverness. A terrace and garden make full use of the surrounding serenity, and discreetly feature what the owners call a 'midge-eating machine', which ought to seal the deal for Highlands regulars. Inside, it's rather more cocoon-like, the dining room a place of dark wood, shuttered windows and evening candlelight. Colin Craig and Lesley Crosfield offer a daily changing dinner menu of five courses plus coffee, based on regional materials cooked with sensitivity and skill. One dinner turned up mousseline of wild halibut with langoustines and lobster in lobster sauce followed by wild mushroom risotto, and then roast saddle of roe deer, alongside candied beetroot, truffled squash and a potato galette in port-boosted game stock sauce. A pause for cheeses is followed by a treat such as citrus soufflé with bitter chocolate ice cream and autumn berries. It all feels beautifully balanced, with great care taken to respect the integrity of ingredients. A very fine wine list has been put together at prices that seem demonstrably fair. There are no notes, but the selections throughout are so unerring as to make pin-sticking a perfectly safe option. The centre of gravity is France. Prices open at £18.

Chef/s: Colin Craig and Lesley Crosfield. **Open:** Tue to Sun D only 7.30 for 8 (1 sitting only). **Closed:** Mon, 3 Jan to 16 Mar, Mon to Wed in Nov and Dec (exc 2 weeks Christmas). **Meals:** Set D £58 (6 courses). **Service:** not inc. **Details:** Cards accepted. 20 seats. No music. No mobile phones. Car parking.

Muir of Ord

The Dower House

Homely Highland hideaway
Highfield, Muir of Ord, IV6 7XN
Tel no: (01463) 870090
www.thedowerhouse.co.uk
Modern British | £42
Cooking score: 2

There is a restful silence round Robyn and Mena Aitchison's early nineteenth-century cottage, which they have run as an unassuming, off-the-beaten track hotel for 24 years. They have much to offer, from comfortable, civilised surroundings and unobtrusive attention to detail to affable service – although Robyn's simply prepared, no-choice dinners are the undoubted star. Cream of chicory soup, fillet of venison with herb relish, and hot raspberry soufflé could easily be dull, but are as well-cooked as one could possibly want. Coffee and Scottish tablet bring proceedings to an end. House wine is £18.

Chef/s: Robyn Aitchison. **Open:** all week D only 7.30 (1 sitting). **Closed:** 25 Dec, 2 weeks Nov. **Meals:** Set D £42. **Service:** not inc. **Details:** Cards accepted. 20 seats. 4 seats outside. No music. No mobile phones. Wheelchair access. Children allowed. Car parking.

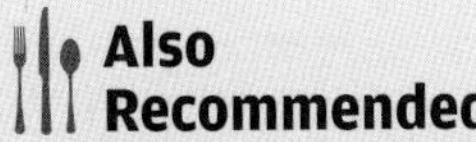

Also Recommended

Also recommended entries are not scored but we think they are worth a visit.

Orkney Islands

The Creel

Stunning local produce, perfectly cooked
Front Road, St Margaret's Hope, Orkney Islands, KW17 2SL
Tel no: (01856) 831311
www.thecreel.co.uk
Modern British | £38
Cooking score: 6

Alan and Joyce Craigie have been running one of our more far-flung restaurants since 1985. They lived over the shop for a few years, before buying up next door and creating three guest rooms for those who've made the journey. And it is certainly a journey worth making. The Orkneys are the last word in remote tranquillity, as the sea view from the dining room will remind you. The seafood on offer here brings a whole new meaning to the word freshness. Not only are there the expected items like crab, scallops, hake and mackerel, but species such as sea witch and torsk also help to broaden the vocabulary. They feature in fixed-price dinner menus that make a virtue of utter simplicity. A crab salad with apple mayonnaise and avocado salsa, or fishcakes served in lobster bisque might start the evening off, ahead of a pairing of roasted ling and steamed lemon sole with puréed cauliflower and garden peas. There's also much great locally grown produce, including fine new potatoes and red fruits, as well as home-baked bannocks and soda bread, and pedigree Scottish cheeses. A carefully composed wine list opens with house Argentinians at £15.
Chef/s: Alan Craigie. **Open:** Tue to Sun D only 7 to 9. **Closed:** Mon, mid-Oct to Apr. **Meals:** Set D £32 (2 courses) to £38. **Service:** not inc. **Details:** Cards accepted. 30 seats. No music. No mobile phones. Wheelchair access. Children allowed. Car parking.

ALSO RECOMMENDED

▲ Dil Se

7 Bridge Street, Kirkwall, Orkney Islands, KW15 1HR
Tel no: (01856) 875242
www.dilserestaurant.co.uk
Indian

Britain's most northerly Indian/Bangladeshi restaurant occupies one of the oldest buildings in Kirkwall. Here you'll find a kitchen making impressive use of island produce – sheek kebab (£5.95) prepared with minced local lamb, and Orkney ice cream served with gulab jamun. The menu dips into different regions of the subcontinent, with king prawn puri among starters, and main courses encompassing chicken shashlik (£12.95) and familiar curry house favourites such as lamb korma. Wines from £11.95. Open all week from 4pm.

Plockton

Plockton Inn

Spanking-fresh seafood hits the spot
Innes Street, Plockton, IV52 8TW
Tel no: (01599) 544222
www.plocktoninn.co.uk
Seafood | £20
Cooking score: 2

£5 OFF £30

'Nothing fancy, but hits the spot', summed up one visitor to this family-run pub-with-rooms near the harbour. Most people are here for the super-fresh seafood, especially locally caught prawns (served hot with garlic butter or cold with Marie Rose sauce) and platters of smoked fish from the pub's smokehouse. Skate with black butter or turbot steamed with spring onions and ginger are other appealing ideas, but if you are in the mood for meat look out for braised venison, haggis and clapshot (a traditional turnip and potato dish) or steak with pickled walnut and mushroom sauce. Homely desserts include sticky toffee pudding. Wines from £13.95.

Chef/s: Mary Gollan. **Open:** all week L 12 to 2.15, D 6 to 9. **Closed:** 25 and 26 Dec. **Meals:** alc (main courses £9 to £18). **Service:** not inc. **Details:** Cards accepted. 60 seats. 20 seats outside. Separate bar. Wheelchair access. Music. Children allowed. Car parking.

Port Appin

Airds Hotel

Flawless professionalism and fine food
Port Appin, PA38 4DF
Tel no: (01631) 730236
www.airds-hotel.com
Modern British | £53
new chef
V

Forget grand sprawling edifices marooned in acres of manicured parkland, the Airds Hotel charms visitors with more modest, homespun attributes – not surprising, given that it started life as a ferry inn by the tranquil shores of Loch Linnhe. Inside, all is cosy and comforting, with a vermilion-walled lounge, snug little bar and conservatory seats for contemplating the view. The long dining room capitalises on those lochside vistas too, and is run with flawless professionalism. As we were going to press, new chef Robert MacPherson arrived from the Isle of Eriska Hotel (see entry), where he was known for his fine country house cooking and dedication to impeccably sourced raw materials. Meanwhile, the varietally arranged wine list promises a user-friendly approach when it comes to food matching. The notes are helpful, prices are far from ghastly and the choice of growers is fine throughout; house suggestions start at £21.50 for a Provence rosé. Reports please.

Chef/s: Robert MacPherson. **Open:** all week L 12 to 1.45, D 7.30 to 9.30. **Closed:** 2 days each week Nov to Jan. **Meals:** Set L £18.95 (2 courses) to £21.95. Set D £53 (5 courses). Sun L £21.95. Tasting menu £70 (7 courses). **Service:** not inc. **Details:** Cards accepted. 32 seats. No music. No mobile phones. Wheelchair access. Children allowed. Car parking.

ALSO RECOMMENDED

▲ The Pierhouse

Port Appin, PA38 4DE
Tel no: (01631) 730302
www.pierhousehotel.co.uk
Seafood

This hotel is spectacularly located by the working pier in Port Appin. The restaurant concentrates mainly on seafood, although carnivores are also catered for. The atmosphere in the Ferry bar and the dining room is informal and cheerful. Cooking is straightforwardly simple and genuine. Starters include Pierhouse seafood chowder (£5.95). Follow with seafood brochette with a shellfish bisque, spring greens and new potatoes, and finish with berry pavlova (£5.50). Open all week, L & D. Wines from £14.50.

Scrabster

The Captain's Galley

Sustainable seafood by the harbour
The Harbour, Scrabster, KW14 7UJ
Tel no: (01847) 894999
www.captainsgalley.co.uk
Seafood | £47
Cooking score: 3

In 2001 Jim and Mary Cowie had the bright idea of turning Scrabster's early-Victorian salmon 'bothy' and ice house into a local restaurant specialising in sustainable seafood from the Highland boats. Good fish deserves respectful treatment and 30 seconds can seem like a lifetime when cooking the stuff; consequently, Jim deliberately stays the rare side of 'medium' ('à point', if you're French; 'sashimi-fresh', if you're from Japan). Frazzled, blisteringly hot dishes have no place here; instead, expect seared fillet of hake with creamed sweetcorn and pea purée, flame-grilled red mullet with Mediterranean-style crushed potatoes and sauce vierge, or gently steamed turbot with clams, mussels, chorizo and bouillabaisse broth. Short rib of Angus beef and haggis with neeps 'n' tatties please the patriots, and there might be coconut pannacotta with local strawberries to finish. Global wines start at £15.95.

Chef/s: Jim Cowie. **Open:** Mon to Sat D only 6.30 to 9. **Closed:** Sun, 25 and 26 Dec, 1 and 2 Jan. **Meals:** Set D £46.50 to £51.50 (4 courses). Tasting menu £55 (7 courses). **Service:** not inc. **Details:** Cards accepted. 25 seats. Separate bar. Wheelchair access. Music. Children allowed. Car parking.

Shieldaig

Tigh an Eilean Hotel

Homespun hospitality
Shieldaig, IV54 8XN
Tel no: (01520) 755251
www.tighaneilean.co.uk
Modern British | £45
Cooking score: 3

Nestled in an unspoilt fishing village overlooking Loch Torridon, this 'house of the island' comes complete with a cottagey feel and views out towards Shieldaig. It's a calm, friendly and homespun set-up, with Cathryn Field on hand when required and husband Christopher working wonders in the kitchen. From the oven-warm, home-baked rolls and complimentary gazpacho to the skilfully crafted petits fours, everything gets an emphatic thumbs-up. Seared hand-dived Hebridean scallops come with green apple and black olives, cannon of Highland estate venison is presented with red cabbage, potato and onion pavé, pot-roasted vegetables and red wine jus, and Braeburn apple tarte Tatin is nicely offset by homemade vanilla ice cream. Wines start at £16.50. Simpler food is served in the Shieldaig Bar & Coastal Kitchen (open all week).

Chef/s: Christopher Field. **Open:** all week D only 7 to 8.30. **Closed:** Nov to Mar. **Meals:** Set D £45. **Service:** not inc. **Details:** Cards accepted. 26 seats. Separate bar. No music. No mobile phones. Wheelchair access. Children allowed. Car parking.

Strontian

Kilcamb Lodge

Graciously welcoming country house
Strontian, PH36 4HY
Tel no: (01967) 402257
www.kilcamblodge.co.uk
Modern European | £50
Cooking score: 4

A venerable, full-dress country house dating back to the 1700s, Kilcamb Lodge is stunningly located far from the madding crowd by the shores of Loch Sunart – with impressive views of mountains in the distance. The past still looms large here, and a mood of gracious, cosseting civility prevails. New chef Gary Phillips is making a brave effort to maintain the standards set by his predecessor, although his presentation can sometimes be too fussy for its own good. Seared Oban scallops with Stornoway black pudding and a truffle and pea purée open proceedings on a promising note, or you might prefer braised oxtail suet pudding with star anise jus. After that, classic Argyll lamb Wellington could share the billing with a fancy combo of venison loin with wild mushroom mousse, a fricassee of red cabbage and sherry sauce. Desserts have included satisfying mango and vanilla pannacotta. The wine list offers sound drinking from £20.50.

Chef/s: Gary Phillips. **Open:** all week L 12 to 2 (3 Sun), D 7.30 to 9.30. **Closed:** 3 Jan to 3 Feb. **Meals:** Set L £14.75 (2 courses) to £17.50. Set D £49.50 (4 courses). Sun L £12.50. **Service:** not inc. **Details:** Cards accepted. 26 seats. Separate bar. No mobile phones. Music. Children allowed. Car parking.

WALES

Glamorgan, Gwent, Mid-Wales, North-East Wales, North-West Wales, West Wales

Cardiff

NEW ENTRY

ffresh

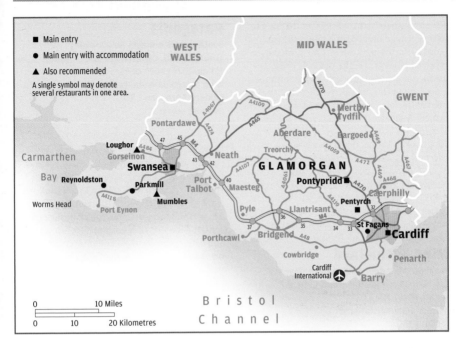

Sleek eatery focusing on Welsh ingredients
The Wales Millennium Centre, Bute Place, Cardiff, CF10 5AL
Tel no: (029) 2063 6465
www.ffresh.org.uk
Modern British | £25
Cooking score: 1

Set in the magnificent Millennium Centre, this airy modern restaurant has floor-to-ceiling glass windows, with views of Cardiff Bay. The décor is sleek and minimalist with an industrial edge (the stainless steel of the kitchen is on full show) and the menu has a similar pared-down simplicity. Shaun Hill from the Walnut Tree, Llanddewi Skirrid (see entry) helped devise it and there's an admirable focus on native ingredients: maybe smoked Welsh Cheddar with pickled carrot salad, chickpeas and shoots, ahead of Brecon venison pie with Tomos Watkin bitter, mashed potato and curly kale. Pud could be orange and chocolate fondant. Wines start at £14.95.

Chef/s: Kurt Fleming. **Open:** Tue to Sun L 12 to 2.30 (4 Sun), Tue to Sat D 5 to 9.30. **Closed:** Mon, 25 Dec. **Meals:** alc (main courses £11 to £19). Set L £14.95 (2 courses) to £17.95. Set D £17.95 (2 courses) to £21.95. Sun L £14.95. **Service:** not inc. **Details:** Cards accepted. 140 seats. 40 seats outside. Separate bar. Wheelchair access. Music. Children allowed.

Garçon! Brasserie Française

Heritage French fare and rapturous views
Mermaid Quay, Cardiff, CF10 5BZ
Tel no: (029) 2049 0990
www.garcon-resto.co.uk
French | £25
Cooking score: 1

A charming French brasserie *en aspic*, Garçon! stands on the Mermaid Quay, with stunning waterfront views to enjoy. The polished wood

floor and smartly attired staff set the tone for some heritage French fare, along the lines of moules marinière, steak tartare, pork cutlets in mustard sauce and – the pièce de résistance – tournedos Rossini properly made with foie gras. Fixed price menus are top value, and you can finish classically with tarte Tatin or crème brûlée. A serviceable French wine list opens at £15.95.

Chef/s: Kevin Wilson. **Open:** all week L 12 to 2.30, Mon to Thu D 6 to 10 (11 Fri and Sat, 5 Sun). **Closed:** 24 to 26 Dec, 1 Jan, first week Jan. **Meals:** alc (main courses £12 to £33). Set L and D £12.95 (2 courses) to £15.95. Sun L £15.95. **Service:** 10% (optional). **Details:** Cards accepted. 90 seats. 32 seats outside. Wheelchair access. Music. Children allowed.

Mint & Mustard

Trailblazing Indian with superb flavours
134 Whitchurch Road, Cardiff, CF14 3LZ
Tel no: (029) 2062 0333
www.mintandmustard.com
Indian | £30
Cooking score: 2

£5 OFF **V**

This contemporary Indian restaurant has a reputation that stretches far beyond its immediate neighbourhood. Diners have praised the clear flavours and the scope of the menu, which manages to embrace favourites like chicken tikka masala as well as innovative and lesser-known dishes such as nandu (crispy soft-shell crab dusted with curry leaves and garlic) followed by tiffin sea bass (pan-seared on curry leaf-infused mash with a mango, ginger and coconut sauce). Plentiful vegetarian options might include paneer tikka and thoran (a traditional Keralan stir-fry). Wines start at £15.

Chef/s: Siddartha Singh Rathore. **Open:** Mon to Sat D only 6 to 11. **Closed:** Sun, 25 and 26 Dec, 1 Jan. **Meals:** alc (main courses £8 to £16). Tasting menu £39 (5 courses). **Service:** not inc. **Details:** Cards accepted. 56 seats. Wheelchair access. Music. Children allowed.

Patagonia

South America meets South Wales
11 Kings Road, Cardiff, CF11 9BZ
Tel no: (029) 2019 0265
www.patagonia-restaurant.co.uk
Modern European | £31
Cooking score: 3

£5 OFF

Now in its ninth year, this charming family-run restaurant is the creation of Joaquin Humaran and Leticia Salina, who met in a Buenos Aires kitchen, then worked their way across Europe before settling in Cardiff. Set in a busy residential area not far from the city centre, Patagonia has a simple, stylish interior and a menu built on excellent international ingredients, notably Argentinian beef – perhaps served with rolled potato, Savoy cabbage and pancetta, roasted vegetables and Malbec jus. Other options include smoked duck salad with raspberry vinaigrette and roasted guinea fowl breast with wild mushroom sauce. Butternut squash, sage and smoked ewes'-milk cheese risotto, followed by homemade pea, porcini, spinach and ricotta rotolo should keep vegetarians happy. Finish with pear frangipane tart. International wines start at £13.90.

Chef/s: Joaquin Humaran. **Open:** Tue to Sat D only 6.30 to 10. **Closed:** Sun, Mon, 25 Dec to 20 Jan, bank hols. **Meals:** Set D £26.90 (2 courses) to £30.90. **Service:** not inc. **Details:** Cards accepted. 42 seats. Wheelchair access. Music. Children allowed.

Woods Brasserie

Local asset with modern menus
The Pilotage Building, Stuart Street, Cardiff, CF10 5BW
Tel no: (029) 2049 2400
www.woods-brasserie.com
Modern European | £50
Cooking score: 3

This popular brasserie occupies a charming old building with plenty of outdoor seating. Inside, an abundance of space and light and judicious splashes of bright colour make for a classy but cool look. The menu keeps pace, offering simple modern dishes such as a brunch salad (crisp air-dried ham, poached egg, black pudding and a zingy tomato dressing) followed by slow-cooked ballottine of local beef with mash, grain-mustard leeks and a rich red wine gravy. Ingredients are largely local but flavours are wide-ranging – Gower coast mussels might come in a Thai green sauce, for instance. Memorable desserts could include a moist chocolate brownie with caramel sauce and vanilla ice cream. A selection of global wines starts at £15.50.

Chef/s: Wesley Hammond. **Open:** all week L 12 to 2 (3 Sun), Mon to Sat D 5.30 to 10. **Closed:** 25 and 26 Dec. **Meals:** alc (main courses £12 to £18). Set L £14.50 (2 courses) to £17.50. Set D £17.95 (2 courses) to £19.95. Sun L £15.95. **Service:** not inc. **Details:** Cards accepted. 90 seats. 80 seats outside. Separate bar. Wheelchair access. Music. Children allowed.

Cowbridge

READERS RECOMMEND

Bar 44

Tapas
44c High Street, Cowbridge, CF71 7AG
Tel no: (01446) 776488
www.bar44.co.uk
'Pleasant tapas bar serving Spanish dishes using a mixture of Spanish and locally sourced ingredients.'

Loughor

ALSO RECOMMENDED

▲ Hurrens Inn on the Estuary

13 Station Road, Loughor, SA4 6TR
Tel no: (01792) 899092
www.hurrens.co.uk
Modern European £5 OFF

Originally a railway station and then a pub, this cottagey building is now an attractive modern restaurant with an easy-going atmosphere. Welcoming young staff keep things well-oiled while the kitchen turns out simple food with big flavours – maybe Thai salmon fishcakes (£5.50) and then Cajun-spiced wild boar with sweet potato mash, red cabbage and balsamic reduction (£16.50) followed by apple and blackberry crumble. Wines start at £13.95. Closed Sun D and Mon.

Mumbles

ALSO RECOMMENDED

▲ Out of the Blue

698 Mumbles Road, Mumbles, SA3 4EH
Tel no: (01792) 361616
www.outoftheblue restaurant.co.uk
Seafood £5 OFF

A smart little restaurant close to the waters that feed its menus, this is a good spot for fresh, sustainably caught seafood – maybe seared scallops on pea purée with crispy pancetta (£8.95) followed by whole plaice pan-fried in fresh herb butter (£16.95) or an extravagant seafood platter. Meat options might include chicken liver parfait with white onion and port jam, and guinea fowl with port-poached baby onions and pancetta. Wines from £12.95. Closed Sun and Mon.

Parkmill

Maes-Yr-Haf

Big-city food from local ingredients
Parkmill, SA3 2EH
Tel no: (01792) 371000
www.maes-yr-haf.com
Modern European | £33
Cooking score: 3

A change of chef at this boutique hotel has not altered the quality of the food, which maintains an unexpectedly metropolitan edge, despite the bucolic surroundings (stunning Three Cliffs Bay is walkable from here). The décor follows suit, with clean lines, lots of mirrors and retro-cool lighting. Attentive staff and slick service keep things well-oiled throughout, while the menu plunders the surrounding larder to offer classic combinations along the lines of carpaccio of

Gower beetroot with Welsh goats' cheese beignet, balsamic and walnut oil, followed by slow-braised shin of Welsh Black beef with smoked bacon, shallots and puréed potato. Desserts such as caramelised banana meringue with sticky toffee pudding play to the comfort zone. A well-spread wine list kicks off at £13.95.

Chef/s: Ben Griffiths. **Open:** all week L 12 to 2, Mon to Sat D 7 to 9. **Closed:** Mon (Nov to Jun), last 2 weeks Jan. **Meals:** alc (main courses £15 to £25). Set L and D £15.95 (2 courses) to £19.95. Sun L £15.20. **Service:** not inc. **Details:** Cards accepted. 44 seats. Separate bar. Wheelchair access. Music. Car parking.

Penarth

READERS RECOMMEND

The Fig Tree

Modern British

The Esplanade, Penarth, CF64 3AU

Tel no: (029) 2070 2512

www.thefigtreepenarth.co.uk

'Food is no-nonsense, local, seasonal fare and very well cooked.'

Pentyrch

NEW ENTRY

Kings Arms

Proper pub with a stylish restaurant

Church Road, Pentyrch, CF15 9QF

Tel no: (029) 2089 0202

www.kingsarmspentyrch.co.uk

Modern British | £25

Cooking score: 2

Padrig Jones once reigned supreme at Le Gallois, the Cardiff restaurant he left in 2008. Now he's cooking up a simpler style of food at the Kings Arms – a traditional pub complete with regulars, a real fire and wonky beams. Its darkly cosy, snug bar opens on to an unexpectedly bright and stylish restaurant with garden views. Food ranges from simple pub fare (ham, egg and chips) to a perfectly seasoned saffron risotto, ahead of confit duck with Savoy cabbage, pancetta, creamed potato and a rich red wine sauce. For dessert, maybe lemon tart with caramel ice cream. House wines from £11.95.

Chef/s: Padrig Jones. **Open:** Tue to Sun L 12 to 2.30 (3 Sun), Tue to Sat D 6 to 9. **Closed:** Mon, 25 to 28 Dec, 1 Jan. **Meals:** alc (main courses £10 to £22). Set L £12.95 (2 courses). Sun L £10.95. **Service:** not inc. **Details:** Cards accepted. 80 seats. 30 seats outside. Separate bar. No mobile phones. Music. Children allowed. Car parking.

Pontypridd

Bunch of Grapes

Laid-back pub with generous platefuls

Ynysangharad Road, Pontypridd, CF37 4DA

Tel no: (01443) 402934

www.bunchofgrapes.org.uk

Modern British | £23

Cooking score: 1

The laid-back style and informality of this 200-year-old, former canal-workers' pub suits its location on the Taff Trail (a walking and cycling route between Merthyr Tydfil and Cardiff) to a T. The bar menu peddles generous plates of ploughman's, burgers or ham, egg and chips, while the restaurant offers vigorously seasonal, uncomplicated dishes such as wood pigeon and oxtail faggots, hay-roasted chicken breast with bubble and squeak, and poached pear with brown sugar ice cream. House wine is £14.30.

Chef/s: Sebastien Vanoni. **Open:** all week L 12 to 2.30 (3 Fri and Sat, 3.30 Sun), Mon to Sat D 6 to 9.30 (10 Fri and Sat). **Meals:** alc (main courses £14 to £25). Sun L £15.50. **Service:** not inc. **Details:** Cards accepted. 66 seats. 24 seats outside. Separate bar. Wheelchair access. Music. Children allowed. Car parking.

Reynoldston

Fairyhill

Special house, special cooking
Reynoldston, SA3 1BS
Tel no: (01792) 390139
www.fairyhill.net
Modern British | £45
Cooking score: 4

A smart, cosy country house hotel in acres of wooded grounds, Fairyhill has hordes of loyal fans. 'This restaurant has never let us down', writes one. 'The ethic at Fairyhill seems to be that the most important and welcome guest they've ever spoken to is the guest they are speaking to at that moment', enthuses another. Central to the operation is gutsy, generous cooking built on superb local ingredients. Typical of the refined yet rustic style are a beautifully balanced beetroot and Pantysgawn goats' cheese salad with pistachio dressing, followed by seared fillet of Welsh beef with slow-cooked ox cheek, braised shin pie, carrot and swede mash and bourguignon sauce. In a similar vein, you could finish with treacle, walnut and almond tart with vanilla ice cream or traditional Welsh rarebit with fruit chutney. Look out for the excellent-value lunch deals. The encyclopaedic wine list covers France with particular reverence and kicks off at £19.50. You can also purchase bottles to take home.

Chef/s: James Hamilton. **Open:** all week L 12 to 2, D 7 to 9. **Closed:** 26 Dec, first 3 weeks Jan. **Meals:** alc (main courses £10 to £30). Set L £15.95 (2 courses) to £19.95. Set D £35 (2 courses) to £45. Sun L £24.50. **Service:** not inc. **Details:** Cards accepted. 60 seats. 40 seats outside. Separate bar. Music. Car parking.

Average Price

The average price listed in main-entry reviews denotes the price of a three-course meal, without wine.

St Fagans

The Old Post Office

Delivering simple but impressive food
Greenwood Lane, St Fagans, CF5 6EL
Tel no: (029) 2056 5400
www.theoldpostofficerestaurant.co.uk
Modern European | £35
Cooking score: 3

£5 OFF

Leafy St Fagans is a sleepy place and this unexpectedly modern restaurant sits right at its heart, cunningly disguised as the post office it once was. Inside, however, it's all clean lines, modern art and minimalism. Start with drinks in the chic little bar or on the sunny terrace with views of the neighbouring church, then move through to the conservatory-style dining room, where smooth service and well-spaced tables get things off to a good start. The food is sprightly and simple: a generous portion of grilled asparagus with a perfectly poached egg impressed at inspection, as did salmon with a clear-flavoured mushroom and prawn ragoût. Classic desserts include sticky toffee pudding and vanilla pannacotta with strawberry salad. Wines start at £17.95.

Chef/s: Simon Kealy. **Open:** Sat and Sun L 12 to 3, Tue to Sat D 6 to 9.30 (7 Sat). **Closed:** Mon, 24 to 27 Dec, 2 weeks Jan, 2 weeks Aug. **Meals:** alc (main courses £17 to £19). Set L £17.95 (2 courses) to £22.95. Set D £20 (2 courses) to £25. Sun L £22.95. **Service:** not inc. **Details:** Cards accepted. 40 seats. 40 seats outside. Separate bar. Wheelchair access. Music. Children allowed. Car parking.

Swansea

Didier & Stephanie

Tasteful French cuisine
56 St Helen's Road, Swansea, SA1 4BE
Tel no: (01792) 655603
French | £30
Cooking score: 4

Didier Suvé and Stephanie Danvel have been purveying their own brand of tasteful French cuisine to the denizens of Swansea for more than a decade, and seem happy to continue in the same caring groove. Stephanie holds sway in the pretty, yellow-walled dining room, while Didier takes care of business in the kitchen. It is all very cosy and accommodating, although the cooking has abundant style and accomplishment beyond its modest intentions. The well-honed repertoire reads like an inventory of bourgeois cuisine – feuilleté of snails and mushrooms, confit duck with shallots, pan-fried scallops with saffron sauce – but earthy themes also come to life in specials such as pig's tail salad with red port vinaigrette or braised shoulder of lamb with thyme. Desserts remain entrenched in the old ways, which means dark chocolate and orange mousse, poached pear in mulled wine and waffles with chestnut cream. Commendable French-accented wines start at £14.90.

Chef/s: Didier Suvé. **Open:** Tue to Sat L 12 to 2, D from 7 onwards. **Closed:** Sun, Mon, Christmas to New Year, 2 weeks summer. **Meals:** alc (main courses £16 to £19). Set L £14.50 (2 courses) to £17.50. Set D £24.10 (2 courses) to £30. **Service:** not inc. **Details:** Cards accepted. 20 seats. No mobile phones. Music. Children allowed.

Hanson at the Chelsea

Haven with on-the-money food
17 St Mary Street, Swansea, SA1 3LH
Tel no: (01792) 464068
www.hansonatthechelsea.co.uk
Modern European | £27
Cooking score: 3

Duck down a lane just off Swansea's wildest street to find this little haven of calm, where friendly staff and simple décor create a relaxed, homely environment. Andrew Hanson made his name cooking seafood and he still does this with aplomb – witness homemade fishcake with cockle and tomato relish, followed by fish in tempura batter with hand-cut chips and tartare sauce – but there are plenty of other options: maybe a deep-fried goats' cheese 'bonbon' on roasted Mediterranean vegetables with olives and sauce vierge, ahead of eight-hour cooked belly pork with scrumpy sauce, sage and onion mash and Pink Lady apple glaze. Finish with honey and whisky bread-and-butter pudding. The wide-ranging wine list kicks off at £12.95.

Chef/s: Andrew Hanson and Gareth Sillman. **Open:** Mon to Sat L 12 to 2, D 7 to 9.30. **Closed:** Sun, first week Oct. **Meals:** alc (main courses £12 to £20). Set L £12.95 (2 courses) to £16.95. Set D £19.95. **Service:** not inc. **Details:** Cards accepted. 40 seats. No mobile phones. Music. Children allowed.

NEW ENTRY

Pant-y-Gwydr Restaurant

Delightful Gallic charmer
Oxford Street, Swansea, SA1 3JG
Tel no: (01792) 455498
www.theph.co.uk
French | £27
Cooking score: 3

'This new Swansea eatery has swept in to this quiet area and taken everyone by surprise', writes one reporter of this bijou French restaurant set in what was once a down-at-heel pub. With 'a delightful French menu and helpful French staff', it has already gathered quite a following – it's wise to book in advance. The interior is all stripped wood and bare tables, with patches of exposed stonework and a mural of Swansea along one wall. Meals are good value, from an opening dish of moules marinière to a main course of slow-cooked belly pork with red cabbage and steamed potatoes, while a list of French classics might include cassoulet, beef bourguignon or poule au pot. Puddings could range from classic crème brûlée to chocolate tart and sorbet with white chocolate mousse. Wines start at £12.80.

Chef/s: Jacques Abdou. **Open:** Tue to Sun L 12 to 2.30, Tue to Sat D 6 to 10.15. **Closed:** Mon, 2 weeks Sept, 1 week Dec. **Meals:** alc (main courses £7 to £25). **Service:** not inc. **Details:** Cards accepted. 40 seats. No mobile phones. Wheelchair access. Music. Children allowed.

Rose Indienne

Raising the Indian bar
73-74 St Helen's Road, Swansea, SA1 4BG
Tel no: (01792) 467000
www.roseindienne.co.uk
Indian | £20
Cooking score: 2

You're spoilt for choice for Indian restaurants on St Helen's Road, but this slick number has raised the game with its vibrant, freshly made food served in arty modern surroundings. Taking inspiration from Northern India, particularly Lucknow in Uttar Pradesh and Amritsar in Punjab, chef Liyakat Ali Khan has created a lengthy menu including impressive seafood offerings – maybe golden fried prawns followed by traditional north Indian fish curry. Signature dishes such as murgh kasoori pasanda (chicken with caramelised onions, tomato, cashew nuts and fenugreek) are worthy of attention, but you'll also find favourites such as onion pakora and lamb rogan josh. Wines start at £11.95.

Chef/s: Liyakat Ali Khan. **Open:** all week L 12 to 2.30 (4 Sun), D 5.30 to 12 (1am Fri and Sat). **Closed:** 25 Dec. **Meals:** alc (main courses £7 to £13). Sun L buffet £8. **Service:** not inc. **Details:** Cards accepted. 108 seats. Separate bar. Wheelchair access. Children allowed.

Slice

Confident pint-sized contender
72-75 Eversley Road, Swansea, SA2 9DE
Tel no: (01792) 290929
www.sliceswansea.co.uk
Modern British | £32
Cooking score: 3

A wedge-shaped building with its seating upstairs and the chef on full view downstairs (wave to him as you walk by), Slice is quirky, welcoming and full of personal touches. Owned and run by Phil Leach and Helen Farmer, it epitomises the axiom that small is beautiful: Phil runs the pint-sized kitchen while Helen is on first-name terms with many of her customers. Suppliers are name-checked on a menu that offers classics like venison pie with parsnip purée, ahead of roast marinated duck breast with fondant potato and port sauce. Desserts such as sticky toffee pudding with butterscotch sauce are equally comforting. A building this small can't accommodate a large cellar, but wines are well-chosen and start at a reasonable £14.

Chef/s: Philip Leach. **Open:** Thur to Sun L 12 to 2, D 6.30 to 9. **Closed:** Mon to Wed, 4 weeks Dec to Jan. **Meals:** Set L £18 (2 courses) to £22. Set D £34. **Service:** not inc. **Details:** Cards accepted. 16 seats. No mobile phones. Music.

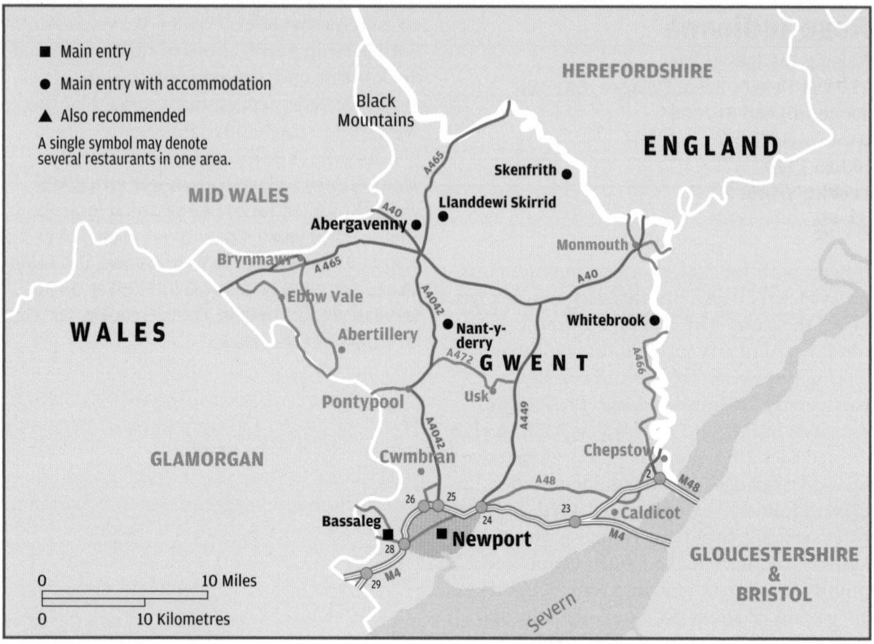

■ Main entry
● Main entry with accommodation
▲ Also recommended
A single symbol may denote several restaurants in one area.

HEREFORDSHIRE
ENGLAND
Black Mountains
MID WALES
WALES
GWENT
GLAMORGAN
GLOUCESTERSHIRE & BRISTOL
Skenfrith
Llanddewi Skirrid
Abergavenny
Monmouth
Brynmawr
Ebbw Vale
Abertillery
Nant-y-derry
Whitebrook
Usk
Pontypool
Cwmbran
Chepstow
Caldicot
Bassaleg
Newport
Severn
A40
A465
A4042
A472
A449
A466
A48
M4
M48
0 10 Miles
0 10 Kilometres

Abergavenny

The Hardwick

Simple comforts and sophisticated treats
Old Raglan Road, Abergavenny, NP7 9AA
Tel no: (01873) 854220
www.thehardwick.co.uk
Modern British | £36
Cooking score: 5

Stephen Terry isn't one to let the grass grow, and visitors to his 'unflashy haven' outside Abergavenny can't fail to notice the addition of accommodation and bright new dining area – a perfect match for the Hardwick's brand of low-beamed, tile-floored rusticity. Given the setting, it's hardly surprising that Terry's cooking is all about generosity and big flavours; he also allows high-quality ingredients to shine without resorting to mannered 'fiff-faff'. Traditionalists who expect their food with a dollop of simple comfort won't be disappointed by steak with béarnaise sauce and all the trimmings or retro chicken Holstein topped with a perfect fried egg, while those who appreciate a touch more sophistication have been well satisfied by crisp breadcrumbed Old Spot pork belly teamed with black pudding, apple and mustard sauce, as well as generous petit salé of duck breast with roasted artichokes and a cleverly balanced dish of Black Mountain salmon with a salmon risotto cake and hints of fennel. To finish, Amalfi lemon crunch offers airy sweetness and citrus tang in equal measure. To drink, there's a substantial choice of classy wines, with easy prices from £17.

Chef/s: Stephen Terry. **Open:** all week L 12 to 3, D 6.30 to 9.30 (9 Sun). **Closed:** 25 Dec. **Meals:** alc (main courses £14 to £25). Set L £20.50 (2 courses) to £25.50. Sun L £22 (2 courses) to £28. **Service:** not inc. **Details:** Cards accepted. 96 seats. Separate bar. No mobile phones. Wheelchair access. Music. Children allowed. Car parking.

Bassaleg

Junction 28

Ex-railway station with eclectic food
Station Approach, Bassaleg, NP10 8LD
Tel no: (01633) 891891
www.junction28.com
Modern European | £30
Cooking score: 2

The décor of this long-running restaurant has changed little over the years (terracotta walls, gilt-framed prints and cane furniture channel a late-80s vibe), but its other stalwart features – good service and an imaginative menu – can be applauded. Gnocchi with cherry tomatoes, rocket, Parmesan and a sweet balsamic dressing impressed at inspection, as did a generous piece of baked hake with French beans, pancetta and sprightly sun-dried tomato pesto, but readers report variable standards, possibly due to an over-long menu. Generous desserts include blackcurrant cheesecake and cranachan. Wines start at £14.95. More reports please.

Chef/s: Simona Bordeianu. **Open:** all week L 12 to 2 (4 Sun), Mon to Sat D 5.30 to 9.30 (9.45 Fri and Sat). **Closed:** 26 Dec, 1 Jan. **Meals:** alc (main courses £11 to £19). Set L £12.95 (2 courses) to £14.95. Set D (until 7) £16.95. Set D (until 9.30) £19.95. Sun L £13.95 (2 courses) to £15.95. **Service:** not inc. **Details:** Cards accepted. 166 seats. Separate bar. Wheelchair access. Music. Children allowed. Car parking.

Llanddewi Skirrid

The Walnut Tree

Famous eatery on top form
Llanddewi Skirrid, NP7 8AW
Tel no: (01873) 852797
www.thewalnuttreeinn.com
Modern British | £37
Cooking score: 6

'This is what every restaurant should strive for,' exhorts one fan, 'brilliant food, warmth, excellence and value'. Shaun Hill and his team are clearly getting it right at the re-energised Walnut Tree, and have created a genuinely unaffected eatery that has city folk jumping in their cars at the first sniff of a getaway (book one of the cottages if you fancy staying over). All of Hill's trademarks are here – matchless seasonal ingredients, generous European input colouring the bare-bones Britishness of the food, and a refreshingly direct approach to flavour. No poncey flourishes, foams or gels disturb the peace, and every plate speaks for itself – goats' cheese gnocchi with chicory and walnuts, monkfish with cucumber and mustard sauce ('beyond reproach'), a glorious dish of hare comprising seared fillet and richly jugged leg, perfectly timed veal sweetbreads with sauerkraut, not forgetting old friends such as hot pheasant pudding with bacon and sage or scallops with lentils and coriander... the hit list goes on and on. Then there are the desserts – a 'stunning' baked apple confection, rhubarb and pistachio meringue, or Portuguese egg tart with Armagnac prunes. Set lunches bring the house down, and the 100-bin wine list offers everything you could wish for, from cannily chosen 'essential' varietals by the glass to 'shining stars' and top-end 'classics' from across the winemaking world. Prices (from £16) are irresistible .

Chef/s: Shaun Hill and Roger Brook. **Open:** Tue to Sat L 12 to 2.30, D 6.30 to 10. **Closed:** Sun, Mon, 1 week Christmas. **Meals:** alc (main courses £12 to £22). Set L £18 (2 courses) to £24. **Service:** not inc. **Details:** Cards accepted. 50 seats. 16 seats outside. Separate bar. No music. Wheelchair access. Children allowed. Car parking.

Nant-y-derry

The Foxhunter

Food that sings with natural flavours
Nant-y-derry, NP7 9DN
Tel no: (01873) 881101
www.thefoxhunter.com
Modern British | £32
Cooking score: 4

It's 11 years since TV chef Matt Tebbutt and his wife Lisa took on this former stationmaster's house and erstwhile pub and decked it out as an informal country restaurant. Local produce is at the heart of things and the food sings with unaffected natural flavours and immediacy, from a game terrine with piccalilli and toasted brioche to crisp lamb's tongue with celeriac rémoulade and mustard vinaigrette. Brecon venison haunch served with salsify, sautéed sprouts, chestnuts and pancetta is a standout main, but fish cookery is equally confident; perhaps sea bream with brown shrimps, red pepper and mussel bourride. Desserts such as warm blood orange and almond sponge served with Seville orange ice cream are true to the season. The zesty wine list is filled with fastidiously chosen bottles at reasonable prices. House wine is £16.75.

Chef/s: Matt Tebbutt. **Open:** Tue to Sun L 12 to 2.30, Tue to Sat D 7 to 9.30. **Closed:** Mon, 25 and 26 Dec. **Meals:** alc (main courses £16 to £21). Set L £19.95 (2 courses) to £24.95. Sun L £26.95. **Service:** not inc. **Details:** Cards accepted. 50 seats. 12 seats outside. Separate bar. Wheelchair access. Music. Children allowed. Car parking.

Newport

The Chandlery

Robust flavours with a local accent

77-78 Lower Dock Street, Newport, NP20 1EH

Tel no: (01633) 256622

www.thechandleryrestaurant.com

Modern European | £37

Cooking score: 4

£5 OFF

Standing aloof from its neighbours on Lower Dock Street, this handsomely restored former chandlery is now a smart two-storey restaurant showcasing the Usk Valley's finest, from Brecon venison and supreme local beef to Monmouthshire air-dried ham. Braised pork belly, confit cheek and chorizo are pressed together in a mightily meaty terrine, while a platter of scallops and Thai fishcakes with lemongrass dressing and sweet chilli sauce points to a dab hand with oriental spices. Robust flavours also show up well in mains such as roast lamb loin with a textbook pithiviers of slow-cooked shoulder, finely diced ratatouille and confit garlic. Double-cooked chips and well-timed vegetables are worth the extra charge, and desserts generally feature a toothsome trio – perhaps a hot brownie with pistachio ice cream alongside a dainty rhubarb and ginger trifle and a vanilla and cherry parfait. The succinct wine list includes 16 by the glass, with bottles from £19.95.

Chef/s: Ryan Mitchell. **Open:** Tue to Sun L 12 to 2.30, Tue to Sat D 6 to 10. **Closed:** Mon. **Meals:** alc (main courses £14 to £25). Set L £14.95 (2 courses) to £17.95. Sun L £15.95 (2 courses) to £18.95. **Service:** not inc. **Details:** Cards accepted. 70 seats. Separate bar. Wheelchair access. Music. Children allowed. Car parking.

Skenfrith

The Bell at Skenfrith

Riverbank inn with intriguing food

Skenfrith, NP7 8UH

Tel no: (01600) 750235

www.skenfrith.co.uk

Modern British | £33

Cooking score: 4

'This is Welsh country style and everything is charming, warm and well kept', raved one reporter. Even so, the view almost steals the show at this remote seventeenth-century hostelry on the banks of the river Monnow. These days it does duty as an inn-with-rooms and Rupert Taylor takes a modern view of things in the kitchen, making the most of the excellent raw materials provided by the surrounding countryside and the inn's own organic kitchen garden. Seasonal menus offer an intriguing array of dishes: ballottine of Cornish mackerel with sweet-and-sour beetroot, for example, or a main course of Welsh beef served with a mini steak-and-kidney pudding, Parmentier potatoes, broccoli purée and braised red cabbage. Treats to finish include an excellent lemon verbena custard slice with filo wafers and verbena granita. William Hutchings' encyclopaedic wine list kicks off with a couple of pages of

recommendations by the glass before cherry-picking from the world cellar. Prices are extremely fair, with bottles starting at £15.
Chef/s: Rupert Taylor. **Open:** all week L 12 to 2.30, D 7 to 9.30 (9 Sun). **Closed:** Tue (Nov to Mar), last week Jan, first week Feb. **Meals:** alc (main courses £14 to £20). Sun L £21 (2 courses) to £25. **Service:** not inc. **Details:** Cards accepted. 60 seats. 30 seats outside. Separate bar. No music. Wheelchair access. Children allowed. Car parking.

Whitebrook

The Crown at Whitebrook

World-class cooking and superlative wine
Whitebrook, NP25 4TX
Tel no: (01600) 860254
www.crownatwhitebrook.co.uk
Modern European | £50
Cooking score: 7
V

Set against a steep hillside in an isolated, straggly village not far from the river Wye, the Crown feels more like an amorous French auberge than a reinvented Welsh inn – although there's nothing homespun about the food on offer here. The best way to experience James Sommerin's world-class cooking is to go for the nine-course tasting extravaganza – an endlessly fascinating surprise package, with nothing given away in advance. One couple who went the whole hog were bowled over by the thrill of it all and marvelled at 'levels of excellence rarely seen these days'. To begin, a teasing amuse-bouche of lobster beignets with garlic purée was swiftly followed by Sommerin's signature take on quail – a parfait on toast, a Scotch egg and poached breast, plus a deep, rich consommé. Next, a fillet of impeccably cooked Cornish mackerel appeared with mackerel tartare, beetroot and white chocolate, while coffee oil lent its smoky aromas to a piece of sublime venison on Savoy cabbage with carrot and cinnamon purée (a strangely tantalising composition that worked beautifully). Meanwhile, smoke of a different sort billowed forth as a black lacquered box was opened to reveal perfumed sea bass with crab lasagne, asparagus and tomato salsa. Finally, two contrasting desserts worked their magic: a reinterpreted 'crumble' involving marinated blackberries, apple compote and vanilla pannacotta with subtly flavoured Parma violet ice cream; also a rich salted chocolate tart with banana and yoghurt ice cream and a peanut espuma. This is a heaven-sent occasion to savour, and it doesn't need to be rushed: recipients have been known to spend four highly pleasurable hours eating their way through Sommerin's cavalcade of revelations. For something quicker – but no less exciting – go for the amazing-value set lunch: start with salt cod brandade, pig's head and sweetcorn, proceed to slow-cooked blade of beef with romanesco, snails and fennel, and finish with a confection of lemon and orange meringue. The superlative wine list ('300 of the most interesting bottles we can lay our hands on') runs all the way from fascinating sherries to gorgeous 'stickies', with pages of classy names and discoveries in between. Half-bottles are generous and house recommendations start at £20 (£5 a glass).
Chef/s: James Sommerin. **Open:** all week L 12 to 2, D 7 to 9. **Closed:** 2 weeks from 24 Dec. **Meals:** Set L £26.50 (2 courses) to £29.50. Set D £49.50. Sun L £29.50. Tasting menu £70 (9 courses). **Service:** not inc. **Details:** Cards accepted. 30 seats. Separate bar. No mobile phones. Music. Car parking.

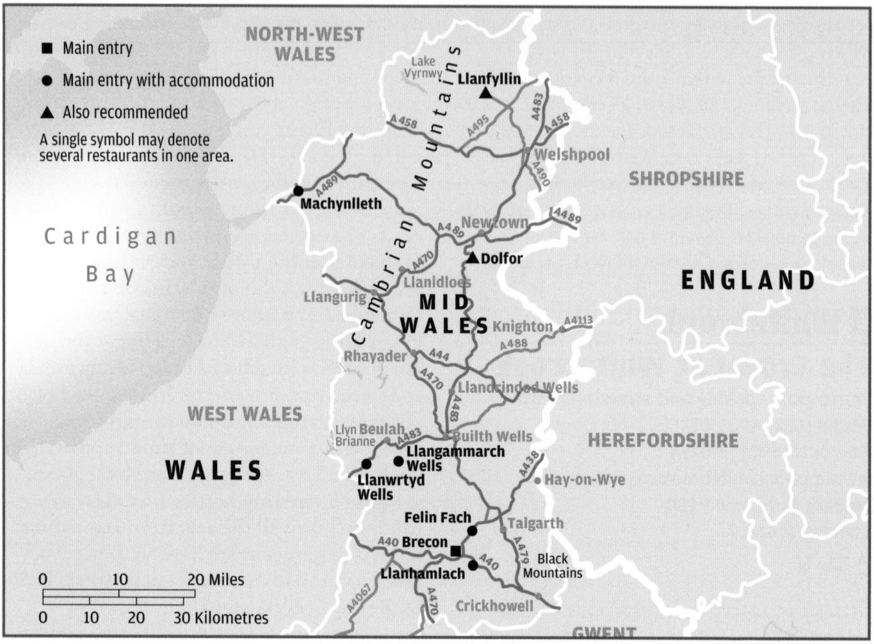

■ Main entry
● Main entry with accommodation
▲ Also recommended
A single symbol may denote several restaurants in one area.

0 10 20 Miles
0 10 20 30 Kilometres

Brecon

Tipple'n'Tiffin

Casual canalside grazing
Canal Wharf, Brecon, LD3 7EW
Tel no: (01874) 611866
Modern British | £22
Cooking score: 1

Beside the canal in Theatr Brycheiniog, this informal restaurant is a popular choice for light lunches and pre-show tapas. The menu is built around small plates and bowls to share; expect a kaleidoscope of dishes made with excellent ingredients, ranging from steak, ale and mushroom pie to crispy duck legs on kumara and butternut squash rösti with apple and onion compote, or chicken tikka skewers with couscous. Finish with classics like treacle tart or summer pudding. Wines start at £12.

Chef/s: Louise Gudsell. **Open:** Mon to Sat L 12 to 2.30 (Sun 11 to 4, Apr to Sept only), D 6 to 9 (exc Sun). **Closed:** 2 weeks Dec. **Meals:** alc (main courses £8 to £12). Set L £10 (2 courses) to £20. Set D £15 (2 courses) to £25. **Service:** not inc. **Details:** Cards accepted. 40 seats. 30 seats outside. Wheelchair access. Music. Children allowed. Car parking.

Dolfor

ALSO RECOMMENDED

▲ The Old Vicarage Dolfor

Dolfor, SY16 4BN
Tel no: (01686) 629051
www.theoldvicaragedolfor.co.uk
Modern European £5 OFF

Helen and Tim Withers are clearly happy in their Victorian vicarage, growing their own produce, looking after free-range hens and working with a network of well-chosen suppliers. Tim's unshowy provincial cooking seems to have found its niche, with a seasonal, organically driven repertoire taking in the likes of Hafod cheese soufflé, pork with prunes, brandy and cream or slow-roast Welsh Black. Fixed-price dinner menus are £30 (£35 for four courses) and wines start at £15. All week, D only. Accommodation.

Felin Fach

The Felin Fach Griffin

Country inn that cheers the soul
Felin Fach, LD3 0UB
Tel no: (01874) 620111
www.thefelinfachgriffin.co.uk
Modern British | £32
Cooking score: 4

All is snug and infectiously hospitable inside this engaging country inn-with-rooms. Comfortable leather sofas and a log fire cheer the soul, and an ever-changing slate of locally brewed ales is an essential part of the picture. The menu is short and to the point. Simplicity is evident in a dish of asparagus with a soft-poached egg, coppa ham and croûtons, and good, tasty flavours come through in a main course of wild rabbit with spinach and ricotta ravioli and grain-mustard cream, and also in hake with buttered spring greens, new potatoes and mushroom cream. For dessert, warm pistachio cake with poached pear and pistachio ice cream is an outright winner. Set menus are really good value and the global wine list is a canny, fairly priced selection, with bottles from £16 and an impressive choice by the glass or carafe.

Chef/s: Ross Bruce. **Open:** all week L 12 to 2 (2.30 Fri to Sun), D 6 to 9 (9.30 Fri and Sat). **Closed:** 24 and 25 Dec, 4 days early Jan. **Meals:** alc (main courses £15 to £20). Set L £16.50 (2 courses) to £19.50. Set D £21.50 (2 courses) to £26.50. Sun L £19.75 (2 courses) to £23.50. **Service:** not inc. **Details:** Cards accepted. 60 seats. 30 seats outside. Separate bar. No mobile phones. Music. Children allowed. Car parking.

Also Recommended

Also recommended entries are not scored but we think they are worth a visit.

Llanfyllin

ALSO RECOMMENDED

▲ Seeds

5 Penybryn Cottages, High Street, Llanfyllin, SY22 5AP
Tel no: (01691) 648604
Modern British

Mark and Felicity Seager's congenial cottage restaurant celebrates its twenty-first birthday in 2012 – and it continues to win praise for uncomplicated, Mediterranean-influenced cooking. Starters tend to be simple ideas such as chestnut mushroom and leek risotto (£4.25), while main courses might include fillet of sea bass on spicy Mediterranean vegetables (£14) or rack of Welsh lamb with Dijon and herb crust. Finish with lemon posset and blackcurrant coulis. House wine is £12. Closed Sun, Mon, and Tue L.

Llangammarch Wells

Lake Country House

A great getaway
Llangammarch Wells, LD4 4BS
Tel no: (01591) 620202
www.lakecountryhouse.co.uk
Modern British | £39
Cooking score: 2

A timbered spa hotel in the heart of rural mid-Wales, Lake Country House is the kind of place in which to get away from it all. The dining room is a soothing enough prospect in itself, with its peachy tones, swagged curtains and smartly dressed tables with fresh posies. A modernised version of country house cooking offers the likes of duck confit with sauerkraut and foie gras mayonnaise, and John Dory in cep velouté with borlotti beans, artichokes and glazed shallots, then perhaps pear tarte Tatin and cinnamon ice cream in a sabayon of advocaat and nutmeg to finish. The wide-ranging wine list starts at £22.

Chef/s: Sean Cullingford. **Open:** all week L 12 to 2, D 7 to 9. **Meals:** Set L £17.50 (2 courses) to £22.50. Set D £38.50 (4 courses). Sun L £22.50. **Service:** not inc. **Details:** Cards accepted. 60 seats. Separate bar. No music. Wheelchair access. Car parking.

Llanhamlach

Peterstone Court

Top ingredients from the family farm
Brecon Road, Llanhamlach, LD3 7YB
Tel no: (01874) 665387
www.peterstone-court.com
Modern British | £32
Cooking score: 4

'We have a 520-square mile back garden' boast the owners of Peterstone Court; in fact, their lovely Georgian manor house backs onto the Brecon Beacons National Park, and the nearby family farm contributes a great deal towards the kitchen's resourceful culinary efforts. Soak up the views from the terrace or the dining room windows while sampling a skilfully rendered plate of Llangynidr mountain lamb or thyme-roasted Glaisfer Sasso chicken (perhaps with homemade white sausage, curly kale and a flageolet bean cassoulet). To begin, there might be goats' cheese beignets with balsamic-glazed beetroot, or seared Cornish scallops with lightly curried raisin vinaigrette, while desserts could herald new season's rhubarb 'crumble trifle' with ginger ice cream, or white chocolate cheesecake with apple sorbet and fritters. Artisan Welsh cheeses are served with handmade Cradoc's biscuits and it is worth checking out the weekly '7 mile dine with wine' menu from the farm. The full list kicks off with a page of 'pouring' selections by the glass or carafe, before cherry-picking from the world cellar. Prices are extremely fair, with bottles starting at £15.30.

Chef/s: Sean Gerrard. **Open:** all week L 12 to 2.30, D 7 to 9.30 (9 Sun). **Meals:** alc (main courses £12 to £18). Set L £12 (2 courses) to £14. Sun L £19 (2 courses) to £22.50. **Service:** not inc. **Details:** Cards accepted. 45 seats. 45 seats outside. Separate bar. Wheelchair access. Music. Children allowed. Car parking.

Llanwrtyd Wells

Carlton Riverside

Deeply relaxing riverside retreat
Irfon Crescent, Llanwrtyd Wells, LD5 4ST
Tel no: (01591) 610248
www.carltonriverside.com
Modern British | £40
Cooking score: 6

£5 OFF

One of the oldest buildings in town, Mary Ann and Alan Gilchrist's smart but homely restaurant-with-rooms sits snug to the river Irfon, with a fine view of its rushing waters from the dining room. Originally a drovers' hostel, it retains an earthy vibe in its cosy cellar bar, where you can order pizza and rub shoulders with the locals. By contrast, the upstairs dining room is a haven of calm and sophistication overseen by Alan, whose 'attentive and personal service' never misses a beat. Mary Ann's cooking is rooted in classical French and European traditions, but toys successfully with elements from further afield – as in a main course of duck breast with duck spring roll, pak choi, rice noodles, oriental-spiced jus and duck scratchings. Choose from the excellent-value Carlton menu where simplicity reigns, or the more adventurous carte, where scallop and crab lasagne with orange butter sauce might precede roast fillet of beef with oxtail and mushroom pithiviers, cottage pie, shallots in red wine, green beans and porcini foam. Desserts range from spiced carpaccio of pineapple with coconut and lime jelly and passion-fruit sorbet to 'excellent' lemon meringue pie. An interesting selection of international wines opens at £15.

Chef/s: Mary Ann Gilchrist. **Open:** Mon to Sat D only 7 to 8.30. **Closed:** Sun, 25 and 26 Dec. **Meals:** Set D £19.50 (2 courses) to £39.50. **Service:** not inc. **Details:** Cards accepted. 20 seats. Separate bar. No mobile phones. Music. Children allowed.

Lasswade Country House

Confident cooking with great views
Station Road, Llanwrtyd Wells, LD5 4RW
Tel no: (01591) 610515
www.lasswadehotel.co.uk
Modern British | £34
Cooking score: 2

Set amid the splendour of the Cambrian Mountains, this is a classic country house hotel with all the elegance and traditional styling that term implies, from a lounge with comfy sofas and a wood-burning stove to a dining room decked out with polished wood furniture and family mementos. Run with plenty of personal touches by Roger and Emma Stevens, it's a comfortable setting for Roger's classically inspired cooking: maybe scallops with pancetta and pea purée followed by roast cannon of Elan Valley organic mutton with leek soufflé, caramelised root vegetables and a Madeira wine reduction. Finish with lavender-scented pannacotta. Wines start at £15.

Chef/s: Roger Stevens. **Open:** all week D only 7.30 to 9. **Closed:** 24 to 27 Dec, bank hols. **Meals:** Set D £34. **Service:** not inc. **Details:** Cards accepted. 20 seats. No music. No mobile phones. Wheelchair access. Children allowed. Car parking.

Machynlleth

The Wynnstay Hotel

Eminently affable Welsh champion
Maengwyn Street, Machynlleth, SY20 8AE
Tel no: (01654) 702941
www.wynnstay-hotel.com
Modern British | £28
Cooking score: 2

'It all starts with ingredients', insists Gareth Johns, co-proprietor and master of the kitchen at this eminently affable market town hotel. Meticulously sourced Welsh ingredients rule here, although there are lots of influences at work: Cardigan fish appears in a spicy Vietnamese pho soup and local duck breast is pointed up with plums and Dulas whimberry sauce, while excellent cuts of meat have made all the difference in melting, slow-cooked beef bourguignon. Artisan regional cheeses go down a treat, and puds such as apple and rhubarb crumble ooze homely comfort. There's also a 'brilliant' bar for beer buffs and a separate wood-fired pizzeria at the back of the hotel. House wine is £13.95.

Chef/s: Gareth Johns. **Open:** all week L 12 to 2, D 6.30 to 9. **Closed:** 1 week around New Year. **Meals:** alc (main courses £12 to £17). Sun L £13.95 (2 courses) to £15.95. **Service:** not inc. **Details:** Cards accepted. 80 seats. 40 seats outside. Separate bar. No music. Wheelchair access. Children allowed. Car parking.

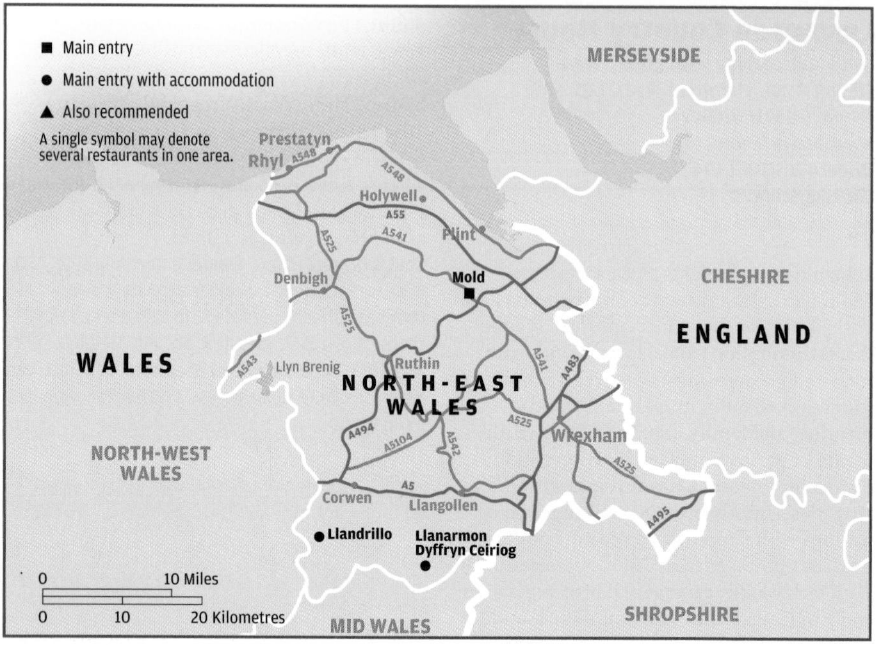

■ Main entry
● Main entry with accommodation
▲ Also recommended
A single symbol may denote several restaurants in one area.

MERSEYSIDE
Prestatyn
Rhyl
Holywell
Plint
Denbigh
Mold
CHESHIRE
ENGLAND
WALES
Llyn Brenig
Ruthin
NORTH-EAST WALES
Wrexham
NORTH-WEST WALES
Corwen
Llangollen
Llandrillo
Llanarmon Dyffryn Ceiriog
0 10 Miles
0 10 20 Kilometres
MID WALES
SHROPSHIRE

Llanarmon Dyffryn Ceiriog

The West Arms Hotel

Remote inn with modern food
Llanarmon Dyffryn Ceiriog, LL20 7LD
Tel no: (01691) 600665
www.thewestarms.co.uk
Modern British | £33
Cooking score: 3

Three centuries ago this remote hostelry in the foothills of the Berwyn Mountains was a refuelling point for drovers trekking their way through the rugged Denbighshire countryside. These days it does duty as an inn-with-rooms – although it still bears witness to years of use, with blackened beams, time-worn flagstone floors and a mighty inglenook dominating the scene. Grant Williams takes a more modern view of things in the kitchen, offering local black pudding glazed with goats' cheese on a crispy bacon and apple salad, or line-caught Anglesey sea bass on tomato and basil salsa with lemongrass butter sauce, as well as rack of Welsh lamb and medallions of beef (with wild mushroom fricassee). Helpings are 'big', but leave space for pud – perhaps lightly set lemon and lime bavarois. Forty wines start at £14.95.

Chef/s: Grant Williams. **Open:** all week L 12 to 2, D 7 to 9. **Meals:** alc (main courses £10 to £20). Set D £27.95 (2 courses) to £32.90. Sun L £16.95. **Service:** 10% (optional). **Details:** Cards accepted. 55 seats. 25 seats outside. Separate bar. Wheelchair access. Music. Children allowed. Car parking.

Please send us your feedback

To register your opinion about any restaurant listed in the Guide, or a new restaurant that you wish to bring to our attention, please visit the web address at the bottom of the page. Your feedback informs the content of the book and will be used to compile next year's reviews.

Llandrillo

Tyddyn Llan

Homely hospitality and unfussy cooking
Llandrillo, LL21 0ST
Tel no: (01490) 440264
www.tyddynllan.co.uk
Modern British | £50
Cooking score: 6

'Unforced hospitality' is a treasured virtue at Bryan and Susan Webb's idyllic Llandrillo retreat, and their appealing Georgian house benefits from homely yet elegant lounges as well as unselfconscious, personal service. Meanwhile, Bryan's cooking follows seasons rather than trends, bringing classical technique to bear on native produce and rejecting frippery in favour of straight and true flavours. Scallops are precision-grilled and pointed up with a perky vegetable relish, while just-pink lamb cutlets might be dressed in springtime garb with peas, broad beans and artichokes. Webb has Welsh blood in his veins and tips his hat to the old country with crisp, greaseless Glamorgan sausages among the canapés and a laverbread beurre blanc accompanying line-caught wild sea bass. But he isn't slavishly patriotic when it comes to sourcing, adding Wirral watercress to a starter of crubeens (stuffed pig's trotters) with piccalilli and dandelion, procuring free-range duck from Madgett's Farm in Gloucestershire and looking to Cornwall for a mighty plateful of dressed crab with fennel and melon salad. Generosity is a byword, and puddings of prune and almond tart or rhubarb fool with Champagne jelly can reach staunchly British proportions. Getting through it all can be 'quite an effort', and there are also signs that Webb is taking his eye off the stove – 'rubbery' deep-fried sweetbreads, excessively creamy sauces and a general lack of flair have dampened the mood for several correspondents. However, everyone should be heartened by the wine list's gentle prices: real care has gone into the choice of growers, half-bottles abound and house selections start at £15 a carafe (£5.75 a glass).

Chef/s: Bryan Webb. **Open:** Fri to Sun L 12.30 to 2, all week D 7 to 9 (9.30 Fri and Sat). **Closed:** last 2 weeks Jan. **Meals:** Set L £28 (2 courses) to £35. Set D £42 (2 courses) to £50. Sun L £35. Tasting menu £70 (8 courses). **Service:** not inc. **Details:** Cards accepted. 40 seats. 10 seats outside. Separate bar. No music. No mobile phones. Wheelchair access. Children allowed. Car parking.

Mold

56 High Street

Smart little seafood restaurant
56 High Street, Mold, CH7 1BD
Tel no: (01352) 759225
www.56highst.co.uk
Seafood | £25
Cooking score: 2

£5 OFF £30

This 'beautiful and intimate' restaurant sits opposite the fourteenth-century church in the heart of Mold. Fresh fish and shellfish are the main focus here: perhaps a bowl of Anglesey moules marinière followed by line-caught wild sea bass fillet with seafood paella or 'beautifully presented and delicious' bouillabaisse. But there are gutsy meat dishes, too, along the lines of roast saddle and leg of wild rabbit (teamed with wild mushroom and sweet pea risotto and red wine sauce). Classic desserts include warm Bakewell tart and fresh fruit pavlova. A modest selection of 'moderately priced' international wines kicks off at £12.50.

Chef/s: Karl Mitchell, Kirsten Robb and Martin Fawcett. **Open:** Tue to Sat L 12 to 3, D 6 to 9.30 (10 Fri and Sat). **Closed:** Sun, Mon, 25 and 26 Dec, bank hols. **Meals:** alc (main courses £12 to £20). Set L £9.95. Set D £10.95. **Service:** not inc. **Details:** Cards accepted. 52 seats. No mobile phones. Wheelchair access. Music. Children allowed.

Abergele

The Kinmel Arms

Serious cooking with Welsh roots

St George, Abergele, LL22 9BP

Tel no: (01745) 832207

www.thekinmelarms.co.uk

Modern British | £27

Cooking score: 4

Owner Tim Watson's paintings cover the cheery yellow walls at this strikingly revamped stone hostelry, which now comes with stained-glass features and a slate-topped bar. The attention to detail is much appreciated, the welcome is as warm as can be and the food 'speaks for itself' – not surprising, given that Welsh roots run deep here and the owners are involved in rearing their own livestock as well as growing exotic vegetables. The kitchen takes up the challenge, baking bread, making preserves and cooking native ingredients with 'flair and flavour' – anything from wild sea bass with Menai Strait mussels to medallions of Kinmel Estate venison with slow-braised shoulder. Other possibilities might include loin of lamb wrapped in Carmarthen ham with glazed beetroot and pea purée, followed by cracking Snowdonian cheeses and skilful desserts such as iced white chocolate and roast plum parfait. Open sandwiches and light, brasserie-style dishes take precedence at lunchtime, and wines kick off with 20 house recommendations from £15.95 (£4 a glass).

Chef/s: Gwyn Roberts. **Open:** Tue to Sat L 12 to 3, D 6.30 to 9.30. **Closed:** Sun, bank hols. **Meals:** alc (main courses £15 to £23). **Service:** not inc. **Details:** Cards accepted. 80 seats. 20 seats outside. Separate bar. Wheelchair access. Music. Children allowed. Car parking.

Average Price

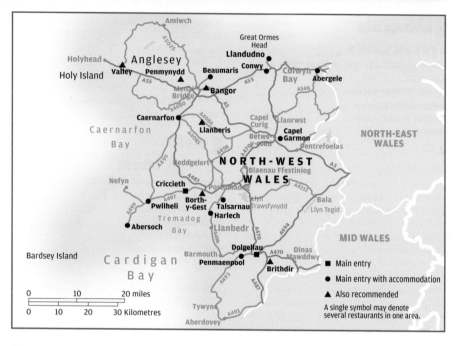

The average price listed in main-entry reviews denotes the price of a three-course meal, without wine.

Abersoch

Porth Tocyn Hotel

Fabulous views and evolving menus
Bwlch Tocyn, Abersoch, LL53 7BU
Tel no: (01758) 713303
www.porthtocynhotel.co.uk
Modern European | £42
Cooking score: 3

The views were a big selling point when the Fletcher-Brewer family acquired this *Good Food Guide* evergreen back in 1948, and the far-reaching vistas across Cardigan Bay are as entrancing as ever. A breezy, animated atmosphere prevails, and a table by the window on a fine evening can help to smooth over any rough edges in the kitchen. Typically, pigeon breast, bacon and hazelnut salad or crab tian with salmon ceviche and confit tomato might precede loin of Welsh lamb with leeks, mushroom duxelle and carrot purée, or halibut fillet in cockle, mussel and clam chowder. Any whiffs of old-fashioned hotel cooking are reinforced by a help-yourself table of Anglo-Welsh cheeses, nostalgic savouries and desserts such as chocolate marquise. Alfresco lunches and reasonably marked-up wines (from £15.95) complete a well-oiled package.

Chef/s: Louise Fletcher-Brewer and Mike Green. **Open:** all week L 12.15 to 2.30, D 7.15 to 9 (9.30 in high season). **Closed:** Nov to just before Easter. **Meals:** Set D £34.50 (2 courses) to £41.50. Sun L £24.50. Light lunch menu. **Service:** not inc. **Details:** Cards accepted. 50 seats. 25 seats outside. Separate bar. No music. No mobile phones. Children allowed. Car parking.

Symbols

Accommodation is available
Three courses for less than £30
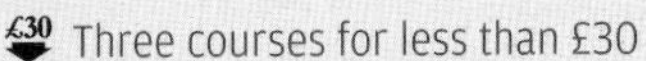
V Separate vegetarian menu
£5-off voucher scheme
Notable wine list

Bangor

ALSO RECOMMENDED

▲ Blue Sky Café

Ambassador Hall, 236 High Street, Bangor, LL57 1PA
Tel no: (01248) 355444
www.blueskybangor.co.uk
International

'I would (and do) recommend this place to anyone visiting this area', noted a regular to this amiable daytime café, where the kitchen's heart is in the right place. Local and seasonal ingredients crop up in everything from breakfasts to Welsh beef burgers served in artisan-baked rolls (£7.45). Praise, too, for homemade falafel with hummus and roasted vegetables (£11.25), grilled ciabatta with dry-cured bacon and organic Perl Wen cheese, and the 'best flapjacks ever'. Wines from £11.25. Open Mon to Sat.

Beaumaris

Ye Olde Bulls Head Inn, Loft Restaurant

Anglesey aristocrat
Castle Street, Beaumaris, LL58 8AP
Tel no: (01248) 810329
www.bullsheadinn.co.uk
Modern British | £42
Cooking score: 5

'Ye Olde' name tag is well deserved, given that the Bulls Head was built in 1472 and 'improved' in 1617; this place is a true Anglesey aristocrat, and it makes the most of its heritage location just a catapult's trajectory from the ancient stone battlements of Beaumaris Castle. When it comes to food, the Bull's gastronomic zenith is the Loft Restaurant, a narrow, raftered dining room squeezed into the eaves of the original building. Striking interiors give it the feel of a trendy eyrie, and chef Hefin Roberts matches the location with some suitably high-flown food. Native Welsh ingredients are woven into the dinner menu

without too much 'land of our fathers' trumpeting, although the results are brilliantly orchestrated. To start, treacle-cured venison harmonises perfectly with blue cheese mousse, celery, pear and walnut salad, while seared king scallop comes with potato, kohlrabi, confit lemon and vanilla crème fraîche. Welsh beef always figures prominently, and lamb might appear as a ginger-rubbed loin in company with braised tongue, celeriac purée and juniper-scented jus. Fish also gets a good outing (brioche-crumbed John Dory with Camembert and chive ravioli, for example), while desserts are marvels of simple artistry such as warm walnut tart with rhubarb ice cream and spiced honey. The auspicious wine list lets rip with some French regional big hitters, but there is ample choice for those who want to branch out into less familiar territory. Classy house selections weigh in at £19.50 (£4.90 a glass).
Chef/s: Hefin Roberts. **Open:** Tue to Sat D only 7 to 9.30 (6.30 Fri and Sat). **Closed:** Sun, Mon, 25 and 26 Dec. **Meals:** Set D £42 (3 courses). **Service:** not inc. **Details:** Cards accepted. 45 seats. Separate bar. No music. No mobile phones. Car parking.

READERS RECOMMEND

Harry's Bistro

Modern European
Henllys, Beaumaris, LL58 8HU
Tel no: (01248) 812976
www.harrysbistro.com
'Simple, straightforward fare, honest and very genuine.'

Borth-y-Gest

ALSO RECOMMENDED

▲ Moorings Bistro

4 Ivy Terrace, Borth-y-Gest, LL49 9TS
Tel no: (01766) 513500
www.mooringsbistroborthygest.com
Modern British

A former ship builder's house with uninterrupted views of Borth-y-Gest Bay and Snowdonia, this is an ideal spot for alfresco dining. Steve Williams does the cooking and his wife Nadya Muir-Williams handles front-of-house with ease. Expect simple classics like mussels marinière (£6.95) followed by grilled sea-bass fillet with char-grilled asparagus (£14.95) or pot-roasted local rabbit with white wine, garlic, herbs and cream. Finish with sticky toffee pudding. House wines from £14.95. Open Wed to Sat D and Sun L.

Brithdir

ALSO RECOMMENDED

▲ Cross Foxes

Brithdir, LL40 2SG
Tel no: (01341) 421001
www.crossfoxes.co.uk
British £5 OFF

Recently rescued from dereliction, this Grade II-listed building is now a stylish all-rounder, offering brasserie-style food throughout the day. The menu takes in everything from tapas platters to well-hung steaks, with dishes such as leek and Perl Las cheese tartlet (£4.95), smoked haddock topped with Welsh rarebit or confit of lamb with honey and rosemary glaze (£14.95) in between. To finish, try lemon tart. Wines from £12.95. Open all week. Accommodation.

Caernarfon

NEW ENTRY

Castell

Revamped Georgian hotel
33 Y Maes, Caernarfon, LL55 2NN
Tel no: (01286) 677970
www.castellcaernarfon.co.uk
Modern British | £30
Cooking score: 2
£5 OFF

Transformed from the former Castle Hotel by Angharad Anwyl, Castell sits at the heart of town, just a stone's throw from thirteenth-century Caernarfon Castle. On the ground floor of the Georgian building there is an open-plan bar with informal but smart dining areas on either side. The flexible à la carte menu suits all tastes (including nibbles, light

bites and starters, sandwiches and panini, as well as substantial main courses and desserts). Soups are a strength and mains might include Welsh lamb with fondant potatoes, redcurrant and port. Finish, perhaps, with bara brith butter pudding and Penderyn whisky ice cream. Wines from £12.95.
Chef/s: Daniel ap Geraint. **Open:** all week L 12 to 3, D 6 to 9.15. **Meals:** alc (main courses £9 to £21). **Service:** not inc. **Details:** Cards accepted. 60 seats. 16 seats outside. Wheelchair access. Music.

Rhiwafallen

Stylish restaurant-with-rooms
Llandwrog, Caernarfon, LL54 5SW
Tel no: (01286) 830172
www.rhiwafallen.co.uk
Modern British | £35
Cooking score: 2

Kate and Rob John put a combined total of 25 years' experience in the restaurant trade to good use when creating this tranquil restaurant-with-rooms. Everything from the décor (neutral shades, rich fabrics, contemporary art) to Rob's cooking shows close attention to detail. Classic techniques meet modern sensibilities on a menu that offers potted hot smoked salmon with corn blini and celeriac rémoulade ahead of a grilled fillet of Welsh beef with horseradish and olive oil mash, sautéed kale with smoked bacon, and green peppercorn sauce. Desserts such as chocolate fudge brownie with banana ice cream and salted butterscotch rack up the comfort factor. Wines start at £15.95.
Chef/s: Robert John. **Open:** Sun L 12 to 2.30, Tue to Sat D 7 to 9. **Closed:** Mon, 25 and 26 Dec. **Meals:** Set D £35 (3 courses). Sun L £19.50. **Service:** not inc. **Details:** Cards accepted. 30 seats. No mobile phones. Music. Car parking.

Also recommended entries are not scored but we think they are worth a visit.

WELSH CHEESES COME OF AGE

Black beef, salt marsh lamb, cockles and laverbread are well-known Welsh specialities, but these days cheese deserves to be added to that list. Historically, cheese was widely made in Wales: it even featured in laws laid down by King Hywel Dda (c. 880-950), stating that cheeses should be divided between husband and wife if they divorced. But by the 1940s, Wales had lost most of its small cheese makers, unable to compete with English factories. Thankfully, Wales now produces enough artisan cheeses to keep a cheeseboard very well stocked.

Gorwydd Caerphilly Made from raw milk. Has a much more developed flavour than the supermarket variety.

Perl Lâs Creamy blue cheese with a clean yet complex flavour.

Y-Fenni Made from mature Cheddar blended with whole-grain mustard and Welsh ale; wonderful melted on toast.

Llanboidy A hard, rinded farmhouse cheese with a smooth, silky texture and rounded, mature flavour.

Celtic Promise A semi-soft cheese with an orange cider-washed rind, pungent aroma and strong, lingering taste.

ALSO RECOMMENDED

▲ Oren

26 Hole in the Wall Street, Caernarfon, LL55 1RF
Tel no: (01286) 674343
Modern European £5 OFF

Dutchman Gert Vos chose orange ('oren' in Welsh) as the name and the design motif for his tiny stone-walled bistro. 'Peasant food' is the gastronomic theme and the menu pulls in ideas from across the globe: typical choices could include veggie samosas, chicken and Kaffir lime soup, spicy turkey and bacon pie and chilli-spiked chocolate cake. You can pick up three courses for £15, with wines starting at £12.20. Check out the regular themed evenings. Open Wed and Thur L, Wed to Sat D.

Capel Garmon

Tan-y-Foel Country House

Skilful cooking in a minimalist farmhouse
Capel Garmon, LL26 0RE
Tel no: (01690) 710507
www.tyfhotel.co.uk
Modern British | £49
Cooking score: 5

The interior of this seventeenth-century farmhouse now has a minimalist, 'slightly Japanese feel', according to one visitor: earthy colours and wall drapes set the mood in the little lounge, while floor-to-ceiling mirrors make the dining room appear larger than it is. Janet Pitman's cooking shows levels of skill and ambition that belie the remote location on the northern fringes of Snowdonia National Park, and she rings the changes every evening offering a couple of choices at each stage. Highlights from recent meals have included halibut poached in red wine with tarragon-creamed leeks, crisp oyster mushrooms and a sauce laced with Merlot, followed by a dish of pink loin and braised shoulder of Welsh lamb served with galette potatoes, rich red wine syrup and creamy onion foam. To finish, there are prettily presented desserts such as caramelised pineapple and ginger lasagne with coconut and mint ice cream and white pepper toffee sauce. Details such as 'exemplary' bread rolls and petits fours are up to the mark, and the globetrotting wine list offers well-bred bottles from £21.

Chef/s: Janet Pitman. **Open:** all week D only 7.30 (1 sitting). **Closed:** Dec, Jan. **Meals:** Set D £49. **Service:** not inc. **Details:** Cards accepted. 10 seats. No music. No mobile phones. Car parking.

Conwy

Dawson's at the Castle Hotel

Hearty crowd-pleasers and classics
High Street, Conwy, LL32 8DB
Tel no: (01492) 582800
www.castlewales.co.uk
Modern British | £30
Cooking score: 2
£5 OFF

Since its refit and re-branding as Dawson's, the Castle Hotel's main eatery has shaken off its rather stuffy and dowdy image in favour of something more upbeat – although dim lighting hardly flatters the much-lauded paintings by renowned Victorian illustrator John Dawson-Watson. The kitchen aims to please, whether you are after roast sirloin of Welsh beef for Sunday lunch or a full-blown, brasserie-style dinner of guinea fowl on bubble and squeak with mustard sauce, chicken korma or seared sea bass with fennel and saffron risotto. For afters, pear tarte Tatin or orange crème brûlée might fit the bill. Similar food is also served in the buzzy and highly popular bar. Wines start at £15.50.

Chef/s: Andrew Nelson and Graham Tinsley. **Open:** all week L 12 to 2, D 7.30 to 9.30 (10 Sat). **Meals:** alc (main courses £15 to £23). Sun L £16.50 (2 courses) to £19.50. **Service:** 10% (optional). **Details:** Cards accepted. 120 seats. 20 seats outside. Separate bar. Music. Children allowed. Car parking.

Criccieth

Tir a Môr

Thriving bistro with comforting food
1-3 Mona Terrace, Criccieth, LL52 0HG
Tel no: (01766) 523084
www.tiramor-criccieth.co.uk
European | £26
Cooking score: 2

Booking is advised at this family-run bistro, set on a street corner not far from the sea. True to its name (which translates as 'land and sea') it offers a good selection of fresh fish alongside other indigenous specialities such as Welsh Black fillet steak with all the trimmings. Cooking is broadly European – think antipasti followed by aubergine cannelloni – but with occasional Eastern influences, as in a starter of Aberdaron crab salad with spring onions, ginger, chilli and mayonnaise, followed by baked monkfish in a light curry sauce. Classic desserts include crème brûlée and tarte aux pommes. Wines from £15.95.
Chef/s: Laurent Hebert. **Open:** Tue to Sat D only 6 to 9.30. **Closed:** Sun, Mon, 23 Dec to mid Feb. **Meals:** alc (main courses £14 to £23). Set D £18.50 (2 courses) to £21.50. **Service:** not inc. **Details:** Cards accepted. 40 seats. Wheelchair access. Music. Children allowed.

Dolgellau

NEW ENTRY

Bwyty Mawddach

Farm-fresh ingredients and a fine view
Llanelltyd, Dolgellau, LL40 2TA
Tel no: (01341) 424020
www.mawddach.com
Modern British | £25
Cooking score: 2

This bar brasserie in a converted farm building combines the traditional and modern, with a minimalist bar on the ground floor and an upstairs dining room with views over the river towards the Cader Idris mountain range. Chef Ifan Dunn was brought up here, and his unfussy cooking is based on produce from his own and neighbouring farms. Begin with warm goats' cheese balls attractively served with beetroot, pine nuts and red wine vinegar. Follow with poached and roasted free-range chicken breast with pan juices and perfectly cooked vegetables. Breads and desserts are homemade; Welsh artisan cheeses are organic. House wines are £14.25.
Chef/s: Ifan Dunn. **Open:** Wed to Sun L 12 to 2.30 (3.30 Sun), Wed to Sat D 6 to 9.30. **Closed:** Mon, Tue, 2 weeks Nov, 1 week Jan, 1 week Apr. **Meals:** alc (main courses £10 to £18). Sun L £12.50 (2 courses) to £16.50. **Service:** not inc. **Details:** Cards accepted. 75 seats. 56 seats outside. Separate bar. Wheelchair access. Music. Children allowed. Car parking.

Dylanwad Da

All-rounder with honest food and wine
2 Ffôs-y-Felin, Dolgellau, LL40 1BS
Tel no: (01341) 422870
www.dylanwad.co.uk
Modern British | £28
Cooking score: 1

Dylan Rowlands' long-serving venue does duty as a café/bar and wine shop during the day, morphing into a relaxed, intimate bistro as night falls. Readers continue to applaud this place for its atmosphere, value and honest cooking – perhaps 'Dolgellau rarebit' with leeks, smoked bacon and apple chutney followed by Welsh lamb in a creamy casserole with roasted almonds. To finish, try cherry cheesecake and don't miss the 'wonderful' homemade chocolates. Dylanwad is also a wine merchant of note, importing bottles directly from Europe and offering terrific value across the board. Drink-in prices start at £15 (£4 a glass).
Chef/s: Dylan Rowlands. **Open:** Tue to Sat L 10 to 3, D 7 to 9. **Closed:** Sun, Mon, Feb. **Meals:** alc (main courses £14 to £19). Set L and D £18.50 (2 courses) to £24. Tasting menu £45. **Service:** not inc. **Details:** Cards accepted. 28 seats. Separate bar. No mobile phones. Music. Children allowed.

Harlech

Castle Cottage

Congenial restaurant-with-rooms
Y Llech, Harlech, LL46 2YL
Tel no: (01766) 780479
www.castlecottageharlech.co.uk
Modern British | £38
Cooking score: 2

£5 OFF

It has been a long-haul labour of love for Glyn and Jacqueline Roberts, who took charge of this sixteenth-century cottage by the castle back in 1989 and have sustained it as a congenial restaurant-with-rooms ever since. Visitors are seldom disappointed, especially when it comes to Glyn's food. His daily menus are stuffed with Welsh produce, from Rhydlewis smoked salmon and Conwy mussels to Carmarthen air-dried ham, local lamb and Coed-y-Brenin venison, but he also finds room for dishes such as smoked duck breast with mango and pine-nut salad or roast porchetta with black pudding, red cabbage and Calvados. For afters, perhaps sticky date sponge. Wines from £15.

Chef/s: Glyn Roberts. **Open:** all week D only 7 to 9. **Closed:** 3 weeks Nov. **Meals:** Set D £38 (3 courses). **Service:** not inc. **Details:** Cards accepted. 40 seats. Separate bar. No mobile phones. Music. Children allowed. Car parking.

Llanberis

ALSO RECOMMENDED

▲ The Peak

86 High Street, Llanberis, LL55 4SU
Tel no: (01286) 872777
www.peakrestaurant.co.uk
Modern British

A 'very unassuming' place serving 'above average' food, the Peak does a good line in internationally-inspired dishes made with excellent Welsh ingredients – maybe Thai fishcakes with sweet chilli (£5.95) followed by Welsh Black ribeye steak with roasted shallot mash and red wine sauce (£16.95) or smoked haddock chowder. Desserts such as bread-and-butter pudding or baked lemon cheesecake round things off nicely. A keenly priced international wine list opens at £12.50 and rarely tops £20. Open all week.

Llandudno

Bodysgallen Hall, The Dining Room

Meticulous, special-occasion food
Llandudno, LL30 1RS
Tel no: (01492) 584466
www.bodysgallen.com
Modern British | £44
Cooking score: 5

V

'Embosomed in woods of noble growth', according to one eighteenth-century historian, Bodysgallen Hall is a rare sight – a full-dress National Trust experience complete with cascading water features, herb-scented box hedges and walled vegetable gardens. And that's before you cross the threshold. Formal meals take place in the the Dining Room, a fastidiously polished space that somehow fits comfortably with Gareth Jones' fiercely contemporary cooking. This is 'special occasion' stuff, methodically and meticulously delivered with all the frills and furbelows of opulent country house dining – although Welsh produce runs like an earthy leitmotif through the food, from stuffed saddle of rabbit with leek, potato and whipped saffron vinaigrette to Bodysgallen summer fruits served with summer berry infusion, sablé breton, yoghurt and lime sorbet. In between, the kitchen might trick out fillet of roe deer with confit red cabbage, a dinky venison and celeriac pie and cocoa-nib sauce, or partner poached fillet of beef with sticky braised short rib and soused carrot. Lunch tones down the luxury and the flamboyance, but readers have been well pleased with the results. The auspicious wine list proves its pedigree with a knowing collection of blue-blooded Bordeaux and Burgundies as well as significant vintages from elsewhere; house

recommendations start at £20. For something easier on the wallet, try the 1620 Bistro in the converted coach house.
Chef/s: Gareth Jones. **Open:** Tue to Sun L 12.30 to 1.45, Tue to Sat D 7 to 9.30. **Closed:** Mon. **Meals:** Set L £19.50 (2 courses) to £22.50. Set D £44. Sun L £30. **Service:** inc. **Details:** Cards accepted. 66 seats. Separate bar. No music. No mobile phones. Wheelchair access. Children allowed. Car parking.

St Tudno Hotel, Terrace Restaurant

Old-school elegance by the sea
Promenade, Llandudno, LL30 2LP
Tel no: (01492) 874411
www.st-tudno.co.uk
Modern British | £31
new chef

£5 OFF

In many ways this is an archetypal seaside hotel of the old school, with views of the promenade, a solid family background and a liking for the safe, comforting things of life. New chef Andy Foster was still settling in as our deadline approached, but few changes are likely on the food front. Expect a mix of mainstream British and European ideas with a goodly helping of local seafood – perhaps line-caught sea bass with a crab fritter, or slow-cooked chicken wrapped in leeks with prune purée, chicken jelly and brioche followed by cinnamon and apple crumble brûlée with apple sorbet. The mammoth wine cellar remains a big selling point, with special sections devoted to cult growers such as Austria's Willi Opitz and d'Arenberg from South Australia. The St Tudno team has travelled the globe in search of quality and value, opening their list with house selections from £16.30 (£4.45 a glass).
Chef/s: Andy Foster. **Open:** all week L 12.30 to 2, D 7 to 9.30 (9 Sun). **Meals:** alc (main courses £16 to £24). Set L £15 (2 courses) to £20. Sun L £19.95. **Service:** not inc. **Details:** Cards accepted. 65 seats. 18 seats outside. Separate bar. No mobile phones. Music. Car parking.

Penmaenpool

Penmaenuchaf Hall

Big helpings of country house grandeur
Penmaenpool, LL40 1YB
Tel no: (01341) 422129
www.penhall.co.uk
Modern British | £43
Cooking score: 2

Sheltering in the foothills of Cader Idris, Penmaenuchaf puts on a lordly show with its grandiose public areas and striking contemporary dining room. The kitchen tries hard and takes full account of the region's produce – witness a trio of Bala lamb comprising herb-crusted best end, a shepherd's pie and a tagine with raisin couscous. Red onion and Perl Lâs cheese tart is a typical opener, while dark chocolate and griottine cherry roulade stands out among the desserts. 'Uneven' cooking is a bugbear, but there are no qualms when it comes to the magnificent, ever-evolving wine list. Mouthwatering names from the USA, Australia and Italy challenge the heavyweight French contingent, with 11 house wines (all at £19.75) offering a wallet-friendly way in.
Chef/s: Justin Pilkington. **Open:** all week L 12 to 2, D 7 to 9.30 (9 Sun). **Meals:** Set L £16.50 (2 courses) to £18.50. Set D £42.50. Sun L £18.75. **Service:** not inc. **Details:** Cards accepted. 35 seats. 16 seats outside. Separate bar. No mobile phones. Wheelchair access. Music. Car parking.

Penmynydd

ALSO RECOMMENDED

▲ Neuadd Lwyd Country House

Penmynydd, LL61 5BX
Tel no: (01248) 715005
www.neuaddlwyd.co.uk
Modern British

With stunning views towards Snowdonia, this smartly converted Victorian rectory, now run as a restaurant-with-rooms, creates a favourable impression with visitors. The dining room makes much of the vista, while the no-choice, four-course menu (£42) makes the most of local and regional ingredients – perhaps Gorau Glas cheese soufflé, Anglesey lamb shank with purées of potato, and pea and mint, Penderyn whisky ice cream teamed with bara brith bread-and-butter pudding, and Anglesey farmhouse cheeses to finish. Wines from £13.95. Open Thur to Sat D only (by arrangement).

Pwllheli

Plas Bodegroes

Landmark country hotel with expert food
Nefyn Road, Pwllheli, LL53 5TH
Tel no: (01758) 612363
www.bodegroes.co.uk
Modern British | £45
Cooking score: 5

Chris and Gunna Chown's rural idyll has been winning fans for over 25 years and shows no signs of flagging. A beautiful, secluded restaurant-with-rooms set in 'glorious countryside' just a mile from the beach, it has a smart and subtly modern dining room (pale walls, artwork, linen-clad tables) plus 'a fine view of the surrounding garden, woods and fields' from the terrace. Chris Chown's cooking favours local ingredients and simple pleasures – maybe ham hock and pig's cheek terrine with piccalilli, followed by char-grilled sirloin of Welsh Black beef with braised blade, fondant potato and onion jus, or grilled fillet of cod with salt cod mash and lemon butter sauce. Occasional international flourishes (roast rump of lamb with char-grilled vegetables and harissa sauce, for instance) are handled well, but readers have mentioned clamouring flavours in some of the more complicated dishes. Desserts such as cinnamon biscuit with rhubarb and apple accompanied by elderflower custard, or orange and Grand Marnier tart with orange sorbet offer sensible flavour combinations. Welsh rarebit on walnut toast with apple salad is a tempting alternative. The illustrious wine list covers France in loving detail, but also roams the globe, rooting out plenty of lesser-known goodies. Half-bottles abound, and around 20 house selections start at £17.
Chef/s: Chris Chown. **Open:** Sun L 12 to 2, Tue to Sat D 6.45 to 9. **Closed:** Mon, 2 Nov to 1 Mar. **Meals:** Set D £45. Sun L £20. **Service:** not inc. **Details:** Cards accepted. 40 seats. Separate bar. No music. No mobile phones. Wheelchair access. Children allowed. Car parking.

ALSO RECOMMENDED

▲ Y Daflod at Tafarn y Fic

Llithfaen, Pwllheli, LL53 6PA
Tel no: (01758) 750473
www.tafarnyfic.com
Modern British

This is a community pub, purchased by a local co-operative in 1988. As you'd expect, Tafarn is a hub for local activities but it's also a good spot for a meal, thanks to self-taught cook Hefina Prichard. Her food is direct, heart-on-sleeve stuff: ham shank terrine with pineapple chutney and parsley and hazelnut pesto (£5.25), then salmon with a parsley crust and sun-dried tomato and harissa sauce (£14), followed by crème brûlée with poached plums in aniseed. Wines from £12.50. Restaurant open Thur to Sat.

Talsarnau

Maes-y-Neuadd

Romantic medieval manor
Talsarnau, LL47 6YA
Tel no: (01766) 780200
www.neuadd.com
Modern European | £35
Cooking score: 3

£5 OFF

Standing amid 85 acres of lush grounds overlooking Cardigan Bay, this gracious medieval manor makes the most of its setting. In fact the hotel's head gardener even gets a name-check on the dinner menu – a reminder that the kitchen relies heavily on his green-fingered skills. Otherwise, Welsh produce makes its presence felt in dishes such as air-dried beef with Parmesan and pickles, hake with crushed root vegetables and laverbread coulis, or duck breast and confit fritter with beetroot fondant. Cheeses are taken seriously and dessert might bring glazed seasonal fruits. Lunches are altogether more casual – perhaps fishcakes or Welsh cawl with dumplings. The wine list is an ever-evolving collection of pedigree bottles from around the globe, with a fruitful Kiwi contingent, some interesting new German names and a strong selection by the glass. For best value, dip into the mini-list of sub-£17.95 offerings.

Chef/s: Peter Jackson and John Owen Jones. **Open:** all week L 12 to 1.45, D 7 to 8.45. **Meals:** alc L (main courses £10 to £15). Set D £35. Sun L £17.95. **Service:** not inc. **Details:** Cards accepted. 65 seats. 20 seats outside. Separate bar. No music. No mobile phones. Wheelchair access. Children allowed. Car parking.

Valley

ALSO RECOMMENDED

▲ The Moody Goose at Cleifiog Uchaf

Spencer Road, Valley, LL65 3AB
Tel no: (01407) 741888
www.cleifioguchaf.co.uk
Modern British £5 OFF

Prydwen and Emyr Parry have done a fine job of converting their sixteenth-century longhouse into a smart restaurant-with-rooms. The kitchen places priority on local produce such as lobster and Anglesey-reared beef, and delivering nicely executed asparagus risotto with Parmesan (£6.25) ahead of char-grilled turbot with lime hollandaise or rump of lamb with flageolet purée and rosé wine jus (£18.50). Finish with a classic lemon tart. Wines from £14.95. Open Tue to Sat D only.

MARY ANN GILCHRIST
Carlton Riverside

What would you cook Great Britain's Olympic Team?
Vegetable risotto, roast rack of Welsh hill lamb, pineapple carpaccio, passion fruit sorbet and coconut and lime jelly.

Do you have a favourite local recipe or ingredient?
The obvious answer is Welsh hill lamb.

What's your favourite tipple?
Campari with Cointreau, fresh orange juice, soda and ice. Tastes harmless but packs a punch!

What's the most ridiculous culinary term you've heard?
A 'rendezvous' of anything.

What's been the worst culinary trend of recent years?
The pricing of bread and vegetables as extras to keep the headline price down. I consider this mean spirited.

And the best?
Tasting menus with recommended wines served by the glass.

What's the best training for a chef?
Personally, I think training on the job.

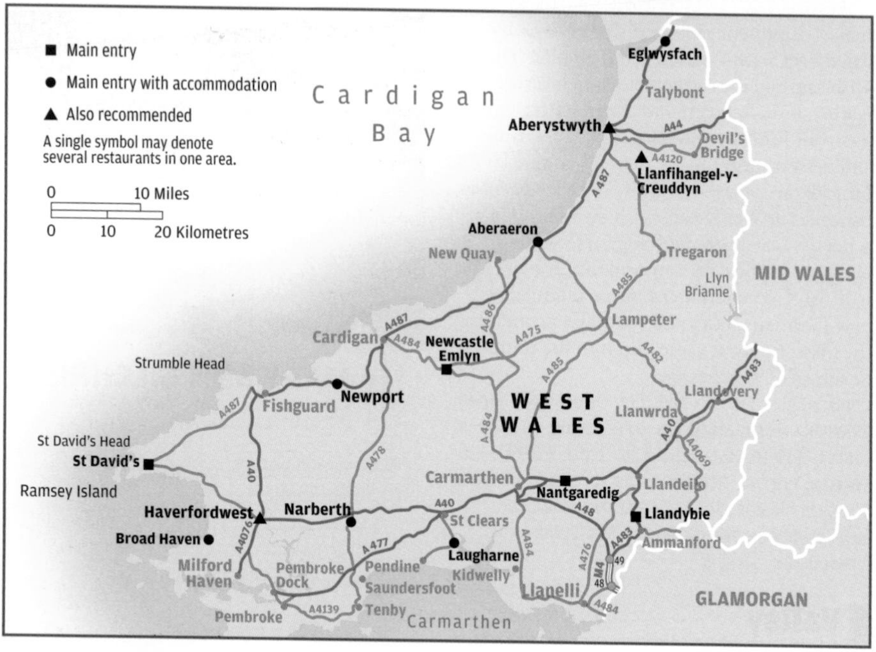

Aberaeron

Harbourmaster

Sleek harbourside hotel
Pen Cei, Aberaeron, SA46 0BT
Tel no: (01545) 570755
www.harbour-master.com
Modern British | £30
Cooking score: 2

This popular boutique hotel has done a good job of establishing itself as a bar and restaurant, and it generally bustles with drinkers and diners. The restaurant is a charming space decked out with seaside blue wood panelling and local artwork and the cooking covers familiar classic-cum-Brit ground, but presentation is modern. Chicken liver parfait with wholemeal toast and chutney got an inspection meal off to a wholesome start, while superbly crisp belly pork with creamy dauphinoise and whole-grain mustard sauce was a nicely balanced main. A light strawberry pavlova with unctuous clotted-cream ice cream is typical of the desserts. The old-school wine list kicks off at £14.50.

Chef/s: Scott Davis. **Open:** all week L 12 to 2.30, D 6 to 9. **Closed:** 25 Dec. **Meals:** alc (main courses £10 to £25). Sun L £16 (2 courses) to £21. **Service:** not inc. **Details:** Cards accepted. 55 seats. 15 seats outside. Separate bar. No music. No mobile phones. Wheelchair access. Children allowed. Car parking.

ALSO RECOMMENDED

▲ Ty Mawr Mansion

Cilcennin, Aberaeron, SA48 8DB
Tel no: (01570) 470033
www.tymawrmansion.co.uk
Modern British

An in-house cinema and the odd ghost or two enhance the dramatic allure of this opulent Georgian mansion deep in the Aeron Valley. Welsh accents colour a menu that might offer well-reported cockle tart and slow-roast venison, as well as ham hock terrine with piccalilli (£8.95), pork tenderloin with leeks, apple cake and black pudding fritter (£20.95), and desserts such as poached pear with ginger ice cream. Cooked breakfasts are a 'tour de force' for overnight guests. Wines from £16.95. Mon to Sat D only.

Aberystwyth

ALSO RECOMMENDED

▲ Treehouse

14 Baker Street, Aberystwyth, SY23 2BJ
Tel no: (01970) 615791
www.treehousewales.co.uk
Global £5 OFF

This relaxed, family-friendly eatery sits above the superb organic food store that supplies all of its ingredients. It operates as a café/bistro/coffee shop, and is open daytimes only, offering everything from breakfast to daily specials such as spicy jerk chicken with Caribbean fruit, bean millet and mixed salads (£8.95) or green Thai vegetable curry with fried tempeh and basmati rice (£6.90). Regular fixtures include quiche and veggie burgers. Wines from £9.95. Open Mon to Sat.

▲ Ultracomida

31 Pier Street, Aberystwyth, SY23 2LN
Tel no: (01970) 630686
www.ultracomida.co.uk
Spanish

A popular deli and restaurant specialising in Spanish food, Ultracomida offers 'excellent service and ambience' and 'spectacular, very reasonable tapas'. Walk through the deli to reach the pleasant restaurant, where a simple daily menu might offer chorizo cooked in red wine, followed by free-range chicken in paprika with crusty bread and salad, plus tarta de Santiago for dessert – all for £13. Typical tapas are smoked mackerel salad and tortilla (£4.20). Wines start at £11.95. A sibling restaurant graces Narberth (see entry). Open all week L, Fri and Sat D.

Broad Haven

The Druidstone

Romantic old house with global food
Broad Haven, SA62 3NE
Tel no: (01437) 781221
www.druidstone.co.uk
Global | £28
Cooking score: 2

For 39 years, the Guide has noted Rod and Jane Bell's competence in feeding the West Wales coast at their hotel perched high on a cliff looking across St Brides Bay. As they approach retirement the reins are being picked up by their son Angus and his wife Beth, but little else has changed. Readers continue to find this a happy, satisfying place, as much taken by the bohemian charm as the generous, interesting cooking – think chunky mulligatawny soup followed by Moroccan fish gratin, pasta con funghi or Caribbean lamb curry, with banoffi pie to finish. Wines from £12.50.

Chef/s: Angus Bell. **Open:** all week L 12.30 to 2.30, D 7 to 9.30. **Meals:** alc (main courses £14 to £20). **Service:** not inc. **Details:** Cards accepted. 60 seats. 30 seats outside. Separate bar. No music. Wheelchair access. Children allowed. Car parking.

Eglwysfach

Ynyshir Hall

Scene-stealing cooking
Eglwysfach, SY20 8TA
Tel no: (01654) 781209
www.ynyshir-hall.co.uk
Modern European | £49
Cooking score: 6

£5 OFF

Ynyshir Hall once belonged to Queen Victoria and you can see why the prospect appealed: rambling gardens merge seamlessly with the wildly beautiful landscape, and public rooms ooze classical elegance – although their walls are now hung with original modern artwork. Meals begin with memorable canapés in the bar, before guests are ushered into the

restaurant – a turquoise-walled room that provides a fitting backdrop for Shane Hughes' scene-stealing cooking. Expect the full quota of extras, from an engaging amuse of celeriac and white bean velouté to a 'sensibly subtle' complimentary course of rock oyster with cucumber jelly, caviar and oyster cappuccino. After that, the kitchen shows its class with a mix of thrillingly imaginative ideas and retakes of classical standards, all underpinned by supreme Welsh produce: poached salmon might be served with asparagus and ravioli of poached egg and cream cheese, while noisettes of lamb could be paraded with asparagus tortellini, crayfish, lamb's tongue and salsify. Sea and land also come together for a stonkingly good dish of sea trout with a tarte Tatin of boudin noir and potato, before a 'refresher' prepares the palate for, say, pitch-perfect warm treacle tart with banana and clotted cream. An expert sommelier is on hand to guide guests through the expansive global wine list, which opens with a stunning choice of house recommendations from £16.
Chef/s: Shane Hughes. **Open:** Wed to Sun L 12 to 1.45, all week D 7 to 8.45. **Meals:** Set L £21.50 (2 courses) to £25. Set D £72.50 (6 courses). Tasting menu L £49, D £90. **Service:** not inc. **Details:** Cards accepted. 35 seats. Separate bar. No mobile phones. Wheelchair access. Music. Children allowed. Car parking.

Haverfordwest

ALSO RECOMMENDED

▲ Black Sheep

Shire Hall, High Street, Haverfordwest, SA61 2BN
Tel no: (01437) 767017
www.blacksheeprestaurant.co.uk
Modern British

You'll find this bustling, unpretentious restaurant upstairs in the Shire Hall in the heart of Haverfordwest. A simple, stylish interior (pale walls, stripped wood, bare tables) sets the tone for hearty, generous dishes made with ingredients from the owners' farm – maybe potted pork with sweet pepper chutney (£4) followed by slow-roasted lamb on sautéed potatoes with a chunky vegetable ratatouille (£12). The homemade cheesecake is a great way to finish. Service is informal and friendly. Wines start at £13. Closed Sun.

▲ The George's

24 Market Street, Haverfordwest, SA61 1NH
Tel no: (01437) 766683
www.thegeorges.uk.com
Eclectic £5 OFF

A popular and idiosyncratic eatery in the heart of Haverfordwest, the George's incorporates a New Age shop, tearoom and restaurant serving robust home cooking and a lengthy selection from the char-grill. Highlights include slow-cooked dishes from around the world – maybe pork and apple casserole (£13.50) – plus homely pies and superfood salads. Finish with homemade treacle and pecan tart (£5.50). Many ingredients come from the restaurant's separate organic walled garden. House wines from £19. Closed Sun and Mon.

Laugharne

The Cors

Quirky and very romantic
Newbridge Road, Laugharne, SA33 4SH
Tel no: (01994) 427219
www.thecors.co.uk
Modern British | £33
Cooking score: 3

Set in a wooded valley bordering a river, the Cors (meaning 'bog' in Welsh) is Nick Priestland's home as well as a restaurant-with-rooms, and it's full of personal touches. The stunning garden – Nick's pride and joy – burgeons with exotic plants, while the house is a rambling Victorian affair whose arty, idiosyncratic interior is perfect for a romantic evening meal. Nick does the cooking as well as the gardening and his menus make the most of local ingredients such as goats' cheese (served on bruschetta with roasted red peppers) or roasted noisettes of lamb with apricot stuffing and caramelised onion gravy. Organic Pembrokeshire Welsh Black beef also puts in

an appearance – maybe a roasted fillet with green peppercorns and red wine jus. A 20-strong wine list kicks off at £14.95.
Chef/s: Nick Priestland. **Open:** Thur to Sun D 7 to 9. **Closed:** Mon to Wed, last two weeks Nov. **Meals:** alc (main courses £15 to £24). **Service:** not inc. **Details:** Cards accepted. 30 seats. 12 seats outside. Separate bar. No mobile phones. Wheelchair access. Music. Car parking.

Llandybie

NEW ENTRY

Valans

Comfort food at its best
29 High Street, Llandybie, SA18 3HX
Tel no: (01269) 851288
www.valans.co.uk
Modern European | £30
Cooking score: 2

Near the church in the village centre, Valans is a hub for locals. A stylish little restaurant with modern furnishings and a crisp red-and-white colour scheme, it offers a please-all menu straddling simple favourites (steak and chips, lunchtime burgers) and more sophisticated fare built on prime local produce – crispy Carmarthen ham, for instance, in a texture-laden salad with diced beetroot and fresh leaves, or tender escalopes of salt marsh lamb with confit shoulder, creamy dauphinoise and redcurrant gravy. A dessert of sticky toffee pudding with ice cream is comfort food at its best. Wines from £12.75.
Chef/s: Dave Vale. **Open:** Tue to Sat L 11.45 to 3 (10.30 Fri), D 7 to 10. **Closed:** Sun, Mon, 24 Dec to 3 Jan. **Meals:** alc (main courses £13 to £22). Weekday set D £10.50 (2 courses) to £14.95. Sat set D £17.95 (2 courses) to £21.50. **Service:** not inc.
Details: Cards accepted. 36 seats. Wheelchair access. Music. Children allowed.

Llanfihangel-y-Creuddyn

ALSO RECOMMENDED

▲ Farmers Arms

Llanfihangel-y-Creuddyn, SY23 4LA
Tel no: (01974) 261275
www.yffarmers.co.uk
Modern British £5 OFF

A food-led pub in the pretty village of Llanfihangel-y-Creuddyn, the Farmers is spick and span, with bare wood floors, whitewashed walls and a wood burner providing warmth on wintry days. Welsh ingredients dominate the menu, but flavours come from far and wide: maybe hot-and-sour chicken soup with homemade bread to start (£4.50) and then local pork sausages with leek and potato mash and onion gravy (£8.50). Finish with Seville orange curd tart with Cointreau cream. Wines start at £13. No food Sun D and Mon.

Nantgaredig

Y Polyn

Simple stuff, superbly done
Capel Dewi, Nantgaredig, SA32 7LH
Tel no: (01267) 290000
www.ypolynrestaurant.co.uk
Modern British | £30
Cooking score: 3

The 200-year-old building was once a toll house, but it's now a modest country pub and restaurant kitted out with a wood-burner in the bar and scrubbed pine tables in the dining room. Meals revolve around set-price menus that never stray into the realms of high art, but offer simple stuff, superbly done. Alongside the rustic styling there's a modern British menu that screams its seasonal and regional credentials via Carmarthen ham (with celeriac roulade), potted Aberdaron crab and fillet of Pembroke pollack (teamed with cannellini beans and chorizo). It also yields duck confit (with Puy lentils and pancetta) and a huge helping of nostalgia in the shape of sherry trifle. House wine is £13.50.

Chef/s: Susan Manson. **Open:** Tue to Sun L 12 to 2 (3 Sat and Sun), Tue to Sat D 7 to 9 (9.30 Fri and Sat). **Closed:** Mon. **Meals:** Set L £12 (2 courses) to £14.50. Set D £24 (2 courses) to £30. Sun L £18.50. **Service:** not inc. **Details:** Cards accepted. 50 seats. 20 seats outside. Separate bar. Wheelchair access. Music. Children allowed. Car parking.

Narberth

The Grove

Accomplished cuisine in an idyllic setting
Molleston, Narberth, SA67 8BX
Tel no: (01834) 860915
www.thegrove-narberth.co.uk
Modern European | £38
Cooking score: 5

A casual but rather gorgeous country house hotel tucked into an unlikely nook of the Pembrokeshire boondocks, the Grove looks a pretty picture with the Preseli Mountains looming on the horizon. Fresh-faced staff keep things friendly, and the Grove's extensive kitchen garden makes a strong seasonal contribution – alongside top-notch local produce and wild pickings. New chef Duncan Barham has raised the restaurant's game considerably, and on inspection his dishes showed a laudable emphasis on textural contrast, vibrant flavours and visual impact. A generous crab salad starter appears as three quenelles of dressed white meat spiked with chives, interleaved with strident saffron snaps and adorned with dried cherry tomatoes, chive flowers and cubes of zesty lime jelly, while clean-flavoured chicken consommé is a simpler concoction embellished with slow-cooked leg meat and shaved radish. Mains show off the kitchen's labour-intensive approach: rose veal is presented on layers of baby broad beans and pickled mousseron mushrooms with foamy blanquette jus; oozing nuggets of fried bone marrow sit atop boulangère potatoes. Puddings are less intricate offerings such as an almond choux bun with praline cream and cherry compote. The 150-bin wine list is a serious read, with knowledgeable notes, competitive mark-ups and a wealth of grape varieties; France is a strong suit, but Italy, New Zealand and elsewhere also have plenty to offer. House selections start at £18 (£5 a glass).

Chef/s: Duncan Barham. **Open:** all week L 12 to 2, D 6 to 9. **Closed:** 9 to 26 Jan. **Meals:** alc (main courses £16 to £26). Set L £19 (2 courses) to £23. Set D £30 (2 courses) to £40. Sun L £25. **Service:** not inc. **Details:** Cards accepted. 55 seats. 20 seats outside. Separate bar. No mobile phones. Music. Children allowed. Car parking.

ALSO RECOMMENDED

▲ Ultracomida

7 High Street, Narberth, SA67 7AR
Tel no: (01834) 861491
www.ultracomida.co.uk
Spanish

You pass through a feast of sights and smells before reaching this simple, rustic-chic tapas bar at the rear of Ultracomida delicatessen. Like its partner in Aberystwyth (see entry) it majors on goods from the deli: Iberian ham (£8.40), fried squid with aïoli and a changing cheeseboard selection (£4.75), as well as comforting French onion soup and tortillas. A nicely annotated Spanish wine list starts at £11.95. Closed Sun.

Newcastle Emlyn

NEW ENTRY

Ludo's at The Coopers

Cosy eatery with generous, imaginative food
Station Road, Newcastle Emlyn, SA38 9BX
Tel no: (01239) 710588
Modern French | £30
Cooking score: 3

Chef-patron Ludovic Dieumegard was previously at the nearby Old Red Cow but has relocated to this cosy stone pub on the edge of town. The interior feels bright and new, with trendy wood and plastic furniture, exposed floors and whitewashed stonework. Ludovic – a one-time *MasterChef* contestant – makes imaginative use of local ingredients in dishes such as Cardigan Bay crab bhaji with sweet chilli sauce. Elsewhere, pan-fried gnocchi with chorizo, Parmesan and spring onion delivers a smart mix of textures and flavours, while a tender piece of fillet steak with sprightly green cabbage, peas and a punchy red wine sauce typifies the generous, unpretentious mains. Memorable desserts include moist pear and almond tart with Amaretto ice cream. Global wines start at £13.95.

Chef/s: Ludovic Dieumegard. **Open:** Wed to Sun L 12 to 2, D 6 to 9. **Closed:** Mon, Tue, 24 to 27 Dec, 1 to 13 Jan. **Meals:** alc (main courses £11 to £21). Set L £10 (2 courses) to £11.50. **Service:** not inc. **Details:** Cards accepted. 40 seats. Music. Children allowed. Car parking.

Newport

Cnapan

Clever home cooking with quality ingredients
East Street, Newport, SA42 0SY
Tel no: (01239) 820575
www.cnapan.co.uk
Modern British | £32
Cooking score: 2

A traditional Georgian residence in the quaint Pembrokeshire town of Newport, Cnapan is a long-running family enterprise where there is 'always a wonderful welcome'. The restaurant (a carpeted room with a Welsh dresser and plenty of ornaments) has a relaxed home-from-home feel. Co-owner Judith Cooper reigns in the kitchen, turning out intelligent home cooking based on the best local ingredients. 'I never refuse the scallops', reports one regular. Other choices include spicy seafood chowder, mains of Welsh Black beef with horseradish dumplings and a peppercorn sauce, and sticky apricot and almond cake with ginger ice cream for dessert. Wines start at £14.50.

Chef/s: Judith Cooper. **Open:** Wed to Mon D only 6.30 to 8.45. **Closed:** Tue, mid Dec to mid Mar. **Meals:** Set D £26 (2 courses) to £32. **Service:** not inc. **Details:** Cards accepted. 35 seats. Separate bar. No mobile phones. Music. Children allowed. Car parking.

Llys Meddyg

Modish, unfussy food
East Street, Newport, SA42 0SY
Tel no: (01239) 820008
www.llysmeddyg.com
Modern British | £33
Cooking score: 4

'Our best-value eating experience of the last few years', enthuses one fan of this stylish yet homely boutique hotel. You can eat in the downstairs bar with its roaring fire and capacious sofas, or upstairs in the smart dining room whose walls are dotted with wonderful original paintings. Either way, expect classy, imaginative cooking using seasonal ingredients that have been bought, shot or foraged locally. Diners have praised the great taste combinations and excellent presentation, and with good reason; an inspection meal included chicken liver parfait with slow-cooked leg and smoked breast in a smoke-filled Kilner jar – a worthwhile piece of showmanship that added wintry depth to impeccable ingredients. A main course of local pheasant breast and leg with parsnip, pancetta, bread sauce and violet potato dumplings followed suit, matching nostalgic charm with modern invention. Desserts such as warm cinnamon doughnuts with apple sorbet perform a similar trick. Wines from a wide-ranging list start at £15.50.

Chef/s: Matt Smith. **Open:** Tue to Sat L 12 to 2.30, D 7 to 9. **Closed:** Sun, Mon. **Meals:** Set L £14.95 (2 courses) to £18.50. Set D £27.50 (2 courses) to £33. **Service:** not inc. **Details:** Cards accepted. 44 seats. 60 seats outside. Separate bar. Music. Children allowed. Car parking.

Also recommended entries are not scored but we think they are worth a visit.

WHAT'S ON TREND?

Here are just some of the ingredients that kept cropping up on our plates this year:

Alexanders - a hollow-stemmed plant that tastes similar to celery and parsley

Kohlrabi - a form of cabbage, the leaves are dwarfed by its globe-like base, which has a texture and flavour similar to turnip and cauliflower

Quince - a relative of apples and pears. In Britain, it is a traditional accompaniment to partridge, or an ingredient in tarts, pies, marmalades and jellies

Rock samphire - an aromatic shrub with long, resinous leaves. Pickled samphire was once so popular that men risked their lives to collect it from coastal cliffs

Sea buckthorn - a small tree that grows on Britain's coastline, and bears clusters of edible orange berries

Sea purslane - found in salt marshes or on seaside dunes, the salty leaves can be eaten raw or cooked

Wild garlic - also known as ramsons or allium. For centuries it was prized by the populace for its strengthening qualities, but disdained by aristocrats. Now it's back on the hottest plates in town

St David's

★ READERS' RESTAURANT OF THE YEAR ★
WALES

Cwtch

Funky, absolutely fabulous family eatery
22 High Street, St David's, SA62 6SD
Tel no: (01437) 720491
www.cwtchrestaurant.co.uk
Modern British | £30
Cooking score: 3

Cwtch's owner Rachael Knott deserves a huge pat on the back for creating an 'absolutely fabulous' family restaurant without resorting to embarrassing clichés or compromise. Eating in this funky yet respectful set-up is 'sheer enjoyment', helped along by genuinely courteous staff and a menu that trumpets sound regional ingredients. To start, home-cured salmon is a must, unless you fancy bursting-with-flavour venison terrine with onion marmalade, or beer-battered herring roes with pickles. After that, slow-roast Pembrokeshire pork belly is a melt-in-the-mouth treat, but fish steals most of the headlines – perhaps local sea bass with laverbread risotto, or hake fillet with sauce vierge and samphire. Desserts also generate much lip-licking appreciation, especially plum, pear and apple crumble topped with clotted cream. Fantastic cocktails and Pen-lon lager supplement the 'boutique' wine list; prices start at £15.

Chef/s: Matt Cox. **Open:** all week D only 6 to 9.30. **Closed:** Sun and Mon (1 Nov to 31 Mar). **Meals:** Set D £24.50 (2 courses) to £30. **Service:** not inc. **Details:** Cards accepted. 50 seats. Wheelchair access. Music. Children allowed.

CHANNEL ISLANDS

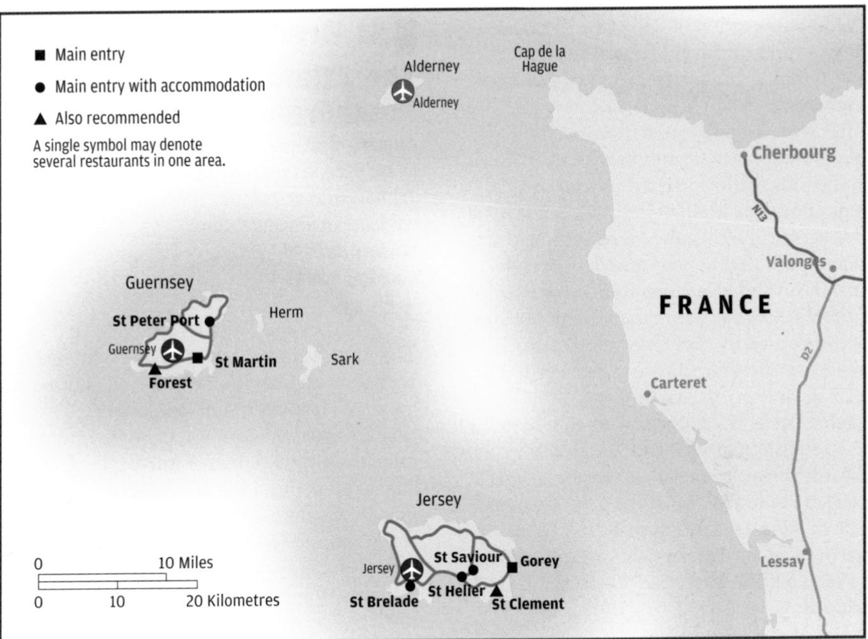

Forest, Guernsey

ALSO RECOMMENDED

▲ Café d'Escalier

Le Gouffre, Forest, Guernsey, GY8 0BN
Tel no: (01481) 264121
Anglo-French £5 OFF

This all-day bistro/brasserie up on the cliffs at Le Gouffre is the energetic little sibling of L'Escalier in St Peter Port, and it promises spectacular views and affordable food for famished families. Local seafood and farm produce show up strongly on the menu, which might run from bowls of bouillabaisse (£4.95) and crab pancakes with lobster bisque (£7.50) to char-grilled steak with mushroom mash and béarnaise (£16). The owners also cook big pans of paella over an open fire, make their own sausages and delight visitors with alfresco afternoon teas. Wines from £15.50. Closed Sun D and Mon.

Gorey, Jersey

Sumas

Scintillating cooking in an enchanting setting
Gorey Hill, St Martin, Gorey, Jersey, JE3 6ET
Tel no: (01534) 853291
www.sumasrestaurant.com
Modern European | £35
Cooking score: 5
£5 OFF

Locations hardly come much more enchanting than this: Sumas is strategically pitched between a picturesque harbour on Jersey's east coast and the hill fortress of Mont Orgueil above. A sister establishment to Longueville Manor (see entry, St Saviour), it offers the same kind of professionally polished service with some equally scintillating cooking, courtesy of Daniel Ward. Seafood is a strength, as might be expected, whether in squid with minted bulghur and a tomato and chorizo compote, or a well-wrought shellfish risotto with avocado purée and a rich, crustacean-based sauce. There is no undue over-complication in either the menu descriptions or the presentations, which are all about highlighting the quality of principal ingredients. Mains might take in Angus beef fillet with curly kale and marrow-bone nuggets, or sea bass with Jerusalem artichokes and confit shallots in a rich red wine reduction. The kitchen pulls out the stops at dessert stage with some inventive ideas: try orange and thyme risotto with poached mandarin and kalamansi sorbet, for example, or praline parfait with caramelised pear in filo, accompanied by Earl Grey jelly. A concise wine list offers fair choice at hearteningly manageable prices, starting at £13.

Chef/s: Daniel Ward. **Open:** all week L 12 to 2.30 (3.30 Sun), Mon to Sat D 6 to 9.30 (Sun in summer). **Closed:** Christmas to mid Jan. **Meals:** alc (main courses £14 to £24). Set L and D £17 (2 courses) to £19.50. Sun L £18.50 (2 courses) to £22.50. **Service:** not inc. **Details:** Cards accepted. 40 seats. 16 seats outside. Wheelchair access. Music. Children allowed.

ALSO RECOMMENDED

▲ Castle Green

La Route de la Côte, Gorey, Jersey, JE3 6DR
Tel no: (01534) 840218
www.castlegreenjersey.co.uk
Modern British £5 OFF

The Jersey Pottery group's loosely based pub operation offers a spectacular location with unbeatable views of Mont Orgueil Castle, as well as something for everyone on the wide-ranging menu. Highlights have included Jersey lobster and crab bisque (£6.75), spicy tempura ribs and king prawns with Asian coleslaw and ginger chilli sauce (£13.50), steak au poivre, and roast apple parfait with hazelnut crunch and caramel sauce to finish. Wines from £14. No food Sun D and Mon.

Also Recommended
Also recommended entries are not scored but we think they are worth a visit.

St Brelade, Jersey

The Atlantic Hotel, Ocean Restaurant

Alluring destination with high-end food
Le Mont de la Pulente, St Brelade, Jersey, JE3 8HE
Tel no: (01534) 744101
www.theatlantichotel.com
Modern British | £60
Cooking score: 4
V

The Atlantic Hotel is an alluring destination with assets aplenty in the shape of amazing sea views, a Hockney-esque pool and a smattering of sub-tropical palm trees for good measure, although there's still an air of 'old school posh' about the place. Done out with maritime colours, artwork and hand-crafted furniture, the swanky Ocean Restaurant takes full advantage of the location, and Mark Jordan's cooking gives island produce an intricate contemporary spin. His signature starter of roasted langoustine tails with caramelised bacon, cauliflower purée and shaved Brazil nuts is pitch-perfect as regards technical know-how, and the high-end style spills over into main courses ranging from fillet of local beef with lobster ravioli, baby vegetables and beef consommé to lemon sole with crab-crushed Jersey Royals, fennel and sauce grenobloise. Desserts often come gilded with intriguing ice creams – honey and lavender with pear tarte Tatin or a Jersey black butter version with nougatine of apple and Calvados, for example. Sommelier Sergio dos Santos presides over an ever-changing 'living' wine list that gives due prominence to global grape varieties, food-matching qualities and classy vintages. House selections start at £24.

Chef/s: Mark Jordan. **Open:** all week L 12.30 to 2.30, D 7 to 10. **Closed:** 2 Jan to 3 Feb. **Meals:** alc £60 (3 courses). Set L £20 (2 courses) to £25. Set D £50. Sun L £30. Tasting menu £75. **Service:** not inc. **Details:** Cards accepted. 60 seats. Separate bar. No mobile phones. Music. Children allowed. Car parking.

ALSO RECOMMENDED

▲ Wayside Café

Le Mont Sohier, St Brelade, Jersey, JE3 8EA
Tel no: (01534) 743915
Global

With its relaxed, informal atmosphere, attentive, hard-working staff, and large decked terrace giving wide-screen views of St Brelade's Bay, you can't beat this beachside café when the sun shines. Orders are taken at the counter during the day (it's a tad more formal in the evening) – perhaps seafood soup with noodles (£5.75) ahead of Thai salad of crispy duck or sea bass with Spanish-style seafood rice (£13.90) plus 'wonderful cakes, pastries, and traditional puddings with a twist'. Wines from £11.95. Open all week.

READERS RECOMMEND

The Oyster Box

Seafood
St Brelade, Jersey, JE3 8EF
Tel no: (01534) 743311
www.oysterbox.co.uk
'A funky restaurant, terrace and beach bar... local sourcing and fantastic views overlooking the bay.'

St Clement, Jersey

ALSO RECOMMENDED

▲ Green Island Restaurant

Green Island, St Clement, Jersey, JE2 6LS
Tel no: (01534) 857787
www.greenisland.je
Seafood £5 OFF

'A nice place to have on your doorstep', commented a visitor to this modern restaurant situated slap bang on the waterfront. Shiny service sets the tone for a feel-good operation and the terrace gets rammed when the sun is out. Oriental duck breast and chicken terrine (£8.50), fillet of local brill with Jersey Royals, local asparagus, baby broad beans and crab bisque sauce (£19.75) and lemon posset with black cherry compote (£6.50) are on the bill of fare. House wine is £14.95. Closed Sun D and Mon.

St Helier, Jersey

Bohemia

A chef at the top of his game
The Club Hotel & Spa, Green Street, St Helier, Jersey, JE2 4UH
Tel no: (01534) 880588
www.bohemiajersey.com
Modern European | £55
Cooking score: 7
V

'A must-do every year', confesses a fan of style-conscious Bohemia – the cool, moneyed restaurant attached to St Helier's ultra-hip Club Hotel & Spa. Ignore the throbbing mayhem in the bar and head straight for the suave, leather-clad dining room, where Shaun Rankin's food elicits drools of delight and wonderment. Here is a chef at the top of his game, with an effortless mastery of contemporary cuisine in all its palate-challenging complexity – although 'modern European' hardly does justice to the creative breadth of the cooking on offer: just consider curry-salted scallops with coconut dhal, onion bhaji, coriander and apple – a sensational starter with 'a real sense of innovation', noted one reader. Rankin also pairs the same bivalves brilliantly with glazed lamb's sweetbreads, spring pea salad and goats' cheese beignets, while emphasising his loyalty to island produce by offering roast local turbot with cockles in sherry vinegar, baby leeks and parsley risotto. Otherwise, intricately conceived ideas are spread across the carte and the kitchen injects some modish pizzazz into classic partnerships – how about a dish of three-hour, free-range duck egg with new season's chanterelles and confit chicken wings, or roast loin of venison bravely supported by a world-larder cavalcade of smoked chocolate tortellini, parsnip purée, Medjool dates and ginger-scented quinoa. To conclude, Rankin's treacle tart with clotted-cream ice cream won fame on TV's Great British Menu, but it's also worth savouring the myriad sensory thrills of 'pear flavours' with warm frangipane, yoghurt sorbet and honeycomb. Given the voguish tone, it's no surprise to find meals interspersed with all manner of teasing amuse-bouches, shot glasses, mid-course refreshers et al. True to form, service is also precise, unfussy and methodical to a fault – even if smiles are sometimes in short supply. The terse wine list looks across the water to France for most of its gems, although exclusive global producers also have their say. Prices start at £15.95 (£5.25 a glass).

Chef/s: Shaun Rankin. **Open:** Mon to Sat L 12 to 2.30, D 6.30 to 10. **Closed:** Sun, 25 Dec 1 Jan. **Meals:** alc (main courses £30 to £34). Set L £18.50 (2 courses) to £21.50. Set D £46 (2 courses) to £55. **Service:** 10%. **Details:** Cards accepted. 52 seats. Separate bar. No mobile phones. Wheelchair access. Music. Children allowed. Car parking.

ALSO RECOMMENDED

▲ The Green Olive

1 Anley Street, St Helier, Jersey, JE2 3QE
Tel no: (01534) 728198
www.greenoliverestaurant.co.uk
Mediterranean £5 OFF

Paul and Anna Le Brocq's 'quiet, intimate' first-floor restaurant specialises in vegetarian, poultry and seafood dishes. 'The lack of steak is unnoticeable with such a veritable feast and variance of dishes on offer,' observed one reader. Typical offerings include local scallops on sweetcorn purée and apricot salsa with pancetta (£8.95), local field mushrooms filled with roast butternut squash, sun-blush tomatoes, roast peppers and asparagus, topped with feta (£12.95) and basil crème brûlée with a strawberry and cream shooter. Wines start at £13.95. Closed Sat L, Sun and Mon.

St Martin, Guernsey

The Auberge

Taste thrills and big flavours
Jerbourg Road, St Martin, Guernsey, GY4 6BH
Tel no: (01481) 238485
www.theauberge.gg
Modern European | £40
Cooking score: 5

The clifftop eyrie occupied by The Auberge is a great spot for spying on the neighbouring Channel Islands, with panoramic views from windows and terrace tables. The inside is designed with a minimum of flounce, making for a cool, smart-casual atmosphere. In keeping with the elevated setting Daniel Green aims high, offering an extensive menu of modern European cooking and a busy presentational style that enhances the excitement. Try scallop tempura in ravigote dressing with beetroot and fennel for starters. That said, there is no bashfulness about serving a plate of oysters au naturel, albeit with eastern garnishes of ginger, chilli, coriander and rice vinegar. Mains include monkfish in a fashionable wrap of Parma ham, with minted pea purée, steamed pak choi and a sauce of black olives, chilli and garlic, or fine beef fillet with pommes Anna, a sweetcorn blini and cep sauce – a more adventurous alternative to one of the ribeye steaks served straight with chunky chips. Dessert might find spiced banana cake alongside blueberry soup and cassis sorbet. Wines start at £17.50.

Chef/s: Daniel Green. **Open:** all week L 12 to 2, D 6.30 to 10. **Closed:** 25 Dec, Jan. **Meals:** alc (main courses £14 to £28). Set L £14.95 (2 courses). Set D £18.95. Sun L £24.95. **Service:** not inc.
Details: Cards accepted. 70 seats. 40 seats outside. Separate bar. Wheelchair access. Music. Children allowed. Car parking.

St Martin, Jersey

READERS RECOMMEND

Feast

Modern European

Gorey Pier, St Martin, Jersey, JE3 6EW
Tel no: (01534) 611118
www.feast.je

'A cross between a French bistro and a beach-side café, with little formality and really friendly staff.'

St Peter Port, Guernsey

La Frégate

Stunning seascapes and detailed dining

Les Cotils, St Peter Port, Guernsey, GY1 1UT
Tel no: (01481) 724624
www.lafregatehotel.com
Modern British | £37
Cooking score: 4

Set high on the hill overlooking St Peter Port harbour, La Frégate is perfectly placed to make the most of fine vistas over the sea. The main frame of the eighteenth-century manor house has been much extended, but a keen eye for décor and updated colours has pulled it all together with a breezy, contemporary look. In the kitchen, care is given to the provenance of supplies and – not surprisingly, considering the location – the menu comes awash with the freshest of seafood; say a starter of scallops with Asian-spiced crabmeat, then grilled local fish with scallops, langoustine and lobster froth. There are non-fish options too – meat might be represented by confit shoulder and pistachio-crusted rack of lamb, served with roasted garlic, fresh pesto and a port jus. Raspberry tart topped with a lime chiboust and served with a white chocolate ice cream might head up desserts. Wines from £17.

Chef/s: Neil Maginnis. **Open:** all week L 12 to 1.45, D 7 to 9.30. **Meals:** alc (main courses £13 to £22). Set L £19.90 (2 courses) to £22.50. Set D £27.90 (2 courses) to £32.50. Sun L £22.50. **Service:** not inc. **Details:** Cards accepted. 75 seats. 20 seats outside. Separate bar. No music. Children allowed. Car parking.

ALSO RECOMMENDED

▲ Da Nello

46 Pollet Street, St Peter Port, Guernsey, GY1 1WF
Tel no: (01481) 721552
www.danello.gg
Italian £5 OFF

Over the last three decades Nello Ciotti's Italian restaurant has become something of a Guernsey institution. He's now passed on the reins to his trusted team, but little will change. 'Simply great food and, moreover, the freshest seafood', remains the beating heart of the business; say local scallops grilled with balsamic syrup and crispy bacon (£15.50) or Guernsey Chancre crab salad. Meat dishes range from beef carpaccio (£7.95) to saltimbocca alla romana. Expect strawberries with zabaglione for dessert and predominantly Italian wines from £19.90. Open all week.

▲ Le Nautique

Quay Steps, St Peter Port, Guernsey, GY1 2LE
Tel no: (01481) 721714
www.lenautiquerestaurant.co.uk
Modern European

Fish gets top billing in Gunter Botzenhardt's busy restaurant overlooking St Peter Port's harbour. There's no fancy menu-speak here, and the broadly contemporary repertoire offers as much local produce as the kitchen can muster, from a cocktail of Guernsey crab (£8.50) to fillet of sea bass with spicy chorizo (£18.50). From a selection of meat dishes, confit roast duckling with caramelised apples and Calvados sauce has raised appreciative murmurs, and among puddings is a good Amaretto parfait. Wines from £16.50. Closed Sat L and Sun.

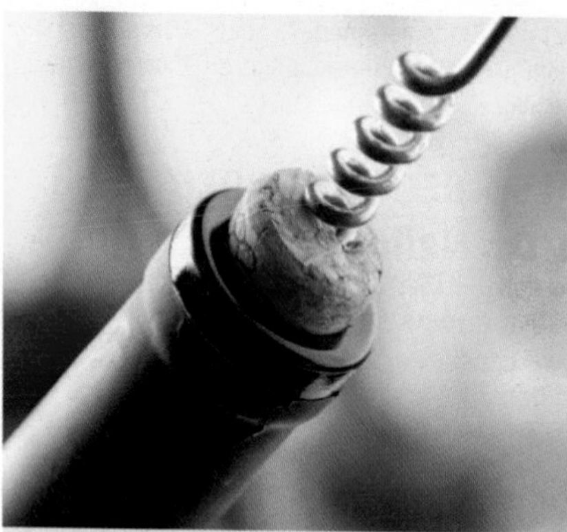

MEASURE FOR MEASURES?

Understanding the measures that glasses of wine are served in becomes more of a challenge with each passing year. As many people prefer to order wine this way rather than by the bottle, either to limit the amount of alcohol consumed or to enjoy a more versatile range of wines, it's an issue that needs clarification.

The two principal measures are 175ml and 250ml, usually sold as standard and large glasses. That's easy enough, as long as you remember that 250ml is one-third of a bottle. If you're drinking something at the upper end of the alcohol range (13.5 to 14 per cent), you're quite possibly consuming far more than you bargained for: drivers beware. Many restaurants and pubs, though, are still offering a rather parsimonious 125ml measure as standard.

In 2011, the government announced its intention to amend the law to permit the sale of smaller measures than 125ml, with the aim of cutting problem drinking. This was met with a degree of public scepticism, and it remains to be seen whether restaurant-goers will broadly accept the idea of drinking ordinary table wines in quantities traditionally suited to sherry and port.

St Saviour, Jersey

Longueville Manor

A beacon of quality
St Saviour, Jersey, JE2 7WF
Tel no: (01534) 725501
www.longuevillemanor.com
Modern British | £55
Cooking score: 5
V

Longueville has been a beacon of quality in the Channel Islands since the Lewis family opened it as a hotel in 1949. Dating back partly to the fourteenth century, it's a handsome, stone-built manor house with all the modern accoutrements, as pleasing in winter when log fires are going as it is when conditions allow for aperitifs on the poolside terrace. Andrew Baird is into his third decade at the kitchen helm, a tenure that has resulted in both consistency and the confidence to move with the culinary times. Seafood shows up especially well, perhaps in the form of grilled scallops that arrive not with the now *de rigueur* vegetable purée, but with a buttery sauce made of the corals, and the bonus of an oyster. The style may be impeccably modern, but there is a sense of working with the grain of ingredients rather than cutting across them: a main course of grilled brill is served on the bone with braised fennel and mustard mash, while a stew of cocoa beans adds depth to roast Angus fillet with ceps and bordelaise sauce. Memorable desserts may include pineapple and ginger pie with lime pannacotta and kiwi sorbet. The wine list is a trove of pedigree names and ripe vintages that looks for value as well as quality. A copious selection by the glass starts at £5, with bottles from £21.

Chef/s: Andrew Baird. **Open:** all week L 12 to 2, D 7 to 10. **Meals:** Set L £20 (2 courses) to £25. Set D £47.50 (2 courses) to £55. Tasting menu £75. **Service:** not inc. **Details:** Cards accepted. 90 seats. 35 seats outside. Separate bar. No music. No mobile phones. Wheelchair access. Children allowed. Car parking.

NORTHERN IRELAND

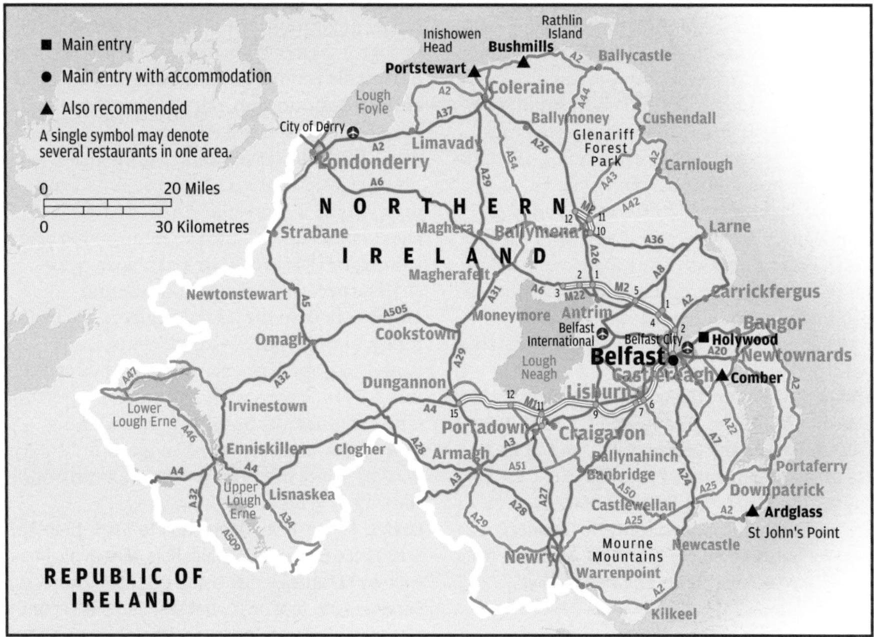

Ardglass, Co Down

ALSO RECOMMENDED

▲ Curran's Seafood Steakhouse

83 Strangford Road, Chapeltown, Ardglass, Co Down, BT30 7SP
Tel no: (028) 4484 1332
www.curransbar.net
International £5 OFF

The kitchen at this large, family-run restaurant draws on local riches from land and sea. Dundrum Bay mussels with cream and white wine (£5.95) or crispy duck salad with hoisin sauce typify the notion of taking local ingredients on a tour of the world's cooking styles. Main courses are a modest assortment embracing seafood gratin, beef lasagne, herb-crusted salmon with white wine sauce (£12.95), and a separate curry menu. Finish with sherry trifle. House wine is £11.95. Open all week.

Belfast, Co Antrim

Cayenne

Sexy fusion sizzler
7 Ascot House, Shaftesbury Square, Belfast, Co Antrim, BT2 7DB
Tel no: (028) 9033 1532
www.cayenne-restaurant.co.uk
Global | £30
Cooking score: 4
V

Belfast's original dream team, Paul and Jeanne Rankin are still keeping up appearances in the city with this fusion sizzler off Shaftesbury Square. True to its red-hot name, Cayenne deals in funky food – but with a cool, streetwise vibe that shows in its arty interiors and glamorous cocktails. Swarms of bright young things flit around the place, lured by its noisy buzz and socialising opportunities, although this isn't simply a lifestyle accessory. The kitchen takes its work seriously, knocking out precise flavours as it backpacks across the globe; expect anything from goats' cheese and potato 'puff pizzas' to chorizo-crusted monkfish or miso cod with mooli salad and sticky sesame rice balls. Supporters have also raved over crunchy salt and chilli squid with slaw and aïoli, veal three ways and the most 'sublime' lobster curry with noodles, as well as textbook hot chocolate fondant and a fascinating combo of buttermilk pudding with rhubarb-tinged rosewater, wild sorrel and hazelnut biscotti. The urbane wine list is as invigorating as the food, with trendy top-end producers in abundance and 'recession-busting' prices across the board. Bottles start at £12 (£4 a glass).

Chef/s: Paul Rankin. **Open:** Wed to Fri, Sun and Mon L 12 to 2.30 (4 Sun), Wed to Mon D 5 to 11 (9 Sun). **Closed:** Tue, 25 and 26 Dec, 1 Jan, 12 and 13 Jul. **Meals:** alc (main courses £18 to £25). Set L £12.50 (2 courses) to £15.50. Set D £15.50 (2 courses) to £18.50. Sun L £12.50. **Service:** 10% (optional). **Details:** Cards accepted. 130 seats. Separate bar. Wheelchair access. Music. Children allowed.

Deanes

Classy Belfast destination
36-40 Howard Street, Belfast, Co Antrim, BT1 6PF
Tel no: (028) 9033 1134
www.michaeldeane.co.uk
Modern European | £37
Cooking score: 5

£5 OFF **V**

Some big foodie names have fallen by the wayside hereabouts, but Michael Deane continues his upward trajectory, with a clutch of eateries in full flow across Belfast (see entries). This self-titled brasserie-style restaurant remains his top priority and it certainly knows how to put on the style, with high ceilings, pinkish-red colour schemes, an open-to-view kitchen and a seafood bar. As the moody jazz soundtrack grooves along, punters get stuck into classy metropolitan plates of 'piglet' (glazed belly pork with roast milk-fed tenderloin, caramelised apple purée and Clonakilty black pudding) or fillet of organic salmon with watercress purée, crispy crab cake and pea shoots. 'Flawless performances' abound: everyone loves the smoked salmon starter (served atop crisp, properly seasoned potato bread with horseradish crème fraîche); readers have also enthused about crisp, salty-skinned duck on a heap of perfectly cooked beans and a special dish of halibut served amid a gorgeous 'abstract green' canvas of foams, purées and drizzled jus. To finish, try soft-centred chocolate cake with broken honeycomb and vanilla, or the three-part 'pear, pear, pear' ('each aspect more delicate, subtle and tantalising than the last'). Service is warm and totally professional, with plenty of lively banter to boot. The exciting global wine list mixes French class with serious pickings from Chile, California, South Africa and other vinous hot spots; 'seasonal suggestions' by the glass or carafe offer the best value, with bottles starting at £23.

Chef/s: Simon Toye. **Open:** Mon to Sat L 12 to 3, D 5.30 to 10. **Closed:** Sun, bank hols. **Meals:** alc (main courses £17 to £25). Set L and D £17.50 (2 courses). **Service:** 10% (optional). **Details:** Cards accepted. 120 seats. Separate bar. Wheelchair access. Music. Children allowed.

Deanes at Queens

Buzzing foodie beacon
1 College Gardens, Belfast, Co Antrim, BT9 6BQ
Tel no: (028) 9038 2111
www.michaeldeane.co.uk
Modern British | £25
Cooking score: 3

'This is highly likeable', writes a reporter of Michael Deane's worthy foodie beacon shining out across College Gardens. The venue is one of a clutch of Deane's Belfast eateries. Hard surfaces mean a fair amount of hullabaloo when it's busy, but staff are vigilant and the brasserie atmosphere works well. The kitchen takes a fairly broad approach: foie gras parfait with pear and saffron chutney, or salt-and-chilli squid with garlic mayo, say. Modest ingredients and simple treatments create main courses such as crisp belly pork with warmed potato salad, creamed celeriac and sage and cider gravy, or chicken with sauté potatoes,

fried onions and garlic and herb butter. End with pannacotta, Eton mess and shortbread, perhaps. There are good-value set deals, and reasonably priced wines from £17.50.
Chef/s: Chris Fearon. **Open:** all week L 12 to 3 (1 to 4 Sun), Mon to Sat D 5.30 to 10 (9 Mon and Tue). **Closed:** 25 and 26 Dec, 1 Jan, Easter Sun and Mon, 12 and 13 Jul. **Meals:** alc (main courses £11 to £20). Set L and D £16.95 (2 courses) to £20. Sun L £22.50. **Service:** 10% (optional). **Details:** Cards accepted. 150 seats. 30 seats outside. Wheelchair access. Music.

The Ginger Bistro

No-frills bistro using fine local produce
7-8 Hope Street, Belfast, Co Antrim, BT12 5EE
Tel no: (028) 9024 4421
www.gingerbistro.com
Modern British | £30
Cooking score: 2

Simon McCance's no-frills bistro with its plain wood tables and saffron-coloured walls achieves the right mix of informality and efficiency. A menu of contemporary dishes, some quite intricately conceived, has been put together using fine local produce from both farm and fishing boat. Tiger prawn tempura with a salsa of red pepper and pineapple and a pickled ginger dressing could be the prelude to pan-roasted hake with mussels and bacon in cock-a-leekie broth, or lamb rump with a mini-shepherd's pie and carrot spaghetti in rosemary jus. A commendable wine list opens with house Sauvignon and Merlot from Chile at £15 (£4.25 a glass).
Chef/s: Simon McCance and Tim Moffett. **Open:** Tue to Sat L 12 to 3, Mon to Sat D 5 to 9.30 (9 Mon, 10 Fri and Sat). **Closed:** Sun, 24 to 26 Dec, May Day, 1 Jan, 11 and 12 July. **Meals:** alc (main courses £13 to £23). **Service:** not inc. **Details:** Cards accepted. 70 seats. Wheelchair access. Music. Children allowed.

James Street South

Assured big-city food
21 James Street South, Belfast, Co Antrim, BT2 7GA
Tel no: (028) 9043 4310
www.jamesstreetsouth.co.uk
Modern European | £28
Cooking score: 5

'Super-cool' is one reader's verdict on this converted linen mill, a fashionable home-from-home for Belfast's smart set since 2003. High arched windows, polished wood floors and contemporary artwork on bare walls add some extra fizz to the trendy ground-floor space, while Niall McKenna's food is pitched at sophisticated, grown-up palates. There are enough foams and jellies to keep the fashion-followers happy, but the kitchen is not about to exploit gimmicks for their own sake; this is seriously considered, intelligent cooking suffused with direct, properly balanced flavours. Organic sea trout might be paired with clams, braised artichoke and ham, while honey-roast duck breast is given texture and richness with figs, radish and 'mustard fruits'; elsewhere, beetroot and new season's asparagus make appropriate bedfellows for a main course of spring lamb. Ingredients are gleaned assiduously from the region's farmers and producers, but dishes never labour the home-grown point – witness saddle of rabbit with truffle and ricotta gnocchi, girolles and onion vinaigrette, or fillet of beef with smoked aubergine and confit potato. Desserts are firmly in the metropolitan mould of white chocolate parfait with poached rhubarb and pistachio, pineapple carpaccio or espresso mousse with plum and Amaretto sorbet. The wine list is a pot-pourri of good stuff from the Old and New Worlds, with prices from £18 (£6.50 a glass).
Chef/s: Stephen Toman. **Open:** Mon to Sat L 12 to 2.45, all week D 5.45 to 10.45 (5.30 to 9 Sun). **Closed:** 25 and 26 Dec, 1 Jan, Easter, 12 Jul. **Meals:** alc (main courses £17 to £22). Set L £14.95 (2 courses) to £16.95. Pre-theatre D £16.95 (2 courses)

to £18.95. **Service:** not inc. **Details:** Cards accepted. 60 seats. Separate bar. Wheelchair access. Music. Children allowed.

Menu by Kevin Thornton

Classy, user-friendly eatery
Fitzwilliam Hotel Belfast, 1-3 Great Victoria Street, Belfast, Co Antrim, BT2 7BQ
Tel no: (028) 9044 2080
www.fitzwilliamhotelbelfast.com
Modern European | £35
Cooking score: 5

V

The Belfast Fitzwilliam's design team certainly went to town when they dreamed up this flagship dining room for celeb chef Kevin Thornton. It's a pared-down look, with blonde wood and high-backed seating upholstered in hunting pink; intimate tables around the sides are supplemented by a refectory-style communal table in the centre, but instead of institutional glare the lighting maintains a discreet level. Patrick Leonard heads up the kitchen as Kevin Thornton's deputy, interpreting his vibrant modern European style with considerable aplomb and fine ingredients. A quail gets the starter treatment in the form of slow-cooked breast, with a pastilla of the legs and a fricassee of artichokes and wild mushrooms in a gamey jus, while scallops can be relied upon these days to turn up with something piggy (a cheek for example) and a purée (such as carrot) in a sauce of red wine. Mains continue the mixing and matching of body parts, with roast loin, knuckle faggot and crispy sweetbread of rose veal, creamily united by Madeira café au lait, or there could be poached sole with a smoked eel stuffing in white wine velouté. An essay on the history of wine opens a resourceful, well-written and exciting list that offers a generous selection by the glass, from £4.25.

Chef/s: Kevin Thornton and Patrick Leonard. **Open:** Sun to Fri L 12.30 to 2.30, all week D 5.30 to 9.30 (10 Fri and Sat). **Meals:** alc (main courses £16 to £28). Set L £10.99 (2 courses) to £15.99. Set D £12.99 (2 courses) to £17.99. Tasting menu £55. **Service:** not inc. **Details:** Cards accepted. 150 seats. Separate bar. Wheelchair access. Music. Children allowed. Car parking.

★ READERS' RESTAURANT OF THE YEAR ★
NORTHERN IRELAND

Molly's Yard

'Secret hideout' with classic bistro cooking
1 College Green Mews, Botanic Avenue, Belfast, Co Antrim, BT7 1LW
Tel no: (028) 9032 2600
www.mollysyard.co.uk
Modern Irish | £27
Cooking score: 3

£5 OFF £30

In the heart of Belfast's university quarter, yet managing to feel far from the madding crowd ('like stepping through the entrance to a secret hideout,' thought one), Molly's Yard is an arm of the family-owned Hilden Brewery operation, hence the house draught beers. With its tiled floor and bare tables, it's an unpretentious venue that produces classic bistro cooking, as well as some stimulating contemporary dishes. An impeccably Northern Irish starter sees a version of eggs Benedict made with potato bread and undyed smoked haddock, and then there may be duck with apple and celeriac rösti, braised red cabbage and vanilla jus to follow. Belgian chocolate brownie with Molly's Chocolate Stout ice cream and chocolate sauce should supply the chocoholic fix. A short, serviceable wine list starts at £13.50.

Chef/s: Ciarán Steele. **Open:** Mon to Sat 12 to 9 (9.30 Fri and Sat). **Closed:** Sun, 25 to 27 Dec, 1 Jan. **Meals:** alc (main courses £13 to £21). **Service:** 10% (optional). **Details:** Cards accepted. 45 seats. 20 seats outside. Wheelchair access. Music. Children allowed.

Mourne Seafood Bar

An exemplary purveyor of local seafood
34-36 Bank Street, Belfast, Co Antrim, BT1 1HL
Tel no: (028) 9024 8544
www.mourneseafood.com
Seafood | £25
Cooking score: 3

A new bar and cookery school are in the pipeline at this exemplary purveyor of local seafood next door to legendary Kelly's Cellars in the heart of Belfast. Carlingford mussels and oysters, Glenarm smoked salmon and beer-battered fish are staples, although the kitchen's eclectic haul might also yield sea bream fillet with fennel and pepper confit or spicy fried cod with crab slaw and Szechuan fries. One devotee happily makes a 70-mile trip to sample the Thai green curry and langoustine risotto, while meat eaters get full satisfaction from slabs of pedigree Dexter ribeye with fries and grilled vegetables. To drink, try the Mourne Oyster Stout, specially produced by the Whitewater Brewery in Kilkeel; there are also some affordable wines from £15.50 (£4.50 a glass). The original MSB is on Main Street, Dundrum BT33 0LU, tel (028) 4375 1377.

Chef/s: Andy Rea. **Open:** all week L 12 to 5 (4 Fri and Sat, 1 to 6 Sun), Tue to Sat D 5 to 9.30 (10.30 Fri and Sat). **Closed:** 24 to 26 Dec, 1 Jan, 17 Mar, Easter. **Meals:** alc (main courses £8 to £17). **Service:** not inc. **Details:** Cards accepted. 70 seats. Wheelchair access. Music. Children allowed.

Nick's Warehouse

Local supplies and good ideas
35 Hill Street, Belfast, Co Antrim, BT1 2LB
Tel no: (028) 9043 9690
www.nickswarehouse.co.uk
Modern British | £30
Cooking score: 3

A veteran provider of hospitality in Belfast's Catherdral Quarter, Nick's Warehouse started life as a bonded warehouse for Bushmills Whiskey. It's now one of the city's more consistent and likeable gastronomic performers. Sean Craig knows his way around the region when it comes to sourcing top-drawer ingredients, and they are perked up with ideas from near and far. Dishes range from Thai-flavoured fishcakes with mango and pineapple salsa to rump of lamb with dauphinoise potatoes, parsnip purée and blackcurrant sauce; from pigeon breast with butternut squash purée, braised red cabbage and red wine sauce to fillet of sea bass with crab linguine, lemon, chilli and basil. The flexible lunch menu (soups, sandwiches, salads, hot dishes) is good value, as is the intelligent global wine list. Bottles from £15.15.

Chef/s: Sean Craig. **Open:** Tue to Sat L 12 to 3, D 5 to 10 (6 Sat). **Closed:** Sun, Mon, 25 to 27 Dec, bank hols, first week Jan. **Meals:** alc (main courses £13 to £23). Set D Tue to Thur £17.95 (2 courses) to £21. **Service:** not inc. **Details:** Cards accepted. 175 seats. Separate bar. Music. Children allowed.

No 27 Talbot Street

Über-cool, with far-and-wide flavours
27 Talbot Street, Belfast, Co Antrim, BT1 2LD
Tel no: (028) 9031 2884
www.no27.co.uk
Modern British | £31
Cooking score: 3

On the site of the old city wall in Belfast's lively Cathedral Quarter, this was once a historic bonded liquor store but is now the epitome of urban cool, with clean lines, an open kitchen, simple modern furnishings and an altogether 'great ambience', helped along by 'excellent service'. The cooking juggles flavours from far and wide, with starters ranging from tom yum soup to risotto with local smoked trout and petits pois. A main course of belly pork (declared by one reader 'the best I ever tasted') might come with cocotte potatoes, spiced red cabbage, button mushrooms and thyme jus, while simpler tastes should be satisfied by char-grilled dry-aged Irish sirloin with home-cut chips and green peppercorn cream. Pud could be white chocolate and blueberry cheesecake with praline-coated vanilla ice cream. A broad selection of wines starts at £15.20.

Chef/s: Alan Higginson. **Open:** Mon to Fri L 12 to 3, Mon to Sat D 6 to 10. **Closed:** Sun, 25 and 26 Dec, 12 and 13 Jul. **Meals:** alc (main courses £14 to £25). Set D £18.95 (2 courses) to £22.95. **Service:** not inc. **Details:** Cards accepted. 78 seats. Separate bar. Wheelchair access. Music. Children allowed.

NEW ENTRY

Zen

Cocktails and capable Japanese food
55-59 Adelaide Street, Belfast, Co Antrim, BT2 8FE
Tel no: (028) 9023 2244
www.zenbelfast.co.uk
Japanese | £25
Cooking score: 2

Zen by name, Zen by nature, this Belfast restaurant brings capable Japanese food, calming vibes and glamorous cocktails to the centre of town. A magnificent Buddha overlooks the softly lit dining room, where mission-statement red chopsticks are neatly arrayed on dark brown tables. There's always a strong showing of sushi and sashimi, teppanyaki and tempura, but it's also worth trying the deep-fried monkfish with a grapefruit 'tangyang' sauce, grilled eel with a honey and BBQ glaze, or sizzling chicken tobanyaki with three kinds of mushrooms. Meanwhile, cut-price lunches suit shoppers and workers on the go. If cocktails don't attract, go for one of the reasonably priced wines (from £15.95). Fusion sibling and robata specialist Zen Two is at 92-94 Lisburn Road, BT9 6AG, tel (028) 9068 7318.

Chef/s: Kim Haut Lee. **Open:** Sun to Fri L 12 to 3 (1.30 Sun), all week D 5 to 11 (12.30 Fri and Sat, 10 Sun). **Closed:** 25 Dec. **Meals:** alc (main courses £10 to £18). Set D £27.95 (4 courses) to £29.95. **Service:** not inc. **Details:** Cards accepted. 190 seats. Wheelchair access. Music. Children allowed.

ALSO RECOMMENDED

▲ Coco

7-11 Linenhall Street, Belfast, Co Antrim, BT2 8AA
Tel no: (028) 9031 1150
www.cocobelfast.com
Modern British

Boutique-chic furnishings and funky artwork help create a 'really fun experience' at this trendy restaurant in the centre of Belfast. It offers 'fine dining without the fuss', pulling together diverse influences on a snappy modern menu. Try tom yum soup (£4.95), lunchtime venison stew and mash, or an evening plate of honey-roast pigeon with plum purée, shiitake mushrooms, noodles, and pain d'épices (£16.50). Wines start at £15.50. Closed Sat L.

READERS RECOMMEND

Shu

Modern European
253 Lisburn Road, Belfast, Co Antrim, BT9 7EN
Tel no: (028) 9038 1655
www.shu-restaurant.com
'A great, buzzing brasserie... a crumble for the table was one of the best I've ever had.'

Bushmills, Co Down

ALSO RECOMMENDED

▲ Tartine at the Distillers Arms

140 Main Street, Bushmills, Co Down, BT57 8QE
Tel no: (028) 2073 1044
www.distillersarms.com
Modern British £5 OFF

In an area 'full of tourist traps and cheap and cheerful Sunday roasts', it's good to know about this Victorian town house and erstwhile pub, now a comfortable modern restaurant. Gary Stewart transforms good raw materials into dishes such as seafood chowder (£4.25), tender slow-braised lamb shank on champ with roast root vegetables and red wine jus (£13.95) or marinated roast topside of venison with port and damson sauce. There are good lunch and dinner set deals, too. Wines from £13.95. Open Sat and Sun L, Wed to Sun D, (all week Jul and Aug).

Comber, Co Down

ALSO RECOMMENDED

▲ The Old Schoolhouse Inn

100 Ballydrain Road, Comber, Co Down, BT23 6EA
Tel no: (028) 9754 1182
www.theoldschoolhouseinn.com
Modern British £5 OFF

The Browns' former schoolhouse stands close to the shores of Strangford Lough. In the kitchen, Avril Brown's evening menu (two/three courses £19.95/£23.95) takes a brasserie jaunt through moules marinière and grilled goats' cheese with apple, wild honey and walnut salad, via fillet of Finnebrogue venison with thyme and claret jus, to desserts such as chocolate tart. House wine is £13.95. Open Mon to Sat, D only.

Holywood, Co Down

The Bay Tree

Fizzing all-dayer
118 High Street, Holywood, Co Down, BT18 9HW
Tel no: (028) 9042 1419
www.baytreeholywood.co.uk
Modern British | £22
Cooking score: 2

The Bay Tree is tucked off Holywood's main street and may not catch the eye of those passing by, but this is a useful address in a busy seaside town. The décor is simple, the service friendly, and the food the star of the all-day show. It's a good spot for breakfast (the cinnamon scones are legendary); lunch brings soup with home-made wheaten bread, salads and casseroles. There's an eclectic choice at dinner, perhaps salad of crispy belly pork with pomegranate, lime and ginger dressing, then spiced coley with potato, spinach and tomato curry. End with Moroccan orange drizzle cake. House wine is £13.95.

Chef/s: Sue Farmer. **Open:** all week L 12 to 3, Mon and Wed to Sat D 5.30 to 9.30. **Closed:** 25 to 27 Dec, 1 Jan. **Meals:** alc (£10 to £19). Set early D £11.50 (2 courses) to £14.50. **Service:** not inc. **Details:** Cards accepted. 60 seats. Music. Children allowed. Car parking.

Portstewart, Co Londonderry

ALSO RECOMMENDED

▲ Preference Brasserie

81 The Promenade, Portstewart, Co Londonderry, BT55 7AF
Tel no: (028) 7083 3959
www.preferencebrasserie.co.uk
Modern European £5 OFF

Neil and Louise Gibson have established this chic brasserie as a serious foodie contender on Portstewart's touristy seafront, matching black leather chairs and modern artwork with a menu of upbeat contemporary dishes. Come here for seared Kilkeel scallops with baby beets and herb salad (£8), homemade tagliatelle, aged fillet of Irish beef with duck-egg béarnaise, or free-range chicken breast with glazed asparagus and truffle-oil hollandaise (£15). For afters, perhaps steamed apple pudding. House French is £16. Open Tue to Sun D only.

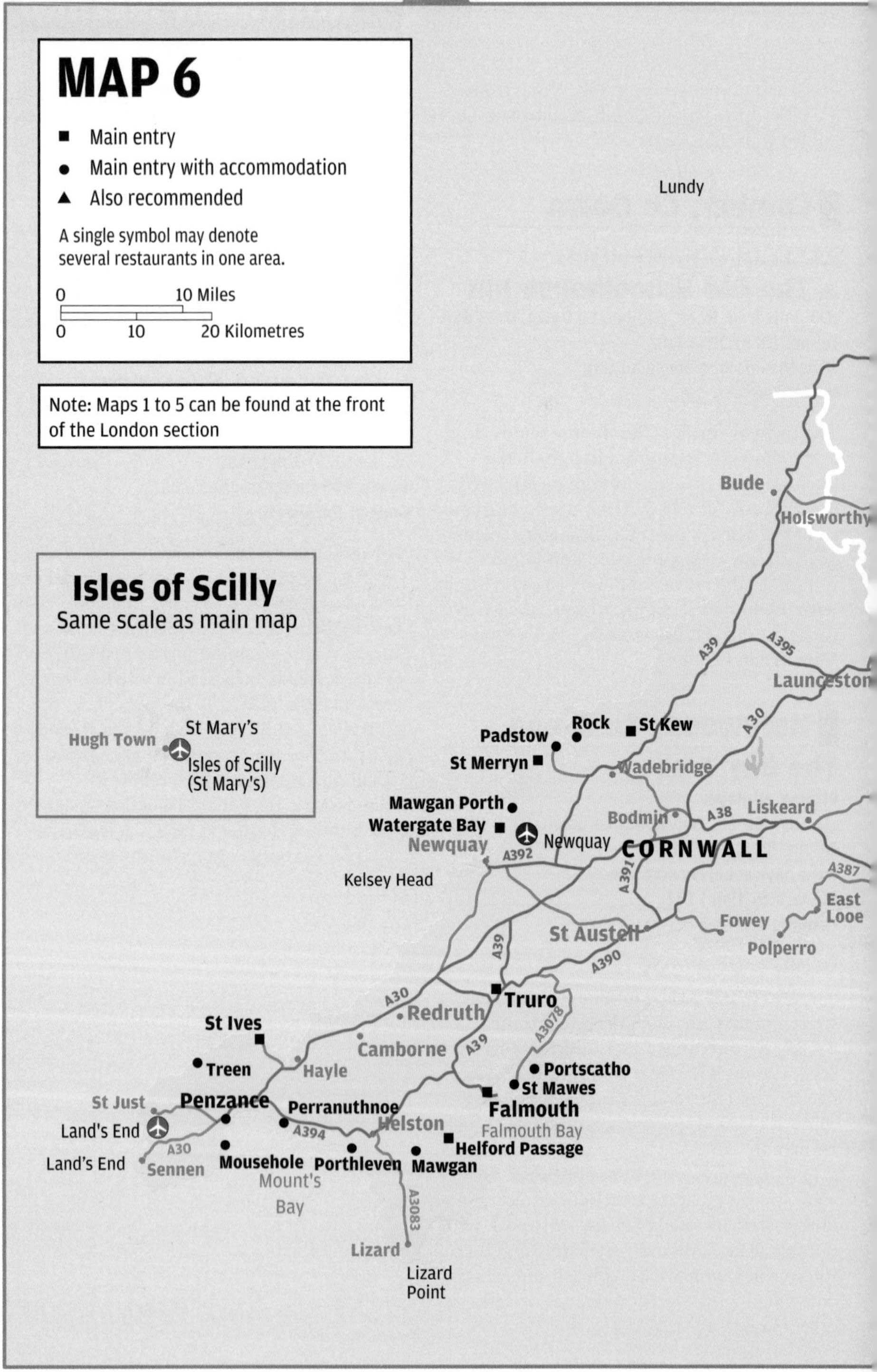

MAP 6
■ Main entry
● Main entry with accommodation
▲ Also recommended
A single symbol may denote several restaurants in one area.
0
10 Miles
0
10
20 Kilometres
Note: Maps 1 to 5 can be found at the front of the London section
Isles of Scilly
Same scale as main map
Hugh Town
St Mary's
Isles of Scilly (St Mary's)
Lundy
Bude
Holsworthy
A39
A395
Launceston
A30
Rock
St Kew
Padstow
St Merryn
Wadebridge
Mawgan Porth
Watergate Bay
Newquay
Newquay
A392
Bodmin
A38
Liskeard
CORNWALL
A387
A391
East Looe
Kelsey Head
Fowey
Polperro
St Austell
A390
A39
A30
Truro
A3078
Redruth
St Ives
Camborne
A39
Portscatho
St Mawes
Treen
Hayle
Falmouth
St Just
Penzance
Perranuthnoe
Land's End
Helston
Falmouth Bay
A394
Helford Passage
Land's End
A30
Sennen
Mousehole
Porthleven
Mawgan
Mount's Bay
A3083
Lizard
Lizard Point

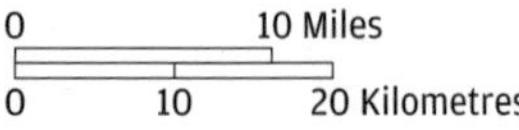

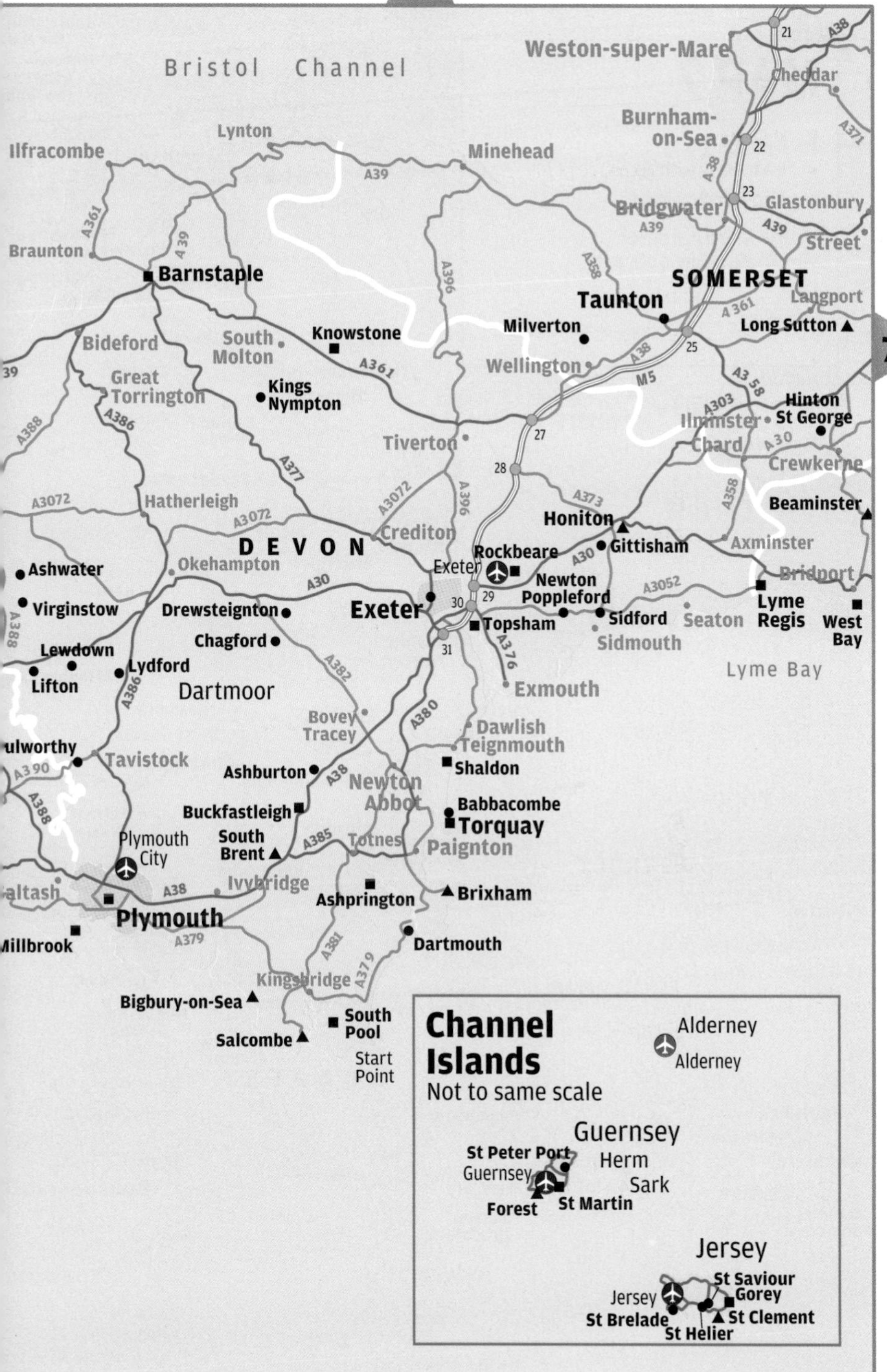
9
7
Bristol Channel
Weston-super-Mare
Cheddar
Burnham-on-Sea
Ilfracombe
Lynton
Minehead
Bridgwater
Glastonbury
Street
Braunton
Barnstaple
SOMERSET
Taunton
Langport
Milverton
Long Sutton
Knowstone
South Molton
Bideford
Wellington
Great Torrington
Kings Nympton
Hinton St George
Ilminster
Chard
Crewkerne
Tiverton
Hatherleigh
Beaminster
Honiton
DEVON
Crediton
Gittisham
Axminster
Ashwater
Okehampton
Rockbeare
Exeter
Bridport
Newton Poppleford
Lyme Regis
West Bay
Virginstow
Drewsteignton
Exeter
Topsham
Sidford
Seaton
Sidmouth
Chagford
Lewdown
Lifton
Lydford
Dartmoor
Lyme Bay
Exmouth
Bovey Tracey
Dawlish
Teignmouth
Tavistock
Shaldon
Ashburton
Newton Abbot
Buckfastleigh
Babbacombe
Torquay
Plymouth City
South Brent
Totnes
Paignton
Ivybridge
Ashprington
Brixham
Plymouth
Millbrook
Dartmouth
Kingsbridge
Bigbury-on-Sea
South Pool
Salcombe
Start Point
Channel Islands
Not to same scale
Alderney
Alderney
Guernsey
St Peter Port
Guernsey
Herm
Sark
Forest
St Martin
Jersey
St Saviour
Gorey
Jersey
St Brelade
St Clement
St Helier
M5
A38
A39
A361
A396
A358
A377
A386
A388
A3072
A30
A303
A373
A3052
A376
A380
A382
A385
A381
A379
A390
A371

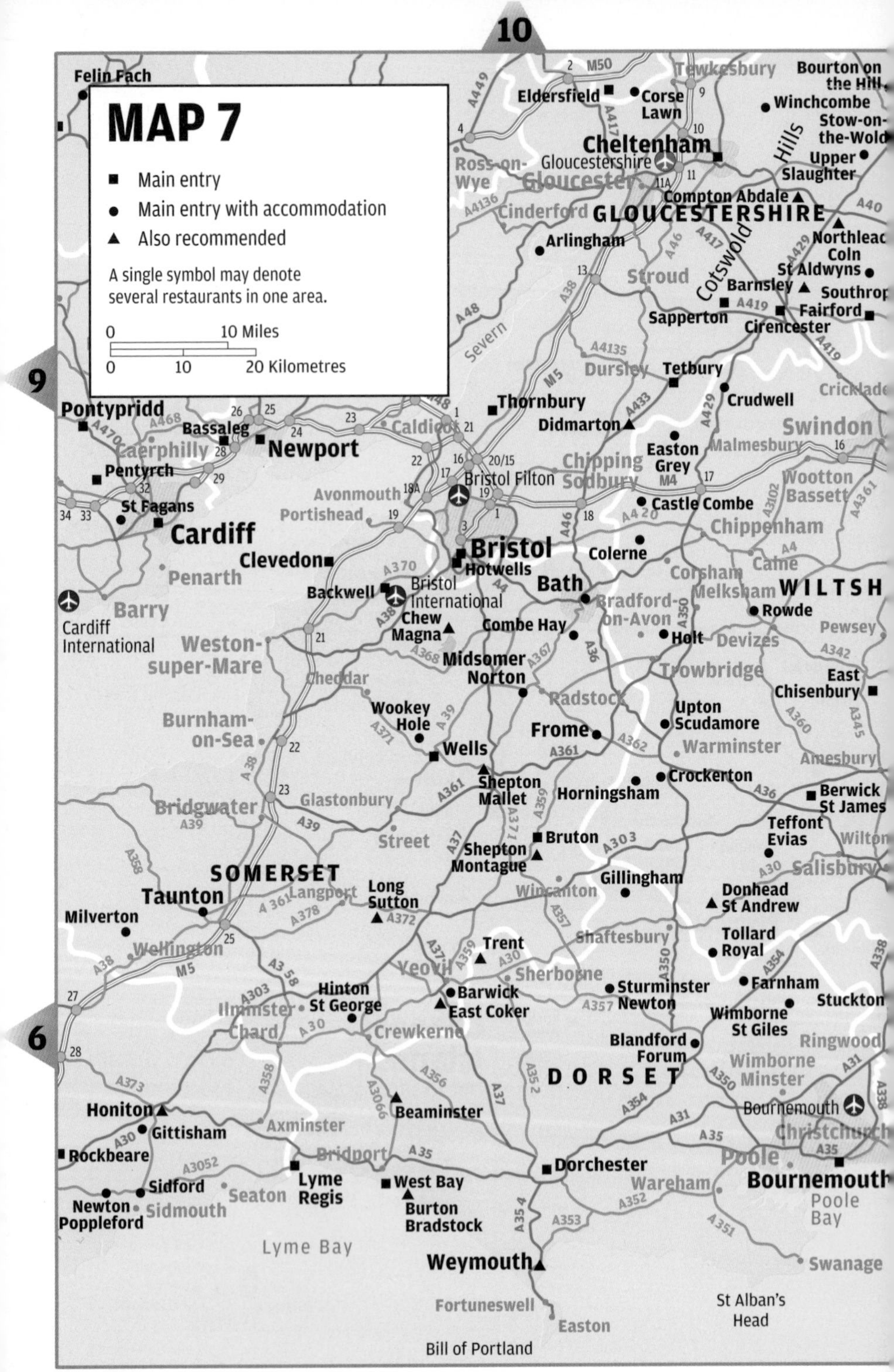

10

MAP 7

- ■ Main entry
- ● Main entry with accommodation
- ▲ Also recommended

A single symbol may denote several restaurants in one area.

0 10 Miles

0 10 20 Kilometres

9

6

Felin Fach
Eldersfield
Corse Lawn
Tewkesbury
Bourton on the Hill
Winchcombe
Stow-on-the-Wold
Cheltenham
Gloucestershire
Ross-on-Wye
Gloucester
Upper Slaughter
Compton Abdale
Cotswold Hills
Cinderford
GLOUCESTERSHIRE
Northleach
Coln St Aldwyns
Arlington
Stroud
Barnsley
Southrop
Sapperton
Fairford
Cirencester
Severn
Dursley
Tetbury
Crudwell
Cricklade
Thornbury
Didmarton
Pontypridd
Bassaleg
Newport
Caldicot
Swindon
Caerphilly
Easton Grey
Malmesbury
Pentyrch
Avonmouth
Bristol Filton
Chipping Sodbury
Wootton Bassett
Portishead
Castle Combe
St Fagans
Cardiff
Chippenham
Bristol
Clevedon
Colerne
Hotwells
Calne
Penarth
Corsham
Backwell
Bristol International
Bath
Melksham
WILTSHIRE
Chew Magna
Bradford-on-Avon
Rowde
Barry
Cardiff International
Combe Hay
Pewsey
Holt
Devizes
Weston-super-Mare
Midsomer Norton
Trowbridge
East Chisenbury
Cheddar
Radstock
Wookey Hole
Upton Scudamore
Burnham-on-Sea
Frome
Wells
Warminster
Amesbury
Shepton Mallet
Crockerton
Horningsham
Berwick St James
Bridgwater
Glastonbury
Teffont Evias
Street
Bruton
Wilton
Shepton Montague
SOMERSET
Gillingham
Salisbury
Long Sutton
Taunton
Langport
Wincanton
Donhead St Andrew
Milverton
Tollard Royal
Wellington
Trent
Shaftesbury
Yeovil
Sherborne
Farnham
Hinton St George
Barwick
Sturminster Newton
Stuckton
Ilminster
East Coker
Wimborne St Giles
Chard
Crewkerne
Blandford Forum
Ringwood
Wimborne Minster
DORSET
Honiton
Beaminster
Bournemouth
Gittisham
Axminster
Christchurch
Rockbeare
Bridport
Dorchester
Poole
Bournemouth
Sidford
Lyme Regis
West Bay
Wareham
Newton Poppleford
Sidmouth
Seaton
Burton Bradstock
Poole Bay
Lyme Bay
Weymouth
Swanage
Fortuneswell
St Alban's Head
Easton
Bill of Portland

11

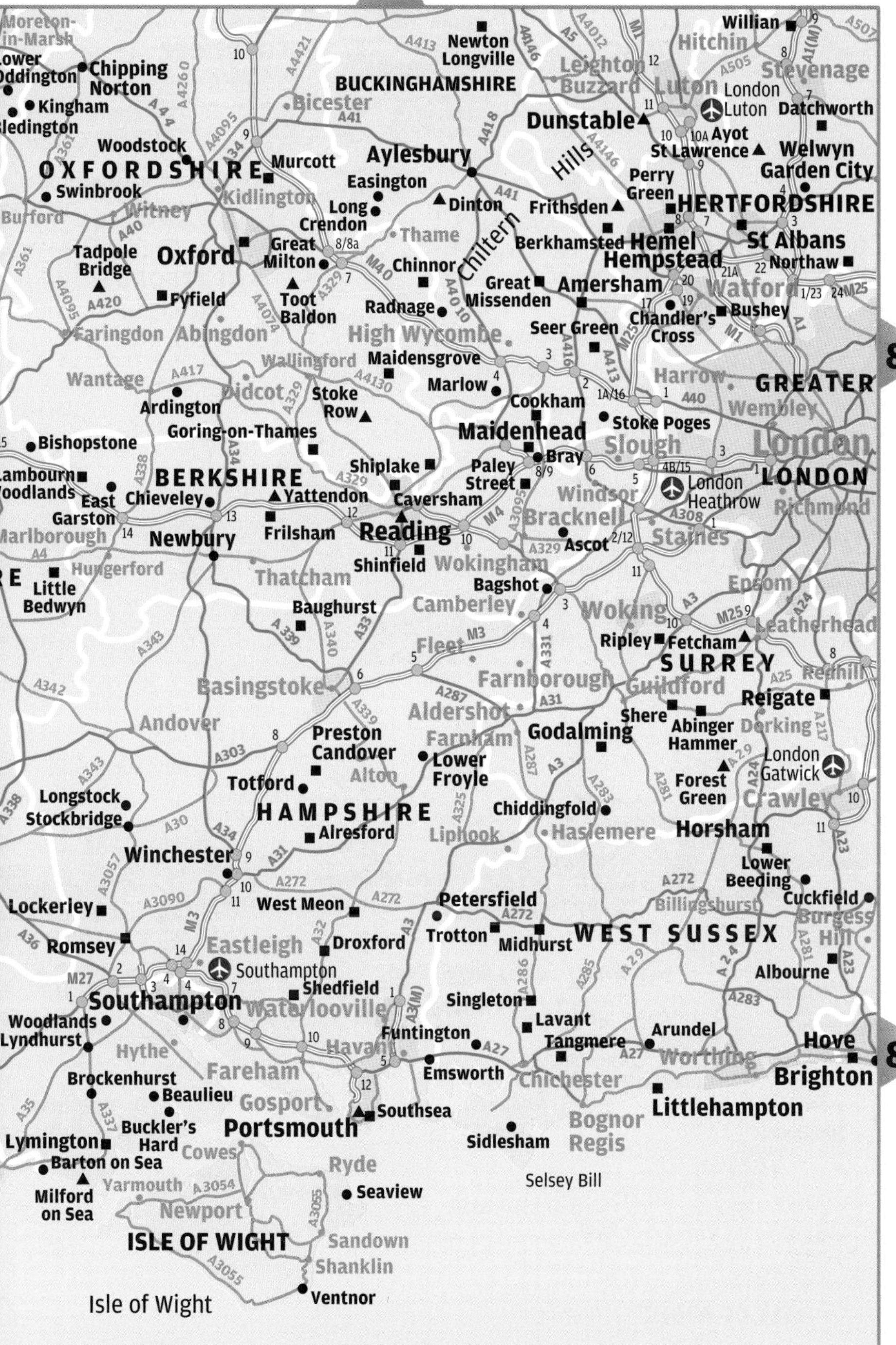
Moreton-in-Marsh
Lower Oddington
Chipping Norton
Kingham
Bledington
Woodstock
OXFORDSHIRE
Swinbrook
Burford
Witney
Kidlington
Murcott
Oxford
Tadpole Bridge
Fyfield
Faringdon
Abingdon
Great Milton
Toot Baldon
Newton Longville
BUCKINGHAMSHIRE
Bicester
Aylesbury
Easington
Long Crendon
Dinton
Thame
Chinnor
Radnage
Chiltern Hills
Leighton Buzzard
Dunstable
Luton
London Luton
Hitchin
Willian
Stevenage
Datchworth
Ayot St Lawrence
Welwyn Garden City
Perry Green
Frithsden
HERTFORDSHIRE
Berkhamsted
Hemel Hempstead
St Albans
Northaw
Great Missenden
Amersham
Watford
Chandler's Cross
Bushey
Seer Green
High Wycombe
Maidensgrove
Wallingford
Wantage
Didcot
Ardington
Stoke Row
Marlow
Cookham
Stoke Poges
Harrow
Wembley
GREATER LONDON
London
Goring-on-Thames
Bishopstone
Lambourn Woodlands
BERKSHIRE
East Garston
Chieveley
Yattendon
Shiplake
Caversham
Maidenhead
Bray
Paley Street
Slough
Windsor
London Heathrow
Richmond
Bracknell
Marlborough
Newbury
Frilsham
Reading
Shinfield
Wokingham
Ascot
Staines
Hungerford
Little Bedwyn
Thatcham
Baughurst
Camberley
Bagshot
Epsom
Woking
Ripley
Fetcham
Leatherhead
SURREY
Fleet
Basingstoke
Farnborough
Aldershot
Guildford
Redhill
Reigate
Shere
Abinger Hammer
Dorking
Andover
Preston Candover
Farnham
Lower Froyle
Godalming
Alton
Totford
Forest Green
London Gatwick
Crawley
Longstock
Stockbridge
HAMPSHIRE
Alresford
Chiddingfold
Liphook
Haslemere
Horsham
Winchester
Lower Beeding
West Meon
Petersfield
Billingshurst
Cuckfield
Lockerley
Burgess Hill
Romsey
Trotton
Midhurst
WEST SUSSEX
Eastleigh
Droxford
Albourne
Southampton
Shedfield
Singleton
Southampton
Waterlooville
Woodlands
Lyndhurst
Lavant
Arundel
Hove
Hythe
Funtington
Tangmere
Havant
Emsworth
Worthing
Brighton
Fareham
Brockenhurst
Chichester
Beaulieu
Gosport
Littlehampton
Southsea
Bognor Regis
Buckler's Hard
Portsmouth
Sidlesham
Lymington
Barton on Sea
Cowes
Ryde
Selsey Bill
Milford on Sea
Yarmouth
Seaview
Newport
ISLE OF WIGHT
Sandown
Shanklin
Ventnor
Isle of Wight
M40
M4
M3
M25
M27
M1
A34
A33
A3
A27
A23
A24
A272

8

8

11

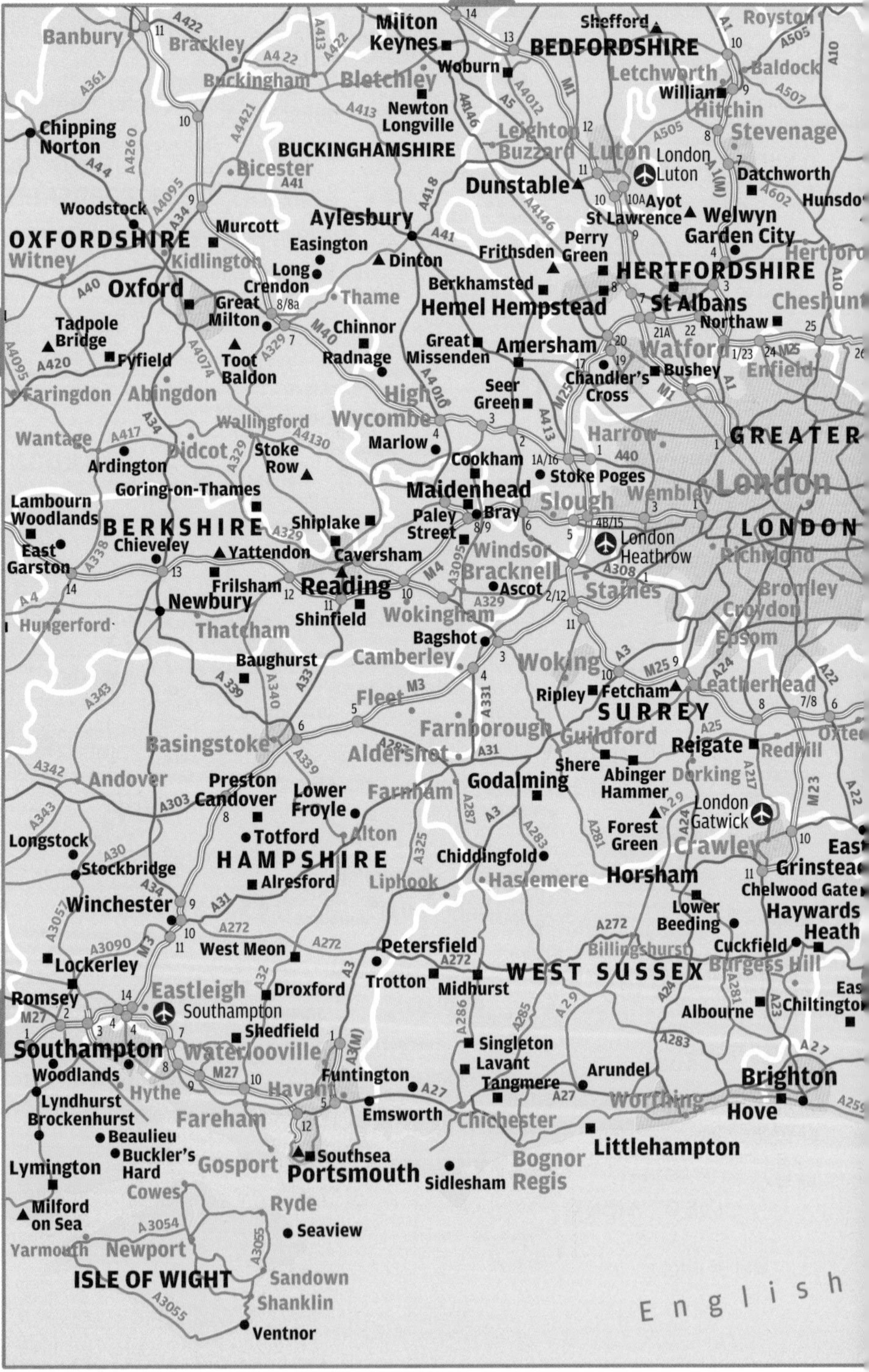

Banbury
Brackley
Milton Keynes
Shefford
Royston
BEDFORDSHIRE
Woburn
Buckingham
Bletchley
Letchworth
Baldock
William
Hitchin
Newton Longville
Chipping Norton
Leighton Buzzard
Luton
Stevenage
BUCKINGHAMSHIRE
London Luton
Bicester
Dunstable
Datchworth
Woodstock
Ayot St Lawrence
Welwyn Garden City
Hunsdon
Murcott
Aylesbury
OXFORDSHIRE
Easington
Perry Green
Witney
Kidlington
Long Crendon
Dinton
Frithsden
HERTFORDSHIRE
Hertford
Oxford
Thame
Berkhamsted
Great Milton
Hemel Hempstead
St Albans
Cheshunt
Tadpole Bridge
Chinnor
Northaw
Fyfield
Toot Baldon
Radnage
Great Missenden
Amersham
Watford
Bushey
Enfield
Chandler's Cross
Faringdon
Abingdon
High Wycombe
Seer Green
Wallingford
Wantage
Didcot
Marlow
Harrow
GREATER
Ardington
Stoke Row
Cookham
Stoke Poges
London
Goring-on-Thames
Maidenhead
Slough
Wembley
Lambourn Woodlands
BERKSHIRE
Shiplake
Paley Street
Bray
LONDON
East Garston
Chieveley
Yattendon
Caversham
Windsor
London Heathrow
Richmond
Frilsham
Reading
Bracknell
Ascot
Staines
Bromley
Newbury
Shinfield
Wokingham
Croydon
Hungerford
Thatcham
Bagshot
Epsom
Baughurst
Camberley
Woking
Ripley
Fetcham
Leatherhead
Fleet
SURREY
Farnborough
Basingstoke
Guildford
Reigate
Oxted
Aldershot
Shere
Abinger Hammer
Redhill
Andover
Preston Candover
Lower Froyle
Farnham
Godalming
Dorking
Forest Green
London Gatwick
Longstock
Totford
Alton
Chiddingfold
Crawley
East Grinstead
Stockbridge
HAMPSHIRE
Alresford
Liphook
Haslemere
Horsham
Chelwood Gate
Winchester
Lower Beeding
Haywards Heath
West Meon
Petersfield
Billingshurst
Cuckfield
Lockerley
Trotton
Midhurst
WEST SUSSEX
Burgess Hill
Eastleigh
Droxford
Romsey
Southampton
Albourne
Chiltington
Shedfield
Singleton
Southampton
Waterlooville
Lavant
Woodlands
Funtington
Arundel
Brighton
Hythe
Havant
Tangmere
Lyndhurst
Worthing
Brockenhurst
Fareham
Emsworth
Chichester
Hove
Beaulieu
Buckler's Hard
Southsea
Littlehampton
Lymington
Gosport
Portsmouth
Bognor Regis
Sidlesham
Cowes
Milford on Sea
Ryde
Seaview
Yarmouth
Newport
ISLE OF WIGHT
Sandown
Shanklin
Ventnor
English

7

7

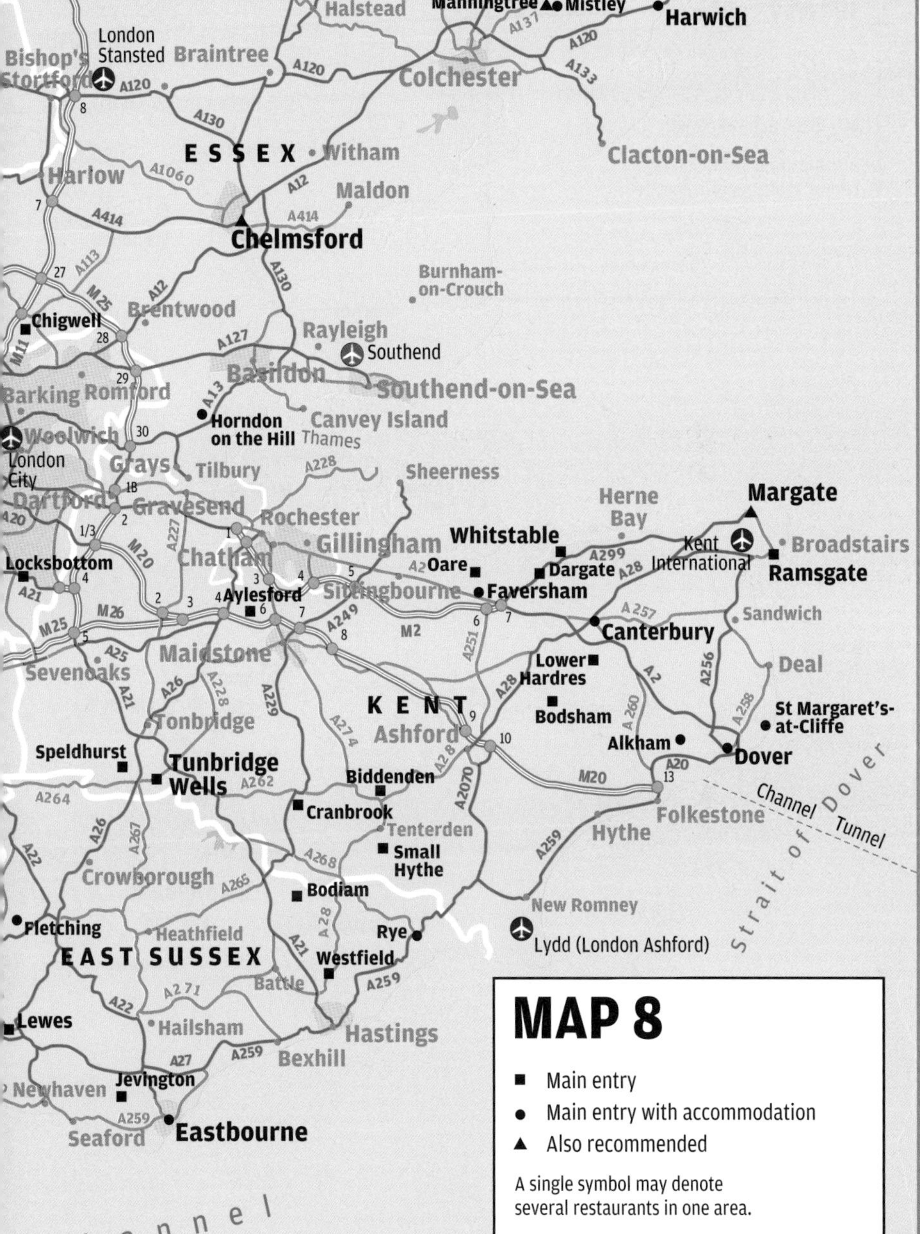

Saffron Walden
Stoke-by-Nayland
Dedham
Felixstowe
Halstead
Manningtree
Mistley
Harwich
London Stansted
Bishop's Stortford
Braintree
Colchester
Clacton-on-Sea
ESSEX
Witham
Harlow
Maldon
Chelmsford
Burnham-on-Crouch
Brentwood
Chigwell
Rayleigh
Southend
Basildon
Southend-on-Sea
Barking
Romford
Horndon on the Hill
Canvey Island
Thames
Woolwich
London City
Grays
Tilbury
Sheerness
Dartford
Gravesend
Rochester
Herne Bay
Margate
Gillingham
Whitstable
Kent International
Broadstairs
Chatham
Locksbottom
Oare
Dargate
Ramsgate
Aylesford
Sittingbourne
Faversham
Sandwich
Canterbury
Sevenoaks
Maidstone
Lower Hardres
Deal
Bodsham
St Margaret's-at-Cliffe
KENT
Tonbridge
Ashford
Alkham
Speldhurst
Tunbridge Wells
Dover
Biddenden
Cranbrook
Folkestone
Channel Tunnel
Tenterden
Hythe
Small Hythe
Strait of Dover
Crowborough
Bodiam
New Romney
Fletching
Heathfield
Rye
Lydd (London Ashford)
EAST SUSSEX
Westfield
Battle
Lewes
Hailsham
Hastings
Bexhill
Newhaven
Jevington
Seaford
Eastbourne
Channel
M11
A10017
A131
A134
A12
A14
A137
A120
A133
A130
A1060
A414
A113
M25
A127
A13
A228
A2
A299
A28
A257
A20
M20
M26
A21
A25
A249
A251
A256
A26
A227
A229
A274
A260
A258
A2070
A262
A264
A267
A268
A259
A22
A265
A271
A27
MAP 8
■ Main entry
● Main entry with accommodation
▲ Also recommended
A single symbol may denote several restaurants in one area.
0 10 Miles
0 10 20 Kilometres

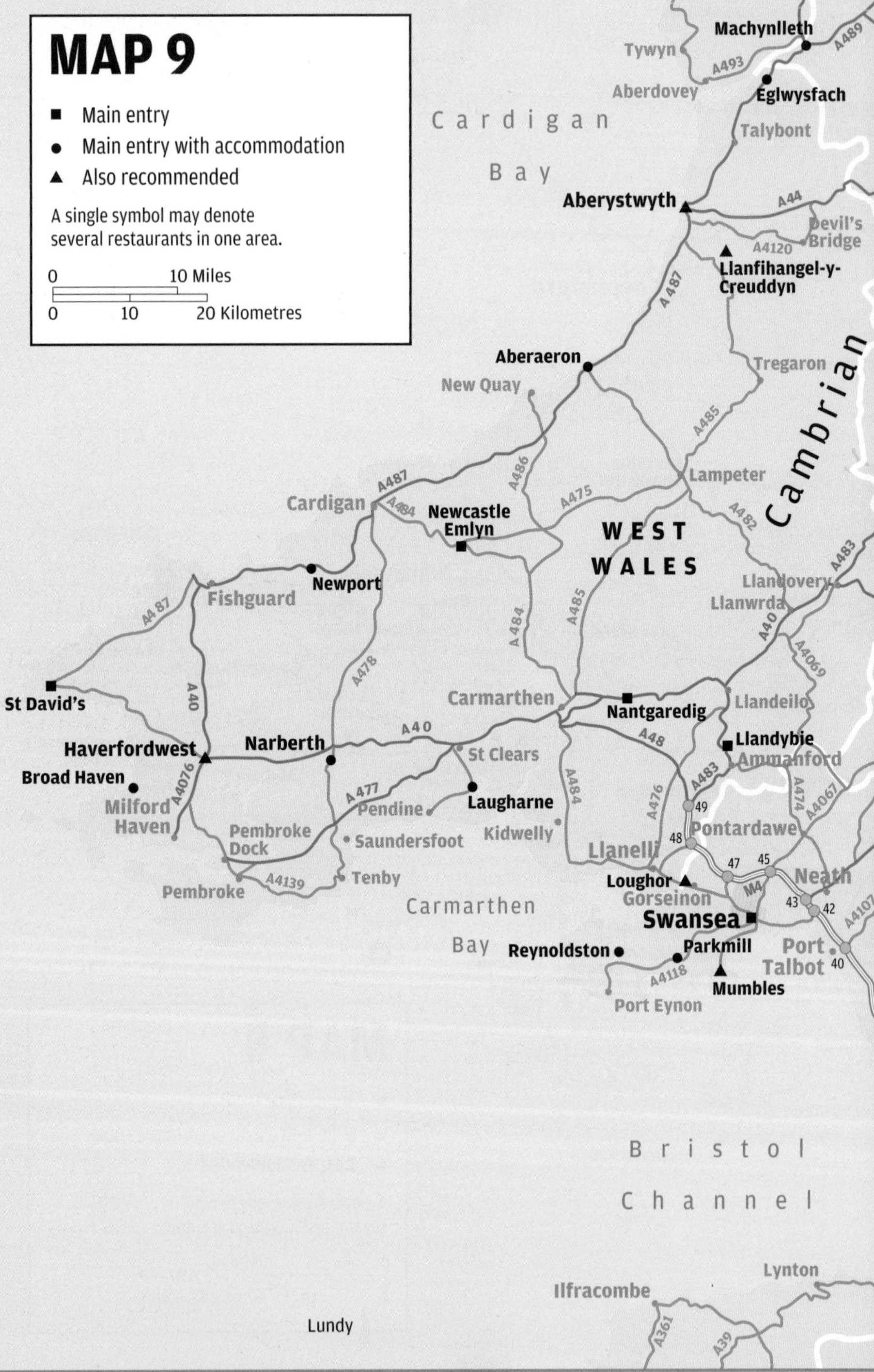
MAP 9
Main entry
Main entry with accommodation
Also recommended
A single symbol may denote several restaurants in one area.
0 10 Miles
0 10 20 Kilometres
Cardigan Bay
Machynlleth
Tywyn
Aberdovey
Eglwysfach
Talybont
Aberystwyth
Devil's Bridge
Llanfihangel-y-Creuddyn
Aberaeron
New Quay
Tregaron
Cambrian
Lampeter
Cardigan
Newcastle Emlyn
WEST WALES
Newport
Fishguard
Llandovery
Llanwrda
St David's
Carmarthen
Nantgaredig
Llandeilo
Haverfordwest
Narberth
St Clears
Llandybie
Ammanford
Broad Haven
Milford Haven
Laugharne
Pendine
Pembroke Dock
Saundersfoot
Kidwelly
Pontardawe
Llanelli
Tenby
Pembroke
Loughor
Gorseinon
Neath
Carmarthen Bay
Swansea
Reynoldston
Parkmill
Port Talbot
Mumbles
Port Eynon
Bristol Channel
Lynton
Ilfracombe
Lundy
A489
A493
A44
A4120
A487
A485
A486
A475
A484
A482
A483
A4 87
A40
A478
A48
A476
A474
A4067
A4069
A4076
A 477
A4139
A4118
M4
A4107
A361
A39
49
48
47
45
43
42
40

10

Mountains
Marton
Minsterley
SHROPSHIRE
Wolverhampton
Newtown
Dolfor
Church Stretton
Bridgnorth
Dudley
Halesowen
Munslow
Wistanstow
Stourbridge
Llanidloes
Llanfair Waterdine
Craven Arms
West Hagley
Kidderminster
Llangurig
MID WALES
Bewdley
Ludlow
Chaddesley Corbett
Knighton
Stourport-on-Severn
Bromsgrove
Rhayader
Ombersley
Droitwich
Llandrindod Wells
Titley
Leominster
Worcester
Kington
Bromyard
Beulah
Builth Wells
Great Malvern
WORCESTER-SHIRE
Llangammarch Wells
Wellington
Pershore
Llanwrtyd Wells
HEREFORDSHIRE
Colwall
Hay-on-Wye
Hereford
Ledbury
Woolhope
Tewkesbury
Talgarth
Eldersfield
Corse Lawn
Brecon
Felin Fach
Cheltenham
Gloucestershire
Llanhamlach
Ross-on-Wye
Gloucester
Skenfrith
Crickhowell
Abergavenny
Llanddewi Skirrid
GLOUCESTERSHIRE
Brynmawr
Monmouth
Cinderford
Arlingham
Whitebrook
Sapperton
Ebbw Vale
Merthyr Tydfil
Nant-y-derry
GWENT
Stroud
Aberdare
Abertillery
Bargoed
Pontypool
Usk
Dursley
Treorchy
Chepstow
Severn
GLAMORGAN
Cwmbran
Tetbury
Maesteg
Pontypridd
Thornbury
Crudwell
Bassaleg
Newport
Caldicot
Didmarton
Malmesbury
Caerphilly
Easton Grey
Pyle
Llantrisant
Pentyrch
Chipping Sodbury
Bristol Filton
Castle Combe
Avonmouth
Bridgend
St Fagans
Portishead
Chippenham
Porthcawl
Cardiff
Bristol
Colerne
Clevedon
Hotwells
Corsham
Cowbridge
Penarth
Bath
Melksham
Backwell
Bristol International
Bradford-on-Avon
Barry
Chew Magna
Cardiff International
Combe Hay
Holt
Weston-super-Mare
Trowbridge
Cheddar
Midsomer Norton
Radstock
Upton Scudamore
Wookey Hole
Burnham-on-Sea
Frome
Warminster
Minehead
Wells
Horningsham
Crockerton
Shepton Mallet
Bridgwater
Glastonbury

10
8
7

12

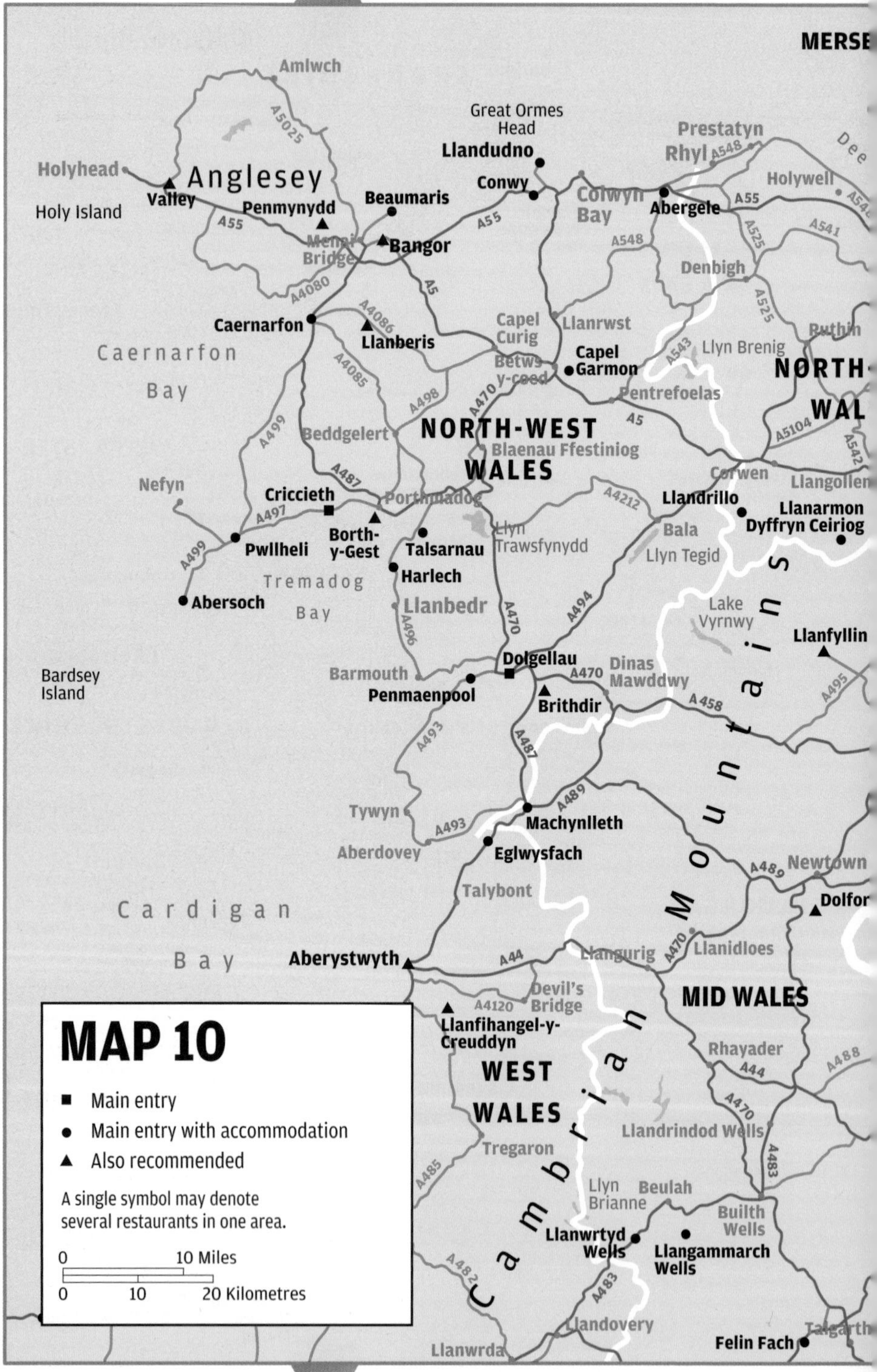
MAP 10
Main entry
Main entry with accommodation
Also recommended
A single symbol may denote several restaurants in one area.
0 10 Miles
0 10 20 Kilometres
Anglesey
Holyhead
Holy Island
Valley
Amlwch
Penmynydd
Beaumaris
Menai Bridge
Bangor
Great Ormes Head
Llandudno
Conwy
Colwyn Bay
Prestatyn
Rhyl
Abergele
Holywell
Denbigh
Ruthin
Caernarfon
Llanberis
Capel Curig
Llanrwst
Capel Garmon
Betws-y-coed
Llyn Brenig
Pentrefoelas
NORTH-EAST WALES
Caernarfon Bay
NORTH-WEST WALES
Beddgelert
Blaenau Ffestiniog
Nefyn
Criccieth
Porthmadog
Borth-y-Gest
Pwllheli
Talsarnau
Harlech
Abersoch
Tremadog Bay
Llanbedr
Llyn Trawsfynydd
Corwen
Llangollen
Llandrillo
Llanarmon Dyffryn Ceiriog
Bala
Llyn Tegid
Lake Vyrnwy
Llanfyllin
Bardsey Island
Barmouth
Penmaenpool
Dolgellau
Brithdir
Dinas Mawddwy
Tywyn
Aberdovey
Machynlleth
Eglwysfach
Talybont
Newtown
Dolfor
Cardigan Bay
Aberystwyth
Llangurig
Llanidloes
Devil's Bridge
Llanfihangel-y-Creuddyn
MID WALES
Rhayader
WEST WALES
Llandrindod Wells
Tregaron
Llyn Brianne
Beulah
Builth Wells
Llanwrtyd Wells
Llangammarch Wells
Cambrian Mountains
Llandovery
Llanwrda
Talgarth
Felin Fach
MERSE
Dee
A5025 A55 A4080 A5 A4086 A4085 A498 A499 A487 A497 A470 A548 A55 A525 A541 A543 A5104 A542 A4212 A494 A496 A458 A495 A493 A489 A470 A44 A4120 A488 A483 A485 A482

9

12

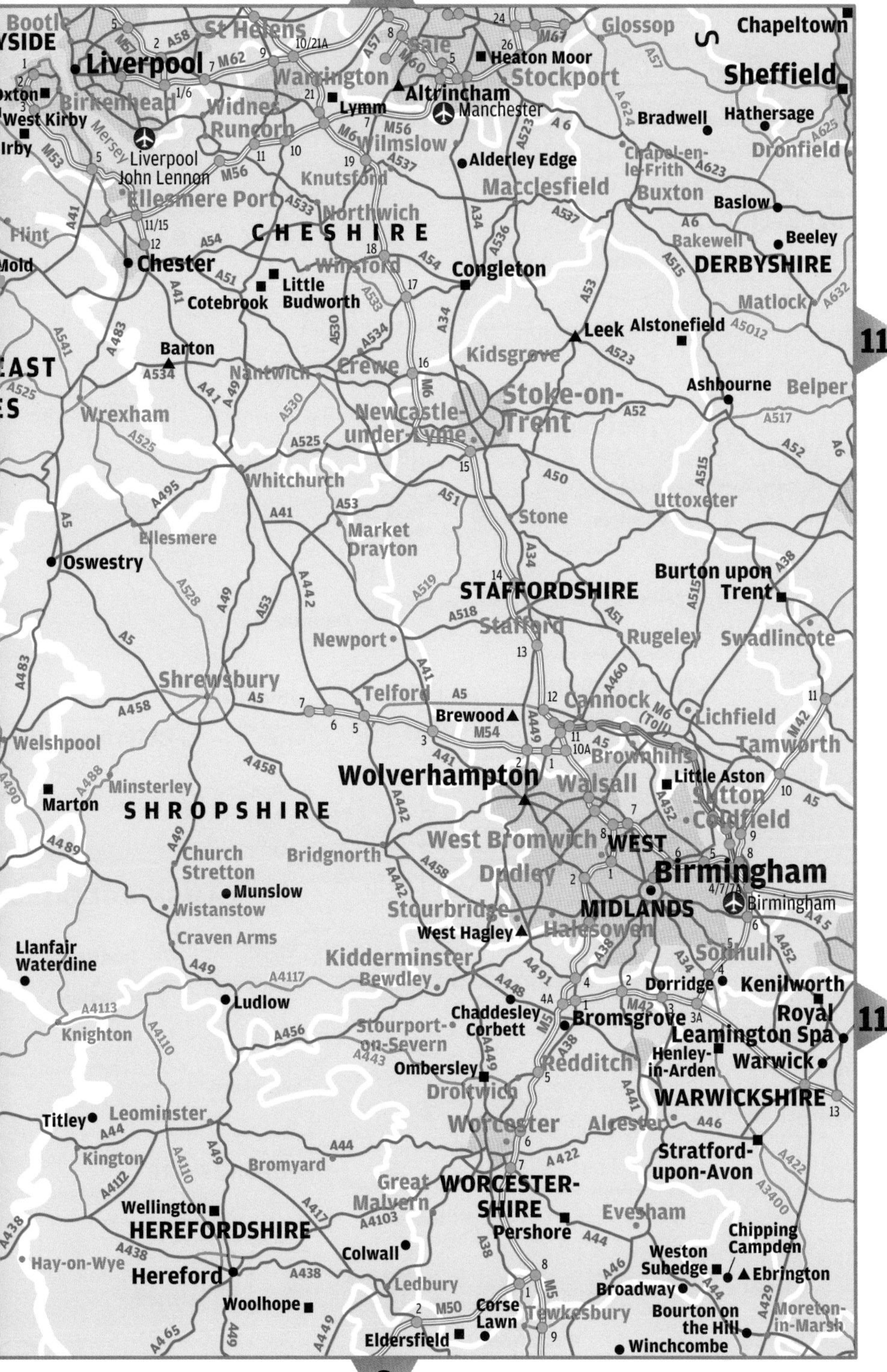
Bootle
Liverpool
St Helens
Warrington
Sale
Heaton Moor
Stockport
Glossop
Chapeltown
Sheffield
Birkenhead
Widnes
Lymm
Altrincham
Manchester
West Kirby
Irby
Runcorn
Wilmslow
Bradwell
Hathersage
Dronfield
Liverpool John Lennon
Mersey
Alderley Edge
Knutsford
Chapel-en-le-Frith
Macclesfield
Buxton
Baslow
Ellesmere Port
Northwich
CHESHIRE
Bakewell
Beeley
Flint
Mold
Chester
Winsford
Congleton
DERBYSHIRE
Cotebrook
Little Budworth
Matlock
Leek
Alstonefield
Barton
Kidsgrove
Crewe
Nantwich
Ashbourne
Belper
Stoke-on-Trent
Newcastle-under-Lyme
Wrexham
Whitchurch
Uttoxeter
Stone
Ellesmere
Market Drayton
Oswestry
STAFFORDSHIRE
Burton upon Trent
Stafford
Newport
Rugeley
Swadlincote
Shrewsbury
Telford
Cannock
Lichfield
Brewood
Welshpool
Tamworth
Brownhills
Wolverhampton
Walsall
Little Aston
Sutton Coldfield
Minsterley
Marton
SHROPSHIRE
West Bromwich
WEST MIDLANDS
Church Stretton
Bridgnorth
Dudley
Birmingham
Munslow
Wistanstow
Stourbridge
Craven Arms
West Hagley
Halesowen
Solihull
Llanfair Waterdine
Kidderminster
Bewdley
Dorridge
Kenilworth
Ludlow
Chaddesley Corbett
Bromsgrove
Royal Leamington Spa
Knighton
Stourport-on-Severn
Henley-in-Arden
Warwick
Ombersley
Redditch
Droitwich
WARWICKSHIRE
Titley
Leominster
Worcester
Alcester
Kington
Bromyard
Stratford-upon-Avon
Great Malvern
WORCESTERSHIRE
Wellington
HEREFORDSHIRE
Pershore
Evesham
Chipping Campden
Colwall
Weston Subedge
Ebrington
Hay-on-Wye
Hereford
Ledbury
Broadway
Woolhope
Corse Lawn
Tewkesbury
Bourton on the Hill
Moreton-in-Marsh
Eldersfield
Winchcombe

11

11

9

13
10
10
8
Rotherham
Maltby
Bawtry
Sheffield
Ridgeway
Dronfield
Chesterfield
DERBYSHIRE
Worksop
Retford
Gainsborough
Market Rasen
Ludford
Louth
Lincoln
Horncastle
Partney
LINCOLNSHIRE
Sutton in Ashfield
Mansfield
Caunton
Newark-on-Trent
Alfreton
NOTTINGHAMSHIRE
Hucknall
Belper
Hough on the Hill
Heanor
Ilkeston
Nottingham
Sleaford
Boston
Darley Abbey
Derby
Langar
Great Gonerby
Grantham
Long Eaton
Plumtree
Stathern
Woolsthrpe by Belvoir
East Midlands
Spalding
Holbeach
Loughborough
Melton Mowbray
Clipsham
Bourne
Ashby de la Zouch
Woodhouse Eaves
Rutland Water
Market Deeping
Coalville
LEICESTERSHIRE
Oakham
Hambleton
Stamford
Easton on the Hill
Leicester
RUTLAND
Peterborough
Wigston
Uppingham
Atherstone
Kibworth Beauchamp
Kibworth Harcourt
Elton
Whittlesey
March
Hinckley
Fotheringhay
Nuneaton
Corby
Bedworth
Market Harborough
Chatteris
Lutterworth
Oundle
CAMBRIDGESHIRE
Coventry
Kettering
Rugby
Keyston
Huntingdon
St Ives
Spaldwick
Hemingford Grey
NORTHAMPTONSHIRE
Royal Leamington Spa
East Haddon
Wellingborough
Rushden
Grafham Water
Warwick
Daventry
Northampton
St Neots
Bolnhurst
WARWICKSHIRE
Roade
Bedford
Towcester
BEDFORDSHIRE
Paulerspury
Old Warden
Biggleswade
Milton Keynes
Royston
Banbury
Brackley
Shefford
Woburn
Letchworth
Baldock
Buckingham
Bletchley
Newton Longville
William
Hitchin
Chipping Norton
BUCKINGHAMSHIRE
Leighton Buzzard
Stevenage

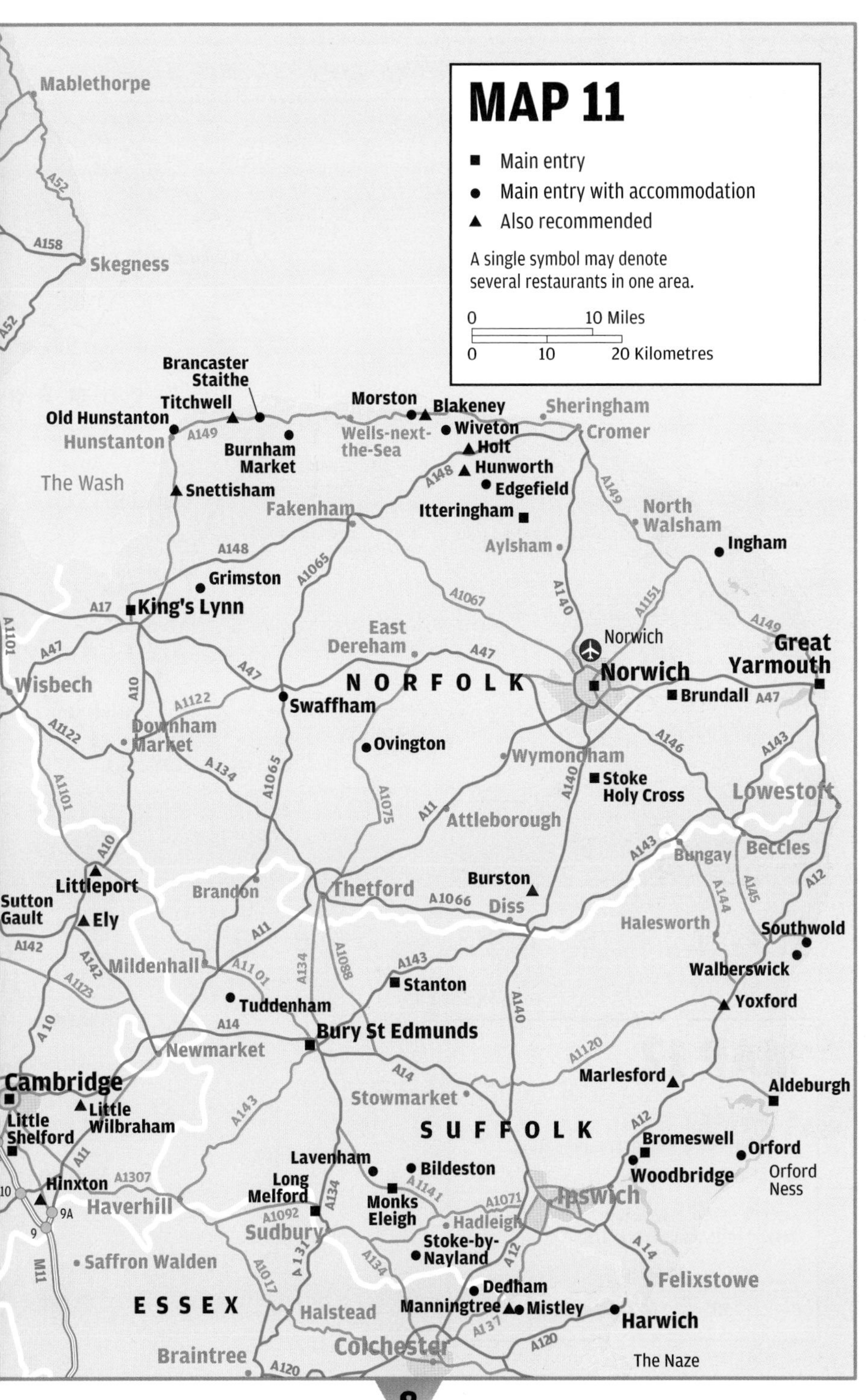
MAP 11
Main entry
Main entry with accommodation
Also recommended
A single symbol may denote several restaurants in one area.
0 10 Miles
0 10 20 Kilometres
Mablethorpe
Skegness
Brancaster Staithe
Titchwell
Old Hunstanton
Hunstanton
Burnham Market
Morston
Blakeney
Wells-next-the-Sea
Wiveton
Sheringham
Cromer
Holt
Hunworth
Edgefield
Itteringham
The Wash
Snettisham
Fakenham
North Walsham
Aylsham
Ingham
Grimston
King's Lynn
Norwich
Great Yarmouth
East Dereham
NORFOLK
Brundall
Wisbech
Swaffham
Downham Market
Ovington
Wymondham
Stoke Holy Cross
Lowestoft
Attleborough
Bungay
Beccles
Littleport
Brandon
Thetford
Burston
Diss
Sutton Gault
Ely
Halesworth
Southwold
Mildenhall
Walberswick
Stanton
Tuddenham
Yoxford
Bury St Edmunds
Newmarket
Cambridge
Marlesford
Aldeburgh
Stowmarket
Little Wilbraham
Little Shelford
SUFFOLK
Bromeswell
Orford
Woodbridge
Orford Ness
Lavenham
Bildeston
Long Melford
Hinxton
Monks Eleigh
Ipswich
Haverhill
Hadleigh
Sudbury
Stoke-by-Nayland
Saffron Walden
Felixstowe
Dedham
ESSEX
Halstead
Manningtree
Mistley
Harwich
Colchester
Braintree
The Naze
A52
A158
A149
A148
A1065
A17
A1101
A47
A10
A1122
A134
A1067
A140
A1151
A146
A143
A1075
A11
A1066
A144
A145
A12
A142
A1123
A1101
A1088
A14
A1120
A1307
A1092
A1141
A1071
A131
A1017
A137
A120
M11
10
9A
9

15

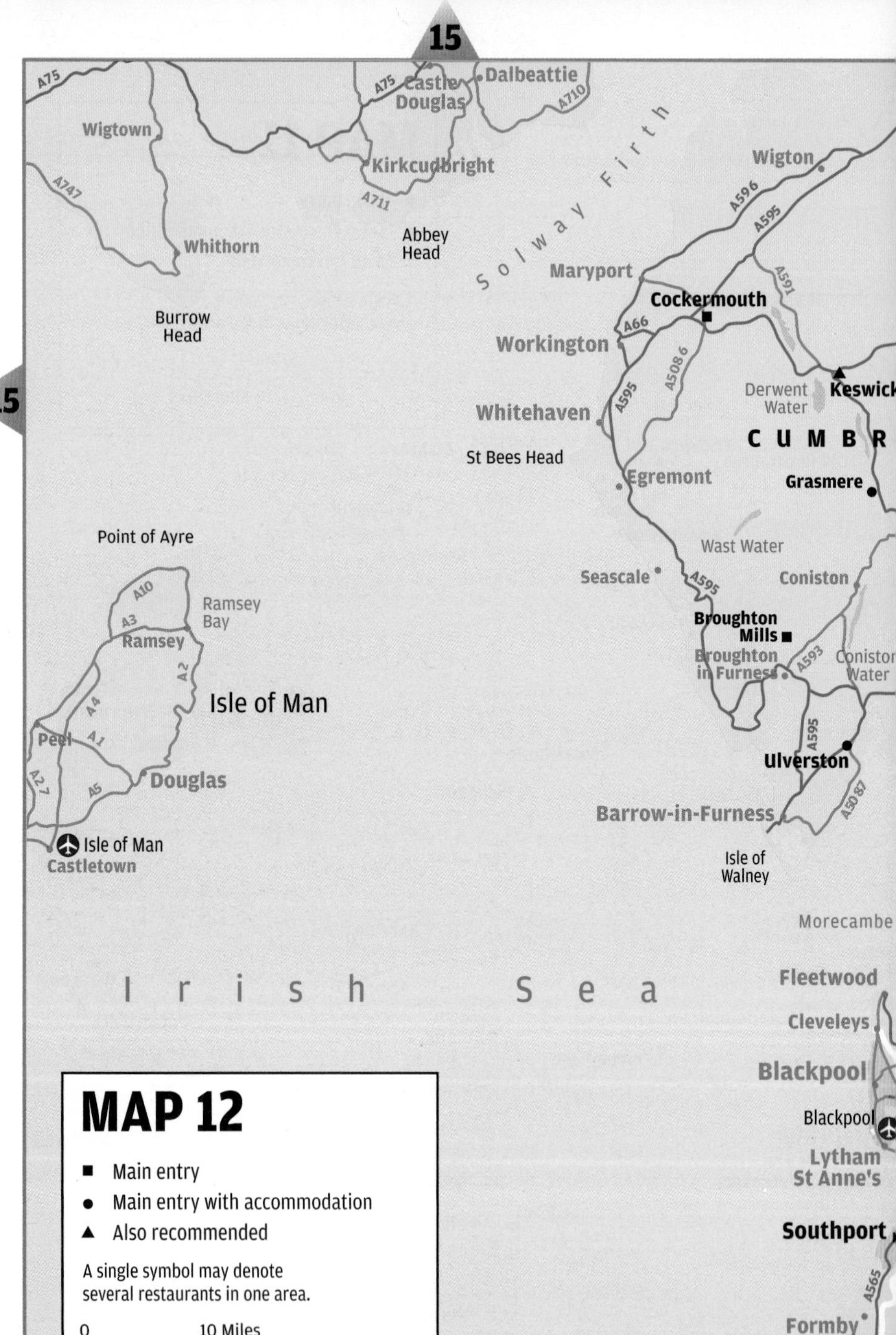

MAP 12

■ Main entry
● Main entry with accommodation
▲ Also recommended

A single symbol may denote several restaurants in one area.

0 10 Miles
0 10 20 Kilometres

10

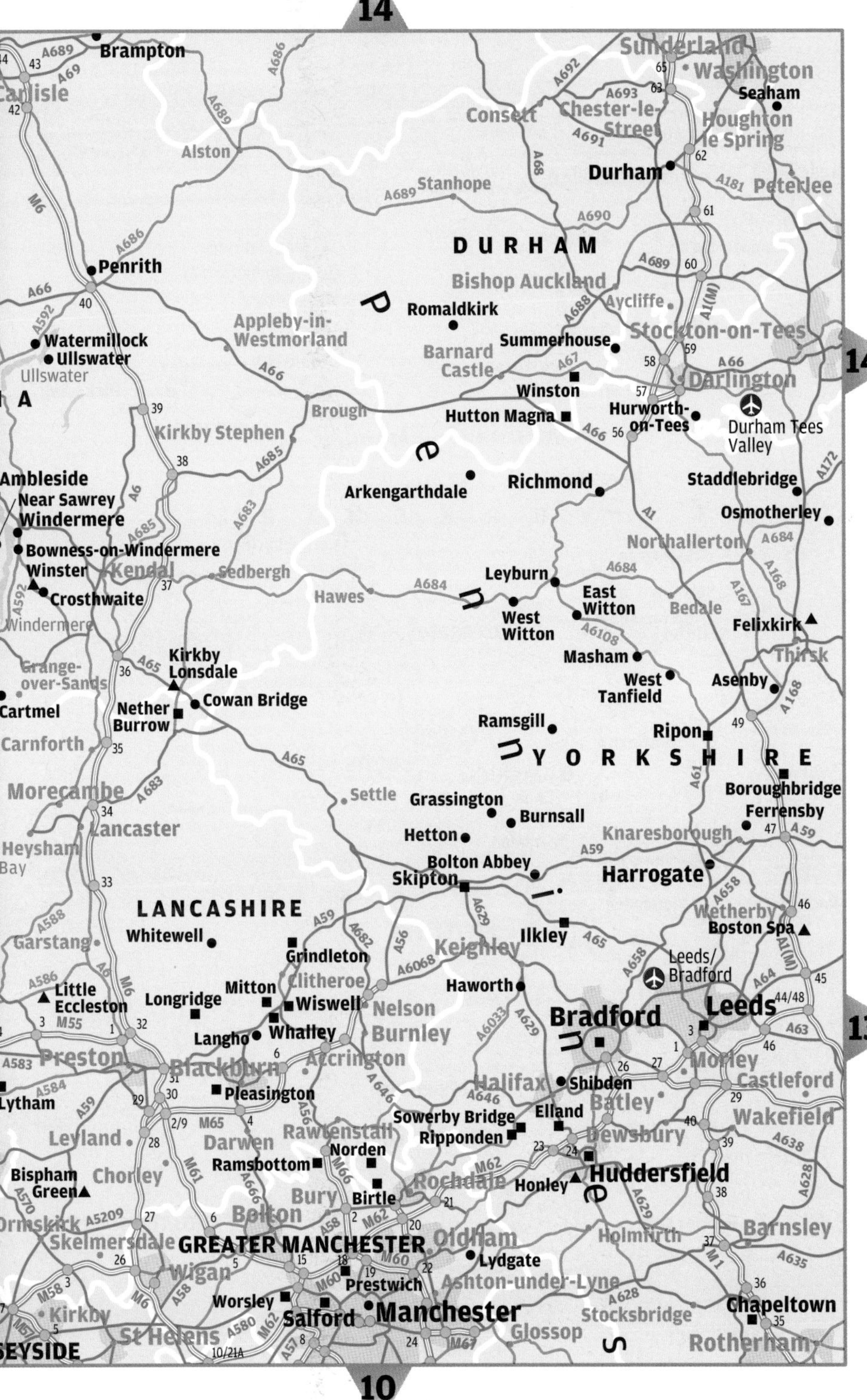
14
Brampton
A689
A69
Carlisle
A686
A689
A692
Sunderland
Washington
Seaham
A693
Chester-le-Street
Consett
A691
Houghton le Spring
Alston
Durham
A68
A181
Peterlee
M6
A689
Stanhope
A690
DURHAM
A686
Penrith
A689
Bishop Auckland
A66
Aycliffe
A1(M)
Romaldkirk
A688
Appleby-in-Westmorland
A592
Watermillock
Ullswater
Ullswater
Summerhouse
Stockton-on-Tees
Barnard Castle
A66
A67
A66
Darlington
14
Winston
A
Brough
Hutton Magna
Hurworth-on-Tees
Durham Tees Valley
Kirkby Stephen
A66
A685
Ambleside
Near Sawrey
Windermere
Arkengarthdale
Richmond
Staddlebridge
A172
A6
A685
A683
A1
Osmotherley
Bowness-on-Windermere
Northallerton
A684
Winster
Kendal
Sedbergh
A684
Leyburn
A684
A168
Crosthwaite
Hawes
A592
East Witton
Bedale
A167
Windermere
West Witton
A6108
Felixkirk
Pennines
Kirkby Lonsdale
Masham
Thirsk
Grange-over-Sands
A65
Cartmel
Nether Burrow
Cowan Bridge
West Tanfield
Asenby
A168
Ramsgill
Ripon
Carnforth
A65
YORKSHIRE
A61
Boroughbridge
Morecambe
A683
Settle
Grassington
Burnsall
Ferrensby
Lancaster
Hetton
Knaresborough
A59
Heysham Bay
Bolton Abbey
A59
Skipton
Harrogate
A658
LANCASHIRE
A588
A59
A629
Wetherby
Boston Spa
Garstang
Whitewell
A682
A56
Keighley
Ilkley
A65
A1(M)
Grindleton
A6068
A658
Leeds/Bradford
A586
Clitheroe
A64
Little Eccleston
A6
M6
Longridge
Mitton
Wiswell
Nelson
Haworth
Leeds
13
Bradford
M55
Langho
Whalley
Burnley
A6033
A629
Morley
A63
A583
Preston
Blackburn
Accrington
Lytham
A584
Pleasington
A646
Halifax
Shibden
Castleford
A59
M65
A56
A646
Batley
Wakefield
Leyland
Darwen
Rawtenstall
Sowerby Bridge
Elland
Ripponden
Dewsbury
A638
Norden
M61
Ramsbottom
M66
M62
Huddersfield
Bispham Green
Chorley
A666
Rochdale
Honley
A628
A570
Bury
Birtle
A629
A5209
Bolton
M62
Ormskirk
A58
Holmfirth
Barnsley
Skelmersdale
GREATER MANCHESTER
Oldham
M1
A635
Wigan
M60
Lydgate
M60
Prestwich
Ashton-under-Lyne
M58
A58
A628
M6
Worsley
Salford
Manchester
Chapeltown
Kirkby
Stocksbridge
M57
St Helens
A580
M62
Glossop
A57
M67
Rotherham
SEYSIDE
10

14
12
12
10
Bishop Auckland
Romaldkirk
Aycliffe
Stockton-on-Tees
Redcar
Middlesbrough
Guisborough
Summerhouse
Barnard Castle
Winston
Darlington
Brough
Hutton Magna
Hurworth-on-Tees
Durham Tees Valley
Kirkby Stephen
Arkengarthdale
Richmond
Staddlebridge
Osmotherley
Northallerton
Leyburn
East Witton
West Witton
Hawes
Bedale
Felixkirk
Helmsley
Sinnington
Pickering
Harome
Masham
West Tanfield
Thirsk
Oldstead
Asenby
Ramsgill
Ripon
Malton
YORKSHIRE
Pennines
Boroughbridge
Settle
Grassington
Burnsall
Hetton
Ferrensby
Newton-on-Ouse
Knaresborough
Bolton Abbey
Skipton
Harrogate
York
Grindleton
Ilkley
Wetherby
Boston Spa
Keighley
Tadcaster
Clitheroe
Haworth
Leeds/ Bradford
Leeds
Nelson
Wiswell
Burnley
Bradford
Selby
Accrington
Morley
Halifax
Shibden
Castleford
Rawtenstall
Sowerby Bridge
Elland
Batley
Wakefield
Goole
Pontefract
Ramsbottom
Ripponden
Dewsbury
Norden
Huddersfield
Thorne
Honley
Bury
Birtle
Rochdale
Bentley
Oldham
Holmfirth
Barnsley
Lydgate
Prestwich
Doncaster
Worsley
Ashton-under-Lyne
Salford
Manchester
Robin Hood
Stocksbridge
Chapeltown
Rotherham
Bawtry
Glossop
Sale
Heaton Moor
Maltby
Gainsborough
Stockport
Sheffield
Altrincham
Manchester
Bradwell
Hathersage
Ridgeway
Worksop
Retford
Wilmslow
Chapel-en-le-Frith
Dronfield
Knutsford
Alderley Edge
NOTTINGHAMSHIRE
Macclesfield
Buxton
Chesterfield
Baslow
Bakewell
Beeley
Congleton
DERBYSHIRE
Mansfield
Caunton
Matlock

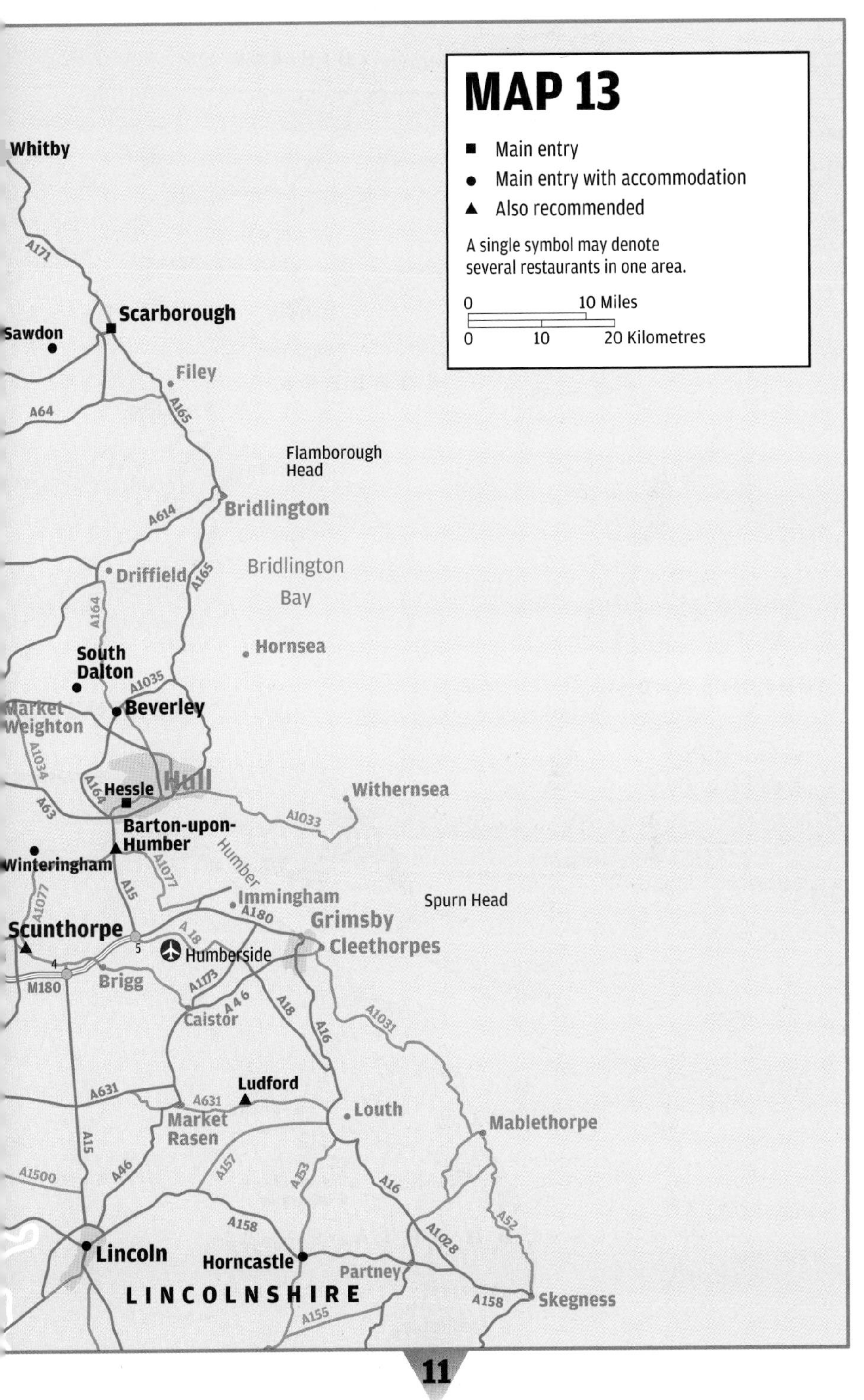
MAP 13
Main entry
Main entry with accommodation
Also recommended
A single symbol may denote several restaurants in one area.
0
10 Miles
0
10
20 Kilometres
Whitby
A171
Scarborough
Sawdon
Filey
A64
A165
Flamborough Head
A614
Bridlington
Bridlington Bay
Driffield
A165
A164
Hornsea
South Dalton
A1035
Beverley
Market Weighton
A1034
Hull
A164
Hessle
A63
Withernsea
A1033
Barton-upon-Humber
Humber
A1077
Winteringham
A15
A1077
Immingham
A180
Spurn Head
Grimsby
Scunthorpe
A18
5
Cleethorpes
Humberside
4
M180
Brigg
A1173
A46
Caistor
A18
A16
A1031
Ludford
A631
A631
Louth
Market Rasen
Mablethorpe
A15
A1500
A46
A157
A153
A16
A52
A1028
A158
Lincoln
Horncastle
Partney
LINCOLNSHIRE
A158
Skegness
A155

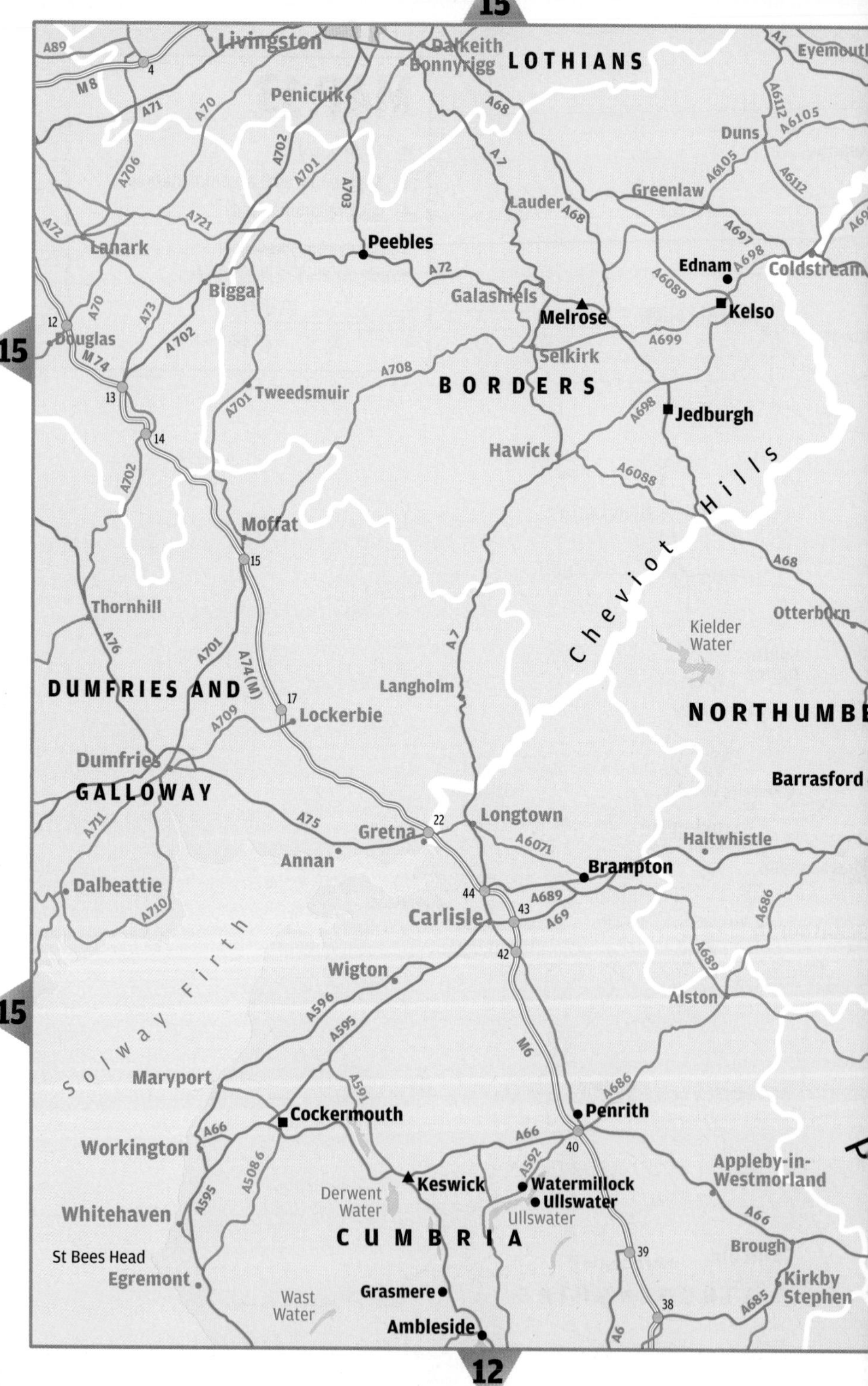
15
15
15
12
LOTHIANS
BORDERS
DUMFRIES AND
GALLOWAY
NORTHUMBE
CUMBRIA
Cheviot Hills
Solway Firth
Livingston
Dalkeith
Bonnyrigg
Eyemouth
Penicuik
Duns
Greenlaw
Lauder
Peebles
Lanark
Ednam
Coldstream
Biggar
Galashiels
Melrose
Kelso
Douglas
Selkirk
Tweedsmuir
Jedburgh
Hawick
Moffat
Thornhill
Kielder Water
Otterburn
Langholm
Lockerbie
Dumfries
Barrasford
Longtown
Gretna
Haltwhistle
Annan
Brampton
Dalbeattie
Carlisle
Wigton
Alston
Maryport
Penrith
Cockermouth
Workington
Appleby-in-Westmorland
Keswick
Watermillock
Ullswater
Derwent Water
Whitehaven
Brough
St Bees Head
Egremont
Kirkby Stephen
Grasmere
Wast Water
Ambleside
A89
M8
A71
A70
A68
A1
A6112
A6105
A702
A706
A701
A703
A7
A721
A72
A697
A698
A6089
A73
A699
M74
A708
A76
A74(M)
A709
A75
A6071
A711
A689
A69
A710
A686
A596
A595
M6
A591
A66
A5086
A592
A685
A6
4
12
13
14
15
17
22
44
43
42
40
39
38

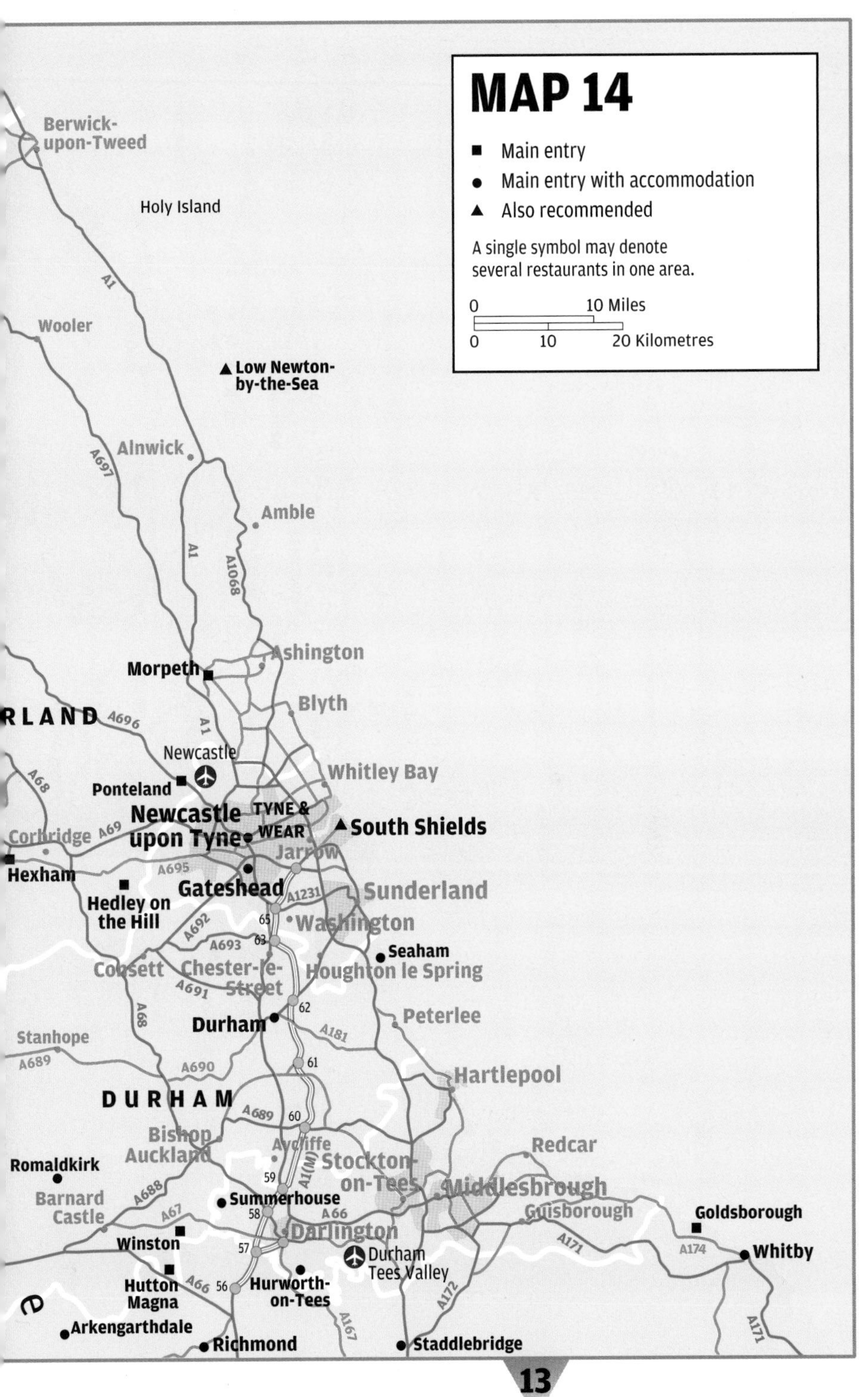
MAP 14
Main entry
Main entry with accommodation
Also recommended
A single symbol may denote several restaurants in one area.
0
10 Miles
0
10
20 Kilometres
Berwick-upon-Tweed
Holy Island
Wooler
Low Newton-by-the-Sea
Alnwick
Amble
Ashington
Morpeth
Blyth
RLAND
Newcastle
Whitley Bay
Ponteland
Newcastle upon Tyne
TYNE & WEAR
South Shields
Corbridge
Jarrow
Hexham
Hedley on the Hill
Gateshead
Sunderland
Washington
Seaham
Consett
Chester-le-Street
Houghton le Spring
Durham
Peterlee
Stanhope
Hartlepool
DURHAM
Bishop Auckland
Aycliffe
Redcar
Romaldkirk
Stockton-on-Tees
Middlesbrough
Barnard Castle
Summerhouse
Guisborough
Goldsborough
Winston
Darlington
Whitby
Durham Tees Valley
Hutton Magna
Hurworth-on-Tees
Arkengarthdale
Richmond
Staddlebridge

Orkney Islands
Mainland
Brough Head
Stronsay
Shapinsay
Finstown
Kirkwall
Stromness
Scapa Flow
Hoy
St Margaret's Hope
South Ronaldsay
Burwick
Pentland Firth
Dunnet Head
Island of Stroma
Duncansby Head
John o'Groats
Scrabster
Thurso
Noss Head
Wick
Shetland Islands
Not to same scale
Herma Ness
Haroldswick
Gutcher
Unst
Belmont
Fetlar
North Roe
Yell
Esha Ness
Hillswick
St Magnus Bay
Ulsta
Papa Stour
Whalsay
Sandness
Mainland
Lerwick
Scalloway
Bressay
Sumburgh
Sumburgh Head
Outer Hebrides
Butt of Lewis
Port of Ness
Barvas
Tolsta Head
Stornoway
Callanish
Isle of Lewis
Kebock Head
Tarbert
Sgarasta Bheag
Harris
Leverburgh
Cape Wrath
Durness
Whiten Head
Melvich
Tongue
Loch Hope
Loch Naver
Altnaharra
Kinbrace
Latheron
Scourie
Point of Stoer
Lochinver
Rubha Coigeach
Inchnadamph
Elphin
Loch Shin
Lairg
Helmsdale
Brora
The Minch
Cailleach Head
Ullapool
Bonar Bridge
Dornoch
Tain
Laide
HIGHLANDS AND ISLANDS
Moray Firth
Gairloch
Loch Maree
Alness
Invergordon
Cromarty
Lossiemouth
Portknockie
Buckie
Banff
Macduff
Fraserburgh
Rattray Head
Elgin
Lochmaddy
North Uist
Benbecula
Stein
Colbost
Uig
Dunvegan
Portree
The Little Minch
Kinlochewe
Garve
Achnasheen
Dingwall
Fortrose
Nairn
Forres
Aberchirder
Mintlaw
Peterhead
Shieldaig
Muir of Ord
Inverness
Tore
Auldearn
Craigellachie
Keith
Turriff
Loch Monar
Beauly
Dufftown
Huntly
Ellon
Raasay
Plockton
Stromeferry
Cannich
Drumnadrochit
Loch Ness
Grantown-on-Spey
Oldmeldrum
Udny Green
Rhynie
Sconser
Scalpay
Skye
Harrapool
Kyle of Lochalsh
Shiel Bridge
Loch Affric
Invermoriston
Carrbridge
GRAMPIAN
Alford
Inverurie
Dyce
South Uist
Lochboisdale
Sleat
Fort Augustus
Aviemore
Aberdeen
Barra
Eriskay
Canna
Armadale
Newtonmore
Kingussie
Grampian Mountains
Ballater
Banchory
Castlebay
Kinloch
Rhum
Mallaig
Loch Quoich
Loch Arkaig
Loch Lochy
Invergarry
Braemar
Stonehaven
Eigg
Muck
Mingulay
Sea of the Hebrides
Galmisdale
Glenfinnan
Spean Bridge
Dalwhinnie
Loch Ericht
Fort William
Blair Atholl
Killiecrankie
Inverbervie
Loch Shiel
Kilchoan
Strontian
Blackwater Reservoir
Loch Rannoch
Loch Tummel
Pitlochry
Kirriemuir
Brechin
Montrose
Coll
Ballachulish

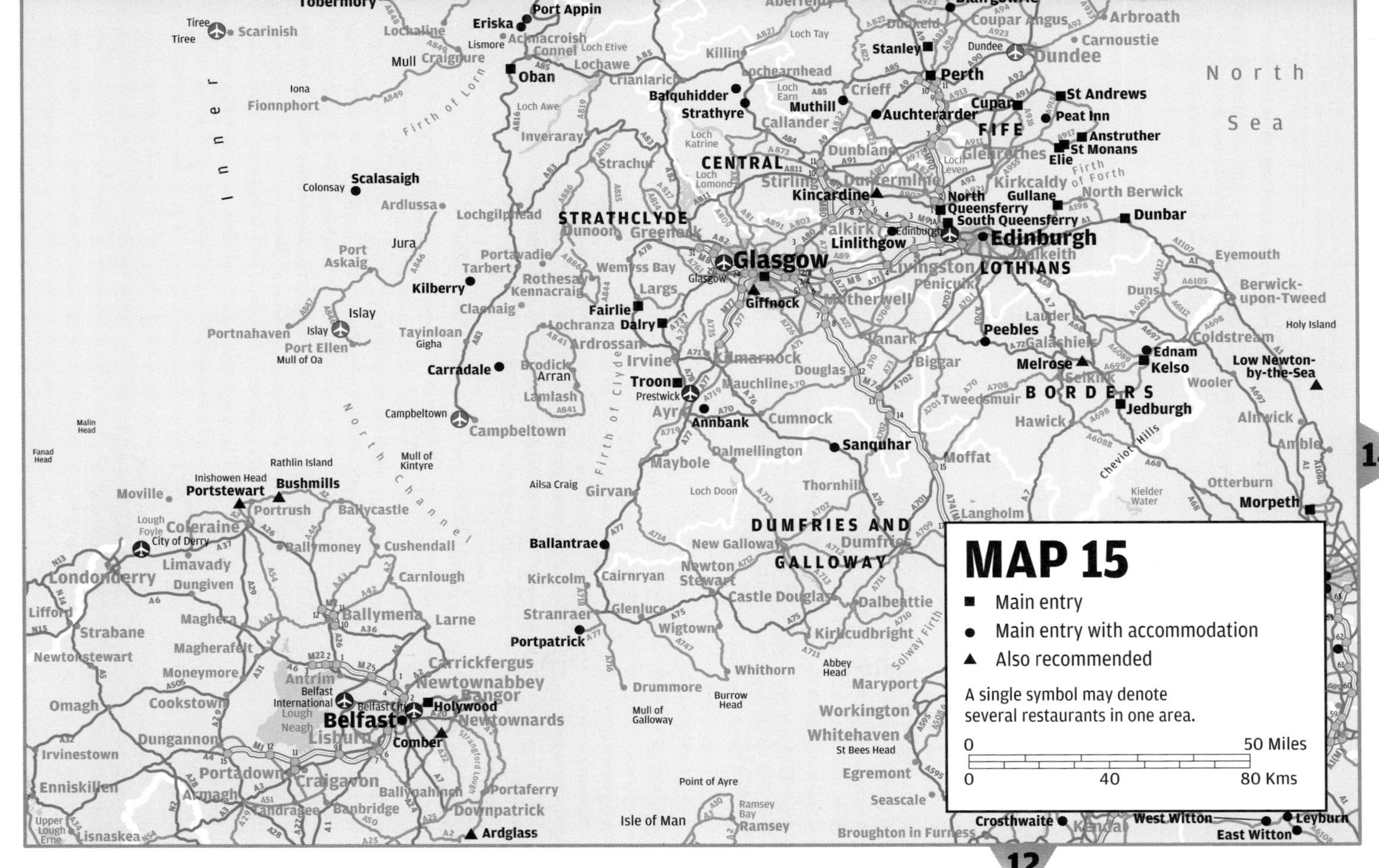
MAP 15
■ Main entry
● Main entry with accommodation
▲ Also recommended
A single symbol may denote several restaurants in one area.
0 50 Miles
0 40 80 Kms
14
12
North Sea
Inner
Firth of Lorn
Firth of Forth
Firth of Clyde
North Channel
Solway Firth
Cheviot Hills
STRATHCLYDE
CENTRAL
FIFE
LOTHIANS
BORDERS
DUMFRIES AND GALLOWAY
Port Appin
Eriska
Oban
Scalasaigh
Colonsay
Kilberry
Carradale
Balquhidder
Strathyre
Muthill
Auchterarder
Stanley
Perth
Cupar
St Andrews
Peat Inn
Anstruther
St Monans
Elie
Kincardine
North Queensferry
South Queensferry
Gullane
Dunbar
Edinburgh
Linlithgow
Glasgow
Giffnock
Fairlie
Dalry
Troon
Annbank
Sanquhar
Peebles
Melrose
Ednam
Kelso
Jedburgh
Low Newton-by-the-Sea
Morpeth
Ballantrae
Portpatrick
Portstewart
Bushmills
Holywood
Belfast
Comber
Ardglass
Crosthwaite
West Witton
Leyburn
East Witton

Note: The INDEX BY TOWN does not include London entries.

Features

Chef (C) and Sommelier (S) Interviews

C

Q

R

S

X

Y

Z

This book couldn't happen without a cast of thousands. Our thanks are due to the following contributors. A full list can be found at www.thegoodfoodguide.co.uk

Mr Cyrus Abadeh
Ms Ydolapo Abbay
Ms Alison Abbott
Miss Carrie Abbott
Miss Harriet Abbott
Mr Mike Abbotts
Miss Sagal Abdillahi
Mrs Patricia Abra
Mr Anthony Abrahams
Mr Alasdair Adam
Mr Keith Adams
Mr Matthew Adams
Ms Susan Adams
Mr Andy Addison
Mr Richard Adey
Mr James Adlem
Mr Jon Adriaenssens
Mrs Beverley Agland
Ms Danielle Ahlquist
Miss Tahsin Ahmed
Miss Hasna Aitissa
Mr Stuart Alder
Mr David Alderson
Mrs Victoria Alderwick
Ms Jean Aldred
Mr Dean Aldridge
Mr Fawaz Alduaij
Mr Rocky Ali
Mrs Karena Allanson
Mrs Andrea Allen
Mr Chris Allen
Mr Henry Allen
Miss Katie Allen
Mr Luke Allen
Dr Margaret Allen
Mr Tom Allen
Mrs Theresa Allen-Gibbs
Mr Frank Allison
Miss Selena Allwood
Ms Maria Aloia
Mr Ian Ambrose
Mr Steve Ambrose-Jones
Mr S Amey
Mr A Amin
Mr Gary Anderson
Mr Ian Anderson
Ms Vickie Anderson
Ms Barbara Anderton
Ms Flora Andrews
Mr Mike Andrews
Mr Philip Andrews
Mrs Victoria Andrews
Mr Max Andrucki
Mr Phi Angell
Mrs Mary Anslow
Ms Martyna Antczak
Mr Steffan Aquarone
Ms Damaris Armstrong
Ms Hilary Armstrong
Mr Ross Arnold
Ms Rebecca Aron
Dr Nicholas Arthur
Mr Michael Ashdown
Ms Lara Ashley
Miss Laura Ashley
Mr Simon Ashley
Ms Maxine Ashman
Ms Caroline Ashton
Mr David Ashton
Mr Dion Ashton
Mr John Ashton
Mrs Karen Ashton
Mr Michael Ashurst
Miss Jo Aspin
Ms Wendy Aspland
Mr Tim Assirati
Mr Stefanos Astin
Ms Margaret Atherton
Miss Amanda Atkinson
Mr Brian Atkinson
Ms Sharlaine Atkinson
Mr Frank Attwood
Mr M Auld
Mrs Michelle Austin
Mr Frank Auton
Dr David Awbery
Mr James Ayres
Mr Simon Ayrton
Mr David Babb
Miss Frances Babirecki
Mr Ram Babu
Ms Patricia Bach
Mr Oliver Badcock

Miss Donia Baddou
Mr Ian Baggott
Mr Michael Bagshaw
Mr Bradley Bahar
Mr Barry Bailey
Mr Kimball Bailey
Mr Paul Bailey
Ms Rita Bailey
Ms Adele Bain
Mr Cameron Baker
Mrs Gail Baker-Bates
Mr David Baley
Mr David Ball
Mr Jason Ball
Ms Lucy Ballands
Mr Daren Balman
Mr Tom Balmer
Ms Sophie Balu
Dr Lisa Bambridge
Mr Graham Banks
Ms Sonia Bannon
Mr Adrian Barber
Mrs Denise Barber
Mrs Kathryn Barber
Miss Kirsty Barber
Mrs Wyn Barber
Mrs Nicola Barclay
Mr Mark Barefoot
Mr Richard Barham
Mrs Beatriz Barker
Mr Brian Barker
Ms Caroline Barker
Mr John Barker
Mr John Barley
Miss Anna Barlow
Mr Chris Barlow
Mr Nick Barlow
Mrs Jane Barnard-Curtis
Mrs Charlotte Barnes
Mr David Barnes
Mr Edward Barnes
Mr Marcus Barnes
Mrs Sue Barnes
Mr David Barnett
Mr Simon Barnett
Ms Helen Barnett-Roberts
Ms Penny Barr
Mr Andrew Barratt
Miss Natalie Barrington
Mr Martin Barron
Mr Hilary Bartlett
Ms Sue Bartlett
Miss Alix Basford
Mrs Loraine Bashforth
Mr Azhar Bashir
Mr Dan Bass
Miss Christina Bassadone
Mrs Geraldine Batchelor
Ms Sarah Bateman
Mr Stuart Bateman
Mrs Alex Bates
Mr John Bates
Mr Ryan Bates
Mr Thomas Bates
Ms Cynthia Battersby
Mr Tim Battle
Miss Amanda Baxter
Mrs Lesley Baxter
Mr Wayne Baxter
Mr Colin Baxter-Jones
Ms Lesley Beach
Mrs Anne Beale
Mrs Sarah Beall
Mr Paul Beard
Ms Emma Beattie
Mr Ken Beattie
Mr Simon Beattie
Ms Deborah Beech
Mr Eitan Beks
Ms Hilary Bell
Mrs Toni Bellord
Mr John Bence
Ms Emma Bennett
Mr Philip Bennett
Mr Roger Bennett
Mr Dominic Benson
Ms Rebecca Benson
Ms Sally Benson
Mr Tim Bent
Miss Katie Bentley
Mr J H P Benyon
Ms Christine Benzie
Mr Mike Benzimra

Mr Antony Berle
Mr Mark Berney
Miss Charlie Berry
Mr David Berry
Mr Simon Berry
Mr Alan Bertram
Miss Alexandra Bertschin
Mr Tom Besant
Ms Justine Besch
Ms Joanna Best
Mrs Dee Beth
Mr Ian Beth
Mr John Bethell
Mr Ian Bethwaite
Ms Janice Beukes
Ms Rebecca Beusmans
Ms Monisha Bharadwaj
Mr Arvind Bhatnagar
Ms Shirley Bibby
Ms Anna Bicheno
Mrs Karen Bickford-Smith
Mr Matthew Biddle
Mr Lyle Bignon
Mrs Erin Bilbao
Mr Geoff Billington
Ms Janet Bingham
Mr Keith Bingham
Mr Lee Bingham
Mrs Kathryn Bingley
Mr Chris and Betty Birch
Mrs Sylvia Birch
Mr Thomas Birch
Miss Daisy Bird
Mrs Debra Birrell
Mr Andrew Birtles
Ms Amanda Bishop
Mrs Corrabeth Bishop
Ms Elaine Bishop
Mr Paul Bishton
Mr Stephen Black
Mr Aaron Blackmore
Ms Suzanne Blacow
Miss Jessica Blair
Ms Louisa Blair
Miss Maggie Blair
Mrs Clare Blake
Miss Helen Blake
Ms Lisa Blake
Ms Nicola Blake
Mr John Blakey
Ms Petra Blazejovska
Mrs Debra Blenkinsop
Mr Steven Bliss
Mr Brian Blissett
Mrs Christine Bloomer
Mrs Sandi Bloomfield
Mr Steve Blore
Mr Stuart Bluck
Mrs Linda Blundell
Ms Eleanor Blyth
Mr Chris Boarland
Mr Andy Boase
Mr Steven Bobasch
Mrs Angela Bobela
Mr Carl Bocock
Mr Andy Boeckstaens
Mr Roger Boissier
Mr Roy Bolan
Mr Adrian Bolton
Ms Julia Bolwell
Ms Angela Bond
Mr Andrew Bone
Mr Matthew Bonnaud
Mrs Claire Bonner
Ms Laura Bonnet
Mr Neil Bonsall
Mr Chris Bonsor
Mrs Judith Booth
Mr Philip Booth
Mr Tony Booth
Miss Charlotte Borgers
Miss Janja Boric
Mr Michael Borlenghi
Mr Stephen Borowiak
Mr Graham Bott
Mr Stephen Botting
Ms Katy Boud
Mr Jim Boulden
Ms Eve Boult
Mr George Boulton
Mrs Una Boulton
Mr Roger Bousfield
Ms Fiona Bowden-Powell

Mr Chris Bowen
Ms Nicola Bowen
Ms Ruth Bowen
Mrs Wendy Bowes
Mrs J Bowis
Ms Melanie Bowman-Oie
Mr David Boyd
Ms Emily Boyd
Mrs Joyce Boyes
Ms Helen Boyle
Mrs Heather Boys
Mr Jonathan Boys
Mrs Louise Boys
Mr Lee Brace
Ms Gill Bracey
Mrs Fiona Braclik
Mr Anthony Bradbury
Mr Neil Bradbury
Mrs Tara Bradford
Mr Chris Bradley
Mrs J Bradley
Mr Neil Bradley
Mr Paul Bradley
Mr Richard Bradley
Mr Matt Bradney
Mr Lucas Brady
Ms Christine Bramham
Mrs Nicky Bramley
Mr Neil Bramwell
Mr Mike Branagan-Harris
Mrs Liz Brand
Ms Sue Branney
Mr Damian Brasher
Mr Alan Braverman
Miss Dominique Brayne
Mrs Judith Brearley
Mr Colin Breckons
Miss Xanthe Breen
Mr Jonathan Brennan
Ms Emma Brett
Ms Karin Brett
Miss Gina Brewer
Mr Roberto Brianti
Ms Nicola Bridgeman
Mr Alan Brierley
Mr Andy Brierley
Mr Thomas Briggs
Mr Peter Brignell
Miss Hannah Brinsden
Ms Amanda Bristol
Miss Louise Brooke
Mrs Helen Brooker
Mrs Om Brooker
Ms Susan Brooker
Mrs Jacky Brookes
Mr Jonathan Brookes
Mrs Polly Brookes
Mrs Caroline Broome
Mrs Judith Brough
Mr Alan Brown
Ms Anne Brown
Mr David Brown
Mr Dominic Brown
Mr Duncan Brown
Miss Lisa Brown
Mrs Lorna Brown
Miss Lynne Brown
Ms Mandy Brown
Mrs Marian Brown
Mrs Sally Brown
Mr Tony Brown
Miss Zara Brown
Mr Tristram Browne
Miss Lucy Brownhill
Mr Robert Bruce
Mr Michael Brunt
Mrs Judy Brunton
Dr Chris Bruton
Mr Dominic Bryan
Mr Robert Bryan
Mrs Martha Bryce
Dr Alice Buchanan
Mrs Lorna Buckle
Mr Alan Buckley
Mr Colin Buckley
Mrs Leanne Bucknor
Mrs Carole Bullock
Mr Max Bullock
Mrs Susan Bullock
Mr David Bullock
Mr Mike Bunce
Mrs Jenny Bunning
Mrs Carole Burch

Mr Clive Burch
Mrs Kath Burdall
Mr Andrew Burge
Mrs Fran Burgess
Ms Nicola Burgess
Mrs Paulette Burgess
Mrs Julie Burgon
Mr Jeremy Burke
Mrs E Burley
Mr Graham Burnett
Mrs Sue Burrows
Mr Antony Bursey
Miss Guin Bursey
Mr Dave Burton
Ms Melva Burton
Mr Owen Burton
Ms Kathryn Busby
Mr Charles Butcher
Miss Felicity Butcher
Mr Mark Butcher
Mrs Michelle Butcher
Ms Sophie Butcher
Mr Thomas Butcher
Mr Luke Butler
Mr Jeremy Buttery
Ms Joanne Byford
Mr Anthony Byrne
Mr Lewis Byrne
Mr Diego Cabeza De Vaca
Mrs Amanda Cadwallader
Mrs Alison Caff
Mr Nicholas Caiger
Mr Grant Calder
Mr Andrew Calman
Mr Ian Cameron
Mr John Camm
Mrs Claire Campbell
Ms Denise Campbell
Mr Glynis Campbell
Mr Ian Campbell
Mr John Campbell
Mr Paul Campbell
Mr Gareth Candy
Mr Daniel Canwell
Miss Chloe Card
Miss Nicolette Card
Mrs Ann Cardwell
Mr Grant Cardwell
Mr Kevin Carmody
Miss Sarah Carmody
Mrs Bettina Carollo
Mr Charlie Carpenter
Miss Michelle Carr
Ms Alice Carrington
Miss Bex Carrington
Ms Kathleen Carroll
Mrs Rebecca Carroll
Mrs Hilary Carruthers
Ms Penny Carruthers
Mr Ewart Carson
Miss Ashleigh Carter
Mr David Carter
Mr Lewis Carter
Mr Mark Carter
Ms Mary Carter
Mr Russell Carter
Miss Suzanne Carter
Ms Ruth Cartwright
Mr Antony Carubia
Mr Mike Carwithen
Mr Jeremy Cassel
Mrs Caroline Casterton
Mr David Castle
Mrs Rebecca Castle
Mr Joseph Catcheside
Mr David Catherall
Miss Michelle Caufield
Mr Jim Cauldrey
Miss Dawn Chadwick
Mr Roy Chadwick
Mrs Nina Challenor
Mr Chris Chamberlain
Mrs Christine Chamberlain
Mr Fred Chamberlain
Miss Julia Chamberlain
Ms Lucy Chamberlain
Mr John Chambers
Mr Arnaud Chanat
Mr Dan Channing Williams
Miss Claire Chant
Ms Samantha Chant-Seeley
Ms Joanne Chapman
Dr Keith Chapman

Miss Mel Chapman
Mr Norman Chapman
Ms Sue Chapman
Ms Tracy Chapman
Mrs Zoe Chapman
Mr Duncan Chappell
Dr Steven Charles
Mrs Joanna Charlton
Mr Steven Charlton
Mrs Chloe Charrington
Mrs Cathy Chattaway
Mrs Sally Chatterjee
Mrs Lyndsey Chatterton
Mr Albert Chau
Mrs Naina Chauhan
Mrs Deb Chester
Mr Matthew Chialton
Miss Emily Chiang
Miss Caroline Chilton
Mrs Gillian Chittenden
Mr Bob Choppen
Mr Rahman Choudhrey
Ms Charlotte Christie
Mrs Jackie Christie
Ms Gill Christy
Mr Michael Cinnamond
Ms Eleanor Clamp
Ms Margaret Clancy
Mrs Mary Clancy
Mrs Alison Clark
Dr Jonathan Clark
Dr Jonathan Clark
Mrs Lisa Clark
Ms Maggie Clark
Mr Peter Clark
Dr Vivienne Clark
Mr John Clarke
Mrs Terri Clarke
Mr Tyler Clarke
Mr Wayne Clarke
Mr Stefan Clasevici
Miss Janetta Clay
Mr John Clayton
Ms Petra Clayton
Mrs Suzanne Clayton
Mr Andrew Clegg
Ms Robyn Clelland
Mrs Sara Clemente-Powell
Ms Rebecca Clements
Mr Russ Clifford
Mr Giles Clinker
Mr Michael Clough
Ms Nicola Clowry
Mrs Margaret Cobbett
Mr John Cockell
Mr Stewart Codd
Mr Jame Cohen
Mrs Mandy Colbourne
Mr Barry Cole
Mr Gareth Cole
Mr Nick Cole
Mrs Sally Cole
Mr John Coleman
Ms Emma Coles
Mr Craig Collantine
Ms Anne Collier
Mr Charles Collins
Miss Diane Collins
Ms Lesley Collins
Mrs Lynne Collins
Miss Tracey Collins
Mr Russ Collinson
Ms Jane Colston
Miss Hayley Colyer
Mr Tom Conlin
Mr Jamie Connolly
Mrs Rachel Connolly
Ms Sara Connolly
Ms Janine Constantin-Russell
Mr Michael Conway
Mrs Elisha Cook
Mrs Lia Cook
Mrs Yvonne Cook
Mr Michael Cool
Ms June Coombes
Ms Aisling Cooper
Ms Emma Cooper
Mrs Gainor Cooper
Mr Martyn Cooper
Mr Peter Cooper
Mr Steve Cooper
Ms Kayleigh Coote
Mr Chris Cope
Mr Peter Corey
Mr Hugh Cornford
Miss Naomi Cornwell
Miss Sarah Corry
Mr Ian Corse
Mrs Rosie Cosby

Mrs Lynn Cosgrove
Mr Derek Cotter
Mr Neil Cotton
Mr Allen Coughlan
Mrs Polly Coulson
Mr Simon Counsell
Ms Clare Coupar
Mrs Gemma Coupar
Mr Robert Coveney
Mr Terry Covington
Mrs J Cowan
Ms Lorna Cowan
Mrs Maureen Cowburn
Mr Ben Cox
Mrs Nicola Cox
Mr Paul Craddock
Mr David Craig
Mrs Diane Craig
Mrs Jennifer Craig
Ms Victoria Craig
Ms Megan Crawford
Mr Sam Crawforde
Miss Penny Craze
Mr Peter Cribb
Mr James Crichton
Mr David Crimble
Mr Etty Criscenti
Ms Sarah Crisp
Mr Andrew Critchley
Miss Nicola Crocker
Mrs Christine Cropper
Miss Gemma Cropper
Mr Mark Crosby
Ms Victoria Crosskey
Mrs Pauline Crossley
Mr Cedric Crouch
Mrs Joanne Crow
Mrs Julie Crow
Mr Peter Crumpton
Dr Chris Cullen
Mrs Marion Cullen
Miss Briony Cullin
Mrs Clare Culliney
Ms Mary Culliney
Mrs Moira Culpan
Mrs Jackie Cummings
Mrs Caroline Cunningham
Mrs Catherine Cunningham
Dr David Cunningham
Ms Joyce Cunningham
Mr Yeohan Cunningham
Ms Gillian Currie
Mr Lachy Curzon
Mr Matthew Cushen
Mr Mike Cushman
Mrs Christina Cutting
Mrs Sheila Cutts
Mr Alexandre Cyrillo Telles
Ms Helen Dagg
Mr J Dagless
Mr Grant Dain
Ms Liza Dale
Mr James Daley
Ms Amber Dalton
Mr John Dalton
Mr David Daniels
Mr Denzil Daniels
Mr Julian Danskin
Mrs Renata Dantas
Dr Owen Darbishire
Mr Stuart Darbyshire
Ms Alison Darling
Mr Daniel Darwood
Mr David Davenport
Dr Meryl Davenport
Mr Matthew Davey
Mr Assas-Silveri David
Mr Brand Davidson
Ms Arlene Davie
Mr Alecxander Davies
Mr Andrew Davies
Mr James Davies
Dr Jo Davies
Ms Kim Davies
Ms Marie Davies
Mr Matt Davies
Ms Molly Davies
Ms Philippa Davies
Miss Sarah Davies
Mr Rob Davinson
Miss Ami Davis
Mrs CL Davis
Mrs Janet Davis
Ms Jenny Davis
Mr John Davis
Mr Martin Davis
Mrs Tina Davis
Mrs Julie Dawson
Miss Shelley Dawson

Mr Ben Day
Mr John Day
Mr Peter Day
Mr Stuart Day
Mr Roger Day
Mrs Marion De Berker
Mr Cameron De Buck
Ms Nora De Donnea
Ms Odette De Sa
Mr Tim Deacon
Mr Michael Dean
Mr Richard Dean
Mrs Karen Delahay
Mr Dave Dempsey
Mr Michael Dempsey
Mr Loic Denesle
Mr Neil Dennis
Mr Steve Denny
Mrs Annie Derrington
Mrs Patricia Derry
Miss Maya Desai
Miss Tamsin Devas
Mr David Devereau
Mr Mike Devereau
Ms Angela Dewey
Mr William Dick
Mrs Surya Dickinson
Mr Tom Dickinson
Mr Justin Dicks
Ms Helen Difrances-comarino
Mr Ken Dine
Ms Kirstine Dinnes
Mr Martin Diplock
Mr Chris Ditchburn
Mr Ashley Ditum
Mr Andrew Divers
Mr Andrew Dixon
Ms Hilary Dixon
Ms Joanne Dixon
Ms Lynda Dixon
Mr Michael Dixon
Mr Ron Dobson
Mr Martin Dodd
Ms Caroline Dodds
Miss Karen Doherty
Ms Mary Doherty
Mr Chris Doig
Ms Julia Domnina
Mr Peter Donaghue
Mr Michael Donaghy
Mr Peter Donelan
Mrs Zuzana Doneley
Miss Amy Donnelly
Ms Fiona Donohoe
Mr Kevin Donovan
Mr Graham Dooley
Mrs Katrina Doran
Mr Alastair Dornan
Miss Sarah Douglas
Miss Elizabeth Dow
Mr Steven Dow
Mr Gilbert Dowding
Mr Neil Dowdney
Ms Hayley Dowling
Mr Bernard Downes
Mr Alistair Doyle
Mr Andrew Drake
Mr Martin Drew
Mr Dave Driver
Mr Derek Driver
Mrs Dianne Drummond
Miss Jayne Dudley
Mrs Gillian Duffy
Ms Susan Duffy
Mr Kevin Duggan
Ms Sarah Dunbavand
Ms Heather Duncan
Mr Jon Duncan
Ms Nicola Duncan
Mr Ross Duncan
Mr David Dundas
Mr Richard Dungworth
Dr Michael Dunn
Mr Bruce Dunnett
Mr Rapahel Duprat
Ms Eva Durham
Mrs Lisa Durrani
Mr Arpan Dutta
Ms Ann Dwyer
Mr John Dwyer
Ms Maria Eade
Mr Simon Eames
Miss Olivia Easby
Mrs Leigh East
Ms Nicola Eastwood
Ms Vivienne Edgecombe
Mr David Edgington
Miss Juliet Edmondson

Mr John Edmonstone
Mr Paul Edmunds
Mr Andrew Edwards
Mr David Edwards
Mrs Helen Edwards
Mr John Edwards
Mrs Karen Edwards
Mrs M Edwards
Mr Osian Edwards
Miss Rebecca Edwards
Mr Stephen Edwards
Mr Alex Egeland
Ms Sarah Eglise
Ms Natasha Egre
Mr Eric Eisenhandler
Miss Charlotte Eland
Mr Mark Elderton
Mrs Amanda Eldridge
Mr Gary Elflett
Ms Penny Elger
Ms Cara Elkin
Mrs Cynthia Elkington
Mr Ray Elks
Mrs Linda Ellis
Mr Ian Ellison
Ms Martine Ellison-Smith
Mr Alan Elson
Mrs Meryl Elwell
Ms Diane Emery
Ms Jane England
Dr Nicholas England
Mr Rob England
Mrs Anne Enoch
Ms Amanda Evans
Miss Carla Evans
Mr Christopher Evans
Mr Dafydd Evans
Mr Gareth Evans
Mrs Jennie Evans
Mr Keith Evans
Mr Leigh Evans
Ms Lisa Evans
Mrs Lynda Evans
Mrs Olga Evans
Mr Paul Evans
Mr Ralph Evans
Ms Sally Evans
Ms Sarah Evans
Miss Sian Evans
Mr Simeon Evans
Mr Alex Eventon
Mrs Sarah Everard
Ms Elaine Everest
Ms Joanna Everett
Mr Petat Fabrice
Mr Stephen Fagan
Mr Tom Fahey
Mrs Lucy Fair
Mr Philip Fairburn
Mr Richard Faircliff
Mr John Fairhurst
Mr Rambaut Fairley
Ms Sarah Falconer
Miss Pippa Farr
Mr Terry Farr
Dr Emma Farrar
Mr Simon Farrimond
Ms Gill Fassnidge
Mr T Fathers
Mrs Barbara Fawcett
Mrs Sue Fawcett
Mr Mark Feinmann
Mr Dominic Fell
Miss Lucy Felton
Ms Charlotte Fenner
Miss Ruth Fenton
Mr Tom Fenwick
Mr John Fereday
Mrs Anne Ferguson
Ms Rosemary Ferguson
Mr Pedro Ferreira
Mr Vinicius Ferreira
Mr Nikolas Fetherston
Mr Anthony Field
Mrs Laura Field
Mr Jeffrey Fieldhouse
Ms Janet Fielding
Mr Rob Fields
Mr Neville Filar
Mr Gustavo Filgueiras
Mr Michael Fincham
Ms Joan Findlay
Mr Nicholas Finley
Mr Michael Finn
Dr Paula Firstbrook
Mrs Linda Fish
Mr Graham Fisher
Mr Leonard Fisher
Mr Rich Fisher

Ms Sioux Fisher
Ms Melissa Fitzgeald
Mr Brian Fitzgerald
Ms Sarah Fitzgerald
Mrs Rosalind Fitz-Gibbon
Ms Jane Fitzsimons
Ms Helen Flather
Mr Kieran Flatt
Mr Glenn Flegg
Ms Caroline Fletcher
Mr Christopher Fletcher
Ms Louise Fletcher
Mr David Flinthill
Mr Simon Flowers-Jones
Mr Kevin Flynn
Ms Anna Foalks
Mr Justin Forbes
Mrs Emma Forbes-Gardener
Mr Andrew Ford
Ms Beverley Ford
Ms Elizabeth Forrest
Mr John Forrester
Mrs Penny Forsyth
Mr John Forth
Mr Gordon Foster
Mr Colin Fountain
Ms Grace Fountain
Mrs Barbara Fowler
Mr John Fowler
Mr Alex Fox
Mrs Hazel Fox
Miss Rachel Fox
Mrs Jane Francis
Mrs Lisa Francis
Mr Vasco Francisco
Mr Simon Frankish
Mr John Fraser
Dr Stephen Fraser
Ms Amanda Freeman
Mrs Pippa Freeman
Mr David Friel
Mr Simon Friend
Ms Kate Frisby
Ms Amanda Frost
Mr Harry Frost
Mrs Lorraine Frost
Miss Silje Frosthammer
Mr David Fryer
Ms Rachel Fryer
Mrs Julie Fuller
Ms Benedetta Fullin
Mrs Deborah Funnell
Mr Stephen Furlong
Ms Sue Furneaux
Mr Neville Furness
Mrs Elizabeth Gadsby
Dr Roger Gadsby
Mrs Victoria Gage
Mr Manish Gajria
Mr Jonathan Gale
Mr Mick Gallagher
Miss Ashleigh Galletta
Ms Dawn Gallienne
Ms Sarah Galloway
Mr Nick Gamble
Mr Tony Gamble
Ms Sally Gane
Ms Heather Garbutt
Mr C Gardiner
Mrs Carla Gardiner
Miss Joanne Gardner
Mrs Lisa Gardner
Mrs Annie Garfoot
Mr Peta Garnavos
Mrs Jan Garner
Mr Tony Garner
Mrs Susan Garnham
Mr Steve Garrett
Miss Asher Garside
Mr Ron Gartside
Ms Laura Garwell
Ms Karen Gaskill
Ms Amanda Gaul
Ms Margaret Geary
Mr Alan Gee
Mr Mark Geffryes
Miss Rebecca Gentle
Dr James Geoghegan
Mrs Donna George
Miss Leanne George
Ms Katie Georgel
Ms Meganne Gerbeau
Mr Stephen Gerrard
Ms Francesca Giangrande
Mrs Elspeth Gibbon
Mrs Ali Gibson
Ms Cressida Gibson
Mr Douglas Gibson
Mr Jock Gibson

Mr Neil Gibson
Mrs Emily Giffard-Taylor
Mrs Dee Gifford
Ms Francesca Gilchrist
Mr Andrew Gill
Mr Chris Gill
Mr Inder Gill
Miss Jodu Gill
Mrs S Gimblett
Miss Helen Gladwell
Ms Sarah Jane Gladwin
Mr Bryan Glastonbury
Mr John Glaze
Ms Tracey Glenn
Mr Clive Glover
Mr Roger Glover
Mr Derek Goddard
Mr Michael Godden
Mr Bruce Godfrey
Mrs Carrie Godfrey
Mrs Maggie Godfrey
Ms Lucy Godwin
Ms Rosanne Goldman
Mr David Goldthorpe
Mr Kevin Golledge
Mr Steve Gomesz
Mr Grant Goodlad
Mr Stephen Goodlife
Ms Jenni Goodman
Mr John Goodman
Mr David Goodship
Mr Andrew Goodwin
Mr Michael Gordge
Mr Rob Gordon
Mrs Susan Gorman
Mr Peter Gorrie
Mr Dan Gostling
Mrs Sarah Gough
Mr Mark Gould
Mr Graham Gouldman
Mr Robert Goundry
Mrs Mary Gower
Mr Ron Gower
Ms Lesley Gowers
Mr Robert Gowland
Mrs Harriet Graeme
Mr Alan Graham
Ms Patricia Graham
Mrs Wendy Graham
Mr David Grant
Mrs Donna Grant
Mrs Christine Granville-Edge
Ms Annette Gray
Ms Annie Gray
Mrs Hazel Gray
Mr John Gray
Mrs Marie Gray
Mr Isaac Gray Cosgrove
Mr Alan Green
Ms Debora Green
Ms Hannah Green
Mr Marcus Green
Mrs Maureen Green
Mrs Pam Green
Dr Rebecca Green
Mr Rupert Green
Mr Terry Green
Mr Tom Green
Mr Tony Green
Mr Tyler Green
Mr Warwick Green
Ms Mary Greener
Mr John Greenhouse
Ms Marilyn Greening
Mrs Anna Greenwood
Mrs Lisa Gregg
Mr John Gregory
Mr Alexander Grell
Ms Alice Grier
Dr Antony Griew
Mr Aled Griffiths
Mr Chris Griffiths
Ms Katie Griffiths
Mrs Maureen Griffiths
Ms Nicola Griffiths
Mrs Elizabeth Griggs
Ms Katrin Groger-Markiel
Mrs Eleanor Grose
Ms Samantha Groves
Mr Tony Grumley-Grennan
Mr Anthony Gubler
Ms Rachael Gudgeon
Ms Linda Gully
Mrs Teri Gumpert
Mr David Gunn
Mr Ian Gunning
Mr Stephen Gunter
Miss Lena Gursli

Ms Timandra Gustafson
Miss Leanda Guy
Ms Carol Gysin
Mr Bill Hackney
Ms Rowena Hackwood
Mr Martin Hadden
Ms Nicola Hague
Mrs Anne Hahndiek
Miss Rumana Haider
Ms Jenny Hailstones
Mr Daniel Haines
Mr Derek Hairon
Miss Liz Hale
Ms Elaine Hall
Mr Graham Hall
Ms Irene Hall
Mr James Hall
Mrs Julie Hall
Mr Roddy Hall
Mrs Sarah Hall
Miss Simona Hall
Mrs Tracy Hall
Miss Sarah Halliday
Ms Anne-Marie Halls
Mrs Sally Halsey
Mr Tom Halsey
Miss Kayleigh Hame
Ms Cate Hamilton
Mr Graham Hamilton
Mrs Jill Hamilton
Ms Judith Hamilton
Miss Bryony Hamilton Kelly
Mrs Caroline Hammond
Ms Kimberley Hammond
Mr David Hancock
Mr Simon Hancock
Mr Noel Handley
Miss Anoushka Hanham
Ms Catherine Hankey
Mr Neil Hanley
Miss Jennifer Hanlon
Ms Nicola Hanmer
Miss Jane Hanson
Mrs Judith Hanson
Mr Mark Hanson
Mr Azimul Haque
Mr Brian Harden
Mrs Claire Harding
Miss Stephanie Hardman
Mr Alexander Hardwidge
Mr Derek Hardy
Mr James Hargraves
Mrs Georgina Hargreaves
Ms Natalie Hargrove
Mrs Marion Harley
Miss Christina Harper
Miss Joan Harper
Mrs Susan Harper
Ms Wendy Harper
Mr Alan Harries
Mrs Laura Harrington
Mr Anthony Paul Harris
Ms Bryony Harris
Mrs Natalie Harris
Mr Neil Harris
Mr Phil Harriss
Mrs Jan Harrison
Ms Jane Harrison
Mrs Sandra Harrison
Mrs Stephanie Harrison
Mr Stuart Harrison
Dr B Harrison
Mr Andrew Hart
Mr Charlie Hart
Mr John Hartley
Ms Katherine Harvey
Miss Susan Harvey
Ms Jenny Hassel
Ms Pamela Hastings
Mr Martin Hatcher
Mr Bryan Hatter
Mr Charles Hawes
Mr Eddie Hawkes
Mr Mark Hawkins
Mr David Hawksmore
Mr Peter Hawksworth
Mr Bob Hawthorne
Ms Elizabeth Hawthorne
Ms Sheena Hay
Mr Andy Hayler
Dr Peter Haynes
Ms Yvonne Haynes
Mr Tim Hayns
Mrs Janine Hayward
Mr Trevor Hayward
Mrs Denise Haywood
Mr Roger Head
Mr Nigel Healey
Mrs Suzanne Heath

Mr Frederic Heathcote
Ms Bronya Heaver
Dr Vanessa Heggie
Mrs Victoria Heine
Mrs Rebecca Helle
Mr Grey Hemingway
Mr Becca Hemmant
Mr Paul Hemsley
Mrs Wendy Hemsworth
Ms Jenny Henderson
Mrs Morag Henderson
Mr Stuart Henderson
Mr Peter Hennessey
Mrs Amy Henry-Morgan
Mr James Hepburn
Mr Max Hepworth-Povey
Mr David Herbert
Mr Roy Herd
Ms Julie Herdman
Miss Amy Herod
Mr Chris Herrieven
Mr Stephen Herriot
Ms Melanie Hesseltine
Ms Ruth Hesketh
Mrs Angela Hewitt
Ms Marie Hewitt
Mr David Hewson
Miss Kate Heyes
Mr Howard Heywood
Ms Jan Hibbert
Ms Louise Hibbert
Ms Jill Hickey
Ms Sue Hickman
Mr Ethan Higgins
Miss Natalie Higgs
Mr Tim Hiles
Mrs A Hill
Ms Julie Hill
Miss Laura Hill
Mr Michael Hill
Mr Nick Hill
Ms Sheelagh Hill
Mr Stanley Hill
Mrs Jane Hillary
Dr Dawn Hillier
Ms Jayne Hills
Mr Tim Hills
Mrs Mary Hilton
Mr Ian Hinckley
Mr Al Hindley
Dr Keith Hine
Mr Simon Hingley
Mr Mark Hirons
Ms Ann Hirst-Smith
Mr Andy Hiskman
Mr John Hitcham
Mr Andy Hobbs
Miss Debz Hobbs-Wyatt
Mr Thomas Hobday
Mr Andrew Hobson
Mrs Margaret Hocking
Miss Margaret Hodge
Mrs Carole Hodges
Mr Peter Hodgetts
Mr Richard Hodson
Mrs Marilyn Hogg
Ms Tracy Hoggarth
Mr Richard Hoile
Mrs Joanne Holcombe
Mr Christopher Holden
Mr James Holden
Dr Kelly Holden
Miss Laura Holden
Mr Rob Holden
Mrs Kate Holdsworth
Ms Rhoda Holehouse
Ms Catherine Holland
Mr William Hollewyn
Mrs Janet Hollingsworth
Mr Jeff Hollingworth
Ms Shelley Hollis
Mr Stephen Holloway
Mr Bob Holmes
Dr Catherine Holmes
Mrs Joy Holmes
Mrs Liz Holmes
Mr Michael Holmes
Mrs Vanessa Holmes
Miss Victoria Holmes
Mrs Mairi Holt
Ms Tanya Holzmann
Mr Bryan Homan
Ms Annie Hon
Mr David Honour
Dr Colette Hood
Mrs Ann Hooker
Mr Josh Hoole
Mr Alex Hope
Mr Robin Hope

Mr Stephen Hope
Mrs Sharon Hopkins
Mr Jonathan Hopkinson
Mr Tim Hopkinson
Mr Liam Horkan
Ms Tracey Horn
Mrs Sue Hornby
Mrs Linda Horne
Ms Michelle Horne
Mr Andrew Howard
Mr Christopher Howard
Mrs Rose Howard
Mr Alan Howarth
Ms Karen Howe
Miss Layla Howe
Ms Diane Howell
Mrs Val Howell
Miss Nicola Howells
Mrs Jennifer Howle
Mrs Helen Hoyle
Mr Thomas Huber
Ms Sharon Huddart
Mr Philip Huddleston
Mr David Hudson
Mrs Deborah Hudson
Mrs Jenny Hudson
Dr Nigel Huggins
Mrs Ann Hughes
Mrs Audrey Hughes
Mr David Hughes
Ms Diane Hughes
Ms Helen Hughes
Mr John Hughes
Mr Michael Hughes
Mr Rob Hughes
Mr Roger Hughes
Mrs Susan Hughes
Mrs Julia Hughes-Roberts
Mrs Victoria Hughson
Dr Ayla Humphrey
Mrs Ann Humphreys
Miss Joanne Humphreys
Mr Marcus Humphries
Mr David Hunt
Ms Katie Hunt
Mr Andrew Hunter
Ms Nicky Hunter
Mr Paul Hunter
Miss Susan Hunton
Miss Emma Hurry
Ms Angela Hurst
Mr Clive Hurt
Mr Anwar Hussain
Mr Israr Hussain
Mrs Jennifer Hutchings
Mrs Jenny Hutchings
Mr Lian Hutchings
Mr Guy Hutchins
Mrs Elen Huws
Mr James Hyde
Mr Stewart Hyde
Mr Martin Ibbotson
Mrs Cheryl Illingworth
Mr Alistair Impey
Mr Carlos Inacio
Miss Samantha Ingarfield
Mr Richard Ingley
Ms Jenny Ingram
Mr Martin Ingram
Ms Alena Ingvarsdottir
Dr M Ip
Dr Alison Irwin
Mr William Iveson
Ms Jacqui Jack
Ms Mary Jack
Mr John Jackaman
Mr David Jackson
Ms Ellie Jackson
Ms Elsie Jackson
Dr Jack Jackson
Miss Jillian Jackson
Miss Rachel Jackson
Ms Amanda Jackson-Stephenson
Mr Peter Jacobs
Mr John Jago
Miss Charlotte James
Mr Jimmy James
Ms Pauline James
Mr Robert Jamieson
Mr Stephen Jamieson
Mr John Jarman
Mr David Jarrad
Miss Caroline Jarvis
Miss Catrina Jarvis
Mr Harish Jaykar
Miss Elise Jeanrenaud
Mr Martin Jeeves
Mr Ian Jefferson

Mr John Jeffery
Mr Richard Jeffries
Mr Alan Jenkins
Mr Guy Jenkins
Mr Ian Jenkins
Mrs R Jenkins
Mr Steven Jenkins
Mr Alaistair Jerrom-Smith
Mr David Jessel
Mr Peter Jessop
Mrs Anna Jester
Mr Tristan Jewitt
Mrs Julia Jeyes
Ms Alison Johns
Mr Andy Johns
Mr Gareth Johns
Mrs Sarah Johns
Ms Caroline Johnson
Ms Cynthia Johnson
Mr David Johnson
Mrs Hayley Johnson
Mr James Johnson
Ms Jenny Johnson
Ms Maria Johnson
Mr Peter Johnson
Miss S D Johnson
Mr W Gordon Johnstone
Mr Darren Jolly
Mr Adrian Jones
Mrs Barbara Jones
Mrs Carey Jones
Mr Clifford Jones
Mr David Jones
Mrs Diana Jones
Ms Ellen Jones
Mrs Georgina Jones
Mrs Hannah Jones
Mrs Hilary Jones
Mr Ian Jones
Mr John Jones
Mrs Judith Jones
Miss Mari Jones
Mr Martin Jones
Mrs Penny Jones
Mr Peter Jones
Mr Phil Jones
Ms Rhiannon Jones
Mr Robin Jones
Ms Sarah Jones
Ms Sharon Jones
Mrs Veronica Jonkman
Ms Joanne-Marie Jordan
Ms Yvonne Joyce
Ms Francine Jury
Mrs Sandra Jury
Mr Simon Jury
Miss Irene Juurlink
Miss Anita Kaczorowska
Mrs Jillian Kammer
Ms Aya Kamoda
Mr Darren Kane
Miss Serena Karp
Mr Richard Katz
Dr Annalise Katz-Summercorn
Ms Liz Kavanagh
Mr Bernard Kay
Ms Gladys Kay
Miss Alice Kearney
Mr Simon Keeling
Mrs Pat Keenan
Mr Len Keighley
Mr Matt Kell
Mr Kevin Kelley
Mr Yann Kelley
Dr Claire Kelly
Mr Denis Kelly
Mr Jacob Kelly
Mrs Lesley Kelly
Miss Louise Kelly
Mrs Sarah Dean Kelly
Mr Philip Kemp
Mrs Suelynn Kemp
Mr John Kennard
Ms Maggie Kennard
Mrs Christelle Kennedy
Mr Nairn Kennedy
Mrs Belinda Kennerley
Miss Sam Kenny
Ms Louise Kenyon
Mr Scott Kerley
Mr Steve Kerns
Mr David Kerr
Mr James Kerr
Mr Jonathan Kerry
Mrs Isabella Kerton
Mr Richard Kettles
Ms Aisha Khan-Evans
Mr William Kidd

THANK YOUS

Mrs Linda Kiddell
Mrs Catheryn Kilgarriff
Mr John Kilgarriff
Ms Amy Kilpin
Mr Andrew King
Mr Graham King
Mrs Jayne King
Ms Judith King
Mr Kevin King
Mr Stuart King
Ms Susan King
Mr Bernard Kinsella
Mrs Olga Kirillova
Ms Amanda Kirk
Mr Robert Kirk
Mr Mark Kirkbride
Mr Jon Kirkup
Mr Ivan Kitchen
Dr Lisa-Marie Kitchen
Ms Ella Kitto
Mrs Suibhan Klejdys
Ms Katherine Knibb
Mr Peter Knibb
Mr Andrew Knight
Mr David Knight
Miss Emily Knight
Mr Mark Knight
Ms Terri Knight
Ms Julie Knighton
Miss Louise Knox
Ms Heather Kohn
Ms Katarzyna Konys-Pieszko
Mr Przemyslaw Koscielak
Mr Ethan Kowalski
Ms Jana Kwasnik
Miss Rosie Kydd
Mr Peter Kyte
Mrs Sue Lacey
Mrs Vanessa Lackford
Mr Keith Lackie
Miss Jag Lagah
Mr Malcolm Laird
Mr Ben Lait
Mrs Carys Lake
Miss Laura Lamb
Mrs Michelle Lamont
Mr Allen Lane
Mr Geoffrey Lang
Mrs Sarah Lang
Miss Gemma Langford
Mr Joss Langford
Mrs Helena Langston
Ms Abigail Langton
Mrs Megan Large
Mr Jonathan Latham
Mr Mike Latter
Mrs Lucie Lattimer
Ms Deborah Laurent
Mr Kenneth Law
Ms Sarah Law
Mrs Amanda Lawrence
Ms Araminta-June Lawson
Mrs Lorraine Lawson
Ms Sarah Lawson
Mrs Colleen Laybourne
Ms Charlotte Le Cras
Robin Leake
Mr Alan Leaman
Mrs Linda Leary
Ms Diana Lebaschi
Ms G Lecoq
Mr Charles Ledigo
Mr Alan Lee
Mrs Diane Lee
Mrs Gloria Lee
Ms Shirley Lee
Mrs Nicole Leech
Mr Peter David Leech
Mr R Lees
Mr Donald Legget
Ms Joan Leighton
Mr Robert Lemon
Mr Andrew Leslau
Mr Brian Lester
Miss Sabine Letort
Ms Daphne Lever
Ms Jane Lewis
Mrs Judy Lewis
Ms Marie Lewis
Ms Maureen Lewis
Dr Simon Lewis
Mrs Sue Lewis
Mrs Victoria Leyland
Ms Heidi Leyshon
Miss Theresa Liddle
Mr R Light
Mr Andy Lightfoot
Mrs Mary Lincoln
Miss Hannah Linday

Mr Steven Lindsay
Ms Adele Lingard
Mr Gerald Lip
Ms Debra Lipscomb
Ms Nicki Little
Ms Anne Littlewood
Ms Joanne Liveston
Ms Claire Livington
Mrs Claire Llewellyn
Mr David Lloyd
Ms Frances Lloyd
Mr Greg Lloyd
Mrs Rebecca Lloyd
Mrs Wendy Lloyd
Mr Antony Lloyd
Mrs Nicola Lloyd-Wiliams
Ms Ros Loakes
Ms Ros Lock
Mrs Linda Locke
Mr Adrian Lockyer
Mrs Julie Logan
Mrs Evelyne Loible
Ms Karen Lombardo
Mr Christopher Long
Mr Michael Long
Mr Steve Long
Mrs Marnie Long-Collins
Mrs Julia Longfellow
Ms Jackie Longley
Ms Samantha Loong
Mr Ken Loos
Mr Fabio Lopez
Mr Adrian Lord
Ms Lucy Lord
Mr Andrew Lovatt
Mr Chris Love
Mr Kenneth Love
Ms Lynn Love
Mr Dan Lovedale
Ms Sanchia Lovell
Ms Tina Lowe
Mrs Adrienne Lowry
Mrs Jade Lowry
Mr Garry Lowther
Mr Antony Lucas
Mrs Helen Lucas
Ms Amy Ludlow
Mr James Ludwig
Mrs Jill Lundberg
Ms Natalie Lundsteen
Mr Mark Lunn
Mr Michael Lunn
Mrs Brigid Lury
Mrs Maureen Lussey
Mr Franz Ernst Lussmann
Mr Martin Lyall
Mr Gary Lygo
Mrs Patricia Lyle
Ms Orly Lyndon
Miss Denise Lyons
Mr Dean Ma
Mr Pete Mabbs
Mr David Macdonald
Mrs Samantha Macdonald
Mr Stuart Macdonald
Mrs Susan Macdonald
Mrs Elizabeth Macdonnell
Ms Marie Machin
Mr Daniel Macintyre
Mr Mark Mackenzie-Charrington
Mrs Susan Mackie
Mr Hugh Mackintosh CBE
Mr Henry Mackley
Mr Alex Maclean
Mrs V Maclean
Ms Ruth Maclennan
Mr Fergus Macleod
Ms Anna Macmillan
Mr David Macphail
Ms Gillian Macrosson
Miss Clare Mactaggart
Mr Gary Madden
Dr George Madden
Ms Eleanor Maidment
Mr Xavier Madjoudj
Mr Monty Magonague
Mrs Helena Magorium
Mr Andrew Maher
Ms Jane Maher
Mr Leo Mahon
Mr Philip Mahoney
Mrs Terry Maidment
Mrs Nina Mair
Ms Sarah Malcolm
Mr John Mallinson
Mr Steve Malpass
Miss Joanna Malsem
Miss Laura Malster

Mr Richard Maltby
Mr Gordon Mann
Mrs Nicola Mann
Mr Michael Manser
Mr Graeme Marchbank
Miss Emily Marchant
Ms Hattie Marjoram
Mr Gavin Markham
Mr Andrew Markland
Mr Laurence Marks
Mrs Margaret Marks
Mr Peter Marks
Dr Charles Markus
Mrs Louise Markus
Mr Gavin Markwick
Mr Chris Marples
Miss Samantha Marriott
Ms Alexandra Marshall
Ms Tina Marshall
Mr Stjohn Marston
Ms Valerie Marston-James
Mr Andrew Martin
Miss Angélique Martin
Mr Francis Martin
Mrs Geraldine Martin
Mr Graham Martin
Mr Grant Martin
Mr James Martin
Ms Janet Martin
Mrs Judith Martin
Ms Marnie Martin
Miss Michelle Martin
Miss Naomi Martin
Mrs Nats Martin
Mr Patrick Martin
Dr Ruth Martin
Miss Elizabeth Masheder
Mr Jeff Maslin
Mr Finlay Mason
Mrs Julie Mason
Ms Nicola Massey
Mr Steve Massey
Mr Sidney Masterson
Mrs Colette Mather
Mr Martin Mather
Mr Stuart Mather
Mr Will Mather
Mrs Louisa Matheson
Mr Stuart Mathieson
Ms Wren Matley
Miss Yvette Mattes
Mr Nikolas Matthew
Miss Amelia Matthews
Ms Claire Matthews
Mr Roy Matthews
Miss Sophie Matthews
Miss Jennifer Maxfield
Ms Lesley Maxwell
Ms Rebecca Maxwell
Mr Anthony May
Mr Chris May
Ms Diana May
Mr Ian May
Mr Kenneth May
Mr Michael May
Mr Colin Mayhead
Mr Andrew Mayne
Mr David Mays
Miss Elizabeth Maze
Miss Sonia McAnea
Mrs Helen McAvoy
Mr Andrew Mcauley
Ms Cheryl Mcbride
Mr Derek Mcbride
Mrs Karen Mcbryde
Mr Mark Mccabe
Miss Sarah Mccaffrey
Mr Sean Mccallion
Ms Jacqueline Mccann
Mrs Laura Mccarten
Miss Jennifer Mccarthy
Mr Patrick Mccarthy
Dr Mike Mccartney
Mrs Kate Mccgwire
Ms Rosalind Mcclure
Mr Andrew Mcconnell
Mr Stephen Mcconnell
Ms Laura Mcconville
Mr Richard Mccowey
Mrs Tina Mccready
Mr Francis Mccullough
Ms Dana Mccusker
Mrs Helen Mcdermott
Ms Louise Mcdonald
Ms Sammy Mcdonald
Mrs Alison Mcdowell
Ms Kasia Mcenery
Mrs Michelle Mcfarland
Ms Tracy Mcgilveray

Mrs Nicola Mcgovern
Ms Rachel Mcgrath
Ms Lizee Mcgraw
Mrs Gillian Mcgregor
Miss Kristina Mcguinness
Mrs Linda Mcguinness
Mrs Ruth Mcguinness
Ms Sara Mcilreavy
Mr Brian Mckay
Mr Clayton Mckenzie
Mr Stuart Mckenzie
Mr Andrew Mckeown
Ms Sandi Mckinnon
Ms Sue Mclaren-Thomson
Mrs Janice Mclaughlin
Ms Anna Mcleod
Mr Phil Mcmahon
Miss Tracy Mcmahon
Mrs Joanne Mcmillan
Mr Lawrence Mcneela
Mr David Mcnulty
Mr Alistair Mcpherson
Ms Briony Mcroberts
Ms Allison Mcsparron-Edwards
Ms Karen Mctigue
Mr Iain Mcwhinnie
Mr Rogan Meadows
Mr Simon Meadows
Mr Paul Meakin
Mrs Lynn Meech
Mrs Jean Meeghan
Mr John Meek
Miss Mahdieh Mehrabi
Mrs Sara Melhado
Ms Irene Mellini
Mr Val Mellini
Mr Jonathan Mellor
Miss Lisa Melvin
Mr Julian Melzack
Mrs Katie Merrick
Mr Peter Merriman
Mrs Teresa Merriott
Miss Anna Merton
Ms Louise Messenger
Mr Laurence Messer
Mr Jeremy Metcalfe
Miss Celine Miani
Mr Assas Michel
Mr Howard Middleton
Mr Iain Middleton
Mr Neil Middleton
Ms Sandie Middleton
Mrs Dee Midgley
Ms Jennifer Miedema
Mr David Miles
Mrs Hayley Miles
Mr Peter Miles
Mr James Millar
Mr Richard Millar
Mrs Debbie Millard
Ms Tara Millbourn
Mr Andy Miller
Ms Barbara Miller
Dr Joanna Miller
Mr Stephen Miller
Ms Valerie Miller
Mr Roy Milligan
Ms Theresa Millington
Miss Grace Mills
Mrs J Mills
Ms Jane Mills
Ms Hazel Millward
Mrs Georgina Milsom
Mr Joris Minne
Ms Christine Mitchell
Mr Daniel Mitchell
Mrs Heather Mitchell
Mr Jonathan Mitchell
Miss Rebecca Mitchell
Mrs Nicky Moffatt
Mr Simon Mogg
Mr Akla Moin
Ms Elaine Mole
Ms Annabella Montagnon
Mrs Debbie Montagnon
Mrs Jennifer Montague
Mrs Liz Montague
Mr Stephen Montgomery
Mrs Karen Moon
Mr Richard Moon
Mrs Alison Mooney
Mr John Mooney
Professor Eric Moonman OBE
Mr Colin Moore
Ms Fiona Moore
Ms Joanne Moore
Mr Michael Moore

Mr Paul Moore
Mr Peter Moore
Ms Susan Moore
Mrs Sue Moorhouse
Ms Susan Moorse
Ms Clare Moran
Ms Sheela Moran
Mr Jack Moreau
Mr David Morehen
Mr Fabio Morello
Mr Martin Morgan
Mr R C Morgan
Ms Rebecca Morgan
Mr Richard Morgan
Mr Terry Morgan
Miss Hannah Morison
Mr Michael Morrice
Miss Amanda Morris
Mrs Colette Morris
Mr Fred Morris
Mr J Morris
Mr John Morris
Miss Lorna Morss
Mrs Jackie Mortimer
Ms Jackie Mortlock
Mr Andrew Morton
Ms Marilyn Moscrip
Mr Keith Moseley
Mrs Anna Mosesson
Miss Jennifer Moss
Ms Josephine Moss
Mr Justin Mote
Mr Michael Moult
Mr Chris Mounsor
Ms Amanda Moxham
Mr John Moy
Ms Hayley Mudge
Mr Martin & Anne Muers
Mr Colin Muir
Mr Diarmuid Mulherin
Ms Karen Mullan
Mr Martin Mulligan
Mr Charles Mullins
Miss Nicola Mundy
Ms Kathy Murdoch
Ms Margo Muris
Mrs Allison Murphy
Miss Anna Murphy
Mr Kieran Murphy
Mr Michael Murphy
Miss Sarah Murphy
Mrs Amanda Murray
Ms Deborah Murray
Mr Iain Murray
Mr Les Murray
Ms Carleen Myatt
Mr Simon Myers
Mr Peter Nahum
Mr Craig Nall
Mr Debal Nandi
Ms Jennifer Nash
Ms Katharine Nash
Miss Naomi Nathan
Mr Nathan Neal
Dr Joanne Neilson
Dr Sue Nelson
Ms Carole Nevitt
Ms Sue Newall
Mr Andy Newbound
Mr Raymond Newell
Ms Sarah Marie Newlove
Mrs Eleanor Newman
Mrs Shirley Newman
Dr Tom Newman
Mr Brooks Newmark
Ms Lesley Newton
Mr Mark Newton
Mr Terence Newton
Ms Alethea Ng
Mr Jeffrey Ng
Mrs Sue Ng
Dr Adam Nicholls
Dr Andrew Nicholls
Mrs Lyn Nicholls
Mr John Nicholson
Mrs Trudy Nicholson
Mr Heath Nickels
Mrs Lousie Nicol
Mr Philip Niesluchowski
Mr David Nightingale
Miss S Nightingale
Mr Rodger Nisbet
Mr Alistair Niven
Mr Andy Niven
Ms Anne-Marie Nixey
Mr Antony Nobes
Ms Gillian Noble
Miss Anna Nolan
Ms Lara Nolan

Mr Peter Nolan
Ms Sonja Noon
Mr Mike Noone
Mr Derek Norfolk
Mrs Elizabeth Beryl Norgrove
Mr George Norrie
Mr David Norris
Mrs Jill North
Ms Penny North
Mr Simon North
Ms Maxine Norton
Miss Carol Nunn
Ms Lisa Nunn
Ms Sue Nursey
Miss Margaret Oakley
Ms Claire Oatridge
Ms Averil O'Boyle
Ms Deborah O'Brien
Ms Kate O'Brien
Ms Jenny O'Brien
Ms Kate O'Brien
Mr Niall O'Brien
Miss Helen O'Connor
Miss Hilary O'Connor
Mr Patrick O'Connor
Mr Graham Oddey
Ms Liz Ogilvie
Ms Caroline Ogden
Ms Catherine Ogden
Mrs Hazel O'Hara
Mr Pauline O'Keeffe
Ms L Oldfield
Mr Mike Oldfield
Mr Tim Oldfield
Miss Victoria Oldfield
Mrs Anne Oldhams
Ms Annabelle Ollis
Ms Katie O'Lone
Miss Susan O'Loughlin
Ms Alleyne Oman
Mrs Hannah O'Neill
Mr Peter O'Neill
Ms Sarah O'Neill
Ms Victoria O'Neill
Mr Dom O'Nions
Mrs Heather Ootam
Ms Kathryn Oram
Mr Peter Orban
Mrs Helen Orchel
Dr Simon Orebi Gann
Mr Michael Orlik
Miss Claire Orme
Mrs Berry O'Rourke
Mr Adrian Ottley
Mr Andrew Owen
Mrs Ann Owen
Miss Mari Owen
Mr Martin Owen
Miss Paula Padilha
Mr Gavin Page
Mr Wallace Paget
Mr Adam Paine
Mrs Naomi Paleschi
Mr Matthew Palk
Miss Michelle Palmares
Mrs Andrea Palmer
Mr Desmond Palmer
Mrs Donna Palmer
Mr John Palmer
Miss Laura Palmer
Ms Rebecca Palmer
Mrs Tracey Palmer
Ms Anna Palosz
Mrs Fiona Pankhurst
Mrs Liz Pardon
Miss Lulu Parent
Mr Andrew Park
Mrs Denise Park
Mrs Heather Parker
Mr David Parker
Ms Catherine Parkin
Mr James Parkin
Miss Liz Parkin
Mr David Parkinson
Mrs Maria Parkinson
Mrs Ruth Parkinson
Mrs Sue Parkinson
Mrs Tessa Parkinson
Mr Andrew Parle
Mr Vince Parry
Mrs Alison Parsons
Mr Christopher Parsons
Dr Quentin Parsons
Mr Luke Pascoe
Mr Neil Pascoe
Mr Stephen Passmore
Dr N Patel
Dr Raj Patel
Mr Robert Paterson
Miss Rachael Patterson
Miss Rachel Patti
Ms Danielle Pauls
Mr Laurence Pawlik
Mr Joseph Paxton
Mr Brent Payne
Miss Rebecca Payne
Mr Tom Payne
Mr Jason Pazour
Mr Spencer Peacock
Miss Katharine M Peake
Mr Colin Pearson
Mr Gary Pearson
Ms Libby Pearson
Mrs Paula Pearson
Mr Nick Peck
Mrs Pamela Peek
Ms Pam Peers
Miss Josephine Pendlebury
Miss Charlotte Penn
Mrs Caroline Pennock
Mr Nigel Pepler
Mr Thomas Peplinski
Mr Dener Pereira
Mr Charles Perkins
Dr John Perkins
Mrs Olwen Perrett
Mr Andrew Perry
Mrs Kirsty Perry
Mr David Pert
Mrs Celia Pestana-Beck
Ms Karlyce Pestello
Ms Beverly Peters
Mr Hans Peters
Mr Steve Peters
Mr Ben Peterson
Mr Greg Pettit
Mrs Tony Pettman
Miss Amy Philip
Mrs Anne Phillips
Mrs Charlotte Phillips
Mrs Diane Phillips
Ms Dorcas Phillips
Mrs Fiona Phillips
Mr Phil Phillips
Mr Thomas Phillips
Mr David Pick
Mr Rob Pickering
Mr Denis Pickett
Mr James Pickford
Mr Ian Pickstock
Ms Christine Pidcock
Mr George Piercy
Miss Juliet Pierrot
Ms Sue Pilling
Miss Melanie Pilsworth
Mrs Sarah Pinnington
Mr Anton Piotrowski
Mr John Pitcairn
Mr David Pitt
Mrs Janet Pitt
Mrs Moira Pitteway
Ms Rebecca Platt
Ms Ellie Player
Mrs Carolyn Plows
Ms Lydia Pluckrose
Miss Sarah Plumley
Mrs Rosalind Plummer
Mrs Sally Plunkett
Ms Sarah Poli
Ms Cheryl Pollard
Ms Mary Pollard
Mr Karol Poniewaz
Mrs Donna Ponsonby
Miss Katrina Poole
Mrs Marie Pope
Mr Mark Pope
Mr Barrie Popkin
Mr Mark Porter
Miss Imke Potgieter
Mr Igor Potje
Mr Chris Potter
Miss R Potter
Miss Teresa Potter
Mr Stephen Povey
Mrs Heather Powell
Miss Joanne Powell
Mr Robert Powell
Mr Rod Power
Mr Ben Prebble
Ms B Prendiville
Mr Colin Prescot
Ms Jane Preston
Ms Kate Preston
Dr Jonathan Price
Miss Natalie Price
Mrs Kathryn Prior
Ms Rita Pritchard-Woollett
Dr Oriel Prizeman
Mrs Clare Prochazka
Mr Chris Proctor
Mr Philip Proffitt
Miss Barbora Prokopova
Mr Mike Prostayko
Ms Maryeve Pudney
Mr Alan Pugh
Mrs Sue Pugsley
Mr Steve Purser
Ms Natasha Puxley
Mr Robert Pye
Mr Alastair Pyke
Ms Jeanne Quigley
Ms Donna Quinn
Mrs Gill Quinn
Ms Rita Quinn
Dr Sarah Quinn
Miss Victoria Quinn
Mr Charles Raab
Ms Gillian Raab
Mrs K Race
Mr Steffen Radespiel
Mr Giorgian Radu
Mr Frank Rae
Mrs Marie-Louisa Raeburn
Dr Tom Rafferty
Ms Lisa Raffles
Mr Abdul Rahman
Mr Limon Rahman
Miss Sharmin Rahman
Mr Narinder Rai
Mrs Bridget Ramsay
Ms Karen Rankine
Mr Ronald Rankine
Dr Joan Ransley
Mrs Wendy Ransom
Ms Cheryle Raphael
Mrs Annette Rasmussen
Mr Alexander Rast
Mrs June Ratcliffe
Ms Patricia Rawlings
Mrs Joanne Ray
Ms Mary Ray
Ms Jan Rayner
Mr Mike Rea
Miss Lydia Read
Ms Jackie Reader
Ms Sally Reardon
Mrs Delphine Recalde
Mrs Christine Redmond
Miss Louise Redvers
Mrs Claire Reece
Mr Brian Reed
Mr Martin Reed
Mrs Nerys Reed
Mr Peter Reed
Ms Emma Rees
Ms Jenni Rees
Mr Gordon Reeves
Mr Timothy Reeves
Mrs Anne-Marie Regnault
Ms Anne Reid
Miss Nicola Reid
Mr Thomas Reid
Miss Grainne Reidy
Ms Louise Reilly
Dr Terry Reilly
Ms Amanda Rencontre
Mrs Ana Rennolds
Mrs Nicola Renshaw
Mrs Victoria Renshaw
Miss Jo Revell
Mr Ronald Reynard
Mr Peter Reynolds
Mr Simon Rhind-Tutt
Mrs Kath Rhodes
Mr Lachlan Rhodes
Ms Debbie Rich
Ms Leanne Richards
Miss Sarah Richards
Mr Andrew Richardson
Mrs Annie Richardson
Ms Ingrid Richardson
Mrs Pamela Richardson
Mr Paul Richardson
Mr Lee Richmond
Mrs Carol Riddick
Miss Jen Ridley
Mr Peter Riedi
Mrs Helen Rigby
Mr Richard Rigby
Mrs Cassandra Rigg
Mr Jake Rigg
Mrs Emma Riley
Mrs Serena Riley
Miss Kerry Rimmer
Mr B J Ripley
Ms Susan Riseley
Mrs Fiona Ritchie
Mr Frank Ritchie
Mr Les Ritchie
Mr Paul Rivett
Ms Lynsey Robbins
Mr Andy Roberts
Mr Ian Roberts
Mr Len Roberts
Ms Lynn Roberts
Miss Naomi Roberts
Mr Peter Roberts
Miss Samantha Roberts
Mr Alasdair Robertson
Mr John Robertson
Mr Warren Robertson
Mr Michael Robertson-Smith
Mr Matthew Robins
Mr Alan Robinson
Mr Irvin Robinson
Mr Peter Robinson
Mr Martyn Robinson-Slater
Mrs Angela Robson
Mr Ben Robson
Mr Brian Robson
Miss Emily Robson
Mrs Kathleen Roche
Mr Noel Roche
Ms Sue Rockingham
Mr A Roddis
Ms Louise Rodwell
Mrs Bernadette Roffe
Ms Christine Rogers
Ms Francesca Rogers
Mrs Jacqui Rogers
Ms Deborah Rogerson
Mr John Rogerson
Mrs Irene Rooney
Ms Kate Rose
Mr Julian Rose-Gibbs
Mr Colin Roth
Mrs Sheree Rotherham
Mr Stephen Rouch
Mr Jim Rouse
Mrs Elaine Rowland
Ms Sarah Rowland
Mr John Rowlands
Mr Richard Rowlands
Mr Wil Rowlands
Mr David Rowley
Ms Rachel Rowley
Miss Samantha Rowley
Mrs Julie Royle
Ms Krysia Rozanska
Mr Justin Ruddock
Mr John Rudkin
Mr Mohammed Ruhel
Mr Antonio Ruiz
Mr Jonathan Runswick-Cole
Miss Bianca Russell
Mr Lee Russell
Mr Richard Russell
Miss Victoria Russell
Mr Adrian Ruthen
Mr Ian Rutherforde-Park
Mr Mike Rutty
Mr Matthew Ryde
Ms Amanda Ryder
Mr Michael Sahota
Mr Dermott Sales
Mr Mark Saliba
Miss Adeline Salim
Mr MJ Salisbury
Mr Keith Salway
Mrs Jumaira Samad
Ms Margaret Sampson
Mr Gerardo Sanchez
Ms Christine Sandiford
Mr Philip Sandiford
Mr Daniel Sangiuseppe
Miss Ernesta Sankauskaite
Miss Charlotte Sankey
Mr Ashley Sansom
Mr R Sansom
Mr Duncan Saunders
Miss Jill Saunders
Mr Peter John Saunders
Mr Nicholas Savage
Mr John Savery
Mr Chris Savory
Mrs Fiona Sawyer
Mr John Sawyer
Ms Sandra Saxony-Burton
Ms Clare Sayer
Miss Jacqui Sayers
Mr Richard Schiessl
Mr Chris Schilling
Mrs Helen Scholey
Mr Dan Scobie
Miss Bertina Scott
Mr George Scott
Mr Richard Scott
Miss V Scott
Ms Sally Scott-Biggs
Mrs Rosalinde Scott-Hodgetts
Mrs Janet Scrafton
Mr Michael Scragg
Ms Gemma Screen
Ms Clare Scullion
Miss Sybille Sculy-Logotheti
Mr Rob Seager
Mr Martin Seah
Mrs Kim Searle
Miss Emma Searle-Barnes
Mrs Muriel Seddon
Mr Trevor Seed
Mr Jonathan Paul Seedall
Miss Carol Seet
Mr David Sefton
Mr Paul Sellers
Miss Vicky Semple
Mrs Alison Senior
Ms Felicia Severns
Mr Phil Sewsamblui
Mrs Vanessa Shallcross
Mr Mitesh Shanbhag
Mr Derek Sharp
Mr William Sharp
Ms Claire Shaughnessy
Mrs Danita Shaw
Mr Duncan Shaw
Ms Monica Shaw
Ms Nicola Shaw
Ms Anna Shawcross
Mr Julian Shawcross
Dr Tony Sheehy
Mr James Sheffield
Mr Martin Shelley
Mr Andrew Shepherd
Mrs Joyce Shepherd
Mr Nicholas Sheppard
Ms Sharon Sheppard
Miss Fallon Sherfield
Mr Richard Sherras
Mr John Sherry
Ms Jill Sherwin
Mrs Catherine Shilling
Mr Wayne Short
Mrs Karen Shufflebotham
Mr Mam Sidke
Mrs Rose Simcock
Mr Alexandros Simitsis
Mr Clive Simkins
Mrs Mary Simmonds
Ms Eleanor Simmons
Mr Chris Simpson
Ms Jennifer Simpson
Mr John Simpson
Ms Juliet Simpson
Mr Paul Simpson
Mr Roger Simpson
Mr Victor Simpson
Mrs Louise Sims
Mrs Ann Sinclair
Mr Adam Singer
Mrs Annie Singh
Mr Kamal Singh
Mr Graham Sivills
Mrs Louise Skillicorn
Mr Staffan Skott
Mrs Kasia Skrzypiec
Mrs Sally Slade
Mrs Carol Slater
Mr Tony Slater
Mr Gary Sleeman
Mr David Sleight
Mr Malcolm Smallwood
Mr Roger Smallwood
Ms Anne Smart
Mr Andy Smith
Ms Anita Smith
Miss Charlotte Smith
Mrs Christine Smith
Mr David Smith
Mrs Fiona Smith
Ms Gaynor Smith
Mr Grant Smith
Ms Heather Smith
Ms Helen Smith
Mr James Smith
Mrs Jan Smith
Mrs Louise Smith
Mr Martin Smith
Mr Matthew Smith
Mr Neil Smith
Mrs Paula Smith
Mr Peter Smith
Mr Phillip Smith
Mr Oliver Smith
Miss Rebecca Smith
Mr Samuel Smith
Dr Sarah Smith

THANK YOUS

Mr Stephen Smith
Ms Tracey Smith
Mr Ken Smythe
Mr Gordon Snell
Mrs Sarah Soames
Mr Paul Soanes
Ms Vera Sokolovski
Mr Paul Somerville
Mr Francesco Sotgiu
Mr John Southall
Ms Lily Southam
Ms Claire Southern
Mrs Patricia Southern
Miss Kelly Southon
Mr Richard Spacey
Mr Alan Spedding
Mr Bradley Speed
Mr Chris Spencer
Mrs Michelle Spencer
Ms Ruth Spencer
Miss Lindsay Spicer
Ms Miranda Spicer
Mrs Heidi Spillman
Mr John Spittle
Mr Christian Spurr
Miss Kerry Spurry
Ms Lucy Stadward
Mrs Margaret Stafford
Miss Kate Stainthorp
Mr Shane Staley
Mr Alan Stalker
Mr Alex Standen
Mr Paul Standley
Mr Simon Stanford
Mrs Nan Stanley
Mrs Sue Stanley
Mrs Jackie Stannard
Mr Javier Stanziola
Ms Rachel Stedman
Mrs Donna Stedmon
Mrs Sarah Steenson
Miss Anna Stefanska
Mrs Gillian Stephens
Mr Andrew Stevens
Ms Christine Stevens
Mrs Jane Stevens
Mrs Laura Stevens
Mr Matthew Stevens
Dr Angela Stevens-King
Dr Andrew Stevenson
Ms Elizabeth Stevenson
Mrs Jennifer Stevenson
Mr Keith Stevenson
Mr Ian Steward
Ms Ann Stewart
Miss Catherine Stewart
Mr Guy Stewart
Mrs Janet Stewart
Mr John Stewart
Mr Ronald Stewart
Mr Ros Stewart
Mr Allen Stidwill
Miss Heather Stobbart
Mr Michael Stobbs
Mr Freddie Stockdale
Ms Amanda Stocker
Ms Hannah Stocking
Mrs Jo Stocks
Mrs Maggie Stocks
Ms Niki Stockton
Miss Alison Stokes
Mrs Jan Stokes
Mr Brian Stone
Mr Colin Stoneman
Mr Richard Strange
Mr G J Stranks
Ms Megan Streb
Mr Madhan Street
Mrs Hilary Strong
Mr Nicholas Stroude
Miss Linda Stuart
Mrs Anne Stubbs
Ms Christine Sturgeon
Ms Emma Sturgess
Mr Orazio Sturniolo
Mr Tom Suffell
Mrs Julie Sullivan
Mr Michael Sullivan
Mr Ben Sulston
Miss Sharon Sulu
Mr Daniel Summers
Mrs Catherine Sutcliffe
Mr Michael Sutcliffe
Mrs Sarah Sutcliffe
Mr David Sutton
Mr Lisa Swain
Ms Sarah Swainbank
Mr Phil Sweeney
Mr David Swift
Mr Joseph Swift

Mr Gary Sykes
Mrs Sara Sylvester
Mr Tony Sylvester
Mr Andrew Symonds
Mr Jonathan Symons
Mrs Leah Taplin
Mrs Jo-Anne Tasker-Heard
Mr Rodney Tatman
Mrs Gina Tattersall
Miss Laura Tattersall
Mrs Judy Tayler-Smith
Mr Andrew Taylor
Mr Ben Taylor
Ms Catherine Taylor
Mr Chris Taylor
Ms Fiona Taylor
Mrs Janet Taylor
Mrs Jean Taylor
Mrs Lisa Taylor
Mrs Margaret Taylor
Mrs Rachel Taylor
Mr Richard Taylor
Mrs Rosline Taylor
Mrs Vanessa Taylor
Ms Leonora Teale
Mr Geoff Tedstone
Mr Robert Templar
Mr Howard Terry
Ms Patricia Terry
Mr Deryck Thake
Mr James Thatcher
Mrs Katherine Theobald
Ms Sara Thom
Mr David Thomas
Ms Emma Thomas
Mr Godfrey Thomas
Mrs Helen Thomas
Ms June Thomas
Mrs Lauren Thomas
Ms Patricia Thomas
Mr Paul Thomas
Mr Richard Thomas
Mr Rob Thomas
Mr Ron Thomas
Mr Ryan Thomas
Ms Stella-Maria Thomas
Ms Brenda Thomason
Mrs Alix Thompson
Mr David Thompson
Ms Helena Thompson
Mr James Thompson
Mrs Jo Thompson
Miss Lauren Thompson
Mr Mark Thompson
Mr Roger Thompson
Ms Rose Thompson
Mr Vaughan Thompson
Ms Julie Thomson
Mrs Sioux Thorn
Mrs Debby Thorne
Mr Julian Thornington
Mr David Thornton
Mr Ian Thornton-Bryar
Mr Alex Thurlow
Mr Bob Thurlow
Ms Karen Thurman
Mrs Heather Thurston
Mr Graham Tidmarsh
Miss Rebecca Tiernan
Mr Lise Tildsley
Mr Nick Tiley
Mr Mark Timberlake
Mr Sam Tims
Mr Darren Tipper
Miss Fiona To
Mr Nigel Tobias
Ms Alice Toby-Brant
Mr Trevor Todd
Mr Michael Tomlinson
Mr Ben Tomsett
Mr Paul Toomer
Ms Stephanie Tortell
Mr Peter Tough
Mr Mike Town
Mr Richard Townson
Mr Michael Trailor
Mrs Rachel Tredwell
Mr Richard Tremayne-Smith
Mr Chris Tremewan
Mr Jonny Trent
Ms Jane Trethewey
Miss Katie Trevis
Ms Sarah Tricks
Mr Christian Troesch
Mr John Troup
Mr John Trowbridge
Ms Kirstie Trudgeon
Mrs Kate Truscott
Mr Matt Tuck
Ms Charlotte Tucker

Mrs Christine Tulip
Mr Neville Tullah
Mr Colin Tunnicliffe
Mr Justin Tunstall
Mr Wojciech Turek
Mr David Turgoose
Ms Charlotte Turland
Mr Billy Turnbull
Mr David Turner
Mr Euan Turner
Mr Fred Turner
Mr John Turner
Ms Louise Turner
Mr Tony Turner
Mr Paul Tursner-Upcott
Mrs Jill Turton
Mr Neil Tweedy
Mr Tony Tween
Mrs Kirsty Tyack-Pearson
Mr Kenneth Underwood
Mr Mark Underwood
Mr Daniel Upton
Miss Gillian Urquhart
Mrs Janice Urquhart
Mrs Caroline Usher
Mr Nik Vaidya
Mr Luciano Valeri
Mr Pim Van Baarsen
Ms Pauline Van Eyk
Mr Howard Van Wijk
Mrs Victoria Van Wyk
Ms Monique Vanni
Mrs Carolyn Varcoe
Mrs Janet Vardy
Mr Gary Varga
Ms Wendy Varley
Ms Deborah Vaudin
Mr Tom Vaughan
Mr Charlie Vaughan-Griffith
Mr Charles Vaughan-Johnson
Mr Ian Venables
Mrs Julie Venables
Mr Stanley Venitt
Mr Martin Verity
Mrs Susan Verity
Mr Philip Vine
Ms Sarah Vine
Miss Ioanna Vlahou
Mr Nigel Voden
Mr Scott Von Poulton
Mrs J Vowles
Dr Benjamin Voyer
Mrs Fran Voykovich
Mr Thomas Wade
Mr Mark Waghorn
Ms Jodie Wagstaff
Mrs Penelope Wake
Mr Warwick Wakefield
Mrs Anest Wales
Mr Brian Walker
Mrs Helen Walker
Dr Joanna Walker
Dr John Walker
Mr Mervyn Walker
Mr William Walker
Mr Andrew Wall
Mr Richard Wall
Miss Demelza Wallace
Mr Ewan Wallace
Mr Frank Wallace
Mrs Joyce Walling
Ms Kerrie Wallis
Ms Noelle Walsh
Ms Yvonne Walsh
Mr Marcus Walters
Mr Adam Waltes
Ms Charlotte Walton
Mrs Elisabeth Walton
Miss Jo Walton
Ms Moira Walton-Dunn
Mr David Ward
Mrs Tammy Ward
Mrs Susan Wardleworth
Ms Wanda Warhaftig
Mrs Sally Warner
Mr Nicolas Warner-Willich
Mr Edward Warnett
Mr Simon Warrington
Miss Jane Warrington-Smith
Miss Natalie Watchman
Miss Elizabeth Waterman
Mrs Fay Waters
Mr John Waters
Mr Dayne Watkins
Mr David Watson
Mr John Watson
Mr Julian Watson
Mr Keith Watson
Mr Kenneth Watson
Mr Peter Watson

Mr William Watson
Mrs Zoe Watters
Mrs Joanne Watts
Mr Denis Waugh
Mrs Alison Waumsley
Mrs Jean Weare
Ms Bryony Weaver
Mrs Helen Webb
Mrs Kathleen Webb
Mrs Patricia Webb
Mrs Karen Webber
Miss Deborah Webster
Miss Eleanor Webster
Ms Penny Webster
Dr Roger Webster
Mrs Michelle Weddell
Mr Richard Weddell
Mr Ashenden Wedderburn
Miss Katie Weeks
Mr Isi Weinberger
Ms Lisa Welbourn
Mr Richard Weller
Mr David Wells
Mr Jamie Welsh
Mr Richard Weremczuk
Ms Megan West
Ms Margaret West
Ms Janet Westman
Ms Sarah Weston
Ms Sarah Wetton
Mr Cameron Weyers
Mr Steven Whalley
Mr Dave Wheat
Mrs Sarah Wheatley
Mr John Wheeler
Mr Oliver Wheeler
Miss Lora Whicher
Mrs Susan Whiston
Mr Philip Whitaker
Mr Bernard White
Ms Carrie White
Mr Dennis White
Mrs Hester White
Mr John White
Miss Julie White
Mrs Melanie White
Ms Ruth White
Mr Tom White
Mr Joe Whiteley
Ms Marion Whitfield
Ms Samantha Whiting
Mr Edward Whittaker
Mr Ian Whittaker
Mrs Sue Whittam
Mr & Mrs Whittle
Miss Claire Whomes
Mr Peter Wicks
Ms Lucy Widenka
Mrs Emma Wilcox
Mr Andrew Wilde
Mr David Wilde
Mr Kyle Wilkes
Dr Chayda Wilkins
Ms Sarah Wilkins
Mr Jon Wilkinson
Mr Nigel Wilkinson
Mr Steve Wilkinson
Ms Tina Wilkinson
Mrs Ruby Joan Wilkinson
Ms Aleksandra Wilkowska
Mr Richard Will
Mr Rupert Willday
Ms Rebecca Willey
Ms Andrea Williams
Mr Anthony Williams
Mr Christian Williams
Mrs Claire Williams
Ms Cristina Williams
Mrs Delith Williams
Mrs Elizabeth Williams
Mr Glyn Williams
Mr Harry Williams
Ms Jackie Williams
Mrs Linda Williams
Miss Lowrian Williams
Mr Martin Williams
Mr Matt Williams
Ms Patricia Williams
Ms Penny Williams
Mr Philip Williams
Ms Ruth Williams
Mr Tom Williams
Ms Abigail Williams
Ms Gill Williamson
Mr Michael Williamson
Mr Julian Willis
Ms Lesley Willis
Mrs Rebecca Willis
Mrs Sophie Willis
Mrs Julie Wills

Mr Michael Wilmore
Ms Abigail Wilson
Mrs Alison Wilson
Mr Andrew Wilson
Ms Anne Wilson
Miss Christina Wilson
Mr Derek Wilson
Mr George Wilson
Ms Geraldine Wilson
Mrs Janis Wilson
Mrs Lisa Wilson
Mrs Marisa Wilson
Mr Matthew Wilson
Mrs Sheila Wilson
Mr Simon Wilson
Mr Edward Wiltshire
Mr Tim Wilyman
Ms Jessica Wimbush
Mr Adam Winchester
Mr John Window
Mr Michael Winfield
Mr Joe Winning
Ms Christine Winstanley
Mr Roger Winstanley
Mrs Lucy Winterbottom
Mr Guy Wisbey
Mrs Molly Wiseman
Mrs Louise Wishart
Ms Kate Witcomb
Mrs Carinne Withey
Ms Rowena Wolton
Miss Charlie Womack
Mrs Sue Womack
Mrs Margaret Wonacott
Miss Alice Wood
Mr Chris Wood
Ms Deborah Wood
Mr Glen Wood
Miss Helen Wood
Ms Kate Wood
Mrs Linda Wood
Mr Philip Wood
Ms Sue Wood
Miss Amelia Woodard
Ms Karen Woodcraft
Mr Matthew Woodford
Ms Julia Woodham
Mr Ronald Woodman
Mr Peter Woods
Mr Colin Woodward
Ms Sara Woodward
Mrs Bridget Woolfall
Mr Thomas Woolfenden
Miss Nicky Woolgar
Mr Alan Woollcombe
Mr David Woolley
Mr Tim Woolmer
Dr David Wootton
Ms Tanya Worsfold
Mrs Margaret Worsley
Mr T Worster
Mr David Wortham
Mr Dave Worthy
Ms Amanda Wragg
Ms Natalie Wragg
Mr Paul Wreglesworth
Ms Marie Wren
Mr Andrew Wright
Miss Angela Wright
Mr David Wright
Ms Debbie Wright
Mr Graham Wright
Mrs Jackie Wright
Mr Will Wright
Mr David Wyatt
Ms Linda Wybar
Ms Andrea Wyper
Mr John Wyper
Miss Erin Wysocki-Jones
Mrs Hilary Yarnall
Mr Chris Yates
Mrs Helen Yates
Dr Roger Yates
Mr John Yearley
Mr Pete Yeo
Mrs Elizabeth Yevtushenko
Mrs Maria Yiannacou
Mr Garvin Yim
Mr Tom Yorath
Miss Jingan Young
Miss Naomi Young
Mr Rob Young
Mr Andy Zadora-Chrzastowski
Mrs Sarah Zanoni
Mr David Zerdin
Ms Catherine Zielicka
Mr Mark Ziles
Mr Paul Zisman

Special thank yous

We would like to extend special thanks to the following people: Kirstie Addis, Iain Barker, Francesca Bashall, Elizabeth Bowden, Andrew Byron, Alex Ellis, Alix Godfree, Natalie Goodrick, Lisa Grey, Alan Grimwade, Ros Mari Grindheim, Ben Kay, Janice Leech, David Mabey, Naomi Maister, Philippa Neville, Angela Newton, Jeffrey Ng, Nicola Parker, John Rowlands, Emma Sturgess, Mark Taylor, Allison Walls, Stuart Walton, Jenny White, Gemma Wilkinson, Blânche Williams and Jane Wilson. And in special memory of a great friend to the Guide, Ms Caroline Ogden.

Picture credits

Illustrations for food and wine features courtesy of Shutterstock.
Laurie Gear courtesy of Snooty Fox Images.

Map credits

Maps designed and produced by Cosmographics Ltd, www.cosmosgraphics.co.uk
UK digital database © Cosmographics Ltd, 2011
Greater London Map © Cosmographics, Ltd, 2011
North and South London maps © Collins Bartholomew, 2011
West, Central and East London maps © BTA (trading as VisitBritain), 2011, produced by Cosmographics Ltd and used with the kind permission of VisitBritain.

Please send updates, queries, menus and wine lists to:
editors@thegoodfoodguide.co.uk or write to:
The Good Food Guide, 2 Marylebone Road, London, NW1 4DF

Please send restaurant feedback to: www.thegoodfoodguide.co.uk/feedback

www.thegoodfoodguide.co.uk
twitter@GoodFoodGuideUK

THE GOOD
FOOD GUIDE
2012
The best restaurants in the UK
BlackBerry

THE GOOD FOOD GUIDE 2012
£5 VOUCHER

THE GOOD FOOD GUIDE 2012
£5 VOUCHER

THE GOOD FOOD GUIDE 2012
£5 VOUCHER

THE GOOD FOOD GUIDE 2012
£5 VOUCHER

THE GOOD FOOD GUIDE 2012
£5 VOUCHER

THE GOOD FOOD GUIDE 2012
£5 VOUCHER

THE GOOD FOOD GUIDE 2012
£5 VOUCHER

THE GOOD FOOD GUIDE 2012
£5 VOUCHER

THE GOOD FOOD GUIDE 2012
£5 VOUCHER

THE GOOD FOOD GUIDE 2012
£5 VOUCHER

THE GOOD FOOD GUIDE 2012
£5 VOUCHERS

TERMS & CONDITIONS
This voucher can only be used in participating restaurants, highlighted by the £5 OFF symbol. It is redeemable against a pre-booked meal for a minimum of two people, provided the customer highlights the intention to use the voucher at the time of booking. Only one voucher may be used per table booked. This voucher may not be used in conjunction with any other scheme.
Offer valid from 08/09/11 to 08/09/12.
For additional terms and conditions, see below.

TERMS & CONDITIONS
This voucher can only be used in participating restaurants, highlighted by the £5 OFF symbol. It is redeemable against a pre-booked meal for a minimum of two people, provided the customer highlights the intention to use the voucher at the time of booking. Only one voucher may be used per table booked. This voucher may not be used in conjunction with any other scheme.
Offer valid from 08/09/11 to 08/09/12.
For additional terms and conditions, see below.

TERMS & CONDITIONS
This voucher can only be used in participating restaurants, highlighted by the £5 OFF symbol. It is redeemable against a pre-booked meal for a minimum of two people, provided the customer highlights the intention to use the voucher at the time of booking. Only one voucher may be used per table booked. This voucher may not be used in conjunction with any other scheme.
Offer valid from 08/09/11 to 08/09/12.
For additional terms and conditions, see below.

TERMS & CONDITIONS
This voucher can only be used in participating restaurants, highlighted by the £5 OFF symbol. It is redeemable against a pre-booked meal for a minimum of two people, provided the customer highlights the intention to use the voucher at the time of booking. Only one voucher may be used per table booked. This voucher may not be used in conjunction with any other scheme.
Offer valid from 08/09/11 to 08/09/12.
For additional terms and conditions, see below.

TERMS & CONDITIONS
This voucher can only be used in participating restaurants, highlighted by the £5 OFF symbol. It is redeemable against a pre-booked meal for a minimum of two people, provided the customer highlights the intention to use the voucher at the time of booking. Only one voucher may be used per table booked. This voucher may not be used in conjunction with any other scheme.
Offer valid from 08/09/11 to 08/09/12.
For additional terms and conditions, see below.

TERMS & CONDITIONS
This voucher can only be used in participating restaurants, highlighted by the £5 OFF symbol. It is redeemable against a pre-booked meal for a minimum of two people, provided the customer highlights the intention to use the voucher at the time of booking. Only one voucher may be used per table booked. This voucher may not be used in conjunction with any other scheme.
Offer valid from 08/09/11 to 08/09/12.
For additional terms and conditions, see below.

TERMS & CONDITIONS
This voucher can only be used in participating restaurants, highlighted by the £5 OFF symbol. It is redeemable against a pre-booked meal for a minimum of two people, provided the customer highlights the intention to use the voucher at the time of booking. Only one voucher may be used per table booked. This voucher may not be used in conjunction with any other scheme.
Offer valid from 08/09/11 to 08/09/12.
For additional terms and conditions, see below.

TERMS & CONDITIONS
This voucher can only be used in participating restaurants, highlighted by the £5 OFF symbol. It is redeemable against a pre-booked meal for a minimum of two people, provided the customer highlights the intention to use the voucher at the time of booking. Only one voucher may be used per table booked. This voucher may not be used in conjunction with any other scheme.
Offer valid from 08/09/11 to 08/09/12.
For additional terms and conditions, see below.

TERMS & CONDITIONS
This voucher can only be used in participating restaurants, highlighted by the £5 OFF symbol. It is redeemable against a pre-booked meal for a minimum of two people, provided the customer highlights the intention to use the voucher at the time of booking. Only one voucher may be used per table booked. This voucher may not be used in conjunction with any other scheme.
Offer valid from 08/09/11 to 08/09/12.
For additional terms and conditions, see below.

TERMS & CONDITIONS
This voucher can only be used in participating restaurants, highlighted by the £5 OFF symbol. It is redeemable against a pre-booked meal for a minimum of two people, provided the customer highlights the intention to use the voucher at the time of booking. Only one voucher may be used per table booked. This voucher may not be used in conjunction with any other scheme.
Offer valid from 08/09/11 to 08/09/12.
For additional terms and conditions, see below.

Vouchers are valid from 8 September 2011 to 8 September 2012. Only one £5 voucher can be used per table booked (for a minimum of 2 people). No photocopies or any other kind of reproduction of vouchers will be accepted. Some participating establishments may exclude certain times, days or menus from the scheme so long as they a) advise customers of the restrictions at the time of booking and b) accept the vouchers at a minimum of 70% of sessions when the restaurant is open. Please note that the number of participating restaurants may vary from time to time.